Bankruptcy Code, Rules and Official Forms

1991 Law School Edition

ST. PAUL, MINN.

WEST PUBLISHING CO.

1991

PREFACE

This pamphlet contains the current Bankruptcy Code, Title 11 of the United States Code, and Bankruptcy Rules and Official Forms. Congress enacted the Bankruptcy Code into positive law by Public Law 95–598, November 6, 1978, 92 Stat. 2549. The Title took effect October 1, 1979, and replaced the existing Title 11, Bankruptcy. Title 11 will appear in this pamphlet as amended through the end of the 1990 Session of Congress.

The Bankruptcy Rules, as adopted by the United States Supreme Court, became effective August 1, 1983 and appear here as amended to January 1, 1991. The Official Forms in this pamphlet became effective September 19, 1986 and appear here as amended to January 1, 1991. Also included in this edition are the Proposed Revised Official Bankruptcy Forms that are scheduled to become effective August 1, 1991.

Reference is made to the "Bankruptcy Highlights" feature by Judge Harold Lavien of Boston, Massachusetts, for a summary of 1990 developments affecting bankruptcy law and practice.

Tables

In this pamphlet four tables have been included:

Table 1 shows the disposition of all sections of former Title 11.

Table 2 shows the derivation of all sections of the new Title 11.

Table 3 shows the disposition of sections of the Bankruptcy Act of 1898, as amended.

Table 4 shows the disposition of former bankruptcy rules and forms.

Also included are Related Provisions of Titles 18 and 28 of the United States Code pertinent to matters relating to Bankruptcy and selected sections of the Internal Revenue Code relating to Federal Tax Lien Statutes.

Historical and Revision Notes

These interpretative and authoritative notes of the House and Senate Committees on the Judiciary contained in House Report No. 95–595 and Senate Report No. 95–989, accompanying the codification of Title 11, are included under appropriate sections.

Library References

This feature is an aid to research which facilitates the finding of pertinent law embodied in the Key Number Digests and Corpus Juris Secundum. These library references are included under appropriate sec-

PREFACE

tions. For bankruptcy research on WESTLAW, see the "WESTLAW Electronic Research Guide" that follows the "Bankruptcy Highlights" feature.

THE PUBLISHER

January, 1991

BANKRUPTCY HIGHLIGHTS

By

George Francis Bason, Jr.
Former United States Bankruptcy Judge
For the District of Columbia

Legislation

After a lull in 1989, Congress came back with a roar in 1990. No less than seven separate statutes, several of them enacted in the last few frantic hours of the 101st Congress, made bankruptcy-law changes. The seven are:

1. P.L. 101–311: *Swap Agreements and Forward Contracts.* Swap agreements and forward contracts are financial instruments used by corporations and financial institutions to hedge their bets on interest and currency-exchange rate fluctuations. The Act (i) adds new definitions in § 101 of the Bankruptcy Code for "margin payment," "settlement payment," "swap agreement" and "swap participant"; (ii) exempts swap-agreement setoffs from the § 362 automatic stay; (iii) exempts swap agreements from the § 365 power to assume or reject executory contracts and (iv) from the § 547 avoiding powers; (v) adds a new § 560 which allows post-petition termination of swap agreements pursuant to a bankruptcy-insolvency-receivership *ipso facto* clause; and (vi) makes technical corrections and clarifications to Bankruptcy Code provisions concerning forward contracts.

2. P.L. 101–508: *Omnibus Budget Reconciliation Act of 1990.* Title III of this Act, entitled the "Student Loan Default Prevention Initiative Act of 1990," includes (i) provisions aimed at preventing educational institutions from avoiding loss of accreditation or licensing status by filing for bankruptcy, by amending §§ 362 and 541 of the Bankruptcy Code; and (ii) a provision amending § 1328(a)(2) of the Code to make student loans nondischargeable in Chapter 13 cases to the same extent as in Chapter 7 cases. Interestingly, the Act contains a sunset provision such that these provisions "shall cease to be effective on October 1, 1996." (Sec. 3008 of P.L. 101–508.)

Title XI of the same Act contains revenue provisions, including provisions pertaining to (i) treatment of stock transactions that constitute distributions (§ 11322, amending § 305(c) of the Internal Revenue Code) and (ii) issuance of debt or stock in satisfaction of indebtedness (§ 11325, amending § 108(c)(10) of the Internal Revenue Code), in bankruptcy cases.

3. P.L. 101–509: *Treasury, Postal Service and General Government Appropriations Act, 1991.* This Act includes provisions that will result in substantial increases in the maximum compensation payable to, and for services rendered as, standing Chapter 12 and 13 trustees, from the present maximum of just under $70,000 per year to a level of over $100,000, plus "the cash value of employment benefits comparable to" the benefits of similarly occupied federal employees.

4. P.L. 101–510: *National Defense Authorization Act of 1991.* This Act renders nondischargeable in bankruptcy (including Chapter 13) (i) an obliga-

tion of an "eligible" medical officer to reimburse the United States pursuant to a reenlistment bonus agreement, if the bankruptcy discharge is entered less than five years after termination of the agreement; and (ii) a military officer's written agreement to remain on active duty in a critical acquisition position for at least one year, unless the bankruptcy discharge occurs more than five years after termination of the agreement.

5. P.L. 101–581: *Criminal Victims Protection Act* ("the MADD law"). This legislation, sponsored and supported by Mothers Against Drunk Driving, offered Congress the opportunity (i) to overturn a Supreme Court decision within less than six months and (ii) to "get tough" with (a) drunk drivers, (b) drug users and (c) "welfare cheats". The law (i) rephrases Code § 523(a)(9) to extend its scope and render nondischargeable any debt "for death or personal injury caused by the debtor's operation of a motor vehicle if such operation was unlawful because the debtor was intoxicated from using alcohol, a drug, or another substance [undefined]"; (ii) amends § 1328(a)(2) so as to make such debts nondischargeable in Chapter 13 as well as in Chapter 7, 11 and 12 cases; and (iii) further amends § 1328(a)(2) so as to make criminal restitution obligations nondischargeable in Chapter 13 as well as other bankruptcy cases. This last provision overturned the Supreme Court's May 29, 1990 opinion in Pa. Dept. of Public Welfare v. Davenport, ___ U.S. ___, 110 S.Ct. 2126, ___ L.Ed.2d ___, holding, in accordance with the plain and unambiguous language of the statute, that a criminal restitution obligation imposed as a condition of probation for welfare fraud was a "debt" as defined in § 101(11) and hence was dischargeable in Chapter 13 as then written.

6. P.L. 101–646: *Crime Control Act.* Just to make doubly sure (let us say), Congress passed the same legislation as Title XXXI of this Act as appears in the MADD law (item 5 above), *i.e.*, rendering nondischargeable under all chapters of the Bankruptcy Code debts arising from drunk driving, driving under the influence of other drugs, and criminal-restitution obligations.

Title XXV of the Crime Control Act, entitled "Banking Law Enforcement," includes a number of provisions limited in their applicability to individuals who have misused their positions of trust and responsibility to financial institutions. These provisions include: (i) making nondischargeable (a) certain debts arising from fraud or defalcation while acting as a fiduciary for a financial institution and (b) certain debts arising from malicious or reckless failure to fulfill a commitment to maintain the capital of a federal depository institution; (ii) relieving a receiver, conservator or liquidator of a federal depository institution from strict compliance in all cases with the requirement to file a nondischargeability complaint within the 60-day period prescribed by former § 523(c), now § 523(c)(1); (iii) eliminating *any* exemption for debts that are for fraud or defalcation or for willful and malicious injury and that are owed by an individual affiliated with an insured depository institution; (iv) eliminating the right to reject any executory contract involving a debt to various stated federal financial regulatory agencies or a commitment to maintain the capital of an insured depository institution; (v) granting a new eighth priority for such a commitment; and

(vi) granting to the Resolution Trust Corp. and the National Credit Union Board a right of recovery of fraudulent conveyances superior to the rights of a bankruptcy trustee or other party.

Title XXXVI of the Crime Control Act, entitled the "Federal Debt Collection Procedures Act of 1990," includes a provision stating that it "shall not be construed to supersede or modify the operation of Title 11," except that it does amend § 523(a)(8) to broaden student-loan nondischargeability to cover any "obligation to repay . . . an educational benefit, scholarship or stipend" and also to extend from five to seven years the period after which such a debt becomes dischargeable.

7. P.L. 101–650: *Judicial Improvements Act.* This Act (i) (a) extends the Bankruptcy Administrator Program (which is in effect only in Alabama and North Carolina in lieu of the United States Trustee Program) for ten more years, until October 1, 2002; (b) grants standing to bankruptcy administrators like that of U.S. trustees; (c) and extends § 105 powers to bankruptcy courts participating in the bankruptcy administrator program; (ii) permits a bankruptcy judge whose term has expired to continue serving for up to six months until the judge's successor is appointed; (iii) authorizes a joint bankruptcy appellate panel for two or more circuits; and (iv) allows bankruptcy judges to render final decisions with respect to abstention and remand determinations, subject to a right of review by appeal to the district court *only* and not to the court of appeals or the Supreme Court.

Supreme Court

(A) *Decisions in 1990*

Meanwhile, the Supreme Court continued its torrid pace of bankruptcy opinions, deciding no less than five such cases in 1990 and remanding one without reaching the merits:

(i) With only Justice Blackmum dissenting, the Court resolved a conflict among the circuits by holding that a bankruptcy court has the authority to order the IRS to apply tax payments made by a Chapter 11 debtor corporation to "trust fund" tax liabilities (*i.e.*, employees' paycheck-withheld income and social security taxes) prior to any non-trust-fund liabilities, thus indirectly benefitting the corporation's principals, who are liable as "responsible individuals" for trust-fund but not for non-trust-fund taxes, if the court determines that this designation is necessary for the success of a reorganization plan. In a broadly worded opinion, after noting that "[t]he Bankruptcy Code does not explicitly authorize" such designations, the Court went on to cite § 1123(b)(5), which grants "residual authority to approve reorganization plans including 'any . . . appropriate provision not inconsistent with the applicable provisions of this title,'" and § 105(a), which authorizes bankruptcy courts to "issue any order, process, or judgment that is necessary or appropriate to carry out the provisions" of the Bankruptcy Code. United States v. Energy Resources Co., Inc., ___ U.S. ___, 110 S.Ct. 2139, 109 L.Ed.2d 580 (1990).

(ii) In Pennsylvania Dept. of Public Welfare v. Davenport, ___ U.S. ___, 110 S.Ct. 2126, 109 L.Ed.2d 588 (1990), the Court held, 7–2, that a restitution order in a criminal case gives rise to a debt that is dischargeable in a Chapter 13 case, even though, as the Court had held in Kelly v. Robinson, 479 U.S. 36, 107 S.Ct. 353, 93 L.Ed.2d 216 (1986), such an obligation is non-dischargeable in a Chapter 7 case under § 523(a)(7), which excepts from discharge (in Chapter 7 but not Chapter 13) any debt that is "a fine, penalty, or forfeiture payable to and for the benefit of a governmental unit, and is not compensation for actual pecuniary loss." As noted above, Congress lost no time in legislatively overruling this decision, not once but twice—in P.L. 101–581, the Criminal Victims Protection Act, and again in P.L. 101–647, the Crime Control Act.

(iii) In Begier v. Internal Revenue Service, ___ U.S. ___, 110 S.Ct. 2258, 110 L.Ed.2d 46 (1990), the Court for the second time in the same term dealt with an issue involving "trust fund" tax payments. (See United States v. Energy Resources Co., Inc., above.) In *Begier*, the Court held without dissent that a trustee in bankruptcy could not recover as a voidable preference "*any* voluntary prepetition payment of trust-fund taxes, regardless of the source of the funds." The Court reasoned that "[t]he debtor's act of voluntarily paying its trust-fund tax obligation therefore is alone sufficient to establish the required nexus between the 'amount' held in trust and the funds paid" so as to satisfy any tracing requirement. 110 S.Ct. at 2267. Justice Scalia concurred in the result though not the reasoning.

(iv) In Pension Benefit Guaranty Corp. v. LTV Corp., ___ U.S. ___, 110 S.Ct. 2668, 110 L.Ed.2d 579 (1990), the Court upheld PBGC's decision requiring LTV to restore certain pension plans which had been terminated in conjunction with LTV's Chapter 11 bankruptcy proceedings, where after the terminations LTV negotiated new pension agreements whereby with the help of PBGC's unwilling contributions the pension-plan participants were restored to substantially the *status quo ante*. The Court upheld PBGC's characterization of the new agreements as "follow-on" plans, even though "[i]t is undisputed that one of LTV Corp.'s principal goals in filing the Chapter 11 petitions was the restructuring of LTV Steel's pension obligations, a goal which could be accomplished if the Plans were terminated and responsibility for the unfunded liabilities was placed on the PBGC." 110 S.Ct. at 2673.

(v) In Langenkamp v. Culp, ___ U.S. ___, 111 S.Ct. 330, ___ L.Ed.2d ___ (1990), the Court reaffirmed, per curiam and without dissent, that its holding in Granfinanciera, S.A. v. Nordberg, 492 U.S. ___, ___, 109 S.Ct. 2782, 2787, 106 L.Ed.2d 26, ___ (1989), that "a person who has not submitted a claim against a bankruptcy estate has a [Seventh Amendment] right to a jury trial when sued by the trustee in bankruptcy to recover an allegedly fraudulent monetary transfer," applies equally in the case of a suit to recover an allegedly preferential monetary transfer. But, the Court went on, persons who *did* file claims against the bankruptcy estate "were not entitled to a jury trial on the trustee's preference action." 111 S.Ct. at 331–332, citing Katchen v. Landy, 382 U.S. 323, 86 S.Ct. 467, 15 L.Ed.2d 391 (1966).

(vi) The question left undecided in both *Granfinanciera* and *Langenkamp*, whether the constitutionally-required jury trial may constitutionally be presided over by a non-Article III bankruptcy judge, is one of two questions that was presented in Insurance Co. of State of Pa. v. Ben Cooper, Inc., cert. granted, 110 S.Ct. 3269 remanded, 111 S.Ct. 425 (1990). The other question presented was whether *post*-petition state-law contract and tort claims fall within the "core" jurisdiction of matters in which Article I bankruptcy judges may constitutionally render final decisions, notwithstanding the Supreme Court's contrary decision in Northern Pipeline Constr. Co. v. Marathon Pipe Line Co., 458 U.S. 50, 102 S.Ct. 2858, 73 L.Ed.2d 598 (1982), with respect to *pre*-petition state-law contract claims. If the Supreme Court decides the second question in the negative, it can again avoid deciding the first question.

The Second Circuit answered both questions affirmatively in its ruling below—In re Ben Cooper, Inc., 896 F.2d 1394 (1990). The circuits are split on the jury-right issue. Disagreeing with the Second Circuit, the Eighth and Tenth Circuits have held that bankruptcy judges may not preside over jury trials. In re United Missouri Bank of Kansas City, N.A., 901 F.2d 1449 (8th Cir.1990); Kriser Steel Corp. v. Frates, 911 F.2d 380 (10th Cir.1990). The First Circuit has held, like the Second, that *post*-petition state-law contract claims are core proceedings. In re Arnold Print Works, Inc., 815 F.2d 165 (1987). The three-sentence remand order failed to decide either issue, instead directing the Court of Appeals to consider a question concerning its "jurisdiction over this case and hence a question about our own jurisdiction."

(B) *Pending Cases in 1991*

Now pending before the Supreme Court for decision are at least two bankruptcy cases:

The first is Owen v. Owen, cert. granted, 110 S.Ct. 2166 (1990), decision below, 877 F.2d 44 (11th Cir.1989), where the question is whether § 522(f) permits a debtor to avoid a judicial lien on property in an opt-out state where the state's exemption law, although exempting property of the same sort, does not include a lien–avoidance provision.

The second case now pending for decision is Grogan v. Garner, cert. granted, 110 S.Ct. 1945 (1990), decision below, 881 F.2d 579 (8th Cir.1989), where the question is whether the standard of proof required to determine fraud for bankruptcy dischargeability purposes is "preponderance of the evidence" (in which event a state court determination of fraud would be binding on the debtor through collateral estoppel) or, as held by the court below, "clear and convincing evidence." *

Pending New Rules

Also pending before the Supreme Court is a proposed complete revision of the Bankruptcy Rules, including even a change of name from "Bankruptcy Rules" to "Federal Rules of Bankruptcy Procedure." The text of these proposed revised Rules appears in West's Bankruptcy Reporter Advance Sheet of October 23, 1990. If as expected the Supreme Court promulgates

---

* The Supreme Court decided Grozan v. Garner, supra, on January 15, 1991 holding unanimously that "preponderance of the evidence" is the correct standard of proof.

these Rules by May 1, 1991, and if as expected Congress takes no action to disapprove them, they will become effective on August 1, 1991.

The proposed new Rules make no radical changes and principally seek to update the Rules with the 1986 Code changes. The former "X" Rules for the U.S. Trustee are discarded and both the former U.S. Trustee Rules and the former Interim Chapter 12 Rules are integrated into the new Rules with all the applicable Chapter 11 Rules made to cover Chapter 12. Several amendments are designed to implement the provisions of the Retiree Benefit Protection Act of 1988, P.L. 100–334; several amendments are simply intended to improve the Rules.

Unless the Supreme Court further amends Rules 5011 and 9027 prior to the new Rules' promulgation, those two Rules will be out of date even before the effective date, because of the provisions in the 1990 Judicial Improvements Act allowing bankruptcy judges to render final decisions with respect to abstention and remand determinations, subject to a right of review by appeal to the district court *only* and not to the court of appeals or the Supreme Court. Based on the prior language of the pertinent statutes (28 U.S.C.A. §§ 1334(c) and 1452(b)), Rules 5011 and 9027 required the awkward procedure, on a motion for abstention or remand, of having the bankruptcy judge hear the motion and make a report and recommendation for final decision by a district judge on de novo review. That awkward procedure no longer serves any useful purpose under the new statute, because review of the bankruptcy judge's decision is now available through appeal to the district court.

A few of the more significant changes in the new Rules are: Rule 1007 does away with the Chapter 13 statement but adds the standard schedules of assets and liabilities and statement of financial affairs for Chapter 13 (as well as Chapter 12) debtors. Rule 2007 provides the procedure for obtaining court approval of the U.S. Trustee's appointment of a Chapter 11 trustee or examiner. Rule 2014 requires a professional seeking appointment to disclose any connection with U.S. Trustee personnel. Rule 2015 deletes the requirement to file a notice in the land records office in every county where the debtor has real estate, leaving the matter to the discretion of the trustee.

Rule 2020 provides that any challenge to any act or failure to act by the U.S. Trustee is to be considered a Rule 9014 contested matter. Rule 4001 clarifies the procedures to be used under Code Section 362 and 363 motions and the notice for settlement agreements. Rule 5002 adds affiliation with the U.S. Trustee to those in the potentially proscribed appointment category. Rule 5009 provides procedures for closing Chapter 7, 12, and 13 cases. Rule 7062 adds an order authorizing assumption or assignment of leases or executory contracts to those exempted from the automatic 10–day stay of F.R.C.P. 62(a).

Rule 8002 preserves a prematurely filed notice of appeal. Rule 9027 requires notice of removal to state whether proceedings are core or non-core and if non-core whether or not consent is given to entry of a final order by the bankruptcy judge. Rule 9027 also, in keeping with the 1988 amendment to 28 U.S.C.A. § 1446(d), removes the bond requirement.

All references to official form numbers are deleted to avoid any references to inconsistently numbered new forms.

Pending New Official Forms

Complementing the pending new Rules discussed above, the Judicial Conference of the United States has adopted a complete revision of the Official Bankruptcy Forms. Under Rule 9009 of the Federal Rules of Bankruptcy Procedure, new forms need not be submitted to the Supreme Court or Congress but are simply promulgated by the Judicial Conference. Nevertheless, the Judicial Conference has delayed the effective date of the new forms until August 1, 1991, so as to coincide with the expected effective date of the proposed new Rules. The new forms appear in West's Bankruptcy Reporter Advance Sheet of October 23, 1990, and are also included at pages 929–1004, infra, of this book.

The forms have been revised, reorganized, and renumbered so that they follow as closely as possible the chronology of a case under the Bankruptcy Code. Thirteen existing forms have been abrogated. The petitions, schedules, and statements, which comprise the basic filing documents in every case under the Bankruptcy Code, have been revised completely, as have the notice of the meeting of creditors and the proof of claim, which also are forms of nearly universal application. Other forms, such as the order of discharge, have merely been renumbered and technical amendments made to conform with the new numbering system. The new forms appear to be a vast improvement.

Fees

The Judicial Conference of the United States, at its September 1990 meeting, added language to clarify that:

Filing fees prescribed by 28 U.S.C. § 1930(a) must be collected when a Bankruptcy Code case is reopened, unless the reopening is to correct an administrative error or for actions related to the debtor's discharge. If a Bankruptcy Code case is reopened for any other purpose, the appropriate fee to be charged is the same as the filing fee in effect for commencing a new case on the date of reopening.

The current schedule of Bankruptcy Fees appears following the text of U.S. Code Title 28, § 1930, infra.

*

WESTLAW® ELECTRONIC RESEARCH GUIDE

1. Coordinating Legal Research with WESTLAW

This *Bankruptcy Code, Rules and Forms* publication provides useful materials relating to bankruptcy law. WESTLAW provides additional resources for research. This Guide is to assist in the effective use of WESTLAW to supplement your bankruptcy research.

2. Databases

A database is an aggregation of documents with one or more features in common. A database may contain statutes, court decisions, administrative materials, or commentaries. Every database has its own identifier. Database identifiers are used to identify the database to be searched. The WESTLAW Directory is a comprehensive listing of databases, with information about each database, and the types of documents each contains.

3. Updating Statutes

A WESTLAW search may be used to ascertain whether a particular section of the United States Code dealing with bankruptcy has been amended after the cut-off date of this pamphlet. Sign on to the FBKR–USC database. Check its most recent update by entering the scope (sc) command and reviewing the information provided. Then, using the desired title number and section number, a query is entered in the following form:

ci(11 +3   362)

This will retrieve section 362 of Title 11 of the United States Code.

4. Updating A Bankruptcy Rule

A WESTLAW search may be used to ascertain whether a particular Bankruptcy Rule has been amended after the cut-off date of this pamphlet. Sign on to the FBKR–USC database, after checking its most recent update, and using the desired rule number, a query is entered in the following form:

ci(Rule +2   1003)

This will retrieve Bankruptcy Rule 1003.

5. Retrieving Cases Citing A Statute

To find cases citing a particular statute, sign on to the Federal Bankruptcy Cases database (FBKR–CS) and using the desired title number and section number, a query is entered in the following form:

(Chapter Title +1 11) "11 U.S.C.***" /5   1123

This will retrieve cases citing section 1123 of Title 11 of the United States Code.

6. Retrieving Cases Citing A Rule

To find cases citing a particular bankruptcy rule, sign on to the Federal Bankruptcy Cases (FBKR–CS) and using the rule, a query is entered in the following form:

"Bankruptcy Rule" Bankr.Proc.Rule /3 1007

This will retrieve Bankruptcy Rule 1007.

7. Key Number Search

WESTLAW may be used to search any topic and key number in West's Key Number System. To retrieve cases with at least one headnote classified to the topic Bankruptcy ☞ 2900(2), sign on to a caselaw database and enter

51k2900(2)

The topic name Bankruptcy is replaced by its numerical equivalent (51) and the ☞ by the letter k. A complete list of topics and their equivalent topic numbers appears at the end of this Guide, is in the WESTLAW Reference Manual and is available in the WESTLAW Directory.

8. Retrieving A Regulation In The Code of Federal Regulations

To find the text of a federal regulation, sign on to FBKR–CFR database. Using the desired citation, a query is entered in the following form:

ci(20 +3 725.603)

This will retrieve section 725.603 of Title 20 of the Code of Federal Regulations.

9. Retrieving A Federal Register Document

To find the text of a Federal Register document, sign on to FBKR–FR database. Using the desired citation, enter a query in the following form:

ci(55 +2 1795)

This will retrieve 55 FR 1795.

10. Using Insta–Cite ® for Case History and Parallel Citations

Insta–Cite ® may be used to find any parallel citations and the history of a case. To view the Insta–Cite history of a displayed case, simply enter the command IC. To view the Insta–Cite history of a selected case, enter a command in this form:

ic 889 F.2d 1104

11. Shepardizing ™ a Case with WESTLAW

To view Shepard's ® Citations for a displayed case, simply enter the command SH. To view Shepard's ® Citations for a selected case, enter a command in this form:

sh 94 B.R. 262

12. Additional Information

The information provided above illustrates some of the ways WESTLAW can complement research using *Bankruptcy Code, Rules and Forms*. However, this brief overview illustrates only some of the power of WESTLAW. The full range of WESTLAW search techniques is available to support your research from this series. Please consult the WESTLAW Reference manual for additional information.

For information about subscribing to WESTLAW, please call 1–800–328–0109.

*

TABLE OF CONTENTS

                                                                                    Page
PREFACE_____ III
BANKRUPTCY HIGHLIGHTS _____ V
WESTLAW ELECTRONIC RESEARCH GUIDE_____ XIII

BANKRUPTCY CODE _____ 1
Chapter
  1. General Provisions _____ 5
  3. Case Administration_____ 37
  5. Creditors, Debtor, and the Estate _____ 115
  7. Liquidation _____ 211
  9. Adjustment of Debts of a Municipality _____ 270
 11. Reorganization_____ 291
 12. Adjustment of Debts of a Family Farmer With Regular Annu-
       al Income _____ 380
 13. Adjustment of Debts of an Individual With Regular Income 400

RELATED PROVISIONS OF U.S. CODE TITLES 18 AND 28____ 429
  Title 18, Crimes and Criminal Procedure_____ 432
  Title 28, Judiciary and Judicial Procedure _____ 441
  Bankruptcy Fees _____ 496

**RULES AND FORMS OF PRACTICE AND PROCEDURE IN
BANKRUPTCY**_____ 503

RULES OF PRACTICE AND PROCEDURE IN BANKRUPTCY__ 509
Part
   I. Commencement of Case; Proceedings Relating to Petition
      and Order for Relief _____ 511
  II. Officers and Administration; Notices; Meetings; Examina-
      tions; Elections; Attorneys and Accountants _____ 536
 III. Claims and Distribution to Creditors and Equity Interest
      Holders; Plans _____ 566
 IV. The Debtor: Duties and Benefits _____ 589
  V. Courts and Clerks_____ 599
 VI. Collection and Liquidation of the Estate _____ 611
VII. Adversary Proceedings _____ 619
VIII. Appeals to District Court or Bankruptcy Appellate Panel 636
 IX. General Provisions _____ 652
  X. United States Trustees _____ 676

OFFICIAL BANKRUPTCY FORMS_____ 685

PROPOSED REVISED OFFICIAL BANKRUPTCY FORMS _____ 787

DISPOSITION TABLES _____ 863

FEDERAL TAX LIEN STATUTES—INTERNAL REVENUE CODE 901

Bankruptcy Code, Rules and Official Forms

*

THE CODE OF THE LAWS OF THE UNITED STATES OF AMERICA

TITLE 11

BANKRUPTCY

Chap.		Sec.
1.	General Provisions	101
3.	Case Administration	301
5.	Creditors, Debtor, and the Estate	501
7.	Liquidation	701
9.	Adjustment of Debts of a Municipality	901
11.	Reorganization	1101
12.	Adjustment of Debts of a Family Farmer With Regular Annual Income	1201
13.	Adjustment of Debts of an Individual With Regular Income	1301

Enacting Clause. Section 101 of Pub.L. 95–598, Title I, Nov. 6, 1978, 92 Stat. 2549, provided in part: "The law relating to bankruptcy is codified and enacted as Title 11 of the United States Code, entitled 'Bankruptcy', and may be cited as 11 U.S.C. § _____."

Repeals. Section 401(a) of Pub.L. 95–598, Title IV, Nov. 6, 1978, 92 Stat. 2682, provided that: "The Bankruptcy Act [act July 1, 1898, ch. 541, 30 Stat. 544, as amended] is repealed."

Effective Dates. Section 402 of Pub.L. 95–598, Title IV, Nov. 6, 1978, 92 Stat. 2682, as amended by Pub.L. 98–249, § 1(a), Mar. 31, 1984, 98 Stat. 116; Pub.L. 98–271, § 1(a), Apr. 30, 1984, 98 Stat. 163; Pub.L. 98–299, § 1(a), May 25, 1984, 98 Stat. 214; Pub.L. 98–325, § 1(a), June 20, 1984, 98 Stat. 268; Pub.L. 98–353, Title I, §§ 113, 121(a), July 10, 1984, 98 Stat. 343, 345; and Pub.L. 98–454, Title X, § 1001, Oct. 5, 1984, 98 Stat. 1745, provided that:

"(a) Except as otherwise provided in this title, this Act shall take effect on October 1, 1979.

"(b) Except as provided in subsections (c) and (d) of this section, the amendments made by title II of this Act shall not be effective. [Pub.L. 98–353, Title I, § 121(a), July 10, 1984, 98 Stat. 345, also amended subsec. (b) by striking out 'June 28, 1984' and inserting in lieu thereof 'the date of enactment of the Bankruptcy Amendments and Federal Judgeship Act of 1984'. (Such Act was enacted on July 10, 1984.) This amendment was not executed to text.]

"(c) The amendments made by sections 210, 214, 219, 220, 222, 224, 225, 228, 229, 235, 244, 245, 246, 249, and 251 of this Act shall take effect on October 1, 1979.

"(d) The amendments made by sections 217, 218, 230, 247, 302, 314(j), 317, 327, 328, 338, and 411 of this Act shall take effect on the date of enactment of this Act.

"(e) [Repealed. Pub.L. 98–454, Title X, § 1001, Oct. 5, 1984, 98 Stat. 1745.]"

[Amendment by section 113 of Pub.L. 98–353 effective on June 27, 1984 pursuant to section 122(c) of Pub.L. 98–353. Amendment by section 121(a) of Pub.L. 98–353 effective on July 10, 1984 pursuant to section 122(a) of Pub.L. 98–353.]

Effective Date of 1984 Amendments. For effective date of amendments by Title I of Pub.L. 98–353, July 10, 1984, 98 Stat. 346, see section 122 of Pub.L. 98–353 set out as an Effective Date of 1984 Amendment note under section 151 of Title 28, Judiciary and Judicial Procedure.

Section 553 of Pub.L. 98–353, Title III, July 10, 1984, 98 Stat. 392, provided that:

"(a) Except as otherwise provided in this section the amendments made by this title [Title III of Pub.L. 98–353] shall become effective to cases filed 90 days after the date of enactment of this Act [July 10, 1984].

"(b) The amendments made by section 426(b) [amending section 303(b)(1) and (h)(1) of this title] shall become effective upon the date of enactment of this Act.

"(c) The amendments made by subtitle J [adding section 1113 of this title] shall become effective as provided in section 541(c) [set out as an Effective Date note under section 1113 of Title 11]."

Short Title of 1984 Amendments. Section 1 of Pub.L. 98–353, July 10, 1984, 98 Stat. 333, provided: "That this Act [enacting sections 557, 558, 559, and 1113 of Title 11, Bankruptcy; sections 151 to 158, 1408 to 1412, and 1452 of Title 28, Judiciary and Judicial Procedure; amending sections 44, 98, 131, 133, 371, 372, 634, 957, 1334, 1360, and 1930 of Title 28; sections 8331, 8334, 8336, 8339, 8341, 8344, 8701, 8706, 8714a, and 8714b of Title 5; Government Organization and Employees, and sections 101, 102, 103, 105, 108, 109, 303, 321, 322, 326, 327, 328, 329, 330, 342, 343, 346, 349, 350, 361, 362, 363, 365, 366, 501, 502, 503, 505, 506, 507, 509, 510, 521, 522, 523, 524, 525, 541, 542, 543, 544, 545, 546, 547, 548, 549, 550, 552, 553, 554, 555, 702, 703, 704, 707, 723, 724, 725, 726, 727, 728, 741, 745, 752, 761, 763, 765, 766, 901, 902, 903, 921, 922, 927, 943, 945, 1102, 1103, 1105, 1106, 1107, 1108, 1112, 1121, 1123, 1124, 1125, 1126, 1127, 1129, 1141, 1142, 1144, 1145, 1146, 1166, 1168, 1169, 1170, 1171, 1173, 1301, 1302, 1304, 1307, 1322, 1324, 1325, 1326, 1328, 1329, 15103, and 151302 of Title 11; Bankruptcy Rules 2002 and 3001, Title 11; and Bankruptcy Form No. 1, Title 11; enacting provisions set out as notes under sections 44, 133, 151, 152, 153, 371, 634, 1334, and 2075 of Title 28; sections 8331 and 8706 of Title 5; and preceding sections 101 and sections 101, 365, and 1113 of Title 11; amending provisions set out as section 581 of Title 28 and preceding section 101 of Title 11; and repealing provisions set out as notes preceding sections 151 and 1471 of Title 28] may be cited as the 'Bankruptcy Amendments and Federal Judgeship Act of 1984'."

Section 361 of Pub.L. 98–353, Title III, July 10, 1984, 98 Stat. 361, provided that: "This subtitle [amending sections 362, 365, and 541 of this title] may be cited as the 'Leasehold Management Bankruptcy Amendments Act of 1983'."

Section 381 of Pub.L. 98–353, Title III, July 10, 1984, 98 Stat. 364, provided that: "This subtitle [amending section 403(e) of Pub.L. 95–598, Nov. 6, 1978, 92 Stat. 2683, set out as a note preceding chapter 1] may be cited as the 'Referees Salary and Expense Fund Act of 1984'."

Short Title of 1986 Amendment. Section 1 of Pub.L. 99–554, § 1, Oct. 27, 1986, 100 Stat. provided: "That this Act [enacting sections 307, and 1201 to 1231 of Title 11, Bankruptcy, and section 589a of Title 28, Judiciary and Judicial Procedure, amending sections 101 to 103, 105, 108, 109, 303, 321, 322, 324, 326, 327, 329, 330, 341, 343, 345 to 348, 362 to 365, 502, 503, 521 to 524, 546 to 549, 554, 557, 701, 703 to 707, 724, 726 to 728, 743, 1102, 1104 to 1106, 1112, 1121, 1129, 1163, 1202, 1302, 1306, 1307, and 1324 to 1326 of Title 11, Bankruptcy Form No. 1, set out in the Appendix to Title 11, and sections 49, 96, 152, 156, 157, 526, 581, 582, 584 to 587, 604, 1334, and 1930 of Title 28, repealing sections 1201 to 1231 and 1501 to 151326 of Title 11, enacting provisions set out as notes under sections 581 and 589 of Title 28, amending provisions set out as a note under section 152 of Title 28, and repealing provisions set out as a note under preceding section 581 of Title 28] may be cited as the 'Bankruptcy Judges, United States Trustees, and Family Farmer Bankruptcy Act of 1986'."

Short Title of 1988 Amendment. Pub.L. 100–334, § 1, June 16, 1988, 102 Stat. 610, provided that: "This Act [enacting section 1114 of this title, amending section 1129 of this title, enacting provisions set out as a note under this section and amending and repealing provisions set as notes under section 1106 of this title] may be cited as the 'Retiree Benefits Bankruptcy Protection Act of 1988'."

Short Title of 1990 Amendment. Pub.L. 101–581, § 1, Nov. 15, 1990, 104 Stat. 2865, provided that: "This Act [amending sections 523 and 1328 of this title and enacting provision set out as a note under section 523 of this title] may be cited as the 'Criminal Victims Protection Act of 1990'."

Pub.L. 101–647, Title III, § 3101, Nov. 29, 1990, 104 Stat. 4916, provided that: "This title [amending sections 523 and 1328 of this title and enacting provisions set out as a note under section 523 of this title] may be cited as the 'Criminal Victims Protection Act of 1990'."

Savings Provisions. Section 403 of Pub.L. 95–598, Title IV, Nov. 6, 1978, 92 Stat. 2683, as amended by Pub.L. 98–353, Title III, § 382, July 10, 1984, 98 Stat. 364, provided that:

"(a) A case commenced under the Bankruptcy Act, and all matters and proceedings in or relating to any such case, shall be conducted and determined under such Act as if this Act had not been enacted, and the substantive rights of parties in connection with any such bankruptcy case, matter, or proceeding shall continue to be governed by the law applicable to such case, matter, or proceeding as if the Act had not been enacted.

"(b) Notwithstanding subsection (a) of this section, sections 1165, 1167, 1168, 1169, and 1171 of title 11 of the United States Code, as enacted by section 101 of this Act, apply to cases pending under section 77 of the Bankruptcy Act (11 U.S.C. 205) on the date of enactment of this Act in which the trustee has not filed a plan of reorganization.

"(c) The repeal made by section 401(a) of this Act does not affect any right of a referee in bankruptcy. United States bankruptcy judge, or survivor of a referee in bankruptcy or United States bankruptcy judge to receive any annuity or other payment under the civil service retirement laws.

"(d) The amendments made by section 314 of this Act do not affect the application of chapter 9, chapter 96, section 2516, section 3057, or section 3284 of title 18 of the United States Code to any act of any person—

"(1) committed before October 1, 1979; or

"(2) committed after October 1, 1979, in connection with a case commenced before such date.

"(e) Notwithstanding subsection (a) of this section—

"(1) a fee may not be charged under section 40c(2)(a) of the Bankruptcy Act in a case pending under such Act after September 30, 1979, to the extent that such fee exceeds $200,000;

"(2) a fee may not be charged under section 40c(2)(b) of the Bankruptcy Act in a case in which the plan is confirmed after September 30, 1978, or in which the final determination as to the amount of such fee is made after September 30, 1979, notwithstanding an earlier confirmation date, to the extent that such fee exceeds $100,000;

"(3) after September 30, 1979, all moneys collected for payment into the referees' salary and expense fund in cases filed under the Bankruptcy Act shall be collected and paid into the general fund of the Treasury; and

"(4) any balance in the referees' salary and expense fund in the Treasury on October 1, 1979, shall be transferred to the general fund of the Treasury and the referees' salary and expense fund account shall be closed."

Separability of Provisions. Section 119 of Pub.L. 98–353, Title I, July 10, 1984, 98 Stat. 344, provided that: "If any provision of this Act [see Short Title of 1984 Amendment note set out above] or the application thereof to any person or circumstance is held invalid, the remainder of this Act, or the application of that provision to persons or circumstances other than those as to which it is held invalid, is not affected thereby."

[For effective date of section 119 of Pub.L. 98–353, see section 122 of Pub.L. 98–353, Title I, July 10, 1984, 98 Stat. 346, set out as an Effective Date of 1984 Amendment note under section 151 of Title 28, Judiciary and Judicial Procedure.]

Section 551 of Pub.L. 98–353, Title III, July 10, 1984, 98 Stat. 391, provided that: "If any provision of this title [Title III of Pub.L. 98–353] or any amendment made by this title, or the application thereof to any person or circumstance is held invalid, the provisions of every other part, and their application shall not be affected thereby."

[For effective date of amendments by Title III of Pub.L. 98–353, see section 553 of Pub.L. 98–353, Title III, July 10, 1984, 98 Stat. 392, set out as an Effective Date of 1984 Amendments note above.]

Legislative History. For legislative history and purpose of Pub.L. 95–598, see 1978 U.S.Code Cong. and Adm.News, p. 5787.

CHAPTER 1—GENERAL PROVISIONS

Sec.
101. Definitions.
102. Rules of construction.
103. Applicability of chapters.
104. Adjustment of dollar amounts.
105. Power of court.
106. Waiver of sovereign immunity.
107. Public access to papers.
108. Extension of time.
109. Who may be a debtor.

---

§ 101. Definitions

In this title—

(1) "accountant" means accountant authorized under applicable law to practice public accounting, and includes professional accounting association, corporation, or partnership, if so authorized;

(2) "affiliate" means—

(A) entity that directly or indirectly owns, controls, or holds with power to vote, 20 percent or more of the outstanding voting securities of the debtor, other than an entity that holds such securities—

(i) in a fiduciary or agency capacity without sole discretionary power to vote such securities; or

(ii) solely to secure a debt, if such entity has not in fact exercised such power to vote;

(B) corporation 20 percent or more of whose outstanding voting securities are directly or indirectly owned, controlled, or held with power to vote, by the debtor, or by an entity that directly or indirectly owns, controls, or holds with power to vote, 20 percent or more of the outstanding voting securities of the debtor, other than an entity that holds such securities—

(i) in a fiduciary or agency capacity without sole discretionary power to vote such securities; or

(ii) solely to secure a debt, if such entity has not in fact exercised such power to vote;

(C) person whose business is operated under a lease or operating agreement by a debtor, or person substantially all of whose property is operated under an operating agreement with the debtor; or

(D) entity that operates the business or substantially all of the property of the debtor under a lease or operating agreement;

(3) "Federal depository institutions regulatory agency" means—

(A) with respect to an insured depository institution (as defined in section 3(c)(2) of the Federal Deposit Insurance Act) for which no

5

conservator or receiver has been appointed, the appropriate Federal banking agency (as defined in section 3(q) of such Act);

(B) with respect to an insured credit union (including an insured credit union for which the National Credit Union Administration has been appointed conservator or liquidating agent), the National Credit Union Administration;

(C) with respect to any insured depository institution for which the Resolution Trust Corporation has been appointed conservator or receiver, the Resolution Trust Corporation; and

(D) with respect to any insured depository institution for which the Federal Deposit Insurance Corporation has been appointed conservator or receiver, the Federal Deposit Insurance Corporation;

(4) "attorney" means attorney, professional law association, corporation, or partnership, authorized under applicable law to practice law;

(5) "claim" means—

(A) right to payment, whether or not such right is reduced to judgment, liquidated, unliquidated, fixed, contingent, matured, unmatured, disputed, undisputed, legal, equitable, secured, or unsecured; or

(B) right to an equitable remedy for breach of performance if such breach gives rise to a right to payment, whether or not such right to an equitable remedy is reduced to judgment, fixed, contingent, matured, unmatured, disputed, undisputed, secured, or unsecured;

(6) "commodity broker" means futures commission merchant, foreign futures commission merchant, clearing organization, leverage transaction merchant, or commodity options dealer, as defined in section 761 of this title, with respect to which there is a customer, as defined in section 761(9) of this title;

(7) "community claim" means claim that arose before the commencement of the case concerning the debtor for which property of the kind specified in section 541(a)(2) of this title is liable, whether or not there is any such property at the time of the commencement of the case;

(8) "consumer debt" means debt incurred by an individual primarily for a personal, family, or household purpose;

(9) "corporation"—

(A) includes—

(i) association having a power or privilege that a private corporation, but not an individual or a partnership, possesses;

(ii) partnership association organized under a law that makes only the capital subscribed responsible for the debts of such association;

(iii) joint-stock company;

(iv) unincorporated company or association; or

(v) business trust; but

(B) does not include limited partnership;

6

(10) "creditor" means—

(A) entity that has a claim against the debtor that arose at the time of or before the order for relief concerning the debtor;

(B) entity that has a claim against the estate of a kind specified in section 348(d), 502(f), 502(g), 502(h) or 502(i) of this title; or

(C) entity that has a community claim;

(11) "custodian" means—

(A) receiver or trustee of any of the property of the debtor, appointed in a case or proceeding not under this title;

(B) assignee under a general assignment for the benefit of the debtor's creditors; or

(C) trustee, receiver, or agent under applicable law, or under a contract, that is appointed or authorized to take charge of property of the debtor for the purpose of enforcing a lien against such property, or for the purpose of general administration of such property for the benefit of the debtor's creditors;

(12) "debt" means liability on a claim;

(13) "debtor" means person or municipality concerning which a case under this title has been commenced;

(14) "disinterested person" means person that—

(A) is not a creditor, an equity security holder, or an insider;

(B) is not and was not an investment banker for any outstanding security of the debtor;

(C) has not been, within three years before the date of the filing of the petition, an investment banker for a security of the debtor, or an attorney for such an investment banker in connection with the offer, sale, or issuance of a security of the debtor;

(D) is not and was not, within two years before the date of the filing of the petition, a director, officer, or employee of the debtor or of an investment banker specified in subparagraph (B) or (C) of this paragraph; and

(E) does not have an interest materially adverse to the interest of the estate or of any class of creditors or equity security holders, by reason of any direct or indirect relationship to, connection with, or interest in, the debtor or an investment banker specified in subparagraph (B) or (C) of this paragraph, or for any other reason;

(15) "entity" includes person, estate, trust, governmental unit, and United States trustee;

(16) "equity security" means—

(A) share in a corporation, whether or not transferable or denominated "stock", or similar security;

(B) interest of a limited partner in a limited partnership; or

(C) warrant or right, other than a right to convert, to purchase, sell, or subscribe to a share, security, or interest of a kind specified in subparagraph (A) or (B) of this paragraph;

(17) "equity security holder" means holder of an equity security of the debtor;

(18) "family farmer" means—

(A) individual or individual and spouse engaged in a farming operation whose aggregate debts do not exceed $1,500,000 and not less than 80 percent of whose aggregate noncontingent, liquidated debts (excluding a debt for the principal residence of such individual or such individual and spouse unless such debt arises out of a farming operation), on the date the case is filed, arise out of a farming operation owned or operated by such individual or such individual and spouse, and such individual or such individual and spouse receive from such farming operation more than 50 percent of such individual's or such individual and spouse's gross income for the taxable year preceding the taxable year in which the case concerning such individual or such individual and spouse was filed; or

(B) corporation or partnership in which more than 50 percent of the outstanding stock or equity is held by one family, or by one family and the relatives of the members of such family, and such family or such relatives conduct the farming operation, and

(i) more than 80 percent of the value of its assets consists of assets related to the farming operation;

(ii) its aggregate debts do not exceed $1,500,000 and not less than 80 percent of its aggregate noncontingent, liquidated debts (excluding a debt for one dwelling which is owned by such corporation or partnership and which a shareholder or partner maintains as a principal residence, unless such debt arises out of a farming operation), on the date the case is filed, arise out of the farming operation owned or operated by such corporation or such partnership; and

(iii) if such corporation issues stock, such stock is not publicly traded;

(19) "family farmer with regular annual income" means family farmer whose annual income is sufficiently stable and regular to enable such family farmer to make payments under a plan under chapter 12 of this title;

(20) "farmer" means (except when such term appears in the term "family farmer") person that received more than 80 percent of such person's gross income during the taxable year of such person immediately preceding the taxable year of such person during which the case under this title concerning such person was commenced from a farming operation owned or operated by such person;

(21) "farming operation" includes farming, tillage of the soil, dairy farming, ranching, production or raising of crops, poultry, or livestock, and production of poultry or livestock products in an unmanufactured state;

(22) "financial institution" means a person that is a commercial or savings bank, industrial savings bank, savings and loan association, or trust company and, when any such person is acting as agent or custodian for a customer in connection with a securities contract, as defined in section 741(7) of this title, such customer;

(23) "foreign proceeding" means proceeding, whether judicial or administrative and whether or not under bankruptcy law, in a foreign country in which the debtor's domicile, residence, principal place of business, or prinicpal assets were located at the commencement of such proceeding, for the purpose of liquidating an estate, adjusting debts by composition, extension, or discharge, or effecting a reorganization;

(24) "foreign representative" means duly selected trustee, administrator, or other representative of an estate in a foreign proceeding;

(25) "forward contract" means a contract (other than a commodity contract) for the purchase, sale, or transfer of a commodity, as defined in section 761(8) of this title, or any similar good, article, service, right, or interest which is presently or in the future becomes the subject of dealing in the forward contract trade, or product or byproduct thereof, with a maturity date more than two days after the date the contract is entered into, including, but not limited to, a repurchase transaction, reverse repurchase transaction, consignment, lease, swap, hedge transaction, deposit, loan, option, allocated transaction, unallocated transaction, or any combination thereof or option thereon;

(26) "forward contract merchant" means a person whose business consists in whole or in part of entering into forward contracts as or with merchants in a commodity, as defined in section 761(8) of this title, or any similar good, article, service, right, or interest which is presently or in the future becomes the subject of dealing in the forward contract trade;

(27) "governmental unit" means United States; State; Commonwealth; District; Territory; municipality; foreign state; department, agency, or instrumentality of the United States (but not a United States trustee while serving as a trustee in a case under this title), a State, a Commonwealth, a District, a Territory, a municipality, or a foreign state; or other foreign or domestic government;

(28) "indenture" means mortgage, deed of trust, or indenture, under which there is outstanding a security, other than a voting-trust certificate, constituting a claim against the debtor, a claim secured by a lien on any of the debtor's property, or an equity security of the debtor;

(29) "indenture trustee" means trustee under an indenture;

(30) "individual with regular income" means individual whose income is sufficiently stable and regular to enable such individual to make payments under a plan under chapter 13 of this title, other than a stockbroker or a commodity broker;

(31) "insider" includes—

    (A) if the debtor is an individual—

        (i) relative of the debtor or of a general partner of the debtor;

        (ii) partnership in which the debtor is a general partner;

        (iii) general partner of the debtor; or

        (iv) corporation of which the debtor is a director, officer, or person in control;

   (B) if the debtor is a corporation—

     (i) director of the debtor;

     (ii) officer of the debtor;

     (iii) person in control of the debtor;

     (iv) partnership in which the debtor is a general partner;

     (v) general partner of the debtor; or

     (vi) relative of a general partner, director, officer, or person in control of the debtor;

   (C) if the debtor is a partnership—

     (i) general partner in the debtor;

     (ii) relative of a general partner in, general partner of, or person in control of the debtor;

     (iii) partnership in which the debtor is a general partner;

     (iv) general partner of the debtor; or

     (v) person in control of the debtor;

   (D) if the debtor is a municipality, elected official of the debtor or relative of an elected official of the debtor;

   (E) affiliate, or insider of an affiliate as if such affiliate were the debtor; and

   (F) managing agent of the debtor;

(32) "insolvent" means—

   (A) with reference to an entity other than a partnership and a municipality, financial condition such that the sum of such entity's debts is greater than all of such entity's property, at a fair valuation, exclusive of—

     (i) property transferred, concealed, or removed with intent to hinder, delay, or defraud such entity's creditors; and

     (ii) property that may be exempted from property of the estate under section 522 of this title;

   (B) with reference to a partnership, financial condition such that the sum of such partnership's debts is greater than the aggregate of, at a fair valuation—

     (i) all of such partnership's property, exclusive of property of the kind specified in subparagraph (A)(i) of this paragraph; and

     (ii) the sum of the excess of the value of each general partner's nonpartnership property, exclusive of property of the kind specified in subparagraph (A) of this paragraph, over such partner's nonpartnership debts; and

   (C) with reference to a municipality, financial condition such that the municipality is—

     (i) generally not paying its debts as they become due unless such debts are the subject of a bona fide dispute; or

     (ii) unable to pay its debts as they become due;

(33) "institution-affiliated party"—

(A) with respect to an insured depository institution (as defined in section 3(c)(2) of the Federal Deposit Insurance Act), has the meaning given it in section 3(u) of the Federal Deposit Insurance Act (12 U.S.C. 1813(u)); and

(B) with respect to an insured credit union, has the meaning given it in section 206(r) of the Federal Credit Union Act (12 U.S.C. 1786(r));

(34) "insured credit union" has the meaning given it in section 101(7) of the Federal Credit Union Act (12 U.S.C. 1752(7));

(35) "insured depository institution"—

(A) has the meaning given it in section 3(c)(2) of the Federal Deposit Insurance Act (12 U.S.C. 1813(c)(2)); and

(B) includes an insured credit union (except in the case of paragraphs (3) and (33)(A) of this subsection);

(36) "judicial lien" means lien obtained by judgment, levy, sequestration, or other legal or equitable process or proceeding;

(37) "lien" means charge against or interest in property to secure payment of a debt or performance of an obligation;

(38) "margin payment" means, for purposes of the forward contract provisions of this title, payment or deposit of cash, a security or other property, that is commonly known in the forward contract trade as original margin, initial margin, maintenance margin, or variation margin, including mark-to-market payments, or variation payments; and

(39) "settlement payment" means, for purposes of the forward contract provisions of this title, a preliminary settlement payment, a partial settlement payment, an interim settlement payment, a settlement payment on account, a final settlement payment, a net settlement payment, or any other similar payment commonly used in the forward contract trade;

(40) "municipality" means political subdivision or public agency or instrumentality of a State;

(41) "person" includes individual, partnership, and corporation, but does not include governmental unit, *Provided, however,* That any governmental unit that acquires an asset from a person as a result of operation of a loan guarantee agreement, or as receiver or liquidating agent of a person, will be considered a person for purposes of section 1102 of this title.

(42) "petition" means petition filed under section 301, 302, 303, or 304 of this title, as the case may be, commencing a case under this title;

(43) "purchaser" means transferee of a voluntary transfer, and includes immediate or mediate transferee of such a transferee;

(44) "railroad" means common carrier by railroad engaged in the transportation of individuals or property or owner of trackage facilities leased by such a common carrier;

(45) "relative" means individual related by affinity or consanguinity within the third degree as determined by the common law, or individual in a step or adoptive relationship within such third degree;

(46) "repo participant" means an entity that, on any day during the period beginning 90 days before the date of the filing of the petition, has an outstanding repurchase agreement with the debtor;

(47) "repurchase agreement" (which definition also applies to a reverse repurchase agreement) means an agreement, including related terms, which provides for the transfer of certificates of deposit, eligible bankers' acceptances, or securities that are direct obligations of, or that are fully guaranteed as to principal and interest by, the United States or any agency of the United States against the transfer of funds by the transferee of such certificates of deposit, eligible bankers' acceptances, or securities with a simultaneous agreement by such transferee to transfer to the transferor thereof certificates of deposit, eligible bankers' acceptances, or securities as described above, at a date certain not later than one year after such transfers or on demand, against the transfer of funds;

(48) "securities clearing agency" means person that is registered as a clearing agency under section 17A of the Securities Exchange Act of 1934 (15 U.S.C. 78q–1) or whose business is confined to the performance of functions of a clearing agency with respect to exempted securities, as defined in section 3(a)(12) of such Act (15 U.S.C. 78c(12)) for the purposes of such section 17A;

(49) "security"—

(A) includes—

(i) note;

(ii) stock;

(iii) treasury stock;

(iv) bond;

(v) debenture;

(vi) collateral trust certificate;

(vii) pre-organization certificate or subscription;

(viii) transferable share;

(ix) voting-trust certificate;

(x) certificate of deposit;

(xi) certificate of deposit for security;

(xii) investment contract or certificate of interest or participation in a profit-sharing agreement or in an oil, gas, or mineral royalty or lease, if such contract or interest is required to be the subject of a registration statement filed with the Securities and Exchange Commission under the provisions of the Securities Act of 1933 (15 U.S.C. 77a et seq.), or is exempt under section 3(b) of such Act (15 U.S.C. 77c(b)) from the requirement to file such a statement;

(xiii) interest of a limited partner in a limited partnership;

(xiv) other claim or interest commonly known as "security"; and

(xv) certificate of interest or participation in, temporary or interim certificate for, receipt for, or warrant or right to subscribe to or purchase or sell, a security; but

(B) does not include—

(i) currency, check, draft, bill of exchange, or bank letter of credit;

(ii) leverage transaction, as defined in section 761(13) of this title;

(iii) commodity futures contract or forward contract;

(iv) option, warrant, or right to subscribe to or purchase or sell a commodity futures contract;

(v) option to purchase or sell a commodity;

(vi) contract or certificate of a kind specified in subparagraph (A)(xii) of this paragraph that is not required to be the subject of a registration statement filed with the Securities and Exchange Commission and is not exempt under section 3(b) of the Securities Act of 1933 (15 U.S.C. 77c(b)) from the requirement to file such a statement; or

(vii) debt or evidence of indebtedness for goods sold and delivered or services rendered;

(50) "security agreement" means agreement that creates or provides for a security interest;

(51) "security interest" means lien created by an agreement;

(52) "State" includes the District of Columbia and Puerto Rico, except for the purpose of defining who may be a debtor under chapter 9 of this title;

(53) "statutory lien" means lien arising solely by force of a statute on specified circumstances or conditions, or lien of distress for rent, whether or not statutory, but does not include security interest or judicial lien, whether or not such interest or lien is provided by or is dependent on a statute and whether or not such interest or lien is made fully effective by statute;

(54) "transfer" means every mode, direct or indirect, absolute or conditional, voluntary or involuntary, of disposing of or parting with property or with an interest in property, including retention of title as a security interest and foreclosure of the debtor's equity of redemption;

(54)[1] "stockbroker" means person—

(A) with respect to which there is a customer, as defined in section 741(2) of this title; and

(B) that is engaged in the business of effecting transactions in securities—

(i) for the account of others; or

(ii) with members of the general public, from or for such person's own account;

(55) "United States", when used in a geographical sense, includes all locations where the judicial jurisdiction of the United States extends, including territories and possessions of the United States;

(55)[1] "swap agreement" means—

(A) an agreement (including terms and conditions incorporated by reference therein) which is a rate swap agreement, basis swap, forward rate agreement, commodity swap, interest rate option, forward foreign exchange agreement, rate cap agreement, rate floor agreement, rate collar agreement, currency swap agreement, cross-currency rate swap agreement, currency option, any other similar agreement (including any option to enter into any of the foregoing);

(B) any combination of the foregoing; or

(C) a master agreement for any of the foregoing together with all supplements;

(56) "intellectual property" means—

(A) trade secret;

(B) invention, process, design, or plant protected under title 35;

(C) patent application;

(D) plant variety;

(E) work of authorship protected under title 17; or

(F) mask work protected under chapter 9 of title 17; to the extent protected by applicable nonbankruptcy law; and

(56)[1] "swap participant" means an entity that, at any time before the filing of the petition, has an outstanding swap agreement with the debtor;

(57) "mask work" has the meaning given it in section 901(a)(2) of title 17.

(57)[1] "timeshare plan" means and shall include that interest purchased in any arrangement, plan, scheme, or similar device, but not including exchange programs, whether by membership, agreement, tenancy in common, sale, lease, deed, rental agreement, license, right to use agreement, or by any other means, whereby a purchaser, in exchange for consideration, receives a right to use accommodations, facilities, or recreational sites, whether improved or unimproved, for a specific period of time less than a full year during any given year, but not necessarily for consecutive years, and which extends for a period of more than three years. A "timeshare interest" is that interest purchased in a timeshare plan which grants the purchaser the right to use and occupy accommodations, facilities, or recreational sites, whether improved or unimproved, pursuant to a timeshare plan.

Pub.L. 95–598, Nov. 6, 1978, 92 Stat. 2549; Pub.L. 97–222, § 1, July 27, 1982, 96 Stat. 235; Pub.L. 98–353, Title III, §§ 391, 401, 421, July 10, 1984, 98 Stat. 364, 366, 367; Pub.L. 99–554, Title II, §§ 201, 251, 283(a), Oct. 27, 1986, 100 Stat. 3097, 3104, 3116; Pub.L. 100–506, § 1(a), Oct. 18, 1988, 102 Stat. 2538; Pub.L. 100–597, § 1, Nov. 3, 1988, 102 Stat. 3028; Pub.L. 101–311, Title I, § 101, Title II, § 201, June 25, 1990, 104 Stat. 267, 269; Pub.L. 101–647, Title XXV, § 2522(e), Nov. 29, 1990, 104 Stat. 4867.

[1] See Codification note below.

Historical and Revision Notes

Notes of Committee on the Judiciary, Senate Report No. 95–989. Section 101 of title 11 contains 40 definitions:

Paragraph (1) defines "accountant" as an accountant authorized under applicable law to practice accounting. The term includes a professional accounting association, corporation, or partnership if applicable law authorizes such a unit to practice accounting.

Paragraph (2) defines "affiliate." An affiliate is an entity with a close relationship to the debtor. It includes a 20 percent parent or subsidiary of the debtor, whether a corporate, partnership, individual, or estate parent.

The use of "directly or indirectly" in subparagraphs (A) and (B) is intended to cover situations in which there is an opportunity to control, and where the existence of that opportunity operates as indirect control.

"Affiliate" is defined primarily for use in the definition of insider, infra, and for use in the chapter 11 reorganization cases. The definition of "affiliate" does not include an entity acting in a fiduciary or agency capacity if the entity does not have the sole discretionary power to vote 20 percent of the voting securities but hold them solely as security and have not exercised the power to vote. This restriction applies to a corporate affiliate under subparagraph (B) of paragraph (2).

Subsections (C) and (D) of paragraph (2) define affiliate also as those persons and entities whose business or substantially all of whose property is operated under a lease or operating agreement by a debtor and whose business or property is more than 50 percent under the control of the debtor.

The definition of "attorney" in paragraph (3) is similar to the definition of accountant.

Paragraph (4) defines "claim." The effect of the definition is a significant departure from present law. Under present law, "claim" is not defined in straight bankruptcy. Instead it is simply used, along with the concept of provability in section 63 of the Bankruptcy Act [former section 103 of this title], to limit the kinds of obligations that are payable in a bankruptcy case. The term is defined in the debtor rehabilitation chapters of present law far more broadly. The definition in paragraph (4) adopts an even broader definition of claim than is found in the present debtor rehabilitation chapters. The definition is any right to payment, whether or not reduced to judgment, liquidated, unliquidated, fixed, contingent, matured, unmatured, disputed, undisputed, legal, equitable, secured, or unsecured. The definition also includes as a claim an equitable right to performance that does not give rise to a right to payment. By this broadest possible definition and by the use of the term throughout the title 11, especially in subchapter I of chapter 5, the bill contemplates that all legal obligations of the debtor, no matter how remote or contingent, will be able to be dealt with in the bankruptcy case. It permits the broadest possible relief in the bankruptcy court.

Paragraph (5) defines "commodity broker" by reference to various terms used and defined in subchapter IV of chapter 7, Commodi-ty Broker Liquidation. The terms are described in connection with section 761, infra.

Paragraph (6) defines "community claim" for those eight States that have community property laws. The definition is keyed to the liability of the debtor's property for a claim against either the debtor or the debtor's spouse. If the debtor's property is liable for a claim against either, that claim is a community claim.

Paragraph (7) defines "consumer debt". The definition is adapted from the definition used in various consumer protection laws. It encompasses only a debt incurred by an individual primarily for a personal, family, or household purpose.

The definition of "corporation" in paragraph (8) is similar to the definition in current law, section 1(8) [former section 1(8) of this title]. The term encompasses any association having the power or privilege that a private corporation, but not an individual or partnership, has; partnership associations organized under a law that makes only the capital subscribed responsible for the debts of the partnership; joint-stock company; unincorporated company or association; and business trust. "Unincorporated association" is intended specifically to include a labor union, as well as other bodies that come under that phrase as used under current law. The exclusion of limited partnerships is explicit, and not left to the case law.

Paragraph (9) [deleted by House amendment] defines "court" as the bankruptcy judge in the district in which the case is pending except in municipal adjustment and railroad reorganization cases, where "court" means the Federal district judge.

Paragraph (10) [now (9)] defines "creditor" to include holders of prepetition claims against the debtor. However, it also encompasses certain holders of claims that are deemed to arise before the date of the filing of the petition, such as those injured by the rejection of an executory contract or unexpired lease, certain investment tax credit recapture claim holders, "involuntary gap" creditors, and certain holders of the right of setoff. The term also includes the holder of a prepetition community claim. A guarantor of or surety for a claim against the debtor is also a creditor, because he holds a contingent claim against the debtor that becomes fixed when he pays the creditor whose claim he has guaranteed or insured.

Paragraph (11) [now (10)] defines "custodian." There is no similar definition in current law. It is defined to facilitate drafting, and means a prepetition liquidator of the debtor's property, such as an assignee for the benefit of creditors, a receiver of the debtor's property, or administrator of the debtor's property. The definition of custodian to include a receiver or trustee is descriptive, and not meant to be limited to court officers with those titles. The definition is intended to include other officers of the court if their functions are substantially similar to those of a receiver or trustee.

"Debt" is defined in paragraph (12) [now (11)] as a liability on a claim. The terms "debt" and "claim" are coextensive: a creditor has a "claim" against the debtor; the debtor owes a "debt" to the creditor. This definition of "debt" and the definition of "claim" on which it is based, proposed 11 U.S.C. 101(4), does not include a transaction such as a policy loan on an insurance policy. Under that kind of transaction, the debtor is not liable to the insurance company for repayment; the amount owed is merely available to the company for setoff against any benefits that become payable under the policy. As such, the loan is not a claim (it is not a right to payment) that the company can assert against the estate; nor is the debtor's obligation a debt (a liability on a claim) that will be discharged under proposed 11 U.S.C. 523 or 524.

Paragraph (13) [now (12)] defines "debtor." Debtor means person or municipality concerning which a case under title 11 has been commenced. This is a change in terminology from present law, which identifies the person by or against whom a petition is filed in a straight bankruptcy liquidation case as the "bankrupt", and a person or municipality that is proceeding under a debtor rehabilitation chapter (chapters VIII through XIII of the Bankruptcy Act) [former sections 201 et seq., 301 et seq., 501 et seq., 701 et seq., 801 et seq. and 1001 et seq. of this title] as a "debtor." The term "debtor" is used for both kinds of cases in this bill, for ease of reference in chapters 1, 3, and 5 (which apply to straight bankruptcy and reorganization cases).

Paragraph (14) [now (13)] defines "disinterested person." The definition is adapted from section 158 of chapter X of current law [former section 558 of this title], though it is expanded and modified in some respects. A person is a disinterested person if the person is not a creditor, equity security holder, or insider; is not and was not an investment banker of the debtor for any outstanding security of the debtor (the change from underwriter in current law to investment banker is to make the term more descriptive and to avoid conflict with the definition of underwriter in section 2(11) of the Securities Act of 1933 (15 U.S.C. 77b(11)) [section 77b(11) of Title 15, Commerce and Trade]; has not been an investment banker for a security of the debtor within 3 years before the date of the filing of the petition (the change from five years to three years here conforms the definition with the statute of limitations in the Securities Act of 1933) [section 77m of Title 15], or an attorney for such an investment banker; is not an insider of the debtor or of such an investment banker; and does not have an interest materially adverse to the estate.

"Entity" is defined, for convenience, in paragraph (15) [now (14)], to include person, estate, trust, and governmental unit. It is the most inclusive of the various defined terms relating to bodies or units.

Paragraph (16) [now (15)] defines "equity security." The term includes a share or stock in a corporation, a limited partner's interest in a limited partnership, and a warrant or right to subscribe to an equity security. The term does not include a security, such as a convertible debenture, that is convertible into equity security, but has not been converted.

Paragraph (17) [now (16)] defines "equity security holder" for convenience as the holder of an equity securing of the debtor.

Paragraph (18) [now (19)] defines "farmer". It encompasses only those persons for whom farming operations contribute 75 percent or more of their total income.

Paragraphs (19) and (20) [now (22) and (23)] define "foreign proceeding" and "foreign representative". A foreign proceeding is a proceeding in another country in which the debtor has some substantial connection for the purpose of liquidating the estate of the debtor or the purpose of financial rehabilitation of the debtor. A foreign representative is the representative of the estate in a foreign proceeding, such as a trustee or administrator.

Paragraph (21) [now (26)] defines "governmental unit" in the broadest sense. The definition encompasses the United States, a State, Commonwealth, District, Territory, municipality, or foreign state, and a department, agency, or instrumentality of any of those entities. "Department, agency, or instrumentality" does not include an entity that owes its existence to State action, such as the granting of a charter or a license but that has no other connection with a State or local government or the Federal Government. The relationship must be an active one in which the department, agency, or instrumentality is actually carrying out some governmental function.

Paragraph (22) [now (27)] defines "indenture." It is similar to the definition of indenture in the Trust Indenture Act of 1939 [section 77aaa et seq. of Title 15, Commerce and Trade]. An indenture is the instrument under which securities, either debt or equity, of the debtor are outstanding.

Paragraph (23) [now (28)] defines "indenture trustee" as the trustee under an indenture.

Paragraph (24) [now (29)] defines "individual with regular income." The effect of this definition, and of its use in section 109(e), is to expand substantially the kinds of individuals that are eligible for relief under chapter 13, Adjustment of Debts of an Individual with Regular Income. Chapter XIII [former section 1001 et seq. of this title] is now available only for wage earners. The definition encompasses all individuals with incomes that are sufficiently stable and regular to enable them to make payments under a chapter 13 plan. Thus, individuals on welfare, social security, fixed pension incomes, or who live on investment incomes, will be able to work out repayment plans with their creditors rather than being forced into straight bankruptcy. Also, self-employed individuals will be eligible to use chapter 13 if they have regular incomes.

However, the definition excludes certain stockbrokers and commodity brokers, in order to prohibit them from proceeding under chapter 13 and avoiding the customer protection provisions of chapter 7.

"Insider", defined in paragraph (25) [now (30)], is a new term. An insider is one who has a sufficiently close relationship with the debtor that his conduct is made subject to closer scrutiny than those dealing at arms length with the debtor. If the debtor is an individual, then a relative of the debtor, a partnership in which the debtor is a general partner, a general partner of the debtor, and a corporation controlled by the debtor are all insiders. If the debtor is a corporation, then a controlling person, a relative of a controlling person, a partnership in which the debtor is a general partner, and a general partner of the debtor are all insiders. If the debtor is a partnership, then a general partner of or in the debtor, a relative of a general partner in

the debtor, and a person in control are all insiders. If the debtor is a municipality, then an elected official of the debtor is an insider. In addition, affiliates of the debtor and managing agents are insiders.

The definition of "insolvent" in paragraph (26) [now (31)] is adopted from section 1(19) of current law [former section 1(19) of this title]. An entity is insolvent if its debts are greater than its assets, at a fair valuation, exclusive of property exempted or fraudulently transferred. It is the traditional bankruptcy balance sheet test of insolvency. For a partnership, the definition is modified to account for the liability of a general partner for the partnership's debts. The difference in this definition from that in current law is in the exclusion of exempt property for all purposes in the definition of insolvent.

Paragraph (27) [now (32)] defines "judicial lien." It is one of three kinds of liens defined in this section. A judicial lien is a lien obtained by judgment, levy, sequestration, or other legal or equitable process or proceeding.

Paragraph (28) [now (33)] defines "lien." The definition is new and is very broad. A lien is defined as a charge against or interest in property to secure payment of a debt or performance of an obligation. It includes inchoate liens. In general, the concept of lien is divided into three kinds of liens: judicial liens, security interests, and statutory liens. Those three categories are mutually exclusive and are exhaustive except for certain common law liens.

Paragraph (29) [now (34)] defines "municipality." The definition is adapted from the terms used in the chapter IX (municipal bankruptcy) amendment to the Bankruptcy Act enacted in 1976 (Pub.L. 94–260) [amending former section 401 et seq. of this title]. That amendment spoke in terms of "political subdivision or public agency or instrumentality of a State". Bankruptcy Act Sec. 84 [former section 404 of this title]. The term municipality is defined by those three terms for convenience. It does not include the District of Columbia or any territories of the United States.

"Person" is defined in paragraph (30) [now (35)]. The definition is a change in wording, but not in substance, from the definition in section 1(23) of the Bankruptcy Act [former section 1(23) of this title]. The definition is also similar to the one contained in 1 U.S.C. sec. 1 [section 1 of Title 1, General Provisions], but is repeated here for convenience and ease of reference. Person includes individual partnership, and corporation. The exclusion of governmental units is made explicit in order to avoid any confusion that may arise if, for example, a municipality is incorporated and thus is legally a corporation as well as governmental unit. The definition does not include an estate or a trust, which are included only in the definition of "entity" in proposed 11 U.S.C. 101(14).

"Petition" is defined for convenience in paragraph (31) [now (36)]. Petition is a petition under section 301, 302, 303, or 304 of the bankruptcy code—that is, a petition that commences a case under title 11.

Paragraph (32) [now (37)] defines purchaser as a transferee of a voluntary transfer, such as a sale or gift, and includes an immediate or mediate transferee of a purchaser.

The definition of "railroad" in paragraph (33) [now (38)] is derived from section 77 of the Bankruptcy Act [former section 205 of this title]. A railroad is a common carrier by railroad engaged in the transportation of individuals or property, or an owner of trackage facilities leased by such a common carrier. The effect of the definition and the use of the term in section 109(d) is to eliminate the limitation now found in section 77 of the Bankruptcy Act [former section 205 of this title] that only railroads engaged in interstate commerce may proceed under the railroad reorganization provisions. The limitation may have been inserted because of a doubt that the commerce power could not reach intrastate railroads. Be that as it may, this bill is enacted under the bankruptcy power.

Paragraph (34) [now (39)] defines "relative" as an individual related by affinity or consanguinity within the third degree as determined by the common law, and includes individuals in a step or adoptive relationship. The definition is similar to current law, but adds the latter phrase. This definition should be applied as of the time when the transaction that it concerns took place. Thus, a former spouse is not a relative, but if, for example, for purposes of the preference section, proposed 11 U.S.C. 547(b)(4)(B), the transferee was a spouse of the debtor at the time of the transfer sought to be avoided, then the transferee would be relative and subject to the insider rules, even if the transferee was no longer married to the debtor at the time of the commencement of the case or at the time of the commencement of the preference recovery proceeding.

Paragraph (35) [now (43)] defines "security." The definition is new and is modeled on the most recent draft of the American Law Institute's proposed securities code, with some exceptions. The interest of a limited partner in a limited partnership is included in order to make sure that everything that is defined as an equity security is also a "security." The definition, as with the definition of "entity", "insider", and "person", is open-ended because the term is not susceptible to precise specification. Thus the courts will be able to use the characterization provided in this definition to treat with new kinds of documents on a flexible basis.

Paragraphs (36) and (37) [now (44) and (45)] defined "security agreement" and "security interest." A security interest is one of the kinds of liens. It is a lien created by an agreement. Security agreement is defined as the agreement creating the security interest. Though these terms are similar to the same terms in the Uniform Commercial Code, article IX, they are broader. For example, the U.C.C. does not cover real property mortgages. Under this definition, such a mortgage is included, as are all other liens created by agreement, even though not covered by the U.C.C. All U.C.C. security interests and security agreements are, however, security interests and security agreements under this definition. Whether a consignment or a lease constitutes a security interest under the bankruptcy code [this title] will depend on whether it constitutes a security interest under applicable State or local law.

Paragraph (38) [now (47)] defines another kind of lien, "statutory lien." The definition, derived from current law, states that a statutory lien is a lien arising solely by force of statute on specified circumstances or conditions and includes a lien of distress for rent (whether statutory, common law, or otherwise). The definition excludes judicial liens and security interests, whether or not they are provided for or are dependent on a statute, and whether or not they are made fully effective by statute. A statutory lien is only one that arises automatically, and is not based on an agreement to give a lien or on judicial action. Mechanics', materialmen's, and warehousemen's liens are examples. Tax liens are also included in the definition of statutory lien.

"Stockbroker" is defined in paragraph (39) [now (48)] as a person engaged in the business of effecting transactions in securities for the account of others or with members of the general public from or for such person's own account, if the person has a customer, as defined. Thus, the definition, derived from a combination of the definitions of "broker" and "dealer" in the Securities Exchange Act of 1934 [section 77b of Title 15, Commerce and Trade], encompasses both brokers and dealers. The definition is used in section 109 and in subchapter III of chapter 7, Stockholder Liquidation. The term does not encompass an employee who acts for a principal that "effects" transaction or deals with the public, because such an employee will not have a "customer".

Paragraph (40) [now (50)] defines "transfer." It is derived and adapted, with stylistic changes, from section 1(30) of the Bankruptcy Act [former section 1(30) of this title]. A transfer is a disposition of an interest in property. The definition of transfer is as broad as possible. Many of the potentially limiting words in current law are deleted, and the language is simplified. Under this definition, any transfer of an interest in property is a transfer, including a transfer of possession, custody, or control even if there is no transfer of title, because possession, custody, and control are interests in property. A deposit in a bank account or similar account is a transfer.

Legislative Statements. Section 101(2) defines "affiliate." The House amendment contains a provision that is a compromise between the definition in the House-passed version of H.R. 8200, subparagraphs (A) and (B) are derived from the Senate amendment and subparagraph (D) is taken from the House bill, while subparagraph (C) represents a compromise, taking the House position with respect to a person whose business is operated under a lease or an operating agreement by the debtor and with respect to a person substantially all of whose property is operated under an operating agreement by the debtor and with respect to a person substantially all of whose property is operated under an operating agreement by the debtor and the Senate position on leased property. Thus, the definition of "affiliate" excludes persons substantially all of whose property is operated under a lease agreement by a debtor, such as a small company which owns equipment all of which is leased to a larger nonrelated company.

Section 101(4)(B) represents a modification of the House-passed bill to include the definition of "claim" a right to an equitable remedy for breach of performance if such breach gives rise to a right to payment. This is intended to cause the liquidation or estimation of contingent rights of payment for which there may

be an alternative equitable remedy with the result that the equitable remedy will be susceptible to being discharged in bankruptcy. For example, in some States, a judgment for specific performance may be satisfied by an alternative right to payment, in the event performance is refused; in that event, the creditor entitled to specific performance would have a "claim" for purposes of a proceeding under title 11.

On the other hand, rights to an equitable remedy for a breach of performance with respect to which such breach does not give rise to a right to payment are not "claims" and would therefore not be susceptible to discharge in bankruptcy.

In a case under chapter 9 to title 11, "claim" does not include a right to payment under an industrial development bond issued by a municipality as a matter of convenience for a third party.

Municipalities are authorized, under section 103(c) of the Internal Revenue Code of 1954, as amended [section 103(c) of Title 26, Internal Revenue Code], to issue tax-exempt industrial development revenue bonds to provide for the financing of certain projects for privately owned companies. The bonds are sold on the basis of the credit of the company on whose behalf they are issued, and the principal, interest, and premium, if any, are payable solely from payments made by the company to the trustee under the bond indenture and do not constitute claims on the tax revenues or other funds of the issuing municipalities. The municipality merely acts as the vehicle to enable the bonds to be issued on a tax-exempt basis. Claims that arise by virtue of these bonds are not among the claims defined by this paragraph and amounts owed by private companies to the holders of industrial development revenue bonds are not to be included among the assets of the municipality that would be affected by the plan.

Section 101(6) defines "community claim" as provided by the Senate amendment in order to indicate that a community claim exists whether or not there is community property in the estate as of the commencement of the case.

Section 101(7) of the House amendment contains a definition of consumer debt identical to the definition in the House bill and Senate amendment. A consumer debt does not include a debt to any extent the debt is secured by real property.

Section 101(9) of the Senate amendment contained a definition of "court." The House amendment deletes the provision as unnecessary in light of the pervasive jurisdiction of a bankruptcy court under all chapters of title 11 as indicated in title II of the House amendment to H.R. 8200.

Section 101(11) defines "debt" to mean liability on a claim, as was contained in the House-passed version of H.R. 8200. The Senate amendment contained language indicating that "debt" does not include a policy loan made by a life insurance company to the debtor. That language is deleted in the House amendment as unnecessary since a life insurance company clearly has no right to have a policy loan repaid by the debtor, although such company does have a right of offset with respect to such policy loan. Clearly, then, a "debt" does not include a policy loan made by a life insurance company. Inclusion of the language contained in the Senate amendment would have required elaboration of other legal relationships not arising by a liability on a claim. Further the language would have required clarification that interest on a policy loan made by a life insurance company is a debt, and that the insurance company does have right to payment to that interest.

Section 101(14) adopts the definition of "entity" contained in the Senate-passed version of H.R. 8200. Since the Senate amendment to H.R. 8200 deleted the U.S. trustee, a corresponding definitional change is made in chapter 15 of the House amendment for U.S. trustees under the pilot program. Adoption by the House amendment of a pilot program for U.S. trustees under chapter 15 requires insertion of "United States trustee" in many sections. Several provisions in chapter 15 of the House amendment that relate to the U.S. trustee were not contained in the Senate amendment in the nature of a substitute.

Section 101(17) defines "farmer," as in the Senate amendment with an income limitation percentage of 80 percent instead of 75 percent.

Section 101(18) contains a new definition of "farming operation" derived from present law and the definition of "farmer" in the Senate amendment. This definition gives a broad construction to the term "farming operation."

Section 101(20) contains a definition of "foreign representative". It clarifies the House bill and Senate amendment by indicating that a foreign representative must be duly selected in a foreign proceeding.

Section 101(35) [now (43)] defines "security" as contained in the Senate amendment. H.R. 8200 as adopted by the House excluded certain commercial notes from the definition of "security", and that exclusion is deleted.

Section 101(40) [now (50)] defines "transfer" as in the Senate amendment. The definition contained in H.R. 8200 as passed by the House included "setoff" in the definition of "transfer". Inclusion of "setoff" is deleted. The effect is that a "setoff" is not subject to being set aside as a preferential "transfer" but will be subject to special rules.

References in Text. The Securities Act of 1933, referred to in par. (49)(xii), is Title I of Act May 27, 1933, c. 38, 48 Stat. 74, which is classified to section 77a et seq. of Title 15, Commerce and Trade.

Section 3(b) of such Act, referred to in par. (49)(xii), is section 3(b) of the Securities Act of 1933, which is classified to section 77c(b) of Title 15.

Codification. Renumbering and conforming amendments by Pub.L. 101–647 failed to take into consideration prior renumbering and conforming amendments by Pub.L. 101–311, thereby resulting in two pars. numbered "(54)", "(55)", "(56)", and "(57)". To accommodate such duplications, the renumberings reflect changes by Pub.L. 101–311 set out first, and Pub.L. 101–647 set out second, but do not reflect the minor conforming amendments.

1986 Amendment. Par. (14). Pub.L. 99–554, § 201(1), substituted "trust, governmental unit, and United States trustee" for "trust, and governmental unit".

Par. (26). Pub.L. 99–554, § 201(2), substituted "of the United States (but not a United States trustee while serving as a trustee in a case under this title), a State" for "of the United States, a State".

See Effective Date of 1986 Amendment, etc., notes set out below.

Effective Date of 1988 Amendments; Application of Amendments. Section 2 of Pub.L. 100–506 provided that:

"(a) Effective Date.—Except as provided in subsection (b), this Act and the amendments made by this Act [enacting par. (52) and par. (53) of this section and section 365(n) of this title] shall take effect on the date of the enactment of this Act [Oct. 18, 1988].

"(b) Application of Amendments.—The amendments made by this Act shall not apply with respect to any case commenced under title 11 of the United States Code [this title] before the date of the enactment of this Act [Oct. 18, 1988]."

Section 12 of Pub.L. 100–597 provided that:

"(a) Effective Date.—Except as provided in subsection (b), this Act and the amendments made by this Act [enacting sections 927 to 929 of this title, amending this section and sections 109, 901, 902, 922, 926 and 943 of this title, and renumbering former section 927 as 930 of this title] shall take effect on the date of the enactment of this Act [Nov. 3, 1988].

"(b) Application of Amendments.—The amendments made by this Act shall not apply with respect to cases commenced under title 11 of the United States Code [this title] before the date of the enactment of this Act [Nov. 3, 1988]."

Effective Date of 1986 Amendments; Savings Provisions; Effective Date of 1986 Amendments for Certain Judicial Districts Not Served by United States Trustees and for Judicial District in Alabama and North Carolina; U.S. Trustee System Fund Deposits in Alabama and North Carolina; Effective Date of Title 11, Chapter 15, Repeal as to Northern District of Alabama; Authority of Certain Estate Administrators in Alabama and North Carolina; Effective Date of 1986 Amendments in Pending Cases Where a U.S. Trustee Not Authorized or Where a Trustee Files Final Report or Plan is Confirmed; Quarterly Fees. Amendment by Pub.L. 99–554 effective 30 days after Oct. 27, 1986, except as otherwise provided for, see section 302(a) of Pub.L. 99–554, set out as a note under section 581 of Title 28, Judiciary and Judicial Procedure.

Amendments by Pub.L. 99–554, § 251, not to apply with respect to cases commenced under Title 11, Bankruptcy, before 30 days after Oct. 27, 1986, see section 302(c)(1) of Pub. L. 99–554, set out as a note under section 581 of Title 28.

Amendment by Pub.L. 99–554, § 201, not to become effective in or with respect to certain specified judicial districts until, or apply to cases while pending in such district before, the expiration of the 270-day period beginning 30 days after Oct. 27, 1986, or of the 30-day period beginning on the date the Attorney General certifies under section 303 of Pub.L. 99–554 the region specified in a paragraph of section 581(a) of Title 28, as amended by section 111(a) of Pub.L. 99–554, that includes such district, whichever occurs first, see sec-

tion 302(d)(1) of Pub.L. 99–554, set out as a note under section 581 of Title 28.

Amendment by Pub.L. 99–554, § 201, not to become effective in or with respect to certain specified judicial districts until, or apply to cases while pending in such district before, the expiration of the 2-year period beginning 30 days after Oct. 27, 1986, or of the 30-day period beginning on the date the Attorney General certifies under section 303 of Pub.L. 99–554 the region specified in a paragraph of section 581(a) of Title 28, as amended by section 111(a) of Pub.L. 99–554, that includes such district, whichever occurs first, see section 302(d)(2) of Pub.L. 99–554, set out as a note under section 581 of Title 28.

Amendment by Pub.L. 99–554, § 201, not to become effective in or with respect to judicial districts established for the States of Alabama and North Carolina until, or apply to cases while pending in such district before, such district elects to be included in a bankruptcy region established in section 581(a) of Title 28, as amended by section 111(a) of Pub.L. 99–554, or Oct. 1, 2002, whichever occurs first, and, except as otherwise provided for, with respect to cases under chapters 7, 11, 12, and 13 of Title 11 commenced before 30 days after Oct. 27, 1986, and pending in a judicial district in the States of Alabama or North Carolina before any election made under section 302(d)(3) (A) of Pub.L. 99–554 by such district becomes effective or Oct. 1, 2002, whichever occurs first, amendments, by Pub.L. 99–554 not to apply until Oct. 1, 2003, or the expiration of the 1-year period beginning on the date such election becomes effective, whichever occurs first, and further, in any judicial district in Alabama or North Carolina not making the election described in section 302(d)(3)(A) of Pub.L. 99–554, any person appointed under regulations issued by the Judicial Conference to administer estates in cases under Title 11 authorized to establish, etc., a panel of private trustees, and to supervise cases and trustees in cases under chapters 7, 11, 12, and 13 of Title 11, until amendments by sections 201 to 231 of Pub.L. 99–554 effective in such district, see section 302(d)(3)(A) to (F), (H), (I) of Pub.L. 99–554, set out as a note under section 581 of Title 28.

Amendment by Pub.L. 99–554, § 201, except as otherwise provided, with respect to cases under chapters 7, 11, 12, and 13 of Title 11 commenced before 30 days after Oct. 27, 1986, and pending in a judicial district referred to in section 581(a) of Title 28, as amended by section 111(a) of Pub.L. 99–554, for which a United States trustee is not authorized before 30 days after Oct. 27, 1986 to be appointed, not applicable until the expiration of the 3-year period beginning on Oct. 27, 1986, or of the 1-year period beginning on the date the Attorney General certifies section 303 of Pub.L. 99–554 the region specified in a paragraph of such section 581(a) that includes, such district, whichever occurs first, see section 302(e)(1), (2) of Pub.L. 99–554, set out as a note under section 581 of Title 28.

See 1986 Amendment notes set out above.

Effective Date of 1984 Amendments. See section 553 of Pub.L. 98–353, Title III, July 10, 1984, 98 Stat. 392, set out as an Effective Date of 1984 Amendment note preceding chapter 1 of Title 11, Bankruptcy.

Separability of Provisions. For separability of provisions of Title III of Pub.L. 98–353, see section 551 of Pub.L. 98–353 set out as a Separability of Provisions note preceding chapter 1 of Title 11, Bankruptcy.

Library References:
C.J.S. Bankruptcy § 2.
West's Key No. Digests, Bankruptcy ⊕2001, 2021, 2022.

WESTLAW Electronic Research
See WESTLAW Electronic Research Guide following the *Bankruptcy Highlights*.

§ 102. Rules of construction

In this title—

(1) "after notice and a hearing", or a similar phrase—

(A) means after such notice as is appropriate in the particular circumstances, and such opportunity for a hearing as is appropriate in the particular circumstances; but

(B) authorizes an act without an actual hearing if such notice is given properly and if—

(i) such a hearing is not requested timely by a party in interest; or

(ii) there is insufficient time for a hearing to be commenced before such act must be done, and the court authorizes such act;

(2) "claim against the debtor" includes claim against property of the debtor;

(3) "includes" and "including" are not limiting;

(4) "may not" is prohibitive, and not permissive;

(5) "or" is not exclusive;

(6) "order for relief" means entry of an order for relief;

(7) the singular includes the plural;

(8) a definition, contained in a section of this title that refers to another section of this title, does not, for the purpose of such reference, affect the meaning of a term used in such other section; and

(9) United States trustee includes a designee of the United States trustee.

Pub.L. 95–598, Nov. 6, 1978, 92 Stat. 2554; Pub.L. 98–353, Title III, § 422, July 10, 1984, 98 Stat. 369; Pub.L. 99–554, Title II, § 202, Oct. 27, 1986, 100 Stat. 3097.

Historical and Revision Notes

Notes of Committee on the Judiciary, Senate Report No. 95–989. Section 102 provides seven rules of construction. Some are derived from current law; others are derived from 1 U.S.C. 1 [section 1 of Title 1, General Provisions]; a few are new. They apply generally throughout proposed title 11. These are terms that are not appropriate for definition, but that require an explanation.

Paragraph (1) defines the concept of "after notice and a hearing." The concept is central to the bill and to the separation of the administrative and judicial functions of bankruptcy judges. The phrase means after such notice as is appropriate in the particular circumstances (to be prescribed by either the Rules of Bankruptcy Procedure or by the court in individual circumstances that the Rules do not cover. In many cases, the Rules will provide for combined notice of several proceedings), and such opportunity for a hearing as is appropriate in the particular circumstances. Thus, a hearing will not be necessary in every instance. If there is no objection to the proposed action, the action may go ahead without court action. This is a significant change from present law, which requires the affirmative approval of the bankruptcy judge for almost every action. The change will permit the bankruptcy judge to stay removed from the administration of the bankruptcy or reorganization case, and to become involved only when there is a dispute about a proposed action, that is, only when there is an objection. The phrase "such opportunity for a hearing as is appropriate in the particular circumstances" is designed to permit the Rules and the courts to expedite or dispense with hearings when speed is essential. The language "or similar phrase" is intended to cover the few instances in the bill where "after notice and a hearing" is interrupted by another phrase, such as "after notice to the debtor and a hearing."

Paragraph (2) specifies that "claim against the debtor" includes claim against property of the debtor. This paragraph is intended to cover nonrecourse loan agreements where the creditor's only rights are against property of the debtor, and not against the debtor personally. Thus, such an agreement would give rise to a claim that would be treated as a claim against the debtor personally, for the purposes of the bankruptcy code [this title].

Paragraph (3) is a codification of American Surety Co. v. Marotta, 287 U.S. 513 (1933) [53 S.Ct. 260, 77 L.Ed. 466]. It specifies that "includes" and "including" are not limiting.

Paragraph (4) specifies that "may not" is prohibitive and not permissive (such as in "might not").

Paragraph (5) specifies that "or" is not exclusive. Thus, if a party "may do (a) or (b)", then the party may do either or both. The party is not limited to a mutually exclusive choice between the two alternatives.

Paragraph (6) makes clear that "order for relief" means entry of an order for relief. If the court orally orders relief, but the order is not entered until a later time, then any time measurements in the bill are from entry, not from the oral order. In a voluntary case, the entry of the order for relief is the filing of the petition commencing the voluntary case.

Paragraph (7) specifies that the singular includes the plural. The plural, however, generally does not include the singular. The bill uses only the singular, even when the item in question most often is found in plural quantities, in order to avoid the confusion possible if both rules of construction applied. When an item is specified in the plural, the plural is intended.

Legislative Statements. Section 102 specifies various rules of construction but is not exclusive. Other rules of construction that are not set out in title 11 are nevertheless intended to be followed in construing the bankruptcy code [this title]. For example, the phrase "on request of a party in interest" or a similar phrase, is used in connection with an action that the court may take in various sections of the Code. The phrase is intended to restrict the court from acting sua sponte. Rules of bankruptcy procedure or court decisions will determine who is a party in interest for the particular purposes of the provision in question, but the court will not be permitted to act on its own.

Although "property" is not construed in this section, it is used consistently throughout the code in its broadest sense, including cash, all interests in property, such as liens, and every kind of consideration including promises to act or forbear to act as in section 548(d).

Section 102(1) expands on a rule of construction contained in H.R. 8200 as passed by the House and in the Senate amendment. The phrase "after notice and a hearing", or a similar phrase, is intended to be construed according to the particular proceeding to mean after such notice as is appropriate in the particular circumstances, and such opportunity, if any, for a hearing as is appropriate in the particular circumstances. If a provision of title 11 authorizes an act to be taken "after notice and a hearing" this means that if appropriate notice is given and no party to whom such notice is sent timely requests a hearing, then the act sought to be taken may be taken without an actual hearing.

In very limited emergency circumstances, there will be insufficient time for a hearing to be commenced before an action must be taken. The action sought to be taken may be taken if authorized by the court at an ex parte hearing of which a record is made in open court. A full hearing after the fact will be available in such an instance.

In some circumstances, such as under section 1128, the bill requires a hearing and the court may act only after a hearing is held. In those circumstances the judge will receive evidence before ruling. In other circumstances, the court may take action "after notice and a hearing," if no party in interest requests a hearing. In that event a court order authorizing the action to be taken is not necessary as the ultimate action taken by the court implies such an authorization.

Section 102(8) is new. It contains a rule of construction indicating that a definition contained in a section in title 11 that refers to another section of title 11 does not, for the purposes of such reference, take the meaning of a term used in the other section. For example, section 522(a)(2) defines "value" for the purposes of section 522. Section 548(d)(2) defines "value" for purposes of section 548. When section 548 is incorporated by reference in section 522, this rule of construction makes clear that the definition of "value" in section 548 governs its meaning in section 522 notwithstanding a different definition of "value" in section 522(a)(2).

1986 Amendment. Par. (9). Pub.L. 99–554, § 202, added par. (9).

See Effective Date of 1986 Amendment, etc., notes set out below.

Effective Date of 1986 Amendments; Effective Date of 1986 Amendments for Certain Judicial Districts Not Served by United States Trustees and for Judicial Districts in Alabama and North Carolina; U.S. Trustee System Fund Deposits in Ala-bama and North Carolina; **Effective Date of Title 11, Chapter 15 Repeal as to Northern District of Alabama; Authority of Certain Estate Administrators in Alabama and North Carolina; Effective Date of 1986 Amendments in Pending Cases Where a U.S. Trustee Not Authorized or Where a Trustee Files Final Report or Plan is Confirmed; Quarterly Fees.** Amendment by Pub.L. 99–554 effective 30 days after Oct. 27, 1986, except as otherwise provided for, see section 302(a) of Pub.L. 99–554, set out as a note under section 581 of Title 28, Judiciary and Judicial Procedure.

Amendment by Pub.L. 99–554, § 202, not to become effective in or with respect to certain specified judicial districts until, or apply to cases while pending in such district before, the expiration of the 270-day period beginning 30 days after Oct. 27, 1986, or of the 30-day period beginning on the date the Attorney General certifies under section 303 of Pub.L. 99–554 the region specified in a paragraph of section 581(a) of Title 28, as amended by section 111(a) of Pub.L. 99–54, that includes such district, whichever occurs first, see section 302(d)(1) of Pub.L. 99–554, set out as a note under section 581 of Title 28.

Amendment by Pub.L. 99–554, § 202, not to become effective in or with respect to certain specified judicial districts until, or apply to cases while pending in such district before, the expiration of the 2-year period beginning 30 days after Oct. 27, 1986, or of the 30-day period beginning on the date the Attorney General certifies under section 303 of Pub.L. 99–554 the region specified in a paragraph of section 581(a) of Title 28, as amended by section 111(a) of Pub.L. 99–554, that includes such district, whichever occurs first, see section 302(d)(2) of Pub.L. 99–554, set out as a note under section 581 of Title 28.

Amendment by Pub.L. 99–554, § 202, not to become effective in or with respect to judicial districts established for the States of Alabama and North Carolina until, or apply to cases while pending in such district before, such district elects to be included in a bankruptcy region established in section 581(a) of Title 28, as amended by section 111(a) of Pub.L. 99–554, or Oct. 1, 2002, whichever occurs first, and, except as otherwise provided for, with respect to cases under chapters 7, 11, 12 and 13 of Title 11 commenced before 30 days after Oct. 27, 1986, and pending in a judicial district in the States of Alabama or North Carolina before any election made under section 302(d)(3) (A) of Pub.L. 99–554 by such district becomes effective or Oct. 1, 2002, whichever occurs first, amendments by Pub.L. 99–554 not to apply until Oct. 1, 2003, or the expiration of the 1-year period beginning on the date such election becomes effective, whichever occurs first, and further, in any judicial district in Alabama or North Carolina not making the election described in section 302(d)(3)(A) of Pub.L. 99–554, any person appointed under regulations issued by the Judicial Conference to administer estates in cases under Title 11 authorized to establish, etc., a panel of private trustees, and to supervise cases and trustees in cases under chapters 7, 11, 12, and 13 of Title 11, until amendments by sections 201 to 231 of Pub.L. 99–554 effective in such district, see section 302(d)(3)(A) to (F), (H), (I) of Pub.L. 99–554, set out as a note under section 581 of Title 28.

Amendment by Pub.L. 99–554, § 202, except as otherwise provided, with respect to cases under chapters 7, 11, 12, and 13 of Title 11 commenced before 30 days after Oct. 27, 1986, and pending in a judicial district referred to in section 581(a) of Title 28, as amended by sec-tion 111(a) of Pub.L. 99–554, for which a United States trustee is not authorized before 30 days after Oct. 27, 1986 to be appointed, not applicable until the expiration of the 3-year period beginning on Oct. 27, 1986, or of the 1-year period beginning on the date the Attorney General certifies under section 303 of Pub.L. 99–554 the region specified in a paragraph of such section 581(a) that includes such district, whichever occurs first, see section 302(e)(1), (2) of Pub.L. 99–554, set out as a note under section 581 of Title 28.

See 1986 Amendment notes set out above.

Effective Date of 1984 Amendments. See section 553 of Pub.L. 98–353, Title III, July 10, 1984, 98 Stat. 392, set out as an Effective Date of 1984 Amendment note preceding chapter 1 of Title 11, Bankruptcy.

Separability of Provisions. For separability of provisions of Title III of Pub.L. 98–353, see section 551 of Pub.L. 98–353 set out as a Separability of Provisions note preceding chapter 1 of Title 11, Bankruptcy.

Library References:

    C.J.S. Bankruptcy § 2.
    West's Key No. Digests, Bankruptcy ⊙=2001, 2021, 2022.

WESTLAW Electronic Research

    See WESTLAW Electronic Research Guide following the *Bankruptcy Highlights.*

§ 103.   Applicability of chapters

    (a) Except as provided in section 1161 of this title, chapters 1, 3, and 5 of this title apply in a case under chapter 7, 11, 12, or 13 of this title.

    (b) Subchapters I and II of chapter 7 of this title apply only in a case under such chapter.

    (c) Subchapter III of chapter 7 of this title applies only in a case under such chapter concerning a stockbroker.

    (d) Subchapter IV of chapter 7 of this title applies only in a case under such chapter concerning a commodity broker.

    (e) Except as provided in section 901 of this title, only chapters 1 and 9 of this title apply in a case under such chapter 9.

    (f) Except as provided in section 901 of this title, subchapters I, II, and III of chapter 11 of this title apply only in a case under such chapter.

    (g) Subchapter IV of chapter 11 of this title applies only in a case under such chapter concerning a railroad.

    (h) Chapter 13 of this title applies only in a case under such chapter.

    (i) Chapter 12 of this title applies only in a case under such chapter.

Pub.L. 95–598, Nov. 6, 1978, 92 Stat. 2555; Pub.L. 97–222, § 2, July 27, 1982, 96 Stat. 235; Pub.L. 98–353, Title III, § 423, July 10, 1984, 98 Stat. 369; Pub.L. 99–554, Title II, § 252, Oct. 27, 1986, 100 Stat. 3104.

Historical and Revision Notes

Notes of Committee on the Judiciary, Senate Report No. 95–989. Section 103 prescribes which chapters of the proposed bankruptcy code apply in various cases. All cases, other than cases ancillary to foreign proceedings, are filed under chapter 7, 9, 11, or 13, the operative chapters of the proposed bankruptcy code [this title]. The general provisions that apply no matter which chapter a case is filed under are found in chapters 1, 3, and 5. Subsection (a) makes this explicit, with an exception for chapter 9. The other provisions, which are self-explanatory, provide the special rules for Stockbroker Liquidations, Commodity Broker Liquidations, Municipal Debt Adjustments, and Railroad Reorganizations.

Effective Date of 1986 Amendments. Savings Provisions; Quarterly Fees. Amendment by Pub.L. 99–554 effective 30 days after Oct. 27, 1986, except as otherwise

provided for, see section 302(a) of Pub.L. 99–554, set out as a note under section 581 of Title 28, Judiciary and Judicial Procedure.

Amendments by Pub.L. 99–554, § 252, not to apply with respect to cases commenced under Title 11, Bankruptcy, before 30 days after Oct. 27, 1986, see section 302(c)(1) of Pub. L. 99–554, set out as a note under section 581 of Title 28.

Effective Date of 1984 Amendments. See section 553 of Pub.L. 98–353, Title III, July 10, 1984, 98 Stat. 392, set out as an Effective Date of 1984 Amendment note preceding chapter 1 of Title 11, Bankruptcy.

Separability of Provisions. For separability of provisions of Title III of Pub.L. 98–353, see section 551 of Pub.L. 98–353 set out as a Separability of Provisions note preceding chapter 1 of Title 11, Bankruptcy.

Cross References

Confirmation in chapter 9 cases upon compliance with provisions of this title made applicable by this section, see section 943.

Meanings of terms in sections made applicable to chapter 9 by this section, see section 901.

Property of estate and trustee defined when used in sections made applicable to cases under chapter 9 by this section, see section 902.

Library References:

C.J.S. Bankruptcy § 37.

West's Key No. Digests, Bankruptcy ⚷2203.

WESTLAW Electronic Research

See WESTLAW Electronic Research Guide following the *Bankruptcy Highlights*.

§ 104.   Adjustment of dollar amounts

The Judicial Conference of the United States shall transmit to the Congress and to the President before May 1, 1985, and before May 1 of every sixth year after May 1, 1985, a recommendation for the uniform percentage adjustment of each dollar amount in this title and in section 1930 of title 28.

Pub.L. 95–598, Nov. 6, 1978, 92 Stat. 2555.

Historical and Revision Notes

Notes of Committee on the Judiciary, Senate Report No. 95–989. This section requires that the Director of the Administrative Office of the U.S. Courts report to Congress and the President before Oct. 1, 1985, and

before May 1 every 6 years thereafter a recommendation for adjustment in dollar amounts found in this title. The Committee feels that regular adjustment of the dollar amounts by the Director will conserve congressional time and yet assure that the relative dollar amounts used in the bill are maintained. Changes in the cost of living should be a significant, but not necessarily the only, factor considered by the Director. The fact that there has been an increase in the cost of living does not necessarily mean that an adjustment of dollar amounts would be needed or warranted.

Notes of Committee on the Judiciary, House Report No. 95–595. This section requires the Judicial Conference to report to the Congress every four years after the effective date of the bankruptcy code any changes that have occurred in the cost of living during the preceding four years, and the appropriate adjustments to the dollar amounts in the bill. The dollar amounts are found primarily in the exemption section (11 U.S.C. 522), the wage priority (11 U.S.C. 507), and the eligibility for chapter 13 (11 U.S.C. 109). This section requires that the Conference recommend uniform percentage changes in these amounts based solely on cost of living changes. The dollar amounts in the bill would not change on that recommendation, absent Congressional veto. Instead, Congress is required to take affirmative action, by passing a law amending

the appropriate section, if it wishes to accomplish the change.

If the Judicial Conference has policy recommendations concerning the appropriate dollar amounts in the bankruptcy code based other than on cost of living considerations there are adequate channels through which it may communicate its views. This section is solely for the housekeeping function of maintaining the dollar amounts in the code at fairly constant real dollar levels.

Legislative Statements. Section 104 represents a compromise between the House bill and the Senate amendment with respect to the adjustment of dollar amounts in title 11. The House amendment authorizes the Judicial Conference of the United States to transmit a recommendation for the uniform percentage of adjustment for each dollar amount in title 11 and in 28 U.S.C.A. 1930 to the Congress and to the President before May 1, 1985, and before May 1 of every sixth year thereafter. The requirement in the House bill that each such recommendation be based only on any change in the cost-of-living increase during the period immediately preceding the recommendation is deleted.

§ 105.   Power of court

(a) The court may issue any order, process, or judgment that is necessary or appropriate to carry out the provisions of this title. No provision of this title providing for the raising of an issue by a party in interest shall be construed to preclude the court from, sua sponte, taking any action or making any determination necessary or appropriate to enforce or implement court orders or rules, or to prevent an abuse of process.

(b) Notwithstanding subsection (a) of this section, a court may not appoint a receiver in a case under this title.

(c) The ability of any district judge or other officer or employee of a district court to exercise any of the authority or responsibilities conferred upon the court under this title shall be determined by reference to the provisions relating to such judge, officer, or employee set forth in title 28. This subsection shall not be interpreted to exclude bankruptcy judges and other officers or employees appointed pursuant to chapter 6 of title 28 from its operation.

Pub.L. 95–598, Nov. 6, 1978, 92 Stat. 2555; Pub.L. 98–353, Title I, § 118, July 10, 1984, 98 Stat. 344; Pub.L. 99–554, Title II, § 203, Oct. 27, 1986, 100 Stat. 3097.

Historical and Revision Notes

Notes of Committee on the Judiciary, Senate Report No. 95–989. Section 105 is derived from section 2a(15) of present law [former section 11a(15) of this title], with two changes. First, the limitation on the power of a bankruptcy judge (the power to enjoin a

court being reserved to the district judge) is removed as inconsistent with the increased powers and jurisdiction of the new bankruptcy court. Second, the bankruptcy judge is prohibited from appointing a receiver in a case under title 11 under any circumstances. The bankruptcy code [this title] has ample provision for the appointment of a trustee when needed. Appointment of a receiver would simply circumvent the established procedures.

This section is also an authorization, as required under 28 U.S.C. 2283 [section 2283 of Title 28, Judiciary and Judicial Procedure], for a court of the United States to stay the action of a State court. As such, Toucey v. New York Life Insurance Company, 314 U.S. 118 (1941) [62 S.Ct. 139, 86 L.Ed. 100, 137 A.L.R. 967], is overruled.

1986 Amendment. Subsec. (a). Pub.L. 99–554, § 203, added "No provision of this title providing for the raising of an issue by a party in interest shall be construed to preclude the court from, sua sponte, taking any action or making any determination necessary or appropriate to enforce or implement court orders or rules, or to prevent an abuse of process" following "of this title".

See Effective Date of 1986 Amendment, etc., notes set out below.

Effective Date of 1986 Amendments; Effective Date of 1986 Amendments for Certain Judicial Districts Not Served by United States Trustees for Judicial Districts in Alabama and North Carolina; U.S. Trustee System Fund Deposits in Alabama and North Carolina; Effective Date of Title 11 Chapter 15 Repeal as to Northern District of Alabama; Authority of Certain Estate Administrators in Alabama and North Carolina; Effective Date of 1986 Amendments in Pending Cases Where a U.S. Trustee Not Authorized or Where a Trustee Files Final Report or Plan is Confirmed; Quarterly Fees. Amendment by Pub.L. 99–554 effective 30 days after Oct. 27, 1986, except as otherwise provided for, see section 302(a) of Pub.L. 99–554, set out as a note under section 581 of Title 28, Judiciary and Judicial Procedure.

Amendment by Pub.L. 99–554, § 203, not to become effective in or with respect to certain specified judicial districts until, or apply to cases while pending in such district before, the expiration of the 270-day period beginning 30 days after Oct. 27, 1986, or of the 30-day period beginning on the date the Attorney General certifies under section 303 of Pub.L. 99–554 the region specified in a paragraph of section 581(a) of Title 28, as amended by section 111(a) of Pub.L. 99–554, that includes such district, whichever occurs first, see section 302(d)(1) of Pub.L. 99–554, set out as a note under section 581 of Title 28.

Amendment by Pub.L. 9–554, § 203, not to become effective in or with respect to certain specified judicial districts until, or apply to cases while pending in such district before, the expiration of the 2-year period beginning 30 days after Oct. 27, 1986, or of the 30-day period beginning on the date the Attorney General certifies under section 303 of Pub.L. 99–554 the region specified in a paragraph of section 581(a) of Title 28, as amended by section 111(a) of Pub.L. 99–554, that includes such district, whichever occurs first, see section 302(d)(2) of Pub.L. 99–554, set out as a note under section 581 of Title 28.

Amendment by Pub.L. 99–554, § 203, not to become effective in or with respect to judicial districts established for the States of Alabama and North Carolina until, or apply to cases while pending in such district before, such district elects to be included in a bankruptcy region established in section 581(a) of Title 28, as amended by section 111(a) of Pub.L. 99–554, or Oct. 1, 2002, whichever occurs first, except that the amendment to subsec. (a) of this section shall become effective as of Dec. 1, 1990, and, except as otherwise provided for, with respect to cases under chapters 7, 11, 12, and 13 of Title 11 commenced before 30 days after Oct. 27, 1986, and pending in a judicial district in the States of Alabama or North Carolina before any election made under section 302(d)(3)(A) of Pub.L. 99–554 by such district becomes effective or Oct. 1, 2002, whichever occurs first, amendments by Pub.L. 99–554 not to apply until Oct. 1, 2003, or the expiration of the 1-year period beginning on the date such election becomes effective, whichever occurs first, and further, in any judicial district in Alabama or North Carolina not making the election described in section 302(d)(3)(A) of Pub.L. 99–554, any person appointed under regulations issued by the Judicial Conference to administer estates in cases under Title 11 authorized to establish, etc., a panel of private trustees, and to supervise cases and trustees in cases under chapters 7, 11, 12, and 13 of Title 11, until amendments by sections 201 to 231 of Pub.L. 99–554 effective in such district, see section 302(d)(3)(A) to (F), (H), (I) of Pub.L. 99–554, set out as a note under section 581 of Title 28.

Amendment by Pub.L. 99–554, § 203 except as otherwise provided, with respect to cases under chapters 7, 11, 12, and 13 of Title 11 commenced before 30 days after Oct. 27, 1986, and pending in a judicial district referred to in section 581(a) of Title 28, as amended by section 111(a) of Pub.L. 99–554, for which a United States trustee is not authorized before 30 days after Oct. 27, 1986 to be appointed, not applicable until the expiration of the 3-year period beginning on Oct. 27, 1986, or of the 1-year period beginning on the date the Attorney General certifies under section 303 of Pub.L. 99–554 the region specified in a paragraph of such section 581(a) that includes such district, whichever occurs first, see section 302(e)(1), (2) of Pub.L. 99–554, set out as a note under section 581 of Title 28.

See 1986 Amendment notes set out above.

Effective Date of 1984 Amendments. For effective date of amendments by Title I of Pub.L. 98–353, see section 122 of Pub.L. 98–353, Title I, July 10, 1984, 98 Stat. 346, set out as an Effective Date of 1984 Amendment note under section 151 of Title 28, Judiciary and Judicial Procedure.

Library References:

C.J.S. Bankruptcy §§ 5, 9, 19, 20.

West's Key No. Digests, Bankruptcy ☞2124–2126.

WESTLAW Electronic Research

See WESTLAW Electronic Research Guide following the *Bankruptcy Highlights*.

§ 106. Waiver of sovereign immunity

(a) A governmental unit is deemed to have waived sovereign immunity with respect to any claim against such governmental unit that is property of the estate and that arose out of the same transaction or occurrence out of which such governmental unit's claim arose.

(b) There shall be offset against an allowed claim or interest of a governmental unit any claim against such governmental unit that is property of the estate.

(c) Except as provided in subsections (a) and (b) of this section and notwithstanding any assertion of sovereign immunity—

(1) a provision of this title that contains "creditor", "entity", or "governmental unit" applies to governmental units; and

(2) a determination by the court of an issue arising under such a provision binds governmental units.

Pub.L. 95–598, Nov. 6, 1978, 92 Stat. 2555.

Historical and Revision Notes

Notes of Committee on the Judiciary, Senate Report No. 95–989. Section 106 provides for a limited waiver of sovereign immunity in bankruptcy cases. Though Congress has the power to waive sovereign immunity for the Federal government completely in bankruptcy cases, the policy followed here is designed to achieve approximately the same result that would prevail outside of bankruptcy. Congress does not, however, have the power to waive sovereign immunity completely with respect to claims of a bankrupt estate against a State, though it may exercise its bankruptcy power through the supremacy clause to prevent or prohibit State action that is contrary to bankruptcy policy.

There is, however, a limited change from the result that would prevail in the absence of bankruptcy; the change is two-fold and is within Congress' power vis-a-vis both the Federal Government and the States. First, the filing of a proof of claim against the estate by a governmental unit is a waiver by that governmental unit of sovereign immunity with respect to compulsory counterclaims, as defined in the Federal Rules of Civil Procedure [Title 28, Judiciary and Judicial Procedure], that is, counterclaims arising out of the same transaction or occurrence. The governmental unit cannot receive a distribution from the estate without subjecting itself to any liability it has to the estate within the confines of a compulsory counterclaim rule. Any other result would be one-sided. The counterclaim by the estate against the governmental unit is without limit.

Second, the estate may offset against the allowed claim of a governmental unit, up to the amount of the governmental unit's claim, any claim that the debtor, and thus the estate, has against the governmental unit, without regard to whether the estate's claim arose out of the same transaction or occurrence as the government's claim. Under this provision, the setoff permitted is only to the extent of the governmental unit's claim. No affirmative recovery is permitted. Subsection (a) governs affirmative recovery.

Though this subsection creates a partial waiver of immunity when the governmental unit files a proof of claim, it does not waive immunity if the debtor or trustee, and not the governmental unit, files proof of a governmental unit's claim under proposed 11 U.S.C. 501(c).

This section does not confer sovereign immunity on any governmental unit that does not already have immunity. It simply recognizes any immunity that exists and prescribes the proper treatment of claims by and against that sovereign.

Legislative Statements. Section 106(c) relating to sovereign immunity is new. The provision indicates that the use of the term "creditor," "entity," or "governmental unit" in title 11 applies to governmental units notwithstanding any assertion of sovereign immunity and that an order of the court binds governmental units. The provision is included to comply with the requirement in case law that an express waiver of sovereign immunity is required in order to be effective. Section 106(c) codifies In re Gwilliam, 519 F.2d 407 (9th Cir., 1975), and In re Dolard, 519 F.2d 282 (9th Cir., 1975), permitting the bankruptcy court to determine the amount and dischargeability of tax liabilities owing by the debtor or the estate prior to or during a bankruptcy case whether or not the governmental unit to which such taxes are owed files a proof of claim. Except as provided in sections 106(a) and (b) subsection (c) is not limited to those issues, but permits the bankruptcy court to bind governmental units on other matters as well. For example, section 106(c) permits a trustee or debtor in possession to assert avoiding powers under title 11 against a governmental unit; contrary language in the House report to H.R. 8200 is thereby overruled.

Library References:

C.J.S. Bankruptcy §§ 15, 245.
West's Key No. Digests, Bankruptcy ☞2679.

WESTLAW Electronic Research

See WESTLAW Electronic Research Guide following the *Bankruptcy Highlights*.

§ 107. Public access to papers

(a) Except as provided in subsection (b) of this section, a paper filed in a case under this title and the dockets of a bankruptcy court are public records and open to examination by an entity at reasonable times without charge.

(b) On request of a party in interest, the bankruptcy court shall, and on the bankruptcy court's own motion, the bankruptcy court may—

    (1) protect an entity with respect to a trade secret or confidential research, development, or commercial information; or

    (2) protect a person with respect to scandalous or defamatory matter contained in a paper filed in a case under this title.

Pub.L. 95–598, Nov. 6, 1978, 92 Stat. 2556.

Historical and Revision Notes

Notes of Committee on the Judiciary, Senate Report No. 95–989. Subsection (a) of this section makes all papers filed in a bankruptcy case and the dockets of the bankruptcy court public and open to examination at reasonable times without charge. "Docket" includes the claims docket, the proceedings docket, and all papers filed in a case.

Subsection (b) permits the court, on its own motion, and requires the court, on the request of a party in interest, to protect trade secrets, confidential research, development, or commercial information, and to protect persons against scandalous or defamatory matter.

Library References:

C.J.S. Records § 35 et seq.
West's Key No. Digests, Records ⟜32.

WESTLAW Electronic Research

See WESTLAW Electronic Research Guide following the *Bankruptcy Highlights.*

§ 108.   Extension of time

(a) If applicable nonbankruptcy law, an order entered in a nonbankruptcy proceeding, or an agreement fixes a period within which the debtor may commence an action, and such period has not expired before the date of the filing of the petition, the trustee may commence such action only before the later of—

(1) the end of such period, including any suspension of such period occurring on or after the commencement of the case; or

(2) two years after the order for relief.

(b) Except as provided in subsection (a) of this section, if applicable nonbankruptcy law, an order entered in a nonbankruptcy proceeding, or an agreement fixes a period within which the debtor or an individual protected under section 1201 or 1301 of this title may file any pleading, demand, notice, or proof of claim or loss, cure a default, or perform any other similar act, and such period has not expired before the date of the filing of the petition, the trustee may only file, cure, or perform, as the case may be, before the later of—

(1) the end of such period, including any suspension of such period occurring on or after the commencement of the case; or

(2) 60 days after the order for relief.

(c) Except as provided in section 524 of this title, if applicable nonbankruptcy law, an order entered in a nonbankruptcy proceeding, or an agreement fixes a period for commencing or continuing a civil action in a court other than a bankruptcy court on a claim against the debtor, or against an individual with respect to which such individual is protected under section 1201 or 1301 of this title, and such period has not expired before the date of the filing of the petition, then such period does not expire until the later of—

(1) the end of such period, including any suspension of such period occurring on or after the commencement of the case; or

(2) 30 days after notice of the termination or expiration of the stay under section 362, 922, 1201, or 1301 of this title, as the case may be, with respect to such claim.

Pub.L. 95–598, Nov. 6, 1978, 92 Stat. 2556; Pub.L. 98–353, Title III, § 424, July 10, 1984, 98 Stat. 369; Pub.L. 99–554, Title II, § 257(b)(1), Oct. 27, 1986, 100 Stat. 3114.

Historical and Revision Notes

Notes of Committee on the Judiciary, Senate Report No. 95–989. Subsections (a) and (b), derived from Bankruptcy Act section 11 [former section 29 of this title], permit the trustee, when he steps into the shoes of the debtor, an extension of time for filing an action or doing some other act that is required to preserve the debtor's rights. Subsection (a) extends any statute of limitation for commencing or continuing an action by the debtor for two years after the date of the order for relief, unless it would expire later. Subsection (b) gives the trustee 60 days to take other actions not covered under subsection (a), such as filing a pleading demand, notice, or proof of claim or loss (such as an insurance claim), unless the period for doing the relevant act expires later than 60 days after the date of the order for relief.

Subsection (c) extends the statute of limitations for creditors. Thus, if a creditor is stayed from commencing or continuing an action against the debtor because of the bankruptcy case, then the creditor is permitted an additional 30 days after notice of the event by which the stay is terminated, whether that event be relief from the automatic stay under proposed 11 U.S.C. 362 or 1301, the closing of the bankruptcy case (which terminates the stay), or the exception from discharge of the debts on which the creditor claims.

In the case of Federal tax liabilities, the Internal Revenue Code [Title 26] suspends the statute of limitations on a tax liability of a taxpayer from running while his assets are in the control or custody of a court and for 6 months thereafter (sec. 6503(b) of the Code) [section 6503(b) of Title 26, Internal Revenue Code]. The amendment applies this rule in a title 11 proceeding. Accordingly, the statute of limitations on collection of a nondischargeable Federal tax liability of a debtor will resume running after 6 months following the end of the period during which the debtor's assets are in the control or custody of the bankruptcy court. This rule will provide the Internal Revenue Service adequate time to collect nondischargeable taxes following the end of title 11 proceedings.

Legislative Statements. The House amendment adopts section 108(c)(1) of the Senate amendment which expressly includes any special suspensions of statutes of limitation periods on collection outside bankruptcy when assets are under the authority of a court. For example, section 6503(b) of the Internal Revenue Code [section 6503(b) of Title 26, Internal Revenue Code] suspends collection of tax liabilities while the debtor's assets are in the control or custody of a court, and for 6 months thereafter. By adopting the language of the Senate amendment, the House amendment insures not only that the period for collection of the taxes outside bankruptcy will not expire during the title 11 proceedings, but also that such period will not expire until at least 6 months thereafter, which is the minimum suspension period provided by the Internal Revenue Code.

Codification. Amendment by Pub.L. 99–554, § 257(b)(2)(B), has been executed to text following "922" as the probable intent of Congress, notwithstanding directory language requiring execution of amendment following "722".

Effective Date of 1986 Amendments; Savings Provisions; Quarterly Fees. Amendment by Pub.L. 99–554 effective 30 days after Oct. 27, 1986, except as otherwise provided for, see section 302(a) of Pub.L. 99–554, set out as a note under section 581 of Title 28, Judiciary and Judicial Procedure.

Amendments by Pub.L. 99–554, § 257(b), not to apply with respect to cases commenced under Title 11, Bankruptcy, before 30 days after Oct. 27, 1986, see section 302(c)(1) of Pub. L. 99–554, set out as a note under section 581 of Title 28.

Effective Date of 1984 Amendments. See section 553 of Pub.L. 98–353, Title III, July 10, 1984, 98 Stat. 392, set out as an Effective Date of 1984 Amendment note preceding chapter 1 of Title 11, Bankruptcy.

Separability of Provisions. For separability of provisions of Title III of Pub.L. 98–353, see section 551 of Pub.L. 98–353 set out as a Separability of Provisions note preceding chapter 1 of Title 11, Bankruptcy.

Library References:

  C.J.S. Bankruptcy § 29.
  West's Key No. Digests, Bankruptcy ☞2132.

WESTLAW Electronic Research

  See WESTLAW Electronic Research Guide following the *Bankruptcy Highlights.*

§ 109. Who may be a debtor

(a) Notwithstanding any other provision of this section, only a person that resides or has a domicile, a place of business, or property in the United States, or a municipality, may be a debtor under this title.

(b) A person may be a debtor under chapter 7 of this title only if such person is not—

(1) a railroad;

(2) a domestic insurance company, bank, savings bank, cooperative bank, savings and loan association, building and loan association, homestead association, credit union, or industrial bank or similar institution which is an insured bank as defined in section 3(h) of the Federal Deposit Insurance Act (12 U.S.C. 1813(h)); or

(3) a foreign insurance company, bank, savings bank, cooperative bank, savings and loan association, building and loan association, homestead association, or credit union, engaged in such business in the United States.

(c) An entity may be a debtor under chapter 9 of this title if and only if such entity—

(1) is a municipality;

(2) is generally authorized to be a debtor under such chapter by State law, or by a governmental officer or organization empowered by State law to authorize such entity to be a debtor under such chapter;

(3) is insolvent;

(4) desires to effect a plan to adjust such debts; and

(5)(A) has obtained the agreement of creditors holding at least a majority in amount of the claims of each class that such entity intends to impair under a plan in a case under such chapter;

(B) has negotiated in good faith with creditors and has failed to obtain the agreement of creditors holding at least a majority in amount of the claims of each class that such entity intends to impair under a plan in a case under such chapter;

(C) is unable to negotiate with creditors because such negotiation is impracticable; or

(D) reasonably believes that a creditor may attempt to obtain a transfer that is avoidable under section 547 of this title.

(d) Only a person that may be a debtor under chapter 7 of this title, except a stockbroker or a commodity broker, and a railroad may be a debtor under chapter 11 of this title.

(e) Only an individual with regular income that owes, on the date of the filing of the petition, noncontingent, liquidated, unsecured debts of less than $100,000 and noncontingent, liquidated, secured debts of less than $350,000, or an individual with regular income and such individual's spouse, except a stockbroker or a commodity broker, that owe, on the date of the filing of the petition, noncontingent, liquidated, unsecured debts that aggregate less than $100,000 and noncontingent, liquidated, secured debts of less than $350,000 may be a debtor under chapter 13 of this title.

(f) Only a family farmer with regular annual income may be a debtor under chapter 12 of this title.

(g) Notwithstanding any other provision of this section, no individual or family farmer may be a debtor under this title who has been a debtor in a case pending under this title at any time in the preceding 180 days if—

(1) the case was dismissed by the court for willful failure of the debtor to abide by orders of the court, or to appear before the court in proper prosecution of the case; or

(2) the debtor requested and obtained the voluntary dismissal of the case following the filing of a request for relief from the automatic stay provided by section 362 of this title.

Pub.L. 95–598, Nov. 6, 1978, 92 Stat. 2557; Pub.L. 97–320, Title VII, § 703(d), Oct. 15, 1982, 96 Stat. 1539; Pub.L. 98–353, Title III, §§ 301, 425, July 10, 1984, 98 Stat. 352, 369; Pub.L. 99–554, Title II, § 253, Oct. 27, 1986, 100 Stat. 3105; Pub.L. 102–597, § 2, Nov. 3, 1988, 102 Stat. 3028.

Historical and Revision Notes

Notes of Committee on the Judiciary, Senate Report No. 95–989. This section specifies eligibility to be a debtor under the bankruptcy laws. The first criterion, found in the current Bankruptcy Act section 2a(1) [former section 11(a)(1) of this title] requires that the debtor reside or have a domicile, a place of business, or property in the United States.

Subsection (b) defines eligibility for liquidation under chapter 7. All persons are eligible except insurance companies, and certain banking institutions. These exclusions are contained in current law. However, the banking institution exception is expanded in light of changes in various banking laws since the current law was last amended on this point. A change is also made to clarify that the bankruptcy laws cover foreign banks and insurance companies not engaged in the banking or insurance business in the United States but having assets in the United States. Banking institutions and insurance companies engaged in business in this country are excluded from liquidation under the bankruptcy laws because they are bodies for which alternate provision is made for their liquidation under various State or Federal regulatory laws. Conversely, when a foreign bank or insurance company is not engaged in the banking or insurance business in the United States, then those regulatory laws do not apply, and the bankruptcy laws are the only ones available for administration of any assets found in the United States.

The first clause of subsection (b) provides that a railroad is not a debtor except where the requirements of section 1174 are met.

Subsection (c) [now (d)] provides that only a person who may be a debtor under chapter 7 and a railroad may also be a debtor under chapter 11, but a stockbroker or commodity broker is eligible for relief only under chapter 7. Subsection (d) [now (e)] establishes dollar limitations on the amount of indebtedness that an individual with regular income can incur and yet file under chapter 13.

Notes of Committee on the Judiciary, House Report No. 95–595. Subsection (c) defines eligibility for chapter 9. Only a municipality that is unable to pay its debts as they mature, and that is not prohibited by State law from proceeding under chapter 9, is permitted to be a chapter 9 debtor. The subsection is derived from Bankruptcy Act § 84 [former section 404 of this title], with two changes. First, section 84 requires that the municipality be "generally authorized to file a petition under this chapter by the legislature, or by a governmental officer or organization empowered by State law to authorize the filing of a petition." The "generally authorized" language is unclear, and has generated a problem for a Colorado Metropolitan District that attempted to use chapter IX [former section 401 et seq. of this title] in 1976. The "not prohibited" language provides flexibility for both the States and the municipalities involved, while protecting State sovereignty as required by Ashton v. Cameron County Water District No. 1, 298 U.S. 513 (1936) [56 S.Ct. 892, 80 L.Ed. 1309, 31 Am.Bankr.Rep.N.S. 96, rehearing denied 57 S.Ct. 5, 299 U.S. 619, 81 L.Ed. 457] and Bekins v. United States, 304 U.S. 27 (1938) [58 S.Ct. 811, 82 L.Ed. 1137, 36

Am.Bankr.Rep.N.S. 187, rehearing denied 58 S.Ct. 1043, 1044, 304 U.S. 589, 82 L.Ed. 1549].

The second change deletes the four prerequisites to filing found in section 84 [former section 404 of this title]. The prerequisites require the municipality to have worked out a plan in advance, to have attempted to work out a plan without success, to fear that a creditor will attempt to obtain a preference, or to allege that prior negotiation is impracticable. The loopholes in those prerequisites are larger than the requirement itself. It was a compromise from pre-1976 chapter IX [former section 401 et seq. of this title] under which a municipality could file only if it had worked out an adjustment plan in advance. In the meantime, chapter IX protection was unavailable. There was some controversy at the time of the enactment of current chapter IX concerning deletion of the pre-negotiation requirement. It was argued that deletion would lead to a rash of municipal bankruptcies. The prerequisites now contained in section 84 were inserted to assuage that fear. They are largely cosmetic and precatory, however, and do not offer any significant deterrent to use of chapter IX. Instead, other factors, such as a general reluctance on the part of any debtor, especially a municipality, to use the bankruptcy laws, operates as a much more effective deterrent against capricious use.

Subsection (d) permits a person that may proceed under chapter 7 to be a debtor under chapter 11, Reorganization, with two exceptions. Railroads, which are excluded from chapter 7, are permitted to proceed under chapter 11. Stockbrokers and commodity brokers, which are permitted to be debtors under chapter 7, are excluded from chapter 11. The special rules for treatment of customer accounts that are the essence of stockbroker and commodity broker liquidations are available only in chapter 7. Customers would be unprotected under chapter 11. The special protective rules are unavailable in chapter 11 because their complexity would make reorganization very difficult at best, and unintelligible at worst. The variety of options available in reorganization cases make it extremely difficult to reorganize and continue to provide the special customer protection necessary in these cases.

Subsection (e) specifies eligibility for chapter 13, Adjustment of Debts of an Individual with Regular Income. An individual with regular income, or an individual with regular income and the individual's spouse, may proceed under chapter 13. As noted in connection with the definition of the term "individual with regular income", this represents a significant departure from current law. The change might have been too great, however, without some limitation. Thus, the debtor (or the debtor and spouse) must have unsecured debts that aggregate less than $100,000, and secured debts that aggregate less than $500,000. These figures will permit the small sole proprietor, for whom a chapter 11 reorganization is too cumbersome a procedure, to proceed under chapter 13. It does not create a presumption that any sole proprietor within that range is better off in chapter 13 than chapter 11. The conversion rules found in section 1307 will govern the appropriateness of the two chapters for any particular individual. The figures merely set maximum limits.

Whether a small business operated by a husband and wife, the so-called "mom and pop grocery store," will be a partnership and thus excluded from chapter 13, or a business owned by an individual, will have to be determined on the facts of each case. Even if partnership papers have not been filed, for example, the issue will be whether the assets of the grocery store are for the benefit of all creditors of the debtor or only for business creditors, and whether such assets may be the subject of a chapter 13 proceeding. The intent of the section is to follow current law that a partnership by estoppel may be adjudicated in bankruptcy and therefore would not prevent a chapter 13 debtor from subjecting assets in such a partnership to the reach of all creditors in a chapter 13 case. However, if the partnership is found to be a partnership by agreement, even informal agreement, then a separate entity exists and the assets of that entity would be exempt from a case under chapter 13.

Legislative Statements. Section 109(b) of the House amendment adopts a provision contained in H.R. 8200 as passed by the House. Railroad liquidations will occur under chapter 11, not chapter 7.

Section 109(c) contains a provision which tracks the Senate amendment as to when a municipality may be a debtor under chapter 11 of title 11. As under the Bankruptcy Act [former Title 11], State law authorization and prepetition negotiation efforts are required.

Section 109(e) represents a compromise between H.R. 8200 as passed by the House and the Senate amendment relating to the dollar amounts restricting eligibility to be a debtor under chapter 13 of title 11. The House amendment adheres to the limit of $100,000 placed on unsecured debts in H.R. 8200 as passed by the House. It adopts a midpoint of $350,000 as a limit on secured claims, a compromise between the level of $500,000 in H.R. 8200 as passed by the House and $200,000 as contained in the Senate amendment.

Effective Date of 1988 Amendment; Application of Amendments. Amendment by Pub.L. 100–597 effective on Nov. 3, 1988, and not applicable to cases commenced under this title prior to such date, see section 12 of Pub.L. 100–597, set out as a note under section 101 of this title.

Effective Date of 1986 Amendments; Savings Provisions; Quarterly Fees. Amendment by Pub.L. 99–554 effective 30 days after Oct. 27, 1986, except as otherwise provided for, see section 302(a) of Pub.L. 99–554, set out as a note under section 581 of Title 28, Judiciary and Judicial Procedure.

Amendments by Pub.L. 99–554, § 253, not to apply with respect to cases commenced under Title 11, Bankruptcy, before 30 days after Oct. 27, 1986, see section 302(c)(1) of Pub. L. 99–554, set out as a note under section 581 of Title 28.

Effective Date of 1984 Amendments. See section 553 of Pub.L. 98–353, Title III, July 10, 1984, 98 Stat. 392, set out as an Effective Date of 1984 Amendment note preceding chapter 1 of Title 11, Bankruptcy.

Separability of Provisions. For separability of provisions of Title III of Pub.L. 98–353, see section 551 of Pub.L. 98–353 set out as a Separability of Provisions note preceding chapter 1 of Title 11, Bankruptcy.

Cross References

Commencement of Chapter 9 cases concerning certain unincorporated tax or special assessment districts, see section 921.

Library References:

C.J.S. Bankruptcy §§ 45–49, 362.
West's Key No. Digests, Bankruptcy ⇐2221–2236.

WESTLAW Electronic Research

See WESTLAW Electronic Research Guide following the *Bankruptcy Highlights*.

CHAPTER 3—CASE ADMINISTRATION

SUBCHAPTER I—COMMENCEMENT OF A CASE

Sec.
301. Voluntary cases.
302. Joint cases.
303. Involuntary cases.
304. Cases ancillary to foreign proceedings.
305. Abstention.
306. Limited appearance.
307. United States trustee.

SUBCHAPTER II—OFFICERS

321. Eligibility to serve as trustee.
322. Qualification of trustee.
323. Role and capacity of trustee.
324. Removal of trustee or examiner.
325. Effect of vacancy.
326. Limitation on compensation of trustee.
327. Employment of professional persons.
328. Limitation on compensation of professional persons.
329. Debtor's transactions with attorneys.
330. Compensation of officers.
331. Interim compensation.

SUBCHAPTER III—ADMINISTRATION

341. Meetings of creditors and equity security holders.
342. Notice.
343. Examination of the debtor.
344. Self-incrimination; immunity.
345. Money of estates.
346. Special tax provisions.
347. Unclaimed property.
348. Effect of conversion.
349. Effect of dismissal.
350. Closing and reopening cases.

SUBCHAPTER IV—ADMINISTRATIVE POWERS

361. Adequate protection.
362. Automatic stay.
363. Use, sale, or lease of property.
364. Obtaining credit.
365. Executory contracts and unexpired leases.
366. Utility service.

1986 Amendment. Pub.L. 99–554, Title II, § 205(b), Oct. 27, 1986, 100 Stat. __, added item 307. See Effective Date of 1986 Amendment, etc., notes set out under such section 307.

SUBCHAPTER I—COMMENCEMENT OF A CASE

§ 301. Voluntary cases

A voluntary case under a chapter of this title is commenced by the filing with the bankruptcy court of a petition under such chapter by an entity that may be a debtor under such chapter. The commencement of a voluntary case under a chapter of this title constitutes an order for relief under such chapter.

Pub.L. 95–598, Nov. 6, 1978, 92 Stat. 2558.

Historical and Revision Notes

Notes of Committee on the Judiciary, Senate Report No. 95–989. Section 301 specifies the manner in which a voluntary bankruptcy case is commenced. The debtor files a petition under this section under the particular operative chapter of the bankruptcy code under which he wishes to proceed. The filing of the petition constitutes an order for relief in the case under that chapter. The section contains no change from current law, except for the use of the phrase "order for relief" instead of "adjudication." The term adjudication is replaced by a less pejorative phrase in light of the clear power of Congress to permit voluntary bankruptcy without the necessity for an adjudication, as under the 1898 act, which was adopted when voluntary bankruptcy was a concept not thoroughly tested.

Legislative Statements. Sections 301, 302, 303, and 304, are all modified in the House amendment to adopt an idea contained in sections 301 and 303 of the Senate amendment requiring a petition commencing a case to be filed with the bankruptcy court. The exception contained in section 301 of the Senate bill relating to cases filed under chapter 9 is deleted. Chapter 9 cases will be handled by a bankruptcy court as are other title 11 cases.

Cross References

Applicability of this section in Chapter 9 cases, see section 901.
Automatic stay, see section 362.
Commencement of chapter 9 cases concerning certain unincorporated tax or special assessment districts, see section 921.
Petition defined, see section 101.
Property of estate, see section 541.

Library References

C.J.S. Bankruptcy § 37.50.
West's Key No. Digests, Bankruptcy ☞2202, 2251.

WESTLAW Electronic Research

See WESTLAW Electronic Research Guide following the *Bankruptcy Highlights*.

§ 302. Joint cases

(a) A joint case under a chapter of this title is commenced by the filing with the bankruptcy court of a single petition under such chapter by an individual that may be a debtor under such chapter and such individual's spouse. The commencement of a joint case under a chapter of this title constitutes an order for relief under such chapter.

(b) After the commencement of a joint case, the court shall determine the extent, if any, to which the debtors' estates shall be consolidated.

Pub.L. 95–598, Nov. 6, 1978, 92 Stat. 2558.

Historical and Revision Notes

Notes of Committee on the Judiciary, Senate Report No. 95–989. A joint case is a voluntary bankruptcy case concerning a wife and husband. Under current law, there is no explicit provision for joint cases. Very often, however, in the consumer debtor context, a husband and wife are jointly liable on their debts, and jointly hold most of their property. A joint case will facilitate consolidation of their estates, to the benefit of both the debtors and their creditors, because the cost of administration will be reduced, and there will be only one filing fee.

Section 302 specifies that a joint case is commenced by the filing of a petition under an appropriate chapter by an individual and that individual's spouse. Thus, one spouse cannot take the other into bankruptcy without the other's knowledge or consent. The filing of the petition constitutes an order for relief under the chapter selected.

Subsection (b) requires the court to determine the extent, if any, to which the estates of the two debtors will be consolidated; that is, assets and liabilities combined in a single pool to pay creditors. Factors that will be relevant in the court's determination include the extent of jointly held property and the amount of jointly-owned debts. The section, of course, is not license to consolidate in order to avoid other provisions of the title to the detriment of either the debtors or their creditors. It is designed mainly for ease of administration.

Cross References

Automatic stay, see section 362.
Petition defined, see section 101.
Property of estate, see section 541.

Library References:

C.J.S. Bankruptcy § 53.
West's Key No. Digests, Bankruptcy ⚷2311.

WESTLAW Electronic Research

See WESTLAW Electronic Research Guide following the *Bankruptcy Highlights*.

§ 303. Involuntary cases

(a) An involuntary case may be commenced only under chapter 7 or 11 of this title, and only against a person, except a farmer, family farmer, or a corporation that is not a moneyed, business, or commercial corporation, that may be a debtor under the chapter under which such case is commenced.

(b) An involuntary case against a person is commenced by the filing with the bankruptcy court of a petition under chapter 7 or 11 of this title—

(1) by three or more entities, each of which is either a holder of a claim against such person that is not contingent as to liability or the subject of a bona fide dispute, or an indenture trustee representing such a holder, if such claims aggregate at least $5,000 more than the value of any lien on property of the debtor securing such claims held by the holders of such claims;

(2) if there are fewer than 12 such holders, excluding any employee or insider of such person and any transferee of a transfer that is voidable under section 544, 545, 547, 548, 549, or 724(a) of this title, by one or more of such holders that hold in the aggregate at least $5,000 of such claims;

(3) if such person is a partnership—

(A) by fewer than all of the general partners in such partnership; or

(B) if relief has been ordered under this title with respect to all of the general partners in such partnership, by a general partner in such partnership, the trustee of such a general partner, or a holder of a claim against such partnership; or

(4) by a foreign representative of the estate in a foreign proceeding concerning such person.

(c) After the filing of a petition under this section but before the case is dismissed or relief is ordered, a creditor holding an unsecured claim that is not contingent, other than a creditor filing under subsection (b) of this section, may join in the petition with the same effect as if such joining creditor were a petitioning creditor under subsection (b) of this section.

(d) The debtor, or a general partner in a partnership debtor that did not join in the petition, may file an answer to a petition under this section.

(e) After notice and a hearing, and for cause, the court may require the petitioners under this section to file a bond to indemnify the debtor for such amounts as the court may later allow under subsection (i) of this section.

(f) Notwithstanding section 363 of this title, except to the extent that the court orders otherwise, and until an order for relief in the case, any business of the debtor may continue to operate, and the debtor may continue to use, acquire, or dispose of property as if an involuntary case concerning the debtor had not been commenced.

(g) At any time after the commencement of an involuntary case under chapter 7 of this title but before an order for relief in the case, the court, on request of a party in interest, after notice to the debtor and a hearing, and if necessary to preserve the property of the estate or to prevent loss to the estate, may order the United States trustee to appoint an interim trustee under section 701 of this title to take possession of the property of the estate and to operate any business of the debtor. Before an order for relief, the debtor may regain possession of property in the possession of a trustee ordered appointed under this subsection if the debtor files such bond as the court requires, conditioned on the debtor's accounting for and delivering to the trustee, if there is an order for relief in the case, such property, or the value, as of the date the debtor regains possession, of such property.

(h) If the petition is not timely controverted, the court shall order relief against the debtor in an involuntary case under the chapter under which the petition was filed. Otherwise, after trial, the court shall order relief against the debtor in an involuntary case under the chapter under which the petition was filed, only if—

(1) the debtor is generally not paying such debtor's debts as such debts become due unless such debts are the subject of a bona fide dispute; or

(2) within 120 days before the date of the filing of the petition, a custodian, other than a trustee, receiver, or agent appointed or authorized to take charge of less than substantially all of the property of the debtor for the purpose of enforcing a lien against such property, was appointed or took possession.

(i) If the court dismisses a petition under this section other than on consent of all petitioners and the debtor, and if the debtor does not waive the right to judgment under this subsection, the court may grant judgment—

    (1) against the petitioners and in favor of the debtor for—

        (A) costs; or

        (B) a reasonable attorney's fee; or

    (2) against any petitioner that filed the petition in bad faith, for—

        (A) any damages proximately caused by such filing; or

        (B) punitive damages.

(j) Only after notice to all creditors and a hearing may the court dismiss a petition filed under this section—

    (1) on the motion of a petitioner;

    (2) on consent of all petitioners and the debtor; or

    (3) for want of prosecution.

(k) Notwithstanding subsection (a) of this section, an involuntary case may be commenced against a foreign bank that is not engaged in such business in the United States only under chapter 7 of this title and only if a foreign proceeding concerning such bank is pending.

Pub.L. 95–598, Nov. 6, 1978, 92 Stat. 2559; Pub.L. 98–353, Title III, §§ 426, 427, July 10, 1984, 98 Stat. 369; Pub.L. 99–554, Title II, §§ 204, 254, 283(b), Oct. 27, 1986, 100 Stat. 3097, 3105, 3116.

Historical and Revision Notes

Notes of Committee on the Judiciary, Senate Report No. 95–989. Section 303 governs the commencement of involuntary cases under title 11. An involuntary case may be commenced only under chapter 7, Liquidation, or chapter 11, Reorganization. Involuntary cases are not permitted for municipalities, because to do so may constitute an invasion of State sovereignty contrary to the 10th amendment, and would constitute bad policy, by permitting the fate of a municipality, governed by officials elected by the people of the municipality, to be determined by a small number of creditors of the municipality. Involuntary chapter 13 cases are not permitted either. To do so would constitute bad policy, because chapter 13 only works when there is a willing debtor that wants to repay his creditors. Short of involuntary servitude, it is difficult to keep a debtor working for his creditors when he does not want to pay them back. See chapter 3, supra.

The exceptions contained in current law that prohibit involuntary cases against farmers, ranchers and eleemosynary institutions are continued. Farmers and ranchers are excepted because of the cyclical nature of their business. One drought year or one year of low prices, as a result of which a farmer is temporarily unable to pay his creditors, should not subject him to involuntary bankruptcy. Eleemosynary institutions, such as churches, schools, and charitable organizations and foundations, likewise are exempt from involuntary bankruptcy.

The provisions for involuntary chapter 11 cases is a slight change from present law, based on the proposed consolidation of the reorganization chapters. Currently, involuntary cases are permitted under chapters X [former section 501 et seq. of this title] and XII [former section 801 et seq. of this title] but not under chapter XI [former section 701 et seq. of this title]. The consolidation requires a single rule for all kinds of reorganization proceedings. Because the assets of an insolvent debtor belong equitably to his creditors, the bill permits involuntary cases in order that creditors may realize on their assets through reorganization as well as through liquidation.

Subsection (b) of the section specifies who may file an involuntary petition. As under current law, if the debtor has more than 12 creditors, three creditors must join in the involuntary petition. The dollar amount limitation is changed from current law to $5,000.

The new amount applies both to liquidation and reorganization cases in order that there not be an artificial difference between the two chapters that would provide an incentive for one or the other. Subsection (b)(1) makes explicit the right of an indenture trustee to be one of the three petitioning creditors on behalf of the creditors the trustee represents under the indenture. If all of the general partners in a partnership are in bankruptcy, then the trustee of a single general partner may file an involuntary petition against the partnership. Finally, a foreign representative may file an involuntary case concerning the debtor in the foreign proceeding, in order to administer assets in this country. This subsection is not intended to overrule Bankruptcy Rule 104(d), which places certain restrictions on the transfer of claims for the purpose of commencing an involuntary case. That Rule will be continued under section 405(d) of this bill [S. 2266].

Subsection (c) permits creditors other than the original petitioning creditors to join in the petition with the same effect as if the joining creditor had been one of the original petitioning creditors. Thus, if the claim of one of the original petitioning creditors is disallowed, the case will not be dismissed for want of three creditors or want of $5,000 in petitioning claims if the joining creditor suffices to fulfill the statutory requirements.

Subsection (d) permits the debtor to file an answer to an involuntary petition. The subsection also permits a general partner in a partnership debtor to answer an involuntary petition against the partnership if he did not join in the petition. Thus, a partnership petition by less than all of the general partners is treated as an involuntary, not a voluntary, petition.

The court may, under subsection (e), require the petitioners to file a bond to indemnify the debtor for such amounts as the court may later allow under subsection (i). Subsection (i) provides for costs, attorneys fees, and damages in certain circumstances. The bonding requirement will discourage frivolous petitions as well as spiteful petitions based on a desire to embarrass the debtor (who may be a competitor of a petitioning creditor) or to put the debtor out of business without good cause. An involuntary petition may put a debtor out of business even if it is without foundation and is later dismissed.

Subsection (f) is both a clarification and a change from existing law. It permits the debtor to continue to operate any business of the debtor and to dispose of property as if the case had not been commenced. The court is permitted, however, to control the debtor's powers under this subsection by appropriate orders, such as where there is a fear that the debtor may attempt to abscond with assets, dispose of them at less than their fair value, or dismantle his business, all to the detriment of the debtor's creditors.

The court may also, under subsection (g), appoint an interim trustee to take possession of the debtor's property and to operate any business of the debtor, pending trial on the involuntary petition. The court may make such an order only on the request of a party in interest, and after notice to the debtor and a hearing. There must be a showing that a trustee is necessary to preserve the property of the estate or to prevent loss to the estate. The debtor may regain possession by posting a sufficient bond.

Subsection (h) provides the standard for an order for relief on an involuntary petition. If the petition is not timely controverted (the Rules of Bankruptcy Procedure will fix time limits), the court orders relief after a trial, only if the debtor is generally unable to pay its debts as they mature, or if the debtor has failed to pay a major portion of his debts as they become due, or if a custodian was appointed during the 90-day period preceding the filing of the petition. The first two tests are variations of the equity insolvency test. They represent the most significant departure from present law concerning the grounds for involuntary bankruptcy, which requires an act of bankruptcy. Proof of the commission of an act of bankruptcy has frequently required a showing that the debtor was insolvent on a "balance-sheet" test when the act was committed. This bill abolishes the concept of acts of bankruptcy.

The equity insolvency test has been in equity jurisprudence for hundreds of years, and though it is new in the bankruptcy context (except in chapter X [former section 501 et seq. of this title]), the bankruptcy courts should have no difficulty in applying it. The third test, appointment of a custodian within ninety days before the petition, is provided for simplicity. It is not a partial re-enactment of acts of bankruptcy. If a custodian of all or substantially all of the property of the debtor has been appointed, this paragraph creates an irrebuttable presumption that the debtor is unable to pay its debts as they mature. Moreover, once a proceeding to liquidate assets has been commenced, the debtor's creditors have an absolute right to have the liquidation (or reorganization) proceed in the bankruptcy court and under the bankruptcy laws with all of the appropriate creditor and debtor protections that those laws provide. Ninety days gives creditors ample time in which to seek bankruptcy liquidation after the appointment of a custodian. If they wait beyond the ninety day period, they are not precluded from filing an involuntary petition. They are simply required to prove equity insolvency rather than the more easily provable custodian test.

Subsection (i) permits the court to award costs, reasonable attorney's fees, or damages if an involuntary petition is dismissed other than by consent of all petitioning creditors and the debtor. The damages that the court may award are those that may be caused by the taking of possession of the debtor's property under subsection (g) or section 1104 of the bankruptcy code [former Title 11]. In addition, if a petitioning creditor filed the petition in bad faith, the court may award the debtor any damages proximately caused by the filing of the petition. These damages may include such items as loss of business during and after the pendency of the case, and so on. "Or" is not exclusive in this paragraph. The court may grant any or all of the damages provided for under the provision. Dismissal in the best interests of credits under section 305(a)(1) would not give rise to a damages claim.

Under subsection (j), the court may dismiss the petition by consent only after giving notice to all creditors. The purpose of the subsection is to prevent collusive settlements among the debtor and the petitioning creditors while other creditors, that wish to see relief ordered with respect to the debtor but that did not participate in the case, are left without sufficient protection.

Subsection (k) governs involuntary cases against foreign banks that are not engaged in business in the United States but that have assets located here. The subsection prevents a foreign bank from being placed into bankruptcy in this country unless a foreign proceeding against the bank is pending. The special protection afforded by this section is needed to prevent creditors from effectively closing down a foreign bank by the commencement of an involuntary bankruptcy case in this country unless that bank is involved in a proceeding under foreign law. An involuntary case commenced under this subsection gives the foreign representative an alternative to commencing a case ancillary to a foreign proceeding under section 304.

Legislative Statements. Section 303(b)(1) is modified to make clear that unsecured claims against the debtor must be determined by taking into account liens securing property held by third parties.

Section 303(b)(3) adopts a provision contained in the Senate amendment indicating that an involuntary petition may be commenced against a partnership by fewer than all of the general partners in such partnership. Such action may be taken by fewer than all of the general partners notwithstanding a contrary agreement between the partners or State or local law.

Section 303(h)(1) in the House amendment is a compromise of standards found in H.R. 8200 as passed by the House and the Senate amendment pertaining to the standards that must be met in order to obtain an order for relief in an involuntary case under title 11. The language specifies that the court will order such relief only if the debtor is generally not paying debtor's debts as they become due.

Section 303(h)(2) reflects a compromise pertaining to section 543 of title 11 relating to turnover of property by a custodian. It provides an alternative test to support an order for relief in an involuntary case. If a custodian, other than a trustee, receiver, or agent appointed or authorized to take charge of less than substantially all of the property of the debtor for the purpose of enforcing a lien against such property, was appointed or took possession within 120 days before the date of the filing of the petition, then the court may order relief in the involuntary case. The test under section 303(h)(2) differs from section 3a(5) of the Bankruptcy Act [former section 21(a)(5) of this title], which requires an involuntary case to be commenced before the earlier of time such custodian was appointed or took possession. The test in section 303(h)(2) authorizes an order for relief to be entered in an involuntary case from the later date on which the custodian was appointed or took possession.

1986 Amendment. Subsec. (g). Pub.L. 99–554, § 204(1), substituted "may order the United States trustee to appoint" for "may appoint".

Subsec. (i)(1)(A). Pub.L. 99–554, § 204(2), substituted "costs; or" for "costs;".

Subsec. (i)(1)(C). Pub.L. 99–554, § 204(2), struck out "(C) any damages proximately caused by the taking of possession of the debtor's property by a trustee appointed under subsection (g) of this section or section 1104 of this title; or".

See Effective Date of 1986 Amendment, etc., notes set out below.

Effective Date of 1986 Amendments; Savings Provisions; Effective Date of 1986 Amendments for Certain Judicial Districts Not Served by United States Trustees and for Judicial Districts in Alabama and North Carolina; U.S. Trustee System Fund Deposits in Alabama and North Carolina; Effective Date of Title 11 Chapter 15 Repeal as to Northern District of Alabama; Authority of Certain Estate Administrators in Alabama and North Carolina; Effective Date of 1986 Amendments in Pending Cases Where a U.S. Trustee Not Authorized or Where a Trustee Files Final Report or Plan is Confirmed; Quarterly Fees. Amendment by Pub.L. 99–554 effective 30 days after Oct. 27, 1986, except as otherwise provided for, see section 302(a) of Pub.L. 99–554, set out as a note under section 581 of Title 28, Judiciary and Judicial Procedure.

Amendments by Pub.L. 99–554, § 254, not to apply with respect to cases commenced under Title 11, Bankruptcy, before 30 days after Oct. 27, 1986, see section 302(c)(1) of Pub. L. 99–554, set out as a note under section 581 of Title 28.

Amendment by Pub.L. 99–554, § 204, not to become effective in or with respect to certain specified judicial districts until, or apply to cases while pending in such district before, the expiration of the 270-day period beginning 30 days after Oct. 27, 1986, or of the 30-day period beginning on the date the Attorney General certifies under section 303 of Pub.L. 99–554 the region specified in a paragraph of section 581(a) of Title 28, as amended by section 111(a) of Pub.L. 99–554, that includes such district, whichever occurs first, see section 302(d)(1) of Pub.L. 99–554, set out as a note under section 581 of Title 28.

Amendment by Pub.L. 99–554, § 204, not to become effective in or with respect to certain specified judicial districts until, or apply to cases while pending in such districts before, the expiration of the 2-year period beginning 30 days after Oct. 27, 1986, or of the 30-day period beginning on the date the Attorney General certifies under section 303 of Pub.L. 99–554 the region specified in a paragraph of section 581(a) of Title 28, as amended by section 111(a) of Pub.L. 99–554, that includes such district, whichever occurs first, see sec-

tion 302(d)(2) of Pub.L. 99–554, set out as a note under section 581 of Title 28.

Amendment by Pub.L. 99–554, § 204, not to become effective in or with respect to judicial districts established for the States of Alabama and North Carolina until, or apply to cases while pending in such district before, such district elects to be included in a bankruptcy region established in section 581(a) of Title 28, as amended by section 111(a) of Pub.L. 99–554, or Oct. 1, 2002, whichever occurs first, and, except as otherwise provided for, with respect to cases under chapters 7, 11, 12, and 13 of Title 11 commenced before 30 days after Oct. 27, 1986, and pending in a judicial district in the States of Alabama or North Carolina before any election made under section 302(d)(3) (A) of Pub.L. 99–554 by such district becomes effective or Oct. 1, 2002, whichever occurs first, amendments by Pub.L. 99–554 not to apply until Oct. 1, 2003, or the expiration of the 1-year period beginning on the date such election becomes effective, whichever occurs first, and further, in any judicial district in Alabama or North Carolina not making the election described in section 302(d)(3)(A) of Pub.L. 99–554, any person appointed under regulations issued by the Judicial Conference to administer estates in cases under Title 11 authorized to establish, etc., a panel of private trustees, and to supervise cases and trustees in cases under chapters 7, 11, 12, and 13 of Title 11, until amendments by sections 201 to 231 of Pub.L. 99–554 effective in such district, see section 302(d)(3)(A) to (F), (H), (I) of Pub.L. 99–554, set out as a note under section 581 of Title 28.

Amendment by Pub.L. 99–554, § 204, except as otherwise provided, with respect to cases under chapters 7, 11, 12, and 13 of Title 11 commenced before 30 days after Oct. 27, 1986, and pending in a judicial district referred to in section 581(a) of Title 28, as amended by section 111(a) of Pub.L. 99–554, for which a United States trustee is not authorized before 30 days after Oct. 27, 1986 to be appointed, not applicable until the expiration of the 3-year period beginning on Oct. 27, 1986, or of the 1-year period beginning on the date the Attorney General certifies under section 303 of Pub.L. 99–554 the region specified in a paragraph of such section 581(a) that includes, such district, whichever occurs first, see section 302(e)(1), (2) of Pub.L. 99–554, set out as a note under section 581 of Title 28.

See 1986 Amendment notes set out above.

Effective Date of 1984 Amendments. See section 553 of Pub.L. 98–353, Title III, July 10,

1984, 98 Stat. 392, set out as an Effective Date of 1984 Amendment note preceding chapter 1 of Title 11, Bankruptcy.

Separability of Provisions. For separability of provisions of Title III of Pub.L. 98–

353, see section 551 of Pub.L. 98–353 set out as a Separability of Provisions note preceding chapter 1 of Title 11, Bankruptcy.

Cross References

Allowance of administrative expenses incurred by creditor filing petition, see section 503.
Automatic stay, see section 362 of this title.
Petition defined, see section 101.
Postpetition transactions, see section 549.
Property of estate, see section 541.
Sharing of compensation between attorneys, see section 504.

Library References:

C.J.S. Bankruptcy §§ 45–47, 56–63.
West's Key No. Digests, Bankruptcy ☞2223, 2229, 2233, 2281–2297.

WESTLAW Electronic Research

See WESTLAW Electronic Research Guide following the *Bankruptcy Highlights*.

§ 304.   Cases ancillary to foreign proceedings

(a) A case ancillary to a foreign proceeding is commenced by the filing with the bankruptcy court of a petition under this section by a foreign representative.

(b) Subject to the provisions of subsection (c) of this section, if a party in interest does not timely controvert the petition, or after trial, the court may—

    (1) enjoin the commencement or continuation of—

        (A) any action against—

            (i) a debtor with respect to property involved in such foreign proceeding; or

            (ii) such property; or

        (B) the enforcement of any judgment against the debtor with respect to such property, or any act or the commencement or continuation of any judicial proceeding to create or enforce a lien against the property of such estate;

    (2) order turnover of the property of such estate, or the proceeds of such property, to such foreign representative; or

    (3) order other appropriate relief.

(c) In determining whether to grant relief under subsection (b) of this section, the court shall be guided by what will best assure an economical and expeditious administration of such estate, consistent with—

    (1) just treatment of all holders of claims against or interests in such estate;

    (2) protection of claim holders in the United States against prejudice and inconvenience in the processing of claims in such foreign proceeding;

    (3) prevention of preferential or fraudulent dispositions of property of such estate;

    (4) distribution of proceeds of such estate substantially in accordance with the order prescribed by this title;

    (5) comity; and

(6) if appropriate, the provision of an opportunity for a fresh start for the individual that such foreign proceeding concerns.

Pub.L. 95–598, Nov. 6, 1978, 92 Stat. 2560.

Historical and Revision Notes

Notes of Committee on the Judiciary, Senate Report No. 95–989. This section governs cases filed in the bankruptcy courts that are ancillary to foreign proceedings. That is, where a foreign bankruptcy case is pending concerning a particular debtor and that debtor has assets in this country, the foreign representative may file a petition under this section, which does not commence a full bankruptcy case, in order to administer assets located in this country, to prevent dismemberment by local creditors of assets located here, or for other appropriate relief. The debtor is given the opportunity to controvert the petition.

Subsection (c) requires the court to consider several factors in determining what relief, if any, to grant. The court is to be guided by what will best assure an economical and expeditious administration of the estate, consistent with just treatment of all creditors and equity security holders; protection of local creditors and equity security holders against prejudice and inconvenience in processing claims and interests in the foreign proceeding; prevention of preferential or fraudulent disposition of property of the estate; distribution of the proceeds of the estate substantially in conformity with the distribution provisions of the bankruptcy code; and, if the debtor is an individual, the provision of an opportunity for a fresh start. These guidelines are designed to give the court the maximum flexibility in handling ancillary cases. Principles of international comity and respect for the judgments and laws of other nations suggest that the court be permitted to make the appropriate orders under all of the circumstances of each case, rather than being provided with inflexible rules.

Legislative Statements. Section 304(b) adopts a provision contained in the Senate amendment with modifications. The provision indicates that if a party in interest does not timely controvert the petition in a case ancillary to a foreign proceeding, or after trial on the merits, the court may take various actions, including enjoining the commencement or continuation of any action against the debtor with respect to property involved in the proceeding, or against the property itself; enjoining the enforcement of any judgment against the debtor or the debtor's property; or the commencement or continuation of any judicial proceeding to create or enforce a lien against the property of the debtor or the estate.

Section 304(c) is modified to indicate that the court shall be guided by considerations of comity in addition to the other factors specified therein.

Cross References
Petition defined, see section 101.

Library References:
C.J.S. Bankruptcy § 39.
West's Key No. Digests, Bankruptcy ⊜2341.

WESTLAW Electronic Research
See WESTLAW Electronic Research Guide following the *Bankruptcy Highlights*.

§ 305. Abstention

(a) The court, after notice and a hearing, may dismiss a case under this title, or may suspend all proceedings in a case under this title, at any time if—

(1) the interests of creditors and the debtor would be better served by such dismissal or suspension; or

(2)(A) there is pending a foreign proceeding; and

(B) the factors specified in section 304(c) of this title warrant such dismissal or suspension.

(b) A foreign representative may seek dismissal or suspension under subsection (a)(2) of this section.

(c) An order under subsection (a) of this section dismissing a case or suspending all proceedings in a case, or a decision not so to dismiss or suspend, is not reviewable by appeal or otherwise by the court of appeals under section 158(d), 1291, or 1292 of this title[1] or by the Supreme Court of the United States under section 1254 of this title.[1]

Pub.L. 95–598, Nov. 6, 1978, 92 Stat. 2561; Pub.L. 101–650, Title III, § 309(a), Dec. 1, 1990, 104 Stat. 5113.

1 See References in Text note below.

Historical and Revision Notes

Notes of Committee on the Judiciary, Senate Report No. 95–989. A principle of the common law requires a court with jurisdiction over a particular matter to take jurisdiction. This section recognizes that there are cases in which it would be appropriate for the court to decline jurisdiction. Abstention under this section, however, is of jurisdiction over the entire case. Abstention from jurisdiction over a particular proceeding in a case is governed by proposed 28 U.S.C. 1471(c). Thus, the court is permitted, if the interests of creditors and the debtor would be better served by dismissal of the case or suspension of all proceedings in the case, to so order. The court may dismiss or suspend under the first paragraph, for example, if an arrangement is being worked out by creditors and the debtor out of court, there is no prejudice to the results of creditors in that arrangement, and an involuntary case has been commenced by a few recalcitrant creditors to provide a basis for future threats to extract full pay-ment. The less expensive out-of-court work-out may better serve the interests in the case. Likewise, if there is pending a foreign proceeding concerning the debtor and the factors specified in proposed 11 U.S.C. 304(c) warrant dismissal or suspension, the court may so act.

Subsection (b) gives a foreign representative authority to appear in the bankruptcy court to request dismissal or suspension. Subsection (c) makes the dismissal or suspension order nonreviewable by appeal or otherwise. The bankruptcy court, based on its experience and discretion is vested with the power of decision.

References in Text. Pub.L. 101–650 amended subsec. (c) by adding references to section 158(d), 1254, 1291, or 1292 of this title. The sections referred to are not set out in this title of the Code, Title 11, Bankruptcy, but in Title 28, Judiciary and Judicial Procedure, where review provisions for the courts of appeals and Supreme Court are found.

Library References:

C.J.S. Bankruptcy § 16; Federal Courts § 10(1) et seq.
West's Key No. Digests, Federal Courts ☞47.

WESTLAW Electronic Research

See WESTLAW Electronic Research Guide following the *Bankruptcy Highlights*.

§ 306. Limited appearance

An appearance in a bankruptcy court by a foreign representative in connection with a petition or request under section 303, 304, or 305 of this title does not submit such foreign representative to the jurisdiction of any court in the United States for any other purpose, but the bankruptcy court may condition any order under section 303, 304, or 305 of this title on compliance by such foreign representative with the orders of such bankruptcy court.

Pub.L. 95–598, Nov. 6, 1978, 92 Stat. 2561.

Historical and Revision Notes

Notes of Committee on the Judiciary, Senate Report No. 95–989. Section 306 permits a foreign representative that is seeking dismissal or suspension under section 305 of an ancillary case or that is appearing in connection with a petition under section 303 or 304 to appear without subjecting himself to the jurisdiction of any other court in the United States, including State courts. The protection is necessary to allow the foreign representative to present his case and the case of the foreign estate, without waiving the normal jurisdictional rules of the foreign country. That is, creditors in this country will still have to seek redress against the foreign estate according to the host country's jurisdictional rules. Any other result would permit local creditors to obtain unfair advantage by filing an involuntary case, thus requiring the foreign representative to appear, and then obtaining local jurisdiction over the representative in connection with his appearance in this country. That kind of bankruptcy law would legalize an ambush technique that has frequently been rejected by the common law in other contexts.

However, the bankruptcy court is permitted under section 306 to condition any relief under section 303, 304, or 305 on the compliance by the foreign representative with the orders of the bankruptcy court. The last provision is not carte blanche to the bankruptcy court to require the foreign representative to submit to jurisdiction in other courts contrary to the general policy of the section. It is designed to enable the bankruptcy court to enforce its own orders that are necessary to the appropriate relief granted under section 303, 304, or 305.

Library References:
C.J.S. Appearances §§ 6, 7, 18, 19, 24, 29.
West's Key No. Digests, Appearance ☞9.

WESTLAW Electronic Research
See WESTLAW Electronic Research Guide following the *Bankruptcy Highlights.*

§ 307. United States trustee

The United States trustee may raise and may appear and be heard on any issue in any case or proceeding under this title but may not file a plan pursuant to section 1121(c) of this title.

Added Pub.L. 99–554, Title II, § 205(a), Oct. 27, 1986, 100 Stat. 3098.

Historical and Revision Notes

Effective Date; Effective Date of 1986 Amendments for Certain Judicial Districts Not Served by United States Trustees and for Judicial Districts in Alabama and North Carolina; U.S. Trustee System Fund Deposits in Alabama and North Carolina; Effective Date of Title 11 Chapter 15 Repeal as to Northern District of Alabama; Authority of Certain Estate Administrators in Alabama and North Carolina; Effective Date of 1986 Amendments in Pending Cases Where a U.S. Trustee Not Authorized or Where a Trustee Files Final Report or Plan is Confirmed; Quarterly Fees. Enactment by Pub.L. 99–554, effective 30 days after Oct. 27, 1986, except as otherwise provided for, see section 302(a) of Pub.L. 99–554, set out as a note under section 581 of Title 28, Judiciary and Judicial Procedure.

Enactment by Pub.L. 99–554, § 205(a), not to become effective in or with respect to certain specified judicial districts until, or apply to cases while pending in such district before, the expiration of the 270-day period beginning 30 days after Oct. 27, 1986, or of the 30-day period beginning on the date the Attorney General certifies under section 303 of Pub.L. 99–554 the region specified in a paragraph of section 581(a) of Title 28, as amended by section 111(a) of Pub.L. 99–554, that includes such district, whichever occurs first, see section 302(d)(1) of Pub.L. 99–554, set out as a note under section 581 of Title 28.

Enactment by Pub.L. 99–554, § 205(a), not to become effective in or with respect to certain specified judicial districts until, or apply to cases while pending in such district before, the expiration of the 2-year period beginning 30 days after Oct. 27, 1986, or of the 30-day period beginning on the date the Attorney General certifies under section 303 of Pub.L. 99–554 the region specified in a paragraph of section 581(a) of Title 28, as amended by section 111(a) of Pub.L. 99–554, that includes such district, whichever occurs first, see section 302(d)(2) of Pub.L. 99–554, set out as a note under section 581 of Title 28.

Enactment by Pub.L. 99–554, § 205(a), not to become effective in or with respect to judicial districts established for the States of Alabama and North Carolina until, or apply to cases while pending in such district before, such district elects to be included in a bankruptcy region established in section 581(a) of Title 28, as amended by section 111(a) of Pub. L. 99–554, or Oct. 1, 2002, whichever occurs first, and, except as otherwise provided for, with respect to cases under chapters 7, 11, 12, and 13 of Title 11 commenced before 30 days after Oct. 27, 1986, and pending in a judicial district in the States of Alabama or North Carolina before an election made under section 302(d)(3)(A) of Pub.L. 99–554 by such district becomes effective or Oct. 1, 2002, whichever occurs first, amendments by Pub.L. 99–554 not to apply until Oct. 1, 2003, or the expiration of the 1-year period beginning on the date such election becomes effective, whichever occurs first, and further, in any judicial district in Alabama or North Carolina not making the election described in section 302(d)(3)(A) of Pub.L. 99–554, any person appointed under regulations issued by the Judicial Conference to administer estates in cases under Title 11 authorized to establish, etc., a panel of private trustees, and to supervise cases and trustees in cases under chapters 7, 11, 12, and 13 of Title 11, until amendments by sections 201 to 231 of Pub.L. 99–554 effective in such district, see section 302(d)(3)(A) to (F), (H), (I), of Pub.L. 99–554, set out as a note under section 581 of Title 28.

Standing. Pub.L. 101–650. Title III, § 317(b), Dec. 1, 1990, 104 Stat. 5115, provided that: "A bankruptcy administrator may raise and may appear and be heard on any issue in any case under title 11, United States Code [this title], but may not file a plan pursuant to section 1121(c) of such title [section 1121(c) of this title]."

Cross References

See 28 U.S.C.A. § 581 et seq., infra.

Library References:

C.J.S. Bankruptcy § 38.
West's Key No. Digests, Bankruptcy ⊗2205.

SUBCHAPTER II—OFFICERS

§ 321.　Eligibility to serve as trustee

(a) A person may serve as trustee in a case under this title only if such person is—

　　(1) an individual that is competent to perform the duties of trustee and, in a case under chapter 7, 12, or 13 of this title, resides or has an office in the judicial district within which the case is pending, or in any judicial district adjacent to such district; or

　　(2) a corporation authorized by such corporation's charter or bylaws to act as trustee, and, in a case under chapter 7, 12, or 13 of this title, having an office in at least one of such districts.

(b) A person that has served as an examiner in the case may not serve as trustee in the case.

(c) The United States trustee for the judicial district in which the case is pending is eligible to serve as trustee in the case if necessary.

Pub.L. 95–598, Nov. 6, 1978, 92 Stat. 2561; Pub.L. 98–353, Title III, § 428, July 10, 1984, 98 Stat. 369; Pub.L. 99–554, Title II, §§ 206, 257(c), Oct. 27, 1986, 100 Stat. 3098, 3114.

Historical and Revision Notes

Notes of Committee on the Judiciary, Senate Report No. 95–989. Section 321 is adapted from current Bankruptcy Act § 45 [former section 73 of this title] and Bankruptcy Rule 209. Subsection (a) specifies that an individual may serve as trustee in a bankruptcy case only if he is competent to perform the duties of trustee and resides or has an office in the judicial district within which the case is pending, or in an adjacent judicial district. A corporation must be authorized by its charter or bylaws to act as trustee, and, for chapter 7 or 13 cases, must have an office in any of the above mentioned judicial districts.

Legislative Statements. Section 321 indicates that an examiner may not serve as a trustee in the case.

1986 Amendment. Subsec. (c). Pub.L. 99–554, § 206, added subsec. (c).

See Effective Date of 1986 Amendment, etc., notes set out below.

Effective Date of 1986 Amendments; Savings Provisions; Effective Date of 1986 Amendments for Certain Judicial Districts Not Served by United States Trustees and for Judicial Districts in Alabama and North Carolina; U.S. Trustee System Fund Deposits in Alabama and North Carolina; Effective Date of Title 11 Chapter 15 Repeal as to Northern District of Alabama; Authority of Certain Estate Administrators in Alabama and North Carolina; Effective Date of 1986 Amendments in Pending Cases Where a U.S. Trustee Not Authorized or Where a Trustee Files Final Report or Plan is Confirmed; Quarterly Fees. Amendment by Pub.L. 99–554 effective 30 days after Oct. 27, 1986, except as otherwise provided for, see section 302(a) of Pub.L. 99–554, set out as a note under section 581 of Title 28, Judiciary and Judicial Procedure.

Amendments by Pub.L. 99–554, § 257(c), not to apply with respect to cases commenced under Title 11, Bankruptcy, before 30 days after Oct. 27, 1986, see section 302(c)(1) of Pub. L. 99–554, set out as a note under section 581 of Title 28.

Amendment by Pub.L. 99–554, § 206, not to become effective in or with respect to certain specified judicial districts until, or apply to cases while pending in such district before, the expiration of the 270-day period beginning 30 days after Oct. 27, 1986, or of the 30-day period beginning on the date the Attorney General certifies under section 303 of Pub.L. 99–554 the region specified in a paragraph of section 581(a) of Title 28, as amended by section 111(a) of Pub.L. 99–554, that includes such district, whichever occurs first, see section 302(d)(1) of Pub.L. 99–554, set out as a note under section 581 of Title 28.

Amendment by Pub.L. 99–554, § 206, not to become effective in or with respect to certain specified judicial districts until, or apply to cases while pending in such district before, the expiration of the 2-year period beginning 30 days after Oct. 27, 1986, or of the 30-day period beginning on the date the Attorney General certifies under section 303 of Pub.L. 99–554 the region specified in a paragraph of section 581(a) of Title 28, as amended by section 111(a) of Pub.L. 99–554, that includes such district, whichever occurs first, see section 302(d)(2) of Pub.L. 99–554, set out as a note under section 581 of Title 28.

Amendment by Pub.L. 99–554, § 206, not to become effective in or with respect to judicial districts established for the States of Alabama and North Carolina until, or apply to cases while pending in such district before, such district elects to be included in a bankruptcy region established in section 581(a) of Title 28, as amended by section 111(a) of Pub.L. 99–554, or Oct. 1, 2002, whichever occurs first, and, except as otherwise provided for, with respect to cases under chapters 7, 11, 12, and 13 of Title 11 commenced before 30 days after Oct. 27, 1986, and pending in a judicial district in the States of Alabama or North Carolina before any election made under section 302(d)(3)(A) of Pub.L. 99–554 by such district becomes effective or Oct. 1, 2002, whichever occurs first, amendments by Pub.L. 99–554 not to apply until Oct. 1, 2003, or the expiration of the 1-year period beginning on the date such election becomes effective whichever occurs first, and further, in any judicial district in Alabama or North Carolina not making the election described in section 302(d)(3)(A) of Pub.L. 99–554, any person appointed under regulations issued by the Judicial Conference to administer estates in cases under Title 11 authorized to establish, etc., a panel of private trustees, and to supervise cases and trustees in cases under chapters 7, 11, 12, and 13 of Title 11, until amendments by sections 201 to 231 of Pub.L. 99–554 effective in such district, see section 302(d)(3)(A) to (F), (H), (I) of Pub.L. 99–554, set out as a note under section 581 of Title 28.

Amendment by Pub.L. 99–554, § 206, except as otherwise provided, with respect to cases under chapters 7, 11, 12, and 13 of Title 11 commenced before 30 days after Oct. 27, 1986, and pending in a judicial district referred to in section 581(a) of Title 28, as amended by section 111(a) of Pub.L. 99–554, for which a United States trustee is not authorized before 30 days after Oct. 27, 1986 to be appointed, not applicable until the expiration of the 3-year period beginning on Oct. 27, 1986, or of the 1-year period beginning on the date the Attorney General certifies under section 303 of

Pub.L. 99–554 the region specified in a paragraph of such section 581(a) that includes, such district, whichever occurs first, see section 302(e)(1), (2) of Pub.L. 99–554, set out as a note under section 581 of Title 28.

See 1986 Amendment notes set out above.

Effective Date of 1984 Amendments. See section 553 of Pub.L. 98–353, Title III, July 10,

1984, 98 Stat. 392, set out as an Effective Date of 1984 Amendment note preceding chapter 1 of Title 11, Bankruptcy.

Separability of Provisions. For separability of provisions of Title III of Pub.L. 98–353, see section 551 of Pub.L. 98–353 set out as a Separability of Provisions note preceding chapter 1 of Title 11, Bankruptcy.

Library References:

C.J.S. Appearances § 40; Bankruptcy § 195.
West's Key No. Digests, Appearance ⚯20; Bankruptcy ⚯3003.

WESTLAW Electronic Research

See WESTLAW Electronic Research Guide following the *Bankruptcy Highlights*.

§ 322. Qualification of trustee

(a) Except as provided in subsection (b)(1), a person selected under section 701, 702, 703, 1104, 1163, 1302, or 1202 of this title to serve as trustee in a case under this title qualifies if before five days after such selection, and before beginning official duties, such person has filed with the court a bond in favor of the United States conditioned on the faithful performance of such official duties.

(b)(1) The United States trustee qualifies wherever such trustee serves as trustee in a case under this title.

(2) The United States trustee shall determine—

(A) the amount of a bond required to be filed under subsection (a) of this section; and

(B) the sufficiency of the surety on such bond.

(c) A trustee is not liable personally or on such trustee's bond in favor of the United States for any penalty or forfeiture incurred by the debtor.

(d) A proceeding on a trustee's bond may not be commenced after two years after the date on which such trustee was discharged.

Pub.L. 95–598, Nov. 6, 1978, 92 Stat. 2562; Pub.L. 98–353, Title III, § 429, July 10, 1984, 98 Stat. 369; Pub.L. 99–554, Title II, §§ 207, 257(d), Oct. 27, 1986, 100 Stat. 3098, 3114.

Historical and Revision Notes

Notes of Committee on the Judiciary, Senate Report No. 95–989. A trustee qualifies in a case by filing, within five days after selection, a bond in favor of the United States, conditioned on the faithful performance of his official duties. This section is derived from the Bankruptcy Act section 50b [former section 78(b) of this title]. The court is required to determine the amount of the bond and the sufficiency of the surety on the bond. Subsection (c), derived from Bankruptcy Act section 50i [former section 78(i) of this title], relieves the trustee from personal liability and from liability on his bond for any penalty or forfeiture incurred by the debtor. Subsection (d),

derived from section 50m [former section 78(m) of this title], fixes a two-year statute of limitations on any action on a trustee's bond. Finally, subsection (e) dispenses with the bonding requirement for the United States trustee.

Legislative Statements. Section 322(a) is modified to include a trustee serving in a railroad reorganization under subchapter IV of chapter 11.

1986 Amendment. Subsec. (a). Pub.L. 99–554, § 207(1), substituted "Except as provided in subsection (b)(1), a person" for "A person".

Subsec. (b). Pub.L. 99–554, § 207(2), added par. (1), designated existing provisions as par. (2), and, as so designated, substituted "The United States trustee" for "The court", "(A) the amount" for "(1) the amount", and "(B) the sufficiency" for "(2) the sufficiency".

See Effective Date of 1986 Amendment, etc., notes set out below.

Effective Date of 1986 Amendments; Savings Provisions; Effective Date of 1986 Amendments for Certain Judicial Districts Not Served by United States Trustees and for Judicial Districts in Alabama and North Carolina; U.S. Trustee System Fund Deposits in Alabama and North Carolina; Effective Date of Title 11 Chapter 15 Repeal as to Northern District of Alabama; Authority of Certain Estate Administrators in Alabama and North Carolina; Effective Date of 1986 Amendments in Pending Cases Where a U.S. Trustee Not Authorized or Where a Trustee Files Final Report or Plan is Confirmed; Quarterly Fees. Amendment by Pub.L. 99–554 effective 30 days after Oct. 27, 1986, except as otherwise provided for, see section 302(a) of Pub.L. 99–554, set out as a note under section 581 of Title 28, Judiciary and Judicial Procedure.

Amendment by Pub.L. 99–554, § 257(d) not to apply with respect to cases commenced under Title 11, Bankruptcy, before 30 days after Oct. 27, 1986, see section 302(c)(1) of Pub. L. 99–554, set out as a note under section 581 of Title 28.

Amendment by Pub.L. 99–554, § 207 not to become effective in or with respect to certain specified judicial districts until, or apply to cases while pending in such district before, the expiration of the 270-day period beginning 30 days after Oct. 27, 1986, or of the 30-day period beginning on the date the Attorney General certifies under section 303 of Pub.L. 99–554 the region specified in a paragraph of section 581(a) of Title 28, as amended by section 111(a) of Pub.L. 99–554, that includes such district, whichever occurs first, see section 302(d)(1) of Pub.L. 99–554, set out as a note under section 581 of Title 28.

Amendment by Pub.L. 99–554, § 207, not to become effective in or with respect to certain specified judicial districts until, or apply to cases while pending in such district before, the expiration of the 2-year period beginning 30 days after Oct. 27, 1986, or of the 30-day period beginning on the date the Attorney General certifies under section 303 of Pub.L. 99–554 the region specified in a paragraph of

section 581(a) of Title 28, as amended by section 111(a) of Pub.L. 99–554, that includes such district, whichever occurs first, see section 302(d)(2) of Pub.L. 99–554, set out as a note under section 581 of Title 28.

Amendment by Pub.L. 99–554, § 207, not to become effective in or with respect to judicial districts established for the States of Alabama and North Carolina until, or apply to cases while pending in such district before, such district elects to be included in a bankruptcy region established in section 581(a) of Title 28, as amended by section 111(a) of Pub.L. 99–554, or Oct. 1, 2002, whichever occurs first, and, except as otherwise provided for, with respect to cases under chapters 7, 11, 12, and 13 of Title 11 commenced before 30 days after Oct. 27, 1986, and pending in a judicial district in the States of Alabama or North Carolina before any election made under section 302(d)(3)(A) of Pub.L. 99–554 by such district becomes effective or Oct. 1, 2002, whichever occurs first, amendments by Pub.L. 99–554 not to apply until Oct. 1, 2003, or the expiration of the 1-year period beginning on the date such election becomes effective, whichever occurs first, and further, in any judicial district in Alabama or North Carolina not making the election described in section 302(d)(3)(A) of Pub.L. 99–554, any person appointed under regulations issued by the Judicial Conference to administer estates in cases under Title 11 authorized to establish, etc., a panel of private trustees, and to supervise cases and trustees in cases under chapters 7, 11, 12, and 13 of Title 11, until amendments by sections 201 to 231 of Pub.L. 99–554 effective in such district, see section 302(d)(3)(A) to (F), (H), (I) of Pub.L. 99–554, set out as a note under section 581 of Title 28.

Amendment by Pub.L. 99–554, § 207, except as otherwise provided, with respect to cases under chapters 7, 11, 12, and 13 of Title 11 commenced before 30 days after Oct. 27, 1986, and pending in a judicial district referred to in section 581(a) of Title 28, as amended by section 111(a) of Pub.L. 99–554, for which a United States trustee is not authorized before 30 days after Oct. 27, 1986 to be appointed, not applicable until the expiration of the 3-year period beginning on Oct. 27, 1986, or of the 1-year period beginning on the date the Attorney General certifies under section 303 of Pub.L. 99–554 the region specified in a paragraph of such section 581(a) that includes, such district, whichever occurs first, see section 302(e)(1), (2) of Pub.L. 99–554, set out as a note under section 581 of Title 28.

See 1986 Amendment notes set out above.

Effective Date of 1984 Amendments. See section 553 of Pub.L. 98–353, Title III, July 10, 1984, 98 Stat. 392, set out as an Effective Date of 1984 Amendment note preceding chapter 1 of Title 11, Bankruptcy.

Separability of Provisions. For separability of provisions of Title III of Pub.L. 98–353, see section 551 of Pub.L. 98–353 set out as a Separability of Provisions note preceding chapter 1 of Title 11, Bankruptcy.

Cross References

Appointment of trustee or examiner upon failure to qualify, see section 1104.
Certain customer transactions affected before qualification of trustee, see section 746.
Debtor in possession defined as debtor except when qualified person is serving as trustee under this section, see section 1101.
Duties of U.S. Trustees, see 28 U.S.C.A. § 586, infra.
Interim trustee, see section 701.
Successor trustee, see section 703.
Trustee in chapter 13 cases, see section 1302.

Library References:

C.J.S. Bankruptcy § 195.
West's Key No. Digests, Bankruptcy ☜3006.

WESTLAW Electronic Research

See WESTLAW Electronic Research Guide following the *Bankruptcy Highlights.*

§ 323. Role and capacity of trustee

(a) The trustee in a case under this title is the representative of the estate.

(b) The trustee in a case under this title has capacity to sue and be sued.
Pub.L. 95–598, Nov. 6, 1978, 92 Stat. 2562.

Historical and Revision Notes

Notes of Committee on the Judiciary, Senate Report No. 95–989. Subsection (a) of this section makes the trustee the representative of the estate. Subsection (b) grants the trustee the capacity to sue and to be sued. If the debtor remains in possession in a chapter 11 case, section 1107 gives the debtor in possession these rights of the trustee: the debtor in possession becomes the representative of the estate, and may sue and be sued. The same applies in a chapter 13 case.

Library References:

C.J.S. Bankruptcy § 197.
West's Key No. Digests, Bankruptcy ☜3008, 3009.

WESTLAW Electronic Research

See WESTLAW Electronic Research Guide following the *Bankruptcy Highlights.*

§ 324. Removal of trustee or examiner

(a) The court, after notice and a hearing, may remove a trustee, other than the United States trustee, or an examiner, for cause.

(b) Whenever the court removes a trustee or examiner under subsection (a) in a case under this title, such trustee or examiner shall thereby be removed in all other cases under this title in which such trustee or examiner is then serving unless the court orders otherwise.
Pub.L. 95–598, Nov. 6, 1978, 92 Stat. 2562; Pub.L. 99–554, Title II, § 208, Oct. 27, 1986, 100 Stat. 3098.

Historical and Revision Notes

Notes of Committee on the Judiciary, Senate Report No. 95–989. This section permits the court, after notice and a hearing, to remove a trustee for cause.

1986 Amendment. Pub.L. 99–554, § 208, designated existing provisions as subsec. (a), and, as so designated, substituted "a trustee, other than the United States trustee, or an examiner" for "a trustee or an examiner", and added subsec. (b).

See Effective Date of 1986 Amendment, etc., notes set out below.

Effective Date of 1986 Amendments; Effective Date of 1986 Amendments for Certain Judicial Districts Not Served by United States Trustees and for Judicial Districts in Alabama and North Carolina; U.S. Trustee System Fund Deposits in Alabama and North Carolina; Effective Date of Title 11 Chapter 15 Repeal as to Northern District of Alabama; Authority of Certain Estate Administrators in Alabama and North Carolina; Effective Date of 1986 Amendments in Pending Cases Where a U.S. Trustee Not Authorized or Where a Trustee Files Final Report or Plan is Confirmed; Quarterly Fees. Amendment by Pub.L. 99–554 effective 30 days after Oct. 27, 1986, except as otherwise provided for, see section 302(a) of Pub.L. 99–554, set out as a note under section 581 of Title 28, Judiciary and Judicial Procedure.

Amendment by Pub.L. 99–554, § 208 not to become effective in or with respect to certain specified judicial districts until, or apply to cases while pending in such district before, the expiration of the 270-day period beginning 30 days after Oct. 27, 1986, or of the 30-day period beginning on the date the Attorney General certifies under section 303 of Pub.L. 99–554 the region specified in a paragraph of section 581(a) of Title 28, as amended by section 111(a) of Pub.L. 99–554, that includes such district, whichever occurs first, see section 302(d)(1) of Pub.L. 99–554, set out as a note under section 581 of Title 28.

Amendment by Pub.L. 99–554, § 208, not to become effective in or with respect to certain specified judicial districts until, or apply to cases while pending in such district before, the expiration of the 2-year period beginning 30 days after Oct. 27, 1986, or of the 30-day period beginning on the date the Attorney General certifies under section 303 of Pub.L. 99–554 the region specified in a paragraph of

section 581(a) of Title 28, as amended by section 111(a) of Pub.L. 99–554, that includes such district, whichever occurs first, see section 302(d)(2) of Pub.L. 99–554, set out as a note under section 581 of Title 28.

Amendment by Pub.L. 99–554, § 208, not to become effective in or with respect to judicial districts established for the States of Alabama and North Carolina until, or apply to cases while pending in such district before, such district elects to be included in a bankruptcy region established in section 581(a) of Title 28, as amended by section 111(a) of Pub.L. 99–554, or Oct. 1, 2002, whichever occurs first, and, except as otherwise provided for, with respect to cases under chapters 7, 11, 12, and 13 of Title 11 commenced before 30 days after Oct. 27, 1986, and pending in a judicial district in the States of Alabama or North Carolina before any election made under section 302(d)(3)(A) of Pub.L. 99–554 by such district becomes effective or Oct. 1, 2002, whichever occurs first, amendments by Pub.L. 99–554 not to apply until Oct. 1, 2003, or the expiration of the 1-year period beginning on the date such election becomes effective, whichever occurs first, and further, in any judicial district in Alabama or North Carolina not making the election described in section 302(d)(3)(A) of Pub.L. 99–554, any person appointed under regulations issued by the Judicial Conference to administer estates in cases under Title 11 authorized to establish, etc., a panel of private trustees, and to supervise cases and trustees in cases under chapters 7, 11, 12, and 13 of Title 11, until amendments by sections 201 to 231 of Pub.L. 99–554 effective in such district, see section 302(d)(3)(A) to (F), (H), (I) of Pub.L. 99–554, set out as a note under section 581 of Title 28.

Amendment by Pub.L. 99–554, § 208, except as otherwise provided, with respect to cases under chapters 7, 11, 12, and 13 of Title 11 commenced before 30 days after Oct. 27, 1986, and pending in a judicial district referred to in section 581(a) of Title 28, as amended by section 111(a) of Pub.L. 99–554, for which a United States trustee is not authorized before 30 days after Oct. 27, 1986 to be appointed, not applicable until the expiration of the 3-year period beginning on Oct. 27, 1986, or of the 1-year period beginning on the date the Attorney General certifies under section 303 of Pub.L. 99–554 the region specified in a paragraph of such section 581(a) that includes, such district, whichever occurs first, see section 302(e)(1), (2) of Pub.L. 99–554, set out as a note under section 581 of Title 28.

See 1986 Amendment notes set out above.

Cross References
Appointment of trustee or examiner upon removal, see section 1104.
Successor trustee, see section 703.

Library References:
C.J.S. Bankruptcy § 196.
West's Key No. Digests, Bankruptcy ☞3007.

WESTLAW Electronic Research
See WESTLAW Electronic Research Guide following the *Bankruptcy Highlights.*

§ 325. Effect of vacancy

A vacancy in the office of trustee during a case does not abate any pending action or proceeding, and the successor trustee shall be substituted as a party in such action or proceeding.

Pub.L. 95–598, Nov. 6, 1978, 92 Stat. 2562.

Historical and Revision Notes

Notes of Committee on the Judiciary, Senate Report No. 95–989. Section 325, derived from Bankruptcy Act section 46 [former section 74 of this title] and Bankruptcy Rule 221(b), specifies that a vacancy in the office of trustee during a case does not abate any pending action or proceeding. The successor trustee, when selected and qualified, is substituted as a party in any pending action or proceeding.

Library References:
C.J.S. Bankruptcy § 196.
West's Key No. Digests, Bankruptcy ☞3007.

WESTLAW Electronic Research
See WESTLAW Electronic Research Guide following the *Bankruptcy Highlights.*

§ 326. Limitation on compensation of trustee

(a) In a case under chapter 7 or 11, the court may allow reasonable compensation under section 330 of this title of the trustee for the trustee's services, payable after the trustee renders such services, not to exceed fifteen percent on the first $1,000 or less, six percent on any amount in excess of $1,000 but not in excess of $3,000, and three percent on any amount in excess of $3,000, upon all moneys disbursed or turned over in the case by the trustee to parties in interest, excluding the debtor, but including holders of secured claims.

(b) In a case under chapter 12 or 13 of this title, the court may not allow compensation for services or reimbursement of expenses of the United States trustee or of a standing trustee appointed under section 586(b) of title 28, but may allow reasonable compensation under section 330 of this title of a trustee appointed under section 1202(a) or 1302(a) of this title for the trustee's services, payable after the trustee renders such services, not to exceed five percent upon all payments under the plan.

(c) If more than one person serves as trustee in the case, the aggregate compensation of such persons for such service may not exceed the maximum compensation prescribed for a single trustee by subsection (a) or (b) of this section, as the case may be.

(d) The court may deny allowance of compensation for services or reimbursement of expenses of the trustee if the trustee failed to make diligent inquiry into facts that would permit denial of allowance under section 328(c) of this title or, with knowledge of such facts, employed a professional person under section 327 of this title.

Pub.L. 95–598, Nov. 6, 1978, 92 Stat. 2562; Pub.L. 98–353, Title III, § 430(a), (b), July 10, 1984, 98 Stat. 369; Pub.L. 99–554, Title II, § 209, Oct. 27, 1986, 100 Stat. 3098.

Historical and Revision Notes

Notes of Committee on the Judiciary, Senate Report No. 95–989. This section is derived in part from section 48c of the Bankruptcy Act [former section 76(c) of this title]. It must be emphasized that this section does not authorize compensation of trustees. This section simply fixes the maximum compensation of a trustee. Proposed 11 U.S.C. 330 authorizes and fixes the standard of compensation. Under section 48c of current law [former section 76(c) of this title], the maximum limits have tended to become minimums in many cases. This section is not intended to be so interpreted. The limits in this section, together with the limitations found in section 330, are to be applied as outer limits, and not as grants or entitlements to the maximum fees specified.

The maximum fee schedule is derived from section 48c(1) of the present act [former section 76(c)(1) of this title], but with a change relating to the bases on which the percentage maxima are computed. The maximum fee schedule is based on decreasing percentages of increasing amounts. The amounts are the amounts of money distributed by the trustee to parties in interest, excluding the debtor, but including secured creditors. These amounts were last amended in 1952. Since then, the cost of living has approximately doubled. Thus, the bases were doubled.

It should be noted that the bases on which the maximum fee is computed includes moneys turned over to secured creditors, to cover the situation where the trustee liquidates property subject to a lien and distributes the proceeds. It does not cover cases in which the trustee simply turns over the property to the secured creditor, nor where the trustee abandons the property and the secured creditor is permitted to foreclose. The provision is also subject to the rights of the secured creditor generally under proposed section 506, especially 506(c). The $150 discretionary fee provision of current law is retained.

Subsection (b) of this section entitles an operating trustee to a reasonable fee, without any limitation based on the maximum provided for a liquidating trustee as in current law, Bankruptcy Act § 48c(2) [former section 76(c)(2) of this title].

Subsection (c) [now (b)] permits a maximum fee of five percent on all payments to creditors under a chapter 13 plan to the trustee appointed in the case.

Subsection (d) [now (c)] provides a limitation not found in current law. Even if more than one trustee serves in the case, the maximum fee payable to all trustees does not change. For example, if an interim trustee is appointed and an elected trustee replaces him, the combined total of the fees payable to the interim trustee and the permanent trustee may not exceed the amount specified in this section. Under current law, very often a receiver receives a full fee and a subsequent trustee also receives a full fee. The resultant "double-dipping", especially in cases in which the receiver and the trustee are the same individual, is detrimental to the interests of creditors, by needlessly increasing the cost of administering bankruptcy estates.

Subsection (e) [now (d)] permits the court to deny compensation to a trustee if the trustee has been derelict in his duty by employing counsel, who is not disinterested.

Legislative Statements. Section 326(a) of the House amendment modifies a provision as contained in H.R. 8200 as passed by the House. The percentage limitation on the fees of a trustee contained in the House bill is retained, but no additional percentage is specified for cases in which a trustee operates the business of the debtor. Section 326(b) of the Senate amendment, is deleted as an unnecessary restatement of the limitation contained in section 326(a) as modified. The provision contained in section 326(a) of the Senate amendment authorizing a trustee to receive a maximum fee of $150 regardless of the availability of assets in the estate is deleted. It will not be necessary in view of the increase in section 326(a) and the doubling of the minimum fee as provided in section 330(b).

Section 326(b) of the House amendment derives from section 326(c) of H.R. 8200 as passed by the House. It is a conforming amendment to indicate a change with respect to the selection of a trustee in a chapter 13 case under section 1302(a) of title 11.

1986 Amendment. Subsec. (b). Pub.L. 99–554, § 209, substituted "under chapter 12 or 13 of this title" for "under chapter 13 of this title", "expenses of the United States trustee or of a standing trustee appointed under section 586(b) of title 28" for "expenses of a standing trustee appointed under section 1302(d) of this title", and "under section 1202(a) or 1302(a) of this title" for "under section 1302(a) of this title".

See Effective Date of 1986 Amendment, etc., notes set out below.

Effective Date of 1986 Amendments; References in Title 11 Section 326(b) to Title 11 Chapter 13 and Section 1302(a) and (d); Effective Date of 1986 Amendments for Certain Judicial Districts Not Served by United States Trustees and for Judicial Districts in Alabama and North Carolina; U.S. Trustee System Fund Deposits in Alabama and North Carolina; Effective Date of Title 11 Chapter 15 Repeal as to Northern District of Alabama; Authority of Certain Estate Administrators in Alabama and North Carolina; Effective Date of 1986 Amendments in Pending Cases Where a U.S. Trustee Not Authorized or Where a Trustee Files Final Report or Plan is Confirmed; Quarterly Fees. Amendment by Pub.L. 99–554 effective 30 days after Oct. 27, 1986, except as otherwise provided for, see section 302(a) of Pub.L. 99–554, set out as a note under section 581 of Title 28, Judiciary and Judicial Procedure.

Until amendments made by section 209 of Pub.L. 99–554 become effective in a district and apply to a case, for purposes of such case any references in subsec. (b) of this section to chapter 13 of this title, to section 1302(d) of this title, or to section 1302(a) of this title deemed references to other provisions of the Code, see section 302(c)(3)(A)(i) to (iii) of Pub.L. 99–554, set out as a note under section 581 of Title 28.

Amendment by Pub.L. 99–554, § 209, not to become effective in or with respect to certain specified judicial districts until, or apply to cases while pending in such district before, the expiration of the 270-day period beginning 30 days after Oct. 27, 1986, or of the 30-day period beginning on the date the Attorney General certifies under section 303 of Pub.L. 99–554 the region specified in a paragraph of section 581(a) of Title 28, as amended by section 111(a) of Pub.L. 99–554, that includes such district, whichever occurs first, see section 302(d)(1) of Pub.L. 99–554, set out as a note under section 581 of Title 28.

Amendment by Pub.L. 99–554, § 209, not to become effective in or with respect to certain specified judicial districts until, or apply to cases while pending in such district before, the expiration of the 2-year period beginning 30 days after Oct. 27, 1986, or of the 30-day period beginning on the date the Attorney General certifies under section 303 of Pub.L. 99–554 the region specified in a paragraph of section 581(a) of Title 28, as amended by section 111(a) of Pub.L. 99–554, that includes such district, whichever occurs first, see section 302(d)(2) of Pub.L. 99–554, set out as a note under section 581 of Title 28.

Amendment by Pub.L. 99–554, § 209, not to become effective in or with respect to judicial districts established for the States of Alabama and North Carolina until, or apply to cases while pending in such district before, such district elects to be included in a bankruptcy region established in section 581(a) of Title 28, as amended by section 111(a) of Pub.L. 99–554, or Oct. 1, 2002, whichever occurs first, and, except as otherwise provided for, with respect to cases under chapters 7, 11, 12, and 13 of Title 11 commenced before 30 days after Oct. 27, 1986, and pending in a judicial district in the States of Alabama or North Carolina before any election made under section 302(d)(3)(A) of Pub.L. 99–554 by such district becomes effective or Oct. 1, 2002, whichever occurs first, amendments by Pub.L. 99–554 not to apply until Oct. 1, 2003, or the expiration of the 1-year period beginning on the date such election becomes effective, whichever occurs first, and further, in any judicial district in Alabama or North Carolina not making the election described in section 302(d)(3)(A) of Pub.L. 99–554, any person appointed under regulations issued by the Judicial Conference to administer estates in cases under Title 11 authorized to establish, etc., a panel of private trustees, and to supervise cases and trustees in cases under chapters 7, 11, 12, and 13 of Title 11, until amendments by sections 201 to 231 of Pub.L. 99–554 effective in such district, see section 302(d)(3)(A) to (F), (H), (I) of Pub.L. 99–554, set out as a note under section 581 of Title 28.

Amendment by Pub.L. 99–554, § 209, except as otherwise provided, with respect to cases under chapters 7, 11, 12, and 13 of Title 11 commenced before 30 days after Oct. 27, 1986, and pending in a judicial district referred to in section 581(a) of Title 28, as amended by section 111(a) of Pub.L. 99–554, for which a United States trustee is not authorized before 30 days after Oct. 27, 1986 to be appointed, not applicable until the expiration of the 3-year period beginning on Oct. 27, 1986, or of the 1-year period beginning on the date the Attor-

ney General certifies under section 303 of Pub.L. 99–554 the region specified in a paragraph of such section 581(a) that includes, such district, whichever occurs first, see section 302(e)(1), (2) of Pub.L. 99–554, set out as a note under section 581 of Title 28.

See 1986 Amendment notes set out above.

Effective Date of 1984 Amendments. See section 553 of Pub.L. 98–353, Title III, July 10, 1984, 98 Stat. 392, set out as an Effective Date of 1984 Amendment note preceding chapter 1 of Title 11, Bankruptcy.

Separability of Provisions. For separability of provisions of Title III of Pub. L. 98–353, see section 551 of Pub. L. 98–353 set out as a Separability of Provisions note preceding chapter 1 of Title 11, Bankruptcy.

Library References:

C.J.S. Bankruptcy § 232.
West's Key No. Digests, Bankruptcy ⊐3152.

WESTLAW Electronic Research

See WESTLAW Electronic Research Guide following the *Bankruptcy Highlights*.

§ 327. Employment of professional persons

(a) Except as otherwise provided in this section, the trustee, with the court's approval, may employ one or more attorneys, accountants, appraisers, auctioneers, or other professional persons, that do not hold or represent an interest adverse to the estate, and that are disinterested persons, to represent or assist the trustee in carrying out the trustee's duties under this title.

(b) If the trustee is authorized to operate the business of the debtor under section 721, 1202 or 1108 of this title, and if the debtor has regularly employed attorneys, accountants, or other professional persons on salary, the trustee may retain or replace such professional persons if necessary in the operation of such business.

(c) In a case under chapter 7, 11 or 12 of this title, a person is not disqualified for employment under this section solely because of such person's employment by or representation of a creditor, unless there is objection by another creditor or the United States trustee, in which case the court shall disapprove such employment if there is an actual conflict of interest.

(d) The court may authorize the trustee to act as attorney or accountant for the estate if such authorization is in the best interest of the estate.

(e) The trustee, with the court's approval, may employ, for a specified special purpose, other than to represent the trustee in conducting the case, an attorney that has represented the debtor, if in the best interest of the estate, and if such attorney does not represent or hold any interest adverse to the debtor or to the estate with respect to the matter on which such attorney is to be employed.

(f) The trustee may not employ a person that has served as an examiner in the case.

Pub.L. 95–598, Nov. 6, 1978, 92 Stat. 2563; Pub.L. 98–353, Title III, § 430(c), July 10, 1984, 98 Stat. 370; Pub.L. 99–554, Title II, §§ 210, 257(e), Oct. 27, 1986, 100 Stat. 3099, 3114.

Historical and Revision Notes

Notes of Committee on the Judiciary, Senate Report No. 95–989. This section authorizes the trustee, subject to the court's approval, to employ professional persons, such as attorneys, accountants, appraisers, and auctioneers, to represent or perform services for the estate. The trustee may employ only disinterested persons that do not hold or represent an interest adverse to the estate.

Subsection (b) is an exception, and authorizes the trustee to retain or replace professional persons that the debtor has employed if necessary in the operation of the debtor's business.

Subsection (c) provides that a professional person is not disqualified for employment solely because of the person's prior employment by or representation of a secured or unsecured creditor.

Subsection (d) permits the court to authorize the trustee, if qualified to act as his own counsel or accountant.

Subsection (e) permits the trustee, subject to the court's approval, to employ for a specified special purpose an attorney that has represented the debtor, if such employment is in the best interest of the estate and if the attorney does not hold or represent an interest adverse to the debtor of the estate with respect to the matter on which he is to be employed. This subsection does not authorize the employment of the debtor's attorney to represent the estate generally or to represent the trustee in the conduct of the bankruptcy case. The subsection will most likely be used when the debtor is involved in complex litigation, and changing attorneys in the middle of the case after the bankruptcy case has commenced would be detrimental to the progress of that other litigation.

Legislative Statements. Section 327(a) of the House amendment contains a technical amendment indicating that attorneys, and perhaps other officers enumerated therein, represent, rather than assist, the trustee in carrying out the trustee's duties.

Section 327(c) represents a compromise between H.R. 8200 as passed by the House and the Senate amendment. The provision states that former representation of a creditor, whether secured or unsecured, will not automatically disqualify a person from being employed by a trustee, but if such person is employed by the trustee, the person may no longer represent the creditor in connection with the case.

Section 327(f) prevents an examiner from being employed by the trustee.

Codification. Amendment by Pub.L. 99–554 § 257(e)(2), has been executed to text following "chapter 7" as the probable intent of Congress, notwithstanding directory language which required amendment to be executed following "section 7".

1986 Amendment. Subsec. (c). Pub.L. 99–554, § 210, substituted "another creditor or the United States trustee, in which case" for "another creditor, in which case".

See Effective Date of 1986 Amendment, etc., notes set out below.

Effective Date of 1986 Amendments; Savings Provisions; Effective Date of 1986 Amendments for Certain Judicial Districts Not Served by United States Trustees and for Judicial Districts in Alabama and North Carolina; U.S. Trustee System Fund Deposits in Alabama and North Carolina; Effective Date of Title 11 Chapter 15 Repeal as to Northern District of Alabama; Authority of Certain Estate Administrators in Alabama and North Carolina; Effective Date of 1986 Amendments in Pending Cases Where a U.S. Trustee Not Authorized or Where a Trustee Files Final Report or Plan is Confirmed; Quarterly Fees. Amendment by Pub.L. 99–554 effective 30 days after Oct. 27, 1986, except as otherwise provided for, see section 302(a) of Pub.L. 99–554, set out as a note under section 581 of Title 28, Judiciary and Judicial Procedure.

Amendments by Pub.L. 99–554, § 257(e), not to apply with respect to cases commenced under Title 11, Bankruptcy, before 30 days after Oct. 27, 1986, see section 302(c)(1) of Pub. L. 99–554, set out as a note under section 581 of Title 28.

Amendment by Pub.L. 99–554, § 210, not to become effective in or with respect to certain specified judicial districts until, or apply to cases while pending in such district before, the expiration of the 270-day period beginning 30 days after Oct. 27, 1986, or of the 30-day period beginning on the date the Attorney General certifies under section 303 of Pub.L. 99–554 the region specified in a paragraph of section 581(a) of Title 28, as amended by section 111(a) of Pub.L. 99–554, that includes such district, whichever occurs first, see section 302(d)(1) of Pub.L. 99–554, set out as a note under section 581 of Title 28.

Amendment by Pub.L. 99–554, § 210, not to become effective in or with respect to certain specified judicial districts until, or apply to cases while pending in such district before, the expiration of the 2-year period beginning 30 days after Oct. 27, 1986, or of the 30-day period beginning on the date the Attorney General certifies under section 303 of Pub.L. 99–554 the region specified in a paragraph of section 581(a) of Title 28, as amended by section 111(a) of Pub.L. 99–554, that includes such district, whichever occurs first, see section 302(d)(2) of Pub.L. 99–554, set out as a note under section 581 of Title 28.

Amendment by Pub.L. 99–554, § 210, not to become effective in or with respect to judicial districts established for the States of Alabama and North Carolina until, or apply to cases while pending in such district before, such district elects to be included in a bankruptcy region established in section 581(a) of Title 28, as amended by section 111(a) of Pub.L. 99–554, or Oct. 1, 2002, whichever occurs first, and, except as otherwise provided for, with respect to cases under chapters 7, 11, 12, and 13 of Title 11 commenced before 30 days after Oct. 27, 1986, and pending in a judicial district in the States of Alabama or North Carolina before any election made under section 302(d)(3)(A) of Pub.L. 99–554 by such district becomes effective or Oct. 1, 2002, whichever occurs first, amendments by Pub.L. 99–554 not to apply until Oct. 1, 2003, or the expiration of the 1-year period beginning on the date such election becomes effective, whichever occurs first, and further, in any judicial district in Alabama or North Carolina not making the election described in section 302(d)(3)(A) of Pub.L. 99–554, any person appointed under regulations issued by the Judicial Conference to administer estates in cases under Title 11 authorized to establish, etc., a panel of private trustees, and to supervise cases and trustees in cases under chapters 7, 11, 12, and 13 of Title 11, until amendments by sections 201 to 231 of Pub.L. 99–554 effective in such district, see section 302(d)(3)(A) to (F), (H), (I) of Pub.L. 99–554, set out as a note under section 581 of Title 28.

Amendment by Pub.L. 99–554, § 210, except as otherwise provided, with respect to cases under chapters 7, 11, 12, and 13 of Title 11 commenced before 30 days after Oct. 27, 1986, and pending in a judicial district referred to in section 581(a) of Title 28, as amended by section 111(a) of Pub.L. 99–554, for which a United States trustee is not authorized before 30 days after Oct. 27, 1986 to be appointed, not applicable until the expiration of the 3-year period beginning on Oct. 27, 1986, or of the 1-year period beginning on the date the Attorney General certifies under section 303 of Pub.L. 99–554 the region specified in a paragraph of such section 581(a) that includes, such district, whichever occurs first, see section 302(e)(1), (2) of Pub.L. 99–554, set out as a note under section 581 of Title 28.

See 1986 Amendment notes set out above.

Effective Date of 1984 Amendments. See section 553 of Pub.L. 98–353, Title III, July 10, 1984, 98 Stat. 392, set out as an Effective Date of 1984 Amendment note preceding chapter 1 of Title 11, Bankruptcy.

Separability of Provisions. For separability of provisions of Title III of Pub.L. 98–353, see section 551 of Pub.L. 98–353 set out as a Separability of Provisions note preceding chapter 1 of Title 11, Bankruptcy.

Cross References

Qualification for employment by debtor in possession despite prior employment or representation, see section 1107.

Library References:

C.J.S. Bankruptcy §§ 231, 234, 238.
West's Key No. Digests, Bankruptcy ⟐3029, 3030.

WESTLAW Electronic Research

See WESTLAW Electronic Research Guide following the *Bankruptcy Highlights*.

§ 328.   Limitation on compensation of professional persons

(a) The trustee, or a committee appointed under section 1102 of this title, with the court's approval, may employ or authorize the employment of a professional person under section 327 or 1103 of this title, as the case may be, on any reasonable terms and conditions of employment, including on a retainer, on an hourly basis, or on a contingent fee basis. Notwithstanding such terms and conditions, the court may allow compensation different from the compensation provided under such terms and conditions after the conclusion of such employment, if such terms and conditions prove to have been improvident in light of developments not capable of being anticipated at the time of the fixing of such terms and conditions.

(b) If the court has authorized a trustee to serve as an attorney or accountant for the estate under section 327(d) of this title, the court may allow compensation for the trustee's services as such attorney or accountant only to the extent that the trustee performed services as attorney or accountant for the estate and not for performance of any of the trustee's duties that are generally performed by a trustee without the assistance of an attorney or accountant for the estate.

(c) Except as provided in section 327(c), 327(e), or 1107(b) of this title, the court may deny allowance of compensation for services and reimbursement of expenses of a professional person employed under section 327 or 1103 of this title if, at any time during such professional person's employment under section 327 or 1103 of this title, such professional person is not a disinterested person, or represents or holds an interest adverse to the interest of the estate with respect to the matter on which such professional person is employed.

Pub.L. 95–598, Nov. 6, 1978, 92 Stat. 2563; Pub.L. 98–353, Title III, § 431, July 10, 1984, 98 Stat. 370.

Historical and Revision Notes

Notes of Committee on the Judiciary, Senate Report No. 95–989. This section, which is parallel to section 326, fixes the maximum compensation allowable to a professional person employed under section 327. It authorizes the trustee, with the court's approval, to employ professional persons on any reasonable terms, including on a retainer, on an hourly or on a contingent fee basis. Subsection (a) further permits the court to allow compensation different from the compensation provided under the trustee's agreement if the prior agreement proves to have been improvident in light of development unanticipatable at the time of the agreement. The court's power includes the power to increase as well as decrease the agreed upon compensation. This provision is permissive, not mandatory, and should not be used by the court if to do so would violate the code of ethics of the professional involved.

Subsection (b) limits a trustee that has been authorized to serve as his own counsel to only one fee for each service. The purpose of permitting the trustee to serve as his own counsel is to reduce costs. It is not included to provide the trustee with a bonus by permitting him to receive two fees for the same service or to avoid the maxima fixed in section 326. Thus, this subsection requires the court to differentiate between the trustee's services as trustee, and his services as trustee's counsel, and to fix compensation accordingly. Services that a trustee normally performs for an estate without assistance of counsel are to be compensated under the limits fixed in section 326. Only services that he performs that are normally performed by trustee's counsel may be compensated under the maxima imposed by this section.

Subsection (c) permits the court to deny compensation for services and reimbursement of expenses if the professional person is not disinterested or if he represents or holds an interest adverse to the estate on the matter on which he is employed. The subsection provides a penalty for conflicts of interest.

Legislative Statements. Section 328(c) adopts a technical amendment contained in the Senate amendment indicating that an attorney for the debtor in possession is not disqualified for compensation for services and reimbursement of expenses simply because of prior representation of the debtor.

Effective Date of 1984 Amendments. See section 553 of Pub.L. 98–353, Title III, July 10, 1984, 98 Stat. 392, set out as an Effective Date of 1984 Amendment note preceding chapter 1 of Title 11, Bankruptcy.

Separability of Provisions. For separability of provisions of Title III of Pub.L. 98–353, see section 551 of Pub.L. 98–353 set out as a Separability of Provisions note preceding chapter 1 of Title 11, Bankruptcy.

Library References:

C.J.S. Bankruptcy §§ 231–238.
West's Key No. Digests, Bankruptcy ⬅3029, 3030, 3155 et seq.

WESTLAW Electronic Research

See WESTLAW Electronic Research Guide following the *Bankruptcy Highlights*.

§ 329. Debtor's transactions with attorneys

(a) Any attorney representing a debtor in a case under this title, or in connection with such a case, whether or not such attorney applies for compensation under this title, shall file with the court a statement of the compensation paid or agreed to be paid, if such payment or agreement was made after one year before the date of the filing of the petition, for services rendered or to be rendered in contemplation of or in connection with the case by such attorney, and the source of such compensation.

(b) If such compensation exceeds the reasonable value of any such services, the court may cancel any such agreement, or order the return of any such payment, to the extent excessive, to—

    (1) the estate, if the property transferred—

        (A) would have been property of the estate; or

        (B) was to be paid by or on behalf of the debtor under a plan under chapter 11, 12 or 13 of this title; or

    (2) the entity that made such payment.

Pub.L. 95–598, Nov. 6, 1978, 92 Stat. 2564; Pub.L. 98–353, Title III, § 432, July 10, 1984, 98 Stat. 370; Pub.L. 99–554, Title II, § 257(c), Oct. 27, 1986, 100 Stat. 3114.

Historical and Revision Notes

Notes of Committee on the Judiciary, Senate Report No. 95–989. This section, derived in large part from current Bankruptcy Act section 60d [former section 96(d) of this title], requires the debtor's attorney to file with the court a statement of the compensation paid or agreed to be paid to the attorney for services in contemplation of and in connection with the case, and the source of the compensation. Payments to a debtor's attorney provide serious potential for evasion of creditor protection provisions of the bankruptcy laws, and serious potential for overreaching by the debtor's attorney, and should be subject to careful scrutiny.

Subsection (b) permits the court to deny compensation to the attorney, to cancel an agreement to pay compensation, or to order the return of compensation paid, if the compensation exceeds the reasonable value of the services provided. The return of payments already made are generally to the trustee for the benefit of the estate. However, if the property would not have come into the estate in any event, the court will order it returned to the entity that made the payment.

The Bankruptcy Commission recommended a provision similar to this that would have also permitted an examination of the debtor's transactions with insiders. S. 236, 94th Cong., 1st sess, sec. 4–311(b) (1975). Its exclusion here is to permit it to be dealt with by the Rules of Bankruptcy Procedure. It is not intended that the provision be deleted entirely, only that the flexibility of the rules is more appropriate for such evidentiary matters.

Effective Date of 1986 Amendments; Savings Provisions; Quarterly Fees. Amendment by Pub.L. 99–554 effective 30 days after Oct. 27, 1986, except as otherwise provided for, see section 302(a) of Pub.L. 99–554, set out as a note under section 581 of Title 28, Judiciary and Judicial Procedure.

Amendments by Pub.L. 99–554, § 257(c), not to apply with respect to cases commenced under Title 11, Bankruptcy, before 30 days after Oct. 27, 1986, see section 302(c)(1) of Pub. L. 99–554, set out as a note under section 581 of Title 28.

Effective Date of 1984 Amendments. See section 553 of Pub.L. 98–353, Title III, July 10, 1984, 98 Stat. 392, set out as an Effective Date of 1984 Amendment note preceding chapter 1 of Title 11, Bankruptcy.

Separability of Provisions. For separability of provisions of Title III, of Pub.L. 98–353, see section 551 of Pub.L. 98–353 set out as a Separability of Provisions note preceding chapter 1 of Title 11, Bankruptcy.

Library References:

C.J.S. Bankruptcy §§ 231, 234, 238.
West's Key No. Digests, Bankruptcy ☞3030.

WESTLAW Electronic Research

See WESTLAW Electronic Research Guide following the *Bankruptcy Highlights*.

§ 330. Compensation of officers

(a) After notice to any parties in interest and to the United States trustee and a hearing, and subject to sections 326, 328, and 329 of this title, the court may award to a trustee, to an examiner, to a professional person employed under section 327 or 1103 of this title, or to the debtor's attorney—

    (1) reasonable compensation for actual, necessary services rendered by such trustee, examiner, professional person, or attorney, as the case may be, and by any paraprofessional persons employed by such trustee, professional person, or attorney, as the case may be, based on the nature, the extent, and the value of such services, the time spent on such services, and the cost of comparable services other than in a case under this title; and

    (2) reimbursement for actual, necessary expenses.

(b) There shall be paid from the filing fee in a case under chapter 7 of this title $45 to the trustee serving in such case, after such trustee's services are rendered.

(c) Unless the court orders otherwise, in a case under chapter 12 or 13 of this title the compensation paid to the trustee serving in the case shall not be less than $5 per month from any distribution under the plan during the administration of the plan.

(d) In a case in which the United States trustee serves as trustee, the compensation of the trustee under this section shall be paid to the clerk of the bankruptcy court and deposited by the clerk into the United States Trustee System Fund established by section 589a of title 28.

Pub.L. 95–598, Nov. 6, 1978, 92 Stat. 2564; Pub.L. 98–353, Title III, §§ 433, 434, July 10, 1984, 98 Stat. 370; Pub.L. 99–554, Title II, §§ 211, 257(f), Oct. 27, 1986, 100 Stat. 3099, 3114.

Historical and Revision Notes

Notes of Committee on the Judiciary, Senate Report No. 95–989. Section 330 authorizes the court to award compensation for services and reimbursement of expenses of officers of the estate, and other professionals. The compensation is to be reasonable, for economy in administration is the basic objective. Compensation is to be for actual necessary services, based on the time spent, the nature, the extent and the value of the services rendered, and the cost of comparable services in nonbankruptcy cases. These are the criteria that have been applied by the courts as analytic aids in defining "reasonable" compensation.

The reference to "the cost of comparable services" in a nonbankruptcy case is not intended as a change of existing law. In a bankruptcy case fees are not a matter for private agreement. There is inherent a "public interest" that "must be considered in awarding fees," Massachusetts Mutual Life Insurance Co. v. Brock, 405 F.2d 429, 432 (C.A.5, 1968), cert. denied, 395 U.S. 906 [89 S.Ct. 1748, 23 L.Ed.2d 220]. An allowance is the result of a balance struck between moderation in the interest of the estate and its security holders and the need to be "generous enough to encourage" lawyers and others to render the necessary and exacting services that bankruptcy cases often require. In re Yale Express System, Inc., 366 F.Supp. 1376, 1381 (S.D.N.Y.1973). The rates for similar kinds of services in private employment is one element, among others, in that balance. Compensation in private employment noted in subsection (a) is a point of reference, not a controlling determinant of what shall be allowed in bankruptcy cases.

One of the major reforms in 1938, especially for reorganization cases, was centralized control over fees in the bankruptcy courts. See Brown v. Gerdes, 321 U.S. 178, 182–184 (1944) [64 S.Ct. 487, 88 L.Ed. 659]; Leiman v. Guttman, 336 U.S. 1, 4–9 (1949) [69 S.Ct. 371, 93 L.Ed. 453]. It was intended to guard against a recurrence of "the many sordid chapters" in "the history of fees in corporate reorganizations." Dickinson Industrial Site, Inc. v. Cowan, 309 U.S. 382, 388 (1940) [60 S.Ct. 595, 84 L.Ed. 819, rehearing denied 60 S.Ct. 806, 309 U.S. 698, 84 L.Ed. 1037]. In the

years since then the bankruptcy bar has flourished and prospered, and persons or merit and quality have not eschewed public service in bankruptcy cases merely because bankruptcy courts, in the interest of economy in administration, have not allowed them compensation that may be earned in the private economy of business or the professions. There is no reason to believe that, in generations to come, their successors will be less persuaded by the need to serve in the public interest because of stronger allures of private gain elsewhere.

Subsection (a) provides for compensation of paraprofessional in order to reduce the cost of administering bankruptcy cases. Paraprofessionals can be employed to perform duties which do not require the full range of skills of a qualified professional. Some courts have not hesitated to recognize paraprofessional services as compensable under existing law. An explicit provision to that effect is useful and constructive.

The last sentence of subsection (a) provides that in the case of a public company—defined in section 1101(3)—the court shall refer, after a hearing, all applications to the Securities and Exchange Commission for a report, which shall be advisory only. In Chapter S [former section 501 et seq. of this title] cases in which the Commission has appeared, it generally filed reports on fee applications. Usually, courts have accorded the SEC's views substantial weight, as representing the opinion of a disinterested agency skilled and experienced in reorganization affairs. The last sentence intends for the advisory assistance of the Commission to be sought only in case of a public company in reorganization under chapter 11.

Subsection (b) reenacts section 249 of Chapter X of the Bankruptcy Act (11 U.S.C. 649) [former section 649 of this title]. It is a codification of equitable principles designed to prevent fiduciaries in the case from engaging in the specified transactions since they are in a position to gain inside information or to shape or influence the course of the reorganization. Wolf v. Weinstein, 372 U.S. 633 (1963) [83 S.Ct. 969, 10 L.Ed.2d 33, rehearing denied 83 S.Ct. 1522, 373 U.S. 928, 10 L.Ed.2d 427]. The statutory bar of compensation and reimbursement is based on the principle that such transactions involve conflicts of interest. Private gain undoubtedly prompts the purchase or sale of claims or stock interests, while the fiduciary's obligation is to render loyal and disinterested service which his position of trust has imposed upon him. Subsection (b) extends to a trustee, his attorney, committees and their attorneys, or any other persons "acting in the case in a representative or fiduciary capacity." It bars compensation to any of the foregoing, who after assuming to act in such capacity has purchased or sold, directly or indirectly, claims against, or stock in the debtor. The bar is absolute. It makes no difference whether the transaction brought a gain or loss, or neither, and the court is not authorized to approve a purchase or sale, before or after the transaction. The exception is for an acquisition or transfer "otherwise" than by a voluntary purchase or sale, such as an acquisition by bequest. See Otis & Co. v. Insurance Bldg. Corp., 110 F.2d 333, 335 (C.A.1, 1940).

Subsection (c) [now (b)] is intended for no asset liquidation cases where minimal compensation for trustees is needed. The sum of $20 will be allowed in each case, which is double the amount provided under current law.

Notes of Committee on the Judiciary, House Report No. 95–595. Section 330 authorizes compensation for services and reimbursement of expenses of officers of the estate. It also prescribes the standards on which the amount of compensation is to be determined. As noted above, the compensation allowable under this section is subject to the maxima set out in sections 326, 328, and 329. The compensation is to be reasonable, for actual necessary services rendered, based on the time, the nature, the extent, and the value of the services rendered, and on the cost of comparable services other than in a case under the bankruptcy code. The effect of the last provision is to overrule In re Beverly Crest Convalescent Hospital, Inc., 548 F.2d 817 (9th Cir.1976, as amended 1977), which set an arbitrary limit on fees payable, based on the amount of a district judge's salary, and other, similar cases that require fees to be determined based on notions of conservation of the estate and economy of administration. If that case were allowed to stand, attorneys that could earn much higher incomes in other fields would leave the bankruptcy arena. Bankruptcy specialists, who enable the system to operate smoothly, efficiently, and expeditiously, would be driven elsewhere, and the bankruptcy field would be occupied by those who could not find other work and those who practice bankrupt-

cy law only occasionally almost as a public service. Bankruptcy fees that are lower than fees in other areas of the legal profession may operate properly when the attorneys appearing in bankruptcy cases do so intermittently, because a low fee in a small segment of a practice can be absorbed by other work. Bankruptcy specialists, however, if required to accept fees in all of their cases that are consistently lower than fees they could receive elsewhere, will not remain in the bankruptcy field.

This subsection provides for reimbursement of actual, necessary expenses. It further provides for compensation of paraprofessionals employed by professional persons employed by the estate of the debtor. The provision is included to reduce the cost of administering bankruptcy cases. In nonbankruptcy areas, attorneys are able to charge for a paraprofessional's time on an hourly basis, and not include it in overhead. If a similar practice does not pertain in bankruptcy cases then the attorney will be less inclined to use paraprofessionals even where the work involved could easily be handled by an attorney's assistant, at much lower cost to the estate. This provision is designed to encourage attorneys to use paraprofessional assistance where possible, and to insure that the estate, not the attorney, will bear the cost, to the benefit of both the estate and the attorneys involved.

Legislative Statements. Section 330(a) contains the standard of compensation adopted in H.R. 8200 as passed by the House rather than the contrary standard contained in the Senate amendment. Attorneys' fees in bankruptcy cases can be quite large and should be closely examined by the court. However bankruptcy legal services are entitled to command the same competency of counsel as other cases. In that light, the policy of this section is to compensate attorneys and other professionals serving in a case under title 11 at the same rate as the attorney or other professional would be compensated for performing comparable services other than in a case under title 11. Contrary language in the Senate report accompanying S. 2266 is rejected, and Massachusetts Mutual Life Insurance Company v. Brock, 405 F.2d 429, 432 (5th Cir.1968) is overruled. Notions of economy of the estate in fixing fees are outdated and have no place in a bankruptcy code.

Section 330(a)(2) of the Senate amendment is deleted although the Securities and Exchange Commission retains a right to file an advisory report under section 1109.

Section 330(b) of the Senate amendment is deleted as unnecessary, as the limitations contained therein are covered by section 328(c) of H.R. 8200 as passed by the House and contained in the House amendment.

Section 330(c) of the Senate amendment providing for a trustee to receive a fee of $20 for each estate from the filing fee paid to the clerk is retained as section 330(b) of the House amendment. The section will encourage private trustees to serve in cases under title 11 and in pilot districts will place less of a burden on the U.S. trustee to serve in no-asset cases.

Section 330(b) of H.R. 8200 as passed by the House is retained by the House amendment as section 330(c) [15330].

1986 Amendment. Subsec. (a). Pub.L. 99–554, § 211(1), substituted "notice to any parties in interest and to the United States trustee and a hearing" for "notice and a hearing".

Subsec. (d). Pub.L. 99–554, § 211(2), added subsec. (d).

See Effective Date of 1986 Amendment, etc., notes set out below.

Effective Date of 1986 Amendments; Savings Provisions; Effective Date of 1986 Amendments for Certain Judicial Districts Not Served by United States Trustees and for Judicial Districts in Alabama and North Carolina; U.S. Trustee System Fund Deposits in Alabama and North Carolina; Effective Date of Title 11 Chapter 15 Repeal as to Northern District of Alabama; Authority of Certain Estate Administrators in Alabama and North Carolina; Effective Date of 1986 Amendments in Pending Cases Where a U.S. Trustee Not Authorized or Where a Trustee Files Final Report or Plan is Confirmed; Quarterly Fees. Amendment by Pub.L. 99–554 effective 30 days after Oct. 27, 1986, except as otherwise provided for, see section 302(a) of Pub.L. 99–554, set out as a note under section 581 of Title 28, Judiciary and Judicial Procedure.

Amendments by Pub.L. 99–554, § 257(f), not to apply with respect to cases commenced under Title 11, Bankruptcy, before 30 days after Oct. 27, 1986, see section 302(c)(1) of Pub. L. 99–554, set out as a note under section 581 of Title 28.

Amendment by Pub.L. 99–554, § 211, not to become effective in or with respect to certain specified judicial districts until, or apply to cases while pending in such district before, the expiration of the 270-day period beginning 30 days after Oct. 27, 1986, or of the 30-day period beginning on the date the Attorney General certifies under section 303 of Pub.L. 99–554 the region specified in a paragraph of section 581(a) of Title 28, as amended by section 111(a) of Pub.L. 99–554, that includes such district, whichever occurs first, see section 302(d)(1) of Pub.L. 99–554, set out as a note under section 581 of Title 28.

Amendment by Pub.L. 99–554, § 211, not to become effective in or with respect to certain specified judicial districts until, or apply to cases while pending in such district before, the expiration of the 2-year period beginning 30 days after Oct. 27, 1986, or of the 30-day period beginning on the date the Attorney General certifies under section 303 of Pub.L. 99–554 the region specified in a paragraph of section 581(a) of Title 28, as amended by section 111(a) of Pub.L. 99–554, that includes such district, whichever occurs first, see section 302(d)(2) of Pub.L. 99–554, set out as a note under section 581 of Title 28.

Amendment by Pub.L. 99–554, § 211, not to become effective in or with respect to judicial districts established for the States of Alabama and North Carolina until, or apply to cases while pending in such district before, such district elects to be included in a bankruptcy region established in section 581(a) of Title 28, as amended by section 111(a) of Pub.L. 99–554, or Oct. 1, 2002, whichever occurs first, and, except as otherwise provided for, with respect to cases under chapters 7, 11, 12, and 13 of Title 11 commenced before 30 days after Oct. 27, 1986, and pending in a judicial district in the States of Alabama or North Carolina before any election made under section 302(d)(3) (A) of Pub.L. 99–554 by such district becomes effective or Oct. 1, 2002, whichever occurs first, amendments by Pub.L. 99–554 not to apply until Oct. 1, 2003, or the expiration of the 1-year period beginning on the date such election becomes effective, whichever occurs first, and further, in any judicial district in Alabama or North Carolina not making the election described in section 302(d)(3)(A) of Pub.L. 99–554, any person appointed under regulations issued by the Judicial Conference to administer estates in cases under Title 11 authorized to establish, etc., a panel of private trustees, and to supervise cases and trustees in cases under chapters 7, 11, 12, and 13 of Title 11, until amendments by sections 201 to 231 of Pub.L. 99–554 effective in such district, see section 302(d)(3)(A) to (F), (H), (I) of Pub.L.

99–554, set out as a note under section 581 of Title 28.

Amendment by Pub.L. 99–554, § 211, except as otherwise provided, with respect to cases under chapters 7, 11, 12, and 13 of Title 11 commenced before 30 days after Oct. 27, 1986, and pending in a judicial district referred to in section 581(a) of Title 28, as amended by section 111(a) of Pub.L. 99–554, for which a United States trustee is not authorized before 30 days after Oct. 27, 1986 to be appointed, not applicable until the expiration of the 3-year period beginning on Oct. 27, 1986, or of the 1-year period beginning on the date the Attorney General certifies under section 303 of Pub.L. 99–554 the region specified in a paragraph of such section 581(a) that includes, such district, whichever occurs first, see section 302(e)(1), (2) of Pub.L. 99–554, set out as a note under section 581 of Title 28.

See 1986 Amendment notes set out above.

Effective Date of 1984 Amendments. See section 553 of Pub.L. 98–353, Title III, July 10, 1984, 98 Stat. 392, set out as an Effective Date of 1984 Amendment note preceding chapter 1 of Title 11, Bankruptcy.

Separability of Provisions. For separability of provisions of Title III of Pub.L. 98–353, see section 551 of Pub.L. 98–353 set out as a Separability of Provisions note preceding chapter 1 of Title 11, Bankruptcy.

Cross References

Debtor in possession's right of compensation, see section 1107.
Officers' compensation as administrative expense, see section 503.

Library References:

C.J.S. Bankruptcy §§ 232–238.
West's Key No. Digests, Bankruptcy ⚷3155 et seq.

WESTLAW Electronic Research

See WESTLAW Electronic Research Guide following the *Bankruptcy Highlights*.

§ 331. Interim compensation

A trustee, an examiner, a debtor's attorney, or any professional person employed under section 327 or 1103 of this title may apply to the court not more than once every 120 days after an order for relief in a case under this title, or more often if the court permits, for such compensation for services rendered before the date of such an application or reimbursement for expenses incurred before such date as is provided under section 330 of this title. After notice and a hearing, the court may allow and disburse to such applicant such compensation or reimbursement.

Pub.L. 95–598, Nov. 6, 1978, 92 Stat. 2564.

Historical and Revision Notes

Notes of Committee on the Judiciary, Senate Report No. 95–989. Section 331 permits trustees and professional persons to apply to the court not more than once every 120 days for interim compensation and reimbursement payments. The court may permit more frequent applications if the circumstances warrant, such as in very large cases where the legal work is extensive and merits more frequent payments. The court is authorized to allow and order disbursement to the applicant of compensation and reimbursement that is otherwise allowable under section 330. The only effect of this section is to remove any doubt that officers of the estate may apply for, and the court may approve, compensation and reimbursement during the case, instead of being required to wait until the end of the case, which in some instances, may be years. The practice of interim compensation is followed in some courts today, but has been subject to some question. This section explicitly authorizes it.

This section will apply to professionals such as auctioneers and appraisers only if they are not paid on a per job basis.

Library References:

C.J.S. Bankruptcy § 235.

West's Key No. Digests, Bankruptcy ⚯3158, 3175.

WESTLAW Electronic Research

See WESTLAW Electronic Research Guide following the *Bankruptcy Highlights*.

SUBCHAPTER III—ADMINISTRATION

§ 341. Meetings of creditors and equity security holders

(a) Within a reasonable time after the order for relief in a case under this title, the United States trustee shall convene and preside at a meeting of creditors.

(b) The United States trustee may convene order a meeting of any equity security holders.

(c) The court may not preside at, and may not attend, any meeting under this section including any final meeting of creditors.

Pub.L. 95–598, Nov. 6, 1978, 92 Stat. 2564; Pub.L. 99–554, Title II, § 212, Oct. 27, 1986, 100 Stat. 3099.

Historical and Revision Notes

Notes of Committee on the Judiciary, Senate Report No. 95–989. Section (a) of this section requires that there be a meeting of creditors within a reasonable time after the order for relief in the case. The Bankruptcy Act [former Title 11] and the current Rules of Bankruptcy Procedure provide for a meeting of creditors, and specify the time and manner of the meeting, and the business to be conducted. This bill leaves those matters to the rules. Under section 405(d) of the bill, the present rules will continue to govern until new rules are promulgated. Thus, pending the adoption of different rules, the present procedure for the meeting will continue.

Subsection (b) authorizes the court to order a meeting of equity security holders in cases where such a meeting would be beneficial or useful, for example, in a chapter 11 reorganization case where it may be necessary for the equity security holders to organize in order to be able to participate in the negotiation of a plan of reorganization.

Subsection (c) makes clear that the bankruptcy judge is to preside at the meeting of creditors.

Legislative Statements. Section 341(c) of the Senate amendment is deleted and a contrary provision is added indicating that the bankruptcy judge will not preside at or attend the first meeting of creditors or equity security holders but a discharge hearing for all individuals will be held at which the judge will preside.

1986 Amendment. Subsec. (a). Pub.L. 99–554, § 212(1), substituted "this title, the United States trustee shall convene and preside at a meeting of creditors" for "this title, there shall be a meeting of creditors".

Subsec. (b). Pub.L. 99–554, § 212(2), substituted "The United States trustee may convene a meeting" for "The court may order a meeting".

Subsec. (c). Pub.L. 99–554, § 212(3), substituted "this section including any final meeting of creditors." for "this section.".

See Effective Date of 1986 Amendment, etc., notes set out below.

Effective Date of 1986 Amendments; Effective Date of 1986 Amendments for Certain Judicial Districts Not Served by United States Trustees and for Judicial Districts in Alabama and North Carolina; U.S. Trustee System Fund Deposits in Alabama and North Carolina; Effective Date of Title 11 Chapter 15 Repeal as to Northern District of Alabama; Authority of Certain Estate Administrators in Alabama and North Carolina; Effective Date of 1986 Amendments in Pending Cases Where a U.S. Trustee Not Authorized or Where a Trustee Files Final Report or Plan is Confirmed; Quarterly Fees. Amendment by Pub.L. 99–554 effective 30 days after Oct. 27,

1986, except as otherwise provided for, see section 302(a) of Pub.L. 99–554, set out as a note under section 581 of Title 28, Judiciary and Judicial Procedure.

Amendment by Pub.L. 99–554, § 212, not to become effective in or with respect to certain specified judicial districts until, or apply to cases while pending in such district before, the expiration of the 270-day period beginning 30 days after Oct. 27, 1986, or of the 30-day period beginning on the date the Attorney General certifies under section 303 of Pub.L. 99–554 the region specified in a paragraph of section 581(a) of Title 28, as amended by section 111(a) of Pub.L. 99–554, that includes such district, whichever occurs first, see section 302(d)(1) of Pub.L. 99–554, set out as a note under section 581 of Title 28.

Amendment by Pub.L. 99–554, § 212, not to become effective in or with respect to certain specified judicial districts until, or apply to cases while pending in such district before, the expiration of the 2-year period beginning 30 days after Oct. 27, 1986, or of the 30-day period beginning on the date the Attorney General certifies under section 303 of Pub.L. 99–554 the region specified in a paragraph of section 581(a) of Title 28, as amended by section 111(a) of Pub.L. 99–554, that includes such district, whichever occurs first, see section 302(d)(2) of Pub.L. 99–554, set out as a note under section 581 of Title 28.

Amendment by Pub.L. 99–554, § 212, not to become effective in or with respect to judicial districts established for the States of Alabama and North Carolina until, or apply to cases while pending in such district before, such district elects to be included in a bankruptcy region established in section 581(a) of Title 28, as amended by section 111(a) of Pub.L. 99–554, or Oct. 1, 2002, whichever occurs first, and, except as otherwise provided for, with respect to cases under chapters 7, 11, 12, and 13 of

Title 11 commenced before 30 days after Oct. 27, 1986, and pending in a judicial district in the States of Alabama or North Carolina before any election made under section 302(d)(3) (A) of Pub.L. 99–554 by such district becomes effective or Oct. 1, 2002, whichever occurs first, amendments by Pub.L. 99–554 not to apply until Oct. 1, 2003, or the expiration of the 1-year period beginning on the date such election becomes effective whichever occurs first, and further, in any judicial district in Alabama or North Carolina not making the election described in section 302(d)(3)(A) of Pub.L. 99–554, any person appointed under regulations issued by the Judicial Conference to administer estates in cases under Title 11 authorized to establish, etc., a panel of private trustees, and to supervise cases and trustees in cases under chapters 7, 11, 12, and 13 of Title 11, until amendments by sections 201 to 231 of Pub.L. 99–554 effective in such district, see section 302(d)(3)(A) to (F), (H), (I) of Pub.L. 99–554, set out as a note under section 581 of Title 28.

Amendment by Pub.L. 99–554, § 212, except as otherwise provided, with respect to cases under chapters 7, 11, 12, and 13 of Title 11 commenced before 30 days after Oct. 27, 1986, and pending in a judicial district referred to in section 581(a) of Title 28, as amended by section 111(a) of Pub.L. 99–554, for which a United States trustee is not authorized before 30 days after Oct. 27, 1986 to be appointed, not applicable until the expiration of the 3-year period beginning on Oct. 27, 1986, or of the 1-year period beginning on the date the Attorney General certifies under section 303 of Pub.L. 99–554 the region specified in a paragraph of such section 581(a) that includes, such district, whichever occurs first, see section 302(e)(1), (2) of Pub.L. 99–554, set out as a note under section 581 of Title 28.

See 1986 Amendment notes set out above.

Cross References
Election of
    Creditors' committee, see section 705.
    Trustee, see section 702.
Inapplicability of this section in railroad reorganization cases, see section 1161.

Library References:
C.J.S. Bankruptcy §§ 193, 373.
West's Key No. Digests, Bankruptcy ⟜3024.

WESTLAW Electronic Research
See WESTLAW Electronic Research Guide following the *Bankruptcy Highlights*.

§ 342.   Notice

(a) There shall be given such notice as is appropriate, including notice to any holder of a community claim, of an order for relief in a case under this title.

(b) Prior to the commencement of a case under this title by an individual whose debts are primarily consumer debts, the clerk shall give written notice to such individual that indicates each chapter of this title under which such individual may proceed.

Pub.L. 95–598, Nov. 6, 1978, 92 Stat. 2565; Pub.L. 98–353, Title III, §§ 302, 435, July 10, 1984, 98 Stat. 352, 370.

Historical and Revision Notes

Notes of Committee on the Judiciary, Senate Report No. 95–989. Subsection (a) of section 342 requires the clerk of the bankruptcy court to give notice of the order for relief. The rules will prescribe to whom the notice should be sent and in what manner notice will be given. The rules already prescribe such things, and they will continue to govern unless changed as provided in section 404(a) of the bill. Due process will certainly require notice to all creditors and equity security holders. State and Federal governmental representatives responsible for collecting taxes will also receive notice. In cases where the debtor is subject to regulation, the regulatory agency with jurisdiction will receive notice. In order to insure maximum notice to all parties in interest, the Rules will include notice by publication in appropriate cases and for appropriate issues. Other notices will be given as appropriate.

Subsections (b) and (c) are derived from section 21g of the Bankruptcy Act [former section 44(g) of this title]. They specify that the trustee may file notice of the commencement of the case in land recording offices in order to give notice of the pendency of the case to potential transferees of the debtor's real property. Such filing is unnecessary in the county in which the bankruptcy case is commenced.

If notice is properly filed, a subsequent purchaser of the property will not be a bona fide purchaser. Otherwise, a purchaser, including a purchaser at a judicial sale, that has no knowledge of the case, is not prevented from obtaining the status of a bona fide purchaser by the mere commencement of the case. "County" is defined in title 1 of the United States Code [section 2 of Title 1, General Provisions] to include other political subdivisions where counties are not used.

Legislative Statements. Section 342(b) and (c) of the Senate amendment are adopted in principle but moved to section 549(c), in lieu of section 342(b) of H.R. 8200 as passed by the House.

Section 342(c) of H.R. 8200 as passed by the House is deleted as a matter to be left to the Rules of Bankruptcy Procedure.

Effective Date of 1984 Amendments. See section 553 of Pub.L. 98–353, Title III, July 10, 1984, 98 Stat. 392, set out as an Effective Date of 1984 Amendment note preceding chapter 1 of Title 11, Bankruptcy.

Separability of Provisions. For separability of provisions of Title III of Pub.L. 98–353, see section 551 of Pub.L. 98–353 set out as a Separability of Provisions note preceding chapter 1 of Title 11, Bankruptcy.

Cross References

Instructions in notice to customers, see section 765.
Net equity defined in relation to payments made by customers to trustee within 60 days after notice, see section 741.
Notice in
    Commodity broker liquidation cases, see section 762.
    Stockbroker liquidation cases, see section 743.

Library References:

C.J.S. Bankruptcy §§ 30, 274, 275.
West's Key No. Digests, Bankruptcy ☞2131, 2900.

WESTLAW Electronic Research

See WESTLAW Electronic Research Guide following the *Bankruptcy Highlights*.

§ 343. Examination of the debtor

The debtor shall appear and submit to examination under oath at the meeting of creditors under section 341(a) of this title. Creditors, any indenture trustee, any trustee or examiner in the case, or the United States trustee may examine the debtor. The United States trustee may administer the oath required under this section.

Pub.L. 95–598, Nov. 6, 1978, 92 Stat. 2565; Pub.L. 98–353, Title III, § 436, July 10, 1984, 98 Stat. 370; Pub.L. 99–554, Title II, § 213, Oct. 27, 1986, 100 Stat. 3099.

Historical and Revision Notes

Notes of Committee on the Judiciary, Senate Report No. 95–989. This section, derived from section 21a of the Bankruptcy Act [former section 44(a) of this title] requires the debtor to appear at the meeting of creditors and submit to examination under oath. The purpose of the examination is to enable creditors and the trustee to determine if assets have improperly been disposed of or concealed or if there are grounds for objection to discharge. The scope of the examination under this section will be governed by the Rules of Bankruptcy Procedure, as it is today. See rules 205(d), 10–213(c), and 11–26. It is expected that the scope prescribed by these rules for liquidation cases, that is, "only the debtor's acts, conduct, or property, or any matter that may affect the administration of the estate, or the debtor's right to discharge" will remain substantially unchanged. In reorganization cases, the examination would be broader, including inquiry into the liabilities and financial condition of the debtor, the operation of his business, and the desirability of the continuance thereof, and other matters relevant to the case and to the formulation of the plan. Examination of other persons in connection with the bankruptcy case is left completely to the rules, just as examination of witnesses in civil cases is governed by the Federal Rules of Civil Procedure [Title 28, Judiciary and Judicial Procedure].

1986 Amendment. Pub.L. 99–554, § 213, substituted "Creditors, any indenture trustee, any trustee or examiner in the case, or the United States trustee may examine the debtor. The United States trustee may administer the oath required under this section." for "Creditors, any indenture trustee, or any trustee or examiner in the case may examine the debtor.".

See Effective Date of 1986 Amendment, etc., notes set out below.

Effective Date of 1986 Amendments; Effective Date of 1986 Amendments for Certain Judicial Districts Not Served by United States Trustees and for Judicial Districts in Alabama and North Carolina; U.S. Trustee System Fund Deposits in Alabama and North Carolina; Effective Date of Title 11, Chapter 15 Repeal as to Northern District of Alabama; Authority of Certain Estate Administrators in Alabama and North Carolina; Effective Date of 1986 Amendments in Pending Cases Where a U.S. Trustee Not Authorized or Where a Trustee Files Final Report or Plan is Confirmed; Quarterly Fees. Amendment by Pub.L. 99–554 effective 30 days after Oct. 27, 1986, except as otherwise provided for, see section 302(a) of Pub.L. 99–554, set out as a note under section 581 of Title 28, Judiciary and Judicial Procedure.

Amendment by Pub.L. 99–554, § 213, not to become effective in or with respect to certain specified judicial districts until, or apply to cases while pending in such district before, the expiration of the 270-day period beginning 30 days after Oct. 27, 1986, or of the 30-day period beginning on the date the Attorney General certifies under section 303 of Pub.L. 99–554 the region specified in a paragraph of section 581(a) of Title 28, as amended by section 111(a) of Pub.L. 99–554, that includes such district, whichever occurs first, see section 302(d)(1) of Pub.L. 99–554, set out as a note under section 581 of Title 28.

Amendment by Pub.L. 99–554, § 213 not to become effective in or with respect to certain specified judicial districts until, or apply to cases while pending in such district before, the expiration of the 2-year period beginning

30 days after Oct. 27, 1986, or of the 30-day period beginning on the date the Attorney General certifies under section 303 of Pub.L. 99–554 the region specified in a paragraph of section 581(a) of Title 28, as amended by section 111(a) of Pub.L. 99–554, that includes such district, whichever occurs first, see section 302(d)(2) of Pub.L. 99–554, set out as a note under section 581 of Title 28.

Amendment by Pub.L. 99–554, § 213 not to become effective in or with respect to judicial districts established for the States of Alabama and North Carolina until, or apply to cases while pending in such district before, such district elects to be included in a bankruptcy region established in section 581(a) of Title 28, as amended by section 111(a) of Pub.L. 99–554, or Oct. 1, 2002, whichever occurs first, and, except as otherwise provided for, with respect to cases under chapters 7, 11, 12, and 13 of Title 11 commenced before 30 days after Oct. 27, 1986, and pending in a judicial district in the States of Alabama or North Carolina before any election made under section 302(d)(3)(A) of Pub.L. 99–554 by such district becomes effective or Oct. 1, 2002, whichever occurs first, amendments by Pub.L. 99–554 not to apply until Oct. 1, 2003, or the expiration of the 1-year period beginning on the date such election becomes effective, whichever occurs first, and further, in any judicial district in Alabama or North Carolina not making the election described in section 302(d)(3)(A) of Pub.L. 99–554, any person appointed under regulations issued by the Judicial Conference to administer estates in cases under Title 11 authorized to establish, etc., a panel of private trustees, and to supervise cases and trustees in cases under chapters 7, 11, 12, and 13 of Title 11, until amendments by sections 201 to 231 of Pub.L. 99–554 effective in such district, see section 302(d)(3)(A) to (F), (H), (I) of Pub.L. 99–554, set out as a note under section 581 of Title 28.

Amendment by Pub.L. 99–554, § 213, except as otherwise provided, with respect to cases under chapters 7, 11, 12, and 13 of Title 11 commenced before 30 days after Oct. 27, 1986, and pending in a judicial district referred to in section 581(a) of Title 28, as amended by section 111(a) of Pub.L. 99–554, for which a United States trustee is not authorized before 30 days after Oct. 27, 1986 to be appointed, not applicable until the expiration of the 3-year period beginning on Oct. 27, 1986, or of the 1-year period beginning on the date the Attorney General certifies under section 303 of Pub.L. 99–554 the region specified in a paragraph of such section 581(a) that includes, such district, whichever occurs first, see section 302(e)(1), (2) of Pub.L. 99–554, set out as a note under section 581 of Title 28.

See 1986 Amendment notes set out above.

Effective Date of 1984 Amendments. See section 553 of Pub.L. 98–353, Title III, July 10, 1984, 98 Stat. 392, set out as an Effective Date of 1984 Amendment note preceding chapter 1 of Title 11, Bankruptcy.

Separability of Provisions. For separability of provisions of Title III of Pub.L. 98–353, see section 551 of Pub.L. 98–353 set out as a Separability of Provisions note preceding chapter 1 of Title 11, Bankruptcy.

Cross References
Inapplicability of this section in railroad reorganization cases, see section 1161.

Library References:
C.J.S. Bankruptcy § 204.
West's Key No. Digests, Bankruptcy ⊃3040–3048.

WESTLAW Electronic Research
See WESTLAW Electronic Research Guide following the *Bankruptcy Highlights*.

§ 344. Self-incrimination; immunity

Immunity for persons required to submit to examination, to testify, or to provide information in a case under this title may be granted under part V of title 18.

Pub.L. 95–598, Nov. 6, 1978, 92 Stat. 2565.

Historical and Revision Notes

Notes of Committee on the Judiciary, Senate Report No. 95–989. Part V of title 18 of the United States Code [section 6001 et seq. of Title 18, Crimes and Criminal Procedure] governs the granting of immunity to witnesses before Federal tribunals. The immunity provided under part V is only use immunity, not transactional immunity. Part V applies to all proceedings before Federal courts, before Federal grand juries, before administrative agencies, and before Congressional committees. It requires the Attorney General or the U.S. attorney to request or to approve any grant of immunity, whether before a court, grand jury, agency, or congressional committee.

This section carries part V [section 6001 et seq. of Title 18, Crimes and Criminal Procedure] over into bankruptcy cases. Thus, for a witness to be ordered to testify before a bankruptcy court in spite of a claim of privilege, the U.S. attorney for the district in which the court sits would have to request from the district court for that district the immunity order. The rule would apply to both debtors, creditors, and any other witnesses in a bankruptcy case. If the immunity were granted, the witness would be required to testify. If not, he could claim the privilege against self-incrimination.

Part V [section 6001 et seq. of Title 18, Crimes and Criminal Procedure] is a significant departure from current law. Under section 7a(10) of the Bankruptcy Act [former section 25(a)(10) of this title] a debtor is required to testify in all circumstances, but any testimony he gives may not be used against him in any criminal proceeding, except testimony given in any hearing on objections to discharge. With that exception, section 7a(10) amounts to a blanket grant of use immunity to all debtors. Immunity for other witnesses in bankruptcy courts today is governed by part V of title 18.

The consequences of a claim of privileges by a debtor under proposed law and under current law differ as well. Under section 14c(6) of current law [former section 32(c)(6) of this title], any refusal to answer a material question approved by the court will result in the denial of a discharge, even if the refusal is based on the privilege against self incrimination. Thus, the debtor is confronted with the choice between losing his discharge and opening himself up to possible criminal prosecution.

Under section 727(a)(6) of the proposed title 11, a debtor is only denied a discharge if he refuses to testify after having been granted immunity. If the debtor claims the privilege and the U.S. attorney does not request immunity from the district courts, then the debtor may refuse to testify and still retain his right to a discharge. It removes the Scylla and Charibdis choice for debtors that exist under the Bankruptcy Act.

References in Text. Part V of title 18, referred to in text, is classified to section 6001 et seq. of Title 18, Crimes and Criminal Procedure.

Cross References

Applicability of this section in chapter 9 cases, see section 901.

Library References:

C.J.S. Witnesses § 439.
West's Key No. Digests, Witnesses ⬳304.

WESTLAW Electronic Research

See WESTLAW Electronic Research Guide following the *Bankruptcy Highlights.*

§ 345. Money of estates

(a) A trustee in a case under this title may make such deposit or investment of the money of the estate for which such trustee serves as will yield the maximum reasonable net return on such money, taking into account the safety of such deposit or investment.

(b) Except with respect to a deposit or investment that is insured or guaranteed by the United States or by a department, agency, or instrumentality of the United States or backed by the full faith and credit of the United States, the trustee shall require from an entity with which such money is deposited or invested—

(1) a bond—

(A) in favor of the United States;

(B) secured by the undertaking of a corporate surety approved by the United States trustee for the district in which the case is pending; and

(C) conditioned on—

(i) a proper accounting for all money so deposited or invested and for any return on such money;

(ii) prompt repayment of such money and return; and

(iii) faithful performance of duties as a depository; or

(2) the deposit of securities of the kind specified in section 9303 of title 31.

(c) An entity with which such moneys are deposited or invested is authorized to deposit or invest such moneys as may be required under this section.

Pub.L. 95–598, Nov. 6, 1978, 92 Stat. 2565; Pub.L. 97–258, § 3(c), Sept. 13, 1982, 96 Stat. 1064; Pub.L. 98–353, Title III, § 437, July 10, 1984, 98 Stat. 370; Pub.L. 99–554, Title II, § 214, Oct. 27, 1986, 100 Stat. 3099.

Historical and Revision Notes

Notes of Committee on the Judiciary, Senate Report No. 95–989. This section is a significant departure from section 61 of the Bankruptcy Act [former section 101 of this title]. It permits a trustee in a bankruptcy case to make such deposit of investment of the money of the estate for which he serves as will yield the maximum reasonable net return on the money, taking into account the safety of such deposit or investment. Under current law, the trustee is permitted to deposit money only with banking institutions. Thus, the trustee is generally unable to secure a high rate of return on money of estates pending distribution, to the detriment of creditors. Under this section, the trustee may make deposits in savings and loans, may purchase government bonds, or make such other deposit or investment as is appropriate. Under proposed 11 U.S.C. 541(a)(6), and except as provided in subsection (c) of this section, any interest or gain realized on the deposit or investment of funds under this section will become property of the estate, and will thus enhance the recovery of creditors.

In order to protect the creditors, subsection (b) requires certain precautions against loss of the money so deposited or invested. The trustee must require from a person with which he deposits or invests money of an estate a bond in favor of the United States secured by approved corporate surety and conditioned on a proper accounting for all money deposited or invested and for any return on such money. Alternately, the trustee may require the deposit of securities of the kind specified in section 15 of title 6 of the United States Code [section 15 of Title 6, Official and Penal Bonds], which governs the posting of security by banks that receive public moneys on deposit. These bonding requirements do not apply to deposits or investments that are insured or guaranteed the United States or a department, agency, or instrumentality of the United States, or that are backed by the full faith and credit of the United States.

These provisions do not address the question of aggregation of funds by a private chapter 13 trustee and are not to be construed as excluding such possibility. The Rules of Bankruptcy Procedure may provide for aggregation under appropriate circumstances and adequate safeguards in cases where there is a significant need, such as in districts in which there is a standing chapter 13 trustee. In such case, the interest or return on the funds would help defray the cost of administering the cases in which the standing trustee serves.

Legislative Statements. The House amendment moves section 345(c) of the House bill to chapter 15 as part of the pilot program for the U.S. trustees. The bond required by section 345(b) may be a blanket bond posted by the financial depository sufficient to cover deposits by trustees in several cases, as is done under current law.

1986 Amendment. Subsec. (b)(1)(B). Pub.L. 99–554, § 214, substituted "approved by the United States trustee for the district" for "approved by the court for the district".

See Effective Date of 1986 Amendment, etc., notes set out below.

Effective Date of 1986 Amendments; Effective Date of 1986 Amendments for Certain Judicial Districts Not Served by United States Trustees and for Judicial Districts in Alabama and North Carolina; U.S. Trustee System Fund Deposits in Alabama and North Carolina; Effective Date of Title 11 Chapter 15 Repeal as to Northern District of Alabama; Authority of Certain Estate Administrators in Alabama and North Carolina; Effective Date of 1986 Amendments in Pending Cases Where a U.S. Trustee Not Authorized or Where a Trustee Files Final Report or Plan is Confirmed; Quarterly Fees. Amendment by Pub.L. 99–554 effective 30 days after Oct. 27, 1986, except as otherwise provided for, see section 302(a) of Pub.L. 99–554, set out as a note under section 581 of Title 28, Judiciary and Judicial Procedure.

Amendment by Pub.L. 99–554, § 214, not to become effective in or with respect to certain specified judicial districts until, or apply to cases while pending in such district before, the expiration of the 270-day period beginning 30 days after Oct. 27, 1986, or of the 30-day period beginning on the date the Attorney General certifies under section 303 of Pub.L. 99–554 the region specified in a paragraph of section 581(a) of Title 28, as amended by section 111(a) of Pub.L. 99–554, that includes such district, whichever occurs first, see section 302(d)(1) of Pub.L. 99–554, set out as a note under section 581 of Title 28.

Amendment by Pub.L. 99–554, § 214, not to become effective in or with respect to certain specified judicial districts until, or apply to cases while pending in such district before, the expiration of the 2-year period beginning 30 days after Oct. 27, 1986, or of the 30-day period beginning on the date the Attorney General certifies under section 303

of Pub.L. 99–554 the region specified in a paragraph of section 581(a) of Title 28, as amended by section 111(a) of Pub.L. 99–554, that includes such district, whichever occurs first, see section 302(d)(2) of Pub.L. 99–554, set out as a note under section 581 of Title 28.

Amendment by Pub.L. 99–554, § 214, not to become effective in or with respect to judicial districts established for the States of Alabama and North Carolina until, or apply to cases while pending in such district before, such district elects to be included in a bankruptcy region established in section 581(a) of Title 28, as amended by section 111(a) of Pub.L. 99–554, or Oct. 1, 2002, whichever occurs first, and, except as otherwise provided for, with respect to cases under chapters 7, 11, 12, and 13 of Title 11 commenced before 30 days after Oct. 27, 1986, and pending in a judicial district in the States of Alabama or North Carolina before any election made under section 302(d)(3)(A) of Pub.L. 99–554 by such district becomes effective or Oct. 1, 2002, whichever occurs first, amendments by Pub.L. 99–554 not to apply until Oct. 1, 2003, or the expiration of the 1-year period beginning on the date such election becomes effective, whichever occurs first, and further, in any judicial district in Alabama or North Carolina not making the election described in section 302(d)(3)(A) of Pub.L. 99–554, any person appointed under regulations issued by the Judicial Conference to administer estates in cases under Title 11 authorized to establish, etc., a panel of private trustees, and to supervise cases and trustees in cases under chapters 7, 11, 12, and 13 of Title 11, until amendments by sections 201 to 231 of Pub.L. 99–554 effective in such district, see section 302(d)(3)(A) to (F), (H), (I) of Pub.L. 99–554, set out as a note under section 581 of Title 28.

Amendment by Pub.L. 99–554, § 214, except as otherwise provided, with respect to cases under chapters 7, 11, 12, and 13 of Title 11 commenced before 30 days after Oct. 27, 1986, and pending in a judicial district referred to in section 581(a) of Title 28, as amended by section 111(a) of Pub.L. 99–554, for which a United States trustee is not authorized before 30 days after Oct. 27, 1986 to be appointed, not applicable until the expiration of the 3-year period beginning on Oct. 27, 1986, or of the 1-year period beginning on the date the Attorney General certifies under section 303 of Pub.L. 99–554 the region specified in a paragraph of such section 581(a) that includes, such district, whichever occurs first, see section 302(e)(1), (2) of Pub.L. 99–554, set out as a note under section 581 of Title 28.

See 1986 Amendment notes set out above.

Effective Date of 1984 Amendments. See section 553 of Pub.L. 98–353, Title III, July 10, 1984, 98 Stat. 392, set out as an Effective Date of 1984 Amendment note preceding chapter 1 of Title 11, Bankruptcy.

Separability of Provisions. For separability of provisions of Title III of Pub.L. 98–353, see section 551 of Pub.L. 98–353 set out as a Separability of Provisions note preceding chapter 1 of Title 11, Bankruptcy.

Library References:

C.J.S. Bankruptcy § 203.
West's Key No. Digests, Bankruptcy ☞3039.

WESTLAW Electronic Research

See WESTLAW Electronic Research Guide following the *Bankruptcy Highlights*.

§ 346. Special tax provisions

(a) Except to the extent otherwise provided in this section, subsections (b), (c), (d), (e), (g), (h), (i), and (j) of this section apply notwithstanding any State or local law imposing a tax, but subject to the Internal Revenue Code of 1954 (26 U.S.C. 1 et seq.).

(b)(1) In a case under chapter 7, 12 or 11 of this title concerning an individual, any income of the estate may be taxed under a State or local law imposing a tax on or measured by income only to the estate, and may not be taxed to such individual. Except as provided in section 728 of this title, if such individual is a partner in a partnership, any gain or loss resulting from a distribution of property from such partnership, or any distributive share of income, gain, loss, deduction, or credit of such individual that is distributed, or considered distributed, from such partnership, after the commencement of the case is gain, loss, income, deduction, or credit, as the case may be, of the estate.

(2) Except as otherwise provided in this section and in section 728 of this title, any income of the estate in such a case, and any State or local tax on or measured by such income, shall be computed in the same manner as the income and the tax of an estate.

(3) The estate in such a case shall use the same accounting method as the debtor used immediately before the commencement of the case.

(c)(1) The commencement of a case under this title concerning a corporation or a partnership does not effect a change in the status of such corporation or partnership for the purposes of any State or local law imposing a tax on or measured by income. Except as otherwise provided in this section and in section 728 of this title, any income of the estate in such case may be taxed only as though such case had not been commenced.

(2) In such a case, except as provided in section 728 of this title, the trustee shall make any tax return otherwise required by State or local law to be filed by or on behalf of such corporation or partnership in the same manner and form as such corporation or partnership, as the case may be, is required to make such return.

(d) In a case under chapter 13 of this title, any income of the estate or the debtor may be taxed under a State or local law imposing a tax on or measured by income only to the debtor, and may not be taxed to the estate.

(e) A claim allowed under section 502(f) or 503 of this title, other than a claim for a tax that is not otherwise deductible or a capital expenditure that is not otherwise deductible, is deductible by the entity to which income of the estate is taxed unless such claim was deducted by another entity, and a deduction for such a claim is deemed to be a deduction attributable to a business.

(f) The trustee shall withhold from any payment of claims for wages, salaries, commissions, dividends, interest, or other payments, or collect, any amount required to be withheld or collected under applicable State or local tax law, and shall pay such withheld or collected amount to the appropriate governmental unit at the time and in the manner required by such tax law, and with the same priority as the claim from which such amount was withheld was paid.

(g)(1) Neither gain nor loss shall be recognized on a transfer—

(A) by operation of law, of property to the estate;

(B) other than a sale, of property from the estate to the debtor; or

(C) in a case under chapter 11 or 12 of this title concerning a corporation, of property from the estate to a corporation that is an affiliate participating in a joint plan with the debtor, or that is a successor to the debtor under the plan, except that gain or loss may be recognized to the same extent that such transfer results in the recognition of gain or loss under section 371 of the Internal Revenue Code of 1954 (26 U.S.C. 371).

(2) The transferee of a transfer of a kind specified in this subsection shall take the property transferred with the same character, and with the transferor's basis, as adjusted under subsection (j)(5) of this section, and holding period.

(h) Notwithstanding sections 728(a) and 1146(a) of this title, for the purpose of determining the number of taxable periods during which the debtor or the estate may use a loss carryover or a loss carryback, the taxable period of the debtor during which the case is commenced is deemed not to have been terminated by such commencement.

(i)(1) In a case under chapter 7, 12, or 11 of this title concerning an individual, the estate shall succeed to the debtor's tax attributes, including—

(A) any investment credit carryover;

(B) any recovery exclusion;

(C) any loss carryover;

(D) any foreign tax credit carryover;

(E) any capital loss carryover; and

(F) any claim of right.

(2) After such a case is closed or dismissed, the debtor shall succeed to any tax attribute to which the estate succeeded under paragraph (1) of this subsection but that was not utilized by the estate. The debtor may utilize such tax attributes as though any applicable time limitations on such utilization by the debtor were suspended during the time during which the case was pending.

(3) In such a case, the estate may carry back any loss of the estate to a taxable period of the debtor that ended before the order for relief under such chapter the same as the debtor could have carried back such loss had the debtor incurred such loss and the case under this title had not been commenced, but the debtor may not carry back any loss of the debtor from a taxable period that ends

after such order to any taxable period of the debtor that ended before such order until after the case is closed.

(j)(1) Except as otherwise provided in this subsection, income is not realized by the estate, the debtor, or a successor to the debtor by reason of forgiveness or discharge of indebtedness in a case under this title.

(2) For the purposes of any State or local law imposing a tax on or measured by income, a deduction with respect to a liability may not be allowed for any taxable period during or after which such liability is forgiven or discharged under this title. In this paragraph, "a deduction with respect to a liability" includes a capital loss incurred on the disposition of a capital asset with respect to a liability that was incurred in connection with the acquisition of such asset.

(3) Except as provided in paragraph (4) of this subsection, for the purpose of any State or local law imposing a tax on or measured by income, any net operating loss of an individual or corporate debtor, including a net operating loss carryover to such debtor, shall be reduced by the amount of indebtedness forgiven or discharged in a case under this title, except to the extent that such forgiveness or discharge resulted in a disallowance under paragraph (2) of this subsection.

(4) A reduction of a net operating loss or a net operating loss carryover under paragraph (3) of this subsection or of basis under paragraph (5) of this subsection is not required to the extent that the indebtedness of an individual or corporate debtor forgiven or discharged—

(A) consisted of items of a deductible nature that were not deducted by such debtor; or

(B) resulted in an expired net operating loss carryover or other deduction that—

(i) did not offset income for any taxable period; and

(ii) did not contribute to a net operating loss in or a net operating loss carryover to the taxable period during or after which such indebtedness was discharged.

(5) For the purposes of a State or local law imposing a tax on or measured by income, the basis of the debtor's property or of property transferred to an entity required to use the debtor's basis in whole or in part shall be reduced by the lesser of—

(A)(i) the amount by which the indebtedness of the debtor has been forgiven or discharged in a case under this title; minus

(ii) the total amount of adjustments made under paragraphs (2) and (3) of this subsection; and

(B) the amount by which the total basis of the debtor's assets that were property of the estate before such forgiveness or discharge exceeds the debtor's total liabilities that were liabilities both before and after such forgiveness or discharge.

(6) Notwithstanding paragraph (5) of this subsection, basis is not required to be reduced to the extent that the debtor elects to treat as taxable income, of the taxable period in which indebtedness is forgiven or discharged, the amount of indebtedness forgiven or discharged that otherwise would be applied in reduction of basis under paragraph (5) of this subsection.

(7) For the purposes of this subsection, indebtedness with respect to which an equity security, other than an interest of a limited partner in a limited partnership, is issued to the creditor to whom such indebtedness was owed, or that is forgiven as a contribution to capital by an equity security holder other than a limited partner in the debtor, is not forgiven or discharged in a case under this title—

(A) to any extent that such indebtedness did not consist of items of a deductible nature; or

(B) if the issuance of such equity security has the same consequences under a law imposing a tax on or measured by income to such creditor as a payment in cash to such creditor in an amount equal to the fair market value of such equity security, then to the lesser of—

(i) the extent that such issuance has the same such consequences; and

(ii) the extent of such fair market value.

Pub.L. 95–598, Nov. 6, 1978, 92 Stat. 2565; Pub.L. 98–353, Title III, § 438, July 10, 1984, 98 Stat. 370; Pub.L. 99–554, Title II, §§ 257(g), 283(c), Oct. 27, 1986, 100 Stat. 3114, 3116.

Historical and Revision Notes

Notes of Committee on the Judiciary, Senate Report No. 95–989. Subsection (a) indicates that subsections (b), (c), (d), (e), (g), (h), (i), and (j) apply notwithstanding any State or local tax law, but are subject to Federal tax law.

Subsection (b)(1) provides that in a case concerning an individual under chapter 7 or 11 of title 11, income of the estate is taxable only to the estate and not to the debtor. The second sentence of the paragraph provides that if such individual is a partner, the tax attributes of the partnership are distributable to the partner's estate rather than to the partner, except to the extent that section 728 of title 11 provides otherwise.

Subsection (b)(2) states a general rule that the estate of an individual is to be taxed as an estate. The paragraph is made subject to the remainder of section 346 and section 728 of title 11.

Subsection (b)(3) requires the accounting method, but not necessarily the accounting period, of the estate to be the same as the method used by the individual debtor.

Subsection (c)(1) states a general rule that the estate of a partnership or a corporated debtor is not a separate entity for tax purposes. The income of the debtor is to be taxed as if the case were not commenced, except as provided in the remainder of section 346 and section 728.

Subsection (c)(2) requires the trustee, except as provided in section 728 of title 11, to file all tax returns on behalf of the partnership or corporation during the case.

Subsection (d) indicates that the estate in a chapter 13 case is not a separate taxable entity and that all income of the estate is to be taxed to the debtor.

Subsection (e) establishes a business deduction consisting of allowed expenses of administration except for tax or capital expenses that are not otherwise deductible. The deduction may be used by the estate when it is a separate taxable entity or by the entity to which the income of the estate is taxed when it is not.

Subsection (f) imposes a duty on the trustee to comply with any Federal, State, or local tax law requiring withholding or collection of taxes from any payment of wages, salaries, commissions, dividends, interest, or other payments. Any amount withheld is to be paid to the taxing authority at the same time and with the same priority as the claim from which such amount withheld was paid.

Subsection (g)(1)(A) indicates that neither gain nor loss is recognized on the transfer by law of property from the debtor or a creditor to the estate. Subparagraph (B) provides a similar policy if the property of the estate is returned from the estate to the debtor other than by a sale of property to debtor. Subparagraph (C) also provides for nonrecognition of gain or loss in a case under chapter 11 if a corporate debtor transfers property to a successor corporation or to an affiliate under a joint plan. An exception is made to enable a taxing authority to cause recognition of gain or loss to the extent provided in IRC section 371 (as amended by section 109 of this bill) [section 371 of Title 26, Internal Revenue Code].

Subsection (g)(2) provides that any of the three kinds of transferees specified in paragraph (1) take the property with the same character, holding period, and basis in the hands of the transferor at the time of such transfer. The transferor's basis may be adjusted under section 346(j)(5) even if the discharge of indebtedness occurs after the transfer of property. Of course, no adjustment will occur if the transfer is from the debtor to the estate or if the transfer is from an entity that is not discharged.

Subsection (h) provides that the creation of the estate of an individual under chapter 7 or 11 of title 11 as a separate taxable entity does not affect the number of taxable years for purposes of computing loss carryovers or carrybacks. The section applies with respect to carryovers or carrybacks of the debtor transferred into the estate under section 346(i)(1) of title 11 or back to the debtor under section 346(i)(2) of title 11.

Subsection (i)(1) states a general rule that an estate that is a separate taxable entity nevertheless succeeds to all tax attributes of the debtor. The six enumerated attributes are illustrative and not exhaustive.

Subsection (i)(2) indicates that attributes passing from the debtor into an estate that is a separate taxable entity will return to the debtor if unused by the estate. The debtor is permitted to use any such attribute as though the case had not been commenced.

Subsection (i)(3) permits an estate that is a separate taxable entity to carryback losses of the estate to a taxable period of the debtor that ended before the case was filed. The estate is treated as if it were the debtor with respect to time limitations and other restrictions. The section makes clear that the debtor may not carryback any loss of his own from a tax year during the pendency of the case to such a period until the case is closed. No tolling of any period of limitation is provided with respect to carrybacks by the debtor of post-petition losses.

Subsection (j) sets forth seven special rules treating with the tax effects of forgiveness or discharge of indebtedness. The terms "forgiveness" and "discharge" are redundant, but

are used to clarify that "discharge" in the context of a special tax provision in title 11 includes forgiveness of indebtedness whether or not such indebtedness is "discharged" in the bankruptcy sense.

Paragraph (1) states the general rule that forgiveness of indebtedness is not taxable except as otherwise provided in paragraphs (2)–(7). The paragraph is patterned after sections 268, 395, and 520 of the Bankruptcy Act [former sections 668, 795, and 920 of this title].

Paragraph (2) disallows deductions for liabilities of a deductible nature in any year during or after the year of cancellation of such liabilities. For the purposes of this paragraph, "a deduction with respect to a liability" includes a capital loss incurred on the disposition of a capital asset with respect to a liability that was incurred in connection with the acquisition of such asset.

Paragraph (3) causes any net operating loss of a debtor that is an individual or corporation to be reduced by any discharge of indebtedness except as provided in paragraphs (2) or (4). If a deduction is disallowed under paragraph (2), then no double counting occurs. Thus, paragraph (3) will reflect the reduction of losses by liabilities that have been forgiven, including deductible liabilities or nondeductible liabilities such as repayment of principal on borrowed funds.

Paragraph (4) specifically excludes two kinds of indebtedness from reduction of net operating losses under paragraph (3) or from reduction of basis under paragraph (5). Subparagraph (A) excludes items of a deductible nature that were not deducted or that could not be deducted such as gambling losses or liabilities for interest owed to a relative of the debtor. Subparagraph (B) excludes indebtedness of a debtor that is an individual or corporation that resulted in deductions which did not offset income and that did not contribute to an unexpired net operating loss or loss carryover. In these situations, the debtor has derived no tax benefit so there is no need to incur an offsetting reduction.

Paragraph (5) provides a two-point test for reduction of basis. The paragraph replaces sections 270, 396, and 522 of the Bankruptcy Act [former sections 670, 796, and 922 of this title]. Subparagraph (A) sets out the maximum amount by which basis may be reduced—the total indebtedness forgiven less adjustments made under paragraph (2) and (3). This avoids double counting. If a deduction is disallowed under paragraph (2) or a carryover is reduced under paragraph (3) then the tax benefit is neutralized, and there is no need to reduce basis. Subparagraph (B) reduces basis to the extent the debtor's total basis of assets before the discharge exceeds total preexisting liabilities still remaining after discharge of indebtedness. This is a "basis solvency" limitation which differs from the usual test of solvency because it measures against the remaining liabilities the benefit aspect of assets, their basis, rather than their value. Paragraph (5) applies so that any transferee of the debtor's property who is required to use the debtor's basis takes the debtor's basis reduced by the lesser of (A) and (B). Thus, basis will be reduced, but never below a level equal to undischarged liabilities.

Paragraph (6) specifies that basis need not be reduced under paragraph (5) to the extent the debtor treats discharged indebtedness as taxable income. This permits the debtor to elect whether to recognize income, which may be advantageous if the debtor anticipates subsequent net operating losses, rather than to reduce basis.

Paragraph (7) establishes two rules excluding from the category of discharged indebtedness certain indebtedness that is exchanged for an equity security issued under a plan or that is forgiven as a contribution to capital by an equity security holder. Subparagraph (A) creates the first exclusion to the extent indebtedness consisting of items not of a deductible nature is exchanged for an equity security, other than the interests of a limited partner in a limited partnership, issued by the debtor or is forgiven as a contribution to capital by an equity security holder. Subparagraph (B) excludes indebtedness consisting of items of a deductible nature, if the exchange of stock for debts has the same effect as a cash payment equal to the value of the equity security, in the amount of the fair market value of the equity security or, if less, the extent to which such exchange has such effect. The two provisions treat the debtor as if it had originally issued stock instead of debt. Subparagraph (B) rectifies the inequity under current law between a cash basis and accrual basis debtor concerning the issuance of stock in exchange for previous services rendered that were of a greater value than the stock. Subparagraph (B) also changes current law by taxing forgiveness of indebtedness to the extent that stock is exchanged for the accrued interest component of a security, because the recipient of such stock would not be regarded as having received money under the *Carman* doctrine.

Legislative Statements. Section 346 of the House amendment, together with sections 728 and 1146, represent special tax provisions applicable in bankruptcy. The policy contained in those sections reflects the policy that should be applied in Federal, State, and local taxes in the view of the House Committee on the Judiciary. The House Ways and Means Committee and the Senate Finance Committee did not have time to process a bankruptcy tax bill during the 95th Congress. It is anticipated that early in the 96th Congress, and before the effective date of the bankruptcy code [this title], the tax committees of Congress will have an opportunity to consider action with respect to amendments to the Internal Revenue Code [Title 26] and the special tax provisions in title 11. Since the special tax provisions are likely to be amended during the first part of the 96th Congress, it is anticipated that the bench and bar will also study and comment on these special tax provisions prior to their revision.

State and local rules. This section provides special tax provisions dealing with the treatment, under State or local, but not Federal, tax law, of the method of taxing bankruptcy estates of individuals, partnerships, and corporations; survival and allocation of tax attributes between the bankrupt and the estate; return filing requirements; and the tax treatment of income from discharge of indebtedness. The Senate bill removed these rules pending adoption of Federal rules on these issues in the next Congress. The House amendment returns the State and local tax rules to section 346 so that they may be studied by the bankruptcy and tax bars who may wish to submit comments to Congress.

Withholding rules. Both the House bill and Senate amendment provide that the trustee is required to comply with the normal withholding rules applicable to the payment of wages and other payments. The House amendment retains this rule for State and local taxes only. The treatment of withholding of Federal taxes will be considered in the next Congress.

Section 726 of the Senate amendment provides that the rule requiring pro rata payment of all expenses within a priority category does not apply to the payment of amounts withheld by a bankruptcy trustee. The purpose of this rule was to insure that the trustee pay the full amount of the withheld taxes to the appropriate governmental tax authority. The House amendment deletes this rule as unnecessary because the existing practice conforms essentially to that rule. If the trustee fails to pay over in full amounts that he withheld, it is a violation of his trustee's duties which would permit the taxing authority to sue the trustee on his bond.

When taxes considered "incurred": The Senate amendment contained rules of general application dealing with when a tax is "incurred" for purposes of the various tax collection rules affecting the debtor and the estate. The House amendment adopts the substance of these rules and transfers them to section 507 of title 11.

Penalty for failure to pay tax. The Senate amendment contains a rule which relieves the debtor and the trustee from certain tax penalties for failure to make timely payment of a tax to the extent that the bankruptcy rules prevent the trustee or the debtor from paying the tax on time. Since most of these penalties relate to Federal taxes, the House amendment deletes these rules pending consideration of Federal tax rules affecting bankruptcy in the next Congress.

References in Text. The Internal Revenue Code of 1954, referred to in subsec. (a), is classified to section 1 et seq. of Title 26, Internal Revenue Code.

Section 371 of the Internal Revenue Code of 1954, referred to in subsec. (g)(1)(C), is classified to section 371 of Title 26.

Effective Date of 1986 Amendments; Savings Provisions; Quarterly Fees. Amendment by Pub.L. 99–554 effective 30 days after Oct. 27, 1986, except as otherwise provided for, see section 302(a) of Pub.L. 99–554, set out as a note under section 581 of Title 28, Judiciary and Judicial Procedure.

Amendments by Pub.L. 99–554, § 257(g), not to apply with respect to cases commenced under Title 11, Bankruptcy, before 30 days after Oct. 27, 1986, see section 302(c)(1) of Pub. L. 99–554, set out as a note under section 581 of Title 28.

Effective Date of 1984 Amendments. See section 553 of Pub.L. 98–353, Title III, July 10, 1984, 98 Stat. 392, set out as an Effective Date of 1984 Amendment note preceding chapter 1 of Title 11, Bankruptcy.

Separability of Provisions. For separability of provisions of Title III of Pub.L. 98–353, see section 551 of Pub.L. 98–353 set out as a Separability of Provisions note preceding chapter 1 of Title 11, Bankruptcy.

Cross References

Request for determination of tax effects of reorganization plan, see section 1146.

Library References:

C.J.S. Taxation § 1094.
West's Key No. Digests, Taxation ⊕1021.

WESTLAW Electronic Research

See WESTLAW Electronic Research Guide following the *Bankruptcy Highlights*.

§ 347. Unclaimed property

(a) Ninety days after the final distribution under section 726, 1226, or 1326 of this title in a case under chapter 7, 12, or 13 of this title, as the case may be, the trustee shall stop payment on any check remaining unpaid, and any remaining property of the estate shall be paid into the court and disposed of under chapter 129 of title 28.

(b) Any security, money, or other property remaining unclaimed at the expiration of the time allowed in a case under chapter 9, 11, or 12 of this title for the presentation of a security or the performance of any other act as a condition to participation in the distribution under any plan confirmed under section 943(b), 1129, 1173, or 1225 of this title, as the case may be, becomes the property of the debtor or of the entity acquiring the assets of the debtor under the plan, as the case may be.

Pub.L. 95–598, Nov. 6, 1978, 92 Stat. 2568; Pub.L. 99–554, Title II, § 257(h), Oct. 27, 1986, 100 Stat. 3114.

Historical and Revision Notes

Notes of Committee on the Judiciary, Senate Report No. 95–989. Section 347 is derived from Bankruptcy Act § 66 [former section 106 of this title]. Subsection (a) requires the trustee to stop payment on any distribution check that is unpaid 90 days after the final distribution in a case under chapter 7 or 13. The unclaimed funds, and any other property of the estate are paid into the court and disposed of under chapter 129 of title 28 [section 2041 et seq. of Title 28, Judiciary and Judicial Procedure], which requires the clerk of court to hold the funds for their owner for 5 years, after which they escheat to the Treasury.

Subsection (b) specifies that any property remaining unclaimed at the expiration of the time allowed in a chapter 9 or 11 case for presentation (exchange) of securities or the performance of any other act as a condition to participation in the plan reverts to the debtor or the entity acquiring the assets of the debtor under the plan. Conditions to participation under a plan include such acts as cashing a check, surrendering securities for cancellation, and so on. Similar provisions are found in sections 96(d) [former section 415(d) of this title] and 205 [former section 605 of this title] of current law.

Legislative Statements. Section 347(a) of the House amendment adopts a comparable provision contained in the Senate amendment instructing the trustee to stop payment on any check remaining unpaid more than 90 days after the final distribution in a case under Chapter 7 or 13. Technical changes are made in section 347(b) to cover distributions in a railroad reorganization.

Effective Date of 1986 Amendments; Savings Provisions; Quarterly Fees. Amendment by Pub.L. 99–554 effective 30 days after Oct. 27, 1986, except as otherwise provided for, see section 302(a) of Pub.L. 99–554, set out as a note under section 581 of Title 28, Judiciary and Judicial Procedure.

Amendments by Pub.L. 99–554, § 257(h), not to apply with respect to cases commenced under Title 11, Bankruptcy, before 30 days after Oct. 27, 1986, see section 302(c)(1) of Pub. L. 99–554, set out as a note under section 581 of Title 28.

Cross References

Applicability of subsec. (b) of this section in chapter 9 cases, see section 901.

Library References:

C.J.S. Bankruptcy §§ 351, 355.
West's Key No. Digests, Bankruptcy ⬥3445.

WESTLAW Electronic Research

See WESTLAW Electronic Research Guide following the *Bankruptcy Highlights.*

§ 348. Effect of conversion

(a) Conversion of a case from a case under one chapter of this title to a case under another chapter of this title constitutes an order for relief under the chapter to which the case is converted, but, except as provided in subsections (b) and (c) of this section, does not effect a change in the date of the filing of the petition, the commencement of the case, or the order for relief.

(b) Unless the court for cause orders otherwise, in sections 701(a), 727(a)(10), 727(b), 728(a), 728(b), 1102(a), 1110(a)(1), 1121(b), 1121(c), 1141(d)(4), 1146(a), 1146(b), 1301(a), 1305(a), 1201(a), 1221, and 1228(a), of this title, "the order for relief under this chapter" in a chapter to which a case has been converted under section 706, 1112, 1307, or 1208 of this title means the conversion of such case to such chapter.

(c) Sections 342 and 365(d) of this title apply in a case that has been converted under section 706, 1112, 1307, or 1208 of this title, as if the conversion order were the order for relief.

(d) A claim against the estate or the debtor that arises after the order for relief but before conversion in a case that is converted under section 1112, 1307, or 1208 of this title, other than a claim specified in section 503(b) of this title, shall be treated for all purposes as if such claim had arisen immediately before the date of the filing of the petition.

(e) Conversion of a case under section 706, 1112, 1307, or 1208 of this title terminates the service of any trustee or examiner that is serving in the case before such conversion.

Pub.L. 95–598, Nov. 6, 1978, 92 Stat. 2568; Pub.L. 99–554, Title II, § 257(i), Oct. 27, 1986, 100 Stat. 3115.

Historical and Revision Notes

Notes of Committee on the Judiciary, Senate Report No. 95–989. This section governs the effect of the conversion of a case from one chapter of the bankruptcy code [this title] to another chapter. Subsection (a) specifies that the date of the filing of the petition, the commencement of the case, or the order for relief are unaffected by conversion, with some exceptions specified in subsections (b) and (c).

Subsection (b) lists certain sections in the operative chapters of the bankruptcy code [this title] in which there is a reference to "the order for relief under this chapter." In those sections, the reference is to be read as a reference to the conversion order if the case has been converted into the particular chapter. Subsection (c) specifies that notice is to be given of the conversion order the same as notice was given of the order for relief, and that the time the trustee (or debtor in possession) has for assuming or rejecting executory contracts recommences, thus giving an opportunity for a newly appointed trustee to familiarize himself with the case.

Subsection (d) provides for special treatment of claims that arise during chapter 11 or 13 cases before the case is converted to a liquidation case. With the exception of claims specified in proposed 11 U.S.C. 503(b) (administrative expenses), preconversion claims are treated the same as prepetition claims.

Subsection (e) provides that conversion of a case terminates the service of any trustee serving in the case prior to conversion.

Legislative Statements. The House amendment adopts section 348(b) of the Senate amendment with slight modifications, as more accurately reflecting sections to which this particular effect of conversion should apply.

Section 348(e) of the House amendment is a stylistic revision of similar provisions contained in H.R. 8200 as passed by the House and in the Senate amendment. Termination of services is expanded to cover any examiner serving in the case before conversion, as done in H.R. 8200 as passed by the House.

Effective Date of 1986 Amendments; Savings Provisions; Quarterly Fees. Amendment by Pub.L. 99–554 effective 30 days after Oct. 27, 1986, except as otherwise provided for, see section 302(a) of Pub.L. 99–554, set out as a note under section 581 of Title 28, Judiciary and Judicial Procedure.

Amendments by Pub.L. 99–554, § 257(i), not to apply with respect to cases commenced under Title 11, Bankruptcy, before 30 days after Oct. 27, 1986, see section 302(c)(1) of Pub. L. 99–554, set out as a note under section 581 of Title 28.

Library References:

C.J.S. Bankruptcy §§ 42, 380, 418, 437.
West's Key No. Digests, Bankruptcy ☞2331, 2332, 3594, 3673, 3717.

WESTLAW Electronic Research

See WESTLAW Electronic Research Guide following the *Bankruptcy Highlights.*

§ 349. Effect of dismissal

(a) Unless the court, for cause, orders otherwise, the dismissal of a case under this title does not bar the discharge, in a later case under this title, of debts that were dischargeable in the case dismissed; nor does the dismissal of a case under this title prejudice the debtor with regard to the filing of a subsequent petition under this title, except as provided in section 109(f) of this title.

(b) Unless the court, for cause, orders otherwise, a dismissal of a case other than under section 742 of this title—

(1) reinstates—

(A) any proceeding or custodianship superseded under section 543 of this title;

(B) any transfer avoided under section 522, 544, 545, 547, 548, 549, or 724(a) of this title, or preserved under section 510(c)(2), 522(i)(2), or 551 of this title; and

(C) any lien voided under section 506(d) of this title;

(2) vacates any order, judgment, or transfer ordered, under section 522(i)(1), 542, 550, or 553 of this title; and

(3) revests the property of the estate in the entity in which such property was vested immediately before the commencement of the case under this title.

Pub.L. 95–598, Nov. 6, 1978, 92 Stat. 2569; Pub.L. 98–353, Title III, § 303, July 10, 1984, 98 Stat. 352.

Historical and Revision Notes

Notes of Committee on the Judiciary, Senate Report No. 95–989. Subsection (a) specifies that unless the court for cause orders otherwise, the dismissal of a case is without prejudice. The debtor is not barred from receiving a discharge in a later case of debts that were dischargeable in the case dismissed. Of course, this subsection refers only to pre-discharge dismissals. If the debtor has already received a discharge and it is not revoked, then the debtor would be barred under section 727(a) from receiving a discharge in a subsequent liquidation case for six years. Dismissal of an involuntary on the merits will generally not give rise to adequate cause so as to bar the debtor from further relief.

Subsection (b) specifies that the dismissal reinstates proceedings or custodianships that were superseded by the bankruptcy case, reinstates avoided transfers, reinstates voided liens, vacates any order, judgment, or transfer ordered as a result of the avoidance of a transfer, and revests the property of the estate in the entity in which the property was vested at the commencement of the case. The court is permitted to order a different result for cause. The basic purpose of the subsection is to undo the bankruptcy case, as far as practicable, and to restore all property rights to the position in which they were found at the commencement of the case. This does not necessarily encompass undoing sales of property from the estate to a good faith purchaser. Where there is a question over the scope of the subsection, the court will make the appropriate orders to protect rights acquired in reliance on the bankruptcy case.

Legislative Statements. Section 349(b)(2) of the House amendment adds a cross reference to section 553 to reflect the new right of recovery of setoffs created under that section. Corresponding changes are made throughout the House amendment.

Effective Date of 1984 Amendments. See section 553 of Pub.L. 98–353, Title III, July 10, 1984, 98 Stat. 392, set out as an Effective Date of 1984 Amendment note preceding chapter 1 of Title 11, Bankruptcy.

Separability of Provisions. For separability of provisions of Title III of Pub.L. 98–353, see section 551 of Pub.L. 98–353 set out as a Separability of Provisions note preceding chapter 1 of Title 11, Bankruptcy.

Cross References

Applicability of this section in chapter 9 cases, see section 901.

Library References:

C.J.S. Bankruptcy §§ 48, 299, 453.
West's Key No. Digests, Bankruptcy ⚖2235, 3275, 3718.

WESTLAW Electronic Research

See WESTLAW Electronic Research Guide following the *Bankruptcy Highlights*.

§ 350. Closing and reopening cases

(a) After an estate is fully administered and the court has discharged the trustee, the court shall close the case.

(b) A case may be reopened in the court in which such case was closed to administer assets, to accord relief to the debtor, or for other cause.

Pub.L. 95–598, Nov. 6, 1978, 92 Stat. 2569; Pub.L. 98–353, Title III, § 439, July 10, 1984, 98 Stat. 370.

Historical and Revision Notes

Notes of Committee on the Judiciary, Senate Report No. 95–989. Subsection (a) requires the court to close a bankruptcy case after the estate is fully administered and the trustee discharged. The Rules of Bankruptcy Procedure will provide the procedure for case closing. Subsection (b) permits reopening of the case to administer assets, to accord relief to the debtor, or for other cause. Though the court may permit reopening of a case so that the trustee may exercise an avoiding power, laches may constitute a bar to an action that has been delayed too long. The case may be reopened in the court in which it was closed.

The rules will prescribe the procedure by which a case is reopened and how it will be conducted after reopening.

Effective Date of 1984 Amendments. See section 553 of Pub.L. 98–353, Title III, July 10, 1984, 98 Stat. 392, set out as an Effective Date of 1984 Amendment note preceding chapter 1 of Title 11, Bankruptcy.

Separability of Provisions. For separability of provisions of Title III of Pub.L. 98–353, see section 551 of Pub.L. 98–353 set out as a Separability of Provisions note preceding chapter 1 of Title 11, Bankruptcy.

Cross References

Applicability of subsec. (b) of this section in chapter 9 cases, see section 901.
Scheduled property deemed abandoned, see section 554.
Successor trustee, see section 703.

Library References:

C.J.S. Bankruptcy § 357.
West's Key No. Digests, Bankruptcy ⚹3444.

WESTLAW Electronic Research

See WESTLAW Electronic Research Guide following the *Bankruptcy Highlights*.

SUBCHAPTER IV—ADMINISTRATIVE POWERS

§ 361. Adequate protection

When adequate protection is required under section 362, 363, or 364 of this title of an interest of an entity in property, such adequate protection may be provided by—

(1) requiring the trustee to make a cash payment or periodic cash payments to such entity, to the extent that the stay under section 362 of this title, use, sale, or lease under section 363 of this title, or any grant of a lien under section 364 of this title results in a decrease in the value of such entity's interest in such property;

(2) providing to such entity an additional or replacement lien to the extent that such stay, use, sale, lease, or grant results in a decrease in the value of such entity's interest in such property; or

(3) granting such other relief, other than entitling such entity to compensation allowable under section 503(b)(1) of this title as an administrative

expense, as will result in the realization by such entity of the indubitable equivalent of such entity's interest in such property.

Pub.L. 95–598, Nov. 6, 1978, 92 Stat. 2569; Pub.L. 98–353, Title III, § 440, July 10, 1984, 98 Stat. 370.

Historical and Revision Notes

Notes of Committee on the Judiciary, Senate Report No. 95–989. Sections 362, 363, and 364 require, in certain circumstances, that the court determine in noticed hearings whether the interest of a secured creditor or co-owner of property with the debtor is adequately protected in connection with the sale or use of property. The interests of which the court may provide protection in the ways described in this section include equitable as well as legal interests. For example, a right to enforce a pledge and a right to recover property delivered to a debtor under a consignment agreement or an agreement of sale or return are interests that may be entitled to protection. This section specifies means by which adequate protection may be provided but, to avoid placing the court in an administrative role, does not require the court to provide it. Instead, the trustee or debtor in possession or the creditor will provide or propose a protection method. If the party that is affected by the proposed action objects, the court will determine whether the protection provided is adequate. The purpose of this section is to illustrate means by which it may be provided and to define the limits of the concept.

The concept of adequate protection is derived from the fifth amendment protection of property interests as enunciated by the Supreme Court. See Wright v. Union Central Life Ins. Co., 311 U.S. 273 (1940) [61 S.Ct. 196, 85 L.Ed. 184, rehearing denied 61 S.Ct. 445, 312 U.S. 711, 85 L.Ed. 1142]; Louisville Joint Stock Land Bank v. Radford, 295 U.S. 555 (1935) [55 S.Ct. 854, 79 L.Ed. 1593].

The automatic stay also provides creditor protection. Without it, certain creditors would be able to pursue their own remedies against the debtor's property. Those who acted first would obtain payment of the claims in preference to and to the detriment of other creditors. Bankruptcy is designed to provide an orderly liquidation procedure under which all creditors are treated equally. A race of diligence by creditors for the debtor's assets prevents that.

Subsection (a) defines the scope of the automatic stay, by listing the acts that are stayed by the commencement of the case. The commencement or continuation, including the issuance of process, of a judicial, administrative or other proceeding against the debtor that was or could have been commenced before the commencement of the bankruptcy case is stayed under paragraph (1). The scope of this paragraph is broad. All proceedings are stayed, including arbitration, administrative, and judicial proceedings. Proceeding in this sense encompasses civil actions and all proceedings even if they are not before governmental tribunals.

The stay is not permanent. There is adequate provision for relief from the stay elsewhere in the section. However, it is important that the trustee have an opportunity to inventory the debtor's position before proceeding with the administration of the case. Undoubtedly the court will lift the stay for proceedings before specialized or nongovernmental tribunals to allow those proceedings to come to a conclusion. Any party desiring to enforce an order in such a proceeding would thereafter have to come before the bankruptcy court to collect assets. Nevertheless, it will often be more appropriate to permit proceedings to continue in their place of origin, when no great prejudice to the bankruptcy estate would result, in order to leave the parties to their chosen forum and to relieve the bankruptcy court from many duties that may be handled elsewhere.

Paragraph (2) stays the enforcement, against the debtor or against property of the estate, of a judgment obtained before the commencement of the bankruptcy case. Thus, execution and levy against the debtors' prepetition property are stayed, and attempts to collect a judgment from the debtor personally are stayed.

Paragraph (3) stays any act to obtain possession of property of the estate (that is, property of the debtor as of the date of the filing of the petition) or property from the estate (property over which the estate has control or possession). The purpose of this provision is to prevent dismemberment of the estate. Liquidation must proceed in an orderly fashion. Any distribution of property must be by the trustee after he has had an opportunity to familiarize himself with the various rights and interests involved and with the property available for distribution.

Paragraph (4) stays lien creation against property of the estate. Thus, taking possession to perfect a lien or obtaining court process is prohibited. To permit lien creation after bankruptcy would give certain creditors preferential treatment by making them secured instead of unsecured.

Paragraph (5) stays any act to create or enforce a lien against property of the debtor, that is, most property that is acquired after the date of the filing of the petition, property that is exempted, or property that does not pass to the estate, to the extent that the lien secures a prepetition claim. Again, to permit postbankruptcy lien creation or enforcement would permit certain creditors to receive preferential treatment. It may also circumvent the debtors' discharge.

Paragraph (6) prevents creditors from attempting in any way to collect a prepetition debt. Creditors in consumer cases occasionally telephone debtors to encourage repayment in spite of bankruptcy. Inexperienced, frightened, or ill-counseled debtors may succumb to suggestions to repay notwithstanding their bankruptcy. This provision prevents evasion of the purpose of the bankruptcy laws by sophisticated creditors.

Paragraph (7) stays setoffs of mutual debts and credits between the debtor and creditors. As with all other paragraphs of subsection (a), this paragraph does not affect the right of creditors. It simply stays its enforcement pending an orderly examination of the debtor's and creditors' rights.

Subsection (b) lists seven exceptions to the automatic stay. The effect of an exception is not to make the action immune from injunction.

The court has ample other powers to stay actions not covered by the automatic stay. Section 105, of proposed title 11, derived from Bankruptcy Act, § 2a(15), [former section 11(a)(15) of this title], grants the power to issue orders necessary or appropriate to carry out the provisions of title 11. The district court and the bankruptcy court as its adjunct have all the traditional injunctive powers of a court of equity, 28 U.S.C. §§ 151 and 164 as proposed in S. 2266, § 201, and 28 U.S.C. § 1334, as proposed in S. 2266, § 216. Stays or injunctions issued under these other sections will not be automatic upon the commencement of the case, but will be granted or issued under the usual rules for the issuance of injunctions. By excepting an act or action from the automatic stay, the bill simply requires that the trustee move the court into action, rather than requiring the stayed party

to request relief from the stay. There are some actions, enumerated in the exceptions, that generally should not be stayed automatically upon the commencement of the case, for reasons of either policy or practicality. Thus, the court will have to determine on a case-by-case basis whether a particular action which may be harming the estate should be stayed.

With respect to stays issued under other powers, or the application of the automatic stay, to governmental actions, this section and the other sections mentioned are intended to be an express waiver of sovereign immunity of the Federal Government, and an assertion of the bankruptcy power over State governments under the supremacy clause notwithstanding a State's sovereign immunity.

The first exception is of criminal proceedings against the debtor. The bankruptcy laws are not a haven for criminal offenders, but are designed to give relief from financial overextension. Thus, criminal actions and proceedings may proceed in spite of bankruptcy.

Paragraph (2) excepts from the stay the collection of alimony, maintenance or support from property that is not property of the estate. This will include property acquired after the commencement of the case, exempted property, and property that does not pass to the estate. The automatic stay is one means of protecting the debtor's discharge. Alimony, maintenance and support obligations are excepted from discharge. Staying collection of them, when not to the detriment of other creditors (because the collection effort is against property that is not property of the estate) does not further that goal. Moreover, it could lead to hardship on the part of the protected spouse or children.

Paragraph (3) excepts any act to perfect an interest in property to the extent that the trustee's rights and powers are limited under section 546(a) of the bankruptcy code. That section permits postpetition perfection of certain liens to be effective against the trustee. If the act of perfection, such as filing, were stayed, the section would be nullified.

Paragraph (4) excepts commencement or continuation of actions and proceedings by governmental units to enforce police or regulatory powers. Thus, where a governmental unit is suing a debtor to prevent or stop violation of fraud, environmental protection, consumer protection, safety, or similar police or regulatory laws, or attempting to fix damages for violation of such a law, the action or proceeding is not stayed under the automatic stay.

Paragraph (5) makes clear that the exception extends to permit an injunction and enforcement of an injunction, and to permit the entry of a money judgment, but does not extend to permit a money enforcement of a money judgment. Since the assets of the debtor are in the possession and control of the bankruptcy court, and since they constitute a fund out of which all creditors are entitled to share, enforcement by a governmental unit of a money judgment would give it preferential treatment to the detriment of all other creditors.

Paragraph (6) excepts the setoff of any mutual debt and claim for commodity transactions.

Paragraph (7) excepts actions by the Secretary of Housing and Urban Development to foreclose or take possession in a case of a loan insured under the National Housing Act [section 1701 et seq. of Title 12, Banks and Banking]. A general exception for such loans is found in current sections 263 [former section 663 of this title] and 517 [former section 917 of this title], the exception allowed by this paragraph is much more limited.

Subsection (c) of section 362 specifies the duration of the automatic stay. Paragraph (1) terminates a stay of an act against property of the estate when the property ceases to be property of the estate, such as by sale, abandonment, or exemption. It does not terminate the stay against property of the debtor if the property leaves the estate and goes to the debtor. Paragraph (2) terminates the stay of any other act on the earliest of the time the case is closed, the time the case is dismissed, or the time a discharge is granted or denied (unless the debtor is a corporation or partnership in a chapter 7 case).

Subsection (c) governs automatic termination of the stay. Subsections (d) through (g) govern termination of the stay by the court on the request of a party in interest.

Subsection (d) requires the court, upon motion of a party in interest, to grant relief from the stay for cause, such as by terminating, annulling, modifying, or conditioning the stay. The lack of adequate protection of an interest in property is one cause for relief, but is not the only cause. Other causes might include the lack of any connection with or interference with the pending bankruptcy case. Generally, proceedings in which the debtor is a fiduciary, or involving postpetition activities of the debtor, need not be stayed because they bear no relationship to the purpose of the automatic stay, which is protection of the debtor and his estate from his creditors.

Upon the court's finding that the debtor has no equity in the property subject to the stay and that the property is not necessary to an effective reorganization of the debtor, the subsection requires the court grant relief from the stay. To aid in this determination, guidelines are established where the property subject to the stay is real property. An exception to "the necessary to an effective reorganization" requirement is made for real property on which no business is being conducted other than operating the real property and activities incident thereto. The intent of this exception is to reach the single-asset apartment type cases which involve primarily tax-shelter investments and for which the bankruptcy laws have provided a too facile method to relay conditions, but not the operating shopping center and hotel cases where attempts at reorganization should be permitted. Property in which the debtor has equity but which is not necessary to an effective reorganization of the debtor should be sold under section 363. Hearings under this subsection are given calendar priority to ensure that court congestion will not unduly prejudice the rights of creditors who may be obviously entitled to relief from the operation of the automatic stay.

Subsection (e) provides protection that is not always available under present law. The subsection sets a time certain within which the bankruptcy court must rule on the adequacy of protection provided for the secured creditor's interest. If the court does not rule within 30 days from a request by motion for relief from the stay, the stay is automatically terminated with respect to the property in question. To accommodate more complex cases, the subsection permits the court to make a preliminary ruling after a preliminary hearing. After a preliminary hearing, the court may continue the stay only if there is a reasonable likelihood that the party opposing relief from the stay will prevail at the final hearing. Because the stay is essentially an injunction, the three stages of the stay may be analogized to the three stages of an injunction. The filing of the petition which gives rise to the automatic stay is similar to a temporary restraining order. The preliminary hearing is similar to the hearing on a preliminary injunction, and the final hearing and order are similar to the hearing and issuance or denial of a permanent injunction. The main difference lies in which party must bring the issue before the court. While in the injunction setting, the party seeking the injunction must prosecute the action, in proceeding for relief from the automatic stay, the enjoined party must move. The difference does not, however, shift the burden of proof. Subsection (g) leaves that burden on the party opposing relief from the stay (that is, on the party seeking continuance of the injunction) on the issue of adequate protection and existence of an equity. It is not, however, intended to be confined strictly to the constitutional requirement. This section and the concept of adequate protection are based as much on policy grounds as on constitutional grounds. Secured creditors should not be deprived of the benefit of their bargain. There may be situations in bankruptcy where giving a secured creditor an absolute right to his bargain may be impossible or seriously detrimental to the policy of the bankruptcy laws. Thus, this section recognizes the availability of alternate means of protecting a secured creditor's interest where such steps are a necessary part of the rehabilitative process. Though the creditor might not be able to retain his lien upon the specific collateral held at the time of filing, the purpose of the section is to insure that the secured creditor receives the value for which he bargained.

The section specifies two exclusive means of providing adequate protection, both of which may require an approximate determination of the value of the protected entity's interest in the property involved. The section does not specify how value is to be determined, nor does it specify when it is to be determined. These matters are left to case-by-case interpretation and development. In light of the restrictive approach of the section to the availability of means of providing adequate protection, this flexibility is important to permit the courts to adapt to varying circumstances and changing modes of financing.

Neither is it expected that the courts will construe the term value to mean, in every case, forced sale liquidation value or full going concern value. There is wide latitude between those two extremes although forced sale liquidation value will be a minimum.

In any particular case, especially a reorganization case, the determination of which entity should be entitled to the difference between the going concern value and the liquidation value must be based on equitable considerations arising from the facts of the case. Finally, the determination of value is binding only for the purposes of the specific hearing and is not to have a res judicata effect.

The first method of adequate protection outlined is the making of cash payments to compensate for the expected decrease in value of the opposing entity's interest. This provision is derived from In re Bermec Corporation, 445

F.2d 367 (2d Cir.1971), though in that case it is not clear whether the payments offered were adequate to compensate the secured creditors for their loss. The use of periodic payments may be appropriate where, for example, the property in question is depreciating at a relatively fixed rate. The periodic payments would be to compensate for the depreciation and might, but need not necessarily, be in the same amount as payments due on the secured obligation.

The second method is the fixing of an additional or replacement lien on other property of the debtor to the extent of the decrease in value or actual consumption of the property involved. The purpose of this method is to provide the protected entity with an alternative means of realizing the value of the original property, if it should decline during the case, by granting an interest in additional property from whose value the entity may realize its loss. This is consistent with the view expressed in Wright v. Union Central Life Ins. Co., 311 U.S. 273 (1940) [61 S.Ct. 196, 85 L.Ed. 184, rehearing denied 61 S.Ct. 445, 312 U.S. 711, 85 L.Ed. 1142], where the Court suggested that it was the value of the secured creditor's collateral, and not necessarily his rights in specific collateral, that was entitled to protection.

The section makes no provision for the granting of an administrative priority as a method of providing adequate protection to an entity as was suggested in In re Yale Express System, Inc., 384 F.2d 990 (2d Cir.1967), because such protection is too uncertain to be meaningful.

Notes of Committee on the Judiciary, House Report No. 95–595. The section specifies four means of providing adequate protection. They are neither exclusive nor exhaustive. They all rely, however, on the value of the protected entity's interest in the property involved. The section does not specify how value is to be determined, nor does it specify when it is to be determined. These matters are left to case-by-case interpretation and development. It is expected that the courts will apply the concept in light of facts of each case and general equitable principles. It is not intended that the courts will develop a hard and fast rule that will apply in every case. The time and method of valuation is not specified precisely, in order to avoid that result. There are an infinite number of variations possible in dealings between debtors and creditors, the law is continually developing, and new ideas are continually being implemented in this field. The flexibility is important to permit the courts to adapt to varying circumstances and changing modes of financing.

Neither is it expected that the courts will construe the term value to mean, in every case, forced sale liquidation value or full going concern value. There is wide latitude between those two extremes. In any particular case, especially a reorganization case, the determination of which entity should be entitled to the difference between the going concern value and the liquidation value must be based on equitable considerations based on the facts of the case. It will frequently be based on negotiation between the parties. Only if they cannot agree will the court become involved.

The first method of adequate protection specified is periodic cash payments by the estate, to the extent of a decrease in value of the opposing entity's interest in the property involved. This provision is derived from In re Yale Express, Inc., 384 F.2d 990 (2d Cir.1967) (though in that case it is not clear whether the payments required were adequate to compensate the secured creditors for their loss). The use of periodic payments may be appropriate, where for example, the property in question is depreciating at a relatively fixed rate. The periodic payments would be to compensate for the depreciation.

The second method is the provision of an additional or replacement lien on other property to the extent of the decrease in value of the property involved. The purpose of this method is to provide the protected entity with a means of realizing the value of the original property, if it should decline during the case, by granting an interest in additional property from whose value the entity may realize its loss.

The third method is the granting of an administrative expense priority to the protected entity to the extent of his loss. This method, more than the others, requires a prediction as to whether the unencumbered assets that will remain if the case if converted from reorganization to liquidation will be sufficient to pay the protected entity in full. It is clearly the most risky, from the entity's perspective, and should be used only when there is relative certainty that administrative expenses will be able to be paid in full in the event of liquidation.

The fourth method gives the parties and the courts flexibility by allowing such other relief as will result in the realization by the protected entity of the value of its interest in the property involved. Under this provision, the courts will be able to adapt to new methods of financing and to formulate protection that is appropriate to the circumstances of the case if none of the other methods would accomplish the desired result. For example, another form of adequate protection might be the guarantee by a third party outside the judicial process of compensation for any loss incurred in the case. Adequate protection might also, in some circumstances, be provided by permitting a secured creditor to bid in his claim at the sale of the property and to offset the claim against the price bid in.

The paragraph also defines, more clearly than the others, the general concept of adequate protection, by requiring such relief as will result in the realization of value. It is the general category, and as such, is defined by the concept involved rather than any particular method of adequate protection.

Legislative Statements. Section 361 of the House amendment represents a compromise between H.R. 8200 as passed by the House and the Senate amendment regarding the issue of "adequate protection" of a secured party. The House amendment deletes the provision found in section 361(3) of H.R. 8200 as passed by the House. It would have permitted adequate protection to be provided by giving the secured party an administrative expense regarding any decrease in the value of such party's collateral. In every case there is the uncertainty that the estate will have sufficient property to pay administrative expenses in full.

Section 361(4) of H.R. 8200 as passed by the House is modified in section 361(3) of the House amendment to indicate that the court may grant other forms of adequate protection, other than an administrative expense, which will result in the realization by the secured creditor of the indubitable equivalent of the creditor's interest in property. In the special instance where there is a reserve fund maintained under the security agreement, such as in the typical bondholder case, indubitable equivalent means that the bondholders would be entitled to be protected as to the reserve fund, in addition to the regular payments needed to service the debt. Adequate protection of an interest of an entity in property is intended to protect a creditor's allowed secured claim. To the extent the protection proves to be inadequate after the fact, the creditor is entitled to a first priority administrative expense under section 503(b).

In the special case of a creditor who has elected application of creditor making an election under section 1111(b)(2), that creditor is entitled to adequate protection of the creditor's interest in property to the extent of the value of the collateral not to the extent of the creditor's allowed secured claim, which is inflated to cover a deficiency as a result of such election.

Effective Date of 1984 Amendments. See section 553 of Pub.L. 98–353, Title III, July 10, 1984, 98 Stat. 392, set out as an Effective Date

of 1984 Amendment note preceding chapter 1 of Title 11, Bankruptcy.

Separability of Provisions. For separability of provisions of Title III of Pub.L. 98–353, see section 551 of Pub.L. 98–353 set out as a Separability of Provisions note preceding chapter 1 of Title 11, Bankruptcy.

Cross References

Applicability of this section in chapter 9 cases, see section 901.

Library References:

C.J.S. Bankruptcy §§ 86–88, 186, 200, 208, 209.
West's Key No. Digests, Bankruptcy ⊙⇒2430–2434, 3035, 3065, 3073.

WESTLAW Electronic Research

See WESTLAW Electronic Research Guide following the *Bankruptcy Highlights*.

§ 362. Automatic stay

(a) Except as provided in subsection (b) of this section, a petition filed under section 301, 302, or 303 of this title, or an application filed under section 5(a)(3) of the Securities Investor Protection Act of 1970 (15 U.S.C. 78eee(a)(3)), operates as a stay, applicable to all entities, of—

(1) the commencement or continuation, including the issuance or employment of process, of a judicial, administrative, or other action or proceeding against the debtor that was or could have been commenced before the commencement of the case under this title, or to recover a claim against the debtor that arose before the commencement of the case under this title;

(2) the enforcement, against the debtor or against property of the estate, of a judgment obtained before the commencement of the case under this title;

(3) any act to obtain possession of property of the estate or of property from the estate or to exercise control over property of the estate;

(4) any act to create, perfect, or enforce any lien against property of the estate;

(5) any act to create, perfect, or enforce against property of the debtor any lien to the extent that such lien secures a claim that arose before the commencement of the case under this title;

(6) any act to collect, assess, or recover a claim against the debtor that arose before the commencement of the case under this title;

(7) the setoff of any debt owing to the debtor that arose before the commencement of the case under this title against any claim against the debtor; and

(8) the commencement or continuation of a proceeding before the United States Tax Court concerning the debtor.

(b) The filing of a petition under section 301, 302, or 303 of this title, or of an application under section 5(a)(3) of the Securities Investor Protection Act of 1970 (15 U.S.C. 78eee(a)(3)), does not operate as a stay—

(1) under subsection (a) of this section, of the commencement or continuation of a criminal action or proceeding against the debtor;

(2) under subsection (a) of this section, of the collection of alimony, maintenance, or support from property that is not property of the estate;

(3) under subsection (a) of this section, of any act to perfect an interest in property to the extent that the trustee's rights and powers are subject to such perfection under section 546(b) of this title or to the extent that such act is accomplished within the period provided under section 547(e)(2)(A) of this title;

(4) under subsection (a)(1) of this section, of the commencement or continuation of an action or proceeding by a governmental unit to enforce such governmental unit's police or regulatory power;

(5) under subsection (a)(2) of this section, of the enforcement of a judgment, other than a money judgment, obtained in an action or proceeding by a governmental unit to enforce such governmental unit's police or regulatory power;

(6) under subsection (a) of this section, of the setoff by a commodity broker, forward contract merchant, stockbroker, financial institutions, or securities clearing agency of any mutual debt and claim under or in connection with commodity contracts, as defined in section 761(4) of this title, forward contracts, or securities contracts, as defined in section 741(7) of this title, that constitutes the setoff of a claim against the debtor for a margin payment, as defined in section 101(34), 741(5), or 761(15) of this title, or settlement payment, as defined in section 101(35) or 741(8) of this title, arising out of commodity contracts, forward contracts, or securities contracts against cash, securities, or other property held by or due from such commodity broker, forward contract merchant, stockbroker, financial institutions, or securities clearing agency to margin, guarantee, secure, or settle commodity contracts, forward contracts, or securities contracts;

(7) under subsection (a) of this section, of the setoff by a repo participant, of any mutual debt and claim under or in connection with repurchase agreements that constitutes the setoff of a claim against the debtor for a margin payment, as defined in section 741(5) or 761(15) of this title, or settlement payment, as defined in section 741(8) of this title, arising out of repurchase agreements against cash, securities, or other property held by or due from such repo participant to margin, guarantee, secure or settle repurchase agreements;

(8) under subsection (a) of this section, of the commencement of any action by the Secretary of Housing and Urban Development to foreclose a mortgage or deed of trust in any case in which the mortgage or deed of trust held by the Secretary is insured or was formerly insured under the National Housing Act and covers property, or combinations of property, consisting of five or more living units;

(9) under subsection (a) of this section, of the issuance to the debtor by a governmental unit of a notice of tax deficiency;

(10) under subsection (a) of this section, of any act by a lessor to the debtor under a lease of nonresidential real property that has terminated by the expiration of the stated term of the lease before the commencement of or during a case under this title to obtain possession of such property; or

(11) under subsection (a) of this section, of the presentment of a negotiable instrument and the giving of notice of and protesting dishonor of such an instrument;

(12) under subsection (a) of this section, after the date which is 90 days after the filing of such petition, of the commencement or continuation, and

conclusion to the entry of final judgment, of an action which involves a debtor subject to reorganization pursuant to chapter 11 of this title and which was brought by the Secretary of Transportation under the Ship Mortgage Act, 1920 (46 App. U.S.C. 911 et seq.) (including distribution of any proceeds of sale) to foreclose a preferred ship or fleet mortgage, or a security interest in or relating to a vessel or vessel under construction, held by the Secretary of Transportation under section 207 or title XI of the Merchant Marine Act, 1936 (46 App. U.S.C. 1117 and 1271 et seq., respectively), or under applicable State law;

(13) under subsection (a) of this section, after the date which is 90 days after the filing of such petition, of the commencement or continuation, and conclusion to the entry of final judgment, of an action which involves a debtor subject to reorganization pursuant to chapter 11 of this title and which was brought by the Secretary of Commerce under the Ship Mortgage Act, 1920 (46 App. U.S.C. 911 et seq.) (including distribution of any proceeds of sale) to foreclose a preferred ship or fleet mortgage in a vessel or a mortgage, deed of trust, or other security interest in a fishing facility held by the Secretary of Commerce under section 207 or title XI of the Merchant Marine Act, 1936 (46 App. U.S.C. 1117 and 1271 et seq., respectively);

(14)[1] under subsection (a) of this section, of the setoff by a swap participant, of any mutual debt and claim under or in connection with any swap agreement that constitutes the setoff of a claim against the debtor for any payment due from the debtor under or in connection with any swap agreement against any payment due to the debtor from the swap participant under or in connection with any swap agreement or against cash, securities, or other property of the debtor held by or due from such swap participant to guarantee, secure or settle any swap agreement.

(14)[1] under subsection (a) of this section, of any action by an accrediting agency regarding the accreditation status of the debtor as an educational institution;

(15) under subsection (a) of this section, of any action by a State licensing body regarding the licensure of the debtor as an educational institution; or

(16) under subsection (a) of this section, of any action by a guaranty agency, as defined in section 435(j) of the Higher Education Act of 1965 (20 U.S.C. 1001 et seq.) or the Secretary of Education regarding the eligibility of the debtor to participate in programs authorized under such Act.

The provisions of paragraphs (12) and (13) of this subsection shall apply with respect to any such petition filed on or before December 31, 1989.

(c) Except as provided in subsections (d), (e), and (f) of this section—

(1) the stay of an act against property of the estate under subsection (a) of this section continues until such property is no longer property of the estate; and

(2) the stay of any other act under subsection (a) of this section continues until the earliest of—

(A) the time the case is closed;

(B) the time the case is dismissed; or

(C) if the case is a case under chapter 7 of this title concerning an individual or a case under chapter 9, 11, 12, or 13 of this title, the time a discharge is granted or denied.

(d) On request of a party in interest and after notice and a hearing, the court shall grant relief from the stay provided under subsection (a) of this section, such as by terminating, annulling, modifying, or conditioning such stay—

(1) for cause, including the lack of adequate protection of an interest in property of such party in interest; or

(2) with respect to a stay of an act against property under subsection (a) of this section, if—

(A) the debtor does not have an equity in such property; and

(B) such property is not necessary to an effective reorganization.

(e) Thirty days after a request under subsection (d) of this section for relief from the stay of any act against property of the estate under subsection (a) of this section, such stay is terminated with respect to the party in interest making such request, unless the court, after notice and a hearing, orders such stay continued in effect pending the conclusion of, or as a result of, a final hearing and determination under subsection (d) of this section. A hearing under this subsection may be a preliminary hearing, or may be consolidated with the final hearing under subsection (d) of this section. The court shall order such stay continued in effect pending the conclusion of the final hearing under subsection (d) of this section if there is a reasonable likelihood that the party opposing relief from such stay will prevail at the conclusion of such final hearing. If the hearing under this subsection is a preliminary hearing, then such final hearing shall be commenced not later than thirty days after the conclusion of such preliminary hearing.

(f) Upon request of a party in interest, the court, with or without a hearing, shall grant such relief from the stay provided under subsection (a) of this section as is necessary to prevent irreparable damage to the interest of an entity in property, if such interest will suffer such damage before there is an opportunity for notice and a hearing under subsection (d) or (e) of this section.

(g) In any hearing under subsection (d) or (e) of this section concerning relief from the stay of any act under subsection (a) of this section—

(1) the party requesting such relief has the burden of proof on the issue of the debtor's equity in property; and

(2) the party opposing such relief has the burden of proof on all other issues.

(h) An individual injured by any willful violation of a stay provided by this section shall recover actual damages, including costs and attorneys' fees, and, in appropriate circumstances, may recover punitive damages.

Pub.L. 95–598, Nov. 6, 1978, 92 Stat. 2570; Pub.L. 97–222, § 3, July 27, 1982, 96 Stat. 235; Pub.L. 98–353, Title III, §§ 304, 363(b), 392, 441, July 10, 1984, 98 Stat. 352, 363, 365, 371; Pub.L. 99–509, Title V, § 5001(a), Oct. 8, 1986, 100 Stat. 1911; Pub.L. 99–554, Title II, §§ 257(j), 283(d), Oct. 27, 1986, 100 Stat. 3115, 3116; Pub.L. 101–311, Title I, § 102, Title II, § 202, June 25, 1990, 104 Stat. 267, 269; Pub.L. 101–508, Title III, § 3007(a)(1), Nov. 5, 1990, 104 Stat. 1388–__.

[1] See Codification note below.

Termination of Amendment

Pub.L. 101–508, § 3008, provided that amendment by Pub.L. 101–508, § 3007(a)(1), amending subsec. (b)(12) to (16) of this section, cease to be effective Oct. 1, 1996. See note below.

Historical and Revision Notes

Notes of Committee on the Judiciary, Senate Report No. 95–989. The automatic stay is one of the fundamental debtor protections provided by the bankruptcy laws. It gives the debtor a breathing spell from his creditors. It stops all collection efforts, all harassment, and all foreclosure actions. It permits the debtor to attempt a repayment or reorganization plan, or simply to be relieved of the financial pressures that drove him into bankruptcy.

The action commenced by the party seeking relief from the stay is referred to as a motion to make it clear that at the expedited hearing under subsection (e), and at hearings on relief from the stay, the only issue will be the lack of adequate protection, the debtor's equity in the property, and the necessity of the property to an effective reorganization of the debtor, or the existence of other cause for relief from the stay. This hearing will not be the appropriate time at which to bring in other issues, such as counterclaims against the creditor, which, although relevant to the question of the amount of the debt, concern largely collateral or unrelated matters. This approach is consistent with that taken in cases such as In re Essex Properties, Ltd., 430 F.Supp. 1112 (N.D.Cal. 1977), that an action seeking relief from the stay is not the assertion of a claim which would give rise to the right or obligation to assert counterclaims. Those counterclaims are not to be handled in the summary fashion that the preliminary hearing under this provision will be. Rather, they will be the subject of more complete proceedings by the trustee to recover property of the estate or to object to the allowance of a claim. However, this would not preclude the party seeking continuance of the stay from presenting evidence on the existence of claims which the court may consider in exercising its discretion. What is precluded is a determination of such collateral claims on the merits at the hearing.

[For additional discussion, see Notes of the Committee on the Judiciary, Senate Report No. 95–989, set out under section 361 of this title.]

Notes of Committee on the Judiciary, House Report No. 95–595. Paragraph (7) [of subsec. (a)] stays setoffs of mutual debts and credits between the debtor and creditors. As with all other paragraphs of subsection (a), this paragraph does not affect the right of creditors. It simply stays its enforcement pending an orderly examination of the debtor's and creditors' rights.

Legislative Statements. Section 362(a)(1) of the House amendment adopts the provision contained in the Senate amendment enjoining the commencement or continuation of a judicial, administrative, or other proceeding to recover a claim against the debtor that arose before the commencement of the case. The provision is beneficial and interacts with section 362(a)(6), which also covers assessment, to prevent harassment of the debtor with respect to pre-petition claims.

Section 362(a)(7) contains a provision contained in H.R. 8200 as passed by the House. The differing provision in the Senate amendment was rejected. It is not possible that a debt owing to the debtor may be offset against an interest in the debtor.

Section 362(a)(8) is new. The provision stays the commencement or continuation of any proceeding concerning the debtor before the U.S. Tax Court.

Section 362(b)(4) indicates that the stay under section 362(a)(1) does not apply to affect the commencement or continuation of an action or proceeding by a governmental unit to enforce the governmental unit's police or regulatory power. This section is intended to be given a narrow construction in order to permit governmental units to pursue actions to protect the public health and safety and not to apply to actions by a governmental unit to protect a pecuniary interest in property of the debtor or property of the estate.

Section 362(b)(6) of the House amendment adopts a provision contained in the Senate amendment restricting the exception to the automatic stay with respect to setoffs to permit only the setoff of mutual debts and claims. Traditionally, the right of setoff has been limited to mutual debts and claims and the lack of the clarifying term "mutual" in H.R. 8200 as passed by the House created an unintentional ambiguity. Section 362(b)(7) of the House amendment permits the issuance of a notice of tax deficiency. The House amendment rejects section 362(b)(7) in the Senate amendment. It would have permitted a particular governmental unit to obtain a pecuniary advantage without a hearing on the merits contrary to the exceptions contained in sections 362(b)(4) and (5).

Section 362(d) of the House amendment represents a compromise between comparable provisions in the House bill and Senate amendment. Under section 362(d)(1) of the House amendment, the court may terminate, annul, modify, or condition the automatic stay for cause, including lack of adequate protection of an interest in property of a secured party. It is anticipated that the Rules of Bankruptcy Procedure will provide that those hearings will receive priority on the calendar. Under section 362(d)(2) the court may alternatively terminate, annul, modify, or condition the automatic stay for cause including inadequate protection for the creditor. The court shall grant relief from the stay if there is no equity and it is not necessary to an effective reorganization of the debtor.

The latter requirement is contained in section 362(d)(2). This section is intended to solve the problem of real property mortgage foreclosures of property where the bankruptcy petition is filed on the eve of foreclosure. The section is not intended to apply if the business of the debtor is managing or leasing real property, such as a hotel operation, even though the debtor has no equity if the property is necessary to an effective reorganization of the debtor. Similarly, if the debtor does have an equity in the property, there is no requirement that the property be sold under section 363 of title 11 as would have been required by the Senate amendment.

Section 362(e) of the House amendment represents a modification of provisions in H.R. 8200 as passed by the House and the Senate amendment to make clear that a final hearing must be commenced within 30 days after a preliminary hearing is held to determine whether a creditor will be entitled to relief from the automatic stay. In order to insure that those hearings will in fact occur within such 30-day period, it is anticipated that the rules of bankruptcy procedure provide that such final hearings receive priority on the court calendar.

Section 362(g) places the burden of proof on the issue of the debtor's equity in collateral on the party requesting relief from the automatic stay and the burden on other issues on the debtor.

An amendment has been made to section 362(b) to permit the Secretary of the Department of Housing and Urban Development to commence an action to foreclose a mortgage or deed of trust. The commencement of such an action is necessary for tax purposes. The section is not intended to permit the continuation of such an action after it is commenced nor is the section to be construed to entitle the Secretary to take possession in lieu of foreclosure.

Sections 362(b)(8) and (9) contained in the Senate amendment are largely deleted in the House amendment. Those provisions add to the list of actions not stayed (a) jeopardy assessments, (b) other assessments, and (c) the issuance of deficiency notices. In the House amendment, jeopardy assessments against property which ceases to be property of the estate is already authorized by section 362(c)(1). Other assessments are specifically stayed under section 362(a)(6), while the issuance of a deficiency notice is specifically permitted. Stay of the assessment and the permission to issue a statutory notice of a tax deficiency will permit the debtor to take his personal tax case to the Tax Court, if the bankruptcy judge authorizes him to do so (as explained more fully in the discussion of section 505.)

References in Text. The National Housing Act, referred to in subsec. (b)(8), is Act June 27, 1934, c. 847, 48 Stat. 1246, which is classified principally to chapter 13 (§ 1701 et seq.) of Title 12, Banks and Banking.

Such Act, referred to in subsec. (b)(16), is the Higher Education Act of 1965, Pub.L. 89–329, as added and amended Pub.L. 99–498, Oct. 17, 1986, 100 Stat. 1278, which is classified principally to chapter 28 (section 1001 et seq.) of Title 20, Education. Section 435(j) of the Act is classified to section 1085(j) of Title 20.

Codification. Renumbering and conforming amendments by Pub.L. 101–647 failed to take into consideration prior renumbering and conforming amendments by Pub.L. 101–311, thereby resulting in two pars. numbered "(14)". To accommodate such duplication, the renumbering reflects changes by Pub.L. 101–311 set out first, and Pub.L. 101–647 set out second, but do not reflect the minor conforming amendments.

Effective and Termination Dates of 1990 Amendment. Section 3007(a)(3) of Pub.L. 101–508 provided that: "The amendments made by this subsection [amending subsec. (b)(12) to (16) of this section and section 541(b)(1) to (3) of this title] shall be effective upon date of enactment of this Act [Nov. 5, 1990]."

Section 3008 of Pub.L. 101–508 provided that: "The amendments made by this subtitle [amending this section, sections 541 and 1328 of this title, and sections 1078, 1078–1, 1078–7, 1085, 1088, and 1091 of Title 20, Education, and enacting provisions set out as notes under this section, and section 1328 of this title, and sections 1001, 1078, 1078–1, 1078–7, 1085, and 1088 of Title 20] shall cease [sic] be effective on October 1, 1966."

Effective Date of 1986 Amendments; Savings Provisions; Quarterly Fees. Amendment by Pub.L. 99–554 effective 30 days after Oct. 27, 1986, except as otherwise provided for, see section 302(a) of Pub.L. 99–554, set out as a note under section 581 of Title 28, Judiciary and Judicial Procedure.

Amendments by Pub.L. 99–554, § 257(j) not to apply with respect to cases commenced under Title 11, Bankruptcy, before 30 days after Oct. 27, 1986, see section 302(c)(1) of Pub. L. 99–554, set out as a note under section 581 of Title 28.

Section 5001(b) of Pub.L. 99–509 provided that: "The amendments made by subsection (a) of this section [amending this section] shall apply only to petitions filed under section 362 of title 11, United States Code, which are made after August 1, 1986."

Effective Date of 1984 Amendments. See section 553 of Pub.L. 98–353, Title III, July 10, 1984, 98 Stat. 392, set out as an Effective Date of 1984 Amendment note preceding chapter 1 of Title 11, Bankruptcy.

Separability of Provisions. For separability of provisions of Title III of Pub.L. 98–353, see section 551 of Pub.L. 98–353 set out as a Separability of Provisions note preceding chapter 1 of Title 11, Bankruptcy.

Cross References

Applicability of this section in chapter 9 cases, see section 901.
Assessment of taxes against estate, see section 505.
Effect of this section on subchapter III of chapter 7, see section 742.
Enforcement of claims against debtor in chapter 9 cases, automatic stay of, see section 922.
Extension of time generally, see section 108.
Priorities, see section 507.
Right of possession of party with security interest in
    Aircraft equipment and vessels, see section 1110.
    Rolling stock equipment, see section 1168.
Setoff, see section 553.
Turnover of property to estate, see section 542.

Library References:

C.J.S. Bankruptcy § 65 et seq.
West's Key No. Digests, Bankruptcy ☞2391 et seq.

WESTLAW Electronic Research

See WESTLAW Electronic Research Guide following the *Bankruptcy Highlights*.

§ 363.   Use, sale, or lease of property

(a) In this section, "cash collateral" means cash, negotiable instruments, documents of title, securities, deposit accounts, or other cash equivalents whenever acquired in which the estate and an entity other than the estate have an interest and includes the proceeds, products, offspring, rents, or profits of property subject to a security interest as provided in section 552(b) of this title, whether existing before or after the commencement of a case under this title.

(b)(1) The trustee, after notice and a hearing, may use, sell, or lease, other than in the ordinary course of business, property of the estate.

(2) If notification is required under subsection (a) of section 7A of the Clayton Act (15 U.S.C. 18a) in the case of a transaction under this subsection, then—

    (A) notwithstanding subsection (a) of such section, such notification shall be given by the trustee; and

(B) notwithstanding subsection (b) of such section, the required waiting period shall end on the tenth day after the date of the receipt of such notification, unless the court, after notice and hearing, orders otherwise.

(c)(1) If the business of the debtor is authorized to be operated under section 721, 1108, 1304, 1203 or 1204 of this title and unless the court orders otherwise, the trustee may enter into transactions, including the sale or lease of property of the estate, in the ordinary course of business, without notice or a hearing, and may use property of the estate in the ordinary course of business without notice or a hearing.

(2) The trustee may not use, sell, or lease cash collateral under paragraph (1) of this subsection unless—

(A) each entity that has an interest in such cash collateral consents; or

(B) the court, after notice and a hearing, authorizes such use, sale, or lease in accordance with the provisions of this section.

(3) Any hearing under paragraph (2)(B) of this subsection may be a preliminary hearing or may be consolidated with a hearing under subsection (e) of this section, but shall be scheduled in accordance with the needs of the debtor. If the hearing under paragraph (2)(B) of this subsection is a preliminary hearing, the court may authorize such use, sale, or lease only if there is a reasonable likelihood that the trustee will prevail at the final hearing under subsection (e) of this section. The court shall act promptly on any request for authorization under paragraph (2)(B) of this subsection.

(4) Except as provided in paragraph (2) of this subsection, the trustee shall segregate and account for any cash collateral in the trustee's possession, custody, or control.

(d) The trustee may use, sell, or lease property under subsection (b) or (c) of this section only to the extent not inconsistent with any relief granted under section 362(c), 362(d), 362(e), or 362(f) of this title.

(e) Notwithstanding any other provision of this section, at any time, on request of an entity that has an interest in property used, sold, or leased, or proposed to be used, sold, or leased, by the trustee, the court, with or without a hearing, shall prohibit or condition such use, sale, or lease as is necessary to provide adequate protection of such interest.

(f) The trustee may sell property under subsection (b) or (c) of this section free and clear of any interest in such property of an entity other than the estate, only if—

(1) applicable nonbankruptcy law permits sale of such property free and clear of such interest;

(2) such entity consents;

(3) such interest is a lien and the price at which such property is to be sold is greater than the aggregate value of all liens on such property;

(4) such interest is in bona fide dispute; or

(5) such entity could be compelled, in a legal or equitable proceeding, to accept a money satisfaction of such interest.

(g) Notwithstanding subsection (f) of this section, the trustee may sell property under subsection (b) or (c) of this section free and clear of any vested or contingent right in the nature of dower or curtesy.

(h) Notwithstanding subsection (f) of this section, the trustee may sell both the estate's interest, under subsection (b) or (c) of this section, and the interest of any co-owner in property in which the debtor had, at the time of the commencement of the case, an undivided interest as a tenant in common, joint tenant, or tenant by the entirety, only if—

(1) partition in kind of such property among the estate and such co-owners is impracticable;

(2) sale of the estate's undivided interest in such property would realize significantly less for the estate than sale of such property free of the interests of such co-owners;

(3) the benefit to the estate of a sale of such property free of the interests of co-owners outweighs the detriment, if any, to such co-owners; and

(4) such property is not used in the production, transmission, or distribution, for sale, of electric energy or of natural or synthetic gas for heat, light, or power.

(i) Before the consummation of a sale of property to which subsection (g) or (h) of this section applies, or of property of the estate that was community property of the debtor and the debtor's spouse immediately before the commencement of the case, the debtor's spouse, or a co-owner of such property, as the case may be, may purchase such property at the price at which such sale is to be consummated.

(j) After a sale of property to which subsection (g) or (h) of this section applies, the trustee shall distribute to the debtor's spouse or the co-owners of such property, as the case may be, and to the estate, the proceeds of such sale, less the costs and expenses, not including any compensation of the trustee, of such sale, according to the interests of such spouse or co-owners, and of the estate.

(k) At a sale under subsection (b) of this section of property that is subject to a lien that secures an allowed claim, unless the court for cause orders otherwise the holder of such claim may bid at such sale, and, if the holder of such claim purchases such property, such holder may offset such claim against the purchase price of such property.

(l) Subject to the provisions of section 365, the trustee may use, sell, or lease property under subsection (b) or (c) of this section, or a plan under chapter 11, 12, or 13 of this title may provide for the use, sale, or lease of property, notwithstanding any provision in a contract, a lease, or applicable law that is conditioned on the insolvency or financial condition of the debtor, on the commencement of a case under this title concerning the debtor, or on the appointment of or the taking possession by a trustee in a case under this title or a custodian, and that effects, or gives an option to effect, a forfeiture, modification, or termination of the debtor's interest in such property.

(m) The reversal or modification on appeal of an authorization under subsection (b) or (c) of this section of a sale or lease of property does not affect the validity of a sale or lease under such authorization to an entity that purchased or leased such property in good faith, whether or not such entity knew of the pendency of the appeal, unless such authorization and such sale or lease were stayed pending appeal.

(n) The trustee may avoid a sale under this section if the sale price was controlled by an agreement among potential bidders at such sale, or may recover from a party to such agreement any amount by which the value of the property sold exceeds the price at which such sale was consummated, and may recover

transmission, or distribution for sale, of electric energy or of natural or synthetic gas for heat, light, or power. This limitation is intended to protect public utilities from being deprived of power sources because of the bankruptcy of a joint owner.

Section 363(k) of the House amendment is derived from the third sentence of section 363(e) of the Senate amendment. The provision indicates that a secured creditor may bid in the full amount of the creditor's allowed claim, including the secured portion and any unsecured portion thereof in the event the creditor is undersecured, with respect to property that is subject to a lien that secures the allowed claim of the sale of the property.

Effective Date of 1986 Amendments; Savings Provisions; Quarterly Fees. Amendment by Pub.L. 99–554 effective 30 days after Oct. 27, 1986, except as otherwise

provided for, see section 302(a) of Pub.L. 99–554, set out as a note under section 581 of Title 28, Judiciary and Judicial Procedure.

Amendments by Pub.L. 99–554, § 257(k), not to apply with respect to cases commenced under Title 11, Bankruptcy, before 30 days after Oct. 27, 1986, see section 302(c)(1) of Pub. L. 99–554, set out as a note under section 581 of Title 28.

Effective Date of 1984 Amendments. See section 553 of Pub.L. 98–353, Title III, July 10, 1984, 98 Stat. 392, set out as an Effective Date of 1984 Amendment note preceding chapter 1 of Title 11, Bankruptcy.

Separability of Provisions. For separability of provisions of Title III of Pub.L. 98–353, see section 551 of Pub.L. 98–353 set out as a Separability of Provisions note preceding chapter 1 of Title 11, Bankruptcy.

Cross References

Continuity of business operation and use, acquisition or disposition of property by debtor, see section 303.
Identical rights and powers of debtor in chapter 13 cases, see section 1303.
Postpetition effect of security interest, see section 552.
Priorities, see section 507.
Right of possession of party with security interest in
    Aircraft equipment and vessels, see section 1110.
    Rolling stock equipment, see section 1168.
Rights and powers of debtor engaged in business, see section 1304.
Sale of property as affecting allowance of claim secured by lien on property of estate, see section 1111.
Sale of property subject to lien securing allowed claim, see section 1129.
Setoff, see section 553.
Turnover of property to estate, see section 542.

Library References:

C.J.S. Bankruptcy §§ 184–187, 207–215, 219–221, 226.
West's Key No. Digests, Bankruptcy ⇔3061 et seq.

WESTLAW Electronic Research

See WESTLAW Electronic Research Guide following the *Bankruptcy Highlights*.

§ 364. Obtaining credit

(a) If the trustee is authorized to operate the business of the debtor under section 721, 1108, 1304, 1203, or 1204 of this title, unless the court orders otherwise, the trustee may obtain unsecured credit and incur unsecured debt in the ordinary course of business allowable under section 503(b)(1) of this title as an administrative expense.

(b) The court, after notice and a hearing, may authorize the trustee to obtain unsecured credit or to incur unsecured debt other than under subsection (a) of this section, allowable under section 503(b)(1) of this title as an administrative expense.

(c) If the trustee is unable to obtain unsecured credit allowable under section 503(b)(1) of this title as an administrative expense, the court, after notice and a hearing, may authorize the obtaining of credit or the incurring of debt—

(1) with priority over any or all administrative expenses of the kind specified in section 503(b) or 507(b) of this title;

(2) secured by a lien on property of the estate that is not otherwise subject to a lien; or

(3) secured by a junior lien on property of the estate that is subject to a lien.

(d)(1) The court, after notice and a hearing, may authorize the obtaining of credit or the incurring of debt secured by a senior or equal lien on property of the estate that is subject to a lien only if—

(A) the trustee is unable to obtain such credit otherwise; and

(B) there is adequate protection of the interest of the holder of the lien on the property of the estate on which such senior or equal lien is proposed to be granted.

(2) In any hearing under this subsection, the trustee has the burden of proof on the issue of adequate protection.

(e) The reversal or modification on appeal of an authorization under this section to obtain credit or incur debt, or of a grant under this section of a priority or a lien, does not affect the validity of any debt so incurred, or any priority or lien so granted, to an entity that extended such credit in good faith, whether or not such entity knew of the pendency of the appeal, unless such authorization and the incurring of such debt, or the granting of such priority or lien, were stayed pending appeal.

(f) Except with respect to an entity that is an underwriter as defined in section 1145(b) of this title, section 5 of the Securities Act of 1933 (15 U.S.C. 77e), the Trust Indenture Act of 1939 (15 U.S.C. 77aaa et seq.), and any State or local law requiring registration for offer or sale of a security or registration or licensing of an issuer of, underwriter of, or broker or dealer in, a security does not apply to the offer or sale under this section of a security that is not an equity security.

Pub.L. 95–598, Nov. 6, 1978, 92 Stat. 2574; Pub.L. 99–554, Title II, § 257(*l*), Oct. 27, 1986, 100 Stat. 3115.

Historical and Revision Notes

Notes of Committee on the Judiciary, Senate Report No. 95–989. This section is derived from provisions in current law governing certificates of indebtedness, but is much broader. It governs all obtaining of credit and incurring of debt by the estate.

Subsection (a) authorizes the obtaining of unsecured credit and the incurring of unsecured debt in the ordinary course of business if the business of the debtor is authorized to be operated under section 721, 1108, or 1304. The debts so incurred are allowable as administrative expenses under section 503(b) (1). The court may limit the estate's ability to incur debt under this subsection.

Subsection (b) permits the court to authorize the trustee to obtain unsecured credit and incur unsecured debts other than in the ordinary course of business, such as in order to wind up a liquidation case, or to obtain a substantial loan in an operating case. Debt incurred under this subsection is allowable as an administrative expense under section 503(b)(1).

Subsection (c) is closer to the concept of certificates of indebtedness in current law. It authorizes the obtaining of credit and the incurring of debt with some special priority, if the trustee is unable to obtain unsecured credit under subsection (a) or (b). The various priorities are (1) with priority over any or all administrative expenses; (2) secured by a lien on unencumbered property of the estate; or (3) secured by a junior lien on encumbered property. The priorities granted under this subsection do not interfere with existing property rights.

Subsection (d) grants the court the authority to authorize the obtaining of credit and the incurring of debt with a superiority, that is a lien on encumbered property that is senior or equal to the existing lien on the property. The court may authorize such a super-priority only if the trustee is otherwise unable to obtain credit, and if there is adequate protection of the original lien holder's interest. Again, the trustee has the burden of proof on the issue of adequate protection.

Subsection (e) provides the same protection for credit extenders pending an appeal of an authorization to incur debt as is provided under section 363(*l*) for purchasers: the credit is not affected on appeal by reversal of the authorization and the incurring of the debt were stayed pending appeal. The protection runs to a good faith lender, whether or not he knew of the pendency of the appeal.

A claim arising as a result of lending or borrowing under this section will be a priority claim, as defined in proposed section 507(a)(1), even if the claim is granted a super-priority over administrative expenses and is to be paid in advance of other first priority claims.

Legislative Statements. Section 364(f) of the House amendment is new. This provision continues the exemption found in section 3(a) (7) of the Securities Act of 1933 [section 77c(a) (7) of Title 15, Commerce and Trade] for certif-icates of indebtedness issued by a trustee in bankruptcy. The exemption applies to any debt security issued under section 364 of title 11. The section does not intend to change present law which exempts such securities from the Trust Indenture Act, 15 U.S.C. 77aaa, et seq. (1976) [section 77aaa et seq. of Title 15].

References in Text. Section 5 of the Securities Act of 1933, referred to in subsec. (f), is classified to section 77e of Title 15, Commerce and Trade.

The Trust Indenture Act of 1939, referred to in subsec. (f), is Title III of Act May 27, 1933, c. 38, as added Aug. 3, 1939, c. 411, 43 Stat. 1149, which is classified to section 77aaa et seq. of Title 15.

Effective Date of 1986 Amendments; Savings Provisions; Quarterly Fees. Amendment by Pub.L. 99–554 effective 30 days after Oct. 27, 1986, except as otherwise provided for, see section 302(a) of Pub.L. 99–554, set out as a note under section 581 of Title 28, Judiciary and Judicial Procedure.

Amendments by Pub.L. 99–554, § 257(*l*), not to apply with respect to cases commenced under Title 11, Bankruptcy, before 30 days after Oct. 27, 1986, see section 302(c)(1) of Pub. L. 99–554, set out as a note under section 581 of Title 28.

Cross References

Applicability of subsecs. (c) to (f) of this section in chapter 9 cases, see section 901.
Priorities, see section 507.
Reversal on appeal of finding of jurisdiction as affecting validity of debt incurred, see section 921.
Rights and powers of debtor engaged in business, see section 1304.

Library References:

C.J.S. Bankruptcy §§ 200–202.
West's Key No. Digests, Bankruptcy ⟿3035–3038.

WESTLAW Electronic Research

See WESTLAW Electronic Research Guide following the *Bankruptcy Highlights.*

§ 365. Executory contracts and unexpired leases

(a) Except as provided in sections 765 and 766 of this title and in subsections (b), (c), and (d) of this section, the trustee, subject to the court's approval, may assume or reject any executory contract or unexpired lease of the debtor.

(b)(1) If there has been a default in an executory contract or unexpired lease of the debtor, the trustee may not assume such contract or lease unless, at the time of assumption of such contract or lease, the trustee—

(A) cures, or provides adequate assurance that the trustee will promptly cure, such default;

(B) compensates, or provides adequate assurance that the trustee will promptly compensate, a party other than the debtor to such contract or lease, for any actual pecuniary loss to such party resulting from such default; and

(C) provides adequate assurance of future performance under such contract or lease.

(2) Paragraph (1) of this subsection does not apply to a default that is a breach of a provision relating to—

(A) the insolvency or financial condition of the debtor at any time before the closing of the case;

(B) the commencement of a case under this title; or

(C) the appointment of or taking possession by a trustee in a case under this title or a custodian before such commencement.

(3) For the purposes of paragraph (1) of this subsection and paragraph (2)(B) of subsection (f), adequate assurance of future performance of a lease of real property in a shopping center includes adequate assurance—

(A) of the source of rent and other consideration due under such lease, and in the case of an assignment, that the financial condition and operating performance of the proposed assignee and its guarantors, if any, shall be similar to the financial condition and operating performance of the debtor and its guarantors, if any, as of the time the debtor became the lessee under the lease;

(B) that any percentage rent due under such lease will not decline substantially;

(C) that assumption or assignment of such lease is subject to all the provisions thereof, including (but not limited to) provisions such as a radius, location, use, or exclusivity provision, and will not breach any such provision contained in any other lease, financing agreement, or master agreement relating to such shopping center; and

(D) that assumption or assignment of such lease will not disrupt any tenant mix or balance in such shopping center.

(4) Notwithstanding any other provision of this section, if there has been a default in an unexpired lease of the debtor, other than a default of a kind specified in paragraph (2) of this subsection, the trustee may not require a lessor to provide services or supplies incidental to such lease before assumption of such lease unless the lessor is compensated under the terms of such lease for any services and supplies provided under such lease before assumption of such lease.

(c) The trustee may not assume or assign any executory contract or unexpired lease of the debtor, whether or not such contract or lease prohibits or restricts assignment of rights or delegation of duties, if—

(1)(A) applicable law excuses a party, other than the debtor, to such contract or lease from accepting performance from or rendering performance to an entity other than the debtor or the debtor in possession whether or not such contract, or lease, prohibits or restricts assignment of rights or delegation of duties; and

(B) such party does not consent to such assumption or assignment; or

(2) such contract is a contract to make a loan, or extend other debt financing or financial accommodations, to or for the benefit of the debtor, or to issue a security of the debtor; or

(3) such lease is of nonresidential real property and has been terminated under applicable nonbankruptcy law prior to the order for relief.

(d)(1) In a case under chapter 7 of this title, if the trustee does not assume or reject an executory contract or unexpired lease of residential real property or of personal property of the debtor within 60 days after the order for relief, or within such additional time as the court, for cause, within such 60-day period, fixes, then such contract or lease is deemed rejected.

(2) In a case under chapter 9, 11, 12, or 13 of this title, the trustee may assume or reject an executory contract or unexpired lease of residential real property or of personal property of the debtor at any time before the confirmation of a plan but the court, on the request of any party to such contract or lease, may order the trustee to determine within a specified period of time whether to assume or reject such contract or lease.

(3) The trustee shall timely perform all the obligations of the debtor, except those specified in section 365(b)(2), arising from and after the order for relief under any unexpired lease of nonresidential real property, until such lease is assumed or rejected, notwithstanding section 503(b)(1) of this title. The court may extend, for cause, the time for performance of any such obligation that arises within 60 days after the date of the order for relief, but the time for performance shall not be extended beyond such 60-day period. This subsection shall not be deemed to affect the trustee's obligations under the provisions of subsection (b) or (f) of this section. Acceptance of any such performance does not constitute waiver or relinquishment of the lessor's rights under such lease or under this title.

(4) Notwithstanding paragraphs (1) and (2), in a case under any chapter of this title, if the trustee does not assume or reject an unexpired lease of nonresidential real property under which the debtor is the lessee within 60 days after the date of the order for relief, or within such additional time as the court, for cause, within such 60-day period, fixes, then such lease is deemed rejected, and the trustee shall immediately surrender such nonresidential real property to the lessor.

(e)(1) Notwithstanding a provision in an executory contract or unexpired lease, or in applicable law, an executory contract or unexpired lease of the debtor may not be terminated or modified, and any right or obligation under such contract or lease may not be terminated or modified, at any time after the commencement of the case solely because of a provision in such contract or lease that is conditioned on—

    (A) the insolvency or financial condition of the debtor at any time before the closing of the case;

    (B) the commencement of a case under this title; or

    (C) the appointment of or taking possession by a trustee in a case under this title or a custodian before such commencement.

(2) Paragraph (1) of this subsection does not apply to an executory contract or unexpired lease of the debtor, whether or not such contract or lease prohibits or restricts assignment of rights or delegation of duties, if—

    (A)(i) applicable law excuses a party, other than the debtor, to such contract or lease from accepting performance from or rendering performance to the trustee or to an assignee of such contract or lease, whether or not such contract or lease prohibits or restricts assignment of rights or delegation of duties; and

    (ii) such party does not consent to such assumption or assignment; or

(B) such contract is a contract to make a loan, or extend other debt financing or financial accommodations, to or for the benefit of the debtor, or to issue a security of the debtor.

(f)(1) Except as provided in subsection (c) of this section, notwithstanding a provision in an executory contract or unexpired lease of the debtor, or in applicable law, that prohibits, restricts, or conditions the assignment of such contract or lease, the trustee may assign such contract or lease under paragraph (2) of this subsection.

(2) The trustee may assign an executory contract or unexpired lease of the debtor only if—

(A) the trustee assumes such contract or lease in accordance with the provisions of this section; and

(B) adequate assurance of future performance by the assignee of such contract or lease is provided, whether or not there has been a default in such contract or lease.

(3) Notwithstanding a provision in an executory contract or unexpired lease of the debtor, or in applicable law that terminates or modifies, or permits a party other than the debtor to terminate or modify, such contract or lease or a right or obligation under such contract or lease on account of an assignment of such contract or lease, such contract, lease, right, or obligation may not be terminated or modified under such provision because of the assumption or assignment of such contract or lease by the trustee.

(g) Except as provided in subsections (h)(2) and (i)(2) of this section, the rejection of an executory contract or unexpired lease of the debtor constitutes a breach of such contract or lease—

(1) if such contract or lease has not been assumed under this section or under a plan confirmed under chapter 9, 11, 12, or 13 of this title, immediately before the date of the filing of the petition; or

(2) if such contract or lease has been assumed under this section or under a plan confirmed under chapter 9, 11, 12, or 13 of this title—

(A) if before such rejection the case has not been converted under section 1112, 1307, or 1208 of this title, at the time of such rejection; or

(B) if before such rejection the case has been converted under section 1112, 1307, or 1208 of this title—

(i) immediately before the date of such conversion, if such contract or lease was assumed before such conversion; or

(ii) at the time of such rejection, if such contract or lease was assumed after such conversion.

(h)(1) If the trustee rejects an unexpired lease of real property of the debtor under which the debtor is the lessor, or a timeshare interest under a timeshare plan under which the debtor is the timeshare interest seller, the lessee or timeshare interest purchaser under such lease or timeshare plan may treat such lease or timeshare plan as terminated by such rejection, where the disaffirmance by the trustee amounts to such a breach as would entitle the lessee or timeshare interest purchaser to treat such lease or timeshare plan as terminated by virtue of its own terms, applicable nonbankruptcy law, or other agreements the lessee or timeshare interest purchaser has made with other parties; or, in the alternative, the lessee or timeshare interest purchaser may remain in possession of the leasehold or timeshare interest under any lease or timeshare plan the term of which has commenced for the balance of such term and for any renewal or extension of such term that is enforceable by such lessee or timeshare interest purchaser under applicable nonbankruptcy law.

(2) If such lessee or timeshare interest purchaser remains in possession as provided in paragraph (1) of this subsection, such lessee or timeshare interest purchaser may offset against the rent reserved under such lease or moneys due for such timeshare interest for the balance of the term after the date of the rejection of such lease or timeshare interest, and any such renewal or extension thereof, any damages occurring after such date caused by the nonperformance of any obligation of the debtor under such lease or timeshare plan after such date, but such lessee or timeshare interest purchaser does not have any rights against the estate on account of any damages arising after such date from such rejection, other than such offset.

(i)(1) If the trustee rejects an executory contract of the debtor for the sale of real property or for the sale of a timeshare interest under a timeshare plan, under which the purchaser is in possession, such purchaser may treat such contract as terminated, or, in the alternative, may remain in possession of such real property or timeshare interest.

(2) If such purchaser remains in possession—

(A) such purchaser shall continue to make all payments due under such contract, but may, offset against such payments any damages occurring after the date of the rejection of such contract caused by the nonperformance of any obligation of the debtor after such date, but such purchaser does not have any rights against the estate on account of any damages arising after such date from such rejection, other than such offset; and

(B) the trustee shall deliver title to such purchaser in accordance with the provisions of such contract, but is relieved of all other obligations to perform under such contract.

(j) A purchaser that treats an executory contract as terminated under subsection (i) of this section, or a party whose executory contract to purchase real property from the debtor is rejected and under which such party is not in possession, has a lien on the interest of the debtor in such property for the recovery of any portion of the purchase price that such purchaser or party has paid.

(k) Assignment by the trustee to an entity of a contract or lease assumed under this section relieves the trustee and the estate from any liability for any breach of such contract or lease occurring after such assignment.

(l) If an unexpired lease under which the debtor is the lessee is assigned pursuant to this section, the lessor of the property may require a deposit or other security for the performance of the debtor's obligations under the lease substantially the same as would have been required by the landlord upon the initial leasing to a similar tenant.

(m) For purposes of this section 365 and sections 541(b)(2) and 362(b)(10), leases of real property shall include any rental agreement to use real property.

(n)(1) If the trustee rejects an executory contract under which the debtor is a licensor of a right to intellectual property, the licensee under such contract may elect—

(A) to treat such contract as terminated by such rejection if such rejection by the trustee amounts to such a breach as would entitle the licensee to treat such contract as terminated by virtue of its own terms, applicable nonbankruptcy law, or an agreement made by the licensee with another entity; or

(B) to retain its rights (including a right to enforce any exclusivity provision of such contract, but excluding any other right under applicable nonbankruptcy law to specific performance of such contract) under such contract and under any agreement supplementary to such contract, to such intellectual property (including any embodiment of such intellectual property to the extent protected by applicable nonbankruptcy law), as such rights existed immediately before the case commenced, for—

(i) the duration of such contract; and

(ii) any period for which such contract may be extended by the licensee as of right under applicable nonbankruptcy law.

(2) If the licensee elects to retain its rights, as described in paragraph (1)(B) of this subsection, under such contract—

(A) the trustee shall allow the licensee to exercise such rights;

(B) the licensee shall make all royalty payments due under such contract for the duration of such contract and for any period described in paragraph (1)(B) of this subsection for which the licensee extends such contract; and

(C) the licensee shall be deemed to waive—

(i) any right of setoff it may have with respect to such contract under this title or applicable nonbankruptcy law; and

(ii) any claim allowable under section 503(b) of this title arising from the performance of such contract.

(3) If the licensee elects to retain its rights, as described in paragraph (1)(B) of this subsection, then on the written request of the licensee the trustee shall—

(A) to the extent provided in such contract, or any agreement supplementary to such contract, provide to the licensee any intellectual property (including such embodiment) held by the trustee; and

(B) not interfere with the rights of the licensee as provided in such contract, or any agreement supplementary to such contract, to such intellectual property (including such embodiment) including any right to obtain such intellectual property (or such embodiment) from another entity.

(4) Unless and until the trustee rejects such contract, on the written request of the licensee the trustee shall—

(A) to the extent provided in such contract or any agreement supplementary to such contract—

(i) perform such contract; or

(ii) provide to the licensee such intellectual property (including any embodiment of such intellectual property to the extent protected by applicable nonbankruptcy law) held by the trustee; and

(B) not interfere with the rights of the licensee as provided in such contract, or any agreement supplementary to such contract, to such intellectual property (including such embodiment), including any right to obtain such intellectual property (or such embodiment) from another entity.

(o) In a case under chapter 11 of this title, the trustee shall be deemed to have assumed (consistent with the debtor's other obligations under section 507), and shall immediately cure any deficit under, any commitment by the debtor to the Federal Deposit Insurance Corporation, the Resolution Trust Corporation, the Director of the Office of Thrift Supervision, the Comptroller of the Currency, or the Board of Governors of the Federal Reserve System, or its predecessors or successors, to maintain the capital of an insured depository institution, and any claim for a subsequent breach of the obligations thereunder shall be entitled to priority under section 507. This subsection shall not extend any commitment that would otherwise be terminated by any act of such an agency.

Pub.L. 95–598, Nov. 6, 1978, 92 Stat. 2574; Pub.L. 98–353, Title III, §§ 362, 402–404, July 10, 1984, 98 Stat. 361, 367; Pub.L. 99–554, Title II, §§ 257(j), (m), 283(e), Oct. 27, 1986, 100 Stat. 3115, 3117; Pub.L. 100–506, § 1(b), Oct. 18, 1988, 102 Stat. 2538; Pub.L. 101–647, Title XXV, § 2522(c), Nov. 29, 1990, 104 Stat. 4866.

Historical and Revision Notes

Notes of Committee on the Judiciary, Senate Report No. 95–989. Subsection (a) of this section authorizes the trustee, subject to the court's approval, to assume or reject an executory contract or unexpired lease. Though there is no precise definition of what contracts are executory, it generally includes contracts on which performance remains due to some extent on both sides. A note is not usually an executory contract if the only performance that remains is repayment. Performance on one side of the contract would have been completed and the contract is no longer executory.

Because of the volatile nature of the commodities markets and the special provisions governing commodity broker liquidations in subchapter IV of chapter 7, the provisions governing distribution in section 765(a) will govern if any conflict between those provisions and the provisions of this section arise.

Subsections (b), (c) and (d) provide limitations on the trustee's powers. Subsection (b) requires the trustee to cure any default in the contract or lease and to provide adequate assurance of future performance if there has been a default, before he may assume. This provision does not apply to defaults under ipso facto or bankruptcy clauses, which is a significant departure from present law.

Subsection (b)(3) permits termination of leases entered into prior to the effective date of this title in liquidation cases if certain other conditions are met.

Subsection (b)(4) prohibits the trustee's assumption of an executory contract requiring the other party to make a loan or deliver equipment to or to issue a security of the debtor. The purpose of this subsection is to make it clear that a party to a transaction which is based upon the financial strength of a debtor should not be required to extend new credit to the debtor whether in the form of loans, lease financing, or the purchase or discount of notes.

Subsection (b)(5) provides that in lease situations common to shopping centers, protections must be provided for the lessor if the trustee assumes the lease, including protection against decline in percentage rents, breach of agreements with other tenants, and preservation of the tenant mix. Protection for tenant mix will not be required in the office building situation.

Subsection (c) prohibits the trustee from assuming or assigning a contract or lease if applicable nonbankruptcy law excuses the other party from performance to someone other than the debtor, unless the other party consents. This prohibition applies only in the situation in which applicable law excuses the other party from performance independent of any restrictive language in the contract or lease itself.

Subsection (d) places time limits on assumption and rejection. In a liquidation case, the trustee must assume within 60 days (or within an additional 60 days, if the court, for cause, extends the time). If not assumed, the contract or lease is deemed rejected. In a rehabilitation case, the time limit is not fixed in the bill. However, if the other party to the contract or lease requests the court to fix a time, the court may specify a time within which the trustee must act. This provision will prevent parties in contractual or lease relationships with the debtor from being left in doubt concerning their status vis-a-vis the estate.

Subsection (e) invalidates ipso facto or bankruptcy clauses. These clauses, protected under present law, automatically terminate the contract or lease, or permit the other contracting party to terminate the contract or lease, in the event of bankruptcy. This frequently hampers rehabilitation efforts. If the trustee may assume or assign the contract under the limitations imposed by the remainder of the section, the contract or lease may be utilized to assist in the debtor's rehabilitation or liquidation.

The unenforcibility of ipso facto or bankruptcy clauses proposed under this section will require the courts to be sensitive to the rights of the nondebtor party to executory contracts and unexpired leases. If the trustee is to assume a contract or lease, the court will have to insure that the trustee's performance under the contract or lease gives the other contracting party the full benefit of his bargain.

This subsection does not limit the application of an ipso facto or bankruptcy clause if a new insolvency or receivership occurs after the bankruptcy case is closed. That is, the clause is not invalidated in toto, but merely made inapplicable during the case for the purposes of disposition of the executory contract or unexpired lease.

Subsection (f) partially invalidates restrictions on assignment of contracts or leases by the trustee to a third party. The subsection imposes two restrictions on the trustee: he must first assume the contract or lease, subject to all the restrictions on assumption found in the section, and adequate assurance of future performance must be provided to the other contracting party. Paragraph (3) of the subsection invalidates contractual provisions that permit termination or modification in the event of an assignment, as contrary to the policy of this subsection.

Subsection (g) defines the time as of which a rejection of an executory contract or unexpired lease constitutes a breach of the contract or lease. Generally, the breach is as of the date immediately preceding the date of the petition. The purpose is to treat rejection claims as prepetition claims. The remainder of the subsection specifies different times for cases that are converted from one chapter to another. The provisions of this subsection are not a substantive authorization to breach or reject an assumed contract. Rather, they prescribe the rules for the allowance of claims in case an assumed contract is breached, or if a case under chapter 11 in which a contract has been assumed is converted to a case under chapter 7 in which the contract is rejected.

Subsection (h) protects real property lessees of the debtor if the trustee rejects an unexpired lease under which the debtor is the lessor (or sublessor). The subsection permits the lessee to remain in possession of the leased property or to treat the lease as terminated by the rejection. The balance of the term of the lease referred to in paragraph (1) will include any renewal terms that are enforceable by the tenant, but not renewal terms if the landlord had an option to terminate. Thus, the tenant will not be deprived of his estate for the term for which he bargained. If the lessee remains in possession, he may offset the rent reserved under the lease against damages caused by the rejection, but does not have any affirmative rights against the estate for any damages after the rejection that result from the rejection.

Subsection (i) gives a purchaser of real property under a land installment sales contract similar protection. The purchaser, if the contract is rejected, may remain in possession or may treat the contract as terminated. If the purchaser remains in possession, he is required to continue to make the payments due, but may offset damages that occur after rejection. The trustee is required to deliver title, but is relieved of all other obligations to perform.

A purchaser that treats the contract as terminated is granted a lien on the property to the extent of the purchase price paid. A party with a contract to purchase land from the debtor has a lien on the property to secure the price already paid, if the contract is rejected and the purchaser is not yet in possession.

Subsection (k) relieves the trustee and the estate of liability for a breach of an assigned contract or lease that occurs after the assignment.

Legislative Statements. Section 365(b)(3) represents a compromise between H.R. 8200 as passed by the House and the Senate amendment. The provision adopts standards contained in section 365(b)(5) of the Senate amendment to define adequate assurance of future performance of a lease of real property in a shopping center.

Section 365(b)(4) of the House amendment indicates that after default the trustee may not require a lessor to supply services or materials without assumption unless the lessor is compensated as provided in the lease.

Section 365(c)(2) and (3) likewise represent a compromise between H.R. 8200 as passed by the House and the Senate amendment. Section 365(c)(2) is derived from section 365(b)(4) of the Senate amendment but does not apply to a contract to deliver equipment as provided in the Senate amendment. As contained in the House amendment, the provision prohibits a trustee or debtor in possession from assuming or assigning an executory contract of the debtor to make a loan, or extend other debt financing or financial accommodations, to or for the benefit of the debtor, or the issuance of a security of the debtor.

Section 365(e) is a refinement of comparable provisions contained in the House bill and Senate amendment. Sections 365(e)(1) and (2) (A) restate section 365(e) of H.R. 8200 as passed by the House. Sections 365(e)(2)(B) expands the section to permit termination of an executory contract or unexpired lease of the debtor if such contract is a contract to make a loan, or extend other debt financing or financial accommodations, to or for the benefit of the debtor, or for the issuance of a security of the debtor.

Characterization of contracts to make a loan, or extend other debt financing or financial accommodations, is limited to the extension of cash or a line of credit and is not intended to embrace ordinary leases or contracts to provide goods or services with payments to be made over time.

Section 365(f) is derived from H.R. 8200 as passed by the House. Deletion of language in section 365(f)(3) of the Senate amendment is done as a matter of style. Restrictions with respect to assignment of an executory contract or unexpired lease are superfluous since the debtor may assign an executory contract or unexpired lease of the debtor only if such contract is first assumed under section 364(f) (2)(A) of the House amendment.

Section 363(h) of the House amendment represents a modification of section 365(h) of the Senate amendment. The House amendment makes clear that in the case of a bankrupt lessor, a lessee may remain in possession for the balance of the term of a lease and any renewal or extension of the term only to the extent that such renewal or extension may be obtained by the lessee without the permission of the landlord or some third party under applicable non-bankruptcy law.

Codification. Amendment to subsec. (c)(1) (A) by Pub.L. 99–554, § 283(e)(1)(*l*), struck out "or an assignee" as the probable intent of Congress, notwithstanding language of amendment requiring "or and assignee" be struck out.

Effective Date of 1988 Amendments; Application of Amendments. Amendment by Pub.L. 100–506 effective Oct. 18, 1988, and not applicable to cases commenced before Oct. 18, 1988, see section 2 of Pub.L. 100–506, set out as a note under section 101 of this title.

Effective Date of 1986 Amendments; Savings Provisions; Quarterly Fees. Amendment by Pub.L. 99–554 effective 30 days after Oct. 27, 1986, except as otherwise provided for, see section 302(a) of Pub.L. 99–554, set out as a note under section 581 of Title 28, Judiciary and Judicial Procedure.

Amendments by Pub.L. 99–554, § 257(j), (m), not to apply with respect to cases commenced under Title 11, Bankruptcy, before 30 days after Oct. 27, 1986, see section 302(c)(1) of Pub.L. 99–554, set out as a note under section 581 of Title 28.

Effective Date of 1984 Amendments. See section 553 of Pub.L. 98–353, Title III, July 10, 1984, 98 Stat. 392, set out as an Effective Date of 1984 Amendment note preceding chapter 1 of Title 11, Bankruptcy.

Separability of Provisions. For separability of provisions of Title III of Pub.L. 98–353, see section 551 of Pub.L. 98–353 set out as a Separability of Provisions note preceding chapter 1 of Title 11, Bankruptcy.

Cross References

Allowance of claims, see section 502.
Applicability of this section in chapter 9 cases, see section 901.
Assumption or rejection of certain executory contracts within reasonable time after order for relief, see section 744.
Collective bargaining agreements, see section 1167.
Effect of rejection of lease of railroad line, see section 1169.
Impairment of claims or interests by plans which cure certain defaults, see section 1124.
Provisions in plan for assumption or rejection of certain executory contracts or unexpired leases, see sections 1123 and 1322.
Right of possession of party with security interest as affected by default
    Aircraft equipment and vessels, see section 1110.
    Rolling stock equipment, see section 1168.
Setoff, see section 553.

Library References:

C.J.S. Bankruptcy §§ 108, 117, 216–230.
West's Key No. Digests, Bankruptcy ⟜3101 et seq.

§ 366. Utility service

(a) Except as provided in subsection (b) of this section, a utility may not alter, refuse, or discontinue service to, or discriminate against, the trustee or the debtor solely on the basis of the commencement of a case under this title or that a debt owed by the debtor to such utility for service rendered before the order for relief was not paid when due.

(b) Such utility may alter, refuse, or discontinue service if neither the trustee nor the debtor, within 20 days after the date of the order for relief, furnishes adequate assurance of payment, in the form of a deposit or other security, for service after such date. On request of a party in interest and after notice and a hearing, the court may order reasonable modification of the amount of the deposit or other security necessary to provide adequate assurance of payment.

Pub.L. 95–598, Nov. 6, 1978, 92 Stat. 2578; Pub.L. 98–353, Title III, § 443, July 10, 1984, 98 Stat. 373.

Historical and Revision Notes

Notes of Committee on the Judiciary, Senate Report No. 95–989. This section gives debtors protection from a cutoff of service by a utility because of the filing of a bankruptcy case. This section is intended to cover utilities that have some special position with respect to the debtor, such as an electric company, gas supplier, or telephone company that is a monopoly in the area so that the debtor cannot easily obtain comparable service from another utility. The utility may not alter, refuse, or discontinue service because of the nonpayment of a bill that would be discharged in the bankruptcy case. Subsection (b) protects the utility company by requiring the trustee or the debtor to provide, within ten days, adequate assurance of payment for service provided after the date of the petition.

Legislative Statements. Section 366 of the House amendment represents a compromise between comparable provisions contained in H.R. 8200 as passed by the House and the Senate amendment. Subsection (a) is modified so that the applicable date is the date of the order for relief rather than the date of the filing of the petition. Subsection (b) contains a similar change but is otherwise derived from section 366(b) of the Senate amendment, with the exception that a time period for continued service of 20 days rather than 10 days is adopted.

Effective Date of 1984 Amendments. See section 553 of Pub.L. 98–353, Title III, July 10, 1984, 98 Stat. 392, set out as an Effective Date of 1984 Amendment note preceding chapter 1 of Title 11, Bankruptcy.

Separability of Provisions. For separability of provisions of Title III of Pub.L. 98–353, see section 551 of Pub.L. 98–353 set out as a Separability of Provisions note preceding chapter 1 of Title 11, Bankruptcy.

Cross References
    Applicability of this section in chapter 9 cases, see section 901.

Library References:
    C.J.S. Bankruptcy §§ 103, 104; Electricity §§ 25, 27; Gas § 19 et seq.; Telegraphs, Telephones, Radio, and Television § 258 et seq.
    West's Key No. Digests, Bankruptcy ⬅️2481, 2482; Electricity ⬅️11(2); Gas ⬅️13(3); Telecommunications ⬅️266.

CHAPTER 5—CREDITORS, DEBTOR, AND THE ESTATE

SUBCHAPTER I—CREDITORS AND CLAIMS

Sec.
501. Filing of proofs of claims or interests.
502. Allowance of claims or interests.
503. Allowance of administrative expenses.
504. Sharing of compensation.
505. Determination of tax liability.
506. Determination of secured status.
507. Priorities.
508. Effect of distribution other than under this title.
509. Claims of codebtors.
510. Subordination.

SUBCHAPTER II—DEBTOR'S DUTIES AND BENEFITS

521. Debtor's duties.
522. Exemptions.
523. Exceptions to discharge.
524. Effect of discharge.
525. Protection against discriminatory treatment.

SUBCHAPTER III—THE ESTATE

541. Property of the estate.
542. Turnover of property to the estate.
543. Turnover of property by a custodian.
544. Trustee as lien creditor and as successor to certain creditors and purchasers.
545. Statutory liens.
546. Limitations on avoiding powers.
547. Preferences.
548. Fraudulent transfers and obligations.
549. Postpetition transactions.
550. Liability of transferee of avoided transfer.
551. Automatic preservation of avoided transfer.
552. Postpetition effect of security interest.
553. Setoff.
554. Abandonment of property of the estate.
555. Contractual right to liquidate a securities contract.
556. Contractual right to liquidate a commodities contract or forward contract.
557. Expedited determination of interests in, and abandonment or other disposition of grain assets.
558. Defenses of the estate.
559. Contractual right to liquidate a repurchase agreement.
560. Contractual right to terminate a swap agreement.

Historical Note

Effective Date of 1984 Amendments. Items 557 to 559 added by Pub.L. 98–353. See section 553 of Pub.L. 98–353, Title III, July 10, 1984, 98 Stat. 392, set out as an Effective Date of 1984 Amendment note preceding chapter 1 of Title 11, Bankruptcy.

Separability of Provisions. For separability of provisions of Title III of Pub.L. 98–353, see section 551 of Pub.L. 98–353 set out as a Separability of Provisions note preceding chapter 1 of Title 11, Bankruptcy.

SUBCHAPTER I—CREDITORS AND CLAIMS

§ 501. Filing of proofs of claims or interests

(a) A creditor or an indenture trustee may file a proof of claim. An equity security holder may file a proof of interest.

(b) If a creditor does not timely file a proof of such creditor's claim, an entity that is liable to such creditor with the debtor, or that has secured such creditor, may file a proof of such claim.

(c) If a creditor does not timely file a proof of such creditor's claim, the debtor or the trustee may file a proof of such claim.

(d) A claim of a kind specified in section 502(e)(2), 502(f), 502(g), 502(h) or 502(i) of this title may be filed under subsection (a), (b), or (c) of this section the same as if such claim were a claim against the debtor and had arisen before the date of the filing of the petition.

Pub.L. 95–598, Nov. 6, 1978, 92 Stat. 2578; Pub.L. 98–353, Title III, § 444, July 10, 1984, 98 Stat. 373.

Historical and Revision Notes

Notes of Committee on the Judiciary, Senate Report No. 95–989. This section governs the means by which creditors and equity security holders present their claims or interests to the court. Subsection (a) permits a creditor to file a proof of claim or interest. An indenture trustee representing creditors may file a proof of claim on behalf of the creditors he represents.

This subsection is permissive only, and does not require filing of a proof of claim by any creditor. It permits filing where some purpose would be served, such as where a claim that appears on a list filed under proposed 11 U.S.C. 924 or 1111 was incorrectly stated or listed as disputed, contingent, or unliquidated, where a creditor with a lien is undersecured and asserts a claim for the balance of the debt owed him (his unsecured claim, as determined under proposed 11 U.S.C. 506(a)), or in a liquidation case where there will be a distribution of assets to the holders of allowed claims. In other instances, such as in no-asset liquidation cases, in situations where a secured creditor does not assert any claim against the estate and a determination of his claim is not made under proposed 11 U.S.C. 506, or in situations where the claim asserted would be subordinated and the creditor would not recover from the estate in any event, filing of a proof of claim may simply not be necessary. The Rules of Bankruptcy Procedure and practice under the law will guide creditors as to when filing is necessary and when it may be dispensed with. In general, however, unless a claim is listed in a chapter 9 or chapter 11 case and allowed as a result of the list, a proof of claim will be a prerequisite to allowance for unsecured claims, including priority claims and the unsecured portion of a claim asserted by the holder of a lien.

The Rules of Bankruptcy Procedure will set the time limits, the form, and the procedure for filing, which will determine whether claims are timely or tardily filed. The rules governing time limits for filing proofs of claims will continue to apply under section 405(d) of the bill. These provide a 6-month-bar date for the filing of tax claims.

Subsection (b) permits a codebtor, surety, or guarantor to file a proof of claim on behalf of the creditor to which he is liable if the creditor does not timely file a proof of claim.

In liquidation and individual repayment plan cases, the trustee or the debtor may file a proof of claim under subsection (c) if the creditor does not timely file. The purpose of this subsection is mainly to protect the debtor if the creditor's claim is nondischargeable. If the creditor does not file, there would be no distribution on the claim, and the debtor would have a greater debt to repay after the case is closed than if the claim were paid in part or in full in the case or under the plan.

Subsection (d) governs the filing of claims of the kind specified in subsections (f), (g), (h), (i), or (j) of proposed 11 U.S.C. 502. The separation of this provision from the other claim-filing provisions in this section is intended to indicate that claims of the kind specified, which do not become fixed or do not arise until after the commencement of the case, must be treated differently for filing purposes such as the bar date for filing claims. The rules will provide for later filing of claims of these kinds.

Subsection (e) gives governmental units (including tax authorities) at least six months following the date for the first meeting of creditors in a chapter 7 or chapter 13 case within which to file proof of claims.

Legislative Statements. The House amendment adopts section 501(b) of the Senate amendment leaving the Rules of Bankruptcy Procedure free to determine where a proof of claim must be filed.

Section 501(c) expands language contained in section 501(c) of the House bill and Senate amendment to permit the debtor to file a proof of claim if a creditor does not timely file a proof of the creditor's claim in a case under title 11.

The House amendment deletes section 501(e) of the Senate amendment as a matter to be left to the rules of bankruptcy procedure. It is anticipated that the rules will enable governmental units, like other creditors, to have a reasonable time to file proofs of claim in bankruptcy cases.

For purposes of section 501, a proof of "interest" includes the interest of a general or limited partner in a partnership, the interest of a proprietor in a sole proprietorship, or the interest of a common or preferred stockholder in a corporation.

Effective Date of 1984 Amendments. See section 553 of Pub.L. 98–353, Title III, July 10, 1984, 98 Stat. 392, set out as an Effective Date of 1984 Amendment note preceding chapter 1 of Title 11, Bankruptcy.

Separability of Provisions. For separability of provisions of Title III of Pub.L. 98–353, see section 551 of Pub.L. 98–353 set out as a Separability of Provisions note preceding chapter 1 of Title 11, Bankruptcy.

Cross References

Applicability of this section in chapter 9 cases, see section 901.
Binding effect of confirmation whether or not claim is filed or deemed filed, see section 944.
Discharge of
     Debtor, see section 1141.
     Liabilities on claims whether or not filed, see section 727.
Distribution of property of estate, see section 726.
Proof of claim deemed filed in
     Chapter 9 cases, see section 925.
     Chapter 11 cases, see section 1111.

Library References:

C.J.S. Bankruptcy § 183.
West's Key No. Digests, Bankruptcy ⊕2895, 2896.

WESTLAW Electronic Research

See WESTLAW Electronic Research Guide following the *Bankruptcy Highlights*.

§ 502.   Allowance of claims or interests

(a) A claim or interest, proof of which is filed under section 501 of this title, is deemed allowed, unless a party in interest, including a creditor of a general partner in a partnership that is a debtor in a case under chapter 7 of this title, objects.

(b) Except as provided in subsections (e)(2), (f), (g), (h) and (i) of this section, if such objection to a claim is made, the court, after notice and a hearing, shall determine the amount of such claim in lawful currency of the United States as of the date of the filing of the petition, and shall allow such claim in such amount except to the extent that—

(1) such claim is unenforceable against the debtor and property of the debtor, under any agreement or applicable law for a reason other than because such claim is contingent or unmatured;

(2) such claim is for unmatured interest;

(3) if such claim is for a tax assessed against property of the estate, such claim exceeds the value of the interest of the estate in such property;

(4) if such claim is for services of an insider or attorney of the debtor, such claim exceeds the reasonable value of such services;

(5) such claim is for a debt that is unmatured on the date of the filing of the petition and that is excepted from discharge under section 523(a)(5) of this title;

(6) if such claim is the claim of a lessor for damages resulting from the termination of a lease of real property, such claim exceeds—

(A) the rent reserved by such lease, without acceleration, for the greater of one year, or 15 percent, not to exceed three years, of the remaining term of such lease, following the earlier of—

(i) the date of the filing of the petition; and

(ii) the date on which such lessor repossessed, or the lessee surrendered, the leased property; plus

(B) any unpaid rent due under such lease, without acceleration, on the earlier of such dates;

(7) if such claim is the claim of an employee for damages resulting from the termination of an employment contract, such claim exceeds—

(A) the compensation provided by such contract, without acceleration, for one year following the earlier of—

(i) the date of the filing of the petition; or

(ii) the date on which the employer directed the employee to terminate, or such employee terminated, performance under such contract; plus

(B) any unpaid compensation due under such contract, without acceleration, on the earlier of such dates; or

(8) such claim results from a reduction, due to late payment, in the amount of an otherwise applicable credit available to the debtor in connection with an employment tax on wages, salaries, or commissions earned from the debtor.

(c) There shall be estimated for purpose of allowance under this section—

(1) any contingent or unliquidated claim, the fixing or liquidation of which, as the case may be, would unduly delay the administration of the case; or

(2) any right to payment arising from a right to an equitable remedy for breach of performance.

(d) Notwithstanding subsections (a) and (b) of this section, the court shall disallow any claim of any entity from which property is recoverable under section 542, 543, 550, or 553 of this title or that is a transferee of a transfer avoidable under section 522(f), 522(h), 544, 545, 547, 548, 549, or 724(a) of this title, unless such entity or transferee has paid the amount, or turned over any such property, for which such entity or transferee is liable under section 522(i), 542, 543, 550, or 553 of this title.

(e)(1) Notwithstanding subsections (a), (b), and (c) of this section and paragraph (2) of this subsection, the court shall disallow any claim for reimbursement or contribution of an entity that is liable with the debtor on or has secured the claim of a creditor, to the extent that—

(A) such creditor's claim against the estate is disallowed;

(B) such claim for reimbursement or contribution is contingent as of the time of allowance or disallowance of such claim for reimbursement or contribution; or

(C) such entity asserts a right of subrogation to the rights of such creditor under section 509 of this title.

(2) A claim for reimbursement or contribution of such an entity that becomes fixed after the commencement of the case shall be determined, and shall be allowed under subsection (a), (b), or (c) of this section, or disallowed under subsection (d) of this section, the same as if such claim had become fixed before the date of the filing of the petition.

(f) In an involuntary case, a claim arising in the ordinary course of the debtor's business or financial affairs after the commencement of the case but before the earlier of the appointment of a trustee and the order for relief shall be determined as of the date such claim arises, and shall be allowed under subsection (a), (b), or (c) of this section or disallowed under subsection (d) or (e) of this section, the same as if such claim had arisen before the date of the filing of the petition.

(g) A claim arising from the rejection, under section 365 of this title or under a plan under chapter 9, 11, 12, or 13 of this title, of an executory contract or unexpired lease of the debtor that has not been assumed shall be determined, and shall be allowed under subsection (a), (b), or (c) of this section or disallowed under subsection (d) or (e) of this section, the same as if such claim had arisen before the date of the filing of the petition.

(h) A claim arising from the recovery of property under section 522, 550, or 553 of this title shall be determined, and shall be allowed under subsection (a), (b), or (c) of this section, or disallowed under subsection (d) or (e) of this section, the same as if such claim had arisen before the date of the filing of the petition.

(i) A claim that does not arise until after the commencement of the case for a tax entitled to priority under section 507(a)(7) of this title shall be determined, and shall be allowed under subsection (a), (b), or (c) of this section, or disallowed under subsection (d) or (e) of this section, the same as if such claim had arisen before the date of the filing of the petition.

(j) A claim that has been allowed or disallowed may be reconsidered for cause. A reconsidered claim may be allowed or disallowed according to the equities of the case. Reconsideration of a claim under this subsection does not affect the validity of any payment or transfer from the estate made to a holder of an allowed claim on account of such allowed claim that is not reconsidered, but if a reconsidered claim is allowed and is of the same class as such holder's claim, such holder may not receive any additional payment or transfer from the estate on account of such holder's allowed claim until the holder of such reconsidered and allowed claim receives payment on account of such claim proportionate in value to that already received by such other holder. This subsection does not alter or modify the trustee's right to recover from a creditor any excess payment or transfer made to such creditor.

Pub.L. 95–598, Nov. 6, 1978, 92 Stat. 2579; Pub.L. 98–353, Title III, § 445, July 10, 1984, 98 Stat. 373; Pub.L. 99–554, Title II, §§ 257(j), 283(f), Oct. 27, 1986, 100 Stat. 3115, 3117.

Historical and Revision Notes

Notes of Committee on the Judiciary, Senate Report No. 95–989. A proof of claim or interest is prima facie evidence of the claim or interest. Thus, it is allowed under subsection (a) unless a party in interest objects. The rules and case law will determine who is a party in interest for purposes of objection to allowance. The case law is well developed on this subject today. As a result of the change in the liability of a general partner's estate for the debts of this partnership, see proposed 11 U.S.C. 723, the category of persons that are parties in interest in the partnership case will be expanded to include a creditor of a partner against whose estate the trustee of the partnership estate may proceed under proposed 11 U.S.C. 723(c).

Subsection (b) prescribes the grounds on which a claim may be disallowed. The court will apply these standards if there is an objection to a proof of claim. The burden of proof on the issue of allowance is left to the Rules of Bankruptcy Procedure. Under the current chapter XIII [former section 1001 et seq. of this title] rules, a creditor is required to prove that his claim is free from usury, rule 13–301. It is expected that the rules will make similar provision for both liquidation and individual repayment plan cases. See Bankruptcy Act § 656(b) [former section 1056(b) of this title]; H.R. 31, 94th Cong., 1st sess., sec. 6–104(a) (1975).

Paragraph (1) requires disallowance if the claim is unenforceable against the debtor for any reason (such as usury, unconscionability, or failure of consideration) other than because it is contingent or unmatured. All such contingent or unmatured claims are to be liquidated by the bankruptcy court in order to afford the debtor complete bankruptcy relief; these claims are generally not provable under present law.

Paragraph (2) requires disallowance to the extent that the claim is for unmatured interest as of the date of the petition. Whether interest is matured or unmatured on the date of bankruptcy is to be determined without reference to any ipso facto or bankruptcy clause in the agreement creating the claim. Interest disallowed under this paragraph includes postpetition interest that is not yet due and payable, and any portion of prepaid interest that represents an original discounting of the claim, yet that would not have been earned on the date of bankruptcy. For example, a claim on a $1,000 note issued the day before bankruptcy would only be allowed to the extent of the cash actually advanced. If the original discount was 10 percent so that the cash advanced was only $900, then notwithstanding the face amount of note, only $900 would be allowed. If $900 was advanced under the note some time before bankruptcy, the interest component of the note would have to be prorated and disallowed to the extent it was for interest after the commencement of the case.

Section 502(b) thus contains two principles of present law. First, interest stops accruing at the date of the filing of the petition, because any claim for unmatured interest is disallowed under this paragraph. Second, bankruptcy operates as the acceleration of the principal amount of all claims against the debtor. One unarticulated reason for this is that the discounting factor for claims after the commencement of the case is equivalent to contractual interest rate on the claim. Thus, this paragraph does not cause disallowance of claims that have not been discounted to a present value because of the irrebuttable presumption that the discounting rate and the contractual interest rate (even a zero interest rate) are equivalent.

Paragraph (3) requires disallowance of a claim to the extent that the creditor may offset the claim against a debt owing to the debtor. This will prevent double recovery, and permit the claim to be filed only for the balance due. This follows section 68 of the Bankruptcy Act [former section 108 of this title].

Paragraph (4) requires disallowance of a property tax claim to the extent that the tax due exceeds the value of the property. This too follows current law to the extent the property tax is ad valorem.

Paragraph (5) prevents overreaching by the debtor's attorneys and concealing of assets by debtors. It permits the court to examine the claim of a debtor's attorney independently of any other provision of this subsection, and to disallow it to the extent that it exceeds the reasonable value of the attorneys' services.

Postpetition alimony, maintenance or support claims are disallowed under paragraph (6). They are to be paid from the debtor's postpetition property, because the claims are nondischargeable.

Paragraph (7), derived from current law, limits the damages allowable to a landlord of the debtor. The history of this provision is set out at length in Oldden v. Tonto Realty Co., 143 F.2d 916 (2d Cir.1944). It is designed to compensate the landlord for his loss while not permitting a claim so large (based on a long-term lease) as to prevent other general unsecured creditors from recovering a dividend from the estate. The damages a landlord may assert from termination of a lease are limited to the rent reserved for the greater of one year or ten percent of the remaining lease term, not to exceed three years, after the earlier of the date of the filing of the petition and the date of surrender or repossession in a chapter 7 case and 3 years lease payments in a chapter 9, 11, or 13 case. The sliding scale

formula for chapter 7 cases is new and designed to protect the long-term lessor. This subsection does not apply to limit administrative expense claims for use of the leased premises to which the landlord is otherwise entitled.

This paragraph will not overrule Oldden, or the proposition for which it has been read to stand: To the extent that a landlord has a security deposit in excess of the amount of his claim allowed under this paragraph, the excess comes into the estate. Moreover, his allowed claim is for his total damages, as limited by this paragraph. By virtue of proposed 11 U.S.C. 506(a) and 506(d), the claim will be divided into a secured portion and an unsecured portion in those cases in which the deposit that the landlord holds is less than his damages. As under Oldden, he will not be permitted to offset his actual damages against his security deposit and then claim for the balance under this paragraph. Rather, his security deposit will be applied in satisfaction of the claim that is allowed under this paragraph.

As used in section 502(b)(7), the phrase "lease of real property" applies only to a "true" or "bona fide" lease and does not apply to financing leases of real property or interests therein, or to leases of such property which are intended as security.

Historically, the limitation on allowable claims of lessors of real property was based on two considerations. First, the amount of the lessor's damages on breach of a real estate lease was considered contingent and difficult to prove. Partly for this reason, claims of a lessor of real estate were not provable prior to the 1934 amendments to the Bankruptcy Act. Second, in a true lease of real property, the lessor retains all risk and benefits as to the value of the real estate at the termination of the lease. Historically, it was, therefore, considered equitable to limit the claims of a real estate lessor.

However, these considerations are not present in "lease financing" transactions where, in substance, the "lease" involves a sale of the real estate and the rental payments are in substance the payment of principal and interest on a secured loan or sale. In a financing lease the lessor is essentially a secured or unsecured creditor (depending upon whether his interest is perfected or not) of the debtor, and the lessor's claim should not be subject to the 502(b)(7) limitation. Financing "leases" are in substance installment sales or loans. The "lessors" are essentially sellers or lenders and should be treated as such for purposes of the bankruptcy law.

Whether a "lease" is true or bona fide lease or, in the alternative, a financing "lease" or a lease intended as security, depends upon the circumstances of each case. The distinction between a true lease and a financing transaction is based upon the economic substance of the transaction and not, for example, upon the locus of title, the form of the transaction or the fact that the transaction is denominated as a "lease". The fact that the lessee, upon compliance with the terms of the lease, becomes or has the option to become the owner of the leased property for no additional consideration or for nominal consideration indicates that the transaction is a financing lease or lease intended as security. In such cases, the lessor has no substantial interest in the leased property at the expiration of the lease term. In addition, the fact that the lessee assumes and discharges substantially all the risks and obligations ordinarily attributed to the outright ownership of the property is more indicative of a financing transaction than of a true lease. The rental payments in such cases are in substance payments of principal and interest either on a loan secured by the leased real property or on the purchase of the leased real property. See, e.g., Financial Accounting Standards Board Statement No. 13 and SEC Reg. S–X, 17 C.F.R. sec. 210.3–16(q) (1977); cf. First National Bank of Chicago v. Irving Trust Co., 74 F.2d 263 (2nd Cir.1934); and Albenda and Lief, "Net Lease Financing Transactions Under the Proposed Bankruptcy Act of 1973," 30 Business Lawyer, 713 (1975).

Paragraph (8) is new. It tracks the landlord limitation on damages provision in paragraph (7) for damages resulting from the breach by the debtor of an employment contract, but limits the recovery to the compensation reserved under an employment contract for the year following the earlier of the date of the petition and the termination of employment.

Subsection (c) requires the estimation of any claim liquidation of which would unduly delay the closing of the estate, such as a contingent claim, or any claim for which applicable law provides only an equitable remedy, such as specific performance. This subsection requires that all claims against the debtor be converted into dollar amounts.

Subsection (d) is derived from present law. It requires disallowance of a claim of a transferee of a voidable transfer in toto if the transferee has not paid the amount or turned over the property received as required under the sections under which the transferee's liability arises.

Subsection (e) also derived from present law, requires disallowance of the claim for reimbursement or contribution of a codebtor, surety or guarantor of an obligation of the debtor, unless the claim of the creditor on such obligation has been paid in full. The provision prevents competition between a creditor and his guarantor for the limited proceeds in the estate.

Subsection (f) specifies that "involuntary gap" creditors receive the same treatment as prepetition creditors. Under the allowance provisions of this subsection, knowledge of the commencement of the case will be irrelevant. The claim is to be allowed "the same as if such claim had arisen before the date of the filing of the petition." Under voluntary petition, proposed 11 U.S.C. 303(f), creditors must be permitted to deal with the debtor and be assured that their claims will be paid. For purposes of this subsection, "creditors" include governmental units holding claims for tax liabilities incurred during the period after the petition is filed and before the earlier of the order for relief or appointment of a trustee.

Subsection (g) gives entities injured by the rejection of an executory contract or unexpired lease, either under section 365 or under a plan or reorganization, a prepetition claim for any resulting damages, and requires that the injured entity be treated as a prepetition creditor with respect to that claim.

Subsection (h) gives a transferee of a setoff that is recovered by one trustee a prepetition claim for the amount recovered.

Subsection (i) answers the nonrecourse loan problem and gives the creditor an unsecured claim for the difference between the value of the collateral and the debt in response to the decision in Great National Life Ins. Co. v. Pine Gate Associates, Ltd., Bankruptcy Case No. B75–4345A (N.D.Ga. Sept. 16, 1977).

The bill, as reported, deletes a provision in the bill as originally introduced (former sec. 502(i)) requiring a tax authority to file a proof of claim for recapture of an investment credit where, during title 11 proceedings, the trustee sells or otherwise disposes of property before the title 11 case began. The tax authority should not be required to submit a formal claim for a taxable event (a sale or other disposition of the asset) of whose occurrence the trustee necessarily knows better than the taxing authority. For procedural purposes, the recapture of investment credit is to be treated as an administrative expense, as to which only a request for payment is required.

Legislative Statements. The House amendment adopts a compromise position in section 502(a) between H.R. 8200, as passed by the House, and the Senate amendment. Section 502(a) has been modified to make clear that a party in interest includes a creditor of a partner in a partnership that is a debtor under chapter 7. Since the trustee of the partnership is given an absolute claim against the estate of each general partner under section 723(c), creditors of the partner must have standing to object to claims against the partnership at the partnership level because no opportunity will be afforded at the partner's level for such objection.

The House amendment contains a provision in section 502(b)(1) that requires disallowance of a claim to the extent that such claim is unenforceable against the debtor and unenforceable against property of the debtor. This is intended to result in the disallowance of any claim for deficiency by an undersecured creditor on a non-recourse loan or under a State antideficiency law, special provision for which is made in section 1111, since neither the debtor personally, nor the property of the debtor is liable for such a deficiency. Similarly claims for usurious interest or which could be barred by an agreement between the creditor and the debtor would be disallowed.

Section 502(b)(7)(A) represents a compromise between the House bill and the Senate amendment. The House amendment takes the provision in H.R. 8200 as passed by the House of Representatives but increases the percentage from 10 to 15 percent.

As used in section 502(b)(7), the phrase "lease of real property" applies only to a "true" or "bona fide" lease and does not apply to financing leases of real property or interests therein, or to leases of such property which are intended as security.

The House amendment adopts section 502(b) (9) of the House bill which disallows any tax claim resulting from a reduction of the Federal Unemployment Tax Act [FUTA] credit (sec. 3302 of the Internal Revenue Code [section 3302 of Title 26, Internal Revenue Code]) on account of a tardy contribution to a State unemployment fund if the contribution is attributable to ways or other compensation paid by the debtor before bankruptcy. The Senate amendment allowed this reduction, but would have subordinated it to other claims in the

distribution of the estate's assets by treating it as a punitive (nonpecuniary loss) penalty. The House amendment would also not bar reduction of the FUTA credit on account of a trustee's late payment of a contribution to a State unemployment fund if the contribution was attributable to a trustee's payment of compensation earned from the estate.

Section 502(c) of the House amendment presents a compromise between similar provisions contained in the House bill and the Senate amendment. The compromise language is consistent with an amendment to the definition of "claim" in section 104(4)(B) of the House amendment and requires estimation of any right to an equitable remedy for breach of performance if such breach gives rise to a right to payment. To the extent language in the House and Senate reports indicate otherwise, such language is expressly overruled.

Section 502(e) of the House amendment contains language modifying a similar section in the House bill and Senate amendment. Section 502(e)(1) states the general rule requiring the court to disallow any claim for reimbursement or contribution of an entity that is liable with the debtor on, or that has secured, the claim of a creditor to any extent that the creditor's claim against the estate is disallowed. This adopts a policy that a surety's claim for reimbursement or contribution is entitled to no better status than the claim of the creditor assured by such surety. Section 502(e)(1)(B) alternatively disallows any claim for reimbursement or contribution by a surety to the extent such claim is contingent as of the time of allowance. Section 502(e)(2) is clear that to the extent a claim for reimbursement or contribution becomes fixed after the commencement of the case that it is to be considered a prepetition claim for purposes of allowance. The combined effect of sections 502(e)(1)(B) and 502(e)(2) is that a surety or codebtor is generally permitted a claim for reimbursement or contribution to the extent the surety or codebtor has paid the assured party at the time of allowance. Section 502(e) (1)(C) alternatively indicates that a claim for reimbursement or contribution of a surety or codebtor is disallowed to the extent the surety or codebtor requests subrogation under section 509 with respect to the rights of the assured party. Thus, the surety or codebtor has a choice; to the extent a claim for contribution or reimbursement would be advantageous, such as in the case where such a claim is secured, a surety or codebtor may opt for reimbursement or contribution under section

502(e). On the other hand, to the extent the claim for such surety or codebtor by way of subrogation is more advantageous, such as where such claim is secured, the surety may elect subrogation under section 509.

The section changes current law by making the election identical in all other respects. To the extent a creditor's claim is satisfied by a surety or codebtor, other creditors should not benefit by the surety's inability to file a claim against the estate merely because such surety or codebtor has failed to pay such creditor's claim in full. On the other hand, to the extent the creditor's claim against the estate is otherwise disallowed, the surety or codebtor should not be entitled to increased rights by way of reimbursement or contribution, to the detriment of competing claims of other unsecured creditors, than would be realized by way of subrogation.

While the foregoing scheme is equitable with respect to other unsecured creditors of the debtor, it is desirable to preserve present law to the extent that a surety or codebtor is not permitted to compete with the creditor he has assured until the assured party's claim has paid in full. Accordingly, section 509(c) of the House amendment subordinates both a claim by way of subrogation or a claim for reimbursement or contribution of a surety or codebtor to the claim of the assured party until the assured party's claim is paid in full.

Section 502(h) of the House amendment expands similar provisions contained in the House bill and the Senate amendment to indicate that any claim arising from the recovery of property under section 522(i), 550, or 553 shall be determined as though it were a prepetition claim.

Section 502(i) of the House amendment adopts a provision contained in section 502(j) of H.R. 8200 as passed by the House but that was not contained in the Senate amendment.

Section 502(i) of H.R. 8200 as passed by the House, but was not included in the Senate amendment, is deleted as a matter to be left to the bankruptcy tax bill next year.

The House amendment deletes section 502(i) of the Senate bill but adopts the policy of that section to a limited extent for confirmation of a plan of reorganization in section 1111(b) of the House amendment.

Section 502(j) of the House amendment is new. The provision codifies section 57k of the Bankruptcy Act [former section 93(k) of this title].

Codification. Amendments by Pub.L. 98–353 § 445(b)(5) to (7) were executed to pars. (3), (5), and (7) as redesignated by par. (4) of section 445(b) as the probable intent of Congress although the directory language specified that the amendment be to pars. (3), (5), and (7) "as redesignated by paragraph (5)".

Effective Date of 1986 Amendments; Savings Provisions; Quarterly Fees. Amendment by Pub.L. 99–554 effective 30 days after Oct. 27, 1986, except as otherwise provided for, see section 302(a) of Pub.L. 99–554, set out as a note under section 581 of Title 28, Judiciary and Judicial Procedure.

Amendments by Pub.L. 99–554, § 257(j) not to apply with respect to cases commenced under Title 11, Bankruptcy, before 30 days after Oct. 27, 1986, see section 302(c)(1) of Pub. L. 99–554, set out as a note under section 581 of Title 28.

Effective Date of 1984 Amendments. See section 553 of Pub.L. 98–353, Title III, July 10, 1984, 98 Stat. 392, set out as an Effective Date of 1984 Amendment note preceding chapter 1 of Title 11, Bankruptcy.

Separability of Provisions. For separability of provisions of Title III of Pub.L. 98–353, see section 551 of Pub.L. 98–353 set out as a Separability of Provisions note preceding chapter 1 of Title 11, Bankruptcy.

Cross References

Acceptance of plan by holders of claims or interests, see section 1126.
Applicability of this section in chapter 9 cases, see section 901.
Binding effect of confirmation whether or not claim is allowed, see section 944.
Certain claims for which partner and partnership are liable, allowance of, see section 723.
Claim defined, see section 101.
Claims secured by lien on property of estate, allowance of, see section 1111.
Creditor as meaning entity having certain claims specified in this section, see section 101.
Deductibility of allowed claim, see section 346.

Discharge of liabilities on claims, see section 727.

Effect of confirmation, see section 1141.

Filing and allowance of postpetition claims, see section 1305.

Liability of exempted property for debtor's debt, see section 522.

Setoff, see section 553.

Trustee as lien creditor and as successor to certain creditors and purchasers, see section 544.

Library References:

C.J.S. Bankruptcy §§ 239–244, 246, 280, 282–286, 351, 356.

West's Key No. Digests, Bankruptcy ⟳2821 et seq., 2921 et seq.

WESTLAW Electronic Research

See WESTLAW Electronic Research Guide following the *Bankruptcy Highlights.*

§ 503. Allowance of administrative expenses

(a) An entity may file a request for payment of an administrative expense.

(b) After notice and a hearing, there shall be allowed administrative expenses, other than claims allowed under section 502(f) of this title, including—

(1)(A) the actual, necessary costs and expenses of preserving the estate, including wages, salaries, or commissions for services rendered after the commencement of the case;

(B) any tax—

(i) incurred by the estate, except a tax of a kind specified in section 507(a)(7) of this title; or

(ii) attributable to an excessive allowance of a tentative carryback adjustment that the estate received, whether the taxable year to which such adjustment relates ended before or after the commencement of the case; and

(C) any fine, penalty, or reduction in credit relating to a tax of a kind specified in subparagraph (B) of this paragraph;

(2) compensation and reimbursement awarded under section 330(a) of this title;

(3) the actual, necessary expenses, other than compensation and reimbursement specified in paragraph (4) of this subsection, incurred by—

(A) a creditor that files a petition under section 303 of this title;

(B) a creditor that recovers, after the court's approval, for the benefit of the estate any property transferred or concealed by the debtor;

(C) a creditor in connection with the prosecution of a criminal offense relating to the case or to the business or property of the debtor;

(D) a creditor, an indenture trustee, an equity security holder, or a committee representing creditors or equity security holders other than a committee appointed under section 1102 of this title, in making a substantial contribution in a case under chapter 9 or 11 of this title; or

(E) a custodian superseded under section 543 of this title, and compensation for the services of such custodian;

(4) reasonable compensation for professional services rendered by an attorney or an accountant of an entity whose expense is allowable under

paragraph (3) of this subsection, based on the time, the nature, the extent, and the value of such services, and the cost of comparable services other than in a case under this title, and reimbursement for actual, necessary expenses incurred by such attorney or accountant;

(5) reasonable compensation for services rendered by an indenture trustee in making a substantial contribution in a case under chapter 9 or 11 of this title, based on the time, the nature, the extent, and the value of such services, and the cost of comparable services other than in a case under this title; and

(6) the fees and mileage payable under chapter 119 of title 28.

Pub.L. 95–598, Nov. 6, 1978, 92 Stat. 2581; Pub.L. 98–353, Title III, § 446, July 10, 1984, 98 Stat. 374; Pub.L. 99–554, Title II, § 283(g), Oct. 27, 1986, 100 Stat. 3117.

Historical and Revision Notes

Notes of Committee on the Judiciary, Senate Report No. 95–989. Subsection (a) of this section permits administrative expense claimants to file with the court a request for payment of an administrative expense. The Rules of Bankruptcy Procedure will specify the time, the form, and the method of such a filing.

Subsection (b) specifies the kinds of administrative expenses that are allowable in a case under the bankruptcy code [this title]. The subsection is derived mainly from section 64a(1) of the Bankruptcy Act [former section 104(a)(1) of this title], with some changes. The actual, necessary costs and expenses of preserving the estate, including wages, salaries, or commissions for services rendered after the order for relief, and any taxes on, measured by, or withheld from such wages, salaries, or commissions, are allowable as administrative expenses.

In general, administrative expenses include taxes which the trustee incurs in administering the debtor's estate, including taxes on capital gains from sales of property by the trustee and taxes on income earned by the estate during the case. Interest on tax liabilities and certain tax penalties incurred by the trustee are also included in this first priority.

Taxes which the Internal Revenue Service may find due after giving the trustee a so-called "quickie" tax refund and later doing an audit of the refund are also payable as administrative expenses. The tax code [Title 26, Internal Revenue Code] permits the trustee of an estate which suffers a net operating loss to carry back the loss against an earlier profit year of the estate or of the debtor and to obtain a tentative refund for the earlier year, subject, however, to a later full audit of the loss which led to the refund. The bill, in effect, requires the Internal Revenue Service to issue a tentative refund to the trustee (whether the refund was applied for by the debtor or by the trustee), but if the refund later proves to have been erroneous in amount, the Service can request that the tax attributable to the erroneous refund be payable by the estate as an administrative expense.

Postpetition payments to an individual debtor for services rendered to the estate are administrative expenses, and are not property of the estate when received by the debtor. This situation would most likely arise when the individual was a sole proprietor and was employed by the estate to run the business after the commencement of the case. An individual debtor in possession would be so employed, for example. See Local Loan v. Hunt, 292 U.S. 234, 243 (1933) [54 S.Ct. 695, 78 L.Ed. 1230].

Compensation and reimbursement awarded officers of the estate under section 330 are allowable as administrative expenses. Actual, necessary expenses, other than compensation of a professional person, incurred by a creditor that files an involuntary petition, by a creditor that recovers property for the benefit of the estate, by a creditor that acts in connection with the prosecution of a criminal offense relating to the case, by a creditor, indenture, trustee, equity security holder, or committee of creditors or equity security holders (other than official committees) that makes a substantial contribution to a reorganization or municipal debt adjustment case, or by a superseded custodian, are all allowable administrative expenses. The phrase "substantial contribution in the case" is derived from Bankruptcy Act §§ 242 and 243 [former sections 642 and 643 of this title]. It does not require a contribution that leads to confirmation of a plan, for in many cases, it will be a substantial contribution if the person involved uncovers facts that would lead to a denial of confirmation, such as fraud in connection with the case.

Paragraph (4) permits reasonable compensation for professional services rendered by an attorney or an accountant of an equity whose expense is compensable under the previous paragraph. Paragraph (5) permits reasonable compensation for an indenture trustee in making a substantial contribution in a reorganization or municipal debt adjustment case. Finally, paragraph (6) permits witness fees and mileage as prescribed under chapter 119 of title 28 [section 1821 et seq. of Title 28, Judiciary and Judicial Procedure].

Legislative Statements. Section 503(a) of the House amendment represents a compromise between similar provisions in the House bill and the Senate amendment by leaving to the Rules of Bankruptcy Procedure the determination of the location at which a request for payment of an administrative expense may be filed. The preamble to section 503(b) of the House bill makes a similar change with respect to the allowance of administrative expenses.

Section 503(b)(1) adopts the approach taken in the House bill as modified by some provisions contained in the Senate amendment. The preamble to section 503(b) makes clear that none of the paragraphs of section 503(b) apply to claims or expenses of the kind specified in section 502(f) that arise in the ordinary course of the debtor's business or financial affairs and that arise during the gap between the commencement of an involuntary case and the appointment of a trustee or the order for relief, whichever first occurs. The remainder of section 503(b) represents a compromise between H.R. 8200 as passed by the House and the Senate amendments. Section 503(b)(3)(E) codifies present law in cases such as Randolph v. Scruggs, 190 U.S. 533, which accords administrative expense status to services rendered by a prepetition custodian or other party to the extent such services actually benefit the estate. Section 503(b)(4) of the House amendment conforms to the provision contained in H.R. 8200 as passed by the House and deletes language contained in the Senate amendment providing a different standard of compensation under section 330 of that amendment.

Effective Date of 1986 Amendments; Savings Provisions; Quarterly Fees. Amendment by Pub.L. 99–554 effective 30 days after Oct. 27, 1986, except as otherwise provided for, see section 302(a) of Pub.L. 99–554, set out as a note under section 581 of Title 28, Judiciary and Judicial Procedure.

Effective Date of 1984 Amendments. See section 553 of Pub.L. 98–353, Title III, July 10, 1984, 98 Stat. 392, set out as an Effective Date of 1984 Amendment note preceding chapter 1 of Title 11, Bankruptcy.

Separability of Provisions. For separability of provisions of Title III of Pub.L. 98–353, see section 551 of Pub.L. 98–353 set out as a Separability of Provisions note preceding chapter 1 of Title 11, Bankruptcy.

Cross References

Adequate protection, other than granting certain administrative expenses, see section 361.
Applicability of this section in chapter 9 cases, see section 901.
Compensation of officers, see section 330.
Deductibility of allowed expense, see section 346.
Effect of conversion, see section 348.
Unsecured debt as administrative expense or having priority over certain administrative expenses, see section 364.

Library References:

C.J.S. Bankruptcy §§ 232, 250–254, 281.
West's Key No. Digests, Bankruptcy ☜2871 et seq.

WESTLAW Electronic Research

See WESTLAW Electronic Research Guide following the *Bankruptcy Highlights*.

§ 504. Sharing of compensation

(a) Except as provided in subsection (b) of this section, a person receiving compensation or reimbursement under section 503(b)(2) or 503(b)(4) of this title may not share or agree to share—

(1) any such compensation or reimbursement with another person; or

(2) any compensation or reimbursement received by another person under such sections.

(b)(1) A member, partner, or regular associate in a professional association, corporation, or partnership may share compensation or reimbursement received under section 503(b)(2) or 503(b)(4) of this title with another member, partner, or regular associate in such association, corporation, or partnership, and may share in any compensation or reimbursement received under such sections by another member, partner, or regular associate in such association, corporation, or partnership.

(2) An attorney for a creditor that files a petition under section 303 of this title may share compensation and reimbursement received under section 503(b)(4) of this title with any other attorney contributing to the services rendered or expenses incurred by such creditor's attorney.

Pub.L. 95–598, Nov. 6, 1978, 92 Stat. 2582.

Historical and Revision Notes

Notes of Committee on the Judiciary, Senate Report No. 95-989. Section 504 prohibits the sharing of compensation, or fee splitting, among attorneys, other professionals, or trustees. The section provides only two exceptions: partners or associates in the same professional association, partnership, or corporation may share compensation inter se; and attorneys for petitioning creditors that join in a petition commencing an involuntary case may share compensation.

Cross References

Applicability of this section in chapter 9 cases, see section 901.

Library References:

C.J.S. Attorney and Client § 174; Contracts §§ 223, 232.
West's Key No. Digests, Attorney and Client ⚖151; Contracts ⚖129(1).

WESTLAW Electronic Research

See WESTLAW Electronic Research Guide following the *Bankruptcy Highlights*.

§ 505. Determination of tax liability

(a)(1) Except as provided in paragraph (2) of this subsection, the court may determine the amount or legality of any tax, any fine or penalty relating to a tax, or any addition to tax, whether or not previously assessed, whether or not paid, and whether or not contested before and adjudicated by a judicial or administrative tribunal of competent jurisdiction.

(2) The court may not so determine—

(A) the amount or legality of a tax, fine, penalty, or addition to tax if such amount or legality was contested before and adjudicated by a judicial or administrative tribunal of competent jurisdiction before the commencement of the case under this title; or

(B) any right of the estate to a tax refund, before the earlier of—

(i) 120 days after the trustee properly requests such refund from the governmental unit from which such refund is claimed; or

(ii) a determination by such governmental unit of such request.

(b) A trustee may request a determination of any unpaid liability of the estate for any tax incurred during the administration of the case by submitting a tax return for such tax and a request for such a determination to the governmental unit charged with responsibility for collection or determination of such tax. Unless such return is fraudulent, or contains a material misrepresentation, the trustee, the debtor, and any successor to the debtor are discharged from any liability for such tax—

(1) upon payment of the tax shown on such return, if—

(A) such governmental unit does not notify the trustee, within 60 days after such request, that such return has been selected for examination; or

(B) such governmental unit does not complete such an examination and notify the trustee of any tax due, within 180 days after such request or within such additional time as the court, for cause, permits;

(2) upon payment of the tax determined by the court, after notice and a hearing, after completion by such governmental unit of such examination; or

(3) upon payment of the tax determined by such governmental unit to be due.

(c) Notwithstanding section 362 of this title, after determination by the court of a tax under this section, the governmental unit charged with responsibility for collection of such tax may assess such tax against the estate, the debtor, or a successor to the debtor, as the case may be, subject to any otherwise applicable law.

Pub.L. 95–598, Nov. 6, 1978, 92 Stat. 2582; Pub.L. 98–353, Title III, § 447, July 10, 1984, 98 Stat. 374.

Historical and Revision Notes

Notes of Committee on the Judiciary, Senate Report No. 95–989. Subsections (a) and (b) are derived, with only stylistic changes, from section 2a(2A) of the Bankruptcy Act [former section 11(a)(2A) of this title]. They permit determination by the bankruptcy court of any unpaid tax liability of the debtor that has not been contested before or adjudicated by a judicial or administrative tribunal of competent jurisdiction before the bankruptcy case, and the prosecution by the trustee of an appeal from an order of such a body if the time for review or appeal has not expired before the commencement of the bankruptcy case. As under current Bankruptcy Act § 2a(2A), Arkansas Corporation Commissioner v. Thompson, 313 U.S. 132 (1941) [61 S.Ct. 888, 85 L.Ed. 1244], remains good law to permit abstention where uniformity of assessment is of significant importance.

Section (c) deals with procedures for obtaining a prompt audit of tax returns filed by the trustee in a liquidation or reorganization case. Under the bill as originally introduced, a trustee who is "in doubt" concerning tax liabilities of the estate incurred during a title 11 proceeding could obtain a discharge from personal liability for himself and the debtor (but not for the debtor or the debtor's successor in a reorganization), provided that certain administrative procedures were followed. The trustee could request a prompt tax audit by the local, State, or Federal governmental unit. The taxing authority would have to notify the trustee and the court within sixty days whether it accepted the return or desired to audit the returns more fully. If an audit were conducted, the tax office would have to notify the trustee of any tax deficiency within 4 months (subject to an extension of time if the court approved). These procedures would apply only to tax years completed on or before the case was closed and for which the trustee had filed a tax return.

The committee bill eliminates the "in doubt" rule and makes mandatory (rather than optional) the trustee's request for a prompt audit of the estate's tax returns. In many cases, the trustee could not be certain that his returns raised no doubt about possible tax issues. In addition, it is desirable not to create a situation where the taxing authority asserts a tax liability against the debtor (as transferee of surplus assets, if any, return to him) after the case is over; in any such situation, the debtor would be called on to defend a tax return which he did not prepare. Under the amendment, all disputes concerning these returns are to be resolved by the bankruptcy court, and both the trustee and the debtor himself do not then face potential post-bankruptcy tax liabilities based on these returns. This result would occur as to the debtor, however, only in a liquidation case.

In a reorganization in which the debtor or a successor to the debtor continues in existence, the trustee could obtain a discharge from personal liability through the prompt audit procedure, but the Treasury could still claim a deficiency against the debtor (or his successor) for additional taxes due on returns filed during the title 11 proceedings.

Legislative Statements. Section 505 of the House amendment adopts a compromise position with respect to the determination of tax liability from the position taken in H.R. 8200 as passed by the House and in the Senate amendment.

Authority of bankruptcy court to rule on merits of tax claims. The House amendment authorizes the bankruptcy court to rule on the merits of any tax claim involving an unpaid tax, fine, or penalty relating to a tax, or any addition to a tax, of the debtor or the estate. This authority applies, in general, whether or not the tax, penalty, fine, or addition to tax had been previously assessed or paid. However, the bankruptcy court will not have jurisdiction to rule on the merits of any tax claim which has been previously adjudicated, in a contested proceeding, before a court of competent jurisdiction. For this purpose, a proceeding in the U.S. Tax Court is to be considered "contested" if the debtor filed a

petition in the Tax Court by the commencement of the case and the Internal Revenue Service had filed an answer to the petition. Therefore, if a petition and answer were filed in the Tax Court before the title II petition was filed, and if the debtor later defaults in the Tax Court, then, under res judicata principles, the bankruptcy court could not then rule on the debtor's or the estate's liability for the same taxes.

The House amendment adopts the rule of the Senate bill that the bankruptcy court can, under certain conditions, determine the amount of tax refund claimed by the trustee. Under the House amendment, if the refund results from an offset or counterclaim to a claim or request for payment by the Internal Revenue Service, or other tax authority, the trustee would not first have to file an administrative claim for refund with the tax authority.

However, if the trustee requests a refund in other situations, he would first have to submit an administrative claim for the refund. Under the House amendment, if the Internal Revenue Service or other tax authority does not rule on the refund claim within 120 days, then the bankruptcy court may rule on the merits of the refund claim.

Under the Internal Revenue Code [Title 26, Internal Revenue Code], a suit for refund of Federal taxes cannot be filed until 6 months after a claim for refund is filed with the Internal Revenue Service (sec. 6532(a) [section 6532(a) of Title 26]). Because of the bankruptcy aim to close the estate as expeditiously as possible, the House amendment shortens to 120 days the period for the Internal Revenue Service to decide the refund claim.

The House amendment also adopts the substance of the Senate bill rule permitting the bankruptcy court to determine the amount of any penalty, whether punitive or pecuniary in nature, relating to taxes over which it has jurisdiction.

Jurisdiction of the tax court in bankruptcy cases. The Senate amendment provided a detailed series of rules concerning the jurisdiction of the U. S. Tax Court, or similar State or local administrative tribunal to determine personal tax liabilities of an individual debtor. The House amendment deletes these specific rules and relies on procedures to be derived from broad general powers of the bankruptcy court.

Under the House amendment, as under present law, a corporation seeking reorganization under chapter 11 is considered to be personally before the bankruptcy court for purposes of giving that court jurisdiction over the debtor's personal liability for a nondischargeable tax.

The rules are more complex where the debtor is an individual under chapter 7, 11, or 13. An individual debtor or the tax authority can, as under section 17c of the present Bankruptcy Act [former section 35(c) of this title], file a request that the bankruptcy court determine the debtor's personal liability for the balance of any nondischargeable tax not satisfied from assets of the estate. The House amendment intends to retain these procedures and also adds a rule staying commencement or continuation of any proceeding in the Tax Court after the bankruptcy petition is filed, unless and until that stay is lifted by the bankruptcy judge under section 362(a)(8). The House amendment also stays assessment as well as collection of a prepetition claim against the debtor (sec. 362(a)(6)). A tax authority would not, however, be stayed from issuing a deficiency notice during the bankruptcy case (sec. (b)(7)). The Senate amendment repealed the existing authority of the Internal Revenue Service to make an immediate assessment of taxes upon bankruptcy (sec. 6871(a) of the code [section 6871(a) of Title 26, Internal Revenue Code]). See section 321 of the Senate bill. As indicated, the substance of that provision, also affecting State and local taxes, is contained in section 362(a)(6) of the House amendment, the statute of limitations is tolled under the House amendment while the bankruptcy case is pending.

Where no proceeding in the Tax Court is pending at the commencement of the bankruptcy case, the tax authority can, under the House amendment, file a claim against the estate for a prepetition tax liability and may also file a request that the bankruptcy court hear arguments and decide the merits of an individual debtor's personal liability for the balance of any nondischargeable tax liability not satisfied from assets of the estate. Bankruptcy terminology refers to the latter type of request as a creditor's complaint to determine the dischargeability of a debt. Where such a complaint is filed the bankruptcy court will have personal jurisdiction over an individual debtor, and the debtor himself would have no access to the Tax Court, or to any other court, to determine his personal liability for nondischargeable taxes.

If a tax authority decides not to file a claim for taxes which would typically occur where there are few, if any, assets in the estate, normally the tax authority would also not request the bankruptcy court to rule on the debtor's personal liability for a nondischargeable tax. Under the House amendment, the tax authority would then have to follow normal procedures in order to collect a nondischargeable tax. For example, in the case of nondischargeable Federal income taxes, the Internal Revenue Service would be required to issue a deficiency notice to an individual debtor, and the debtor could then file a petition in the Tax Court—or a refund suit in a district court—as the forum in which to litigate his personal liability for a nondischargeable tax.

Under the House amendment, as under present law, an individual debtor can also file a complaint to determine dischargeability. Consequently, where the tax authority does not file a claim or a request that the bankruptcy court determine dischargeability of a specific tax liability, the debtor could file such a request on his own behalf, so that the bankruptcy court would then determine both the validity of the claim against assets in the estate and also the personal liability of the debtor for any nondischargeable tax.

Where a proceeding is pending in the Tax Court at the commencement of the bankruptcy case, the commencement of the bankruptcy case automatically stays further action in the Tax Court case unless and until the stay is lifted by the bankruptcy court. The Senate amendment repealed a provision of the Internal Revenue case barring a debtor from filing a petition in the Tax Court after commencement of a bankruptcy case (sec. 6871(b) of the code) [section 6871(b) of Title 26, Internal Revenue Code]. See section 321 of the Senate bill. As indicated earlier, the equivalent of the code amendment is embodied in section 362(a)(8) of the House amendment, which automatically stays commencement or continuation of any proceeding in the Tax Court until the stay is lifted or the case is terminated. The stay will permit sufficient time for the bankruptcy trustee to determine if he desires to join the Tax Court proceeding on behalf of the estate. Where the trustee chooses to join the Tax Court proceeding, it is expected that he will seek permission to intervene in the Tax Court case and then request that the stay on the Tax Court proceeding be lifted. In such a case, the merits of the tax liability will be determined by the Tax Court, and its decision will bind both the individual debtor as to any taxes which are nondischargeable and the trustee as to the tax claim against the estate.

Where the trustee does not want to intervene in the Tax Court, but an individual debtor wants to have the Tax Court determine the amount of his personal liability for nondischargeable taxes, the debtor can request the bankruptcy court to lift the automatic stay on existing Tax Court proceedings. If the stay is lifted and the Tax Court reaches its decision before the bankruptcy court's decision on the tax claim against the estate, the decision of the Tax Court would bind the bankruptcy court under principles of res judicata because the decision of the Tax Court affected the personal liability of the debtor. If the trustee does not wish to subject the estate to the decision of the Tax Court if the latter court decides the issues before the bankruptcy court rules, the trustee could resist the lifting of the stay on the existing Tax Court proceeding. If the Internal Revenue Service had issued a deficiency notice to the debtor before the bankruptcy case began, but as of the filing of the bankruptcy petition the 90-day period for filing in the Tax Court was still running, the debtor would be automatically stayed from filing a petition in the Tax Court. If either the debtor or the Internal Revenue Service then files a complaint to determine dischargeability in the bankruptcy court, the decision of the bankruptcy court would bind both the debtor and the Internal Revenue Service.

The bankruptcy judge could, however, lift the stay on the debtor to allow him to petition the Tax Court, while reserving the right to rule on the tax authority's claim against assets of the estate. The bankruptcy court could also, upon request by the trustee, authorize the trustee to intervene in the Tax Court for purposes of having the estate also governed by the decision of the Tax Court.

In essence, under the House amendment, the bankruptcy judge will have authority to determine which court will determine the merits of the tax claim both as to claims against the estate and claims against the debtor concerning his personal liability for nondischargeable taxes. Thus, if the Internal Revenue Service, or a State or local tax authority, files a petition to determine dischargeability, the bankruptcy judge can either rule on the merits of the claim and continue the stay on any pending Tax Court proceeding or lift the stay on the Tax Court and hold the dischargeability complaint in abeyance. If he rules on the merits of the complaint before the decision of the Tax Court is reached, the bankruptcy court's decision would bind the debtor as to nondischargeable taxes and the Tax Court would be governed by that decision under principles of res judicata. If the bankruptcy judge does not rule on the merits of the complaint before the decision of the Tax Court is reached, the bankruptcy court will be bound by the decision of the Tax Court as it affects the amount of any claim against the debtor's estate.

If the Internal Revenue Service does not file a complaint to determine dischargeability and the automatic stay on a pending Tax Court proceeding is not lifted, the bankruptcy court could determine the merits of any tax claim against the estate. That decision will not bind the debtor personally because he would not have been personally before the bankruptcy court unless the debtor himself asks the bankruptcy court to rule on his personal liability. In any such situation where no party filed a dischargeability petition, the debtor would have access to the Tax Court to determine his personal liability for a nondischargeable tax debt. While the Tax Court in such a situation could take into account the ruling of the bankruptcy court on claims against the estate in deciding the debtor's personal liability, the bankruptcy court's ruling would not bind the Tax Court under principles of res judicata, because the debtor, in that situation would not have been personally before the bankruptcy court.

If neither the debtor nor the Internal Revenue Service files a claim against the estate or a request to rule on the debtor's personal liability, any pending tax court proceeding would be stayed until the closing of the bankruptcy case, at which time the stay on the tax court would cease and the tax court case could continue for purposes of deciding the merits of the debtor's personal liability for nondischargeable taxes.

Audit of trustee's returns. Under both bills, the bankruptcy court could determine the amount of any administrative period taxes. The Senate amendment, however, provided for an expedited audit procedure which was mandatory in some cases. The House amendment (sec. 505(b)), adopts the provision of the House bill allowing the trustee discretion in all cases whether to ask the Internal Revenue Service, or State or local tax authority for a prompt audit of his returns on behalf of the estate. The House amendment, however, adopts the provision of the Senate bill permitting a prompt audit only on the basis of tax returns filed by the trustee for completed taxable periods. Procedures for a prompt audit set forth in the Senate bill are also adopted in modified form.

Under the procedure, before the case can be closed, the trustee may request a tax audit by the local, State or Federal tax authority of all tax returns filed by the trustee. The taxing authority would have to notify the trustee and the bankruptcy court within 60 days whether it accepts returns or desires to audit the returns more fully. If an audit is conducted, the taxing authority would have to notify the trustee of tax deficiency within 180 days after the original request, subject to extensions of time if the bankruptcy court approves. If the trustee does not agree with the results of the audit, the trustee could ask the bankruptcy court to resolve the dispute. Once the trustee's tax liability for administration period taxes has thus been determined, the legal effect in a case under chapter 7 or 11 would be to discharge the trustee and any predecessor of the trustee, and also the debtor, from any further liability for these taxes.

The prompt audit procedure would not be available with respect to any tax liability as to which any return required to be filed on behalf of the estate is not filed with the proper tax authority. The House amendment also specifies that a discharge of the trustee or the debtor which would otherwise occur will not be granted, or will be void if the return filed on behalf of the estate reflects fraud or material misrepresentation of facts.

For purposes of the above prompt audit procedures, it is intended that the tax authority with which the request for audit is to be filed is, as to Federal taxes, the office of the District Director in the district where the bankruptcy case is pending.

Under the House amendment, if the trustee does not request a prompt audit, the debtor would not be discharged from possible transferee liability if any assets are returned to the debtor.

Assessment after decision. As indicated above, the commencement of a bankruptcy case automatically stays assessment of any tax (sec. 362(a)(6)). However, the House amendment provides (sec. 505(c)) that if the bankruptcy court renders a final judgment with regard to any tax (under the rules discussed above), the tax authority may then make an assessment (if permitted to do so under otherwise applicable tax law) without waiting for termination of the case or confirmation of a reorganization plan.

Trustee's authority to appeal tax cases. The equivalent provision in the House bill (sec. 505(b)) and in the Senate bill (sec. 362(h)) authorizing the trustee to prosecute an appeal or review of a tax case are deleted as unnecessary. Section 541(a) of the House amendment provides that property of the estate is to include all legal or equitable interests of the debtor. These interests include the debtor's causes of action, so that the specific provisions of the House and Senate bills are not needed.

Effective Date of 1984 Amendments. See section 553 of Pub.L. 98–353, Title III, July 10, 1984, 98 Stat. 392 set out as an Effective Date of 1984 Amendment note preceding chapter 1 of Title 11, Bankruptcy.

Separability of Provisions. For separability of provisions of Title III of Pub.L. 98–353, see section 551 of Pub.L. 98–353 set out as a Separability of Provisions note preceding chapter 1 of Title 11, Bankruptcy.

Library References:

C.J.S. Bankruptcy § 242.
West's Key No. Digests, Bankruptcy ⊛2830.

WESTLAW Electronic Research

See WESTLAW Electronic Research Guide following the *Bankruptcy Highlights*.

§ 506. Determination of secured status

(a) An allowed claim of a creditor secured by a lien on property in which the estate has an interest, or that is subject to setoff under section 553 of this title, is a secured claim to the extent of the value of such creditor's interest in the estate's interest in such property, or to the extent of the amount subject to setoff, as the case may be, and is an unsecured claim to the extent that the value of such creditor's interest or the amount so subject to setoff is less than the amount of such allowed claim. Such value shall be determined in light of the purpose of the valuation and of the proposed disposition or use of such property, and in conjunction with any hearing on such disposition or use or on a plan affecting such creditor's interest.

(b) To the extent that an allowed secured claim is secured by property the value of which, after any recovery under subsection (c) of this section, is greater than the amount of such claim, there shall be allowed to the holder of such claim, interest on such claim, and any reasonable fees, costs, or charges provided for under the agreement under which such claim arose.

(c) The trustee may recover from property securing an allowed secured claim the reasonable, necessary costs and expenses of preserving, or disposing of, such property to the extent of any benefit to the holder of such claim.

(d) To the extent that a lien secures a claim against the debtor that is not an allowed secured claim, such lien is void, unless—

    (1) such claim was disallowed only under section 502(b)(5) or 502(e) of this title; or

    (2) such claim is not an allowed secured claim due only to the failure of any entity to file a proof of such claim under section 501 of this title.

Pub.L. 95–598, Nov. 6, 1978, 92 Stat. 2583; Pub.L. 98–353, Title III, § 448, July 10, 1984, 98 Stat. 374.

Historical and Revision Notes

Notes of Committee on the Judiciary, Senate Report No. 95–989. Subsection (a) of this section separates an undersecured creditor's claim into two parts: He has a secured claim to the extent of the value of his collateral; and he has an unsecured claim for the balance of his claim. The subsection also provides for the valuation of claims which involve setoffs under section 553. While courts will have to determine value on a case-by-case basis, the subsection makes it clear that valuation is to be determined in light of the purpose of the valuation and the proposed disposition or use of the subject property. This determination shall be made in conjunction with any hearing on such disposition or use of property or on a plan affecting the creditor's interest. To illustrate, a valuation early in the case in a proceeding under sections 361–363 would not be binding upon the debtor or creditor at the time of confirmation of the plan. Throughout the bill, references to secured claims are only to the claim determined to be secured under this subsection, and not to the full amount of the creditor's claim. This provision abolishes the use of the terms "secured creditor" and "unsecured creditor" and substitutes in their places the terms "secured claim" and "unsecured claim."

Subsection (b) codifies current law by entitling a creditor with an oversecured claim to any reasonable fees (including attorney's fees), costs, or charges provided under the agreement under which the claim arose. These fees, costs, and charges are secured claims to the extent that the value of the collateral exceeds the amount of the underlying claim.

Subsection (c) also codifies current law by permitting the trustee to recover from property the value of which is greater than the sum of the claims secured by a lien on that property the reasonable, necessary costs and expenses of preserving, or disposing of, the property. The recovery is limited to the extent of any benefit to the holder of such claim.

Subsection (d) provides that to the extent a secured claim is not allowed, its lien is void unless the holder had neither actual notice nor knowledge of the case, the lien was not listed by the debtor in a chapter 9 or 11 case or such claim was disallowed only under section 502(e).

Notes of Committee on the Judiciary, House Report No. 95–595. Subsection (d) permits liens to pass through the bankruptcy case unaffected. However, if a party in interest requests the court to determine and allow or disallow the claim secured by the lien under section 502 and the claim is not allowed, then the lien is void to the extent that the claim is not allowed. The voiding provision does not apply to claims disallowed only under section 502(e), which requires disallowance of certain claims against the debtor by a codebtor, surety, or guarantor for contribution or reimbursement.

Legislative Statements. Section 506(a) of the House amendment adopts the provision contained in the Senate amendment and rejects a contrary provision as contained in H.R. 8200 as passed by the House. The provision contained in the Senate amendment and adopted by the House amendment recognizes that an amount subject to set-off is sufficient to recognize a secured status in the holder of such right. Additionally a determination of what portion of an allowed claim is secured and what portion is unsecured is binding only for the purpose for which the determination is made. Thus determinations for purposes of adequate protection is not binding for purposes of "cram down" on confirmation in a case under chapter 11.

Section 506(b) of the House amendment adopts language contained in the Senate amendment and rejects language contained in H.R. 8200 as passed by the House. If the security agreement between the parties provides for attorneys' fees, it will be enforceable under title 11, notwithstanding contrary law, and is recoverable from the collateral after any recovery under section 506(c).

Section 506(c) of the House amendment was contained in H.R. 8200 as passed by the House and adopted, verbatim, in the Senate amendment. Any time the trustee or debtor in possession expends money to provide for the reasonable and necessary cost and expenses of preserving or disposing of a secured creditor's collateral, the trustee or debtor in possession is entitled to recover such expenses from the secured party or from the property securing an allowed secured claim held by such party.

Section 506(d) of the House amendment is derived from H.R. 8200 as passed by the House and is adopted in lieu of the alternative test provided in section 506(d) of the Senate amendment. For purposes of section 506(d) of the House amendment, the debtor is a party in interest.

The House amendment deletes section 506(d)(3) of the Senate amendment, which insures that a tax lien securing a nondischargeable tax claim is not voided because a tax authority with notice or knowledge of the bankruptcy case fails to file a claim for the liability (as it may elect not to do, if it is clear there are insufficient assets to pay the liability). Since the House amendment retains section 506(d) of the House bill that a lien is not voided unless a party in interest has requested that the court determine and allow or disallow the claim, provision of the Senate amendment is not necessary.

Effective Date of 1984 Amendments. See section 553 of Pub.L. 98–353, Title III, July 10, 1984, 98 Stat. 392, set out as an Effective Date of 1984 Amendment note preceding chapter 1 of Title 11, Bankruptcy.

Separability of Provisions. For separability of provisions of Title III of Pub.L. 98–353, see section 551 of Pub.L. 98–353 set out as a Separability of Provisions note preceding chapter 1 of Title 11, Bankruptcy.

Cross References

Applicability of this section in chapter 9 cases, see section 901.
Automatic preservation of avoided transfer, see section 551.
Claims secured by lien on property of estate, see section 1111.
Effect of dismissal, see section 349.
Liability of exempted property for debtor's debt, see section 522.
Postpetition effect of security interest, see section 552.

Library References:

C.J.S. Bankruptcy § 246.
West's Key No. Digests, Bankruptcy ⬅2931.

WESTLAW Electronic Research

See WESTLAW Electronic Research Guide following the *Bankruptcy Highlights*.

§ 507. Priorities

(a) The following expenses and claims have priority in the following order:

(1) First, administrative expenses allowed under section 503(b) of this title, and any fees and charges assessed against the estate under chapter 123 of title 28.

(2) Second, unsecured claims allowed under section 502(f) of this title.

(3) Third, allowed unsecured claims for wages, salaries, or commissions, including vacation, severance, and sick leave pay—

(A) earned by an individual within 90 days before the date of the filing of the petition or the date of the cessation of the debtor's business, whichever occurs first; but only

(B) to the extent of $2,000 for each such individual.

(4) Fourth, allowed unsecured claims for contributions to an employee benefit plan—

(A) arising from services rendered within 180 days before the date of the filing of the petition or the date of the cessation of the debtor's business, whichever occurs first; but only

(B) for each such plan, to the extent of—

(i) the number of employees covered by each such plan multiplied by $2,000; less

(ii) the aggregate amount paid to such employees under paragraph (3) of this subsection, plus the aggregate amount paid by the estate on behalf of such employees to any other employee benefit plan.

(5) Fifth, allowed unsecured claims of persons—

(A) engaged in the production or raising of grain, as defined in section 557(b)(1) of this title, against a debtor who owns or operates a grain storage facility, as defined in section 557(b)(2) of this title, for grain or the proceeds of grain, or

(B) engaged as a United States fisherman against a debtor who has acquired fish or fish produce from a fisherman through a sale or conversion, and who is engaged in operating a fish produce storage or processing facility—

but only to the extent of $2,000 for each such individual.

(6) Sixth, allowed unsecured claims of individuals, to the extent of $900 for each such individual, arising from the deposit, before the commencement of the case, of money in connection with the purchase, lease, or rental of property, or the purchase of services, for the personal, family, or household use of such individuals, that were not delivered or provided.

(7) Seventh, allowed unsecured claims of governmental units; only to the extent that such claims are for—

(A) a tax on or measured by income or gross receipts—

(i) for a taxable year ending on or before the date of the filing of the petition for which a return, if required, is last due, including extensions, after three years before the date of the filing of the petition;

(ii) assessed within 240 days, plus any time plus 30 days during which an offer in compromise with respect to such tax that was made within 240 days after such assessment was pending, before the date of the filing of the petition; or

(iii) other than a tax of a kind specified in section 523(a)(1)(B) or 523(a)(1)(C) of this title, not assessed before, but assessable, under applicable law or by agreement, after, the commencement of the case;

(B) a property tax assessed before the commencement of the case and last payable without penalty after one year before the date of the filing of the petition;

(C) a tax required to be collected or withheld and for which the debtor is liable in whatever capacity;

(D) an employment tax on a wage, salary, or commission of a kind specified in paragraph (3) of this subsection earned from the debtor before the date of the filing of the petition, whether or not actually paid before such date, for which a return is last due, under applicable law or under any extension, after three years before the date of the filing of the petition;

(E) an excise tax on—

(i) a transaction occurring before the date of the filing of the petition for which a return, if required, is last due, under applicable law or under any extension, after three years before the date of the filing of the petition; or

(ii) if a return is not required, a transaction occurring during the three years immediately preceding the date of the filing of the petition;

(F) a customs duty arising out of the importation of merchandise—

(i) entered for consumption within one year before the date of the filing of the petition;

(ii) covered by an entry liquidated or reliquidated within one year before the date of the filing of the petition; or

(iii) entered for consumption within four years before the date of the filing of the petition but unliquidated on such date, if the Secretary of the Treasury certifies that failure to liquidate such entry was due to an investigation pending on such date into assessment of antidumping or countervailing duties or fraud, or if information needed for the proper appraisement or classification of such merchandise was not available to the appropriate customs officer before such date; or

(G) a penalty related to a claim of a kind specified in this paragraph and in compensation for actual pecuniary loss.

(8) Eighth, allowed unsecured claims based upon any commitment by the debtor to the Federal Deposit Insurance Corporation, the Resolution Trust Corporation, the Director of the Office of Thrift Supervision, the Comptroller of the Currency, or the Board of Governors of the Federal Reserve System, or their predecessors or successors, to maintain the capital of an insured depository institution.

(b) If the trustee, under section 362, 363, or 364 of this title, provides adequate protection of the interest of a holder of a claim secured by a lien on property of the debtor and if, notwithstanding such protection, such creditor has a claim allowable under subsection (a)(1) of this section arising from the stay of action against such property under section 362 of this title, from the use, sale, or lease of such property under section 363 of this title, or from the granting of a lien under section 364(d) of this title, then such creditor's claim under such subsection shall have priority over every other claim allowable under such subsection.

(c) For the purpose of subsection (a) of this section, a claim of a governmental unit arising from an erroneous refund or credit of a tax has the same priority as a claim for the tax to which such refund or credit relates.

(d) An entity that is subrogated to the rights of a holder of a claim of a kind specified in subsection (a)(3), (a)(4), (a)(5), or (a)(6) of this section is not subrogated to the right of the holder of such claim to priority under such subsection.

Pub.L. 95–598, Nov. 6, 1978, 92 Stat. 2583; Pub.L. 98–353, Title III, §§ 350, 449, July 10, 1984, 98 Stat. 358, 374; Pub.L. 101–647, Title XXV, § 2522(d), Nov. 29, 1990, 104 Stat. 4867.

Historical and Revision Notes

Notes of Committee on the Judiciary, Senate Report No. 95–989. Section 507 specifies the kinds of claims that are entitled to priority in distribution, and the order of their priority. Paragraph (1) grants first priority to allowed administrative expenses and to fees and charges assessed against the estate under chapter 123 of title 28 [section 1911 et seq. of Title 28, Judiciary and Judicial Procedure]. Taxes included as administrative expenses under section 503(b)(1) of the bill generally receive the first priority, but the bill makes certain qualifications: Examples of these specially treated claims are the estate's liability for recapture of an investment tax credit claimed by the debtor before the title 11 case (this liability receives sixth priority) and the estate's employment tax liabilities on wages earned before, but paid after, the petition was filed (this liability generally receives the same priority as the wages).

"Involuntary gap" creditors, granted first priority under current law, are granted second priority by paragraph (2). This priority, covering claims arising in the ordinary course of the debtor's business or financial affairs after a title 11 case has begun but before a trustee is appointed or before the order for relief, includes taxes incurred during the conduct of such activities.

Paragraph (3) expands and increases the wage priority found in current section 64a(2) [former section 104(a)(2) of this title]. The amount entitled to priority is raised from $600 to $1800. The former figure was last adjusted in 1926. Inflation has made it nearly meaningless, and the bill brings it more than up to date. The three month limit of current law is retained, but is modified to run from the earlier of the date of the filing of the petition or the date of the cessation of the debtor's business. The priority is expanded to cover vacation, severance, and sick leave pay. The bill adds to the third priority so-called "trust fund" taxes, that is, withheld income taxes and the employees' share of the social security or railroad retirement taxes, but only to the extent that the wages on which taxes are imposed are themselves entitled to third priority.

The employer's share, the employment tax and the employer's share of the social security or railroad retirement tax on third priority compensation, is also included in the third priority category, but only if, and to the extent that the wages and related trust fund taxes have first been paid in full. Because of the claimants urgent need for their wages in the typical cases, the employer's taxes should not be paid before the wage claims entitled to priority, as well as the related trust fund taxes, are fully paid.

Paragraph (4) overrules United States v. Embassy Restaurant, 359 U.S. 29 (1958) [79 S.Ct. 554, 3 L.Ed.2d 601], which held that fringe benefits were not entitled to wage priority status. The bill recognizes the realities of labor contract negotiations, where fringe benefits may be substituted for wage demands. The priority granted is limited to claims for contributions to employee benefit plans such as pension plans, health or life insurance plans, and others, arising from services rendered within 120 days before the commencement of the case or the date of cessation of the debtor's business, whichever occurs first. The dollar limit placed on the total of all contributions payable under this paragraph is equal to the difference between the maximum allowable priority under paragraph (3), $1,800, times the number of employees covered by the plan less the actual distributions under paragraph (3) with respect to these employees.

Paragraph (5) is a new priority for consumer creditors—those who have deposited money in connection with the purchase, lease, or rental of property, or the purchase of services, for their personal, family, or household use, that were not delivered or provided. The priority amount is not to exceed $600. In order to reach only those persons most deserving of this special priority, it is limited to individuals whose adjustable gross income from all sources derived does not exceed $20,000. See Senate Hearings, testimony of Prof. Vern Countryman, at pp. 848–849. The income of the husband and wife should be aggregated for the purposes of the $20,000 limit if either or both spouses assert such a priority claim.

The sixth priority is for certain taxes. Priority is given to income taxes for a taxable year that ended on or before the date of the filing of the petition, if the last due date of the return for such year occurred not more than 3 years immediately before the date on which the petition was filed (§ 507(a)(6)(A)(i)). For the purposes of this rule, the last due date of the return is the last date under any extension of time to file the return which the taxing authority may have granted the debtor.

Employment taxes and transfer taxes (including gift, estate, sales, use and other excise taxes) are also given sixth priority if the transaction or event which gave rise to the tax occurred before the petition date, provided that the required return or report of such tax liabilities was last due within 3 years before the petition was filed or was last due after the petition date (§ 507(a)(6)(A)(ii)). The employment taxes covered under this rule are the employer's share of the social security and railroad retirement taxes and required employer payments toward unemployment insurance.

Priority is given to income taxes and other taxes of a kind described in section 507(a)(6)(A)(i) and (ii) which the Federal, State, or local tax authority had assessed within 3 years after the last due date of the return, that is, including any extension of time to file the return, if the debtor filed in title 11 within 240 days after the assessment was made (§ 507(a)(6)(B)(i)). This rule may bring into the sixth priority the debtor's tax liability for some taxable years which would not qualify for priority under the general three-year rule of section 507(a)(6)(A).

The sixth priority category also includes taxes which the tax authority was barred by law from assessing or collecting at any time during the 300 days before the petition under title 11 was filed (§ 507(a)(6)(B)(ii)). In the case of certain Federal taxes, this preserves a priority for tax liabilities for years more than three years before the filing of the petition where the debtor and the Internal Revenue Service were negotiating over an audit of the debtor's returns or were engaged in litigation in the Tax Court. In such situations, the tax law prohibits the service's right to assess a tax deficiency until ninety days after the service sends the taxpayer a deficiency letter or, if the taxpayer files a petition in the Tax Court during that 90-day period, until the outcome of the litigation. A similar priority exists in present law, except that the taxing authority is allowed no time to assess and collect the taxes after the restrictions on assessment (discussed above) are lifted. Some taxpayers have exploited this loophole by filing in bankruptcy immediately after the end of the 90-day period or immediately after the close of Tax Court proceedings. The bill remedies this defect by preserving a priority for taxes the assessment of which was barred by law by giving the tax authority 300 days within which to make the assessment after the lifting of the bar and then to collect or file public notice of its tax lien. Thus, if a taxpayer files a title 11 petition at any time during that 300-day period, the tax deficiency will be entitled to priority. If the petition is filed more than 300 days after the restriction on assessment was lifted, the taxing authority will not have priority for the tax deficiency.

Taxes for which an offer in compromise was withdrawn by the debtor, or rejected by a governmental unit, within 240 days before the petition date (§ 507(a)(6)(B)(iii)) will also receive sixth priority. This rule closes a loophole under present law under which, following an assessment of tax, some taxpayers have submitted a formal offer in compromise, dragged out negotiations with the taxing authority until the tax liability would lose priority under the three-year priority period of present law, and then filed in bankruptcy before the governmental unit could take collection steps.

Also included are certain taxes for which no return or report is required by law (§ 507(a)(6)(C)), if the taxable transaction occurred within three years before the petition was filed.

Taxes (not covered by the third priority) which the debtor was required by law to withhold or collect from others and for which he is liable in any capacity, regardless of the age of the tax claims (§ 507(a)(6)(D)) are included. This category covers the so-called "trust fund" taxes, that is, income taxes which an employer is required to withhold from the pay of his employees, the employees' shares of social security and railroad retirement taxes, and also Federal unemployment insurance. This category also includes excise taxes which a seller of goods or services is required to collect from a buyer and pay over to a taxing authority.

This category also covers the liability of a responsible corporate officer under the Internal Revenue Code [Title 26] for income taxes or for the employees' share of employment taxes which, under the tax law, the employer was required to withhold from the wages of employees. This priority will operate where a person found to be a responsible officer has himself filed a petition under title 11, and the priority covers the debtor's liability as an officer under the Internal Revenue Code [Title 26] regardless of the age of the tax year to which the tax relates.

The priority rules under the bill governing employment taxes can be summarized as follows: In the case of wages earned and actually paid before the petition under title 11 was filed, the liability for the employees' share of the employment taxes, regardless of the prepetition year in which the wages were earned and paid. The employer's share of employment taxes on all wages earned and paid before the petition receive sixth priority; generally, these taxes will be those for which a return was due within three years before the petition. With respect to wages earned by employees before the petition but actually paid by the trustee after the title 11 case commenced, taxes required to be withheld receives the same priority as the wages themselves. Thus, the employees' share of taxes on third priority wages also receives third priority. Taxes on the balance of such wages receive no priority and are collectible only as general claims because the wages themselves are payable only as general claims and liability for the taxes arises only to the extent the wages are actually paid. The employer's share of employment taxes on third priority wages earned before the petition but paid after the petition was filed receives third priority, but only if the wages in this category have first been paid in full. Assuming there are sufficient funds to pay third priority wages

and the related employer taxes in full, the employer's share of taxes on the balance of wage payments becomes a general claim (because the wages themselves are payable as general claims). Both the employees' and the employer's share of employment taxes on wages earned and paid after the petition was filed receive first priority as administrative expenses.

Also covered by this sixth priority are property taxes required to be assessed within 3 years before the filing of the petition (§ 507(a)(6)(E)).

Taxes attributable to a tentative carry-back adjustment received by the debtor before the petition was filed, such as a "quickie refund" received under section 6411 of the Internal Revenue Code [section 6411 of Title 26, Internal Revenue Code] (§ 507(a)(6)(F)) are included. However, the tax claim against the debtor will rein a prepetition loss year for which the tax return was last due, including extensions, within 3 years before the petition was filed.

Taxes resulting from a recapture, occasioned by a transfer during bankruptcy, of a tax credit or deduction taken during an earlier tax year (§ 507(a)(6)(G)) are included. A typical example occurs when there is a sale by the trustee of depreciable property during the case and depreciation deductions taken in prepetition years are subject to recapture under section 1250 of the Code [section 1250 of Title 26, Internal Revenue Code].

Taxes owed by the debtor as a transferee of assets from another person who is liable for a tax, if the tax claim against the transferor would have received priority in a chapter 11 case commenced by the transferor within 1 year before the date of the petition filed by the transferee (§ 507(a)(6)(H)), are included.

Also included are certain tax payments required to have been made during the 1 year immediately before the petition was filed, where the debtor had previously entered into a deferred payment agreement (including an offer in compromise) to pay an agreed liability in periodic installments but had become delinquent in one or more installments before the petition was filed (§ 507(a)(6)(I)). This priority covers all types of deferred or part payment agreements. The priority covers only installments which first became due during the 1 year before the petition but which remained unpaid at the date of the petition. The priority does not come into play, however, if before the case began or during the case, the debtor and the taxing authority agree to a further extension of time to pay the delinquent amounts.

Certain tax-related liabilities which are not true taxes or which are not collected by regular assessment procedures (§ 507(a)(6)(J)) are included. One type of liability covered in this category is the liability under section 3505 of the Internal Revenue Code [section 3505 of Title 26, Internal Revenue Code] of a lender who pays wages directly to employees of another employer or who supplies funds to an employer for the payment of wages. Another is the liability under section 6332 of the Internal Revenue Code [section 6332 of Title 26, Internal Revenue Code] of a person who fails to turn over money or property of the taxpayer in response to a levy. Since the taxing authority must collect such a liability from the third party by suit rather than normal assessment procedures, an extra year is added to the normal 3-year priority periods. If a suit was commenced by the taxing authority within the four-year period and before the petition was filed, the priority is also preserved, provided that the suit had not terminated more than 1 year before the date of the filing of the petition.

Also included are certain unpaid customs duties which have not grown unreasonably "stale" (§ 507(a)(6)(K)). These include duties on imports entered for consumption within 3 years before the filing of the petition if the duties are still unliquidated on the petition date. If an import entry has been liquidated (in general, liquidation is in an administrative determination of the value and tariff rate of the item) or reliquidated, within two years of the filing of the petition the customs liability is given priority. If the Secretary of the Treasury certifies that customs duties were not liquidated because of an investigation into possible assessment of antidumping or countervailing duties, or because of fraud penalties, duties not liquidated for this reason during the five years before the importer filed under title 11 also will receive priority.

Subsection (a) of this section also provides specifically that interest on sixth priority tax claims accrued before the filing of the petition is also entitled to sixth priority.

Subsection (b) of this section provides that any fine or penalty which represents compensation for actual pecuniary loss of a governmental unit, and which involves a tax liability entitled to sixth priority, is to receive the same priority.

Subsection (b) also provides that a claim arising from an erroneous refund or credit of tax is to be given the same priority as the tax to which the refund or credit relates.

Legislative Statements. Section 507(a)(3) of the House amendment represents a compromise dollar amount and date for the priority between similar provisions contained in H.R. 8200 as passed by the House and the Senate amendments. A similar compromise is contained in section 507(a)(4).

Section 507(a)(5) represents a compromise on amount between the priority as contained in H.R. 8200 as passed by the House and the Senate amendment. The Senate provision for limiting the priority to consumers having less than a fixed gross income is deleted.

Section 507(a)(6) of the House amendment represents a compromise between similar provisions contained in H.R. 8200 as passed by the House and the Senate amendment.

Section 507(b) of the House amendment is new and is derived from the compromise contained in the House amendment with respect to adequate protection under section 361. Subsection (b) provides that to the extent adequate protection of the interest of a holder of a claim proves to be inadequate, then the creditor's claim is given priority over every other allowable claim entitled to distribution under section 507(a). Section 507(b) of the Senate amendment is deleted.

Section 507(c) of the House amendment is new. Section 507(d) of the House amendment prevents subrogation with respect to priority for certain priority claims. Subrogation with respect to priority is intended to be permitted for administrative claims and claims arising during the gap period.

Under the House amendment, taxes receive priority as follows:

First, Administration expenses: The amendment generally follows the Senate amendment in providing expressly that taxes incurred during the administration of the estate share the first priority given to administrative expenses generally. Among the taxes which receives first priority, as defined in section 503, are the employees' and the employer's shares of employment taxes on wages earned and paid after the petition is filed. Section 503(b)(1) also includes in administration expenses a tax liability arising from an excessive allowance by a tax authority of a "quickie refund" to the estate. (In the case of Federal taxes, such refunds are allowed under special rules based on net operating loss carrybacks (sec. 6411 of the Internal Revenue Code) [section 6411 of Title 26, Internal Revenue Code]).

An exception is made to first priority treatment for taxes incurred by the estate with regard to the employer's share of employment taxes on wages earned from the debtor before the petition but paid from the estate after the petition has been filed. In this situation, the employer's tax receives either sixth priority or general claim treatment.

The House amendment also adopts the provisions of the Senate amendment which include in the definition of administrative expenses under section 503 any fine, penalty (including "additions to tax" under applicable tax laws) or reduction in credit imposed on the estate.

Second. "Involuntary gap" claims: "Involuntary gap" creditors are granted second priority by paragraph (2) of section 507(a). This priority includes tax claims arising in the ordinary course of the debtor's business or financial affairs after he has been placed involuntarily in bankruptcy but before a trustee is appointed or before the order for relief.

Third. Certain taxes on prepetition wages: Wage claims entitled to third priority are for compensation which does not exceed $2,000 and was earned during the 90 days before the filing of the bankruptcy petition or the cessation of the debtor's business. Certain employment taxes receive third priority in payment from the estate along with the payment of wages to which the taxes relate. In the case of wages earned before the filing of the petition, but paid by the trustee (rather than by the debtor) after the filing of the petition, claims or the employees' share of the employment taxes (withheld income taxes and the employees' share of the social security or railroad retirement tax) receive third priority to the extent the wage claims themselves are entitled to this priority.

In the case of wages earned from and paid by the debtor before the filing of the petition, the employer's share of the employment taxes on these wages paid by the debtor receives sixth priority or, if not entitled to that priority, are treated only as general claims. Under the House amendment, the employer's share of employment taxes on wages earned by employees of the debtor, but paid by the trustee after the filing of the bankruptcy petition, will also receive sixth priority to the extent that claims for the wages receive third priority. To the extent the claims for wages do not receive third priority, but instead are treated only as general claims, claims for the employer's share of the employment taxes attributable to those wages will also be treated as general claims. In calculating the amounts payable as general wage claims, the trustee must pay the employer's share of employment taxes on such wages.

Sixth priority. The House amendment modifies the provisions of both the House bill and Senate amendment in the case of sixth priority taxes. Under the amendment, the following Federal, State and local taxes are included in the sixth priority:

First. Income and gross receipts taxes incurred before the date of the petition for which the last due date of the return, including all extensions of time granted to file the return, occurred within 3 years before the date on which the petition was filed, or after the petition date. Under this rule, the due date of the return, rather than the date on which the taxes were assessed, determines the priority.

Second. Income and gross receipts taxes assessed at any time within 240 days before the petition date. Under this rule, the date on which the governmental unit assesses the tax, rather than the due date of the return, determines the priority.

If, following assessment of a tax, the debtor submits an offer in compromise to the governmental unit, the House amendment provides that the 240-day period is to be suspended for the duration of the offer and will resume running after the offer is withdrawn or rejected by the governmental unit, but the tax liability will receive priority if the title 11 petition is filed during the balance of the 240-day period or during a minimum of 30 days after the offer is withdrawn or rejected. This rule modifies a provision of the Senate amendment dealing specifically with offers in compromise. Under the modified rule, if, after the assessment, an offer in compromise is submitted by the debtor and is still pending (without having been accepted or rejected) at the date on which a title 11 petition is filed, the underlying liability will receive sixth priority. However, if an assessment of a tax liability is made but the tax is not collected within 240 days, the tax will not receive priority under section 507(a)(6)(A)(i) and the debtor cannot revive a priority for that tax by submitting an offer in compromise.

Third. Income and gross receipts taxes not assessed before the petition date but still permitted, under otherwise applicable tax laws, to be assessed. Thus, for example, a prepetition tax liability is to receive sixth priority under this rule if, under the applicable statute of limitations, the tax liability can still be assessed by the tax authority. This rule also covers situations referred to in section 507(a)(6)(B)(ii) of the Senate amendment where the assessment or collection of a tax was prohibited before the petition pending exhaustion of judicial or administrative remedies, except that the House amendment eliminates the 300-day limitation of the Senate bill. So, for example, if before the petition a debtor was engaged in litigation in the Tax Court, during which the Internal Revenue Code [Title 26] bars the Internal Revenue Service from assessing or collecting the tax, and if the tax court decision is made in favor of the Service before the petition under title 11 is filed, thereby lifting the restrictions on assessment and collection, the tax liability will receive sixth priority even if the tax authority does not make an assessment within 300 days before the petition (provided, of course, that the statute of limitations on assessment has not expired by the petition date).

In light of the above categories of the sixth priority, and tax liability of the debtor (under the Internal Revenue Code [Title 26] or State or local law) as a transferee of property from another person will receive sixth priority without the limitations contained in the Senate amendment so long as the transferee liability had not been assessed by the tax authority by the petition date but could still have been assessed by that date under the applicable tax statute of limitations or, if the transferee liability had been assessed before the petition, the assessment was made no more than 240 days before the petition date.

Also in light of the above categories, the treatment of prepetition tax liabilities arising from an excessive allowance to the debtor of a tentative carryback adjustment, such as a "quickie refund" under section 6411 of the Internal Revenue Code [section 6411 of Title 26, Internal Revenue Code], is revised as follows: If the tax authority has assessed the additional tax before the petition, the tax liability will receive priority if the date of assessment was within 240 days before the petition date. If the tax authority had not assessed the additional tax by the petition, the tax liability will still receive priority so long as, on the petition date, assessment of the liability is not barred by the statute of limitations.

Fourth. Any property tax assessed before the commencement of the case and last payable without penalty within 1 year before the petition, or thereafter.

Fifth. Taxes which the debtor was required by law to withhold or collect from others and for which he is liable in any capacity, regardless of the age of the tax claims. This category covers the so-called "trust fund" taxes, that is, income taxes which an employer is required to withhold from the pay of his employees, and the employees' share of social security taxes.

In addition, this category includes the liability of a responsible officer under the Internal Revenue Code (sec. 6672 [section 6672 of Title 26, Internal Revenue Code]) for income taxes or for the employees' share of social security taxes which that officer was responsible for withholding from the wages of employees and paying to the Treasury, although he was not himself the employer. This priority will operate when a person found to be a responsible officer has himself filed in title 11, and the priority will cover the debtor's responsible officer liability regardless of the age of the tax year to which the tax relates. The U.S. Supreme Court has interpreted present law to require the same result as will be reached under this rule. U.S. v. Sotelo, 436 U.S. 268 (1978) [98 S.Ct. 1795, 56 L.Ed.2d 275, rehearing denied 98 S.Ct. 3126, 438 U.S. 907, 57 L.Ed.2d 1150].

This category also includes the liability under section 3505 of the Internal Revenue Code [section 3505 of Title 26, Internal Revenue Code] of a taxpayer who loans money for the payment of wages or other compensation.

Sixth. The employer's share of employment taxes on wages paid before the petition and on third-priority wages paid postpetition by the estate. The priority rules under the House amendment governing employment taxes can thus be summarized as follows: Claims for the employees' shares of employment taxes attributable to wages both earned and paid before the filing of the petition are to receive sixth priority. In the case of employee wages earned, but not paid, before the filing of the bankruptcy petition, claims for the employees' share of employment taxes receive third priority to the extent the wages themselves receive third priority. Claims which relate to wages earned before the petition, but not paid before the petition (and which are not entitled to the third priority under the rule set out above), will be paid as general claims. Since the related wages will receive no priority, the related employment taxes would also be paid as nonpriority general claims.

The employer's share of the employment taxes on wages earned and paid before the bankruptcy petition will receive sixth priority to the extent the return for these taxes was last due (including extensions of time) within 3 years before the filing of the petition, or was due after the petition was filed. Older tax claims of this nature will be payable as general claims. In the case of wages earned by employees before the petition, but actually paid by the trustee (as claims against the estate) after the title 11 case commenced, the employer's share of the employment taxes on third priority wages will be payable as sixth priority claims and the employer's taxes on prepetition wages which are treated only as general claims will be payable only as general claims. In calculating the amounts payable as general wage claims, the trustee must pay the employer's share of employment taxes on such wages. The House amendment thus deletes the provision of the Senate amendment that certain employer taxes receive third priority and are to be paid immediately after payment of third priority wages and the employees' shares of employment taxes on those wages.

In the case of employment taxes relating to wages earned and paid after the petition, both the employees' shares and the employer's share will receive first priority as administration expenses of the estate.

Seventh. Excise taxes on transactions for which a return, if required, is last due, under otherwise applicable law or under any extension of time to file the return, within 3 years before the petition was filed, or thereafter. If a return is not required with regard to a particular excise tax, priority is given if the transaction or event itself occurred within 3 years before the date on which the title 11 petition was filed. All Federal, State or local taxes generally considered or expressly treated as excises are covered by this category, including sales taxes, estate and gift taxes, gasoline and special fuel taxes, and wagering and truck taxes.

Eighth. Certain unpaid customs duties. The House amendment covers in this category duties on imports entered for consumption within 1 year before the filing of the petition, but which are still unliquidated on the petition date; duties covered by an entry liquidated or reliquidated within 1 year before the petition date; and any duty on merchandise entered for consumption within 4 years before the petition but not liquidated on the petition date, if the Secretary of the Treasury or his delegate certifies that duties were not liquidated because of possible assessment of antidumping or countervailing duties or fraud penalties.

For purposes of the above priority rules, the House amendment adopts the provision of the Senate bill that any tax liability which, under otherwise applicable tax law, is collectible in the form of a "penalty," is to be treated in the same manner as a tax liability. In bankruptcy terminology, such tax liabilities are referred to as pecuniary loss penalties. Thus, any tax liability which under the Internal Revenue Code [Title 26] or State or local tax law is payable as a "penalty," in addition to the liability of a responsible person under section 6672 of the Internal Revenue Code [section 6672 of Title 26, Internal Revenue Code] will be entitled to the priority which the liability would receive if it were expressly labeled as a "tax" under the applicable tax law. However, a tax penalty which is punitive in nature is given subordinated treatment under section 726(a)(4).

The House amendment also adopts the provision of the Senate amendment that a claim arising from an erroneous refund or credit of tax, other than a "quickie refund," is to receive the same priority as the tax to which the refund or credit relates.

The House amendment deletes the express provision of the Senate amendment that a tax liability is to receive sixth priority if it satisfies any one of the subparagraphs of section 507(a)(6) even if the liability fails to satisfy the terms of one or more other subparagraphs. No change of substance is intended by the deletion, however, in light of section 102(5) of the House amendment, providing a rule of construction that the word "or" is not intended to be exclusive.

The House amendment deletes from the express priority categories of the Senate amendment the priority for a debtor's liability as a third party for failing to surrender property or to pay an obligation in response to a levy for taxes of another, and the priority for amounts provided for under deferred payment agreements between a debtor and the tax authority.

The House amendment also adopts the substance of the definition in section 346(a) the Senate amendment of when taxes are to be considered "incurred" except that the House amendment applies these definitions solely for purposes of determining which category of section 507 tests the priority of a particular tax liability. Thus, for example, the House amendment contains a special rule for the treatment of taxes under the 45-day exception to the preference rules under section 547 and the definitions of when a tax is incurred for priority purposes are not to apply to such preference rules. Under the House amendment, for purposes of the priority rules, a tax on income for a particular period is to be considered "incurred" on the last day of the period. A tax on or measured by some event, such as the payment of wages or a transfer by reason of death or gift, or an excise tax on a sale or other transaction, is to be considered "incurred" on the date of the transaction or event.

References in Text. Chapter 123 of title 28, referred to in subsec. (a)(1), is classified to section 1911 et seq. of Title 28, Judiciary and Judicial Procedure.

Effective Date of 1984 Amendments. See section 553 of Pub.L. 98–353, Title III, July 10, 1984, 98 Stat. 392, set out as an Effective Date of 1984 Amendment note preceding chapter 1 of Title 11, Bankruptcy.

Separability of Provisions. For separability of provisions of Title III of Pub.L. 98–353, see section 551 of Pub.L. 98–353 set out as a Separability of Provisions note preceding chapter 1 of Title 11, Bankruptcy.

Cross References

Applicability of subsec. (a)(1) of this section in chapter 9 cases, see section 901.

Confirmation upon payment of administrative expenses, fees, and charges, see section 943.

Designation by plan of classes of claims, see section 1123.

Distribution of
    Certain estate property subject to liens, see section 724.
    Customer property in commodity broker liquidation cases, see section 766.
    Customer property in stockbroker liquidation cases, see section 752.
    Property of estate, see section 726.

Tax or customs duty excepted from discharge, see section 523.

Time of payment of administrative expenses, fees and charges in Chapter 13 cases, see section 1326.

Treatment of certain claims as affecting confirmation of plan, see section 1129.

Unsecured debt having priority over certain administrative expenses, see section 364.

Library References:

C.J.S. Bankruptcy §§ 255 et seq., 351, 353.

West's Key No. Digests, Bankruptcy ⟷2951 et seq.

WESTLAW Electronic Research

See WESTLAW Electronic Research Guide following the *Bankruptcy Highlights*.

§ 508.   Effect of distribution other than under this title

(a) If a creditor receives, in a foreign proceeding, payment of, or a transfer of property on account of, a claim that is allowed under this title, such creditor may not receive any payment under this title on account of such claim until each of the other holders of claims on account of which such holders are entitled to share equally with such creditor under this title has received payment under this title equal in value to the consideration received by such creditor in such foreign proceeding.

(b) If a creditor of a partnership debtor receives, from a general partner that is not a debtor in a case under chapter 7 of this title, payment of, or a transfer of property on account of, a claim that is allowed under this title and that is not secured by a lien on property of such partner, such creditor may not receive any payment under this title on account of such claim until each of the other holders of claims on account of which such holders are entitled to share equally with

such creditor under this title has received payment under this title equal in value to the consideration received by such creditor from such general partner.
Pub.L. 95–598, Nov. 6, 1978, 92 Stat. 2585.

Historical and Revision Notes

Notes of Committee on the Judiciary, Senate Report No. 95–989. This section prohibits a creditor from receiving any distribution in the bankruptcy case if he has received payment of a portion of his claim in a foreign proceeding, until the other creditors in the bankruptcy case in this country that are entitled to share equally with that creditor have received as much as he has in the foreign proceeding.

Legislative Statements. Section 508(b) of the House amendment is new and provides an identical rule with respect to a creditor of a partnership who receives payment from a partner, to that of a creditor of a debtor who receives a payment in a foreign proceeding involving the debtor.

Library References:

C.J.S. Bankruptcy § 267.
West's Key No. Digests, Bankruptcy ⟜2964.

WESTLAW Electronic Research

See WESTLAW Electronic Research Guide following the *Bankruptcy Highlights.*

§ 509.   Claims of codebtors

(a) Except as provided in subsection (b) or (c) of this section, an entity that is liable with the debtor on, or that has secured, a claim of a creditor against the debtor, and that pays such claim, is subrogated to the rights of such creditor to the extent of such payment.

(b) Such entity is not subrogated to the rights of such creditor to the extent that—

    (1) a claim of such entity for reimbursement or contribution on account of such payment of such creditor's claim is—

        (A) allowed under section 502 of this title;

        (B) disallowed other than under section 502(e) of this title; or

        (C) subordinated under section 510 of this title; or

    (2) as between the debtor and such entity, such entity received the consideration for the claim held by such creditor.

(c) The court shall subordinate to the claim of a creditor and for the benefit of such creditor an allowed claim, by way of subrogation under this section, or for reimbursement or contribution, of an entity that is liable with the debtor on, or that has secured, such creditor's claim, until such creditor's claim is paid in full, either through payments under this title or otherwise.

Pub.L. 95–598, Nov. 6, 1978, 92 Stat. 2585; Pub.L. 98–353, Title III, § 450, July 10, 1984, 98 Stat. 375.

Historical and Revision Notes

Notes of Committee on the Judiciary, Senate Report No. 95–989. Section 509 deals with codebtors generally, and is in addition to the disallowance provision in section

502(e). This section is based on the notion that the only rights available to a surety, guarantor, or comaker are contribution, reimbursement, and subrogation. The right that applies in a particular situation will depend on the agreement between the debtor and the codebtor, and on whether and how payment was made by the codebtor to the creditor. The claim of a surety or codebtor for contribution or reimbursement is discharged even if the claim is never filed, as is any claim for subrogation even if the surety or codebtor chooses to file a claim for contribution or reimbursement instead.

Subsection (a) subrogates the codebtor (whether as a codebtor, surety, or guarantor) to the rights of the creditor, to the extent of any payment made by the codebtor to the creditor. Whether the creditor's claim was filed under section 501(a) or 501(b) is irrelevant. The right of subrogation will exist even if the primary creditor's claim is allowed by virtue of being listed under proposed 11 U.S.C. 924 or 1111, and not by reason of a proof of claim.

Subsection (b) permits a subrogated codebtor to receive payments in the bankruptcy case only if the creditor has been paid in full, either through payments under the bankruptcy code or otherwise.

Legislative Statements. Section 509 of the House amendment represents a substantial revision of provisions contained in H.R. 8200 as passed by the House and in the Senate amendment. Section 509(a) states a general rule that a surety or co-debtor is subrogated to the rights of a creditor assured by the surety or co-debtor to the extent the surety or co-debtor pays such creditor. Section 509(b)

states a general exception indicating that subrogation is not granted to the extent that a claim of a surety or co-debtor for reimbursement or contribution is allowed under section 502 or disallowed other than under section 502(e). Additionally, section 509(b)(1)(C) provides that such claims for subrogation are subordinated to the extent that a claim of the surety or co-debtor for reimbursement or contribution is subordinated under section 510(a) (1) or 510(b). Section 509(b)(2) reiterates the well-known rule that prevents a debtor that is ultimately liable on the debt from recovering from a surety or a co-debtor. Although the language in section 509(b)(2) focuses in terms of receipt of consideration, legislative history appearing elsewhere indicates that an agreement to share liabilities should prevail over an agreement to share profits throughout title 11. This is particularly important in the context of co-debtors who are partners. Section 509(c) subordinates the claim of a surety or co-debtor to the claim of an assured creditor until the creditor's claim is paid in full.

Effective Date of 1984 Amendments. See section 553 of Pub.L. 98–353, Title III, July 10, 1984, 98 Stat. 392, set out as an Effective Date of 1984 Amendment note preceding chapter 1 of Title 11, Bankruptcy.

Separability of Provisions. For separability of provisions of Title III of Pub.L. 98–353, see section 551 of Pub.L. 98–353 set out as a Separability of Provisions note preceding chapter 1 of Title 11, Bankruptcy.

Cross References

Applicability of this section in chapter 9 cases, see section 901.

Library References:

C.J.S. Bankruptcy § 241.
West's Key No. Digests, Bankruptcy ⚖2823.

WESTLAW Electronic Research

See WESTLAW Electronic Research Guide following the *Bankruptcy Highlights*.

§ 510. Subordination

(a) A subordination agreement is enforceable in a case under this title to the same extent that such agreement is enforceable under applicable nonbankruptcy law.

(b) For the purpose of distribution under this title, a claim arising from rescission of a purchase or sale of a security of the debtor or of an affiliate of the debtor, for damages arising from the purchase or sale of such a security, or for reimbursement or contribution allowed under section 502 on account of such a claim, shall be subordinated to all claims or interests that are senior to or equal the claim or interest represented by such security, except that if such security is common stock, such claim has the same priority as common stock.

(c) Notwithstanding subsections (a) and (b) of this section, after notice and a hearing, the court may—

(1) under principles of equitable subordination, subordinate for purposes of distribution all or part of an allowed claim to all or part of another allowed claim or all or part of an allowed interest to all or part of another allowed interest; or

(2) order that any lien securing such a subordinated claim be transferred to the estate.

Pub.L. 95–598, Nov. 6, 1978, 92 Stat. 2586; Pub.L. 98–353, Title III, § 451, July 10, 1984, 98 Stat. 375.

Historical and Revision Notes

Notes of Committee on the Judiciary, Senate Report No. 95–989. Subsection (a) requires the court to enforce subordination agreements. A subordination agreement will not be enforced, however, in a reorganization case in which the class that is the beneficiary of the agreement has accepted, as specified in proposed 11 U.S.C. 1126, a plan that waives their rights under the agreement. Otherwise, the agreement would prevent just what chapter 11 contemplates: that seniors may give up rights to juniors in the interest of confirmation of a plan and rehabilitation of the debtor. The subsection also requires the court to subordinate in payment any claim for rescission of a purchase or sale of a security of the debtor or of an affiliate, or for damages arising from the purchase or sale of such a security, to all claims and interests that are senior to the claim or interest represented by the security. Thus, the later subordination varies with the claim or interest involved. If the security is a debt instrument, the damages or rescission claim will be granted the status of a general unsecured claim. If the security is an equity security, the damages or rescission claim is subordinated to all creditors and treated the same as the equity security itself.

Subsection (b) authorizes the bankruptcy court, in ordering distribution of assets, to subordinate all or any part of any claim to all or any part of another claim, regardless of the priority ranking of either claim. In addition, any lien securing such a subordinated claim may be transferred to the estate. The bill provides, however, that any subordination ordered under this provision must be based on principles of equitable subordination. These principles are defined by case law, and have generally indicated that a claim may normally be subordinated only if its holder is guilty of misconduct. As originally introduced, the bill provided specifically that a tax claim may not be subordinated on equitable grounds. The bill deletes this express exception, but the effect under the amendment should be much the same in most situations since, under the judicial doctrine of equitable subordination, a tax claim would rarely be subordinated.

Legislative Statements. Section 510(c)(1) of the House amendment represents a compromise between similar provisions in the House bill and Senate amendment. After notice and a hearing, the court may, under principles of equitable subordination, subordinate for purposes of distribution all or part of an allowed claim to all or part of another allowed claim or all or part of an allowed interest to all or part of another allowed interest. As a matter of equity, it is reasonable that a court subordinate claims to claims and interests to interests. It is intended that the term "principles of equitable subordination" follow existing case law and leave to the courts development of this principle. To date, under existing law, a claim is generally subordinated only if holder of such claim is guilty of inequitable conduct, or the claim itself is of a status susceptible to subordination, such as a penalty or a claim for damages arising from the purchase or sale of a security of the debtor. The fact that such a claim may be secured is of no consequence to the issue of subordination. However, it is inconceivable that the status of a claim as a secured claim could ever be grounds for justifying equitable subordination.

Since the House amendment authorizes subordination of claims only under principles of equitable subordination, and thus incorporates principles of existing case law, a tax claim would rarely be subordinated under this provision of the bill.

Section 511 of the Senate amendment is deleted. Its substance is adopted in section 502(b)(9) of the House amendment which reflects an identical provision contained in H.R. 8200 as passed by the House.

Effective Date of 1984 Amendments. See section 553 of Pub.L. 98–353, Title III, July 10,

1984, 98 Stat. 392, set out as an Effective Date of 1984 Amendment note preceding chapter 1 of Title 11, Bankruptcy.

Separability of Provisions. For separability of provisions of Title III of Pub.L. 98–353, see section 551 of Pub.L. 98–353 set out as a Separability of Provisions note preceding chapter 1 of Title 11, Bankruptcy.

Cross References

Applicability of this section in chapter 9 cases, see section 901.
Certain customer claims, subordination of, see section 747.
Confirmation of plan, see section 1129.
Distribution of,
    Customer property, see section 752.
    Property of estate, see section 726.
Effect of dismissal, see section 349.
Property of estate, see section 541.
Property recoverable by trustee as exempt, see section 522.
Unpaid portion of certain claims as entitled to distribution, see section 766.

Library References:

C.J.S. Bankruptcy §§ 264–266, 351.
West's Key No. Digests, Bankruptcy ⬥2967–2970.

WESTLAW Electronic Research

See WESTLAW Electronic Research Guide following the *Bankruptcy Highlights.*

SUBCHAPTER II—DEBTOR'S DUTIES AND BENEFITS

§ 521. Debtor's duties

The debtor shall—

(1) file a list of creditors, and unless the court orders otherwise, a schedule of assets and liabilities, a schedule of current income and current expenditures, and a statement of the debtor's financial affairs;

(2) if an individual debtor's schedule of assets and liabilities includes consumer debts which are secured by property of the estate—

    (A) within thirty days after the date of the filing of a petition under chapter 7 of this title or on or before the date of the meeting of creditors, whichever is earlier, or within such additional time as the court, for cause, within such period fixes, the debtor shall file with the clerk a statement of his intention with respect to the retention or surrender of such property and, if applicable, specifying that such property is claimed as exempt, that the debtor intends to redeem such property, or that the debtor intends to reaffirm debts secured by such property;

    (B) within forty-five days after the filing of a notice of intent under this section, or within such additional time as the court, for cause, within such forty-five day period fixes, the debtor shall perform his intention with respect to such property, as specified by subparagraph (A) of this paragraph; and

(C) nothing in subparagraphs (A) and (B) of this paragraph shall alter the debtor's or the trustee's rights with regard to such property under this title;

(3) if a trustee is serving in the case, cooperate with the trustee as necessary to enable the trustee to perform the trustee's duties under this title;

(4) if a trustee is serving in the case, surrender to the trustee all property of the estate and any recorded information, including books, documents, records, and papers, relating to property of the estate, whether or not immunity is granted under section 344 of this title; and

(5) appear at the hearing required under section 524(d) of this title.

Pub.L. 95–598, Nov. 6, 1978, 92 Stat. 2586; Pub.L. 98–353, Title III, §§ 305, 452, July 10, 1984, 98 Stat. 352, 375; Pub.L. 99–554, Title II, § 283(h), Oct. 27, 1986, 100 Stat. 3117.

Historical and Revision Notes

Notes of Committee on the Judiciary, Senate Report No. 95–989. This section lists three duties of the debtor in a bankruptcy case. The Rules of Bankruptcy Procedure will specify the means of carrying out these duties. The first duty is to file with the court a list of creditors and, unless the court orders otherwise, a schedule of assets and liabilities and a statement of his financial affairs. Second, the debtor is required to cooperate with the trustee as necessary to enable the trustee to perform the trustee's duties. Finally, the debtor must surrender to the trustee all property of the estate, and any recorded information, including books, documents, records, and papers, relating to property of the estate. This phrase "recorded information, including books, documents, records, and papers," has been used here and throughout the bill as a more general term, and includes such other forms of recorded information as data in computer storage or in other machine readable forms.

The list in this section is not exhaustive of the debtor's duties. Others are listed elsewhere in proposed title 11, such as in section 343, which requires the debtor to submit to examination, or in the Rules of Bankruptcy Procedure, as continued by § 404(a) of S. 2266, such as the duty to attend any hearing on discharge, Rule 402(2).

Legislative Statements. Section 521 of the House amendment modifies a comparable provision contained in the House bill and Senate amendment. The Rules of Bankruptcy Procedure should provide where the list of creditors is to be filed. In addition, the debtor is required to attend the hearing on discharge under section 524(d).

Codification. Amendment by Pub.L. 98–353 § 452 was executed to par. (4) as the probable intent of Congress although the directory language specified that the amendment be to par. (3) "as redesignated in section 305 [of Pub.L. 98–353]".

Effective Date of 1986 Amendments; Savings Provisions; Quarterly Fees. Amendment by Pub.L. 99–554 effective 30 days after Oct. 27, 1986, except as otherwise provided for, see section 302(a) of Pub.L. 99–554, set out as a note under section 581 of Title 28, Judiciary and Judicial Procedure.

Effective Date of 1984 Amendments. See section 553 of Pub.L. 98–353, Title III, July 10, 1984, 98 Stat. 392, set out as an Effective Date of 1984 Amendment note preceding chapter 1 of Title 11, Bankruptcy.

Separability of Provisions. For separability of provisions of Title III of Pub.L. 98–353, see section 551 of Pub.L. 98–353 set out as a Separability of Provisions note preceding chapter 1 of Title 11, Bankruptcy.

Cross References

Filing of list, schedule and statement by trustee, see section 1106.
Proof of claim or interest deemed filed if scheduled, see section 1111.

Property scheduled but unadministered before close of case deemed abandoned, see section 554.

Library References:

C.J.S. Bankruptcy §§ 44, 184, 186, 191.

West's Key No. Digests, Bankruptcy ⊕2321 et seq., 3022, 3063.

WESTLAW Electronic Research

See WESTLAW Electronic Research Guide following the *Bankruptcy Highlights.*

§ 522. Exemptions   *NH Rev. Stat. Ann 511:2 (1983)*

(a) In this section— *(State supercedes Federal)*

(1) "dependent" includes spouse, whether or not actually dependent; and

(2) "value" means fair market value as of the date of the filing of the petition or, with respect to property that becomes property of the estate after such date, as of the date such property becomes property of the estate.

(b) Notwithstanding section 541 of this title, an individual debtor may exempt from property of the estate the property listed in either paragraph (1) or, in the alternative, paragraph (2) of this subsection. In joint cases filed under section 302 of this title and individual cases filed under section 301 or 303 of this title by or against debtors who are husband and wife, and whose estates are ordered to be jointly administered under Rule 1015(b) of the Bankruptcy Rules, one debtor may not elect to exempt property listed in paragraph (1) and the other debtor elect to exempt property listed in paragraph (2) of this subsection. If the parties cannot agree on the alternative to be elected, they shall be deemed to elect paragraph (1), where such election is permitted under the law of the jurisdiction where the case is filed. Such property is—

(1) property that is specified under subsection (d) of this section, unless the State law that is applicable to the debtor under paragraph (2)(A) of this subsection specifically does not so authorize; or, in the alternative,

(2)(A) any property that is exempt under Federal law, other than subsection (d) of this section, or State or local law that is applicable on the date of the filing of the petition at the place in which the debtor's domicile has been located for the 180 days immediately preceding the date of the filing of the petition, or for a longer portion of such 180-day period than in any other place; and

(B) any interest in property in which the debtor had, immediately before the commencement of the case, an interest as a tenant by the entirety or joint tenant to the extent that such interest as a tenant by the entirety or joint tenant is exempt from process under applicable nonbankruptcy law.

(c) Unless the case is dismissed, property exempted under this section is not liable during or after the case for any debt of the debtor that arose, or that is determined under section 502 of this title as if such debt had arisen, before the commencement of the case, except—

(1) a debt of a kind specified in section 523(a)(1) or 523(a)(5) of this title;

(2) a debt secured by a lien that is—

(A)(i) not avoided under subsection (f) or (g) of this section or under section 544, 545, 547, 548, 549, or 724(a) of this title; and

151

(ii) not void under section 506(d) of this title; or

(B) a tax lien, notice of which is properly filed; or

(3) a debt of a kind specified in section 523(a)(4) or 523(a)(6) of this title owed by an institution-affiliated party of an insured depository institution to a Federal depository institutions regulatory agency acting in its capacity as conservator, receiver, or liquidating agent for such institution.

(d) The following property may be exempted under subsection (b)(1) of this section:

(1) The debtor's aggregate interest, not to exceed $7,500 in value, in real property or personal property that the debtor or a dependent of the debtor uses as a residence, in a cooperative that owns property that the debtor or a dependent of the debtor uses as a residence, or in a burial plot for the debtor or a dependent of the debtor.

(2) The debtor's interest, not to exceed $1,200 in value, in one motor vehicle.

(3) The debtor's interest, not to exceed $200 in value in any particular item or $4,000 in aggregate value, in household furnishings, household goods, wearing apparel, appliances, books, animals, crops, or musical instruments, that are held primarily for the personal, family, or household use of the debtor or a dependent of the debtor.

(4) The debtor's aggregate interest, not to exceed $500 in value, in jewelry held primarily for the personal, family, or household use of the debtor or a dependent of the debtor.

(5) The debtor's aggregate interest in any property, not to exceed in value $400 plus up to $3,750 of any unused amount of the exemption provided under paragraph (1) of this subsection.

(6) The debtor's aggregate interest, not to exceed $750 in value, in any implements, professional books, or tools, of the trade of the debtor or the trade of a dependent of the debtor.

(7) Any unmatured life insurance contract owned by the debtor, other than a credit life insurance contract.

(8) The debtor's aggregate interest, not to exceed in value $4,000 less any amount of property of the estate transferred in the manner specified in section 542(d) of this title, in any accrued dividend or interest under, or loan value of, any unmatured life insurance contract owned by the debtor under which the insured is the debtor or an individual of whom the debtor is a dependent.

(9) Professionally prescribed health aids for the debtor or a dependent of the debtor.

(10) The debtor's right to receive—

(A) a social security benefit, unemployment compensation, or a local public assistance benefit;

(B) a veterans' benefit;

(C) a disability, illness, or unemployment benefit;

(D) alimony, support, or separate maintenance, to the extent reasonably necessary for the support of the debtor and any dependent of the debtor;

    (E) a payment under a stock bonus, pension, profitsharing, annuity, or similar plan or contract on account of illness, disability, death, age, or length of service, to the extent reasonably necessary for the support of the debtor and any dependent of the debtor, unless—

        (i) such plan or contract was established by or under the auspices of an insider that employed the debtor at the time the debtor's rights under such plan or contract arose;

        (ii) such payment is on account of age or length of service; and

        (iii) such plan or contract does not qualify under section 401(a), 403(a), 403(b), 408, or 409 of the Internal Revenue Code of 1954 (26 U.S.C. 401(a), 403(a), 403(b), 408, or 409).

  (11) The debtor's right to receive, or property that is traceable to—

    (A) an award under a crime victim's reparation law;

    (B) a payment on account of the wrongful death of an individual of whom the debtor was a dependent, to the extent reasonably necessary for the support of the debtor and any dependent of the debtor;

    (C) a payment under a life insurance contract that insured the life of an individual of whom the debtor was a dependent on the date of such individual's death, to the extent reasonably necessary for the support of the debtor and any dependent of the debtor;

    (D) a payment, not to exceed $7,500, on account of personal bodily injury, not including pain and suffering or compensation for actual pecuniary loss, of the debtor or an individual of whom the debtor is a dependent; or

    (E) a payment in compensation of loss of future earnings of the debtor or an individual of whom the debtor is or was a dependent, to the extent reasonably necessary for the support of the debtor and any dependent of the debtor.

  (e) A waiver of an exemption executed in favor of a creditor that holds an unsecured claim against the debtor is unenforceable in a case under this title with respect to such claim against property that the debtor may exempt under subsection (b) of this section. A waiver by the debtor of a power under subsection (f) or (h) of this section to avoid a transfer, under subsection (g) or (i) of this section to exempt property, or under subsection (i) of this section to recover property or to preserve a transfer, is unenforceable in a case under this title.

  (f) Notwithstanding any waiver of exemptions, the debtor may avoid the fixing of a lien on an interest of the debtor in property to the extent that such lien impairs an exemption to which the debtor would have been entitled under subsection (b) of this section, if such lien is—

  (1) a judicial lien; or

  (2) a nonpossessory, nonpurchase-money security interest in any—

    (A) household furnishings, household goods, wearing apparel, appliances, books, animals, crops, musical instruments, or jewelry that are held primarily for the personal, family, or household use of the debtor or a dependent of the debtor;

      (B) implements, professional books, or tools, of the trade of the debtor or the trade of a dependent of the debtor; or

      (C) professionally prescribed health aids for the debtor or a dependent of the debtor.

  (g) Notwithstanding sections 550 and 551 of this title, the debtor may exempt under subsection (b) of this section property that the trustee recovers under section 510(c)(2), 542, 543, 550, 551, or 553 of this title, to the extent that the debtor could have exempted such property under subsection (b) of this section if such property had not been transferred, if—

      (1)(A) such transfer was not a voluntary transfer of such property by the debtor; and

      (B) the debtor did not conceal such property; or

      (2) the debtor could have avoided such transfer under subsection (f)(2) of this section.

  (h) The debtor may avoid a transfer of property of the debtor or recover a setoff to the extent that the debtor could have exempted such property under subsection (g)(1) of this section if the trustee had avoided such transfer, if—

      (1) such transfer is avoidable by the trustee under section 544, 545, 547, 548, 549, or 724(a) of this title or recoverable by the trustee under section 553 of this title; and

      (2) the trustee does not attempt to avoid such transfer.

  (i)(1) If the debtor avoids a transfer or recovers a setoff under subsection (f) or (h) of this section, the debtor may recover in the manner prescribed by, and subject to the limitations of, section 550 of this title, the same as if the trustee had avoided such transfer, and may exempt any property so recovered under subsection (b) of this section.

  (2) Notwithstanding section 551 of this title, a transfer avoided under section 544, 545, 547, 548, 549, or 724(a) of this title, under subsection (f) or (h) of this section, or property recovered under section 553 of this title, may be preserved for the benefit of the debtor to the extent that the debtor may exempt such property under subsection (g) of this section or paragraph (1) of this subsection.

  (j) Notwithstanding subsections (g) and (i) of this section, the debtor may exempt a particular kind of property under subsections (g) and (i) of this section only to the extent that the debtor has exempted less property in value of such kind than that to which the debtor is entitled under subsection (b) of this section.

  (k) Property that the debtor exempts under this section is not liable for payment of any administrative expense except—

      (1) the aliquot share of the costs and expenses of avoiding a transfer of property that the debtor exempts under subsection (g) of this section, or of recovery of such property, that is attributable to the value of the portion of such property exempted in relation to the value of the property recovered; and

      (2) any costs and expenses of avoiding a transfer under subsection (f) or (h) of this section, or of recovery of property under subsection (i)(1) of this section, that the debtor has not paid.

(*l*) The debtor shall file a list of property that the debtor claims as exempt under subsection (b) of this section. If the debtor does not file such a list, a dependent of the debtor may file such a list, or may claim property as exempt from property of the estate on behalf of the debtor. Unless a party in interest objects, the property claimed as exempt on such list is exempt.

(m) Subject to the limitation in subsection (b), this section shall apply separately with respect to each debtor in a joint case.

Pub.L. 95–598, Nov. 6, 1978, 92 Stat. 2586; Pub.L. 98–353, Title III, §§ 306, 453, July 10, 1984, 98 Stat. 353, 375; Pub.L. 99–554, Title II, § 283(i), Oct. 27, 1986, 100 Stat. 3117; Pub.L. 101–647, Title XXV, § 2522(b), Nov. 29, 1990, 104 Stat. 4866.

Historical and Revision Notes

Notes of Committee on the Judiciary, Senate Report No. 95–989. Subsection (a) of this section defines two terms: "dependent" includes the debtor's spouse, whether or not actually dependent; and "value" means fair market value as of the date of the filing of the petition.

Subsection (b) tracts current law. It permits a debtor the exemptions to which he is entitled under other Federal law and the law of the State of his domicile. Some of the items that may be exempted under Federal laws other than title 11 include:

Foreign Service Retirement and Disability payments, 22 U.S.C. 1104 [section 1104 of Title 22, Foreign Relations and Intercourse];

Social security payments, 42 U.S.C. 407 [section 407 of Title 42, The Public Health and Welfare];

Injury or death compensation payments from war risk hazards, 42 U.S.C. 1717 [section 1717 of Title 42];

Wages of fishermen, seamen, and apprentices, 46 U.S.C. 601 [section 601 of Title 46, Shipping];

Civil service retirement benefits, 5 U.S.C. 729, 2265 [sections 729 and 2265 of Title 5, Government Organization and Employees];

Longshoremen's and Harbor Workers' Compensation Act death and disability benefits, 33 U.S.C. 916 [section 916 of Title 33, Navigation and Navigable Waters];

Railroad Retirement Act annuities and pensions, 45 U.S.C. 228(L) [former section 228*l* of Title 45, Railroads];

Veterans benefits, 45 U.S.C. 352(E) [section 352(e) of Title 45];

Special pensions paid to winners of the Congressional Medal of Honor, 38 U.S.C. 3101 [section 3101 of Title 38, Veterans' Benefits]; and

Federal homestead lands on debts contracted before issuance of the patent, 43 U.S.C. 175 [section 175 of Title 43, Public Lands].

He may also exempt an interest in property in which the debtor had an interest as a tenant by the entirety or joint tenant to the extent that interest would have been exempt from process under applicable nonbankruptcy law.

Under proposed section 541, all property of the debtor becomes property of the estate, but the debtor is permitted to exempt certain property from property of the estate under this section. Property may be exempted even if it is subject to a lien, but only the unencumbered portion of the property is to be counted in computing the "value" of the property for the purposes of exemption.

As under current law, the debtor will be permitted to convert nonexempt property into exempt property before filing a bankruptcy petition. The practice is not fraudulent as to creditors, and permits the debtor to make full use of the exemptions to which he is entitled under the law.

Subsection (c) insulates exempt property from prepetition claims other than tax claims (whether or not dischargeable), and other than alimony, maintenance, or support claims that are excepted from discharge. The bankruptcy discharge does not prevent enforcement of valid liens. The rule of Long v. Bullard, 117 U.S. 617 (1886) [6 S.Ct. 917, 29 L.Ed. 1004], is accepted with respect to the enforcement of valid liens on nonexempt property as well as on exempt property. Cf. Louisville Joint

Stock Land Bank v. Radford, 295 U.S. 555, 583 (1935) [55 S.Ct. 854].

Subsection (c)(3) permits the collection of dischargeable taxes from exempt assets. Only assets exempted from levy under Section 6334 of the Internal Revenue Code [section 6334 of Title 26, Internal Revenue Code] or under applicable state or local tax law cannot be applied to satisfy these tax claims. This rule applies to prepetition tax claims against the debtor regardless of whether the claims do or do not receive priority and whether they are dischargeable or nondischargeable. Thus, even if a tax is dischargeable vis-a-vis the debtor's after-acquired assets, it may nevertheless be collectible from exempt property held by the estate. (Taxes incurred by the debtor's estate which are collectible as first priority administrative expenses are not collectible from the debtor's estate which are collectible as first priority administrative expenses are not collectible from the debtor's exempt assets.)

Subsection (d) protects the debtor's exemptions, either Federal or State, by making unenforceable in a bankruptcy case a waiver of exemptions or a waiver of the debtor's avoiding powers under the following subsections.

Subsection (e) protects the debtor's exemptions, his discharge, and thus his fresh start by permitting him to avoid certain liens on exempt property. The debtor may avoid a judicial lien on any property to the extent that the property could have been exempted in the absence of the lien, and may similarly avoid a nonpurchase-money security interest in certain household and personal goods. The avoiding power is independent of any waiver of exemptions.

Subsection (f) gives the debtor the ability to exempt property that the trustee recovers under one of the trustee's avoiding powers if the property was involuntarily transferred away from the debtor (such as by the fixing of a judicial lien) and if the debtor did not conceal the property. The debtor is also permitted to exempt property that the trustee recovers as the result of the avoiding of the fixing of certain security interests to the extent that the debtor could otherwise have exempted the property.

Subsection (g) provides that if the trustee does not exercise an avoiding power to recover a transfer of property that would be exempt, the debtor may exercise it and exempt the property, if the transfer was involuntary and the debtor did not conceal the property. If

the debtor wishes to preserve his right to pursue any action under this provision, then he must intervene in any action brought by the trustee based on the same cause of action. It is not intended that the debtor be given an additional opportunity to avoid a transfer or that the transferee should have to defend the same action twice. Rather, the section is primarily designed to give the debtor the rights the trustee could have, but has not, pursued. The debtor is given no greater rights under this provision than the trustee, and thus, the debtor's avoiding powers under proposed sections 544, 545, 547, and 548, are subject to proposed 546, as are the trustee's powers.

These subsections are cumulative. The debtor is not required to choose which he will use to gain an exemption. Instead, he may use more than one in any particular instance, just as the trustee's avoiding powers are cumulative.

Subsection (h) permits recovery by the debtor of property transferred by an avoided transfer from either the initial or subsequent transferees. It also permits preserving a transfer for the benefit of the debtor. In either event, the debtor may exempt the property recovered or preserved.

Subsection (i) makes clear that the debtor may exempt property under the avoiding subsections (f) and (h) only to the extent he has exempted less property than allowed under subsection (b).

Subsection (j) makes clear that the liability of the debtor's exempt property is limited to the debtor's aliquot share of the costs and expenses recovery of property that the trustee recovers and the debtor later exempts, and any costs and expenses of avoiding a transfer by the debtor that the debtor has not already paid.

Subsection (k) requires the debtor to file a list of property that he claims as exempt from property of the estate. Absent an objection to the list, the property is exempted. A dependent of the debtor may file it and thus be protected if the debtor fails to file the list.

Subsection (l) provides the rule for a joint case.

Notes of Committee on the Judiciary, House Report No. 95–595. Subsection (a) of this section defines two terms: "dependent" includes the debtor's spouse, whether or not actually dependent; and "value" means fair market value as of the date of the filing of the petition.

Subsection (b), the operative subsection of this section, is a significant departure from present law. It permits an individual debtor in a bankruptcy case a choice between exemption systems. The debtor may choose the Federal exemptions prescribed in subsection (d), or he may choose the exemptions to which he is entitled under other Federal law and the law of the State of his domicile. If the debtor chooses the latter, some of the items that may be exempted under other Federal laws include:

—Foreign Service Retirement and Disability payments, 22 U.S.C. 1104 [section 1104 of Title 22, Foreign Relations and Intercourse];

—Social security payments, 42 U.S.C. 407 [section 407 of Title 42, The Public Health and Welfare];

—Injury or death compensation payments from war risk hazards, 42 U.S.C. 1717 [section 1717 of Title 42];

—Wages of fishermen, seamen, and apprentices, 46 U.S.C. 601 [section 601 of Title 46, Shipping];

—Civil service retirement benefits, 5 U.S.C. 729, 2265 [sections 729, 2265 of Title 5, Government Organization and Employees];

—Longshoremen's and Harbor Workers' Compensation Act death and disability benefits, 33 U.S.C. 916 [section 916 of Title 33, Navigation and Navigable Waters];

—Railroad Retirement Act annuities and pensions, 45 U.S.C. 228(*l*) [231m]; [former section 228*l* of Title 45, Railroads];

—Veterans benefits, 45 U.S.C. 352(E) [section 352(e) of Title 45];

—Special pensions paid to winners of the Congressional Medal of Honor, 38 U.S.C. 3101 [section 3101 of Title 38, Veterans' Benefits]; and

—Federal homestead lands on debts contracted before issuance of the patent, 43 U.S.C. 175 [section 175 of Title 43, Public Lands].

He may also exempt an interest in property in which the debtor had an interest as a tenant by the entirety or joint tenant to the extent that interest would have been exempt from process under applicable nonbankruptcy law. The Rules will provide for the situation where the debtor's choice of exemption, Federal or State, was improvident and should be changed, for example, where the court has ruled against the debtor with respect to a major exemption.

Under proposed 11 U.S.C. 541, all property of the debtor becomes property of the estate, but the debtor is permitted to exempt certain property from property of the estate under this section. Property may be exempted even if it is subject to a lien, but only the unencumbered portion of the property is to be counted in computing the "value" of the property for the purposes of exemption. Thus, for example, a residence worth $30,000 with a mortgage of $25,000 will be exemptable to the extent of $5,000. This follows current law. The remaining value of the property will be dealt with in the bankruptcy case as is any interest in property that is subject to a lien.

As under current law, the debtor will be permitted to convert nonexempt property into exempt property before filing a bankruptcy petition. See Hearings, pt. 3, at 1355–58. The practice is not fraudulent as to creditors and permits the debtor to make full use of the exemptions to which he is entitled under the law.

Subsection (c) insulates exempt property from prepetition claims, except tax and alimony, maintenance, or support claims that are excepted from discharge. The bankruptcy discharge will not prevent enforcement of valid liens. The rule of Long v. Bullard, 117 U.S. 617 (1886) [6 S.Ct. 917, 29 L.Ed. 1004], is accepted with respect to the enforcement of valid liens on nonexempt property as well as on exempt property. Cf. Louisville Joint Stock Land Bank v. Radford, 295 U.S. 555, 583 (1935) [55 S.Ct. 854].

Subsection (d) specifies the Federal exemptions to which the debtor is entitled. They are derived in large part from the Uniform Exemptions Act, promulgated by the Commissioners of Uniform State Laws in August, 1976. Eleven categories of property are exempted. First is a homestead to the extent of $10,000, which may be claimed in real or personal property that the debtor or a dependent of the debtor uses as a residence. Second, the debtor may exempt a motor vehicle to the extent of $1500. Third, the debtor may exempt household goods, furnishings, clothing, and similar household items, held primarily for the personal, family, or household use of the debtor or a dependent of the debtor. "Animals" includes all animals, such as pets, livestock, poultry, and fish, if they are held primarily for personal, family or household use. The limitation for third category items is $300 on any particular item. The debtor may also exempt up to $750 of personal jewelry.

Paragraph (5) permits the exemption of $500, plus any unused amount of the homestead exemption, in any property, in order not to discriminate against the nonhomeowner. Paragraph (6) grants the debtor up to $1000 in implements, professional books, or tools, of the trade of the debtor or a dependent. Paragraph (7) exempts a life insurance contract, other than a credit life insurance contract, owned by the debtor. This paragraph refers to the life insurance contract itself. It does not encompass any other rights under the contract, such as the right to borrow out the loan value. Because of this provision, the trustee may not surrender a life insurance contract, which remains property of the debtor if he chooses the Federal exemptions. Paragraph (8) permits the debtor to exempt up to $5000 in loan value in a life insurance policy owned by the debtor under which the debtor or an individual of whom the debtor is a dependent is the insured. The exemption provided by this paragraph and paragraph (7) will also include the debtor's rights in a group insurance certificate under which the insured is an individual of whom the debtor is a dependent (assuming the debtor has rights in the policy that could be exempted) or the debtor. A trustee is authorized to collect the entire loan value on every life insurance policy owned by the debtor as property of the estate. First, however, the debtor will choose which policy or policies under which the loan value will be exempted. The $5000 figure is reduced by the amount of any automatic premium loan authorized after the date of the filing of the petition under section 542(d). Paragraph (9) exempts professionally prescribed health aids.

Paragraph (10) exempts certain benefits that are akin to future earnings of the debtor. These include social security, unemployment compensation, or public assistance benefits, veteran's benefits, disability, illness, or unemployment benefits, alimony, support, or separate maintenance (but only to the extent reasonably necessary for the support of the debtor and any dependents of the debtor), and benefits under a certain stock bonus, pension, profitsharing, annuity or similar plan based on illness, disability, death, age or length of service. Paragraph (11) allows the debtor to exempt certain compensation for losses. These include crime victim's reparation benefits, wrongful death benefits (with a reasonably necessary for support limitation), life in-

surance proceeds (same limitation), compensation for bodily injury, not including pain and suffering ($10,000 limitation), and loss of future earnings payments (support limitation). This provision in subparagraph (D) (11) is designed to cover payments in compensation of actual bodily injury, such as the loss of a limb, and is not intended to include the attendant costs that accompany such a loss, such as medical payments, pain and suffering, or loss of earnings. Those items are handled separately by the bill.

Subsection (e) protects the debtor's exemptions, either Federal or State, by making unenforceable in a bankruptcy case a waiver of exemptions or a waiver of the debtor's avoiding powers under the following subsections.

Subsection (f) protects the debtor's exemptions, his discharge, and thus his fresh start by permitting him to avoid certain liens on exempt property. The debtor may avoid a judicial lien on any property to the extent that the property could have been exempted in the absence of the lien, and may similarly avoid a nonpurchase-money security interest in certain household and personal goods. The avoiding power is independent of any waiver of exemptions.

Subsection (g) gives the debtor the ability to exempt property that the trustee recovers under one of the trustee's avoiding powers if the property was involuntarily transferred away from the debtor (such as by the fixing of a judicial lien) and if the debtor did not conceal the property. The debtor is also permitted to exempt property that the trustee recovers as the result of the avoiding of the fixing of certain security interests to the extent that the debtor could otherwise have exempted the property.

If the trustee does not pursue an avoiding power to recover a transfer of property that would be exempt, the debtor may pursue it and exempt the property, if the transfer was involuntary and the debtor did not conceal the property. If the debtor wishes to preserve his right to pursue an action under this provision, then he must intervene in any action brought by the trustee based on the same cause of action. It is not intended that the debtor be given an additional opportunity to avoid a transfer or that the transferee have to defend the same action twice. Rather, the section is primarily designed to give the debtor the rights the trustee could have pursued if the trustee chooses not to pursue them. The debtor is given no greater rights under this provision than the trustee, and thus the debtor's avoiding powers under proposed 11 U.S.C. 544, 545, 547, and 548, are subject to proposed 11 U.S.C. 546, as are the trustee's powers.

These subsections are cumulative. The debtor is not required to choose which he will use to gain an exemption. Instead, he may use more than one in any particular instance, just as the trustee's avoiding powers are cumulative.

Subsection (i) permits recovery by the debtor of property transferred in an avoided transfer from either the initial or subsequent transferees. It also permits preserving a transfer for the benefit of the debtor. Under either case the debtor may exempt the property recovered or preserved.

Subsection (k) makes clear that the debtor's aliquot share of the costs and expenses [for] recovery of property that the trustee recovers and the debtor later exempts, and any costs and expenses of avoiding a transfer by the debtor that the debtor has not already paid.

Subsection (*l*) requires the debtor to file a list of property that he claims as exempt from property of the estate. Absent an objection to the list, the property is exempted. A dependent of the debtor may file it and thus be protected if the debtor fails to file the list.

Subsection (m) requires the clerk of the bankruptcy court to give notice of any exemptions claimed under subsection (*l*), in order that parties in interest may have an opportunity to object to the claim.

Subsection (n) provides the rule for a joint case: each debtor is entitled to the Federal exemptions provided under this section or to the State exemptions, whichever the debtor chooses.

Legislative Statements. Section 522 of the House amendment represents a compromise on the issue of exemptions between the position taken in the House bill, and that taken in the Senate amendment. Dollar amounts specified in section 522(d) of the House bill have been reduced from amounts as contained in H.R. 8200 as passed by the House. The States may, by passing a law, determine whether the Federal exemptions will apply as an alternative to State exemptions in bankruptcy cases.

Section 522(c)(1) tracks the House bill and provides that dischargeable tax claims may not be collected out of exempt property.

Section 522(f)(2) is derived from the Senate amendment restricting the debtor to avoidance of nonpossessory, nonpurchase money security interests.

Section 522(c)(1) of the House amendment adopts a provision contained in the House bill that dischargeable taxes cannot be collected from exempt assets. This changes present law, which allows collection of dischargeable taxes from exempt property, a rule followed in the Senate amendment. Nondischargeable taxes, however, will continue to the [be] collectable out of exempt property. It is anticipated that in the next session Congress will review the exemptions from levy currently contained in the Internal Revenue Code [Title 26] with a view to increasing the exemptions to more realistic levels.

References in Text. Sections 401(a), 403(a), 403(b), 408, and 409 of the Internal Revenue Code of 1954, referred to in subsec. (d)(10)(E), are classified to sections 401(a), 403(a), 403(b), 408, and 409 of Title 26, Internal Revenue Code.

Effective Date of 1986 Amendments; Savings Provisions; Quarterly Fees. Amendment by Pub.L. 99–554 effective 30 days after Oct. 27, 1986, except as otherwise provided for, see section 302(a) of Pub.L. 99–554, set out as a note under section 581 of Title 28, Judiciary and Judicial Procedure.

Effective Date of 1984 Amendments. See section 553 of Pub.L. 98–353, Title III, July 10, 1984, 98 Stat. 392, set out as an Effective Date of 1984 Amendment note preceding chapter 1, of Title 11, Bankruptcy.

Separability of Provisions. For separability of provisions of Title III of Pub.L. 98–353, see section 551 of Pub.L. 98–353 set out as a Separability of Provisions note preceding chapter 1 of Title 11, Bankruptcy.

Cross References

Allowance of claims or interests, see section 502.

Automatic preservation of avoided transfer, see section 551.

Effect of dismissal, see section 349.

Insolvent as meaning financial condition wherein entity's debts are greater than entity's property exclusive of property that may be exempted under this section, see section 101.

Provisions in plan for use, sale or lease of exempt property, see section 1123.

Redemption, see section 722.
Turnover of property to estate, see section 542.

Library References:

C.J.S. Bankruptcy § 172 et seq.
West's Key No. Digests, Bankruptcy ⊕2761 et seq.

WESTLAW Electronic Research

See WESTLAW Electronic Research Guide following the *Bankruptcy Highlights.*

§ 523. Exceptions to discharge

(a) A discharge under section 727, 1141, 1228(a), 1228(b), or 1328(b) of this title does not discharge an individual debtor from any debt—

(1) for a tax or a customs duty—

(A) of the kind and for the periods specified in section 507(a)(2) or 507(a)(7) of this title, whether or not a claim for such tax was filed or allowed;

(B) with respect to which a return, if required—

(i) was not filed; or

(ii) was filed after the date on which such return was last due, under applicable law or under any extension, and after two years before the date of the filing of the petition; or

(C) with respect to which the debtor made a fraudulent return or willfully attempted in any manner to evade or defeat such tax;

(2) for money, property, services, or an extension, renewal, or refinancing of credit, to the extent obtained by—

(A) false pretenses, a false representation, or actual fraud, other than a statement respecting the debtor's or an insider's financial condition;

(B) use of a statement in writing—

(i) that is materially false;

(ii) respecting the debtor's or an insider's financial condition;

(iii) on which the creditor to whom the debtor is liable for such money, property, services, or credit reasonably relied; and

(iv) that the debtor caused to be made or published with intent to deceive; or

(C) for purposes of subparagraph (A) of this paragraph, consumer debts owed to a single creditor and aggregating more than $500 for "luxury goods or services" incurred by an individual debtor on or within forty days before the order for relief under this title, or cash advances aggregating more than $1,000 that are extensions of consumer credit under an open end credit plan obtained by an individual debtor on or within twenty days before the order for relief under this title, are presumed to be nondischargeable; "luxury goods or services" do not include goods or services reasonably acquired for the support or maintenance of the debtor or a dependent of the debtor; an extension of consumer credit under an open end credit plan is to be defined for purposes of this subparagraph as it is defined in the Consumer Credit Protection Act (15 U.S.C. 1601 et seq.);

(3) neither listed nor scheduled under section 521(1) of this title, with the name, if known to the debtor, of the creditor to whom such debt is owed, in time to permit—

(A) if such debt is not of a kind specified in paragraph (2), (4), or (6) of this subsection, timely filing of a proof of claim, unless such creditor had notice or actual knowledge of the case in time for such timely filing; or

(B) if such debt is of a kind specified in paragraph (2), (4), or (6) of this subsection, timely filing of a proof of claim and timely request for a determination of dischargeability of such debt under one of such paragraphs, unless such creditor had notice or actual knowledge of the case in time for such timely filing and request;

(4) for fraud or defalcation while acting in a fiduciary capacity, embezzlement, or larceny;

(5) to a spouse, former spouse, or child of the debtor, for alimony to, maintenance for, or support of such spouse or child, in connection with a separation agreement, divorce decree or other order of a court of record, determination made in accordance with state or territorial law by a governmental unit, or property settlement agreement, but not to the extent that—

(A) such debt is assigned to another entity, voluntarily, by operation of law, or otherwise (other than debts assigned pursuant to section 402(a)(26) of the Social Security Act, or any such debt which has been assigned to the Federal Government or to a State or any political subdivision of such State); or

(B) such debt includes a liability designated as alimony, maintenance, or support, unless such liability is actually in the nature of alimony, maintenance, or support;

(6) for willful and malicious injury by the debtor to another entity or to the property of another entity;

(7) to the extent such debt is for a fine, penalty, or forfeiture payable to and for the benefit of a governmental unit, and is not compensation for actual pecuniary loss, other than a tax penalty—

(A) relating to a tax of a kind not specified in paragraph (1) of this subsection; or

(B) imposed with respect to a transaction or event that occurred before three years before the date of the filing of the petition;

(8) for an educational loan made, insured, or guaranteed by a governmental unit, or made under any program funded in whole or in part by a governmental unit or a nonprofit institution, unless—

(A) such loan first became due before five years (exclusive of any applicable suspension of the repayment period) before the date of the filing of the petition; or

(B) excepting such debt from discharge under this paragraph will impose an undue hardship on the debtor and the debtor's dependents;

(9) for death or personal injury caused by the debtor's operation of a motor vehicle if such operation was unlawful because the debtor was intoxicated from using alcohol, a drug, or another substance;

(10) that was or could have been listed or scheduled by the debtor in a prior case concerning the debtor under this title or under the Bankruptcy Act in which the debtor waived discharge, or was denied a discharge under section 727(a)(2), (3), (4), (5), (6), or (7) of this title, or under section 14c(1), (2), (3), (4), (6), or (7) of such Act;

(11) provided in any final judgment, unreviewable order, or consent order or decree entered in any court of the United States or of any State, issued by a Federal depository institutions regulatory agency, or contained in any settlement agreement entered into by the debtor, arising from any act of fraud or defalcation while acting in a fiduciary capacity committed with respect to any depository institution or insured credit union; or

(12) for malicious or reckless failure to fulfill any commitment by the debtor to a Federal depository institutions regulatory agency to maintain the capital of an insured depository institution, except that this paragraph shall not extend any such commitment which would otherwise be terminated due to any act of such agency.

(b) Notwithstanding subsection (a) of this section, a debt that was excepted from discharge under subsection (a)(1), (a)(3), or (a)(8) of this section, under section 17a(1), 17a(3), or 17a(5) of the Bankruptcy Act, under section 439A of the Higher Education Act of 1965 (20 U.S.C. 1087-3), or under section 733(g) of the Public Health Service Act (42 U.S.C. 294f) in a prior case concerning the debtor under this title, or under the Bankruptcy Act, is dischargeable in a case under this title unless, by the terms of subsection (a) of this section, such debt is not dischargeable in the case under this title.

(c)(1) Except as provided in subsection (a)(3)(B) of this section, the debtor shall be discharged from a debt of a kind specified in paragraph (2), (4), or (6) of subsection (a) of this section, unless, on request of the creditor to whom such debt is owed, and after notice and a hearing, the court determines such debt to be excepted from discharge under paragraph (2), (4), or (6), as the case may be, of subsection (a) of this section.

(2) Paragraph (1) shall not apply in the case of a Federal depository institutions regulatory agency seeking, in its capacity as conservator, receiver, or liquidating agent for an insured depository institution, to recover a debt described in subsection (a)(2), (a)(4), (a)(6), or (a)(11) owed to such institution by an institution-affiliated party unless the receiver, conservator, or liquidating agent was appointed in time to reasonably comply, or for a Federal depository institutions regulatory agency acting in its corporate capacity as a successor to such receiver, conservator, or liquidating agent to reasonably comply, with subsection (a)(3)(B) as a creditor of such institution-affiliated party with respect to such debt.

(d) If a creditor requests a determination of dischargeability of a consumer debt under subsection (a)(2) of this section, and such debt is discharged, the court shall grant judgment in favor of the debtor for the costs of, and a reasonable attorney's fee for, the proceeding if the court finds that the position of the creditor was not substantially justified, except that the court shall not award such costs and fees if special circumstances would make the award unjust.

(e) Any institution-affiliated party of a depository institution or insured credit union shall be considered to be acting in a fiduciary capacity with respect to the purposes of subsection (a)(4) or (11).

Pub.L. 95–598, Nov. 6, 1978, 92 Stat. 2590; Pub.L. 96–56, § 3, Aug. 14, 1979, 93 Stat. 387; Pub.L. 97–35, Title XXIII, § 2334(b), Aug. 13, 1981, 95 Stat. 863; Pub. L. 98–353, Title III, §§ 307, 371, 454, July 10, 1984, 98 Stat. 353, 364, 375; Pub.L. 99–554, Title II, §§ 257(n), 281, 283(j), Oct. 27, 1986, 100 Stat. 3115–3117; Pub.L. 101–581, § 2(a), Nov. 15, 1990, 104 Stat. 2865; Pub.L. 101–647, Title XXV, § 2522(a), Title XXXI, § 3102, Title XXXVI, § 3621, Nov. 29, 1990, 104 Stat. 4865, 4866, 4916, 4964, 4965.

Amendment of Subsec. (a)(8)

Pub.L. 101–647, Title XXXVI, §§ 3621, 3631, Nov. 29, 1990, 104 Stat. 4964, 4965, provided that, effective 180 days after Nov. 29, 1990, and except as provided, subsec. (a)(8) is amended as follows:

(1) by striking "for an educational" and all that follows through "unless", and inserting the following: "for an educational benefit overpayment or loan made, insured or guaranteed by a governmental unit, or made under any program funded in whole or in part by a governmental unit or nonprofit institution, or for an obligation to repay funds received as an educational benefit, scholarship or stipend, unless"; and

(2) by amending subparagraph (A) to read as follows:

"(A) such loan, benefit, scholarship, or stipend overpayment first became due more than 7 years (exclusive of any applicable suspension of the repayment period) before the date of the filing of the petition; or".

Historical and Revision Notes

Notes of Committee on the Judiciary, Senate Report No. 95–989. This section specifies which of the debtor's debts are not discharged in a bankruptcy case, and certain procedures for effectuating the section. The provision in Bankruptcy Act § 17c [former section 35(c) of this title] granting the bankruptcy courts jurisdiction to determine dischargeability is deleted as unnecessary, in view of the comprehensive grant of jurisdiction prescribed in proposed 28 U.S.C. 1334(b), which is adequate to cover the full jurisdiction that the bankruptcy courts have today over dischargeability and related issues under Bankruptcy Act § 17c [former section 35(c) of this title]. The Rules of Bankruptcy Procedure will specify, as they do today, who may request determinations of dischargeability, subject, of course, to proposed 11 U.S.C. 523(c), and when such a request may be made. Proposed 11 U.S.C. 350, providing for reopening of cases, provides one possible procedure for a determination of dischargeability and related issues after a case is closed.

Subsection (a) lists nine kinds of debts excepted from discharge. Taxes that are excepted from discharge are set forth in paragraph (1). These include claims against the debtor which receive priority in the second, third and sixth categories (§ 507(a)(3)(B) and (C) and (6)). These categories include taxes for which the tax authority failed to file a claim against the estate or filed its claim late. Whether or not the taxing authority's claim is secured will also not affect the claim's nondischargeability if the tax liability in question is otherwise entitled to priority.

Also included in the nondischargeable debts are taxes for which the debtor had not filed a required return as of the petition date, or for which a return had been filed beyond its last permitted due date (§ 523(a)(1)(B)). For this purpose, the date of the tax year to which the return relates is immaterial. The late return rule applies, however, only to the late returns filed within three years before the petition was filed, and to late returns filed after the petition in title 11 was filed. For this purpose, the taxable year in question need not be one or more of the three years immediately preceding the filing of the petition.

Tax claims with respect to which the debtor filed a fraudulent return, entry or invoice, or fraudulently attempted to evade or defeat any tax (§ 523(a)(1)(C)) are included. The date of the taxable year with regard to which the fraud occurred is immaterial.

Also included are tax payments due under an agreement for deferred payment of taxes, which a debtor had entered into with the Internal Revenue Service (or State or local tax authority) before the filing of the petition and which relate to a prepetition tax liability (§ 523(a)(1)(D)) are also nondischargeable. This classification applies only to tax claims which would have received priority under section 507(a) if the taxpayer had filed a title 11 petition on the date on which the deferred payment agreement was entered into. This rule also applies only to installment payments which become due during and after the commencement of the title 11 case. Payments which had become due within one year before the filing of the petition receive sixth priority, and will be nondischargeable under the general rule of section 523(a)(1)(A).

The above categories of nondischargeability apply to customs duties as well as to taxes.

Paragraph (2) provides that as under Bankruptcy Act § 17a(2) [former section 35(a)(2) of this title], a debt for obtaining money, property, services, or a refinancing extension or renewal of credit by false pretenses, a false representation, or actual fraud, or by use of a statement in writing respecting the debtor's financial condition that is materially false, on which the creditor reasonably relied, and which the debtor made or published with intent to deceive, is excepted from discharge. This provision is modified only slightly from current section 17a(2) [former section 35(a)(2) of this title]. First, "actual fraud" is added as a ground for exception from discharge. Second, the creditor must not only have relied on a false statement in writing, but the reliance must have been reasonable. This codifies case law construing present section 17a(2) [former section 35(a)(2) of this title]. Third, the phrase "in any manner whatsoever" that appears in current law after "made or published" is deleted as unnecessary, the word "published" is used in the same sense that it is used in defamation cases.

Unscheduled debts are excepted from discharge under paragraph (3). The provision, derived from section 17a(3) [former section 35(a)(3) of this title], follows current law, but clarifies some uncertainties generated by the case law construing 17a(3) [former section 35(a)(3) of this title]. The debt is excepted from discharge if it was not scheduled in time to permit timely action by the creditor to protect his rights, unless the creditor had notice or actual knowledge of the case.

Paragraph (4) excepts debts for fraud incurred by the debtor while acting in a fiduciary capacity or for defalcation, embezzlement, or misappropriation.

Paragraph (5) provides that debts for willful and malicious conversion or injury by the debtor to another entity or the property of another entity are nondischargeable. Under this paragraph "willful" means deliberate or intentional. To the extent that Tinker v. Colwell, 139 U.S. 473 (1902) [24 S.Ct. 505, 48 L.Ed. 754, 11 Am.Bankr.Rep. 568], held that a less strict standard is intended, and to the extent that other cases have relied on *Tinker* to apply a "reckless disregard" standard, they are overruled.

Paragraph (6) excepts from discharge debts to a spouse, former spouse, or child of the debtor for alimony to, maintenance for, or support of the spouse or child. This language, in combination with the repeal of section 456(b) of the Social Security Act (42 U.S.C. 656(b)) [section 656(b) of Title 42, The Public Health and Welfare] by section 326 of the bill, will apply to make nondischargeable only alimony, maintenance, or support owed directly to a spouse or dependent. What constitutes alimony, maintenance, or support, will be determined under the bankruptcy law, not State law. Thus, cases such as In re Waller, 494 F.2d 447 (6th Cir.1974), are overruled, and the result in cases such as Fife v. Fife, 1 Utah 2d 281, 265 P.2d 642 (1952) is followed. The proviso, however, makes nondischargeable any debts resulting from an agreement by the debtor to hold the debtor's spouse harmless on joint debts, to the extent that the agreement is in payment of alimony, maintenance, or support of the spouse, as determined under bankruptcy law considerations as to whether a particular agreement to pay money to a spouse is actually alimony or a property settlement.

Paragraph (7) makes nondischargeable certain liabilities for penalties including tax penalties if the underlying tax with respect to which the penalty was imposed is also nondischargeable (sec. 523(a)(7)). These latter liabilities cover those which, but are penal in nature, as distinct from so-called "pecuniary loss" penalties which, in the case of taxes, involve basically the collection of a tax under the label of a "penalty." This provision differs from the bill as introduced, which did not link the nondischarge of a tax penalty with the treatment of the underlying tax. The amended provision reflects the existing position of the Internal Revenue Service as to tax penalties imposed by the Internal Revenue Code [Title 26] (Rev.Rul. 68–574, 1968–2 C.B. 595).

Paragraph (8) follows generally current law and excerpts from discharge student loans until such loans have been due and owing for five years. Such loans include direct student loans as well as insured and guaranteed loans. This provision is intended to be self-executing and the lender or institution is not required to file a complaint to determine the nondischargeability of any student loan.

Paragraph (9) excepts from discharge debts that the debtor owed before a previous bankruptcy case concerning the debtor in which the debtor was denied a discharge other than on the basis of the six-year bar.

Subsection (b) of this section permits discharge in a bankruptcy case of an unscheduled debt from a prior case. This provision is carried over from Bankruptcy Act § 17b [former section 35(b) of this title]. The result dictated by the subsection would probably not be different if the subsection were not included. It is included nevertheless for clarity.

Subsection (c) requires a creditor who is owed a debt that may be excepted from discharge under paragraph (2), (4), or (5), (false statements, defalcation or larceny misappropriation, or willful and malicious injury) to initiate proceedings in the bankruptcy court for an exception to discharge. If the creditor does not act, the debt is discharged. This provision does not change current law.

Subsection (d) is new. It provides protection to a consumer debtor that dealt honestly with a creditor who sought to have a debt excepted from discharge on the ground of falsity in the incurring of the debt. The debtor may be awarded costs and a reasonable attorney's fee for the proceeding to determine the dischargeability of a debt under subsection (a)(2), if the court finds that the proceeding was frivolous or not brought by its creditor in good faith.

The purpose of the provision is to discourage creditors from initiating proceedings to obtaining a false financial statement exception to discharge in the hope of obtaining a settlement from an honest debtor anxious to save attorney's fees. Such practices impair the debtor's fresh start and are contrary to the spirit of the bankruptcy laws.

Notes of Committee on the Judiciary, House Report No. 95–595. Subsection (a) lists eight kinds of debts excepted from discharge. Taxes that are entitled to priority are excepted from discharge under paragraph (1). In addition, taxes with respect to which the debtor made a fraudulent return or willfully attempted to evade or defeat, or with respect to which a return (if required) was not filed or was not filed after the due date and after one year before the bankruptcy case are excepted from discharge. If the taxing authority's claim has been disallowed, then it would be barred by the more modern rules of collateral estoppel from reasserting that claim against the debtor after the case was closed. See Plumb, The Tax Recommendations of the Commission on the Bankruptcy Laws: Tax Procedures, 88 Harv.L.Rev. 1360, 1388 (1975).

As under Bankruptcy Act § 17a(2) [former section 35(a)(2) of this title], a debt for obtaining money, property, services, or an extension or renewal of credit by false pretenses, a false representation, or actual fraud, or by use of a statement in writing respecting the debtor's financial condition that is materially false, on which the creditor reasonably relied, and that the debtor made or published with intent to deceive, is excepted from discharge. This provision is modified only slightly from current section 17a(2). First, "actual fraud" is added as a grounds for exception from discharge. Second, the creditor must not only have relied on a false statement in writing, the reliance must have been reasonable. This codifies case law construing this provision. Third, the phrase "in any manner whatsoever" that appears in current law after "made or published" is deleted as unnecessary. The word "published" is used in the same sense that it is used in slander actions.

Unscheduled debts are excepted from discharge under paragraph (3). The provision, derived from section 17a(3) [former section 35(a)(3) of this title], follows current law, but clarifies some uncertainties generated by the case law construing 17a(3). The debt is excepted from discharge if it was not scheduled in time to permit timely action by the creditor to protect his rights, unless the creditor had notice or actual knowledge of the case.

Paragraph (4) excepts debts for embezzlement or larceny. The deletion of willful and malicious conversion from § 17a(2) [former section 35(a)(2) of this title] of the Bankruptcy Act is not intended to effect a substantive change. The intent is to include in the category of non-dischargeable debts a conversion under which the debtor willfully and maliciously intends to borrow property for a short period of time with no intent to inflict injury but on which injury is in fact inflicted.

Paragraph (5) excepts from discharge debts to a spouse, former spouse, or child of the debtor for alimony to, maintenance for, or support of, the spouse or child. This language, in combination with the repeal of section 456(b) of the Social Security Act (42 U.S.C. 656(b)) [former section 656(b) of Title 42, The Public Health and Welfare] by section 327 of the bill, will apply to make nondischargeable only alimony, maintenance, or support owed directly to a spouse or dependent. See Hearings, pt. 2, at 942. What constitutes alimony, maintenance, or support, will be determined under the bankruptcy laws, not State law. Thus, cases such as In re Waller, 494 F.2d 447 (6th Cir.1974); Hearings, pt. 3, at 1308–10, are overruled, and the result in cases such as Fife v. Fife, 1 Utah 2d 281, 265 P.2d 642 (1952) is followed. This provision will, however, make nondischargeable any debts resulting from an agreement by the debtor to hold the debtor's spouse harmless on joint debts, to the extent that the agreement is in payment of alimony, maintenance, or support of the spouse, as determined under bankruptcy law considerations that are similar to considerations of whether a particular agreement to pay money to a spouse is actually alimony or a property settlement. See Hearings, pt. 3, at 1287–1290.

Paragraph (6) excepts debts for willful and malicious injury by the debtor to another person or to the property of another person. Under this paragraph, "willful" means deliberate or intentional. To the extent that Tinker v. Colwell, 193 U.S. 473 (1902) [24 S.Ct. 505, 48 L.Ed. 754, 11 Am.Bankr.Rep. 568], held that a looser standard is intended, and to the extent that other cases have relied on Tinker to apply a "reckless disregard" standard, they are overruled.

Paragraph (7) excepts from discharge a debt for a fine, penalty, or forfeiture payable to and for the benefit of a governmental unit, that is not compensation for actual pecuniary loss.

Paragraph (8) [now (9)] excepts from discharge debts that the debtor owed before a previous bankruptcy case concerning the debt-

or in which the debtor was denied a discharge other than on the basis of the six-year bar.

Subsection (b) of this section permits discharge in a bankruptcy case of an unscheduled debt from a prior case. This provision is carried over from Bankruptcy Act § 17b [former section 35(b) of this title]. The result dictated by the subsection would probably not be different if the subsection were not included. It is included nevertheless for clarity.

Subsection (c) requires a creditor who is owed a debt that may be expected from discharge under paragraph (2), (4), or (6) (false statements, embezzlement or larceny, or willful and malicious injury) to initiate proceedings in the bankruptcy court for an exception to discharge. If the creditor does not act, the debt is discharged. This provision does not change current law.

Subsection (d) is new. It provides protection to a consumer debtor that dealt honestly with a creditor who sought to have a debt excepted from discharge on grounds of falsity in the incurring of the debt. The debtor is entitled to costs of and a reasonable attorney's fee for the proceeding to determine the dischargeability of a debt under subsection (a)(2), if the creditor initiated the proceeding and the debt was determined to be dischargeable. The court is permitted to award any actual pecuniary loss that the debtor may have suffered as a result of the proceeding (such as loss of a day's pay). The purpose of the provision is to discourage creditors from initiating false financial statement exception to discharge actions in the hopes of obtaining a settlement from an honest debtor anxious to save attorney's fees. Such practices impair the debtor's fresh start.

Legislative Statements. Section 523(a)(1) represents a compromise between the position taken in the House bill and the Senate amendment. Section 523(a)(2) likewise represents a compromise between the position taken in the House bill and the Senate amendment with respect to the false financial statement exception to discharge. In order to clarify that a "renewal of credit" includes a "refinancing of credit", explicit reference to a refinancing of credit is made in the preamble to section 523(a)(2). A renewal of credit or refinancing of credit that was obtained by a false financial statement within the terms of section 523(a)(2) is nondischargeable. However, each of the provisions of section 523(a)(2) must be proved. Thus, under section 523(a)(2)(A) a creditor must prove that the debt was obtained by false pretenses, a false representation, or actual fraud, other than a statement respecting the debtor's or an insider's financial condition. Subparagraph (A) is intended to codify current case law e.g., Neal v. Clark, 95 U.S. 704 (1887) [24 L.Ed. 586], which interprets "fraud" to mean actual or positive fraud rather than fraud implied in law. Subparagraph (A) is mutually exclusive from subparagraph (B). Subparagraph (B) pertains to the so-called false financial statement. In order for the debt to be nondischargeable, the creditor must prove that the debt was obtained by the use of a statement in writing (i) that is materially false; (ii) respecting the debtor's or an insider's financial condition; (iii) on which the creditor to whom the debtor is liable for obtaining money, property, services, or credit reasonably relied; (iv) that the debtor caused to be made or published with intent to deceive. Section 523(a)(2)(B)(iv) is not intended to change from present law since the statement that the debtor causes to be made or published with the intent to deceive automatically includes a statement that the debtor actually makes or publishes with an intent to deceive. Section 523(a)(2)(B) is explained in the House report. Under section 523(a)(2)(B)(i) a discharge is barred only as to that portion of a loan with respect to which a false financial statement is materially false.

In many cases, a creditor is required by state law to refinance existing credit on which there has been no default. If the creditor does not forfeit remedies or otherwise rely to his detriment on a false financial statement with respect to existing credit, then an extension, renewal, or refinancing of such credit is nondischargeable only to the extent of the new money advanced; on the other hand, if an existing loan is in default or the creditor otherwise reasonably relies to his detriment on a false financial statement with regard to an existing loan, then the entire debt is nondischargeable under section 523(a)(2)(B). This codifies the reasoning expressed by the second circuit in In re Danns, 558 F.2d 114 (2d Cir. 1977).

Section 523(a)(3) of the House amendment is derived from the Senate amendment. The provision is intended to overrule Birkett v. Columbia Bank, 195 U.S. 345 (1904) [25 S.Ct. 38, 49 L.Ed. 231, 12 Am.Bankr.Rep. 691].

Section 523(a)(4) of the House amendment represents a compromise between the House bill and the Senate amendment.

Section 523(a)(5) is a compromise between the House bill and the Senate amendment.

The provision excepts from discharge a debt owed to a spouse, former spouse or child of the debtor, in connection with a separation agreement, divorce decree, or property settlement agreement, for alimony to, maintenance for, or support of such spouse or child but not to the extent that the debt is assigned to another entity. If the debtor has assumed an obligation of the debtor's spouse to a third party in connection with a separation agreement, property settlement agreement, or divorce proceeding, such debt is dischargeable to the extent that payment of the debt by the debtor is not actually in the nature of alimony, maintenance, or support of debtor's spouse, former spouse, or child.

Section 523(a)(6) adopts the position taken in the House bill and rejects the alternative suggested in the Senate amendment. The phrase "willful and malicious injury" covers a willful and malicious conversion.

Section 523(a)(7) of the House amendment adopts the position taken in the Senate amendment and rejects the position taken in the House bill. A penalty relating to a tax cannot be nondischargeable unless the tax itself is nondischargeable.

Section 523(a)(8) represents a compromise between the House bill and the Senate amendment regarding educational loans. This provision is broader than current law which is limited to federally insured loans. Only educational loans owing to a governmental unit or a nonprofit institution of higher education are made nondischargeable under this paragraph.

Section 523(b) is new. The section represents a modification of similar provisions contained in the House bill and the Senate amendment.

Section 523(c) of the House amendment adopts the position taken in the Senate amendment.

Section 523(d) represents a compromise between the position taken in the House bill and the Senate amendment on the issue of attorneys' fees in false financial statement complaints to determine dischargeability. The provision contained in the House bill permitting the court to award damages is eliminated. The court must grant the debtor judgment or a reasonable attorneys' fee unless the granting of judgment would be clearly inequitable.

The House amendment retains the basic categories of nondischargeable tax liabilities contained in both bills, but restricts the time limits on certain nondischargeable taxes. Under the amendment, nondischargeable taxes cover taxes entitled to priority under section 507(a)(6) of title 11 and, in the case of individual debtors under chapters 7, 11, or 13, tax liabilities with respect to which no required return had been filed or as to which a late return had been filed if the return became last due, including extensions, within 2 years before the date of the petition or became due after the petition or as to which the debtor made a fraudulent return, entry or invoice or fraudulently attempted to evade or defeat the tax.

In the case of individuals in liquidation under chapter 7 or in reorganization under chapter 11 of title 11, section 1141(d)(2) incorporates by reference the exceptions to discharge continued in section 523. Different rules concerning the discharge of taxes where a partnership or corporation reorganizes under chapter 11, apply under section 1141.

The House amendment also deletes the reduction rule contained in section 523(e) of the Senate amendment. Under that rule, the amount of an otherwise nondischargeable tax liability would be reduced by the amount which a governmental tax authority could have collected from the debtor's estate if it had filed a timely claim against the estate but which it did not collect because no such claim was filed. This provision is deleted in order not to effectively compel a tax authority to file claim against the estate in "no asset" cases, along with a dischargeability petition. In no-asset cases, therefore, if the tax authority is not potentially penalized by failing to file a claim, the debtor in such cases will have a better opportunity to choose the prepayment forum, bankruptcy court or the Tax Court, in which to litigate his personal liability for a nondischargeable tax.

The House amendment also adopts the Senate amendment provision limiting the nondischargeability of punitive tax penalties, that is, penalties other than those which represent collection of a principal amount of tax liability through the form of a "penalty." Under the House amendment, tax penalties which are basically punitive in nature are to be nondischargeable only if the penalty is computed by reference to a related tax liability which is nondischargeable or, if the amount of the penalty is not computed by reference to a tax liability, the transaction or event giving rise to the penalty occurred during the 3-year period ending on the date of the petition.

References in Text. Section 402(a)(26) of the Social Security Act, referred to in subsec. (a)(5)(A), is classified to section 602(a)(26) of Title 42, The Public Health and Welfare.

Section 14c(1), (2), (3), (4), (6), and (7) of the Bankruptcy Act, referred to in subsec. (a)(10), was classified to former section 32(c)(1), (2), (3), (4), (6), and (7) of this title, respectively.

The Bankruptcy Act, referred to in subsecs. (a)(10) and (b), is act July 1, 1898, ch. 541, 30 Stat. 544, as amended, which was classified generally to former Title 11, Bankruptcy.

Section 17a(1), 17a(3), and 17a(5) of the Bankruptcy Act, referred to in subsec. (b) was classified to former section 35(a)(1), 35(a)(3) and 35(a)(5) of this title, respectively.

Section 439A of the Higher Education Act of 1965, referred to in subsec. (b), is classified to section 1087-3 of Title 20, Education.

Section 733(g) of the Public Health Services Act, referred to in subsec. (b), is classified to section 294f of Title 42, The Public Health and Welfare.

Codification. Pub.L. 101-581 and Pub.L. 101-647, § 3102(a), made identical amendments to subsec. (a)(9) of this section.

Effective Dates of 1990 Amendments. Section 4 of Pub.L. 101-581 provided that:

"(a) Effective Date.—This Act and the amendments made by this Act [amending this section and section 1328 of this title] shall take effect on the date of the enactment of this Act [Nov. 15, 1990].

"(b) Application of Amendments. The amendments made by this Act shall not apply with respect to cases commenced under title 11 of the United States Code [this title] before the date of the enactment of this Act [Nov. 5, 1990.]"

Section 3104 of Pub.L. 101-647 provided that:

"(a) Effective Date.—This title and the amendments made by this title [amending this section and section 1328 of this title] shall take effect on the date of the enactment of this Act [Nov. 29, 1990].

"(b) Application of Amendments.—The amendments made by this title shall not apply with respect to cases commenced under title 11 of the United States Code [this title] before the date of the enactment of this Act [Nov. 29, 1990]."

Effective Date of 1986 Amendments; Savings Provisions; Quarterly Fees. Amendment by Pub.L. 99–554 effective 30 days after Oct. 27, 1986, except as otherwise provided for, see section 302(a) of Pub.L. 99–554, set out as a note under section 581 of Title 28, Judiciary and Judicial Procedure.

Amendments by Pub.L. 99–554, § 257(n), not to apply with respect to cases commenced under Title 11, Bankruptcy, before 30 days after Oct. 27, 1986, see section 302(c)(1) of Pub. L. 99–554, set out as a note under section 581 of Title 28.

Effective Date of 1984 Amendments. See section 553 of Pub.L. 98–353, Title III, July 10, 1984, 98 Stat. 392, set out as an Effective Date of 1984 Amendment note preceding chapter 1 of Title 11, Bankruptcy.

Effective Date of 1981 Amendment. Amendment by Pub.L. 97–35 effective Aug. 13, 1981, see section 2334(c) of Pub.L. 97–35.

Separability of Provisions. For separability of provisions of Title III of Pub.L. 98–353, see section 551 of Pub.L. 98–353 set out as a Separability of Provisions note preceding chapter 1 of Title 11, Bankruptcy.

Cross References

Disallowance of claim to extent claim is for unmatured debt and excepted from discharge as debt for alimony, maintenance or support, see section 502.
Discharge, see section 727.
Effect of confirmation, see section 1141.
Extent of priorities for unsecured claims of governmental units, see section 507.

Library References:

C.J.S. Bankruptcy § 172 et seq.
West's Key No. Digests, Bankruptcy ⇒2761 et seq.

WESTLAW Electronic Research

See WESTLAW Electronic Research Guide following the *Bankruptcy Highlights*.

§ 524. Effect of discharge

(a) A discharge in a case under this title—

(1) voids any judgment at any time obtained, to the extent that such judgment is a determination of the personal liability of the debtor with respect to any debt discharged under section 727, 944, 1141, 1228, or 1328 of this title, whether or not discharge of such debt is waived;

(2) operates as an injunction against the commencement or continuation of an action, the employment of process, or an act, to collect, recover or offset any such debt as a personal liability of the debtor, whether or not discharge of such debt is waived; and

(3) operates as an injunction against the commencement or continuation of an action, the employment of process, or an act, to collect or recover from, or offset against, property of the debtor of the kind specified in section 541(a)(2) of this title that is acquired after the commencement of the case, on account of any allowable community claim, except a community claim that is excepted from discharge under section 523, 1228(a)(1), or 1328(c)(1) of this title, or that would be so excepted, determined in accordance with the provisions of sections 523(c) and 523(d) of this title, in a case concerning the debtor's spouse commenced on the date of the filing of the petition in the case concerning the debtor, whether or not discharge of the debt based on such community claim is waived.

(b) Subsection (a)(3) of this section does not apply if—

(1)(A) the debtor's spouse is a debtor in a case under this title, or a bankrupt or a debtor in a case under the Bankruptcy Act, commenced within six years of the date of the filing of the petition in the case concerning the debtor; and

(B) the court does not grant the debtor's spouse a discharge in such case concerning the debtor's spouse; or

(2)(A) the court would not grant the debtor's spouse a discharge in a case under chapter 7 of this title concerning such spouse commenced on the date of the filing of the petition in the case concerning the debtor; and

(B) a determination that the court would not so grant such discharge is made by the bankruptcy court within the time and in the manner provided for a determination under section 727 of this title of whether a debtor is granted a discharge.

(c) An agreement between a holder of a claim and the debtor, the consideration for which, in whole or in part, is based on a debt that is dischargeable in a case under this title is enforceable only to any extent enforceable under applicable nonbankruptcy law, whether or not discharge of such debt is waived, only if—

(1) such agreement was made before the granting of the discharge under section 727, 1141, 1228, or 1328 of this title;

(2) such agreement contains a clear and conspicuous statement which advises the debtor that the agreement may be rescinded at any time prior to discharge or within sixty days after such agreement is filed with the court, whichever occurs later, by giving notice of rescission to the holder of such claim;

(3) such agreement has been filed with the court and, if applicable, accompanied by a declaration or an affidavit of the attorney that represented the debtor during the course of negotiating an agreement under this subsection, which states that such agreement—

(A) represents a fully informed and voluntary agreement by the debtor; and

(B) does not impose an undue hardship on the debtor or a dependent of the debtor;

(4) the debtor has not rescinded such agreement at any time prior to discharge or within sixty days after such agreement is filed with the court, whichever occurs later, by giving notice of rescission to the holder of such claim;

(5) the provisions of subsection (d) of this section have been complied with; and

(6)(A) in a case concerning an individual who was not represented by an attorney during the course of negotiating an agreement under this subsection, the court approves such agreement as—

(i) not imposing an undue hardship on the debtor or a dependent of the debtor; and

(ii) in the best interest of the debtor.

(B) Subparagraph (A) shall not apply to the extent that such debt is a consumer debt secured by real property.

(d) In a case concerning an individual, when the court has determined whether to grant or not to grant a discharge under section 727, 1141, 1228, or 1328 of this title, the court may hold a hearing at which the debtor shall appear in person. At any such hearing, the court may inform the debtor that a discharge has been granted or the reason why a discharge has not been granted. If a discharge has been granted and if the debtor desires to make an agreement of the kind specified in subsection (c) of this section, then the court shall hold a hearing at which the debtor shall appear in person and at such hearing the court shall

(1) inform the debtor—

(A) that such an agreement is not required under this title, under nonbankruptcy law, or under any agreement not made in accordance with the provisions of subsection (c) of this section; and

(B) of the legal effect and consequences of—

(i) an agreement of the kind specified in subsection (c) of this section; and

(ii) a default under such an agreement;

(2) determine whether the agreement that the debtor desires to make complies with the requirements of subsection (c)(6) of this section, if the consideration for such agreement is based in whole or in part on a consumer debt that is not secured by real property of the debtor.

(e) Except as provided in subsection (a)(3) of this section, discharge of a debt of the debtor does not affect the liability of any other entity on, or the property of any other entity for, such debt.

(f) Nothing contained in subsection (c) or (d) of this section prevents a debtor from voluntarily repaying any debt.

Pub.L. 95–598, Nov. 6, 1978, 92 Stat. 2592; Pub.L. 98–353, Title III, §§ 308, 455, July 10, 1984, 98 Stat. 354, 376; Pub.L. 99–554, Title II, §§ 257(o), 282, 283(k), Oct. 27, 1986, 100 Stat. 3115–3117.

Historical and Revision Notes

Notes of Committee on the Judiciary, Senate Report No. 95–989. Subsection (a) specifies that a discharge in a bankruptcy case voids any judgment to the extent that it is a determination of the personal liability of the debtor with respect to a prepetition debt, and operates as an injunction against the commencement or continuation of an action, the employment of process, or any act, including telephone calls, letters, and personal contacts, to collect, recover, or offset any discharged debt as a personal liability of the debtor, or from property of the debtor, whether or not the debtor has waived discharge of the debt involved. The injunction is to give complete effect to the discharge and to eliminate any doubt concerning the effect of the discharge as a total prohibition on debt collection efforts. This paragraph has been expanded over a comparable provision in Bankruptcy Act § 14f [former section 32(f) of this title] to cover any act to collect, such as dunning by telephone or letter, or indirectly through friends, relatives, or employers, harassment, threats of repossession, and the like. The change is consonant with the new policy forbidding binding reaffirmation agreements under proposed 11 U.S.C. 524(b), and is intended to insure that once a debt is discharged, the debtor will not be pressured in any way to repay it. In effect, the discharge extinguishes the debt, and creditors may not attempt to avoid that. The language "whether or not discharge of such debt is waived" is intended to prevent waiver of discharge of a particular debt from defeating the purposes of this section. It is directed at waiver of discharge of a particular debt, not waiver of discharge in toto as permitted under section 727(a)(9).

Subsection (a) also codifies the split discharge for debtors in community property states. If community property was in the estate and community claims were discharged, the discharge is effective against community creditors of the non-debtor spouse as well as of the debtor spouse.

Subsection (b) gives further effect to the discharge. It prohibits reaffirmation agreements after the commencement of the case with respect to any dischargeable debt. The prohibition extends to agreements the consideration for which in whole or in part is based on a dischargeable debt, and it applies whether or not discharge of the debt involved in the agreement has been waived. Thus, the prohibition on reaffirmation agreements extends to debts that are based on discharged debts. Thus, "second generation" debts, which included all or a part of a discharged debt could not be included in any new agreement for new money. This subsection will not have any effect on reaffirmations of debts discharged under the Bankruptcy Act [former Title 11]. It will only apply to discharges granted if commenced under the new title 11 bankruptcy code.

Subsection (c) grants an exception to the anti-reaffirmation provision. It permits reaffirmation in connection with the settlement of a proceeding to determine the dischargeability of the debt being reaffirmed, or in connection with a redemption agreement permitted under section 722. In either case, the reaffirmation agreement must be entered into in good faith and must be approved by the court.

Subsection (d) provides the discharge of the debtor does not affect co-debtors or guarantors.

Legislative Statements. Section 524(a) of the House amendment represents a compromise between the House bill and the Senate amendment. Section 524(b) of the House amendment is new, and represents standards clarifying the operation of section 524(a)(3) with respect to community property.

Sections 524(c) and (d) represent a compromise between the House bill and Senate amendment on the issue of reaffirmation of a debt discharged in bankruptcy. Every affirmation to be enforceable must be approved by the court, and any debtor may rescind a reaffirmation for 30 days from the time the reaffirmation becomes enforceable. If the debtor is an individual the court must advise the debtor of various effects of reaffirmation at a hearing. In addition, to any extent the debt is a consumer debt that is not secured by real property of the debtor reaffirmation is permitted only if the court approves the reaffirmation agreement, before granting a discharge under section 727, 1141, or 1328, as not imposing a hardship on the debtor or a dependent of the debtor and in the best interest of the debtor; alternatively, the court may approve an agreement entered into in good faith that is in settlement of litigation of a complaint to determine dischargeability or that is entered into in connection with redemption under section 722. The hearing on discharge under section 524(d) will be held whether or not the debtor desires to reaffirm any debts.

Effective Date of 1986 Amendment; Savings Provisions; Quarterly Fees. Amendment by Pub.L. 99–554 effective 30 days after Oct. 27, 1986, except as otherwise provided for, see section 302(a) of Pub.L. 99–554, set out as a note under section 581 of Title 28, Judiciary and Judicial Procedure.

Amendments by Pub.L. 99–554, § 257(*o*), not to apply with respect to cases commenced under Title 11, Bankruptcy, before 30 days after Oct. 27, 1986, see section 302(c)(1) of Pub. L. 99–554, set out as a note under section 581 of Title 28.

Effective Date of 1984 Amendments. See section 553 of Pub.L. 98–353, Title III, July 10, 1984, 98 Stat. 392, set out as an Effective Date of 1984 Amendment note preceding chapter 1 of Title 11, Bankruptcy.

Separability of Provisions. For separability of provisions of Title III of Pub.L. 98–353, see section 551 of Pub.L. 98–353 set out as a Separability of Provisions note preceding chapter 1 of Title 11, Bankruptcy.

Cross References

Applicability of subsec. (a)(1), (2) of this section in chapter 9 cases, see section 901.
Extension of time generally, see section 108.

§ 525. Protection against discriminatory treatment

(a) Except as provided in the Perishable Agricultural Commodities Act, 1930 (7 U.S.C. 499a–499s), the Packers and Stockyards Act, 1921 (7 U.S.C. 181–229), and section 1 of the Act entitled "An Act making appropriations for the Department of Agriculture for the fiscal year ending June 30, 1944, and for other purposes," approved July 12, 1943 (57 Stat. 422; 7 U.S.C. 204), a governmental unit may not deny, revoke, suspend, or refuse to renew a license, permit, charter, franchise, or other similar grant to, condition such a grant to, discriminate with respect to such a grant against, deny employment to, terminate the employment of, or discriminate with respect to employment against, a person that is or has been a debtor under this title or a bankrupt or a debtor under the Bankruptcy Act, or another person with whom such bankrupt or debtor has been associated, solely because such bankrupt or debtor is or has been a debtor under this title or a bankrupt or debtor under the Bankruptcy Act, has been insolvent before the commencement of the case under this title, or during the case but before the debtor is granted or denied a discharge, or has not paid a debt that is dischargeable in the case under this title or that was discharged under the Bankruptcy Act.

(b) No private employer may terminate the employment of, or discriminate with respect to employment against, an individual who is or has been a debtor under this title, a debtor or bankrupt under the Bankruptcy Act, or an individual associated with such debtor or bankrupt, solely because such debtor or bankrupt—

    (1) is or has been a debtor under this title or a debtor or bankrupt under the Bankruptcy Act;

    (2) has been insolvent before the commencement of a case under this title or during the case but before the grant or denial of a discharge; or

    (3) has not paid a debt that is dischargeable in a case under this title or that was discharged under the Bankruptcy Act.

Pub.L. 95–598, Nov. 6, 1978, 92 Stat. 2593; Pub.L. 98–353, Title III, § 309, July 10, 1984, 98 Stat. 354.

Historical and Revision Notes

Notes of Committee on the Judiciary, Senate Report No. 95–989. This section is additional debtor protection. It codifies the result of Perez v. Campbell, 402 U.S. 637 (1971) [91 S.Ct. 1704, 29 L.Ed.2d 233], which held that a State would frustrate the Congressional policy of a fresh start for a debtor if it were permitted to refuse to renew a drivers license because a tort judgment resulting from an automobile accident had been unpaid as a result of a discharge in bankruptcy.

Notwithstanding any other laws, section 525 prohibits a governmental unit from denying, revoking, suspending, or refusing to renew a license, permit, charter, franchise, or other similar grant to, from conditioning such a grant to, from discrimination with respect to such a grant against, deny employment to, terminate the employment of, or discriminate with respect to employment against, a person that is or has been a debtor or that is or has been associated with a debtor. The prohibition extends only to discrimination or other action based solely on the basis of the bankruptcy, on the basis of insolvency before or during bankruptcy prior to a determination of discharge, or on the basis of nonpayment of a debt discharged in the bankruptcy case (the Perez situation). It does not prohibit consideration of other factors, such as future financial responsibility or ability, and does not prohibit imposition of requirements such as net capital rules, if applied nondiscriminatorily.

In addition, the section is not exhaustive. The enumeration of various forms of discrimination against former bankrupts is not intended to permit other forms of discrimination. The courts have been developing the Perez rule. This section permits further development to prohibit actions by governmental or quasi-governmental organizations that perform licensing functions, such as a State bar association or a medical society, or by other organizations that can seriously affect the debtors' livelihood or fresh start, such as exclusion from a union on the basis of discharge of a debt to the union's credit union.

The effect of the section, and of further interpretations of the Perez rule, is to strengthen the anti-reaffirmation policy found in section 524(b). Discrimination based solely on nonpayment could encourage reaffirmations, contrary to the expressed policy.

The section is not so broad as a comparable section proposed by the Bankruptcy Commission, S. 236, 94th Cong., 1st Sess. § 4–508

(1975), which would have extended the prohibition to any discrimination, even by private parties. Nevertheless, it is not limiting either, as noted. The courts will continue to mark the contours of the anti-discrimination provision in pursuit of sound bankruptcy policy.

References in Text. The Perishable Agricultural Commodities Act, 1930, referred to in text, is Act June 10, 1930, c. 436, 46 Stat. 531, which is classified principally to chapter 20A [section 499a et seq.] of Title 7, Agriculture.

The Packers and Stockyards Act, 1921, referred to in text, is Act Aug. 15, 1921, c. 64, 42 Stat. 159, which is classified principally to chapter 9 [section 181 et seq.] of Title 7.

Section 1 of the Act entitled "An Act making appropriations for the Department of Agriculture for the fiscal year ending June 30, 1944, and for other purposes", approved July 12, 1943, referred to in text, is classified to section 204 of Title 7.

Effective Date of 1984 Amendments. See section 553 of Pub.L. 98–353, Title III, July 10, 1984, 98 Stat. 392, set out as an Effective Date of 1984 Amendment note preceding chapter 1 of Title 11, Bankruptcy.

Separability of Provisions. For separability of provisions of Title III of Pub.L. 98–353, see section 551 of Pub.L. 98–353 set out as a Separability of Provisions note preceding chapter 1 of Title 11, Bankruptcy.

Library References:

    C.J.S. Bankruptcy §§ 2, 97, 98.
    West's Key No. Digests, Bankruptcy ⊜2363–2366.

WESTLAW Electronic Research

    See WESTLAW Electronic Research Guide following the *Bankruptcy Highlights*.

SUBCHAPTER III—THE ESTATE

§ 541. Property of the estate

(a) The commencement of a case under section 301, 302, or 303 of this title creates an estate. Such estate is comprised of all the following property, wherever located and by whomever held:

    (1) Except as provided in subsections (b) and (c)(2) of this section, all legal or equitable interests of the debtor in property as of the commencement of the case.

    (2) All interests of the debtor and the debtor's spouse in community property as of the commencement of the case that is—

(A) under the sole, equal, or joint management and control of the debtor; or

(B) liable for an allowable claim against the debtor, or for both an allowable claim against the debtor and an allowable claim against the debtor's spouse, to the extent that such interest is so liable.

(3) Any interest in property that the trustee recovers under section 329(b), 363(n), 543, 550, 553, or 723 of this title.

(4) Any interest in property preserved for the benefit of or ordered transferred to the estate under section 510(c) or 551 of this title.

(5) Any interest in property that would have been property of the estate if such interest had been an interest of the debtor on the date of the filing of the petition, and that the debtor acquires or becomes entitled to acquire within 180 days after such date—

(A) by bequest, devise, or inheritance;

(B) as a result of a property settlement agreement with the debtor's spouse, or of an interlocutory or final divorce decree; or

(C) as a beneficiary of a life insurance policy or of a death benefit plan.

(6) Proceeds, product, offspring, rents, or profits of or from property of the estate, except such as are earnings from services performed by an individual debtor after the commencement of the case.

(7) Any interest in property that the estate acquires after the commencement of the case.

(b) Property of the estate does not include—

(1) any power that the debtor may exercise solely for the benefit of an entity other than the debtor;

(2) any interest of the debtor as a lessee under a lease of nonresidential real property that has terminated at the expiration of the stated term of such lease before the commencement of the case under this title, and ceases to include any interest of the debtor as a lessee under a lease of nonresidential real property that has terminated at the expiration of the stated term of such lease during the case; or

(3) any eligibility of the debtor to participate in programs authorized under the Higher Education Act of 1965 (20 U.S.C. 1001 et seq.; 42 U.S.C. 2751 et seq.), or any accreditation status or State licensure of the debtor as an educational institution.

(c)(1) Except as provided in paragraph (2) of this subsection, an interest of the debtor in property becomes property of the estate under subsection (a)(1), (a)(2), or (a)(5) of this section notwithstanding any provision in an agreement, transfer instrument, or applicable nonbankruptcy law—

(A) that restricts or conditions transfer of such interest by the debtor; or

(B) that is conditioned on the insolvency or financial condition of the debtor, on the commencement of a case under this title, or on the appointment of or taking possession by a trustee in a case under this title or a custodian before such commencement and that effects or gives an option to effect a forfeiture, modification, or termination of the debtor's interest in property.

(2) A restriction on the transfer of a beneficial interest of the debtor in a trust that is enforceable under applicable nonbankruptcy law is enforceable in a case under this title.

(d) Property in which the debtor holds, as of the commencement of the case, only legal title and not an equitable interest, such as a mortgage secured by real property, or an interest in such a mortgage, sold by the debtor but as to which the debtor retains legal title to service or supervise the servicing of such mortgage or interest, becomes property of the estate under subsection (a)(1) or (2) of this section only to the extent of the debtor's legal title to such property, but not to the extent of any equitable interest in such property that the debtor does not hold.

Pub.L. 95–598, Nov. 6, 1978, 92 Stat. 2594; Pub.L. 98–353, Title III, §§ 363(a), 456, July 10, 1984, 98 Stat. 363, 376; Pub.L. 101–508, Title III, § 3007(a)(2), Nov. 5, 1990, 104 Stat. 1388–____.

Termination of Amendment

Pub.L. 101–508, § 3008, provided that amendment by Pub.L. 101–508, § 3007(a)(2), amending subsec. (b) of this section, to cease to be effective Oct. 1, 1996. See note under section 362 of this title.

Historical and Revision Notes

Notes of Committee on the Judiciary, Senate Report No. 95–989. This section defines property of the estate, and specifies what property becomes property of the estate. The commencement of a bankruptcy case creates an estate. Under paragraph (1) of subsection (a), the estate is comprised of all legal or equitable interest of the debtor in property, wherever located, as of the commencement of the case. The scope of this paragraph is broad. It includes all kinds of property, including tangible or intangible property, causes of action (see Bankruptcy Act § 70a(6) [former section 110(a)(6) of this title]), and all other forms of property currently specified in section 70a of the Bankruptcy Act § 70a [former section 110(a) of this title], as well as property recovered by the trustee under section 542 of proposed title 11, if the property recovered was merely out of the possession of the debtor, yet remained "property of the debtor." The debtor's interest in property also includes "title" to property, which is an interest, just as are a possessory interest, or leasehold interest, for example. The result of Segal v. Rochelle, 382 U.S. 375 (1966) [86 S.Ct. 511, 15 L.Ed.2d 428], is followed, and the right to a refund is property of the estate.

Though this paragraph will include choses in action and claims by the debtor against others, it is not intended to expand the debt-or's rights against others more than they exist at the commencement of the case. For example, if the debtor has a claim that is barred at the time of the commencement of the case by the statute of limitations, then the trustee would not be able to pursue that claim, because he too would be barred. He could take no greater rights than the debtor himself had. But see proposed 11 U.S.C. 108, which would permit the trustee a tolling of the statute of limitations if it had not run before the date of the filing of the petition.

Paragraph (1) has the effect of overruling Lockwood v. Exchange Bank, 190 U.S. 294 (1903) [23 S.Ct. 751, 47 L.Ed. 1061, 10 Am. Bankr.Rep. 107], because it includes as property of the estate all property of the debtor, even that needed for a fresh start. After the property comes into the estate, then the debtor is permitted to exempt it under proposed 11 U.S.C. 522, and the court will have jurisdiction to determine what property may be exempted and what remains as property of the estate. The broad jurisdictional grant in proposed 28 U.S.C. 1334 would have the effect of overruling Lockwood independently of the change made by this provision.

Paragraph (1) also has the effect of overruling Lines v. Frederick, 400 U.S. 18 (1970) [91 S.Ct. 113, 27 L.Ed.2d 124].

Situations occasionally arise where property ostensibly belonging to the debtor will actually not be property of the debtor, but will be held in trust for another. For example, if the debtor has incurred medical bills that were covered by insurance, and the insurance company had sent the payment of the bills to the debtor before the debtor had paid the bill for which the payment was reimbursement, the payment would actually be held in constructive trust for the person to whom the bill was owed. This section and proposed 11 U.S.C. 545 also will not affect various statutory provisions that give a creditor of the debtor a lien that is valid outside as well as inside bankruptcy, or that creates a trust fund for the benefit of a creditor of the debtor. See Packers and Stockyards Act § 206, 7 U.S.C. 196 [section 196 of Title 7, Agriculture].

Bankruptcy Act § 8 [former section 26 of this title] has been deleted as unnecessary. Once the estate is created, no interests in property of the estate remain in the debtor. Consequently, if the debtor dies during the case, only property exempted from property of the estate or acquired by the debtor after the commencement of the case and not included as property of the estate will be available to the representative of the debtor's probate estate. The bankruptcy proceeding will continue in rem with respect to property of the state, and the discharge will apply in personam to relieve the debtor, and thus his probate representative, of liability for dischargeable debts.

The estate also includes the interests of the debtor and the debtor's spouse in community property, subject to certain limitations; property that the trustee recovers under the avoiding powers; property that the debtor acquires by bequest, devise, inheritance, a property settlement agreement with the debtor's spouse, or as the beneficiary of a life insurance policy within 180 days after the petition; and proceeds, product, offspring, rents, and profits of or from property of the estate, except such as are earning from services performed by an individual debtor after the commencement of the case. Proceeds here is not used in a confining sense, as defined in the Uniform Commercial Code, but is intended to be a broad term to encompass all proceeds of property of the estate. The conversion in form of property of the estate does not change its character as property of the estate.

Subsection (b) excludes from property of the estate any power, such as a power of appointment, that the debtor may exercise solely for the benefit of an entity other than the debtor. This changes present law which excludes powers solely benefiting other persons but not other entities.

Subsection (c) invalidates restrictions on the transfer of property of the debtor, in order that all of the interests of the debtor in property will become property of the estate. The provisions invalidated are those that restrict or condition transfer of the debtor's interest, and those that are conditioned on the insolvency or financial condition of the debtor, on the commencement of a bankruptcy case, or on the appointment of a custodian of the debtor's property. Paragraph (2) of subsection (c), however, preserves restrictions on a transfer of a spendthrift trust that the restriction is enforceable nonbankruptcy law to the extent of the income reasonably necessary for the support of a debtor and his dependents.

Subsection (d) [now (e)], derived from section 70c of the Bankruptcy Act [former section 110(c) of this title], gives the estate the benefit of all defenses available to the debtor as against an entity other than the estate, including such defenses as statutes of limitations, statutes of frauds, usury, and other personal defenses, and makes waiver by the debtor after the commencement of the case ineffective to bind the estate.

Section 541(e) [now (d)] confirms the current status under the Bankruptcy Act [former Title 11] of bona fide secondary mortgage market transactions as the purchase and sale of assets. Mortgages or interests in mortgages sold in the secondary market should not be considered as part of the debtor's estate. To permit the efficient servicing of mortgages or interests in mortgages the seller often retains the original mortgage notes and related documents, and the purchaser records under State recording statutes the purchaser's ownership of the mortgages or interests in mortgages purchased. Section 541(e) makes clear that the seller's retention of the mortgage documents and the purchaser's decision not to record do not impair the asset sale character of secondary mortgage market transactions. The committee notes that in secondary mortgage market transactions the parties may characterize their relationship as one of trust, agency, or independent contractor. The characterization adopted by the parties should not affect the statutes in bankruptcy on bona fide secondary mortgage market purchases and sales.

Legislative Statements. Section 541(a)(7) is new. The provision clarifies that any interest in property that the estate acquires after the commencement of the case is property of the estate; for example, if the estate enters into a contract, after the commencement of the case, such a contract would be property of the estate. The addition of this provision by the House amendment merely clarifies that section 541(a) is an all-embracing definition which includes charges on property, such as liens held by the debtor on property of a third party, or beneficial rights and interests that the debtor may have in property of another. However, only the debtor's interest in such property becomes property of the estate. If the debtor holds bare legal title or holds property in trust for another, only those rights which the debtor would have otherwise had emanating from such interest pass to the estate under section 541. Neither this section nor section 545 will affect various statutory provisions that give a creditor a lien that is valid both inside and outside bankruptcy against a bona fide purchaser of property from the debtor, or that creates a trust fund for the benefit of creditors meeting similar criteria. See Packers and Stockyards Act § 206, 7 U.S.C. 196 (1976) [section 196 of Title 7, Agriculture].

Section 541(c)(2) follows the position taken in the House bill and rejects the position taken in the Senate amendment with respect to income limitations on a spend-thrift trust.

Section 541(d) of the House amendment is derived from section 541(e) of the Senate amendment and reiterates the general principle that where the debtor holds bare legal title without any equitable interest, that the estate acquires bare legal title without any equitable interest in the property. The purpose of section 541(d) as applied to the secondary mortgage market is identical to the purpose of section 541(e) of the Senate amendment and section 541(d) will accomplish the same result as would have been accomplished by section 541(e). Even if a mortgage seller retains for purposes of servicing legal title to mortgages or interests in mortgages sold in the secondary mortgage market, the trustee would be required by section 541(d) to turn over the mortgages or interests in mortgages to the purchaser of those mortgages.

The seller of mortgages in the secondary mortgage market will often retain the original mortgage notes and related documents and the seller will not endorse the notes to reflect the sale to the purchaser. Similarly, the purchaser will often not record the purchaser's ownership of the mortgages or interests in mortgages under State recording statutes. These facts are irrelevant and the seller's retention of the mortgage documents and the purchaser's decision not to record do not change the trustee's obligation to turn the mortgages or interests in mortgages over to the purchaser. The application of section 541(d) to secondary mortgage market transactions will not be affected by the terms of the servicing agreement between the mortgage servicer and the purchaser of the mortgages. Under section 541(d), the trustee is required to recognize the purchaser's title to the mortgages or interests in mortgages and to turn this property over to the purchaser. It makes no difference whether the servicer and the purchaser characterize their relationship as one of trust, agency, or independent contractor.

The purpose of section 541(d) as applied to the secondary mortgage market is therefore to make certain that secondary mortgage market sales as they are currently structured are not subject to challenge by bankruptcy trustees and that purchasers of mortgages will be able to obtain the mortgages or interests in mortgages which they have purchased from trustees without the trustees asserting that a sale of mortgages is a loan from the purchaser to the seller.

Thus, as section 541(a)(1) clearly states, the estate is comprised of all legal or equitable interests of the debtor in property as of the commencement of the case. To the extent such an interest is limited in the hands of the debtor, it is equally limited in the hands of the estate except to the extent that defenses which are personal against the debtor are not effective against the estate.

The Senate amendment provided that property of the estate does not include amounts held by the debtor as trustee and any taxes withheld or collected from others before the commencement of the case. The House amendment removes these two provisions. As to property held by the debtor as a trustee, the House amendment provides that property of the estate will include whatever interest the debtor held in the property at the commencement of the case. Thus, where the debtor held only legal title to the property and the beneficial interest in that property belongs to another, such as exists in the case of property held in trust, the property of the estate includes the legal title, but not the beneficial interest in the property.

As to withheld taxes, the House amendment deletes the rule in the Senate bill as unnecessary since property of the estate does not include the beneficial interest in property held by the debtor as a trustee. Under the Internal Revenue Code of 1954 (section 7501 [section 7501 of Title 26, Internal Revenue Code]), the amounts of withheld taxes are held to be a special fund in trust for the United States. Where the Internal Revenue Service can demonstrate that the amounts of taxes withheld are still in the possession of the debtor at the commencement of the case, then if a trust is created, those amounts are not property of the estate. Compare In re Shakesteers Coffee Shops, 546 F.2d 821 (9th Cir.1976) with In re Glynn Wholesale Building Materials, Inc. (S.D.Ga.1978) and In re Progress Tech Colleges, Inc., 42 Aftr 2d 78–5573 (S.D.Ohio 1977).

Where it is not possible for the Internal Revenue Service to demonstrate that the amounts of taxes withheld are still in the possession of the debtor at the commencement of the case, present law generally includes amounts of withheld taxes as property of the estate. See, e.g., United States v. Randall, 401 U.S. 513 (1973) [91 S.Ct. 991, 28 L.Ed.2d 273] and In re Tamasha Town and Country Club, 483 F.2d 1377 (9th Cir.1973). Nonetheless, a serious problem exists where "trust fund taxes" withheld from others are held to be property of the estate where the withheld amounts are commingled with other assets of the debtor. The courts should permit the use of reasonable assumptions under which the Internal Revenue Service, and other tax authorities, can demonstrate that amounts of withheld taxes are still in the possession of the debtor at the commencement of the case. For example, where the debtor had commingled that amount of withheld taxes in his general checking account, it might be reasonable to assume that any remaining amounts in that account on the commencement of the case are the withheld taxes. In addition, Congress may consider future amendments to the Internal Revenue Code making clear that amounts of withheld taxes are held by the debtor in a trust relationship and, consequently, that such amounts are not property of the estate.

Effective and Termination Dates of 1990 Amendment. Amendment by Pub.L. 101–508, § 3007(a)(2), effective Nov. 5, 1990, see section 3007(a)(3) of Pub.L. 101–508, set out as a note under section 362 of this title.

Amendment by Pub.L. 101–508, § 3007(a)(2), to cease to be effective Oct. 1, 1996, see section 3008 of Pub.L. 101–508, set out as a note under section 362 of this title.

Effective Date of 1984 Amendments. See section 553 of Pub.L. 98–353, Title III, July 10, 1984, 98 Stat. 392, set out as an Effective Date of 1984 Amendment note preceding chapter 1 of Title 11, Bankruptcy.

Separability of Provisions. For separability of provisions of Title III of Pub.L. 98–353, see section 551 of Pub.L. 98–353 set out as a Separability of Provisions note preceding chapter 1 of Title 11, Bankruptcy.

Cross References
Community claim defined, see section 101.
Distribution of property of estate, see section 726.
Effect of discharge, see section 524.
Exemptions, see section 522.
Property of estate in chapter 13 cases, see section 1306.
Special tax provisions concerning estates of partners and partnerships, see section 728.

Library References:
C.J.S. Bankruptcy § 105 et seq.
West's Key No. Digests, Bankruptcy ☞2491 et seq.

WESTLAW Electronic Research
See WESTLAW Electronic Research Guide following the *Bankruptcy Highlights.*

§ 542. Turnover of property to the estate
(a) Except as provided in subsection (c) or (d) of this section, an entity, other than a custodian, in possession, custody, or control, during the case, of property that the trustee may use, sell, or lease under section 363 of this title, or that the debtor may exempt under section 522 of this title, shall deliver to the trustee,

and account for, such property or the value of such property, unless such property is of inconsequential value or benefit to the estate.

(b) Except as provided in subsection (c) or (d) of this section, an entity that owes a debt that is property of the estate and that is matured, payable on demand, or payable on order, shall pay such debt to, or on the order of, the trustee, except to the extent that such debt may be offset under section 553 of this title against a claim against the debtor.

(c) Except as provided in section 362(a)(7) of this title, an entity that has neither actual notice nor actual knowledge of the commencement of the case concerning the debtor may transfer property of the estate, or pay a debt owing to the debtor, in good faith and other than in the manner specified in subsection (d) of this section, to an entity other than the trustee, with the same effect as to the entity making such transfer or payment as if the case under this title concerning the debtor had not been commenced.

(d) A life insurance company may transfer property of the estate or property of the debtor to such company in good faith, with the same effect with respect to such company as if the case under this title concerning the debtor had not been commenced, if such transfer is to pay a premium or to carry out a nonforfeiture insurance option, and is required to be made automatically, under a life insurance contract with such company that was entered into before the date of the filing of the petition and that is property of the estate.

(e) Subject to any applicable privilege, after notice and a hearing, the court may order an attorney, accountant, or other person that holds recorded information, including books, documents, records, and papers, relating to the debtor's property or financial affairs, to to[1] turn over or disclose such recorded information to the trustee.

Pub.L. 95–598, Nov. 6, 1978, 92 Stat. 2595; Pub.L. 98–353, Title III, § 457, July 10, 1984, 98 Stat. 376.

[1] So in original.

Historical and Revision Notes

Notes of Committee on the Judiciary, Senate Report No. 95–989. Subsection (a) of this section requires anyone holding property of the estate on the date of the filing of the petition, or property that the trustee may use, sell, or lease under section 363, to deliver it to the trustee. The subsection also requires an accounting. The holder of property of the estate is excused from the turnover requirement of this subsection if the property held is of inconsequential value to the estate. However, this provision must be read in conjunction with the remainder of the subsection, so that if the property is of inconsequential monetary value, yet has a significant use value for the estate, the holder of the property would not be excused from turnover.

Subsection (b) requires an entity that owes money to the debtor as of the date of the petition, or that holds money payable on demand or payable on order, to pay the money to the order of the trustee. An exception is made to the extent that the entity has a valid right of setoff, as recognized by section 553.

Subsection (c) provides an exception to subsections (a) and (b). It protects an entity that has neither actual notice nor actual knowledge of the case and that transfers, in good faith, property that is deliverable or payable to the trustee to someone other than to the estate or on order of the estate. This subsection codifies the result of Bank of Marin v. England, 385 U.S. 99 (1966) [87 S.Ct. 274, 17 L.Ed.2d 197], but does not go so far as to permit bank setoff in violation of the automatic stay, proposed 11 U.S.C. 362(a)(7), even if the bank offsetting the debtor's balance has no knowledge of the case.

Subsection (d) protects life insurance companies that are required by contract to make automatic premium loans from property that might otherwise be property of the estate.

Subsection (e) requires an attorney, accountant, or other professional that holds recorded information relating to the debtor's property or financial affairs, to surrender it to the trustee. This duty is subject to any applicable claim of privilege, such as attorney-client privilege. It is a new provision that deprives accountants and attorneys of the leverage that they have today, under State law lien provisions, to receive payment in full ahead of other creditors when the information they hold is necessary to the administration of the estate.

Legislative Statements. Section 542(a) of the House amendment modifies similar provisions contained in the House bill and the Senate amendment treating with turnover of property to the estate. The section makes clear that any entity, other than a custodian, is required to deliver property of the estate to the trustee or debtor in possession whenever such property is acquired by the entity during the case, if the trustee or debtor in possession may use, sell, or lease the property under section 363, or if the debtor may exempt the property under section 522, unless the property is of inconsequential value or benefit to the estate. This section is not intended to require

an entity to deliver property to the trustee if such entity has obtained an order of the court authorizing the entity to retain possession, custody or control of the property.

The House amendment adopts section 542(c) of the House bill in preference to a similar provision contained in section 542(c) of the Senate amendment. Protection afforded by section 542(c) applies only to the transferor or payor and not to a transferee or payee receiving a transfer or payment, as the case may be. Such transferee or payee is treated under section 549 and section 550 of title 11.

The extent to which the attorney client privilege is valid against the trustee is unclear under current law and is left to be determined by the courts on a case by case basis.

Effective Date of 1984 Amendments. See section 553 of Pub.L. 98–353, Title III, July 10, 1984, 98 Stat. 392, set out as an Effective Date of 1984 Amendment note preceding chapter 1, of Title 11, Bankruptcy.

Separability of Provisions. For separability of provisions of Title III of Pub.L. 98–353, see section 551 of Pub.L. 98–353 set out as a Separability of Provisions note preceding chapter 1 of Title 11, Bankruptcy.

Cross References

Disallowance of claims of entity from which property is recoverable, see section 502.
Exemptions, see section 522.

Library References:

C.J.S. Bankruptcy §§ 184–187.
West's Key No. Digests, Bankruptcy ⊜3063–3066.

WESTLAW Electronic Research

See WESTLAW Electronic Research Guide following the *Bankruptcy Highlights*.

§ 543. Turnover of property by a custodian

(a) A custodian with knowledge of the commencement of a case under this title concerning the debtor may not make any disbursement from, or take any action in the administration of, property of the debtor, proceeds, product, offspring, rents, or profits of such property, or property of the estate, in the possession, custody, or control of such custodian, except such action as is necessary to preserve such property.

(b) A custodian shall—

(1) deliver to the trustee any property of the debtor held by or transferred to such custodian, or proceeds, product, offspring, rents, or profits of such property, that is in such custodian's possession, custody, or control on the date that such custodian acquires knowledge of the commencement of the case; and

(2) file an accounting of any property of the debtor, or proceeds, product, offspring, rents, or profits of such property, that, at any time, came into the possession, custody, or control of such custodian.

(c) The court, after notice and a hearing, shall—

(1) protects all entities to which a custodian has become obligated with respect to such property or proceeds, product, offspring, rents, or profits of such property;

(2) provide for the payment of reasonable compensation for services rendered and costs and expenses incurred by such custodian; and

(3) surcharge such custodian, other than an assignee for the benefit of the debtor's creditors that was appointed or took possession more than 120 days before the date of the filing of the petition, for any improper or excessive disbursement, other than a disbursement that has been made in accordance with applicable law or that has been approved, after notice and a hearing, by a court of competent jurisdiction before the commencement of the case under this title.

(d) After notice and hearing, the bankruptcy court—

(1) may excuse compliance with subsection (a), (b), or (c) of this section, if the interests of creditors and, if the debtor is not insolvent, of [1] equity security holders would be better served by permitting a custodian to continue in possession, custody, or control of such property, and

(2) shall excuse compliance with subsections (a) and (b)(1) of this section if the custodian is an assignee for the benefit of the debtor's creditors that was appointed or took possession more than 120 days before the date of the filing of the petition, unless compliance with such subsections is necessary to prevent fraud or injustice.

Pub.L. 95–598, Nov. 6, 1978, 92 Stat. 2595; Pub.L. 98–353, Title III, § 458, July 10, 1984, 98 Stat. 376.

[1] So in original. Probably should be "if".

Historical and Revision Notes

Notes of Committee on the Judiciary, Senate Report No. 95–989. This section requires a custodian appointed before the bankruptcy case to deliver to the trustee and to account for property that has come into his possession, custody, or control as a custodian. "Property of the debtor" in section (a) includes property that was property of the debtor at the time the custodian took the property, but the title to which passed to the custodian. The section requires the court to protect any obligations incurred by the custodian, provide for the payment of reasonable compensation for services rendered and costs and expenses incurred by the custodian, and to surcharge the custodian for any improper or excessive disbursement, unless it has been approved by a court of competent jurisdiction. Subsection (d) reinforces the general abstention policy in section 305 by permitting the bankruptcy court to authorize the custodianship to proceed notwithstanding this section.

Legislative Statements. Section 543(a) is a modification of similar provisions contained in the House bill and the Senate amendment. The provision clarifies that a custodian may always act as is necessary to preserve property of the debtor. Section 543(c)(3) excepts from surcharge a custodian that is an assignee for the benefit of creditors, who was appointed or took possession before 120 days before the date of the filing of the petition, whichever is later. The provision also prevents a custodian from being surcharged in connection with payments made in accordance with applicable law.

Effective Date of 1984 Amendments. See section 553 of Pub.L. 98–353, Title III, July 10, 1984, 98 Stat. 392, set out as an Effective Date of 1984 Amendment note preceding chapter 1 of Title 11, Bankruptcy.

Separability of Provisions. For separability of provisions of Title III of Pub.L. 98–

353, see section 551 of Pub.L. 98–353 set out as a Separability of Provisions note preceding chapter 1 of Title 11, Bankruptcy.

Cross References

Administrative expenses of superseded custodians, see section 503.

Disallowance of claims of entity from which property is recoverable, see section 502.

Effect of dismissal, see section 349.

Order of payment on claims for expenses of superseded custodians, see section 726.

Property recoverable by trustee as exempt, see section 522.

Library References:

C.J.S. Bankruptcy § 185.

West's Key No. Digests, Bankruptcy ⊗⇒3064.

WESTLAW Electronic Research

See WESTLAW Electronic Research Guide following the *Bankruptcy Highlights.*

§ 544. Trustee as lien creditor and as successor to certain creditors and purchasers

(a) The trustee shall have, as of the commencement of the case, and without regard to any knowledge of the trustee or of any creditor, the rights and powers of, or may avoid any transfer of property of the debtor or any obligation incurred by the debtor that is voidable by—

(1) a creditor that extends credit to the debtor at the time of the commencement of the case, and that obtains, at such time and with respect to such credit, a judicial lien on all property on which a creditor on a simple contract could have obtained such a judicial lien, whether or not such a creditor exists;

(2) a creditor that extends credit to the debtor at the time of the commencement of the case, and obtains, at such time and with respect to such credit, an execution against the debtor that is returned unsatisfied at such time, whether or not such a creditor exists; or

(3) a bona fide purchaser of real property, other than fixtures, from the debtor, against whom applicable law permits such transfer to be perfected, that obtains the status of a bona fide purchaser and has perfected such transfer at the time of the commencement of the case, whether or not such a purchaser exists.

(b) The trustee may avoid any transfer of an interest of the debtor in property or any obligation incurred by the debtor that is voidable under applicable law by a creditor holding an unsecured claim that is allowable under section 502 of this title or that is not allowable only under section 502(e) of this title.

Pub.L. 95–598, Nov. 6, 1978, 92 Stat. 2596; Pub.L. 98–353, Title III, § 459, July 10, 1984, 98 Stat. 377.

Historical and Revision Notes

Notes of Committee on the Judiciary, Senate Report No. 95–989. Subsection (a) is the "strong arm clause" of current law, now found in Bankruptcy Act § 70c [former section 110(c) of this title]. It gives the trustee the rights of a creditor on a simple contract with a judicial lien on the property of the debtor as of the date of the petition; of a creditor with a writ of execution against the property of the debtor unsatisfied as of the date of the petition; and a bona fide purchaser of the real property of the debtor as of the date of the petition. "Simple contract" as used here is derived from Bankruptcy Act § 60a(4) [former section 96(a)(4) of this title]. The third status, that of a bona fide purchaser of real property, is new.

Subsection (b) is derived from current section 70e [former section 110(e) of this title]. It gives the trustee the rights of actual unsecured creditors under applicable law to void transfers. It follows Moore v. Bay, 284 U.S. 4 (1931) [52 S.Ct. 3, 76 L.Ed. 133, 18 Am.Bankr. Rep.N.S. 675], and overrules those cases that hold section 70e [former section 110(e) of this title] gives the trustee the rights of secured creditors.

Legislative Statements. Section 544(a)(3) modifies similar provisions contained in the House bill and Senate amendment so as not to require a creditor to perform the impossible in order to perfect his interest. Both the lien creditor test in section 544(a)(1), and the bona fide purchaser test in section 544(a)(3) should not require a transferee to perfect a transfer against an entity with respect to which applicable law does not permit perfection. The avoiding powers under section 544(a)(1), (2), and (3) are new. In particular, section 544(a)(1) overrules Pacific Finance Corp. v. Edwards, 309 F.2d 224 (9th Cir. 1962), and In re Federals, Inc., 553 F.2d 509 (6th Cir. 1977), insofar as those cases held that the trustee did not have the status of a creditor who extended credit immediately prior to the commencement of the case.

The House amendment deletes section 544(c) of the House bill.

Effective Date of 1984 Amendments. See section 553 of Pub.L. 98–353, Title III, July 10, 1984, 98 Stat. 392, set out as an Effective Date of 1984 Amendment note preceding chapter 1 of Title 11, Bankruptcy.

Separability of Provisions. For separability of provisions of Title III of Pub.L. 98–353, see section 551 of Pub.L. 98–353 set out as a Separability of Provisions note preceding chapter 1 of Title 11, Bankruptcy.

Cross References

Applicability of this section in chapter 9 cases, see section 901.

Appointment of trustee upon debtor's refusal to pursue cause of action under this section, see section 926.

Commencement of involuntary cases by transferees of voidable transfers, see section 303.

Disallowance of claims of entity that is transferee of avoidable transfer, see section 502.

Effect of dismissal, see section 349.

Exemptions, see section 522.

Voidable transfers in

Commodity broker liquidation cases, see section 764.

Stockbroker liquidation cases, see section 749.

Library References:

C.J.S. Bankruptcy §§ 123, 124, 126, 134, 180.

West's Key No. Digests, Bankruptcy ⚷2512–2516, 2701–2705.

WESTLAW Electronic Research

See WESTLAW Electronic Research Guide following the *Bankruptcy Highlights*.

§ 545. Statutory liens

The trustee may avoid the fixing of a statutory lien on property of the debtor to the extent that such lien—

(1) first becomes effective against the debtor—

(A) when a case under this title concerning the debtor is commenced;

(B) when an insolvency proceeding other than under this title concerning the debtor is commenced;

(C) when a custodian is appointed or authorized to take or takes possession;

(D) when the debtor becomes insolvent;

(E) when the debtor's financial condition fails to meet a specified standard; or

(F) at the time of an execution against property of the debtor levied at the instance of an entity other than the holder of such statutory lien;

(2) is not perfected or enforceable at the time of the commencement of the case against a bona fide purchaser that purchases such property at the time of the commencement of the case, whether or not such a purchaser exists;

(3) is for rent; or

(4) is a lien of distress for rent.

Pub.L. 95–598, Nov. 6, 1978, 92 Stat. 2597; Pub.L. 98–353, Title III, § 460, July 10, 1984, 98 Stat. 377.

Historical and Revision Notes

Notes of Committee on the Judiciary, Senate Report No. 95–989. This section permits the trustee to avoid the fixing of certain statutory liens. It is derived from subsection 67(b) [former section 107(b) of this title] and 67(c) [former section 107(c) of this title] of present law. Liens that first become effective on the bankruptcy or insolvency of the debtor are voidable by the trustee. Liens that are not perfected or enforceable on the date of the petition against a bona fide purchaser are voidable. If a transferee is able to perfect under section 546(a) and that perfection relates back to an earlier date, then in spite of the filing of the bankruptcy petition, the trustee would not be able to defeat the lien, because the lien would be perfected and enforceable against a bona fide purchaser that purchased the property on the date of the filing of the petition. Finally, a lien for rent or of distress for rent is voidable, whether the lien is a statutory lien or a common law lien of distress for rent. See proposed 11 U.S.C. 101(37); Bankruptcy Act § 67(c)(1)(C) [former section 107(c)(1)(C) of this title]. The trustee may avoid a lien under this section even if the lien has been enforced by sale before the commencement of the case. To that extent, Bankruptcy Act § 67(c)(5) [former section 107(c)(5) of this title] is not followed.

Subsection (b) limits the trustee's power to avoid tax liens under Federal, state, or local law. For example, under § 6323 of the Internal Revenue Code [section 6323 of Title 26,

Internal Revenue Code]. Once public notice of a tax lien has been filed, the Government is generally entitled to priority over subsequent lienholders. However, certain purchasers who acquire an interest in certain specific kinds of personal property will take free of an existing filed tax lien attaching to such property. Among the specific kinds of personal property which a purchaser can acquire free of an existing tax lien (unless the buyer knows of the existence of the lien) are stocks and securities, motor vehicles, inventory, and certain household goods. Under the present Bankruptcy Act (§ 67(c)(1) [former section 107(c)(1) of this title]), the trustee may be viewed as a bona fide purchaser, so that he can take over any such designated items free of tax liens even if the tax authority has perfected its lien. However, the reasons for enabling a bona fide purchaser to take these kinds of assets free of an unfiled tax lien, that is, to encourage free movement at these assets in general commerce, do not apply to a trustee in a title 11 case, who is not in the same position as an ordinary bona fide purchaser as to such property. The bill accordingly adds a new subsection (b) to sec. 545 providing, in effect, that a trustee in bankruptcy does not have the right under this section to take otherwise specially treated items of personal property free of a tax lien filed before the filing of the petition.

Legislative Statements. Section 545 of the House amendment modifies similar provisions contained in the House bill and Senate amendment to make clear that a statutory lien may be avoided under section 545 only to the extent the lien violates the perfection standards of section 545. Thus a Federal tax lien is invalid under section 545(2) with respect to property specified in sections 6323(b) and (c) of the Internal Revenue Code of 1954 [sections 6323(b) and (c) of Title 26, Internal Revenue Code]. As a result of this modification, section 545(b) of the Senate amendment is deleted as unnecessary.

The House amendment retains the provision of section 545(2) of the House bill giving the trustee in a bankruptcy case the same power which a bona fide purchaser has to take over certain kinds of personal property despite the existence of a tax lien covering that property. The amendment thus retains present law, and deletes section 545(b) of the Senate amendment which would have no longer allowed the trustee to step into the shoes of a bona fide purchaser for this purpose.

Effective Date of 1984 Amendments. See section 553 of Pub.L. 98–353, Title III, July 10, 1984, 98 Stat. 392, set out as an Effective Date of 1984 Amendment note preceding chapter 1 of Title 11, Bankruptcy.

Separability of Provisions. For separability of provisions of Title III of Pub.L. 98–353, see section 551 of Pub.L. 98–353 set out as a Separability of Provisions note preceding chapter 1 of Title 11, Bankruptcy.

Cross References
Applicability of this section in chapter 9 cases, see section 901.

Appointment of trustee upon debtor's refusal to pursue cause of action under this section, see section 926.

Commencement of involuntary cases by transferees of voidable transfers, see section 303.

Disallowance of claims of entity that is a transferee of an avoidable transfer, see section 502.

Effect of dismissal, see section 349.

Exemptions, see section 522.

Voidable transfers in

    Commodity broker liquidation cases, see section 764.

    Stockbroker liquidation cases, see section 749.

Library References:
C.J.S. Bankruptcy § 130.

West's Key No. Digests, Bankruptcy ⇐2580–2582.

WESTLAW Electronic Research
See WESTLAW Electronic Research Guide following the *Bankruptcy Highlights*.

§ 546. Limitations on avoiding powers

(a) An action or proceeding under section 544, 545, 547, 548, or 553 of this title may not be commenced after the earlier of—

    (1) two years after the appointment of a trustee under section 702, 1104, 1163, 1302, or 1202 of this title; or

    (2) the time the case is closed or dismissed.

(b) The rights and powers of a trustee under sections 544, 545, and 549 of this title are subject to any generally applicable law that permits perfection of an interest in property to be effective against an entity that acquires rights in such property before the date of such perfection. If such law requires seizure of such property or commencement of an action to accomplish such perfection, and such property has not been seized or such action has not been commenced before the date of the filing of the petition, such interest in such property shall be perfected by notice within the time fixed by such law for such seizure or commencement.

(c) Except as provided in subsection (d) of this section, the rights and powers of a trustee under sections 544(a), 545, 547, and 549 of this title are subject to any statutory or common-law right of a seller of goods that has sold goods to the debtor, in the ordinary course of such seller's business, to reclaim such goods if the debtor has received such goods while insolvent, but—

(1) such a seller may not reclaim any such goods unless such seller demands in writing reclamation of such goods before ten days after receipt of such goods by the debtor; and

(2) the court may deny reclamation to a seller with such a right of reclamation that has made such a demand only if the court—

(A) grants the claim of such a seller priority as a claim of a kind specified in section 503(b) of this title; or

(B) secures such claim by a lien.

(d) In the case of a seller who is a producer of grain sold to a grain storage facility, owned or operated by the debtor, in the ordinary course of such seller's business (as such terms are defined in section 557 of this title) or in the case of a United States fisherman who has caught fish sold to a fish processing facility owned or operated by the debtor in the ordinary course of such fisherman's business, the rights and powers of the trustee under sections 544(a), 545, 547, and 549 of this title are subject to any statutory or common law right of such producer or fisherman to reclaim such grain or fish if the debtor has received such grain or fish while insolvent, but—

(1) such producer or fisherman may not reclaim any grain or fish unless such producer or fisherman demands, in writing, reclamation of such grain or fish before ten days after receipt thereof by the debtor; and

(2) the court may deny reclamation to such a producer or fisherman with a right of reclamation that has made such a demand only if the court secures such claim by a lien.

(e) Notwithstanding sections 544, 545, 547, 548(a)(2), and 548(b) of this title, the trustee may not avoid a transfer that is a margin payment, as defined in section 101(34), 741(5), or 761(15) of this title, or settlement payment, as defined in section 101(35) or 741(8) of this title, made by or to a commodity broker, forward contract merchant, stockbroker, financial institution, or securities clearing agency, that is made before the commencement of the case, except under section 548(a)(1) of this title.

(f) Notwithstanding sections 544, 545, 547, 548(a)(2), and 548(b) of this title, the trustee may not avoid a transfer that is a margin payment, as defined in section 741(5) or 761(15) of this title, or settlement payment, as defined in section 741(8) of this title, made by or to a repo participant, in connection with a repurchase agreement and that is made before the commencement of the case, except under section 548(a)(1) of this title.

(g) Notwithstanding sections 544, 545, 547, 548(a)(2) and 548(b) of this title, the trustee may not avoid a transfer under a swap agreement, made by or to a swap participant, in connection with a swap agreement and that is made before the commencement of the case, except under section 548(a)(1) of this title.

Pub.L. 95–598, Nov. 6, 1978, 92 Stat. 2597; Pub.L. 97–222, § 4, July 27, 1982, 96 Stat. 236; Pub.L. 98–353, Title III, §§ 351, 393, 461, July 10, 1984, 98 Stat. 359, 365, 377; Pub.L. 99–554, Title II, §§ 257(d), 283(*l*), Oct. 27, 1986, 100 Stat. 3114,

3117; Pub.L. 101–311, Title I, § 103, Title II, § 203, June 25, 1990, 104 Stat. 268, 269.

Historical and Revision Notes

Notes of Committee on the Judiciary, Senate Report No. 95–989. The trustee's rights and powers under certain of the avoiding powers are limited by section 546. First, if an interest holder against whom the trustee would have rights still has, under applicable nonbankruptcy law, and as of the date of the petition, the opportunity to perfect his lien against an intervening interest holder, then he may perfect his interest against the trustee. If applicable law requires seizure for perfection, then perfection is by notice to the trustee instead. The rights granted to a creditor under this subsection prevail over the trustee only if the transferee has perfected the transfer in accordance with applicable law, and that perfection relates back to a date that is before the commencement of the case.

The phrase "generally applicable law" relates to those provisions of applicable law that apply both in bankruptcy cases and outside of bankruptcy cases. For example, many State laws, under the Uniform Commercial Code, permit perfection of a purchase-money security interest to relate back to defeat an earlier levy by another creditor if the former was perfected within ten days of delivery of the property. U.C.C. § 9–301(2). Such perfection would then be able to defeat an intervening hypothetical judicial lien creditor on the date of the filing of the petition. The purpose of the subsection is to protect, in spite of the surprise intervention of a bankruptcy petition, those whom State law protects by allowing them to perfect their liens or interests as of an effective date that is earlier than the date of perfection. It is not designed to give the States an opportunity to enact disguised priorities in the form of liens that apply only in bankruptcy case.

Subsection (b) specifies that the trustee's rights and powers under the strong arm clause, the successor to creditors provision, the preference section, and the postpetition transaction section are all subject to any statutory or common-law right of a seller, in the ordinary course of business, of goods to the debtor to reclaim the goods if the debtor received the goods on credit while insolvent. The seller must demand reclamation within ten days after receipt of the goods by the debtor. As under nonbankruptcy law, the right is subject to any superior rights of secured creditors. The purpose of the provision is to recognize, in part, the validity of section 2–702 of the Uniform Commercial Code, which has generated much litigation, confusion, and divergent decisions in different circuits. The right is subject, however, to the power of the court to deny reclamation and protect the seller by granting him a priority as an administrative expense for his claim arising out of the sale of the goods.

Subsection (c) [now (a)] adds a statute of limitations to the use by the trustee of the avoiding powers. The limitation is two years after his appointment, or the time the case is closed or dismissed, whichever, occurs later.

Legislative Statements. Section 546(a) of the House amendment is derived from section 546(c) of the Senate amendment. Section 546(c) of the House amendment is derived from section 546(b) of the Senate amendment. It applies to receipt of goods on credit as well as by cash sales. The section clarifies that a demand for reclamation must be made in writing anytime before 10 days after receipt of the goods by the debtor. The section also permits the court to grant the reclaiming creditor a lien or an administrative expense in lieu of turning over the property.

Effective Date of 1986 Amendments; Savings Provisions; Quarterly Fees. Amendment by Pub.L. 99–554, effective 30 days after Oct. 27, 1986, except as otherwise provided for, see section 302(a) of Pub.L. 99–554, set out as a note under section 581 of Title 28, Judiciary and Judicial Procedure.

Amendments by Pub.L. 99–554, § 257(d), not to apply with respect to cases commenced under Title 11, Bankruptcy, before 30 days after Oct. 27, 1986, see section 302(c)(1) of Pub.L. 99–554, set out as a note under section 581 of Title 28.

Effective Date of 1984 Amendments. See section 553 of Pub.L. 98–353, Title III, July 10, 1984, 98 Stat. 392, set out as an Effective Date of 1984 Amendment note preceding chapter 1 of Title 11, Bankruptcy.

Separability of Provisions. For separability of provisions of Title III of Pub.L. 98–353, see section 551 of Pub.L. 98–353, set out as a Separability of Provisions note preceding chapter 1 of Title 11, Bankruptcy.

§ 547.   Preferences

(a) In this section—

(1) "inventory" means personal property leased or furnished, held for sale or lease, or to be furnished under a contract for service, raw materials, work in process, or materials used or consumed in a business, including farm products such as crops or livestock, held for sale or lease;

(2) "new value" means money or money's worth in goods, services, or new credit, or release by a transferee of property previously transferred to such transferee in a transaction that is neither void nor voidable by the debtor or the trustee under any applicable law, including proceeds of such property, but does not include an obligation substituted for an existing obligation;

(3) "receivable" means right to payment, whether or not such right has been earned by performance; and

(4) a debt for a tax is incurred on the day when such tax is last payable without penalty, including any extension.

(b) Except as provided in subsection (c) of this section, the trustee may avoid any transfer of an interest of the debtor in property—

(1) to or for the benefit of a creditor;

(2) for or on account of an antecedent debt owed by the debtor before such transfer was made;

(3) made while the debtor was insolvent;

(4) made—

(A) on or within 90 days before the date of the filing of the petition; or

(B) between ninety days and one year before the date of the filing of the petition, if such creditor at the time of such transfer was an insider; and

(5) that enables such creditor to receive more than such creditor would receive if—

(A) the case were a case under chapter 7 of this title;

(B) the transfer had not been made; and

(C) such creditor received payment of such debt to the extent provided by the provisions of this title.

(c) The trustee may not avoid under this section a transfer—

(1) to the extent that such transfer was—

(A) intended by the debtor and the creditor to or for whose benefit such transfer was made to be a contemporaneous exchange for new value given to the debtor; and

(B) in fact a substantially contemporaneous exchange;

(2) to the extent that such transfer was—

(A) in payment of a debt incurred by the debtor in the ordinary course of business or financial affairs of the debtor and the transferee;

(B) made in the ordinary course of business or financial affairs of the debtor and the transferee; and

(C) made according to ordinary business terms;

(3) that creates a security interest in property acquired by the debtor—

(A) to the extent such security interest secures new value that was—

(i) given at or after the signing of a security agreement that contains a description of such property as collateral;

(ii) given by or on behalf of the secured party under such agreement;

(iii) given to enable the debtor to acquire such property; and

(iv) in fact used by the debtor to acquire such property; and

(B) that is perfected on or before 10 days after the debtor receives possession of such property;

(4) to or for the benefit of a creditor, to the extent that, after such transfer, such creditor gave new value to or for the benefit of the debtor—

(A) not secured by an otherwise unavoidable security interest; and

(B) on account of which new value the debtor did not make an otherwise unavoidable transfer to or for the benefit of such creditor;

(5) that creates a perfected security interest in inventory or a receivable or the proceeds of either, except to the extent that the aggregate of all such transfers to the transferee caused a reduction, as of the date of the filing of the petition and to the prejudice of other creditors holding unsecured claims, of any amount by which the debt secured by such security interest exceeded the value of all security interests for such debt on the later of—

(A)(i) with respect to a transfer to which subsection (b)(4)(A) of this section applies, 90 days before the date of the filing of the petition; or

(ii) with respect to a transfer to which subsection (b)(4)(B) of this section applies, one year before the date of the filing of the petition; or

(B) the date on which new value was first given under the security agreement creating such security interest;

(6) that is the fixing of a statutory lien that is not avoidable under section 545 of this title; or

(7) if, in a case filed by an individual debtor whose debts are primarily consumer debts, the aggregate value of all property that constitutes or is affected by such transfer is less than $600.

(d) The trustee may avoid a transfer of an interest in property of the debtor transferred to or for the benefit of a surety to secure reimbursement of such a surety that furnished a bond or other obligation to dissolve a judicial lien that would have been avoidable by the trustee under subsection (b) of this section. The liability of such surety under such bond or obligation shall be discharged to the extent of the value of such property recovered by the trustee or the amount paid to the trustee.

(e)(1) For the purposes of this section—

(A) a transfer of real property other than fixtures, but including the interest of a seller or purchaser under a contract for the sale of real property, is perfected when a bona fide purchaser of such property from the debtor against whom applicable law permits such transfer to be perfected cannot acquire an interest that is superior to the interest of the transferee; and

(B) a transfer of a fixture or property other than real property is perfected when a creditor on a simple contract cannot acquire a judicial lien that is superior to the interest of the transferee.

(2) For the purposes of this section, except as provided in paragraph (3) of this subsection, a transfer is made—

(A) at the time such transfer takes effect between the transferor and the transferee, if such transfer is perfected at, or within 10 days after, such time;

(B) at the time such transfer is perfected, if such transfer is perfected after such 10 days; or

(C) immediately before the date of the filing of the petition, if such transfer is not perfected at the later of—

(i) the commencement of the case; or

(ii) 10 days after such transfer takes effect between the transferor and the transferee.

(3) For the purposes of this section, a transfer is not made until the debtor has acquired rights in the property transferred.

(f) For the purposes of this section, the debtor is presumed to have been insolvent on and during the 90 days immediately preceding the date of the filing of the petition.

(g) For the purposes of this section, the trustee has the burden of proving the avoidability of a transfer under subsection (b) of this section, and the creditor or party in interest against whom recovery or avoidance is sought has the burden of proving the nonavoidability of a transfer under subsection (c) of this section.

Pub.L. 95–598, Nov. 6, 1978, 92 Stat. 2597; Pub.L. 98–353, Title III, §§ 310, 462, July 10, 1984, 98 Stat. 355, 377; Pub.L. 99–554, Title II, § 283(m), Oct. 27, 1986, 100 Stat. 3117.

Historical and Revision Notes

Notes of Committee on the Judiciary, Senate Report No. 95–989. This section is a substantial modification of present law. It modernizes the preference provisions and brings them more into conformity with commercial practice and the Uniform Commercial Code.

Subsection (a) contains three definitions. Inventory, new value, and receivable are defined in their ordinary senses, but are defined to avoid any confusion or uncertainty surrounding the terms.

Subsection (b) is the operative provision of this section. It authorizes the trustee to avoid a transfer if five conditions are met. These are the five elements of a preference action. First, the transfer must be to or for the benefit of a creditor. Second, the transfer must be for or on account of an antecedent debt owed by the debtor before the transfer was made. Third, the transfer must have been made when the debtor was insolvent. Fourth, the transfer must have been made during the 90 days immediately preceding the commencement of the case. If the transfer was to an insider, the trustee may avoid the transfer if it was made during the period that begins one year before the filing of the petition and ends 90 days before the filing, if the insider to whom the transfer was made had reasonable cause to believe the debtor was insolvent at the time the transfer was made.

Finally, the transfer must enable the creditor to whom or for whose benefit it was made to receive a greater percentage of his claim than he would receive under the distributive provisions of the bankruptcy code. Specifically, the creditor must receive more than he would if the case were a liquidation case, if the transfer had not been made, and if the creditor received payment of the debt to the extent provided by the provisions of the code [this title].

The phrasing of the final element changes the application of the greater percentage test from that employed under current law. Under this language, the court must focus on the relative distribution between classes as well as the amount that will be received by the members of the class of which the creditor is a member. The language also requires the court to focus on the allowability of the claim for which the preference was made. If the claim would have been entirely disallowed, for example, then the test of paragraph (5) will be met, because the creditor would have received nothing under the distributive provisions of the bankruptcy code [this title].

The trustee may avoid a transfer of a lien under this section even if the lien has been enforced by sale before the commencement of the case.

Subsection (b)(2) of this section in effect exempts from the preference rules payments by the debtor of tax liabilities, regardless of their priority status.

Subsection (c) contains exceptions to the trustee's avoiding power. If a creditor can qualify under any one of the exceptions, then he is protected to that extent. If he can qualify under several, he is protected by each to the extent that he can qualify under each.

The first exception is for a transfer that was intended by all parties to be a contemporaneous exchange for new value, and was in fact substantially contemporaneous. Normally, a check is a credit transaction. However, for the purposes of this paragraph, a transfer involving a check is considered to be "intended to be contemporaneous", and if the check is presented for payment in the normal course of affairs, which the Uniform Commercial Code specifies as 30 days, U.C.C. § 3–503(2)(a), that will amount to a transfer that is "in fact substantially contemporaneous."

The second exception protects transfers in the ordinary course of business (or of financial affairs, where a business is not involved) transfers. For the case of a consumer, the paragraph uses the phrase "financial affairs" to include such nonbusiness activities as payment of monthly utility bills. If the debt on account of which the transfer was made was incurred in the ordinary course of both the debtor and the transferee, if the transfer was made not later than 45 days after the debt was incurred, if the transfer itself was made in the ordinary course of both the debtor and the transferee, and if the transfer was made according to ordinary business terms, then the transfer is protected. The purpose of this exception is to leave undisturbed normal financial relations, because it does not detract from the general policy of the preference section to discourage unusual action by either the debtor or his creditors during the debtor's slide into bankruptcy.

The third exception is for enabling loans in connection with which the debtor acquires the property that the loan enabled him to purchase after the loan is actually made.

The fourth exception codifies the net result rule in section 60c of current law [former section 96(c) of this title]. If the creditor and the debtor have more than one exchange during the 90-day period, the exchanges are netted out according to the formula in paragraph (4). Any new value that the creditor advances must be unsecured in order for it to qualify under this exception.

Paragraph (5) codifies the improvement in position test, and thereby overrules such cases as DuBay v. Williams, 417 F.2d 1277 (C.A.9, 1966), and Grain Merchants of Indiana, Inc. v. Union Bank and Savings Co., 408 F.2d 209 (C.A.7, 1969). A creditor with a security interest in a floating mass, such as inventory or accounts receivable, is subject to preference attack to the extent he improves his position during the 90-day period before bankruptcy. The test is a two-point test, and requires determination of the secured creditor's position 90 days before the petition and on the date of the petition. If new value was first given after 90 days before the case, the date on which it was first given substitutes for the 90-day point.

Paragraph (6) excepts statutory liens validated under section 545 from preference attack. It also protects transfers in satisfaction of such liens, and the fixing of a lien under section 365(j), which protects a vendee whose contract to purchase real property from the debtor is rejected.

Subsection (d), derived from section 67a of the Bankruptcy Act [former section 107(a) of this title] permits the trustee to avoid a transfer to reimburse a surety that posts a bond to dissolve a judicial lien that would have been avoidable under this section. The second sentence protects the surety from double liability.

Subsection (e) determines when a transfer is made for the purposes of the preference section. Paragraph (1) defines when a transfer is perfected. For real property, a transfer is perfected when it is valid against a bona fide purchaser. For personal property and fixtures, a transfer is perfected when it is valid against a creditor on a simple contract that obtains a judicial lien after the transfer is perfected. "Simple contract" as used here is derived from Bankruptcy Act § 60a(4) [former section 96(a)(4) of this title]. Paragraph (2) specifies that a transfer is made when it takes effect between the transferor and the transferee if it is perfected at or within 10 days after that time. Otherwise, it is made when the transfer is perfected. If it is not perfected before the commencement of the case, it is made immediately before the commencement of the case. Paragraph (3) specifies that a transfer is not made until the debtor has acquired rights in the property transferred. This provision, more than any other in the section, overrules DuBay and Grain Merchants, and in combination with subsection (b)(2), overrules In re King-Porter Co., 446 F.2d 722 (5th Cir. 1971).

Subsection (e) is designed to reach the different results under the 1962 version of Article 9 of the U.C.C. and under the 1972 version because different actions are required under each version in order to make a security agreement effective between the parties.

Subsection (f) creates a presumption of insolvency for the 90 days preceding the bankruptcy case. The presumption is as defined in Rule 301 of the Federal Rules of Evidence [Title 28, Judiciary and Judicial Procedure] made applicable in bankruptcy cases by sections 224 and 225 of the bill. The presumption requires the party against whom the presumption exists to come forward with some evidence to rebut the presumption, but the burden of proof remains on the party in whose favor the presumption exists.

Legislative Statements. No limitation is provided for payments to commodity brokers as in section 766 of the Senate amendment other than the amendment to section 548 of title 11. Section 547(c)(2) protects most payments.

Section 547(b)(2) of the House amendment adopts a provision contained in the House bill and rejects an alternative contained in the Senate amendment relating to the avoidance of a preferential transfer that is payment of a tax claim owing to a governmental unit. As provided, section 106(c) of the House amendment overrules contrary language in the House report with the result that the Government is subject to avoidance of preferential transfers.

Contrary to language contained in the House report, payment of a debt by means of a check is equivalent to a cash payment, unless the check is dishonored. Payment is considered to be made when the check is delivered for purposes of sections 547(c)(1) and (2).

Section 547(c)(6) of the House bill is deleted and is treated in a different fashion in section 553 of the House amendment.

Section 547(c)(6) represents a modification of a similar provision contained in the House bill and Senate amendment. The exception relating to satisfaction of a statutory lien is deleted. The exception for a lien created under title 11 is deleted since such a lien is a statutory lien that will not be avoidable in a subsequent bankruptcy.

Section 547(e)(1)(B) is adopted from the House bill and Senate amendment without change. It is intended that the simple contract test used in this section will be applied as under section 544(a)(1) not to require a creditor to perfect against a creditor on a simple contract in the event applicable law makes such perfection impossible. For example, a purchaser from a debtor at an improperly noticed bulk sale may take subject to the rights of a creditor on a simple contract of the debtor for 1 year after the bulk sale. Since the purchaser cannot perfect against such a creditor on a simple contract, he should not be held responsible for failing to do the impossible. In the event the debtor goes into bankruptcy within a short time after the bulk sale, the trustee should not be able to use the avoiding powers under section 544(a)(1) or 547 merely because State law has made some transfers of personal property subject to the rights of a creditor on a simple contract to acquire a judicial lien with no opportunity to perfect against such a creditor.

The House amendment deletes from the category of transfers on account of antecedent debts which may be avoided under the preference rules, section 547(b)(2), the exception in the Senate amendment for taxes owed to governmental authorities. However, for purposes of the "ordinary course" exception to the pref-erence rules contained in section 547(c)(2), the House amendment specifies that the 45-day period referred to in section 547(c)(2)(B) is to begin running, in the case of taxes from the last due date, including extensions, of the return with respect to which the tax payment was made.

Effective Date of 1986 Amendments; Savings Provisions; Quarterly Fees. Amendment by Pub.L. 99–554, effective 30 days after Oct. 27, 1986, except as otherwise provided for, see section 302(a) of Pub.L. 99–554, set out as a note under section 581 of Title 28, Judiciary and Judicial Procedure.

Effective Date of 1984 Amendments. See section 553 of Pub.L. 98–353, Title III, July 10, 1984, 98 Stat. 392, set out as an Effective Date of 1984 Amendment note preceding chapter 1 of Title 11, Bankruptcy.

Separability of Provisions. For separability of provisions of Title III of Pub.L. 98–353, see section 551 of Pub.L. 98–353 set out as a Separability of Provisions note preceding chapter 1 of Title 11, Bankruptcy.

Cross References

Applicability of this section in chapter 9 cases, see section 901.

Appointment of trustee upon debtor's refusal to pursue cause of action under this section, see section 926.

Commencement of involuntary cases by transferees of voidable transfers, see section 303.

Disallowance of claims of entity that is transferee of avoidable transfer, see section 502.

Effect of dismissal, see section 349.

Exemptions, see section 522.

Voidable transfers in

Commodity broker liquidation cases, see section 764.

Stockbroker liquidation cases, see section 749.

Library References:

C.J.S. Bankruptcy § 135 et seq.

West's Key No. Digests, Bankruptcy ☞2601 et seq.

WESTLAW Electronic Research

See WESTLAW Electronic Research Guide following the *Bankruptcy Highlights*.

§ 548. Fraudulent transfers and obligations

(a) The trustee may avoid any transfer of an interest of the debtor in property, or any obligation incurred by the debtor, that was made or incurred on or within one year before the date of the filing of the petition, if the debtor voluntarily or involuntarily—

(1) made such transfer or incurred such obligation with actual intent to hinder, delay, or defraud any entity to which the debtor was or became, on

or after the date that such transfer was made or such obligation was incurred, indebted; or

(2)(A) received less than a reasonably equivalent value in exchange for such transfer or obligation; and

(B)(i) was insolvent on the date that such transfer was made or such obligation was incurred, or became insolvent as a result of such transfer or obligation;

(ii) was engaged in business or a transaction, or was about to engage in business or a transaction, for which any property remaining with the debtor was an unreasonably small capital; or

(iii) intended to incur, or believed that the debtor would incur, debts that would be beyond the debtor's ability to pay as such debts matured.

(b) The trustee of a partnership debtor may avoid any transfer of an interest of the debtor in property, or any obligation incurred by the debtor, that was made or incurred on or within one year before the date of the filing of the petition, to a general partner in the debtor, if the debtor was insolvent on the date such transfer was made or such obligation was incurred, or became insolvent as a result of such transfer or obligation.

(c) Except to the extent that a transfer or obligation voidable under this section is voidable under section 544, 545, or 547 of this title, a transferee or obligee of such a transfer or obligation that takes for value and in good faith has a lien on or may retain any interest transferred or may enforce any obligation incurred, as the case may be, to the extent that such transferee or obligee gave value to the debtor in exchange for such transfer or obligation.

(d)(1) For the purposes of this section, a transfer is made when such transfer is so perfected that a bona fide purchaser from the debtor against whom applicable law permits such transfer to be perfected cannot acquire an interest in the property transferred that is superior to the interest in such property of the transferee, but if such transfer is not so perfected before the commencement of the case, such transfer is made immediately before the date of the filing of the petition.

(2) In this section—

(A) "value" means property, or satisfaction or securing of a present or antecedent debt of the debtor, but does not include an unperformed promise to furnish support to the debtor or to a relative of the debtor;

(B) a commodity broker, forward contract merchant, stockbroker, financial institution, or securities clearing agency that receives a margin payment, as defined in section 101(34), 741(5) or 761(15) of this title, or settlement payment, as defined in section 101(35) or 741(8) of this title, takes for value to the extent of such payment;

(C) a repo participant that receives a margin payment, as defined in section 741(5) or 761(15) of this title, or settlement payment, as defined in section 741(8) of this title, in connection with a repurchase agreement, takes for value to the extent of such payment; and

(D) a swap participant that receives a transfer in connection with a swap agreement takes for value to the extent of such transfer.

Pub.L. 95–598, Nov. 6, 1978, 92 Stat. 2600; Pub.L. 97–222, § 5, July 27, 1982, 96 Stat. 236; Pub.L. 98–353, Title III, §§ 394, 463, July 10, 1984, 98 Stat. 365, 378;

Pub.L. 99–554, Title II, § 283(n), Oct. 27, 1986, 100 Stat. 3117; Pub.L. 101–311, Title I, § 104, Title II, § 204, June 25, 1990, 104 Stat. 268, 269.

Historical and Revision Notes

Notes of Committee on the Judiciary, Senate Report No. 95–989. This section is derived in large part from section 67d of the Bankruptcy Act [former section 107(d) of this title]. It permits the trustee to avoid transfers by the debtor in fraud of his creditors. Its history dates from the statute of 13 Eliz. c. 5 (1570).

The trustee may avoid fraudulent transfers or obligations if made with actual intent to hinder, delay, or defraud a past or future creditor. Transfers made for less than a reasonably equivalent consideration are also vulnerable if the debtor was or thereby becomes insolvent, was engaged in business with an unreasonably small capital, or intended to incur debts that would be beyond his ability to repay.

The trustee of a partnership debtor may avoid any transfer of partnership property to a partner in the debtor if the debtor was or thereby became insolvent.

If a transferee's only liability to the trustee is under this section, and if he takes for value and in good faith, then subsection (c) grants him a lien on the property transferred, or other similar protection.

Subsection (d) specifies that for the purposes of fraudulent transfer section, a transfer is made when it is valid against a subsequent bona fide purchaser. If not made before the commencement of the case, it is considered made immediately before then. Subsection (d) also defines "value" to mean property, or the satisfaction or securing of a present or antecedent debt, but does not include an unperformed promise to furnish support to the debtor or a relative of the debtor.

Legislative Statements. Section 548(d)(2) is modified to reflect general application of a provision contained in section 766 of the Senate amendment with respect to commodity brokers. In particular, section 548(d)(2)(B) of the House amendment makes clear that a commodity broker who receives a margin payment is considered to receive the margin payment in return for "value" for purposes of section 548.

Effective Date of 1986 Amendments; Savings Provisions; Quarterly Fees. Amendment by Pub.L. 99–554, effective 30 days after Oct. 27, 1986, except as otherwise provided for, see section 302(a) of Pub.L. 99–554, set out as a note under section 581 of Title 28, Judiciary and Judicial Procedure.

Effective Date of 1984 Amendments. See section 553 of Pub.L. 98–353, Title III, July 10, 1984, 98 Stat. 392, set out as an Effective Date of 1984 Amendment note preceding chapter 1 of Title 11, Bankruptcy.

Separability of Provisions. For separability of provisions of Title III of Pub.L. 98–353, see section 551 of Pub.L. 98–353 set out as a Separability of Provisions note preceding chapter 1 of Title 11, Bankruptcy.

Cross References

Applicability of this section in chapter 9 cases, see section 901.

Appointment of trustee upon debtor's refusal to pursue cause of action under this section, see section 926.

Commencement of involuntary cases by transferees of voidable transfers, see section 303.

Disallowance of claims of entity that is transferee of avoidable transfer, see section 502.

Effect of dismissal, see section 349.

Exemptions, see section 522.

Voidable transfers in,

    Commodity broker liquidation cases, see section 764.

    Stockbroker liquidation cases, see section 749.

Library References:

C.J.S. Bankruptcy § 152 et seq.

West's Key No. Digests, Bankruptcy ⚖2641 et seq.

§ 549. Postpetition transactions

(a) Except as provided in subsection (b) or (c) of this section, the trustee may avoid a transfer of property of the estate—

(1) that occurs after the commencement of the case; and

(2)(A) that is authorized only under section 303(f) or 542(c) of this title; or

(B) that is not authorized under this title or by the court.

(b) [1] In an involuntary case, a transfer made after the commencement of such case but before the order for relief to the extent any value, including services, but not including satisfaction or securing of a debt that arose before the commencement of the case, is given after the commencement of the case in exchange for such transfer, notwithstanding any notice or knowledge of the case that the transferee has.

(c) The trustee may not avoid under subsection (a) of this section a transfer of real property to a good faith purchaser without knowledge of the commencement of the case and for present fair equivalent value unless a copy or notice of the petition was filed, where a transfer of such real property may be recorded to perfect such transfer, before such transfer is so perfected that a bona fide purchaser of such property, against whom applicable law permits such transfer to be perfected, could not acquire an interest that is superior to the interest of such good faith purchaser. A good faith purchaser without knowledge of the commencement of the case and for less than present fair equivalent value has a lien on the property transferred to the extent of any present value given, unless a copy or notice of the petition was so filed before such transfer was so perfected.

(d) An action or proceeding under this section may not be commenced after the earlier of—

(1) two years after the date of the transfer sought to be avoided; or

(2) the time the case is closed or dismissed.

Pub.L. 95–598, Nov. 6, 1978, 92 Stat. 2601; Pub.L. 98–353, Title III, § 464, July 10, 1984, 98 Stat. 379; Pub.L. 99–554, Title II, § 283(*o*), Oct. 27, 1986, 100 Stat. 3117.

[1] See Codification note below.

Historical and Revision Notes

Notes of Committee on the Judiciary, Senate Report No. 95–989. This section modifies section 70d of current law [former section 110(d) of this title]. It permits the trustee to avoid transfers of property that occur after the commencement of the case. The transfer must either have been unauthorized, or authorized under a section that protects only the transferor. Subsection (b) protects "involuntary gap" transferees to the extent of any value (including services, but not including satisfaction of a debt that arose before the commencement of the case), given after commencement in exchange for the transfer. Notice or knowledge of the transfer-ee is irrelevant in determining whether he is protected under this provision.

Legislative Statements. Section 549 of the House amendment has been redrafted in order to incorporate sections 342(b) and (c) of the Senate amendment. Those sections have been consolidated and redrafted in section 549(c) of the House amendment. Section 549(d) of the House amendment adopts a provision contained in section 549(c) of the Senate amendment.

Codification. Section 464(a)(3) to (5) of Pub.L. 98–353 (H.R. 5174) purported to amend subsec. (a) of this section. Par. (3) directed that "made" be substituted for "that occurs".

Par. (4) directed that "to the extent" be substituted for "is valid against the trustee to the extent of". Par. (5) directed that "is" be inserted before "given".

The predecessor bill to H.R. 5174 was S. 445. Section 361 of the predecessor bill set out the amendments to subsecs. (a) and (b) of this section in such a manner that indicated that Congress did not intend to amend subsec. (a) of this section by Pub.L. 98–353 § 464(a)(3) to (5).

S. 445, § 361, contained subsecs. (a), (b), and (c). Only subsecs. (a) and (b) thereof are pertinent here. Such subsecs. (a) and (b) read as follows:

SEC. 361. (a) Section 549(a) of title 11 of the United States Code is amended—

(1) by striking out "(b) and (c)" and inserting in lieu thereof "(b) or (c)"; and

(2) in paragraph (2)(A), by inserting "only" after "authorized".

(b) Section 549(b) of title 11 of the United States Code is amended by—

(1) inserting "the trustee may not avoid under subsection (a) of this section," after "involuntary case,";

(2) striking out "that occurs" and inserting in lieu thereof "made";

(3) striking out "is valid against the trustee to the extent of" and inserting in lieu thereof "to the extent"; and

(4) inserting "is" before "given".

Section 464 of Pub.L. 98–353 contained subsecs. (a) and (c); no subsec. (b) appeared therein. Only subsec. (a) is pertinent here. Subsec. (a) read as follows:

SEC. 464. (a) Section 549(a) of title 11 of the United States Code is amended—

(1) by striking out "(b) and (c)" and inserting in lieu thereof "(b) or (c)"; and

(2) in paragraph (2)(A), by inserting "only" after "authorized".

(3) striking out "that occurs" and inserting in lieu thereof "made";

(4) striking out "is valid against the trustee to the extent of" and inserting in lieu thereof "to the extent"; and

(5) inserting "is" before "given".

A comparison thus reveals that Congress had intended subsec. (b)(1) to (4) of section 361 of S. 445 to amend subsec. (b) of this section and to restrict to subsec. (b) of this section the amendments directed to be made by Pub.L. 98–353 § 464(a)(3) to (5). Accordingly, the amendments specified by Pub.L. 98–353 § 464(a)(3) to (5) were not executed to subsec. (a) of this section. Nor were the amendments specified by Pub.L. 98–353 § 464(a)(3) to (5) executed to subsec. (b) of this section as the probable intent of Congress since this would result in an unintelligible provision being set out as subsec. (b) absent the unenacted amendments which appeared only in the predecessor bill, i.e., S. 445, § 361(b)(1) and (2).

Such amendments were later effectuated by Pub.L. 99–554.

Effective Date of 1986 Amendments; Savings Provisions; Quarterly fees. Amendment by Pub.L. 99–554 effective 30 days after Oct. 27, 1986, except as otherwise provided for, see section 302(a) of Pub.L. 99–554, set out as a note under section 581 of Title 28, Judiciary and Judicial Procedure.

Effective Date of 1984 Amendments. See section 553 of Pub.L. 98–353, Title III, July 10, 1984, 98 Stat. 392, set out as an Effective Date of 1984 Amendment note preceding chapter 1 of Title 11, Bankruptcy.

Separability of Provisions. For separability of provisions of Title III of Pub.L. 98–353, see section 551 of Pub.L. 98–353 set out as a Separability of Provisions note preceding chapter 1 of Title 11, Bankruptcy.

Cross References

Applicability of subsecs. (a), (c) and (d) of this section in chapter 9 cases, see section 901.

Appointment of trustee upon debtor's refusal to pursue cause of action under this section, see section 926.

Commencement of involuntary cases by transferees of voidable transfers, see section 303.

Disallowance of claims of entity that is transferee of avoidable transfer, see section 502.

Effect of dismissal, see section 349.

Exemptions, see section 522.

Voidable transfers in,
    Commodity broker liquidation cases, see section 764.
    Stockbroker liquidation cases, see section 749.

Library References:
C.J.S. Bankruptcy § 131.
West's Key No. Digests, Bankruptcy ⊗2588.

WESTLAW Electronic Research
See WESTLAW Electronic Research Guide following the *Bankruptcy Highlights.*

§ 550. Liability of transferee of avoided transfer

(a) Except as otherwise provided in this section, to the extent that a transfer is avoided under section 544, 545, 547, 548, 549, 553(b), or 724(a) of this title, the trustee may recover, for the benefit of the estate, the property transferred, or, if the court so orders, the value of such property, from—

    (1) the initial transferee of such transfer or the entity for whose benefit such transfer was made; or

    (2) any immediate or mediate transferee of such initial transferee.

(b) The trustee may not recover under section (a)(2) of this section from—

    (1) a transferee that takes for value, including satisfaction or securing of a present or antecedent debt, in good faith, and without knowledge of the voidability of the transfer avoided; or

    (2) any immediate or mediate good faith transferee of such transferee.

(c) The trustee is entitled to only a single satisfaction under subsection (a) of this section.

(d)(1) A good faith transferee from whom the trustee may recover under subsection (a) of this section has a lien on the property recovered to secure the lesser of—

    (A) the cost, to such transferee, of any improvement made after the transfer, less the amount of any profit realized by or accruing to such transferee from such property; and

    (B) any increase in the value of such property as a result of such improvement, of the property transferred.

(2) In this subsection, "improvement" includes—

    (A) physical additions or changes to the property transferred;

    (B) repairs to such property;

    (C) payment of any tax on such property;

    (D) payment of any debt secured by a lien on such property that is superior or equal to the rights of the trustee; and

    (E) preservation of such property.

(e) An action or proceeding under this section may not be commenced after the earlier of—

    (1) one year after the avoidance of the transfer on account of which recovery under this section is sought; or

    (2) the time the case is closed or dismissed.

Pub.L. 95–598, Nov. 6, 1978, 92 Stat. 2601; Pub.L. 98–353, Title III, § 465, July 10, 1984, 98 Stat. 379.

Historical and Revision Notes

Notes of Committee on the Judiciary, Senate Report No. 95–989. Section 550 prescribes the liability of a transferee of an avoided transfer, and enunciates the separation between the concepts of avoiding a transfer and recovering from the transferee. Subsection (a) permits the trustee to recover from the initial transferee of an avoided transfer or from any immediate or mediate transferee of the initial transferee. The words "to the extent that" in the lead in to this subsection are designed to incorporate the protection of transferees found in proposed 11 U.S.C. 549(b) and 548(c). Subsection (b) limits the liability of an immediate or mediate transferee of the initial transferee if such secondary transferee takes for value, in good faith and without knowledge of the voidability of the transfer. An immediate or mediate good faith transferee of a protected secondary transferee is also shielded from liability. This subsection is limited to the trustee's right to recover from subsequent transferees under subsection (a)(2). It does not limit the trustee's rights against the initial transferee under subsection (a)(1). The phrase "good faith" in this paragraph is intended to prevent a transferee from whom the trustee could recover from transferring the recoverable property to an innocent transferee, and receiving a retransfer from him, that is, "washing" the transaction through an innocent third party. In order for the transferee to be excepted from liability under this paragraph, he himself must be a good faith transferee. Subsection (c) is a further limitation on recovery. It specifies that the trustee is entitled to only one satisfactory, under subsection (a), even if more than one transferee is liable.

Subsection (d) protects good faith transferees, either initial or subsequent, to the extent of the lesser of the cost of any improvement the transferee makes in the transferred property and the increase in value of the property as a result of the improvement. Paragraph (2) of the subsection defines improvement to include physical additions or changes to the property, repairs, payment of taxes on the property, payment of a debt secured by a lien on the property, discharge of a lien on the property, and preservation of the property.

Subsection (e) establishes a statute of limitations on avoidance by the Trustee. The limitation is one year after the avoidance of the transfer or the time the case is closed or dismissed, whichever is earlier.

Legislative Statements. Section 550(a)(1) of the House amendment has been modified in order to permit recovery from an entity for whose benefit an avoided transfer is made in addition to a recovery from the initial transferee of the transfer. Section 550(c) would still apply, and the trustee is entitled only to a single satisfaction. The liability of a transferee under section 550(a) applies only "to the extent that a transfer is avoided". This means that liability is not imposed on a transferee to the extent that a transferee is protected under a provision such as section 548(c) which grants a good faith transferee for value of a transfer that is avoided only as a fraudulent transfer, a lien on the property transferred to the extent of value given.

Section 550(b) of the House amendment is modified to indicate that value includes satisfaction or securing of a present antecedent debt. This means that the trustee may not recover under subsection (a)(2) from a subsequent transferee that takes for "value", provided the subsequent transferee also takes in good faith and without knowledge of the transfer avoided.

Section 550(e) of the House amendment is derived from section 550(e) of the Senate amendment.

Effective Date of 1984 Amendments. See section 553 of Pub.L. 98–353, Title III, July 10, 1984, 98 Stat. 392, set out as an Effective Date of 1984 Amendment note preceding chapter 1 of Title 11, Bankruptcy.

Separability of Provisions. For separability of provisions of Title III of Pub.L. 98–353, see section 551 of Pub.L. 98–353 set out as a Separability of Provisions note preceding chapter 1 of Title 11, Bankruptcy.

Cross References

Allowance of claims or interests, see section 502.

Applicability of this section in chapter 9 cases, see section 901.

Appointment of trustee upon debtor's refusal to pursue cause of action under this
section, see section 926.

Effect of dismissal, see section 349.

Exemptions, see section 522.

Library References:

C.J.S. Bankruptcy § 134.

West's Key No. Digests, Bankruptcy ☞2701–2729.

WESTLAW Electronic Research

See WESTLAW Electronic Research Guide following the *Bankruptcy Highlights*.

§ 551.   Automatic preservation of avoided transfer

Any transfer avoided under section 522, 544, 545, 547, 548, 549, or 724(a) of
this title, or any lien void under section 506(d) of this title, is preserved for the
benefit of the estate but only with respect to property of the estate.

Pub.L. 95–598, Nov. 6, 1978, 92 Stat. 2602.

Historical and Revision Notes

**Notes of Committee on the Judiciary,
Senate Report No. 95–989.** This section is a
change from present law. It specifies that
any avoided transfer is automatically preserved for the benefit of the estate. Under
current law, the court must determine whether or not the transfer should be preserved.
The operation of the section is automatic, unlike current law, even though preservation
may not benefit the estate in every instance.
A preserved lien may be abandoned by the
trustee under proposed 11 U.S.C. 554 if the
preservation does not benefit the estate. The
section as a whole prevents junior lienors
from improving their position at the expense
of the estate when a senior lien is avoided.

Legislative Statements. Section 551 is
adopted from the House bill and the alternative in the Senate amendment is rejected.
The section is clarified to indicate that a
transfer avoided or a lien that is void is preserved for the benefit of the estate, but only
with respect to property of the estate. This
prevents the trustee from asserting an avoided tax lien against after acquired property of
the debtor.

Cross References

Applicability of this section in chapter 9 cases, see section 901.

Effect of dismissal, see section 349.

Exemptions, see section 522.

Library References:

C.J.S. Bankruptcy § 133.

West's Key No. Digests, Bankruptcy ☞2706.

WESTLAW Electronic Research

See WESTLAW Electronic Research Guide following the *Bankruptcy Highlights*.

§ 552.   Postpetition effect of security interest

(a) Except as provided in subsection (b) of this section, property acquired by
the estate or by the debtor after the commencement of the case is not subject to
any lien resulting from any security agreement entered into by the debtor before
the commencement of the case.

(b) Except as provided in sections 363, 506(c), 522, 544, 545, 547, and 548 of
this title, if the debtor and an entity entered into a security agreement before
the commencement of the case and if the security interest created by such

security agreement extends to property of the debtor acquired before the commencement of the case and to proceeds, product, offspring, rents, or profits of such property, then such security interest extends to such proceeds, product, offspring, rents, or profits acquired by the estate after the commencement of the case to the extent provided by such security agreement and by applicable non-bankruptcy law, except to any extent that the court, after notice and a hearing and based on the equities of the case, orders otherwise.

Pub.L. 95–598, Nov. 6, 1978, 92 Stat. 2602; Pub.L. 98–353, Title III, § 466, July 10, 1984, 98 Stat. 380.

Historical and Revision Notes

Notes of Committee on the Judiciary, Senate Report No. 95–989. Under the Uniform Commercial Code, article 9, creditors may take security interests in after-acquired property. Section 552 governs the effect of such a prepetition security interest in postpetition property. It applies to all security interests as defined in section 101(37) of the bankruptcy code [this title] not only to U.C.C. security interests.

As a general rule, if a security agreement is entered into before the commencement of the case, then property that the estate acquires is not subject to the security interest created by a provision in the security agreement extending the security interest to after-acquired property. Subsection (b) provides an important exception consistent with the Uniform Commercial Code. If the security agreement extends to proceeds, product, offspring, rents, or profits of the property in question, then the proceeds would continue to be subject to the security interest pursuant to the terms of the security agreement and provisions of applicable law, except to the extent that where the estate acquires the proceeds at the expense of other creditors holding unsecured claims, the expenditure resulted in an improvement in the position of the secured party.

The exception covers the situation where raw materials, for example, are converted into inventory, or inventory into accounts, at some expense to the estate, thus depleting the fund available for general unsecured creditors, but is limited to the benefit inuring to the secured party thereby. Situations in which the estate

incurs expense in simply protecting collateral are governed by 11 U.S.C. 506(c). In ordinary circumstances, the risk of loss in continued operations will remain with the estate.

Legislative Statements. Section 552(a) is derived from the House bill and the alternative provision in the Senate amendment is rejected. Section 552(b) represents a compromise between the House bill and the Senate amendment. Proceeds coverage, but not after acquired property clauses, are valid under title 11. The provision allows the court to consider the equities in each case. In the course of such consideration the court may evaluate any expenditures by the estate relating to proceeds and any related improvement in position of the secured party. Although this section grants a secured party a security interest in proceeds, product, offspring, rents, or profits, the section is explicitly subject to other sections of title 11. For example, the trustee or debtor in possession may use, sell, or lease proceeds, product, offspring, rents or profits under section 363.

Effective Date of 1984 Amendments. See section 553 of Pub.L. 98–353, Title III, July 10, 1984, 98 Stat. 392, set out as an Effective Date of 1984 Amendment note preceding chapter 1 of Title 11, Bankruptcy.

Separability of Provisions. For separability of provisions of Title III of Pub.L. 98–353, see section 551 of Pub.L. 98–353 set out as a Separability of Provisions note preceding chapter 1 of Title 11, Bankruptcy.

Cross References

    Applicability of this section in chapter 9 cases, see section 901.

Library References:

    C.J.S. Bankruptcy § 121.

    West's Key No. Digests, Bankruptcy ⚷2573.

§ 553. Setoff

(a) Except as otherwise provided in this section and in sections 362 and 363 of this title, this title does not affect any right of a creditor to offset a mutual debt owing by such creditor to the debtor that arose before the commencement of the case under this title against a claim of such creditor against the debtor that arose before the commencement of the case, except to the extent that—

(1) the claim of such creditor against the debtor is disallowed other than under section 502(b)(3) of this title;

(2) such claim was transferred, by an entity other than the debtor, to such creditor—

(A) after the commencement of the case; or

(B)(i) after 90 days before the date of the filing of the petition; and

(ii) while the debtor was insolvent; or

(3) the debt owed to the debtor by such creditor was incurred by such creditor—

(A) after 90 days before the date of the filing of the petition;

(B) while the debtor was insolvent; and

(C) for the purpose of obtaining a right of setoff against the debtor.

(b)(1) Except with respect to a setoff of a kind described in section 362(b)(6), 362(b)(7), 362(b)(14), 365(h)(2), or 365(i)(2) of this title, if a creditor offsets a mutual debt owing to the debtor against a claim against the debtor on or within 90 days before the date of the filing of the petition, then the trustee may recover from such creditor the amount so offset to the extent that any insufficiency on the date of such setoff is less than the insufficiency on the later of—

(A) 90 days before the date of the filing of the petition; and

(B) the first date during the 90 days immediately preceding the date of the filing of the petition on which there is an insufficiency.

(2) In this subsection, "insufficiency" means amount, if any, by which a claim against the debtor exceeds a mutual debt owing to the debtor by the holder of such claim.

(c) For the purposes of this section, the debtor is presumed to have been insolvent on and during the 90 days immediately preceding the date of the filing of the petition.

Pub.L. 95–598, Nov. 6, 1978, 92 Stat. 2602; Pub.L. 98–353, Title III, §§ 395, 467, July 10, 1984, 98 Stat. 365, 380; Pub.L. 101–311, Title I, § 105, June 25, 1990, 104 Stat. 268.

Historical and Revision Notes

Notes of Committee on the Judiciary, Senate Report No. 95–989. This section preserves, with some changes, the right of setoff in bankruptcy cases now found in section 68 of the Bankruptcy Act [former section 108 of this title]. One exception to the right is the auto-matic stay, discussed in connection with proposed 11 U.S.C. 362. Another is the right of the trustee to use property under section 363 that is subject to a right of setoff.

The section states that the right of setoff is unaffected by the bankruptcy code [this title] except to the extent that the creditor's claim is disallowed, the creditor acquired (other than from the debtor) the claim during the 90 days preceding the case while the debtor was insolvent, the debt being offset was incurred for the purpose of obtaining a right of setoff, while the debtor was insolvent and during the 90-day prebankruptcy period, or the creditor improved his position in the 90-day period (similar to the improvement in position test found in the preference section 547(c)(5)). Only the last exception is an addition to current law.

As under section 547(f), the debtor is presumed to have been insolvent during the 90 days before the case.

Legislative Statements. Section 553 of the House amendment is derived from a similar provision contained in the Senate amendment, but is modified to clarify application of a two-point test with respect to setoffs.

Effective Date of 1984 Amendments. See section 553 of Pub.L. 98–353, Title III, July 10, 1984, 98 Stat. 392, set out as an Effective Date of 1984 Amendment note preceding chapter 1 of Title 11, Bankruptcy.

Separability of Provisions. For separability of provisions of Title III of Pub.L. 98–353, see section 551 of Pub.L. 98–353 set out as a Separability of Provisions note preceding chapter 1 of Title 11, Bankruptcy.

Cross References

> Allowance of claims or interests, see section 502.
> Applicability of this section in chapter 9 cases, see section 901.
> Determination of secured status, see section 506.
> Effect of dismissal, see section 349.
> Recovered property as exempt, see section 522.

Library References:

> C.J.S. Bankruptcy §§ 164 et seq., 245.
> West's Key No. Digests, Bankruptcy ⟲2671–2680.

WESTLAW Electronic Research

> See WESTLAW Electronic Research Guide following the *Bankruptcy Highlights*.

§ 554. Abandonment of property of the estate

(a) After notice and a hearing, the trustee may abandon any property of the estate that is burdensome to the estate or that is of inconsequential value and benefit to the estate.

(b) On request of a party in interest and after notice and a hearing, the court may order the trustee to abandon any property of the estate that is burdensome to the estate or that is of inconsequential value and benefit to the estate.

(c) Unless the court orders otherwise, any property scheduled under section 521(1) of this title not otherwise administered at the time of the closing of a case is abandoned to the debtor and administered for purposes of section 350 of this title.

(d) Unless the court orders otherwise, property of the estate that is not abandoned under this section and that is not administered in the case remains property of the estate.

Pub.L. 95–598, Nov. 6, 1978, 92 Stat. 2603; Pub.L. 98–353, Title III, § 468, July 10, 1984, 98 Stat. 380; Pub.L. 99–554, Title II, § 283(p), Oct. 27, 1986, 100 Stat. 3118.

Historical and Revision Notes

Notes of Committee on the Judiciary, Senate Report No. 95–989. Under this sec- tion the court may authorize the trustee to abandon any property of the estate that is burdensome to the estate or that is of inconsequential value to the estate. Abandonment, may be to any party with a possessory interest in the property abandoned. In order to aid administration of the case, subsection (b) deems the court to have authorized abandonment of any property that is scheduled under section 521(1) and that is not administered before the case is closed. That property is deemed abandoned to the debtor. Subsection (c) specifies that if property is neither abandoned nor administered it remains property of the estate.

Legislative Statements. Section 554(b) is new and permits a party in interest to request the court to order the trustee to abandon property of the estate that is burdensome to the estate or that is of inconsequential value to the estate.

Effective Date of 1986 Amendments; Savings Provisions; Quarterly Fees. Amendment by Pub.L. 99–554 effective 30 days after Oct. 27, 1986, except as otherwise provided for, see section 302(a) of Pub.L. 99–554, set out as a note under section 581 of Title 28, Judiciary and Judicial Procedure.

Effective Date of 1984 Amendments. See section 553 of Pub.L. 98–353, Title III, July 10, 1984, 98 Stat. 392, set out as an Effective Date of 1984 Amendment note preceding chapter 1 of Title 11, Bankruptcy.

Separability of Provisions. For separability of provisions of Title III of Pub.L. 98–353, see section 551 of Pub.L. 98–353 set out as a Separability of Provisions note preceding chapter 1 of Title 11, Bankruptcy.

Cross References

Redemption, see section 722.

Library References:

C.J.S. Bankruptcy §§ 188, 189.
West's Key No. Digests, Bankruptcy ⟜3131 et seq.

WESTLAW Electronic Research

See WESTLAW Electronic Research Guide following the *Bankruptcy Highlights.*

§ 555. Contractual right to liquidate a securities contract

The exercise of a contractual right of a stockbroker, financial institution, or securities clearing agency to cause the liquidation of a securities contract, as defined in section 741(7), because of a condition of the kind specified in section 365(e)(1) of this title shall not be stayed, avoided, or otherwise limited by operation of any provision of this title or by order of a court or administrative agency in any proceeding under this title unless such order is authorized under the provisions of the Securities Investor Protection Act of 1970 (15 U.S.C. 78aaa et seq.) or any statute administered by the Securities and Exchange Commission. As used in this section, the term "contractual right" includes a right set forth in a rule or bylaw of a national securities exchange, a national securities association, or a securities clearing agency.

Added Pub.L. 97–222, § 6(a), July 27, 1982, 96 Stat. 236; Pub.L. 98–353, Title III, § 469, July 10, 1984, 98 Stat. 380.

References in Text. The Securities Investor Protection Act of 1970 (15 U.S.C. 78aaa et seq.), referred to in text, is Pub.L. 91–598, Dec. 30, 1970, 84 Stat. 1636, which is classified generally to chapter 2B–1 (§ 78aaa et seq.) of Title 15, Commerce and Trade.

Effective Date of 1984 Amendments. See section 553 of Pub.L. 98–353, Title III, July 10,

1984, 98 Stat. 392, set out as an Effective Date of 1984 Amendment note preceding chapter 1 of Title 11, Bankruptcy.

Separability of Provisions. For separability of provisions of Title III of Pub.L. 98–353, see section 551 of Pub.L. 98–353 set out as a Separability of Provisions note preceding chapter 1 of Title 11, Bankruptcy.

§ 556. Contractual right to liquidate a commodities contract or forward contract

The contractual right of a commodity broker or forward contract merchant to cause the liquidation of a commodity contract, as defined in section 761(4), or forward contract because of a condition of the kind specified in section 365(e)(1) of this title, and the right to a variation or maintenance margin payment received from a trustee with respect to open commodity contracts or forward contracts, shall not be stayed, avoided, or otherwise limited by operation of any provision of this title or by the order of a court in any proceeding under this title. As used in this section, the term "contractual right" includes a right set forth in a rule or bylaw of a clearing organization or contract market or in a resolution of the governing board thereof and a right, whether or not evidenced in writing, arising under common law, under law merchant or by reason of normal business practice.

Added Pub.L. 97–222, § 6(a), July 27, 1982, 96 Stat. 236; Pub.L. 101–311, Title II, § 205, June 25, 1990, 104 Stat. 270.

§ 557. Expedited determination of interests in, and abandonment or other disposition of grain assets

(a) This section applies only in a case concerning a debtor that owns or operates a grain storage facility and only with respect to grain and the proceeds of grain. This section does not affect the application of any other section of this title to property other than grain and proceeds of grain.

(b) In this section—

(1) "grain" means wheat, corn, flaxseed, grain sorghum, barley, oats, rye, soybeans, other dry edible beans, or rice;

(2) "grain storage facility" means a site or physical structure regularly used to store grain for producers, or to store grain acquired from producers for resale; and

(3) "producer" means an entity which engages in the growing of grain.

(c)(1) Notwithstanding sections 362, 363, 365, and 554 of this title, on the court's own motion the court may, and on the request of the trustee or an entity that claims an interest in grain or the proceeds of grain the court shall, expedite the procedures for the determination of interests in and the disposition of grain and the proceeds of grain, by shortening to the greatest extent feasible such time periods as are otherwise applicable for such procedures and by establishing, by order, a timetable having a duration of not to exceed 120 days for the completion of the applicable procedure specified in subsection (d) of this section. Such time periods and such timetable may be modified by the court, for cause, in accordance with subsection (f) of this section.

206

(2) The court shall determine the extent to which such time periods shall be shortened, based upon—

(A) any need of an entity claiming an interest in such grain or the proceeds of grain for a prompt determination of such interest;

(B) any need of such entity for a prompt disposition of such grain;

(C) the market for such grain;

(D) the conditions under which such grain is stored;

(E) the costs of continued storage or disposition of such grain;

(F) the orderly administration of the estate;

(G) the appropriate opportunity for an entity to assert an interest in such grain; and

(H) such other considerations as are relevant to the need to expedite such procedures in the case.

(d) The procedures that may be expedited under subsection (c) of this section include—

(1) the filing of and response to—

(A) a claim of ownership;

(B) a proof of claim;

(C) a request for abandonment;

(D) a request for relief from the stay of action against property under section 362(a) of this title;

(E) a request for determination of secured status;

(F) a request for determination of whether such grain or the proceeds of grain—

(i) is property of the estate;

(ii) must be turned over to the estate; or

(iii) may be used, sold, or leased; and

(G) any other request for determination of an interest in such grain or the proceeds of grain;

(2) the disposition of such grain or the proceeds of grain, before or after determination of interests in such grain or the proceeds of grain, by way of—

(A) sale of such grain;

(B) abandonment;

(C) distribution; or

(D) such other method as is equitable in the case;

(3) subject to sections 701, 702, 703, 1104, 1202, and 1302 of this title, the appointment of a trustee or examiner and the retention and compensation of any professional person required to assist with respect to matters relevant to the determination of interests in or disposition of such grain or the proceeds of grain; and

(4) the determination of any dispute concerning a matter specified in paragraph (1), (2), or (3) of this subsection.

(e)(1) Any governmental unit that has regulatory jurisdiction over the operation or liquidation of the debtor or the debtor's business shall be given notice of any request made or order entered under subsection (c) of this section.

(2) Any such governmental unit may raise, and may appear and be heard on, any issue relating to grain or the proceeds of grain in a case in which a request is made, or an order is entered, under subsection (c) of this section.

(3) The trustee shall consult with such governmental unit before taking any action relating to the disposition of grain in the possession, custody, or control of the debtor or the estate.

(f) The court may extend the period for final disposition of grain or the proceeds of grain under this section beyond 120 days if the court finds that—

(1) the interests of justice so require in light of the complexity of the case; and

(2) the interests of those claimants entitled to distribution of grain or the proceeds of grain will not be materially injured by such additional delay.

(g) Unless an order establishing an expedited procedure under subsection (c) of this section, or determining any interest in or approving any disposition of grain or the proceeds of grain, is stayed pending appeal—

(1) the reversal or modification of such order on appeal does not affect the validity of any procedure, determination, or disposition that occurs before such reversal or modification, whether or not any entity knew of the pendency of the appeal; and

(2) neither the court nor the trustee may delay, due to the appeal of such order, any proceeding in the case in which such order is issued.

(h)(1) The trustee may recover from grain and the proceeds of grain the reasonable and necessary costs and expenses allowable under section 503(b) of this title attributable to preserving or disposing of grain or the proceeds of grain, but may not recover from such grain or the proceeds of grain any other costs or expenses.

(2) Notwithstanding section 326(a) of this title, the dollar amounts of money specified in such section include the value, as of the date of disposition, of any grain that the trustee distributes in kind.

(i) In all cases where the quantity of a specific type of grain held by a debtor operating a grain storage facility exceeds ten thousand bushels, such grain shall be sold by the trustee and the assets thereof distributed in accordance with the provisions of this section.

Added Pub.L. 98–353, Title III, § 352(a), July 10, 1984, 98 Stat. 359; Pub.L. 99–554, Title II, § 257(p), Oct. 27, 1986, 100 Stat. 3115.

Effective Date of 1986 Amendments; Savings Provisions; Quarterly Fees. Amendment by Pub.L. 99–554 effective 30 days after Oct. 27, 1986, except as otherwise provided for, see section 302(a) of Pub.L. 99–554, set out as a note under section 581 of Title 28, Judiciary and Judicial Procedure.

Amendments by Pub.L. 99–554, § 257(p), not to apply with respect to cases commenced under Title 11, Bankruptcy, before 30 days after Oct. 27, 1986, see section 302(c)(1) of Pub.

L. 99–554, set out as a note under section 581 of Title 28.

Effective Date. See section 553 of Pub.L. 98–353, Title III, July 10, 1984, 98 Stat. 392, set out as an Effective Date of 1984 Amendment note preceding chapter 1 of Title 11, Bankruptcy.

Separability of Provisions. For separability of provisions of Title III of Pub.L. 98–353, see section 551 of Pub.L. 98–353 set out as a Separability of Provisions note preceding chapter 1 of Title 11, Bankruptcy.

Library References:

C.J.S. Bankruptcy §§ 171, 258.
West's Key No. Digests, Bankruptcy ☞2744.

§ 558. Defenses of the estate

The estate shall have the benefit of any defense available to the debtor as against any entity other than the estate, including statutes of limitation, statutes of frauds, usury, and other personal defenses. A waiver of any such defense by the debtor after the commencement of the case does not bind the estate.

Added Pub.L. 98–353, Title III, § 470(a), July 10, 1984, 98 Stat. 380.

Effective Date. See section 553 of Pub.L. 98–353, Title III, July 10, 1984, 98 Stat. 392, set out as an Effective Date of 1984 Amendment note preceding chapter 1 of Title 11, Bankruptcy.

Separability of Provisions. For separability of provisions of Title III of Pub.L. 98–353, see section 551 of Pub.L. 98–353 set out as a Separability of Provisions note preceding chapter 1 of Title 11, Bankruptcy.

Library References:

C.J.S. Bankruptcy § 27.
West's Key No. Digests, Bankruptcy ☞2152.

§ 559. Contractual right to liquidate a repurchase agreement

The exercise of a contractual right of a repo participant to cause the liquidation of a repurchase agreement because of a condition of the kind specified in section 365(e)(1) of this title shall not be stayed, avoided, or otherwise limited by operation of any provision of this title or by order of a court or administrative agency in any proceeding under this title, unless, where the debtor is a stockbroker or securities clearing agency, such order is authorized under the provisions of the Securities Investor Protection Act of 1970 (15 U.S.C. 78aaa et seq.) or any statute administered by the Securities and Exchange Commission. In the event that a repo participant liquidates one or more repurchase agreements with a debtor and under the terms of one or more such agreements has agreed to deliver assets subject to repurchase agreements to the debtor, any excess of the market prices received on liquidation of such assets (or if any such assets are not disposed of on the date of liquidation of such repurchase agreements, at the prices available at the time of liquidation of such repurchase agreements from a generally recognized source or the most recent closing bid quotation from such a source) over the sum of the stated repurchase prices and all expenses in connection with the liquidation of such repurchase agreements shall be deemed property of the estate, subject to the available rights of setoff. As used in this section, the term "contractual right" includes a right set forth in a rule or bylaw, applicable to each party to the repurchase agreement, of a national securities exchange, a national securities association, or a securities clearing agency, and a right, whether or not evidenced in writing, arising under common law, under law merchant or by reason of normal business practice.

Added Pub.L. 98–353, Title III, § 396(a), July 10, 1984, 98 Stat. 366.

References in Text. The Securities Investor Protection Act of 1970 (15 U.S.C. 78aaa et seq.), referred to in text, is Pub.L. 91–598, Dec. 30, 1970, 84 Stat. 1636, as amended, which is classified generally to chapter 2B–1 (§ 78aaa et seq.) of Title 15, Commerce and Trade.

Effective Date. See section 553 of Pub.L. 98–353, Title III, July 10, 1984, 98 Stat. 392, set out as an Effective Date of 1984 Amendment note preceding chapter 1 of Title 11, Bankruptcy.

Separability of Provisions. For separability of provisions of Title III of Pub.L. 98–353, see section 551 of Pub.L. 98–353 set out as a Separability of Provisions note preceding chapter 1 of Title 11, Bankruptcy.

Library References:
C.J.S. Bankruptcy § 99.
West's Key No. Digests, Bankruptcy ⬅2367.

§ 560. Contractual right to terminate a swap agreement

The exercise of any contractual right of any swap participant to cause the termination of a swap agreement because of a condition of the kind specified in section 365(e)(1) of this title or to offset or net out any termination values or payment amounts arising under or in connection with any swap agreement shall not be stayed, avoided, or otherwise limited by operation of any provision of this title or by order of a court or administrative agency in any proceeding under this title. As used in this section, the term "contractual right" includes a right, whether or not evidenced in writing, arising under common law, under law merchant, or by reason of normal business practice.

Added Pub.L. 101–311, Title I, § 106(a), June 25, 1990, 104 Stat. 268.

CHAPTER 7—LIQUIDATION

SUBCHAPTER I—OFFICERS AND ADMINISTRATION

Sec.
701. Interim trustee.
702. Election of trustee.
703. Successor trustee.
704. Duties of trustee.
705. Creditors' committee.
706. Conversion
707. Dismissal.

SUBCHAPTER II—COLLECTION, LIQUIDATION, AND DISTRIBUTION OF THE ESTATE

721. Authorization to operate business.
722. Redemption.
723. Rights of partnership trustee against general partners.
724. Treatment of certain liens.
725. Disposition of certain property.
726. Distribution of property of the estate.
727. Discharge.
728. Special tax provisions.

SUBCHAPTER III—STOCKBROKER LIQUIDATION

741. Definitions for this subchapter.
742. Effect of section 362 of this title in this subchapter.
743. Notice.
744. Executory contracts.
745. Treatment of accounts.
746. Extent of customer claims.
747. Subordination of certain customer claims.
748. Reduction of securities to money.
749. Voidable transfers.
750. Distribution of securities.
751. Customer name securities.
752. Customer property.

SUBCHAPTER IV—COMMODITY BROKER LIQUIDATION

761. Definitions for the subchapter.
762. Notice to the Commission and right to be heard.
763. Treatment of accounts.
764. Voidable transfers.
765. Customer instructions.
766. Treatment of customer property.

Cross References

Amount received for claim through liquidation under this chapter as standard for confirmation requirement in
Chapter 11 cases, see section 1129.
Chapter 13 cases, see section 1325.

Amount received for claim through liquidation under this chapter as standard for discharge requirement under chapter 13, see section 1328.

Chapters 1, 3 and 5 of this title applicable in case under this chapter, see section 103.

Commencement of involuntary cases, see section 303.

Conversion to this chapter from
Chapter 11, see section 1112.
Chapter 13, see section 1307.

Denial of discharge under this chapter as affecting operation of injunction, see section 524.

Distribution of certain proceeds and property under this chapter as requirement for confirmation of plan, see section 1173.

Duration of automatic stay in case concerning an individual under this chapter, see section 362.

Effect of distribution other than under this title, see section 508.

Eligibility to serve as trustee, see section 321.

Employment of professional persons, see section 327.

Executory contracts and unexpired leases, see section 365.

Limitation on compensation of trustee, see section 326.

Liquidation in railroad reorganization case as if under this chapter, see section 1174.

Objection to allowance of claims by creditor of partner in partnership that is debtor under this chapter, see section 502.

Payment of trustee from filing fee, see section 330.

Persons who may be debtors under this chapter, see section 109.

Property of estate in cases converted from chapter 13, see section 1306.

Recommendation by trustee of conversion from chapter 11 to this chapter, see section 1106.

Special tax provisions, see section 346.

Stay of action against chapter 13 codebtor in cases converted to this chapter, see section 1301.

Transfers enabling creditor to receive more than under this chapter, see section 547.

Unclaimed property, see section 347.

Effective Date of 1984 Amendments. Item 703 added by Pub.L. 98–353. See section 553 of Pub.L. 98–353, Title III, July 10, 1984, 98 Stat. 392, set out as an Effective Date of 1984 Amendment note preceding chapter 1 of Title 11, Bankruptcy.

Separability of Provisions. For separability of provisions of Title III of Pub.L. 98–353, see section 551 of Pub.L. 98–353 set out as a Separability of Provisions note preceding chapter 1 of Title 11, Bankruptcy.

SUBCHAPTER I—OFFICERS AND ADMINISTRATION

Cross References

Subchapter applicable only in case under this chapter, see section 103.

§ 701. Interim trustee

(a)(1) Promptly after the order for relief under this chapter, the United States trustee shall appoint one disinterested person that is a member of the panel of private trustees established under section 586(a)(1) of title 28 or that is serving as trustee in the case immediately before the order for relief under this chapter to serve as interim trustee in the case.

(2) If none of the members of such panel is willing to serve as interim trustee in the case, then the United States trustee may serve as interim trustee in the case.

(b) The service of an interim trustee under this section terminates when a trustee elected or designated under section 702 of this title to serve as trustee in the case qualifies under section 322 of this title.

(c) An interim trustee serving under this section is a trustee in a case under this title.

Pub.L. 95–598, Nov. 6, 1978, 92 Stat. 2604; Pub.L. 99–554, Title II, § 215, Oct. 27, 1986, 100 Stat. 3100.

Historical and Revision Notes

Notes of Committee on the Judiciary, Senate Report No. 95–989. This section requires the court to appoint an interim trustee. The appointment must be made from the panel of private trustees established and maintained by the Director of the Administrative Office under proposed 28 U.S.C. 604(e).

Subsection (a) requires the appointment of an interim trustee to be made promptly after the order for relief, unless a trustee is already serving in the case, such as before a conversion from a reorganization to a liquidation case.

Subsection (b) specifies that the appointment of an interim trustee expires when the permanent trustee is elected or designated under section 702.

Subsection (c) makes clear that an interim trustee is a trustee in a case under the bankruptcy code [this title].

Subsection (d) provides that in a commodity broker case where speed is essential the interim trustee must be appointed by noon of the business day immediately following the order for relief.

Legislative Statements. The House amendment deletes section 701(d) of the Senate amendment. It is anticipated that the Rules of Bankruptcy Procedure will require the appointment of an interim trustee at the earliest practical moment in commodity broker bankruptcies, but no later than noon of the day after the date of the filing of the petition, due to the volatility of such cases.

1986 Amendment. Subsec. (a). Pub.L. 99–554, § 215, designated existing provisions as par. (1), and, as so designated, substituted "the United States trustee shall appoint" for "the court shall appoint", "586(a)(1)" for "604(f)", "that is serving" for "that was serving", and added par. (2).

See Effective Date of 1986 Amendment, etc., notes set out below.

Effective Date of 1986 Amendments; Effective Date of 1986 Amendments for Certain Judicial Districts Not Served by United States Trustees and for Judicial Districts in Alabama and North Carolina; U.S. Trustee System Fund Deposits in Alabama and North Carolina; Effective Date of Title 11, Chapter 15 Repeal as to Northern District of Alabama; Authority of Certain Estate Administrators in Alabama and North Carolina; Effective Date of 1986 Amendments in Pending Cases Where a U.S. Trustee Not Authorized or Where a Trustee Files Final Report or Plan is Confirmed; Quarterly Fees. Amendment by Pub.L. 99–554 effective 30 days after Oct. 27, 1986, except as otherwise provided for, see section 302(a) of Pub.L. 99–554, set out as a note under section 581 of Title 28, Judiciary and Judicial Procedure.

Amendment by Pub.L. 99–554, § 215, not to become effective in or with respect to certain specified judicial districts until, or apply to cases while pending in such district before, the expiration of the 270-day period beginning 30 days after Oct. 27, 1986, or of the 30-day period beginning on the date the Attorney General certifies under section 303 of Pub.L. 99–554 the region specified in a paragraph of section 581(a) of Title 28, as amended by section 111(a) of Pub.L. 99–554, that includes such district, whichever occurs first, see section 302(d)(1) of Pub.L. 99–554, set out as a note under section 581 of Title 28.

Amendment by Pub.L. 99–554, § 215, not to become effective in or with respect to certain specified judicial districts until, or apply to cases while pending in such district before, the expiration of the 2-year period beginning 30 days after Oct. 27, 1986, or of the 30-day period beginning on the date the Attorney

General certifies under section 303 of Pub.L. 99–554 the region specified in a paragraph of section 581(a) of Title 28, as amended by section 111(a) of Pub.L. 99–554, that includes such district, whichever occurs first, see section 302(d)(2) of Pub.L. 99–554, set out as a note under section 581 of Title 28.

Amendment by Pub.L. 99–554, § 215, not to become effective in or with respect to judicial districts established for the States of Alabama and North Carolina until, or apply to cases while pending in such district before, such district elects to be included in a bankruptcy region established in section 581(a) of Title 28, as amended by section 111(a) of Pub.L. 99–554, or Oct. 1, 2002, whichever occurs first, and, except as otherwise provided for, with respect to cases under chapters 7, 11, 12, and 13 of Title 11 commenced before 30 days after Oct. 27, 1986, and pending in a judicial district in the States of Alabama or North Carolina before any election made under section 302(d)(3)(A) of Pub.L. 99–554 by such district becomes effective or Oct. 1, 2002, whichever occurs first, amendments by Pub.L. 99–554 not to apply until Oct. 1, 2003, or the expiration of the 1-year period beginning on the date such election becomes effective, whichever occurs first, and further, in any judicial district in Alabama or North Carolina not making the election described in section 302(d)(3)(A) of

Pub.L. 99–554, any person appointed under regulations issued by the Judicial Conference to administer estates in cases under Title 11 authorized to establish, etc., a panel of private trustees, and to supervise cases and trustees in cases under chapters 7, 11, 12, and 13 of Title 11, until amendments by sections 201 to 231 of Pub.L. 99–554 effective in such district, see section 302(d)(3)(A) to (F), (H), (I) of Pub.L. 99–554, set out as a note under section 581 of Title 28.

Amendment by Pub.L. 99–554, § 215, except as otherwise provided, with respect to cases under chapters 7, 11, 12, and 13 of Title 11 commenced before 30 days after Oct. 27, 1986, and pending in a judicial district referred to in section 581(a) of Title 28, as amended by section 111(a) of Pub.L. 99–554, for which a United States trustee is not authorized before 30 days after Oct. 27, 1986 to be appointed, not applicable until the expiration of the 3-year period beginning on Oct. 27, 1986, or of the 1-year period beginning on the date the Attorney General certifies under section 303 of Pub.L. 99–554 the region specified in a paragraph of such section 581(a) that includes, such district, whichever occurs first, see section 302(e)(1)(2) of Pub.L. 99–554, set out as a note under section 581 of Title 28.

See 1986 Amendment notes set out above.

Cross References

Appointment of interim trustee after commencement of involuntary case, see section 303.

Disinterested person defined, see section 101.

Effect of conversion, see section 348.

Qualification of trustee, see section 322.

Library References:

C.J.S. Bankruptcy § 195.

West's Key No. Digests, Bankruptcy ⟸3002.

WESTLAW Electronic Research

See WESTLAW Electronic Research Guide following the *Bankruptcy Highlights*.

§ 702. Election of trustee

(a) A creditor may vote for a candidate for trustee only if such creditor—

(1) holds an allowable, undisputed, fixed, liquidated, unsecured claim of a kind entitled to distribution under section 726(a)(2), 726(a)(3), 726(a)(4), 752(a), 766(h), or 766(i) of this title;

(2) does not have an interest materially adverse, other than an equity interest that is not substantial in relation to such creditor's interest as a creditor, to the interest of creditors entitled to such distribution; and

(3) is not an insider.

(b) At the meeting of creditors held under section 341 of this title, creditors may elect one person to serve as trustee in the case if election of a trustee is requested by creditors that may vote under subsection (a) of this section, and that hold at least 20 percent in amount of the claims specified in subsection (a)(1) of this section that are held by creditors that may vote under subsection (a) of this section.

(c) A candidate for trustee is elected trustee if—

(1) creditors holding at least 20 percent in amount of the claims of a kind specified in subsection (a)(1) of this section that are held by creditors that may vote under subsection (a) of this section vote; and

(2) such candidate receives the votes of creditors holding a majority in amount of claims specified in subsection (a)(1) of this section that are held by creditors that vote for a trustee.

(d) If a trustee is not elected under this section, then the interim trustee shall serve as trustee in the case.

Pub.L. 95–598, Nov. 6, 1978, 92 Stat. 2604; Pub.L. 97–222, § 7, July 27, 1982, 96 Stat. 237; Pub.L. 98–353, Title III, § 472, July 10, 1984, 98 Stat. 380.

Historical and Revision Notes

Notes of Committee on the Judiciary, Senate Report No. 95–989. Subsection (a) of this section specifies which creditors may vote for a trustee. Only a creditor that holds an allowable, undisputed, fixed, liquidated, unsecured claim that is not entitled to priority, that does not have an interest materially adverse to the interest of general unsecured creditors, and that is not an insider may vote for a trustee. The phrase "materially adverse" is currently used in the Rules of Bankruptcy Procedure, rule 207(d). The application of the standard requires a balancing of various factors, such as the nature of the adversity. A creditor with a very small equity position would not be excluded from voting solely because he holds a small equity in the debtor. The Rules of Bankruptcy Procedure also currently provide for temporary allowance of claims, and will continue to do so for the purposes of determining who is eligible to vote under this provision.

Subsection (b) permits creditors at the meeting of creditors to elect one person to serve as trustee in the case. Creditors holding at least 20 percent in amount of the claims specified in the preceding paragraph must request election before creditors may elect a trustee. Subsection (c) specifies that a candidate for trustee is elected trustee if creditors holding at least 20 percent in amount of those claims actually vote, and if the candidate receives a majority in amount of votes actually cast.

Subsection (d) specifies that if a trustee is not elected, then the interim trustee becomes the permanent trustee and serves in the case permanently.

Legislative Statements. The House amendment adopts section 702(a)(2) of the Senate amendment. An insubstantial equity interest does not disqualify a creditor from voting for a candidate for trustee.

Effective Date of 1984 Amendments. See section 553 of Pub.L. 98–353, Title III, July 10, 1984, 98 Stat. 392, set out as an Effective Date of 1984 Amendment note preceding chapter 1 of Title 11, Bankruptcy.

Separability of Provisions. For separability of provisions of Title III of Pub.L. 98–353, see section 551 of Pub.L. 98–353 set out as a Separability of Provisions note preceding chapter 1 of Title 11, Bankruptcy.

Cross References

Insider defined, see section 101.
Qualification of trustee, see section 322.
Time for bringing action, see section 546.

§ 703.   Successor trustee

(a) If a trustee dies or resigns during a case, fails to qualify under section 322 of this title, or is removed under section 324 of this title, creditors may elect, in the manner specified in section 702 of this title, a person to fill the vacancy in the office of trustee.

(b) Pending election of a trustee under subsection (a) of this section, if necessary to preserve or prevent loss to the estate, the United States trustee may appoint an interim trustee in the manner specified in section 701(a).

(c) If creditors do not elect a successor trustee under subsection (a) of this section or if a trustee is needed in a case reopened under section 350 of this title, then the United States trustee—

(1) shall appoint one disinterested person that is a member of the panel of private trustees established under section 586(a)(1) of title 28 to serve as trustee in the case; or

(2) may, if none of the disinterested members of such panel is willing to serve as trustee, serve as trustee in the case.

Pub.L. 95–598, Nov. 6, 1978, 92 Stat. 2605; Pub.L. 98–353, Title III, § 473, July 10, 1984, 98 Stat. 381; Pub.L. 99–554, Title II, § 216, Oct. 27, 1986, 100 Stat. 3100.

Historical and Revision Notes

Notes of Committee on the Judiciary, Senate Report No. 95–989. If the office of trustee becomes vacant during the case, this section makes provision for the selection of a successor trustee. The office might become vacant through death, resignation, removal, failure to qualify under section 322 by posting bond, or the reopening of a case. If it does, creditors may elect a successor in the same manner as they may elect a trustee under the previous section. Pending the election of a successor, the court may appoint an interim trustee in the usual manner if necessary to preserve or prevent loss to the estate. If creditors do not elect a successor, or if a trustee is needed in a reopened case, then the court appoints a disinterested member of the panel of private trustees to serve.

1986 Amendment. Subsec. (b). Pub.L. 99–554, § 216, substituted "the United States trustee may appoint" for "the court may appoint" and "manner specified in section 701(a)" for "manner and subject to the provisions of section 701 of this title".

Subsec. (c). Pub.L. 99–554, § 216, substituted "this section or" for "this section, or", "then the United States trustee" for "then the court", designated part of existing provisions as par. (1), and, as so designated, substituted "586(a)(1)" for "604(f)", "in the case; or" for "in the case.", and added par. (2).

See Effective Date of 1986 Amendment, etc., notes set out below.

Effective Date of 1986 Amendments; Effective Date of 1986 Amendments for Certain Judicial Districts Not Served by United States Trustees and for Judicial Districts in Alabama and North Carolina; U.S. Trustee System Fund Deposits in Alabama and North Carolina; Effective Date of Title 11, Chapter 15 Repeal as to Northern District of Alabama; Authority of Certain Estate Administrators in Alabama and North Carolina; Effective Date of 1986 Amendments in Pending Cases Where a U.S. Trustee Not Authorized or Where a Trustee Files Final Report or Plan is Confirmed; Quarterly Fees. Amendment by

Pub.L. 99–554 effective 30 days after Oct. 27, 1986, except as otherwise provided for, see section 302(a) of Pub.L. 99–554, set out as a note under section 581 of Title 28, Judiciary and Judicial Procedure.

Amendment by Pub.L. 99–554, § 216, not to become effective in or with respect to certain specified judicial districts until, or apply to cases while pending in such district before, the expiration of the 270-day period beginning 30 days after Oct. 27, 1986, or of the 30-day period beginning on the date the Attorney General certifies under section 303 of Pub.L. 99–554 the region specified in a paragraph of section 581(a) of Title 28, as amended by section 111(a) of Pub.L. 99–554, that includes such district, whichever occurs first, see section 302(d)(1) of Pub.L. 99–554, set out as a note under section 581 of Title 28.

Amendment by Pub.L. 99–554, § 216, not to become effective in or with respect to certain specified judicial districts until, or apply to cases while pending in such district before, the expiration of the 2-year period beginning 30 days after Oct. 27, 1986, or of the 30-day period beginning on the date the Attorney General certifies under section 303 of Pub.L. 99–554 the region specified in a paragraph of section 581(a) of Title 28, as amended by section 111(a) of Pub.L. 99–554, that includes such district, whichever occurs first, see section 302(d)(2) of Pub.L. 99–554, set out as a note under section 581 of Title 28.

Amendment by Pub.L. 99–554, § 216, not to become effective in or with respect to judicial districts established for the States of Alabama and North Carolina until, or apply to cases while pending in such district before, such district elects to be included in a bankruptcy region established in section 581(a) of Title 28, as amended by section 111(a) of Pub.L. 99–554, or Oct. 1, 2002, whichever occurs first, and, except as otherwise provided for, with respect to cases under chapters 7, 11, 12, and 13 of Title 11 commenced before 30 days after Oct. 27, 1986, and pending in a judicial district in the States of Alabama or North Carolina before any election made under section 302(d)(3) (A) of Pub.L. 99–554 by such district becomes

effective or Oct. 1, 2002, whichever occurs first, amendments by Pub.L. 99–554 not to apply until Oct. 1, 2003, or the expiration of the 1-year period beginning on the date such election becomes effective, whichever occurs first, and further, in any judicial district in Alabama or North Carolina not making the election described in section 302(d)(3)(A) of Pub.L. 99–554, any person appointed under regulations issued by the Judicial Conference to administer estates in cases under Title 11 authorized to establish, etc., a panel of private trustees, and to supervise cases and trustees in cases under chapters 7, 11, 12, and 13 of Title 11, until amendments by sections 201 to 231 of Pub.L. 99–554 effective in such district, see section 302(d)(3)(A) to (F), (H), (I) of Pub.L. 99–554, set out as a note under section 581 of Title 28.

Amendment by Pub.L. 99–554, § 216, except as otherwise provided, with respect to cases under chapters 7, 11, 12, and 13 of Title 11 commenced before 30 days after Oct. 27, 1986, and pending in a judicial district referred to in section 581(a) of Title 28, as amended by section 111(a) of Pub.L. 99–554, for which a United States trustee is not authorized before 30 days after Oct. 27, 1986 to be appointed, not applicable until the expiration of the 3-year period beginning on Oct. 27, 1986, or of the 1-year period beginning on the date the Attorney General certifies under section 303 of Pub.L. 99–554 the region specified in a paragraph of such section 581(a) that includes, such district, whichever occurs first, see section 302(e)(1), (2) of Pub.L. 99–554, set out as a note under section 581 of Title 28.

See 1986 Amendment notes set out above.

Effective Date of 1984 Amendments. See section 553 of Pub.L. 98–353, Title III, July 10, 1984, 98 Stat. 392, set out as an Effective Date of 1984 Amendment note preceding chapter 1 of Title 11, Bankruptcy.

Separability of Provisions. For separability of provisions of Title III of Pub.L. 98–353, see section 551 of Pub.L. 98–353 set out as a Separability of Provisions note preceding chapter 1 of Title 11, Bankruptcy.

Cross References

    Effect of vacancy in office of trustee, see section 325.

    Qualification of trustee, see section 322.

Library References:

    C.J.S. Bankruptcy § 196.

    West's Key No. Digests, Bankruptcy ⟸3007.

§ 704. Duties of trustee

The trustee shall—

(1) collect and reduce to money the property of the estate for which such trustee serves, and close such estate as expeditiously as is compatible with the best interests of parties in interest;

(2) be accountable for all property received;

(3) ensure that the debtor shall perform his intention as specified in section 521(2)(B) of this title;

(4) investigate the financial affairs of the debtor;

(5) if a purpose would be served, examine proofs of claims and object to the allowance of any claim that is improper;

(6) if advisable, oppose the discharge of the debtor;

(7) unless the court orders otherwise, furnish such information concerning the estate and the estate's administration as is requested by a party in interest;

(8) if the business of the debtor is authorized to be operated, file with the court, with the United States trustee, and with any governmental unit charged with responsibility for collection or determination of any tax arising out of such operation, periodic reports and summaries of the operation of such business, including a statement of receipts and disbursements, and such other information as, with the United States trustee or the court requires; and

(9) make a final report and file a final account of the administration of the estate with the court and with the United States trustee.

Pub.L. 95–598, Nov. 6, 1978, 92 Stat. 2605; Pub.L. 98–353, Title III, §§ 311(a), 474, July 10, 1984, 98 Stat. 355, 381; Pub.L. 99–554, Title II, § 217, Oct. 27, 1986, 100 Stat. 3100.

Historical and Revision Notes

Notes of Committee on the Judiciary, Senate Report No. 95–989. The essential duties of the trustee are enumerated in this section. Others, or elaborations on these, may be prescribed by the Rules of Bankruptcy Procedure to the extent not inconsistent with those prescribed by this section. The duties are derived from section 47a of the Bankruptcy Act [former section 75(a) of this title].

The trustee's principal duty is to collect and reduce to money the property of the estate for which he serves, and to close up the estate as expeditiously as is compatible with the best interests of parties in interest. He must be accountable for all property received, and must investigate the financial affairs of the debtor. If a purpose would be served (such as if there are assets that will be distributed), the

trustee is required to examine proofs of claims and object to the allowance of any claim that is improper. If advisable, the trustee must oppose the discharge of the debtor, which is for the benefit of general unsecured creditors whom the trustee represents.

The trustee is responsible to furnish such information concerning the estate and its administration as is requested by a party in interest. If the business of the debtor is authorized to be operated, then the trustee is required to file with governmental units charged with the responsibility for collection or determination of any tax arising out of the operation of the business periodic reports and summaries of the operation, including a statement of receipts and disbursements, and such other information as the court requires. He is required to give constructive notice of the commencement of the case in the manner specified under section 342(b).

Legislative Statements. Section 704(8) of the Senate amendment is deleted in the House amendment. Trustees should give constructive notice of the commencement of the case in the manner specified under section 549(c) of title 11.

1986 Amendment. Par. (8). Pub.L. 99–554, § 217(1), substituted "with the court, with the United States trustee, and with" for "with the court and with" and "information as the United States trustee or the court" for "information as the court".

Par. (9). Pub.L. 99–554, § 217(2), substituted "with the court and with the United States trustee." for "with the court.".

See Effective Date of 1986 Amendment, etc., notes set out below.

Effective Date of 1986 Amendments; Effective Date of 1986 Amendments for Certain Judicial Districts Not Served by United States Trustees and for Judicial Districts in Alabama and North Carolina; U.S. Trustee System Fund Deposits in Alabama and North Carolina; Effective Date of Title 11 Chapter 15 Repeal as to Northern District of Alabama; Authority of Certain Estate Administrators in Alabama and North Carolina; Effective Date of 1986 Amendments in Pending Cases Where a U.S. Trustee Not Authorized or Where a Trustee Files Final Report or Plan is Confirmed; Quarterly Fees. Amendment by Pub.L. 99–554 effective 30 days after Oct. 27, 1986, except as otherwise provided for, see section 302(a) of Pub.L. 99–554, set out as a note under section 581 of Title 28, Judiciary and Judicial Procedure.

Amendment by Pub.L. 99–554, § 217, not to become effective in or with respect to certain specified judicial districts until, or apply to cases while pending in such district before, the expiration of the 270-day period beginning 30 days after Oct. 27, 1986, or of the 30-day period beginning on the date the Attorney General certifies under section 303 of Pub.L. 99–554 the region specified in a paragraph of section 581(a) of Title 28, as amended by section 111(a) of Pub.L. 99–554, that includes such district, whichever occurs first, see section 302(d)(1) of Pub.L. 99–554, set out as a note under section 581 of Title 28.

Amendment by Pub.L. 99–554, § 217, not to become effective in or with respect to certain specified judicial districts until, or apply to cases while pending in such district before, the expiration of the 2-year period beginning 30 days after Oct. 27, 1986, or of the 30-day period beginning on the date the Attorney General certifies under section 303 of Pub.L. 99–554 the region specified in a paragraph of section 581(a) of Title 28, as amended by section 111(a) of Pub.L. 99–554, that includes such district, whichever occurs first, see section 302(d)(2) of Pub.L. 99–554, set out as a note under section 581 of Title 28.

Amendment by Pub.L. 99–554, § 217, not to become effective in or with respect to judicial districts established for the States of Alabama and North Carolina until, or apply to cases while pending in such district before, such district elects to be included in a bankruptcy region established in section 581(a) of Title 28, as amended by section 111(a) of Pub.L. 99–554, or Oct. 1, 2002, whichever occurs first, and, except as otherwise provided for, with respect to cases under chapters 7, 11, 12, and 13 of Title 11 commenced before 30 days after Oct. 27, 1986, and pending in a judicial district in the States of Alabama or North Carolina before any election made under section 302(d)(3) (A) of Pub.L. 99–554 by such district becomes effective or Oct. 1, 2002, whichever occurs first, amendments by Pub.L. 99–554 not to apply until Oct. 1, 2003, or the expiration of the 1-year period beginning on the date such election becomes effective, whichever occurs first, and further, in any judicial district in Alabama or North Carolina not making the election described in section 302(d)(3)(A) of Pub.L. 99–554, any person appointed under regulations issued by the Judicial Conference to administer estates in cases under Title 11 authorized to establish, etc., a panel of private trustees, and to supervise cases and trustees in cases under chapters 7, 11, 12, and 13 of Title 11, until amendments by sections 201 to 231 of Pub.L. 99–554 effective in such district, see section 302(d)(3)(A) to (F), (H), (I) of Pub.L. 99–554, set out as a note under section 581 of Title 28.

Amendment by Pub.L. 99–554, § 217, except as otherwise provided, with respect to cases under chapters 7, 11, 12, and 13 of Title 11 commenced before 30 days after Oct. 27, 1986, and pending in a judicial district referred to in section 581(a) of Title 28, as amended by section 111(a) of Pub.L. 99–554, for which a United States trustee is not authorized before 30 days after Oct. 27, 1986 to be appointed, not applicable until the expiration of the 3-year period beginning on Oct. 27, 1986, or of the 1-year period beginning on the date the Attorney General certifies under section 303 of Pub.L. 99–554 the region specified in a paragraph of such section 581(a) that includes, such district, whichever occurs first, see section 302(e)(1), (2) of Pub.L. 99–554, set out as a note under section 581 of Title 28.

See 1986 Amendment notes set out above.

Effective Date of 1984 Amendments. See section 553 of Pub.L. 98–353, Title III, July 10,

1984, 98 Stat. 392, set out as an Effective Date of 1984 Amendment note preceding chapter 1 of Title 11, Bankruptcy.

Separability of Provisions. For separability of provisions of Title III of Pub.L. 98–353, see section 551 of Pub.L. 98–353 set out as a Separability of Provisions note preceding chapter 1 of Title 11, Bankruptcy.

Cross References

Duties of trustee in
    Chapter 11 cases, see section 1106.
    Chapter 13 cases, see section 1302.
Filing of reports and summaries by debtor engaged in business, see section 1304.

Library References:

C.J.S. Bankruptcy § 197.
West's Key No. Digests, Bankruptcy ⟸3008.

WESTLAW Electronic Research

See WESTLAW Electronic Research Guide following the *Bankruptcy Highlights*.

§ 705. Creditors' committee

(a) At the meeting under section 341(a) of this title, creditors that may vote for a trustee under section 702(a) of this title may elect a committee of not fewer than three, and not more than eleven, creditors, each of whom holds an allowable unsecured claim of a kind entitled to distribution under section 726(a) (2) of this title.

(b) A committee elected under subsection (a) of this section may consult with the trustee or the United States trustee in connection with the administration of the estate, make recommendations to the trustee or the United States trustee respecting the performance of the trustee's duties, and submit to the court or the United States trustee any question affecting the administration of the estate.

Pub.L. 95–598, Nov. 6, 1978, 92 Stat. 2605; Pub.L. 99–554, Title II, § 218, Oct. 27, 1986, 100 Stat. 3100.

Historical and Revision Notes

Notes of Committee on the Judiciary, Senate Report No. 95–989. This section is derived from section 44b of the Bankruptcy Act [former section 72(b) of this title] without substantial change. It permits election by general unsecured creditors of a committee of not fewer than 3 members and not more than 11 members to consult with the trustee in connection with the administration of the estate, to make recommendations to the trustee respecting the performance of his duties, and to submit to the court any question affecting the administration of the estate. There is no provision for compensation or reimbursement of its counsel.

Legislative Statements. Section 705(a) of the House amendment adopts a provision contained in the Senate amendment that limits a committee of creditors to not more than 11; the House bill contained no maximum limitation.

1986 Amendment. Subsec. (b). Pub.L. 99–554, § 218, substituted "with the trustee or the United States trustee in connection" for "with the trustee in connection", "to the trustee or the United States trustee respecting" for "to the trustee respecting", and "to the court or the United States trustee any question" for "to the court any question".

See Effective Date of 1986 Amendment, etc., notes set out below.

Effective Date of 1986 Amendments; Effective Date of 1986 Amendments for Certain Judicial Districts Not Served by United States Trustees and for Judicial Districts in Alabama and North Carolina; U.S. Trustee System Fund Deposits in Alabama and North Carolina; Effective Date of Title 11 Chapter 15 Repeal as to Northern District of Alabama; Authority of Certain Estate Administrators in Alabama and North Carolina; Effective Date of 1986 Amendments in Pending Cases Where a U.S. Trustee Not Authorized or Where a Trustee Files Final Report or Plan is Confirmed; Quarterly Fees. Amendment by Pub.L. 99–554 effective 30 days after Oct. 27, 1986, except as otherwise provided for, see section 302(a) of Pub.L. 99–554, set out as a note under section 581 of Title 28, Judiciary and Judicial Procedure.

Amendment by Pub.L. 99–554, § 218, not to become effective in or with respect to certain specified judicial districts until, or apply to cases while pending in such district before, the expiration of the 270-day period beginning 30 days after Oct. 27, 1986, or of the 30-day period beginning on the date the Attorney General certifies under section 303 of Pub.L. 99–554 the region specified in a paragraph of section 581(a) of Title 28, as amended by section 111(a) of Pub.L. 99–554, that includes such district, whichever occurs first, see section 302(d)(1) of Pub.L. 99–554, set out as a note under section 581 of Title 28.

Amendment by Pub.L. 99–554, § 218, not to become effective in or with respect to certain specified judicial districts until, or apply to cases while pending in such district before, the expiration of the 2-year period beginning 30 days after Oct. 27, 1986, or of the 30-day period beginning on the date the Attorney General certifies under section 303 of Pub.L. 99–554 the region specified in a paragraph of section 581(a) of Title 28, as amended by section 111(a) of Pub.L. 99–554, that includes such district, whichever occurs first, see section 302(d)(2) of Pub.L. 99–554, set out as a note under section 581 of Title 28.

Amendment by Pub.L. 99–554, § 218, not to become effective in or with respect to judicial districts established for the States of Alabama and North Carolina until, or apply to cases while pending in such district before, such district elects to be included in a bankruptcy region established in section 581(a) of Title 28, as amended by section 111(a) of Pub.L. 99–554, or Oct. 1, 2002, whichever occurs first, and, except as otherwise provided for, with respect to cases under chapters 7, 11, 12, and 13 of Title 11 commenced before 30 days after Oct. 27, 1986, and pending in a judicial district in the States of Alabama or North Carolina before any election made under section 302(d)(3)(A) of Pub.L. 99–554 by such district becomes effective or Oct. 1, 2002, whichever occurs first, amendments by Pub.L. 99–554 not to apply until Oct. 1, 2003, or the expiration of the 1-year period beginning on the date such election becomes effective, whichever occurs first, and further, in any judicial district in Alabama or North Carolina not making the election described in section 302(d)(3)(A) of Pub.L. 99–554, any person appointed under regulations issued by the Judicial Conference to administer estates in cases under Title 11 authorized to establish, etc., a panel of private trustees, and to supervise cases and trustees in cases under chapters 7, 11, 12, and 13 of Title 11, until amendments by sections 201 to 231 of Pub.L. 99–554 effective in such district, see section 302(d)(3)(A) to (F), (H), (I) of Pub.L. 99–554, set out as a note under section 581 of Title 28.

Amendment by Pub.L. 99–554, § 218, except as otherwise provided, with respect to cases under chapters 7, 11, 12, and 13 of Title 11 commenced before 30 days after Oct. 27, 1986, and pending in a judicial district referred to in section 581(a) of Title 28, as amended by section 111(a) of Pub.L. 99–554, for which a United States trustee is not authorized before 30 days after Oct. 27, 1986 to be appointed, not applicable until the expiration of the 3-year period beginning on Oct. 27, 1986, or of the 1-year period beginning on the date the Attorney General certifies under section 303 of Pub.L. 99–554 the region specified in a paragraph of such section 581(a) that includes, such district, whichever occurs first, see section 302(e)(1), (2) of Pub.L. 99–554, set out as a note under section 581 of Title 28.

See 1986 Amendment notes set out above.

Cross References

Appointment of creditors' and equity security holders' committees in Chapter 11 cases, see section 1102.

Powers and duties of committees in chapter 11 cases, see section 1103.

Library References:

C.J.S. Bankruptcy §§ 193, 373.

West's Key No. Digests, Bankruptcy ⚷3024.

WESTLAW Electronic Research

See WESTLAW Electronic Research Guide following the *Bankruptcy Highlights*.

§ 706. Conversion

(a) The debtor may convert a case under this chapter to a case under chapter 11, 12, or 13 of this title at any time, if the case has not been converted under section 1112, 1307, or 1208 of this title. Any waiver of the right to convert a case under this subsection is unenforceable.

(b) On request of a party in interest and after notice and a hearing, the court may convert a case under this chapter to a case under chapter 11 of this title at any time.

(c) The court may not convert a case under this chapter to a case under chapter 12 or 13 of this title unless the debtor requests such conversion.

(d) Notwithstanding any other provision of this section, a case may not be converted to a case under another chapter of this title unless the debtor may be a debtor under such chapter.

Pub.L. 95–598, Nov. 6, 1978, 92 Stat. 2606; Pub.L. 99–554, Title II, § 257(q), Oct. 27, 1986, 100 Stat. 3115.

Historical and Revision Notes

Notes of Committee on the Judiciary, Senate Report No. 95–989. Subsection (a) of this section gives the debtor the one-time absolute right of conversion of a liquidation case to a reorganization or individual repayment plan case. If the case has already once been converted from chapter 11 or 13 to chapter 7, then the debtor does not have that right. The policy of the provision is that the debtor should always be given the opportunity to repay his debts, and a waiver of the right to convert a case is unenforceable.

Subsection (b) permits the court, on request of a party in interest and after notice and a hearing, to convert the case to chapter 11 at any time. The decision whether to convert is left in the sound discretion of the court, based on what will most inure to the benefit of all parties in interest.

Subsection (c) is part of the prohibition against involuntary chapter 13 cases, and prohibits the court from converting a case to chapter 13 without the debtor's consent.

Subsection (d) reinforces section 109 by prohibiting conversion to a chapter unless the debtor is eligible to be a debtor under that chapter.

Legislative Statements. Section 706(a) of the House amendment adopts a provision contained in the Senate amendment indicating that a waiver of the right to convert a case under section 706(a) is unenforceable. The explicit reference in title 11 forbidding the waiver of certain rights is not intended to imply that other rights, such as the right to file a voluntary bankruptcy case under section 301, may be waived.

Section 706 of the House amendment adopts a similar provision contained in H.R. 8200 as passed by the House. Competing proposals contained in section 706(c) and section 706(d) of the Senate amendment are rejected.

Effective Date of 1986 Amendments; Savings Provisions; Quarterly Fees. Amendment by Pub.L. 99–554 effective 30 days after Oct. 27, 1986, except as otherwise provided for, see section 302(a) of Pub.L. 99–554, set out as a note under section 581 of Title 28, Judiciary and Judicial Procedure.

Amendments by Pub.L. 99–554, § 257(q), not to apply with respect to cases commenced under Title 11, Bankruptcy, before 30 days after Oct. 27, 1986, see section 302(c)(1) of Pub. L. 99–554, set out as a note under section 581 of Title 28.

Cross References

Conversion or dismissal of
    Chapter 11 cases, see section 1112.
    Chapter 13 cases, see section 1307.
Effect of conversion, see section 348.
Termination of debtor's taxable period, see section 1146.

Library References:

C.J.S. Bankruptcy § 42.
West's Key No. Digests, Bankruptcy ⟱2331, 2332.

WESTLAW Electronic Research

See WESTLAW Electronic Research Guide following the *Bankruptcy Highlights*.

§ 707. Dismissal

(a) The court may dismiss a case under this chapter only after notice and a hearing and only for cause, including—

    (1) unreasonable delay by the debtor that is prejudicial to creditors;

    (2) nonpayment of any fees or charges required under chapter 123 of title 28; and

    (3) failure of the debtor in a voluntary case to file, within fifteen days or such additional time as the court may allow after the filing of the petition commencing such case, the information required by paragraph (1) of section 521, but only on a motion by the United States trustee.

(b) After notice and a hearing, the court, on its own motion or on a motion by the United States Trustee, but not at the request or suggestion of any party in interest, may dismiss a case filed by an individual debtor under this chapter whose debts are primarily consumer debts if it finds that the granting of relief would be a substantial abuse of the provisions of this chapter. There shall be a presumption in favor of granting the relief requested by the debtor.

Pub.L. 95–598, Nov. 6, 1978, 92 Stat. 2606; Pub.L. 98–353, Title III, §§ 312, 475, July 10, 1984, 98 Stat. 355, 381; Pub.L. 99–554, Title II, § 219, Oct. 27, 1986, 100 Stat. 3100.

Historical and Revision Notes

Notes of Committee on the Judiciary, Senate Report No. 95–989. This section authorizes the court to dismiss a liquidation case only for cause, such as unreasonable delay by the debtor that is prejudicial to creditors or nonpayment of any fees and charges required under chapter 123 of title 28 [section 1911 et seq. of Title 28, Judiciary and Judicial Procedure]. These causes are not exhaustive, but merely illustrative. The section does not contemplate, however, that the ability of the debtor to repay his debts in whole or in part constitutes adequate cause for dismissal. To permit dismissal on that ground would be to enact a non-uniform mandatory chapter 13, in lieu of the remedy of bankruptcy.

Legislative Statements. Section 707 of the House amendment indicates that the court may dismiss a case only after notice and a hearing.

References in Text. Chapter 123 of title 28, referred to in par. (2), is classified to section 1911 et seq. of Title 28, Judiciary and Judicial Procedure.

1986 Amendment. Subsec. (a)(3). Pub.L. 99–554, § 219(a), added par. (3).

Subsec. (b). Pub.L. 99–554, § 219(b), substituted "motion or on a motion by the United States trustee, but not" for "motion and not".

See Effective Date of 1986 Amendment, etc., notes set out below.

Effective Date of 1986 Amendments; Effective Date of 1986 Amendments for Certain Judicial Districts Not Served by Unit-

ed States Trustees and for Judicial Districts in Alabama and North Carolina; U.S. Trustee System Fund Deposits in Alabama and North Carolina; Effective Date of Title 11 Chapter 15 Repeal as to Northern District of Alabama; Authority of Certain Estate Administrators in Alabama and North Carolina; Effective Date of 1986 Amendments in Pending Cases Where a U.S. Trustee Not Authorized or Where a Trustee Files Final Report or Plan is Confirmed; Quarterly Fees. Amendment by Pub.L. 99–554 effective 30 days after Oct. 27, 1986, except as otherwise provided for, see section 302(a) of Pub.L. 99–554, set out as a note under section 581 of Title 28, Judiciary and Judicial Procedure.

Amendment by Pub.L. 99–554, § 219, not to become effective in or with respect to certain specified judicial districts until, or apply to cases while pending in such district before, the expiration of the 270-day period beginning 30 days after Oct. 27, 1986, or of the 30-day period beginning on the date the Attorney General certifies under section 303 of Pub.L. 99–554 the region specified in a paragraph of section 581(a) of Title 28, as amended by section 111(a) of Pub.L. 99–554, that includes such district, whichever occurs first, see section 302(d)(1) of Pub.L. 99–554, set out as a note under section 581 of Title 28.

Amendment by Pub.L. 99–554, § 219, not to become effective in or with respect to certain specified judicial districts until, or apply to cases while pending in such district before, the expiration of the 2-year period beginning 30 days after Oct. 27, 1986, or of the 30-day period beginning on the date the Attorney General certifies under section 303 of Pub.L. 99–554 the region specified in a paragraph of section 581(a) of Title 28, as amended by section 111(a) of Pub.L. 99–554, that includes such district, whichever occurs first, see section 302(d)(2) of Pub.L. 99–554, set out as a note under section 581 of Title 28.

Amendment by Pub.L. 99–554, § 219, not to become effective in or with respect to judicial districts established for the States of Alabama and North Carolina until, or apply to cases while pending in such district before, such district elects to be included in a bankruptcy region established in section 581(a) of Title 28, as amended by section 111(a) of Pub.L. 99–554, or Oct. 1, 2002, whichever occurs first, and, except as otherwise provided for, with respect to cases under chapters 7, 11, 12, and 13 of Title 11 commenced before 30 days after Oct. 27, 1986, and pending in a judicial district in

the States of Alabama or North Carolina before any election made under section 302(d)(3)(A) of Pub.L. 99–554 by such district becomes effective or Oct. 1, 2002, whichever occurs first, amendments by Pub.L. 99–554 not to apply until Oct. 1, 2003, or the expiration of the 1-year period beginning on the date such election becomes effective, whichever occurs first, and further, in any judicial district in Alabama or North Carolina not making the election described in section 302(d)(3)(A) of Pub.L. 99–554, any person appointed under regulations issued by the Judicial Conference to administer estates in cases under Title 11 authorized to establish, etc., a panel of private trustees, and to supervise cases and trustees in cases under chapters 7, 11, 12, and 13 of Title 11, until amendments by sections 201 to 231 of Pub.L. 99–554 effective in such district, see section 302(d)(3)(A) to (F), (H), (I) of Pub.L. 99–554, set out as a note under section 581 of Title 28.

Amendment by Pub.L. 99–554, § 219, except as otherwise provided, with respect to cases under chapters 7, 11, 12, and 13 of Title 11 commenced before 30 days after Oct. 27, 1986, and pending in a judicial district referred to in section 581(a) of Title 28, as amended by section 111(a) of Pub.L. 99–554, for which a United States trustee is not authorized before 30 days after Oct. 27, 1986 to be appointed, not applicable until the expiration of the 3-year period beginning on Oct. 27, 1986, or of the 1-year period beginning on the date the Attorney General certifies under section 303 of Pub.L. 99–554 the region specified in a paragraph of such section 581(a) that includes, such district, whichever occurs first, see section 302(e)(1), (2) of Pub.L. 99–554, set out as a note under section 581 of Title 28.

See 1986 Amendment notes set out above.

Effective Date of 1984 Amendments. See section 553 of Pub.L. 98–353, Title III, July 10, 1984, 98 Stat. 392, set out as an Effective Date of 1984 Amendment note preceding chapter 1 of Title 11, Bankruptcy.

Separability of Provisions. For separability of provisions of Title III of Pub.L. 98–353, see section 551 of Pub.L. 98–353 set out as a Separability of Provisions note preceding chapter 1 of Title 11, Bankruptcy.

Rules Promulgated by Supreme Court. United States Supreme Court to prescribe general rules implementing the practice and procedure to be followed under subsec. (b) of this section, with section 2075 of Title 28, Judiciary and Judicial Procedure, to apply with respect to such general rules, see section 320 of Pub.L. 98–353, set out as a note under section 2075 of Title 28, Judiciary and Judicial Procedure.

Cross References

Conversion or dismissal of
    Chapter 11 cases, see section 1112.
    Chapter 13 cases, see section 1307.
Dismissal of chapter 9 cases, see section 927.
Effect of dismissal, see section 349.

Library References:

C.J.S. Bankruptcy §§ 54, 55, 61–63.
West's Key No. Digests, Bankruptcy ⟜2259–2264, 2295.

WESTLAW Electronic Research

See WESTLAW Electronic Research Guide following the *Bankruptcy Highlights*.

SUBCHAPTER II—COLLECTION, LIQUIDATION, AND DISTRIBUTION OF THE ESTATE

§ 721. Authorization to operate business

The court may authorize the trustee to operate the business of the debtor for a limited period, if such operation is in the best interest of the estate and consistent with the orderly liquidation of the estate.

Pub.L. 95–598, Nov. 6, 1978, 92 Stat. 2606.

Historical and Revision Notes

Notes of Committee on the Judiciary, Senate Report No. 95–989. This section is derived from section 2a(5) of the Bankruptcy Act [former section 11(a)(5) of this title]. It permits the court to authorize the operation of any business of the debtor for a limited period, if the operation is in the best interest of the estate and consistent with orderly liquidation of the estate. An example is the operation of a watch company to convert watch movements and cases into completed watches which will bring much higher prices than the component parts would have brought.

Cross References

Authorization to operate business in chapter 11 cases, see section 1108.
Debtor engaged in business in chapter 13 cases, see section 1304.
Executory contracts and unexpired leases, see section 365.
Executory contracts in stockbroker liquidation cases, see section 744.
Obtaining credit, see section 364.
Retention or replacement of professional persons, see section 327.
Treatment of accounts in
    Stockbroker liquidation cases, see section 745.
    Commodity broker liquidation cases, see section 763.
Use, sale or lease of property, see section 363.
Utility service, see section 366.

Library References:

C.J.S. Bankruptcy § 199.
West's Key No. Digests, Bankruptcy ⟜3025.

WESTLAW Electronic Research

See WESTLAW Electronic Research Guide following the *Bankruptcy Highlights*.

§ 722.   Redemption

An individual debtor may, whether or not the debtor has waived the right to redeem under this section, redeem tangible personal property intended primarily for personal, family, or household use, from a lien securing a dischargeable consumer debt, if such property is exempted under section 522 of this title or has been abandoned under section 554 of this title, by paying the holder of such lien the amount of the allowed secured claim of such holder that is secured by such lien.

Pub.L. 95–598, Nov. 6, 1978, 92 Stat. 2606.

Historical and Revision Notes

Notes of Committee on the Judiciary, Senate Report No. 95–989. This section is new and is broader than rights of redemption under the Uniform Commercial Code. It authorizes an individual debtor to redeem tangible personal property intended primarily for personal, family, or household use, from a lien securing a nonpurchase money dischargeable consumer debt. It applies only if the debtor's interest in the property is exempt or has been abandoned.

This right to redeem is a very substantial change from current law. To prevent abuses such as may occur when the debtor deliberately allows the property to depreciate in value, the debtor will be required to pay the fair market value of the goods or the amount of the claim if the claim is less. The right is personal to the debtor and not assignable.

Notes of Committee on the Judiciary, House Report No. 95–595. The right to redeem extends to the whole of the property, not just the debtor's exempt interest in it. Thus, for example, if a debtor owned a $2,000 car, subject to a $1,200 lien, the debtor could exempt his $800 interest in the car. The debtor is permitted a $1,500 exemption in a car, proposed 11 U.S.C. 522(d)(2). This section permits him to pay the holder of the lien $1,200 and redeem the entire car, not just the remaining $700 of his exemption. The redemption is accomplished by paying the holder of the lien the amount of the allowed claim secured by the lien. The provision amounts to a right of first refusal for the debtor in consumer goods that might otherwise be repossessed. The right of redemption under this section is not waivable.

Legislative Statements. Section 722 of the House amendment adopts the position taken in H.R. 8200 as passed by the House and rejects the alternative contained in section 722 of the Senate amendment.

Cross References

Effect of discharge on certain agreements providing for redemption, see section 524.

Library References:

C.J.S. Bankruptcy §§ 111, 112.
West's Key No. Digests, Bankruptcy ⬷3034.

WESTLAW Electronic Research

See WESTLAW Electronic Research Guide following the *Bankruptcy Highlights*.

§ 723.   Rights of partnership trustee against general partners

(a) If there is a deficiency of property of the estate to pay in full all claims which are allowed in a case under this chapter concerning a partnership and with respect to which a general partner of the partnership is personally liable, the trustee shall have a claim against such general partner for the full amount of the deficiency.

(b) To the extent practicable, the trustee shall first seek recovery of such deficiency from any general partner in such partnership that is not a debtor in a case under this title. Pending determination of such deficiency, the court may order any such partner to provide the estate with indemnity for, or assurance of payment of, any deficiency recoverable from such partner, or not to dispose of property.

(c) Notwithstanding section 728(c) of this title, the trustee has a claim against the estate of each general partner in such partnership that is a debtor in a case under this title for the full amount of all claims of creditors allowed in the case concerning such partnership. Notwithstanding section 502 of this title, there shall not be allowed in such partner's case a claim against such partner on which both such partner and such partnership are liable, except to any extent that such claim is secured only by property of such partner and not by property of such partnership. The claim of the trustee under this subsection is entitled to distribution in such partner's case under section 726(a) of this title the same as any other claim of a kind specified in such section.

(d) If the aggregate that the trustee recovers from the estates of general partners under subsection (c) of this section is greater than any deficiency not recovered under subsection (b) of this section, the court, after notice and a hearing, shall determine an equitable distribution of the surplus so recovered, and the trustee shall distribute such surplus to the estates of the general partners in such partnership according to such determination.

Pub.L. 95–598, Nov. 6, 1978, 92 Stat. 2606; Pub.L. 98–353, Title III, § 476, July 10, 1984, 98 Stat. 381.

Historical and Revision Notes

Notes of Committee on the Judiciary, Senate Report No. 95–989. This section is a significant departure from present law. It repeals the jingle rule, which, for ease of administration, denied partnership creditors their rights against general partners by permitting general partners' individual creditors to share in their estates first to the exclusion of partnership creditors. The result under this section more closely tracks generally applicable partnership law, without a significant administrative burden.

Subsection (a) specifies that each general partner in a partnership debtor is liable to the partnership's trustee for any deficiency of partnership property to pay in full all administrative expenses and all claims against the partnership.

Subsection (b) requires the trustee to seek recovery of the deficiency from any general partner that is not a debtor in a bankruptcy case. The court is empowered to order that partner to indemnify the estate or not to dispose of property pending a determination of the deficiency. The language of the subsection is directed to cases under the bankruptcy code [this title]. However, if, during the early stages of the transition period, a partner in a partnership is proceeding under the Bankruptcy Act [former Title 11] while the partnership is proceeding under the bankruptcy code [this title], the trustee should not first seek recovery against the Bankruptcy Act partner. Rather, the Bankruptcy Act partner should be deemed for the purposes of this section and the rights of the trustee to be proceeding under title 11.

Subsection (c) requires the partnership trustee to seek recovery of the full amount of the deficiency from the estate of each general partner that is a debtor in a bankruptcy case. The trustee will share equally with the partners' individual creditors in the assets of the partners' estates. Claims of partnership creditors who may have filed against the partner will be disallowed to avoid double counting.

Subsection (d) provides for the case where the total recovery from all of the bankrupt general partners is greater than the deficiency of which the trustee sought recovery. This case would most likely occur for a partnership with a large number of general partners. If the situation arises, the court is required to determine an equitable redistribution of the surplus to the estate of the general partners. The determination will be based on factors such as the relative liability of each of the general partners under the partnership agreement and the relative rights of each of the general partners in the profits of the enterprise under the partnership agreement.

Legislative Statements. Section 723(c) of the House amendment is a compromise between similar provisions contained in the House bill and Senate amendment. The section makes clear that the trustee of a partnership has a claim against each general partner for the full amount of all claims of creditors allowed in the case concerning the partnership. By restricting the trustee's rights to claims of "creditors," the trustee of the partnership will not have a claim against the general partners for administrative expenses or claims allowed in the case concerning the partnership. As under present law, sections of the Bankruptcy Act applying to codebtors and sureties apply to the relationship of a partner with respect to a partnership debtor. See sections 501(b), 502(e), 506(d)(2), 509, 524(d), and 1301 of title 11.

Effective Date of 1984 Amendments. See section 553 of Pub.L. 98–353, Title III, July 10, 1984, 98 Stat. 392, set out as an Effective Date of 1984 Amendment note preceding chapter 1 of Title 11, Bankruptcy.

Separability of Provisions. For separability of provisions of Title III of Pub.L. 98–353, see section 551 of Pub.L. 98–353 set out as a Separability of Provisions note preceding chapter 1 of Title 11, Bankruptcy.

Cross References

Property of estate, see section 541.

Library References:

C.J.S. Bankruptcy §§ 118, 119.
West's Key No. Digests, Bankruptcy ⟶2559.

WESTLAW Electronic Research

See WESTLAW Electronic Research Guide following the *Bankruptcy Highlights*.

§ 724. Treatment of certain liens

(a) The trustee may avoid a lien that secures a claim of a kind specified in section 726(a)(4) of this title.

(b) Property in which the estate has an interest and that is subject to a lien that is not avoidable under this title and that secures an allowed claim for a tax, or proceeds of such property, shall be distributed—

    (1) first, to any holder of an allowed claim secured by a lien on such property that is not avoidable under this title and that is senior to such tax lien;

    (2) second, to any holder of a claim of a kind specified in section 507(a)(1), 507(a)(2), 507(a)(3), 507(a)(4), 507(a)(5), or 507(a)(b) of this title, to the extent of the amount of such allowed tax claim that is secured by such tax lien;

    (3) third, to the holder of such tax lien, to any extent that such holder's allowed tax claim that is secured by such tax lien exceeds any amount distributed under paragraph (2) of this subsection;

    (4) fourth, to any holder of an allowed claim secured by a lien on such property that is not avoidable under this title and that is junior to such tax lien;

    (5) fifth, to the holder of such tax lien, to the extent that such holder's allowed claim secured by such tax lien is not paid under paragraph (3) of this subsection; and

    (6) sixth, to the estate.

(c) If more than one holder of a claim is entitled to distribution under a particular paragraph of subsection (b) of this section, distribution to such holders under such paragraph shall be in the same order as distribution to such holders would have been other than under this section.

(d) A statutory lien the priority of which is determined in the same manner as the priority of a tax lien under section 6323 of the Internal Revenue Code of 1954 (26 U.S.C. 6323) shall be treated under subsection (b) of this section the same as if such lien were a tax lien.

Pub.L. 95–598, Nov. 6, 1978, 92 Stat. 2607; Pub.L. 98–353, Title III, § 477, July 10, 1984, 98 Stat. 381; Pub.L. 99–554, Title II, § 283(r), Oct. 27, 1986, 100 Stat. 3118.

Historical and Revision Notes

Notes of Committee on the Judiciary, Senate Report No. 95–989. Subsection (a) of section 724 permits the trustee to avoid a lien that secures a fine, penalty, forfeiture, or multiple, punitive, or exemplary damages claim to the extent that the claim is not compensation for actual pecuniary loss. The subsection follows the policy found in section 57j of the Bankruptcy Act [former section 93(j) of this title] of protecting unsecured creditors from the debtor's wrongdoing, but expands the protection afforded. The lien is made voidable rather than void in chapter 7, in order to permit the lien to be revived if the case is converted to chapter 11 under which penalty liens are not voidable. To make the lien void would be to permit the filing of a chapter 7, the voiding of the lien, and the conversion to a chapter 11, simply to avoid a penalty lien, which should be valid in a reorganization case.

Subsection (b) governs tax liens. This provision retains the rule of present bankruptcy law (§ 67(c)(3) of the Bankruptcy Act [former section 107(c)(3) of this title]) that a tax lien on personal property, if not avoidable by the trustee, is subordinated in payment to unsecured claims having a higher priority than unsecured tax claims. Those other claims may be satisfied from the amount that would otherwise have been applied to the tax lien, and any excess of the amount of the lien is then applied to the tax. Any personal property (or sale proceeds) remaining is to be used to satisfy claims secured by liens which are junior to the tax lien. Any proceeds remaining are next applied to pay any unpaid balance of the tax lien.

Subsection (d) specifies that any statutory lien whose priority is determined in the same manner as a tax lien is to be treated as a tax lien under this section, even if the lien does not secure a claim for taxes. An example is the ERISA lien.

Notes of Committee on the Judiciary, House Report No. 95–595. Subsection (b) governs tax liens. It is derived from section 67(c)(3) of the Bankruptcy Act [former section 107(c)(3) of this title], without substantial modification in result. It subordinates tax liens to administrative expense and wage claims, and solves certain circuity of liens problems that arise in connection with the subordination. The order of distribution of property subject to a tax lien is as follows: First, to holders of liens senior to the tax lien; second, to administrative expenses, wage claims, and consumer creditors that are granted priority, but only to the extent of the amount of the allowed tax claim secured by the lien. In other words, the priority claimants step into the shoes of the tax collector. Third, to the tax claimant, to the extent that priority claimants did not use up his entire claim. Fourth, to junior holders. Fifth, to the tax collector to the extent that he was not paid under paragraph (3). Finally, any remaining property goes to the estate. The result of these provisions are to leave senior and junior lienors and holders of unsecured claims undisturbed. If there are any liens that are equal in status to the tax lien, they share pari passu with the tax lien under the distribution provisions of this subsection.

Legislative Statements. Section 724 of the House amendment adopts the provision taken in the House bill and rejects the provision taken in the Senate amendment. In effect, a tax claim secured by a lien is treated as a claim between the fifth and sixth priority in a case under chapter 7 rather than as a secured claim.

The House amendment modifies present law by requiring the subordination of tax liens on both real and personal property to the payment of claims having a priority. This means that assets are to be distributed from the debtor's estate to pay higher priority claims before the tax claims are paid, even though the tax claims are properly secured. Under present law and the Senate amendment only tax liens on personal property, but not on real property, are subordinated to the payment of claims having a priority above the priority for tax claims.

References in Text. Section 6323 of the Internal Revenue Code of 1954, referred to in subsec. (d), is classified to section 6323 of Title 26, Internal Revenue Code.

Effective Date of 1986 Amendments; Quarterly Fees. Amendment by Pub.L. 99–554 effective 30 days after Oct. 27, 1986, ex-

cept as otherwise provided for, see section 302(a) of Pub.L. 99–554, set out as a note under section 581 of Title 28, Judiciary and Judicial Procedure.

Effective Date of 1984 Amendments. See section 553 of Pub.L. 98–353, Title III, July 10, 1984, 98 Stat. 392, set out as an Effective Date of 1984 Amendment note preceding chapter 1 of Title 11, Bankruptcy.

Separability of Provisions. For separability of provisions of Title III of Pub.L. 98–353, see section 551 of Pub.L. 98–353 set out as a Separability of Provisions note preceding chapter 1 of Title 11, Bankruptcy.

Cross References

Automatic preservation of avoided transfer, see section 551.

Commencement of involuntary cases by transferees of voidable transfers, see section 303.

Disallowance of claims of entity that is transferee of avoidable transfer, see section 502.

Effect of dismissal, see section 349.

Exemptions, see section 522.

Liability of transferee of avoided transfer, see section 550.

Voidable transfers in

    Commodity broker liquidation cases, see section 764.

    Stockholder liquidation cases, see section 749.

Library References:

C.J.S. Bankruptcy §§ 123, 134, 215.

West's Key No. Digests, Bankruptcy ⇒2701, 3078(2).

WESTLAW Electronic Research

See WESTLAW Electronic Research Guide following the *Bankruptcy Highlights*.

§ 725. Disposition of certain property

After the commencement of a case under this chapter, but before final distribution of property of the estate under section 726 of this title, the trustee, after notice and a hearing, shall dispose of any property in which an entity other than the estate has an interest, such as a lien, and that has not been disposed of under another section of this title.

Pub.L. 95–598, Nov. 6, 1978, 92 Stat. 2607; Pub.L. 98–353, Title III, § 478, July 10, 1984, 98 Stat. 381.

Historical and Revision Notes

Notes of Committee on the Judiciary, Senate Report No. 95–989. This section requires the court to determine the appropriate disposition of property in which the estate and an entity other than the estate have an interest. It would apply, for example, to property subject to a lien or property co-owned by the estate and another entity. The court must make the determination with respect to property that is not disposed of under another

section of the bankruptcy code, such as by abandonment under section 554, by sale or distribution under 363, or by allowing foreclosure by a secured creditor by lifting the stay under section 362. The purpose of the section is to give the court appropriate authority to ensure that collateral or its proceeds is returned to the proper secured creditor, that consigned or bailed goods are returned to the consignor or bailor and so on. Current law is curiously silent on this point, though case law has grown to fill the void. The section is in lieu of a section that would direct a certain distribution to secured creditors. It gives the court greater flexibility to meet the circumstances, and it is broader, permitting disposition of property subject to a co-ownership interest.

Legislative Statements. Section 725 of the House amendment adopts the substance contained in both the House bill and Senate amendment but transfers an administrative function to the trustee in accordance with the general thrust of this legislation to separate the administrative and the judicial functions where appropriate.

Effective Date of 1984 Amendments. See section 553 of Pub.L. 98–353, Title III, July 10, 1984, 98 Stat. 392, set out as an Effective Date of 1984 Amendment note preceding chapter 1 of Title 11, Bankruptcy.

Separability of Provisions. For separability of provisions of Title III of Pub.L. 98–353, see section 551 of Pub.L. 98–353 set out as a Separability of Provisions note preceding chapter 1 of Title 11, Bankruptcy.

Library References:

C.J.S. Bankruptcy §§ 355, 356.
West's Key No. Digests, Bankruptcy ☞3441.

WESTLAW Electronic Research

See WESTLAW Electronic Research Guide following the *Bankruptcy Highlights.*

§ 726. Distribution of property of the estate

(a) Except as provided in section 510 of this title, property of the estate shall be distributed—

(1) first, in payment of claims of the kind specified in, and in the order specified in, section 507 of this title;

(2) second, in payment of any allowed unsecured claim, other than a claim of a kind specified in paragraph (1), (3), or (4) of this subsection, proof of which is—

(A) timely filed under section 501(a) of this title;

(B) timely filed under section 501(b) or 501(c) of this title; or

(C) tardily filed under section 501(a) of this title, if—

(i) the creditor that holds such claim did not have notice or actual knowledge of the case in time for timely filing of a proof of such claim under section 501(a) of this title; and

(ii) proof of such claim is filed in time to permit payment of such claim;

(3) third, in payment of any allowed unsecured claim proof of which is tardily filed under section 501(a) of this title, other than a claim of the kind specified in paragraph (2)(C) of this subsection;

(4) fourth, in payment of any allowed claim, whether secured or unsecured, for any fine, penalty, or forfeiture, or for multiple, exemplary, or punitive damages, arising before the earlier of the order for relief or the appointment of a trustee, to the extent that such fine, penalty, forfeiture, or damages are not compensation for actual pecuniary loss suffered by the holder of such claim;

(5) fifth, in payment of interest at the legal rate from the date of the filing of the petition, on any claim paid under paragraph (1), (2), (3), or (4) of this subsection; and

(6) sixth, to the debtor.

(b) Payment on claims of a kind specified in paragraph (1), (2), (3), (4), (5), (6) or (7) of section 507(a) of this title, or in paragraph (2), (3), (4), or (5) of subsection (a) of this section, shall be made pro rata among claims of the kind specified in each such particular paragraph, except that in a case that has been converted to this chapter under section 1112 ¹ 1208, or 1307 of this title, a claim allowed under section 503(b) of this title incurred under this chapter after such conversion has priority over a claim allowed under section 503(b) of this title incurred under any other chapter of this title or under this chapter before such conversion and over any expenses of a custodian superseded under section 543 of this title.

(c) Notwithstanding subsections (a) and (b) of this section, if there is property of the kind specified in section 541(a)(2) of this title, or proceeds of such property, in the estate, such property or proceeds shall be segregated from other property of the estate, and such property or proceeds and other property of the estate shall be distributed as follows:

(1) Claims allowed under section 503 of this title shall be paid either from property of the kind specified in section 541(a)(2) of this title, or from other property of the estate, as the interest of justice requires.

(2) Allowed claims, other than claims allowed under section 503 of this title, shall be paid in the order specified in subsection (a) of this section, and, with respect to claims of a kind specified in a particular paragraph of section 507 of this title or subsection (a) of this section, in the following order and manner:

(A) First, community claims against the debtor or the debtor's spouse shall be paid from property of the kind specified in section 541(a) (2) of this title, except to the extent that such property is solely liable for debts of the debtor.

(B) Second, to the extent that community claims against the debtor are not paid under subparagraph (A) of this paragraph, such community claims shall be paid from property of the kind specified in section 541(a) (2) of this title that is solely liable for debts of the debtor.

(C) Third, to the extent that all claims against the debtor including community claims against the debtor are not paid under subparagraph (A) or (B) of this paragraph such claims shall be paid from property of the estate other than property of the kind specified in section 541(a)(2) of this title.

(D) Fourth, to the extent that community claims against the debtor or the debtor's spouse are not paid under subparagraph (A), (B), or (C) of this paragraph, such claims shall be paid from all remaining property of the estate.

Pub.L. 95–598, Nov. 6, 1978, 92 Stat. 2608; Pub.L. 98–353, Title III, § 479, July 10, 1984, 98 Stat. 381; Pub.L. 99–554, Title II, §§ 257(r), 283(s), Oct. 27, 1986, 100 Stat. 3115, 3118.

¹ So in original. Probably should be followed by a comma.

Historical and Revision Notes

Notes of Committee of the Judiciary, Senate Report No. 95–989. This section is the general distribution section for liquidation cases. It dictates the order in which distribution of property of the estate, which has usually been reduced to money by the trustee under the requirements of section 704(1).

First, property is distributed among priority claimants, as determined by section 507, and in the order prescribed by section 507. Second, distribution is to general unsecured creditors. This class excludes priority creditors and the two classes of subordinated creditors specified below. The provision is written to permit distribution to creditors that tardily file claims if their tardiness was due to lack of notice or knowledge of the case. Though it is in the interest of the estate to encourage timely filing, when tardy filing is not the result of a failure to act by the creditor, the normal subordination penalty should not apply. Third distribution is to general unsecured creditors who tardily file. Fourth distribution is to holders of fine, penalty, forfeiture, or multiple, punitive, or exemplary damage claims. More of these claims are disallowed entirely under present law. They are simply subordinated here.

Paragraph (4) provides that punitive penalties, including prepetition tax penalties, are subordinated to the payment of all other classes of claims, except claims for interest accruing during the case. In effect, these penalties are payable out of the estate's assets only if and to the extent that a surplus of assets would otherwise remain at the close of the case for distribution back to the debtor.

Paragraph (5) provides that postpetition interest on prepetition claims is also to be paid to the creditor in a subordinated position. Like prepetition penalties, such interest will be paid from the estate only if and to the extent that a surplus of assets would otherwise remain for return to the debtor at the close of the case.

This section also specifies that interest accrued on all claims (including priority and nonpriority tax claims) which accrued before the date of the filing of the title 11 petition is to be paid in the same order of distribution of the estate's assets as the principal amount of the related claims.

Any surplus is paid to the debtor under paragraph (6).

Subsection (b) follows current law. It specifies that claims within a particular class are to be paid pro rata. This provision will apply, of course, only when there are inadequate funds to pay the holders of claims of a particular class in full. The exception found in the section, which also follows current law, specifies that liquidation administrative expenses are to be paid ahead of reorganization administrative expenses if the case has been converted from a reorganization case to a liquidation case, or from an individual repayment plan case to a liquidation case.

Subsection (c) governs distributions in cases in which there is community property and other property of the estate. The section requires the two kinds of property to be segregated. The distribution is as follows: First, administrative expenses are to be paid, as the court determines on any reasonable equitable basis, from both kinds of property. The court will divide administrative expenses according to such factors as the amount of each kind of property in the estate, the cost of preservation and liquidation of each kind of property, and whether any particular administrative expenses are attributable to one kind of property or the other. Second, claims are to be paid as provided under subsection (a) (the normal liquidation case distribution rules) in the following order and manner: First, community claims against the debtor or the debtor's spouse are paid from community property, except such as is liable solely for the debts of the debtor.

Second, community claims against the debtor, to the extent not paid under the first provision, are paid from community property that is solely liable for the debts of the debtor. Third, community claims, to the extent they remain unpaid, and all other claims against the debtor, are paid from noncommunity property. Fourth, if any community claims against the debtor or the debtor's spouse remain unpaid, they are paid from whatever property remains in the estate. This would occur if community claims against the debtor's spouse are large in amount and most of the estate's property is property solely liable, under nonbankruptcy law, for debts of the debtor.

The marshalling rules in this section apply only to property of the estate. However, they will provide a guide to the courts in the interpretation of proposed 11 U.S.C. 725, relating to distribution of collateral, in cases in which there is community property. If a secured creditor has a lien on both community and noncommunity property, the marshalling rules here—by analogy would dictate that the creditor be satisfied first out of community property, and then out of separate property.

Legislative Statements. Section 726(a)(4) adopts a provision contained in the Senate amendment subordinating prepetition penalties and penalties arising in the involuntary gap period to the extent the penalties are not compensation for actual pecuniary laws.

The House amendment deletes a provision following section 726(a)(6) of the Senate amendment providing that the term "claim" includes interest due owed before the date of the filing of the petition as unnecessary since a right to payment for interest due is a right to payment which is within the definition of "claim" in section 101(4) of the House amendment.

Effective Date of 1986 Amendments; Savings Provisions; Quarterly Fees.

Amendment by Pub.L. 99–554 effective 30 days after Oct. 27, 1986, except as otherwise provided for, see section 302(a) of Pub.L. 99–554, set out as a note under section 581 of Title 28, Judiciary and Judicial Procedure.

Amendments by Pub.L. 99–554, § 257(r), not to apply with respect to cases commenced under Title 11, Bankruptcy, before 30 days after Oct. 27, 1986, see section 302(c)(1) of Pub. L. 99–554, set out as a note under section 581 of Title 28.

Effective Date of 1984 Amendments. See section 553 of Pub.L. 98–353, Title III, July 10, 1984, 98 Stat. 392, set out as an Effective Date of 1984 Amendment note preceding chapter 1 of Title 11, Bankruptcy.

Separability of Provisions. For separability of provisions of Title III of Pub.L. 98–353, see section 551 of Pub.L. 98–353 set out as a Separability of Provisions note preceding chapter 1 of Title 11, Bankruptcy.

Cross References

Customer property, distribution in
   Commodity broker liquidation cases, see section 766.
   Stockbroker liquidation cases, see section 752.
Distribution in chapter 11 cases, see section 1143.
Distribution of securities in stockbroker liquidation cases, see section 750.
Election of creditors holding certain claims entitled to distribution to creditors' committee, see section 705.
Election of trustee by creditors holding claims entitled to distribution, see section 702.
Payment stopped on checks remaining unpaid 90 days after final distribution, see section 347.

Library References:

C.J.S. Bankruptcy §§ 351–353.
West's Key No. Digests, Bankruptcy ☞3442, 3443.

WESTLAW Electronic Research

See WESTLAW Electronic Research Guide following the *Bankruptcy Highlights*.

§ 727. Discharge

(a) The court shall grant the debtor a discharge, unless—

   (1) the debtor is not an individual;

   (2) the debtor, with intent to hinder, delay, or defraud a creditor or an officer of the estate charged with custody of property under this title, has transferred, removed, destroyed, mutilated, or concealed, or has permitted to be transferred, removed, destroyed, mutilated, or concealed—

      (A) property of the debtor, within one year before the date of the filing of the petition; or

      (B) property of the estate, after the date of the filing of the petition;

(3) the debtor has concealed, destroyed, mutilated, falsified, or failed to keep or preserve any recorded information, including books, documents, records, and papers, from which the debtor's financial condition or business transactions might be ascertained, unless such act or failure to act was justified under all of the circumstances of the case;

(4) the debtor knowingly and fraudulently, in or in connection with the case—

    (A) made a false oath or account;

    (B) presented or used a false claim;

    (C) gave, offered, received, or attempted to obtain money, property, or advantage, or a promise of money, property, or advantage, for acting or forbearing to act; or

    (D) withheld from an officer of the estate entitled to possession under this title, any recorded information, including books, documents, records, and papers, relating to the debtor's property or financial affairs;

(5) the debtor has failed to explain satisfactorily, before determination of denial of discharge under this paragraph, any loss of assets or deficiency of assets to meet the debtor's liabilities;

(6) the debtor has refused, in the case—

    (A) to obey any lawful order of the court, other than an order to respond to a material question or to testify;

    (B) on the ground of privilege against self-incrimination, to respond to a material question approved by the court or to testify, after the debtor has been granted immunity with respect to the matter concerning which such privilege was invoked; or

    (C) on a ground other than the properly invoked privilege against self-incrimination, to respond to a material question approved by the court or to testify;

(7) the debtor has committed any act specified in paragraph (2), (3), (4), (5), or (6) of this subsection, on or within one year before the date of the filing of the petition, or during the case, in connection with another case, under this title or under the Bankruptcy Act, concerning an insider;

(8) the debtor has been granted a discharge under this section, under section 1141 of this title, or under section 14, 371, or 476 of the Bankruptcy Act, in a case commenced within six years before the date of the filing of the petition;

(9) the debtor has been granted a discharge under section 1228 or 1328 of this title, or under section 660 or 661 of the Bankruptcy Act, in a case commenced within six years before the date of the filing of the petition, unless payments under the plan in such case totaled at least—

    (A) 100 percent of the allowed unsecured claims in such case; or

    (B)(i) 70 percent of such claims; and

    (ii) the plan was proposed by the debtor in good faith, and was the debtor's best effort; or

(10) the court approves a written waiver of discharge executed by the debtor after the order for relief under this chapter.

(b) Except as provided in section 523 of this title, a discharge under subsection (a) of this section discharges the debtor from all debts that arose before the date of the order for relief under this chapter, and any liability on a claim that is determined under section 502 of this title as if such claim had arisen before the commencement of the case, whether or not a proof of claim based on any such debt or liability is filed under section 501 of this title, and whether or not a claim based on any such debt or liability is allowed under section 502 of this title.

(c)(1) The trustee, a creditor, or the United States trustee may object to the granting of a discharge under subsection (a) of this section.

(2) On request of a party in interest, the court may order the trustee to examine the acts and conduct of the debtor to determine whether a ground exists for denial of discharge.

(d) On request of the trustee, a creditor, or the United States trustee, and after notice and a hearing, the court shall revoke a discharge granted under subsection (a) of this section if—

(1) such discharge was obtained through the fraud of the debtor, and the requesting party did not know of such fraud until after the granting of such discharge;

(2) the debtor acquired property that is property of the estate, or became entitled to acquire property that would be property of the estate, and knowingly and fraudulently failed to report the acquisition of or entitlement to such property, or to deliver or surrender such property to the trustee; or

(3) the debtor committed an act specified in subsection (a)(6) of this section.

(e) The trustee, a creditor, or the United States trustee may request a revocation of a discharge—

(1) under subsection (d)(1) of this section within one year after such discharge is granted; or

(2) under subsection (d)(2) or (d)(3) of this section before the later of—

(A) one year after the granting of such discharge; and

(B) the date the case is closed.

Pub.L. 95–598, Nov. 6, 1978, 92 Stat. 2609; Pub.L. 98–353, Title III, § 480, July 10, 1984, 98 Stat. 382; Pub.L. 99–554, Title II, §§ 220, 257(s), Oct. 27, 1986, 100 Stat. 3101, 3116.

Historical and Revision Notes

Notes of Committee on the Judiciary, Senate Report No. 95–989. This section is the heart of the fresh start provisions of the bankruptcy law. Subsection (a) requires the court to grant a debtor a discharge unless one of nine conditions is met. The first condition is that the debtor is not an individual. This is a change from present law, under which corporations and partnerships may be discharged in liquidation cases, though they rarely are. The change in policy will avoid trafficking in corporate shells and in bankrupt partnerships.

"Individual" includes a deceased individual, so that if the debtor dies during the bankruptcy case, he will nevertheless be released from his debts, and his estate will not be liable for them. Creditors will be entitled to only one satisfaction—from the bankruptcy estate and not from the probate estate.

The next three grounds for denial of discharge center on the debtor's wrongdoing in or in connection with the bankruptcy case. They are derived from Bankruptcy Act § 14c [former section 32(c) of this title]. If the debtor, with intent to hinder, delay, or defraud his creditors or an officer of the estate, has transferred, removed, destroyed, mutilated, or concealed, or has permitted any such action with respect to, property of the debtor within the year preceding the case, or property of the estate after the commencement of the case, then the debtor is denied discharge. The debtor is also denied discharge if he has concealed, destroyed, mutilated, falsified, or failed to keep or preserve any books and records from which his financial condition might be ascertained, unless the act or failure to act was justified under all the circumstances of the case. The fourth ground for denial of discharge is the commission of a bankruptcy crime, although the standard of proof is preponderance of the evidence rather than proof beyond a reasonable doubt. These crimes include the making of a false oath or account, the use or presentation of a false claim, the giving or receiving of money for acting or forbearing to act, and the withholding from an officer of the estate entitled to possession of books and records relating to the debtor's financial affairs.

The fifth ground for denial of discharge is the failure of the debtor to explain satisfactorily any loss of assets or deficiency of assets to meet the debtor's liabilities. The sixth ground concerns refusal to testify. It is a change from present law, under which the debtor may be denied discharge for legitimately exercising his right against self-incrimination. Under this provision, the debtor may be denied discharge if he refuses to obey any lawful order of the court, or if he refuses to testify after having been granted immunity or after improperly invoking the constitutional privilege against self-incrimination.

The seventh ground for denial of discharge is the commission of an act specified in grounds two through six during the year before the debtor's case in connection with another bankruptcy case concerning an insider.

The eighth ground for denial of discharge is derived from § 14c(5) of the Bankruptcy Act [former section 32(c)(5) of this title]. If the debtor has been granted a discharge in a case commenced within 6 years preceding the present bankruptcy case, he is denied discharge. This provision, which is no change from current law with respect to straight bankruptcy, is the 6-year bar to discharge. Discharge under chapter 11 will bar a discharge for 6 years. As under current law, confirmation of a composition wage earner plan under chapter 13 is a basis for invoking the 6-year bar.

The ninth ground is approval by the court of a waiver of discharge.

Subsection (b) specifies that the discharge granted under this section discharges the debtor from all debts that arose before the date of the order for relief. It is irrelevant whether or not a proof of claim was filed with respect to the debt, and whether or not the claim based on the debt was allowed.

Subsection (c) permits the trustee, or a creditor, to object to discharge. It also permits the court, on request of a party in interest, to order the trustee to examine the acts and conduct of the debtor to determine whether a ground for denial of discharge exists.

Subsection (d) requires the court to revoke a discharge already granted in certain circumstances. If the debtor obtained the discharge through fraud, if he acquired and concealed property of the estate, or if he refused to obey a court order or to testify, the discharge is to be revoked.

Subsection (e) permits the trustee or a creditor to request revocation of a discharge within 1 year after the discharge is granted, on the grounds of fraud, and within one year of discharge or the date of the closing of the case, whichever is later, on other grounds.

Legislative Statements. Sections 727(a)(8) and (9) of the House amendment represent a compromise between provisions contained in section 727(a)(8) of the House bill and Senate amendment. Section 727(a)(8) of the House amendment adopts section 727(a)(8) of the House bill. However, section 727(a)(9) of the House amendment contains a compromise based on section 727(a)(8) of the Senate amendment with respect to the circumstances under which a plan by way of composition under Chapter XIII of the Bankruptcy Act [former section 1001 et seq. of this title] should be a bar to discharge in a subsequent proceeding under title 11. The paragraph provides that a discharge under section 660 or 661 of the Bankruptcy Act [former sections 1060 and 1061 of this title] or section 1328 of title 11 in a case commenced within 6 years before the date of the filing of the petition in a subsequent case, operates as a bar to discharge unless, first, payments under the plan totaled at least 100 percent of the allowed unsecured claims in the case; or second, payments under the plan totaled at least 70 percent of the allowed unsecured claims in the case and the plan was proposed by the debtor in good faith and was the debtor's best effort.

It is expected that the Rules of Bankruptcy Procedure will contain a provision permitting the debtor to request a determination of whether a plan is the debtor's "best effort" prior to confirmation of a plan in a case under chapter 13 of title 11. In determining whether a plan is the debtor's "best effort" the court will evaluate several factors. Different facts and circumstances in cases under chapter 13 operate to make any rule of thumb of limited usefulness. The court should balance the debtor's assets, including family income, health insurance, retirement benefits, and other wealth, a sum which is generally determinable, against the foreseeable necessary living expenses of the debtor and the debtor's dependents, which unfortunately is rarely quantifiable. In determining the expenses of the debtor and the debtor's dependents, the court should consider the stability of the debtor's employment, if any, the age of the debtor, the number of the debtor's dependents and their ages, the condition of equipment and tools necessary to the debtor's employment or to the operation of his business, and other foreseeable expenses that the debtor will be required to pay during the period of the plan, other than payments to be made to creditors under the plan.

Section 727(a)(10) of the House amendment clarifies a provision contained in section 727(a)(9) of the House bill and Senate amendment indicating that a discharge may be barred if the court approves a waiver of discharge executed in writing by the debtor after the order for relief under chapter 7.

Section 727(b) of the House amendment adopts a similar provision contained in the Senate amendment modifying the effect of discharge. The provision makes clear that the debtor is discharged from all debts that arose before the date of the order for relief under chapter 7 in addition to any debt which is determined under section 502 as if it were a prepetition claim. Thus, if a case is converted from chapter 11 or chapter 13 to a case under chapter 7, all debts prior to the time of conversion are discharged, in addition to debts determined after the date of conversion of a kind specified in section 502, that are to be determined as prepetition claims. This modification is particularly important with respect to an individual debtor who files a petition under chapter 11 or chapter 13 of title 11 if the case is converted to chapter 7. The logical result of the House amendment is to equate the result that obtains whether the case is converted from another chapter to chapter 7, or whether the other chapter proceeding is dismissed and a new case is commenced by filing a petition under chapter 7.

References in Text. Sections 14, 371, and 476 of the Bankruptcy Act, referred to in subsec. (a)(8), were classified to former sections 32, 771 and 876 of this title, respectively.

Sections 660 and 661 of the Bankruptcy Act, referred to in subsec. (a)(9), were classified to former sections 1060 and 1061 of this title, respectively.

1986 Amendment. Subsec. (c)(1). Pub.L. 99–554, § 220, substituted "The trustee, a creditor, or the United States trustee may object" for "The trustee or a creditor may object".

Subsec. (d). Pub.L. 99–554, § 220, substituted ", a creditor, or the United States trustee," for "or a creditor,".

Subsec. (d)(2). Pub.L. 99–554, § 220, substituted "acquisition of or entitlement to such property" for "acquisition of, or entitlement to, such property".

Subsec. (e). Pub.L. 99–554, § 220, substituted "The trustee, a creditor, or the United States trustee may" for "The trustee or a creditor may".

Subsec. (e)(1). Pub.L. 99–554, § 220, substituted "section within" for "section, within" and "discharge is granted" for "discharge was granted".

Subsec. (e)(2). Pub.L. 99–554, § 220, substituted "section before" for "section, before", and in subpar. (A) "discharge; and" for "discharge; or".

See Effective Date of 1986 Amendment, etc., notes set out below.

Effective Date of 1986 Amendments; Savings Provisions; Effective Date of 1986 Amendments for Certain Judicial Districts Not Served by United States Trustees and for Judicial Districts in Alabama and North Carolina; U.S. Trustee System Fund Deposits in Alabama and North Carolina; Effective Date of Title 11 Chapter 15 Repeal as to Northern District of Alabama; Authority of Certain Estate Administrators in Alabama and North Carolina; Effective Date of 1986 Amendments in Pending Cases Where a U.S. Trustee Not Authorized or Where a Trustee Files Final Report or Plan is Confirmed; Quarterly Fees. Amendment by Pub.L. 99–554 effective 30 days after Oct. 27, 1986, except as otherwise provided for, see section 302(a) of Pub.L.

99–554, set out as a note under section 581 of Title 28, Judiciary and Judicial Procedure.

Amendments by Pub.L. 99–554, § 257(5), not to apply with respect to cases commenced under Title 11, Bankruptcy, before 30 days after Oct. 27, 1986, see section 302(c)(1) of Pub.L. 99–554, set out as a note under section 581 of Title 28.

Amendment by Pub.L. 99–554, § 220 not to become effective in or with respect to certain specified judicial districts until, or apply to cases while pending in such district before, the expiration of the 270-day period beginning 30 days after Oct. 27, 1986, or of the 30-day period beginning on the date the Attorney General certifies under section 303 of Pub.L. 99–554 the region specified in a paragraph of section 581(a) of Title 28, as amended by section 111(a) of Pub.L. 99–554, that includes such district, whichever occurs first, see section 302(d)(1) of Pub.L. 99–554, set out as a note under section 581 of Title 28.

Amendment by Pub.L. 99–554, § 220, not to become effective in or with respect to certain specified judicial districts until, or apply to cases while pending in such district before, the expiration of the 2-year period beginning 30 days after Oct. 27, 1986, or of the 30-day period beginning on the date the Attorney General certifies under section 303 of Pub.L. 99–554 the region specified in a paragraph of section 581(a) of Title 28, as amended by section 111(a) of Pub.L. 99–554, that includes such district, whichever occurs first, see section 302(d)(2) of Pub.L. 99–554, set out as a note under section 581 of Title 28.

Amendment by Pub.L. 99–554, § 220, not to become effective in or with respect to judicial districts established for the States of Alabama and North Carolina until, or apply to cases while pending in such district before, such district elects to be included in a bankruptcy region established in section 581(a) of Title 28, as amended by section 111(a) of Pub.L. 99–554, or Oct. 1, 2002, whichever occurs first, and, except as otherwise provided for, with respect to cases under chapters 7, 11, 12, and 13 of Title 11 commenced before 30 days after Oct. 27, 2002, and pending in a judicial district in the States of Alabama or North Carolina be-

fore any election made under section 302(d)(3)(A) of Pub.L. 99–554 by such district becomes effective or Oct. 1, 2002, whichever occurs first, amendments by Pub.L. 99–554 not to apply until Oct. 1, 2003, or the expiration of the 1-year period beginning on the date such election becomes effective, whichever occurs first, and further, in any judicial district in Alabama or North Carolina not making the election described in section 302(d)(3)(A) of Pub.L. 99–554, any person appointed under regulations issued by the Judicial Conference to administer estates in cases under Title 11 authorized to establish, etc., a panel of private trustees, and to supervise cases and trustees in cases under chapters 7, 11, 12, and 13 of Title 11, until amendments by sections 201 to 231 of Pub.L. 99–554 effective in such district, see section 302(d)(3)(A) to (F), (H), (I) of Pub.L. 99–554, set out as a note under section 581 of Title 28.

Amendment by Pub.L. 99–554, § 220, except as otherwise provided, with respect to cases under chapters 7, 11, 12, and 13 of Title 11 commenced before 30 days after Oct. 27, 1986, and pending in a judicial district referred to in section 581(a) of Title 28, as amended by section 111(a) of Pub.L. 99–554, for which a United States trustee is not authorized before 30 days after Oct. 27, 1986 to be appointed, not applicable until the expiration of the 3-year period beginning on Oct. 27, 1986, or of the 1-year period beginning on the date the Attorney General certifies under section 303 of Pub.L. 99–554 the region specified in a paragraph of such section 581(a) that includes, such district, whichever occurs first, see section 302(e)(1)(2) of Pub.L. 99–554, set out as a note under section 581 of Title 28.

See 1986 Amendment notes set out above.

Effective Date of 1984 Amendments. See section 553 of Pub.L. 98–353, Title III, July 10, 1984, 98 Stat. 392, set out as an Effective Date of 1984 Amendment note preceding chapter 1 of Title 11, Bankruptcy.

Separability of Provisions. For separability of provisions of Title III of Pub.L. 98–353, see section 551 of Pub.L. 98–353 set out as a Separability of Provisions note preceding chapter 1 of Title 11, Bankruptcy.

Cross References

Confirmation of plan as affecting discharge in
Chapter 9 cases, see section 944.
Chapter 11 cases, see section 1141.
Discharge in Chapter 13 cases, see section 1328.
Duty of trustee to oppose discharge, see section 704.

Effect of
　Conversion, see section 348.
　Discharge, see section 524.
Exceptions to discharge, see section 523.

Library References:

C.J.S. Bankruptcy § 288 et seq.
West's Key No. Digests, Bankruptcy ☞3271 et seq.

WESTLAW Electronic Research

See WESTLAW Electronic Research Guide following the *Bankruptcy Highlights*.

§ 728. Special tax provisions

(a) For the purposes of any State or local law imposing a tax on or measured by income, the taxable period of a debtor that is an individual shall terminate on the date of the order for relief under this chapter, unless the case was converted under section 1112 or 1208 of this title.

(b) Notwithstanding any State or local law imposing a tax on or measured by income, the trustee shall make tax returns of income for the estate of an individual debtor in a case under this chapter or for a debtor that is a corporation in a case under this chapter only if such estate or corporation has net taxable income for the entire period after the order for relief under this chapter during which the case is pending. If such entity has such income, or if the debtor is a partnership, then the trustee shall make and file a return of income for each taxable period during which the case was pending after the order for relief under this chapter.

(c) If there are pending a case under this chapter concerning a partnership and a case under this chapter concerning a partner in such partnership, a governmental unit's claim for any unpaid liability of such partner for a State or local tax on or measured by income, to the extent that such liability arose from the inclusion in such partner's taxable income of earnings of such partnership that were not withdrawn by such partner, is a claim only against such partnership.

(d) Notwithstanding section 541 of this title, if there are pending a case under this chapter concerning a partnership and a case under this chapter concerning a partner in such partnership, then any State or local tax refund or reduction of tax of such partner that would have otherwise been property of the estate of such partner under section 541 of this title—

　(1) is property of the estate of such partnership to the extent that such tax refund or reduction of tax is fairly apportionable to losses sustained by such partnership and not reimbursed by such partner; and

　(2) is otherwise property of the estate of such partner.

Pub.L. 95–598, Nov. 6, 1978, 92 Stat. 2611; Pub.L. 98–353, Title III, § 481, July 10, 1984, 98 Stat. 382; Pub.L. 99–554, Title II, § 257(t), Oct. 27, 1986, 100 Stat. 3116.

Historical and Revision Notes

Notes of Committee on the Judiciary, Senate Report No. 95–989. Section 728 of title 11 applies only to state and local taxation. This provision contains four subsections which embody special tax provisions that apply in a case under chapter 7. Subsection (a) terminates the taxable year of an individual debtor on the date of the order for relief under chapter 7 of title 11. The date of termination of the individual's taxable year is the date on which the estate first becomes a separate taxable entity. If the case was originally filed under chapter 11 of title 11, then the estate would have been made a separate taxable entity on the date of the order for relief under that chapter. In the rare case of a multiple conversion, then the date of the order for relief under the first chapter under which the estate was a separate taxable entity is controlling.

Subsection (b) permits the trustee of the estate of an individual debtor or a corporation in a case under chapter 7 of title 11 to make a tax return only if the estate or corporation has net taxable income for the entire case. If the estate or corporation has net taxable income at the close of the case, then the trustee files an income tax return for each tax year during which the case was pending. The trustee of a partnership debtor must always file returns for each such taxable period.

Subsection (c) sets forth a marshalling rule pertaining to tax claims against a partner and a partnership in a case under chapter 7 of title 11. To the extent that the income tax liability arose from the inclusion of undistributed earnings in the partner's taxable income, the court is required to disallow the tax claim against the partner's estate and to allow such claim against the partnership estate. No burden is placed on the taxing authority; the taxing authority should file a complete proof of claim in each case and the court will execute the marshalling. If the partnership's assets are insufficient to satisfy partnership creditors in full, then section 723(c) of title 11 will apply, notwithstanding this subsection, to allow any unsatisfied tax claims to be asserted by the partnership trustee against the estate of the partner. The marshalling rule under this subsection applies only for purposes of allowance and distribution. Thus the tax claim may be nondischargeable with respect to an individual partner.

Subsection (d) requires the court to apportion any tax refund or reduction of tax between the estate of a partner and the estate of his partnership. The standard of apportionment entitles the partnership estate to receive that part of the tax refund or reduction that is attributable to losses sustained by the partnership that were deducted by the partner but for which the partner never reimbursed the partnership. The partner's estate receives any part not allocated to the partnership estate. The section applies notwithstanding section 541 of title 11, which includes the partner's right to a tax refund or to reduction of tax as property of the partner's estate.

Legislative Statements. Section 728 of the House amendment adopts a provision contained in the House bill that was deleted by the Senate amendment.

Liquidations. The House bill contained special tax provisions concerning the treatment of liquidations cases for State and local tax laws. These provisions deal with the taxable years of an individual debtor, return-filing requirements, and rules allocating State and local tax liabilities and refunds between a bankrupt partner and the partnership of which he is a member. The Senate amendment deleted these rules pending consideration of the Federal tax treatment of bankruptcy in the next Congress. The House amendment returns these provisions to the bill in order that they may be studied by the bankruptcy and tax bars who may wish to submit comments to Congress in connection with its consideration of these provisions in the next Congress.

Effective Date of 1986 Amendments; Savings Provisions; Quarterly Fees. Amendment by Pub.L. 99–554 effective 30 days after Oct. 27, 1986, except as otherwise provided for, see section 302(a) of Pub.L. 99–554, set out as a note under section 581 of Title 28, Judiciary and Judicial Procedure.

Amendments by Pub.L. 99–554, § 257(t), not to apply with respect to cases commenced under Title 11, Bankruptcy, before 30 days after Oct. 27, 1986, see section 302(c)(1) of Pub. L. 99–554, set out as a note under section 581 of Title 28.

Effective Date of 1984 Amendments. See section 553 of Pub.L. 98–353, Title III, July 10, 1984, 98 Stat. 392, set out as an Effective Date of 1984 Amendment note preceding chapter 1 of Title 11, Bankruptcy.

Separability of Provisions. For separability of provisions of Title III of Pub.L. 98–353, see section 551 of Pub.L. 98–353 set out as a Separability of Provisions note preceding chapter 1 of Title 11, Bankruptcy.

SUBCHAPTER III—STOCKBROKER LIQUIDATION

§ 741. Definitions for this subchapter

In this subchapter—

(1) "Commission" means Securities and Exchange Commission;

(2) "customer" includes—

(A) entity with whom a person deals as principal or agent and that has a claim against such person on account of a security received, acquired, or held by such person in the ordinary course of such person's business as a stockbroker, from or for the securities account or accounts of such entity—

(i) for safekeeping;

(ii) with a view to sale;

(iii) to cover a consummated sale;

(iv) pursuant to a purchase;

(v) as collateral under a security agreement; or

(vi) for the purpose of effecting registration of transfer; and

(B) entity that has a claim against a person arising out of—

(i) a sale or conversion of a security received, acquired, or held as specified in subparagraph (A) of this paragraph; or

(ii) a deposit of cash, a security, or other property with such person for the purpose of purchasing or selling a security;

(3) "customer name security" means security—

(A) held for the account of a customer on the date of the filing of the petition by or on behalf of the debtor;

(B) registered in such customer's name on such date or in the process of being so registered under instructions from the debtor; and

(C) not in a form transferable by delivery on such date;

(4) "customer property" means cash, security, or other property, and proceeds of such cash, security, or property, received, acquired, or held by or

for the account of the debtor, from or for the securities account of a customer—

    (A) including—

        (i) property that was unlawfully converted from and that is the lawful property of the estate;

        (ii) a security held as property of the debtor to the extent such security is necessary to meet a net equity claim of a customer based on a security of the same class and series of an issuer;

        (iii) resources provided through the use or realization of a customer's debit cash balance or a debit item includible in the Formula for Determination of Reserve Requirement for Brokers and Dealers as promulgated by the Commission under the Securities Exchange Act of 1934 (15 U.S.C. 78a et seq.); and

        (iv) other property of the debtor that any applicable law, rule, or regulation requires to be set aside or held for the benefit of a customer, unless including such property as customer property would not significantly increase customer property; but

    (B) not including—

        (i) a customer name security delivered to or reclaimed by a customer under section 751 of this title; or

        (ii) property to the extent that a customer does not have a claim against the debtor based on such property;

    (5) "margin payment" means payment or deposit of cash, a security, or other property, that is commonly known to the securities trade as original margin, initial margin, maintenance margin, or variation margin, or as a mark-to-market payment, or that secures an obligation of a participant in a securities clearing agency;

    (6) "net equity" means, with respect to all accounts of a customer that such customer has in the same capacity—

    (A)(i) aggregate dollar balance that would remain in such accounts after the liquidation, by sale or purchase, at the time of the filing of the petition, of all securities positions in all such accounts, except any customer name securities of such customer; minus

        (ii) any claim of the debtor against such customer in such capacity that would have been owing immediately after such liquidation; plus

    (B) any payment by such customer to the trustee, within 60 days after notice under section 342 of this title, of any business related claim of the debtor against such customer in such capacity;

    (7) "securities contract" means contract for the purchase, sale, or loan of a security, including an option for the purchase or sale of a security, certificate of deposit, or group or index of securities (including any interest therein or based on the value thereof), or any option entered into on a national securities exchange relating to foreign currencies, or the guarantee of any settlement of cash or securities by or to a securities clearing agency;

    (8) "settlement payment" means a preliminary settlement payment, a partial settlement payment, an interim settlement payment, a settlement

payment on account, a final settlement payment, or any other similar payment commonly used in the securities trade; and

(9) "SIPC" means Securities Investor Protection Corporation.

Pub.L. 95–598, Nov. 6, 1978, 92 Stat. 2611; Pub.L. 97–222, § 8, July 27, 1982, 96 Stat. 237; Pub.L. 98–353, Title III, § 482, July 10, 1984, 98 Stat. 382.

Historical and Revision Notes

Notes of Committee on the Judiciary, Senate Report No. 95–989. Section 741 sets forth definitions for subchapter III of chapter 7.

Paragraph (1) defines "Commission" to mean the Securities and Exchange Commission.

Paragraph (2) defines "customer" to include anybody that interacts with the debtor in a capacity that concerns securities transactions. The term embraces cash or margin customers of a broker or dealer in the broadest sense.

Paragraph (3) defines "customer name security" in a restrictive fashion to include only non-transferrable securities that are registered, or in the process of being registered in a customer's own name. The securities must not be endorsed by the customer and the stockbroker must not be able to legally transfer the securities by delivery, by a power of attorney, or otherwise.

Paragraph (4) defines "customer property" to include all property of the debtor that has been segregated for customers or property that should have been segregated but was unlawfully converted. Clause (i) refers to customer property not properly segregated by the debtor or customer property converted and then recovered so as to become property of the estate. Unlawfully converted property that has been transferred to a third party is excluded until it is recovered as property of the estate by virtue of the avoiding powers. The concept excludes customer name securities that have been delivered to or reclaimed by a customer and any property properly belonging to the stockholder, such as money deposited by a customer to pay for securities that the stockholder has distributed to such customer.

Paragraph (5) [now (6)] defines "net equity" to establish the extent to which a customer will be entitled to share in the single and separate fund. Accounts of a customer are aggregated and offset only to the extent the accounts are held by the customer in the same capacity. Thus, a personal account is separate from an account held as trustee. In a community property state an account held for the community is distinct from an account held as separate property.

The net equity is computed by liquidating all securities positions in the accounts and crediting the account with any amount due to the customer. Regardless of the actual dates, if any, of liquidation, the customer is only entitled to the liquidation value at the time of the filing of the petition. To avoid double counting, the liquidation value of customer name securities belonging to a customer is excluded from net equity. Thus, clause (ii) includes claims against a customer resulting from the liquidation of a security under clause (i). The value of a security on which trading has been suspended at the time of the filing of the petition will be estimated. Once the net liquidation value is computed, any amount that the customer owes to the stockbroker is subtracted including any amount that would be owing after the hypothetical liquidation, such as brokerage fees. Debts owed by the customer to the debtor, other than in a securities related transaction, will not reduce the net equity of the customer. Finally, net equity is increased by any payment by the customer to the debtor actually paid within 60 days after notice. The principal reason a customer would make such a payment is to reclaim customer name securities under § 751.

Paragraph (6) defines "1934 Act" to mean the Securities Exchange Act of 1934 [section 78a et seq. of Title 15, Commerce and Trade].

Paragraph (7) [now (9)] defines "SIPC" to mean the Securities Investor Protection Corporation.

Legislative Statements. Section 741(6) of the House bill and Senate amendment is deleted by the House amendment since the defined term is used only in section 741(4)(A)(iii). A corresponding change is made in that section.

References in Text. The Securities Exchange Act of 1934, referred to in par. (4)(A), is Act June 6, 1934, c. 404, 48 Stat. 881, which is classified to section 78a et seq. of Title 15, Commerce and Trade.

Effective Date of 1984 Amendments. See section 553 of Pub.L. 98–353, Title III, July 10, 1984, 98 Stat. 392, set out as an Effective Date of 1984 Amendment note preceding chapter 1 of Title 11, Bankruptcy.

Separability of Provisions. For separability of provisions of Title III of Pub.L. 98–353, see section 551 of Pub.L. 98–353 set out as a Separability of Provisions note preceding chapter 1 of Title 11, Bankruptcy.

Cross References

Definitions applicable in
    Cases under this title, see section 101.
    Chapter 9 cases, see section 902.
    Commodity broker liquidation cases, see section 761.
    Railroad reorganization cases, see section 1162.
    Reorganization cases, see section 1101.
Stockbroker defined, see section 101.

Library References:

C.J.S. Bankruptcy §§ 358–360; Securities Regulation § 6.
West's Key No. Digests, Bankruptcy ⬅3461; Securities Regulation ⬅185.10–185.21.

WESTLAW Electronic Research

See WESTLAW Electronic Research Guide following the *Bankruptcy Highlights.*

§ 742. Effect of section 362 of this title in this subchapter

Notwithstanding section 362 of this title, SIPC may file an application for a protective decree under the Securities Investor Protection Act of 1970 (15 U.S.C. 78aaa et seq.). The filing of such application stays all proceedings in the case under this title unless and until such application is dismissed. If SIPC completes the liquidation of the debtor, then the court shall dismiss the case.

Pub.L. 95–598, Nov. 6, 1978, 92 Stat. 2613; Pub.L. 97–222, § 9, July 27, 1982, 96 Stat. 237.

Historical and Revision Notes

Notes of Committee on the Judiciary, Senate Report No. 95–989. Section 742 indicates that the automatic stay does not prevent SIPC from filing an application for a protective decree under SIPA. If SIPA does file such an application, then all bankruptcy proceedings are suspended until the SIPC action is completed. If SIPC completes liquidation of the stockbroker then the bankruptcy case is dismissed.

Legislative Statements. Section 742 of the House amendment deletes a sentence contained in the Senate amendment requiring the trustee in an interstate stock-brokerage liquidation to comply with the provisions of subchapter IV of chapter 7 if the debtor is also a commodity broker. The House amendment expands the requirement to require the SIPC trustee to perform such duties, if the debtor is a commodity broker, under section 7(b) of the Securities Investor Protection Act [section 78ggg(b) of Title 15, Commerce and Trade]. The requirement is deleted from section 742 since the trustee of an intrastate stockbroker will be bound by the provisions of subchapter IV of chapter 7 if the debtor is also a commodity broker by reason of section 103 of title 11.

References in Text. The Securities Investor Protection Act of 1970, referred to in text, is Pub.L. 91–598, Dec. 30, 1970, 84 Stat. 1636, which is classified to section 78aaa et seq. of Title 15, Commerce and Trade.

Cross References

Automatic stay of enforcement of claims against debtor in chapter 9 cases, see section 922.
Effect of dismissal, see section 349.
Stay of action against codebtor in chapter 13 cases, see section 1301.

Library References:

C.J.S. Bankruptcy §§ 358–360; Securities Regulation § 6.
West's Key No. Digests, Bankruptcy ⇐3461; Securities Regulation ⇐185.10–185.21.

WESTLAW Electronic Research

See WESTLAW Electronic Research Guide following the *Bankruptcy Highlights.*

§ 743. Notice

The clerk shall give the notice required by section 342(a) of this title to SIPC and to the Commission.

Pub.L. 95–598, Nov. 6, 1978, 92 Stat. 2613.

Historical and Revision Notes

Notes of Committee on the Judiciary, Senate Report No. 95–989. Section 743 requires that notice of the order for relief be given to SIPC and to the SEC in every stockbroker case.

Codification. Pub.L. 99–554, Title II, § 283(t), Oct. 27, 1986, 100 Stat. ___, provided that this section is amended by striking out "(d)", which amendment was incapable of execution in view of present language of text.

Effective Date of 1986 Amendments; Quarterly Fees. Amendment by Pub.L. 99–554 effective 30 days after Oct. 27, 1986, except as otherwise provided for, see section 302(a) of Pub.L. 99–554, set out as a note under section 581 of Title 28, Judiciary and Judicial Procedure.

Cross References

Notice in chapter 9 cases, see section 923.
Notice to the Commodity Futures Trading Commission, see section 762.

Library References:

C.J.S. Bankruptcy §§ 358–360; Securities Regulation § 6.
West's Key No. Digests, Bankruptcy ⇐3461; Securities Regulation 185.10–185.21.

WESTLAW Electronic Research

See WESTLAW Electronic Research Guide following the *Bankruptcy Highlights.*

§ 744. Executory contracts

Notwithstanding section 365(d)(1) of this title, the trustee shall assume or reject, under section 365 of this title, any executory contract of the debtor for the purchase or sale of a security in the ordinary course of the debtor's business, within a reasonable time after the date of the order for relief, but not to exceed 30 days. If the trustee does not assume such a contract within such time, such contract is rejected.

Pub.L. 95–598, Nov. 6, 1978, 92 Stat. 2613; Pub.L. 97–222, § 10, July 27, 1982, 96 Stat. 238.

Historical and Revision Notes

Notes of Committee on the Judiciary, Senate Report No. 95–989. Section 744 instructs the court to give the trustee a reasonable time, not to exceed 30 days, to assume or reject any executory contract of the stockbroker to buy or sell securities. Any contract not assumed within the time fixed by the court is considered to be rejected.

Cross References

Effect of rejection of lease of railroad line, see section 1169.

Library References:

> C.J.S. Bankruptcy §§ 358–360; Securities Regulation § 6.
> West's Key No. Digests, Bankruptcy ☞3461; Securities Regulation ☞185.10–185.21.

WESTLAW Electronic Research

> See WESTLAW Electronic Research Guide following the *Bankruptcy Highlights*.

§ 745. Treatment of accounts

(a) Accounts held by the debtor for a particular customer in separate capacities shall be treated as accounts of separate customers.

(b) If a stockbroker or a bank holds a customer net equity claim against the debtor that arose out of a transaction for a customer of such stockbroker or bank, each such customer of such stockbroker or bank shall be treated as a separate customer of the debtor.

(c) Each trustee's account specified as such on the debtor's books, and supported by a trust deed filed with, and qualified as such by, the Internal Revenue Service, and under the Internal Revenue Code of 1954 (26 U.S.C. 1 et seq.), shall be treated as a separate customer account for each beneficiary under such trustee account.

Pub.L. 95–598, Nov. 6, 1978, 92 Stat. 2613; Pub.L. 97–222, § 11, July 27, 1982, 96 Stat. 238; Pub.L. 98–353, Title III, § 483, July 10, 1984, 98 Stat. 383.

Historical and Revision Notes

Notes of Committee on the Judiciary, Senate Report No. 95–989. Section 745(a) indicates that each account held by a customer in a separate capacity is to be considered a separate account. This prevents the offset of accounts held in different capacities.

Subsection (b) indicates that a bank or another stockbroker that is a customer of a debtor is considered to hold its customers accounts in separate capacities. Thus a bank or other stockbroker is not treated as a mutual fund for purposes of bulk investment. This protects unrelated customers of a bank or other stockholder from having their accounts offset.

1982 Amendment. Subsec. (c). Pub.L. 97–222, substituted "Each" for "A."

Subsection (c) effects the same result with respect to a trust so that each beneficiary is treated as the customer of the debtor rather than the trust itself. This eliminates any doubt whether a trustee holds a personal account in a separate capacity from his trustee's account.

References in Text. The Internal Revenue Code of 1954, referred to in subsec. (c), is classified to section 1 et seq. of Title 26, Internal Revenue Code.

Effective Date of 1984 Amendments. See section 553 of Pub.L. 98–353, Title III, July 10, 1984, 98 Stat. 392, set out as an Effective Date of 1984 Amendment note preceding chapter 1 of Title 11, Bankruptcy.

Separability of Provisions. For separability of provisions of Title III of Pub.L. 98–353, see section 551 of Pub.L. 98–353 set out as a Separability of Provisions note preceding chapter 1 of Title 11, Bankruptcy.

Cross References

> Treatment of accounts in commodity broker liquidation cases, see section 763.
> Stockbroker defined, see section 101.

Library References:

> C.J.S. Bankruptcy §§ 358–360; Securities Regulation § 6.
> West's Key No. Digests, Bankruptcy ☞3461; Securities Regulation ☞185.10–185.21.

WESTLAW Electronic Research

> See WESTLAW Electronic Research Guide following the *Bankruptcy Highlights*.

§ 746. Extent of customer claims

(a) If, after the date of the filing of the petition, an entity enters into a transaction with the debtor, in a manner that would have made such entity a customer had such transaction occurred before the date of the filing of the petition, and such transaction was entered into by such entity in good faith and before the qualification under section 322 of this title of a trustee, such entity shall be deemed a customer, and the date of such transaction shall be deemed to be the date of the filing of the petition for the purpose of determining such entity's net equity.

(b) An entity does not have a claim as a customer to the extent that such entity transferred to the debtor cash or a security that, by contract, agreement, understanding, or operation of law, is—

(1) part of the capital of the debtor; or

(2) subordinated to the claims of any or all creditors.

Pub.L. 95–598, Nov. 6, 1978, 92 Stat. 2613; Pub.L. 97–222, § 12, July 27, 1982, 96 Stat. 238.

Historical and Revision Notes

Notes of Committee on the Judiciary, Senate Report No. 95–989. Section 746(a) protects entities who deal in good faith with the debtor after the filing of the petition and before a trustee is appointed by deeming such entities to be customers. The principal application of this section will be in an involuntary case before the order for relief, because § 701(b) requires prompt appointment of an interim trustee after the order for relief.

Subsection (b) indicates that an entity who holds securities that are either part of the capital of the debtor or that are subordinated to the claims of any creditor of the debtor is not a customer with respect to those securities. This subsection will apply when the stockbroker has sold securities in itself to the customer or when the customer has otherwise placed such securities in an account with the stockbroker.

Cross References

Allowance of claims or interests, see section 502.

Library References:

C.J.S. Bankruptcy §§ 358–360; Securities Regulation § 6.

West's Key No. Digests, Bankruptcy ⟐3461; Securities Regulation ⟐185.10–185.21.

WESTLAW Electronic Research

See WESTLAW Electronic Research Guide following the *Bankruptcy Highlights.*

§ 747. Subordination of certain customer claims

Except as provided in section 510 of this title, unless all other customer net equity claims have been paid in full, the trustee may not pay in full or pay in part, directly or indirectly, any net equity claim of a customer that was, on the date the transaction giving rise to such claim occurred—

(1) an insider;

(2) a beneficial owner of at least five percent of any class of equity securities of the debtor, other than—

    (A) nonconvertible stock having fixed preferential dividend and liquidation rights; or

    (B) interests of limited partners in a limited partnership;

(3) a limited partner with a participation of at least five percent in the net assets or net profits of the debtor; or

(4) an entity that, directly or indirectly, through agreement or otherwise, exercised or had the power to exercise control over the management or policies of the debtor.

Pub.L. 95–598, Nov. 6, 1978, 92 Stat. 2613; Pub.L. 97–222, § 13, July 27, 1982, 96 Stat. 238.

Historical and Revision Notes

Notes of Committee on the Judiciary, Senate Report No. 95–989. Section 747 subordinates to other customer claims, all claims of a customer who is an insider, a five percent owner of the debtor, or otherwise in control of the debtor.

Cross References

Insider defined, see section 101.

Library References:

C.J.S. Bankruptcy § 451 et seq.; Securities Regulation § 6.
West's Key No. Digests, Bankruptcy ⟳345; Securities Regulation ⟳4.

WESTLAW Electronic Research

See WESTLAW Electronic Research Guide following the *Bankruptcy Highlights.*

§ 748. Reduction of securities to money

As soon as practicable after the date of the order for relief, the trustee shall reduce to money, consistent with good market practice, all securities held as property of the estate, except for customer name securities delivered or reclaimed under section 751 of this title.

Pub.L. 95–598, Nov. 6, 1978, 92 Stat. 2614.

Historical and Revision Notes

Notes of Committee on the Judiciary, Senate Report No. 95–989. Section 748 requires the trustee to liquidate all securities, except for customer name securities, of the estate in a manner consistent with good market practice. The trustee should refrain from flooding a thin market with a large percentage of shares in any one issue. If the trustee holds restricted securities or securities in which trading has been suspended, then the trustee must arrange to liquidate such securities in accordance with the securities laws. A private placement may be the only exemption available with the customer of the debtor the best prospect for such a placement. The subsection does not permit such a customer to bid in his net equity as part of the purchase price; a contrary result would permit a customer to receive a greater percentage on his net equity claim than other customers.

Cross References

Reduction of certain securities and property to money in commodity broker liquidation cases, see section 766.

Library References:

C.J.S. Bankruptcy §§ 358–360; Securities Regulation § 6.
West's Key No. Digests, Bankruptcy ⟳3461; Securities Regulation ⟳185.10–185.21.

WESTLAW Electronic Research

See WESTLAW Electronic Research Guide following the *Bankruptcy Highlights.*

§ 749. Voidable transfers

(a) Except as otherwise provided in this section, any transfer of property that, but for such transfer, would have been customer property, may be avoided by the trustee, and such property shall be treated as customer property, if and to the extent that the trustee avoids such transfer under section 544, 545, 547, 548, or 549 of this title. For the purpose of such sections, the property so transferred shall be deemed to have been property of the debtor and, if such transfer was made to a customer or for a customer's benefit, such customer shall be deemed, for the purposes of this section, to have been a creditor.

(b) Notwithstanding sections 544, 545, 547, 548, and 549 of this title, the trustee may not avoid a transfer made before five days after the order for relief if such transfer is approved by the Commission by rule or order, either before or after such transfer, and if such transfer is—

    (1) a transfer of a securities contract entered into or carried by or through the debtor on behalf of a customer, and of any cash, security, or other property margining or securing such securities contract; or

    (2) the liquidation of a securities contract entered into or carried by or through the debtor on behalf of a customer.

Pub.L. 95–598, Nov. 6, 1978, 92 Stat. 2614; Pub.L. 97–222, § 14, July 27, 1982, 96 Stat. 238.

Historical and Revision Notes

Notes of Committee on the Judiciary, Senate Report No. 95–989. Section 749 indicates that if the trustee avoids a transfer, property recovered is customer property to any extent it would have been customer property but for the transfer. The section clarifies that a customer who receives a transfer of property of the debtor is a creditor and that property in a customer's account is property of a creditor for purposes of the avoiding powers.

Cross References

Voidable transfers in commodity broker liquidation cases, see section 764.

Library References:

C.J.S. Bankruptcy §§ 358–360; Securities Regulation § 6.
West's Key No. Digests, Bankruptcy ☞3461; Securities Regulation ☞185.10–185.21.

WESTLAW Electronic Research

See WESTLAW Electronic Research Guide following the *Bankruptcy Highlights*.

§ 750. Distribution of securities

The trustee may not distribute a security except under section 751 of this title.

Pub.L. 95–598, Nov. 6, 1978, 92 Stat. 2614.

Historical and Revision Notes

Notes of Committee on the Judiciary, Senate Report No. 95–989. Section 750 forbids the trustee from distributing a security other than a customer name security. The term "distribution" refers to a distribution to customers in satisfaction of net equity claims and is not intended to preclude the trustee from liquidating securities under proposed 11 U.S.C. 748.

Cross References

Distribution of property of estate, see section 726.
Distribution in chapter 11 cases, see section 1143.

Library References:

C.J.S. Bankruptcy §§ 358–360; Securities Regulation § 6.
West's Key No. Digests, Bankruptcy ⚋3461; Securities Regulation ⚋185.10–185.21.

WESTLAW Electronic Research

See WESTLAW Electronic Research Guide following the *Bankruptcy Highlights*.

§ 751.   Customer name securities

The trustee shall deliver any customer name security to or on behalf of the customer entitled to such security, unless such customer has a negative net equity. With the approval of the trustee, a customer may reclaim a customer name security after payment to the trustee, within such period as the trustee allows, of any claim of the debtor against such customer to the extent that such customer will not have a negative net equity after such payment.

Pub.L. 95–598, Nov. 6, 1978, 92 Stat. 2614.

Historical and Revision Notes

Notes of Committee on the Judiciary, Senate Report No. 95–989. Section 751 requires the trustee to deliver a customer name security to the customer entitled to such security unless the customer has a negative net equity. The customer's net equity will be negative when the amount owed by the customer to the stockbroker exceeds the liquidation value of the noncustomer name securities in the customer's account. If the customer is a net debtor of the stockbroker, then the trustee may permit the customer to repay debts to the stockbroker so that the customer will no longer be in debt to the stockbroker. If the customer refuses to pay such amount, then the court may order the customer to endorse the security in order that the trustee may liquidate such property.

Library References:

C.J.S. Bankruptcy §§ 358–360; Securities Regulation § 6.
West's Key No. Digests, Bankruptcy ⚋3461; Securities Regulation ⚋185.10–185.21.

WESTLAW Electronic Research

See WESTLAW Electronic Research Guide following the *Bankruptcy Highlights*.

§ 752.   Customer property

(a) The trustee shall distribute customer property ratably to customers on the basis and to the extent of such customers' allowed net equity claims and in priority to all other claims, except claims of the kind specified in section 507(a)(1) of this title that are attributable to the administration of such customer property.

(b)(1) The trustee shall distribute customer property in excess of that distributed under subsection (a) of this section in accordance with section 726 of this title.

(2) Except as provided in section 510 of this title, if a customer is not paid the full amount of such customer's allowed net equity claim from customer property, the unpaid portion of such claim is a claim entitled to distribution under section 726 of this title.

(c) Any cash or security remaining after the liquidation of a security interest created under a security agreement made by the debtor, excluding property excluded under section 741(4)(B) of this title, shall be apportioned between the general estate and customer property in the same proportion as the general estate of the debtor and customer property were subject to such security interest.

Pub.L. 95–598, Nov. 6, 1978, 92 Stat. 2614; Pub.L. 97–222, § 15, July 27, 1982, 96 Stat. 238; Pub.L. 98–353, Title III, § 484, July 10, 1984, 98 Stat. 383.

Historical and Revision Notes

Notes of Committee on the Judiciary, Senate Report No. 95–989. Section 752(a) requires the trustee to distribute customer property to customers based on the amount of their net equity claims. Customer property is to be distributed in priority to all claims except expenses of administration entitled to priority under § 507(1). It is anticipated that the court will apportion such administrative claims on an equitable basis between the general estate and the customer property of the debtor.

Subsection (b)(1) indicates that in the event customer property exceeds customers net equity claims and administrative expenses, the excess pours over into the general estate. This event would occur if the value of securities increased dramatically after the order for relief but before liquidation by the trustee. Subsection (b)(2) indicates that the unpaid portion of a customer's net equity claim is entitled to share in the general estate as an unsecured claim unless subordinated by the court under proposed 11 U.S.C. 501. A net equity claim of a customer that is subordinated under section 747 is entitled to share in distribution under section 726(a)(2) unless subordinated under section 510 independently of the subordination under section 747.

Subsection (c) provides for apportionment between customer property and the general estate of any equity of the debtor in property

remaining after a secured creditor liquidates a security interest. This might occur if a stockbroker hypothecates securities of his own and of his customers if the value of the hypothecated securities exceeds the debt owed to the secured party. The apportionment is to be made according to the ratio of customer property and general property of the debtor that comprised the collateral. The subsection refers to cash and securities of customers to include any customer property unlawfully converted by the stockbroker in the course of such a transaction. The apportionment is made subject to section 741(4)(B) to insure that property in a customer's account that is owed to the stockbroker will not be considered customer property. This recognizes the right of the stockbroker to withdraw money that has been erroneously placed in a customer's account or that is otherwise owing to the stockbroker.

Effective Date of 1984 Amendments. See section 553 of Pub. L. 98–353, Title III, July 10, 1984, 98 Stat. 392, set out as an Effective Date of 1984 Amendment note preceding chapter 1 of Title 11, Bankruptcy.

Separability of Provisions. For separability of provisions of Title III of Pub. L. 98–353, see section 551 of Pub. L. 98–353 set out as a Separability of Provisions note preceding chapter 1 of Title 11, Bankruptcy.

Cross References

Distribution in chapter 11 cases, see section 1143.
Distribution of
    Customer property in commodity broker liquidation cases, see section 766.
    Property of estate, see section 726.
Priorities, see section 507.

Library References:

C.J.S. Bankruptcy §§ 358–360; Securities Regulation § 6.
West's Key No. Digests, Bankruptcy ⟐3461; Securities Regulation ⟐185.10–185.21.

WESTLAW Electronic Research

See WESTLAW Electronic Research Guide following the *Bankruptcy Highlights.*

SUBCHAPTER IV—COMMODITY BROKER LIQUIDATION

Cross References

Powers and duties of trustee in investor protection liquidation proceedings, see section 78fff–1 of Title 15, Commerce and Trade.

Subchapter generally applicable only in case under chapter concerning commodity broker, see section 103.

§ 761. Definitions for the subchapter

In this subchapter—

(1) "Act" means Commodity Exchange Act (7 U.S.C. 1 et seq.);

(2) "clearing organization" means organization that clears commodity contracts made on, or subject to the rules of, a contract market or board of trade;

(3) "Commission" means Commodity Futures Trading Commission;

(4) "commodity contract" means—

(A) with respect to a futures commission merchant, contract for the purchase or sale of a commodity for future delivery on, or subject to the rules of, a contract market or board of trade;

(B) with respect to a foreign futures commission merchant, foreign future;

(C) with respect to a leverage transaction merchant, leverage transaction;

(D) with respect to a clearing organization, contract for the purchase or sale of a commodity for future delivery on, or subject to the rules of, a contract market or board of trade that is cleared by such clearing organization, or commodity option traded on, or subject to the rules of, a contract market or board of trade that is cleared by such clearing organization; or

(E) with respect to a commodity options dealer, commodity option;

(5) "commodity option" means agreement or transaction subject to regulation under section 4c(b) of the Act (7 U.S.C. 6c(b));

(6) "commodity options dealer" means person that extends credit to, or that accepts cash, a security, or other property from, a customer of such person for the purchase or sale of an interest in a commodity option;

(7) "contract market" means board of trade designated as a contract market by the Commission under the Act;

(8) "contract of sale", "commodity", "future delivery", "board of trade", and "futures commission merchant" have the meanings assigned to those terms in the Act;

(9) "customer" means—

(A) with respect to a futures commission merchant—

(i) entity for or with whom such futures commission merchant deals and that holds a claim against such futures commission merchant on account of a commodity contract made, received, acquired, or held by or through such futures commission merchant in the ordinary course of such futures commission merchant's business as a futures commission merchant from or for the commodity futures account of such entity; or

(ii) entity that holds a claim against such futures commission merchant arising out of—

(I) the making, liquidation, or change in the value of a commodity contract of a kind specified in clause (i) of this subparagraph;

(II) a deposit or payment of cash, a security, or other property with such futures commission merchant for the purpose of making or margining such a commodity contract; or

(III) the making or taking of delivery on such a commodity contract;

(B) with respect to a foreign futures commission merchant—

(i) entity for or with whom such foreign futures commission merchant deals and that holds a claim against such foreign futures commission merchant on account of a commodity contract made, received, acquired, or held by or through such foreign futures commission merchant in the ordinary course of such foreign futures commission merchant's business as a foreign futures commission merchant from or for the foreign futures account of such entity; or

(ii) entity that holds a claim against such foreign futures commission merchant arising out of—

(I) the making, liquidation, or change in value of a commodity contract of a kind specified in clause (i) of this subparagraph;

(II) a deposit or payment of cash, a security, or other property with such foreign futures commission merchant for the purpose of making or margining such a commodity contract; or

(III) the making or taking of delivery on such a commodity contract;

(C) with respect to a leverage transaction merchant—

(i) entity for or with whom such leverage transaction merchant deals and that holds a claim against such leverage transaction merchant on account of a commodity contract engaged in by or with such leverage transaction merchant in the ordinary course of such leverage transaction merchant's business as a leverage transaction merchant from or for the leverage account of such entity; or

(ii) entity that holds a claim against such leverage transaction merchant arising out of—

(I) the making, liquidation, or change in value of a commodity contract of a kind specified in clause (i) of this subparagraph;

(II) a deposit or payment of cash, a security, or other property with such leverage transaction merchant for the purpose of entering into or margining such a commodity contract; or

  (III) the making or taking of delivery on such a commodity contract;

 (D) with respect to a clearing organization, clearing member of such clearing organization with whom such clearing organization deals and that holds a claim against such clearing organization on account of cash, a security, or other property received by such clearing organization to margin, guarantee, or secure a commodity contract in such clearing member's proprietary account or customers' account; or

 (E) with respect to a commodity options dealer—

  (i) entity for or with whom such commodity options dealer deals and that holds a claim on account of a commodity contract made, received, acquired, or held by or through such commodity options dealer in the ordinary course of such commodity options dealer's business as a commodity options dealer from or for the commodity options account of such entity; or

  (ii) entity that holds a claim against such commodity options dealer arising out of—

   (I) the making of, liquidation of, exercise of, or a change in value of, a commodity contract of a kind specified in clause (i) of this subparagraph; or

   (II) a deposit or payment of cash, a security, or other property with such commodity options dealer for the purpose of making, exercising, or margining such a commodity contract;

 (10) "customer property" means cash, a security, or other property, or proceeds of such cash, security, or property, received, acquired, or held by or for the account of the debtor, from or for the account of a customer—

 (A) including—

  (i) property received, acquired, or held to margin, guarantee, secure, purchase, or sell a commodity contract;

  (ii) profits or contractual or other rights accruing to a customer as a result of a commodity contract;

  (iii) an open commodity contract;

  (iv) specifically identifiable customer property;

  (v) warehouse receipt or other document held by the debtor evidencing ownership of or title to property to be delivered to fulfill a commodity contract from or for the account of a customer;

  (vi) cash, a security, or other property received by the debtor as payment for a commodity to be delivered to fulfill a commodity contract from or for the account of a customer;

  (vii) a security held as property of the debtor to the extent such security is necessary to meet a net equity claim based on a security of the same class and series of an issuer;

  (viii) property that was unlawfully converted from and that is the lawful property of the estate; and

(ix) other property of the debtor that any applicable law, rule, or regulation requires to be set aside or held for the benefit of a customer, unless including such property as customer property would not significantly increase customer property; but

(B) not including property to the extent that a customer does not have a claim against the debtor based on such property;

(11) "foreign future" means contract for the purchase or sale of a commodity for future delivery on, or subject to the rules of, a board of trade outside the United States;

(12) "foreign futures commission merchant" means entity engaged in soliciting or accepting orders for the purchase or sale of a foreign future or that, in connection with such a solicitation or acceptance, accepts cash, a security, or other property, or extends credit to margin, guarantee, or secure any trade or contract that results from such a solicitation or acceptance;

(13) "leverage transaction" means agreement that is subject to regulation under section 19 of the Commodity Exchange Act (7 U.S.C. 23), and that is commonly known to the commodities trade as a margin account, margin contract, leverage account, or leverage contract;

(14) "leverage transaction merchant" means person in the business of engaging in leverage transactions;

(15) "margin payment" means payment or deposit of cash, a security, or other property, that is commonly known to the commodities trade as original margin, initial margin, maintenance margin, or variation margin, including mark-to-market payments, settlement payments, variation payments, daily settlement payments, and final settlement payments made as adjustments to settlement prices;

(16) "member property" means customer property received, acquired, or held by or for the account of a debtor that is a clearing organization, from or for the proprietary account of a customer that is a clearing member of the debtor; and

(17) "net equity" means, subject to such rules and regulations as the Commission promulgates under the Act, with respect to the aggregate of all of a customer's accounts that such customer has in the same capacity—

(A) the balance remaining in such customer's accounts immediately after—

(i) all commodity contracts of such customer have been transferred, liquidated, or become identified for delivery; and

(ii) all obligations of such customer in such capacity to the debtor have been offset; plus

(B) the value, as of the date of return under section 766 of this title, of any specifically identifiable customer property actually returned to such customer before the date specified in subparagraph (A) of this paragraph; plus

(C) the value, as of the date of transfer, of—

(i) any commodity contract to which such customer is entitled that is transferred to another person under section 766 of this title; and

(ii) any cash, security, or other property of such customer transferred to such other person under section 766 of this title to margin or secure such transferred commodity contract.

Pub.L. 95–598, Nov. 6, 1978, 92 Stat. 2615; Pub.L. 27–222, § 16, July 27, 1982, 96 Stat. 238; Pub.L. 98–353, Title III, § 485, July 10, 1984, 98 Stat. 383.

Historical and Revision Notes

Notes of Committee on the Judiciary, Senate Report No. 95–989. Paragraph (1) defines "Act" to mean the Commodity Exchange Act [section 1 et seq. of Title 7, Agriculture].

Paragraph (2) defines "clearing organization" to mean an organization that clears (i. e., matches purchases and sales) commodity futures contracts made on or subject to the rules of a contract market or commodity options transactions made on or subject to the rules of a commodity option exchange. Although commodity option trading on exchanges is currently prohibited, it is anticipated that CFTC may permit such trading in the future.

Paragraphs (3) and (4) define terms "Commission" and "commodity futures contract".

Paragraph (5) [now (4)] defines "commodity contract" to mean a commodity futures contract (§ 761(4)), a commodity option (§ 761(6)), or a leverage contract (§ 761(15)).

Paragraph (6) [now (5)] defines "commodity option" by reference to section 4c(b) of the Commodity Exchange Act [section 6c(b) of Title 7, Agriculture].

Paragraphs (7) [now (6)], (8) [now (7)], and (9) [now (8)], define "commodity options dealer," "contract market," "contract of sale," "commodity," "future delivery," "board of trade," and "futures commission merchant."

Paragraph (10) [now (9)] defines the term "customer" to mean with respect to a futures commission merchant or a foreign futures commission merchant, the entity for whom the debtor carries a commodity futures contract or foreign future, or with whom such a contract is carried (such as another commodity broker), or from whom the debtor has received, acquired, or holds cash, securities, or other property arising out of or connected with specified transactions involving commodity futures contracts or foreign futures. This section also defines "customer" in the context of leverage transaction merchants, clearing organizations, and commodity options dealers. Persons associated with a commodity broker,

such as its employees, officers, or partners, may be customers under this definition.

The definition of "customer" serves to isolate that class of persons entitled to the protection subchapter IV provides to customers. In addition, section 101(5) defines "commodity broker" to mean a futures commission merchant, foreign futures commission merchant, clearing organization, leverage transaction merchant, or commodity options dealer, with respect to which there is a customer. Accordingly, the definition of customer also serves to designate those entities which must utilize chapter 7 and are precluded from reorganizing under chapter 11.

Paragraph (11) [now (10)] defines "customer property" to mean virtually all property or proceeds thereof, received, acquired, or held by or for the account of the debtor for a customer arising out of or in connection with a transaction involving a commodity contract.

Paragraph (12) defines "distribution share" to mean the amount to which a customer is entitled under section 765(a).

Paragraphs (13) [now (11)], (14) [now (12)], (15) [now (13)], and (16) [now (14)], define "foreign future," "foreign futures commission merchant," "leverage transaction," and "leverage transaction merchant."

Paragraph (17) [now (15)] defines "margin payment" to mean a payment or deposit commonly known to the commodities trade as original margin, initial margin, or variation margin.

Paragraph (18) [now (16)] defines "member property."

Paragraph (19) [now (17)] defines "net equity" to be the sum of (A) the value of all customer property remaining in a customer's account immediately after all commodity contracts of such customer have been transferred, liquidated, or become identified for delivery and all obligations of such customer to the debtor have been offset (such as margin payments, whether or not called, and brokerage commissions) plus (B) the value of specifically identifiable customer property previously returned to the customer by the trustee, plus (C) if the trustee has transferred any commodity contract to which the customer is entitled or any margin or security for such contract, the value of such contract and margin or security. Net equity, therefore, will be the total amount of customer property to which a customer is entitled as of the date of the filing of the bankruptcy petition, although valued at subsequent dates. The Commission is given authority to promulgate rules and regulations to further refine this definition.

Notes of Committee on the Judiciary, House Report No. 95–595. Paragraph (8) [now (4)] is a dynamic definition of "contractual commitment". The definition will vary depending on the character of the debtor in each case. If the debtor is a futures commission merchant or a clearing organization, then subparagraphs (A) and (D) indicate that the definition means a contract of sale of a commodity for future delivery on a contract market. If the debtor is a foreign futures commission merchant, a leverage transaction merchant, or a commodity options dealer, then subparagraphs (B), (C), and (E) indicate that the definition means foreign future, leverage transaction, or commodity option, respectively.

Paragraph (9) defines "customer" in a similar style. It is anticipated that a debtor with multifaceted characteristics will have separate estates for each different kind of customer. Thus, a debtor that is a leverage transaction merchant and a commodity options, dealer would have separate estates for the leverage transaction customers and for the options customers, and a general estate for other creditors. Customers for each kind of commodity broker, except the clearing organization, arise from either of two relationships. In subparagraphs (A), (B), (C), and (E), clause (i) treats with customers to the extent of contractual commitments with the debtor in either a broker or a dealer relationship. Clause (ii) treats with customers to the extent of proceeds from contractual commitments or deposits for the purpose of making contractual commitments. The customer of the clearing organization is a member with a proprietary or customers' account.

Paragraph (10) defines "customer property" to include all property in customer accounts and property that should have been in those accounts but was diverted through conversion or mistake. Clause (i) refers to customer property not properly segregated by the debtor or customer property converted and then recovered so as to become property of the estate. Clause (vii) is intended to exclude property that would cost more to recover from a third party than the value of the property itself. Subparagraph (B) excludes property in a customer's account that belongs to the commodity broker, such as a contract placed in the account by error, or cash due the broker for a margin payment that the broker has made.

Paragraph (15) [now (17)] defines "net equity" to include the value of all contractual commitments at the time of liquidation or transfer less any obligations owed by the customer to the debtor, such as brokerage fees. In addition, the term includes the value of any specifically identifiable property as of the date of return to the customer and the value of any customer property transferred to another commodity broker as of the date of transfer. This definition places the risk of market fluctuations on the customer until commitments leave the estate.

Legislative Statements. Subchapter IV of chapter 7 represents a compromise between similar chapters in the House bill and Senate amendment. Section 761(2) of the House amendment defines "clearing organization" to cover an organization that clears commodity contracts on a contract market or a board of trade; the expansion of the definition is intended to include clearing organizations that clear commodity options. Section 761(4) of the House amendment adopts the term "commodity contract" as used in section 761(5) of the Senate amendment but with the more precise substantive definitions contained in section 761(8) of the House bill. The definition is modified to insert "board of trade" to cover commodity options. Section 761(5) of the House amendment adopts the definition contained in section 761(6) of the Senate amendment in preference to the definition contained in section 761(4) of the House bill which erroneously included onions. Section 761(9) of the House amendment represents a compromise between similar provisions contained in section 761(10) of the Senate amendment and section 761(9) of the House bill. The compromise adopts the substance contained in the House bill and adopts the terminology of "commodity contract" in lieu of "contractual commitment" as suggested in the Senate amendment. Section 761(10) of the House amendment represents a compromise between similar sections in the House bill and Senate amendment regarding the definition of "customer property." The definition of "distribution share" contained in section 761(12) of the Senate amendment is deleted as unnecessary. Section 761(12) of the House amendment adopts a definition of "foreign futures commission merchant" similar to the definition contained in section 761(14) of the Senate amendment. The definition is modified to cover either an entity engaged in soliciting orders or the purchase or sale of a foreign future, or an entity that accepts cash, a security, or other property for credit in connection with such a solicitation or acceptance. Section 761(13) of the House amendment adopts a definition of "leverage transaction" identical to the definition contained in section 761(15) of the Senate amendment. Section 761(15) of the House amendment adopts the definition of "margin payment" contained in section 761(17) of the Senate amendment. Section 761(17) of the House amendment adopts a definition of "net equity" derived from section 761(15) of the House bill.

References in Text. The Commodity Exchange Act, referred to in pars. (1), (7), (8), and

(17), is Act Sept. 21, 1922, c. 369, 42 Stat. 998, which is classified to section 1 et seq. of Title 7, Agriculture.

Section 4c(b) of the Commodity Exchange Act, referred to in par. (5), is classified to section 6c(b) of Title 7.

Section 19 of the Commodity Exchange Act, referred to in par. (13), is classified to section 23 of Title 7.

Effective Date of 1984 Amendments. See section 553 of Pub. L. 98–353, Title III, July 10, 1984, 98 Stat. 392, set out as an Effective Date of 1984 Amendment note preceding chapter 1 of Title 11, Bankruptcy.

Separability of Provisions. For separability of provisions of Title III of Pub. L. 98–353, see section 551 of Pub. L. 98–353 set out as a Separability of Provisions note preceding chapter 1 of Title 11, Bankruptcy.

Cross References

　　Commodity broker defined, see section 101.
　　Definitions applicable in
　　　　Chapter 9 cases, see section 902.
　　　　Railroad reorganization cases, see section 1162.
　　　　Reorganization cases, see section 1101.
　　　　Stockbroker liquidation cases, see section 741.
　　Reception of margin payments by commodity brokers or forward contract merchants
　　　　as taking for value, see section 548.
　　Security as not including leverage transaction as defined in this section, see section
　　　　101.

Library References:

　　C.J.S. Bankruptcy §§ 358–360; Exchanges § 11; Securities Regulation § 6.
　　West's Key No. Digests, Bankruptcy ⬥3461; Exchanges ⬥12; Securities Regulation
　　　　⬥185.10–185.21.

WESTLAW Electronic Research

　　See WESTLAW Electronic Research Guide following the *Bankruptcy Highlights.*

§ 762.　Notice to the Commission and right to be heard

　　(a) The clerk shall give the notice required by section 342 of this title to the Commission.

　　(b) The Commission may raise and may appear and be heard on any issue in a case under this chapter.

Pub.L. 95–598, Nov. 6, 1978, 92 Stat. 2618.

Historical and Revision Notes

Notes of Committee on the Judiciary, Senate Report No. 95–989. Section 762 provides that the Commission shall be given such notice as is appropriate of an order for relief

in a bankruptcy case and that the Commission may raise and may appear and may be heard on any issue in case involving a commodity broker liquidation.

Cross References

Notice in chapter 9 cases, see section 923.

Notice to Security Investor Protection Corporation and Securities and Exchange Commission, see section 743.

Library References:

C.J.S. Bankruptcy §§ 358–360; Securities Regulation § 6.

West's Key No. Digests, Bankruptcy ⊕3461; Securities Regulation ⊕185.10–185.21.

WESTLAW Electronic Research

See WESTLAW Electronic Research Guide following the *Bankruptcy Highlights*.

§ 763.   Treatment of accounts

(a) Accounts held by the debtor for a particular customer in separate capacities shall be treated as accounts of separate customers.

(b) A member of a clearing organization shall be deemed to hold such member's proprietary account in a separate capacity from such member's customers' account.

(c) The net equity in a customer's account may not be offset against the net equity in the account of any other customer.

Pub.L. 95–598, Nov. 6, 1978, 92 Stat. 2618; Pub.L. 98–353, Title III, § 486, July 10, 1984, 98 Stat. 383.

Historical and Revision Notes

Notes of Committee on the Judiciary, Senate Report No. 95–989. Section 763 provides for separate treatment of accounts held in separate capacities. A deficit in one account held for a customer may not be offset against the net equity in another account held by the same customer in a separate capacity or held by another customer.

Effective Date of 1984 Amendments. See section 553 of Pub. L. 98–353, Title III, July 10, 1984, 98 Stat. 392, set out as an Effective Date of 1984 Amendment note preceding chapter 1 of Title 11, Bankruptcy.

Separability of Provisions. For separability of provisions of Title III of Pub. L. 98–353, see section 551 of Pub. L. 98–353 set out as a Separability of Provisions note preceding chapter 1 of Title 11, Bankruptcy.

Cross References

Treatment of accounts in stockholder liquidation cases, see section 745.

Library References:

C.J.S. Bankruptcy §§ 358–360; Exchanges § 11.

West's Key No. Digests, Bankruptcy ⊕3461; Exchanges ⊕12.

WESTLAW Electronic Research

See WESTLAW Electronic Research Guide following the *Bankruptcy Highlights*.

§ 764.   Voidable transfers

(a) Except as otherwise provided in this section, any transfer by the debtor of property that, but for such transfer, would have been customer property, may be avoided by the trustee, and such property shall be treated as customer property, if and to the extent that the trustee avoids such transfer under section 544, 545, 547, 548, 549, or 724(a) of this title. For the purpose of such sections, the property so transferred shall be deemed to have been property of the debtor, and, if such transfer was made to a customer or for a customer's benefit, such customer shall be deemed, for the purposes of this section, to have been a creditor.

(b) Notwithstanding sections 544, 545, 547, 548, 549, and 724(a) of this title, the trustee may not avoid a transfer made before five days after the order for relief, if such transfer is approved by the Commission by rule or order, either before or after such transfer, and if such transfer is—

(1) a transfer of a commodity contract entered into or carried by or through the debtor on behalf of a customer, and of any cash, securities, or other property margining or securing such commodity contract; or

(2) the liquidation of a commodity contract entered into or carried by or through the debtor on behalf of a customer.

Pub.L. 95–598, Nov. 6, 1978, 92 Stat. 2618; Pub.L. 97–222, § 17, July 27, 1982, 96 Stat. 240; Pub.L. 98–353, Title III, § 487, July 10, 1984, 98 Stat. 383.

Historical and Revision Notes

Notes of Committee on the Judiciary, Senate Report No. 95–989. Section 764 permits the trustee to void any transfer of property that, except for such transfer, would have been customer property, to the extent permitted under section 544, 545, 547, 548, 549, or 724(a).

Notes of Committee on the Judiciary, House Report No. 95–595. Section 764 indicates the extent to which the avoiding powers may be used by the trustee under subchapter IV of chapter 7. If property recovered would have been customer property if never transferred, then subsection (a) indicates that it will be so treated when recovered.

Subsection (b) prohibits avoiding any transaction that occurs before or within five days after the petition if the transaction is approved by the Commission and concerns an open contractual commitment. This enables the Commission to exercise its discretion to protect the integrity of the market by insuring that transactions cleared with other brokers

will not be undone on a preference or a fraudulent transfer theory.

Subsection (c) insulates variation margin payments and other deposits from the avoiding powers except to the extent of actual fraud under section 548(a)(1). This facilitates prepetition transfers and protects the ordinary course of business in the market.

Legislative Statements. Section 764 of the House amendment is derived from the House bill.

Effective Date of 1984 Amendments. See section 553 of Pub.L. 98–353, Title III, July 10, 1984, 98 Stat. 392, set out as an Effective Date of 1984 Amendment note preceding chapter 1 of Title 11, Bankruptcy.

Separability of Provisions. For separability of provisions of Title III of Pub.L. 98–353, see section 551 of Pub. L. 98–353 set out as a Separability of Provisions note preceding chapter 1 of Title 11, Bankruptcy.

Cross References

Voidable transfers in stockbroker liquidation cases, see section 749.

Library References:

C.J.S. Bankruptcy §§ 358–360; Securities Regulation § 6.
West's Key No. Digests, Bankruptcy ⚷3461; Securities Regulation ⚷185.10–185.21.

WESTLAW Electronic Research

See WESTLAW Electronic Research Guide following the *Bankruptcy Highlights*.

§ 765. Customer instructions

(a) The notice required by section 342 of this title to customers shall instruct each customer—

(1) to file a proof of such customer's claim promptly, and to specify in such claim any specifically identifiable security, property, or commodity contract; and

(2) to instruct the trustee of such customer's desired disposition, including transfer under section 766 of this title or liquidation, of any commodity contract specifically identified to such customer.

(b) The trustee shall comply, to the extent practicable, with any instruction received from a customer regarding such customer's desired disposition of any commodity contract specifically identified to such customer. If the trustee has transferred, under section 766 of this title, such a commodity contract, the trustee shall transmit any such instruction to the commodity broker to whom such commodity contract was so transferred.

Pub.L. 95–598, Nov. 6, 1978, 92 Stat. 2619; Pub.L. 97–222, § 18, July 27, 1982, 96 Stat. 240; Pub.L. 98–353, Title III, § 488, July 10, 1984, 98 Stat. 383.

Historical and Revision Notes

Notes of Committee on the Judiciary, House Report No. 95–595. Section 765(a) indicates that a customer must file a proof of claim, including any claim to specifically identifiable property, within such time as the court fixes.

Legislative Statements. Sections 765 and 766 of the House amendment represent a consolidation and redraft of sections 765, 766, 767, and 768 of the House bill and sections 765, 766, 767, and 768 of the Senate amendment. [For additional information see Historical and Revision Notes under section 766.] In particular, section 765(a) of the House amendment is derived from section 765(a) of the House bill and section 767(a) of the Senate amendment. Under section 765(a) of the House amendment customers are notified of the opportunity to immediately file proofs of claim and to identify specifically identifiable securities, property, or commodity contracts.

The customer is also afforded an opportunity to instruct the trustee regarding the customer's desires concerning disposition of the customer's commodity contracts. Section 767(b) makes clear that the trustee must comply with instructions received to the extent practicable, but in the event the trustee has transferred commodity contracts to a commodity broker, such instructions shall be forwarded to the broker.

Effective Date of 1984 Amendments. See section 553 of Pub.L. 98–353, Title III, July 10, 1984, 98 Stat. 392, set out as an Effective Date of 1984 Amendment note preceding chapter 1 of Title 11, Bankruptcy.

Separability of Provisions. For separability of provisions of Title III of Pub.L. 98–353, see section 551 of Pub.L. 98–353 set out as a Separability of Provisions note preceding chapter 1 of Title 11, Bankruptcy.

Cross References

Executory contracts and unexpired leases, see section 365.

Library References:

C.J.S. Bankruptcy §§ 358–360; Exchanges § 11.
West's Key No. Digests, Bankruptcy ⚮3461; Exchanges ⚮12.

WESTLAW Electronic Research

See WESTLAW Electronic Research Guide following the *Bankruptcy Highlights*.

§ 766. Treatment of customer property

(a) The trustee shall answer all margin calls with respect to a specifically identifiable commodity contract of a customer until such time as the trustee returns or transfers such commodity contract, but the trustee may not make a margin payment that has the effect of a distribution to such customer of more than that to which such customer is entitled under subsection (h) or (i) of this section.

(b) The trustee shall prevent any open commodity contract from remaining open after the last day of trading in such commodity contract, or into the first day on which notice of intent to deliver on such commodity contract may be tendered, whichever occurs first. With respect to any commodity contract that has remained open after the last day of trading in such commodity contract or with respect to which delivery must be made or accepted under the rules of the contract market on which such commodity contract was made, the trustee may operate the business of the debtor for the purpose of—

(1) accepting or making tender of notice of intent to deliver the physical commodity underlying such commodity contract;

(2) facilitating delivery of such commodity; or

(3) disposing of such commodity if a party to such commodity contract defaults.

(c) The trustee shall return promptly to a customer any specifically identifiable security, property, or commodity contract to which such customer is entitled, or shall transfer, on such customer's behalf, such security, property, or commodity contract to a commodity broker that is not a debtor under this title, subject to such rules or regulations as the Commission may prescribe, to the extent that the value of such security, property, or commodity contract does not exceed the amount to which such customer would be entitled under subsection (h) or (i) of this section if such security, property, or commodity contract were not returned or transferred under this subsection.

(d) If the value of a specifically identifiable security, property, or commodity contract exceeds the amount to which the customer of the debtor is entitled under subsection (h) or (i) of this section, then such customer to whom such security, property, or commodity contract is specifically identified may deposit cash with the trustee equal to the difference between the value of such security, property, or commodity contract and such amount, and the trustee then shall—

(1) return promptly such security, property, or commodity contract to such customer; or

(2) transfer, on such customer's behalf, such security, property, or commodity contract to a commodity broker that is not a debtor under this title, subject to such rules or regulations as the Commission may prescribe.

(e) Subject to subsection (b) of this section, the trustee shall liquidate any commodity contract that—

(1) is identified to a particular customer and with respect to which such customer has not timely instructed the trustee as to the desired disposition of such commodity contract;

(2) cannot be transferred under subsection (c) of this section; or

(3) cannot be identified to a particular customer.

(f) As soon as practicable after the commencement of the case, the trustee shall reduce to money, consistent with good market practice, all securities and other property, other than commodity contracts, held as property of the estate, except for specifically identifiable securities or property distributable under subsection (h) or (i) of this section.

(g) The trustee may not distribute a security or other property except under subsection (h) or (i) of this section.

(h) Except as provided in subsection (b) of this section, the trustee shall distribute customer property ratably to customers on the basis and to the extent of such customers' allowed net equity claims, and in priority to all other claims, except claims of a kind specified in section 507(a)(1) of this title that are attributable to the administration of customer property. Such distribution shall be in the form of—

    (1) cash;

    (2) the return or transfer, under subsection (c) or (d) of this section, of specifically identifiable customer securities, property, or commodity contracts; or

    (3) payment of margin calls under subsection (a) of this section.

Notwithstanding any other provision of this subsection, a customer net equity claim based on a proprietary account, as defined by Commission rule, regulation, or order, may not be paid either in whole or in part, directly or indirectly, out of customer property unless all other customer net equity claims have been paid in full.

(i) If the debtor is a clearing organization, the trustee shall distribute—

    (1) customer property, other than member property, ratably to customers on the basis and to the extent of such customers' allowed net equity claims based on such customers' accounts other than proprietary accounts, and in priority to all other claims, except claims of a kind specified in section 507(a)(1) of this title that are attributable to the administration of such customer property; and

    (2) member property ratably to customers on the basis and to the extent of such customers' allowed net equity claims based on such customers' proprietary accounts, and in priority to all other claims, except claims of a kind specified in section 507(a)(1) of this title that are attributable to the administration of member property or customer property.

(j)(1) The trustee shall distribute customer property in excess of that distributed under subsection (h) or (i) of this section in accordance with section 726 of this title.

(2) Except as provided in section 510 of this title, if a customer is not paid the full amount of such customer's allowed net equity claim from customer property, the unpaid portion of such claim is a claim entitled to distribution under section 726 of this title.

Pub.L. 95–598, Nov. 6, 1978, 92 Stat. 2619; Pub.L. 97–222, § 19, July 27, 1982, 96 Stat. 240; Pub.L. 98–353, Title III, § 489, July 10, 1984, 98 Stat. 383.

Historical and Revision Notes

Notes of Committee on the Judiciary, Senate Report No. 95–989. Subsection (a) of this section [subsec. (a) of section 765 of S.Bill (now subsec. (h) of this section)] provides that with respect to liquidation of commodity brokers which are not clearing organizations, the trustee shall distribute customer property to customers on the basis and to the extent of such customers' allowed net equity claims, and in priority to all other claims. This section grants customers' claims first priority in the distribution of the estate. Subsection (b) [subsec. (b) of section 765 of S.Bill (now subsec. (i) of this section)] grants the same priority to member property and other customer property in the liquidation of a clearing organization. A fundamental purpose of these provisions is to ensure that the property entrusted by customers to their brokers will not be subject to the risks of the broker's business and will be available for disbursement to customers if the broker becomes bankrupt.

As a result of section 765 [section 765 of S.Bill (now subsecs. (h) and (i) of this section)], a customer need not trace any funds in order to avoid treatment as a general creditor as was required by the Seventh Circuit in In re Rosenbaum Grain Corporation [C.A.7, 1940, 112 F.2d 315].

Section 767 [section 767 of S.Bill (now this section)] sets forth the procedures to be followed by the trustee. It should be emphasized that many of the duties imposed on the trustee are required to be discharged by the trustee immediately upon his appointment. The earlier these duties are discharged the less potential market disruption can result.

The initial duty of the trustee is to endeavor to transfer to another commodity broker or brokers all identified customer accounts together with the customer property margining such accounts, to the extent the trustee deems appropriate. Although it is preferable for all such accounts to be transferred, exigencies may dictate a partial transfer. The requirement that the value of the accounts and property transferred not exceed the customer's distribution share may necessitate a slight delay until the trustee can submit to the court, for its disapproval, an estimate of each customer's distribution share pursuant to section 768 [section 768 of S.Bill (omitted)].

Subsection (c) [subsec. (c) of section 767 of S.Bill (now subsec. (e) of this section)] provides that contemporaneously with the estimate of the distribution share and the transfer of identified customer accounts and property, subsection (c) provides that the trustee should make arrangements for the liquidation of all commodity contracts maintained by the debtor that are not identifiable to specific customers. These contracts would, of course, include all such contracts held in the debtor's proprietory account.

At approximately the same time, the trustee should notify each customer of the debtor's bankruptcy and instruct each customer immediately to submit a claim including any claim to a specifically identifiable security or other property, and advise the trustee as to the desired disposition of commodity contracts carried by the debtor for the customer.

This requirement is placed upon the trustee to insure that producers who have hedged their production in the commodities market are allowed the opportunity to preserve their positions. The theory of the commodity market is that it exists for producers and buyers of commodities and not for the benefit of the speculators whose transactions now comprise the overwhelming majority of trades. Maintenance of positions by hedges may require them to put up additional margin payments in the hours and days following the commodity broker bankruptcy, which they may be unable or unwilling to do. In such cases, their positions will be quickly liquidated by the trustee, but they must have the opportunity to make those margin payments before they are summarily liquidated out of the market to the detriment of their growing crop. The failure of the customer to advise the trustee as to disposition of the customer's commodity contract will not delay a transfer of a contract pursuant to subsection (b) [subsec. (b) of section 767 of S.Bill] so long as the contract can otherwise be identified to the customer. Nor will the failure of the customer to submit a claim prevent the customer from recovering the net equity in that customer's account, absent a claim the customer cannot participate in the determination of the net equity in the account.

If the customer submits instructions pursuant to subsection (a) [subsec. (a) of section 767 of S.Bill (now subsec. (a) of section 765 of this title)] after the customer's commodity contracts are transferred to another commodity broker, the trustee must transmit the instruction to the transferee. If the customer's commodity contracts are not transferred before the customer's instructions are received, the trustee must attempt to comply with the instruction, subject to the provisions of section 767(d) [section 767(d) of S.Bill (now subsec. (e) of this section)].

Under subsection (d) [subsec. (d) of section 767 of S.Bill (now subsec. (e) of this section)], the trustee has discretion to liquidate any commodity contract carried by the debtor at any time. This discretion must be exercised with restraint in such cases, consistent with the purposes of this subchapter and good business practices. The committee intends that hedged accounts will be given special consideration before liquidation as discussed in connection with subsection (c) [subsec. (c) of section 767 of S.Bill (now subsec. (e) of this section)].

Subsection (e) [subsec. (e) of section 767 of S.Bill (now subsecs. (c) and (d) of this section)] instructs the trustee as to the disposition of any security or other property, not disposed of pursuant to subsection (b) or (d) [subsecs. (b) or (d) of section 767 of S.Bill], that is specifically identifiable to a customer and to which the customer is entitled. Such security or other property must be returned to the customer or promptly transferred to another commodity broker for the benefit of the customer. If the value of the security or other property retained or transferred, together with any other distribution made by the trustee to or on behalf of the customer, exceeds the customer's distribution share the customer must deposit cash with the trustee equal to that difference before the return or transfer of the security or other property.

Subsection (f) [subsec. (f) of section 767 of S.Bill (now subsec. (a) of this section)] requires the trustee to answer margin calls on specifically identifiable customer commodity contracts, but only to the extent that the margin payment, together with any other distribution made by the trustee to or on behalf of the customer, does not exceed the customer's distribution share.

Subsection (g) [subsec. (g) of section 767 of S.Bill (now subsec. (b) of this section)] requires the trustee to liquidate all commodity futures contracts prior to the close of trading in that contract, or the first day on which notice of intent to deliver on that contract may be tendered, whichever occurs first. If the customer desires that the contract be kept open for delivery, the contract should be transferred to another commodity broker pursuant to subsection (b) [subsec. (b) of section 767 of S.Bill].

If for some reason the trustee is unable to transfer a contract on which delivery must be made or accepted and is unable to close out such contract, the trustee is authorized to operate the business of the debtor for the purpose of accepting or making tender of notice of intent to deliver the physical commodity underlying the contract, facilitating delivery of the physical commodity or disposing of the physical commodity in the event of a default. Any property received, not previously held, by the trustee in connection with its operation of the business of the debtor for these purposes, is not by the terms of this subchapter specifically included in the definition of customer property.

Finally, subsection (h) [subsec. (h) of section 767 of S.Bill (now subsec. (f) of this section)]

requires the trustee to liquidate the debtor's estate as soon as practicable and consistent with good market practice, except for specifically identifiable securities or other property distributable under subsection (e) [subsec. (e) of section 767 of S.Bill (now subsecs. (c) and (d) of this section)].

Section 768 [section 768 of S.Bill (omitted)] is an integral part of the commodity broker liquidation procedures outlined in section 767 [section 767 of S.Bill (now this section)]. Prompt action by the trustee to transfer or liquidate customer commodity contracts is necessary to protect customers, the debtor's estate, and the marketplace generally. However, transfers of customer accounts and property valued in excess of the customer's distribution share are prohibited. Since a determination of the customer's distribution share requires a determination of the customer's net equity and the total dollar value of customer property held by or for the account of the debtor, it is possible that the customer's distribution share will not be determined, and thus the customer's contracts and property will not be transferred, on a timely basis. To avoid this problem, and to expedite transfers of customer property, section 768 permits the trustee to make distributions to customers in accordance with a preliminary estimate of the debtor's customer property and each customer's distribution share.

It is acknowledged that the necessity for prompt action may not allow the trustee to assemble all relevant facts before such an estimate is made. However, the trustee is expected to develop as accurate an estimate as possible based on the available facts. Further, in order to permit expeditious action, section 768 [section 768 of S.Bill (omitted)] does not require that notice be given to customers or other creditors before the court approves or disapproves the estimate. Nor does section 768 require that customer claims be received pursuant to section 767(a) [section 767(a) of S.Bill (now section 765(a) of this title)] before the trustee may act upon and in accordance with the estimate. If the estimate is inaccurate, the trustee is absolved of liability for a distribution which exceeds the customer's actual distribution share so long as the distribution did not exceed the customer's estimated distribution share. However, a trustee may have a claim back against a customer who received more than its actual distribution share.

Section 769 [section 769 of S.Bill (omitted)] codifies the holding in Board of Trade v. Johnson [Ill.1924, 44 S.Ct. 232, 264 U.S. 1], by validating the bylaws, rules or regulations of a contract market or clearing organization regarding the application of the proceeds derived from the sale of the debtor's membership in the contract market or clearing organization.

This section [section 770 of S.Bill (omitted)] is designed to preclude any court from issuing any order preventing, staying, or otherwise prohibiting the exercise by a commodity broker of a contractual right to liquidate or transfer a commodity contract. The committee is particularly concerned that clearing organizations not be stricted in their power to close out undermargined accounts.

Notes of Committee on the Judiciary, House Report No. 95–595. Subsection (c) [subsec. (c) of section 765 of H. Bill (now subsec. (e) of this section)] sets forth the general rule requiring the trustee to liquidate contractual commitments that are either not specifically identifiable or with respect to which a customer has not instructed the trustee during the time fixed by the court. Subsection (d) [subsec. (d) of section 765 of H. Bill (now subsec. (b) of this section)] indicates an exception to the time limits in the rule by requiring the trustee to liquidate any open contractual commitment before the last day of trading or the first day during which delivery may be demanded, whichever first occurs, if transfer cannot be effectuated.

Section 766(a) [section 766(a) of H.Bill (now subsec. (g) of this section)] indicates that the trustee may distribute securities or other property only under section 768 [section 768 of H.Bill (now subsecs. (a) and (c) of this section)]. This does not preclude a distribution of cash under section 767(a) [section 767(a) of H.Bill (now subsec. (h) of this section)] or distribution of any excess customer property under section 767(c) [section 767(c) of H.Bill (now subsec. (j) of this section)] to the general estate.

Subsection (b) [subsec. (b) of section 766 of H.Bill (now subsec. (f) of this section)] indicates that the trustee shall liquidate all securities and other property that is not specifically identifiable property as soon as practicable after the commencement of the case and in accordance with good market practice. If securities are restricted or trading has been suspended, the trustee will have to make an exempt sale or file a registration statement. In the event of a private placement, a customer is not entitled to "bid in" his net equity claim. To do so would enable him to receive a greater percentage recovery than other customers.

Section 767(a) [section 767(a) of H.Bill (now subsec. (h) of this section)] provides for the trustee to distribute customer property pro rata according to customers' net equity claims. The court will determine an equitable portion of customer property to pay administrative expenses. Paragraphs (2) and (3) indicate that the return of specifically identifiable property constitutes a distribution of net equity.

Subsection (b) [subsec. (b) of section 767 of H.Bill (now subsec. (i) of this section)] indicates that if the debtor is a clearing organization, customer property is to be segregated into customers' accounts and proprietary accounts and distributed accordingly without offset. This protects a member's customers from having their claims offset against the member's proprietary account. Subsection (c) (1) [subsec. (c)(1) of section 767 of H.Bill (now subsec. (j)(1) of this section)] indicates that any excess customer property will pour over into the general estate. This unlikely event would occur only if customers fail to file proofs of claim. Subsection (c)(2) [subsec. (c)(2) of section 767 of H.Bill (now subsec. (j)(2) of this section)] indicates that to the extent customers are not paid in full, they are entitled to share in the general estate as unsecured creditors, unless subordinated by the court under proposed 11 U.S.C. 510.

Section 768(a) [section 768(a) of H.Bill (now subsec. (c) of this section)] requires the trustee to return specifically identifiable property to the extent that such distribution will not exceed a customer's net equity claim. Thus, if the customer owes money to a commodity broker, this will be offset under section 761(15)(A)(ii) [now section 761(17)(A)(ii)]. If the value of the specifically identifiable property exceeds the net equity claim, then the customer may deposit cash with the trustee to make up the difference after which the trustee may return or transfer the customer's property.

Subsection (c) [subsec. (c) of section 768 of H.Bill (now subsec. (a) of this section)] permits the trustee to answer all margin calls, to the extent of the customer's net equity claim, with respect to any specifically identifiable open contractual commitment. It should be noted that any payment under subsections (a) or (c) [subsecs. (a) or (c) of section 768 of H.Bill (now subsecs. (a) and (c) of this section)] will be considered a reduction of the net equity claim under section 767(a) [section 767(a) of H.Bill (now subsec. (h) of this section)]. Thus the customer's net equity claim is a dynamic amount that varies with distributions of specifically identifiable property or margin payments on such property. This approach differs from the priority given to specifically identifiable property under subchapter III of chapter 7 by limiting the priority effect to a right to receive specific property as part of, rather than in addition to, a ratable share of customer property. This policy is designed to protect the small customer who is unlikely to have property in specifically identifiable form as compared with the professional trader. The CFTC is authorized to make rules defining specifically identifiable property under section 302 of the bill, in title III.

Legislative Statements. Section 766(a) of the House amendment is derived from section 768(c) of the House bill and section 767(f) of the Senate amendment. Section 766(b) of the House amendment is derived from section 765(d) of the House bill, and section 767(g) of the Senate amendment. Section 766(c) of the House amendment is derived from section 768(a) of the House bill and section 767(e) of the Senate amendment. Section 766(d) of the House amendment is derived from section 768(b) of the House bill and the second sentence of section 767(e) of the Senate amendment.

Section 766(e) of the House amendment is derived from section 765(c) of the House bill and sections 767(c) and (d) of the Senate amendment. The provision clarifies that the trustee may liquidate a commodity contract only if the commodity contract cannot be transferred to a commodity broker under section 766(c), cannot be identified to a particular customer, or has been identified with respect to a particular customer, but with respect to which the customer's instructions have not been received.

Section 766(f) of the House amendment is derived from section 766(b) of the House bill and section 767(h) of the Senate amendment. The term "all securities and other property" is not intended to include a commodity contract. Section 766(g) of the House amendment is derived from section 766(a) of the House bill. Section 766(h) of the House amendment is derived from section 767(a) of the House bill and section 765(a) of the Senate amendment. In order to induce private trustees to undertake the difficult and risky job of liquidating a commodity broker, the House amendment contains a provision insuring that a pro rata share of administrative claims will be paid. The provision represents a compromise between the position taken in the House bill, subordinating customer property to all expenses of administration, and the position taken in the Senate amendment requiring the distribution of customer property in advance of any expenses of administration. The position in the Senate amendment is rejected since customers, in any event, would have to pay a brokerage commission or fee in the ordinary course of business. The compromise provision requires customers to pay only those administrative expenses that are attributable to the administration of customer property.

Section 766(i) of the House amendment is derived from section 767(b) of the House bill and contains a similar compromise with respect to expenses of administration as the compromise detailed in connection with section 766(h) of the House amendment. Section 766(j) of the House amendment is derived from section 767(c) of the House bill. No counterpart is contained in the Senate amendment. The provision takes account of the rare case where the estate has customer property in excess of customer claims and administrative expenses attributable to those claims. The section also specifies that to the extent a customer is not paid in full out of customer property, that the unpaid claim will be treated the same as any other general unsecured creditor.

Section 768 of the Senate amendment was deleted from the House amendment as unwise. The provision in the Senate amendment would have permitted the trustee to distribute customer property based upon an estimate of value of the customer's account, with no provision for recapture of excessive disbursements. Moreover, the section would have exonerated the trustee from any liability for such an excessive disbursement. Furthermore, the section is unclear with respect to the customer's rights in the event the trustee makes a distribution less than the share to which the customer is entitled. The provision is deleted in the House amendment so that this difficult problem may be handled on a case-by-case basis by the courts as the facts and circumstances of each case require.

Section 769 of the Senate amendment is deleted in the House amendment as unnecessary. The provision was intended to codify Board of Trade v. Johnson, 264 U.S. 1 (1924) [Ill.1924, 44 S.Ct. 232]. Board of Trade against Johnson, is codified in section 363(f) of the House amendment which indicates the only five circumstances in which property may be sold free and clear of an interest in such property of an entity other than the estate.

Section 770 of the Senate amendment is deleted in the House amendment as unnecessary. That section would have permitted commodity brokers to liquidate commodity contracts, notwithstanding any contrary order of the court. It would require an extraordinary circumstance, such as a threat to the national security, to enjoin a commodity broker from liquidating a commodity contract. However, in those circumstances, an injunction must prevail. Failure of the House amendment to incorporate section 770 of the Senate amendment does not imply that the automatic stay prevents liquidation of commodity contracts by commodity brokers. To the contrary, whenever by contract, or otherwise, a commodity broker is entitled to liquidate a posi-

tion as a result of a condition specified in a contract, other than a condition or default of the kind specified in section 365(b)(2) of title 11, the commodity broker may engage in such liquidation. To this extent, the commodity broker's contract with his customer is treated no differently than any other contract under section 365 of title 11.

Effective Date of 1984 Amendments. See section 553 of Pub.L. 98–353, Title III, July 10, 1984, 98 Stat. 392, set out as an Effective Date of 1984, Amendment note preceding chapter 1 of Title 11, Bankruptcy.

Separability of Provisions. For separability of provisions of Title III of Pub.L. 98–353, see section 551 of Pub.L. 98–353 set out as a Separability of Provisions note preceding chapter 1 of Title 11, Bankruptcy.

Cross References

Distribution in chapter 11 cases, see section 1143.
Distribution of
    Customer property in stockbroker liquidation cases, see section 752.
    Property of estate, see section 726.
Executory contracts and unexpired leases, see section 365.

Library References:

C.J.S. Bankruptcy §§ 358–360; Exchanges § 11; Securities Regulation § 6.
West's Key No. Digests, Bankruptcy ☜3461; Exchanges ☜12; Securities Regulation
    ☜185.10–185.21.

WESTLAW Electronic Research

See WESTLAW Electronic Research Guide following the *Bankruptcy Highlights*.

CHAPTER 9—ADJUSTMENT OF DEBTS OF A MUNICIPALITY

SUBCHAPTER I—GENERAL PROVISIONS

Sec.
901. Applicability of other sections of this title.
902. Definitions for this chapter.
903. Reservation of State power to control municipalities.
904. Limitation on jurisdiction and powers of court.

SUBCHAPTER II—ADMINISTRATION

921. Petition and proceedings relating to petition.
922. Automatic stay of enforcement of claims against the debtor.
923. Notice.
924. List of creditors.
925. Effect of list of claims.
926. Avoiding powers.
927. Limitation on recourse.
928. Post petition effect of security interest.
929. Municipal leases.
930. Dismissal.

SUBCHAPTER III—THE PLAN

941. Filing of plan.
942. Modification of plan.
943. Confirmation.
944. Effect of confirmation.
945. Continuing jurisdiction and closing of the case.
946. Effect of exchange of securities before the date of the filing of the petition.

Cross References

Allowance of administrative expenses of substantial contributors in cases under this chapter, see section 503.

Chapter 1 of this title and this chapter solely applicable in cases under this chapter except as provided in section 901, see section 103.

Claims arising from rejection of executory contracts or unexpired leases under this chapter's plans, see section 502.

Duration of automatic stay, see section 362.

Entities which may be debtors under this chapter, see section 109.

Executory contracts and unexpired leases, see section 365.

SUBCHAPTER I—GENERAL PROVISIONS

§ 901. Applicability of other sections of this title

(a) Sections 301, 344, 347(b), 349, 350(b), 361, 362, 364(c), 364(d), 364(e), 364(f), 365, 366, 501, 502, 503, 504, 506, 507(a)(1), 509, 510, 524(a)(1), 524 (a)(2), 544, 545, 546, 547, 548, 549(a), 549(c), 549(d), 550, 551, 552, 553, 557, 1102, 1103, 1109, 1111(b), 1122, 1123(a)(1), 1123(a)(2), 1123(a)(3), 1123(a)(4), 1123(a)(5), 1123(b), 1124,

1125, 1126(a), 1126(b), 1126(c), 1126(e), 1126(f), 1126(g), 1127(d), 1128, 1129(a)(2), 1129(a)(3), 1129(a)(6), 1129(a)(8), 1129(a)(10), 1129(b)(1), 1129(b)(2)(A), 1129(b)(2)(B), 1142(b), 1143, 1144, and 1145 of this title apply in a case under this chapter.

(b) A term used in a section of this title made applicable in a case under this chapter by subsection (a) of this section or section 103(e) of this title has the meaning defined for such term for the purpose of such applicable section, unless such term is otherwise defined in section 902 of this title.

(c) A section made applicable in a case under this chapter by subsection (a) of this section that is operative if the business of the debtor is authorized to be operated is operative in a case under this chapter.

Pub.L. 95–598, Nov. 6, 1978, 92 Stat. 2621; Pub.L. 98–353, Title III, §§ 353, 490, July 10, 1984, 98 Stat. 361, 383; Pub.L. 100–597, § 3, Nov. 3, 1988, 102 Stat. 3028.

Historical and Revision Notes

Notes of Committee on the Judiciary, House Report No. 95–595. Section 901 makes applicable appropriate provisions of other chapters of proposed title 11. The general rule set out in section 103(e) is that only the provisions of chapters 1 and 9 apply in a chapter 9 case. Section 901 is the exception, and specifies other provisions that do apply. They are as follows:

§ 301. Voluntary cases. Application of this section makes clear, as under current chapter IX [former section 401 et seq. of this title], that a municipal case can be commenced only by the municipality itself. There are no involuntary chapter 9 cases.

§ 344. Self-incrimination; immunity. Application of this section is of no substantive effect for the administration of the case, but merely provides that the general rules in part V of title 18 [section 6001 et seq. of Title 18, Crimes and Criminal Procedure] govern immunity.

§ 347(b). Unclaimed property. This provision currently appears in section 96(d) of chapter IX [former section 416(d) of this title].

§ 349. Effect of dismissal. This section governs the effect of a dismissal of a chapter 9 case. It provides in substance that rights that existed before the case that were disturbed by the commencement of the case are reinstated. This section does not concern grounds for dismissal, which are found in section 926.

§ 361. Adequate protection. Section 361 provides the general standard for the protection of secured creditors whose property is used in a case under title 11. Its importance lies in its application to sections 362 and 364.

§ 362. Automatic stay. The automatic stay provisions of the general portions of the title are incorporated into chapter 9. There is an automatic stay provided in current Bankruptcy Act § 85(e) [former section 405(e) of this title]. The thrust of section 362 is the same as that of section 85(e), but, of course, its application in chapter 9 is modernized and drafted to conform with the stay generally applicable under the bankruptcy code. An additional part of the automatic stay applicable only to municipal cases is included in section 922.

§§ 364(c), 364(d), 364(e). Obtaining credit. This section governs the borrowing of money by a municipality in reorganization. It is narrower than a comparable provision in current law, section 82(b)(2) [former section 402(b)(2) of this title]. The difference lies mainly in the removal under the bill of the authority of the court to supervise borrowing by the municipality in instances in which none of the special bankruptcy powers are involved. That is, if a municipality could borrow money outside of the bankruptcy court, then it should have the same authority in bankruptcy court, under the doctrine of Ashton v. Cameron Water District No. 1, 298 U.S. 513 (1936) [Tex.1936, 56 S.Ct. 892, 80 L.Ed. 1309, 31 Am.Bankr.Rep.N.S. 96, rehearing denied 57 S.Ct. 5, 299 U.S. 619, 81 L.Ed. 457] and National League of Cities v. Usery, 426 U.S. 833 (1976) [Dist.Col.1976, 96 S.Ct. 2465, 49 L.Ed.2d 245, on remand 429 F.Supp. 703]. Only when the municipality needs special authority, such as subordination of existing liens, or special priority for the borrowed funds, will the court become involved in the authorization.

§ 365. Executory contracts and unexpired leases. The applicability of section 365 incorporates the general power of a bankruptcy court to authorize the assumption or rejection of executory contracts or unexpired leases found in other chapters of the title. This section is comparable to section 82(b)(1) [former section 402(b)(1) of this title] of current law.

§ 366. Utility service. This section gives a municipality the same authority as any other debtor with respect to continuation of utility service during the proceeding, provided adequate assurance of future payment is provided. No comparable explicit provision is found in current law, although the case law seems to support the same result.

§ 501. Filing of proofs of claims. This section permits filing of proofs of claims in a chapter 9 case. Note, however, that section 924 permits listing of creditors' claims, as under chapter 11 and under section 85(b) of chapter IX [former section 405(b) of this title].

§ 502. Allowance of claims. This section applies the general allowance rules to chapter 9 cases. This is no change from current law.

§ 503. Administrative expenses. Administrative expenses as defined in section 503 will be paid in a chapter 9 case, as provided under section 89(1) of current law [former section 409(1) of this title].

§ 504. Sharing of compensation. There is no comparable provision in current law. However, this provision applies generally throughout the proposed law, and will not affect the progress of the case, only the interrelations between attorneys and other professionals that participate in the case.

§ 506. Determination of secured status. Section 506 specifies that claims secured by a lien should be separated, to the extent provided, into secured and unsecured claims. It applies generally. Current law follows this result, though there is no explicit provision.

§ 507(1). Priorities. Paragraph (1) of section 507 requires that administrative expenses be paid first. This rule will apply in chapter 9 cases. It is presently found in section 89(1) [former section 409(1) of this title]. The two other priorities presently found in section 89 [former section 409 of this title] have been deleted. The second for claims arising within 3 months before the case is commenced, is deleted from the statute, but may be within the court's equitable power to award, under the case of Fosdick v. Schall, 99 U.S. 235 (1878) [25 L.Ed. 339]. Leaving the provision to the courts permits greater flexibility, as under railroad cases, than an absolute three-month rule. The third priority under current law, for claims which are entitled to priority under the laws of the United States, is deleted because of the proposed amendment to section 3466 of the Revised Statutes contained in section 321(a) of title III of the bill, which previously has given the United States an absolute first priority in Chapter X [former section 501 et seq. of this title] and section 77 [former section 205 of this title] cases. Because the priority rules are regularized and brought together in the bankruptcy laws by this bill, the need for incorporation of priorities elsewhere specified is eliminated.

§ 509. Claims of codebtors. This section provides for the treatment of sureties, guarantors, and codebtors. The general rule of postponement found in the other chapters will apply in chapter 9. This section adopts current law.

§ 510. Subordination of claims. This section permits the court to subordinate, on equitable grounds, any claim, and requires enforcement of contractual subordination agreements, and subordination of securities rescission claims. The section recognizes the inherent equitable power of the court under current law, and the practice followed with respect to contractual provisions.

§ 547. Preferences. Incorporation of section 547 will permit the debtor to recover preferences. This power will be used primarily when those who gave the preferences have been replaced by new municipal officers or when creditors coerced preferential payments. Unlike Bankruptcy Act § 85(h) [former section 405(h) of this title], the section does not permit the appointment of a trustee for the purpose of pursuing preferences. Moreover, this bill does not incorporate the other avoiding powers of a trustee for chapter 9, found in current section 85(h).

§ 550. Liability of transfers. Incorporation of this section is made necessary by the incorporation of the preference section, and permits recovery by the debtor from a transferee of an avoided preference.

§ 551. Automatic preservation of avoided transfer. Application of section 551 requires preservation of any avoided preference for the benefit of the estate.

§ 552. Postpetition effect of security interest. This section will govern the applicability after the commencement of the case of security interests granted by the debtor before the commencement of the case.

§ 553. Setoff. Under current law, certain setoff is stayed. Application of this section preserves that result, though the setoffs that are permitted under section 553 are better defined than under present law. Application of this section is necessary to stay the setoff and to provide the offsetting creditor with the protection to which he is entitled under present law.

§ 1122. Classification of claims. This section is derived from current section 88(b) [former section 408(b) of this title], and is substantially similar.

§ 1123(a)(1)–(4), (b). Contents of plan. The general provisions governing contents of a chapter 11 plan are made applicable here, with two exceptions relating to the rights of stockholders, which are not applicable in chapter 9 cases. This section expands current law by specifying the contents of a plan in some detail. Section 91 of current law [former section 411 of this title] speaks only in general terms. The substance of the two sections is substantially the same, however.

§ 1124. Impairment of claims. The confirmation standards adopted in chapter 9 are the same as those of chapter 11. This changes current chapter IX [former section 401 et seq. of this title], which requires compliance with the fair and equitable rule. The greater flexibility of proposed chapter 11 is carried over into chapter 9, for there appears to be no reason why the confirmation standards for the two chapters should be different, or why the elimination of the fair and equitable rule from corporate reorganizations should not be followed in municipal debt adjustments. The current chapter IX rule is based on the confirmation rules of current chapter X. The change in the latter suggests a corresponding change in the former. Section 1124 is one part of the new confirmation standard. It defines impairment, for use in section 1129.

§ 1125. Postpetition disclosure and solicitation. The change in the confirmation standard necessitates a corresponding change in the disclosure requirements for solicitation of acceptances of a plan. Under current chapter IX [former section 401 et seq. of this title] there is no disclosure requirement. Incorporation of section 1125 will insure that creditors receive adequate information before they are required to vote on a plan.

§ 1126(a), (b), (c), (e), (f), (g). Acceptance of plan. Section 1126 incorporates the cur-

rent chapter IX [former section 401 et seq. of this title] acceptance requirement: two-thirds in amount and a majority in number, Bankruptcy Act § 92 [former section 412 of this title]. Section 1125 permits exclusion of certain acceptances from the computation if the acceptances were obtained in bad faith or, unlike current law, if there is a conflict of interest motivating the acceptance.

§ 1127(d). Modification of plan. This section governs the change of a creditor's vote on the plan after a modification is proposed. It is derived from current section 92(e) [former section 410(e) of this title].

§ 1128. Hearing on confirmation. This section requires a hearing on the confirmation of the plan, and permits parties in interest to object. It is the same as Bankruptcy Act §§ 93 [former section 413 of this title] and 94(a) [former section 414(a) of this title], though the provision, comparable to section 206 of current chapter X [former section 606 of this title], permitting a labor organization to appear and be heard on the economic soundness of the plan, has been deleted as more appropriate for the Rules.

§ 1129(a)(2), (3), (8), (b)(1), (2). Confirmation of plan. This section provides the boilerplate language that the plan be proposed in good faith and that it comply with the provisions of the chapter, and also provides the financial standard for confirmation, which replaces the fair and equitable rule. See 1124, supra.

§ 1142(b). Execution of plan. Derived from Bankruptcy Act § 96(b) [former section 416(b) of this title], this section permits the court to order execution and delivery of instruments in order to execute the plan.

§ 1143. Distribution. This section is the same in substance as section 96(d) [former section 416(d) of this title], which requires presentment or delivery of securities within five years, and bars creditors that do not act within that time.

§ 1144. Revocation of order of confirmation. This section permits the court to revoke the order of confirmation and the discharge if the confirmation of the plan was procured by fraud. There is no comparable provision in current chapter IX [former section 401 et seq. of this title].

Legislative Statements. Chapter 9 of the House amendment represents a compromise between chapter 9 of the House bill and 9 of the Senate amendment. In most respects this chapter follows current law with respect to the adjustment of debts of a municipality. Stylistic changes and minor substantive revisions have been made in order to conform this chapter with other new chapters of the bankruptcy code [this title]. There are few major differences between the House bill and the Senate amendment on this issue. Section 901 indicates the applicability of other sections of title 11 in cases under chapter 9. Included are sections providing for creditors' committees under sections 1102 and 1103.

Effective Date of 1988 Amendment; Application of Amendments. Amendment by Pub.L. 100–597 effective on Nov. 3, 1988, and not applicable to cases commenced under this title prior to such date, see section 12 of Pub.L. 100–597, set out as a note under section 101 of this title.

Effective Date of 1984 Amendments. See section 553 of Pub.L. 98–353, Title III, July 10, 1984, 98 Stat. 392, set out as an Effective Date of 1984 Amendment note preceding chapter 1 of Title 11, Bankruptcy.

Separability of Provisions. For separability of provisions of Title III of Pub.L. 98–353, see section 551 of Pub.L. 98–353 set out as a Separability of Provisions note preceding chapter 1 of Title 11, Bankruptcy.

Cross References

     Confirmation in chapter 9 cases upon compliance with provisions of this title made applicable by this section, see section 943.

Library References:

     C.J.S. Bankruptcy §§ 361–367.
     West's Key No. Digests, Bankruptcy ⟨⟩3481.

WESTLAW Electronic Research

     See WESTLAW Electronic Research Guide following the *Bankruptcy Highlights*.

§ 902.   Definitions for this chapter

In this chapter—

     (1) "property of the estate", when used in a section that is made applicable in a case under this chapter by section 103(e) or 901 of this title, means property of the debtor;

     (2) "special revenues" means—

         (A) receipts derived from the ownership, operation, or disposition of projects or systems of the debtor that are primarily used or intended to be used primarily to provide transportation, utility, or other services, including the proceeds of borrowings to finance the projects or systems;

         (B) special excise taxes imposed on particular activities or transactions;

         (C) incremental tax receipts from the benefited area in the case of tax-increment financing;

         (D) other revenues or receipts derived from particular functions of the debtor, whether or not the debtor has other functions; or

         (E) taxes specifically levied to finance one or more projects or systems, excluding receipts from general property, sales, or income taxes (other than tax-increment financing) levied to finance the general purposes of the debtor;

     (3) "special tax payer" means record owner or holder of legal or equitable title to real property against which a special assessment or special tax has been levied the proceeds of which are the sole source of payment of an obligation issued by the debtor to defray the cost of an improvement relating to such real property;

(4) "special tax payer affected by the plan" means special tax payer with respect to whose real property the plan proposes to increase the proportion of special assessments or special taxes referred to in paragraph (2) of this section assessed against such real property; and

(5) "trustee", when used in a section that is made applicable in a case under this chapter by section 103(e) or 901 of this title, means debtor, except as provided in section 926 of this title.

Pub.L. 95–598, Nov. 6, 1978, 92 Stat. 2622; Pub.L. 98–353, Title III, § 491, July 10, 1984, 98 Stat. 383; Pub.L. 100–597, § 4, Nov. 3, 1988, 102 Stat. 3028.

Historical and Revision Notes

Notes of Committee on the Judiciary, Senate Report No. 95–989. There are six definitions for use in chapter 9. Paragraph (1) defines what claims are included in a chapter 9 case and adopts the definition now found in section 81(1). All claims against the petitioner generally will be included, with one significant exception. Municipalities are authorized, under section 103(c) of the Internal Revenue Code of 1954 [section 103(c) of Title 26, Internal Revenue Code], as amended, to issue tax-exempt industrial development revenue bonds to provide for the financing of certain projects for privately owned companies. The bonds are sold on the basis of the credit of the company on whose behalf they are issued, and the principal, interest, and premium, if any, are payable solely from payments made by the company to the trustee under the bond indenture and do not constitute claims on the tax revenues or other funds of the issuing municipalities. The municipality merely acts as the vehicle to enable the bonds to be issued on a tax-exempt basis. Claims that arise by virtue of these bonds are not among the claims defined by this paragraph and amounts owed by private companies to the holders of industrial development revenue bonds are not to be included among the assets of the municipality that would be affected by the plan. See Cong. Record, 94th Cong., 1st Sess. H.R. 12073 (statement by Mr. Don Edwards, floor manager of the bill in the House). Paragraph (2) defines the court which means the federal district court or federal district judge before which the case is pending. Paragraph (3) [now (1)] specifies that when the term "property of the estate" is used in a section in another chapter made applicable in chapter 9 cases, the term means "property of the debtor". Paragraphs (4) [now (2)] and (5) [now (3)] adopt the definition of "special taxpayer affected by the plan" that appears in current sections 81(10) [former section 401(10) of this title] and 81(11) [former section 401(11) of this

title] of the Bankruptcy Act. Paragraph (6) provides that "trustee" means "debtor" when used in conjunction with chapter 9.

Notes of Committee on the Judiciary, House Report No. 95–595. There are only four definitions for use only in chapter 9. The first specifies that when the term "property of the estate" is used in a section in another chapter made applicable in chapter 9 cases, the term will mean "property of the debtor". Paragraphs (2) and (3) adopt the definition of "special taxpayer affected by the plan" that appears in current sections 81(10) [former section 401(10) of this title] and 81(11) [former section 401(11) of this title]. Paragraph (4) provides for "trustee" the same treatment as provided for "property of the estate", specifying that it means "debtor" when used in conjunction with chapter 9.

Legislative Statements. Section 902(2) of the Senate amendment is deleted since the bankruptcy court will have jurisdiction over all cases under chapter 9. The concept of a claim being materially and adversely affected reflected in section 902(1) of the Senate amendment has been deleted and replaced with the new concept of "impairment" set forth in section 1124 of the House amendment and incorporated by reference into chapter 9.

Effective Date of 1988 Amendment; Application of Amendments. Amendment by Pub.L. 100–597 effective on Nov. 3, 1988, and not applicable to cases commenced under this title prior to such date, see section 12 of Pub.L. 100–597, set out as a note under section 101 of this title.

Effective Date of 1984 Amendments. See section 553 of Pub.L. 98–353, Title III, July 10, 1984, 98 Stat. 392, set out as an Effective Date of 1984 Amendment note preceding chapter 1 of Title 11, Bankruptcy.

Separability of Provisions. For separability of provisions of Title III of Pub.L. 98–353, see section 551 of Pub.L. 98–353 set out as

a Separability of Provisions note preceding
chapter 1 of Title 11, Bankruptcy.

Cross References
Definitions applicable in
　Cases under this title, see section 101.
　Commodity broker liquidation cases, see section 761.
　Railroad reorganization cases, see section 1162.
　Reorganization cases, see section 1101.
　Stockbroker liquidation cases, see section 741.

Library References:
C.J.S. Bankruptcy §§ 361–367.
West's Key No. Digests, Bankruptcy ⊕=3481.

WESTLAW Electronic Research
See WESTLAW Electronic Research Guide following the *Bankruptcy Highlights*.

§ 903.　Reservation of State power to control municipalities

This chapter does not limit or impair the power of a State to control, by legislation or otherwise, a municipality of or in such State in the exercise of the political or governmental powers of such municipality, including expenditures for such exercise, but—

(1) a State law prescribing a method of composition of indebtedness of such municipality may not bind any creditor that does not consent to such composition; and

(2) a judgment entered under such a law may not bind a creditor that does not consent to such composition.

Pub.L. 95–598, Nov. 6, 1978, 92 Stat. 2622; Pub.L. 98–353, Title III, § 492, July 10, 1984, 98 Stat. 383.

Historical and Revision Notes

Notes of Committee on the Judiciary, Senate Report No. 95–989. Section 903 is derived, with stylistic changes, from section 83 of current Chapter IX [former section 403 of this title]. It sets forth the primary authority of a State, through its constitution, laws, and other powers, over its municipalities. The proviso in section 83, prohibiting State composition procedures for municipalities, is retained. Deletion of the provision would "permit all States to enact their own versions of Chapter IX [former section 401 et seq. of this title]", Municipal Insolvency, 50 Am.Bankr. L.J. 55, 65, which would frustrate the constitutional mandate of uniform bankruptcy laws. Constitution of the United States, Art. I, Sec. 8.

This section provides that the municipality can consent to the court's orders in regard to use of its income or property. It is contemplated that such consent will be required by the court for the issuance of certificates of indebtedness under section 364(c). Such consent could extend to enforcement of the conditions attached to the certificates or the municipal services to be provided during the proceedings.

Legislative Statements. Section 903 of the House amendment represents a stylistic revision of section 903 of the Senate amendment. To the extent section 903 of the House bill would have changed present law, such section is rejected.

Effective Date of 1984 Amendments. See section 553 of Pub.L. 98–353, Title III, July 10, 1984, 98 Stat. 392, set out as an Effective Date of 1984 Amendment note preceding chapter 1, of Title 11, Bankruptcy.

Separability of Provisions. For separability of provisions of Title III of Pub.L. 98–353, see section 551 of Pub.L. 98–353 set out as a Separability of Provisions note preceding chapter 1 of Title 11, Bankruptcy.

§ 904.   Limitation on jurisdiction and powers of court

Notwithstanding any power of the court, unless the debtor consents or the plan so provides, the court may not, by any stay, order, or decree, in the case or otherwise, interfere with—

(1) any of the political or governmental powers of the debtor;

(2) any of the property or revenues of the debtor; or

(3) the debtor's use or enjoyment of any income-producing property.

Pub.L. 95–598, Nov. 6, 1978, 92 Stat. 2622.

Historical and Revision Notes

Notes of Committee on the Judiciary, Senate Report No. 95–989. This section adopts the policy of section 82(c) of current law [former section 402(c) of this title]. The only change in this section from section 82(c) is to conform the section to the style and cross-references of S. 2266.

Notes of Committee on the Judiciary, House Report No. 95–595. This section adopts the policy of section 82(c) of current law [former section 402(c) of this title]. The Usery case underlines the need for this limitation on the court's powers. The only change in this section from section 82(c) is to conform the section to the style and cross-references of H.R. 8200. This section makes clear that the court may not interfere with the choices a municipality makes as to what services and benefits it will provide to its inhabitants.

SUBCHAPTER II—ADMINISTRATION

Effective Date of 1984 Amendments. Subchapter II spelling corrected by Pub.L. 98–353. See section 553 of Pub.L. 98–353, Title III, July 10, 1984, 98 Stat. 392, set out as an Effective Date of 1984 Amendment note preceding chapter 1 of Title 11, Bankruptcy.

Separability of Provisions. For separability of provisions of Title III of Pub.L. 98–353, see section 551 of Pub.L. 98–353 set out as a Separability of Provisions note preceding chapter 1 of Title 11, Bankruptcy.

§ 921.   Petition and proceedings relating to petition

(a) Notwithstanding sections 109(d) and 301 of this title, a case under this chapter concerning an unincorporated tax or special assessment district that does not have such district's own officials is commenced by the filing under section 301 of this title of a petition under this chapter by such district's governing authority or the board or body having authority to levy taxes or assessments to meet the obligations of such district.

(b) The chief judge of the court of appeals for the circuit embracing the district in which the case is commenced shall designate the bankruptcy judge to conduct the case.

(c) After any objection to the petition, the court, after notice and a hearing, may dismiss the petition if the debtor did not file the petition in good faith or if the petition does not meet the requirements of this title.

(d) If the petition is not dismissed under subsection (c) of this section, the court shall order relief under this chapter.

(e) The court may not, on account of an appeal from an order for relief, delay any proceeding under this chapter in the case in which the appeal is being taken; nor shall any court order a stay of such proceeding pending such appeal. The reversal on appeal of a finding of jurisdiction does not affect the validity of any debt incurred that is authorized by the court under section 364(c) or 364(d) of this title.

Pub.L. 95–598, Nov. 6, 1978, 92 Stat. 2622; Pub.L. 98–353, Title III, § 494, July 10, 1984, 98 Stat. 383.

Historical and Revision Notes

Notes of Committee on the Judiciary, House Report No. 95–595. Subsection (a) is derived from section 85(a) [former section 405(a) of this title], second sentence, of current law. There is no substantive change in the law. The subsection permits a municipality that does not have its own officers to be moved into chapter 9 by the action of the body or board that has authority to levy taxes for the municipality.

Subsection (b) permits a party in interest to object to the filing of the petition not later than 15 days after notice. This provision tracks the third sentence of section 85(a) [former section 405(a) of this title], except that the provision for publication in section 85(a) is left to the Rules (See Rule 9–14 [Rules of Bankruptcy Procedure, this title]), and therefore the determinative date is left less definite.

Subsection (c) permits the court to dismiss a petition not filed in good faith or not filed in compliance with the requirements of the chapter. This provision is the fourth sentence of section 85(a) [former section 405(a) of this title].

Subsection (d) [now (e)] directs the court to order relief on the petition if it does not dismiss the case under subsection (c).

Subsection (e) [now (f)] contains the fifth and sixth sentences of section 85(a) [former section 405(a) of this title].

Legislative Statements. Section 905 of the Senate amendment is incorporated as section 921(b) of the House amendment with the difference that the chief judge of the circuit embracing the district in which the case is commenced designates a bankruptcy judge to conduct the case in lieu of a district judge as under present law. It is intended that a municipality may commence a case in any district in which the municipality is located, as under present law. Section 906 of the Senate amendment has been adopted in substance in section 109(c) of the House amendment.

Effective Date of 1984 Amendments. See section 553 of Pub.L. 98–353, Title III, July 10, 1984, 98 Stat. 392, set out as an Effective Date of 1984 Amendment note preceding chapter 1 of Title 11, Bankruptcy.

Separability of Provisions. For separability of provisions of Title III of Pub.L. 98–353, see section 551 of Pub.L. 98–353 set out as a Separability of Provisions note preceding chapter 1 of Title 11, Bankruptcy.

Library References:

C.J.S. Bankruptcy §§ 361–367.

West's Key No. Digests, Bankruptcy ⬡3481.

WESTLAW Electronic Research

See WESTLAW Electronic Research Guide following the *Bankruptcy Highlights.*

§ 922. Automatic stay of enforcement of claims against the debtor

(a) A petition filed under this chapter operates as a stay, in addition to the stay provided by section 362 of this title, applicable to all entities, of—

    (1) the commencement or continuation, including the issuance or employment of process, of a judicial, administrative, or other action or proceeding against an officer or inhabitant of the debtor that seeks to enforce a claim against the debtor; and

    (2) the enforcement of a lien on or arising out of taxes or assessments owed to the debtor.

(b) Subsections (c), (d), (e), (f), and (g) of section 362 of this title apply to a stay under subsection (a) of this section the same as such subsections apply to a stay under section 362(a) of this title.

(c) If the debtor provides, under section 362, 364, or 922 of this title, adequate protection of the interest of the holder of a claim secured by a lien on property of the debtor and if, notwithstanding such protection such creditor has a claim arising from the stay of action against such property under section 362 or 922 of this title or from the granting of a lien under section 364(d) of this title, then such claim shall be allowable as an administrative expense under section 503(b) of this title.

(d) Notwithstanding section 362 of this title and subsection (a) of this section, a petition filed under this chapter does not operate as a stay of application of pledged special revenues in a manner consistent with section 927 of this title to payment of indebtedness secured by such revenues.

Pub.L. 95–598, Nov. 6, 1978, 92 Stat. 2623; Pub.L. 98–353, Title III, § 495, July 10, 1984, 98 Stat. 384; Pub.L. 100–597, § 5, Nov. 3, 1988, 102 Stat. 3029.

Historical and Revision Notes

Notes of Committee on the Judiciary, House Report No. 95–595. The automatic stay provided under section 362 of title 11 is incomplete for a municipality, because there is the possibility of action by a creditor against an officer or inhabitant of the municipality to collect taxes due the municipality. Section 85(e)(1) of current chapter IX [former section 405(e)(1) of this title] stays such actions. Section 922 carries over that protection into the proposed chapter 9. Subsection (b) applies the provisions for relief from the stay that apply generally in section 362 to the stay under section 922.

Effective Date of 1988 Amendment; Application of Amendments. Amendment by Pub.L. 100–597 effective on Nov. 3, 1988, and not applicable to cases commenced under this title prior to such date, see section 12 of Pub.L. 100–597, set out as a note under section 101 of this title.

Effective Date of 1984 Amendments. See section 553 of Pub.L. 98–353, Title III, July 10, 1984, 98 Stat. 392, set out as an Effective Date of 1984 Amendment note preceding chapter 1 of Title 11, Bankruptcy.

Separability of Provisions. For separability of provisions of Title III of Pub.L. 98–353, see section 551 of Pub.L. 98–353 set out as a Separability of Provisions note preceding chapter 1 of Title 11, Bankruptcy.

Cross References

Effect of section 362 of this title in stockbroker liquidation cases, see section 742.

Extension of time generally, see section 108.

Stay of action against codebtor in chapter 13 cases, see section 1301.

Library References:

C.J.S. Bankruptcy §§ 361–367.

West's Key No. Digests, Bankruptcy ⬤⟳3481.

WESTLAW Electronic Research

See WESTLAW Electronic Research Guide following the *Bankruptcy Highlights*.

§ 923. Notice

There shall be given notice of the commencement of a case under this chapter, notice of an order for relief under this chapter, and notice of the dismissal of a case under this chapter. Such notice shall also be published at least once a week for three successive weeks in at least one newspaper of general circulation published within the district in which the case is commenced, and in such other newspaper having a general circulation among bond dealers and bondholders as the court designates.

Pub.L. 95–598, Nov. 6, 1978, 92 Stat. 2623.

Historical and Revision Notes

Notes of Committee on the Judiciary, House Report No. 95–595. The notice provisions in section 923 are significantly more sparse than those provided under section 85(d) of chapter IX [former section 405(d) of this title]. The exact contours of the notice to be given under chapter 9 are left to the Rules [Rules of Bankruptcy Procedure, this title]. Because the Rules deal with notice in a municipal case (Rule 9–14), and because section 405(d) of title IV of the bill continues those Rules in effect to the extent not inconsistent with the bill, the notice provisions of current law and Rules would continue to apply.

Legislative Statements. Section 923 of the House amendment represents a compromise with respect to the notice provisions contained in comparable provisions of the House bill and Senate amendment. As a general matter, title 11 leaves most procedural issues to be determined by the Rules of Bankruptcy Procedure. Section 923 of the House amendment contains certain important aspects of procedure that have been retained from present law. It is anticipated that the Rules of Bankruptcy Procedure will adopt rules similar to the present rules for chapter IX of the Bankruptcy Act [former section 401 et seq. of this title].

Cross References

Notice of order for relief, see section 342.

Notice to
  Commodity Futures Trading Commission, see section 762.
  Security Investor Protection Corporation and Securities and Exchange Commission, see section 743.

Library References:

C.J.S. Bankruptcy §§ 361–367.

West's Key No. Digests, Bankruptcy ⬤⟳3481.

WESTLAW Electronic Research

See WESTLAW Electronic Research Guide following the *Bankruptcy Highlights*.

§ 924.   List of creditors

The debtor shall file a list of creditors.

Pub.L. 95–598, Nov. 6, 1978, 92 Stat. 2623.

Historical and Revision Notes

Notes of Committee on the Judiciary, Senate Report No. 95–989. This section adopts the provision presently contained in section 85(b) of Chapter IX [former section 405(b) of this title]. A list of creditors, as complete and accurate as practicable, must be filed with the court.

Notes of Committee on the Judiciary, House Report No. 95–595. This section directs the debtor to file a list of creditors with the court. A comparable provision is presently contained in section 85(b) of chapter IX [former section 405(b) of this title]. The Rules, [Rules of Bankruptcy Procedure, this title], in Rule 9–7, copy the provisions of sec-

tion 85(b), with additional matter. As noted above, section 405(d) of title IV will continue those Rules in effect. Because the form, time of filing, and nature of the list, are procedural matters that may call for some flexibility, those details have been left to the Rules.

Legislative Statements. Section 924 of the House amendment is derived from section 924 of the House bill with the location of the filing of the list of creditors to be determined by the rules of bankruptcy procedure. The detailed requirements of section 724 [924] of the Senate bill are anticipated to be incorporated in the rules of bankruptcy procedure.

Cross References

Duty of
  Debtor to file list of creditors, see section 521.
  Trustee to file list of creditors in chapter 11 cases, see section 1106.

Library References:

C.J.S. Bankruptcy §§ 361–367.
West's Key No. Digests, Bankruptcy ⊕3481.

WESTLAW Electronic Research

See WESTLAW Electronic Research Guide following the *Bankruptcy Highlights*.

§ 925.   Effect of list of claims

A proof of claim is deemed filed under section 501 of this title for any claim that appears in the list filed under section 924 of this title, except a claim that is listed as disputed, contingent, or unliquidated.

Pub.L. 95–598, Nov. 6, 1978, 92 Stat. 2623.

Historical and Revision Notes

Notes of Committee on the Judiciary, Senate Report No. 95–989. Section 926 [now section 925] follows the policy contained in section 88(a) of the present Act [former section 408(a) of this title], though certain details are left to the Rules. The language of section 926 is the same as that of proposed 11 U.S.C. 1111, which applies in chapter 11 cases. The list of creditors filed under section 924 is given

weight as prima facie evidence of the claims listed (except claims that are listed as disputed, contingent, or unliquidated), which are deemed filed under section 501, obviating the need for listed creditors to file proofs of claim.

Legislative Statements. Section 925 of the Senate amendment regarding venue and fees has been deleted.

Library References:

C.J.S. Bankruptcy §§ 361–367.
West's Key No. Digests, Bankruptcy ⊕3481.

§ 926. Avoiding powers

(a) If the debtor refuses to pursue a cause of action under section 544, 545, 547, 548, 549(a), or 550 of this title, then on request of a creditor, the court may appoint a trustee to pursue such cause of action.

(b) A transfer of property of the debtor to or for the benefit of any holder of a bond or note, on account of such bond or note, may not be avoided under section 547 of this title.

Pub.L. 95–598, Nov. 6, 1978, 92 Stat. 2623; Pub.L. 100–597, § 6, Nov. 3, 1988, 102 Stat. 3029.

Historical and Revision Notes

Notes of Committee on the Judiciary, Senate Report No. 95–989. This section adopts current section 85(h) [former section 405(h) of this title] which provides for a trustee to be appointed for the purpose of pursuing an action under an avoiding power, if the debtor refuses to do so. This section is necessary because a municipality might, by reason of political pressure or desire for future good relations with a particular creditor or class of creditors, make payments to such creditors in the days preceding the petition to the detriment of all other creditors. No change in the elected officials of such a city would automatically occur upon filing of the petition, and it might be very awkward for those same officials to turn around and demand the return of the payments following the filing of the petition. Hence, the need for a trustee for such purpose.

The general avoiding powers are incorporated by reference in section 901 and are broader than under current law. Preferences, fraudulent conveyances, and other kinds of transfers will thus be voidable.

Incorporated by reference also is the power to accept or reject executory contracts and leases (section 365). Within the definition of executory contracts are collective bargaining agreements between the city and its employees. Such contracts may be rejected despite contrary State laws. Courts should readily allow in the municipality's reorganization and the rejection of such contracts where they are burdensome, the rejection will aid in consideration of the equities of each case. On the last point, "[e]quities in favor of the city in chapter 9 will be far more compelling than the equities in favor of the employer in chapter 11. Onerous employment obligations may prevent a city from balancing its budget for some time. The prospect of an unbalanced budget may preclude judicial confirmation of the plan. Unless a city can reject its labor contracts, lack of funds may force cutbacks in police, fire, sanitation, and welfare services, imposing hardships on many citizens. In addition, because cities in the past have often seemed immune to the constraint of "profitability" faced by private businesses, their wage contracts may be relatively more onerous than those in the private sector." Executory Contracts and Municipal Bankruptcy, 85 Yale L.J. 957, 965 (1976) (footnote omitted). Rejection of the contracts may require the municipalities to renegotiate such contracts by state collective bargaining laws. It is intended that the power to reject collective bargaining agreements will pre-empt state termination provisions, but not state collective bargaining laws. Thus, a city would not be required to maintain existing employment terms during the renegotiation period.

Legislative Statements. Section 926 of the House amendment is derived from section 928 of the Senate bill. The provision enables creditors to request the court to appoint a trustee to pursue avoiding powers if the debtor refuses to exercise those powers. Section 901 of the House amendment makes a corresponding change to incorporate avoiding powers included in the Senate amendment, but excluded from the House bill.

Effective Date of 1988 Amendment; Application of Amendments. Amendment by Pub.L. 100–597 effective on Nov. 3, 1988, and not applicable to cases commenced under this title prior to such date, see section 12 of Pub.L. 100–597, set out as a note under section 101 of this title.

§ 927. Limitation on recourse

The holder of a claim payable solely from special revenues of the debtor under applicable nonbankruptcy law shall not be treated as having recourse against the debtor on account of such claim pursuant to section 1111(b) of this title.

Added Pub.L. 100–597, § 7(2), Nov. 3, 1988, 102 Stat. 3029.

Historical and Revision Notes

Effective Date; Application of Amendments. Enactment by Pub.L. 100–597 effective on Nov. 3, 1988, and not applicable to cases commenced under this title prior to such date, see section 12 of Pub.L. 100–597, set out as a note under section 101 of this title.

§ 928. Post petition effect of security interest

(a) Notwithstanding section 552(a) of this title and subject to subsection (b) of this section, special revenues acquired by the debtor after the commencement of the case shall remain subject to any lien resulting from any security agreement entered into by the debtor before the commencement of the case.

(b) Any such lien on special revenues, other than municipal betterment assessments, derived from a project or system shall be subject to the necessary operating expenses of such project or system, as the case may be.

Added Pub.L. 100–597, § 8, Nov. 3, 1988, 102 Stat. 3029.

Historical and Revision Notes

Effective Date; Application of Amendments. Enactment by Pub.L. 100–597 effective on Nov. 3, 1988, and not applicable to cases commenced under this title prior to such date, see section 12 of Pub.L. 100–597, set out as a note under section 101 of this title.

§ 929. Municipal leases

A lease to a municipality shall not be treated as an executory contract or unexpired lease for the purposes of section 365 or 502(b)(6) of this title solely by reason of its being subject to termination in the event the debtor fails to appropriate rent.

Added Pub.L. 100–597, § 9, Nov. 3, 1988, 102 Stat. 3030.

Historical and Revision Notes

Effective Date; Application of Amendments. Enactment by Pub.L. 100–597 effective on Nov. 3, 1988, and not applicable to cases commenced under this title prior to such date, see section 12 of Pub.L. 100–597, set out as a note under section 101 of this title.

§ 930. Dismissal

(a) After notice and a hearing, the court may dismiss a case under this chapter for cause, including—

(1) want of prosecution;

(2) unreasonable delay by the debtor that is prejudicial to creditors;

(3) failure to propose a plan within the time fixed under section 941 of this title;

(4) if a plan is not accepted within any time fixed by the court;

(5) denial of confirmation of a plan under section 943(b) of this title and denial of additional time for filing another plan or a modification of a plan; or

(6) if the court has retained jurisdiction after confirmation of a plan—

(A) material default by the debtor with respect to a term of such plan; or

(B) termination of such plan by reason of the occurrence of a condition specified in such plan.

(b) The court shall dismiss a case under this chapter if confirmation of a plan under this chapter is refused.

Pub.L. 95–598, Nov. 6, 1978, 92 Stat. 2623, formerly § 927; Pub.L. 98–353, Title III, § 496, July 10, 1984, 98 Stat. 384; renumbered § 930, Pub.L. 100–597, § 7(1), Nov. 3, 1988, 102 Stat. 3029.

Historical and Revision Notes

Notes of Committee on the Judiciary, Senate Report No. 95–989. Section 927 conforms to section 98 [former section 418 of this title] of current law. The Section permits dismissal by the court for unreasonable delay by the debtor, failure to propose a plan, failure of acceptance of a plan, or default by the debtor under a conformed plan. Mandatory dismissal is required if confirmation is refused.

Legislative Statements. Section 927(b) of the House amendment is derived from section 927(b) of the Senate bill. The provision requires mandatory dismissal if confirmation of a plan is refused.

The House amendment deletes section 929 of the Senate amendment as unnecessary since the bankruptcy court has original exclusive jurisdiction of all cases under chapter 9.

The House amendment deletes section 930 of the Senate amendment and incorporates section 507(a)(1) by reference.

Effective Date of 1988 Amendment; Application of Amendments. Amendment by Pub.L. 100–597 effective on Nov. 3, 1988, and not applicable to cases commenced under this title prior to such date, see section 12 of Pub.L. 100–597, set out as a note under section 101 of this title.

Effective Date of 1984 Amendments. See section 553 of Pub.L. 98–353, Title III, July 10, 1984, 98 Stat. 392, set out as an Effective Date of 1984 Amendment note preceding chapter 1 of Title 11, Bankruptcy.

Separability of Provisions. For separability of provisions of Title III of Pub.L. 98–353, see section 551 of Pub.L. 98–353 set out as a Separability of Provisions note preceding chapter 1 of Title 11, Bankruptcy.

Cross References

Conversion or dismissal of
> Chapter 11 cases, see section 1112.
> Chapter 13 cases, see section 1307.

Dismissal of chapter 7 cases, see section 707.

Effect of dismissal, see section 349.

Library References:

C.J.S. Bankruptcy § 365.

West's Key No. Digests, Bankruptcy ⬦3481.

WESTLAW Electronic Research

See WESTLAW Electronic Research Guide following the *Bankruptcy Highlights*.

SUBCHAPTER III—THE PLAN

§ 941. Filing of plan

The debtor shall file a plan for the adjustment of the debtor's debts. If such a plan is not filed with the petition, the debtor shall file such a plan at such later time as the court fixes.

Pub.L. 95–598, Nov. 6, 1978, 92 Stat. 2624.

Historical and Revision Notes

Notes of Committee on the Judiciary, Senate Report No. 95–989. Section 941 gives the debtor the exclusive right to propose a plan, and directs that the debtor propose one either with the petition or within such time as the court directs. The section follows section 90(a) of current law [former section 410(a) of this title].

Cross References

Dismissal for failure to timely propose plan, see section 927.

Filing of plan in chapter 13 cases, see section 1321.

Who may file a plan in chapter 11 cases, see section 1121.

Library References:

C.J.S. Bankruptcy § 366.

West's Key No. Digests, Bankruptcy ⬦3481.

WESTLAW Electronic Research

See WESTLAW Electronic Research Guide following the *Bankruptcy Highlights*.

§ 942. Modification of plan

The debtor may modify the plan at any time before confirmation, but may not modify the plan so that the plan as modified fails to meet the requirements of this chapter. After the debtor files a modification, the plan as modified becomes the plan.

Pub.L. 95–598, Nov. 6, 1978, 92 Stat. 2624.

Historical and Revision Notes

Notes of Committee on the Judiciary, Senate Report No. 95–989. Section 942 permits the debtor to modify the plan at any time before confirmation, as does section 90(a) of current law [former section 410(a) of this title].

Legislative Statements. The House amendment deletes section 942 of the Senate amendment in favor of incorporating section

1125 by cross-reference. Similarly, the House amendment does not incorporate sections 944 or 945 of the Senate amendment since incorporation of several sections in chapter 11 in section 901 is sufficient.

Cross References

Modification of plan after confirmation in chapter 13 cases, see section 1329.
Modification of plan before confirmation in chapter 13 cases, see section 1323.
Modification of plan in chapter 11 cases, see section 1127.

Library References:

C.J.S. Bankruptcy § 366.
West's Key No. Digests, Bankruptcy ⟝3481.

WESTLAW Electronic Research

See WESTLAW Electronic Research Guide following the *Bankruptcy Highlights*.

§ 943. Confirmation

(a) A special tax payer may object to confirmation of a plan.

(b) The court shall confirm the plan if—

(1) the plan complies with the provisions of this title made applicable by sections 103(e) and 901 of this title;

(2) the plan complies with the provisions of this chapter;

(3) all amounts to be paid by the debtor or by any person for services or expenses in the case or incident to the plan have been fully disclosed and are reasonable;

(4) the debtor is not prohibited by law from taking any action necessary to carry out the plan;

(5) except to the extent that the holder of a particular claim has agreed to a different treatment of such claim, the plan provides that on the effective date of the plan each holder of a claim of a kind specified in section 507(a)(1) of this title will receive on account of such claim cash equal to the allowed amount of such claim;

(6) any regulatory or electoral approval necessary under applicable nonbankruptcy law in order to carry out any provision of the plan has been obtained, or such provision is expressly conditioned on such approval; and

(7) the plan is in the best interests of creditors and is feasible.

Pub.L. 95–598, Nov. 6, 1978, 92 Stat. 2624; Pub.L. 98–353, Title III, § 497, July 10, 1984, 98 Stat. 384; Pub.L. 100–597, § 10, Nov. 3, 1988, 102 Stat. 3030.

Historical and Revision Notes

Notes of Committee on the Judiciary, Senate Report No. 95–989. Section 946 [now this section] is adopted from current section 94 [former section 414 of this title]. The test for confirmation is whether or not the plan is fair and equitable and feasible. The fair and equitable test tracts current chapter X [former section 501 et seq. of this title] and is known as the strict priority rule. Creditors must be provided, under the plan, the going concern value of their claims. The going concern value contemplates a "comparison of revenues and expenditures taking into account the taxing power and the extent to which tax increases are both necessary and feasible" Municipal Insolvency, supra, at p. 64, and is intended to provide more of a return to creditors than the liquidation value if the city's assets could be liquidated like those of a private corporation.

Notes of Committee on the Judiciary, House Report No. 95–595. In addition to the confirmation requirements incorporated from section 1129 by section 901, this section specifies additional requirements. Paragraph (1) requires compliance with the provisions of the title made applicable in chapter 9 cases. This provision follows section 94(b)(2) [former section 414(b)(2) of this title]. Paragraph (2) requires compliance with the provisions of chapter 9, as does section 94(b)(2) [former section 414(b)(2) of this title]. Paragraph (3) adopts section 94(b)(4) [former section 414(b)(4) of this title], requiring disclosure and reasonableness of all payments to be made in connection with the plan or the case. Paragraph (4), copied from section 92(b)(6) [former section 414(b)(6) of this title], requires that the debtor not be prohibited by law from taking any action necessary to carry out the plan. Paragraph (5) departs from current law by requiring that administrative expenses be paid in full, but not necessarily in cash. Finally, paragraph (6) requires that the plan be in the best interest of creditors and feasible. The best interest test was deleted in section 94(b)(1) of current chapter IX [former section 414(b)(1) of this title] from previous chapter IX [former section 401 et seq. of this title], because it was redundant with the fair and equitable rule. However, this bill proposes a new confirmation standard generally for reorganization, one element of which is the best interest of creditors test; see section 1129(a)(7). In that section, the test is phrased in terms of liquidation of the debtor. Because that is not possible in a municipal case, the test here is phrased in its more traditional form, using the words of art "best interest of creditors." The best interest of creditors test here is in addition to the financial standards imposed on the plan by section 1129(a)(8) and 1129(b), just as those provisions are in addition to the comparable best interest test in chapter 11, 11 U.S.C. 1129(a)(7). The feasibility requirement, added in the revision of chapter IX [former section 401 et seq. of this title] last year, is retained.

Legislative Statements. Section 943(a) of the House amendment makes clear that a special taxpayer may object to confirmation of a plan. Section 943(b) of the House amendment is derived from section 943 of the House bill respecting confirmation of a plan under chapter 9. It must be emphasized that these standards of confirmation are in addition to standards in section 1129 that are made applicable to chapter 9 by section 901 of the House

amendment. In particular, if the requirements of section 1129(a)(8) are not complied with, then the proponent may request application of section 1129(b). The court will then be required to confirm the plan if it complies with the "fair and equitable" test and is in the best interests of creditors. The best interests of creditors test does not mean liquidation value as under chapter XI of the Bankruptcy Act [former section 701 et seq. of this title]. In making such a determination, it is expected that the court will be guided by standards set forth in Kelley v. Everglades Drainage District, 319 U.S. 415 (1943) [Fla.1943, 63 S.Ct. 1141, 87 L.Ed. 1485, rehearing denied 63 S.Ct. 1444, 320 U.S. 214, 87 L.Ed. 1851, motion denied 64 S.Ct. 783, 321 U.S. 754, 88 L.Ed. 1054] and Fano v. Newport Heights Irrigation Dist., 114 F.2d 563 (9th Cir.1940), as under present law, the bankruptcy court should make findings as detailed as possible to support a conclusion that this test has been met. However, it must be emphasized that unlike current law, the fair and equitable test under section 1129(b) will not apply if section 1129(a) (8) has been satisfied in addition to the other confirmation standards specified in section 943 and incorporated by reference in section 901 of the House amendment. To the extent that American United Mutual Life Insurance Co. v. City of Avon Park, 311 U.S. 138 (1940) [Fla.1940, 61 S.Ct. 157, 85 L.Ed. 91, 136 A.L.R. 860, rehearing denied 61 S.Ct. 395, 311 U.S. 730, 85 L.Ed. 475] and other cases are to the contrary, such cases are overruled to that extent.

Effective Date of 1988 Amendment; Application of Amendments. Amendment by Pub.L. 100–597 effective on Nov. 3, 1988, and not applicable to cases commenced under this title prior to such date, see section 12 of Pub.L. 100–597, set out as a note under section 101 of this title.

Effective Date of 1984 Amendments. See section 553 of Pub.L. 98–353, Title III, July 10, 1984, 98 Stat. 392, set out as an Effective Date of 1984 Amendment note preceding chapter 1 of Title 11, Bankruptcy.

Separability of Provisions. For separability of provisions of Title III of Pub.L. 98–353, see section 551 of Pub.L. 98–353 set out as a Separability of Provisions note preceding chapter 1 of Title 11, Bankruptcy.

Cross References

Confirmation hearing in
    Chapter 11 cases, see section 1128.
    Chapter 13 cases, see section 1324.
Confirmation of plan in
    Chapter 13 cases, see section 1325.
    Railroad reorganization cases, see section 1173.
    Reorganization cases, see section 1129.
Dismissal for denial of confirmation of plan, see section 927.
Unclaimed property, see section 347.

Library References:

C.J.S. Bankruptcy § 367.
West's Key No. Digests, Bankruptcy ⊕3481.

WESTLAW Electronic Research

See WESTLAW Electronic Research Guide following the *Bankruptcy Highlights*.

§ 944. Effect of confirmation

(a) The provisions of a confirmed plan bind the debtor and any creditor, whether or not—

    (1) a proof of such creditor's claim is filed or deemed filed under section 501 of this title;

    (2) such claim is allowed under section 502 of this title; or

    (3) such creditor has accepted the plan.

(b) Except as provided in subsection (c) of this section, the debtor is discharged from all debts as of the time when—

    (1) the plan is confirmed;

    (2) the debtor deposits any consideration to be distributed under the plan with a disbursing agent appointed by the court; and

    (3) the court has determined—

        (A) that any security so deposited will constitute, after distribution, a valid legal obligation of the debtor; and

        (B) that any provision made to pay or secure payment of such obligation is valid.

(c) The debtor is not discharged under subsection (b) of this section from any debt—

    (1) excepted from discharge by the plan or order confirming the plan; or

    (2) owed to an entity that, before confirmation of the plan, had neither notice nor actual knowledge of the case.

Pub.L. 95–598, Nov. 6, 1978, 92 Stat. 2624.

Historical and Revision Notes

Notes of Committee on the Judiciary, Senate Report No. 95–989. Subsection (a) makes the provisions of a confirmed plan binding on the debtor and creditors. It is derived from section 95(a) of chapter 9 [former section 415(a) of this title].

Subsections (b) and (c) provide for the discharge of a municipality. The discharge is essentially the same as that granted under section 95(b) of the Bankruptcy Act [former section 415(b) of this title].

§ 945. Continuing jurisdiction and closing of the case

(a) The court may retain jurisdiction over the case for such period of time as is necessary for the successful implementation of the plan.

(b) Except as provided in subsection (a) of this section, the court shall close the case when administration of the case has been completed.

Pub.L. 95–598, Nov. 6, 1978, 92 Stat. 2625; Pub.L. 98–353, Title III, § 498, July 10, 1984, 98 Stat. 384.

Historical and Revision Notes

Notes of Committee on the Judiciary, Senate Report No. 95–989. Section 948 [now this section] permits the court to retain jurisdiction over the case to ensure successful execution of the plan. The provision is the same as that found in section 96(e) of Chapter 9 of the present Act [former section 416(e) of this title].

Effective Date of 1984 Amendments. See section 553 of Pub.L. 98–353, Title III, July 10, 1984, 98 Stat. 392, set out as an Effective Date of 1984 Amendment note preceding chapter 1 of Title 11, Bankruptcy.

Separability of Provisions. For separability of provisions of Title III of Pub.L. 98–353, see section 551 of Pub.L. 98–353 set out as a Separability of Provisions note preceding chapter 1 of Title 11, Bankruptcy.

§ 946. Effect of exchange of securities before the date of the filing of the petition

The exchange of a new security under the plan for a claim covered by the plan, whether such exchange occurred before or after the date of the filing of the petition, does not limit or impair the effectiveness of the plan or of any provision of this chapter. The amount and number specified in section 1126(c) of this title include the amount and number of claims formerly held by a creditor that has participated in any such exchange.

Pub.L. 95–598, Nov. 6, 1978, 92 Stat. 2625.

Historical and Revision Notes

Notes of Committee on the Judiciary, Senate Report No. 95–989. This section, which follows section 97 of current law [former section 417 of this title], permits an exchange of a security before the case is filed to constitute an acceptance of the plan if the exchange was under a proposal that later becomes the plan.

Legislative Statements. The House amendment deletes section 950 of the Senate amendment as unnecessary. The constitutionality of chapter 9 of the House amendment is beyond doubt.

Library References:

    C.J.S. Bankruptcy §§ 361–367.

    West's Key No. Digests, Bankruptcy ⚷3481.

WESTLAW Electronic Research

    See WESTLAW Electronic Research Guide following the *Bankruptcy Highlights*.

CHAPTER 11—REORGANIZATION

SUBCHAPTER I—OFFICERS AND ADMINISTRATION

Sec.
1101. Definitions for this chapter.
1102. Creditors' and equity security holders' committees.
1103. Powers and duties of committees.
1104. Appointment of trustee or examiner.
1105. Termination of trustee's appointment.
1106. Duties of trustee and examiner.
1107. Rights, powers, and duties of debtor in possession.
1108. Authorization to operate business.
1109. Right to be heard.
1110. Aircraft equipment and vessels.
1111. Claims and interests.
1112. Conversion or dismissal.
1113. Rejection of collective bargaining agreements.
1114. Payment of insurance benefits to retired employees.

SUBCHAPTER II—THE PLAN

1121. Who may file a plan.
1122. Classification of claims or interests.
1123. Contents of plan.
1124. Impairment of claims or interests.
1125. Postpetition disclosure and solicitation.
1126. Acceptance of plan.
1127. Modification of plan.
1128. Confirmation hearing.
1129. Confirmation of plan.

SUBCHAPTER III—POSTCONFIRMATION MATTERS

1141. Effect of confirmation.
1142. Implementation of plan.
1143. Distribution.
1144. Revocation of an order of confirmation.
1145. Exemption from securities laws.
1146. Special tax provisions.

SUBCHAPTER IV—RAILROAD REORGANIZATION

1161. Inapplicability of other sections.
1162. Definition.
1163. Appointment of trustee.
1164. Right to be heard.
1165. Protection of the public interest.
1166. Effect of subtitle IV of title 49 and of Federal, State, or local regulations.
1167. Collective bargaining agreements.
1168. Rolling stock equipment.
1169. Effect of rejection of lease of railroad line.
1170. Abandonment of railroad line.
1171. Priority claims.

Sec.
1172.   Contents of plan.
1173.   Confirmation of plan.
1174.   Liquidation.

Historical and Revision Notes

Legislative Statements. Chapter 11 of the House amendment is derived in large part from chapter 11 as contained in the House bill. Unlike chapter 11 of the Senate amendment, chapter 11 of the House amendment does not represent an extension of chapter X of current law [former section 501 et seq. of this title] or any other chapter of the Bankruptcy Act. Rather chapter 11 of the House amendment takes a new approach consolidating subjects dealt with under chapters VIII, X, XI, and XII of the Bankruptcy Act [former sections 201 et seq., 501 et seq., 701 et seq. and 801 et seq. of this title, respectively]. The new consolidated chapter 11 contains no special procedure for companies with public debt or equity security holders. Instead, factors such as the standard to be applied to solicitation of acceptances of a plan of reorganization are left to be determined by the court on a case-by-case basis. In order to insure that adequate investigation of the debtor is conducted to determine fraud or wrongdoing on the part of present management, an examiner is required to be appointed in all cases in which the debtor's fixed, liquidated, and unsecured debts, other than debts for goods, services, or taxes, or owing to an insider, exceed $5 million. This should adequately represent the needs of public security holders in most cases. However, in addition, section 1109 of the House amendment enables both the Securities and Exchange Commission and any party in interest who is creditor, equity security holder, indenture trustee, or any committee representing creditors or equity security holders to raise and appear and be heard on any issue in a case under chapter 11. This will enable the bankruptcy court to evaluate all sides of a position and to determine the public interest. This approach is sharply contrasted to that under chapter X of present law in which the public interest is often determined only in terms of the interest of public security holders. The advisory role of the Securities and Exchange Commission will enable the court to balance the needs of public security holders against equally important public needs relating to the economy, such as employment and production, and other factors such as the public health and safety of the people or protection of the national interest. In this context, the new chapter 11 deletes archaic rules contained in certain chapters of present law such as the requirement of an approval hearing and the prohibition of prepetition solicitation. Such requirements were written in an age before the enactment of the Trust Indenture Act [section 77aaa et seq. of Title 15, Commerce and Trade] and the development of securities laws had occurred. The benefits of these provisions have long been outlived but the detriment of the provisions served to frustrate and delay effective reorganization in those chapters of the Bankruptcy Act in which such provisions applied. Chapter 11 thus represents a much needed revision of reorganization laws. A brief discussion of the history of this important achievement is useful to an appreciation of the monumental reform embraced in chapter 11.

Under the existing Bankruptcy Act, debtors seeking reorganization may choose among three reorganization chapters, chapter X [former section 501 et seq. of this title], chapter XI [former section 701 et seq. of this title], and chapter XII [former section 801 et seq. of this title]. Individuals and partnerships may file under chapter XI or, if they own property encumbered by mortgage liens, they may file under chapter XII. A corporation may file under either chapter X or chapter XI, but is ineligible to file under chapter XII. Chapter X was designed to facilitate the pervasive reorganization of corporations whose creditors include holders of publicly issued debt securities. Chapter XI, on the other hand, was designed to permit smaller enterprises to negotiate composition or extension plans with their unsecured creditors. The essential differences between chapters X and XI are as follows. Chapter X mandates that, first, an independent trustee be appointed and assume management control from the officers and directors of the debtor corporation; second, the Securities and Exchange Commission must be afforded an opportunity to participate both as an adviser to the court and as a representative of the interests of public security holders; third, the court must approve any proposed plan of reorganization, and prior to such approval, acceptances of creditors and shareholders may not be solicited; fourth, the court must apply the absolute priority rule; and fifth, the court has the power to affect, and grant the debtor a discharge in respect of, all types of claims, whether secured or unsecured and whether arising by reason of fraud or breach of contract.

The Senate amendment consolidates chapters X [former section 501 et seq. of this title], XI [former section 701 et seq. of this title], and XII [former section 801 et seq. of this title], but establishes a separate and distinct reorganization procedure for "public companies." The special provisions applicable to "public companies" are tantamount to the codification of chapter X of the existing Bankruptcy Act and thus result in the creation of a "two-track system." The narrow definition of the term "public company" would require many businesses which could have been rehabilitated under chapter XI to instead use the more cumbersome procedures of chapter X, whether needed or not.

The special provisions of the Senate amendment applicable to a "public company" are as follows:

(a) Section 1101(3) defines a "public company" as a debtor who, within 12 months prior to the filing of the petition, had outstanding $5 million or more in debt and had not less than 1000 security holders;

(b) Section 1104(a) requires the appointment of a disinterested trustee irrespective of whether creditors support such appointment and whether there is cause for such appointment;

(c) Section 1125(f) prohibits the solicitation of acceptances of a plan of reorganization prior to court approval of such plan even though the solicitation complies with all applicable securities laws;

(d) Section 1128(a) requires the court to conduct a hearing on any plan of reorganization proposed by the trustee or any other party;

(e) Section 1128(b) requires the court to refer any plans "worthy of consideration" to the Securities and Exchange Commission for their examination and report, prior to court approval of a plan; and

(f) Section 1128(c) and section 1130(a)(7) requires the court to approve a plan or plans which are "fair and equitable" and comply with the other provisions of chapter 11.

The record of the Senate hearings on S. 2266 and the House hearings on H.R. 8200 is replete with evidence of the failure of the reorganization provisions of the existing Bankruptcy Act to meet the needs of insolvent corporations in today's business environment. Chapter X [former section 501 et seq. of this title] was designed to impose rigid and formalized procedures upon the reorganization of corporations and, although designed to protect public creditors, has often worked to the detriment of such creditors. As the House report has noted:

The negative results under chapter X [former section 501 et seq. of this title] have resulted from the stilted procedures, under which management is always ousted and replaced by an independent trustee, the courts and the Securities and Exchange Commission examine the plan of reorganization in great detail, no matter how long that takes, and the court values the business, a time consuming and inherently uncertain procedure.

The House amendment deletes the "public company" exception, because it would codify the well recognized infirmities of chapter X [former section 501 et seq. of this title], because it would extend the chapter X approach to a large number of new cases without regard to whether the rigid and formalized procedures of chapter X are needed, and because it is predicated upon the myth that provisions similar to those contained in chapter X are necessary for the protection of public investors. Bankruptcy practice in large reorganization cases has also changed substantially in the 40 years since the Chandler Act [the 1938 amendment of the Bankruptcy Act] was enacted. This change is, in large part, attributable to the pervasive effect of the Federal Securities laws and the extraordinary success of the Securities and Exchange Commission in sensitizing both management and members of the bar to the need for full disclosure and fair dealing in transactions involving publicly held securities.

It is important to note that Congress passed the Chandler Act [the 1938 amendment of the Bankruptcy Act] prior to enactment of the Trust Indenture Act of 1939 [section 77aaa et seq. of Title 15, Commerce and Trade] and prior to the definition and enforcement of the disclosure requirements of the Securities Act of 1933 [section 77(a) et seq. of Title 15] and the Securities Exchange Act of 1934 [section 78a et seq. of Title 15]. The judgments made by the 75th Congress in enacting the Chandler Act are not equally applicable to the financial markets of 1978. First of all, most public debenture holders are neither weak nor unsophisticated investors. In most cases, a significant portion of the holders of publicly issued debentures are sophisticated institutions, acting for their own account or as trustees for investment funds, pension funds, or private trusts. In addition, debenture holders, sophisticated, and unsophisticated alike, are represented by indenture trustees, qualified under section 77ggg of the Trust Indenture Act [section 77ggg of Title 15, Commerce and Trade]. Given the high standard of care to which indenture trustees are bound, they are invariably active and sophisticated participants in efforts to rehabilitate corporate debtors in distress.

It is also important to note that in 1938 when the Chandler Act was enacted, public investors commonly held senior, not subordinated, debentures and corporations were very often privately owned. In this environment, the absolute priority rule protected debenture holders from an erosion of their position in favor of equity holders. Today, however, if there are public security holders in a case, they are likely to be holders of subordinated debentures and equity and thus the application of the absolute priority rule under chapter X [former section 501 et seq. of this title] leads to the exclusion, rather than the protection, of the public.

The primary problem posed by chapter X [former section 501 et seq. of this title] is delay. The modern corporation is a complex and multifaceted entity. Most corporations do not have a significant market share of the lines of business in which they compete. The success, and even the survival, of a corporation in contemporary markets depends on three elements: First, the ability to attract and hold skilled management; second, the ability to obtain credit; and third, the corporation's ability to project to the public an image of vitality. Over and over again, it is demonstrated that corporations which must avail themselves of the provisions of the Bankruptcy Act suffer appreciable deterioration if they are caught in a chapter X proceeding for any substantial period of time.

There are exceptions to this rule. For example, King Resources filed a chapter X [former section 501 et seq. of this title] petition in the District of Colorado and it emerged from such proceeding as a solvent corporation. The debtor's new found solvency was not, however,

so much attributable to a brilliant rehabilitation program conceived by a trustee, but rather to a substantial appreciation in the value of the debtor's oil and uranium properties during the pendency of the proceedings.

Likewise, Equity Funding is always cited as an example of a successful chapter X [former section 501 et seq. of this title] case. But it should be noted that in Equity Funding there was no question about retaining existing management. Rather, Equity Funding involved fraud on a grand scale. Under the House amendment with the deletion of the mandatory appointment of a trustee in cases involving "public companies," a bankruptcy judge, in a case like Equity Funding, would presumably have little difficulty in concluding that a trustee should be appointed under section 1104(6).

While I will not undertake to list the chapter X [former section 501 et seq. of this title] failures, it is important to note a number of cases involving corporations which would be "public companies" under the Senate amendment which have successfully skirted the shoals of chapter X and confirmed plans of arrangement in chapter XI [former section 701 et seq. of this title]. Among these are Daylin, Inc. ("Daylin") and Colwell Mortgage Investors ("Colwell").

Daylin filed a chapter XI [former section 701 et seq. of this title] petition on February 26, 1975, and confirmed its plan of arrangement on October 20, 1976. The success of its turnaround is best evidenced by the fact that it had consolidated net income of $6,473,000 for the first three quarters of the 1978 fiscal year.

Perhaps the best example of the contrast between chapter XI [former section 701 et seq. of this title] and chapter X [former section 501 et seq. of this title] is the recent case of In Re Colwell Mortgage Investors. Colwell negotiated a recapitalization plan with its institutional creditors, filed a proxy statement with the Securities and Exchange Commission, and solicited consents of its creditors and shareholders prior to filing its chapter XI petition. Thereafter, Colwell confirmed its plan of arrangement 41 days after filing its chapter XI petition. This result would have been impossible under the Senate amendment since Colwell would have been a "public company."

There are a number of other corporations with publicly held debt which have successfully reorganized under chapter XI [former section 701 et seq. of this title]. Among these are National Mortgage Fund (NMF), which filed a chapter XI petition in the northern district of Ohio on June 30, 1976. Prior to commencement of the chapter XI proceeding, NMF filed a proxy statement with the Securities and Exchange Commission and solicited acceptances to a proposed plan of arrangement. The NMF plan was subsequently confirmed on December 14, 1976. The Securities and Exchange Commission did not file a motion under section 328 of the Bankruptcy Act [former section 728 of this title] to transfer the case to chapter X [former section 501 et seq. of this title] and a transfer motion which was filed by private parties was denied by the court.

While there are other examples of large publicly held companies which have successfully reorganized in chapter XI [former section 701 et seq. of this title], including Esgrow, Inc. (C.D.Cal. 73–02510), Sherwood Diversified Services Inc. (S.D.N.Y. 73–B–213), and United Merchants and Manufacturers, Inc. (S.D.N.Y. 77–B–1513), the numerous successful chapter XI cases demonstrate two points: first, the complicated and time-consuming provisions of chapter X [former section 501 et seq. of this title] are not always necessary for the successful reorganization of a company with publicly held debt, and second, the more flexible provisions in chapter XI permit a debtor to obtain relief under the Bankruptcy Act in significantly less time than is required to confirm a plan of reorganization under chapter X of the Bankruptcy Act.

One cannot overemphasize the advantages of speed and simplicity to both creditors and debtors. Chapter XI [former section 701 et seq. of this title] allows a debtor to negotiate a plan outside of court and, having reached a settlement with a majority in number and amount of each class of creditors, permits the debtor to bind all unsecured creditors to the terms of the arrangement. From the perspective of creditors, early confirmation of a plan of arrangement: first, generally reduces administrative expenses which have priority over the claims of unsecured creditors; second, permits creditors to receive prompt distributions on their claims with respect to which interest does not accrue after the filing date; and third, increases the ultimate recovery on creditor claims by minimizing the adverse effect on the business which often accompanies efforts to operate an enterprise under the protection of the Bankruptcy Act.

Although chapter XI [former section 701 et seq. of this title] offers the corporate debtor flexibility and continuity of management, successful rehabilitation under chapter XI is oft-en impossible for a number of reasons. First, chapter XI does not permit a debtor to "affect" secured creditors or shareholders, in the absence of their consent. Second, whereas a debtor corporation in chapter X [former section 501 et seq. of this title], upon the consummation of the plan or reorganization, is discharged from all its debts and liabilities, a corporation in chapter XI may not be able to get a discharge in respect of certain kinds of claims including fraud claims, even in cases where the debtor is being operated under new management. The language of chapter 11 in the House amendment solves these problems and thus increases the utility and flexibility of the new chapter 11, as compared to chapter XI of the existing Bankruptcy Act.

Those who would urge the adoption of a two-track system have two major obstacles to meet. First, the practical experience of those involved in business rehabilitation cases, practitioners, debtors, and bankruptcy judges, has been that the more simple and expeditious procedures of chapter XI [former section 701 et seq. of this title] are appropriate in the great majority of cases. While attempts have been made to convince the courts that a chapter X [former section 501 et seq. of this title] proceeding is required in every case where public debt is present, the courts have categorically rejected such arguments. Second, chapter X has been far from a success. Of the 991 chapter X cases filed during the period of January 1, 1967, through December 31, 1977, only 664 have been terminated. Of those cases recorded as "terminated," only 140 resulted in consummated plans. This 21 percent success rate suggests one of the reasons for the unpopularity of chapter X.

In summary, it has been the experience of the great majority of those who have testified before the Senate and House subcommittees that a consolidated approach to business rehabilitation is warranted. Such approach is adopted in the House amendment.

Having discussed the general reasons why chapter 11 of the House amendment is sorely needed, a brief discussion of the differences between the House bill, Senate amendment, and the House amendment is in order. Since chapter 11 of the House amendment rejects the concept of separate treatment for a public company, sections 1101(3), 1104(a), 1125(f), 1128, and 1130(a)(7) of the Senate amendment have been deleted.

Effective Date of 1984 Amendments. Items 1113 and 1142 added by Pub.L. 98–353. See section 553 of Pub.L. 98–353, Title III,

July 10, 1984, 98 Stat. 392, set out as an Effective Date of 1984 Amendment note preceding chapter 1 of Title 11, Bankruptcy.

Separability of Provisions. For separability of provisions of Title III of Pub.L. 98–

353, see section 551 of Pub.L. 98–353 set out as a Separability of Provisions note preceding chapter 1 of Title 11, Bankruptcy.

Cross References

Allowance of administrative expenses of substantial contributors to cases under this chapter, see section 503.

Chapters 1, 3, and 5 of this title applicable in cases under this chapter except as provided in section 1161 of this title, see section 103.

Claims arising from rejection under chapter plans of executory contracts or unexpired leases, see section 502.

Commencement of involuntary cases, see section 303.

Conversion to this chapter from
Chapter 7, see section 706.
Chapter 13, see section 1307.

Duration of automatic stay, see section 362.

Employment of professional persons, see section 327.

Executory contracts and unexpired leases, see section 365.

Limitation on compensation of trustee, see section 326.

Persons who may be debtors under this chapter, see section 109.

Property of estate in cases converted from chapter 13, see section 1306.

Return of excessive attorney compensation if transferred property was to be paid by debtor under plan under this chapter, see section 329.

Special tax provisions, see sections 346.

Stay of action against chapter 13 codebtor in cases converted to this chapter, see section 1301.

Unclaimed property, see section 347.

Use, sale or lease of property under plan under this chapter, see section 363.

WESTLAW Electronic Research

See WESTLAW Electronic Research Guide following the *Bankruptcy Highlights*.

SUBCHAPTER I—OFFICERS AND ADMINISTRATION

Cross References

Subchapter applicable only in case under this chapter except as provided in section 901, see section 103.

§ 1101. Definitions for this chapter

In this chapter—

(1) "debtor in possession" means debtor except when a person that has qualified under section 322 of this title is serving as trustee in the case;

(2) "substantial consummation" means—

(A) transfer of all or substantially all of the property proposed by the plan to be transferred;

(B) assumption by the debtor or by the successor to the debtor under the plan of the business or of the management of all or substantially all of the property dealt with by the plan; and

(C) commencement of distribution under the plan.

Pub.L. 95–598, Nov. 6, 1978, 92 Stat. 2626.

Historical and Revision Notes

Note of Committee on the Judiciary, Senate Report No. 95–989. This section contains definitions of three terms that are used in chapter 11. Paragraph (1) defines debtor in possession to mean the debtor, except when a trustee who has qualified in serving in the case.

Paragraph (2), derived from section 229a of current law [former section 629(a) of this title], defines substantial consummation. Substantial consummation of a plan occurs when transfer of all or substantially all of the property proposed by the plan to be transferred is actually transferred; when the debtor (or its successor) has assumed the business of the debtor or the management of all or substantially all of the property dealt with by the plan; and when distribution under the plan has commenced.

Paragraph (3) defines for purposes of Chapter 11 a public company to mean "a debtor who, within 12 months prior to the filing of a petition for relief under this chapter, had outstanding liabilities of $5 million or more, exclusive of liabilities for goods, services, or taxes and not less than 1,000 security holders." There are, as noted, special safeguards for public investors related to the reorganization of a public company, as so defined.

Both requirements must be met: (1) liabilities, excluding tax obligations and trade liabilities, must be $5 million or more; and (2) the number of holders of securities, debt or equity, or both, must be not less than 1,000. The amount and number are to be determined as of any time within 12 months prior to the filing of the petition for reorganization.

Cross References

Definitions applicable in
    Cases under this title, see section 101.
    Chapter 9 cases, see section 902.
    Commodity broker liquidation cases, see section 761.
    Railroad reorganization cases, see section 1162.
    Stockbroker liquidation cases, see section 741.

Library References:

C.J.S. Bankruptcy § 368 et seq.
West's Key No. Digests, Bankruptcy ☞3501 et seq.

WESTLAW Electronic Research

See WESTLAW Electronic Research Guide following the *Bankruptcy Highlights*.

§ 1102.   Creditors' and equity security holders' committees

(a)(1) As soon as practicable after the order for relief under chapter 11 of this title, the United States trustee shall appoint a committee of creditors holding unsecured claims and may appoint additional committees of creditors or of equity security holders as the United States trustee deems appropriate.

(2) On request of a party in interest, the court may order the appointment of additional committees of creditors or of equity security holders if necessary to assure adequate representation of creditors or of equity security holders. The United States trustee shall appoint any such committee.

(b)(1) A committee of creditors appointed under subsection (a) of this section shall ordinarily consist of the persons, willing to serve, that hold the seven largest claims against the debtor of the kinds represented on such committee, or of the members of a committee organized by creditors before the commencement of the case under this chapter, if such committee was fairly chosen and is representative of the different kinds of claims to be represented.

(2) A committee of equity security holders appointed under subsection (a)(2) of this section shall ordinarily consist of the persons, willing to serve, that hold

the seven largest amounts of equity securities of the debtor of the kinds represented on such committee.

Pub.L. 95–598, Nov. 6, 1978, 92 Stat. 2626; Pub.L. 98–353, Title III, § 499, July 10, 1984, 98 Stat. 384; Pub.L. 99–554, Title II, § 221, Oct. 27, 1986, 100 Stat. 3101.

Historical and Revision Notes

Notes of Committee on the Judiciary, Senate Report No. 95–989. This section provides for the election and appointment of committees. Subsection (c) provides that this section does not apply in case of a public company, as to which a trustee, appointed under section 1104(a) will have responsibility to administer the estate and to formulate a plan as provided in section 1106(a).

There is no need for the election or appointment of committees for which the appointment of a trustee is mandatory. In the case of a public company there are likely to be several committees, each representing a different class of security holders and seeking authority to retain accountants, lawyers, and other experts, who will expect to be paid. If in the case of a public company creditors or stockholders wish to organize committees, they may do so, as authorized under section 1109(a). Compensation and reimbursement will be allowed for contributions to the reorganization pursuant to section 503(b)(3) and (4).

Notes of Committee on the Judiciary, House Report No. 95–595. This section provides for the appointment of creditors' and equity security holders' committees, which will be the primary negotiating bodies for the formulation of the plan of reorganization. They will represent the various classes of creditors and equity security holders from which they are selected. They will also provide supervision of the debtor in possession and of the trustee, and will protect their constituents' interests.

Subsection (a) requires the court to appoint at least one committee. That committee is to be composed of creditors holding unsecured claims. The court is authorized to appoint such additional committees as are necessary to assure adequate representation of creditors and equity security holders. The provision will be relied upon in cases in which the debtor proposes to affect several classes of debt or equity holders under the plan, and in which they need representation.

Subsection (b) contains precatory language directing the court to appoint the persons holding the seven largest claims against the debtor of the kinds represented on a creditors' committee, or the members of a prepetition committee organized by creditors before the order for relief under chapter 11. The court may continue prepetition committee members only if the committee was fairly chosen and is representative of the different kinds of claims to be represented. The court is restricted to the appointment of persons in order to exclude governmental holders of claims or interests.

Paragraph (2) of subsection (b) requires similar treatment for equity security holders' committees. The seven largest holders are normally to be appointed, but the language is only precatory.

Subsection (c) authorizes the court, on request of a party in interest, to change the size or the membership of a creditors' or equity security holders' committee if the membership of the committee is not representative of the different kinds of claims or interests to be represented. This subsection is intended, along with the nonbinding nature of subsection (b), to afford the court latitude in appointing a committee that is manageable and representative in light of the circumstances of the case.

Legislative Statements. Section 1102(a) of the House amendment adopts a compromise between the House bill and Senate amendment requiring appointment of a committee of creditors holding unsecured claims by the court; the alternative of creditor committee election is rejected.

Section 1102(b) of the House amendment represents a compromise between the House bill and the Senate amendment by preventing the appointment of creditors who are unwilling to serve on a creditors committee.

1986 Amendment. Subsec. (a)(1). Pub.L. 99–554, § 221(1), substituted "under chapter 11 of this title, the United States trustee shall appoint" for "under this chapter, the court shall appoint" and added "and may appoint additional committees of creditors or of equity security holders as the United States trustee deems appropriate." following "unsecured claims".

Subsec. (a)(2). Pub.L. 99–554, § 221(1), substituted "The United States trustee shall appoint" for "The court shall appoint".

Subsec. (c). Pub.L. 99–554, § 221(2), struck out subsec. (c) which read as follows: "On request of a party in interest and after notice and a hearing, the court may change the membership or the size of a committee appointed under subsection (a) of this section if the membership of such committee is not representative of the different kinds of claims or interests to be represented.".

See Effective Date of 1986 Amendment, etc., notes set out below.

Effective Date of 1986 Amendments; Effective Date of 1986 Amendments for Certain Judicial Districts Not Served by United States Trustees and for Judicial Districts in Alabama and North Carolina; U.S. Trustee System Fund Deposits in Alabama and North Carolina; Effective Date of Title 11 Chapter 15 Repeal as to Northern District of Alabama; Authority of Certain Estate Administrators in Alabama and North Carolina; Effective Date of 1986 Amendments in Pending Cases Where a U.S. Trustee Not Authorized or Where a Trustee Files Final Report or Plan is Confirmed; Quarterly Fees. Amendment by Pub.L. 99–554 effective 30 days after Oct. 27, 1986, except as otherwise provided for, see section 302(a) of Pub.L. 99–554, set out as a note under section 581 of Title 28, Judiciary and Judicial Procedure.

Amendment by Pub.L. 99–554, § 221, not to become effective in or with respect to certain specified judicial districts until, or apply to cases while pending in such district before, the expiration of the 270–day period beginning 30 days after Oct. 27, 1986, or of the 30–day period beginning on the date the Attorney General certifies under section 303 of Pub.L. 99–554 the region specified in a paragraph of section 581(a) of Title 28, as amended by section 111(a) of Pub.L. 99–554, that includes such district, whichever occurs first, see section 302(d)(1) of Pub.L. 99–554, set out as a note under section 581 of Title 28.

Amendment by Pub.L. 99–554, § 221, not to become effective in or with respect to certain specified judicial districts until, or apply to cases while pending in such district before, the expiration of the 2–year period beginning 30 days after Oct. 27, 1986, or of the 30–day period beginning on the date the Attorney

General certifies under section 303 of Pub.L. 99–554 the region specified in a paragraph of section 581(a) of Title 28, as amended by section 111(a) of Pub.L. 99–554, that includes such district, whichever occurs first, see section 302(d)(2) of Pub.L. 99–554, set out as a note under section 581 of Title 28.

Amendment by Pub.L. 99–554, § 221, not to become effective in or with respect to judicial districts established for the States of Alabama and North Carolina until, or apply to cases while pending in such district before, such district elects to be included in a bankruptcy region established in section 581(a) of Title 28, as amended by section 111(a) of Pub.L. 99–554, or Oct. 1, 2002, whichever occurs first, and, except as otherwise provided for, with respect to cases under chapters 7, 11, 12, and 13 of Title 11 commenced before 30 days after Oct. 27, 1986, and pending in a judicial district in the States of Alabama or North Carolina before any election made under section 302(d)(3)(A) of Pub.L. 99–554 by such district becomes effective or Oct. 1, 2002, whichever occurs first, amendments by Pub.L. 99–554 not to apply until Oct. 1, 2003, or the expiration of the 1–year period beginning on the date such election becomes effective, whichever occurs first, and further, in any judicial district in Alabama or North Carolina not making the election described in section 302(d)(3)(A) of Pub.L. 99–554, any person appointed under regulations issued by the Judicial Conference to administer estates in cases under Title 11 authorized to establish, etc., a panel of private trustees, and to supervise cases and trustees in cases under chapters 7, 11, 12, and 13 of Title 11, until amendments by sections 201 to 231 of Pub.L. 99–554 effective in such district, see section 302(d)(3)(A) to (F), (H), (I) of Pub.L. 99–554, set out as a note under section 581 of Title 28.

Amendment by Pub.L. 99–554, § 221, except as otherwise provided, with respect to cases under chapters 7, 11, 12, and 13 of Title 11 commenced before 30 days after Oct. 27, 1986, and pending in a judicial district referred to in section 581(a) of Title 28, as amended by section 111(a) of Pub.L. 99–554, for which a United States trustee is not authorized before 30 days after Oct. 27, 1986 to be appointed, not applicable until the expiration of the 3–year period beginning on Oct. 27, 1986, or of the 1–year period beginning on the date the Attorney General certifies under section 303 of Pub.L. 99–554 the region specified in a paragraph of such section 581(a) that includes, such district, whichever occurs first, see section 302(e)(1), (2) of Pub.L. 99–554, set out as a note under section 581 of Title 28.

See 1986 Amendment notes set out above.

Effective Date of 1984 Amendments. See section 553 of Pub.L. 98–353, Title III, July 10, 1984, 98 Stat. 392, set out as an Effective Date of 1984 Amendment note preceding chapter 1 of Title 11, Bankruptcy.

Separability of Provisions. For separability of provisions of Title III of Pub.L. 98–353, see section 551 of Pub.L. 98–353 set out as a Separability of Provisions note preceding chapter 1 of Title 11, Bankruptcy.

Cross References

Applicability of this section in chapter 9 cases, see section 901.

Creditors' committees in chapter 7 cases, see section 705.

Disallowance of administrative expenses for creditors' and equity security holders' committees, see section 503.

Effect of conversion, see section 348.

Inapplicability of subsec. (a)(1) of this section to railroad reorganization cases, see section 1161.

Limitation on compensation of professional persons, see section 328.

Library References:

C.J.S. Bankruptcy §§ 193, 373.

West's Key No. Digests, Bankruptcy ⬯3024.

WESTLAW Electronic Research

See WESTLAW Electronic Research Guide following the *Bankruptcy Highlights*.

§ 1103. Powers and duties of committees

(a) At a scheduled meeting of a committee appointed under section 1102 of this title, at which a majority of the members of such committee are present, and with the court's approval, such committee may select and authorize the employment by such committee of one or more attorneys, accountants, or other agents, to represent or perform services for such committee.

(b) An attorney or accountant employed to represent a committee appointed under section 1102 of this title may not, while employed by such committee, represent any other entity having an adverse interest in connection with the case. Representation of one or more creditors of the same class as represented by the committee shall not per se constitute the representation of an adverse interest.

(c) A committee appointed under section 1102 of this title may—

(1) consult with the trustee or debtor in possession concerning the administration of the case;

(2) investigate the acts, conduct, assets, liabilities, and financial condition of the debtor, the operation of the debtor's business and the desirability of the continuance of such business, and any other matter relevant to the case or to the formulation of a plan;

(3) participate in the formulation of a plan, advise those represented by such committee of such committee's determinations as to any plan formulated, and collect and file with the court acceptances or rejections of a plan;

(4) request the appointment of a trustee or examiner under section 1104 of this title; and

(5) perform such other services as are in the interest of those represented.

(d) As soon as practicable after the appointment of a committee under section 1102 of this title, the trustee shall meet with such committee to transact such business as may be necessary and proper.

Pub.L. 95–598, Nov. 6, 1978, 92 Stat. 2627; Pub.L. 98–353, Title III, §§ 324, 500, July 10, 1984, 98 Stat. 358, 384.

Historical and Revision Notes

Notes of Committee on the Judiciary, Senate Report No. 95–989. This section defines the powers and duties of a committee elected or appointed under section 1102.

Under subsection (a) the committee may, if authorized by the court, employ one or more attorneys, accountants, or other agents to represent or perform services for the committee. Normally one attorney should suffice; more than one may be authorized for good cause. The same considerations apply to the services of others, if the need for any at all is demonstrated.

Under subsections (c) and (d) the committee, like any party in interest, may confer with the trustee or debtor regarding the administration of the estate; may advise the court on the need for a trustee under section 1104(b). The committee may investigate matters specified in paragraph (2) of subsection (c), but only if authorized by the court and if no trustee or examiner is appointed.

Effective Date of 1984 Amendments. See section 553 of Pub.L. 98–353, Title III, July 10, 1984, 98 Stat. 392, set out as an Effective Date of 1984 Amendment note preceding chapter 1 of Title 11, Bankruptcy.

Separability of Provisions. For separability of provisions of Title III of Pub.L. 98–353, see section 551 of Pub.L. 98–353 set out as a Separability of Provisions note preceding chapter 1 of Title 11, Bankruptcy.

Cross References

Applicability of this section in chapter 9 cases, see section 901.
Compensation of officers, see section 330.
Creditors' committees in chapter 7 cases, see section 705.
Interim compensation for professional persons, see section 331.
Limitation on compensation of professional persons, see section 328.

Library References:

C.J.S. Bankruptcy §§ 193, 373.
West's Key No. Digests, Bankruptcy ⊛3024.

WESTLAW Electronic Research

See WESTLAW Electronic Research Guide following the *Bankruptcy Highlights*.

§ 1104.　Appointment of trustee or examiner

(a) At any time after the commencement of the case but before confirmation of a plan, on request of a party in interest or the United States trustee, and after notice and a hearing, the court shall order the appointment of a trustee—

(1) for cause, including fraud, dishonesty, incompetence, or gross mismanagement of the affairs of the debtor by current management, either before or after the commencement of the case, or similar cause, but not including the number of holders of securities of the debtor or the amount of assets or liabilities of the debtor; or

(2) if such appointment is in the interests of creditors, any equity security holders, and other interests of the estate, without regard to the

number of holders of securities of the debtor or the amount of assets or liabilities of the debtor.

(b) If the court does not order the appointment of a trustee under this section, then at any time before the confirmation of a plan, on request of a party in interest or the United States trustee, and after notice and a hearing, the court shall order the appointment of an examiner to conduct such an investigation of the debtor as is appropriate, including an investigation of any allegations of fraud, dishonesty, incompetence, misconduct, mismanagement, or irregularity in the management of the affairs of the debtor of or by current or former management of the debtor, if—

(1) such appointment is in the interests of creditors, any equity security holders, and other interests of the estate; or

(2) the debtor's fixed, liquidated, unsecured debts, other than debts for goods, services, or taxes, or owing to an insider, exceed $5,000,000.

(c) If the court orders the appointment of a trustee or an examiner, if a trustee or an examiner dies or resigns during the case or is removed under section 324 of this title, or if a trustee fails to qualify under section 322 of this title, then the United States trustee, after consultation with parties in interest, shall appoint, subject to the court's approval, one disinterested person other than the United States trustee to serve as trustee or examiner, as the case may be, in the case.

Pub.L. 95–598, Nov. 6, 1978, 92 Stat. 2627; Pub.L. 99–554, Title II, § 222, Oct. 27, 1986, 100 Stat. 3102.

Historical and Revision Notes

Notes of Committee on the Judiciary, Senate Report No. 95–989. Subsection (a) provides for the mandatory appointment of a disinterested trustee in the case of a public company, as defined in section 1101(3), within 10 days of the order for relief, or of a successor, in the event of a vacancy, as soon as practicable.

Section 156 of chapter X (11 U.S.C. 516) [former section 516 of this title] requires the appointment of a disinterested trustee if the debtor's liabilities are $250,000 or over. Section 1104(a) marks a substantial change. The appointment of a trustee is mandatory only for a public company, which under section 1101(3), has $5 million in liabilities, excluding tax and trade obligations, and 1,000 security holders. In view of past experience, cases involving public companies will under normal circumstances probably be relatively few in number but of vast importance in terms of public investor interest.

In case of a nonpublic company, the appointment or election of a trustee is discretionary if the interests of the estate and its security holders would be served thereby. A test based on probable costs and benefits of a trusteeship is not practical. The appointment may be made at any time prior to confirmation of the plan.

In case of a nonpublic company, if no trustee is appointed, the court may under subsection (c) appoint an examiner, if the appointment would serve the interests of the estate and security holders. The purpose of his appointment is specified in section 1106(b).

Notes of Committee on the Judiciary, House Report No. 95–595. Subsection (a) of this section governs the appointment of trustees in reorganization cases. The court is permitted to order the appointment of one trustee at any time after the commencement of the case if a party in interest so requests. The court may order appointment only if the protection afforded by a trustee is needed and the costs and expenses of a trustee would not be disproportionately higher than the value of the protection afforded.

The protection afforded by a trustee would be needed, for example, in cases where the current management of the debtor has been fraudulent or dishonest, or has grossly mismanaged the company, or where the debtor's management has abandoned the business. A trustee would not necessarily be needed to investigate misconduct of former management of the debtor, because an examiner appointed under this section might well be able to serve that function adequately without displacing the current management. Generally, a trustee would not be needed in any case where the protection afforded by a trustee could equally be afforded by an examiner. Though the device of examiner appears in current chapter X [former section 501 et seq. of this title], it is rarely used because of the nearly absolute presumption in favor of the appointment of a trustee. Its use here will give the courts, debtors, creditors, and equity security holders greater flexibility in handling the affairs of an insolvent debtor, permitting the court to tailor the remedy to the case.

The second test, relating to the costs and expenses of a trustee, is not intended to be a strict cost/benefit analysis. It is included to require the court to have due regard for any additional costs or expenses that the appointment of a trustee would impose on the estate.

Subsection (b) permits the court, at any time after the commencement of the case and on request of a party in interest, to order the appointment of an examiner, if the court has not ordered the appointment of a trustee. The examiner would be appointed to conduct such an investigation of the debtor as is appropriate under the particular circumstances of the case, including an investigation of any allegations of fraud, dishonesty, or gross mismanagement of the debtor of or by current or former management of the debtor. The standards for the appointment of an examiner are the same as those for the appointment of a trustee: the protection must be needed, and the costs and expenses must not be disproportionately high.

By virtue of proposed 11 U.S.C. 1109, an indenture trustee and the Securities and Exchange Commission will be parties in interest for the purpose of requesting the appointment of a trustee or examiner.

Subsection (c) directs that the United States trustee actually select and appoint the trustee or examiner ordered appointed under this section. The United States trustee is required to consult with various parties in interest before selecting and appointing a trustee. He is not bound to select one of the members of the panel of private trustees established under proposed 28 U.S.C. 586(a)(1) which exists only for the purpose of providing trustees for chapter 7 cases. Neither is he precluded from selecting a panel member if the member is qualified to serve as chapter 11 trustee. Appointment by the United States trustee will remove the court from the often criticized practice of appointing an officer that will appear in litigation before the court against an adverse party.

Legislative Statements. Section 1104 of the House amendment represents a compromise between the House bill and the Senate amendment concerning the appointment of a trustee or examiner. The method of appointment rather than election, is derived from the House bill; the two alternative standards of appointment are derived with modifications from the Senate amendment, instead of the standard stated in the House bill. For example, if the current management of the debtor gambled away rental income before the filing of the petition, a trustee should be appointed after the petition, whether or not postpetition mismanagement can be shown. However, under no circumstances will cause include the number of security holders of the debtor or the amount of assets or liabilities of the debtor. The standard also applies to the appointment of an examiner in those circumstances in which mandatory appointment, as previously detailed, is not required.

1986 Amendment. Subsec. (a). Pub.L. 99–554, § 222(1), added "or the United States trustee" following "party in interest".

Subsec. (b). Pub.L. 99–554, § 222(2), added "or the United States trustee" following "party in interest".

Subsec. (c). Pub.L. 99–554, § 222(3), substituted "the United States trustee after consultation with parties in interest, shall appoint, subject to the court's approval, one disinterested person other than the United States trustee to serve" for "the court shall appoint one disinterested person to serve".

See Effective Date of 1986 Amendment, etc., notes set out below.

Effective Date of 1986 Amendments; Savings Provisions; Effective Date of 1986 Amendments for Certain Judicial Districts Not Served by United States Trustees and for Judicial Districts in Alabama and North Carolina; U.S. Trustee System Fund Deposits in Alabama and North Carolina; Effective Date of Title 11 Chapter 15 Repeal as to Northern District of Alabama; Authority of Certain Estate Administrators in Alabama and North Carolina; Effective Date of 1986 Amendments in Pending Cases Where a U.S. Trustee Not Authorized or Where a Trustee Files Final

Report or Plan is Confirmed; Quarterly Fees. Amendment by Pub.L. 99–554 effective 30 days after Oct. 27, 1986, except as otherwise provided for, see section 302(a) of Pub.L. 99–554, set out as a note under section 581 of Title 28, Judiciary and Judicial Procedure.

Amendment by Pub.L. 99–554, § 222, not to become effective in or with respect to certain specified judicial districts until, or apply to cases while pending in such district before, the expiration of the 270-day period beginning 30 days after Oct. 27, 1986, or of the 30-day period beginning on the date the Attorney General certifies under section 303 of Pub.L. 99–554 the region specified in a paragraph of section 581(a) of Title 28, as amended by section 111(a) of Pub.L. 99–554, that includes such district, whichever occurs first, see section 302(d)(1) of Pub.L. 99–554, set out as a note under section 581 of Title 28.

Amendment by Pub.L. 99–554, § 222 not to become effective in or with respect to certain specified judicial districts until, or apply to cases while pending in such district before, the expiration of the 2-year period beginning 30 days after Oct. 27, 1986, or of the 30-day period beginning on the date the Attorney General certifies under section 303 of Pub.L. 99–554 the region specified in a paragraph of section 581(a) of Title 28, as amended by section 111(a) of Pub.L. 99–554, that includes such district, whichever occurs first, see section 302(d)(2) of Pub.L. 99–554, set out as a note under section 581 of Title 28.

Amendment by Pub.L. 99–554, § 222, not to become effective in or with respect to judicial districts established for the States of Alabama and North Carolina until, or apply to cases while pending in such district before, such district elects to be included in a bankruptcy region established in section 581(a) of Title 28, as amended by section 111(a) of Pub.L. 99–554, or Oct. 1, 2002, whichever occurs first, and, except as otherwise provided for, with respect to cases under chapters 7, 11, 12, and 13 of Title 11 commenced before 30 days after Oct. 27, 1986, and pending in a judicial district in the States of Alabama or North Carolina before any election made under section 302(d)(3)(A) of Pub.L. 99–554 by such district becomes effective or Oct. 1, 2002, whichever occurs first, amendments by Pub.L. 99–554 not to apply until Oct. 1, 2003, or the expiration of the 1-year period beginning on the date such election becomes effective, whichever occurs first, and further, in any judicial district in Alabama or North Carolina not making the election described in section 302(d)(3)(A) of Pub.L. 99–554, any person appointed under regulations issued by the Judicial Conference to administer estates in cases under Title 11 authorized to establish, etc., a panel of private trustees, and to supervise cases and trustees in cases under chapters 7, 11, 12, and 13 of Title 11, until amendments by sections 201 to 231 of Pub.L. 99–554 effective in such district, see section 302(d)(3)(A) to (F), (H), (I) of Pub.L. 99–554, set out as a note under section 581 of Title 28.

Amendment by Pub.L. 99–554, § 222, except as otherwise provided, with respect to cases under chapters 7, 11, 12, and 13 of Title 11 commenced before 30 days after Oct. 27, 1986, and pending in a judicial district referred to in section 581(a) of Title 28, as amended by section 111(a) of Pub.L. 99–554, for which a United States trustee is not authorized before 30 days after Oct. 27, 1986 to be appointed, not applicable until the expiration of the 3-year period beginning on Oct. 27, 1986, or of the 1-year period beginning on the date the Attorney General certifies under section 303 of Pub.L. 99–554 the region specified in a paragraph of such section 581(a) that includes, such district, whichever occurs first, see section 302(e)(1), (2) of Pub.L. 99–554 set out as a note under section 581 of Title 28.

See 1986 Amendment notes set out above.

Cross References

Appointment of trustee in
    Chapter 13 cases, see section 1302.
    Railroad reorganization cases, see section 1163.
Election of trustee, see section 702.
Grant of damages to debtor proximately caused by trustee taking possession of debtor's property, see section 303.
Inapplicability of this section to
    Railroad reorganization cases, see section 1161.
Qualification of trustee, see section 322.
Time for bringing action, see section 546.

§ 1105. Termination of trustee's appointment

At any time before confirmation of a plan, on request of a party in interest or the United States trustee, and after notice and a hearing, the court may terminate the trustee's appointment and restore the debtor to possession and management of the property of the estate and of the operation of the debtor's business.

Pub.L. 95–598, Nov. 6, 1978, 92 Stat. 2628; Pub.L. 98–353, Title III, § 501, July 10, 1984, 98 Stat. 384; Pub.L. 99–554, Title II, § 223, Oct. 27, 1986, 100 Stat. 3102.

Historical and Revision Notes

Notes of Committee on the Judiciary, Senate Report No. 95–989. This section authorizes the court to terminate the trustee's appointment and to restore the debtor to possession and management of the property of the estate and to operation of the debtor's business. Section 1104(a) provides that this section does not apply in the case of a public company, for which the appointment of a trustee is mandatory.

Notes of Committee on the Judiciary, House Report No. 95–595. This section authorizes the court to terminate the trustee's appointment and to restore the debtor to possession and management of the property of the estate, and to operation of the debtor's business. This section would permit the court to reverse its decision to order the appointment of a trustee in light of new evidence.

1986 Amendment. Pub.L. 99–554, § 223, added "or the United States trustee" following "party in interest".

See Effective Date of 1986 Amendment, etc., notes set out below.

Effective Date of 1986 Amendments; Effective Date of 1986 Amendments for Certain Judicial Districts Not Served by United States Trustees and for Judicial Districts in Alabama and North Carolina; U.S. Trustee System Fund Deposits in Alabama and North Carolina; Effective Date of Title 11 Chapter 15 Repeal as to Northern District of Alabama; Authority of Certain Estate Administrators in Alabama and North Carolina; Effective Date of 1986 Amendments in Pending Cases Where a

U.S. Trustee Not Authorized or Where a Trustee Files Final Report or Plan is Confirmed; Quarterly Fees. Amendment by Pub.L. 99–554 effective 30 days after Oct. 27, 1986, except as otherwise provided for, see section 302(a) of Pub.L. 99–554, set out as a note under section 581 of Title 28, Judiciary and Judicial Procedure.

Amendment by Pub.L. 99–554, § 223, not to become effective in or with respect to certain specified judicial districts until, or apply to cases while pending in such district before, the expiration of the 270-day period beginning 30 days after Oct. 27, 1986, or of the 30-day period beginning on the date the Attorney General certifies under section 303 of Pub.L. 99–554 the region specified in a paragraph of section 581(a) of Title 28, as amended by section 111(a) of Pub.L. 99–554, that includes such district, whichever occurs first, see section 302(d)(1) of Pub.L. 99–554, set out as a note under section 581 of Title 28.

Amendment by Pub.L. 99–554, § 223, not to become effective in or with respect to certain specified judicial districts until, or apply to cases while pending in such district before, the expiration of the 2-year period beginning 30 days after Oct. 27, 1986, or of the 30-day period beginning on the date the Attorney General certifies under section 303 of Pub.L. 99–554 the region specified in a paragraph of section 581(a) of Title 28, as amended by section 111(a) of Pub.L. 99–554, that includes such district, whichever occurs first, see section 302(d)(2) of Pub.L. 99–554, set out as a note under section 581 of Title 28.

Amendment by Pub.L. 99–554, § 223, not to become effective in or with respect to judicial districts established for the States of Alabama and North Carolina until, or apply to cases while pending in such district before, such district elects to be included in a bankruptcy region established in section 581(a) of Title 28, as amended by section 111(a) of Pub.L. 99–554, or Oct. 1, 2002, whichever occurs first, and, except as otherwise provided for, with respect to cases under chapters 7, 11, 12, and 13 of Title 11 commenced before 30 days after Oct. 27, 1986, and pending in a judicial district in the States of Alabama or North Carolina before any election made under section 302(d)(3) (A) of Pub.L. 99–554 by such district becomes effective or Oct. 1, 2002, whichever occurs first, amendments by Pub.L. 99–554 not to apply until Oct. 1, 2003, or the expiration of the 1-year period beginning on the date such election becomes effective, whichever occurs first, and further, in any judicial district in Alabama or North Carolina not making the election described in section 302(d)(3)(A) of Pub.L. 99–554, any person appointed under regulations issued by the Judicial Conference to administer estates in cases under Title 11 authorized to establish, etc., a panel of private trustees, and to supervise cases and trustees in cases under chapters 7, 11, 12, and 13 of Title 11, until amendments by sections 201 to 231 of Pub.L. 99–554 effective in such district, see section 302(d)(3)(A) to (F), (H), (I) of Pub.L.

99–554, set out as a note under section 581 of Title 28.

Amendment by Pub.L. 99–554, § 223, except as otherwise provided, with respect to cases under chapters 7, 11, 12, and 13 of Title 11 commenced before 30 days after Oct. 27, 1986, and pending in a judicial district referred to in section 581(a) of Title 28, as amended by section 111(a) of Pub.L. 99–554, for which a United States trustee is not authorized before 30 days after Oct. 27, 1986 to be appointed, not applicable until the expiration of the 3-year period beginning on Oct. 27, 1986, or of the 1-year period beginning on the date the Attorney General certifies under section 303 of Pub.L. 99–554 the region specified in a paragraph of such section 581(a) that includes, such district, whichever occurs first, see section 302(e)(1), (2) of Pub.L. 99–554, set out as a note under section 581 of Title 28.

See 1986 Amendment notes set out above.

Effective Date of 1984 Amendments. See section 553 of Pub.L. 98–353, Title III, July 10, 1984, 98 Stat. 392, set out as an Effective Date of 1984 Amendment note preceding chapter 1 of Title 11, Bankruptcy.

Separability of Provisions. For separability of provisions of Title III of Pub.L. 98–353, see section 551 of Pub.L. 98–353 set out as a Separability of Provisions note preceding chapter 1 of Title 11, Bankruptcy.

Cross References

Effect of vacancy in office of trustee, see section 325.
Inapplicability of this section to Railroad reorganization cases, see section 1161.
Removal of trustee, see section 324.

Library References:

C.J.S. Bankruptcy § 196.
West's Key No. Digests, Bankruptcy ⬥3007.

WESTLAW Electronic Research

See WESTLAW Electronic Research Guide following the *Bankruptcy Highlights*.

§ 1106.   Duties of trustee and examiner

(a) A trustee shall—

    (1) perform the duties of a trustee specified in sections 704(2), 704(5), 704(7), 704(8), and 704(9) of this title;

    (2) if the debtor has not done so, file the list, schedule, and statement required under section 521(1) of this title;

    (3) except to the extent that the court orders otherwise, investigate the acts, conduct, assets, liabilities, and financial condition of the debtor, the operation of the debtor's business and the desirability of the continuance of

such business, and any other matter relevant to the case or to the formulation of a plan;

(4) as soon as practicable—

(A) file a statement of any investigation conducted under paragraph (3) of this subsection, including any fact ascertained pertaining to fraud, dishonesty, incompetence, misconduct, mismanagement, or irregularity in the management of the affairs of the debtor, or to a cause of action available to the estate; and

(B) transmit a copy or a summary of any such statement to any creditors' committee or equity security holders' committee, to any indenture trustee, and to such other entity as the court designates;

(5) as soon as practicable, file a plan under section 1121 of this title, file a report of why the trustee will not file a plan, or recommend conversion of the case to a case under chapter 7, 12, or 13 of this title or dismissal of the case;

(6) for any year for which the debtor has not filed a tax return required by law, furnish, without personal liability, such information as may be required by the governmental unit with which such tax return was to be filed, in light of the condition of the debtor's books and records and the availability of such information; and

(7) after confirmation of a plan, file such reports as are necessary or as the court orders.

(b) An examiner appointed under section 1104(c) of this title shall perform the duties specified in paragraphs (3) and (4) of subsection (a) of this section, and, except to the extent that the court orders otherwise, any other duties of the trustee that the court orders the debtor in possession not to perform.

Pub.L. 95–598, Nov. 6, 1978, 92 Stat. 2628; Pub.L. 98–353, Title III, §§ 311(b)(1), 502, July 10, 1984, 98 Stat. 355, 384; Pub.L. 99–554, Title II, § 257(c), Oct. 27, 1986, 100 Stat. 3114.

Historical and Revision Notes

Notes of Committee on the Judiciary, Senate Report No. 95–989. Subsection (a) of this section prescribes the trustee's duties. He is required to perform the duties of a trustee in a liquidation case specified in section 704(2), (4), (6), (7), (8), and (9). These include reporting and informational duties, and accountability for all property received. Paragraph (2) of this subsection requires the trustee to file with the court, if the debtor has not done so, the list of creditors, schedule of assets and liabilities, and statement of affairs required under section 521(1).

Paragraph (3) of S. 1106 requires the trustee to investigate the acts, conduct, assets, liabilities, and financial condition of the debtor, the operation of the debtor's business, and the desirability of the continuance of the business, and any other matter relevant to the case or to the formulation of a plan. Paragraph (4) requires the trustee to report the results of his investigation to the court and to creditors' committees, equity security holders' committees, indenture trustees and any other entity the court designates.

Paragraph (5) requires the trustee to file a plan or to report why a plan cannot be formulated, or to recommend conversion to liquidation or to an individual repayment plan case, or dismissal. It is anticipated that the trustee will consult with creditors and other parties in interest in the formulation of a plan, just as the debtor in possession would.

Paragraph (6) [now (7)] requires final reports by the trustee, as the court orders.

Subsection (b) gives the trustee's investigative duties to an examiner, if one is appointed. The court is authorized to give the examiner additional duties as the circumstances warrant.

Paragraphs (3), (4), and (5) of subsection (a) are derived from sections 165 and 169 of chapter X (11 U.S.C. 565, 569) [former sections 565 and 569 of this title, respectively].

Effective Date of 1986 Amendments; Savings Provisions; Quarterly Fees. Amendment by Pub.L. 99–554 effective 30 days after Oct. 27, 1986, except as otherwise provided for, see section 302(a) of Pub.L. 99–554, set out as a note under section 581 of Title 28, Judiciary and Judicial Procedure.

Amendments by Pub.L. 99–554, § 257(c), not to apply with respect to cases commenced under Title 11, Bankruptcy, before 30 days after Oct. 27, 1986, see section 302(c)(1) of Pub. L. 99–554, set out as a note under section 581 of Title 28.

Effective Date of 1984 Amendments. See section 553 of Pub.L. 98–353, Title III, July 10, 1984, 98 Stat. 392, set out as an Effective Date of 1984 Amendment note preceding chapter 1 of Title 11, Bankruptcy.

Separability of Provisions. For separability of provisions of Title III of Pub.L. 98–353, see section 551 of Pub.L. 98–353 set out as a Separability of Provisions note preceding chapter 1 of Title 11, Bankruptcy.

Payment of Benefits to Retired Former Employees; Covered Benefits and Employees; Payments, Procedures, Etc. Pub.L. 99–591, Title I, § 101(b) [Title VI, § 608], Oct. 30, 1986, 99 Stat. 3341–74, as amended Pub.L. 100–41, May 15, 1987, 101 Stat. 309; Pub.L. 100–99, Aug. 18, 1987, 101 Stat. 716; Pub.L. 100–334, § 3(a), June 16, 1988, 102 Stat. 613, provided that:

"(a)(1) Subject to paragraphs (2), (3), (4), and (5), and notwithstanding title 11 of the United States Code [this title] the trustee shall pay benefits to retired former employees under a plan, fund, or program maintained or established by the debtor prior to filing a petition (through the purchase of insurance or otherwise) for the purpose of providing medical, surgical, or hospital care benefits, or benefits in the event of sickness, accident, disability, or death.

"(2) The level of benefits required to be paid by this subsection may be modified prior to confirmation of a plan under section 1129 of such title [section 1129 of this title] if—

"(A) the trustee and an authorized representative of the former employees with respect to whom such benefits are payable agree to the modification of such benefit payments; or

"(B) the court finds that a modification proposed by the trustee meets the standards of section 1113(b)(1)(A) of such title [section 1113(b)(1)(A) of this title] and the balance of the equities clearly favors the modification.

"If such benefits are covered by a collective bargaining agreement, the authorized representative shall be the labor organization that is signatory to such collective bargaining agreement unless there is a conflict of interest.

"(3) The trustee shall pay benefits in accordance with this subsection until—

"(A) the dismissal of the case involved; or

"(B) the effective date of a plan confirmed under section 1129 of such title which provides for the continued payment after confirmation of the plan of all such benefits at the level established under paragraph (2) of this subsection, at any time prior to the confirmation of the plan, for the duration of the period the debtor (as defined in such title) has obligated itself to provide such benefits.

"(4) No such benefits paid between the filing of a petition in a case covered by this section and the time a plan confirmed under section 1129 of such title with respect to such case becomes effective shall be deducted or offset from the amount allowed as claims for any benefits which remain unpaid, or from the amount to be paid under the plan with respect to such claims for unpaid benefits, whether such claims for unpaid benefits are based upon or arise from a right to future benefits or from any benefit not paid as a result of modifications allowed pursuant to this section.

"(5) No claim for benefits covered by this section shall be limited by section 502(b)(7) of such title [section 502(b)(7) of this title].

"(b)(1) Notwithstanding any provision of title 11 of the United States Code [this title], the trustee shall pay an allowable claim of any person for a benefit paid—

"(A) before the filing of the petition under title 11 of the United States Code; and

"(B) directly or indirectly to a retired former employee under a plan, fund, or program described in subsection (a)(1);

if, as determined by the court, such person is entitled to recover from such employee, or any provider of health care to such employee, directly or indirectly, the amount of such benefit for which such person receives no payment from the debtor.

"(2) For purposes of paragraph (1), the term 'provider of health care' means a person who—

"(A) is the direct provider of health care (including a physician, dentist, nurse, podiatrist, optometrist, physician assistant, or ancillary personnel employed under the supervision of a physician); or

"(B) administers a facility or institution (including a hospital, alcohol and drug abuse treatment facility, outpatient facility, or health maintenance organization) in which health care is provided.

"(c) This section is effective with respect to cases commenced under chapter 11, of title 11, United States Code [this chapter], in which a plan for reorganization has not been confirmed by the court and in which any such benefit is still being paid on Octo-ber 2, 1986, and in cases that become subject to chapter 11, title 11, United States Code, after October 2, 1986 and before the date of the enactment of the Retiree Benefits Bankruptcy Protection Act of 1988 [June 16, 1988].

"(d) This section shall not apply during any period in which a case is subject to chapter 7, title 11, United States Code [11 U.S.C.A. § 701 et seq.]."

[A similar provision to Pub.L. 99–591 but not amended by subsequent law was enacted by Pub.L. 99–500, Title I, § 101(b) [Title VI, § 608], Oct. 18, 1986, 100 Stat. 1783–74.]

Payment of Certain Benefits to Retired Former Employees. Pub.L. 99–656, § 2, Nov. 14, 1986, 100 Stat. 3668, as amended Pub.L. 100–41, May 15, 1987, 101 Stat. 309; Pub.L. 100–99, Aug. 18, 1987, 101 Stat. 716, which related to payment of benefits by bankruptcy trustee until Oct. 15, 1987, to retired former employees in enumerated instances, was repealed by Pub.L. 100–334, § 3(b), June 16, 1988, 102 Stat. 614.

Cross References

Additional duties of trustees in chapter 13 cases, see section 1302.

Library References:

C.J.S. Bankruptcy §§ 197, 376.
West's Key No. Digests, Bankruptcy ⚷3008, 3627.

WESTLAW Electronic Research

See WESTLAW Electronic Research Guide following the *Bankruptcy Highlights*.

§ 1107. Rights, powers, and duties of debtor in possession

(a) Subject to any limitations on a trustee serving in a case under this chapter, and to such limitations or conditions as the court prescribes, a debtor in possession shall have all the rights, other than the right to compensation under section 330 of this title, and powers, and shall perform all the functions and duties, except the duties specified in sections 1106(a)(2), (3), and (4) of this title, of a trustee serving in a case under this chapter.

(b) Notwithstanding section 327(a) of this title, a person is not disqualified for employment under section 327 of this title by a debtor in possession solely because of such person's employment by or representation of the debtor before the commencement of the case.

Pub.L. 95–598, Nov. 6, 1978, 92 Stat. 2628; Pub.L. 98–353, Title III, § 503, July 10, 1984, 98 Stat. 384.

Historical and Revision Notes

Notes of Committee on the Judiciary, Senate Report No. 95–989. This section places a debtor in possession in the shoes of a trustee in every way. The debtor is given the rights and powers of a chapter 11 trustee. He is required to perform the functions and duties of a chapter 11 trustee (except the investigative duties). He is also subject to any limitations on a chapter 11 trustee, and to such other limitations and conditions as the court prescribes cf. Wolf v. Weinstein, 372 U.S. 633, 649–650 (1963).

Legislative Statements. The House amendment adopts section 1107(b) of the Senate amendment which clarifies a point not covered by the House bill.

Effective Date of 1984 Amendments. See section 553 of Pub.L. 98–353, Title III, July 10, 1984, 98 Stat. 392, set out as an Effective Date of 1984 Amendment note preceding chapter 1 of Title 11, Bankruptcy.

Separability of Provisions. For separability of provisions of Title III of Pub.L. 98–353, see section 551 of Pub.L. 98–353 set out as a Separability of Provisions note preceding chapter 1 of Title 11, Bankruptcy.

Cross References

Debtor engaged in business in chapter 13 cases, see section 1304.
Debtor's duties, see section 521.
Inapplicability of this section in railroad reorganization cases, see section 1161.
Limitation on compensation of professional persons, see section 328.
Rights and powers of debtor in chapter 13 cases, see section 1303.
Trustee's duties in chapter 7 cases, see section 704.

Library References:

C.J.S. Bankruptcy § 374.
West's Key No. Digests, Bankruptcy ⚖3622.

WESTLAW Electronic Research

See WESTLAW Electronic Research Guide following the *Bankruptcy Highlights*.

§ 1108. Authorization to operate business

Unless the court, on request of a party in interest and after notice and a hearing, orders otherwise, the trustee may operate the debtor's business.

Pub.L. 95–598, Nov. 6, 1978, 92 Stat. 2629; Pub.L. 98–353, Title III, § 504, July 10, 1984, 98 Stat. 384.

Historical and Revision Notes

Notes of Committee on the Judiciary, Senate Report No. 95–989. This section permits the debtor's business to continue to be operated, unless the court orders otherwise. Thus, in a reorganization case, operation of the business will be the rule, and it will not be necessary to go to the court to obtain an order authorizing operation.

Notes of Committee on the Judiciary, House Report No. 95–595. This section does not presume that a trustee will be appointed to operate the business of the debtor. Rather, the power granted to trustee under this section is one of the powers that a debtor in possession acquires by virtue of proposed 11 U.S.C. 1107.

Legislative Statements. The House amendment adopts section 1108 of the House bill in preference to the style of an identical

substantive provision contained in the Senate amendment. Throughout Title 11 references to a "trustee" is read to include other parties under various sections of the bill. For example, section 1107 applies to give the debtor in possession all the rights and powers of a trustee in a case under chapter 11; this includes the power of the trustee to operate the debtor's business under section 1108.

Effective Date of 1984 Amendments. See section 553 of Pub.L. 98–353, Title III, July 10, 1984, 98 Stat. 392, set out as an Effective Date of 1984 Amendment note preceding chapter 1 of Title 11, Bankruptcy.

Separability of Provisions. For separability of provisions of Title III of Pub.L. 98–353, see section 551 of Pub.L. 98–353 set out as a Separability of Provisions note preceding chapter 1 of Title 11, Bankruptcy.

Cross References

Authorization to operate business in chapter 7 cases, see section 721.
Executory contracts and unexpired leases, see section 365.
Executory contracts in stockbroker liquidation cases, see section 744.
Obtaining credit, see section 364.
Retention or replacement of professional persons, see section 327.
Treatment of accounts in
    Commodity broker liquidation cases, see section 763.
    Stockbroker liquidation cases, see section 745.
Use, sale or lease of property, see section 363.
Utility service, see section 366.

Library References:

C.J.S. Bankruptcy § 199.
West's Key No. Digests, Bankruptcy ⟜3025, 3026.

WESTLAW Electronic Research

See WESTLAW Electronic Research Guide following the *Bankruptcy Highlights*.

§ 1109. Right to be heard

(a) The Securities and Exchange Commission may raise and may appear and be heard on any issue in a case under this chapter, but the Securities and Exchange Commission may not appeal from any judgment, order, or decree entered in the case.

(b) A party in interest, including the debtor, the trustee, a creditors' committee, an equity security holders' committee, a creditor, an equity security holder, or any indenture trustee, may raise and may appear and be heard on any issue in a case under this chapter.

Pub.L. 95–598, Nov. 6, 1978, 92 Stat. 2629.

Historical and Revision Notes

Notes of Committee on the Judiciary, Senate Report No. 95–989. Subsection (a) provides, in unqualified terms, that any creditor, equity security holder, or an indenture trustee shall have the right to be heard as a party in interest under this chapter in person, by an attorney, or by a committee. It is derived from section 206 of chapter X (11 U.S.C. 606) [former section 606 of this title].

Subsection (b) provides that the Securities and Exchange Commission may appear by filing an appearance in a case of a public company and may appear in other cases if authorized or requested by the court. As a party in interest in either case, the Commission may raise and be heard on any issue. The Commission may not appeal from a judgment, order, or decree in a case, but may participate in any appeal by any other party in interest. This is the present law under section 208 of chapter X (11 U.S.C. 608) [former section 608 of this title].

Notes of Committee on the Judiciary, House Report No. 95–595. Section 1109 au-thorizes the Securities and Exchange Commission and any indenture trustee to intervene in the case at any time on any issue. They may raise an issue or may appear and be heard on an issue that is raised by someone else. The section, following current law, denies the right of appeal to the Securities and Exchange Commission. It does not, however, prevent the Commission from joining or participating in an appeal taken by a true party in interest. The Commission is merely prevented from initiating the appeal in any capacity.

Legislative Statements. Section 1109 of the House amendment represents a compromise between comparable provisions in the House bill and Senate amendment. As previously discussed the section gives the Securities and Exchange Commission the right to appear and be heard and to raise any issue in a case under chapter 11; however, the Securities and Exchange Commission is not a party in interest and the Commission may not appeal from any judgment, order, or decree entered in the case. Under section 1109(b) a party in interest, including the debtor, the trustee, creditors committee, equity securities holders committee, a creditor, an equity security holder, or an indentured trustee, may raise and may appear and be heard on any issue in a case under chapter 11. Section 1109(c) of the Senate amendment has been moved to subchapter IV pertaining to Railroad Reorganizations.

Cross References

Applicability of this section in chapter 9 cases, see section 901.

Right of Commodity Futures Trading Commission to be heard, see section 762.

Right of Interstate Commerce Commission, Department of Transportation, and State or local regulatory commission to be heard in railroad reorganization, see section 1164.

Library References:

C.J.S. Bankruptcy § 38.

West's Key No. Digests, Bankruptcy ⚷2205.

WESTLAW Electronic Research

See WESTLAW Electronic Research Guide following the *Bankruptcy Highlights*.

§ 1110.   Aircraft equipment and vessels

(a) The right of a secured party with a purchase-money equipment security interest in, or of a lessor or conditional vendor of, whether as trustee or otherwise, aircraft, aircraft engines, propellers, appliances, or spare parts, as defined in section 101 of the Federal Aviation Act of 1958 (49 U.S.C. 1301), or vessels of the United States, as defined in subsection B(4) of the Ship Mortgage Act, 1920 (46 U.S.C. 911(4)), that are subject to a purchase-money equipment security interest granted by, leased to, or conditionally sold to, a debtor that is an air carrier operating under a certificate of convenience and necessity issued by the Civil Aeronautics Board, or a water carrier that holds a certificate of public convenience and necessity or permit issued by the Interstate Commerce Commission, as the case may be, to take possession of such equipment in compliance with the provisions of a purchase-money equipment security agreement, lease, or conditional sale contract, as the case may be, is not affected by section 362 or 363 of this title or by any power of the court to enjoin such taking of possession, unless—

    (1) before 60 days after the date of the order for relief under this chapter, the trustee, subject to the court's approval, agrees to perform all obligations of the debtor that become due on or after such date under such security agreement, lease, or conditional sale contract, as the case may be; and

    (2) any default, other than a default of a kind specified in section 365(b)(2) of this title, under such security agreement, lease, or conditional sale contract, as the case may be—

        (A) that occurred before such date is cured before the expiration of such 60-day period; and

        (B) that occurs after such date is cured before the later of—

            (i) 30 days after the date of such default; and

            (ii) the expiration of such 60-day period.

(b) The trustee and the secured party, lessor, or conditional vendor, as the case may be, whose right to take possession is protected under subsection (a) of this section may agree, subject to the court's approval, to extend the 60-day period specified in subsection (a)(1) of this section.

Pub.L. 95–598, Nov. 6, 1978, 92 Stat. 2629.

Historical and Revision Notes

Notes of Committee on the Judiciary, Senate Report No. 95–989. This section, to a large degree, preserves the protection given lessors and conditional vendors of aircraft to a certificated air carrier or of vessels to a certificated water carrier under section 116(5) and 116(6) of present Chapter X [former sections 516(5) and 516(6) of this title]. It is modified to conform with the consolidation of Chapters X [former section 501 et seq. of this title] and XI [former section 701 et seq. of this title] and with the new chapter 11 generally. It is also modified to give the trustee in a reorganization case an opportunity to continue in possession of the equipment in question by curing defaults and by making the required lease or purchase payments. This removes the absolute veto power over a reorganization that lessors and conditional vendors have under present law, while entitling them to protection of their investment.

The section overrides the automatic stay or any power of the court to enjoin taking of possession of certain leased, conditionally sold, or liened equipment, unless, the trustee agrees to perform the debtor's obligations and cures all prior defaults (other than defaults under ipso facto or bankruptcy clauses) within 60 days after the order for relief. The trustee and the equipment financer are permitted to extend the 60-day period by agreement. During the first 60 days, the automatic stay will apply to prevent foreclosure unless the creditor gets relief from the stay.

The effect of this section will be the same if the debtor has granted the security interest to the financer or if the debtor is leasing equipment from a financer that has leveraged the lease and leased the equipment subject to a security interest of a third party.

Legislative Statements. Section 1110 of the House amendment adopts an identical

provision contained in the House bill without modifications contained in the Senate amendment. This section protects a limited class of financiers of aircraft and vessels and is intended to be narrowly construed to prevent secured parties or lessors from gaining the protection of the section unless the interest of such lessor or secured party is explicitly enumerated therein. It should be emphasized that under section 1110(a) a debtor in possession or trustee is given 60 days after the order for relief in a case under chapter 11, to have an opportunity to comply with the provisions of section 1110(a).

During this time the automatic stay will apply and may not be lifted prior to the expiration of the 60-day period. Under section 1110(b), the debtor and secured party or lessor are given an opportunity to extend the 60-day period, but no right to reduce the period is intended. It should additionally be noted that under section 1110(a) the trustee or debtor in possession is not required to assume the executory contract or unexpired lease under section 1110; rather, if the trustee or debtor in possession complies with the requirements of section 1110(a), the trustee or debtor in possession is entitled to retain the aircraft or vessels subject to the normal requirements of section 365. The discussion regarding aircraft and vessels likewise applies with respect to railroad rolling stock in a railroad reorganization under section 1168.

References in Text. Section 101 of the Federal Aviation Act of 1958, referred to in subsec. (a), is classified to section 1301 of Title 49, Transportation.

Subsection B(4) of the Ship Mortgage Act, 1920, referred to in subsec. (a), is classified to section 911(4) of Title 46, Shipping.

Cross References

Effect of conversion, see section 348.
Rights of certain secured parties in rolling stock equipment, see section 1168.

Library References:

C.J.S. Bankruptcy § 370.
West's Key No. Digests, Bankruptcy ⟐3504.

WESTLAW Electronic Research

See WESTLAW Electronic Research Guide following the *Bankruptcy Highlights*.

§ 1111. Claims and interests

(a) A proof of claim or interest is deemed filed under section 501 of this title for any claim or interest that appears in the schedules filed under section 521(1) or 1106(a)(2) of this title, except a claim or interest that is scheduled as disputed, contingent, or unliquidated.

(b)(1)(A) A claim secured by a lien on property of the estate shall be allowed or disallowed under section 502 of this title the same as if the holder of such claim had recourse against the debtor on account of such claim, whether or not such holder has such recourse, unless—

(i) the class of which such claim is a part elects, by at least two-thirds in amount and more than half in number of allowed claims of such class, application of paragraph (2) of this subsection; or

(ii) such holder does not have such recourse and such property is sold under section 363 of this title or is to be sold under the plan.

(B) A class of claims may not elect application of paragraph (2) of this subsection if—

(i) the interest on account of such claims of the holders of such claims in such property is of inconsequential value; or

(ii) the holder of a claim of such class has recourse against the debtor on account of such claim and such property is sold under section 363 of this title or is to be sold under the plan.

(2) If such an election is made, then notwithstanding section 506(a) of this title, such claim is a secured claim to the extent that such claim is allowed.

Pub.L. 95–598, Nov. 6, 1978, 92 Stat. 2630.

Historical and Revision Notes

Notes of Committee on the Judiciary, Senate Report No. 95–989. This section dispenses with the need for every creditor and equity security holder to file a proof of claim or interest in a reorganization case. Usually the debtor's schedules are accurate enough that they will suffice to determine the claims or interests allowable in the case. Thus, the section specifies that any claim or interest included on the debtor's schedules is deemed filed under section 501. This does not apply to claims or interests that are scheduled as disputed, contingent, or unliquidated.

Legislative Statements. A discussion of section 1111(b) of the House amendment is best considered in the context of confirmation and will therefore, be discussed in connection with section 1129.

Cross References

Applicability of subsec. (b) of this section in chapter 9 cases, see section 901.
Effect of list of claims in chapter 9 cases, see section 925.
Election as affecting confirmation of plan, see section 1129.
Filing and allowance of postpetition claims in chapter 9 cases, see section 1305.

Library References:

C.J.S. Bankruptcy §§ 239–244, 351, 354.
West's Key No. Digests, Bankruptcy ⚬=2821 et seq.

WESTLAW Electronic Research
See WESTLAW Electronic Research Guide following the *Bankruptcy Highlights*.

§ 1112. Conversion or dismissal

(a) The debtor may convert a case under this chapter to a case under chapter 7 of this title unless—

(1) the debtor is not a debtor in possession;

(2) the case originally was commenced as an involuntary case under this chapter; or

(3) the case was converted to a case under this chapter other than on the debtor's request.

(b) Except as provided in subsection (c) of this section, on request of a party in interest or the United States trustee, and after notice and a hearing, the court may convert a case under this chapter to a case under chapter 7 of this title or may dismiss a case under this chapter, whichever is in the best interest of creditors and the estate, for cause, including—

(1) continuing loss to or diminution of the estate and absence of a reasonable likelihood of rehabilitation;

(2) inability to effectuate a plan;

(3) unreasonable delay by the debtor that is prejudicial to creditors;

(4) failure to propose a plan under section 1121 of this title within any time fixed by the court;

(5) denial of confirmation of every proposed plan and denial of a request made for additional time for filing another plan or a modification of a plan;

(6) revocation of an order of confirmation under section 1144 of this title, and denial of confirmation of another plan or a modified plan under section 1129 of this title;

(7) inability to effectuate substantial consummation of a confirmed plan;

(8) material default by the debtor with respect to a confirmed plan;

(9) termination of a plan by reason of the occurrence of a condition specified in the plan; or

(10) nonpayment of any fees or charges required under chapter 123 of title 28.

(c) The court may not convert a case under this chapter to a case under chapter 7 of this title if the debtor is a farmer or a corporation that is not a moneyed, business, or commercial corporation, unless the debtor requests such conversion.

(d) The court may convert a case under this chapter to a case under chapter 12 or 13 of this title only if—

(1) the debtor requests such conversion;

(2) the debtor has not been discharged under section 1141(d) of this title; and

(3) if the debtor requests conversion to chapter 12 of this title, such conversion is equitable.

(e) Except as provided in subsections (c) and (f), the court, on request of the United States trustee, may convert a case under this chapter to a case under

315

chapter 7 of this title or may dismiss a case under this chapter, whichever is in the best interest of creditors and the estate if the debtor in a voluntary case fails to file, within fifteen days after the filing of the petition commencing such case or such additional time as the court may allow, the information required by paragraph (1) of section 521, including a list containing the names and addresses of the holders of the twenty largest unsecured claims (or of all unsecured claims if there are fewer than twenty unsecured claims), and the approximate dollar amounts of each of such claims.

(f) Notwithstanding any other provision of this section, a case may not be converted to a case under another chapter of this title unless the debtor may be a debtor under such chapter.

Pub.L. 95–598, No. 6, 1978, 92 Stat. 2630; Pub.L. 98–353, Title III, § 505, July 10, 1984, 98 Stat. 384; Pub.L. 99–554, Title II, §§ 224, 256, Oct. 27, 1986, 100 Stat. 3102, 3114.

Historical and Revision Notes

Notes of Committee on the Judiciary, Senate Report No. 95–989. This section brings together all of the conversion and dismissal rules for chapter 11 cases. Subsection (a) gives the debtor an absolute right to convert a voluntarily commenced chapter 11 case in which the debtor remains in possession to a liquidation case.

Subsection (b) gives wide discretion to the court to make an appropriate disposition of the case sua sponte or upon motion of a party in interest, or the court is permitted to convert a reorganization case to a liquidation case or to dismiss the case, whichever is in the best interest of creditors and the estate, but only for cause. Cause may include the continuing loss to or diminution of the estate of an insolvent debtor, the absence of a reasonable likelihood of rehabilitation, the inability to effectuate a plan, unreasonable delay by the debtor that is prejudicial to creditors, failure to file a plan within the appropriate time limits, denial of confirmation and any opportunity to modify or propose a new plan, revocation of confirmation and denial of confirmation of a modified plan, inability to effectuate substantial consummation of a confirmed plan, material default by the debtor under the plan, and termination of the plan by reason of the occurrence of a condition specified in the plan. This list is not exhaustive. The court will be able to consider other factors as they arise, and to use its equitable powers to reach an appropriate result in individual cases. The power of the court to act sua sponte should be used sparingly and only in emergency situations.

Subsection (c) prohibits the court from converting a case concerning a farmer or an eleemosynary institution to a liquidation case unless the debtor consents.

Subsection (d) prohibits conversion of a reorganization case to a chapter 13 case unless the debtor requests conversion and his discharge has not been granted or has been revoked.

Subsection (e) reinforces section 109 by prohibiting conversion of a chapter 11 case to a case under another chapter proceedings under which the debtor is not permitted to proceed.

Legislative Statements. Section 1112 of the House amendment represents a compromise between the House bill and Senate amendment with respect to the factors constituting cause for conversion of a case to chapter 7 or dismissal. The House amendment combines two separate factors contained in section 1112(b)(1) and section 1112(b)(2) of the Senate amendment. Section 1112(b)(1) of the House amendment permits the court to convert a case to a case under chapter 7 or to dismiss the case if there is both a continuing loss to or diminution of the estate and the absence of a reasonable likelihood of rehabilitation; requiring both factors to be present simultaneously represents a compromise from the House bill which eliminated both factors from the list of causes enumerated.

Sections 1112(c) and 1112(d) of the House amendment is derived from the House bill which differs from the Senate amendment only as a matter of style.

1986 Amendment. Subsec. (b). Pub.L. 99–554, § 224(1)(A), added "or the United States trustee" following "party in interest".

Subsec. (b)(10). Pub.L. 99–554, § 224(1)(B)–(D), added par. (10).

Subsec. (e). Pub.L. 99–554, § 224(3), added subsec. (e). Former subsec. (e) was redesignated (f).

Subsec. (f). Pub.L. 99–554, § 224(2), redesignated former subsec. (e) as (f).

See Effective Date of 1986 Amendment, etc., notes set out below.

Effective Date of 1986 Amendments; Savings; Effective Date of 1986 Amendments for Certain Judicial Districts Not Served by United States Trustees and for Judicial Districts in Alabama and North Carolina; U.S. Trustee System Fund Deposits in Alabama and North Carolina; Effective Date of Title 11 Chapter 15 Repeal as to Northern District of Alabama; Authority of Certain Estate Administrators in Alabama and North Carolina; Effective Date of 1986 Amendments in Pending Cases Where a U.S. Trustee Not Authorized or Where a Trustee Files Final Report or Plan is Confirmed; Quarterly Fees. Amendment by Pub.L. 99–554 effective 30 days after Oct. 27, 1986, except as otherwise provided for, see section 302(a) of Pub.L. 99–554, set out as a note under section 581 of Title 28, Judiciary and Judicial Procedure.

Amendments by Pub.L. 99–554, § 256, not to apply with respect to cases commenced under Title 11, Bankruptcy, before 30 days after Oct. 27, 1986, see section 302(c)(1) of Pub. L. 99–554, set out as a note under section 581 of Title 28.

Amendment by Pub.L. 99–554, § 224, not to become effective in or with respect to certain specified judicial districts until, or apply to cases while pending in such district before, the expiration of the 270-day period beginning 30 days after Oct. 27, 1986, or of the 30-day period beginning on the date the Attorney General certifies under section 303 of Pub.L. 99–554 the region specified in a paragraph of section 581(a) of Title 28, as amended by section 111(a) of Pub.L. 99–554, that includes such district, whichever occurs first, see section 302(d)(1) of Pub.L. 99–554, set out as a note under section 581 of Title 28.

Amendment by Pub.L. 99–554, § 224, not to become effective in or with respect to certain specified judicial districts until, or apply to cases while pending in such district before, the expiration of the 2-year period beginning 30 days after Oct. 27, 1986, or of the 30-day period beginning on the date the Attorney General certifies under section 303 of Pub.L. 99–554 the region specified in a paragraph of section 581(a) of Title 28, as amended by section 111(a) of Pub.L. 99–554, that includes such district, whichever occurs first, see section 302(d)(2) of Pub.L. 99–554, set out as a note under section 581 of Title 28.

Amendment by Pub.L. 99–554, § 224, not to become effective in or with respect to judicial districts established for the States of Alabama and North Carolina until, or apply to cases while pending in such district before, such district elects to be included in a bankruptcy region established in section 581(a) of Title 28, as amended by section 111(a) of Pub.L. 99–554, or Oct. 1, 2002, whichever occurs first, and, except as otherwise provided for, with respect to cases under chapters 7, 11, 12, and 13 of Title 11 commenced before 30 days after Oct. 27, 1986, and pending in a judicial district in the States of Alabama or North Carolina before any election made under section 302(d)(3) (A) of Pub.L. 99–554 by such district becomes effective or Oct. 1, 2002, whichever occurs first, amendments by Pub.L. 99–554 not to apply until Oct. 1, 2003, or the expiration of the 1-year period beginning on the date such election becomes effective, whichever occurs first, and further, in any judicial district in Alabama or North Carolina not making the election described in section 302(d)(3)(A) of Pub.L. 99–554, any person appointed under regulations issued by the Judicial Conference to administer estates in cases under Title 11 authorized to establish, etc., a panel of private trustees, and to supervise cases and trustees in cases under chapters 7, 11, 12, and 13 of Title 11, until amendments by sections 201 to 231 of Pub.L. 99–554 effective in such district, see section 302(d)(3)(A) to (F), (H), (I) of Pub.L. 99–554, set out as a note under section 581 of Title 28.

Amendment by Pub.L. 99–554, § 224, except as otherwise provided, with respect to cases under chapters 7, 11, 12, and 13 of Title 11 commenced before 30 days after Oct. 27, 1986, and pending in a judicial district referred to in section 581(a) of Title 28, as amended by section 111(a) of Pub.L. 99–554, for which a United States trustee is not authorized before 30 days after Oct. 27, 1986 to be appointed, not applicable until the expiration of the 3-year period beginning on Oct. 27, 1986, or of the 1-year period beginning on the date the Attorney General certifies under section 303 of Pub.L. 99–554 the region specified in a paragraph of such section 581(a) that includes, such district, whichever occurs first, see section 302(e)(1), (2) of Pub.L. 99–554, set out as a note under section 581 of Title 28.

See 1986 Amendment notes set out above.

Effective Date of 1984 Amendments. See section 553 of Pub.L. 98–353, Title III, July 10, 1984, 98 Stat. 392, set out as an Effective Date of 1984 Amendment note preceding chapter 1 of Title 11, Bankruptcy.

Separability of provisions. For separability of provisions of Title III of Pub.L. 98–353, see section 551 of Pub.L. 98–353 set out as a Separability of Provisions note preceding chapter 1 of Title 11, Bankruptcy.

Cross References

Conversion of
> Chapter 7 cases, see section 706.
> Chapter 13 cases, see section 1307.

Dismissal of
> Chapter 7 cases, see section 707.
> Chapter 9 cases, see section 927.
> Chapter 13 cases where not converted under this section, see section 1307.

Distribution of property of estate converted to chapter 7, see section 726.

Effect of conversion, see section 348.

Effect of dismissal, see section 349.

Executory contracts and unexpired leases, see section 365.

Liquidation of estate in railroad reorganization cases, see section 1174.

Termination of debtor's taxable period for cases converted to chapter 7, see section 728.

Library References:

C.J.S. Bankruptcy §§ 377, 379, 380.
West's Key No. Digests, Bankruptcy ⇔3592–3594.

WESTLAW Electronic Research

See WESTLAW Electronic Research Guide following the *Bankruptcy Highlights*.

§ 1113. Rejection of collective bargaining agreements

(a) The debtor in possession, or the trustee if one has been appointed under the provisions of this chapter, other than a trustee in a case covered by subchapter IV of this chapter and by title I of the Railway Labor Act, may assume or reject a collective bargaining agreement only in accordance with the provisions of this section.

(b)(1) Subsequent to filing a petition and prior to filing an application seeking rejection of a collective bargaining agreement, the debtor in possession or trustee (hereinafter in this section, "trustee" shall include a debtor in possession), shall—

(A) make a proposal to the authorized representative of the employees covered by such agreement, based on the most complete and reliable information available at the time of such proposal, which provides for those necessary modifications in the employees benefits and protections that are necessary to permit the reorganization of the debtor and assures that all creditors, the debtor and all of the affected parties are treated fairly and equitably; and

(B) provide, subject to subsection (d)(3), the representative of the employees with such relevant information as is necessary to evaluate the proposal.

(2) During the period beginning on the date of the making of a proposal provided for in paragraph (1) and ending on the date of the hearing provided for in subsection (d)(1), the trustee shall meet, at reasonable times, with the

authorized representative to confer in good faith in attempting to reach mutually satisfactory modifications of such agreement.

(c) The court shall approve an application for rejection of a collective bargaining agreement only if the court finds that—

(1) the trustee has, prior to the hearing, made a proposal that fulfills the requirements of subsection (b)(1);

(2) the authorized representative of the employees has refused to accept such proposal without good cause; and

(3) the balance of the equities clearly favors rejection of such agreement.

(d)(1) Upon the filing of an application for rejection the court shall schedule a hearing to be held not later than fourteen days after the date of the filing of such application. All interested parties may appear and be heard at such hearing. Adequate notice shall be provided to such parties at least ten days before the date of such hearing. The court may extend the time for the commencement of such hearing for a period not exceeding seven days where the circumstances of the case, and the interests of justice require such extension, or for additional periods of time to which the trustee and representative agree.

(2) The court shall rule on such application for rejection within thirty days after the date of the commencement of the hearing. In the interests of justice, the court may extend such time for ruling for such additional period as the trustee and the employees' representative may agree to. If the court does not rule on such application within thirty days after the date of the commencement of the hearing, or within such additional time as the trustee and the employees' representative may agree to, the trustee may terminate or alter any provisions of the collective bargaining agreement pending the ruling of the court on such application.

(3) The court may enter such protective orders, consistent with the need of the authorized representative of the employee to evaluate the trustee's proposal and the application for rejection, as may be necessary to prevent disclosure of information provided to such representative where such disclosure could compromise the position of the debtor with respect to its competitors in the industry in which it is engaged.

(e) If during a period when the collective bargaining agreement continues in effect, and if essential to the continuation of the debtor's business, or in order to avoid irreparable damage to the estate, the court, after notice and a hearing, may authorize the trustee to implement interim changes in the terms, conditions, wages, benefits, or work rules provided by a collective bargaining agreement. Any hearing under this paragraph shall be scheduled in accordance with the needs of the trustee. The implementation of such interim changes shall not render the application for rejection moot.

(f) No provision of this title shall be construed to permit a trustee to unilaterally terminate or alter any provisions of a collective bargaining agreement prior to compliance with the provisions of this section.

Added Pub.L. 98–353, Title III, § 541(a), July 10, 1984, 98 Stat. 390.

Historical and Revision Notes

References in Text. The Railway Labor Act, referred to in subsec. (a), is Act May 20, 1926, c. 347, 44 Stat. 577, as amended, which is classified principally to chapter 8 (§ 151 et seq.) of Title 45, Railroads.

Effective Date. Section 541(c) of Pub. L. 98–353, Title III, July 10, 1984, 98 Stat. 391, provided that: "The amendments made by this section [adding section 1113 of this title] shall become effective upon the date of enactment of this Act [July 10, 1984]; provided that this section shall not apply to cases filed under title 11 of the United States Code which were commenced prior to the date of enactment of this section."

For effective date of amendments by Title III of Pub. L. 98–353, see section 553 of Pub. L. 98–353, Title III, July 10, 1984, 98 Stat. 392, set out as an Effective Date of 1984 Amendment note preceding chapter 1 of Title 11, Bankruptcy.

Separability of Provisions. For separability of provisions of Title III of Pub. L. 98–353, see section 551 of Pub. L. 98–353 set out as a Separability of Provisions note preceding chapter 1 of Title 11, Bankruptcy.

Library References:

C.J.S. Bankruptcy §§ 224, 225.
West's Key No. Digests, Bankruptcy ⊕3108, 3113.

§ 1114. Payment of insurance benefits to retired employees

(a) For purposes of this section, the term "retiree benefits" means payments to any entity or person for the purpose of providing or reimbursing payments for retired employees and their spouses and dependents, for medical, surgical, or hospital care benefits, or benefits in the event of sickness, accident, disability, or death under any plan, fund, or program (through the purchase of insurance or otherwise) maintained or established in whole or in part by the debtor prior to filing a petition commencing a case under this title.

(b)(1) For purposes of this section, the term "authorized representative" means the authorized representative designated pursuant to subsection (c) for persons receiving any retiree benefits covered by a collective bargaining agreement or subsection (d) in the case of persons receiving retiree benefits not covered by such an agreement.

(2) Committees of retired employees appointed by the court pursuant to this section shall have the same rights, powers, and duties as committees appointed under sections 1102 and 1103 of this title for the purpose of carrying out the purposes of sections 1114 and 1129(a)(13) and, as permitted by the court, shall have the power to enforce the rights of persons under this title as they relate to retiree benefits.

(c)(1) A labor organization shall be, for purposes of this section, the authorized representative of those persons receiving any retiree benefits covered by any collective bargaining agreement to which that labor organization is signatory, unless (A) such labor organization elects not to serve as the authorized representative of such persons, or (B) the court, upon a motion by any party in interest, after notice and hearing, determines that different representation of such persons is appropriate.

(2) In cases where the labor organization referred to in paragraph (1) elects not to serve as the authorized representative of those persons receiving any retiree benefits covered by any collective bargaining agreement to which that labor organization is signatory, or in cases where the court, pursuant to paragraph (1) finds different representation of such persons appropriate, the court,

upon a motion by any party in interest, and after notice and a hearing, shall appoint a committee of retired employees if the debtor seeks to modify or not pay the retiree benefits or if the court otherwise determines that it is appropriate, from among such persons, to serve as the authorized representative of such persons under this section.

(d) The court, upon a motion by any party in interest, and after notice and a hearing, shall appoint a committee of retired employees if the debtor seeks to modify or not pay the retiree benefits or if the court otherwise determines that it is appropriate, to serve as the authorized representative, under this section, of those persons receiving any retiree benefits not covered by a collective bargaining agreement.

(e)(1) Notwithstanding any other provision of this title, the debtor in possession, or the trustee if one has been appointed under the provisions of this chapter (hereinafter in this section "trustee" shall include a debtor in possession), shall timely pay and shall not modify any retiree benefits, except that—

    (A) the court, on motion of the trustee or authorized representative, and after notice and a hearing, may order modification of such payments, pursuant to the provisions of subsections (g) and (h) of this section, or

    (B) the trustee and the authorized representative of the recipients of those benefits may agree to modification of such payments,

after which such benefits as modified shall continue to be paid by the trustee.

(2) Any payment for retiree benefits required to be made before a plan confirmed under section 1129 of this title is effective has the status of an allowed administrative expense as provided in section 503 of this title.

(f)(1) Subsequent to filing a petition and prior to filing an application seeking modification of the retiree benefits, the trustee shall—

    (A) make a proposal to the authorized representative of the retirees, based on the most complete and reliable information available at the time of such proposal, which provides for those necessary modifications in the retiree benefits that are necessary to permit the reorganization of the debtor and assures that all creditors, the debtor and all of the affected parties are treated fairly and equitably; and

    (B) provide, subject to subsection (k)(3), the representative of the retirees with such relevant information as is necessary to evaluate the proposal.

(2) During the period beginning on the date of the making of a proposal provided for in paragraph (1), and ending on the date of the hearing provided for in subsection (k)(1), the trustee shall meet, at reasonable times, with the authorized representative to confer in good faith in attempting to reach mutually satisfactory modifications of such retiree benefits.

(g) The court shall enter an order providing for modification in the payment of retiree benefits if the court finds that—

    (1) the trustee has, prior to the hearing, made a proposal that fulfills the requirements of subsection (f);

    (2) the authorized representative of the retirees has refused to accept such proposal without good cause; and

    (3) such modification is necessary to permit the reorganization of the debtor and assures that all creditors, the debtor, and all of the affected

parties are treated fairly and equitably, and is clearly favored by the balance of the equities;

except that in no case shall the court enter an order providing for such modification which provides for a modification to a level lower than that proposed by the trustee in the proposal found by the court to have complied with the requirements of this subsection and subsection (f): *Provided, however,* That at any time after an order is entered providing for modification in the payment of retiree benefits, or at any time after an agreement modifying such benefits is made between the trustee and the authorized representative of the recipients of such benefits, the authorized representative may apply to the court for an order increasing those benefits which order shall be granted if the increase in retiree beneftis sought is consistent with the standard set forth in paragraph (3): *Provided further,* That neither the trustee nor the authorized representative is precluded from making more than one motion for a modification order governed by this subsection.

(h)(1) Prior to a court issuing a final order under subsection (g) of this section, if essential to the continuation of the debtor's business, or in order to avoid irreparable damage to the estate, the court, after notice and a hearing, may authorize the trustee to implement interim modifications in retiree benefits.

(2) Any hearing under this subsection shall be scheduled in accordance with the needs of the trustee.

(3) The implementation of such interim changes does not render the motion for modification moot.

(i) No retiree benefits paid between the filing of the petition and the time a plan confirmed under section 1129 of this title becomes effective shall be deducted or offset from the amounts allowed as claims for any benefits which remain unpaid, or from the amounts to be paid under the plan with respect to such claims for unpaid benefits, whether such claims for unpaid benefits are based upon or arise from a right to future unpaid benefits or from any benefits not paid as a result of modifications allowed pursuant to this section.

(j) No claim for retiree benefits shall be limited by section 502(b)(7) of this title.

(k)(1) Upon the filing of an application for modifying retiree benefits, the court shall schedule a hearing to be held not later than fourteen days after the date of the filing of such application. All interested parties may appear and be heard at such hearing. Adequate notice shall be provided to such parties at least ten days before the date of such hearing. The court may extend the time for the commencement of such hearing for a period not exceeding seven days where the circumstances of the case, and the interests of justice require such extension, or for additional periods of time to which the trustee and the authorized representative agree.

(2) The court shall rule on such application for modification within ninety days after the date of the commencement of the hearing. In the interests of justice, the court may extend such time for ruling for such additional period as the trustee and the authorized representative may agree to. If the court does not rule on such application within ninety days after the date of the commencement of the hearing, or within such additional time as the trustee and the authorized representative may agree to, the trustee may implement the proposed modifications pending the ruling of the court on such application.

(3) The court may enter such protective orders, consistent with the need of the authorized representative of the retirees to evaluate the trustee's proposal and the application for modification, as may be necessary to prevent disclosure of information provided to such representative where such disclosure could compromise the position of the debtor with respect to its competitors in the industry in which it is engaged.

(l) This section shall not apply to any retiree, or the spouse or dependents of such retiree, if such retiree's gross income for the twelve months preceding the filing of the bankruptcy petition equals or exceeds $250,000, unless such retiree can demonstrate to the satisfaction of the court that he is unable to obtain health, medical, life, and disability coverage for himself, his spouse, and his dependents who would otherwise be covered by the employer's insurance plan, comparable to the coverage provided by the employer on the day before the filing of a petition under this title.

Added Pub.L. 100–334, § 2(a), June 16, 1988, 102 Stat. 610.

Effective Date; Application of Amendments. Section 4 of Pub.L. 100–334 provided that:

"(a) General Effective Date.—Except as provided in subsection (b), this Act and the amendments made by this Act [enacting this section, amending section 1129 of this title, enacting provisions set out as notes under this section, and amending and repealing provisions set out as notes under

section 1106 of this title] shall take effect on the date of the enactment of this Act [June 16, 1988].

"(b) Application of Amendments.—The amendments made by section 2 [enacting this section and amending section 1129 of this title] shall not apply with respect to cases commenced under title 11 of the United States Code [this title] before the date of the enactment of this Act [June 16, 1988]."

SUBCHAPTER II—THE PLAN

§ 1121. Who may file a plan

(a) The debtor may file a plan with a petition commencing a voluntary case, or at any time in a voluntary case or an involuntary case.

(b) Except as otherwise provided in this section, only the debtor may file a plan until after 120 days after the date of the order for relief under this chapter.

(c) Any party in interest, including the debtor, the trustee, a creditors' committee, an equity security holders' committee, a creditor, an equity security holder, or any indenture trustee, may file a plan if and only if—

(1) a trustee has been appointed under this chapter;

(2) the debtor has not filed a plan before 120 days after the date of the order for relief under this chapter; or

(3) the debtor has not filed a plan that has been accepted, before 180 days after the date of the order for relief under this chapter, by each class of claims or interests that is impaired under the plan.

(d) On request of a party in interest made within the respective periods specified in subsections (b) and (c) of this section and after notice and a hearing, the court may for cause reduce or increase the 120-day period or the 180-day period referred to in this section.

Pub.L. 95–598, Nov. 6, 1978, 92 Stat. 2631; Pub.L. 98–353, Title III, § 506, July 10, 1984, 98 Stat. 385; Pub.L. 99–554, Title II, § 283(u), Oct. 27, 1986, 100 Stat. 3118.

Historical and Revision Notes

Notes of Committee on the Judiciary, Senate Report No. 95–989. Subsection (a) permits the debtor to file a reorganization plan with a petition commencing a voluntary case or at any time during a voluntary or involuntary case.

Subsection (b) gives the debtor the exclusive right to file a plan during the first 120 days of the case. There are exceptions, however, enumerated in subsection (c). If a trustee has been appointed, if the debtor does not meet the 120-day deadline, or if the debtor fails to obtain the required consent within 180 days after the filing of the petition, any party in interest may purpose a plan. This includes the debtor, the trustee, a creditors' committee, an equity security holders' committee, a creditor, an equity security holder, and an indenture trustee. The list is not exhaustive. In the case of a public company, a trustee is appointed within 10 days of the petition. In such a case, for all practical purposes, any party in interest may file a plan.

Subsection (d) permits the court, for cause, to increase or reduce the 120-day and 180-day periods specified. Since, the debtor has an exclusive privilege for 6 months during which others may not file a plan, the granted extension should be based on a showing of some promise of probable success. An extension should not be employed as a tactical device to put pressure on parties in interest to yield to a plan they consider unsatisfactory.

Legislative Statements. Section 1121 of the House amendment is derived from section 1121 of the House bill; section 1121(c)(1) will be satisfied automatically in a case under subchapter IV of title 11.

Effective Date of 1986 Amendments; Quarterly Fees. Amendment by Pub.L. 99–554 effective 30 days after Oct. 27, 1986, except as otherwise provided for, see section 302(a) of Pub.L. 99–554, set out as a note under section 581 of Title 28, Judiciary and Judicial Procedure.

Effective Date of 1984 Amendments. See section 553 of Pub. L. 98–353, Title III, July 10, 1984, 98 Stat. 392, set out as an Effective Date of 1984 Amendment note preceding chapter 1, of Title 11, Bankruptcy.

Separability of Provisions. For separability of provisions of Title III of Pub. L. 98–353, see section 551 of Pub. L. 98–353 set out as a Separability of Provisions note preceding chapter 1 of Title 11, Bankruptcy.

Cross References

Effect of conversion, see section 348.
Failure to propose plan as cause for conversion or dismissal, see section 1112.
Filing of plan by trustee, see section 1106.
Filing of plan in
    Chapter 9 cases, see section 941.
    Chapter 13 cases, see section 1321.

Library References:

C.J.S. Bankruptcy § 382.
West's Key No. Digests, Bankruptcy ⬤⟞3533–3535.

WESTLAW Electronic Research

See WESTLAW Electronic Research Guide following the *Bankruptcy Highlights.*

§ 1122.   Classification of claims or interests

(a) Except as provided in subsection (b) of this section, a plan may place a claim or an interest in a particular class only if such claim or interest is substantially similar to the other claims or interests of such class.

(b) A plan may designate a separate class of claims consisting only of every unsecured claim that is less than or reduced to an amount that the court approves as reasonable and necessary for administrative convenience.

Pub.L. 95–598, Nov. 6, 1978, 92 Stat. 2631.

Historical and Revision Notes

Notes of Committee on the Judiciary, Senate Report No. 95–989. This section codifies current case law surrounding the classification of claims and equity securities. It requires classification based on the nature of the claims or interests classified, and permits inclusion of claims or interests in a particular class only if the claim or interest being included is substantially similar to the other claims or interests of the class.

Subsection (b), also a codification of existing practice, contains an exception. The plan may designate a separate class of claims consisting only of every unsecured claim that is less than or reduced to an amount that the court approves as reasonable and necessary for administrative convenience.

Cross References

Applicability of this section in chapter 9 cases, see section 901.
Contents of plan, see section 1322.
Filing and allowance of postpetition claims in chapter 13 cases, see section 1305.
Filing of proofs of claims or interests, see section 501.

Library References:

C.J.S. Bankruptcy § 386.
West's Key No. Digests, Bankruptcy ⟨⇒3550.

WESTLAW Electronic Research

See WESTLAW Electronic Research Guide following the *Bankruptcy Highlights.*

§ 1123.   Contents of plan

(a) Notwithstanding any otherwise applicable nonbankruptcy law, a plan shall—

(1) designate, subject to section 1122 of this title, classes of claims, other than claims of a kind specified in section 507(a)(1), 507(a)(2), or 507(a)(7) of this title, and classes of interests;

(2) specify any class of claims or interests that is not impaired under the plan;

(3) specify the treatment of any class of claims or interests that is impaired under the plan;

(4) provide the same treatment for each claim or interest of a particular class, unless the holder of a particular claim or interest agrees to a less favorable treatment of such particular claim or interest;

(5) provide adequate means for the plan's implementation, such as—

(A) retention by the debtor of all or any part of the property of the estate;

(B) transfer of all or any part of the property of the estate to one or more entities, whether organized before or after the confirmation of such plan;

(C) merger or consolidation of the debtor with one or more persons;

(D) sale of all or any part of the property of the estate, either subject to or free of any lien, or the distribution of all or any part of the property of the estate among those having an interest in such property of the estate;

(E) satisfaction or modification of any lien;

(F) cancellation or modification of any indenture or similar instrument;

(G) curing or waiving of any default;

(H) extension of a maturity date or a change in an interest rate or other term of outstanding securities;

(I) amendment of the debtor's charter; or

(J) issuance of securities of the debtor, or of any entity referred to in subparagraph (B) or (C) of this paragraph, for cash, for property, for existing securities, or in exchange for claims or interests, or for any other appropriate purpose;

(6) provide for the inclusion in the charter of the debtor, if the debtor is a corporation, or of any corporation referred to in paragraph (5)(B) or (5)(C) of this subsection, of a provision prohibiting the issuance of nonvoting equity securities, and providing, as to the several classes of securities possessing voting power, an appropriate distribution of such power among such classes, including, in the case of any class of equity securities having a preference over another class of equity securities with respect to dividends, adequate provisions for the election of directors representing such preferred class in the event of default in the payment of such dividends; and

(7) contain only provisions that are consistent with the interests of creditors and equity security holders and with public policy with respect to the manner of selection of any officer, director, or trustee under the plan and any successor to such officer, director, or trustee.

(b) Subject to subsection (a) of this section, a plan may—

(1) impair or leave unimpaired any class of claims, secured or unsecured, or of interests;

(2) subject to section 365 of this title, provide for the assumption, rejection, or assignment of any executory contract or unexpired lease of the debtor not previously rejected under such section;

(3) provide for—

(A) the settlement or adjustment of any claim or interest belonging to the debtor or to the estate; or

(B) the retention and enforcement by the debtor, by the trustee, or by a representative of the estate appointed for such purpose, of any such claim or interest;

(4) provide for the sale of all or substantially all of the property of the estate, and the distribution of the proceeds of such sale among holders of claims or interests; and

(5) include any other appropriate provision not inconsistent with the applicable provisions of this title.

(c) In a case concerning an individual, a plan proposed by an entity other than the debtor may not provide for the use, sale, or lease of property exempted under section 522 of this title, unless the debtor consents to such use, sale, or lease.

Pub.L. 95–598, Nov. 6, 1978, 92 Stat. 2631; Pub.L. 98–353, Title III, § 507, July 10, 1984, 98 Stat. 385.

Historical and Revision Notes

Notes of Committee on the Judiciary, Senate Report No. 95–989. Subsection (a) specifies what a plan of reorganization must contain. The plan must designate classes of claims and interests, and specify, by class, the claims or interests that are unimpaired under the plan. Priority claims are not required to be classified because they may not have arisen when the plan is filed. The plan must provide the same treatment for each claim or interest of a particular class, unless the holder of a particular claim or interest agrees to a different, but not better, treatment of his claim or interest.

Paragraph (3) applies to claims, not creditors. Thus, if a creditor is undersecured, and thus has a secured claim and an unsecured claim, this paragraph will be applied independently to each of his claims.

Paragraph (4) of subsection (a) is derived from section 216 of chapter X [former section 616 of this title] with some modifications. It requires the plan to provide adequate means for the plans execution. These means may include retention by the debtor of all or any part of the property of the estate, transfer of all or any part of the property of the estate to one or more entities, whether organized pre- or postconfirmation, merger or consolidation of the debtor with one or more persons, sale and distribution of all or any part of the property of the estate, satisfaction or modification of any lien, cancellation or modification of any indenture or similar instrument, curing or waiving of any default, extension of maturity dates or change in interest rates of securities, amendment of the debtor's charter, and issuance of securities.

Subparagraph (C), as it applies in railroad cases, has the effect of overruling St. Joe Paper Co. v. Atlantic Coast Line R.R., 347 U.S. 298 (1954). [Fla.1954, 74 S.Ct. 574, 98 L.Ed. 710, rehearing denied 74 S.Ct. 734, 347 U.S. 980, 98 L.Ed. 1118]. It will allow the trustee or creditors to propose a plan of merger with another railroad without the consent of the debtor, and the debtor will be bound under proposed 11 U.S.C. 1141(a). See Hearings, pt. 3, at 1616. "Similar instrument" referred to in subparagraph (F) might include a deposit with an agent for distribution, other than an indenture trustee, such as an agent under an agreement in a railroad conditional sale or lease financing agreement.

Paragraphs (5) and (6) and subsection (b) are derived substantially from Section 216 of Chapter X (11 U.S.C. 616) [former section 616 of this title]. Paragraph (5) requires the plan to prohibit the issuance of nonvoting equity securities, and to provide for an appropriate distribution of voting power among the various classes of equity securities. Paragraph (6) requires that the plan contain only provisions that are consistent with the interests of creditors and equity security holders, and with public policy with respect to the selection of officers, directors, and trustees, and their successors.

Subsection (b) specifies the matters that the plan may propose. The plan may impair or leave unimpaired any claim or interest. The plan may provide for the assumption or rejection of executory contracts or unexpired leases not previously rejected under section 365. The plan may also provide for the treatment of claims by the debtor against other entities that are not settled before the confirmation of the plan. The plan may propose settlement or adjustment of any claim or equity security belonging to the estate, or may propose retention and enforcement of such claim or interest by the debtor or by an agent appointed for that purpose.

The plan may also propose the sale of all or substantially all of the property of the estate, and the distribution of the proceeds of the sale among creditors and equity security holders. This would be a liquidating plan. The subsection permits the plan to include any other appropriate provision not inconsistent with the applicable provisions of the bankruptcy code.

Subsection (c) protects an individual debtor's exempt property by prohibiting its use, sale, or lease under a plan proposed by someone other than the debtor, unless the debtor consents.

Legislative Statements. Section 1123 of the House amendment represents a compromise between similar provisions in the House bill and Senate amendment. The section has been clarified to clearly indicate that both secured and unsecured claims, or either of them, may be impaired in a case under title 11. In addition assumption or rejection of an executory contract under a plan must comply with section 365 of title 11. Moreover, section 1123(a)(1) has been substantively modified to permit classification of certain kinds of priority claims. This is important for purposes of confirmation under section 1129(a)(9).

Section 1123(a)(5) of the House amendment is derived from a similar provision in the House bill and Senate amendment but deletes the language pertaining to "fair upset price" as an unnecessary restriction. Section 1123 is also intended to indicate that a plan may provide for any action specified in section 1123 in the case of a corporation without a resolution of the board of directors. If the plan is confirmed, then any action proposed in the plan may be taken notwithstanding any otherwise applicable nonbankruptcy law in accordance with section 1142(a) of title 11.

Effective Date of 1984 Amendments. See section 553 of Pub. L. 98–353, Title III, July 10, 1984, 98 Stat. 392, set out as an Effective Date of 1984 Amendment note preceding chapter 1, of Title 11, Bankruptcy.

Separability of Provisions. For separability of provisions of Title III of Pub. L. 98–353, see section 551 of Pub. L. 98–353 set out as a Separability of Provisions note preceding chapter 1 of Title 11, Bankruptcy.

Cross References

Applicability of subsecs. (a)(1) to (5) and (b) of this section in chapter 9 cases, see section 901.
Contents of plan filed in
    Chapter 13 cases, see section 1322.
    Railroad reorganization cases, see section 1172.

Library References:

C.J.S. Bankruptcy § 385 et seq.
West's Key No. Digests, Bankruptcy ⊖3548 et seq.

WESTLAW Electronic Research

See WESTLAW Electronic Research Guide following the *Bankruptcy Highlights*.

§ 1124. Impairment of claims or interests

Except as provided in section 1123(a)(4) of this title, a class of claims or interests is impaired under a plan unless, with respect to each claim or interest of such class, the plan—

(1) leaves unaltered the legal, equitable, and contractual rights to which such claim or interest entitles the holder of such claim or interest;

(2) notwithstanding any contractual provision or applicable law that entitles the holder of such claim or interest to demand or receive accelerated payment of such claim or interest after the occurrence of a default—

(A) cures any such default that occurred before or after the commencement of the case under this title, other than a default of a kind specified in section 365(b)(2) of this title;

(B) reinstates the maturity of such claim or interest as such maturity existed before such default;

(C) compensates the holder of such claim or interest for any damages incurred as a result of any reasonable reliance by such holder on such contractual provision or such applicable law; and

(D) does not otherwise alter the legal, equitable, or contractual rights to which such claim or interest entitles the holder of such claim or interest; or

(3) provides that, on the effective date of the plan, the holder of such claim or interest receives, on account of such claim or interest, cash equal to—

(A) with respect to a claim, the allowed amount of such claim; or

(B) with respect to an interest, if applicable, the greater of—

(i) any fixed liquidation preference to which the terms of any security representing such interest entitle the holder of such interest; or

(ii) any fixed price at which the debtor, under the terms of such security, may redeem such security from such holder.

Pub.L. 95–598, Nov. 6, 1978, 92 Stat. 2633; Pub.L. 98–353, Title III, § 508, July 10, 1984, 98 Stat. 385.

Historical and Revision Notes

Notes of Committee on the Judiciary, Senate Report No. 95–989. The basic concept underlying this section is not new. It rests essentially on Section 107 of Chapter X (11 U.S.C. 507) [former section 507 of this title], which states that creditors or stockholders or any class thereof "shall be deemed to be 'affected' by a plan only if their or its interest shall be materially and adversely affected thereby."

This section is designed to indicate when contractual rights of creditors or interest holders are not materially affected. It specifies three ways in which the plan may leave a claim or interest unimpaired.

First, the plan may propose not to alter the legal, equitable, or contractual rights to which the claim or interest entitled its holder.

Second, a claim or interest is unimpaired by curing the effect of a default and reinstating the original terms of an obligation when maturity was brought on or accelerated by the default. The intervention of bankruptcy and the defaults represent a temporary crisis which the plan of reorganization is intended to clear away. The holder of a claim or interest who under the plan is restored to his original position, when others receive less or get nothing at all, is fortunate indeed and has no cause to complain. Curing of the default and the assumption of the debt in accordance with its terms is an important reorganization technique for dealing with a particular class of claims, especially secured claims.

Third, a claim or interest is unimpaired if the plan provides for their payment in cash. In the case of a debt liability, the cash payment is for the allowed amount of the claim, which does not include a redemption premium. If it is an equity security with a fixed liquidation preference, such as a preferred stock, the allowed amount is such liquidation preference, with no redemption premium. With respect to any other equity security, such as a common stock, cash payment must be equal to the "value of such holder's interest in the debtor."

Section 1124 does not include payment "in property" other than cash. Except for a rare case, claims or interests are not by their terms payable in property, but a plan may so provide and those affected thereby may accept or reject the proposed plan. They may not be forced to accept a plan declaring the holders' claims or interests to be "unimpaired."

Notes of Committee on the Judiciary, House Report No. 95–595. Second, the plan is permitted to reinstate a claim or interest and thus leave it unimpaired. Reinstatement consists of curing any default (other than a default under an ipso facto or bankruptcy clause) and reinstatement of the maturity of the claim or interest. Further, the plan may not otherwise alter any legal, equitable, or contractual right to which the claim or interest entitles its holder.

Third, the plan may leave a claim or interest unimpaired by paying its amount in full other than in securities of the debtor, an affiliate of the debtor participating in a joint plan, or a successor to the debtor. These securities are excluded because determination of their value would require a valuation of the business being reorganized. Use of them to pay a creditor or equity security holder without his consent may be done only under section 1129(b) and only after a valuation of the debtor. Under this paragraph, the plan must pay the allowed amount of the claim in full, in cash or other property, or, in the case of an equity security, must pay the greatest of any fixed liquidation preference to which the terms of the equity security entitle its holder, any fixed price at which the debtor, under the terms of the equity security may redeem such equity security, and the value, as of the effective date of the plan, of the holder's interest in the debtor. The value of the holder's interest need not be determined precisely by valuing the debtor's business if such value is clearly below redemption or liquidation preference values. If such value would require a full-scale valuation of the business, then such interest should be treated as impaired. But, if the debtor corporation is clearly insolvent, then the value of the common stock holder's interest in the debtor is zero, and offering them nothing under the plan of reorganization will not impair their rights.

"Value as of the effective date of the plan," as used in paragraph (3) and in proposed 11 U.S.C. 1179(a)(7)(B), 1129(a)(9), 1129(b), 1172(2), 1325(a)(4), 1325(a)(5)(B), and 1328(b), indicates that the promised payment under the plan must be discounted to present value as of the effective date of the plan. The discounting should be based only on the unpaid balance of the amount due under the plan, until that amount, including interest, is paid in full.

Legislative Statements. Section 1124 of the House amendment is derived from a similar provision in the House bill and Senate amendment. The section defines the new concept of "impairment" of claims or interests; the concept differs significantly from the concept of "materially and adversely affected" under the Bankruptcy Act. Section 1124(3) of the House amendment provides that a holder of a claim or interest is not impaired, if the plan provides that the holder will receive the allowed amount of the holder's claim, or in the case of an interest with a fixed liquidation preference or redemption price, the greater of

such price. This adopts the position contained in the House bill and rejects the contrary standard contained in the Senate amendment.

Section 1124(3) of the House amendment rejects a provision contained in section 1124(3)(B)(iii) of the House bill which would have considered a class of interest not to be impaired by virtue of the fact that the plan provided cash or property for the value of the holder's interest in the debtor.

The effect of the House amendment is to permit an interest not to be impaired only if the interest has a fixed liquidation preference or redemption price. Therefore, a class of interests such as common stock, must either accept a plan under section 1129(a)(8), or the plan must satisfy the requirements of section 1129(b)(2)(C) in order for a plan to be confirmed.

A compromise reflected in section 1124(2)(C) of the House amendment indicates that a class of claims is not impaired under the circumstances of section 1124(2) if damages are paid to rectify reasonable reliance engaged in by the holder of a claim or interest arising from the prepetition breach of a contractual provision, such as an ipso facto or bankruptcy clause, or law. Where the rights of third parties are concerned, such as in the case of lease premises which have been rerented to a third party, it is not intended that there will be adequate damages to compensate the third party.

Effective Date of 1984 Amendments. See section 553 of Pub. L. 98–353, Title III, July 10, 1984, 98 Stat. 392, set out as an Effective Date of 1984 Amendment note preceding chapter 1 of Title 11, Bankruptcy.

Separability of Provisions. For separability of provisions of Title III of Pub. L. 98–353, see section 551 of Pub. L. 98–353 set out as a Separability of Provisions note preceding chapter 1 of Title 11, Bankruptcy.

Cross References

    Allowance of claims or interests, see section 502.
    Applicability of this section in chapter 9 cases, see section 901.
    Claims and interests generally, see section 1111.
    Filing of proofs of claims or interests, see section 501.

Library References:

    C.J.S. Bankruptcy §§ 383, 384.
    West's Key No. Digests, Bankruptcy ☞3536, 3537.

WESTLAW Electronic Research

    See WESTLAW Electronic Research Guide following the *Bankruptcy Highlights.*

§ 1125.   Postpetition disclosure and solicitation

(a) In this section—

(1) "adequate information" means information of a kind, and in sufficient detail, as far as is reasonably practicable in light of the nature and history of the debtor and the condition of the debtor's books and records, that would enable a hypothetical reasonable investor typical of holders of claims or interests of the relevant class to make an informed judgment about the plan, but adequate information need not include such information about any other possible or proposed plan; and

(2) "investor typical of holders of claims or interests of the relevant class" means investor having—

(A) a claim or interest of the relevant class;

(B) such a relationship with the debtor as the holders of other claims or interests of such class generally have; and

(C) such ability to obtain such information from sources other than the disclosure required by this section as holders of claims or interest in such class generally have.

(b) An acceptance or rejection of a plan may not be solicited after the commencement of the case under this title from a holder of a claim or interest with respect to such claim or interest, unless, at the time of or before such solicitation, there is transmitted to such holder the plan or a summary of the plan, and a written disclosure statement approved, after notice and a hearing, by the court as containing adequate information. The court may approve a disclosure statement without a valuation of the debtor or an appraisal of the debtor's assets.

(c) The same disclosure statement shall be transmitted to each holder of a claim or interest of a particular class, but there may be transmitted different disclosure statements, differing in amount, detail, or kind of information, as between classes.

(d) Whether a disclosure statement required under subsection (b) of this section contains adequate information is not governed by any otherwise applicable nonbankruptcy law, rule, or regulation, but an agency or official whose duty is to administer or enforce such a law, rule, or regulation may be heard on the issue of whether a disclosure statement contains adequate information. Such an agency or official may not appeal from, or otherwise seek review of, an order approving a disclosure statement.

(e) A person that solicits acceptance or rejection of a plan, in good faith and in compliance with the applicable provisions of this title, or that participates, in good faith and in compliance with the applicable provisions of this title, in the offer, issuance, sale, or purchase of a security, offered or sold under the plan, of the debtor, of an affiliate participating in a joint plan with the debtor, or of a newly organized successor to the debtor under the plan, is not liable, on account of such solicitation or participation, for violation of any applicable law, rule, or regulation governing solicitation of acceptance or rejection of a plan or the offer, issuance, sale, or purchase of securities.

Pub.L. 95–598, Nov. 6, 1978, 92 Stat. 2633; Pub.L. 98–353, Title III, § 509, July 10, 1984, 98 Stat. 385.

Historical and Revision Notes

Notes of Committee on the Judiciary, Senate Report No. 95–989. This section extends disclosure requirements in connection with solicitations to all cases under chapter 11. Heretofore this subject was dealt with by the Bankruptcy Act mainly in the special contexts of railroad reorganizations and chapter X [former section 501 et seq. of this title] cases.

Subsection (a) defines (1) the subject matter of disclosure as "adequate information" and relates the standard of adequacy to an (2) "investor typical of holders or claims or interests of the relevant class." "Investor" is used broadly here, for it will almost always include a trade creditor to other creditors who originally had no investment intent or interest. It refers to the investment-type decision by those called upon to accept a plan to modify their claims or interests, which typically will involve acceptance of new securities or of a cash payment in lieu thereof.

Both the kind and form of information are left essentially to the judicial discretion of the court, guided by the specification in subparagraph (a)(1) that it be of a kind and in sufficient detail that a reasonable and typical investor can make an informed judgment about the plan. The information required will necessarily be governed by the circumstances of the case.

Reporting and audit standards devised for solvent and continuing businesses do not necessarily fit a debtor in reorganization. Subsection (a)(1) expressly incorporates consideration of the nature and history of the debtor and the condition of its books and records into the determination of what is reasonably practicable to supply. These factors are particularly pertinent to historical data and to discontinued operations of no future relevance.

A plan is necessarily predicated on knowledge of the assets and liabilities being dealt with and on factually supported expectations as to the future course of the business sufficient to meet the feasibility standard in section 1130(a)(11) of this title. It may thus be necessary to provide estimates or judgments for that purpose. Yet it remains practicable to describe, in such detail as may be relevant and needed, the basis for the plan and the data on which supporters of the plan rely.

Subsection (b) establishes the jurisdiction of the court over this subject by prohibiting solicitation of acceptance or rejection of a plan after the commencement of the case, unless the person solicited receives, before or at the time of the solicitation, a written disclosure statement approved by the court, after notice and hearing, as containing adequate information. As under present law, determinations of value, by appraisal or otherwise, are not required if not needed to accomplish the purpose specified in subsection (a)(1).

Subsection (c) requires that the same disclosure statement be transmitted to each member of a class. It recognizes that the information needed for an informed judgment about the plan may differ among classes. A class whose rights under the plan center on a particular fund or asset would have no use for an extensive description of other matters that could not affect them.

Subsection (d) relieves the court of the need to follow any otherwise applicable Federal or state law in determining the adequacy of the information contained in the disclosure statement submitted for its approval. It authorizes an agency or official, Federal or state, charged with administering cognate laws so preempted to advise the court on the adequacy of proposed disclosure statement. But they are not authorized to appeal the court's decision.

Solicitations with respect to a plan do not involve just mere requests for opinions. Acceptance of the plan vitally affects creditors and shareholders, and most frequently the solicitation involves an offering of securities in exchange for claims or interests. The present bankruptcy statute has exempted such offerings under each of its chapters from the registration and disclosure requirements of the Securities Act of 1933 [former section 77a et seq. of Title 15, Commerce and Trade], an exemption also continued by section 1145(a)(2) of this title. The extension of the disclosure requirements to all chapter 11 cases justifies the coordinate extension of these exemptions. By the same token, no valid purpose is served not to exempt from the requirements of similar state laws in a matter under the exclusive jurisdiction of the Federal bankruptcy laws.

Subsection (e) exonerates any person who, in good faith and in compliance with this title, solicits or participates in the offer, issuance, sale or purchase, under the plan, of a security from any liability, on account of such solicitation or participation, for violation of any law, rule, or regulation governing the offer, issuance, sale, or purchase of securities. This exoneration is coordinate with the exemption from Federal or State registration or licensing requirements provided by section 1145 of this title.

In the nonpublic case, the court, when approving the disclosure statement, has before it the texts of the plan, a proposed disclosure document, and such other information the plan proponents and other interested parties may present at the hearing. In the final analysis the exoneration which subsection (e) grants must depend on the good faith of the plan proponents and of those who participate in the preparation of the disclosure statement and in the solicitation. Subsection (e) does not affect civil or criminal liability for defects and inadequacies that are beyond the limits of the exoneration that good faith provides.

Section 1125 applies to public companies as well, subject to the qualifications of subsection (f). In case of a public company no solicitations of acceptance is permitted unless authorized by the court upon or after approval of the plan pursuant to section 1128(c). In addition to the documents specified in subsection (b), subsection (f) requires transmission of the opinion and order of the court approving the plan and, if filed, the advisory report of the Securities and Exchange Commission or a summary thereof prepared by the Commission.

Notes of Committee on the Judiciary, House Report No. 95–595. This section is new. It is the heart of the consolidation of the various reorganization chapters found in current law. It requires disclosure before solicitation of acceptances of a plan or reorganization.

Subsection (a) contains two definitions. First, "adequate information" is defined to mean information of a kind, and in sufficient detail, as far as is reasonably practical in light of the nature and history of the debtor and the condition of the debtor's books and records, that would enable a hypothetical reasonable investor typical of holders of claims or interests of the relevant class to make an informed judgment about the plan. Second, "investor typical of holders of claims or interests of the relevant class" is defined to mean an investor having a claim or interest of the relevant class, having such a relationship with the debtor as the holders of other claims or interests of the relevant class have, and having such ability to obtain information from sources other than the disclosure statement as holders of claims or interests of the relevant

class have, and having such ability to obtain information from sources other than the disclosure statement as holders of claims or interests of the relevant class have. That is, the hypothetical investor against which the disclosure is measured must not be an insider if other members of the class are not insiders, and so on. In other words, the adequacy of disclosure is measured against the typical investor, not an extraordinary one.

The Supreme Court's rulemaking power will not extend to rulemaking that will prescribe what constitutes adequate information. That standard is a substantive standard. Precisely what constitutes adequate information in any particular instance will develop on a case-by-case basis. Courts will take a practical approach as to what is necessary under the circumstances of each case, such as the cost of preparation of the statements, the need for relative speed in solicitation and confirmation, and, of course, the need for investor protection. There will be a balancing of interests in each case. In reorganization cases, there is frequently great uncertainty. Therefore the need for flexibility is greatest.

Subsection (b) is the operative subsection. It prohibits solicitation of acceptances or rejections of a plan after the commencement of the case unless, at the time of the solicitation or before, there is transmitted to the solicitee the plan or a summary of the plan, and a written disclosure statement approved by the court as containing adequate information. The subsection permits approval of the statement without the necessity of a valuation of the debtor or an appraisal of the debtor's assets. However, in some cases, a valuation or appraisal will be necessary to develop adequate information. The court will be able to determine what is necessary in light of the facts and circumstances of each particular case.

Subsection (c) requires that the same disclosure statement go to all members of a particular class, but permits different disclosure to different classes.

Subsection (d) excepts the disclosure statements from the requirements of the securities laws (such as section 14 of the 1934 Act [section 78n of Title 15, Commerce and Trade] and section 5 of the 1933 Act [section 77e of Title 15]), and from similar State securities laws (blue sky laws, for example). The subsection permits an agency or official whose duty is to administer or enforce such laws (such as the Securities and Exchange Commission or State Corporation Commissioners) to appear and be heard on the issue of whether a disclosure statement contains adequate information, but the agencies and officials are not granted the right of appeal from an adverse determination in any capacity. They may join in an appeal by a true party in interest, however.

Subsection (e) is a safe harbor provision, and is necessary to make the exemption provided by subsection (d) effective. Without it, a creditor that solicited an acceptance or rejection in reliance on the court's approval of a disclosure statement would be potentially liable under antifraud sections designed to enforce the very sections of the securities laws from which subsection (d) excuses compliance. The subsection protects only persons that solicit in good faith and in compliance with the applicable provisions of the reorganization chapter. It provides protection from legal liability as well as from equitable liability based on an injunctive action by the SEC [Securities and Exchange Commission] or other agency or official.

Legislative Statements. Section 1125 of the House amendment is derived from section 1125 of the House bill and Senate amendment

except with respect to section 1125(f) of the Senate amendment. It will not be necessary for the court to consider the report of the examiner prior to approval of a disclosure statement. The investigation of the examiner is to proceed on an independent basis from the procedure of the reorganization under chapter 11. In order to ensure that the examiner's report will be expeditious and fair, the examiner is precluded from serving as a trustee in the case or from representing a trustee if a trustee is appointed, whether the case remains in chapter 11 or is converted to chapter 7 or 13.

Effective Date of 1984 Amendments. See section 553 of Pub. L. 98–353, Title III, July 10, 1984, 98 Stat. 392, set out as an Effective Date of 1984 Amendment note preceding chapter 1 of Title 11, Bankruptcy.

Separability of Provisions. For separability of provisions of Title III of Pub. L. 98–353, see section 551 of Pub. L. 98–353 set out as a Separability of Provisions note preceding chapter 1 of Title 11, Bankruptcy.

Cross References

Applicability of this section in chapter 9 cases, see section 901.
Exemption from securities laws of certain transactions in which disclosure statements are provided, see section 1145.

Library References:

C.J.S. Bankruptcy §§ 399, 400; Securities Regulation §§ 94, 132, 228, 237.
West's Key No. Digests, Bankruptcy ☞3539, 3540; Securities Regulation ☞101 et seq., 291 et seq.

WESTLAW Electronic Research

See WESTLAW Electronic Research Guide following the *Bankruptcy Highlights.*

§ 1126. Acceptance of plan

(a) The holder of a claim or interest allowed under section 502 of this title may accept or reject a plan. If the United States is a creditor or equity security holder, the Secretary of the Treasury may accept or reject the plan on behalf of the United States.

(b) For the purposes of subsections (c) and (d) of this section, a holder of a claim or interest that has accepted or rejected the plan before the commencement of the case under this title is deemed to have accepted or rejected such plan, as the case may be, if—

    (1) the solicitation of such acceptance or rejection was in compliance with any applicable nonbankruptcy law, rule, or regulation governing the adequacy of disclosure in connection with such solicitation; or

    (2) if there is not any such law, rule, or regulation, such acceptance or rejection was solicited after disclosure to such holder of adequate information, as defined in section 1125(a) of this title.

(c) A class of claims has accepted a plan if such plan has been accepted by creditors, other than any entity designated under subsection (e) of this section, that hold at least two-thirds in amount and more than one-half in number of the allowed claims of such class held by creditors, other than any entity designated under subsection (e) of this section, that have accepted or rejected such plan.

(d) A class of interests has accepted a plan if such plan has been accepted by holders of such interests, other than any entity designated under subsection (e) of this section, that hold at least two-thirds in amount of the allowed interests of such class held by holders of such interests, other than any entity designated under subsection (e) of this section, that have accepted or rejected such plan.

(e) On request of a party in interest, and after notice and a hearing, the court may designate any entity whose acceptance or rejection of such plan was not in good faith, or was not solicited or procured in good faith or in accordance with the provisions of this title.

(f) Notwithstanding any other provision of this section, a class that is not impaired under a plan, and each holder of a claim or interest of such class, are conclusively presumed to have accepted the plan, and solicitation of acceptances with respect to such class from the holders of claims or interests of such class is not required.

(g) Notwithstanding any other provision of this section, a class is deemed not to have accepted a plan if such plan provides that the claims or interests of such class do not entitle the holders of such claims or interests to receive or retain any property under the plan on account of such claims or interests.

Pub.L. 95–598, Nov. 6, 1978, 92 Stat. 2634; Pub.L. 98–353, Title III, § 510, July 10, 1984, 98 Stat. 386.

Historical and Revision Notes

Notes of Committee on the Judiciary, Senate Report No. 95–989. Subsection (a) of this section permits the holder of a claim or interest allowed under section 502 to accept or reject a proposed plan of reorganization. The subsection also incorporates a provision now found in section 199 of chapter X [former section 599 of this title] that authorizes the Secretary of the Treasury to accept or reject a plan on behalf of the United States when the United States is a creditor or equity security holder.

Subsection (b) governs acceptances and rejections of plans obtained before commencement of a reorganization for a nonpublic company. Paragraph (3) expressly states that subsection (b) does not apply to a public company.

Prepetition solicitation is a common practice under chapter XI [former section 701 et seq. of this title] today, and chapter IX [former section 401 et seq. of this title] current makes explicit provision for it. Section 1126(b) counts a prepetition acceptance or rejection toward the required amounts and number of acceptances only if the solicitation of the acceptance or rejection was in compliance with any applicable nonbankruptcy law, rule, or regulation governing the adequacy of disclosure in connection with such solicitation. If there is not any such applicable law, rule, or regulation, then the acceptance or rejection is counted only if it was solicited after disclosure of adequate information, to the holder, as defined in section 1125(a)(1). This permits the court to ensure that the requirements of section 1125 are not avoided by prepetition solicitation.

Subsection (c) specifies the required amount and number of acceptances for a class of creditors. A class of creditors has accepted a plan if at least two-thirds in amount and more than one-half in number of the allowed claims of the class that are voted are cast in favor of the plan. The amount and number are computed on the basis of claims actually voted for or against the plan, not as under chapter X [former section 501 et seq. of this title] on the basis of the allowed claims in the class. Subsection (f) excludes from all these calculations claims not voted in good faith, and claims procured or solicited not in good faith or not in accordance with the provisions of this title.

Subsection (c) requires that the same disclosure statement be transmitted to each member of a class. It recognizes that the information needed for an informed judgment about the plan may differ among classes. A class whose rights under the plan center on a particular fund or asset would have no use for an extensive description of other matters that could not affect them.

Subsection (d) relieves the court of the need to follow any otherwise applicable Federal or state law in determining the adequacy of the information contained in the disclosure statement submitted for its approval. It authorizes an agency or official, Federal or state, charged with administering cognate laws so pre-empted to advise the court on the adequacy of proposed disclosure statement. But they are not authorized to appeal the court's decision.

Solicitations with respect to a plan do not involve just mere requests for opinions. Acceptance of the plan vitally affects creditors and shareholders, and most frequently the solicitation involves an offering of securities in exchange for claims or interests. The present Bankruptcy Act has exempted such offerings under each of its chapters from the registration and disclosure requirements of the Securities Act of 1933 [sections 77f, 77g, and 77j of Title 15, Commerce and Trade], an exemption also continued by section 1145 of this title. The extension of the disclosure requirements to all chapter 11 cases is justified by the integration of the separate chapters into the single chapter 11. By the same token, no valid purpose is served by failing to provide exemption from the requirements of similar state laws in a matter under the exclusive jurisdiction of the Federal bankruptcy laws.

Under subsection (d), with respect to a class of equity securities, it is sufficient for acceptance of the plan if the amount of securities voting for the plan is at least two-thirds of the total actually voted.

Subsection (e) provides that no acceptances are required from any class whose claims or interests are unimpaired under the plan or in the order confirming the plan.

Subsection (g) provides that any class denied participation under the plan is conclusively deemed to have rejected the plan. There is obviously no need to submit a plan for a vote by a class that is to receive nothing. But under subsection (g) the excluded class is like a class that has not accepted, and is a dissenting class for purposes of confirmation under section 1130.

Legislative Statements. Section 1126 of the House amendment deletes section 1126(e) as contained in the House bill. Section 105 of the bill constitutes sufficient power in the court to designate exclusion of a creditor's claim on the basis of a conflict of interest. Section 1126(f) of the House amendment adopts a provision contained in section 1127(f) of the Senate bill indicating that a class that is not impaired under a plan is deemed to have accepted a plan and solicitation of acceptances from such class is not required.

Effective Date of 1984 Amendments. See section 553 of Pub.L. 98–353, Title III, July 10, 1984, 98 Stat. 392, set out as an Effective Date of 1984 Amendment note preceding chapter 1 of Title 11, Bankruptcy.

Separability of Provisions. For separability of provisions of Title III of Pub.L. 98–353, see section 551 of Pub.L. 98–353 set out as a Separability of Provisions note preceding chapter 1 of Title 11, Bankruptcy.

Cross References

Amount and number of claims within class as including claims formerly held by certain creditors, see section 946.
Applicability of subsecs. (a) to (c) and (e) to (g) of this section in chapter 9 cases, see section 901.

Library References:

C.J.S. Bankruptcy §§ 401–405.
West's Key No. Digests, Bankruptcy ⊙—3541–3547.

WESTLAW Electronic Research

See WESTLAW Electronic Research Guide following the *Bankruptcy Highlights*.

§ 1127. Modification of plan

(a) The proponent of a plan may modify such plan at any time before confirmation, but may not modify such plan so that such plan as modified fails to meet the requirements of sections 1122 and 1123 of this title. After the proponent of a plan files a modification of such plan with the court, the plan as modified becomes the plan.

(b) The proponent of a plan or the reorganized debtor may modify such plan at any time after confirmation of such plan and before substantial consummation of such plan, but may not modify such plan so that such plan as modified fails to meet the requirements of sections 1122 and 1123 of this title. Such plan as modified under this subsection becomes the plan only if circumstances warrant such modification and the court, after notice and a hearing, confirms such plan as modified, under section 1129 of this title.

(c) The proponent of a modification shall comply with section 1125 of this title with respect to the plan as modified.

(d) Any holder of a claim or interest that has accepted or rejected a plan is deemed to have accepted or rejected, as the case may be, such plan as modified, unless, within the time fixed by the court, such holder changes such holder's previous acceptance or rejection.

Pub.L. 95–598, Nov. 6, 1978, 92 Stat. 2635; Pub.L. 98–353, Title III, § 511, July 10, 1984, 98 Stat. 386.

Historical and Revision Notes

Notes of Committee on the Judiciary, Senate Report No. 95–989. Under subsection (a) the proponent may file a proposal to modify a plan prior to confirmation. In the case of a public company the modifying proposal may be filed prior to approval.

Subsection (b) provides that a party in interest eligible to file a plan may file instead of a plan a proposal to modify a plan filed by another. Under subsection (c) a party in interest objecting to some feature of a plan may submit a proposal to modify the plan to meet the objection.

After a plan has been confirmed, but before its substantial consummation, a plan may be modified by leave of court, which subsection (d) provides shall be granted for good cause. Subsection (e) provides that a proposal to modify a plan is subject to the disclosure requirements of section 1125 and as provided in subsection (f). It provides that a creditor or stockholder who voted for or against a plan is deemed to have accepted or rejected the modifying proposal. But if the modification materially and adversely affects any of their interests, they must be afforded an opportunity to change their vote in accordance with the disclosure and solicitation requirements of section 1125.

Under subsection (g) a plan, if modified prior to confirmation, shall be confirmed if it meets the requirements of section 1130.

Notes of Committee on the Judiciary, House Report No. 95–595. Subsection (a) permits the proponent of a plan to modify it at any time before confirmation, subject, of course, to the requirements of sections 1122 and 1123, governing classification and contents of a plan. After the proponent of a plan files a modification with the court, the plan as modified becomes the plan, and is to be treated the same as an original plan.

Subsection (b) permits modification of a plan after confirmation under certain circumstances. The modification must be proposed before substantial consummation of the plan. The requirements of sections 1122 and 1123 continue to apply. The plan as modified under this subsection becomes the plan only if the court confirms the plan as modified under section 1129 and the circumstances warrant the modification.

Subsection (c) requires the proponent of a modification to comply with the disclosure provisions of section 1125. Of course, if the modification were sufficiently minor, the court might determine that additional disclosure was not required under the circumstances.

Subsection (d) simplifies modification procedure by deeming any creditor or equity security holder that has already accepted or rejected the plan to have accepted or rejected the modification, unless, within the time fixed by the court, the creditor or equity security holder changes this previous acceptance or rejection.

Legislative Statements. Section 1127(a) of the House amendment adopts a provision contained in the House bill permitting only the proponent of a plan to modify the plan and

rejecting the alternative of open modification contained in the Senate amendment.

Effective Date of 1984 Amendments. See section 553 of Pub.L. 98–353, Title III, July 10, 1984, 98 Stat. 392, set out as an Effective Date of 1984 Amendment note preceding chapter 1 of Title 11, Bankruptcy.

Separability of Provisions. For separability of provisions of Title III of Pub.L. 98–353, see section 551 of Pub.L. 98–353, set out as a Separability of Provisions note preceding chapter 1 of Title 11, Bankruptcy.

Cross References

Applicability of subsec. (d) of this section in chapter 9 cases, see section 901.
Modification of plan filed in chapter 9 cases, see section 942.
Modification of plan filed in chapter 13 cases,
    After confirmation, see section 1329.
    Before confirmation, see section 1323.

Library References:

C.J.S. Bankruptcy § 410.
West's Key No. Digests, Bankruptcy ⬦3569.

WESTLAW Electronic Research

See WESTLAW Electronic Research Guide following the *Bankruptcy Highlights.*

§ 1128. Confirmation hearing

(a) After notice, the court shall hold a hearing on confirmation of a plan.

(b) A party in interest may object to confirmation of a plan.

Pub.L. 95–598, Nov. 6, 1978, 92 Stat. 2635.

Historical and Revision Notes

Notes of Committee on the Judiciary, Senate Report No. 95–989. Subsection (a) requires that there be a hearing in every case on the confirmation of the plan. Notice is required.

Subsection (b) permits any party in interest to object to the confirmation of the plan. The

Securities and Exchange Commission and indenture trustees, as parties in interest under section 1109, may object to confirmation of the plan.

Cross References

Applicability of this section in chapter 9 cases, see section 901.
Confirmation hearing in chapter 13 cases, see section 1324.
Right to be heard in cases under this chapter, see section 1109.

Library References:

C.J.S. Bankruptcy § 406.
West's Key No. Digests, Bankruptcy ⬦3566.

WESTLAW Electronic Research

See WESTLAW Electronic Research Guide following the *Bankruptcy Highlights.*

§ 1129. Confirmation of plan

(a) The court shall confirm a plan only if all of the following requirements are met:

(1) The plan complies with the applicable provisions of this title.

(2) The proponent of the plan complies with the applicable provisions of this title.

(3) The plan has been proposed in good faith and not by any means forbidden by law.

(4) Any payment made or to be made by the proponent, by the debtor, or by a person issuing securities or acquiring property under the plan, for services or for costs and expenses in or in connection with the case, or in connection with the plan and incident to the case, has been approved by, or is subject to the approval of, the court as reasonable;

(5)(A)(i) The proponent of the plan has disclosed the identity and affiliations of any individual proposed to serve, after confirmation of the plan, as a director, officer, or voting trustee of the debtor, an affiliate of the debtor participating in a joint plan with the debtor, or a successor to the debtor under the plan; and

(ii) the appointment to, or continuance in, such office of such individual, is consistent with the interests of creditors and equity security holders and with public policy; and

(B) the proponent of the plan has disclosed the identity of any insider that will be employed or retained by the reorganized debtor, and the nature of any compensation for such insider.

(6) Any governmental regulatory commission with jurisdiction, after confirmation of the plan, over the rates of the debtor has approved any rate change provided for in the plan, or such rate change is expressly conditioned on such approval.

(7) With respect to each impaired class of claims or interests—

(A) each holder of a claim or interest of such class—

(i) has accepted the plan; or

(ii) will receive or retain under the plan on account of such claim or interest property of a value, as of the effective date of the plan, that is not less than the amount that such holder would so receive or retain if the debtor were liquidated under chapter 7 of this title on such date; or

(B) if section 1111(b)(2) of this title applies to the claims of such class, each holder of a claim of such class will receive or retain under the plan on account of such claim property of a value, as of the effective date of the plan, that is not less than the value of such holder's interest in the estate's interest in the property that secures such claims.

(8) With respect to each class of claims or interests—

(A) such class has accepted the plan; or

(B) such class is not impaired under the plan.

(9) Except to the extent that the holder of a particular claim has agreed to a different treatment of such claim, the plan provides that—

(A) with respect to a claim of a kind specified in section 507(a)(1) or 507(a)(2) of this title, on the effective date of the plan, the holder of such claim will receive on account of such claim cash equal to the allowed amount of such claim;

(B) with respect to a class of claims of a kind specified in section 507(a)(3), 507(a)(4), 507(a)(5) or 507(a)(6) of this title, each holder of a claim of such class will receive—

(i) if such class has accepted the plan, deferred cash payments of a value, as of the effective date of the plan, equal to the allowed amount of such claim; or

(ii) if such class has not accepted the plan, cash on the effective date of the plan equal to the allowed amount of such claim; and

(C) with respect to a claim of a kind specified in section 507(a)(7) of this title, the holder of such claim will receive on account of such claim deferred cash payments, over a period not exceeding six years after the date of assessment of such claim, of a value, as of the effective date of the plan, equal to the allowed amount of such claim.

(10) If a class of claims is impaired under the plan, at least one class of claims that is impaired under the plan has accepted the plan, determined without including any acceptance of the plan by any insider.

(11) Confirmation of the plan is not likely to be followed by the liquidation, or the need for further financial reorganization, of the debtor or any successor to the debtor under the plan, unless such liquidation or reorganization is proposed in the plan.

(12) All fees payable under section 1930, as determined by the court at the hearing on confirmation of the plan, have been paid or the plan provides for the payment of all such fees on the effective date of the plan.

(13) The plan provides for the continuation after its effective date of payment of all retiree benefits, as that term is defined in section 1114 of this title, at the level established pursuant to subsection (e)(1)(B) or (g) of section 1114 of this title, at any time prior to confirmation of the plan, for the duration of the period the debtor has obligated itself to provide such benefits.

(b)(1) Notwithstanding section 510(a) of this title, if all of the applicable requirements of subsection (a) of this section other than paragraph (8) are met with respect to a plan, the court, on request of the proponent of the plan, shall confirm the plan notwithstanding the requirements of such paragraph if the plan does not discriminate unfairly, and is fair and equitable, with respect to each class of claims or interests that is impaired under, and has not accepted, the plan.

(2) For the purpose of this subsection, the condition that a plan be fair and equitable with respect to a class includes the following requirements:

(A) With respect to a class of secured claims, the plan provides—

(i)(I) that the holders of such claims retain the liens securing such claims, whether the property subject to such liens is retained by the debtor or transferred to another entity, to the extent of the allowed amount of such claims; and

(II) that each holder of a claim of such class receive on account of such claim deferred cash payments totaling at least the allowed amount of such claim, of a value, as of the effective date of the plan, of at least the value of such holder's interest in the estate's interest in such property;

(ii) for the sale, subject to section 363(k) of this title, of any property that is subject to the liens securing such claims, free and clear of such liens, with such liens to attach to the proceeds of such sale, and the treatment of such liens on proceeds under clause (i) or (iii) of this subparagraph; or

(iii) for the realization by such holders of the indubitable equivalent of such claims.

(B) With respect to a class of unsecured claims—

(i) the plan provides that each holder of a claim of such class receive or retain on account of such claim property of a value, as of the effective date of the plan, equal to the allowed amount of such claim; or

(ii) the holder of any claim or interest that is junior to the claims of such class will not receive or retain under the plan on account of such junior claim or interest any property.

(C) With respect to a class of interests—

(i) the plan provides that each holder of an interest of such class receive or retain on account of such interest property of a value, as of the effective date of the plan, equal to the greatest of the allowed amount of any fixed liquidation preference to which such holder is entitled, any fixed redemption price to which such holder is entitled, or the value of such interest; or

(ii) the holder of any interest that is junior to the interests of such class will not receive or retain under the plan on account of such junior interest any property.

(c) Notwithstanding subsections (a) and (b) of this section and except as provided in section 1127(b) of this title, the court may confirm only one plan, unless the order of confirmation in the case has been revoked under section 1144 of this title. If the requirements of subsections (a) and (b) of this section are met with respect to more than one plan, the court shall consider the preferences of creditors and equity security holders in determining which plan to confirm.

(d) Notwithstanding any other provision of this section, on request of a party in interest that is a governmental unit, the court may not confirm a plan if the principal purpose of the plan is the avoidance of taxes or the avoidance of the application of section 5 of the Securities Act of 1933 (15 U.S.C. 77e). In any hearing under this subsection, the governmental unit has the burden of proof on the issue of avoidance.

Pub.L. 95–598, Nov. 6, 1978, 92 Stat. 2635; Pub.L. 98–353, Title III, § 512, July 10, 1984, 98 Stat. 386; Pub.L. 99–554, Title II, §§ 225, 283(v), Oct. 27, 1986, 100 Stat. 3102, 3118; Pub.L. 100–334, § 2(b), June 16, 1988, 102 Stat. 613.

Historical and Revision Notes

Notes of Committee on the Judiciary, Senate Report No. 95–989. Subsection (a) enumerates the requirement governing confirmation of a plan. The court is required to confirm a plan if and only if all of the requirements are met.

Paragraph (1) requires that the plan comply with the applicable provisions of chapter 11, such as sections 1122 and 1123, governing classification and contents of plan.

Paragraph (2) requires that the proponent of the plan comply with the applicable provisions of chapter 11, such as section 1125 regarding disclosure.

Paragraph (3) requires that the plan have been proposed in good faith, and not by any means forbidden by law.

Paragraph (4) is derived from section 221 of chapter X [former section 621 of this title]. It requires that any payment made or promised by the proponent, the debtor, or person issuing securities or acquiring property under the plan, for services or for costs and expenses in, or in connection with the case, or in connection with the plan and incident to the case, be disclosed to the court. In addition, any payment made before confirmation must have been reasonable, and any payment to be fixed after confirmation must be subject to the approval of the court as reasonable.

Paragraph (5) is also derived from section 221 of chapter X [former section 621 of this title]. It requires the plan to disclose the identity and affiliations of any individual proposed to serve, after confirmation, as a director, officer, or voting trustee of the reorganized debtor. The appointment to or continuance in one of these offices by the individual must be consistent with the interests of creditors and equity security holders and with public policy. The plan must also disclose the identity of any insider that will be employed or retained by the reorganized debtor, and the nature of any compensation to be paid to the insider.

Paragraph (6) permits confirmation only if any regulatory commission that will have jurisdiction over the debtor after confirmation of the plan has approved any rate change provided for in the plan, as an alternative, the rate change may be conditioned on such approval.

Paragraph (7) provides that in the case of a public company the court shall confirm the plan if it finds the plan to be fair and equitable and the plan either (1) has been accepted by classes of claims or interests as provided in section 1126, or (2), if not so accepted, satisfies the requirements of subsection (b) of this section.

Paragraphs (8) and (9) apply only in nonpublic cases. Paragraph (8) does not apply the fair and equitable standards in two situations. The first occurs if there is unanimous consent of all affected holders of claims and interests. It is also sufficient for purposes of confirmation if each holder of a claim or interest receives or retains consideration of a value, as of the effective date of the plan, that is not less than each would have or receive if the debtor were liquidated under chapter 7 of this title. This standard adapts the test of "best interest of creditors" as interpreted by the courts under chapter XI [former section 701 et seq. of this title]. It is given broader application in chapter 11 of this title since a plan under chapter 11 may affect not only unsecured claims but secured claims and stock as well.

Under paragraph (9)(A), if a class of claims or interests has not accepted the plan, the court will confirm the plan if, for the dissenting class and any class of equal rank, the negotiated plan provides in value no less than under a plan that is fair and equitable. Such review and determination are not required for any other classes that accepted the plan.

Paragraph 9(A) would permit a senior creditor to adjust his participation for the benefit of stockholders. In such a case, junior creditors, who have not been satisfied in full, may not object if, absent the "give-up", they are receiving all that a fair and equitable plan would give them. To illustrate, suppose the estate is valued at $1.5 million and claims and stock are:

	Claims and stock (millions)	Equity (millions)
(1) Senior debt	$1.2	$1.2
(2) Junior debt	.5	.3
(3) Stock	(¹)	—
Total	1.7	1.5

¹ No value.

Under the plan, the senior creditor gives up $100,000 in value for the benefit of stockholders as follows:

	Millions
(1) Senior debt	$1.1
(2) Junior debt	.3

If the junior creditors dissent, the court may nevertheless confirm the plan since under the fair and equitable standard they had an equity of only $300,000 and the allocation to equity security holders did not affect them.

Paragraph 9(A) provides a special alternative with respect to secured claims. A plan may be confirmed against a dissenting class of secured claims if the plan or order of confirmation provides for the realization of their security (1) by the retention of the property subject to such security; (2) by a sale of the property and transfer of the claim to the proceeds of sale if the secured creditors were permitted to bid at the sale and set off against the purchase price up to the allowed amount of their claims; or (3) by such other method that will assure them the realization of the indubitable equivalent of the allowed amount of their secured claims. The indubitable equivalent language is intended to follow the strict approach taken by Judge Learned Hand in In Re Murel Holding Corp. 7, 5 F.2d 941 (2nd Cir.1935).

Paragraph (9)(B) provides that, if a class of claims or interests is excluded from participation under the plan, the court may nevertheless confirm the plan if it determines that no class on a parity with or junior to such participates under the plan. In the previous illustration, no confirmation would be permitted if the negotiated plan would grant a participation to stockholders but nothing for junior creditors. As noted elsewhere, by reason of section 1126(g), an excluded class is a dissenting class under section 1130.

Paragraph (10) states that, to be confirmed, the plan must provide that each holder of a claim under section 507 will receive property, as therein noted, of a value equal to the allowed amount of the claim. There are two exceptions: (A) The holder thereof may agree to a different settlement in part or in whole; (B) where a debtor's business is reorganized under chapter 11, this provision requires that taxes entitled to priority (including administrative claims or taxes) must be paid in cash not later than 120 days after the plan is confirmed, unless the Secretary of the Treasury agrees to other terms or kinds of payment. The bill, as introduced, required full payment in cash within 60 days after the plan is confirmed.

Paragraph (11) requires a determination regarding feasibility of the plan. It is a slight elaboration of the law that has developed in the application of the word "feasible" in Chapter X of the present Act [former section 501 et seq. of this title].

Paragraph (12) requires that at least one class must accept the plan, but any claims or interests held by insiders are not to be included for purposes of determining the number and amount of acceptances.

Subsection (b) provides that if, in the case of a public company, the plan meets the requirements of subsection (a) (except paragraphs (8) and (9) which do not apply to such a company), the court is to confirm the plan if the plan or the order of confirmation provides adequate protection for the realization of the value of the claims or interests of each class not accepting the plan. The intent is to incorporate inclusively, as a guide to the meaning of subsection (a) the provisions of section 216(7) (11 U.S.C. 616(7)) [former section 616(7) of this title] with respect to claims and section 216(8) (11 U.S.C. 616(8)) [former section 616(8) of this title] with respect to equity security interests.

Under subsection (c) the court may confirm only one plan, unless the order of confirmation has been revoked under section 1144. If the requirements for confirmation are met with respect to more than one plan, the court shall consider the preferences of creditors and stockholders in deciding which plan to confirm.

Subsection (d) provides that the bankruptcy court may not confirm a plan of reorganization if its principal purpose is the avoidance of taxes or the avoidance of section 5 of the Securities Act of 1933 (15 U.S.C. 77e) [section 77e of Title 15, Commerce and Trade]. This rule modifies a similar provision of present law (section 269 of the Bankruptcy Act) [former section 669 of this title].

Notes of Committee on the Judiciary, House Report No. 95–595. Paragraph (7) incorporates the former "best interest of creditors" test found in chapter 11, but spells out precisely what is intended. With respect to each class, the holders of the claims or interests of that class must receive or retain under the plan on account of those claims or interest property of a value, as of the effective date of the plan, that is not less than the amount that they would so receive or retain if the debtor were liquidated under chapter 7 on the effective date of the plan.

In order to determine the hypothetical distribution in a liquidation, the court will have to consider the various subordination provisions of proposed 11 U.S.C. 510, 726(a)(3), 726(a)(4), and the postponement provisions of proposed 11 U.S.C. 724. Also applicable in appropriate cases will be the rules governing partnership distributions under proposed 11 U.S.C. 723, and distributions of community property under proposed 11 U.S.C. 726(c). Under subparagraph (A), a particular holder is permitted to accept less than liquidation value, but his acceptance does not bind the class.

Property under subparagraph (B) may include securities of the debtor. Thus, the provision will apply in cases in which the plan is confirmed under proposed 11 U.S.C. 1129(b).

Paragraph (8) is central to the confirmation standards. It requires that each class either have accepted the plan or be unimpaired.

Paragraph (9) augments the requirements of paragraph (8) by requiring payment of each priority claim in full. It permits payments over time and payment other than in cash, but payment in securities is not intended to be permitted without consent of the priority claimant even if the class has consented. It also permits a particular claimant to accept less than full payment.

Subsection (b) permits the court to confirm a plan notwithstanding failure of compliance with paragraph (8) of subsection (a). The plan must comply with all other paragraphs of subsection (a), including paragraph (9). This subsection contains the so-called cramdown. It requires simply that the plan meet certain standards of fairness to dissenting creditors or equity security holders. The general principle of the subsection permits confirmation notwithstanding nonacceptance by an impaired class if that class and all below it in priority are treated according to the absolute priority rule. The dissenting class must be paid in full before any junior class may share under the plan. If it is paid in full, then junior classes may share. Treatment of classes of secured creditors is slightly different because they do not fall in the priority ladder, but the principle is the same.

Specifically, the court may confirm a plan over the objection of a class of secured claims if the members of that class are unimpaired or if they are to receive under the plan property of a value equal to the allowed amount of their secured claims, as determined under proposed 11 U.S.C. 506(a). The property is to be valued as of the effective date of the plan, thus recognizing the time-value of money. As used throughout this subsection, "property" includes both tangible and intangible property, such as a security of the debtor or a successor to the debtor under a reorganization plan.

The court may confirm over the dissent of a class of unsecured claims, including priority claims, only if the members of the class are unimpaired, if they will receive under the plan property of a value equal to the allowed amount of their unsecured claims, or if no class junior will share under the plan. That is, if the class is impaired, then they must be paid in full or, if paid less than in full, then no class junior may receive anything under the plan. This codifies the absolute priority rule from the dissenting class on down.

With respect to classes of equity, the court may confirm over a dissent if the members of the class are unimpaired, if they receive their liquidation preference or redemption rights, if any, or if no class junior shares under the plan. This, too, is a codification of the absolute priority rule with respect to equity. If a partnership agreement subordinates limited partners to general partners to any degree, then the general principles of paragraph (3) of this subsection would apply to prevent the general partners from being squeezed out.

One requirement applies generally to all classes before the court may confirm under this subsection. No class may be paid more than in full.

The partial codification of the absolute priority rule here is not intended to deprive senior creditor of compensation for being required to take securities in the reorganized debtor that are of an equal priority with the securities offered to a junior class. Under current law, seniors are entitled to compensation for their loss of priority, and the increased risk put upon them by being required to give up their priority will be reflected in a lower value of the securities given to them than the value of comparable securities given to juniors that have not lost a priority position.

Finally, the proponent must request use of this subsection. The court may not confirm notwithstanding nonacceptance unless the proponent requests and the court may then confirm only if subsection (b) is complied with. The court may not rewrite the plan.

A more detailed explanation follows:

The test to be applied by the court is set forth in the various paragraphs of section 1129(b). The elements of the test are new departing from both the absolute priority rule and the best interests of creditors tests found under the Bankruptcy Act. The court is not permitted to alter the terms of the plan. It must merely decide whether the plan complies with the requirements of section 1129(b). If so, the plan is confirmed, if not the plan is denied confirmation.

The procedure followed is simple. The court examines each class of claims or interests designated under section 1123(a)(1) to see if the requirements of section 1129(b) are met. If the class is a class of secured claims, then paragraph (1) contains two tests that must be complied with in order for confirmation to occur. First, under subparagraph (A), the court must be able to find that the consideration given under the plan on account of the secured claim does not exceed the allowed amount of the claim. This condition is not prescribed as a matter of law under section 1129(a), because if the secured claim is compensated in securities of the debtor, a valuation of the business would be necessary to determine the value of the consideration. While section 1129(a) does not contemplate a valuation of the debtor's business, such a valuation will almost always be required under section 1129(b) in order to determine the value of the consideration to be distributed under the plan. Once the valuation is performed, it becomes a simple matter to impose the criterion that no claim will be paid more than in full.

Application of the test under subparagraph (A) also requires a valuation of the consideration "as of the effective date of the plan". This contemplates a present value analysis that will discount value to be received in the future; of course, if the interest rate paid is equivalent to the discount rate used, the present value and face future value will be identical. On the other hand, if no interest is proposed to be paid, the present value will be less than the face future value. For example, consider an allowed secured claim of $1,000 in a class by itself. One plan could propose to pay $1,000 on account of this claim as of the effective date of the plan. Another plan could propose to give a note with a $1,000 face amount due five years after the effective date of the plan on account of this claim. A third plan could propose to give a note in a face amount of $1,000 due five years from the effective date of the plan plus six percent annual interest commencing on the effective date of the plan on account of this claim. The first plan clearly meets the requirements of subparagraph (A) because the amount received on account of the second claim has an equivalent present value as of the effective date of the plan equal to the allowed amount of such claim.

The second plan also meets the requirements of subparagraph (A) because the present value of the five years note as of the effective date of the plan will never exceed the allowed amount of the secured claim; the higher the discount rate, the less present value the note will have. Whether the third plan complies with subparagraph (A) depends on whether the discount rate is less than six percent. Normally, the interest rate used in the plan will be prima facie evidence of the discount rate because the interest rate will reflect an arms length determination of the risk of the security involved and feasibility considerations will tend to understate interest payments. If the court found the discount rate to be greater than or equal to the interest rate used in the plan, then subparagraph (A) would be complied with because the value of the note as of the effective date of the plan would not exceed the allowed amount of the second claim. If, however, the court found the discount rate to be less than the interest rate proposed under the plan, then the present value of the note would exceed $1,000 and the plan would fail of confirmation. On the other hand, it is important to recognize that the future principal amount of a note in excess of the allowed amount of a secured claim may have a present value less than such allowed amount, if the interest rate under the plan is correspondingly less than the discount rate.

Even if the requirements of subparagraph (A) are complied with, the class of secured claims must satisfy one of the three clauses in paragraph (B) in order to pass muster. It is sufficient for confirmation if the class has accepted the plan, or if the claims of the class are unimpaired, or if each holder of a secured claim in the class will receive property of a value as of the effective date of the plan equal to the allowed amount of such claim (unless he has agreed to accept less). It is important to note that under section 506(a), the allowed amount of the secured claim will not include any extent to which the amount of such claim exceeds the value of the property securing such claim. Thus, instead of focusing on secured creditors or unsecured creditors, the statute focuses on secured claims and unsecured claims.

After the court has applied paragraph (1) to each class of secured claims, it then applies paragraph (2) to each class of unsecured claims. Again two separate components must be tested. Subparagraph (A) is identical with the test under section 1129(b)(1)(A) insofar as the holder of an unsecured claim is not permitted to receive property of a value as of the effective date of the plan on account of such claim that is greater than the allowed amount of such claim. In addition, subparagraph (B) requires compliance with one of four conditions. The conditions in clauses (i)–(iii) mirror the conditions of acceptance unimpairment, or full value found in connection with secured claims in section 1129(b)(1)(B).

The condition contained in section 1129(b)(2)(B)(iv) provides another basis for confirming the plan with respect to a class of unsecured claims. It will be of greatest use when an impaired class that has not accepted the plan is to receive less than full value under the plan. The plan may be confirmed under clause (iv) in those circumstances if the class is not unfairly discriminated against with respect to equal classes and if junior classes will receive nothing under the plan. The second criterion is the easier to understand. It is designed to prevent a senior class from giving up consideration to a junior class unless every intermediate class consents, is paid in full, or is unimpaired. This gives intermediate creditors a great deal of leverage in negotiating with senior or secured creditors who wish to have a plan that gives value to equity. One aspect of this test that is not obvious is that whether one class is senior, equal, or junior to another class is relative and not absolute. Thus from the perspective of trade creditors holding unsecured claims, claims of senior and subordinated debentures may be entitled to share on an equal basis with the trade claims. However, from the perspective of the senior unsecured debt, the subordinated debentures are junior.

This point illustrates the lack of precision in the first criterion which demands that a class not be unfairly discriminated against with respect to equal classes. From the perspective of unsecured trade claims, there is no unfair discrimination as long as the total consideration given all other classes of equal rank does not exceed the amount that would result from an exact aliquot distribution. Thus if trade creditors, senior debt, and subordinate debt are each owed $100 and the plan proposes to pay the trade debt $15, the senior debt $30, and the junior debt $0, the plan would not unfairly discriminate against the trade debt nor would any other allocation of consideration under the plan between the senior and junior debt be unfair as to the trade debt as long as the aggregate consideration is less than $30. The senior debt could take $25 and give up $5 to the junior debt and the trade debt would have no cause to complain because

as far as it is concerned the junior debt is an equal class.

However, in this latter case the senior debt would have been unfairly discriminated against because the trade debt was being unfairly over-compensated; of course the plan would also fail unless the senior debt was unimpaired, received full value, or accepted the plan, because from its perspective a junior class received property under the plan. Application of the test from the perspective of senior debt is best illustrated by the plan that proposes to pay trade debt $15, senior debt $25, and junior debt $0. Here the senior debt is being unfairly discriminated against with respect to the equal trade debt even though the trade debt receives less than the senior debt. The discrimination arises from the fact that the senior debt is entitled to the rights of the junior debt which in this example entitle the senior debt to share on a 2:1 basis with the trade debt.

Finally, it is necessary to interpret the first criterion from the perspective of subordinated debt. The junior debt is subrogated to the rights of senior debt once the senior debt is paid in full. Thus, while the plan that pays trade debt $15, senior debt $25, and junior debt $0 is not unfairly discriminatory against the junior debt, a plan that proposes to pay trade debt $55, senior debt $100, and junior debt $1, would be unfairly discriminatory. In order to avoid discriminatory treatment against the junior debt, at least $10 would have to be received by such debt under those facts.

The criterion of unfair discrimination is not derived from the fair and equitable rule or from the best interests of creditors test. Rather it preserves just treatment of a dissenting class from the class's own perspective.

If each class of secured claims satisfies the requirements of section 1129(b)(1) and each class of unsecured claims satisfies the requirements of section 1129(b)(2), then the court must still see if each class of interests satisfies section 1129(b)(3) before the plan may be confirmed. Again, two separate criteria must be met. Under subparagraph (A) if the interest entitles the holder thereof to a fixed liquidation preference or if such interest may be redeemed at a fixed price, then the holder of such interest must not receive under the plan on account of such interest property of a value as of the effective date of the plan greater than the greater of these two values of the interest. Preferred stock would be an example of an interest likely to have liquidation preference or redemption price.

If an interest such as most common stock or the interest of a general partnership has neither a fixed liquidation preference nor a fixed redemption price, then the criterion in subparagraph (A) is automatically fulfilled. In addition subparagraph (B) contains five clauses that impose alternative conditions of which at least one must be satisfied in order to warrant confirmation. The first two clauses contain requirements of acceptance or unimpairment similar to the first two clauses in paragraphs (1)(B) and (2)(B). Clause (iii) is similar to the unimpairment test contained in section 1124(3)(B), except that it will apply to cover the issuance securities of the debtor of a value as of the effective date of the plan equal to the greater of any fixed liquidation preference or redemption price. The fourth clause allows confirmation if junior interests are not compensated under the plan and the fifth clause allows confirmation if there are no junior interests. These clauses recognized that as long as senior classes receive no more than full payment, the objection of a junior class will not defeat confirmation unless a class junior to it is receiving value under the plan and the objecting class is impaired. While a determination of impairment may be made under section 1124(3)(B)(iii) without a precise valuation of the business when common stock is clearly under water, once section 1129(b) is used, a more detailed valuation is a necessary byproduct. Thus, if no property is given to a holder of an interest under the plan, the interest should be clearly worthless in order to find unimpairment under section 1124(3)(B)(iii) and section 1129(a)(8); otherwise, since a class of interests receiving no property is deemed to object under section 1126(g), the more precise valuation of section 1129(b) should be used.

If all of the requirements of section 1129(b) are complied with, then the court may confirm the plan subject to other limitations such as those found in section 1129(a) and (d).

Subsection (c) of section 1129 governs confirmation when more than one plan meets the requirements of the section. The court must consider the preferences of creditors and equity security holders in determining which plan to confirm.

Subsection (d) requires the court to deny confirmation if the principal purpose of the plan is the avoidance of taxes (through use of sections 346 and 1146, and applicable provisions of State law or the Internal Revenue Code [Title 26] governing bankruptcy reorganizations) or the avoidance of section 5 of the Securities Act of 1933 [section 77e of Title 15, Commerce and Trade] (through use of section 1145).

Legislative Statements. Section 1129 of the House amendment relates to confirmation of a plan in a case under chapter 11. Section 1129(a)(3) of the House amendment adopts the position taken in the Senate amendment and section 1129(a)(5) takes the position adopted in the House bill. Section 1129(a)(7) adopts the position taken in the House bill in order to insure that the dissenting members of an accepting class will receive at least what they would otherwise receive under the best interest of creditors test; it also requires that even the members of a class that has rejected the plan be protected by the best interest of creditors test for those rare cramdown cases where a class of creditors would receive more on liquidation than under reorganization of the debtor. Section 1129(a)(7)(C) is discussed in connection with section 1129(b) and section 1111(b). Section 1129(a)(8) of the House amendment adopts the provision taken in the House bill which permits confirmation of a plan as to a particular class without resort to the fair and equitable test if the class has accepted a plan or is unimpaired under the plan.

Section 1129(a)(9) represents a compromise between a similar provision contained in the House bill and the Senate amendment. Under subparagraph (A) claims entitled to priority under section 507(a)(1) or (2) are entitled to receive cash on the effective date of the plan equal to the amount of the claim. Under subparagraph (B) claims entitled to priority under section 507(a)(3), (4), or (5), are entitled to receive deferred cash payments of a present value as of the effective date of the plan equal to the amount of the claims if the class has accepted the plan or cash payments on the effective date of the plan otherwise. Tax claims entitled to priority under section 507(a)(6) of different governmental units may not be contained in one class although all claims of one such unit may be combined and such unit may be required to take deferred cash payments over a period not to exceed 6 years after the date of assessment of the tax with the present value equal to the amount of the claim.

Section 1129(a)(10) is derived from section 1130(a)(12) of the Senate amendment.

Section 1129(b) is new. Together with section 1111(b) and section 1129(a)(7)(C), this section provides when a plan may be confirmed, notwithstanding the failure of an impaired class to accept the plan under section 1129(a) (8). Before discussing section 1129(b) an understanding of section 1111(b) is necessary. Section 1111(b)(1), the general rule that a secured claim is to be treated as a recourse claim in chapter 11 whether or not the claim is nonrecourse by agreement or applicable law. This preferred status for a nonrecourse loan terminates if the property securing the loan is sold under section 363 or is to be sold under the plan.

The preferred status also terminates if the class of which the secured claim is a part elects application of section 1111(b)(2). Section 1111(b)(2) provides that an allowed claim is a secured claim to the full extent the claim is allowed rather than to the extent of the collateral as under section 506(a). A class may elect application of paragraph (2) only if the security is not of inconsequential value and, if the creditor is a recourse creditor, the collateral is not sold under section 363 or to be sold under the plan. Sale of property under section 363 or under the plan is excluded from treatment under section 1111(b) because of the secured party's right to bid in the full amount of his allowed claim at any sale of collateral under section 363(k) of the House amendment.

As previously noted, section 1129(b) sets forth a standard by which a plan may be confirmed notwithstanding the failure of an impaired class to accept the plan.

Paragraph (1) makes clear that this alternative confirmation standard, referred to as "cram down," will be called into play only on the request of the proponent of the plan. Under this cramdown test, the court must confirm the plan if the plan does not discriminate unfairly, and is "fair and equitable," with respect to each class of claims or interests that is impaired under, and has not accepted, the plan. The requirement of the House bill that a plan not "discriminate unfairly" with respect to a class is included for clarity; the language in the House report interpreting that requirement, in the context of subordinated debentures, applies equally under the requirements of section 1129(b)(1) of the House amendment.

Although many of the factors interpreting "fair and equitable" are specified in paragraph (2), others, which were explicated in the description of section 1129(b) in the House report, were omitted from the House amendment to avoid statutory complexity and because they would undoubtedly be found by a

court to be fundamental to "fair and equitable" treatment of a dissenting class. For example, a dissenting class should be assured that no senior class receives more than 100 percent of the amount of its claims. While that requirement was explicitly included in the House bill, the deletion is intended to be one of style and not one of substance.

Paragraph (2) provides guidelines for a court to determine whether a plan is fair and equitable with respect to a dissenting class. It must be emphasized that the fair and equitable requirement applies only with respect to dissenting classes. Therefore, unlike the fair and equitable rule contained in chapter X [former section 501 et seq. of this title] and section 77 of the Bankruptcy Act [former section 205 of this title] under section 1129(b)(2), senior accepting classes are permitted to give up value to junior classes as long as no dissenting intervening class receives less than the amount of its claims in full. If there is no dissenting intervening class and the only dissent is from a class junior to the class to which value have been given up, then the plan may still be fair and equitable with respect to the dissenting class, as long as no class senior to the dissenting class has received more than 100 percent of the amount of its claims.

Paragraph (2) contains three subparagraphs, each of which applies to a particular kind of class of claims or interests that is impaired and has not accepted the plan. Subparagraph (A) applies when a class of secured claims is impaired and has not accepted the plan. The provision applies whether or not section 1111(b) applies. The plan may be crammed down notwithstanding the dissent of a secured class only if the plan complies with clause (i), (ii), or (iii).

Clause (i) permits cramdown if the dissenting class of secured claims will retain its lien on the property whether the property is retained by the debtor or transferred. It should be noted that the lien secures the allowed secured claim held by such holder. The meaning of "allowed secured claim" will vary depending on whether section 1111(b)(2) applies to such class.

If section 1111(b)(2) applies then the "electing" class is entitled to have the entire allowed amount of the debt related to such property secured by a lien even if the value of the collateral is less than the amount of the debt. In addition, the plan must provide for the holder to receive, on account of the allowed secured claims, payments, either present or deferred, of a principal face amount equal to the amount of the debt and of a present value equal to the value of the collateral.

For example, if a creditor loaned $15,000,000 to a debtor secured by real property worth $18,000,000 and the value of the real property had dropped to $12,000,000 by the date when the debtor commenced a proceeding under chapter 11, the plan could be confirmed notwithstanding the dissent of the creditor as long as the lien remains on the collateral to secure a $15,000,000 debt, the face amount of present or extended payments to be made to the creditor under the plan is at least $15,000,000, and the present value of the present or deferred payments is not less than $12,000,000. The House report accompanying the House bill described what is meant by "present value".

Clause (ii) is self explanatory. Clause (iii) requires the court to confirm the plan notwithstanding the dissent of the electing secured class if the plan provides for the realization by the secured class of the indubitable equivalents of the secured claims. The standard of "indubitable equivalents" is taken from In re Murel Holding Corp., 75 F.2d 941 (2d Cir.1935) (Learned Hand, Jr.).

Abandonment of the collateral to the creditor would clearly satisfy indubitable equivalence, as would a lien on similar collateral. However, present cash payments less than the secured claim would not satisfy the standard because the creditor is deprived of an opportunity to gain from a future increase in value of the collateral. Unsecured notes as to the secured claim or equity securities of the debtor would not be the indubitable equivalent. With respect to an oversecured creditor, the secured claim will never exceed the allowed claim.

Although the same language applies, a different result pertains with respect to a class of secured claims to which section 1111(b)(2) does not apply. This will apply to all claims secured by a right of setoff. The court must confirm the plan notwithstanding the dissent of such a class of secured claims if any of three alternative requirements is met. Under clause (i) the plan may be confirmed if the class retains a right of setoff or a lien securing the allowed secured claims of the class and the holders will receive payments of a present value equal to the allowed amount of their secured claims. Contrary to electing classes of secured creditors who retain a lien under subparagraph (A)(i)(I) to the extent of the en-

tire claims secured by such lien, nonelecting creditors retain a lien on collateral only to the extent of their allowed secured claims and not to the extent of any deficiency, and such secured creditors must receive present or deferred payments with a present value equal to the allowed secured claim, which in turn is only the equivalent of the value of the collateral under section 506(a).

Any deficiency claim of a nonelecting class of secured claims is treated as an unsecured claim and is not provided for under subparagraph (A). The plan may be confirmed under clause (ii) if the plan proposes to sell the property free and clear of the secured party's lien as long as the lien will attach to the proceeds and will receive treatment under clause (i) or (iii). Clause (iii) permits confirmation if the plan provides for the realization by the dissenting nonelecting class of secured claims of the indubitable equivalent of the secured claims of such class.

Contrary to an "electing" class to which section 1111(b)(2) applies, the nonelecting class need not be protected with respect to any future appreciation cured claim of such a class is never undersecured by reason of section 506(a). Thus the lien secures only the value of interest of such creditor in the collateral. To the extent deferred payments exceed that amount, they represent interest. In the event of a subsequent default, the portion of the face amount of deferred payments representing unaccrued interest will not be secured by the lien.

Subparagraph (B) applies to a dissenting class of unsecured claims. The court must confirm the plan notwithstanding the dissent of a class of impaired unsecured claims if the plan provides for such claims to receive property with a present value equal to the allowed amount of the claims. Unsecured claims may receive any kind of "property," which is used in its broadest sense, as long as the present value of the property given to the holders of unsecured claims is equal to the allowed amount of the claims. Some kinds of property, such as securities, may require difficult valuations by the court; in such circumstances the court need only determine that there is a reasonable likelihood that the property given the dissenting class of impaired unsecured claims equals the present value of such allowed claims.

Alternatively, under clause (ii), the court must confirm the plan if the plan provides that holders of any claims or interests junior to the interests of the dissenting class of impaired unsecured claims will not receive any property under the plan on account of such junior claims or interests. As long as senior creditors have not been paid more than in full, and classes of equal claims are being treated so that the dissenting class of impaired unsecured claims is not being discriminated against unfairly, the plan may be confirmed if the impaired class of unsecured claims receives less than 100 cents on the dollar (or nothing at all) as long as no class junior to the dissenting class receives anything at all. Such an impaired dissenting class may not prevent confirmation of a plan by objection merely because a senior class has elected to give up value to a junior class that is higher in priority than the impaired dissenting class of unsecured claims as long as the above safeguards are met.

Subparagraph (C) applies to a dissenting class of impaired interests. Such interests may include the interests of general or limited partners in a partnership, the interests of a sole proprietor in a proprietorship, or the interest of common or preferred stockholders in a corporation. If the holders of such interests are entitled to a fixed liquidation preference or fixed redemption price on account of such interests then the plan may be confirmed notwithstanding the dissent of such class of interests as long as it provides the holders property of a present value equal to the greatest of the fixed redemption price, or the value of such interests. In the event there is no fixed liquidation preference or redemption price, then the plan may be confirmed as long as it provides the holders of such interests property of a present value equal to the value of such interests. If the interests are "under water" then they will be valueless and the plan may be confirmed notwithstanding the dissent of that class of interests even if the plan provides that the holders of such interests will not receive any property on account of such interests.

Alternatively, under clause (ii), the court must confirm the plan notwithstanding the dissent of a class of interests if the plan provides that holders of any interests junior to the dissenting class of interests will not receive or retain any property on account of such junior interests. Clearly, if there are no junior interests junior to the class of dissenting interests, then the condition of clause (ii) is satisfied. The safeguards that no claim or interest receive more than 100 percent of the allowed amount of such claim or interest and that no class be discriminated against unfairly

will insure that the plan is fair and equitable with respect to the dissenting class of interests.

Except to the extent of the treatment of secured claims under subparagraph (A) of this statement, the House report remains an accurate description of confirmation of section 1129(b). Contrary to the example contained in the Senate report, a senior class will not be able to give up value to a junior class over the dissent of an intervening class unless the intervening class receives the full amount, as opposed to value, of its claims or interests.

One last point deserves explanation with respect to the admittedly complex subject of confirmation. Section 1129(a)(7)(C) in effect exempts secured creditors making an election under section 1111(b)(2) from application of the best interest of creditors test. In the absence of an election the amount such creditors receive in a plan of liquidation would be the value of their collateral plus any amount recovered on the deficiency in the case of a recourse loan. However, under section 1111(b)(2), the creditors are given an allowed secured claim to the full extent the claim is allowed and have no unsecured deficiency. Since section 1129(b)(2)(A) makes clear that an electing class need receive payments of a present value only equal to the value of the collateral, it is conceivable that under such a "cram down" the electing creditors would receive nothing with respect to their deficiency. The advantage to the electing creditors is that they have a lien securing the full amount of the allowed claim so that if the value of the collateral increases after the case is closed, the deferred payments will be secured claims. Thus it is both reasonable and necessary to exempt such electing class from application of section 1129(a)(7) as a logical consequence of permitting election under section 1111(b)(2).

Section 1131 of the Senate amendment is deleted as unnecessary in light of the protection given a secured creditor under section 1129(b) of the House amendment.

Payment of taxes in reorganizations. Under the provisions of section 1141 as revised by the House amendment, an individual in reorganization under chapter 11 will not be discharged from any debt, including prepetition tax liabilities, which are nondischargeable under section 523. Thus, an individual debtor whose plan of reorganization is confirmed under chapter 11 will remain liable for prepetition priority taxes, as defined in section 507, and for tax liabilities which receive no priority but are nondischargeable under section 523, including no return, late return, and fraud liabilities.

In the case of a partnership or a corporation in reorganization under chapter 11 of title 11, section 1141(d)(1) of the House amendment adopts a provision limiting the taxes that must be provided for in a plan before a plan can be confirmed to taxes which receive priority under section 507. In addition, the House amendment makes dischargeable, in effect, tax liabilities attributable to no return, late return, or fraud situations. The amendment thus does not adopt a shareholder continuity test such as was contained in section 1141(d)(2)(A)(iii) of the Senate amendment. However, the House amendment amends section 1106, relating to duties of the trustee, to require the trustee to furnish, on request of a tax authority and without personal liability, information available to the trustee concerning potential prepetition tax liabilities for unfiled returns of the debtor. Depending on the condition of the debtor's books and records, this information may include schedules and files available to the business. The House amendment also does not prohibit a tax authority from disallowing any tax benefit claimed after the reorganization if the item originated in a deduction, credit, or other item improperly reported before the reorganization occurred. It may also be appropriate for the Congress to consider in the future imposing civil or criminal liability on corporate officers for preparing a false or fraudulent tax return. The House amendment also contemplates that the Internal Revenue Service will monitor the relief from liabilities under this provision and advise the Congress if, and to the extent, any significant tax abuse may be resulting from the provision.

Medium of payment of taxes. Federal, State, and local taxes incurred during the administration period of the estate, and during the "gap" period in an involuntary case, are to be paid solely in cash. Taxes relating to third priority wages are to be paid, under the general rules, in cash on the effective date of the plan, if the class has not accepted the plan, in an amount equal to the allowed amount of the claim. If the class has accepted the plan, the taxes must be paid in cash but the payments must be made at the time the wages are paid which may be paid in deferred periodic installments having a value, on the effective date of the plan, equal to the allowed amount of the tax claims. Prepetition taxes entitled to sixth priority under section 507(a)(6) also must be paid in cash, but the plan may

also permit the debtor whether a corporation, partnership, or an individual, to pay the allowed taxes in installments over a period not to exceed 6 years following the date on which the tax authority assesses the tax liability, provided the value of the deferred payments representing principal and interest, as of the effective date of the plan, equals the allowed amount of the tax claim.

The House amendment also modifies the provisions of both bills dealing with the time when tax liabilities of a debtor in reorganization may be assessed by the tax authority. The House amendment follows the Senate amendment in deleting the limitation in present law under which a priority tax assessed after a reorganization plan is confirmed must be assessed within 1 year after the date of the filing of the petition. The House amendment specifies broadly that after the bankruptcy court determines the liability of the estate for a prepetition tax or for an administration period tax, the governmental unit may thereafter assess the tax against the estate, debtor, or successor to the debtor. The party to be assessed will, of course, depend on whether the case is under chapter 7, 11, or 13, whether the debtor is an individual, partnership, or a corporation, and whether the court is determining an individual debtor's personal liability for a nondischargeable tax. Assessment of the tax may only be made, however, within the limits of otherwise applicable law, such as the statute of limitations under the tax law.

Tax avoidance purpose. The House bill provided that no reorganization plan may be approved if the principal purpose of the plan is the avoidance of taxes. The Senate amendment modified the rule so that the bankruptcy court need make a determination of tax avoidance purpose only if it is asked to do so by the appropriate tax authority. Under the Senate amendment, if the tax authority does not request the bankruptcy court to rule on the purpose of the plan, the tax authority would not be barred from later asserting a tax avoidance motive with respect to allowance of a deduction or other tax benefit claimed after the reorganization. The House amendment adopts the substance of the Senate amendment, but does not provide a basis by which a tax authority may collaterally attack confirmation of a plan of reorganization other than under section 1144.

1986 Amendment. Subsec. (a)(12). Pub.L. 99–554, § 225, added par. (12).

See Effective Date of 1986 Amendment, etc., notes set out below.

Effective Date of 1988 Amendment; Application of Amendments. Amendment by Pub.L. 100–334 adding subsec. (a)(13) effective on June 16, 1988 and not applicable to cases commenced under this title before June 16, 1988, see section 4 of Pub.L. 100–334, set out as a note under section 1114 of this title.

Effective Date of 1986 Amendments; Effective Date of 1986 Amendments for Certain Judicial Districts Not Served by United States Trustees and for Judicial Districts in Alabama and North Carolina; U.S. Trustee System Fund Deposits in Alabama and North Carolina; Effective Date of Title 11 Chapter 15 Repeal as to Northern District of Alabama; Authority of Certain Estate Administrators in Alabama and North Carolina; Effective Date of 1986 Amendments in Pending Cases Where a U.S. Trustee Not Authorized or Where a Trustee Files Final Report or Plan is Confirmed; Quarterly Fees. Amendment by Pub.L. 99–554 effective 30 days after Oct. 27, 1986, except as otherwise provided for, see section 302(a) of Pub.L. 99–554, set out as a note under section 581 of Title 28, Judiciary and Judicial Procedure.

Amendment by Pub.L. 99–554, § 225, not to become effective in or with respect to certain specified judicial districts until, or apply to cases while pending in such district before, the expiration of the 270-day period beginning 30 days after Oct. 27, 1986, or of the 30-day period beginning on the date the Attorney General certifies under section 303 of Pub.L. 99–554 the region specified in a paragraph of section 581(a) of Title 28, as amended by section 111(a) of Pub.L. 99–554, that includes such district, whichever occurs first, see section 302(d)(1) of Pub.L. 99–554, set out as a note under section 581 of Title 28.

Amendment by Pub.L. 99–554, § 225, not to become effective in or with respect to certain specified judicial districts until, or apply to cases while pending in such district before, the expiration of the 2-year period beginning 30 days after Oct. 27, 1986, or of the 30-day period beginning on the date the Attorney General certifies under section 303 of Pub.L. 99–554 the region specified in a paragraph of section 581(a) of Title 28, as amended by section 111(a) of Pub.L. 99–554, that includes such district, whichever occurs first, see section 302(d)(2) of Pub.L. 99–554, set out as a note under section 581 of Title 28.

Amendment by Pub.L. 99–554, § 225, not to become effective in or with respect to judicial districts established for the States of Alabama and North Carolina until, or apply to cases while pending in such district before, such district elects to be included in a bankruptcy region established in section 581(a) of Title 28, as amended by section 111(a) of Pub.L. 99–554, or Oct. 1, 2002, whichever occurs first, and, except as otherwise provided for, with respect to cases under chapters 7, 11, 12, and 13 of Title 11 commenced before 30 days after Oct. 27, 1986, and pending in a judicial district in the States of Alabama or North Carolina before any election made under section 302(d)(3)(A) of Pub.L. 99–554 by such district becomes effective or Oct. 1, 2002, whichever occurs first, amendments by Pub.L. 99–554 not to apply until Oct. 1, 2003, or the expiration of the 1-year period beginning on the date such election becomes effective, whichever occurs first, and further, in any judicial district in Alabama or North Carolina not making the election described in section 302(d)(3)(A) of Pub.L. 99–554, any person appointed under regulations issued by the Judicial Conference to administer estates in cases under Title 11 authorized to establish, etc., a panel of private trustees, and to supervise cases and trustees in cases under chapters 7, 11, 12, and 13 of Title 11, until amendments by sections 201 to 231 of Pub.L. 99–554 effective in such district, see section 302(d)(3)(A) to (F), (H), (I) of Pub.L. 99–554, set out as a note under section 581 of Title 28.

Amendment by Pub.L. 99–554, § 225, except as otherwise provided, with respect to cases under chapters 7, 11, 12, and 13 of Title 11 commenced before 30 days after Oct. 27, 1986, and pending in a judicial district referred to in section 581(a) of Title 28, as amended by section 111(a) of Pub.L. 99–554, for which a United States trustee is not authorized before 30 days after Oct. 27, 1986 to be appointed, not applicable until the expiration of the 3-year period beginning on Oct. 27, 1986, or of the 1-year period beginning on the date the Attorney General certifies under section 303 of Pub.L. 99–554 the region specified in a paragraph of such section 581(a) that includes, such district, whichever occurs first, see section 302(e)(1), (2) of Pub.L. 99–554, set out as a note under section 581 of Title 28.

See 1986 Amendment notes set out above.

Effective Date of 1984 Amendments. See section 553 of Pub.L. 98–353, Title III, July 10, 1984, 98 Stat. 392, set out as an Effective Date of 1984 Amendment note preceding chapter 1 of Title 11, Bankruptcy.

Separability of Provisions. For separability of provisions of Title III of Pub.L. 98–

353, see section 551 of Pub.L. 98–353 set out as
a Separability of Provisions note preceding
chapter 1 of Title 11, Bankruptcy.

Cross References
Applicability of subsecs. (a)(2), (3), (8), (10), and (b)(1), (2)(A), (2)(B) of this section in
    chapter 9 cases, see section 901.
Confirmation of plan in
    Chapter 9 cases, see section 943.
    Chapter 13 cases, see section 1325.
    Railroad reorganization cases, see section 1173.
Denial of confirmation of plan as cause for conversion or dismissal, see section 1112.
Effect of confirmation in cases under this chapter, see section 1141.
Inapplicability of subsecs. (a)(7) and (c) of this section in railroad reorganization cases,
    see section 1161.
Revocation of order of confirmation in cases under this chapter, see section 1144.
Special tax provisions for certain dispositions of securities or instruments under
    confirmed plan, see section 1146.
Unclaimed property, see section 347.

Library References:
C.J.S. Bankruptcy § 385 et seq.
West's Key No. Digests, Bankruptcy ☞3548 et seq.

WESTLAW Electronic Research
See WESTLAW Electronic Research Guide following the *Bankruptcy Highlights*.

SUBCHAPTER III—POSTCONFIRMATION MATTERS

§ 1141.   Effect of confirmation

(a) Except as provided in subsections (d)(2) and (d)(3) of this section, the provisions of a confirmed plan bind the debtor, any entity issuing securities under the plan, any entity acquiring property under the plan, and any creditor, equity security holder, or general partner in the debtor, whether or not the claim or interest of such creditor, equity security holder, or general partner is impaired under the plan and whether or not such creditor, equity security holder, or general partner has accepted the plan.

(b) Except as otherwise provided in the plan or the order confirming the plan, the confirmation of a plan vests all of the property of the estate in the debtor.

(c) Except as provided in subsections (d)(2) and (d)(3) of this section and except as otherwise provided in the plan or in the order confirming the plan, after confirmation of a plan, the property dealt with by the plan is free and clear of all claims and interests of creditors, equity security holders, and of general partners in the debtor.

(d)(1) Except as otherwise provided in this subsection, in the plan, or in the order confirming the plan, the confirmation of a plan—

    (A) discharges the debtor from any debt that arose before the date of such confirmation, and any debt of a kind specified in section 502(g), 502(h), or 502(i) of this title, whether or not—

        (i) a proof of the claim based on such debt is filed or deemed filed under section 501 of this title;

(ii) such claim is allowed under section 502 of this title; or

(iii) the holder of such claim has accepted the plan; and

(B) terminates all rights and interests of equity security holders and general partners provided for by the plan.

(2) The confirmation of a plan does not discharge an individual debtor from any debt excepted from discharge under section 523 of this title.

(3) The confirmation of a plan does not discharge a debtor if—

(A) the plan provides for the liquidation of all or substantially all of the property of the estate;

(B) the debtor does not engage in business after consummation of the plan; and

(C) the debtor would be denied a discharge under section 727(a) of this title if the case were a case under chapter 7 of this title.

(4) The court may approve a written waiver of discharge executed by the debtor after the order for relief under this chapter.

Pub.L. 95–598, Nov. 6, 1978, 92 Stat. 2638; Pub.L. 98–353, Title III, § 513, July 10, 1984, 98 Stat. 387.

Historical and Revision Notes

Notes of Committee on the Judiciary, Senate Report No. 95–989. Subsection (a) of this section makes the provisions of a confirmed plan binding on the debtor, any entity issuing securities under the plan, any entity acquiring property under the plan, and any creditor, equity security holder, or general partner in the debtor, whether or not the claim or interest of the creditor, equity security holder, or partner is impaired under the plan and whether or not he has accepted the plan. There are two exceptions, enumerated in paragraph (2) and (3) of subsection (d).

Unless the plan or the order confirming the plan provides otherwise, the confirmation of a plan vests all of the property of the estate in the debtor and releases it from all claims and interests of creditors, equity security holders and general partners.

Subsection (d) contains the discharge for a reorganized debtor. Paragraph (1) specifies that the confirmation of a plan discharges the debtor from any debt that arose before the date of the order for relief unless the plan or the order confirming the plan provides otherwise. The discharge is effective against those claims whether or not proof of the claim is filed (or deemed filed), and whether or not the claim is allowed. The discharge also terminates all rights and interests of equity security holders and general partners provided for by the plan. The paragraph permits the plan or the order confirming the plan to provide

otherwise, and excepts certain debts from the discharge as provided in paragraphs (2) and (3).

Paragraph (2) of subsection (d) makes clear what taxes remain nondischargeable in the case of a corporate debtor emerging from a reorganization under chapter 11. Nondischargeable taxes in such a reorganization are the priority taxes (under section 507) and tax payments which come due during and after the proceeding under a deferred or part-payment agreement which the debtor had entered into with the tax authority before the bankruptcy proceedings began. On the other hand, a corporation which is taken over by its creditors through a plan of reorganization will not continue to be liable for nonpriority taxes arising from the corporation's prepetition fraud, failure to file a return, or failure to file a timely return, since the creditors who take over the reorganized company should not bear the burden of acts for which the creditors were not at fault.

Paragraph (3) specifies that the debtor is not discharged by the confirmation of a plan if the plan is a liquidating plan and if the debtor would be denied discharge in a liquidation case under section 727. Specifically, if all or substantially all of the distribution under the plan is of all or substantially all of the property of the estate or the proceeds of it, if the business, if any, of the debtor does not continue, and if the debtor would be denied a discharge under section 727 (such as if the debtor were not an individual or if he had committed an act that would lead to a denial of discharge), the chapter 11 discharge is not granted.

Paragraph (4) authorizes the court to approve a waiver of discharge by the debtor.

Notes of Committee on the Judiciary, House Report No. 95–595. Paragraph (2) [of subsec. (d)] makes applicable to an individual debtor the general exceptions to discharge that are enumerated in section 523(a) of the bankruptcy code [this title].

Legislative Statements. Section 1141(d) of the House amendment is derived from a comparable provision contained in the Senate amendment. However, section 1141(d)(2) of the House amendment is derived from the House bill as preferable to the Senate amendment. It is necessary for a corporation or partnership undergoing reorganization to be able to present its creditors with a fixed list of liabilities upon which the creditors or third parties can make intelligent decisions. Retaining an exception for discharge with respect to nondischargeable taxes would leave an undesirable uncertainty surrounding reorganizations that is unacceptable. Section 1141(d)(3) is derived from the Senate amendment. Section 1141(d)(4) is likewise derived from the Senate amendment.

Effective Date of 1984 Amendments. See section 553 of Pub.L. 98–353, Title III, July 10, 1984, 98 Stat. 392, set out as an Effective Date of 1984 Amendment note preceding chapter 1 of Title 11, Bankruptcy.

Separability of Provisions. For separability of provisions of Title III of Pub.L. 98–353, see section 551 of Pub.L. 98–353 set out as a Separability of Provisions note preceding chapter 1 of Title 11, Bankruptcy.

Cross References

Confirmation of plan filed under this chapter, see section 1129.
Discharge under chapter 7, see section 727.
Effect of confirmation of plans filed in
　　Chapter 9 cases, see section 944.
　　Chapter 13 cases, see section 1327.
Effect of conversion, see section 348.
Effect of discharge, see section 524.
Exceptions to discharge, see section 523.
Failure of discharge as cause for conversion, see section 1112.

Library References:

C.J.S. Bankruptcy §§ 407, 408.
West's Key No. Digests, Bankruptcy ⬦3568(1–3).

WESTLAW Electronic Research

See WESTLAW Electronic Research Guide following the *Bankruptcy Highlights*.

§ 1142. Implementation of plan

(a) Notwithstanding any otherwise applicable nonbankruptcy law, rule, or regulation relating to financial condition, the debtor and any entity organized or to be organized for the purpose of carrying out the plan shall carry out the plan and shall comply with any orders of the court.

(b) The court may direct the debtor and any other necessary party to execute or deliver or to join in the execution or delivery of any instrument required to effect a transfer of property dealt with by a confirmed plan, and to perform any other act, including the satisfaction of any lien, that is necessary for the consummation of the plan.

Pub.L. 95–598, Nov. 6, 1978, 92 Stat. 2639; Pub.L. 98–353, Title III, § 514, July 10, 1984, 98 Stat. 387.

Effective Date of 1984 Amendments. See section 553 of Pub.L. 98–353, Title III, July 10, 1984, 98 Stat. 392, set out as an Effective Date

of 1984 Amendment note preceding chapter 1
of Title 11, Bankruptcy.

Separability of Provisions. For separability of provisions of Title III of Pub.L. 98–

353, see section 551 of Pub.L. 98–353 set out as
a Separability of Provisions note preceding
chapter 1 of Title 11, Bankruptcy.

Cross References

Applicability of subsec. (b) of this section in chapter 9 cases, see section 901.

Library References:

C.J.S. Bankruptcy § 409.
West's Key No. Digests, Bankruptcy ⏀3570.

WESTLAW Electronic Research

See WESTLAW Electronic Research Guide following the *Bankruptcy Highlights*.

§ 1143.　Distribution

If a plan requires presentment or surrender of a security or the performance of any other act as a condition to participation in distribution under the plan, such action shall be taken not later than five years after the date of the entry of the order of confirmation. Any entity that has not within such time presented or surrendered such entity's security or taken any such other action that the plan requires may not participate in distribution under the plan.

Pub.L. 95–598, Nov. 6, 1978, 92 Stat. 2639.

Historical and Revision Notes

Notes of Committee on the Judiciary, Senate Report No. 95–989. Section 1143 fixes a 5-year limitation on presentment or surrender of securities or the performance of any other act that is a condition to participation in distribution under the plan. The 5 years runs from the date of the entry of the order of confirmation. Any entity that does not take the appropriate action within the 5-year period is barred from participation in the distribution under the plan.

Cross References

Applicability of this section in chapter 9 cases, see section 901.
Distribution of property of estate in chapter 7 cases, see section 726.
Distribution of securities in stockbroker liquidation cases, see section 750.

Library References:

C.J.S. Bankruptcy §§ 351, 352.
West's Key No. Digests, Bankruptcy ⏀3442.

WESTLAW Electronic Research

See WESTLAW Electronic Research Guide following the *Bankruptcy Highlights*.

§ 1144.　Revocation of an order of confirmation

On request of a party in interest at any time before 180 days after the date of the entry of the order of confirmation, and after notice and a hearing, the court may revoke such order if and only if such order was procured by fraud. An order under this section revoking an order of confirmation shall—

(1) contain such provisions as are necessary to protect any entity acquiring rights in good faith reliance on the order of confirmation; and

(2) revoke the discharge of the debtor.

Pub.L. 95–598, Nov. 6, 1978, 92 Stat. 2639; Pub.L. 98–353, Title III, § 515, July 10, 1984, 98 Stat. 387.

Historical and Revision Notes

Notes of Committee on the Judiciary, Senate Report No. 95–989. If an order of confirmation was procured by fraud, then the court may revoke the order on request of a party in interest if the request is made before 180 days after the date of the entry of the order of confirmation. The order revoking the order of confirmation must revoke the discharge of the debtor, and contain such provisions as are necessary to protect any entity acquiring rights in good faith reliance on the order of confirmation.

Effective Date of 1984 Amendments. See section 553 of Pub.L. 98–353, Title III, July 10, 1984, 98 Stat. 392, set out as an Effective Date of 1984 Amendment note preceding chapter 1 of Title 11, Bankruptcy.

Separability of Provisions. For separability of provisions of Title III of Pub.L. 98–353, see section 551 of Pub.L. 98–353 set out as a Separability of Provisions note preceding chapter 1 of Title 11, Bankruptcy.

Cross References

Applicability of this section in chapter 9 cases, see section 901.
Confirmation of one plan as affected by revocation, see section 1129.
Revocation of confirmation order as cause for conversion or dismissal, see section 1112.
Revocation of order of confirmation in chapter 13 cases, see section 1330.

Library References:

C.J.S. Bankruptcy § 411.
West's Key No. Digests, Bankruptcy ⟐3569.

WESTLAW Electronic Research

See WESTLAW Electronic Research Guide following the *Bankruptcy Highlights*.

§ 1145. Exemption from securities laws

(a) Except with respect to an entity that is an underwriter as defined in subsection (b) of this section, section 5 of the Securities Act of 1933 (15 U.S.C. 77e) and any State or local law requiring registration for offer or sale of a security or registration or licensing of an issuer of, underwriter of, or broker or dealer in, a security does not apply to—

    (1) the offer or sale under a plan of a security of the debtor, of an affiliate participating in a joint plan with the debtor, or of a successor to the debtor under the plan—

        (A) in exchange for a claim against, an interest in, or a claim for an administrative expense in the case concerning, the debtor or such affiliate; or

        (B) principally in such exchange and partly for cash or property;

    (2) the offer of a security through any warrant, option, right to subscribe, or conversion privilege that was sold in the manner specified in paragraph (1) of this subsection, or the sale of a security upon the exercise of such a warrant, option, right, or privilege;

    (3) the offer or sale, other than under a plan, of a security of an issuer other than the debtor or an affiliate, if—

        (A) such security was owned by the debtor on the date of the filing of the petition;

(B) the issuer of such security is—

(i) required to file reports under section 13 or 15(d) of the Securities Exchange Act of 1934 (15 U.S.C. 78m or 78o(d)); and

(ii) in compliance with the disclosure and reporting provision of such applicable section; and

(C) such offer or sale is of securities that do not exceed—

(i) during the two-year period immediately following the date of the filing of the petition, four percent of the securities of such class outstanding on such date; and

(ii) during any 180-day period following such two-year period, one percent of the securities outstanding at the beginning of such 180-day period; or

(4) a transaction by a stockbroker in a security that is executed after a transaction of a kind specified in paragraph (1) or (2) of this subsection in such security and before the expiration of 40 days after the first date on which such security was bona fide offered to the public by the issuer or by or through an underwriter, if such stockbroker provides, at the time of or before such transaction by such stockbroker, a disclosure statement approved under section 1125 of this title, and, if the court orders, information supplementing such disclosure statement.

(b)(1) Except as provided in paragraph (2) of this subsection and except with respect to ordinary trading transactions of an entity that is not an issuer, an entity is an underwriter under section 2(11) of the Securities Act of 1933 (15 U.S.C. 77b(11)), if such entity—

(A) purchases a claim against, interest in, or claim for an administrative expense in the case concerning, the debtor, if such purchase is with a view to distribution of any security received or to be received in exchange for such a claim or interest;

(B) offers to sell securities offered or sold under the plan for the holders of such securities;

(C) offers to buy securities offered or sold under the plan from the holders of such securities, if such offer to buy is—

(i) with a view to distribution of such securities; and

(ii) under an agreement made in connection with the plan, with the consummation of the plan, or with the offer or sale of securities under the plan; or

(D) is an issuer, as used in such section 2(11), with respect to such securities.

(2) An entity is not an underwriter under section 2(11) of the Securities Act of 1933 or under paragraph (1) of this subsection with respect to an agreement that provides only for—

(A)(i) the matching or combining of fractional interests in securities offered or sold under the plan into whole interests; or

(ii) the purchase or sale of such fractional interests from or to entities receiving such fractional interests under the plan; or

(B) the purchase or sale for such entities of such fractional or whole interests as are necessary to adjust for any remaining fractional interests after such matching.

(3) An entity other than an entity of the kind specified in paragraph (1) of this subsection is not an underwriter under section 2(11) of the Securities Act of 1933 with respect to any securities offered or sold to such entity in the manner specified in subsection (a)(1) of this section.

(c) An offer or sale of securities of the kind and in the manner specified under subsection (a)(1) of this section is deemed to be a public offering.

(d) The Trust Indenture Act of 1939 (15 U.S.C. 77aaa et seq.) does not apply to a note issued under the plan that matures not later than one year after the effective date of the plan.

Pub.L. 95–598, Nov. 6, 1978, 92 Stat. 2639; Pub.L. 98–353, Title III, § 516, July 10, 1984, 98 Stat. 387.

Historical and Revision Notes

Notes of Committee on the Judiciary, Senate Report No. 95–989. This section, derived from similar provisions found in sections 264, 393, and 518 of the Bankruptcy Act [former sections 664, 793, and 918 of this title], provides a limited exemption from the securities laws for securities issued under a plan of reorganization and for certain other securities. Subsection (a) exempts from the requirements of section 5 of the Securities Act of 1933 [section 77e of Title 15, Commerce and Trade] and from any State or local law requiring registration or licensing of an issuer of, underwriter of, or broker or dealer in, a security, the offer or sale of certain securities.

Paragraph (1) of subsection (a) exempts the offer or sale under section 364 of any security that is not an equity security or convertible into an equity security. This paragraph is designed to facilitate the issuance of certificates of indebtedness, and should be read in light of the amendment made in section 306 of title III to section 3(a)(7) of the 1933 act [section 77c(a)(7) of Title 15, Commerce and Trade].

Paragraph (2) of subsection (a) exempts the offer or sale of any security of the debtor, a successor to the debtor, or an affiliate in a joint plan, distributed under a plan if such security is exchanged in principal part for securities of the debtor or for allowed claims or administrative expenses. This exemption is carried over from present law, except as to administrative claims, but is limited to prevent distribution of securities to other than claim holders or equity security holders of the debtor or the estate.

Paragraph (3) of subsection (a) exempts the offer or sale of any security that arises from the exercise of a subscription right or from the exercise of a conversion privilege when such subscription right or conversion privilege was issued under a plan. This exemption is necessary in order to enhance the marketability of subscription rights or conversion privileges, including warrants, offered or sold under a plan. This is present law.

Paragraph (4) of subsection (a) exempts sales of portfolio securities, excluding securities of the debtor or its affiliate, owned by the debtor on the date of the filing of the petition. The purpose of this exemption is to allow the debtor or trustee to sell or distribute, without allowing manipulation schemes, restricted portfolio securities held or acquired by the debtor. Subparagraph (B) of section 1145(a)(4) limits the exemption to securities of a company that is required to file reports under section 13 of the Securities Act [section 78m of Title 15, Commerce and Trade] and that is in compliance with all requirements for the continuance of trading those securities. This limitation effectively prevents selling into the market "cats and dogs" of a nonreporting company. Subparagraph (C) places a limitation on the amount of restricted securities that may be distributed. During the case, the trustee may sell up to 4 percent of each class of restricted securities at any time during the first 2 years and 1 percent during any 180-day period thereafter. This relaxation of the resale rules for debtors in holding restricted securities is similar to but less extensive than the relaxation in SEC [Securities and Exchange Commission] Rule 114(c)(3)(v) for the estates of deceased holders of securities.

Paragraph (5) contains an exemption for brokers and dealers (stockbrokers, as defined in title 11) akin to the exemption provided by section 4(3)(A) of the Securities Act of 1933 [section 77d(3)(A) of Title 15, Commerce and Trade]. Instead of being required to supply a prospectus, however, the stockbroker is required to supply the approved disclosure statement, and if the court orders, information supplementing the disclosure statement. Under present law, the stockholder is not required to supply anything.

Subsection (b) is new. The subsection should be read in light of the amendment in section 306 of Title III to the 1933 act [section 77a et seq. of Title 15, Commerce and Trade]. It specifies the standards under which a creditor, equity security holder, or other entity acquiring securities under the plan may resell them. The Securities Act places limitations on sales by underwriters. This subsection defines who is an underwriter, and thus restricted, and who is free to resell. Paragraph (1) enumerates real underwriters that participate in a classical underwriting. A person is an underwriter if he purchases a claim against, interest in, or claim for an administrative expense in the case concerning, the debtor, with a view to distribution or interest. This provision covers the purchase of a certificate of indebtedness issued under proposed 11 U.S.C. 364 and purchased from the debtor, if the purchase of the certificate was with a view to distribution.

A person is also an underwriter if he offers to sell securities offered or sold under the plan for the holders of such securities, or offers to buy securities offered or sold under the plan from the holders of such securities, if the offer to buy is with a view to distribution of the securities and under an agreement made in connection with the plan, with the consummation of the plan or with the offer or sale of securities under the plan. Finally, a person is an underwriter if he is an issuer, as used in section 2(11) of the Securities Act of 1933 [section 77b(11) of Title 15, Commerce and Trade].

Paragraph (2) of subsection (b) exempts from the definition of underwriter any entity to the extent that any agreement that would bring the entity under the definition in paragraph (1) provides only for the matching combination of fractional interests in the covered securities or the purchase or sale of fractional interests. This paragraph and paragraph (1)

are modeled after former rule 133 of the Securities and Exchange Commission.

Paragraph (3) specifies that if an entity is not an underwriter under the provisions of paragraph (1), as limited by paragraph (2), then the entity is not an underwriter for the purposes of the Securities Act of 1933 [section 77a et seq. of Title 15, Commerce and Trade] with respect to the covered securities, that is, those offered or sold in an exempt transaction specified in subsection (a)(2). This makes clear that the current definition of underwriter in section 2(11) of the Securities Act of 1933 [section 77b(11) of Title 15] does not apply to such a creditor. The definition in that section technically applies to any person that purchases securities with "a view to distribution." If literally applied, it would prevent any creditor in a bankruptcy case from selling securities received without filing a registration statement or finding another exemption.

Subsection (b) is a first run transaction exemption and does not exempt a creditor that, for example, some years later becomes an underwriter by reacquiring securities originally issued under a plan.

Subsection (c) makes an offer or sale of securities under the plan in an exempt transaction (as specified in subsection (a)(2)) a public offering, in order to prevent characterization of the distribution as a "private placement" which would result in restrictions, under rule 144 of the SEC [Securities and Exchange Commission] on the resale of the securities.

Legislative Statements. Section 1145 of the House amendment deletes a provision contained in section 1145(a)(1) of the House bill in favor of a more adequate provision contained in section 364(f) of the House amendment. In addition, section 1145(d) has been added to indicate that the Trust Indenture Act [section 77aaa et seq. of Title 15, Commerce and Trade] does not apply to a commercial note issued under a plan, if the note matures not later than 1 year after the effective date of the plan. Some commercial notes receive such an exemption under 304(a)(4) of the Trust Indenture Act of 1939 (15 U.S.C. § 77ddd(a)(4)) [section 77ddd(a)(4) of Title 15] and others may receive protection by incorporation by reference into the Trust Indenture Act of securities exempt under section 3a(3), (7), (9), or (10) of the Securities Act of 1933 [section 77c(a)(3), (7), (9) and (10) of Title 15, respectively].

In light of the amendments made to the Securities Act of 1933 [section 77a et seq. of

Title 15, Commerce and Trade] in title III of the House amendment to H.R. 8200, a specific exemption from the Trust Indenture Act [section 77aaa et seq. of Title 15, Commerce and Trade] is required in order to create certainty regarding plans of reorganization. Section 1145(d) is not intended to imply that commercial notes issued under a plan that matures more than 1 year after the effective date of the plan or automatically covered by the Trust Indenture Act of 1939 since such notes may fall within another exemption thereto.

One other point with respect to Section 1145 deserves comment. Section 1145(a)(3) grants a debtor in possession or trustee in chapter 11 an extremely narrow portfolio security exemption from section 5 of the Securities Act of 1933 [section 77e of Title 15, Commerce and Trade] or any comparable State law. The provision was considered by Congress and adopted after much study. The exemption is reasonable and is more restrictive than comparable provisions under the Securities Act [section 77a et seq. of Title 15, Commerce and Trade] relating to the estates of decedents. Subsequent to passage of H.R. 8200 by the House of Representatives, the Securities and Exchange Commission promulgated Rule 148 to treat with this problem under existing law. Members of Congress received opinions from attorneys indicating dissatisfaction with the Commission's rule although the rule has been amended, the ultimate limitation of 1 percent promulgated by the Commission is wholly unacceptable.

The Commission rule would permit a trustee or debtor in possession to distribute securities at the rate of 1 percent every 6 months. Section 1145(a)(3) permits the trustee to distribute 4 percent of the securities during the 2-year period immediately following the date of the filing of the petition. In addition, the security must be of a reporting company under section 13 of the Securities and Exchange Act of 1934 [section 78m of Title 15, Commerce and Trade], and must be in compliance with all applicable requirements for the continuing of trading in the security on the date that the trustee offers or sells the security.

With these safeguards the trustee or debtor in possession should be able to distribute 4 percent of the securities of a class at any time during the 2-year period immediately following the date of the filing of the petition in the interests of expediting bankruptcy administration. The same rationale that applies in expeditiously terminating decedents' estates applies no less to an estate under title 11.

References in Text. Section 5 of the Securities Act of 1933, referred to in subsec. (a), is classified to section 77e of Title 15, Commerce and Trade.

Section 13 of the Securities Exchange Act of 1934, referred to in subsec. (a)(3)(B)(i), is classified to section 78m of Title 15.

The Trust Indenture Act of 1939, referred to in subsec. (d), is Title III of Act May 27, 1933, c. 38, as added Aug. 3, 1939, c. 411, 53 Stat. 1149, which is classified to section 77aaa et seq. of Title 15.

Effective Date of 1984 Amendments. See section 553 of Pub.L. 98–353, Title III, July 10, 1984, 98 Stat. 392, set out as an Effective Date of 1984 Amendment note preceding chapter 1 of Title 11, Bankruptcy.

Separability of Provisions. For separability of provisions of Title III of Pub.L. 98–353, see section 551 of Pub.L. 98–353 set out as a Separability of Provisions note preceding chapter 1 of Title 11, Bankruptcy.

Cross References

Applicability of term "security" to offers or sales under section 364 to underwriters, see section 364.
Applicability of this section in chapter 9 cases, see section 901.

Library References:

C.J.S. Securities Regulation §§ 3, 22, 36, 194, 195, 201.
West's Key No. Digests, Securities Regulation ⬤⊃18.10 et seq., 35.11 et seq., 247, 248.

WESTLAW Electronic Research

See WESTLAW Electronic Research Guide following the *Bankruptcy Highlights*.

§ 1146. Special tax provisions

(a) For the purposes of any State or local law imposing a tax on or measured by income, the taxable period of a debtor that is an individual shall terminate on the date of the order for relief under this chapter, unless the case was converted under section 706 of this title.

(b) The trustee shall make a State or local tax return of income for the estate of an individual debtor in a case under this chapter for each taxable period after the order for relief under this chapter during which the case is pending.

(c) The issuance, transfer, or exchange of a security, or the making or delivery of an instrument of transfer under a plan confirmed under section 1129 of this title, may not be taxed under any law imposing a stamp tax or similar tax.

(d) The court may authorize the proponent of a plan to request a determination, limited to questions of law, by a State or local governmental unit charged with responsibility for collection or determination of a tax on or measured by income, of the tax effects, under section 346 of this title and under the law imposing such tax, of the plan. In the event of an actual controversy, the court may declare such effects after the earlier of—

(1) the date on which such governmental unit responds to the request under this subsection; or

(2) 270 days after such request.

Pub.L. 95–598, Nov. 6, 1978, 92 Stat. 2641; Pub.L. 98–353, Title III, § 517, July 10, 1984, 98 Stat. 388.

Historical and Revision Notes

Notes of Committee on the Judiciary, Senate Report No. 95–989. Section 1146 provides special tax rules applicable to Title 11 reorganizations. Subsection (a) provides that the taxable period of an individual debtor terminates on the date of the order for relief, unless the case has been converted into a reorganization from a liquidation proceeding.

Subsection (b) requires the trustee of the estate of an individual debtor in a reorganization to file a tax return for each taxable period while the case is pending after the order for relief. For corporations in chapter 11, the trustee is required to file the tax returns due while the case is pending (sec. 346(c)(2)).

Subsection (c) exempts from Federal, State, or local stamp taxes the issuance, transfer, or exchange of a security, or the making or delivery of an instrument of transfer under a plan. This subsection is derived from section 267 of the present Bankruptcy Act [former section 667 of this title].

Subsection (d) permits the court to authorize the proponent of a reorganization plan to request from the Internal Revenue Service (or State or local tax authority) an advance ruling on the tax effects of the proposed plan. If a ruling is not obtained within 270 days after

the request was made, or if a ruling is obtained but the proponent of the plan disagrees with the ruling, the bankruptcy court may resolve the dispute and determine the tax effects of the proposed plan.

Subsection (e) provides that prepetition taxes which are nondischargeable in a reorganization, and all taxes arising during the administration period of the case, may be assessed and collected from the debtor or the debtor's successor in a reorganization (see sec. 505(c) of the bill).

Notes of Committee on the Judiciary, House Report No. 95–595. Section 1146 of title 11 specifies five subsections which embody special tax provisions that apply in a case under chapter 11 of title 11. Subsection (a) indicates that the tax year of an individual debtor terminates on the date of the order for relief under chapter 11. Termination of the taxable year of the debtor commences the tax period of the estate. If the case was converted from chapter 7 of title 11 then the estate is created as a separate taxable entity dating from the order for relief under chapter 7. If multiple conversion of the case occurs, then the estate is treated as a separate taxable entity on the date of the order for relief under the first chapter under which the estate is a separate taxable entity.

Subsection (d) permits the court to authorize the proponent of a plan to request a taxing authority to declare the tax effects of such plan. In the event of an actual controversy, the court may declare the tax effects of the plan of reorganization at any time after the earlier of action by such taxing authority or 270 days after the request. Such a declaration, unless appealed, becomes a final judgment and binds any tax authority that was requested by the proponent to determine the tax effects of the plan.

Legislative Statements. Section 1146 of the House amendment represents a compromise between the House bill and Senate amendment.

The House bill provided rules on the effect of bankruptcy on the taxable year of the debtor and on tax return filing requirements for State and local taxes only. The House bill also exempted from State or local stamp taxes the issuance, transfer, or exchange of a security, or the making or delivery of an instrument of transfer under a plan. The House bill also authorized the bankruptcy court to declare the tax effects of a reorganization plan after the proponent of the plan had requested a ruling from State or local tax authority and either had received an unfavorable ruling or the tax authority had not issued a ruling within 270 days.

The Senate amendment deleted the rules concerning the taxable years of the debtor and tax return filing requirements since the Federal rules were to be considered in the next Congress. It broadened the rule exempting transfers of securities to include Federal stamp or similar taxes, if any. In addition, the Senate amendment deleted the provision which permitted the bankruptcy court to determine the tax effects of a plan.

The House amendment retains the State and local rules in the House bill with one modification. Under the House amendment, the power of the bankruptcy court to declare the tax effects of the plan is limited to issues of law and not to questions of fact such as the allowance of specific deductions. Thus, the bankruptcy court could declare whether the reorganization qualified for taxfree status under State or local tax rules, but it could not declare the dollar amount of any tax attributes that survive the reorganization.

Effective Date of 1984 Amendments. See section 553 of Pub.L. 98–353, Title III, July 10, 1984, 98 Stat. 392, set out as an Effective Date of 1984 Amendment note preceding chapter 1 of Title 11, Bankruptcy.

Separability of Provisions. For separability of provisions of Title III of Pub.L. 98–353, see section 551 of Pub.L. 98–353 set out as a Separability of Provisions note preceding chapter 1 of Title 11, Bankruptcy.

Cross References

Determination of
Number of taxable periods during which debtor may use loss carryover or carryback, see section 346.
Tax liability, see section 505.
Effect of conversion, see section 348.
Special tax provisions in chapter 7 cases, see section 728.

Library References:

C.J.S. Taxation §§ 1079 et seq., 1094, 1100, 1102.
West's Key No. Digests, Taxation ⊕105½, 982, 1021, 1079.

WESTLAW Electronic Research

See WESTLAW Electronic Research Guide following the *Bankruptcy Highlights.*

SUBCHAPTER IV—RAILROAD REORGANIZATION

§ 1161. Inapplicability of other sections

Sections 341, 343, 1102(a)(1), 1104, 1105, 1107, 1129(a)(7), and 1129(c) of this title do not apply in a case concerning a railroad.

Pub.L. 95–598, Nov. 6, 1978, 92 Stat. 2641.

Historical and Revision Notes

Notes of Committee on the Judiciary, Senate Report No. 95–989. This section makes inapplicable sections of the bill which are either inappropriate in railroad reorganizations, or relate to matters which are otherwise dealt with in subchapter IV.

Cross References

Applicability of other sections of this title to chapter 9 cases, see section 901.

Library References:

C.J.S. Bankruptcy § 37.
West's Key No. Digests, Bankruptcy ☜2203.

WESTLAW Electronic Research

See WESTLAW Electronic Research Guide following the *Bankruptcy Highlights*.

§ 1162. Definition

In this subchapter, "Commission" means Interstate Commerce Commission.

Pub.L. 95–598, Nov. 6, 1978, 92 Stat. 2641.

Historical and Revision Notes

Notes of Committee on the Judiciary, Senate Report No. 95–989. Two definitions are provided: That "Commission" means the Interstate Commerce Commission, and that "person" includes a governmental unit for purposes of the subchapter. The latter definition is made necessary because governmental unit is excluded from the definition of person in section 101(30).

Legislative Statements. Section 1162 of the House amendment is derived from section 1162(1) of the Senate bill.

Cross References

Definitions applicable in
    Cases under this chapter, see section 1101.
    Cases under this title, see section 101.
    Chapter 9 cases, see section 902.
    Commodity broker liquidation cases, see section 761.
    Stockbroker liquidation cases, see section 741.

WESTLAW Electronic Research

See WESTLAW Electronic Research Guide following the *Bankruptcy Highlights*.

§ 1163. Appointment of trustee

As soon as practicable after the order for relief the Secretary of Transportation shall submit a list of five disinterested persons that are qualified and willing to serve as trustees in the case. The United States trustee shall appoint one of such persons to serve as trustee in the case.

Pub.L. 95–598, Nov. 6, 1978, 92 Stat. 2641; Pub.L. 99–554, Title II, § 226, Oct. 27, 1986, 100 Stat. 3102.

Historical and Revision Notes

Notes of Committee on the Judiciary, Senate Report No. 95–989. Requires the court to appoint a trustee in every case. Since the trustee may employ whatever help he needs, multiple trusteeships are unnecessary and add to the cost of administration. The present requirement of section 77(c)(1) [former section 205(c)(1) of this title] that the trustee be approved by the Interstate Commerce Commission is unnecessary, since the trustee will be selected either from the panel established under section 606(f) of title 28 [section 606(f) of Title 28, Judiciary and Judicial Procedure], or someone certified by the Director of the Administrative Office of the United States Courts as qualified to become a member of that panel.

Legislative Statements. Section 1163 of the House amendment represents a compromise between the House bill and Senate amendment with respect to the appointment of a trustee in a railroad reorganization. As soon as practicable after the order for relief, the Secretary of Transportation is required to submit a list of five disinterested persons who are qualified to serve as trustee and the court will then appoint one trustee from the list to serve as trustee in the case.

The House amendment deletes section 1163 of the Senate amendment in order to cover intrastate railroads in a case under subchapter IV of chapter 11. The bill does not confer jurisdiction on the Interstate Commerce Commission with respect to intrastate railroads.

1986 Amendment. Pub.L. 99–554, § 226, substituted "relief the Secretary" for "relief, the Secretary" and "The United States trustee shall appoint" for "The court shall appoint".

See Effective Date of 1986 Amendment, etc., notes set out below.

Effective Date of 1986 Amendments; Effective Date of 1986 Amendments for Certain Judicial Districts Not Served by United States Trustees and for Judicial Districts in Alabama and North Carolina; U.S. Trustee System Fund Deposits in Alabama and North Carolina; Effective Date of Title 11 Chapter 15 Repeal as to Northern District of Alabama; Authority of Certain Estate Administrators in Alabama and North Carolina; Effective Date of 1986 Amendments in Pending Cases Where a U.S. Trustee Not Authorized or Where a Trustee Files Final Report or Plan is Confirmed; Quarterly Fees. Amendment by Pub.L. 99–554 effective 30 days after Oct. 27, 1986, except as otherwise provided for, see section 302(a) of Pub.L. 99–554, set out as a note under section 581 of Title 28, Judiciary and Judicial Procedure.

Amendment by Pub.L. 99–554, § 226, not to become effective in or with respect to certain specified judicial districts until, or apply to cases while pending in such district before,

the expiration of the 270-day period beginning 30 days after Oct. 27, 1986, or of the 30-day period beginning on the date the Attorney General certifies under section 303 of Pub.L. 99–554 the region specified in a paragraph of section 581(a) of Title 28, as amended by section 111(a) of Pub.L. 99–554, that includes such district, whichever occurs first, see section 302(d)(1) of Pub.L. 99–554, set out as a note under section 581 of Title 28.

Amendment by Pub.L. 99–554, § 226, not to become effective in or with respect to certain specified judicial districts until, or apply to cases while pending in such district before, the expiration of the 2-year period beginning 30 days after Oct. 27, 1986, or of the 30-day period beginning on the date the Attorney General certifies under section 303 of Pub.L. 99–554 the region specified in a paragraph of section 581(a) of Title 28, as amended by section 111(a) of Pub.L. 99–554, that includes such district, whichever occurs first, see section 302(d)(2) of Pub.L. 99–554, set out as a note under section 581 of Title 28.

Amendment by Pub.L. 99–554, § 226, not to become effective in or with respect to judicial districts established for the States of Alabama and North Carolina until, or apply to cases while pending in such district before, such district elects to be included in a bankruptcy region established in section 581(a) of Title 28, as amended by section 111(a) of Pub.L. 99–554, or Oct. 1, 2002, whichever occurs first, and, except as otherwise provided for, with respect to cases under chapters 7, 11, 12, and 13 of Title 11 commenced before 30 days after Oct. 27, 1986, and pending in a judicial district in the States of Alabama or North Carolina before any election made under section 302(d)(3)(A) of Pub.L. 99–554 by such district becomes effective or Oct. 1, 2002, whichever occurs first, amendments by Pub.L. 99–554 not to apply until Oct. 1, 2003, or the expiration of the 1-year period beginning on the date such election becomes effective, whichever occurs first, and further, in any judicial district in Alabama or North Carolina not making the election described in section 302(d)(3)(A) of Pub.L. 99–554, any person appointed under regulations issued by the Judicial Conference to administer estates in cases under Title 11 authorized to establish, etc., a panel of private trustees, and to supervise cases and trustees in cases under chapters 7, 11, 12, and 13 of Title 11, until amendments by sections 201 to 231 of Pub.L. 99–554 effective in such district, see section 302(d)(3)(A) to (F), (H), (I) of Pub.L.

§ 1163　　　　　　　　BANKRUPTCY CODE　　　　　　　Title 11

99–554, set out as a note under section 581 of Title 28.

Amendment by Pub.L. 99–554, § 226, except as otherwise provided, with respect to cases under chapters 7, 11, 12, and 13 of Title 11 commenced before 30 days after Oct. 27, 1986, and pending in a judicial district referred to in section 581(a) of Title 28, as amended by section 111(a) of Pub.L. 99–554, for which a United States trustee is not authorized before 30 days after Oct. 27, 1986 to be appointed, not applicable until the expiration of the 3-year period beginning on Oct. 27, 1986, or of the 1-year period beginning on the date the Attorney General certifies under section 303 of Pub.L. 99–554 the region specified in a paragraph of such section 581(a) that includes, such district, whichever occurs first, see section 302(e)(1), (2) of Pub.L. 99–554, set out as a note under section 581 of Title 28.

See 1986 Amendment notes set out above.

Library References:

C.J.S. Bankruptcy § 195.
West's Key No. Digests, Bankruptcy ⚷3004.

§ 1164. Right to be heard

The Commission, the Department of Transportation, and any State or local commission having regulatory jurisdiction over the debtor may raise and may appear and be heard on any issue in a case under this chapter, but may not appeal from any judgment, order, or decree entered in the case.
Pub.L. 95–598, Nov. 6, 1978, 92 Stat. 2641.

Historical and Revision Notes

Notes of Committee on the Judiciary, House Report No. 95–595. This section gives the same right to raise, and appear and be heard on, any issue in a railroad reorganization case to the Interstate Commerce Commission, the Department of Transportation, and any State or local commission having regulatory jurisdiction over the debtor as is given to the SEC [Securities and Exchange Commission] and indenture trustees under section 1109 in ordinary reorganization cases. The right of appeal is denied the ICC [Interstate Commerce Commission], the Department of Transportation, and State and local regulatory agencies, the same as it is denied the SEC.

Legislative Statements. Section 1164 of the Senate amendment is deleted as a matter to be left to the Rules of Bankruptcy Procedure. It is anticipated that the rules will require a petition in a railroad reorganization to be filed with the Interstate Commerce Commission and the Secretary of Transportation in a case concerning an interstate railroad.

Section 1164 of the House amendment is derived from section 1163 of the House bill. The section makes clear that the Interstate Commerce Commission, the Department of Transportation, and any State or local commission having regulatory jurisdiction over the debtor may raise and appear and be heard on any issue in a case under subchapter IV of chapter 11, but may not appeal from any judgment, order, or decree in the case. As under section 1109 of title 11, such intervening parties are not parties in interest.

Cross References

Right of Commodity Futures Trading Commission to be heard, see section 762.
Right of Securities and Exchange Commission and party in interest to be heard in case under this chapter, see section 1109.
Right to be heard in cases under this chapter, see section 1109.

Library References:

C.J.S. Bankruptcy § 38.
West's Key No. Digests, Bankruptcy ⚷2205.

WESTLAW Electronic Research

See WESTLAW Electronic Research Guide following the *Bankruptcy Highlights*.

366

§ 1165. Protection of the public interest

In applying sections 1166, 1167, 1169, 1170, 1171, 1172, 1173, and 1174 of this title, the court and the trustee shall consider the public interest in addition to the interests of the debtor, creditors, and equity security holders.

Pub.L. 95–598, Nov. 6, 1978, 92 Stat. 2641.

Historical and Revision Notes

Notes of Committee on the Judiciary, Senate Report No. 95–989. Section 1165 requires the court, in consideration of the relief to be granted upon the filing of an involuntary petition, to take into account the "public interest" in the preservation of the debtor's rail service. This is an important factor in railroad reorganization, which distinguishes them from other business reorganizations. Hence, this section modifies the provisions in sections 303 and 305 that govern generally when the business of a debtor may continue to operate, when relief under the Act sought should be granted, and when the petition should be dismissed.

Legislative Statements. Section 1165 of the House amendment represents a modification of sections 1165 and 1167 of the Senate amendment requiring the court and the trustee to consider the broad, general public interest in addition to the interests of the debtor, creditors, and equity security holders in applying specific sections of the subchapter.

Savings Provisions. Section to apply to cases pending under section 77 of the Bankruptcy Act [section 205 of former Title 11] on Nov. 6, 1978, in which the trustee had not filed a plan of reorganization, see section 403(b) of Pub.L. 95–598, set out preceding section 101 of this title.

Library References:

C.J.S. Bankruptcy § 412.
West's Key No. Digests, Bankruptcy ⊙3651.

WESTLAW Electronic Research

See WESTLAW Electronic Research Guide following the *Bankruptcy Highlights*.

§ 1166. Effect of subtitle IV of title 49 and of Federal, State, or local regulations

Except with respect to abandonment under section 1170 of this title, or merger, modification of the financial structure of the debtor, or issuance or sale of securities under a plan, the trustee and the debtor are subject to the provisions of subtitle IV of title 49 that are applicable to railroads, and the trustee is subject to orders of any Federal, State, or local regulatory body to the same extent as the debtor would be if a petition commencing the case under this chapter had not been filed, but—

(1) any such order that would require the expenditure, or the incurring of an obligation for the expenditure, of money from the estate is not effective unless approved by the court; and

(2) the provisions of this chapter are subject to section 601(b) of the Regional Rail Reorganization Act of 1973 (45 U.S.C. 791(b)).

Pub.L. 95–598, Nov. 6, 1978, 92 Stat. 2642; Pub.L. 97–449, § 5(a)(2), Jan. 12, 1983, 96 Stat. 2442; Pub.L. 98–353, Title III, § 518, July 10, 1984, 98 Stat. 388.

Historical and Revision Notes

Notes of Committee on the Judiciary, Senate Report No. 95–989. Section 1168 [now this section] makes the trustee subject to the Interstate Commerce Act [section 10101 et seq. of Title 49, Transportation] and to lawful orders of the Interstate Commerce Commission, the U.S. Department of Transportation, and State and regulatory bodies. The approval of the court is required, however, if the order requires the expenditure of money or the incurring of an expenditure other than the payment of certain interline accounts. The limitation of "lawful orders" of State commissions to those involving "safety, location of tracks, and terminal facilities," which is contained in present section 77(c)(2) [former section 205(c)(2) of this title], is eliminated.

Subsection (1) further provides that the debtor must pay in cash all amounts owed other carriers for current balances owed for interline freight, passenger and per diem, including incentive per diem, for periods both prior and subsequent to the filing of the petition, without the necessity of court approval.

Subsection (2) makes the provisions of the chapter subject to section 601(b) of the Regional Rail Reorganization Act [section 791(b) of Title 45, Railroad], which excludes the Interstate Commerce Commission from any participation in the reorganization of certain northeast railroads that have transferred their rail properties to Consolidated Rail Corporation (Conrail).

Notes of Committee on the Judiciary, House Report No. 95–595. Section 1164 [now 1166] makes the debtor railroad subject to the provisions of the Interstate Commerce Act [section 10101 et seq. of Title 49, Transportation] that are applicable to railroads, and the trustees subject to the orders of the Interstate Commerce Commission to the same extent as the debtor would have been if the case had not been commenced. There are several exceptions. The section does not apply with respect to abandonment of rail lines, which is provided for under section 1169, or with respect to merger under a plan, modification of the financial structure of the debtor by reason of the plan, or the issuance or sale of securities under a plan. Further, the orders of the

ICC [Interstate Commerce Commission] are not effective if the order would require the expenditure or the incurring of an obligation for the expenditure of money from the estate, unless approved by the court, and the provisions of this chapter are subject to section 601(b) of the Regional Rail Reorganization Act of 1973 [section 791(b) of Title 45, Railroads].

The same rules apply with respect to Federal, State, or local regulations. The trustee is subject to the orders of a Federal, State, or local regulatory body to the same extent as the debtor would be if the case had not been commenced. However, any order that would require the expenditure, or the incurring of an obligation for the expenditure, of money is not effective under [until] approved by the court.

Legislative Statements. Section 1166 of the House amendment is derived from sections 1164 and 1165 of the House bill. An alternative proposal contained in section 1168(1) of the Senate bill is rejected as violative of the principle or equal treatment of all creditors under title 11.

References in Text. Section 601(b) of the Regional Rail Reorganization Act of 1973, referred to in text, is classified to section 791(b) of Title 45, Railroads.

Codification. Pub.L. 98–353 enacted identical amendment as Pub.L. 97–449 previously executed to text.

Effective Date of 1984 Amendments. See section 553 of Pub.L. 98–353, Title III, July 10, 1984, 98 Stat. 392, set out as an Effective Date of 1984 Amendment note preceding chapter 1 of Title 11, Bankruptcy.

Separability of Provisions. For separability of provisions of Title III of Pub.L. 98–353, see section 551 of Pub.L. 98–353 set out as a Separability of Provisions note preceding chapter 1 of Title 11, Bankruptcy.

§ 1167.   Collective bargaining agreements

Notwithstanding section 365 of this title, neither the court nor the trustee may change the wages or working conditions of employees of the debtor established by a collective bargaining agreement that is subject to the Railway Labor

Act (45 U.S.C. 151 et seq.) except in accordance with section 6 of such Act (45 U.S.C. 156).

Pub.L. 95–598, Nov. 6, 1978, 92 Stat. 2642.

Historical and Revision Notes

Notes of Committee on the Judiciary, Senate Report No. 95–989. Section 1176 [now this section] is derived from present section 77(n) [former section 205(n) of this title]. It provides that notwithstanding the general section governing the rejection of executory contracts (section 365), neither the court nor the trustee may change the wages or working conditions of employees of the debtor established by a collective bargaining agreement that is subject to the Railway Labor Act [section 151 et seq. of Title 45, Railroads], except in accordance with section 6 of that Act [section 156 of Title 45]. As reported by the subcommittee this section provided that wages and salaries of rail employees could not be affected by the trustee, but that work rules could be rejected by the trustee. The reorganization court was given the authority to review the trustee's decisions and to settle any disputes arising from the rejection. This provision was withdrawn by the full committee, and hearings will be conducted next year by the Human Resources Committee in the area of rail labor contracts and the trustee's ability to reject them in a bankruptcy situation.

References in Text. The Railway Labor Act, referred to in text, is Act May 20, 1926, c. 347, 44 Stat. 577, which is classified to section 151 et seq. of Title 45, Railroads.

Section 6 of the Railway Labor Act, referred to in text, is classified to section 156 of Title 45.

Savings Provisions. Section to apply to cases pending under section 77 of the Bankruptcy Act [section 205 of former Title 11] on Nov. 6, 1978, in which the trustee had not filed a plan of reorganization, see section 403(b) of Pub. L. 95–598, set out preceding section 101 of this title.

Cross References

Authorization of trustee to operate business, see section 1108.

Library References:

C.J.S. Bankruptcy §§ 224, 225.
West's Key No. Digests, Bankruptcy ⟐3108, 3113.

WESTLAW Electronic Research

See WESTLAW Electronic Research Guide following the *Bankruptcy Highlights.*

§ 1168. Rolling stock equipment

(a) The right of a secured party with a purchase-money equipment security interest in, or of a lessor or conditional vendor of, whether as trustee or otherwise, rolling stock equipment or accessories used on such equipment, including superstructures and racks, that are subject to a purchase-money equipment security interest granted by, leased to, or conditionally sold to, the debtor to take possession of such equipment in compliance with the provisions of a purchase-money equipment security agreement, lease, or conditional sale contract, as the case may be, is not affected by section 362 or 363 of this title or by any power of the court to enjoin such taking of possession, unless—

    (1) before 60 days after the date of the commencement of a case under this chapter, the trustee, subject to the court's approval, agrees to perform all obligations of the debtor under such security agreement, lease, or conditional sale contract, as the case may be; and

(2) any default, other than a default of a kind specified in section 365(b)(2) of this title, under such security agreement, lease, or conditional sale contract, as the case may be—

(A) that occurred before such date and is an event of default therewith is cured before the expiration of such 60-day period; and

(B) that occurs or becomes an event of default after such date is cured before the later of—

(i) 30 days after the date of such default or event of default; and

(ii) the expiration of such 60-day period.

(b) The trustee and the secured party, lessor, or conditional vendor, as the case may be, whose right to take possession is protected under subsection (a) of this section, may agree, subject to the court's approval, to extend the 60-day period specified in subsection (a)(1) of this section.

Pub.L. 95–598, Nov. 6, 1978, 92 Stat. 2642; Pub.L. 98–353, Title III, § 519, July 10, 1984, 98 Stat. 388.

Historical and Revision Notes

Notes of Committee on the Judiciary, Senate Report No. 95–989. Section 1175 [now this section] continues the protection accorded in present section 77(j) [former section 205(j) of this title] to the rights of holders of purchase-money equipment security, and of lessors or conditional vendors of railroad rolling stock, but accords to the trustee a limited period within which to assume the debtor's obligation and to cure any defaults. The rights of such lenders are not affected by the automatic stay and related provisions of sections 362 and 363, or by any power of the court, unless (1) within 60 days after the commencement of the case (or such longer period as may be agreed to by the secured party, lessor or conditional vendor) the trustees, with the approval of the court, agrees to perform all of the debtor's obligations under the security agreement, lease or conditional sale contract, and (2) all defaults are cured within the 60-day period.

Defaults described in section 365(b)(2)—defaults which are breaches of provisions relating to the insolvency or financial condition of the debtor, or the commencement of a case under this title, or the appointment of a trustee—are for obvious reasons, excepted.

Notes of Committee on the Judiciary, House Report No. 95–595. This section, derived with changes from the last sentence of present section 77(j) [former section 205(j) of this title], protects the interests of rolling stock equipment financers, while providing the trustee with some opportunity to cure defaults, agree to make payments, and retain and use the equipment. The provision is parallel to section 1110, concerning aircraft equipment and vessels.

Legislative Statements. Section 1168 of the House amendment incorporates a provision contained in section 1166 of the House bill instead of the provision contained in section 1175 of the Senate amendment for the reasons stated in connection with the discussion of section 1110 of the House amendment.

Effective Date of 1984 Amendments. See section 553 of Pub.L. 98–353, Title III, July 10, 1984, 98 Stat. 392, set out as an Effective Date of 1984 Amendment note preceding chapter 1 of Title 11, Bankruptcy.

Separability of Provisions. For separability of provisions of Title III of Pub.L. 98–353, see section 551 of Pub.L. 98–353 set out as a Separability of Provisions note preceding chapter 1 of Title 11, Bankruptcy.

Savings Provisions. Section to apply to cases pending under section 77 of the Bankruptcy Act [section 205 of former Title 11] on Nov. 6, 1978, in which the trustee had not filed a plan of reorganization, see section 403(b) of Pub. L. 95–598, set out preceding section 101 of this title.

Cross References

Rights of certain secured parties in aircraft equipment and vessels, see section 1110.

Library References:
C.J.S. Bankruptcy § 413.
West's Key No. Digests, Bankruptcy ⟜3654.

WESTLAW Electronic Research
See WESTLAW Electronic Research Guide following the *Bankruptcy Highlights.*

§ 1169. Effect of rejection of lease of railroad line

(a) Except as provided in subsection (b) of this section, if a lease of a line of railroad under which the debtor is the lessee is rejected under section 365 of this title, and if the trustee, within such time as the court fixes, and with the court's approval, elects not to operate the leased line, the lessor under such lease, after such approval, shall operate the line.

(b) If operation of such line by such lessor is impracticable or contrary to the public interest, the court, on request of such lessor, and after notice and a hearing, shall order the trustee to continue operation of such line for the account of such lessor until abandonment is ordered under section 1170 of this title, or until such operation is otherwise lawfully terminated, whichever occurs first.

(c) During any such operation, such lessor is deemed a carrier subject to the provisions of subtitle IV of title 49 that are applicable to railroads.

Pub.L. 95–598, Nov. 6, 1978, 92 Stat. 2643; Pub.L. 97–449, § 5(a)(3), Jan. 12, 1983, 96 Stat. 2442; Pub.L. 98–353, Title III, § 520, July 10, 1984, 98 Stat. 388.

Historical and Revision Notes

Notes of Committee on the Judiciary, Senate Report No. 95–989. Section 1177 [now this section] continues, essentially without change, the provisions relating to the rejection by the trustee of a lease of a line of railroad now contained in section 77(c)(6) [former section 205(c)(6) of this title]. Subsection (a) requires the lessor of a line of railroad to operate it if the lease is rejected by the trustee and the trustee, with the approval of the court, elects not to operate the leased line. Subsection (b), however, further provides that if operation by the lessor is impractical or contrary to the public interest, the court shall require the trustee to operate the line for the account of the lessor until the operation is lawfully terminated. Subsection (c) provides that during such operation, the lessor is a carrier subject to the Interstate Commerce Act [section 10101 et seq. of Title 49, Transportation].

Legislative Statements. Section 1169 of the Senate amendment is deleted from the House amendment as unnecessary since 28 U.S.C. 1407 [section 1407 of Title 28, Judiciary and Judicial Procedure] treating with the judicial panel on multi-district litigation will apply by its terms to cases under title 11.

References in Text. The Interstate Commerce Act, referred to in subsec. (c), was formerly set out as section 1 et seq. of Title 49, Transportation, prior to the revision of Title 49 by Pub.L. 95–473, Oct. 13, 1978, 92 Stat. 1337, and is now covered by section 10101 et seq. of Title 49.

Codification. Pub.L. 98–353 enacted identical amendment as Pub.L. 97–449 previously executed to text.

Effective Date of 1984 Amendments. See section 553 of Pub.L. 98–353, Title III, July 10, 1984, 98 Stat. 392, set out as an Effective Date of 1984 Amendment note preceding chapter 1 of Title 11, Bankruptcy.

Separability of Provisions. For separability of provisions of Title III of Pub.L. 98–353, see section 551 of Pub.L. 98–353 set out as a Separability of Provisions note preceding chapter 1 of Title 11, Bankruptcy.

Savings Provisions. Section to apply to cases pending under section 77 of the Bankruptcy Act [section 205 of former Title 11] on Nov. 6, 1978, in which the trustee had not filed a plan of reorganization, see section 403(b) of Pub. L. 95–598, set out preceding section 101 of this title.

Cross References

Executory contracts in stockbroker liquidation cases, see section 744.

Library References:

C.J.S. Bankruptcy §§ 227, 229.
West's Key No. Digests, Bankruptcy ⚮3115.

WESTLAW Electronic Research

See WESTLAW Electronic Research Guide following the *Bankruptcy Highlights*.

§ 1170. Abandonment of railroad line

(a) The court, after notice and a hearing, may authorize the abandonment of all or a portion of a railroad line if such abandonment is—

(1)(A) in the best interest of the estate; or

(B) essential to the formulation of a plan; and

(2) consistent with the public interest.

(b) If, except for the pendency of the case under this chapter, such abandonment would require approval by the Commission under a law of the United States, the trustee shall initiate an appropriate application for such abandonment with the Commission. The court may fix a time within which the Commission shall report to the court on such application.

(c) After the court receives the report of the Commission, or the expiration of the time fixed under subsection (b) of this section, whichever occurs first, the court may authorize such abandonment, after notice to the Commission, the Secretary of Transportation, the trustee, any party in interest that has requested notice, any affected shipper or community, and any other entity prescribed by the court, and a hearing.

(d)(1) Enforcement of an order authorizing such abandonment shall be stayed until the time for taking an appeal has expired, or, if an appeal is timely taken, until such order has become final.

(2) If an order authorizing such abandonment is appealed, the court, on request of a party in interest, may authorize suspension of service on a line or a portion of a line pending the determination of such appeal, after notice to the Commission, the Secretary of Transportation, the trustee, any party in interest that has requested notice, any affected shipper or community, and any other entity prescribed by the court, and a hearing. An appellant may not obtain a stay of the enforcement of an order authorizing such suspension by the giving of a supersedeas bond or otherwise, during the pendency of such appeal.

(e)(1) In authorizing any abandonment of a railroad line under this section, the court shall require the rail carrier to provide a fair arrangement at least as protective of the interests of employees as that established under section 11347 of title 49.

(2) Nothing in this subsection shall be deemed to affect the priorities or timing of payment of employee protection which might have existed in the absence of this subsection.

Pub.L. 95–598, Nov. 6, 1978, 92 Stat. 2643; Pub.L. 96–448, Title II, § 227(a), Oct. 14, 1980, 94 Stat. 1931; Pub.L. 98–353, Title III, § 521, July 10, 1984, 98 Stat. 388.

Historical and Revision Notes

Notes of Committee on the Judiciary, Senate Report No. 95–989. Subsection (a) of section 1178 [now this section] permits the court to authorize the abandonment of a railroad line if the abandonment is consistent with the public interest and either in the best interest of the estate or essential to the formulation of a plan. This avoids the normal abandonment requirements of generally applicable railroad regulatory law.

Subsection (b) permits some participation by the Interstate Commerce Commission in the abandonment process. The Commission's role, however, is only advisory. The Commission will represent the public interest, while the trustee and various creditors and equity security holders will represent the interests of those who have invested money in the enterprise. The court will balance the various interests and make an appropriate decision. The subsection specifies that if, except for the pendency of the railroad reorganization case, the proposed abandonment would require Commission approval, then the trustee, with the approval of the court, must initiate an application for the abandonment with the Commission. The court may then fix a time within which the Commission must report to the court on the application.

Subsection (c) permits the court to act after it has received the report of the Commission or the time fixed under subsection (b) has expired, whichever occurs first. The court may then authorize the abandonment after notice and a hearing. The notice must go to the Commission, the Secretary of Transportation, the trustee, and party in interest that has requested notice, any affected shipper or community, and any other entity that the court specifies.

Subsection (d) stays the enforcement of an abandonment until the time for taking an appeal has expired, or if an appeal has been taken, until the order has become final. However, the court may, and after notice and a hearing, on request of a party in interest authorize termination of service on the line or a portion of the line pending the determination of the appeal. The notice required is the same as that required under subsection (c). If the court authorizes termination of service pending determination of the appeal, an appellant may not obtain a stay of the enforcement of the order authorizing termination, either by the giving of a supersedeas bond or otherwise, during the pendency of the appeal.

Effective Date of 1984 Amendments. See section 553 of Pub.L. 98–353, Title III, July 10, 1984, 98 Stat. 392, set out as an Effective Date of 1984 Amendment note preceding chapter 1 of Title 11, Bankruptcy.

Effective Date of 1980 Amendment. Amendment by Pub.L. 96–448 effective Oct. 1, 1980, see section 710(a) of Pub.L. 96–448, set out as a note under section 10101 of Title 49, Transportation.

Separability of Provisions. For separability of provisions of Title III of Pub.L. 98–353, see section 551 of Pub.L. 98–353 set out as a Separability of Provisions note preceding chapter 1 of Title 11, Bankruptcy.

Cross References

Abandonment of property of estate, see section 554.

Library References:

C.J.S. Bankruptcy § 414.
West's Key No. Digests, Bankruptcy ⚷3653.

WESTLAW Electronic Research

See WESTLAW Electronic Research Guide following the *Bankruptcy Highlights*.

§ 1171. Priority claims

(a) There shall be paid as an administrative expense any claim of an individual or of the personal representative of a deceased individual against the debtor or the estate, for personal injury to or death of such individual arising out of the operation of the debtor or the estate, whether such claim arose before or after the commencement of the case.

(b) Any unsecured claim against the debtor that would have been entitled to priority if a receiver in equity of the property of the debtor had been appointed by a Federal court on the date of the order for relief under this title shall be entitled to the same priority in the case under this chapter.

Pub.L. 95–598, Nov. 6, 1978, 92 Stat. 2643; Pub.L. 98–353, Title III, § 522, July 10, 1984, 98 Stat. 388.

Historical and Revision Notes

Notes of Committee on the Judiciary, House Report No. 95–595. This section is derived from current law. Subsection (a) grants an administrative expense priority to the claim of any individual (or of the personal representative of a deceased individual) against the debtor or the estate for personal injury to or death of the individual arising out of the operation of the debtor railroad or the estate, whether the claim arose before or after commencement of the case. The priority under current law, found in section 77(n) [former section 205(n) of this title], applies only to employees of the debtor. This subsection expands the protection provided.

Subsection (b) follows present section 77(b) of the Bankruptcy Act [former section 205(b) of this title] by giving priority to any unsecured claims that would be entitled to priority if a receiver in equity of the property of the debtor had been appointed by a Federal court on the date of the order for relief under the bankruptcy laws. As under current law, the courts will determine the precise contours of the priority recognized by this subsection in each case.

Legislative Statements. Section 1171 of the House amendment is derived from section 1170 of the House bill in lieu of section 1173(a)(9) of the Senate amendment.

Effective Date of 1984 Amendments. See section 553 of Pub.L. 98–353, Title III, July 10, 1984, 98 Stat. 392, set out as an Effective Date of 1984 Amendment note preceding chapter 1 of Title 11, Bankruptcy.

Separability of Provisions. For separability of provisions of Title III of Pub.L. 98–353, see section 551 of Pub.L. 98–353 set out as a Separability of Provisions note preceding chapter 1 of Title 11, Bankruptcy.

Savings Provisions. Section to apply to cases pending under section 77 of the Bankruptcy Act [section 205 of former Title 11] on Nov. 6, 1978, in which the trustee had not filed a plan of reorganization, see section 403(b) of Pub. L. 95–598, set out preceding section 101 of this title.

Cross References

Allowance of administrative expenses, see section 503.
Priorities, see section 507.

Library References:

C.J.S. Bankruptcy §§ 250, 260, 353, 354.
West's Key No. Digests, Bankruptcy ⚮2871, 2965.

WESTLAW Electronic Research

See WESTLAW Electronic Research Guide following the *Bankruptcy Highlights.*

§ 1172.   Contents of plan

(a) In addition to the provisions required or permitted under section 1123 of this title, a plan—

    (1) shall specify the extent to and the means by which the debtor's rail service is proposed to be continued, and the extent to which any of the debtor's rail service is proposed to be terminated; and

    (2) may include a provision for—

        (A) the transfer of any or all of the operating railroad lines of the debtor to another operating railroad; or

(B) abandonment of any railroad line in accordance with section 1170 of this title.

(b) If, except for the pendency of the case under this chapter, transfer of, or operation of or over, any of the debtor's rail lines by an entity other than the debtor or a successor to the debtor under the plan would require approval by the Commission under a law of the United States, then a plan may not propose such a transfer or such operation unless the proponent of the plan initiates an appropriate application for such a transfer or such operation with the Commission and, within such time as the court may fix, not exceeding 180 days, the Commission, with or without a hearing, as the Commission may determine, and with or without modification or condition, approves such application, or does not act on such application. Any action or order of the Commission approving, modifying, conditioning, or disapproving such application is subject to review by the court only under sections 706(2)(A), 706(2)(B), 706(2)(C), and 706(2)(D) of title 5.

(c)(1) In approving an application under subsection (b) of this section, the Commission shall require the rail carrier to provide a fair arrangement at least as protective of the interests of employees as that established under section 11347 of title 49.

(2) Nothing in this subsection shall be deemed to affect the priorities or timing of payment of employee protection which might have existed in the absence of this subsection.

Pub.L. 95–598, Nov. 6, 1978, 92 Stat. 2644; Pub.L. 96–448, Title II, § 227(b), Oct. 14, 1980, 94 Stat. 1931.

Historical and Revision Notes

Notes of Committee on the Judiciary, Senate Report No. 95–989. Section 1170 [now this section] adds to the general provisions required or permitted in reorganization plans by section 1123. Subsection (1) requires that a reorganization plan under the railroad subchapter specify the means by which the value of the claims of creditors and the interests of equity holders which are materially and adversely affected by the plan are to be realized. Subsection (2) permits a plan to include provisions for the issuance of warrants. Subsection (3) requires that the plan provide for fixed charges by probable earnings for their payment. Subsection (4) requires that the plan specify the means by which, and the extent to which, the debtor's rail service is to be continued, and shall identify any rail service to be terminated. Subsection (5) permits other appropriate provisions not inconsistent with the chapter. With the exception of subsection (4), the requirements are comparable to those of present section 77(b) [former section 205(b) of this title] subsection (4) emphasizes the public interest in the preservation of rail transportation.

Notes of Committee on the Judiciary, House Report No. 95–595. A plan in a railroad reorganization case may include provisions in addition to those required and permitted under an ordinary reorganization plan. It may provide for the transfer of any or all of the operating railroad lines of the debtor to another operating railroad.

Paragraph (1) contemplates a liquidating plan for the debtor's rail lines, much as occurred in the Penn Central case by transfer of operating lines to Con Rail. Such a liquidating plan is not per se contrary to the public interest, and the court will have to determine on a case-by-case basis, with the guidance of the Interstate Commerce Commission and of other parties in interest, whether the particular plan proposed is in the public interest, as required under proposed 11 U.S.C. 1172(3).

The plan may also provide for abandonment in accordance with section 1169, governing abandonment generally. Neither of these provisions in a plan, transfer or abandonment of lines, requires ICC approval. Confirmation of the plan by the court authorizes the debtor to comply with the plan in accordance with section 1142(a) notwithstanding any bankruptcy law to the contrary.

Legislative Statements. Section 1172 of the House amendment is derived from section 1171 of the House bill in preference to section 1170 of the Senate amendment with the exception that section 1170(4) of the Senate amendment is incorporated into section 1172(a)(1) of the House amendment.

Section 1172(b) of the House amendment is derived from section 1171(c) of the Senate amendment. The section gives the Interstate Commerce Commission the exclusive power to approve or disapprove the transfer of, or operation of or over, any of the debtor's rail lines over which the Commission has jurisdiction, subject to review under the Administrative Procedures Act [sections 551 et seq. and 701 et seq. of Title 5, Government Organization and Employees]. The section does not apply to a transfer of railroad lines to a successor of the debtor under a plan of reorganization by merger or otherwise.

The House amendment deletes section 1171(a) of the Senate amendment as a matter to be determined by the Rules of Bankruptcy Procedure. It is anticipated that the rules will specify the period of time, such as 18 months, within which a trustee must file with the court a proposed plan of reorganization for the debtor or a report why a plan cannot be formulated. Incorporation by reference of section 1121 in section 1161 of title 11 means that a party in interest will also have a right to file a plan of reorganization. This differs from the position taken in the Senate amendment which would have permitted the Interstate Commerce Commission to file a plan of reorganization.

Effective Date of 1980 Amendment. Amendment by Pub.L. 96–448 effective Oct. 1, 1980, see section 710(a) of Pub.L. 96–448, set out as a note under section 10101 of Title 49, Transportation.

Cross References
Contents of plan filed in chapter 13 cases, see section 1322.

Library References:
C.J.S. Bankruptcy § 415.
West's Key No. Digests, Bankruptcy ⊜3652.

WESTLAW Electronic Research
See WESTLAW Electronic Research Guide following the *Bankruptcy Highlights*.

§ 1173. Confirmation of plan

(a) The court shall confirm a plan if—

(1) the applicable requirements of section 1129 of this title have been met;

(2) each creditor or equity security holder will receive or retain under the plan property of a value, as of the effective date of the plan, that is not less than the value of property that each such creditor or equity security holder would so receive or retain if all of the operating railroad lines of the debtor were sold, and the proceeds of such sale, and the other property of the estate, were distributed under chapter 7 of this title on such date;

(3) in light of the debtor's past earnings and the probable prospective earnings of the reorganized debtor, there will be adequate coverage by such prospective earnings of any fixed charges, such as interest on debt, amortization of funded debt, and rent for leased railroads, provided for by the plan; and

(4) the plan is consistent with the public interest.

(b) If the requirements of subsection (a) of this section are met with respect to more than one plan, the court shall confirm the plan that is most likely to maintain adequate rail service in the public interest.

Pub.L. 95–598, Nov. 6, 1978, 92 Stat. 2644; Pub.L. 98–353, Title III, § 523, July 10, 1984, 98 Stat. 388.

Historical and Revision Notes

Notes of Committee on the Judiciary, Senate Report No. 95–989. Section 1173 adapts the provisions dealing with reorganization plans generally contained in section 1130 to the particular requirements of railroad reorganization plans, as set out in present section 77(e) [former section 205(e) of this title]. Subsection (a) specifies the findings which the court must make before approving a plan: (1) The plan complies with the applicable provisions of the chapter; (2) the proponent of the plan complies with the applicable provisions of the chapter; (3) the plan has been proposed in good faith; (4) any payments for services or for costs or expenses in connection with the case or the plan are disclosed to the court and are reasonable, or, if to be paid later, are subject to the approval of the court as reasonable; (5) the proponent of the plan has disclosed the identity and affiliations of the individuals who will serve as directors, officers, or voting trustees, such appointments or continuations in office are consistent with the interests of creditors, equity security holders, and the proponent the public, and has disclosed the identity and compensation of any insider who will be employed or retained under the plan; (6) that rate changes proposed in the plan have been approved by the appropriate regulatory commission, or that the plan is contingent on such approval; (7) that confirmation of the plan is not likely to be followed by further reorganization or liquidation, unless it is contemplated by the plan; (8) that the plan, if there is more than one, is the one most likely to maintain adequate rail service and (9) that the plan provides the priority traditionally accorded by section 77(b) [former section 205(b) of this title] to claims by rail creditors for necessary services rendered during the 6 months preceding the filing of the petition in bankruptcy.

Subsection (b) continues the present power of the court in section 77(e) [former section 205(e) of this title] to confirm a plan over the objections of creditors or equity security holders who are materially and adversely affected. The subsection also confirms the authority of the court to approve a transfer of all or part of a debtor's property or its merger over the objections of equity security holders if it finds (1) that the "public interest" in continued rail transportation outweighs any adverse effect on creditors and equity security holders, and (2) that the plan is fair and equitable, affords due recognition to the rights of each class, and does not discriminate unfairly against any class.

Subsection (c) permits modification of a plan confirmed by a final order only for fraud.

Notes of Committee on the Judiciary, House Report No. 95–595. This section requires the court to confirm a plan if the applicable requirements of section 1129 (relating to confirmation of reorganization plans generally) are met, if the best interest test is met, and if the plan is compatible with the public interest.

The test in this paragraph is similar to the test prescribed for ordinary corporate reorganizations. However, since a railroad cannot liquidate its assets and sell them for scrap to satisfy its creditors, the test focuses on the value of the railroad as a going concern. That is, the test is based on what the assets, sold as operating rail lines, would bring.

The public interest requirement, found in current law, will now be decided by the court, with the ICC [Interstate Commerce Commission] representing the public interest before the court, rather than in the first instance by the ICC. Liquidation of the debtor is not, per se, contrary to the public interest.

Legislative Statements. Section 1173 of the House amendment concerns confirmation of a plan of railroad reorganization and is derived from section 1172 of the House bill as modified. In particular, section 1173(a)(3) of the House amendment is derived from section 1170(3) of the Senate amendment. Section 1173(b) is derived from section 1173(a)(8) of the Senate amendment.

Effective Date of 1984 Amendments. See section 553 of Pub.L. 98–353, Title III, July 10, 1984, 98 Stat. 392, set out as an Effective Date of 1984 Amendment note preceding chapter 1 of Title 11, Bankruptcy.

Separability of Provisions. For separability of provisions of Title III of Pub.L. 98–353, see section 551 of Pub.L. 98–353 set out as a Separability of Provisions note preceding chapter 1 of Title 11, Bankruptcy.

Cross References

Confirmation of plan in
    Chapter 9 cases, see section 943.
    Chapter 13 cases, see section 1325.
Effect of confirmation in cases under this chapter, see section 1141.
Revocation of order of confirmation in cases under this chapter, see section 1144.
Unclaimed property, see section 347.

Library References:

C.J.S. Bankruptcy § 415.
West's Key No. Digests, Bankruptcy ☞3652.

WESTLAW Electronic Research

See WESTLAW Electronic Research Guide following the *Bankruptcy Highlights.*

§ 1174. Liquidation

On request of a party in interest and after notice and a hearing, the court may, or, if a plan has not been confirmed under section 1173 of this title before five years after the date of the order for relief, the court shall, order the trustee to cease the debtor's operation and to collect and reduce to money all of the property of the estate in the same manner as if the case were a case under chapter 7 of this title.

Pub.L. 95–598, Nov. 6, 1978, 92 Stat. 2644.

Historical and Revision Notes

Notes of Committee on the Judiciary, Senate Report No. 95–989. Section 1174 permits the court to convert the case to a liquidation under chapter 7 if the court finds that the debtor cannot be reorganized, or if various time limits specified in the subchapter are not met. Section 77 [former section 205 of this title] does not authorize a liquidation of a railroad under the Bankruptcy Act. If the railroad is not reorganizable, the only action open to the court is to dismiss the petition, which would in all likelihood be followed by a State court receivership, with all of its attendant disadvantages. If reorganization is impossible, the debtor should be liquidated under the Bankruptcy Act.

Legislative Statements. Section 1174 of the House amendment represents a compromise between the House bill and Senate amendment on the issue of liquidation of a railroad. The provision permits a party in interest at any time to request liquidation. In addition, if a plan has not been confirmed under section 1173 of the House amendment before 5 years after the date of order for relief, the court must order the trustee to cease the debtor's operation and to collect and reduce to money all of the property of the estate in the same manner as if the case were a case under chapter 7 of title 11. The approach differs from the conversion to chapter 7 under section 1174 of the Senate bill in order to make special provisions contained in subchapter IV of chapter 11 applicable to liquidation. However, maintaining liquidation in the context of chapter 11 is not intended to delay liquidation of the railroad to a different extent than if the case were converted to chapter 7.

Although the House amendment does not adopt provisions contained in sections 1170(1), (2), (3), or (5), of the Senate amendment such provisions are contained explicitly or implicitly in section 1123 of the House amendment.

Cross References

Conversion of
    Chapter 7 cases, see section 706.
    Chapter 11 cases, see section 1112.
    Chapter 13 cases, see section 1307.

Dismissal of
    Chapter 7 cases, see section 707.
    Chapter 9 cases, see section 927.
    Chapter 11 cases, see section 1112.
    Chapter 13 cases, see section 1307.

Library References:
C.J.S. Bankruptcy § 387.
West's Key No. Digests, Bankruptcy ⟿3651.

WESTLAW Electronic Research
See WESTLAW Electronic Research Guide following the *Bankruptcy Highlights*.

CHAPTER 12—ADJUSTMENT OF DEBTS OF A FAMILY FARMER WITH REGULAR ANNUAL INCOME

SUBCHAPTER I—OFFICERS, ADMINISTRATION, AND THE ESTATE

Sec.
1201. Stay of action against codebtor.
1202. Trustee.
1203. Rights and powers of debtor.
1204. Removal of debtor as debtor in possession.
1205. Adequate protection.
1206. Sales free of interests.
1207. Property of the estate.
1208. Conversion or dismissal.

SUBCHAPTER II—THE PLAN

1221. Filing of plan.
1222. Contents of plan.
1223. Modification of plan before confirmation.
1224. Confirmation hearing.
1225. Confirmation of plan.
1226. Payments.
1227. Effect of confirmation.
1228. Discharge.
1229. Modification of plan after confirmation.
1230. Revocation of an order of confirmation.
1231. Special tax provisions.

Repeal of Chapter and Savings Provisions

Pub.L. 99–554, Title III, § 302(f), Oct. 27, 1986, 100 Stat. 3124, repealed this chapter on Oct. 1, 1993, and all cases commenced or pending under chapter 12 of title 11, United States Code, and all matters and proceedings in or relating to such cases, conducted and determined under such chapter as if such chapter had not been repealed, and substantive rights of parties in connection with such cases, matters, and proceedings shall continue to be governed under the laws applicable to such cases, matters, and proceedings as if such chapter had not been repealed.

SUBCHAPTER I—OFFICERS, ADMINISTRATION, AND THE ESTATE

§ 1201. Stay of action against codebtor

(a) Except as provided in subsections (b) and (c) of this section, after the order for relief under this chapter, a creditor may not act, or commence or continue any civil action, to collect all or any part of a consumer debt of the debtor from any individual that is liable on such debt with the debtor, or that secured such debt, unless—

(1) such individual became liable on or secured such debt in the ordinary course of such individual's business; or

(2) the case is closed, dismissed, or converted to a case under chapter 7 of this title.

(b) A creditor may present a negotiable instrument, and may give notice of dishonor of such an instrument.

(c) On request of a party in interest and after notice and a hearing, the court shall grant relief from the stay provided by subsection (a) of this section with respect to a creditor, to the extent that—

(1) as between the debtor and the individual protected under subsection (a) of this section, such individual received the consideration for the claim held by such creditor;

(2) the plan filed by the debtor proposes not to pay such claim; or

(3) such creditor's interest would be irreparably harmed by continuation of such stay.

(d) Twenty days after the filing of a request under subsection (c)(2) of this section for relief from the stay provided by subsection (a) of this section, such stay is terminated with respect to the party in interest making such request, unless the debtor or any individual that is liable on such debt with the debtor files and serves upon such party in interest a written objection to the taking of the proposed action.

Added Pub.L. 99–554, Title II, § 255, Oct. 27, 1986, 100 Stat. 3105.

Repeal of Section and Savings Provisions

Pub.L. 99–554, Title III, § 302(f), Oct. 27, 1986, 100 Stat. 3124, repealed this section on Oct. 1, 1993, and all cases commenced or pending under chapter 12 of title 11, United States Code, and all matters and proceedings in or relating to such cases, conducted and determined under such chapter as if such chapter had not been repealed, and substantive rights of parties in connection with such cases, matters, and proceedings shall continue to be governed under the laws applicable to such cases, matters, and proceedings as if such chapter had not been repealed.

Historical Notes

Effective Date; Savings Provisions; Quarterly Fees. Enactment by Pub.L. 99–554 effective 30 days after Oct. 27, 1986, except as otherwise provided for, see section 302(a) of Pub.L. 99–554, set out as a note under section 581 of Title 28, Judiciary and Judicial Procedure.

Enactment by Pub.L. 99–554, § 255, not to apply with respect to cases commenced under Title 11, Bankruptcy, before 30 days after Oct. 27, 1986, see section 302(c)(1) of Pub.L. 99–554, set out as a note under section 581 of Title 28.

Library References:

C.J.S. Bankruptcy § 65 et seq.
West's Key No. Digests, Bankruptcy ⚙2391 et seq.

§ 1202.   Trustee

(a) If the United States trustee has appointed an individual under section 586(b) of title 28 to serve as standing trustee in cases under this chapter and if such individual qualifies as a trustee under section 322 of this title, then such individual shall serve as trustee in any case filed under this chapter. Otherwise, the United States trustee shall appoint one disinterested person to serve as trustee in the case or the United States trustee may serve as trustee in the case if necessary.

(b) The trustee shall—

(1) perform the duties specified in sections 704(2), 704(3), 704(5), 704(6), 704(7) and 704(9) of this title;

(2) perform the duties specified in section 1106(a)(3) and 1106(a)(4) of this title if the court, for cause and on request of a party in interest, the trustee, or the United States trustee, so orders;

(3) appear and be heard at any hearing that concerns—

(A) the value of property subject to a lien;

(B) confirmation of a plan;

(C) modification of the plan after confirmation; or

(D) the sale of property of the estate;

(4) ensure that the debtor commences making timely payments required by a confirmed plan; and

(5) if the debtor ceases to be a debtor in possession, perform the duties specified in sections 704(8), 1106(a)(1), 1106(a)(2), 1106(a)(6), 1106(a)(7), and 1203.

Added Pub.L. 99–554, Title II, § 255, Oct. 27, 1986, 100 Stat. 3106, and amended Pub.L. 99–554, Title II, § 227, Oct. 27, 1986, 100 Stat. 3103.

Repeal of Section and Savings Provisions

Pub.L. 99–554, Title III, § 302(f), Oct. 27, 1986, 100 Stat. 3124, repealed this section on Oct. 1, 1993, and all cases commenced or pending under chapter 12 of title 11, United States Code, and all matters and proceedings in or relating to such cases, conducted and determined under such chapter as if such chapter had not been repealed, and substantive rights of parties in connection with such cases, matters, and proceedings shall continue to be governed under the laws applicable to such cases, matters, and proceedings as if such chapter had not been repealed.

Historical Note

1986 Amendment. Subsecs. (c) and (d). Pub.L. 99–554, § 227, struck out subsecs. (c) and (d) which read as follows:

"(c) If the number of cases under this chapter commenced in a particular judicial district so warrants, the court may appoint one or more individuals to serve as standing trustee for such district in cases under this chapter.

"(d)(1) A court that has appointed an individual under subsection (a) of this section to serve as standing trustee in cases under this chapter shall set for such individual—

"(A) a maximum annual compensation not to exceed the lowest annual rate of basic pay in effect for grade GS–16 of the General Schedule prescribed under section 5332 of title 5; and

"(B) a percentage fee not to exceed the sum of—

"(i) not to exceed ten percent of the payments made under the plan of such debtor, with respect to payments in an aggregate amount not to exceed $450,000; and "(ii) three percent of payments made under the plan of such debtor, with respect to payments made after the aggregate amount of payments made under the plan exceeds $450,000;

based on such maximum annual compensation and the actual, necessary expenses incurred by such individual as standing trustee.

"(2) Such individual shall collect such percentage fee from all payments under plans in the cases under this chapter for which such individual serves as standing trustee. Such individual shall pay annually to the Treasury—

"(A) any amount by which the actual compensation received by such individual exceeds five percent of all such payments made under plans in cases under this chapter for which such individual serves as standing trustee; and

"(B) any amount by which the percentage fee fixed under paragraph (1)(B) of this subsection for all such cases exceeds—

"(i) such individual's actual compensation for such cases, as adjusted under subparagraph (A) of this paragraph; plus

"(ii) the actual, necessary expenses incurred by such individual as standing trustee in such cases.".

See Effective Date, etc., notes set out below.

Effective Date; Effective Date of 1986 Amendments; Savings Provisions; References in Title 11 Section 326(b) to Title 11 Chapter 13 and Section 1302(a) and (d); References in Title 11 Section 1202(a) to United States Trustee; Effective Date of 1986 Amendments for Certain Judicial Districts Not Served by United States Trustees and for Judicial Districts in Alabama and North Carolina; U.S. Trustee System Fund Deposits in Alabama and North Carolina; Effective Date of Title 11 Chapter 15 Repeal as to Northern District of Alabama; Authority of Certain Estate Administrators in Alabama and North Carolina; Effective Date of 1986 Amendments in Pending Cases Where a U.S. Trustee Not Authorized or Where a Trustee Files Final Report or Plan is Confirmed; Quarterly Fees; Effective Date and Savings Provisions for Repeal of Title 11 Chapter 12. Enactment by Pub.L. 99–554 effective 30 days after Oct. 27, 1986, except as otherwise provided for, see section 302(a) of Pub.L. 99–554, set

out as a note under section 581 of Title 28, Judiciary and Judicial Procedure.

Enactment by Pub.L. 99–554, § 255, not to apply with respect to cases commenced under Title 11, Bankruptcy, before 30 days after Oct. 27, 1986, see section 302(c)(1) of Pub.L. 99–554, set out as a note under section 581 of Title 28.

Enactment by section 255 of Pub.L. 99–554 to take effect 30 days after Oct. 27, 1986, and before amendment made by section 227 of Pub.L. 99–554, striking out subsecs. (c) and (d) of this section, see section 302(c)(2) of Pub.L. 99–554, set out as a note under section 581 of Title 28.

Until amendments made by section 227 of Pub.L. 99–554 become effective in a district and apply to a case, for purposes of such case any references in subsec. (a) of this section to the United States trustee or to section 586(b) of Title 28, Judiciary and Judicial Procedure, deemed references, respectively, to the court or subsec. (c) of this section, see section 302(c)(3)(B)(i), (i) of Pub.L. 99–554, set out as a note under section 581 of Title 28.

Amendment by Pub.L. 99–554, § 227, not to become effective in or with respect to certain specified judicial districts until, or apply to cases while pending in such district before, the expiration of the 270-day period beginning 30 days after Oct. 27, 1986, or of the 30-day period beginning on the date the Attorney General certifies under section 303 of Pub.L. 99–554 the region specified in a paragraph of section 581(a) of Title 28, as amended by section 111(a) of Pub.L. 99–554, that includes such district, whichever occurs first, see section 302(d)(1) of Pub.L. 99–554, set out as a note under section 581 of Title 28.

Amendment by Pub.L. 99–554, § 227, not to become effective in or with respect to certain specified judicial districts until, or apply to cases while pending in such district before, the expiration of the 2-year period beginning 30 days after Oct. 27, 1986, or of the 30-day period beginning on the date the Attorney General certifies under section 303 of Pub.L. 99–554 the region specified in a paragraph of section 581(a) of Title 28, as amended by section 111(a) of Pub.L. 99–554, that includes such district, whichever occurs first, see section 302(d)(2) of Pub.L. 99–554, set out as a note under section 581 of Title 28.

Amendment by Pub.L. 99–554, § 227, not to become effective in or with respect to judicial districts established for the States of Alabama and North Carolina until, or apply to cases while pending in such district before, such district elects to be included in a bankruptcy region established in section 581(a) of Title 28, as amended by section 111(a) of Pub.L. 99–554, or Oct. 1, 2002, whichever occurs first, and, except as otherwise provided for, with respect to cases under chapters 7, 11, 12, and 13 of Title 11 commenced before 30 days after Oct. 27, 1986, and pending in a judicial district in the States of Alabama or North Carolina before any election made under section 302(d)(3) (A) of Pub.L. 99–554 by such district becomes effective or Oct. 1, 2002, whichever occurs first, amendments by Pub.L. 99–554 not to apply until Oct. 1, 2003, or the expiration of the 1-year period beginning on the date such election becomes effective, whichever occurs first, and further, in any judicial district in Alabama or North Carolina not making the election described in section 302(d)(3)(A) of Pub.L. 99–554, any person appointed under regulations issued by the Judicial Conference to administer estates in cases under Title 11 authorized to establish, etc., a panel of private trustees, and to supervise cases and trustees in cases under chapters 7, 11, 12, and 13 of

Title 11, until amendments by sections 201 to 231 of Pub.L. 99–554 becomes effective in such district, see section 302(d)(3)(A) to (F), (H), (I) of Pub.L. 99–554, set out as a note under section 581 of Title 28.

Amendment by Pub.L. 99–554, § 227, except as otherwise provided, with respect to cases under chapters 7, 11, 12, and 13 of Title 11 commenced before 30 days after Oct. 27, 1986, and pending in a judicial district referred to in section 581(a) of Title 28, as amended by section 111(a) of Pub.L. 99–554, for which a United States trustee is not authorized before 30 days after Oct. 27, 1986 to be appointed, not applicable until the expiration of the 3-year period beginning on Oct. 27, 1986, or of the 1-year period beginning on the date the Attorney General certifies under section 303 of Pub.L. 99–554 the region specified in a paragraph of such section 581(a) that includes, such district, whichever occurs first, see section 302(e)(1), (2) of Pub.L. 99–554, set out as a note under section 581 of Title 28.

See 1986 Amendment notes set out above.

Library References:
C.J.S. Bankruptcy § 417.
West's Key No. Digests, Bankruptcy ⚷3672.

§ 1203.   Rights and powers of debtor

Subject to such limitations as the court may prescribe, a debtor in possession shall have all the rights, other than the right to compensation under section 330, and powers, and shall perform all the functions and duties, except the duties specified in paragraphs (3) and (4) of section 1106(a), of a trustee serving in a case under chapter 11, including operating the debtor's farm.

Added Pub.L. 99–554, Title II, § 255, Oct. 27, 1986, 100 Stat. 3107.

Repeal of Section and Savings Provisions

Pub.L. 99–554, Title III, § 302(f), Oct. 27, 1986, 100 Stat. 3124, repealed this section on Oct. 1, 1993, and all cases commenced or pending under chapter 12 of title 11, United States Code, and all matters and proceedings in or relating to such cases, conducted and determined under such chapter as if such chapter had not been repealed, and substantive rights of parties in connection with such cases, matters, and proceedings shall continue to be governed under the laws applicable to such cases, matters, and proceedings as if such chapter had not been repealed.

Historical Note

Effective Date; Savings Provisions; Quarterly Fees. Enactment by Pub.L. 99–554 effective 30 days after Oct. 27, 1986, except as otherwise provided for, see section 302(a) of Pub.L. 99–554, set out as a note

under section 581 of Title 28, Judiciary and Judicial Procedure.

Enactment by Pub.L. 99–554, § 255, not to apply with respect to cases commenced under Title 11, Bankruptcy, before 30 days after Oct.

27, 1986, see section 302(c)(1) of Pub.L. 99–554, set out as a note under section 581 of Title 28.

§ 1204. Removal of debtor as debtor in possession

(a) On request of a party in interest, and after notice and a hearing, the court shall order that the debtor shall not be a debtor in possession for cause, including fraud, dishonesty, incompetence, or gross mismanagement of the affairs of the debtor, either before or after the commencement of the case.

(b) On request of a party in interest, and after notice and a hearing, the court may reinstate the debtor in possession.

Added Pub.L. 99–554, Title II, § 255, Oct. 27, 1986, 100 Stat. 3107.

Repeal of Section and Savings Provisions

Pub.L. 99–554, Title III, § 302(f), Oct. 27, 1986, 100 Stat. 3124, repealed this section on Oct. 1, 1993, and all cases commenced or pending under chapter 12 of title 11, United States Code, and all matters and proceedings in or relating to such cases, conducted and determined under such chapter as if such chapter had not been repealed, and substantive rights of parties in connection with such cases, matters, and proceedings shall continue to be governed under the laws applicable to such cases, matters, and proceedings as if such chapter had not been repealed.

Historical Note

Effective Date; Savings Provisions; Quarterly Fees. Enactment by Pub.L. 99–554 effective 30 days after Oct. 27, 1986, except as otherwise provided for, see section 302(a) of Pub.L. 99–554, set out as a note under section 581 of Title 28, Judiciary and Judicial Procedure.

Enactment by Pub.L. 99–554, § 255, not to apply with respect to cases commenced under Title 11, Bankruptcy, before 30 days after Oct. 27, 1986, see section 302(c)(1) of Pub.L. 99–554, set out as a note under section 581 of Title 28.

§ 1205. Adequate protection

(a) Section 361 does not apply in a case under this chapter.

(b) In a case under this chapter, when adequate protection is required under section 362, 363, or 364 of this title of an interest of an entity in property, such adequate protection may be provided by—

(1) requiring the trustee to make a cash payment or periodic cash payments to such entity, to the extent that the stay under section 362 of this title, use, sale, or lease under section 363 of this title, or any grant of a lien under section 364 of this title results in a decrease in the value of property securing a claim or of an entity's ownership interest in property;

(2) providing to such entity an additional or replacement lien to the extent that such stay, use, sale, lease, or grant results in a decrease in the value of property securing a claim or of an entity's ownership interest in property;

(3) paying to such entity for the use of farmland the reasonable rent customary in the community where the property is located, based upon the rental value, net income, and earning capacity of the property; or

(4) granting such other relief, other than entitling such entity to compensation allowable under section 503(b)(1) of this title as an administrative expense, as will adequately protect the value of property securing a claim or of such entity's ownership interest in property.

Added Pub.L. 99–554, Title II, § 255, Oct. 27, 1986, 100 Stat. 3107.

Repeal of Section and Savings Provisions

Pub.L. 99–554, Title III, § 302(f), Oct. 27, 1986, 100 Stat. 3124, repealed this section on Oct. 1, 1993, and all cases commenced or pending under chapter 12 of title 11, United States Code, and all matters and proceedings in or relating to such cases, conducted and determined under such chapter as if such chapter had not been repealed, and substantive rights of parties in connection with such cases, matters, and proceedings shall continue to be governed under the laws applicable to such cases, matters, and proceedings as if such chapter had not been repealed.

Historical Note

Effective Date; Savings Provisions; Quarterly Fees. Enactment by Pub.L. 99–554 effective 30 days after Oct. 27, 1986, except as otherwise provided for, see section 302(a) of Pub.L. 99–554, set out as a note under section 581 of Title 28, Judiciary and Judicial Procedure.

Enactment by Pub.L. 99–554, § 255, not to apply with respect to cases commenced under Title 11, Bankruptcy, before 30 days after Oct. 27, 1986, see section 302(c)(1) of Pub.L. 99–554, set out as a note under section 581 of Title 28.

Library References:
C.J.S. Bankruptcy §§ 86–88, 186, 200, 208, 209.
West's Key No. Digests, Bankruptcy ⬅2430–2434, 3035, 3065, 3073.

§ 1206. Sales free of interests

After notice and a hearing, in addition to the authorization contained in section 363(f), the trustee in a case under this chapter may sell property under section 363(b) and (c) free and clear of any interest in such property of an entity other than the estate if the property is farmland or farm equipment, except that the proceeds of such sale shall be subject to such interest.

Added Pub.L. 99–554, Title II, § 255, Oct. 27, 1986, 100 Stat. 3108.

Repeal of Section and Savings Provisions

Pub.L. 99–554, Title III, § 302(f), Oct. 27, 1986, 100 Stat. 3124, repealed this section on Oct. 1, 1993, and all cases commenced or pending under chapter 12 of title 11, United States Code, and all matters and proceedings in or relating to such cases, conducted and determined under such chapter as if such chapter had not been repealed, and substantive rights of parties in connection with such cases, matters, and proceedings shall continue to be governed under the laws applicable to such cases, matters, and proceedings as if such chapter had not been repealed.

Historical Note

Effective Date; Savings Provisions; Quarterly Fees. Enactment by Pub.L. 99–554 effective 30 days after Oct. 27, 1986, except as otherwise provided for, see section 302(a) of Pub.L. 99–554, set out as a note under section 581 of Title 28, Judiciary and Judicial Procedure.

Enactment by Pub.L. 99–554, § 255, not to apply with respect to cases commenced under Title 11, Bankruptcy, before 30 days after Oct. 27, 1986, see section 302(c)(1) of Pub.L. 99–554, set out as a note under section 581 of Title 28.

Library References:

C.J.S. Bankruptcy §§ 208, 209.
West's Key No. Digests, Bankruptcy ⚬⇒3073.

§ 1207. Property of the estate

(a) Property of the estate includes, in addition to the property specified in section 541 of this title—

(1) all property of the kind specified in such section that the debtor acquires after the commencement of the case but before the case is closed, dismissed, or converted to a case under chapter 7 of this title, whichever occurs first; and

(2) earnings from services performed by the debtor after the commencement of the case but before the case is closed, dismissed, or converted to a case under chapter 7 of this title, whichever occurs first.

(b) Except as provided in section 1204, a confirmed plan, or an order confirming a plan, the debtor shall remain in possession of all property of the estate.

Added Pub.L. 99–554, Title II, § 255, Oct. 27, 1986, 100 Stat. 3108.

Repeal of Section and Savings Provisions

Pub.L. 99–554, Title III, § 302(f), Oct. 27, 1986, 100 Stat. 3124, repealed this section on Oct. 1, 1993, and all cases commenced or pending under chapter 12 of title 11, United States Code, and all matters and proceedings in or relating to such cases, conducted and determined under such chapter as if such chapter had not been repealed, and substantive rights of parties in connection with such cases, matters, and proceedings shall continue to be governed under the laws applicable to such cases, matters, and proceedings as if such chapter had not been repealed.

Historical Note

Effective Date; Savings Provisions; Quarterly Fees. Enactment by Pub.L. 99–554 effective 30 days after Oct. 27, 1986, except as otherwise provided for, see section 302(a) of Pub.L. 99–554, set out as a note under section 581 of Title 28, Judiciary and Judicial Procedure.

Enactment by Pub.L. 99–554, § 255, not to apply with respect to cases commenced under Title 11, Bankruptcy, before 30 days after Oct. 27, 1986, see section 302(c)(1) of Pub.L. 99–554, set out as a note under section 581 of Title 28.

§ 1208. Conversion or dismissal

(a) The debtor may convert a case under this chapter to a case under chapter 7 of this title at any time. Any waiver of the right to convert under this subsection is unenforceable.

(b) On request of the debtor at any time, if the case has not been converted under section 706 or 1112 of this title, the court shall dismiss a case under this chapter. Any waiver of the right to dismiss under this subsection is unenforceable.

(c) On request of a party in interest, and after notice and a hearing, the court may dismiss a case under this chapter for cause, including—

(1) unreasonable delay, or gross mismanagement, by the debtor that is prejudicial to creditors;

(2) nonpayment of any fees and charges required under chapter 123 of title 28;

(3) failure to file a plan timely under section 1221 of this title;

(4) failure to commence making timely payments required by a confirmed plan;

(5) denial of confirmation of a plan under section 1225 of this title and denial of a request made for additional time for filing another plan or a modification of a plan;

(6) material default by the debtor with respect to a term of a confirmed plan;

(7) revocation of the order of confirmation under section 1230 of this title, and denial of confirmation of a modified plan under section 1229 of this title;

(8) termination of a confirmed plan by reason of the occurrence of a condition specified in the plan; or

(9) continuing loss to or diminution of the estate and absence of a reasonable likelihood of rehabilitation.

(d) On request of a party in interest, and after notice and a hearing, the court may dismiss a case under this chapter or convert a case under this chapter to a case under chapter 7 of this title upon a showing that the debtor has committed fraud in connection with the case.

(e) Notwithstanding any other provision of this section, a case may not be converted to a case under another chapter of this title unless the debtor may be a debtor under such chapter.

Added Pub.L. 99–554, Title II, § 255, Oct. 27, 1986, 100 Stat. 3108.

Repeal of Section and Savings Provisions

Pub.L. 99–554, Title III, § 302(f), Oct. 27, 1986, 100 Stat. 3124, repealed this section on Oct. 1, 1993, and all cases commenced or pending under chapter 12 of title 11, United States Code, and all matters and proceedings in or relating to such cases, conducted and determined under such chapter as if such chapter had not been repealed, and substantive rights of parties in connection with such cases, matters, and proceedings shall continue to be governed under the laws applicable to such cases, matters, and proceedings as if such chapter had not been repealed.

Historical Note

Effective Date; Savings Provisions; Quarterly Fees. Enactment by Pub.L. 99–554 effective 30 days after Oct. 27, 1986, except as otherwise provided for, see section 302(a) of Pub.L. 99–554, set out as a note under section 581 of Title 28, Judiciary and Judicial Procedure.

Enactment by Pub.L. 99–554, § 255, not to apply with respect to cases commenced under Title 11, Bankruptcy, before 30 days after Oct. 27, 1986, see section 302(c)(1) of Pub.L. 99–554, set out as a note under section 581 of Title 28.

Library References:

C.J.S. Bankruptcy § 418.
West's Key No. Digests, Bankruptcy ⇐3673.

SUBCHAPTER II—THE PLAN

§ 1221. Filing of plan

The debtor shall file a plan not later than 90 days after the order for relief under this chapter, except that the court may extend such period if an extension is substantially justified.

Added Pub.L. 99–554, Title II, § 255, Oct. 27, 1986, 100 Stat. 3109.

Repeal of Section and Savings Provisions

Pub.L. 99–554, Title III, § 302(f), Oct. 27, 1986, 100 Stat. 3124, repealed this section on Oct. 1, 1993, and all cases commenced or pending under chapter 12 of title 11, United States Code, and all matters and proceedings in or relating to such cases, conducted and determined under such chapter as if such chapter had not been repealed, and substantive rights of parties in connection with such cases, matters, and proceedings shall continue to be governed under the laws applicable to such cases, matters, and proceedings as if such chapter had not been repealed.

Historical Note

Effective Date; Savings Provisions; Quarterly Fees. Enactment by Pub.L. 99–554 effective 30 days after Oct. 27, 1986, except as otherwise provided for, see section 302(a) of Pub.L. 99–554, set out as a note under section 581 of Title 28, Judiciary and Judicial Procedure.

Enactment by Pub.L. 99–554, § 255, not to apply with respect to cases commenced under Title 11, Bankruptcy, before 30 days after Oct. 27, 1986, see section 302(c)(1) of Pub.L. 99–554, set out as a note under section 581 of Title 28.

Library References:

C.J.S. Bankruptcy §§ 419, 420.
West's Key No. Digests, Bankruptcy ⇐3681.

§ 1222.   Contents of plan

(a) The plan shall—

(1) provide for the submission of all or such portion of future earnings or other future income of the debtor to the supervision and control of the trustee as is necessary for the execution of the plan;

(2) provide for the full payment, in deferred cash payments, of all claims entitled to priority under section 507 of this title, unless the holder of a particular claim agrees to a different treatment of such claim; and

(3) if the plan classifies claims and interests, provide the same treatment for each claim or interest within a particular class unless the holder of a particular claim or interest agrees to less favorable treatment.

(b) Subject to subsections (a) and (c) of this section, the plan may—

(1) designate a class or classes of unsecured claims, as provided in section 1122 of this title, but may not discriminate unfairly against any class so designated; however, such plan may treat claims for a consumer debt of the debtor if an individual is liable on such consumer debt with the debtor differently than other unsecured claims;

(2) modify the rights of holders of secured claims, or of holders of unsecured claims, or leave unaffected the rights of holders of any class of claims;

(3) provide for the curing or waiving of any default;

(4) provide for payments on any unsecured claim to be made concurrently with payments on any secured claim or any other unsecured claim;

(5) provide for the curing of any default within a reasonable time and maintenance of payments while the case is pending on any unsecured claim or secured claim on which the last payment is due after the date on which the final payment under the plan is due;

(6) subject to section 365 of this title, provide for the assumption, rejection, or assignment of any executory contract or unexpired lease of the debtor not previously rejected under such section;

(7) provide for the payment of all or part of a claim against the debtor from property of the estate or property of the debtor;

(8) provide for the sale of all or any part of the property of the estate or the distribution of all or any part of the property of the estate among those having an interest in such property;

(9) provide for payment of allowed secured claims consistent with section 1225(a)(5) of this title, over a period exceeding the period permitted under section 1222(c);

(10) provide for the vesting of property of the estate, on confirmation of the plan or at a later time, in the debtor or in any other entity; and

(11) include any other appropriate provision not inconsistent with this title.

(c) Except as provided in subsections (b)(5) and (b)(9), the plan may not provide for payments over a period that is longer than three years unless the court for cause approves a longer period, but the court may not approve a period that is longer than five years.

Added Pub.L. 99–554, Title II, § 255, Oct. 27, 1986, 100 Stat. 3109.

Repeal of Section and Savings Provisions

Pub.L. 99–554, Title III, § 302(f), Oct. 27, 1986, 100 Stat. 3124, repealed this section on Oct. 1, 1993, and all cases commenced or pending under chapter 12 of title 11, United States Code, and all matters and proceedings in or relating to such cases, conducted and determined under such chapter as if such chapter had not been repealed, and substantive rights of parties in connection with such cases, matters, and proceedings shall continue to be governed under the laws applicable to such cases, matters, and proceedings as if such chapter had not been repealed.

Historical Note

Effective Date; Savings Provisions; Quarterly Fees. Enactment by Pub.L. 99–554 effective 30 days after Oct. 27, 1986, except as otherwise provided for, see section 302(a) of Pub.L. 99–554, set out as a note under section 581 of Title 28, Judiciary and Judicial Procedure.

Enactment by Pub.L. 99–554, § 255, not to apply with respect to cases commenced under Title 11, Bankruptcy, before 30 days after Oct. 27, 1986, see section 302(c)(1) of Pub.L. 99–554, set out as a note under section 581 of Title 28.

Library References:

C.J.S. Bankruptcy §§ 419, 421–425, 427, 430.
West's Key No. Digests, Bankruptcy ☞3682.

§ 1223. Modification of plan before confirmation

(a) The debtor may modify the plan at any time before confirmation, but may not modify the plan so that the plan as modified fails to meet the requirements of section 1222 of this title.

(b) After the debtor files a modification under this section, the plan as modified becomes the plan.

(c) Any holder of a secured claim that has accepted or rejected the plan is deemed to have accepted or rejected, as the case may be, the plan as modified, unless the modification provides for a change in the rights of such holder from what such rights were under the plan before modification, and such holder changes such holder's previous acceptance or rejection.

Added Pub.L. 99–554, Title II, § 255, Oct. 27, 1986, 100 Stat. 3110.

Repeal of Section and Savings Provisions

Pub.L. 99–554, Title III, § 302(f), Oct. 27, 1986, 100 Stat. 3124, repealed this section on Oct. 1, 1993, and all cases commenced or pending under chapter 12 of title 11, United States Code, and all matters and proceedings in or relating to such cases, conducted and determined under such chapter as if such chapter had not been repealed, and substantive rights of parties in connection with such cases, matters, and proceedings shall continue to be governed under the laws applicable to such cases, matters, and proceedings as if such chapter had not been repealed.

§ 1224. Confirmation hearing

After expedited notice, the court shall hold a hearing on confirmation of the plan. A party in interest, the trustee, or the United States trustee may object to the confirmation of the plan. Except for cause, the hearing shall be concluded not later than 45 days after the filing of the plan.

Added Pub.L. 99–554, Title II, § 255, Oct. 27, 1986, 100 Stat. 3110.

Repeal of Section and Savings Provisions

Pub.L. 99–554, Title III, § 302(f), Oct. 27, 1986, 100 Stat. 3124, repealed this section on Oct. 1, 1993, and all cases commenced or pending under chapter 12 of title 11, United States Code, and all matters and proceedings in or relating to such cases, conducted and determined under such chapter as if such chapter had not been repealed, and substantive rights of parties in connection with such cases, matters, and proceedings shall continue to be governed under the laws applicable to such cases, matters, and proceedings as if such chapter had not been repealed.

§ 1225. Confirmation of plan

(a) Except as provided in subsection (b), the court shall confirm a plan if—

(1) the plan complies with the provisions of this chapter and with the other applicable provisions of this title;

(2) any fee, charge, or amount required under chapter 123 of title 28, or by the plan, to be paid before confirmation, has been paid;

(3) the plan has been proposed in good faith and not by any means forbidden by law;

(4) the value, as of the effective date of the plan, of property to be distributed under the plan on account of each allowed unsecured claim is not less than the amount that would be paid on such claim if the estate of the debtor were liquidated under chapter 7 of this title on such date;

(5) with respect to each allowed secured claim provided for by the plan—

(A) the holder of such claim has accepted the plan;

(B)(i) the plan provides that the holder of such claim retain the lien securing such claim; and

(ii) the value, as of the effective date of the plan, of property to be distributed by the trustee or the debtor under the plan on account of such claim is not less than the allowed amount of such claim; or

(C) the debtor surrenders the property securing such claim to such holder; and

(6) the debtor will be able to make all payments under the plan and to comply with the plan.

(b)(1) If the trustee or the holder of an allowed unsecured claim objects to the confirmation of the plan, then the court may not approve the plan unless, as of the effective date of the plan—

(A) the value of the property to be distributed under the plan on account of such claim is not less than the amount of such claim; or

(B) the plan provides that all of the debtor's projected disposable income to be received in the three-year period, or such longer period as the court may approve under section 1222(c), beginning on the date that the first payment is due under the plan will be applied to make payments under the plan.

(2) For purposes of this subsection, "disposable income" means income which is received by the debtor and which is not reasonably necessary to be expended—

(A) for the maintenance or support of the debtor or a dependent of the debtor; or

(B) for the payment of expenditures necessary for the continuation, preservation, and operation of the debtor's business.

(c) After confirmation of a plan, the court may order any entity from whom the debtor receives income to pay all or any part of such income to the trustee.

Added Pub.L. 99–554, Title II, § 255, Oct. 27, 1986, 100 Stat. 3110.

Repeal of Section and Savings Provisions

Pub.L. 99–554, Title III, § 302(f), Oct. 27, 1986, 100 Stat. 3124, repealed this section on Oct. 1, 1993, and all cases commenced or pending under chapter 12 of title 11, United States Code, and all matters and proceedings in or relating to such cases, conducted and determined under such chapter as if such chapter had not been repealed, and substantive rights of parties in connection with such cases, matters, and proceedings shall continue to be governed under the laws applicable to such cases, matters, and proceedings as if such chapter had not been repealed.

Historical Note

Effective Date; Savings Provisions; Quarterly Fees. Enactment by Pub.L. 99–554 effective 30 days after Oct. 27, 1986, except as otherwise provided for, see section 302(a) of Pub.L. 99–554, set out as a note under section 581 of Title 28, Judiciary and Judicial Procedure.

Enactment by Pub.L. 99–554, § 255, not to apply with respect to cases commenced under Title 11, Bankruptcy, before 30 days after Oct. 27, 1986, see section 302(c)(1) of Pub.L. 99–554, set out as a note under section 581 of Title 28.

Library References:

C.J.S. Bankruptcy §§ 428, 429.
West's Key No. Digests, Bankruptcy ☞3683.

§ 1226. Payments

(a) Payments and funds received by the trustee shall be retained by the trustee until confirmation or denial of confirmation of a plan. If a plan is confirmed, the trustee shall distribute any such payment in accordance with the plan. If a plan is not confirmed, the trustee shall return any such payments to the debtor, after deducting—

(1) any unpaid claim allowed under section 503(b) of this title; and

(2) if a standing trustee is serving in the case, the percentage fee fixed for such standing trustee.

(b) Before or at the time of each payment to creditors under the plan, there shall be paid—

(1) any unpaid claim of the kind specified in section 507(a)(1) of this title; and

(2) if a standing trustee appointed under section 1202(d) of this title is serving in the case, the percentage fee fixed for such standing trustee under section 1202(e) of this title.

(c) Except as otherwise provided in the plan or in the order confirming the plan, the trustee shall make payments to creditors under the plan.

Added Pub.L. 99–554, Title II, § 255, Oct. 27, 1986, 100 Stat. 3111.

Repeal of Section and Savings Provisions

Pub.L. 99–554, Title III, § 302(f), Oct. 27, 1986, 100 Stat. 3124, repealed this section on Oct. 1, 1993, and all cases commenced or pending under chapter 12 of title 11, United States Code, and all matters and proceedings in or relating to such cases, conducted and determined under such chapter as if such chapter had not been repealed, and substantive rights of parties in connection with such cases, matters, and proceedings shall continue to be governed under the laws applicable to such cases, matters, and proceedings as if such chapter had not been repealed.

Historical Note

References in Text. Section 1202(d) and (e) of this title, referred to in subsec. (b)(2) do not exist. Such section 1202 only contains subsecs. (a) and (b).

Reference to section 1202(e) probably should be a reference to section 586(e)(1)(B of Title 28, Judiciary and Judicial Procedure, since the provisions relating to percentage fees for standing trustees are set forth in section 586 of Title 28.

Effective Date; Savings Provisions; Quarterly Fees. Enactment by Pub.L. 99–554 effective 30 days after Oct. 27, 1986, ex-cept as otherwise provided for, see section 302(a) of Pub.L. 99–554, set out as a note under section 581 of Title 28, Judiciary and Judicial Procedure.

Enactment by Pub.L. 99–554, § 255, not to apply with respect to cases commenced under Title 11, Bankruptcy, before 30 days after Oct. 27, 1986, see section 302(c)(1) of Pub.L. 99–554, set out as a note under section 581 of Title 28.

Library References:

C.J.S. Bankruptcy §§ 426, 429.
West's Key No. Digests, Bankruptcy ⬅3685.

§ 1227. Effect of confirmation

(a) Except as provided in section 1228(a) of this title, the provisions of a confirmed plan bind the debtor, each creditor, each equity security holder, and each general partner in the debtor, whether or not the claim of such creditor, such equity security holder, or such general partner in the debtor is provided for by the plan, and whether or not such creditor, such equity security holder, or such general partner in the debtor has objected to, has accepted, or has rejected the plan.

(b) Except as otherwise provided in the plan or the order confirming the plan, the confirmation of a plan vests all of the property of the estate in the debtor.

(c) Except as provided in section 1228(a) of this title and except as otherwise provided in the plan or in the order confirming the plan, the property vesting in the debtor under subsection (b) of this section is free and clear of any claim or interest of any creditor provided for by the plan.

Added Pub.L. 99–554, Title II, § 255, Oct. 27, 1986, 100 Stat. 3112.

Repeal of Section and Savings Provisions

Pub.L. 99–554, Title III, § 302(f), Oct. 27, 1986, 100 Stat. 3124, repealed this section on Oct. 1, 1993, and all cases commenced or pending under chapter 12 of title 11, United States Code, and all matters and proceedings in or relating to such cases, conducted and determined under such chapter as if such chapter had not been repealed, and substantive rights of parties in connection with such cases, matters, and proceedings shall continue to be governed under the laws applicable to such cases, matters, and proceedings as if such chapter had not been repealed.

Historical Note

Effective Date; Savings Provisions; Quarterly Fees. Enactment by Pub.L. 99–554 effective 30 days after Oct. 27, 1986, ex-cept as otherwise provided for, see section 302(a) of Pub.L. 99–554, set out as a note under section 581 of Title 28, Judiciary and Judicial Procedure.

Enactment by Pub.L. 99–554, § 255, not to apply with respect to cases commenced under Title 11, Bankruptcy, before 30 days after Oct. 27, 1986, see section 302(c)(1) of Pub.L. 99–554, set out as a note under section 581 of Title 28.

Library References:

C.J.S. Bankruptcy §§ 428, 429.
West's Key No. Digests, Bankruptcy ☞3683.

§ 1228.   Discharge

(a) As soon as practicable after completion by the debtor of all payments under the plan, other than payments to holders of allowed claims provided for under section 1222(b)(5) or 1222(b)(10) of this title, unless the court approves a written waiver of discharge executed by the debtor after the order for relief under this chapter, the court shall grant the debtor a discharge of all debts provided for by the plan allowed under section 503 of this title or disallowed under section 502 of this title, except any debt—

(1) provided for under section 1222(b)(5) or 1222(b)(10) of this title; or

(2) of the kind specified in section 523(a) of this title.

(b) At any time after the confirmation of the plan and after notice and a hearing, the court may grant a discharge to a debtor that has not completed payments under the plan only if—

(1) the debtor's failure to complete such payments is due to circumstances for which the debtor should not justly be held accountable;

(2) the value, as of the effective date of the plan, of property actually distributed under the plan on account of each allowed unsecured claim is not less than the amount that would have been paid on such claim if the estate of the debtor had been liquidated under chapter 7 of this title on such date; and

(3) modification of the plan under section 1229 of this title is not practicable.

(c) A discharge granted under subsection (b) of this section discharges the debtor from all unsecured debts provided for by the plan or disallowed under section 502 of this title, except any debt—

(1) provided for under section 1222(b)(5) or 1222(b)(10) of this title; or

(2) of a kind specified in section 523(a) of this title.

(d) On request of a party in interest before one year after a discharge under this section is granted, and after notice and a hearing, the court may revoke such discharge only if—

(1) such discharge was obtained by the debtor through fraud; and

(2) the requesting party did not know of such fraud until after such discharge was granted.

(e) After the debtor is granted a discharge, the court shall terminate the services of any trustee serving in the case.

Added Pub.L. 99–554, Title II, § 255, Oct. 27, 1986, 100 Stat. 3112.

Repeal of Section and Savings Provisions

Pub.L. 99–554, Title III, § 302(f), Oct. 27, 1986, 100 Stat. 3124, repealed this section on Oct. 1, 1993, and all cases commenced or pending under chapter 12 of title 11, United States Code, and all matters and proceedings in or relating to such cases, conducted and determined under such chapter as if such chapter had not been repealed, and substantive rights of parties in connection with such cases, matters, and proceedings shall continue to be governed under the laws applicable to such cases, matters, and proceedings as if such chapter had not been repealed.

Historical Note

Effective Date; Savings Provisions; Quarterly Fees. Enactment by Pub.L. 99–554 effective 30 days after Oct. 27, 1986, except as otherwise provided for, see section 302(a) of Pub.L. 99–554, set out as a note under section 581 of Title 28, Judiciary and Judicial Procedure.

Enactment by Pub.L. 99–554, § 255, not to apply with respect to cases commenced under Title 11, Bankruptcy, before 30 days after Oct. 27, 1986, see section 302(c)(1) of Pub.L. 99–554, set out as a note under section 581 of Title 28.

Library References:

C.J.S. Bankruptcy § 432.
West's Key No. Digests, Bankruptcy ⟜3674.

§ 1229.   Modification of plan after confirmation

(a) At any time after confirmation of the plan but before the completion of payments under such plan, the plan may be modified, on request of the debtor, the trustee, or the holder of an allowed unsecured claim, to—

    (1) increase or reduce the amount of payments on claims of a particular class provided for by the plan;

    (2) extend or reduce the time for such payments; or

    (3) alter the amount of the distribution to a creditor whose claim is provided for by the plan to the extent necessary to take account of any payment of such claim other than under the plan.

(b)(1) Sections 1222(a), 1222(b), and 1223(c) of this title and the requirements of section 1225(a) of this title apply to any modification under subsection (a) of this section.

(2) The plan as modified becomes the plan unless, after notice and a hearing, such modification is disapproved.

(c) A plan modified under this section may not provide for payments over a period that expires after three years after the time that the first payment under the original confirmed plan was due, unless the court, for cause, approves a longer period, but the court may not approve a period that expires after five years after such time.

Added Pub.L. 99–554, Title II, § 255, Oct. 27, 1986, 100 Stat. 3113.

Repeal of Section and Savings Provisions

Pub.L. 99–554, Title III, § 302(f), Oct. 27, 1986, 100 Stat. 3124, repealed this section on Oct. 1, 1993, and all cases commenced or pending under chapter 12 of title 11, United States Code, and all matters and proceedings in or relating to such cases, conducted and determined under such chapter as if such chapter had not been repealed, and substantive rights of parties in connection with such cases, matters, and proceedings shall continue to be governed under the laws applicable to such cases, matters, and proceedings as if such chapter had not been repealed.

Historical Note

Effective Date; Savings Provisions; Quarterly Fees. Enactment by Pub.L. 99-554 effective 30 days after Oct. 27, 1986, except as otherwise provided for, see section 302(a) of Pub.L. 99-554, set out as a note under section 581 of Title 28, Judiciary and Judicial Procedure.

Enactment by Pub.L. 99-554, § 255 not to apply with respect to cases commenced under Title 11, Bankruptcy, before 30 days after Oct. 27, 1986, see section 302(c)(1) of Pub.L. 99-554, set out as a note under section 581 of Title 28.

Library References:

C.J.S. Bankruptcy §§ 430, 431.
West's Key No. Digests, Bankruptcy ⟹3684.

§ 1230. Revocation of an order of confirmation

(a) On request of a party in interest at any time within 180 days after the date of the entry of an order of confirmation under section 1225 of this title, and after notice and a hearing, the court may revoke such order if such order was procured by fraud.

(b) If the court revokes an order of confirmation under subsection (a) of this section, the court shall dispose of the case under section 1207 of this title, unless, within the time fixed by the court, the debtor proposes and the court confirms a modification of the plan under section 1229 of this title.

Added Pub.L. 99-554, Title II, § 255, Oct. 27, 1986, 100 Stat. 3113.

Repeal of Section and Savings Provisions

Pub.L. 99-554, Title III, § 302(f), Oct. 27, 1986, 100 Stat. 3124, repealed this section on Oct. 1, 1993, and all cases commenced or pending under chapter 12 of title 11, United States Code, and all matters and proceedings in or relating to such cases, conducted and determined under such chapter as if such chapter had not been repealed, and substantive rights of parties in connection with such cases, matters, and proceedings shall continue to be governed under the laws applicable to such cases, matters, and proceedings as if such chapter had not been repealed.

Historical Note

Effective Date; Savings Provisions; Quarterly Fees. Enactment by Pub.L. 99-554 effective 30 days after Oct. 27, 1986, except as otherwise provided for, see section 302(a) of Pub.L. 99-554, set out as a note under section 581 of Title 28, Judiciary and Judicial Procedure.

Enactment by Pub.L. 99-554, § 255, not to apply with respect to cases commenced under Title 11, Bankruptcy, before 30 days after Oct. 27, 1986, see section 302(c)(1) of Pub.L. 99-554, set out as a note under section 581 of Title 28.

Library References:

C.J.S. Bankruptcy §§ 430, 431.
West's Key No. Digests, Bankruptcy ⟹3684.

§ 1231. Special tax provisions

(a) For the purpose of any State or local law imposing a tax on or measured by income, the taxable period of a debtor that is an individual shall terminate on the date of the order for relief under this chapter, unless the case was converted under section 706 of this title.

(b) The trustee shall make a State or local tax return of income for the estate of an individual debtor in a case under this chapter for each taxable period after the order for relief under this chapter during which the case is pending.

(c) The issuance, transfer, or exchange of a security, or the making or delivery of an instrument of transfer under a plan confirmed under section 1225 of this title, may not be taxed under any law imposing a stamp tax or similar tax.

(d) The court may authorize the proponent of a plan to request a determination, limited to questions of law, by a State or local governmental unit charged with responsibility for collection or determination of a tax on or measured by income, of the tax effects, under section 346 of this title and under the law imposing such tax, of the plan. In the event of an actual controversy, the court may declare such effects after the earlier of—

(1) the date on which such governmental unit responds to the request under this subsection; or

(2) 270 days after such request.

Added Pub.L. 99–554, Title II, § 255, Oct. 27, 1986, 100 Stat. 3113.

Repeal of Section and Savings Provisions

Pub.L. 99–554, Title III, § 302(f), Oct. 27, 1986, 100 Stat. 3124, repealed this section on Oct. 1, 1993, and all cases commenced or pending under chapter 12 of title 11, United States Code, and all matters and proceedings in or relating to such cases, conducted and determined under such chapter as if such chapter had not been repealed, and substantive rights of parties in connection with such cases, matters, and proceedings shall continue to be governed under the laws applicable to such cases, matters, and proceedings as if such chapter had not been repealed.

Historical Note

Effective Date; Savings Provisions; Quarterly Fees. Enactment by Pub.L. 99–554 effective 30 days after Oct. 27, 1986, except as otherwise provided for, see section 302(a) of Pub.L. 99–554, set out as a note under section 581 of Title 28, Judiciary and Judicial Procedure.

Enactment by Pub.L. 99–554, § 255, not to apply with respect to cases commenced under Title 11, Bankruptcy, before 30 days after Oct. 27, 1986, see section 302(c)(1) of Pub.L. 99–554, set out as a note under section 581 of Title 28.

Library References:

C.J.S. Taxation §§ 1107, 1108.
West's Key No. Digests, Taxation ⚲1094, 1100, 1102.

CHAPTER 13—ADJUSTMENT OF DEBTS OF AN INDIVIDUAL WITH REGULAR INCOME

SUBCHAPTER I—OFFICERS, ADMINISTRATION, AND THE ESTATE

Sec.
1301. Stay of action against codebtor.
1302. Trustee.
1303. Rights and powers of debtor.
1304. Debtor engaged in business.
1305. Filing and allowance of postpetition claims.
1306. Property of the estate.
1307. Conversion or dismissal.

SUBCHAPTER II—THE PLAN

1321. Filing of plan.
1322. Contents of plan.
1323. Modification of plan before confirmation.
1324. Confirmation hearing.
1325. Confirmation of plan.
1326. Payments.
1327. Effect of confirmation.
1328. Discharge.
1329. Modification of plan after confirmation.
1330. Revocation of an order of confirmation.

Cross References

Chapter applicable only in cases under this chapter, see section 103.

Chapters 1, 3 and 5 of this title applicable in cases under this chapter, see section 103.

Claims arising from rejection of executory contracts or unexpired leases by plans under this chapter, see section 502.

Conversion from
   Chapter 7, see section 706.
   Chapter 11, see section 1112.

Duration of automatic stay, see section 362.

Eligibility to serve as trustee, see section 321.

Executory contracts and unexpired leases, see section 365.

Individual with regular income defined, see section 101.

Individuals who may be debtors under this chapter, see section 109.

Limitation on compensation of trustee, see section 326.

Recommendation by trustee of conversion from chapter 11 to this chapter, see section 1106.

Return of excessive attorney compensation if transferred property was to be paid by debtor under plan under this chapter, see section 329.

Special tax provisions, see section 346.

SUBCHAPTER I—OFFICERS, ADMINISTRATION, AND THE ESTATE

§ 1301. Stay of action against codebtor

(a) Except as provided in subsections (b) and (c) of this section, after the order for relief under this chapter, a creditor may not act, or commence or continue any civil action, to collect all or any part of a consumer debt of the debtor from any individual that is liable on such debt with the debtor, or that secured such debt, unless—

    (1) such individual became liable on or secured such debt in the ordinary course of such individual's business; or

    (2) the case is closed, dismissed, or converted to a case under chapter 7 or 11 of this title.

(b) A creditor may present a negotiable instrument, and may give notice of dishonor of such an instrument.

(c) On request of a party in interest and after notice and a hearing, the court shall grant relief from the stay provided by subsection (a) of this section with respect to a creditor, to the extent that—

    (1) as between the debtor and the individual protected under subsection (a) of this section, such individual received the consideration for the claim held by such creditor;

    (2) the plan filed by the debtor proposes not to pay such claim; or

    (3) such creditor's interest would be irreparably harmed by continuation of such stay.

(d) Twenty days after the filing of a request under subsection (c)(2) of this section for relief from the stay provided by subsection (a) of this section, such stay is terminated with respect to the party in interest making such request, unless the debtor or any individual that is liable on such debt with the debtor files and serves upon such party in interest a written objection to the taking of the proposed action.

Pub.L. 95–598, Nov. 6, 1978, 92 Stat. 2645; Pub.L. 98–353, Title III, §§ 313, 524, July 10, 1984, 98 Stat. 355, 388.

Historical and Revision Notes

Notes of Committee on the Judiciary, Senate Report No. 95–989. Subsection (a) automatically stays the holder of a claim based on a consumer debt of the chapter 13 debtor from acting or proceeding in any way, except as authorized pursuant to subsections (b) and (c), against an individual or the property of an individual liable with the chapter 13 debtor, unless such codebtor became liable in the ordinary course of his business, or unless the case is closed, dismissed, or converted to another chapter.

Under the terms of the agreement with the codebtor who is not in bankruptcy, the creditor has a right to collect all payments to the extent they are not made by the debtor at the time they are due. To the extent to which a chapter 13 plan does not propose to pay a creditor his claims, the creditor may obtain relief from the court from the automatic stay and collect such claims from the codebtor. Conversely, a codebtor obtains the benefit of any payments made to the creditor under the plan. If a debtor defaults on scheduled payments under the plan, then the codebtor would be liable for the remaining deficiency; otherwise, payments not made under the plan may never be made by the codebtor. The obligation of the codebtor to make the creditor whole at the time payments are due remains.

The automatic stay under this section pertains only to the collection of a consumer debt, defined by section 101(7) of this title to mean a debt incurred by an individual primarily for a personal, family, or household purpose. Therefore, not all debts owed by a chapter 13 debtor will be subject to the stay of the codebtor, particularly those business debts incurred by an individual with regular income, as defined by section 101(24) of this title, engaged in business, that is permitted by virtue of section 109(b) and section 1304 to obtain chapter 13 relief.

Subsection (b) excepts the giving of notice of dishonor of a negotiable instrument from the reach of the codebtor stay.

Under subsection (c), if the codebtor has property out of which the creditor's claim can be satisfied, the court can grant relief from the stay absent the transfer of a security interest in that property by the codebtor to the creditor. Correspondingly, if there is reasonable cause to believe that property is about to be disposed of by the codebtor which could be used to satisfy his obligation to the creditor, the court should lift the stay to allow the creditor to perfect his rights against such property. Likewise, if property is subject to rapid depreciation or decrease in value the stay should be lifted to allow the creditor to protect his rights to reach such property. Otherwise, the creditor's interest would be irreparably harmed by such stay. Property which could be used to satisfy the claim could be disposed of or encumbered and placed beyond the reach of the creditor. The creditor should be allowed to protect his rights to reach property which could satisfy his claim and prevent its erosion in value, disposal, or encumbrance.

Notes of Committee on the Judiciary, House Report No. 95–595. This section is new. It is designed to protect a debtor operating under a chapter 13 individual repayment plan case by insulating him from indirect pressures from his creditors exerted through friends or relatives that may have cosigned an obligation of the debtor. The protection is limited, however, to ensure that the creditor involved does not lose the benefit of the bargain he made for a cosigner. He is entitled to full compensation, including any interest, fees, and costs provided for by the agreement under which the debtor obtained his loan. The creditor is simply required to share with other creditors to the extent that the debtor will repay him under the chapter 13 plan.

The creditor is delayed, but his substantive rights are not affected.

Subsection (a) is the operative subsection. It stays action by a creditor after an order for relief under chapter 13. The creditor may not act, or commence or continue any civil action, to collect all or any part of a consumer debt of the debtor from any individual that is liable on such debt with the debtor, or that has secured the debt, unless the individual became liable or secured the debt in the ordinary course of his business, or the case is closed, dismissed, or converted to chapter 7 or 11.

Subsection (b) permits the creditor, notwithstanding the stay, to present a negotiable instrument and to give notice of dishonor of the instrument, in order to preserve his substantive rights against the codebtor as required by applicable nonbankruptcy law.

Subsection (c) requires the court to grant relief from the stay in certain circumstances. The court must grant relief to the extent that the debtor does not propose to pay, under the plan, the amount owed to the creditor. The court must also grant relief to the extent that the debtor was really the codebtor in the transaction, that is, to the extent that the nondebtor party actually received the consideration for the claim held by the creditor. Finally, the court must grant relief to the extent that the creditor's interest would be irreparably harmed by the stay, for example, where the codebtor filed bankruptcy himself, or threatened to leave the locale, or lost his job.

Legislative Statements. Section 1301 of the House amendment is identical with the provision contained in section 1301 of the House bill and adopted by the Senate amendment. Section 1301(c)(1) indicates that a basis for lifting the stay is that the debtor did not receive consideration for the claim by the creditor, or in other words, the debtor is really the "codebtor." As with other sections in title 11, the standard of receiving consideration is a general rule, but where two co-debtors have agreed to share liabilities in a different manner than profits it is the individual who does not ultimately bear the liability that is protected by the stay under section 1301.

Effective Date of 1984 Amendments. See section 553 of Pub.L. 98–353, Title III, July 10, 1984, 98 Stat. 392, set out as an Effective Date of 1984 Amendment note preceding chapter 1 of Title 11, Bankruptcy.

Separability of Provisions. For separability of provisions of Title III of Pub.L. 98–353, see section 551 of Pub.L. 98–353 set out as a Separability of Provisions note preceding chapter 1 of Title 11, Bankruptcy.

Cross References

Automatic stay, see section 362.

Automatic stay of enforcement of claims against debtor in chapter 9 cases, see section 922.

Claims of codebtors, see section 509.

Effect of conversion, see section 348.

Effect of section 362 of this title in stockbroker liquidation cases, see section 742.

Extension of time generally, see section 108.

Library References:

C.J.S. Bankruptcy § 65 et seq.

West's Key No. Digests, Bankruptcy ⊕2391 et seq.

WESTLAW Electronic Research

See WESTLAW Electronic Research Guide following the *Bankruptcy Highlights*.

§ 1302. Trustee

(a) If the United States trustee appoints an individual under section 586(b) of title 28 to serve as standing trustee in cases under this chapter and if such individual qualifies under section 322 of this title, then such individual shall serve as trustee in the case. Otherwise, the United States trustee shall appoint one disinterested person to serve as trustee in the case or the United States trustee may serve as a trustee in the case.

(b) The trustee shall—

(1) perform the duties specified in sections 704(2), 704(3), 704(4), 704(5), 704(6), 704(7), and 704(9) of this title;

(2) appear and be heard at any hearing that concerns—

(A) the value of property subject to a lien;

(B) confirmation of a plan; or

(C) modification of the plan after confirmation;

(3) dispose of, under regulations issued by the Director of the Administrative Office of the United States Courts, moneys received or to be received in a case under chapter XIII of the Bankruptcy Act; and

(4) advise, other than on legal matters, and assist the debtor in performance under the plan; and

(5) ensure that the debtor commences making timely payments under section 1326 of this title.

(c) If the debtor is engaged in business, then in addition to the duties specified in subsection (b) of this section, the trustee shall perform the duties specified in sections 1106(a)(3) and 1106(a)(4) of this title.

Pub.L. 95–598, Nov. 6, 1978, 92 Stat. 2645; Pub.L. 98–353, Title III, §§ 314, 525, July 10, 1984, 98 Stat. 356, 388; Pub.L. 99–554, Title II, §§ 228, 283(w), Oct. 27, 1986, 100 Stat. 3103, 3118.

Historical and Revision Notes

Notes of Committee on the Judiciary, Senate Report No. 95–989. The principal administrator in a chapter 13 case is the chapter 13 trustee. Experience under chapter XIII of the Bankruptcy Act [former section 1001 et seq. of this title] has shown that the more efficient and effective wage earner programs have been conducted by standing chapter XIII trustees who exercise a broad range of responsibilities in both the design and the effectuation of debtor plans.

Subsection (a) provides administrative flexibility by permitting the bankruptcy judge to appoint an individual from the panel of trustees established pursuant to 28 U.S.C. § 604(f) and qualified under section 322 of title 11, either to serve as a standing trustee in all chapter 13 cases filed in the district or a portion thereof, or to serve in a single case.

Subsection (b)(1) makes it clear that the chapter 13 trustee is no mere disbursing agent of the monies paid to him by the debtor under the plan [section 1322 (a)(1)], by imposing upon him certain relevant duties of a liquidation trustee prescribed by section 704 of this title.

Subsection (b)(2) requires the chapter 13 trustee to appear before and be heard by the bankruptcy court whenever the value of property secured by a lien or the confirmation or modification of a plan after confirmation as provided by sections 1323–1325 is considered by the court.

Subsection (b)(3) requires the chapter 13 trustee to advise and counsel the debtor while under chapter 13, except on matters more appropriately left to the attorney for the debtor. The chapter 13 trustee must also assist the debtor in performance under the plan by attempting to tailor the requirements of the plan to the changing needs and circumstances of the debtor during the extension period.

Subsection (c) imposes on the trustee in a chapter 13 case filed by a debtor engaged in business the investigative and reporting duties normally required of a chapter 11 debtor or trustee as prescribed by section 1106(a)(3) and (4).

Legislative Statements. Section 1302 of the House amendment adopts a provision contained in the Senate amendment instead of the position taken in the House bill. Sections 1302(d) and (e) are modeled on the standing trustee system contained in the House bill with the court assuming supervisory functions in districts not under the pilot program.

Codification. Section 525(b)(1) of Pub.L. 98–353 purported to amend subsec. (e) in paragraph (4), by striking out "fix" and inserting in lieu thereof "set for such individual". The amendment was not capable of execution in that no par. (4) has been enacted in subsec. (e). The amendment was executed to par. (1) as the probable intent of Congress.

Section 283(w) of Pub.L. 99–554 amended subsec. (e)(1) of this section by substituting "set for such individual" for "fix", and section 228(2) of Pub.L. 99–554 struck out such subsection (e).

1986 Amendment. Subsec. (a). Pub.L. 99–554, § 228(1), substituted "If the United States trustee appoints" for "If the court has appointed", "section 586(b) of title 28" for "subsection (d) of this section", and "the United States trustee shall appoint one disinterested person to serve as trustee in the case or the United States trustee may serve as a trustee in the case" for "the court shall appoint a person to serve as trustee in the case".

Subsecs. (d) and (e). Pub.L. 99–554, § 228(2), struck out subsecs. (d) and (e) which read as follows:

"(d) If the number of cases under this chapter commenced in a particular judicial district so warrant, the court may appoint one or more individuals to serve as standing trustee for such district in cases under this chapter.

"(e)(1) A court that has appointed an individual under subsection (d) of this section to serve as standing trustee in cases under this chapter shall set for such individual—

"(A) a maximum annual compensation, not to exceed the lowest annual rate of basic pay in effect for grade GS–16 of the General Schedule prescribed under section 5332 of title 5; and

"(B) a percentage fee, not to exceed ten percent, based on such maximum annual compensation and the actual, necessary expenses incurred by such individual as standing trustee.

"(2) Such individual shall collect such percentage fee from all payments under plans in the cases under this chapter for which such individual serves as standing trustee. Such individual shall pay annually to the Treasury—

"(A) any amount by which the actual compensation received by such individual exceeds five percent of all such payments made under plans in cases under this chapter for which such individual serves as standing trustee; and

"(B) any amount by which the percentage fee fixed under paragraph (1)(B) of this subsection for all such cases exceeds—

"(i) such individual's actual compensation for such cases, as adjusted under subparagraph (A) of this paragraph; plus

"(ii) the actual, necessary expenses incurred by such individual as standing trustee in such cases.".

See Effective Date of 1986 Amendment, etc., notes set out below.

Effective Date of 1986 Amendments; References in Title 11 Section 326(b) to Title 11 Chapter 13 and Section 1302(a) and (d); Effective Date of 1986 Amendments for Certain Judicial Districts Not Served by United States Trustees and for Judicial Districts in Alabama and North Carolina; U.S. Trustee System Fund Deposits in Alabama and North Carolina; Effective Date of Title 11 Chapter 15 Repeal as to Northern District of Alabama; Authority of Certain Estate Administrators in Alabama and North Carolina; Effective Date of 1986 Amendments in Pending Cases Where a U.S. Trustee Not Authorized or Where a Trustee Files Final Report or Plan is Confirmed; Quarterly Fees. Amendment by Pub.L. 99–554 effective 30 days after Oct. 27, 1986, except as otherwise provided for, see section 302(a) of Pub.L. 99–554, set out as a note under section 581 of Title 28, Judiciary and Judicial Procedure.

Amendment by Pub.L. 99–554, § 228, not to become effective in or with respect to certain specified judicial districts until, or apply to cases while pending in such district before, the expiration of the 270-day period beginning 30 days after Oct. 27, 1986, or of the 30-day period beginning on the date the Attorney General certifies under section 303 of Pub.L. 99–554 the region specified in a paragraph of section 581(a) of Title 28, as amended by section 111(a) of Pub.L. 99–554, that includes such district, whichever occurs first, see section 302(d)(1) of Pub.L. 99–554, set out as a note under section 581 of Title 28.

Amendment by Pub.L. 99–554, § 228, not to become effective in or with respect to certain specified judicial districts until, or apply to cases while pending in such district before,

the expiration of the 2-year period beginning 30 days after Oct. 27, 1986, or of the 30-day period beginning on the date the Attorney General certifies under section 303 of Pub.L. 99–554 the region specified in a paragraph of section 581(a) of Title 28, as amended by section 111(a) of Pub.L. 99–554, that includes such district, whichever occurs first, see section 302(d)(2) of Pub.L. 99–554, set out as a note under section 581 of Title 28.

Amendment by Pub.L. 99–554, § 228, not to become effective in or with respect to judicial districts established for the States of Alabama and North Carolina until, or apply to cases while pending in such district before, such district elects to be included in a bankruptcy region established in section 581(a) of Title 28, as amended by section 111(a) of Pub.L. 99–554, or Oct. 1, 2002, whichever occurs first, and, except as otherwise provided for, with respect to cases under chapters 7, 11, 12, and 13 of Title 11 commenced before 30 days after Oct. 27, 1986, and pending in a judicial district in the States of Alabama or North Carolina before any election made under section 302(d)(3)(A) of Pub.L. 99–554 by such district becomes effective or Oct. 1, 2002, whichever occurs first, amendments by Pub.L. 99–554 not to apply until Oct. 1, 2003, or the expiration of the 1-year period beginning on the date such election becomes effective, whichever occurs first, and further, in any judicial district in Alabama or North Carolina not making the election described in section 302(d)(3)(A) of Pub.L. 99–554, any person appointed under regulations issued by the Judicial Conference to administer estates in cases under Title 11 authorized to establish, etc., a panel of private trustees, and to supervise cases and trustees in cases under chapters 7, 11, 12, and 13 of Title 11, until amendments by sections 201 to 231 of Pub.L. 99–554 effective in such district, see section 302(d)(3)(A) to (F), (H), (I) of Pub.L. 99–554, set out as a note under section 581 of Title 28.

Amendment by Pub.L. 99–554, § 228, except as otherwise provided, with respect to cases under chapters 7, 11, 12, and 13 of Title 11 commenced before 30 days after Oct. 27, 1986, and pending in a judicial district referred to in section 581(a) of Title 28, as amended by section 111(a) of Pub.L. 99–554, for which a United States trustee is not authorized before 30 days after Oct. 27, 1986 to be appointed, not applicable until the expiration of the 3-year period beginning on Oct. 27, 1986, or of the 1-year period beginning on the date the Attorney General certifies under section 303 of

Pub.L. 99–554 the region specified in a paragraph of such section 581(a) that includes, such district, whichever occurs first, see section 302(e)(1), (2) of Pub.L. 99–554, set out as a note under section 581 of Title 28.

See 1986 Amendment notes set out above.

Effective Date of 1984 Amendments. See section 553 of Pub.L. 98–353, Title III, July 10, 1984, 98 Stat. 392, set out as an Effective Date of 1984 Amendment note preceding chapter 1 of Title 11, Bankruptcy.

Separability of Provisions. For separability of provisions of Title III of Pub.L. 98–353, see section 551 of Pub.L. 98–353 set out as a Separability of Provisions note preceding chapter 1 of Title 11, Bankruptcy.

Cross References

Appointment of trustee in
     Chapter 11 cases, see section 1104.
     Railroad reorganization cases, see section 1163.
Compensation of officers, see section 330.
Election of trustee, see section 702.
Eligibility to serve as trustee, see section 321.
Limitation on compensation of trustee, see section 326.
Qualification of trustee, see section 322.
Removal of trustee, see section 324.
Role and capacity of trustee, see section 323.
Time of bringing action, see section 546.
Time of payment of percentage fee fixed for standing trustee, see section 1326.

Library References:

C.J.S. Bankruptcy § 435 et seq.
West's Key No. Digests, Bankruptcy ☞3703.

WESTLAW Electronic Research

See WESTLAW Electronic Research Guide following the *Bankruptcy Highlights*.

§ 1303.   Rights and powers of debtor

Subject to any limitations on a trustee under this chapter, the debtor shall have, exclusive of the trustee, the rights and powers of a trustee under sections 363(b), 363(d), 363(e), 363(f), and 363(*l*), of this title.

Pub.L. 95–598, Nov. 6, 1978, 92 Stat. 2646.

Historical and Revision Notes

Notes of Committee on the Judiciary, Senate Report No. 95–989. A chapter 13 debtor is vested with the identical rights and powers, and is subject to the same limitations in regard to their exercise, as those given a liquidation trustee by virtue of section 363(b), (d), (e), (f), and (h) of title 11, relating to the sale, use or lease of property.

Legislative Statements. Section 1303 of the House amendment specifies rights and powers that the debtor has exclusive of the trustees. The section does not imply that the debtor does not also possess other powers concurrently with the trustee. For example, although section 1323 is not specified in section 1303, certainly it is intended that the debtor has the power to sue and be sued.

Cross References

Rights, powers and duties of debtor in possession in chapter 11 cases, see section 1107.

Library References:

C.J.S. Bankruptcy § 435.
West's Key No. Digests, Bankruptcy ☞3703.

§ 1304.   Debtor engaged in business

(a) A debtor that is self-employed and incurs trade credit in the production of income from such employment is engaged in business.

(b) Unless the court orders otherwise, a debtor engaged in business may operate the business of the debtor and, subject to any limitations on a trustee under sections 363(c) and 364 of this title and to such limitations or conditions as the court prescribes, shall have, exclusive of the trustee, the rights and powers of the trustee under such sections.

(c) A debtor engaged in business shall perform the duties of the trustee specified in section 704(8) of this title.

Pub.L. 95–598, Nov. 6, 1978, 92 Stat. 2646; Pub.L. 98–353, Title III, §§ 311(b)(2), 526, July 10, 1984, 98 Stat. 355, 389.

Historical and Revision Notes

Notes of Committee on the Judiciary, Senate Report No. 95–989. Increased access to the simpler, speedier, and less expensive debtor relief provisions of chapter 13 is accomplished by permitting debtors engaged in business to proceed under chapter 13, provided their income is sufficiently stable and regular to permit compliance with a chapter 13 plan [section 101(24)] and that the debtor (or the debtor and spouse) do not owe liquidated, noncontingent unsecured debts of $50,000, or liquidated, noncontingent secured debts of $200,000 (§ 109(d)).

Section 1304(a) states that a self-employed individual who incurs trade credit in the production of income is a debtor engaged in business.

Subsection (b) empowers a chapter 13 debtor engaged in business to operate his business, subject to the rights, powers and limitations that pertain to a trustee under section 363(c) and 364 of title 11, and subject to such further

limitations and conditions as the court may prescribe.

Subsection (c) requires a chapter 13 debtor engaged in business to file with the court certain financial statements relating to the operation of the business.

Legislative Statements. Section 1304(b) of the House amendment adopts the approach taken in the comparable section of the Senate amendment as preferable to the position taken in the House bill.

Effective Date of 1984 Amendments. See section 553 of Pub.L. 98–353, Title III, July 10, 1984, 98 Stat. 392, set out as an Effective Date of 1984 Amendment note preceding chapter 1 of Title 11, Bankruptcy.

Separability of Provisions. For separability of provisions of Title III of Pub.L. 98–353, see section 551 of Pub.L. 98–353 set out as a Separability of Provisions note preceding chapter 1 of Title 11, Bankruptcy.

Cross References

Authorization of trustee to operate business in
    Chapter 7 cases, see section 721.
    Chapter 11 cases, see section 1108.
Obtaining credit, see section 364.
Rights, powers and duties of debtor in possession in chapter 11 cases, see section 1107.
Use, sale or lease of property, see section 363.

Library References:

C.J.S. Bankruptcy §§ 199, 435.
West's Key No. Digests, Bankruptcy ⟐3026, 3703.

§ 1305.   Filing and allowance of postpetition claims

(a) A proof of claim may be filed by any entity that holds a claim against the debtor—

(1) for taxes that become payable to a governmental unit while the case is pending; or

(2) that is a consumer debt, that arises after the date of the order for relief under this chapter, and that is for property or services necessary for the debtor's performance under the plan.

(b) Except as provided in subsection (c) of this section, a claim filed under subsection (a) of this section shall be allowed or disallowed under section 502 of this title, but shall be determined as of the date such claim arises, and shall be allowed under section 502(a), 502(b), or 502(c) of this title, or disallowed under section 502(d) or 502(e) of this title, the same as if such claim had arisen before the date of the filing of the petition.

(c) A claim filed under subsection (a)(2) of this section shall be disallowed if the holder of such claim knew or should have known that prior approval by the trustee of the debtor's incurring the obligation was practicable and was not obtained.

Pub.L. 95–598, Nov. 6, 1978, 92 Stat. 2647.

Historical and Revision Notes

Notes of Committee on the Judiciary, Senate Report No. 95–989. Section 1305, exclusively applicable in chapter 13 cases, supplements the provisions of sections 501–511 of title 11, dealing with the filing and allowance of claims. Sections 501–511 apply in chapter 13 cases by virtue of section 103(a) of this title. Section 1305(a) provides for the filing of a proof of claim for taxes and other obligations incurred after the filing of the chapter 13 case. Subsection (b) prescribes that section 502 of title 11 governs the allowance of section 1305(a) claims, except that its standards shall be applied as of the date of allowance of the claim, rather than the date of filing of the petition. Subsection (c) requires the disallowance of a postpetition claim for property or services necessary for the debtor's performance under the plan, if the holder of the claim knew or should have known that prior approval by the trustee of the debtor's incurring of the obligation was practicable and was not obtained.

Subsection (d) is the successor to section 656(b) of the Bankruptcy Act [former section 1056(b) of this title]. Section 1305(d) recognizes the inequity to chapter 13 debtors and their creditors alike of permitting a usurious or other invalid claim to share in distributions under the chapter 13 plan. It is envisioned that appropriate rules will be adopted mandating procedures for assuring the provision of proof by a chapter 13 creditor that the claim is free from any charge forbidden by applicable law, including usury.

Legislative Statements. Section 1305(a)(2) of the House amendment modifies similar provisions contained in the House and Senate bills by restricting application of the paragraph to a consumer debt. Debts of the debtor that are not consumer debts should not be subjected to section 1305(c) or section 1328(d) of the House amendment.

Section 1305(b) of the House amendment represents a technical modification of similar provisions contained in the House bill and Senate amendment.

The House amendment deletes section 1305(d) of the Senate amendment as unnecessary. Section 502(b)(1) is sufficient to disallow any claim to the extent the claim represents the usurious interest or any other charge forbidden by applicable law. It is anticipated that the Rules of Bankruptcy Procedure may require a creditor filing a proof of claim in a case under chapter 13 to include an affirmative statement as contemplated by section 1305(d) of the Senate amendment.

Cross References

Allowance and filing of claims and interests in chapter 11 cases, see section 1111.

Discharge of certain consumer debts, see section 1328.

Effect of conversion, see section 348.

Filing of proofs of claims or interests, see section 501.

Provisions in plans for payment of claims, see section 1322.

Library References:

C.J.S. Bankruptcy § 240.

West's Key No. Digests, Bankruptcy ☞2832.

WESTLAW Electronic Research

See WESTLAW Electronic Research Guide following the *Bankruptcy Highlights.*

§ 1306. Property of the estate

(a) Property of the estate includes, in addition to the property specified in section 541 of this title—

(1) all property of the kind specified in such section that the debtor acquires after the commencement of the case but before the case is closed, dismissed, or converted to a case under chapter 7, 11, or 12 of this title, whichever occurs first; and

(2) earnings from services performed by the debtor after the commencement of the case but before the case is closed, dismissed, or converted to a case under chapter 7, 11, or 12 of this title, whichever occurs first.

(b) Except as provided in a confirmed plan or order confirming a plan, the debtor shall remain in possession of all property of the estate.

Pub.L. 95–598, Nov. 6, 1978, 92 Stat. 2647; Pub.L. 99–554, Title II, § 257(u), Oct. 27, 1986, 100 Stat. 3116.

Historical and Revision Notes

Notes of Committee on the Judiciary, Senate Report No. 95–989. Section 541 is expressly made applicable to chapter 13 cases by section 103(a). Section 1306 broadens the definition of property of the estate for chapter 13 purposes to include all property acquired and all earnings from services performed by the debtor after the commencement of the case.

Subsection (b) nullifies the effect of section 521(3), otherwise applicable, by providing that a chapter 13 debtor need not surrender possession of property of the estate, unless required by the plan or order of confirmation.

Legislative Statements. Section 1306(a)(2) adopts a provision contained in the Senate amendment in preference to a similar provision contained in the House bill.

Effective Date of 1986 Amendments; Savings Provisions. References in Title 11 Section 326(b) to Title 11 Chapter 13 and Section 1302(a) and (d); Quarterly Fees. Amendment by Pub.L. 99–554 effective 30 days after Oct. 27, 1986, except as otherwise provided for, see section 302(a) of Pub.L. 99–554, set out as a note under section 581 of Title 28, Judiciary and Judicial Procedure.

Amendments by Pub.L. 99–554, § 257(u), not to apply with respect to cases commenced under Title 11, Bankruptcy, before 30 days after Oct. 27, 1986, see section 302(c)(1) of Pub. L. 99–554, set out as a note under section 581 of Title 28.

Library References:

C.J.S. Bankruptcy §§ 120, 122.

West's Key No. Digests, Bankruptcy ☞2558.

WESTLAW Electronic Research

See WESTLAW Electronic Research Guide following the *Bankruptcy Highlights.*

§ 1307. Conversion or dismissal

(a) The debtor may convert a case under this chapter to a case under chapter 7 of this title at any time. Any waiver of the right to convert under this subsection is unenforceable.

(b) On request of the debtor at any time, if the case has not been converted under section 706, 1112, or 1208 of this title, the court shall dismiss a case under this chapter. Any waiver of the right to dismiss under this subsection is unenforceable.

(c) Except as provided in subsection (e) of this section, on request of a party in interest or the United States trustee and after notice and a hearing, the court may convert a case under this chapter to a case under chapter 7 of this title, or may dismiss a case under this chapter, whichever is in the best interests of creditors and the estate, for cause, including—

(1) unreasonable delay by the debtor that is prejudicial to creditors;

(2) nonpayment of any fees and charges required under chapter 123 of title 28;

(3) failure to file a plan timely under section 1321 of this title;

(4) failure to commence making timely payments under section 1326 of this title;

(5) denial of confirmation of a plan under section 1325 of this title and denial of a request made for additional time for filing another plan or a modification of a plan;

(6) material default by the debtor with respect to a term of a confirmed plan;

(7) revocation of the order of confirmation under section 1330 of this title, and denial of confirmation of a modified plan under section 1329 of this title;

(8) termination of a confirmed plan by reason of the occurrence of a condition specified in the plan other than completion of payments under the plan;

(9) only on request of the United States trustee, failure of the debtor to file, within fifteen days, or such additional time as the court may allow, after the filing of the petition commencing such case, the information required by paragraph (1) of section 521; or

(10) only on request of the United States trustee, failure to timely file the information required by paragraph (2) of section 521.

(d) Except as provided in subsection (e) of this section, at any time before the confirmation of a plan under section 1325 of this title, on request of a party in interest or the United States trustee and after notice and a hearing, the court may convert a case under this chapter to a case under chapter 11 or 12 of this title.

(e) The court may not convert a case under this chapter to a case under chapter 7, 11, or 12 of this title if the debtor is a farmer, unless the debtor requests such conversion.

410

(f) Notwithstanding any other provision of this section, a case may not be converted to a case under another chapter of this title unless the debtor may be a debtor under such chapter.

Pub.L. 95–598, Nov. 6, 1978, 92 Stat. 2647; Pub.L. 98–353, Title III, §§ 315, 527, July 10, 1984, 98 Stat. 356, 389; Pub.L. 99–554, Title II, §§ 229, 257(v), Oct. 27, 1986, 100 Stat. 3103, 3116.

Historical and Revision Notes

Notes of Committee on the Judiciary, Senate Report No. 95–989. Subsections (a) and (b) confirm, without qualification, the rights of a chapter 13 debtor to convert the case to a liquidating bankruptcy case under chapter 7 of title 11, at any time, or to have the chapter 13 case dismissed. Waiver of any such right is unenforceable. Subsection (c) specifies various conditions for the exercise of the power of the court to convert a chapter 13 case to one under chapter 7 or to dismiss the case. Subsection (d) deals with the conversion of a chapter 13 case to one under chapter 11. Subsection (e) prohibits conversion of the chapter 13 case filed by a farmer to chapter 7 or 11 except at the request of the debtor. No case is to be converted from chapter 13 to any other chapter, unless the debtor is an eligible debtor under the new chapter.

Notes of Committee on the Judiciary, House Report No. 95–595. Subsection (f) reinforces section 109 by prohibiting conversion to a chapter under which the debtor is not eligible to proceed.

Legislative Statements. Section 1307(a) is derived from the Senate amendment in preference to a comparable provision contained in the House bill.

References in Text. Chapter 123 of title 28, referred to in subsec. (c)(2) of this title, is classified to section 1911 et seq. of Title 28, Judiciary and Judicial Procedure.

1986 Amendment. Subsec. (c). Pub.L. 99–554, § 229(1)(A), added "or the United States trustee" following "party in interest".

Subsec. (c)(9), (10). Pub.L. 99–554, § 229(1) (B)–(D), added pars. (9) and (10).

Subsec. (d). Pub.L. 99–554, § 229(2), added "or the United States trustee" following "party in interest".

See Effective Date of 1986 Amendment, etc., notes set out below.

Effective Date of 1986 Amendments; Savings Provisions; References in Title 11 Section 326(b) to Title 11 Chapter 13 and Section 1302(a) and (d); Effective Date of

1986 Amendments for Certain Judicial Districts Not Served by United States Trustees and for Judicial Districts in Alabama and North Carolina; U.S. Trustee System Fund Deposits in Alabama and North Carolina; Effective Date of Title 11 Chapter 15 Repeal as to Northern District of Alabama; Authority of Certain Estate Administrators in Alabama and North Carolina; Effective Date of 1986 Amendments in Pending Cases Where a U.S. Trustee Not Authorized or Where a Trustee Files Final Report or Plan is Confirmed; Quarterly Fees. Amendment by Pub.L. 99–554 effective 30 days after Oct. 27, 1986, except as otherwise provided for, see section 302(a) of Pub.L. 99–554, set out as a note under section 581 of Title 28, Judiciary and Judicial Procedure.

Amendments by Pub.L. 99–554, § 257(v), not to apply with respect to cases commenced under Title 11, Bankruptcy, before 30 days after Oct. 27, 1986, see section 302(c)(1) of Pub. L. 99–554, set out as a note under section 581 of Title 28.

Amendment by Pub.L. 99–554, § 229, not to become effective in or with respect to certain specified judicial districts until, or apply to cases while pending in such district before, the expiration of the 270-day period beginning 30 days after Oct. 27, 1986, or of the 30-day period beginning on the date the Attorney General certifies under section 303 of Pub.L. 99–554 the region specified in a paragraph of section 581(a) of Title 28, as amended by section 111(a) of Pub.L. 99–554, that includes such district, whichever occurs first, see section 302(d)(1) of Pub.L. 99–554, set out as a note under section 581 of Title 28.

Amendment by Pub.L. 99–554, § 229, not to become effective in or with respect to certain specified judicial districts until, or apply to cases while pending in such district before, the expiration of the 2-year period beginning 30 days after Oct. 27, 1986, or of the 30-day period beginning on the date the Attorney General certifies under section 303 of Pub.L. 99–554 the region specified in a paragraph of section 581(a) of Title 28, as amended by section 111(a) of Pub.L. 99–554, that includes such district, whichever occurs first, see section 302(d)(2) of Pub.L. 99–554, set out as a note under section 581 of Title 28.

Amendment by Pub.L. 99–554, § 229, not to become effective in or with respect to judicial districts established for the States of Alabama and North Carolina until, or apply to cases while pending in such district before, such district elects to be included in a bankruptcy region established in section 581(a) of Title 28, as amended by section 111(a) of Pub.L. 99–554, or Oct. 1, 2002, whichever occurs first, and, except as otherwise provided for, with respect to cases under chapters 7, 11, 12, and 13 of Title 11 commenced before 30 days after Oct. 27, 1986, and pending in a judicial district in the States of Alabama or North Carolina before any election made under section 302(d)(3)(A) of Pub.L. 99–554 by such district becomes effective or Oct. 1, 2002, whichever occurs first, amendments by Pub.L 99–554 not to apply, until Oct. 1, 2003, or the expiration of the 1-year period beginning on the date such election becomes effective, whichever occurs first, and, further, in any judicial district in Alabama or North Carolina not making the election described in section 302(d)(3)(A) of Pub.L. 99–554, any person appointed under regulations issued by the Judicial Conference to administer estates in cases under Title 11 authorized to establish, etc., a panel of private trustees, and to supervise cases and trustees in cases under chapters 7, 11, 12, and 13 of Title 11, until amendments by sections 201 to

231 of Pub.L. 99–554 effective in such district, see section 302(d)(3)(A) to (F), (H), (I) of Pub.L. 99–554, set out as a note under section 581 of Title 28.

Amendment by Pub.L. 99–554, § 229 except as otherwise provided, with respect to cases under chapters 7, 11, 12, and 13 of Title 11 commenced before 30 days after Oct. 27, 1986, and pending in a judicial district referred to in section 581(a) of Title 28, as amended by section 111(a) of Pub.L. 99–554, for which a United States trustee is not authorized before 30 days after Oct. 27, 1986 to be appointed, not applicable until the expiration of the 3-year period beginning on Oct. 27, 1986, or of the 1-year period beginning on the date the Attorney General certifies under section 303 of Pub.L. 99–554 the region specified in a paragraph of such section 581(a) that includes, such district, whichever occurs first, see section 302(e)(1), (2) of Pub.L 99–554, set out as a note under section 581 of Title 28.

See 1986 Amendment notes set out above.

Effective Date of 1984 Amendments. See section 553 of Pub.L. 98–353, Title III, July 10, 1984, 98 Stat. 392, set out as an Effective Date of 1984 Amendment note preceding chapter 1 of Title 11, Bankruptcy.

Separability of Provisions. For separability of provisions of Title III of Pub.L. 98–353, see section 551 of Pub.L. 98–353 set out as a Separability of Provisions note preceding chapter 1 of Title 11, Bankruptcy.

Cross References

    Conversion from chapter 7, see section 706.
    Conversion or dismissal upon revocation of order of confirmation, see section 1330.
    Dismissal of
        Chapter 7 cases, see section 707.
        Chapter 9 cases, see section 927.
    Distribution of property of estate converted to chapter 7, see section 726.
    Effect of
        Conversion, see section 348.
        Dismissal, see section 349.
    Executory contracts and unexpired leases, see section 365.
    Liquidation of estate in railroad reorganization cases, see section 1174.

Library References:

    C.J.S. Bankruptcy §§ 436, 437.
    West's Key No. Digests, Bankruptcy ⊂⇒3716, 3717.

WESTLAW Electronic Research

    See WESTLAW Electronic Research Guide following the *Bankruptcy Highlights.*

SUBCHAPTER II—THE PLAN

§ 1321. Filing of plan

The debtor shall file a plan.

Pub.L. 95–598, Nov. 6, 1978, 92 Stat. 2648.

Historical and Revision Notes

Notes of Committee on the Judiciary, Senate Report No. 95–989. Chapter 13 con- templates the filing of a plan only by the debtor.

Cross References

Conversion or dismissal for failure to timely file plan, see section 1307.
Filing of plan in chapter 9 cases, see section 941.
Who may file plan in chapter 11 cases, see section 1121.

Library References:

C.J.S. Bankruptcy § 438.
West's Key No. Digests, Bankruptcy ⚏3704.

WESTLAW Electronic Research

See WESTLAW Electronic Research Guide following the *Bankruptcy Highlights.*

§ 1322. Contents of plan

(a) The plan shall—

(1) provide for the submission of all or such portion of future earnings or other future income of the debtor to the supervision and control of the trustee as is necessary for the execution of the plan;

(2) provide for the full payment, in deferred cash payments, of all claims entitled to priority under section 507 of this title, unless the holder of a particular claim agrees to a different treatment of such claim; and

(3) if the plan classifies claims, provide the same treatment for each claim within a particular class.

(b) Subject to subsections (a) and (c) of this section, the plan may—

(1) designate a class or classes of unsecured claims, as provided in section 1122 of this title, but may not discriminate unfairly against any class so designated; however, such plan may treat claims for a consumer debt of the debtor if an individual is liable on such consumer debt with the debtor differently than other unsecured claims;

(2) modify the rights of holders of secured claims, other than a claim secured only by a security interest in real property that is the debtor's principal residence, or of holders of unsecured claims, or leave unaffected the rights of holders of any class of claims;

(3) provide for the curing or waiving of any default;

(4) provide for payments on any unsecured claim to be made concurrently with payments on any secured claim or any other unsecured claim;

(5) notwithstanding paragraph (2) of this subsection, provide for the curing of any default within a reasonable time and maintenance of payments while the case is pending on any unsecured claim or secured claim on

which the last payment is due after the date on which the final payment under the plan is due;

(6) provide for the payment of all or any part of any claim allowed under section 1305 of this title;

(7) subject to section 365 of this title, provide for the assumption, rejection, or assignment of any executory contract or unexpired lease of the debtor not previously rejected under such section;

(8) provide for the payment of all or part of a claim against the debtor from property of the estate or property of the debtor;

(9) provide for the vesting of property of the estate, on confirmation of the plan or at a later time, in the debtor or in any other entity; and

(10) include any other appropriate provision not inconsistent with this title.

(c) The plan may not provide for payments over a period that is longer than three years, unless the court, for cause, approves a longer period, but the court may not approve a period that is longer than five years.

Pub.L. 95–598, Nov. 6, 1978, 92 Stat. 2648; Pub.L. 98–355, Title III, §§ 316, 528, July 10, 1984, 98 Stat. 356, 389.

Historical and Revision Notes

Notes of Committee on the Judiciary, Senate Report No. 95–989. Chapter 13 is designed to serve as a flexible vehicle for the repayment of part or all of the allowed claims of the debtor. Section 1322 emphasizes that purpose by fixing a minimum of mandatory plan provisions.

Subsection (a) requires that the plan submit whatever portion of the future income of the debtor is necessary to implement the plan to the control of the trustee, mandates payment in full of all section 507 priority claims, and requires identical treatment for all claims of a particular class.

Subsection (b) permits a chapter 13 plan to (1) divide unsecured claims not entitled to priority under section 507 into classes in the manner authorized for chapter 11 claims; (2) modify the rights of holders of secured and unsecured claims, except claims wholly secured by real estate mortgages; (3) cure or waive any default; (4) propose payments on unsecured claims concurrently with payments on any secured claim or any other class of unsecured claims; (5) provide for curing any default on any secured or unsecured claim on which the final payment is due after the proposed final payment under the plan; (6) provide for payment of any allowed postpetition claim; (7) assume or reject any previously unrejected executory contract or unexpired lease of the debtor; (8) propose the payment of all or any part of any claim from property of the estate or of the debtor; (9) provide for the vesting of property of the estate; and (10) include any other provision not inconsistent with other provisions of title 11.

Subsection (c) limits the payment period under the plan to 3 years, except that a 4-year payment period may be permitted by the court.

Legislative Statements. Section 1322(b)(2) of the House amendment represents a compromise agreement between similar provisions in the House bill and Senate amendment. Under the House amendment, the plan may modify the rights of holders of secured claims other than a claim secured by a security interest in real property that is the debtor's principal residence. It is intended that a claim secured by the debtor's principal residence may be treated with under section 1322(b)(5) of the House amendment.

Section 1322(c) adopts a 5-year period derived from the House bill in preference to a 4-year period contained in the Senate amendment. A conforming change is made in section 1329(c) adopting the provision in the House bill in preference to a comparable provision in the Senate amendment.

Tax payments in wage earner plans. The House bill provided that a wage earner plan had to provide that all priority claims would be paid in full. The Senate amendment contained a special rule in section 1325(c) requiring that Federal tax claims must be paid in cash, but that such tax claims can be paid in deferred cash installments under the general rules applicable to the payment of debts in a wage earner plan, unless the Internal Revenue Service negotiates with the debtor for some different medium or time for payment of the tax liability.

The House bill adopts the substance of the Senate amendment rule under section 1322(a)(2) of the House amendment. A wage earner plan must provide for full payment in deferred cash payments, of all priority claims, unless the holder of a particular claim agrees with a different treatment of such claim.

Effective Date of 1984 Amendments. See section 553 of Pub.L. 98–353, Title III, July 10, 1984, 98 Stat. 392, set out as an Effective Date of 1984 Amendment note preceding chapter 1 of Title 11, Bankruptcy.

Separability of Provisions. For separability of provisions of Title III of Pub.L. 98–353, see section 551 of Pub.L. 98–353 set out as a Separability of Provisions note preceding chapter 1 of Title 11, Bankruptcy.

Cross References
Contents of plan filed in
Chapter 11 cases, see section 1123.
Railroad reorganization cases, see section 1172.

Library References:
C.J.S. Bankruptcy §§ 438–445, 447.
West's Key No. Digests, Bankruptcy ☞3705–3712.

WESTLAW Electronic Research
See WESTLAW Electronic Research Guide following the *Bankruptcy Highlights.*

§ 1323.   Modification of plan before confirmation

(a) The debtor may modify the plan at any time before confirmation, but may not modify the plan so that the plan as modified fails to meet the requirements of section 1322 of this title.

(b) After the debtor files a modification under this section, the plan as modified becomes the plan.

(c) Any holder of a secured claim that has accepted or rejected the plan is deemed to have accepted or rejected, as the case may be, the plan as modified, unless the modification provides for a change in the rights of such holder from what such rights were under the plan before modification, and such holder changes such holder's previous acceptance or rejection.

Pub.L. 95–598, Nov. 6, 1978, 92 Stat. 2649.

Historical and Revision Notes

Notes of Committee on the Judiciary, Senate Report No. 95–989. The debtor is permitted to modify the plan before confirmation without court approval so long as the modified plan, which becomes the plan on filing, complies with the requirements of section 1322.

The original acceptance or rejection of a plan by the holder of a secured claim remains binding unless the modified plan changes the rights of the holder and the holder withdraws or alters its earlier acceptance or rejection.

Cross References
Modification of plan filed in
Chapter 9 cases, see section 942.
Chapter 11 cases, see section 1127.

§ 1324. Confirmation hearing

After notice, the court shall hold a hearing on confirmation of the plan. A party in interest may object to confirmation of the plan.

Pub.L. 95–598, Nov. 6, 1978, 92 Stat. 2649; Pub.L. 98–353, Title III, § 529, July 10, 1984, 98 Stat. 389; Pub.L. 99–554, Title II, § 283(x), Oct. 27, 1986, 100 Stat. 3118.

Historical and Revision Notes

Notes of Committee on the Judiciary, Senate Report No. 95–989. Any party in interest may object to the confirmation of a plan, as distinguished from merely rejecting a plan. An objection to confirmation is predicated on failure of the plan or the procedures employed prior to confirmation to conform with the requirements of chapter 13. The bankruptcy judge is required to provide notice and an opportunity for hearing any such objection to confirmation.

Effective Date of 1986 Amendments; Savings Provisions. References in Title 11 Section 326(b) to Title 11 Chapter 13 and Section 1302(a) and (d); Quarterly Fees. Amendment by Pub.L. 99–554 effective 30 days after Oct. 27, 1986, except as otherwise provided for, see section 302(a) of Pub.L. 99–554, set out as a note under section 581 of Title 28, Judiciary and Judicial Procedure.

Effective Date of 1984 Amendments. See section 553 of Pub.L. 98–353, Title III, July 10, 1984, 98 Stat. 392, set out as an Effective Date of 1984 Amendment note preceding chapter 1 of Title 11, Bankruptcy.

Separability of Provisions. For separability of provisions of Title III of Pub.L. 98–353, see section 551 of Pub.L. 98–353 set out as a Separability of Provisions note preceding chapter 1 of Title 11, Bankruptcy.

§ 1325. Confirmation of plan

(a) Except as provided in subsection (b), the court shall confirm a plan if—

(1) the plan complies with the provisions of this chapter and with the other applicable provisions of this title;

(2) any fee, charge, or amount required under chapter 123 of title 28, or by the plan, to be paid before confirmation, has been paid;

(3) the plan has been proposed in good faith and not by any means forbidden by law;

(4) the value, as of the effective date of the plan, of property to be distributed under the plan on account of each allowed unsecured claim is not

less than the amount that would be paid on such claim if the estate of the debtor were liquidated under chapter 7 of this title on such date;

(5) with respect to each allowed secured claim provided for by the plan—

(A) the holder of such claim has accepted the plan;

(B)(i) the plan provides that the holder of such claim retain the lien securing such claim; and

(ii) the value, as of the effective date of the plan, of property to be distributed under the plan on account of such claim is not less than the allowed amount of such claim; or

(C) the debtor surrenders the property securing such claim to such holder; and

(6) the debtor will be able to make all payments under the plan and to comply with the plan.

(b)(1) If the trustee or the holder of an allowed unsecured claim objects to the confirmation of the plan, then the court may not approve the plan unless, as of the effective date of the plan—

(A) the value of the property to be distributed under the plan on account of such claim is not less than the amount of such claim; or

(B) the plan provides that all of the debtor's projected disposable income to be received in the three-year period beginning on the date that the first payment is due under the plan will be applied to make payments under the plan.

(2) For purposes of this subsection, "disposable income" means income which is received by the debtor and which is not reasonably necessary to be expended—

(A) for the maintenance or support of the debtor or a dependent of the debtor; and

(B) if the debtor is engaged in business, for the payment of expenditures necessary for the continuation, preservation, and operation of such business.

(c) After confirmation of a plan, the court may order any entity from whom the debtor receives income to pay all or any part of such income to the trustee.

Pub.L. 95–598, Nov. 6, 1978, 92 Stat. 2649; Pub.L. 98–353, Title III, §§ 317, 530, July 10, 1984, 98 Stat. 356, 389; Pub.L. 99–554, Title II, § 283(y), Oct. 27, 1986, 100 Stat. 3118.

Historical and Revision Notes

Notes of Committee on the Judiciary, Senate Report No. 95–989. The bankruptcy court must confirm a plan if (1) the plan satisfies the provisions of chapter 13 and other applicable provisions of title 11; (2) it is proposed in good faith; (3) it is in the best interests of creditors, and defined by subsection (a) (4) of Section 1325; (4) it has been accepted by the holder of each allowed secured claim provided for the plan or where the holder of any such secured claim is to receive value under the plan not less than the amount of the allowed secured claim, or where the debtor surrenders to the holder the collateral securing any such allowed secured claim; (5) the plan is feasible; and (6) the requisite fees and charges have been paid.

Subsection (b) authorizes the court to order an entity, as defined by Section 101(15), to pay any income of the debtor to the trustee. Any governmental unit is an entity subject to such an order.

Legislative Statements. Section 1325(a)(5) (B) of the House amendment modifies the House bill and Senate amendment to significantly protect secured creditors in chapter 13. Unless the secured creditor accepts the plan, the plan must provide that the secured creditor retain the lien securing the creditor's allowed secured claim in addition to receiving value, as of the effective date of the plan of property to be distributed under the plan on account of the claim not less than the allowed amount of the claim. To this extent, a secured creditor in a case under chapter 13 is treated identically with a recourse creditor under section 1111(b)(1) of the House amendment except that the secured creditor in a case under chapter 13 may receive any property of a value as of the effective date of the plan equal to the allowed amount of the creditor's secured claim rather than being restricted to receiving deferred cash payments. Of course, the secured creditors' lien only secures the value of the collateral and to the extent property is distributed of a present value equal to the allowed amount of the creditor's secured claim the creditor's lien will have been satisfied in full. Thus the lien created under section 1325(a)(5)(B)(i) is effective only to secure deferred payments to the extent of the amount of the allowed secured claim. To the extent the deferred payments exceed the value of the allowed amount of the secured claim and the debtor subsequently defaults, the lien will not secure unaccrued interest represented in such deferred payments.

References in Text. Chapter 123 of title 28, referred to in subsec. (a)(2), is classified to section 1911 et seq. of Title 28, Judiciary and Judicial Procedure.

Effective Date of 1986 Amendments; References in Title 11 Section 326(b) to Title 11 Chapter 13 and Section 1302(a) and (d); Quarterly Fees. Amendment by Pub.L. 99–554 effective 30 days after Oct. 27, 1986, except as otherwise provided for, see section 302(a) of Pub.L. 99–554, set out as a note under section 581 of Title 28, Judiciary and Judicial Procedure.

Effective Date of 1984 Amendments. See section 553 of Pub.L. 98–353, Title III, July 10, 1984, 98 Stat. 392, set out as an Effective Date of 1984 Amendment note preceding chapter 1 of Title 11, Bankruptcy.

Separability of Provisions. For separability of provisions of Title III of Pub.L. 98–353, see section 551 of Pub.L. 98–353 set out as a Separability of Provisions note preceding chapter 1 of Title 11, Bankruptcy.

Cross References

Confirmation of plan in
    Chapter 9 cases, see section 943.
    Chapter 11 cases, see section 1129.
    Railroad reorganization cases, see section 1173.
Conversion or dismissal, see section 1307.

Library References:

C.J.S. Bankruptcy § 438 et seq.
West's Key No. Digests, Bankruptcy ⬬3705–3715.

WESTLAW Electronic Research

See WESTLAW Electronic Research Guide following the *Bankruptcy Highlights*.

§ 1326. Payments

(a)(1) Unless the court orders otherwise, the debtor shall commence making the payments proposed by a plan within 30 days after the plan is filed.

(2) A payment made under this subsection shall be retained by the trustee until confirmation or denial of confirmation of a plan. If a plan is confirmed, the trustee shall distribute any such payment in accordance with the plan. If a plan is not confirmed, the trustee shall return any such payment to the debtor, after deducting any unpaid claim allowed under section 503(b) of this title.

(b) Before or at the time of each payment to creditors under the plan, there shall be paid—

(1) any unpaid claim of the kind specified in section 507(a)(1) of this title; and

(2) if a standing trustee appointed under section 586(b) of title 28 is serving in the case, the percentage fee fixed for such standing trustee under section 586(e)(1)(B) of title 28.

(c) Except as otherwise provided in the plan or in the order confirming the plan, the trustee shall make payments to creditors under the plan.

Pub.L. 95–598, Nov. 6, 1978, 92 Stat. 2650; Pub.L. 98–353, Title III, §§ 318(a), 531, July 10, 1984, 98 Stat. 357, 389; Pub.L. 99–554, Title II, §§ 230, 283(z), Oct. 27, 1986, 100 Stat. 3103, 3118.

Historical and Revision Notes

Notes of Committee on the Judiciary, Senate Report No. 95–989. Section 1326 supplements the priorities provisions of section 507. Subsection (a) requires accrued costs of administration and filing fees, as well as fees due the chapter 13 trustee, to be disbursed before payments to creditors under the plan. Subsection (b) makes it clear that the chapter 13 trustee is normally to make distribution to creditors of the payments made under the plan by the debtor.

Notes of Committee on the Judiciary, House Report No. 95–595. Subsection (a) requires that before or at the time of each payment any outstanding administrative expenses [and] any percentage fee due for a private standing chapter 13 trustee be paid in full.

Legislative Statements. Section 1326(a)(2) of the House amendment adopts a comparable provision contained in the House bill providing for standing trustees.

1986 Amendment. Subsec. (b)(2). Pub.L. 99–554, § 230, substituted "586(b) of title 28" for "1302(d) of this title" and "586(e)(1)(B) of title 28" for "1302(e) of this title".

See Effective Date of 1986 Amendment, etc., notes set out below.

Effective Date of 1986 Amendments; References in Title 11 Section 326(b) to Title 11 Chapter 13 and Section 1302(a) and (d); Effective Date of 1986 Amendments for Certain Judicial Districts Not Served by United States Trustees and for Judicial Districts in Alabama and North Carolina; U.S. Trustee System Fund Deposits in Alabama and North Carolina; Effective Date of Title 11 Chapter 15 Repeal as to Northern District of Alabama; Authority of Certain Estate Administrators in Alabama and North Carolina; Effective Date of 1986 Amendments in Pending Cases Where a

U.S. Trustee Not Authorized or Where a Trustee Files Final Report or Plan is Confirmed; Quarterly Fees. Amendment by Pub.L. 99–554 effective 30 days after Oct. 27, 1986, except as otherwise provided for, see section 302(a) of Pub.L. 99–554, set out as a note under section 581 of Title 28, Judiciary and Judicial Procedure.

Amendment by Pub.L. 99–554, § 230, not to become effective in or with respect to certain specified judicial districts until, or apply to cases while pending in such district before, the expiration of the 270-day period beginning 30 days after Oct. 27, 1986, or of the 30-day period beginning on the date the Attorney General certifies under section 303 of Pub.L. 99–554 the region specified in a paragraph of section 581(a) of Title 28, as amended by section 111(a) of Pub.L. 99–554, that includes such district, whichever occurs first, see section 302(d)(1) of Pub.L. 99–554, set out as a note under section 581 of Title 28.

Amendment by Pub.L. 99–554, § 230, not to become effective in or with respect to certain specified judicial districts until, or apply to cases while pending in such district before, the expiration of the 2-year period beginning 30 days after Oct. 27, 1986, or of the 30-day period beginning on the date the Attorney General certifies under section 303 of Pub.L. 99–554 the region specified in a paragraph of section 581(a) of Title 28, as amended by section 111(a) of Pub.L. 99–554, that includes such district, whichever occurs first, see section 302(d)(2) of Pub.L. 99–554, set out as a note under section 581 of Title 28.

Amendment by Pub.L. 99–554, § 230, not to become effective in or with respect to judicial districts established for the States of Alabama and North Carolina until, or apply to cases while pending in such district before, such district elects to be included in a bankruptcy region established in section 581(a) of Title 28, as amended by section 111(a) of Pub.L. 99–554, or Oct. 1, 2002, whichever occurs first, and, except as otherwise provided for, with respect to cases under chapters 7, 11, 12, and 13 of Title 11 commenced before 30 days after Oct. 27, 1986, and pending in a judicial district in the States of Alabama or North Carolina before any election made under section 302(d)(3)(A) of Pub.L. 99–554 by such district becomes effective or Oct. 1, 2002, whichever occurs first, amendments by Pub.L. 99–554 not to apply until Oct. 1, 2003, or the expiration of the 1-year period beginning on the date such election becomes effective, whichever occurs first, and further, in any judicial district in Alabama or North Carolina not making the election described in section 302(d)(3)(A) of Pub.L. 99–554, any person appointed under regulations issued by the Judicial Conference to administer estates in cases under Title 11 authorized to establish, etc., a panel of private trustees, and to supervise cases and trustees in cases under chapters 7, 11, 12, and 13 of Title 11, until amendments by sections 201 to 231 of Pub.L. 99–554 effective in such district, see section 302(d)(3)(A) to (F), (H), (I) of Pub.L. 99–554, set out as a note under section 581 of Title 28.

Amendment by Pub.L. 99–554, § 230 except as otherwise provided, with respect to cases under chapters 7, 11, 12, and 13 of Title 11 commenced before 30 days after Oct. 27, 1986, and pending in a judicial district referred to in section 581(a) of Title 28, as amended by section 111(a) of Pub.L. 99–554, for which a United States trustee is not authorized before 30 days after Oct. 27, 1986 to be appointed, not applicable until the expiration of the 3-year period beginning on Oct. 27, 1986, or of the 1-year period beginning on the date the Attorney General certifies under section 303 of Pub.L. 99–554 the region specified in a paragraph of such section 581(a) that includes, such district, whichever occurs first, see section 302(e)(1), (2) of Pub.L. 99–554, set out as a note under section 581 of Title 28.

See 1986 Amendment notes set out above.

Effective Date of 1984 Amendments. See section 553 of Pub.L. 98–353, Title III, July 10, 1984, 98 Stat. 392, set out as an Effective Date of 1984 Amendment note preceding chapter 1 of Title 11, Bankruptcy.

Separability of Provisions. For separability of provisions of Title III of Pub.L. 98–353, see section 551 of Pub.L. 98–353 set out as a Separability of Provisions note preceding chapter 1 of Title 11, Bankruptcy.

Cross References

Payment stopped on checks remaining unpaid 90 days after final distribution, see section 347.

Library References:

C.J.S. Bankruptcy § 438.
West's Key No. Digests, Bankruptcy ⟜3704.

WESTLAW Electronic Research

See WESTLAW Electronic Research Guide following the *Bankruptcy Highlights*.

§ 1327. Effect of confirmation

(a) The provisions of a confirmed plan bind the debtor and each creditor, whether or not the claim of such creditor is provided for by the plan, and whether or not such creditor has objected to, has accepted, or has rejected the plan.

(b) Except as otherwise provided in the plan or the order confirming the plan, the confirmation of a plan vests all of the property of the estate in the debtor.

(c) Except as otherwise provided in the plan or in the order confirming the plan, the property vesting in the debtor under subsection (b) of this section is free and clear of any claim or interest of any creditor provided for by the plan.

Pub.L. 95–598, Nov. 6, 1978, 92 Stat. 2650.

Historical and Revision Notes

Notes of Committee on the Judiciary, Senate Report No. 95–989. Subsection (a) binds the debtor and each creditor to the provisions of a confirmed plan, whether or not the claim of the creditor is provided for by the plan and whether or not the creditor has accepted, rejected, or objected to the plan. Unless the plan itself or the order confirming the plan otherwise provides, confirmation is deemed to vest all property of the estate in the debtor, free and clear of any claim or interest of any creditor provided for by the plan.

Cross References

Effect of confirmation in
 Chapter 9 cases, see section 944.
 Chapter 11 cases, see section 1141.

Library References:

C.J.S. Bankruptcy § 450.
West's Key No. Digests, Bankruptcy ⟜3715.

WESTLAW Electronic Research

See WESTLAW Electronic Research Guide following the *Bankruptcy Highlights.*

§ 1328. Discharge

(a) As soon as practicable after completion by the debtor of all payments under the plan, unless the court approves a written waiver of discharge executed by the debtor after the order for relief under this chapter, the court shall grant the debtor a discharge of all debts provided for by the plan or disallowed under section 502 of this title, except any debt—

(1) provided for under section 1322(b)(5) of this title;

(2) of the kind specified in paragraph (5) or (8) of section 523(a) or 523(a)(9) [1] of this title; or

(3) for restitution included in a sentence on the debtor's conviction of a crime.

(b) At any time after the confirmation of the plan and after notice and a hearing, the court may grant a discharge to a debtor that has not completed payments under the plan only if—

(1) the debtor's failure to complete such payments is due to circumstances for which the debtor should not justly be held accountable;

(2) the value, as of the effective date of the plan, of property actually distributed under the plan on account of each allowed unsecured claim is not less than the amount that would have been paid on such claim if the estate of the debtor had been liquidated under chapter 7 of this title on such date; and

(3) modification of the plan under section 1329 of this title is not practicable.

(c) A discharge granted under subsection (b) of this section discharges the debtor from all unsecured debts provided for by the plan or disallowed under section 502 of this title, except any debt—

(1) provided for under section 1322(b)(5) of this title; or

(2) of a kind specified in section 523(a) of this title.

(d) Notwithstanding any other provision of this section, a discharge granted under this section does not discharge the debtor from any debt based on an allowed claim filed under section 1305(a)(2) of this title if prior approval by the trustee of the debtor's incurring such debt was practicable and was not obtained.

(e) On request of a party in interest before one year after a discharge under this section is granted, and after notice and a hearing, the court may revoke such discharge only if—

(1) such discharge was obtained by the debtor through fraud; and

(2) the requesting party did not know of such fraud until after such discharge was granted.

Pub.L. 95–598, Nov. 6, 1978, 92 Stat. 2650; Pub.L. 98–353, Title III, § 532, July 10, 1984, 98 Stat. 389; Pub.L. 101–508, § 3007(b), Nov. 5, 1990, 104 Stat. 1388–__;[1] Pub.L. 101–581, §§ 2(b), 3, Nov. 15, 1990, 104 Stat. 2865; Pub.L. 101–647, Title XXXI, §§ 3102(b), 3103, Nov. 29, 1990, 104 Stat. 4916.

[1] See Codification note below.

Termination of Amendment

Pub.L. 101–508, § 3008, provided that amendment by Pub.L. 101–508, § 3007(b)(1), amending subsec. (a)(2) of this section, to cease to be effective Oct. 1, 1996. See note under section 362 of this title.

Historical and Revision Notes

Notes of Committee on the Judiciary, Senate Report No. 95–989. The court is to enter a discharge, unless waived, as soon as practicable after completion of payments under the plan. The debtor is to be discharged of all debts provided for by the plan or disallowed under section 502, except a debt provided for under the plan the last payment on which was not due until after the completion of the plan, or a debt incurred for willful and malicious conversion of or injury to the property or person of another.

Subsection (b) is the successor to Bankruptcy Act Section 661 [former section 1061 of this title]. This subsection permits the bankruptcy judge to grant the debtor a discharge at any time after confirmation of a plan, if the court determines, after notice and hearing, that the failure to complete payments under the plan is due to circumstances for which the debtor should not justly be held accountable, the distributions made to each creditor under the plan equal in value the amount that would have been paid to the creditor had the estate been liquidated under chapter 7 of title 11 at the date of the hearing under this subsection, and that modification of the plan is impracticable. The discharge granted under subsection (b) relieves the debtor from all unsecured debts provided for by the plan or disallowed under section 502, except nondis-

chargeable debts described in section 523(a) of title 11 or debts of the type covered by section 1322(b)(5).

Subsection (d) excepts from any chapter 13 discharge a debt based on an allowed section 1305(a)(2) postpetition claim, if prior trustee approval of the incurring of the debt was practicable but was not obtained.

A chapter 13 discharge obtained through fraud and before the moving party gained knowledge of the fraud may be revoked by the court under subsection (e), after notice and hearing, at the request of any party in interest made within 1 year after the discharge was granted.

Legislative Statements. Section 1328(a) adopts a provision contained in the Senate amendment permitting the court to approve a waiver of discharge by the debtor. It is anticipated that such a waiver must be in writing executed after the order for relief in a case under chapter 13.

Codification. Pub.L. 101–581 and Pub.L. 101–647, Title XXXI, §§ 3102(b) and 3103, made identical amendments to subsec. (a) of this section. See, also note below.

Amendments by Pub.L. 101–581 and Pub.L. 101–647 which both inserted "or 523(a)(9)" following "523(a)(5)" were incapable of literal execution in view of prior amendment by

Pub.L. 101–508 which substituted "paragraph (5) or (8) of section 523(a)" for "section 523(a)(5)", thereby deleting language subsequently amended. The amendments have been editorially executed according to the probable intent of Congress.

Effective and Termination Dates of 1990 Amendments. Amendment by Pub.L. 101–581, §§ 2(b) and 3 effective Nov. 15, 1990, see section 4 of Pub.L. 101–581, set out as a note under section 523 of this title. [For effective date of identical amendments by Pub.L. 101–647, see, also, section 3104 of Pub.L. 101–647, set out as a note under section 523 of this title.]

Section 3007(b)(2) of Pub.L. 101–508 provided that: "The amendment made by paragraph (1) [amending subsec. (a)(2) of this section] shall not apply to any case under the provi-sions of title 11, United States Code [this title], commenced before the date of the enactment of this Act [Nov. 5, 1990]."

Amendment by Pub.L. 101–508, § 3007(a)(2), to cease to be effective Oct. 1, 1996, see section 3008, set out as a note under section 362 of this title.

Effective Date of 1984 Amendments. See section 553 of Pub.L. 98–353, Title III, July 10, 1984, 98 Stat. 392, set out as an Effective Date of 1984 Amendment note preceding chapter 1 of Title 11, Bankruptcy.

Separability of Provisions. For separability of provisions of Title III of Pub.L. 98–353, see section 551 of Pub.L. 98–353 set out as a Separability of Provisions note preceding chapter 1 of Title 11, Bankruptcy.

Cross References

Discharge in Chapter 7 cases, see section 727.
Effect of
    Conversion, see section 348.
    Discharge, see section 524.
Exceptions to discharge, see section 523.

Library References:

C.J.S. Bankruptcy § 453.
West's Key No. Digests, Bankruptcy ⬅3718.

WESTLAW Electronic Research

See WESTLAW Electronic Research Guide following the *Bankruptcy Highlights.*

§ 1329. Modification of plan after confirmation

(a) At any time after confirmation of the plan but before the completion of payments under such plan, the plan may be modified, upon request of the debtor, the trustee, or the holder of an allowed unsecured claim, to—

    (1) increase or reduce the amount of payments on claims of a particular class provided for by the plan;

    (2) extend or reduce the time for such payments; or

    (3) alter the amount of the distribution to a creditor whose claim is provided for by the plan to the extent necessary to take account of any payment of such claim other than under the plan.

(b)(1) Sections 1322(a), 1322(b), and 1323(c) of this title and the requirements of section 1325(a) of this title apply to any modification under subsection (a) of this section.

(2) The plan as modified becomes the plan unless, after notice and a hearing, such modification is disapproved.

(c) A plan modified under this section may not provide for payments over a period that expires after three years after the time that the first payment under the original confirmed plan was due, unless the court, for cause, approves a longer period, but the court may not approve a period that expires after five years after such time.

Pub.L. 95–598, Nov. 6, 1978, 92 Stat. 2651; Pub.L. 98–353, Title III, §§ 319, 533, July 10, 1984, 98 Stat. 357, 389.

Historical and Revision Notes

Notes of Committee on the Judiciary, Senate Report No. 95–989. At any time prior to the completion of payments under a confirmed plan, the plan may be modified, after notice and hearing, to change the amount of payments to creditors or a particular class of creditors and to extend or reduce the payment period. A modified plan may not contain any provision which could not be included in an original plan as prescribed by section 1322. A modified plan may not call for payments to be made beyond four years as measured from the date of the commencement of payments under the original plan.

Effective Date of 1984 Amendments. See section 553 of Pub.L. 98–353, Title III, July 10, 1984, 98 Stat. 392, set out as an Effective Date of 1984 Amendment note preceding chapter 1 of Title 11, Bankruptcy.

Separability of Provisions. For separability of provisions of Title III of Pub.L. 98–353, see section 551 of Pub.L. 98–353 set out as a Separability of Provisions note preceding chapter 1 of Title 11, Bankruptcy.

Cross References

Conversion or dismissal upon denial of confirmation of modified plan, see section 1307.
Modification of plan in
Chapter 9 cases, see section 942.
Chapter 11 cases, see section 1127.

Library References:

C.J.S. Bankruptcy § 451.
West's Key No. Digests, Bankruptcy ⟞3715.

WESTLAW Electronic Research

See WESTLAW Electronic Research Guide following the *Bankruptcy Highlights*.

§ 1330.　Revocation of an order of confirmation

(a) On request of a party in interest at any time within 180 days after the date of the entry of an order of confirmation under section 1325 of this title, and after notice and a hearing, the court may revoke such order if such order was procured by fraud.

(b) If the court revokes an order of confirmation under subsection (a) of this section, the court shall dispose of the case under section 1307 of this title, unless, within the time fixed by the court, the debtor proposes and the court confirms a modification of the plan under section 1329 of this title.

Pub.L. 95–598, Nov. 6, 1978, 92 Stat. 2651.

Historical and Revision Notes

Notes of Committee on the Judiciary, Senate Report No. 95–989. The court may revoke an order of confirmation procured by fraud, after notice and hearing, on application of a party in interest filed within 180 days after the entry of the order. Thereafter, unless a modified plan is confirmed, the court is to convert or dismiss the chapter 13 case as provided in section 1307.

Legislative Statements. Section 1331 of the House bill and Senate amendment is deleted in the House amendment.

Section 1331 of title 11 of the House bill and the comparable provisions in sections 1322 and 1327(d) of the Senate amendment, pertaining to assessment and collection of taxes in wage earner plans, are deleted, and the governing rule is placed in section 505(c) of the House amendment. The provisions of both bills allowing assessment and collection of taxes after confirmation of the wage-earner plan are modified to allow assessment and collection after the court fixes the fact and amount of a tax liability, including adminis-trative period taxes, regardless of whether this occurs before or after confirmation of the plan. The provision of the House bill limiting the collection of taxes to those assessed before one year after the filing of the petition is eliminated, thereby leaving the period of limitations on assessment of these nondischargeable tax liabilities the usual period provided by the Internal Revenue Code [Title 26].

Cross References

Conversion or dismissal upon revocation of order of confirmation, see section 1307.

Revocation of order of confirmation in chapter 11 cases, see section 1144.

Library References:

C.J.S. Bankruptcy § 452.

West's Key No. Digests, Bankruptcy ⬖3715.

WESTLAW Electronic Research

See WESTLAW Electronic Research Guide following the *Bankruptcy Highlights.*

CHAPTER 15—UNITED STATES TRUSTEES

§§ 1501 to 151326. Repealed. Pub.L. 99–554, Title II, § 231, Oct. 27, 1986, 100 Stat. 3103. See 28 U.S.C.A. § 581 et seq. (infra).

Historical Notes

Section 1501, Pub.L. 95–598, Nov. 6, 1978, 92 Stat. 2652, set forth applicability of chapter.

Section 15101, Pub.L. 95–598, Nov. 6, 1978, 92 Stat. 2652, defined terms "entity" and "governmental unit".

Section 15102, Pub.L. 95–598, Nov. 6, 1978, 92 Stat. 2652, set forth rule of construction.

Section 15103, Pub.L. 95–598, Nov. 6, 1978, 92 Stat. 2652; Pub.L. 98–353, Title III, §§ 311(b)(3), 318(b), July 10, 1984, 98 Stat. 355, 357, set forth applicability of subchapters and sections.

Section 15303, Pub.L. 95–598, Nov. 6, 1978, 92 Stat. 2653, set forth provisions relating to involuntary cases.

Section 15321, Pub.L. 95–598, Nov. 6, 1978, 92 Stat. 2653, related to eligibility to serve as trustee.

Section 15322, Pub.L. 95–598, Nov. 6, 1978, 92 Stat. 2653, related to qualifications of trustees.

Section 15324, Pub.L. 95–598, Nov. 6, 1978, 92 Stat. 2653, related to removal of trustee or examiner.

Section 15326, Pub.L. 95–598, Nov. 6, 1978, 92 Stat. 2653, related to limitation on compensation of trustees.

Section 15330, Pub.L. 95–598, Nov. 6, 1978, 92 Stat. 2653, set forth compensation of officers.

Section 15343, Pub.L. 95–598, Nov. 6, 1978, 92 Stat. 2653, related to examination of the debtor.

Section 15345, Pub.L. 95–598, Nov. 6, 1978, 92 Stat. 2654; Pub.L. 97–258, § 3(c), Sept. 13, 1982, 96 Stat. 1064, related to money of estates.

Section 15701, Pub.L. 95–598, Nov. 6, 1978, 92 Stat. 2654, related to appointment, etc., of interim trustee.

Section 15703, Pub.L. 95–598, Nov. 6, 1978, 92 Stat. 2654, related to successor trustee.

Section 15704, Pub.L. 95–598, Nov. 6, 1978, 92 Stat. 2655, related to duties of trustees.

Section 15727, Pub.L. 95–598, Nov. 6, 1978, 92 Stat. 2655, set forth provisions relating to discharge under section 727(a) of this title.

Section 151102, Pub.L. 95–598, Nov.6, 1978, 92 Stat. 2655, set forth provisions relating to creditors' and equity security holders' committees.

Section 151104, Pub.L. 95–598, Nov. 6, 1978, 92 Stat. 2655, related to appointment of trustee or examiner in reorganization matters.

Section 151105, Pub.L. 95–598, Nov. 6, 1978, 92 Stat. 2656, related to termination of trustee's appointment.

Section 151163, Pub.L. 95–598, Nov. 6, 1978, 92 Stat. 2656, related to appointment of trustee.

Section 151302, Pub.L. 95–598, Nov. 6, 1978, 92 Stat. 2656; Pub.L. 98–353, Title III, §§ 311(b)(4), 534, July 10, 1984, 98 Stat. 355, 390, related to functions of trustee with respect to adjustment of debts of an individual with regular income.

Section 151326, Pub.L. 95–598, Nov. 6, 1978, 92 Stat. 2657, set forth provisions relating to payments.

Effective Date of Repeal. Repeal by Pub. L. 99–554 effective 30 days after Oct. 27, 1986, except as otherwise provided for, see section 302 of Pub.L. 99–554, set out as a note under section 581 of Title 28, Judiciary and Judicial Procedure.

Repeal not applicable in or with respect to Northern District of Alabama until March 1, 1987, or the effective date of any election made under section 302(d)(3)(A) of Pub.L. 99–554, see section 302(d)(3)(H) of Pub.L. 99–554, set out as a note under section 581 of Title 28.

Repeal of Chapter by Pub.L. 95–598, § 408(c). Pub.L. 95–598, Title IV, § 408(c), Nov. 6, 1978, 92 Stat. 2687, as amended Pub.L. 98–166, Title II, § 200, Nov. 28, 1983, 97 Stat. 1081; Pub.L. 98–353, Title III, § 323, July 10, 1984, 98 Stat. 358; Pub.L. 99–429, Sept. 30, 1986, 100 Stat. 985, provided that, effective Nov. 10, 1986, this chapter is repealed.

Pub.L. 99–500, Title I, § 101(b) [Title II, § 200], Oct. 18, 1986, 100 Stat. 1783–45, and

Pub.L. 99–591, Title I, § 101(b) [Title II, § 200], Oct. 30, 1986, 100 Stat. 3341–45 provided that, effective immediately before November 10, 1986, section 408(c) of the Act of November 6, 1978 (Public Law 95–598; 92 Stat. 2687), is amended by striking out "November 10, 1986" and inserting in lieu thereof "September 30, 1987". Such amendment was incapable of execution in view of the prior amendment of such section 408(c) by section 307(a) of Pub.L. 99–554, effective Oct. 27, 1986, pursuant to section 302(b) of Pub.L. 99–554, and in view of the repeal of section 408(c) by section 307(b) of Pub.L. 99–554.

Cross References

See 28 U.S.C.A. § 581 et seq., infra.

*

RELATED PROVISIONS
OF
U.S. CODE TITLES 18 AND 28

TITLE 18—CRIMES AND CRIMINAL PROCEDURE

CHAPTER 9—BANKRUPTCY

Sec.
151. Definition.
152. Concealment of assets; false oaths and claims; bribery.
153. Embezzlement by trustee or officer.
154. Adverse interest and conduct of officers.
155. Fee agreements in cases under Title 11 and receiverships.

CHAPTER 96—RACKETEER INFLUENCED AND CORRUPT
ORGANIZATIONS

1961. Definitions.

CHAPTER 119—WIRE INTERCEPTION AND INTERCEPTION OF ORAL
COMMUNICATIONS

2516. Authorization for interception of wire, oral, or electronic communications.

CHAPTER 203—ARREST AND COMMITMENT

3057. Bankruptcy investigations.

CHAPTER 213—LIMITATIONS

3284. Concealment of bankrupt's assets.

PART V—IMMUNITY OF WITNESSES

6001. Definitions.

TITLE 28—JUDICIARY AND JUDICIAL PROCEDURE

PART I—ORGANIZATIONS OF COURTS

CHAPTER 6—BANKRUPTCY JUDGES

151. Designation of bankruptcy courts.
152. Appointment of bankruptcy judges.
153. Salaries; character of service.
154. Division of businesses; chief judge.
155. Temporary transfer of bankruptcy judges.
156. Staff; expenses.
157. Procedures.
158. Appeals.

RELATED PROVISIONS

CHAPTER 17—RESIGNATION AND RETIREMENT OF JUSTICES AND JUDGES

Sec.
372. Retirement for disability; substitute judge on failure to retire; judicial discipline.

CHAPTER 21—GENERAL PROVISIONS APPLICABLE TO COURTS AND JUDGES

455. Disqualification of justice, judge, or magistrate.

PART II—DEPARTMENT OF JUSTICE

CHAPTER 39—UNITED STATES TRUSTEES

581. United States trustees.
582. Assistant United States trustees.
583. Oath of office.
584. Official stations.
585. Vacancies.
586. Duties; supervision by Attorney General.
587. Salaries.
588. Expenses.
589. Staff and other employees.
589a. United States Trustee System Fund.

PART III—COURT OFFICERS AND EMPLOYEES

CHAPTER 41—ADMINISTRATIVE OFFICE OF UNITED STATES COURT

604. Duties of Director generally.

CHAPTER 44—ARBITRATION

651. Authorization of arbitration.
652. Jurisdiction.
653. Powers of arbitrator; arbitration hearing.
654. Arbitration award and judgment.
655. Trial de novo.
656. Certification of arbitrators.
657. Compensation of arbitrators.
658. District courts that may authorize arbitration.

CHAPTER 57—GENERAL PROVISIONS APPLICABLE TO COURT OFFICERS AND EMPLOYEES

959. Trustees and receivers suable; management; State laws.

PART IV—JURISDICTION AND VENUE

CHAPTER 85—DISTRICT COURTS; JURISDICTION

1334. Bankruptcy cases and proceedings.

CHAPTER 87—DISTRICT COURTS; VENUE

1408. Venue of cases under Title 11.
1409. Venue of proceedings arising under Title 11 or arising in or related to cases under Title 11.

U.S. CODE TITLES

Sec.
1410. Venue of cases ancillary to foreign proceedings.
1411. Jury trials.
1412. Change of venue.

CHAPTER 89—DISTRICT COURTS; REMOVAL OF CASES FROM STATE COURTS

1452. Removal of claims related to bankruptcy cases.

PART V—PROCEDURE

CHAPTER 123—FEES AND COSTS

1930. Bankruptcy fees.

[Miscellaneous Fee Schedule]

CHAPTER 131—RULES OF COURTS

2075. Bankruptcy rules.

TITLE 18

CRIMES AND CRIMINAL PROCEDURE

CHAPTER 9—BANKRUPTCY

Sec.
151. Definition.
152. Concealment of assets; false oaths and claims; bribery.
153. Embezzlement by trustee or officer.
154. Adverse interest and conduct of officers.
155. Fee agreements in cases under Title 11 and receiverships.

---

§ 151. Definition

As used in this chapter, the term "debtor" means a debtor concerning whom a petition has been filed under title 11.

June 25, 1948, c. 645, 62 Stat. 689; Nov. 6, 1978, Pub.L. 95–598, Title III, § 314(b) (1), 92 Stat. 2676.

§ 152. Concealment of assets; false oaths and claims; bribery

Whoever knowingly and fraudulently conceals from a custodian, trustee, marshal, or other officer of the court charged with the control or custody of property, or from creditors in any case under title 11, any property belonging to the estate of a debtor; or

Whoever knowingly and fraudulently makes a false oath or account in or in relation to any case under title 11; or

Whoever knowingly and fraudulently makes a false declaration, certificate, verification, or statement under penalty of perjury as permitted under section 1746 of title 28, United States Code, in or in relation to any case under title 11; or

Whoever knowingly and fraudulently presents any false claim for proof against the estate of a debtor, or uses any such claim in any case under title 11, personally, or by agent, proxy, or attorney, or as agent, proxy, or attorney; or

Whoever knowingly and fraudulently receives any material amount of property from a debtor after the filing of a case under title 11, with intent to defeat the provisions of title 11; or

Whoever knowingly and fraudulently gives, offers, receives or attempts to obtain any money or property, remuneration, compensation, reward, advantage, or promise thereof, for acting or forbearing to act in any case under title 11; or

Whoever, either individually or as an agent or officer of any person or corporation, in contemplation of a case under title 11 by or against him or any other person or corporation, or with intent to defeat the provisions of title 11, knowingly and fraudulently transfers or conceals any of his property or the property of such other person or corporation; or

Whoever, after the filing of a case under title 11 or in contemplation thereof, knowingly and fraudulently conceals, destroys, mutilates, falsifies, or makes a false entry in any recorded information, including books, documents, records, and papers, relating to the property or financial affairs of a debtor; or

Whoever, after the filing of a case under title 11, knowingly and fraudulently withholds from a custodian, trustee, marshal, or other officer of the court entitled to its possession, any recorded information, including books, documents, records, and papers, relating to the property or financial affairs of a debtor.

Shall be fined not more than $5,000 or imprisoned not more than five years, or both.

June 25, 1948, c. 645, 62 Stat. 689; June 12, 1960, Pub.L. 86–519, § 2, 74 Stat. 217; Sept. 2, 1960, Pub.L. 86–701, 74 Stat. 753; Oct. 18, 1976, Pub.L. 94–550, § 4, 90 Stat. 2535; Nov. 6, 1978, Pub.L. 95–598, Title III, § 314(a), (c), 92 Stat. 2676, 2677; Nov. 18, 1988, Pub.L. 100–690, Title VII, § 7017, 102 Stat. 4395.

§ 153.   Embezzlement by trustee or officer

Whoever knowingly and fraudulently appropriates to his own use, embezzles, spends, or transfers any property or secretes or destroys any document belonging to the estate of a debtor which came into his charge as trustee, custodian, marshal, or other officer of the court, shall be fined not more than $5,000 or imprisoned not more than five years, or both.

June 25, 1948, c. 645, 62 Stat. 690; Nov. 6, 1978, Pub.L. 95–598, Title III, § 314(a) (1), (d)(1), (2), 92 Stat. 2676, 2677.

§ 154.   Adverse interest and conduct of officers

Whoever, being a custodian, trustee, marshal, or other officer of the court, knowingly purchases, directly or indirectly, any property of the estate of which he is such officer in a case under title 11; or

Whoever being such officer, knowingly refuses to permit a reasonable opportunity for the inspection of the documents and accounts relating to the affairs of estates in his charge by parties in interest when directed by the court to do so—

Shall be fined not more than $500, and shall forfeit his office, which shall thereupon become vacant.

June 25, 1948, c. 645, 62 Stat. 690; Nov. 6, 1978, Pub.L. 95–598, Title III, § 314(a) (2), (e)(1), (2), 92 Stat. 2676, 2677.

§ 155.   Fee agreements in cases under Title 11 and receiverships

Whoever, being a party in interest, whether as a debtor, creditor, receiver, trustee or representative of any of them, or attorney for any such party in interest, in any receivership or case under title 11 in any United States court or under its supervision, knowingly and fraudulently enters into any agreement, express or implied, with another such party in interest or attorney for another such party in interest, for the purpose of fixing the fees or other compensation to be paid to any party in interest or to any attorney for any party in interest for services rendered in connection therewith, from the assets of the estate, shall be fined not more than $5,000 or imprisoned not more than one year, or both.

June 25, 1948, c. 645, 62 Stat. 690; May 24, 1949, c. 139, § 4, 63 Stat. 90; Nov. 6, 1978, Pub.L. 95–598, Title III, § 314(f)(1), (2), 92 Stat. 2677.

CHAPTER 96—RACKETEER INFLUENCED AND CORRUPT ORGANIZATIONS

§ 1961. Definitions

As used in this chapter—

(1) "racketeering activity" means (A) any act or threat involving murder, kidnaping, gambling, arson, robbery, bribery, extortion, dealing in obscene matter, or dealing in narcotic or other dangerous drugs, which is chargeable under State law and punishable by imprisonment for more than one year; (B) any act which is indictable under any of the following provisions of title 18, United States Code: Section 201 (relating to bribery), section 224 (relating to sports bribery), sections 471, 472, and 473 (relating to counterfeiting), section 659 (relating to theft from interstate shipment) if the act indictable under section 659 is felonious, section 664 (relating to embezzlement from pension and welfare funds), sections 891–894 (relating to extortionate credit transactions), section 1029 (relating to fraud and related activity in connection with access devices), section 1084 (relating to the transmission of gambling information), section 1341 (relating to mail fraud), section 1343 (relating to wire fraud), section 1344 (relating to financial institution fraud), sections 1461–1465 (relating to obscene matter), section 1503 (relating to obstruction of justice), section 1510 (relating to obstruction of criminal investigations), section 1511 (relating to the obstruction of State or local law enforcement), section 1512 (relating to tampering with a witness, victim, or an informant), section 1513 (relating to retaliating against a witness, victim, or an informant), section 1951 (relating to interference with commerce, robbery, or extortion), section 1952 (relating to racketeering), section 1953 (relating to interstate transportation of wagering paraphernalia), section 1954 (relating to unlawful welfare fund payments), section 1955 (relating to the prohibition of illegal gambling businesses), section 1956 (relating to the laundering of monetary instruments), section 1957 (relating to engaging in monetary transactions in property derived from specified unlawful activity), section 1958 (relating to use of interstate commerce facilities in the commission of murder-for-hire), sections 2251–2252 (relating to sexual exploitation of children), sections 2312 and 2313 (relating to interstate transportation of stolen motor vehicles), sections 2314 and 2315 (relating to interstate transportation of stolen property), section 2321 (relating to trafficking in certain motor vehicles or motor vehicle parts), sections 2341–2346 (relating to trafficking in contraband cigarettes), sections 2421–24 (relating to white slave traffic), (C) any act which is indictable under title 29, United States Code, section 186 (dealing with restrictions on payments and loans to labor organizations) or section 501(c) (relating to embezzlement from union funds), or (D) any offense involving fraud connected with a case under title 11, fraud in the sale of securities, or the felonious manufacture, importation, receiving, concealment, buying, selling, or otherwise dealing in narcotic or other dangerous drugs, punishable under any law of the United States, or (E) any act which is indictable under the Currency and Foreign Transactions Reporting Act;

(2) "State" means any State of the United States, the District of Columbia, the Commonwealth of Puerto Rico, any territory or possession of the United States, any political subdivision, or any department, agency, or instrumentality thereof;

(3) "person" includes any individual or entity capable of holding a legal or beneficial interest in property;

(4) "enterprise" includes any individual, partnership, corporation, association, or other legal entity, and any union or group of individuals associated in fact although not a legal entity;

(5) "pattern of racketeering activity" requires at least two acts of racketeering activity, one of which occurred after the effective date of this chapter and the last of which occurred within ten years (excluding any period of imprisonment) after the commission of a prior act of racketeering activity;

(6) "unlawful debt" means a debt (A) incurred or contracted in gambling activity which was in violation of the law of the United States, a State or political subdivision thereof, or which is unenforceable under State or Federal law in whole or in part as to principal or interest because of the laws relating to usury, and (B) which was incurred in connection with the business of gambling in violation of the law of the United States, a State or political subdivision thereof, or the business of lending money or a thing of value at a rate usurious under State or Federal law, where the usurious rate is at least twice the enforceable rate;

(7) "racketeering investigator" means any attorney or investigator so designated by the Attorney General and charged with the duty of enforcing or carrying into effect this chapter;

(8) "racketeering investigation" means any inquiry conducted by any racketeering investigator for the purpose of ascertaining whether any person has been involved in any violation of this chapter or of any final order, judgment, or decree of any court of the United States, duly entered in any case or proceeding arising under this chapter;

(9) "documentary material" includes any book, paper, document, record, recording, or other material; and

(10) "Attorney General" includes the Attorney General of the United States, the Deputy Attorney General of the United States, the Associate Attorney General of the United States, any Assistant Attorney General of the United States, or any employee of the Department of Justice or any employee of any department or agency of the United States so designated by the Attorney General to carry out the powers conferred on the Attorney General by this chapter. Any department or agency so designated may use in investigations authorized by this chapter either the investigative provisions of this chapter or the investigative power of such department or agency otherwise conferred by law.

Added Pub.L. 91–452, Title IX, § 901(a), Oct. 15, 1970, 84 Stat. 941, and amended Pub.L. 95–575, § 3(c), Nov. 2, 1978, 92 Stat. 2465; Pub.L. 95–598, Title III, § 314(g), Nov. 6, 1978, 92 Stat. 2677; Pub.L. 98–473, Title II, §§ 901(g), 1020, Oct. 12, 1984, 98 Stat. 2136, 2143; Pub.L. 98–547, Title II, § 205, Oct. 25, 1984, 98 Stat. 2770; Pub.L. 99–570, Title I, § 1365(b), Oct. 27, 1986, 100 Stat. 3207–35; Pub.L. 99–646, § 50(a), Nov. 10, 1986, 100 Stat. 3605; Pub.L. 100–690, Title VII,

§§ 7013, 7019(c), 7032, 7054, 7514, Nov. 18, 1988, 102 Stat. 4395, 4396, 4398, 4402, 4489; Pub.L. 101–73, Title IX, § 968, Aug. 9, 1989, 103 Stat. 506; Pub.L. 101–647, Title XXXV, § 3560, Nov. 29, 1990, 104 Stat. 4927.

CHAPTER 119—WIRE INTERCEPTION AND INTERCEPTION OF ORAL COMMUNICATIONS

§ 2516. Authorization for interception of wire, oral, or electronic communications

(1) The Attorney General, Deputy Attorney General, Associate Attorney General, or any Assistant Attorney General, any acting Assistant Attorney General, or any Deputy Assistant Attorney General in the Criminal Division specially designated by the Attorney General, may authorize an application to a Federal judge of competent jurisdiction for, and such judge may grant in conformity with section 2518 of this chapter an order authorizing or approving the interception of wire or oral communications by the Federal Bureau of Investigation, or a Federal agency having responsibility for the investigation of the offense as to which the application is made, when such interception may provide or has provided evidence of—

(a) any offense punishable by death or by imprisonment for more than one year under sections 2274 through 2277 of title 42 of the United States Code (relating to the enforcement of the Atomic Energy Act of 1954), section 2284 of title 42 of the United States Code (relating to sabotage of nuclear facilities or fuel), or under the following chapters of this title: chapter 37 (relating to espionage), chapter 105 (relating to sabotage), chapter 115 (relating to treason), chapter 102 (relating to riots), chapter 65 (relating to malicious mischief, chapter 111 (relating to destruction of vessels), or chapter 81 (relating to piracy);

(b) a violation of section 186 or section 501(c) of title 29, United States Code (dealing with restrictions on payments and loans to labor organizations), or any offense which involves murder, kidnapping, robbery, or extortion, and which is punishable under this title;

(c) any offense which is punishable under the following sections of this title: section 201 (bribery of public officials and witnesses), section 215 (relating to bribery of bank officials), section 224 (bribery in sporting contests), subsection (d), (e), (f), (g), (h), or (i) of section 844 (unlawful use of explosives), section 1032 (relating to concealment of assets), section 1084 (transmission of wagering information), section 751 (relating to escape), section 1014 (relating to loans and credit applications generally; renewals and discounts), sections 1503, 1512, and 1513 (influencing or injuring an officer, juror, or witness generally), section 1510 (obstruction of criminal investigations), section 1511 (obstruction of State or local law enforcement), section 1751 (Presidential and Presidential staff assassination, kidnaping, and assault), section 1951 (interference with commerce by threats or violence), section 1952 (interstate and foreign travel or transportation in aid of racketeering enterprises), section 1958 (relating to use of interstate commerce facilities in the commission of murder for hire), section 1959 (relating to violent crimes in aid of racketeering activity), section 1954 (offer, acceptance, or solicitation to influence operations of employee benefit plan), section

1955 (prohibition of business enterprises of gambling), section 1956 (laundering of monetary instruments), section 1957 (relating to engaging in monetary transactions in property derived from specified unlawful activity), section 659 (theft from interstate shipment), section 664 (embezzlement from pension and welfare funds), section 1343 (fraud by wire, radio, or television), section 1344 (relating to bank fraud), sections 2251 and 2252 (sexual exploitation of children), sections 2312, 2313, 2314, and 2315 (interstate transportation of stolen property), section 2321 (relating to trafficking in certain motor vehicles or motor vehicle parts), section 1203 (relating to hostage taking), section 1029 (relating to fraud and related activity in connection with access devices), section 3146 (relating to penalty for failure to appear), section 3521(b)(3) (relating to witness relocation and assistance), section 32 (relating to destruction of aircraft or aircraft facilities), section 1963 (violations with respect to racketeer influenced and corrupt organizations), section 115 (relating to threatening or retaliating against a Federal official), and section 1341 (relating to mail fraud), or section 351 (violations with respect to congressional, Cabinet, or Supreme Court assassinations, kidnaping, and assault), section 831 (relating to prohibited transactions involving nuclear materials), section 33 (relating to destruction of motor vehicles or motor vehicle facilities), section 175 (relating to biological weapons), or section 1992 (relating to wrecking trains);

(d) any offense involving counterfeiting punishable under section 471, 472, or 473 of this title;

(e) any offense involving fraud connected with a case under title 11 or the manufacture, importation, receiving, concealment, buying, selling, or otherwise dealing in narcotic drugs, marihuana, or other dangerous drugs, punishable under any law of the United States;

(f) any offense including extortionate credit transactions under sections 892, 893, or 894 of this title;

(g) a violation of section 5322 of title 31, United States Code (dealing with the reporting of currency transactions);

(h) any felony violation of sections 2511 and 2512 (relating to interception and disclosure of certain communications and to certain intercepting devices) of this title;

(i) any felony violation of chapter 71 (relating to obscenity) of this title;

(j) any violation of section 11(c)(2) of the Natural Gas Pipeline Safety Act of 1968 (relating to destruction of a natural gas pipeline) or section 902(i) or (n) of the Federal Aviation Act of 1958 (relating to aircraft piracy);

(k) any criminal violation of section 2778 of title 22 (relating to the Arms Export Control Act);

(l) the location of any fugitive from justice from an offense described in this section; or

(m) any felony violation of sections 922 and 924 of title 18, United States Code (relating to firearms);

(n) any violation of section 5861 of the Internal Revenue Code of 1986 (relating to firearms); and

(o) any conspiracy to commit any offense described in any subparagraph of this paragraph.

(2) The principal prosecuting attorney of any State, or the principal prosecuting attorney of any political subdivision thereof, if such attorney is authorized by a statute of that State to make application to a State court judge of competent jurisdiction for an order authorizing or approving the interception of wire, oral, or electronic communications, may apply to such judge for, and such judge may grant in conformity with section 2518 of this chapter and with the applicable State statute an order authorizing, or approving the interception of wire, oral, or electronic communications by investigative or law enforcement officers having responsibility for the investigation of the offense as to which the application is made, when such interception may provide or has provided evidence of the commission of the offense of murder, kidnapping, gambling, robbery, bribery, extortion, or dealing in narcotic drugs, marihuana or other dangerous drugs, or other crime dangerous to life, limb, or property, and punishable by imprisonment for more than one year, designated in any applicable State statute authorizing such interception, or any conspiracy to commit any of the foregoing offenses.

(3) Any attorney for the Government (as such term is defined for the purposes of the Federal Rules of Criminal Procedure) may authorize an application to a Federal judge of competent jurisdiction for, and such judge may grant, in conformity with section 2518 of this title, an order authorizing or approving the interception of electronic communications by an investigative or law enforcement officer having responsibility for the investigation of the offense as to which the application is made, when such interception may provide or has provided evidence of any Federal felony.

Added Pub.L. 90–351, Title III, § 802, June 19, 1968, 82 Stat. 216, and amended Pub.L. 91–452, Title VIII, § 810, Title IX, § 902(a), Title XI, § 1103, Oct. 15, 1970, 84 Stat. 940, 947, 959; Pub.L. 91–644, Title IV, § 16, Jan. 2, 1971, 84 Stat. 1891; Pub.L. 95–598, Title III, § 314(h), Nov. 6, 1978, 92 Stat. 2677; Pub.L. 97–285, §§ 2(e), 4(e), Oct. 6, 1982, 96 Stat. 1220, 1221; Pub.L. 98–292, § 8, May 21, 1984, 98 Stat. 206; Pub.L. 98–473, Title II, § 1203(c), Oct. 12, 1984, 98 Stat. 2152; Pub.L. 99–508, Title I, §§ 101(c)(1)(A), 104, 105, Oct. 21, 1986, 100 Stat. 1851, 1855; Pub.L. 99–570, Title I, § 1365(c), Oct. 27, 1986, 100 Stat. 3207–35; Pub.L. 100–690, Title VI, § 6461, Title VII, §§ 7036, 7053(d), 7525, Nov. 18, 1988, 102 Stat. 4374, 4499, 4402, 4502; Pub.L. 101–298, § 3(b), May 22, 1990, 104 Stat. 203; Pub.L. 101–647, Title XXV, § 2531, Title XXXV, § 3568, Nov. 29, 1990, 104 Stat. 4879, 4928.

Historical Note

References in Text. Section 11(c)(2) of the Natural Gas Pipeline Safety Act of 1968, referred to in par. (1)(j), is classified to section 1679a(c)(2) of the Appendix to Title 49, Transportation.

Section 902(i) or (n) of the Federal Aviation Act of 1958, referred to in par. (1)(j), is classified to section 1472(i) or (n) of the Appendix to Title 49.

Codification. Pub.L. 101–647, §§ 2531(3) and 3568, made substantially similar amendments to subsec. (1)(j) of this section and amendment by section 3568 of Pub.L. 101–647

has been executed to text as the probable intent of Congress, and notwithstanding impossibility of execution in view of amendment by section 2531(3) which struck out language assumed still to be in text in amendment by section 3568.

Effective Date of 1986 Amendment. Amendment of section effective 90 days after Oct. 21, 1986, and, in the case of conduct pursuant to a court order or extension, applicable only with respect to court orders or extensions made after Title I of Pub.L. 99–508 takes effect, except that any interception pursuant to par. (2) of this section which would be valid and lawful without regard to the amendments made by this Title I of Pub.L. 99–508 shall be valid and lawful notwithstanding such amendments if such interception occurs during the period beginning on the date such amendments take effect and ending on the earlier of the day before the date of the taking effect of State law conforming to the applicable State statute with chapter 119 of title 18, United States Code, as so amended; or the date two years after Oct. 21, 1986, and amendments made by section 104 of Pub.L. 99–508 effective on Oct. 21, 1986, see section 111 of Pub.L. 99–508.

CHAPTER 203—ARREST AND COMMITMENT

§ 3057. Bankruptcy investigations

(a) Any judge, receiver, or trustee having reasonable grounds for believing that any violation under chapter 9 of this title or other laws of the United States relating to insolvent debtors, receiverships or reorganization plans has been committed, or that an investigation should be had in connection therewith, shall report to the appropriate United States attorney all the facts and circumstances of the case, the names of the witnesses and the offense or offenses believed to have been committed. Where one of such officers has made such report, the others need not do so.

(b) The United States attorney thereupon shall inquire into the facts and report thereon to the judge, and if it appears probable that any such offense has been committed, shall without delay, present the matter to the grand jury, unless upon inquiry and examination he decides that the ends of public justice do not require investigation or prosecution, in which case he shall report the facts to the Attorney General for his direction.

June 25, 1948, c. 645, 62 Stat. 818; May 24, 1949, c. 139, § 48, 63 Stat. 96; Nov. 6, 1978, Pub.L. 95–598, Title III, § 314(i), 92 Stat. 2677.

CHAPTER 213—LIMITATIONS

§ 3284. Concealment of bankrupt's assets

The concealment of assets of a debtor in a case under Title 11 shall be deemed to be a continuing offense until the debtor shall have been finally discharged or a discharge denied, and the period of limitations shall not begin to run until such final discharge or denial of discharge.

June 25, 1948, c. 645, 62 Stat. 828; Nov. 6, 1978, Pub.L. 95–598, Title III, § 314(k), 92 Stat. 2678.

PART V—IMMUNITY OF WITNESSES

§ 6001. Definitions

As used in this part—

(1) "agency of the United States" means any executive department as defined in section 101 of title 5, United States Code, a military department as defined in section 102 of title 5, United States Code, the Atomic Energy Commission, the China Trade Act registrar appointed under 53 Stat. 1432 (15 U.S.C. sec. 143), the Civil Aeronautics Board, the Commodity Futures Trading Commission, the Federal Communications Commission, the Federal

Deposit Insurance Corporation, the Federal Maritime Commission, the Federal Power Commission, the Federal Trade Commission, the Interstate Commerce Commission, the National Labor Relations Board, the National Transportation Safety Board, the Railroad Retirement Board, an arbitration board established under 48 Stat. 1193 (45 U.S.C. sec. 157), the Securities and Exchange Commission, the Subversive Activities Control Board, or a board established under 49 Stat. 31 (15 U.S.C. sec. 715d);

(2) "other information" includes any book, paper, document, record, recording, or other material;

(3) "proceeding before an agency of the United States" means any proceeding before such an agency with respect to which it is authorized to issue subpenas and to take testimony or receive other information from witnesses under oath; and

(4) "court of the United States" means any of the following courts: the Supreme Court of the United States, a United States court of appeals, a United States district court established under chapter 5, title 28, United States Code, a United States bankruptcy court established under chapter 6, title 28, United States Code, the District of Columbia Court of Appeals, the Superior Court of the District of Columbia, the District Court of Guam, the District Court of the Virgin Islands, the United States Claims Court, the Tax Court of the United States, the Court of International Trade, and the Court of Military Appeals.

Added Pub.L. 91–452, Title II, § 201(a), Oct. 15, 1970, 84 Stat. 926, and amended Pub.L. 95–405, § 25, Sept. 30, 1978, 92 Stat. 877; Pub.L. 95–598, Title III, § 314(*l*), Nov. 6, 1978, 92 Stat. 2678; Pub.L. 96–417, Title VI, § 601(1), Oct. 10, 1980, 94 Stat. 1744; Pub.L. 97–164, Title I, § 164(1), Apr. 2, 1982, 96 Stat. 50.

TITLE 28

JUDICIARY AND JUDICIAL PROCEDURE

PART I—ORGANIZATION OF COURTS

CHAPTER 6—BANKRUPTCY JUDGES

Sec.
151. Designation of bankruptcy courts.
152. Appointment of bankruptcy judges.
153. Salaries; character of service.
154. Division of businesses; chief judge.
155. Temporary transfer of bankruptcy judges.
156. Staff; expenses.
157. Procedures.
158. Appeals.

---

§ 151. Designation of bankruptcy courts

In each judicial district, the bankruptcy judges in regular active service shall constitute a unit of the district court to be known as the bankruptcy court for that district. Each bankruptcy judge, as a judicial officer of the district court, may exercise the authority conferred under this chapter with respect to any action, suit, or proceeding and may preside alone and hold a regular or special session of the court, except as otherwise provided by law or by rule or order of the district court.

Added Pub.L. 98–353, Title I, § 104(a), July 10, 1984, 98 Stat. 336.

Historical Note

Effective Date of 1984 Amendments. Section 122 of Pub.L. 98–353, July 10, 1984, 98 Stat. 346, provided that:

"(a) Except as otherwise provided in this section, this title and the amendments made by this title [Title I of Pub.L. 98–353, enacting sections 151 to 158, 1408 to 1412, and 1452 of Title 28, Judiciary and Judicial Procedure; amending sections 372, 634, 957, 1334, 1360, and 1930 of Title 28, sections 8331, 8334, 8336, 8339, 8341, and 8344 of Title 5, Government Organization and Employees; and section 105 of Title 11, Bankruptcy; enacting provisions set out as notes under sections 151, 152, 153, 634, and 1334 of Title 28 and section 8331 of Title 5; and repealing provisions set out as notes preceding sections 151 and 1471 of Title 28] shall take effect on the date of the enactment of this Act [July 10, 1984].

"(b) Section 1334(c)(2) of title 28, United States Code, and section 1411(a) of title 28, United States Code, as added by this Act, shall not apply with respect to cases under title 11 of the United States Code [Title 11, Bankruptcy] that are pending on the date of enactment of this Act [July 10, 1984], or to proceedings arising in or related to such cases.

"(c) Sections 108(b) [set out as a note under section 634 of Title 28], 113 [amending section 402(b) of Pub.L. 95–598, set out as a note preceding chapter 1 of Title 11, Bankruptcy], and 121(e) [set out as a note below] shall take effect on June 27, 1984."

Term of Office of Bankruptcy Judges Serving on March 31, 1984. Section 2 of Pub.L. 98–249, Mar. 31, 1984, 98 Stat. 116, provided that: "The term of office of any bankruptcy judge who was serving on March

441

31, 1984 and of any bankruptcy judge who is serving on the date of the enactment of this Act [Mar. 31, 1984] is extended to and shall expire on May 1, 1984."

Term of Office of Bankruptcy Judges Serving on April 30, 1984. Section 2 of Pub. L. 98–271, Apr. 30, 1984, 98 Stat. 163, provided that: "The term of office of any bankruptcy judge who was serving on April 30, 1984, and of any bankruptcy judge who is serving on the date of the enactment of this Act [Apr. 30, 1984] is extended to and shall expire on May 25, 1984."

Term of Office of Bankruptcy Judges Serving on May 25, 1984. Section 2 of Pub. L. 98–299, May 25, 1984, 98 Stat. 214, provided that: "The term of office of any bankruptcy judge who was serving on May 25, 1984, and of any bankruptcy judge who is serving on the date of the enactment of this Act [May 25, 1984] is extended to and shall expire on June 20, 1984."

Term of Office of Bankruptcy Judges Serving on June 20, 1984. Section 2 of Pub. L. 98–325, June 20, 1984, 98 Stat. 268, provided that: "The term of office of any bankruptcy judge who was serving on June 20, 1984, and of any bankruptcy judge who is serving on the date of the enactment of this Act [June 20, 1984] is extended to and shall expire on June 27, 1984."

Term of Office of Bankruptcy Judges Serving on June 27, 1984. Section 121(e) of Pub.L. 98–353, July 10, 1984, 98 Stat. 346, provided that: "The term of office of any bankruptcy judge who was serving on June 27, 1984, is extended to and shall expire at the end of the day of enactment of this Act [July 10, 1984]."

[Section 121(e) of Pub.L. 98–353 effective June 27, 1984, see section 122(c) of Pub.L. 98–353, set out as an Effective Date note above.]

§ 152. Appointment of bankruptcy judges

(a)(1) The United States court of appeals for the circuit shall appoint bankruptcy judges for the judicial districts established in paragraph (2) in such numbers as are established in such paragraph. Such appointments shall be made after considering the recommendations of the Judicial Conference submitted pursuant to subsection (b). Each bankruptcy judge shall be appointed for a term of fourteen years, subject to the provisions of subsection (e). However, upon the expiration of the term, a bankruptcy judge may, with the approval of the judicial council of the circuit, continue to perform the duties of the office until the earlier of the date which is 180 days after the expiration of the term or the date of the appointment of a successor. Bankruptcy judges shall serve as judicial officers of the United States district court established under Article III of the Constitution.

(2) The bankruptcy judges appointed pursuant to this section shall be appointed for the several judicial districts as follows:

Districts	Judges
Alabama:	
Northern	5
Middle	2
Southern	2
Alaska	2
Arizona	5
Arkansas:	
Eastern and Western	3
California:	
Northern	9
Eastern	6
Central	19
Southern	4
Colorado	5
Connecticut	2
Delaware	1

Districts	Judges
District of Columbia	1
Florida:	
Northern	1
Middle	4
Southern	3
Georgia:	
Northern	6
Middle	2
Southern	2
Hawaii	1
Idaho	2
Illinois:	
Northern	10
Central	3
Southern	1
Indiana:	
Northern	3
Southern	4
Iowa:	
Northern	2
Southern	2
Kansas	4
Kentucky:	
Eastern	2
Western	3
Louisiana:	
Eastern	2
Middle	1
Western	3
Maine	2
Maryland	3
Massachusetts	4
Michigan:	
Eastern	4
Western	3
Minnesota	4
Mississippi:	
Northern	1
Southern	2
Missouri:	
Eastern	3
Western	3
Montana	1
Nebraska	2
Nevada	3
New Hampshire	1
New Jersey	7
New Mexico	2
New York:	
Northern	2
Southern	7
Eastern	6
Western	3

Districts	Judges
North Carolina:	
Eastern	2
Middle	2
Western	2
North Dakota	1
Ohio:	
Northern	8
Southern	7
Oklahoma:	
Northern	2
Eastern	1
Western	3
Oregon	5
Pennsylvania:	
Eastern	3
Middle	2
Western	4
Puerto Rico	2
Rhode Island	1
South Carolina	2
South Dakota	2
Tennessee:	
Eastern	3
Middle	2
Western	3
Texas:	
Northern	5
Eastern	2
Southern	6
Western	4
Utah	3
Vermont	1
Virginia:	
Eastern	4
Western	3
Washington:	
Eastern	2
Western	5
West Virginia:	
Northern	1
Southern	1
Wisconsin:	
Eastern	4
Western	2
Wyoming	1

(3) Whenever a majority of the judges of any court of appeals cannot agree upon the appointment of a bankruptcy judge, the chief judge of such court shall make such appointment.

(4) The judges of the district courts for the territories shall serve as the bankruptcy judges for such courts. The United States court of appeals for the circuit within which such a territorial district court is located may appoint bankruptcy judges under this chapter for such district if authorized to do so by the Congress of the United States under this section.

(b)(1) The Judicial Conference of the United States shall, from time to time, and after considering the recommendations submitted by the Director of the Administrative Office of the United States Courts after such Director has consulted with the judicial council of the circuit involved, determine the official duty stations of bankruptcy judges and places of holding court.

(2) The Judicial Conference shall, from time to time, submit recommendations to the Congress regarding the number of bankruptcy judges needed and the districts in which such judges are needed.

(c) Each bankruptcy judge may hold court at such places within the judicial district, in addition to the official duty station of such judge, as the business of the court may require.

(d) With the approval of the Judicial Conference and of each of the judicial councils involved, a bankruptcy judge may be designated to serve in any district adjacent to or near the district for which such bankruptcy judge was appointed.

(e) A bankruptcy judge may be removed during the term for which such bankruptcy judge is appointed, only for incompetence, misconduct, neglect of duty, or physical or mental disability and only by the judicial council of the circuit in which the judge's official duty station is located. Removal may not occur unless a majority of all of the judges of such council concur in the order of removal. Before any order of removal may be entered, a full specification of charges shall be furnished to such bankruptcy judge who shall be accorded an opportunity to be heard on such charges.

Added Pub.L. 98–353, Title I, § 104(a), July 10, 1984, 98 Stat. 336, and amended Pub.L. 99–554, Title I, § 101, Oct. 27, 1986, 100 Stat. 3088; Pub.L 100–587, Nov. 3, 1988, 102 Stat. 2982; Pub.L 101–650, Title III, § 304, Dec. 1, 1990, 104 Stat. 5105.

Historical Note

Effective Date of 1986 Amendment. Amendment by Pub.L. 99–554 effective on Oct. 27, 1986, see section 302(b) of Pub.L. 99–554, set out as a note under section 581 of this title.

Effective Date. For effective date of amendments by Title I of Pub.L. 98–353, see section 122 of Pub.L. 98–353, Title I, July 10, 1984, 98 Stat. 346, set out as an Effective Date of 1984 Amendment note under section 151 of Title 28, Judiciary and Judicial Procedure.

Extension and Termination of Term of Office of Part-Time Bankruptcy Judge Serving on July 2, 1986, In District of Oregon, Western District of Michigan, and Eastern District of Oklahoma. Pub.L. 99–349, Title I, c. II, July 2, 1986, 100 Stat. 718, provided that: "Notwithstanding the provisions of section 106(b)(1) of the Bankruptcy Amendments and Federal Judgeship Act of 1984 [section 106(b)(1) of Pub.L. 98–353, set out as a note under this section], a bankruptcy judge serving on a part-time basis on the date of enactment of this Act [July 2, 1986] may continue to serve as a part-time judge for such district until December 31, 1986, or until such time as a full-time bankruptcy judge for such

district is appointed, whichever is earlier: *Provided,* That these provisions shall apply only to part-time bankruptcy judges serving in the district of Oregon, the western district of Michigan, and the eastern district of Oklahoma."

Extension and Termination of Term of Office of Bankruptcy Judge and Part-Time Bankruptcy Judge Serving on July 10, 1984; Practice of Law by Part-Time Bankruptcy Judge. Section 106 of Pub.L. 98–353 provided that:

"(a) Notwithstanding section 152 of title 28, United States Code, as added by this Act, the term of office of a bankruptcy judge who is serving on the date of enactment of this Act [July 10, 1984] is extended to and expires four years after the date such bankruptcy judge was last appointed to such office or on October 1, 1986, whichever is later.

"(b)(1) Notwithstanding section 153(a) of title 28, United States Code, as added by this Act, and notwithstanding subsection (a) of this section [subsec. (a) of this note], a bankruptcy judge serving on a part-time basis on the date of enactment of this Act may continue to serve on such basis for a period not to exceed two years from the date of enactment of this Act.

"(2) Notwithstanding the provisions of section 153(b) of title 28, United States Code, a bankruptcy judge serving on a part-time basis may engage in the practice of law but may not engage in any other practice, business, occupation, or employment inconsistent with the expeditious, proper, and impartial performance of such bankruptcy judge's duties as a judicial officer. The Judicial Conference of the United States may promulgate appropriate rules and regulations to implement this paragraph."

[For effective date of section 106 of Pub.L. 98–353, see section 122 of Pub.L. 98–353, Title I, July 10, 1984, 98 Stat. 346, set out as an Effective Date of 1984 Amendment note under section 151 of Title 28, Judiciary and Judicial Procedure.]

Appointment to Fill Vacancies; Nominations; Qualifications. Section 120 of Pub.L. 98–353, Title I, July 10, 1984, 98 Stat. 344, as amended by Pub.L. 99–554, Title I, § 102, Oct. 27, 1986, 100 Stat. 3089, provided that:

"(a)(1) Whenever a court of appeals is authorized to fill a vacancy that occurs on a bankruptcy court of the United States, such court of appeals shall appoint to fill that vacancy a person whose character, experience, ability, and impartiality qualify such person to serve in the Federal judiciary.

"(2) It is the sense of the Congress that the courts of appeals should consider for appointment under section 152 of title 28, United States Code, to the first vacancy which arises after the date of the enactment of this Act [July 10, 1984] in the office of each bankruptcy judge, the bankruptcy judge who holds such office immediately before such vacancy arises, if such bankruptcy judge requests to be considered for such appointment.

"(b) The judicial council of the circuit involved shall assist the court of appeals by evaluating potential nominees and by recommending to such court for consideration for appointment to each vacancy on the bankruptcy court persons who are qualified to be bankruptcy judges under regulations prescribed by the Judicial Conference of the United States. In the case of the first vacancy which arises after the date of the enactment of this Act [July 10, 1984] in the office of each

bankruptcy judge, such potential nominees shall include the bankruptcy judge who holds such office immediately before such vacancy arises, if such bankruptcy judge requests to be considered for such appointment and the judicial council determines that such judge is qualified under subsection (c) of this section to continue to serve. Such potential nominees shall receive consideration equal to that given all other potential nominees for such position.

"(c) Before transmitting to the court of appeals the names of the persons the judicial council for the circuit deems best qualified to fill any existing vacancy, the judicial council shall have determined that—

"(1) public notice of such vacancy has been given and an effort has been made, in the case of each such vacancy, to identify qualified candidates, without regard to race, color, sex, religion, or national origin,

"(2) such persons are members in good standing of at least one State bar, the District of Columbia bar, or the bar of the Commonwealth of Puerto Rico, and members in good standing of every other bar of which they are members,

"(3) such persons possess, and have a reputation for, integrity and good character,

"(4) such persons are of sound physical and mental health,

"(5) such persons possess and have demonstrated commitment to equal justice under law,

"(6) such persons possess and have demonstrated outstanding legal ability and competence, as evidenced by substantial legal experience, ability to deal with complex legal problems, aptitude for legal scholarship and writing, and familiarity with courts and court processes, and

"(7) such persons [sic] demeanor, character, and personality indicate that they would exhibit judicial temperament if appointed to the position of United States bankruptcy judge."

[For effective date of section 120 of Pub.L. 98–353, see section 122 of Pub.L. 98–353, Title I, July 10, 1984, 98 Stat. 346, set out as an Effective Date of 1984 Amendment note under section 151 of Title 28, Judiciary and Judicial Procedure.]

§ 153. Salaries; character of service

(a) Each bankruptcy judge shall serve on a full-time basis and shall receive as full compensation for his services, a salary at an annual rate that is equal to 92 percent of the salary of a judge of the district court of the United States as determined pursuant to section 135, to be paid at such times as the Judicial Conference of the United States determines.

(b) A bankruptcy judge may not engage in the practice of law and may not engage in any other practice, business, occupation, or employment inconsistent with the expeditious, proper, and impartial performance of such bankruptcy judge's duties as a judicial officer. The Conference may promulgate appropriate rules and regulations to implement this subsection.

(c) Each individual appointed under this chapter shall take the oath or affirmation prescribed by section 453 of this title before performing the duties of the office of bankruptcy judge.

(d) A bankruptcy judge appointed under this chapter shall be exempt from the provisions of subchapter I of chapter 63 of title 5.

Added Pub.L. 98–353, Title I, § 104(a), July 10, 1984, 98 Stat. 338; and amended Pub.L. 100–202, § 101(a) [Title IV, § 408(a)], Dec. 22, 1987, 101 Stat. 1329–26; Pub.L. 100–702, Title X, § 1003(a)(1), Nov. 19, 1988, 102 Stat. 4665.

Historical Note

Effective Date of 1987 Amendment. Section 101 (a) [Title IV, § 408(d)] of Pub.L. 100–202 provided that: "This section [amending this section, section 634 of this title, and section 356 of title 2, The Congress] shall become effective October 1, 1988, and any salary affected by the provisions of this section shall be adjusted at the beginning of the first applicable pay period commencing on or after such date of enactment."

Effective Date. For effective date of amendments by Title I of Pub.L. 98–353, see section 122 of Pub.L. 98–353, Title I, July 10, 1984, 98 Stat. 346, set out as an Effective Date of 1984 Amendment note under section 151 of Title 28, Judiciary and Judicial Procedure.

Transition Provisions. Section 1003(b) of Pub.L. 100–702 provided that:

"(1) If an individual who is exempted from the Leave Act by operation of amendments under this section [amending this section and sections 156, 631, 634, 712, 752, and 794 of this title] and who was previously subject to the provisions of subchapter I of chapter 63 of Title 5, United States Code [section 6301 et seq. of Title 5, Government Organization and Employees] without a break in service, again becomes subject to this subchapter on completion of his service as an exempted officer, the unused annual leave and sick leave standing to his credit when he was exempted from this sub-

chapter is deemed to have remained to his credit.

"(2) In computing an annuity under section 8339 of Title 5, United States Code [section 8339 of Title 5], the total service of a person specified in paragraph (1) of this subsection who retired on an immediate annuity or dies leaving a survivor or survivors entitled to an annuity includes, without regard to the limitations imposed by subsection (f) of section 8339 of title 5, United States Code, the days of unused sick leave standing to his credit when he was exempted from subchapter I of chapter 63 of title 5, United States Code, except that these days will not be counted in determining average pay or annuity eligibility."

Continuation of Salaries of Bankruptcy Judges in Effect on June 27, 1984. Section 105(a) of Pub.L. 98–353, July 10, 1984, 98 Stat. 342, provided that: "The salary of a bankruptcy judge in effect on June 27, 1984, shall remain in effect until changed as a result of a determination or adjustment made pursuant to section 153(a) of title 28, United States Code, as added by this Act."

[For effective date of section 105 of Pub.L. 98–353, see section 122 of Pub.L. 98–353, Title I, July 10, 1984, 98 Stat. 346, set out as an Effective Date of 1984 Amendment note under section 151 of Title 28, Judiciary and Judicial Procedure.]

§ 154. Division of businesses; chief judge

(a) Each bankruptcy court for a district having more than one bankruptcy judge shall by majority vote promulgate rules for the division of business among the bankruptcy judges to the extent that the division of business is not otherwise provided for by the rules of the district court.

(b) In each district court having more than one bankruptcy judge the district court shall designate one judge to serve as chief judge of such bankruptcy court. Whenever a majority of the judges of such district court cannot agree upon the designation as chief judge, the chief judge of such district court shall make such designation. The chief judge of the bankruptcy court shall ensure that the rules of the bankruptcy court and of the district court are observed and that the business of the bankruptcy court is handled effectively and expeditiously.

Added Pub.L. 98–353, Title I, § 104(a), July 10, 1984, 98 Stat. 339.

Historical Note

Effective Date. For effective date of amendments by Title I of Pub.L. 98–353, see section 122 of Pub.L. 98–353, Title I, July 10, 1984, 98 Stat. 346, set out as an Effective Date of 1984 Amendment note under section 151 of Title 28, Judiciary and Judicial Procedure.

§ 155. Temporary transfer of bankruptcy judges

(a) A bankruptcy judge may be transferred to serve temporarily as a bankruptcy judge in any judicial district other than the judicial district for which such bankruptcy judge was appointed upon the approval of the judicial council of each of the circuits involved.

(b) A bankruptcy judge who has retired may, upon consent, be recalled to serve as a bankruptcy judge in any judicial district by the judicial council of the circuit within which such district is located. Upon recall, a bankruptcy judge may receive a salary for such service in accordance with regulations promulgated by the Judicial Conference of the United States, subject to the restrictions on the payment of an annuity in section 377 of this title or in subchapter III of chapter 83, and chapter 84, of title 5 which are applicable to such judge.

Added Pub.L. 98–353, Title I, § 104(a), July 10, 1984, 98 Stat. 339, and amended Pub.L. 99–651, Title II, § 202(a), Nov. 14, 1986, 100 Stat. 3648; Pub.L. 100–659, § 4(a), Nov. 15, 1988, 102 Stat. 3918.

Historical Note

Effective Date of 1988 Amendment. Section 9 of Pub.L. 100–659 provided that the amendments by Pub.L. 100–659 shall take effect on Nov. 15, 1988, and shall apply to bankruptcy judges and magistrates who retire on or after Nov. 15, 1988, with special election provisions for bankruptcy judges, etc., who left office on or after July 31, 1987, and before Nov. 15, 1988.

Effective Date of 1986 Amendment. Section 203 of Pub.L. 99–651 provided that

amendment of subsec. (b) by Pub.L. 99–651 is effective Jan. 1, 1987.

Effective Date. For effective date of amendments by Title I of Pub.L. 98–353, see section 122 of Pub.L. 98–353, Title I, July 10, 1984, 98 Stat. 346, set out as an Effective Date of 1984 Amendment note under section 151 of Title 28, Judiciary and Judicial Procedure.

§ 156. Staff; expenses

(a) Each bankruptcy judge may appoint a secretary, a law clerk, and such additional assistants as the Director of the Administrative Office of the United States Courts determines to be necessary. A law clerk appointed under this section shall be exempt from the provisions of subchapter I of chapter 63 of title 5, unless specifically included by the appointing judge or by local rule of court.

(b) Upon certification to the judicial council of the circuit involved and to the Director of the Administrative Office of the United States Courts that the number of cases and proceedings pending within the jurisdiction under section 1334 of this title within a judicial district so warrants, the bankruptcy judges for such district may appoint an individual to serve as clerk of such bankruptcy court. The clerk may appoint, with the approval of such bankruptcy judges, and in such number as may be approved by the Director, necessary deputies, and may remove such deputies with the approval of such bankruptcy judges.

(c) Any court may utilize facilities or services, either on or off the court's premises, which pertain to the provision of notices, dockets, calendars, and other administrative information to parties in cases filed under the provisions of title 11, United States Code, where the costs of such facilities or services are paid for out of the assets of the estate and are not charged to the United States. The utilization of such facilities or services shall be subject to such conditions and limitations as the pertinent circuit council may prescribe.

(d) No office of the bankruptcy clerk of court may be consolidated with the district clerk of court office without the prior approval of the Judicial Conference and the Congress.

(e) In a judicial district where a bankruptcy clerk has been appointed pursuant to subsection (b), the bankruptcy clerk shall be the official custodian of the records and dockets of the bankruptcy court.

(f) For purposes of financial accountability in a district where a bankruptcy clerk has been certified, such clerk shall be accountable for and pay into the Treasury all fees, costs, and other monies collected by such clerk except uncollected fees not required by an Act of Congress to be prepaid. Such clerk shall make returns thereof to the Director of the Administrative Office of the United States Courts and the Director of the Executive Office For United States Trustees, under regulations prescribed by such Directors.

Added Pub.L. 98–353, Title I, § 104(a), July 10, 1984, 98 Stat. 339, and amended Pub.L. 99–554, Title I, §§ 103, 142, 144(a), Oct. 27, 1986, 100 Stat. 3090, 3096; Pub.L. 100–702, Title X, § 1003(a)(3), Nov. 19, 1988, 102 Stat. 4665.

Historical Note

Effective Date of 1986 Amendment. Amendment of subsec. (d) by Pub.L. 99–554 effective on Oct. 27, 1986, see section 302(b) of Pub.L. 99–554, set out as a note under section 581 of this title.

Amendment of subsecs. (e) and (f) by Pub.L. 99–554 effective 30 days after Oct. 27, 1986, except as otherwise provided for, see section 302(a) of Pub.L. 99–554, set out as a note under section 581 of this title.

Effective Date. For effective date of amendments by Title I of Pub.L. 98–353, see section 122 of Pub.L. 98–353, Title I, July 10, 1984, 98 Stat. 346, set out as an Effective Date of 1984 Amendment note under section 151 of Title 28, Judiciary and Judicial Procedure.

§ 157. Procedures

(a) Each district court may provide that any or all cases under title 11 and any or all proceedings arising under title 11 or arising in or related to a case under title 11 shall be referred to the bankruptcy judges for the district.

(b)(1) Bankruptcy judges may hear and determine all cases under title 11 and all core proceedings arising under title 11, or arising in a case under title 11, referred under subsection (a) of this section, and may enter appropriate orders and judgments, subject to review under section 158 of this title.

(2) Core proceedings include, but are not limited to—

(A) matters concerning the administration of the estate;

(B) allowance or disallowance of claims against the estate or exemptions from property of the estate, and estimation of claims or interests for the purposes of confirming a plan under chapter 11, 12, or 13 of title 11 but not the liquidation or estimation of contingent or unliquidated personal injury tort or wrongful death claims against the estate for purposes of distribution in a case under title 11;

(C) counterclaims by the estate against persons filing claims against the estate;

(D) orders in respect to obtaining credit;

(E) orders to turn over property of the estate;

(F) proceedings to determine, avoid, or recover preferences;

(G) motions to terminate, annul, or modify the automatic stay;

(H) proceedings to determine, avoid, or recover fraudulent conveyances;

(I) determinations as to the dischargeability of particular debts;

(J) objections to discharges;

(K) determinations of the validity, extent, or priority of liens;

(L) confirmations of plans;

(M) orders approving the use or lease of property, including the use of cash collateral;

(N) orders approving the sale of property other than property resulting from claims brought by the estate against persons who have not filed claims against the estate; and

(O) other proceedings affecting the liquidation of the assets of the estate or the adjustment of the debtor-creditor or the equity security holder relationship, except personal injury tort or wrongful death claims.

(3) The bankruptcy judge shall determine, on the judge's own motion or on timely motion of a party, whether a proceeding is a core proceeding under this subsection or is a proceeding that is otherwise related to a case under title 11. A determination that a proceeding is not a core proceeding shall not be made solely on the basis that its resolution may be affected by State law.

(4) Non-core proceedings under section 157(b)(2)(B) of title 28, United States Code, shall not be subject to the mandatory abstention provisions of section 1334(c)(2).

(5) The district court shall order that personal injury tort and wrongful death claims shall be tried in the district court in which the bankruptcy case is pending, or in the district court in the district in which the claim arose, as determined by the district court in which the bankruptcy case is pending.

(c)(1) A bankruptcy judge may hear a proceeding that is not a core proceeding but that is otherwise related to a case under title 11. In such proceeding, the bankruptcy judge shall submit proposed findings of fact and conclusions of law to the district court, and any final order or judgment shall be entered by the district judge after considering the bankruptcy judge's proposed findings and conclusions and after reviewing de novo those matters to which any party has timely and specifically objected.

(2) Notwithstanding the provisions of paragraph (1) of this subsection, the district court, with the consent of all the parties to the proceeding, may refer a proceeding related to a case under title 11 to a bankruptcy judge to hear and determine and to enter appropriate orders and judgments, subject to review under section 158 of this title.

(d) The district court may withdraw, in whole or in part, any case or proceeding referred under this section, on its own motion or on timely motion of any party, for cause shown. The district court shall, on timely motion of a party, so withdraw a proceeding if the court determines that resolution of the proceeding requires consideration of both title 11 and other laws of the United States regulating organizations or activities affecting interstate commerce.

Added Pub.L. 98–353, Title I, § 104(a), July 10, 1984, 98 Stat. 340, and amended Pub.L. 99–554, Title I, §§ 143, 144(b), Oct. 27, 1986, 100 Stat. 3096.

Historical Note

Effective Date of 1986 Amendment. Amendment by Pub.L. 99–554 effective 30 days after Oct. 27, 1986, except as otherwise provided for, see section 302(a) of Pub.L. 99–554, set out as a note under section 581 of this title.

Effective Date. For effective date of amendments by Title I of Pub.L. 98–353, see section 122 of Pub.L. 98–353, Title I, July 10, 1984, 98 Stat. 346, set out as an Effective Date of 1984 Amendment note under section 151 of Title 28, Judiciary and Judicial Procedure.

§ 158. Appeals

(a) The district courts of the United States shall have jurisdiction to hear appeals from final judgments, orders, and decrees, and, with leave of the court, from interlocutory orders and decrees, of bankruptcy judges entered in cases and proceedings referred to the bankruptcy judges under section 157 of this title. An appeal under this subsection shall be taken only to the district court for the judicial district in which the bankruptcy judge is serving.

(b)(1) The judicial council of a circuit may establish a bankruptcy appellate panel, comprised of bankruptcy judges from districts within the circuit, to hear and determine, upon the consent of all the parties, appeals under subsection (a) of this section.

(2) If authorized by the Judicial Conference of the United States, the judicial councils of 2 or more circuits may establish a joint bankruptcy appellate panel comprised of bankruptcy judges from the districts within the circuits for which such panel is established, to hear and determine, upon the consent of all the parties, appeals under subsection (a) of this section.

(3) No appeal may be referred to a panel under this subsection unless the district judges for the district, by majority vote, authorize such referral of appeals originating within the district.

(4) A panel established under this section shall consist of three bankruptcy judges, provided a bankruptcy judge may not hear an appeal originating within a district for which the judge is appointed or designated under section 152 of this title.

(c) An appeal under subsections (a) and (b) of this section shall be taken in the same manner as appeals in civil proceedings generally are taken to the courts of appeals from the district courts and in the time provided by Rule 8002 of the Bankruptcy Rules.

(d) The courts of appeals shall have jurisdiction of appeals from all final decisions, judgments, orders, and decrees entered under subsections (a) and (b) of this section.

Added Pub.L. 98–353, Title I, § 104(a), July 10, 1984, 98 Stat. 341, and amended Pub.L 101–650, Title III, § 305, Dec. 1, 1990, 104 Stat. 5105.

Historical Note

Effective Date. For effective date of amendments by Title I of Pub.L. 98–353, see section 122 of Pub.L. 98–353, Title I, July 10, 1984, 98 Stat. 346, set out as an Effective Date of 1984 Amendment note under section 151 of Title 28, Judiciary and Judicial Procedure.

CHAPTER 17—RESIGNATION AND RETIREMENT OF JUSTICES AND JUDGES

§ 372. Retirement for disability; substitute judge on failure to retire; judicial discipline

(a) Any justice or judge of the United States appointed to hold office during good behavior who becomes permanently disabled from performing his duties may retire from regular active service, and the President shall, by and with the advice and consent of the Senate, appoint a successor.

Any justice or judge of the United States desiring to retire under this section shall certify to the President his disability in writing.

Whenever an associate justice of the Supreme Court, a chief judge of a circuit or the chief judge of the Court of International Trade, desires to retire under this section, he shall furnish to the President a certificate of disability signed by the Chief Justice of the United States.

A circuit or district judge, desiring to retire under this section, shall furnish to the President a certificate of disability signed by the chief judge of his circuit.

A judge of the Court of International Trade desiring to retire under this section, shall furnish to the President a certificate of disability signed by the chief judge of his court.

Each justice or judge retiring under this section after serving ten years continuously or otherwise shall, during the remainder of his lifetime, receive the salary of the office. A justice or judge retiring under this section who has served less than ten years in all shall, during the remainder of his lifetime, receive one-half the salary of the office.

(b) Whenever any judge of the United States appointed to hold office during good behavior who is eligible to retire under this section does not do so and a certificate of his disability signed by a majority of the members of the Judicial Council of his circuit in the case of a circuit or district judge, or by the Chief Justice of the United States in the case of the Chief Judge of the Court of International Trade, or by the chief judge of his court in the case of a judge of the Court of International Trade, is presented to the President and the President finds that such judge is unable to discharge efficiently all the duties of his office by reason of permanent mental or physical disability and that the appointment of an additional judge is necessary for the efficient dispatch of business, the

President may make such appointment by and with the advice and consent of the Senate. Whenever any such additional judge is appointed, the vacancy subsequently caused by the death, resignation, or retirement of the disabled judge shall not be filled. Any judge whose disability causes the appointment of an additional judge shall, for purpose of precedence, service [1] as chief judge, or temporary performance of the duties of that office, be treated as junior in commission to the other judges of the circuit, district, or court.

(c)(1) Any person alleging that a circuit, district, or bankruptcy judge, or a magistrate, has engaged in conduct prejudicial to the effective and expeditious administration of the business of the courts, or alleging that such a judge or magistrate is unable to discharge all the duties of office by reason of mental or physical disability, may file with the clerk of the court of appeals for the circuit a written complaint containing a brief statement of the facts constituting such conduct.

(2) Upon receipt of a complaint filed under paragraph (1) of this subsection, the clerk shall promptly transmit such complaint to the chief judge of the circuit, or, if the conduct complained of is that of the chief judge, to that circuit judge in regular active service next senior in date of commission (hereafter, for purposes of this subsection only, included in the term "chief judge"). The clerk shall simultaneously transmit a copy of the complaint to the judge or magistrate whose conduct is the subject of the complaint.

(3) After expeditiously reviewing a complaint, the chief judge, by written order stating his reasons, may—

(A) dismiss the complaint, if he finds it to be (i) not in conformity with paragraph (1) of this subsection, (ii) directly related to the merits of a decision or procedural ruling, or (iii) frivolous; or

(B) conclude the proceeding if he finds that appropriate corrective action has been taken.

The chief judge shall transmit copies of his written order to the complainant and to the judge or magistrate whose conduct is the subject of the complaint.

(4) If the chief judge does not enter an order under paragraph (3) of this subsection, such judge shall promptly—

(A) appoint himself and equal numbers of circuit and district judges of the circuit to a special committee to investigate the facts and allegations contained in the complaint;

(B) certify the complaint and any other documents pertaining thereto to each member of such committee; and

(C) provide written notice to the complainant and the judge or magistrate whose conduct is the subject of the complaint of the action taken under this paragraph.

(5) Each committee appointed under paragraph (4) of this subsection shall conduct an investigation as extensive as it considers necessary, and shall expeditiously file a comprehensive written report thereon with the judicial council of the circuit. Such report shall present both the findings of the investigation and the committee's recommendations for necessary and appropriate action by the judicial council of the circuit.

(6) Upon receipt of a report filed under paragraph (5) of this subsection, the judicial council—

(A) may conduct any additional investigation which it considers to be necessary;

(B) shall take such action as is appropriate to assure the effective and expeditious administration of the business of the courts within the circuit, including, but not limited to, any of the following actions:

(i) directing the chief judge of the district of the magistrate whose conduct is the subject of the complaint to take such action as the judicial council considers appropriate;

(ii) certifying disability of a judge appointed to hold office during good behavior whose conduct is the subject of the complaint, pursuant to the procedures and standards provided under subsection (b) of this section;

(iii) requesting that any such judge appointed to hold office during good behavior voluntarily retire, with the provision that the length of service requirements under section 371 of this title shall not apply;

(iv) ordering that, on a temporary basis for a time certain, no further cases be assigned to any judge or magistrate whose conduct is the subject of a complaint;

(v) censuring or reprimanding such judge or magistrate by means of private communication;

(vi) censuring or reprimanding such judge or magistrate by means of public announcement; or

(vii) ordering such other action as it considers appropriate under the circumstances, except that (I) in no circumstances may the council order removal from office of any judge appointed to hold office during good behavior, and (II) any removal of a magistrate shall be in accordance with section 631 of this title and any removal of a bankruptcy judge shall be in accordance with section 152 of this title; and

(C) shall immediately provide written notice to the complainant and to such judge or magistrate of the action taken under this paragraph.

(7)(A) In addition to the authority granted under paragraph (6) of this subsection, the judicial council may, in its discretion, refer any complaint under this subsection, together with the record of any associated proceedings and its recommendations for appropriate action, to the Judicial Conference of the United States.

(B) In any case in which the judicial council determines, on the basis of a complaint and an investigation under this subsection, or on the basis of information otherwise available to the council, that a judge appointed to hold office during good behavior has engaged in conduct—

(i) which might constitute one or more grounds for impeachment under article I of the Constitution; or

(ii) which, in the interest of justice, is not amenable to resolution by the judicial council,

the judicial council shall promptly certify such determination, together with any complaint and a record of any associated proceedings, to the Judicial Conference of the United States.

(C) A judicial council acting under authority of this paragraph shall, unless contrary to the interests of justice, immediately submit written notice to the complainant and to the judge or magistrate whose conduct is the subject of the action taken under this paragraph.

(8) Upon referral or certification of any matter under paragraph (7) of this subsection, the Judicial Conference, after consideration of the prior proceedings and such additional investigation as it considers appropriate, shall by majority vote take such action, as described in paragraph (6)(B) of this subsection, as it considers appropriate. If the Judicial Conference concurs in the determination of the council, or makes its own determination, that consideration of impeachment may be warranted, it shall so certify and transmit the determination and the record of proceedings to the House of Representatives for whatever action the House of Representatives considers to be necessary.

(9)(A) In conducting any investigation under this subsection, the judicial council, or a special committee appointed under paragraph (4) of this subsection, shall have full subpoena powers as provided in section 332(d) of this title.

(B) In conducting any investigation under this subsection, the Judicial Conference, or a standing committee appointed by the Chief Justice under section 331 of this title, shall have full subpoena powers as provided in that section.

(10) A complainant, judge, or magistrate aggrieved by a final order of the chief judge under paragraph (3) of this subsection may petition the judicial council for review thereof. A complainant, judge, or magistrate aggrieved by an action of the judicial council under paragraph (6) of this subsection may petition the Judicial Conference of the United States for review thereof. The Judicial Conference, or the standing committee established under section 331 of this title, may grant a petition filed by a complainant, judge, or magistrate under this paragraph. Except as expressly provided in this paragraph, all orders and determinations, including denials of petitions for review, shall be final and conclusive and shall not be judicially reviewable on appeal or otherwise.

(11) Each judicial council and the Judicial Conference may prescribe such rules for the conduct of proceedings under this subsection, including the processing of petitions for review, as each considers to be appropriate. Such rules shall contain provisions requiring that—

    (A) adequate prior notice of any investigation be given in writing to the judge or magistrate whose conduct is the subject of the complaint;

    (B) the judge or magistrate whose conduct is the subject of the complaint be afforded an opportunity to appear (in person or by counsel) at proceedings conducted by the investigating panel, to present oral and documentary evidence, to compel the attendance of witnesses or the production of documents, to cross-examine witnesses, and to present argument orally or in writing; and

    (C) the complainant be afforded an opportunity to appear at proceedings conducted by the investigating panel, if the panel concludes that the complainant could offer substantial information.

Any such rule shall be made or amended only after giving appropriate public notice and an opportunity for comment. Any rule promulgated under this subsection shall be a matter of public record, and any such rule promulgated by a judicial council may be modified by the Judicial Conference.

(12) No judge or magistrate whose conduct is the subject of an investigation under this subsection shall serve upon a special committee appointed under paragraph (4) of this subsection, upon a judicial council, upon the Judicial

Conference, or upon the standing committee established under section 331 of this title, until all related proceedings under this subsection have been finally terminated.

(13) No person shall be granted the right to intervene or to appear as amicus curiae in any proceeding before a judicial council or the Judicial Conference under this subsection.

(14) All papers, documents, and records of proceedings related to investigations conducted under this subsection shall be confidential and shall not be disclosed by any person in any proceeding unless—

(A) the judicial council of the circuit, the Judicial Conference of the United States, or the Senate or the House of Representatives by resolution, releases any such material which is believed necessary to an impeachment investigation or trial of a judge under article I of the Constitution; or

(B) authorized in writing by the judge or magistrate who is the subject to the complaint and by the chief judge of the circuit, the Chief Justice, or the chairman of the standing committee established under section 331 of this title.

(15) Each written order to implement any action under paragraph (6)(B) of this subsection, which is issued by a judicial council, the Judicial Conference, or the standing committee established under section 331 of this title, shall be made available to the public through the appropriate clerk's office of the court of appeals for the circuit. Unless contrary to the interests of justice, each such order issued under this paragraph shall be accompanied by written reasons therefor.

(16) Except as expressly provided in this subsection, nothing in this subsection shall be construed to affect any other provision of this title, the Federal Rules of Civil Procedure, the Federal Rules of Criminal Procedure, the Federal Rules of Appellate Procedure, or the Federal Rules of Evidence.

(17) The United States Claims Court, the Court of International Trade, and the Court of Appeals for the Federal Circuit shall each prescribe rules, consistent with the foregoing provisions of this subsection, establishing procedures for the filing of complaints with respect to the conduct of any judge of such court and for the investigation and resolution of such complaints. In investigating and taking action with respect to any such complaint, each such court shall have the powers granted to a judicial council under this subsection.

June 25, 1948, c. 646, 62 Stat. 903; May 24, 1949, c. 139, § 67, 63 Stat. 99; Feb. 10, 1954, c. 6, § 4(a), 68 Stat. 13; Sept. 2, 1957, Pub.L. 85–261, 71 Stat. 586; Oct. 10, 1980, Pub.L. 96–417, Title V, § 501(9), 94 Stat. 1742; Oct. 15, 1980, Pub.L. 96–458, § 3(a), (b), 94 Stat. 2036, 2040; Apr. 2, 1982, Pub.L. 97–164, Title I, § 112, 96 Stat. 29; July 10, 1984, Pub.L. 98–353, Title I, § 107, 98 Stat. 342; Nov. 19, 1988, Pub.L. 100–702, Title IV, § 403(c), 102 Stat. 4651.

[1] So in original.

Amendment of Subsec. (c)

Pub.L. 101–650, Title IV, §§ 402, 407, Dec. 1, 1990, 104 Stat. 5122, 5124, provided that, effective 90 days after Dec. 1, 1990, subsec. (c) is amended as follows:

(a) Identification of Complaints by Chief Judge.—Paragraph (1) of section 372(c) of title 28, United States Code, is amended by adding at the end thereof the following: "In the interests of the effective and expeditious administration of the business of the courts and on the basis of information available to the chief judge of the circuit, the chief judge may, by written order stating reasons therefor, identify a complaint for purposes of this subsection and thereby dispense with filing of a written complaint.".

(b) Membership of Special Investigative Committees.—Paragraph (4) of section 372(c) of such title is amended by adding at the end thereof the following: "A judge appointed to a special committee under this paragraph may continue to serve on that committee after becoming a senior judge or, in the case of the chief judge of the circuit, after his or her term as chief judge terminates under subsection (a)(3) or (c) of section 45 of this title. If a judge appointed to a committee under this paragraph dies, or retires from office under section 371(a) of this title, while serving on the committee, the chief judge of the circuit may appoint another circuit or district judge, as the case may be, to the committee.".

(c) Public Availability of Impeachment Recommendation.—(1) Paragraph (8) of section 372(c) of such title is amended by adding at the end thereof the following sentence: "Upon receipt of the determination and record of proceedings in the House of Representatives, the Clerk of the House of Representatives shall make available to the public the determination and any reasons for the determination.".

(2) Paragraph (14) of such section is amended—

(A) by striking out "All" and inserting in lieu thereof "Except as provided in paragraph (8), all";

(B) by striking out "unless" and inserting in lieu thereof "except to the extent that";

(C) in subparagraph (B) by inserting "such disclosure is" before "authorized";

(D) by redesignating subparagraphs (A) and (B) as subparagraphs (B) and (C), respectively; and

(E) by inserting the following new subparagraph (A) immediately before subparagraph (B) (as so redesignated):

"(A) the judicial council of the circuit in its discretion releases a copy of a report of a special investigative committee under paragraph (5) to the complainant whose complaint initiated the investigation by that special committee and to the judge or magistrate whose conduct is the subject of the complaint;".

(d) Impeachment Recommendations With Respect to Convicted Judges.— Section 372(c) of such title is further amended in paragraph (8)—

(1) by inserting "(A)" after "(8)"; and

(2) by adding at the end thereof the following:

"(B) If a judge or magistrate has been convicted of a felony and has exhausted all means of obtaining direct review of the conviction, or the time for seeking further direct review of the conviction has passed and no such review has been sought, the Judicial Conference may, by majority vote and without referral or certification under paragraph (7), transmit to the House of Representatives a determination that consideration of impeachment may be warranted, together with appropriate court records, for whatever action the House of Representatives considers to be necessary.".

(e) Rules by Judicial Conference and Judicial Councils.—Paragraph (11) of section 372(c) of such title is amended by adding at the end thereof the following: "No rule promulgated under this subsection may limit the period of time within which a person may file a complaint under this subsection.".

(f) Conclusion of Proceedings by Chief Judge.—Paragraph (3)(B) of section 372(c) of such title is amended by inserting before the period the following: "or that action on the complaint is no longer necessary because of intervening events".

(g) Dismissal of Complaints by Judicial Councils.—Paragraph (6) of section 372(c) of such title is amended—

    (1) by striking out "and" at the end of subparagraph (B);

    (2) by redesignating subparagraph (C) as subparagraph (D); and

    (3) by inserting after subparagraph (B) the following:

"(C) may dismiss the complaint; and".

(h) Reimbursement for Expenses and Attorneys' Fees.—Section 372(c) of such title is further amended—

    (1) by redesignating paragraphs (16) and (17) as paragraphs (17) and (18); and

    (2) by inserting after paragraph (15) the following new paragraph:

"(16) Upon the request of a judge or magistrate whose conduct is the subject of a complaint under this subsection, the judicial council may, if the complaint has been finally dismissed under paragraph (6)(C), recommend that the Director of the Administrative Office of the United States Courts award reimbursement, from funds appropriated to the Federal judiciary, for those reasonable expenses, including attorneys' fees, incurred by that judge or magistrate during the investigation which would not have been incurred but for the requirements of this subsection.".

(i) Technical Corrections.—(1) Paragraph (7)(B) of section 372(c) of such title is amended—

    (A) by striking out "has engaged in conduct" and inserting in lieu thereof "may have engaged in conduct"; and

    (B) in clause (i) by striking out "article I" and inserting in lieu thereof "article II".

(2) Paragraph (14)(C) of such section, as redesignated by subsection (c)(2)(D) of this section, is amended by striking out "subject to the complaint" and inserting in lieu thereof "subject of the complaint".

Historical Note

National Commission on Judicial Impeachment. Sections 408 to 418 of Pub.L. 101-650 provided that:

"Sec. 408. Short title.

"This subtitle [subtitle II of title IV of Pub.L. 101-650, this note] may be cited as the 'National Commission on Judicial Discipline and Removal Act'.

"Sec. 409. Establishment.

"There is hereby established a commission to be known as the 'National Commission on Judicial Discipline and Removal' (hereafter in this subtitle referred to as the 'Commission').

"Sec. 410. Duties of commission.

"The duties of the Commission are—

"(1) to investigate and study the problems and issues involved in the tenure (including discipline and removal) of an article III judge;

"(2) to evaluate the advisability of proposing alternatives to current arrangements with respect to such problems and issues, including alternatives for discipline or removal of judges that would require amendment to the Constitution; and

"(3) to prepare and submit to the Congress, the Chief Justice of the United States, and the President a report in accordance with section 415.

"Sec. 411. Membership.

"(a) Number and appointment.—The Commission shall be composed of 13 members as follows:

"(1) Three appointed by the President pro tempore of the Senate.

"(2) Three appointed by the Speaker of the House of Representatives.

"(3) Three appointed by the Chief Justice of the United States.

"(4) Three appointed by the President.

"(5) One appointed by the Conference of Chief Justices of the States of the United States.

"(b) Term.—Members of the Commission shall be appointed for the life of the Commission.

"(c) Quorum.—Six members of the Commission shall constitute a quorum, but a lesser number may conduct meetings.

"(d) Chairman.—The members of the Commission shall select one of the members to be the Chairman.

"(e) Appointment Deadline.—The first appointments made under subsection (a) shall be made within 60 days after the date of the enactment of this Act [Dec. 1, 1990].

"(f) First meeting.—The first meeting of the Commission shall be called by the Chairman and shall be held within 90 days after the date of the enactment of this Act [Dec. 1, 1990].

"(g) Vacancy.—A vacancy on the Commission resulting from the death or resignation of a member shall not affect its powers and shall be filled in the same manner in which the original appointment was made.

"(h) Continuation of membership.—If any member of the Commission who was appointed to the Commission as a Member of Congress or as an officer or employee of a government leaves that office, or if any member of the Commission who was appointed from persons who are not officers or employees of a government becomes an officer or employee of a government, the member may continue as a member of the Commission for not longer than the 90-day period beginning on the date the member leaves that office or becomes such an officer or employee, as the case may be.

"Sec. 412. Compensation of the commission.

"(a) Pay.—(1) Except as provided in paragraph (2), each member of the Commission who is not otherwise employed by the United States Government shall be entitled to receive the daily equivalent of the annual rate of basic pay payable for GS-18 of the General Schedule under section 5332 of title 5, United States Code [section 5332 of Title 5, Government Organization and Employees], for each day (including travel time) during which he or she is engaged in the actual performance of duties as a member of the Commission.

"(2) A member of the Commission who is an officer or employee of the United States Government shall serve without additional compensation.

"(b) Travel.—All members of the Commission shall be reimbursed for travel, subsistence, and other necessary expenses incurred by them in the performance of their duties.

"Sec. 413. Director and staff of commission; experts and consultants.

"(a) Director.—The Commission shall, without regard to section 5311(b) of title 5, United States Code [section 5311(b) of Titled 5], have a Director who shall be appointed by the Chairman and who shall be paid at a rate not to exceed the rate of basic pay payable for level V of the Executive Schedule under section 5316 of such title [section 5316 of Title 5].

"(b) Staff.—The Chairman of the Commission may appoint and fix the pay of such additional personnel as the Chairman finds necessary to enable the Commission to carry out its duties. Such personnel may be appointed without regard to the provisions of title 5, United States Code [Title 5], governing appointments in the competitive service, and may be paid without regard to the provisions of chapter 51 and subchapter III of chapter 53 of such title [section 5101 et seq. and section 5331 et seq. of Title 5] relating to classification and General Schedule pay rates, except that the annual rate of pay for any individual so appointed may not exceed a rate equal to the annual rate of basic pay payable for GS–18 of the General Schedule under section 5332 of such title [section 5332 of Title 5].

"(c) Experts and Consultants.—The Commission may procure temporary and intermittent services of experts and consultants under section 3109(b) of title 5, United States Code [section 3109(b) of Title 5].

"Sec. 414. Powers of Commission.

"(a) Hearings and sessions.—The Commission or, on authorization of the Commission, a member of the Commission may, for the purpose of carrying out this subtitle, hold such hearings, sit and act at such times and places, take such testimony, and receive such evidence, as the Commission considers appropriate. The Commission may administer oaths or affirmations to witnesses appearing before it.

"(b) Obtaining official data.—The Commission may secure directly from any department, agency, or entity within the executive or judicial branch of the Federal Government information necessary to enable it to carry out this subtitle. Upon request of the Chairman of the Commission, the head of such department or agency shall furnish such information to the Commission.

"(c) Facilities and support services.— The Administrator of General Services shall provide to the Commission on a reimbursable basis such facilities and support services as the Commission may request. Upon request of the Commission, the head of any Federal agency is authorized to make any of the facilities and services of such agency available to the Commission to assist the Commission in carrying out its duties under this subtitle.

"(d) Expenditures and contracts.—The Commission or, on authorization of the Commission, a member of the Commission may make expenditures and enter into contracts for the procurement of such supplies, services, and property as the Commission or member considers appropriate for the purposes of carrying out the duties of the Commission. Such expenditures and contracts may be made only to such extent or in such amounts as are provided in appropriation Acts.

"(e) Mails.—The Commission may use the United States mails in the same manner and under the same conditions as other departments and agencies of the United States.

"(f) Gifts.—The Commission may accept, use, and dispose of gifts or donations of services or property.

"Sec. 415. Report.

"The Commission shall submit to each House of Congress, the Chief Justice of the United States, and the President a report not later than one year after the date of its first meeting. The report shall contain a detailed statement of the findings and conclusions of the Commission, together with its recommendations for such legislative or administrative action as it considers appropriate.

"Sec. 416. Termination.

"The Commission shall cease to exist on the date 30 days after the date it submits its report to the President and the Congress under section 415.

"Sec. 417. Authorization of appropriations.

"There is authorized to be appropriated the sum of $750,000 to carry out the provisions of this subtitle.

"Sec. 418. Effective date.

"This subtitle shall take effect on the date of the enactment of this Act [Dec. 1, 1990]."

CHAPTER 21—GENERAL PROVISIONS APPLICABLE TO COURTS AND JUDGES

§ 455.   Disqualification of justice, judge, or magistrate

(a) Any justice, judge, or magistrate of the United States shall disqualify himself in any proceeding in which his impartiality might reasonably be questioned.

(b) He shall also disqualify himself in the following circumstances:

(1) Where he has a personal bias or prejudice concerning a party, or personal knowledge of disputed evidentiary facts concerning the proceeding;

(2) Where in private practice he served as a lawyer in the matter in controversy, or a lawyer with whom he previously practiced law served during such association as a lawyer concerning the matter, or the judge or such lawyer has been a material witness concerning it;

(3) Where he has served in governmental employment and in such capacity participated as counsel, adviser or material witness concerning the proceeding or expressed an opinion concerning the merits of the particular case in controversy;

(4) He knows that he, individually or as a fiduciary, or his spouse or minor child residing in his household, has a financial interest in the subject matter in controversy or in a party to the proceeding, or any other interest that could be substantially affected by the outcome of the proceeding;

(5) He or his spouse, or a person within the third degree of relationship to either of them, or the spouse of such a person:

(i) Is a party to the proceeding, or an officer, director, or trustee of a party;

(ii) Is acting as a lawyer in the proceeding;

(iii) Is known by the judge to have an interest that could be substantially affected by the outcome of the proceeding;

(iv) Is to the judge's knowledge likely to be a material witness in the proceeding.

(c) A judge should inform himself about his personal and fiduciary financial interests, and make a reasonable effort to inform himself about the personal financial interests of his spouse and minor children residing in his household.

(d) For the purposes of this section the following words or phrases shall have the meaning indicated:

(1) "proceeding" includes pretrial, trial, appellate review, or other stages of litigation;

(2) the degree of relationship is calculated according to the civil law system;

(3) "fiduciary" includes such relationships as executor, administrator, trustee, and guardian;

(4) "financial interest" means ownership of a legal or equitable interest, however small, or a relationship as director, adviser, or other active participant in the affairs of a party, except that:

(i) Ownership in a mutual or common investment fund that holds securities is not a "financial interest" in such securities unless the judge participates in the management of the fund;

(ii) An office in an educational, religious, charitable, fraternal, or civic organization is not a "financial interest" in securities held by the organization;

(iii) The proprietary interest of a policyholder in a mutual insurance company, of a depositor in a mutual savings association, or a similar proprietary interest, is a "financial interest" in the organization only if the outcome of the proceeding could substantially affect the value of the interest;

(iv) Ownership of government securities is a "financial interest" in the issuer only if the outcome of the proceeding could substantially affect the value of the securities.

(e) No justice, judge, or magistrate shall accept from the parties to the proceeding a waiver of any ground for disqualification enumerated in subsection (b). Where the ground for disqualification arises only under subsection (a), waiver may be accepted provided it is preceded by a full disclosure on the record of the basis for disqualification.

(f) Notwithstanding the preceding provisions of this section, if any justice, judge, magistrate, or bankruptcy judge to whom a matter has been assigned would be disqualified, after substantial judicial time has been devoted to the matter, because of the appearance or discovery, after the matter was assigned to him or her, that he or she individually or as a fiduciary, or his or her spouse or minor child residing in his or her household, has a financial interest in a party (other than an interest that could be substantially affected by the outcome), disqualification is not required if the justice, judge, magistrate, bankruptcy judge, spouse or minor child, as the case may be, divests himself or herself of the interest that provides the grounds for the disqualification.

June 25, 1948, c. 646, 62 Stat. 908; Dec. 5, 1974, Pub.L. 93–512, § 1, 88 Stat. 1609; Nov. 6, 1978, Pub.L. 95–598, Title II, § 214(a), (b), 92 Stat. 2661; Pub.L. 100–702, Title X, § 1007, Nov. 19, 1988, 102 Stat. 4667.

PART II—DEPARTMENT OF JUSTICE

CHAPTER 39—UNITED STATES TRUSTEES

Sec.
581. United States trustees.
582. Assistant United States trustees.
583. Oath of office.
584. Official stations.
585. Vacancies.
586. Duties; supervision by Attorney General.
587. Salaries.
588. Expenses.
589. Staff and other employees.
589a. United States Trustee System Fund.

United States Trustee Pilot; Repeal of Bankruptcy Provisions Relating to United States Trustees. Pub.L. 95–598, Title IV, § 408, Nov. 6, 1978, 92 Stat. 2687, as amended Pub.L. 98–166, Title II, § 200, Nov. 28, 1983, 97 Stat. 1081; Pub.L. 98–353, Title III, § 323, July 10, 1984, 98 Stat. 358; Pub.L. 99–429, Sept. 30, 1986, 100 Stat. 985; Pub.L. 99–554, Title III, § 307(a), Oct. 27, 1986, 100 Stat. 3125, which provided that the Attorney General conduct such studies and surveys as necessary to evaluate the needs, feasibility, and effectiveness of the United States trustee system, and report the result of such studies and surveys to the Congress, the President, and the Judicial Conference of the United States, beginning on or before January 3, 1980, and annually thereafter during the transition period; that not later then January 3, 1984, the Attorney General report to the Congress, to the President, and the Judicial Conference of the United States, as to the feasibility, projected annual cost and effectiveness of the United States trustee system, as determined on the basis of the studies and surveys respecting the operation of the United States trustee system in the districts, together with recommendations as to the desirability and method of proceeding with implementation of the United States trustee system in all judicial districts of the United States; and that chapter 15 of title 11 of the United States Code [section 1501 et seq. of Title 11, Bankruptcy] and chapter 39 of title 28 of the United States Code [this chapter] are repealed, and all references to the United States trustee contained in title 28 of the United States Code [this title] are deleted, as of 30 days after the effective date of the Bankruptcy Judges, United States Trustees, and Family Farmer Bankruptcy Act of 1986 [see section 302 of Pub.L. 99–554, set out as a note under section 581 of this title], with service of any United States trustee, of any assistant United States trustee, and of any employee employed or appointed under the authority of such chapter 39 is terminated on such date, was repealed by Pub.L. 99–554, Title III, § 307(b), Oct. 27, 1986, 100 Stat. 3125.

[For effective date of repeal, see section 302 of Pub.L. 99–554, set out as a note under section 581 of Title 28.]

Pub.L. 99–500, Title I, § 101(b) [Title II, § 200], Oct. 18, 1986, 100 Stat. 1783–45, and Pub.L. 99–591, Title I, § 101(b) [Title II, § 200], Oct. 30, 1986, 100 Stat. 3341–45, provided that, effective immediately before November 10, 1986, section 408(c) of the Act of November 6, 1978 (Public Law 95–598; 92 Stat. 2687), is amended by striking out "November 10, 1986" and inserting in lieu thereof "September 30, 1987". Such amendment was incapable of execution in view of the prior Amendment of such section 408(c) by section 307(a) of Pub.L. 99–554, effective Oct. 27, 1986, pursuant to section 302(b) of Pub.L. 99–554, and in view of the repeal of section 408(c) by section 307(b) of Pub.L. 99–554.

§ 581. United States trustees

(a) The Attorney General shall appoint one United States trustee for each of the following regions composed of Federal judicial districts (without regard to section 451):

(1) The judicial districts established for the States of Maine, Massachusetts, New Hampshire, and Rhode Island.

(2) The judicial districts established for the States of Connecticut, New York, and Vermont.

(3) The judicial districts established for the States of Delaware, New Jersey, and Pennsylvania.

(4) The judicial districts established for the States of Maryland, North Carolina, South Carolina, Virginia, and West Virginia and for the District of Columbia.

(5) The judicial districts established for the States of Louisiana and Mississippi.

(6) The Northern District of Texas and the Eastern District of Texas.

(7) The Southern District of Texas and the Western District of Texas.

(8) The judicial districts established for the States of Kentucky and Tennessee.

(9) The judicial districts established for the States of Michigan and Ohio.

(10) The Central District of Illinois and the Southern District of Illinois; and the judicial districts established for the State of Indiana.

(11) The Northern District of Illinois; and the judicial districts established for the State of Wisconsin.

(12) The judicial districts established for the States of Minnesota, Iowa, North Dakota, and South Dakota.

(13) The judicial districts established for the States of Arkansas, Nebraska, and Missouri.

(14) The District of Arizona.

(15) The Southern District of California; and the judicial districts established for the State of Hawaii, and for Guam and the Commonwealth of the Northern Mariana Islands.

(16) The Central District of California.

(17) The Eastern District of California and the Northern District of California; and the judicial district established for the State of Nevada.

(18) The judicial districts established for the States of Alaska, Idaho (exclusive of Yellowstone National Park), Montana (exclusive of Yellowstone National Park), Oregon, and Washington.

(19) The judicial districts established for the States of Colorado, Utah, and Wyoming (including those portions of Yellowstone National Park situated in the States of Montana and Idaho).

(20) The judicial districts established for the States of Kansas, New Mexico, and Oklahoma.

(21) The judicial districts established for the States of Alabama, Florida, and Georgia and for the Commonwealth of Puerto Rico and the Virgin Islands of the United States.

(b) Each United States trustee shall be appointed for a term of five years. On the expiration of his term, a United States trustee shall continue to perform the duties of his office until his successor is appointed and qualifies.

(c) Each United States trustee is subject to removal by the Attorney General.

Added Pub.L. 95–598, Title II, § 224(a), Nov. 6, 1978, 92 Stat. 2662, and amended Pub.L. 99–554, Title I, § 111(a)-(c), Oct. 27, 1986, 100 Stat. 3090, 3091.

Historical Note

Short Title of 1986 Amendment. For short title of Pub.L. 99–554 as the "Bankruptcy Judges, United States Trustees, and Family Farmer Bankruptcy Act of 1986", see section 1 of Pub.L. 99–554, set out as a note preceding section 101 of Title 11, Bankruptcy.

Incumbent United States Trustee. Sections 301, 302(b), of Pub.L. 99–554 eff. Oct. 27, 1986, provided that:

"(a) Area for Which Appointed. Notwithstanding any paragraph of section 581(a) of title 28, United States Code, as in effect before the effective date of this Act [section 581(a) of Title 28, Judiciary and Judicial Procedure prior to amendment by Pub.L. 99–554], a United States trustee serving in such office on the effective date of this Act [see section 302 of Pub.L. 99–554, set out as a note under section 581 of Title 28] shall serve the remaining term of such office as United States trustee for the region specified in a paragraph of such section, as amended by this Act, that includes the site at which the primary official station of the United States trustee is located immediately before the effective date of this Act.

"(b) Term of Office. Notwithstanding section 581(b) of title 28, United States Code, as in effect before the effective date of this Act [section 581(b) of Title 28, prior to amendment by Pub.L. 99–554], the term of office of any United States trustee serving in such office on the date of the enactment of this Act [Oct. 27, 1986] shall expire—

"(1) 2 years after the expiration date of such term of office under such section, as so in effect, or

"(2) 4 years after the date of the enactment of this Act [Oct. 27, 1986], whichever occurs first."

Effective Date of 1986 Amendments; Savings Provisions; References in Title 11 Section 326(b) to Title 11 Chapter 13 and Section 1302(a) and (d); References in Title 11 Section 1202(a) to United States Trustee; Effective Date of 1986 Amendments for Certain Judicial Districts Not Served by U.S. Trustees and for Judicial Districts in Alabama and North Carolina; U.S. Trustee System Fund Deposits in Alabama and North Carolina; Effective Date of Title 11 Chapter 15 Repeal as to Northern District

of Alabama; Authority of Certain Estate Administrators in Alabama and North Carolina; Effective Date of 1986 Amendments in Pending Cases Where a U.S. Trustee Not Authorized or Where a Trustee Files Final Report or Plan is Confirmed; Quarterly Fees; Effective Date and Savings Provisions for Repeal of Title 11 Chapter 12. Section 302 of Pub.L. 99–554 as amended by Pub.L. 101–650, Title III, § 317(a), (c), Dec. 1, 1990, 104 Stat. 5115, 5116, provided that:

"(a) General Effective Date. Except as provided in subsections (b), (c), (d), (e), and (f), this Act and the amendments made by this Act [see Short Title of 1986 Amendment note set out preceding section 101 of Title 11, Bankruptcy] shall take effect 30 days after the date of the enactment of this Act [Oct. 27, 1986].

"(b) Amendments Relating to Bankruptcy Judges and Incumbent United States Trustees. Subtitle A of title I [amending sections 152 and 156 of Title 28, Judiciary and Judicial Procedure and provisions set out as a note under section 152 of Title 28], and sections 301 [set out as a note under section 581 of Title 28] and 307(a) [amending provisions set out as a note preceding section 581 of Title 28], shall take effect on the date of the enactment of this Act [Oct. 27, 1986].

"(c) Amendments Relating to Family Farmers. (1) The amendments made by subtitle B of title II [enacting sections 1201 to 1231 of Title 11, Bankruptcy, and amending sections 101, 103, 108, 109, 303, 321, 322, 327, 329, 330, 346, 347, 348, 362, 363, 364, 365, 502, 523, 524, 546, 557, 706, 726, 727, 728, 1106, 1112, 1306, and 1307 of Title 11] shall not apply with respect to cases commenced under title 11 of the United States Code [Title 11] before the effective date of this Act [this section].

"(2) Section 1202 of title 11 of the United States Code (as added by the amendment made by section 255 of this Act) [section 1202 of Title 11] shall take effect on the effective date of this Act [this section] and before the amendment made by section 227 of this Act [striking out sections 1202(c) and (d) of Title 11].

"(3) Until the amendments made by subtitle A of title II of this Act [enacting section 307 of Title 11, amending sections 101, 102, 105, 303, 321, 322, 324, 326, 327, 330, 341, 343, 345, 701, 703, 704, 705, 707, 727, 1102, 1104, 1105, 1112, 1129, 1163, 1202, 1302, 1307, and 1326 of Title 11, and repealing sections 1501 to 151326 of Title 11] become

effective in a district and apply to a case, for purposes of such case—

"(A)(i) any reference in section 326(b) of title 11 of the United States Code [section 326(b) of Title 11] to chapter 13 of title 11 of the United States Code [section 1301 et seq. of Title 11] shall be deemed to be a reference to chapter 12 or chapter 13 of title 11 of the United States Code [section 1201 et seq. or 1301 et seq. of Title 11].

"(ii) any reference in such section 326(b) [section 326(b) of Title 11] to section 1302(d) of title 11 of the United States Code [section 1302(d) of Title 11] shall be deemed to be a reference to section 1302(d) of title 11 of the United States Code [section 1302(d) of Title 11] or section 586(b) of title 28 of the United States Code [section 586(b) of Title 28], and

"(iii) any reference in such section 326(b) [section 326(b) of Title 11] to section 1302(a) of title 11 of the United States Code [section 1302(a) of Title 11] shall be deemed to be a reference to section 1202(a) or section 1302(a) of title 11 of the United States Code [section 1202(a) or 1302(a) of Title 11], and

"(B)(i) the first two references in section 1202(a) of title 11 of the United States Code (as added by the amendment made by section 255 of this Act) [section 1202(a) of Title 11] to the United States trustee shall be deemed to be a reference to the court, and

"(ii) any reference in such section 1202(a) [section 1202(a) of Title 11] to section 586(b) of title 28 of the United States Code [section 586(b) of Title 28] shall be deemed to be a reference to section 1202(c) of title 11 of the United States Code (as so added) [section 1202(c) of Title 11].

"(d) Application of Amendments to Judicial Districts.

"(1) Certain Regions Not Currently Served by United States Trustees. (A) The amendments made by subtitle A of title II of this Act [enacting section 307 of Title 11, amending sections 101, 102, 105, 303, 321, 322, 324, 326, 327, 330, 341, 343, 345, 701, 703, 704, 705, 707, 727, 1102, 1104, 1105, 1112, 1129, 1163, 1202, 1302, 1307, and 1326 of Title 11, and repealing sections 1501 to 151326 of Title 11], and section 1930(a)(6) of title 28 of the United States Code (as added by section 117(4) of this Act) [section 1930(a)(6) of Title 28], shall not—

"(i) become effective in or with respect to a judicial district specified in subparagraph (B) until, or

"(ii) apply to cases while pending in such district before, the expiration of the 270-day period beginning on the effective date of this Act [this section] or of the 30-day period beginning on the date the Attorney General certifies under section 303 of this Act [set out as a note under section 581 of Title 28] the region specified in a paragraph of section 581(a) of Title 28, United States Code, as amended by section 111(a) of this Act [section 581(a) of Title 28], that includes such district, whichever occurs first.

"(B) Subparagraph (A) applies to the following:

"(i) The judicial district established for the Commonwealth of Puerto Rico.

"(ii) The District of Connecticut.

"(iii) The judicial districts established for the State of New York (other than the Southern District of New York).

"(iv) The District of Vermont.

"(v) The judicial districts established for the State of Pennsylvania.

"(vi) The judicial district established for the Virgin Islands of the United States.

"(vii) The District of Maryland.

"(viii) The judicial districts established for the State of North Carolina.

"(ix) The District of South Carolina.

"(x) The judicial districts established for the State of West Virginia.

"(xi) The Western District of Virginia.

"(xii) The Eastern District of Texas.

"(xiii) The judicial districts established for the State of Wisconsin.

"(xiv) The judicial districts established for the State of Iowa.

"(xv) The judicial districts established for the State of New Mexico.

"(xvi) The judicial districts established for the State of Oklahoma.

"(xvii) The District of Utah.

"(xviii) The District of Wyoming (including those portions of Yellowstone National Park situated in the States of Montana and Idaho).

"(xix) The judicial districts established for the State of Alabama.

"(xx) The judicial districts established for the State of Florida.

"(xxi) The judicial districts established for the State of Georgia.

"(2) Certain Remaining Judicial Districts Not Currently Served by United States Trustees. (A) The amendments made by subtitle A of title II of this Act [enacting section 307 of Title 11, amending sections 101, 102, 105, 303, 321, 322, 324, 326, 327, 330, 341, 343, 345, 701, 703, 704, 705, 707, 727, 1102, 1104, 1105, 1112, 1129, 1163, 1202, 1302, 1307, and 1326 of Title 11, and repealing sections 1501 to 151326 of Title 11], and section 1930(a)(6) of title 28 of the United States Code (as added by section 117(4) of this Act) [section 1930(a)(6) of Title 28], shall not—

"(i) become effective in or with respect to a judicial district specified in subparagraph (B), until, or

"(ii) apply to cases while pending in such district before, the expiration of the 2-year period beginning on the effective date of this Act [this section] or of the 30-day period beginning on the date the Attorney General certifies under section 303 of this Act [set out as a note under section 581 of Title 28] the region specified in a paragraph of section 581(a) of title 28, United States Code, as amended by section 111(a) of this Act [section 581(a) of Title 28], that includes such district, whichever occurs first.

"(B) Subparagraph (A) applies to the following:

"(i) The judicial districts established for the State of Louisiana.

"(ii) The judicial districts established for the State of Mississippi.

"(iii) The Southern District of Texas and the Western District of Texas.

"(iv) The judicial districts established for the State of Kentucky.

"(v) The judicial districts established for the State of Tennessee.

"(vi) The judicial districts established for the State of Michigan.

"(vii) The judicial districts established for the State of Ohio.

"(viii) The judicial districts established for the State of Illinois (other than the Northern District of Illinois).

"(ix) The judicial districts established for the State of Indiana.

"(x) The judicial districts established for the State of Arkansas.

"(xi) The judicial districts established for the State of Nebraska.

"(xii) The judicial districts established for the State of Missouri.

"(xiii) The District of Arizona.

"(xiv) The District of Hawaii.

"(xv) The judicial district established for Guam.

"(xvi) The judicial district established for the Commonwealth of the Northern Mariana Islands.

"(xvii) The judicial districts established for the State of California (other than the Central District of California).

"(xviii) The District of Nevada.

"(xix) The District of Alaska.

"(xx) The District of Idaho.

"(xxi) The District of Montana.

"(xxii) The District of Oregon.

"(xxiii) The judicial districts established for the State of Washington.

"(3) Judicial Districts for the States of Alabama and North Carolina. (A) Notwithstanding paragraphs (1) and (2), and any other provision of law, the amendments made by subtitle A of title II of this Act [enacting section 307 of Title 11, amending sections 101, 102, 105, 303, 321, 322, 324, 326, 327, 330, 341, 343, 345, 701, 703, 704, 705, 707, 727, 1102, 1104, 1105, 1112, 1129, 1163, 1202, 1302, 1307, and 1326 of Title 11, and repealing sections 1501 to 151326 of Title 11], and section 1930(a)(6) of title 28 of the United States Code (as added by section 117(4) of this Act) [section 1930(a)(6) of Title 28], shall not—

"(i) become effective in or with respect to a judicial district specified in subparagraph (E) until, or

"(ii) apply to cases while pending in such district before, such district elects to be included in a bankruptcy region established in section 581(a) of Title 28, United States Code, as amended by section 111(a) of this Act [section 581(a) of Title 28], or October 1, 2002, whichever occurs first, except that the amendment to section 105(a) of title 11, United States Code, shall become effective as of the date of the enactment of the Feder-

al Courts Study Committee Implementation Act of 1990.

"(B) Any election under subparagraph (A) shall be made upon a majority vote of the chief judge of such district and each bankruptcy judge in such judicial district in favor of such election.

"(C) Notice that an election has been made under subparagraph (A) shall be given, not later than 10 days after such election, to the Attorney General and the appropriate Federal Circuit Court of Appeals for such district.

"(D) Any election made under subparagraph (A) shall become effective on the date the amendments made by subtitle A of title II of this Act become effective in the region that includes such district or 30 days after the Attorney General receives the notice required under subparagraph (C), whichever occurs later.

"(E) Subparagraph (A) applies to the following:

"(i) The judicial districts established for the State of Alabama.

"(ii) The judicial districts established for the State of North Carolina.

"(F)(i) Subject to clause (ii), with respect to cases under chapters 7, 11, 12, and 13 of title 11, United States Code [sections 701 et seq., 1101 et seq., 1201 et seq., and 1301 et seq., respectively, of Title 11]—

"(I) commenced before the effective date of this Act [this section], and

"(II) pending in a judicial district in the State of Alabama or the State of North Carolina before any election made under subparagraph (A) by such district becomes effective or October 1, 2002, whichever occurs first,

the amendments made by section 113 [amending section 586 of Title 28] and subtitle A of title II of this Act, and section 1930(a)(6) of title 28 of the United States Code (as added by section 117(4) of this Act), shall not apply until October 1, 2003, or the expiration of the 1-year period beginning on the date such election becomes effective, whichever occurs first.

"(ii) For purposes of clause (i), the amendments made by section 113 and subtitle A of title II of this Act, and section 1930(a)(6) of title 28 of the United States Code (as added by section 117(4) of this Act), shall not apply with respect to a case under chapter 7, 11, 12, or 13 of title 11, United States Code, if—

"(I) the trustee in the case files the final report and account of administration of the estate, required under section 704 of such title [section 704 of Title 11], or

"(II) a plan is confirmed under section 1129, 1225, or 1325 of such title [section 1129, 1225, or 1325 of Title 11, respectively],

before October 1, 2003, or the expiration of the 1-year period beginning on the date such election becomes effective, whichever occurs first.

"(G) Notwithstanding section 589a of title 28, United States Code, as added by section 115 of this Act [section 589a of Title 28], funds collected as a result of the amendments made by section 117 of this Act [amending section 1930 of Title 28], in a judicial district in the State of Alabama or the State of North Carolina under section 1930(a) of title 28, United States Code, before the date the amendments made by subtitle A of title II of this Act take effect in such district shall be deposited in the general receipts of the Treasury.

"(H) The repeal made by section 231 of this Act [repealing section 1501 et seq. of Title 11] shall not apply in or with respect to the Northern District of Alabama until March 1, 1987, or the effective date of any election made under subparagraph (A) by such district, whichever occurs first.

"(I) In any judicial district in the State of Alabama or the State of North Carolina that has not made the election described in subparagraph (A), any person who is appointed under regulations issued by the Judicial Conference of the United States to administer estates in cases under title 11 of the United States Code may—

"(i) establish, maintain, and supervise a panel of private trustees that are eligible and available to serve as trustees in cases under title 11, United States Code, and

"(ii) supervise the administration of cases and trustees in cases under chapters 7, 11, 12, and 13 of title 11, United States Code,

until the amendments made by subtitle A of title II take effect in such district.

"(e) Application of United States Trustee System and Quarterly Fees to Certain Cases.

"(1) In general. Subject to paragraph (2), with respect to cases under chapters 7, 11, 12, and 13 of title 11, United States Code [sections 701 et seq., 1101 et seq., 1201 et seq., and 1301 et seq., respectively, of Title 11]—

"(A) commenced before the effective date of this Act [this section], and

"(B) pending in a judicial district referred to in section 581(a) of title 28, United States Code, as amended by section 111(a) of this Act [section 581(a) of Title 11], for which a United States trustee is not authorized before the effective date of this Act [this section] to be appointed,

the amendments made by section 113 [amending section 586 of Title 28] and subtitle A of title II of this Act [enacting section 307 of Title 11, amending sections 101, 102, 105, 303, 321, 322, 324, 326, 327, 330, 341, 343, 345, 701, 703, 704, 705, 707, 727, 1102, 1104, 1105, 1112, 1129, 1163, 1202, 1302, 1307, and 1326 of Title 11, and repealing sections 1501 to 151326 of Title 11], and section 1930(a)(6) of title 28 of the United States Code (as added by section 117(4) of this Act) [section 1930(a)(6) of Title 28], shall not apply until the expiration of the 3-year period beginning on the effective date of this Act [this section] or of the 1-year period beginning on the date the Attorney General certifies under section 303 of this Act [set out as a note under section 581 of Title 28], the region specified in a paragraph of such section 581(a), as so amended, that includes such district, whichever occurs first.

"(2) Amendments inapplicable. For purposes of paragraph (1), the amendments made by section 113 and subtitle A of title II of this Act, and section 1930(a)(6) of title 28 of the United States Code (as added by section 117(4) of this Act), shall not apply with respect to a case under chapter 7, 11, 12, or 13 of title 11, United States Code, if—

"(A) the trustee in the case files the final report and account of administration of the estate, required under section 704 of such title [section 704 of Title 11], or

"(B) a plan is confirmed under section 1129, 1225, or 1325 of such title [section 1129, 1225, or 1325 of Title 11, respectively],

before the expiration of the 3-year period, or the expiration of the 1-year period, specified in paragraph (1), whichever occurs first.

"(3) Rule of Construction Regarding Fees for Cases. This Act [see Short Title of 1986 Amendment note set out preceding 101 of Title 11] and the amendments made by section 117(4) of this Act [amending section 1930(a)(5), (6) of Title 28] shall not be construed to require the payment of a fee under paragraph (6) of section 1930(a) of Title 28, United States Code, in a case under Title 11 of the United States Code for any conduct or period occurring before such paragraph becomes effective in the district in which such case is pending.

"(f) Repeal of Chapter 12 of Title 11. Chapter 12 of title 11 of the United States Code [section 1201 et seq. of Title 11] is repealed on October 1, 1993. All cases commenced or pending under chapter 12 of title 11, United States Code, and all matters and proceedings in or relating to such cases, shall be conducted and determined under such chapter as if such chapter had not been repealed. The substantive rights of parties in connection with such cases, matters, and proceedings shall continue to be governed under the laws applicable to such cases, matters, and proceedings as if such chapter had not been repealed."

Certification of Judicial Districts; Notice and Publication of Certification. Section 303 of Pub.L. 99–554 provided that:

"(a) Certification by Attorney General. The Attorney General may certify in writing a region specified in a paragraph of section 581(a) of title 28, United States Code (other than paragraph (16)), as amended by section 111(a) of this Act [section 581(a) of Title 28, Judiciary and Judicial Procedure], to the appropriate court of appeals of the United States, for the purpose of informing such court that certain amendments made by this Act [Pub.L. 99–554] will become effective in accordance with section 302 of this Act [set out as a note under section 581 of Title 28].

"(b) Notice and Publication of Certification. Whenever the Attorney General transmits a certification under subsection (a), the Attorney General shall simultaneously—

"(1) transmit a copy of such certification to the Speaker of the House of Repre-

sentatives and to the President pro tempore of the Senate, and

"(2) publish such certification in the Federal Register."

Administrative Provisions. Section 304 of Pub.L. 99–554 provided that:

"(a) Cooperative Arrangements. The Attorney General and the Director of the Administrative Office of the United States Courts may enter into agreements under which United States trustees may—

"(1) use—

"(A) the services, equipment, personnel, records, reports, and data compilations, in any form, of the courts of the United States, and

"(B) the facilities of such courts, and

"(2) cooperate in the use by the courts of the United States of—

"(A) the services, equipment, personnel, records, reports, and data compilations, in any form, of United States trustees, and

"(B) the facilities of such trustees,

to prevent duplication during the 2-year period beginning on the effective date of this Act [see section 302 of Pub.L. 99–554, set out as a note under section 581 of Title 28, Judiciary and Judicial Procedure].

"(b) Information and Documents Relating to Bankruptcy Cases and United States Trustees. The Director of the Administrative Office of the United States Courts shall make available to United States trustees, at the request of the Attorney General and on a continuing basis, all records, reports, and data compilations relating to—

"(1) cases and proceedings under title 11 of the United States Code [Title 111, Bankruptcy], and

"(2) the duties of United States trustees under titles 11 and 28 of the United States Code [Titles 11 and 28]."

Application of Certain Bankruptcy Rules. Section 305 of Pub.L. 99–554 provided that:

"(a) Rules Relating to the United States Trustee System. If a United States trustee is not authorized, before the effective date of this Act [see section 302 of Pub.L. 99–554, set out as a note under section 581 of Title 28, Judiciary and Judicial Procedure], to be appointed for a judicial district referred to in section 581(a) of title 28, United States Code, as amended by section 111(a) of this Act [section 581(a) of Title 28], then part X of the Bankruptcy Rules [set out in Title 11, Bankruptcy] shall not apply to cases in such district until the amendments made by subtitle A of title II of this Act [Pub.L. 99–554, Title II, §§ 201 to 231] become effective under section 302 of this Act in such district.

"(b) Rules Relating to Chapter 12 of Title 11. The rules prescribed under section 2075 of title 28, United States Code [section 2075 of Title 28], and in effect on the date of the enactment of this Act [Oct. 27, 1986] shall apply to cases filed under chapter 12 of title 11, United States Code [this chapter], to the extent practicable and not inconsistent with the amendments made by title II of this Act [Pub.L. 99–554, Title II, §§ 201 to 283]."

Salary of Incumbent United States Trustee. Section 306 of Pub.L. 99–554 provided that:

"For service as a United States trustee in the period beginning on the effective date of this Act [see section 302 of Pub.L. 99–554, set out as a note under section 581 of Title 28, Judiciary and Judicial Procedure] and ending on the expiration under section 301 of this Act [set out as a note under section 581 of Title 28] of their respective terms of office, the salary payable to United States trustees serving in such offices on the effective date of this Act shall be fixed in accordance with section 587 of title 28, United States Code, as amended by section 114(a) of this Act [section 587 of Title 28]."

Preservation of United States Trustee System During Pendency of Legislation Repealer. Section 307 of Pub.L. 99–554 provided that:

"(a) Temporary Delay of Repeal of United States Trustee System. Effective immediately before November 10, 1986, section 408(c) of the Act of November 6, 1978 (Pub. L. 95–598; 92 Stat. 2687) [formerly set out as a note preceding section 581 of Title 28, Judiciary and Judicial Procedure], is amended by striking out 'November 10, 1986' and inserting in lieu thereof '30 days after the effective date of the Bankruptcy Judges, United States Trustees, and Family Farmer Bankruptcy Act of 1986'.

"(b) Conforming Amendment. Section 408 of the Act of November 6, 1978 (Pub.L. 95–598; 92 Stat. 2687) [formerly set out as a note preceding section 581 of Title 28, Judiciary and Judicial Procedure], is repealed."

[Section 302(b) of Pub.L. 99–554 provided in part that the amendment by subsec. (a) is effective Oct. 27, 1986.]

Consideration of Current Private Trustees for Appointment by United States Trustees. Section 308 of Pub.L. 99–554 provided that:

"(a) Trustees in Bankruptcy Cases Under Chapter 7. It is the sense of the Congress that individuals who are serving before the effective date of this Act [see section 302 of Pub.L. 99–554, set out as a note under section 581 of Title 28, Judiciary and Judicial Procedure], as trustees in cases under chapter 7 of title 11, United States Code [section 701 et seq. of Title 11, Bankruptcy], should be considered by United States trustees for appointment under section 586(a)(1) of title 28, United States Code [section 586(a)(1) of Title 28], to the panels of private trustees that are established as a result of the amendments made by this Act [see Short Title of 1986 Amendment note preceding section 101 of Title 11].

"(b) Standing Trustees in Bankruptcy Cases Under Chapter 13. It is the sense of the Congress that individuals who are serving before the effective date of this Act [see section 302 of Pub.L. 99–554, set out as a note under section 581 of Title 28], as standing trustees in cases under chapter 13 of title 11, United States Code [section 1301 et seq. of Title 11], should be considered by the United States trustees for appointment under section 586(b) of title 28, United States Code [section 586(b) of Title 28], as standing trustees who are appointed as a result of the amendments made by this Act [see note preceding section 101 of Title 11]."

Appointment of United States Trustees by Attorney General. Section 309 of Pub.L. 99–554 provided that:

"It is the sense of the Congress that individuals otherwise qualified who are serving, before the effective date of this Act [see section 302 of Pub.L. 99–554, set out as a note under section 581 of Title 28, Judiciary and Judicial Procedure], as estate administrators under title 11 of the United States Code [Title 11, Bankruptcy] should be considered by the Attorney General for appointment under sections 581 and 582 of title 28, United States Code [sections 581 and 582 of Title 28], to new positions of United States trustee and assistant United States trustee resulting from the amendments made by this Act [see Short Title of 1986 Amendment note set out preceding section 101 of Title 11]."

Electronic Case Management Demonstration Project. Section 310 of Pub.L. 99–554 provided that:

"(a) Establishment of Project. Not later than 1 year after the effective date of this Act [see section 302 of Pub.L. 99–584, set out as a note under section 581 of Title 28, Judiciary and Judicial Procedure], the Director of the Executive Office for United States Trustees, in consultation with the Director of the Administrative Office of the United States Courts, shall establish an electronic case management demonstration project to be carried out in 3 Federal judicial districts that have a sufficiently large and varied bankruptcy caseload so as to provide a meaningful evaluation of the cost and effectiveness of such system. A contract for such project shall be awarded—

"(1) on the basis of competitive bids submitted by qualified nongovernmental entities that are able to design an automated joint information system for use by the United States courts and by United States trustees, and

"(2) in accordance with the Federal Property and Administrative Services Act of 1949, the Office of Federal Procurement Policy Act, and title 31 of the United States Code [Act June 30, 1949, ch. 288, 63 Stat. 377, Pub.L. 93–400, Aug. 30, 1974, 88 Stat. 796, and Title 31, Money and Finance, respectively].

"(b) Study by General Accounting Office. Not later than 1 year after the electronic case management system begins to operate in all of the judicial districts participating in the demonstration project carried out under subsection (a), the General Accounting Office shall conduct a study to compare the cost and effectiveness of such system with the cost and effectiveness of case management systems used in Federal judicial districts that are not participating in such project.

"(c) Term of Project. The demonstration project required by subsection (a) shall be carried out until—

"(1) the expiration of the 2-year period beginning on the date the electronic case management system begins to operate in all of the judicial districts participating in such project, or

"(2) legislation is enacted to extend, expand, modify, or terminate the operation of such project,

whichever occurs first.

"(d) Use by Clerks of the Courts. The electronic case management system demonstrated under the project required by subsection (a) shall provide the clerk of court in each district in which such system is operated, with a means of—

"(1) maintaining a complete electronic case file of all relevant information contained in petitions and schedules (and any amendments thereto) relating to debtors in cases under title 11 of the United States Code [Title 11, Bankruptcy], including—

"(A) a complete list of creditors in each such case, as listed by the debtor,

"(B) a complete list of assets scheduled by the debtor, the value of such asset, and any action taken by the trustee or debtor in possession with regard to such asset during the pendency of such case,

"(C) a complete list of debts and, with respect to each debt—

"(i) any priority of such debt under title 11 of the United States Code,

"(ii) whether such debt is secured or unsecured, and

"(iii) whether such debt is contingent or noncontingent, and

"(D) the debtor's statements of current expenses and income, and

"(2) maintaining all calendars and dockets and producing all notices required to be sent in cases under title 11 of the United States Code.

"(e) Use by United States Trustees. The electronic case management system demonstrated under the project required by subsection (a) shall provide, at a minimum, the United States trustee in each district in which such system is operated with—

"(1) complete electronic case files which contain, in addition to the information listed in subsection (d), records of case openings, case closings, hearings, and the filing of all motions, trustee appointments, pleadings, and responses, as well as a record of the responses by the United States trustee to those motions, trustee appointments, and pleadings,

"(2) a means to generate standardized forms for motions, appointments, pleadings, and responses,

"(3) a means to generate standard management reports and letters on an exception basis,

"(4) a means to maintain accounting records, reports, and information required to be maintained by debtors in possession and trustees in cases under title 11 of the United States Code,

"(5) a means to calculate and record distribution to creditors, final applications and orders for distribution, and final case closing reports, and

"(6) a means to monitor the payment of filing and other required fees.

"(f) Availability to Certain Governmental Entities. Unlimited access to information maintained in the electronic case management system demonstrated under the project required by subsection (a) shall be provided at no charge to the following:

"(1) The Congress.

"(2) The Executive Office for the United States Trustees.

"(3) The Administrative Office of the United States Courts.

"(4) The clerks of the courts in judicial districts in which such system is operated and persons who review case information, in accordance with section 107(a) of title 11, United States Code [section 107(a) of Title 11], in the offices of the clerks.

"(5) The judges on the bankruptcy and district courts in districts in which such system is operated.

"(6) Trustees in cases pending in districts in which such system is operated.

"(g) Fees for Other Users. (1) The entity which is awarded a contract to provide the electronic case management system demonstrated under this project may, under guidelines established by the Director of the Executive Office for the United States Trustees in the provisions of such contract, collect reasonable fees from assets of the estate of the debtor in bankruptcy for providing notices and services to the court and trustees under the demonstration project.

"(2) Access to information maintained in electronic case files pursuant to the demonstration project may be provided to persons other than those specified in subsection (f), but such access shall be limited to viewing such information only. A reasonable charge for such access may be collected by the entity which is awarded a contract under this section, in accordance with the guidelines established by the Director of the Executive Office for the United States Trustees in such contract. A reasonable portion of any charge so collected may be required by the Director to be remitted to the Executive Office for United States Trustees and deposited in the United States Trustee System Fund established in section 589a of title 28, United States Code [section 589a of Title 28].

"(h) Security. Access provided under subsection (f) to an entity or an individual shall be subject to such security limitations as may be imposed by the Congress or the head of the affected entity."

Cases Pending, Under the Bankruptcy Act. Section 311 of Pub.L. 99–554 provided that:

"At the end of one calendar year following the date the amendments made by subtitle A of title II of this Act [amendments by Pub.L. 99–554, Title II, §§ 201 to 231, which were approved Oct. 27, 1986] take effect in a district in which any case is still pending under the Bankruptcy Act [section 1 et seq. of former Title 11, Bankruptcy], the district court shall withdraw the reference of any such case and, after notice and a hearing, determine the status of the case. Such case shall be remanded to the bankruptcy judge with such instructions as are necessary for the prompt closing of the case and with a requirement that a progress report on the case be provided by the bankruptcy judge after such interval as the district court deems appropriate."

§ 582.   Assistant United States trustees

(a) The Attorney General may appoint one or more assistant United States trustees in any region when the public interest so requires.

(b) Each assistant United States trustee is subject to removal by the Attorney General.

Added Pub.L. 95–598, Title II, § 224(a), Nov. 6, 1978, 92 Stat. 2663 and amended Pub.L. 99–554, Title I, § 111(d), Oct. 27, 1986, 100 Stat. 3091.

Effective Date of 1986 Amendment. Amendment by Pub.L. 99–554 effective 30 days after Oct. 27, 1986, except as otherwise provided for, see section 302(a) of Pub.L. 99–554, set out as a note under section 581 of this title.

Appointment of United States Trustees by Attorney General. Appointment of Unit- ed States Trustees by the Attorney General of individuals serving before effective date of Pub.L. 99–554, see section 309 of Pub.L. 99–554, set out as a note under section 581 of Title 28, Judiciary and Judicial Procedure.

§ 583.   Oath of office

Each United States trustee and assistant United States trustee, before taking office, shall take an oath to execute faithfully his duties.

Added Pub.L. 95–598, Title II, § 224(a), Nov. 6, 1978, 92 Stat. 2663.

§ 584.   Official stations

The Attorney General may determine the official stations of the United States trustees and assistant United States trustees within the regions for which they were appointed.

Added Pub.L. 95–598, Title II, § 224(a), Nov. 6, 1978, 92 Stat. 2663, and amended Pub.L. 99–554, Title I, § 144(d), Oct. 27, 1986, 100 Stat. 3096.

Effective Date of 1986 Amendment. Amendment by Pub.L. 99–554 effective 30 days after Oct. 27, 1986, except as otherwise provided for, see section 302(a) of Pub.L. 99–554, set out as a note under section 581 of this title.

§ 585.   Vacancies

(a) The Attorney General may appoint an acting United States trustee for a region in which the office of the United States trustee is vacant. The individual so appointed may serve until the date on which the vacancy is filled by appointment under section 581 of this title or by designation under subsection (b) of this section.

(b) The Attorney General may designate a United States trustee to serve in not more than two regions for such time as the public interest requires.

Added Pub.L. 95–598, Title II, § 224(a), Nov. 6, 1978, 92 Stat. 2663, and amended Pub.L. 99–554, Title I, § 112, Oct. 27, 1986, 100 Stat. 3091.

Effective Date of 1986 Amendment. Amendment by Pub.L. 99–554 effective 30 days after Oct. 27, 1986, except as otherwise provided for, see section 302(a) of Pub.L. 99–554, set out as a note under section 581 of this title.

§ 586.   Duties; supervision by Attorney General

(a) Each United States trustee, within the region for which such United States trustee is appointed, shall—

(1) establish, maintain, and supervise a panel of private trustees that are eligible and available to serve as trustees in cases under chapter 7 of title 11;

(2) serve as and perform the duties of a trustee in a case under title 11 when required under title 11 to serve as trustee in such a case;

(3) supervise the administration of cases and trustees in cases under chapter 7, 11, or 13 of title 11 by, whenever the United States trustee considers it to be appropriate—

(A) monitoring applications for compensation and reimbursement filed under section 330 of title 11 and, whenever the United States trustee deems it to be appropriate, filing with the court comments with respect to any of such applications;

(B) monitoring plans and disclosure statements filed in cases under chapter 11 of title 11 and filing with the court, in connection with hearings under sections 1125 and 1128 of such title, comments with respect to such plans and disclosure statements;

(C) monitoring plans filed under chapters 12 and 13 of title 11 and filing with the court, in connection with hearings under sections 1224, 1229, 1324, and 1329 of such title, comments with respect to such plans;

(D) taking such action as the United States trustee deems to be appropriate to ensure that all reports, schedules, and fees required to be filed under title 11 and this title by the debtor are properly and timely filed;

(E) monitoring creditors' committees appointed under title 11;

(F) notifying the appropriate United States attorney of matters which relate to the occurrence of any action which may constitute a crime under the laws of the United States and, on the request of the United States attorney, assisting the United States attorney in carrying out prosecutions based on such action;

(G) monitoring the progress of cases under title 11 and taking such actions as the United States trustee deems to be appropriate to prevent undue delay in such progress; and

(H) monitoring applications filed under section 327 of title 11 and, whenever the United States trustee deems it to be appropriate, filing with the court comments with respect to the approval of such applications;

(4) deposit or invest under section 345 of title 11 money received as trustee in cases under title 11;

(5) perform the duties prescribed for the United States trustee under title 11 and this title, and such duties consistent with title 11 and this title as the Attorney General may prescribe; and

(6) make such reports as the Attorney General directs.

(b) If the number of cases under chapter 12 or 13 of title 11 commenced in a particular region so warrants, the United States trustee for such region may, subject to the approval of the Attorney General, appoint one or more individuals to serve as standing trustee, or designate one or more assistant United States trustees to serve in cases under such chapter. The United States trustee for such region shall supervise any such individual appointed as standing trustee in the performance of the duties of standing trustee.

(c) Each United States trustee shall be under the general supervision of the Attorney General, who shall provide general coordination and assistance to the United States trustees.

(d) The Attorney General shall prescribe by rule qualifications for membership on the panels established by United States trustees under paragraph (a)(1) of this section, and qualifications for appointment under subsection (b) of this section to serve as standing trustee in cases under chapter 12 or 13 of title 11. The Attorney General may not require that an individual be an attorney in order to qualify for appointment under subsection (b) of this section to serve as standing trustee in cases under chapter 12 or 13 of title 11.

(e)(1) The Attorney General, after consultation with a United States trustee that has appointed an individual under subsection (b) of this section to serve as standing trustee in cases under chapter 12 or 13 of title 11, shall fix—

    (A) a maximum annual compensation for such individual consisting of—

        (i) an amount not to exceed the highest annual rate of basic pay in effect for level V of the Executive Schedule; and

        (ii) the cash value of employment benefits comparable to the employment benefits provided by the United States to individuals who are employed by the United States at the same rate of basic pay to perform similar services during the same period of time; and

    (B) a percentage fee not to exceed—

        (i) in the case of a debtor who is not a family farmer, ten percent; or

        (ii) in the case of a debtor who is a family farmer, the sum of—

            (I) not to exceed ten percent of the payments made under the plan of such debtor, with respect to payments in an aggregate amount not to exceed $450,000; and

            (II) three percent of payments made under the plan of such debtor, with respect to payments made after the aggregate amount of payments made under the plan exceeds $450,000;

based on such maximum annual compensation and the actual, necessary expenses incurred by such individual as standing trustee.

(2) Such individual shall collect such percentage fee from all payments received by such individual under plans in the cases under chapter 12 or 13 of title 11 for which such individual serves as standing trustee. Such individual shall pay to the United States trustee, and the United States trustee shall deposit in the United States Trustee System Fund—

    (A) any amount by which the actual compensation of such individual exceeds 5 per centum upon all payments received under plans in cases under chapter 12 or 13 of title 11 for which such individual serves as standing trustee; and

    (B) any amount by which the percentage for all such cases exceeds—

        (i) such individual's actual compensation for such cases, as adjusted under subparagraph (A) of paragraph (1); plus

        (ii) the actual, necessary expenses incurred by such individual as standing trustee in such cases. Subject to the approval of the Attorney General, any or all of the interest earned from the deposit of payments under plans by such individual may be utilized to pay actual, necessary expenses without regard to the percentage limitation contained in subparagraph (d)(1)(B) of this section.

Added Pub.L. 95–598, Title II, § 224(a), Nov. 6, 1978, 92 Stat. 2663, and amended Pub.L. 99–554, Title I, § 113, Oct. 27, 1986, 100 Stat. 3091; Pub.L. 101–509, Title I, § 110(a) Nov. 5, 1990, 104 Stat. 1452.

Historical Note

1986 Amendment. Subsec. (a). Pub.L. 99–554, § 113(a)(1), substituted "within the region for which such United States trustee is appointed shall" for "within his district, shall".

Subsec. (a)(3). Pub.L. 99–554, § 113(a)(2)(A), substituted "of title 11 by, whenever the United States trustee considers it to be appropriate—" for "of title 11;".

Subsec. (a)(3)(A) to (H). Pub.L. 99–554, § 113(a)(2)(B), added subpars. (A) to (H).

Subsec. (a)(5). Pub.L. 99–554, § 113(a)(3), added "and this title, and such duties consistent with title 11 and this title as the Attorney General may prescribe" following "under title 11".

Subsec. (b). Pub.L. 99–554, § 113(b), substituted "under chapter 12 or 13" for "under chapter 13", "particular region so warrants, the" for "particular judicial district so warrant", "trustee for such region may" for "trustee for such district may", "assistant United States trustees to serve in cases" for "assistant United States trustee, in cases", and "trustee for such region shall" for "trustee for such district shall".

Subsec. (d). Pub.L. 99–554, § 113(c), substituted "paragraph (a)(1)" for "subsection (a)(1)" and "chapter 12 or 13" for "chapter 13" wherever appearing in text.

Subsec. (e)(1). Pub.L. 99–554, § 113(c), substituted "chapter 12 or 13" for "chapter 13", in subpar. (A) substituted "the annual rate" for "the lowest annual rate", and "for step 1 of grade" for "for grade", and in subpar. (B) substituted "a percentage fee not to exceed—" for "a percentage fee, not to exceed ten percent," and added cls. (i) and (ii).

Subsec. (e)(2). Pub.L. 99–554, § 113(c), added "received by such individual" following "from all payments", substituted "chapter 12 or 13" for "chapter 13" and "shall deposit in the United States Trustee System Fund" for "shall pay to the Treasury".

Subsec. (e)(2)(A). Pub.L. 99–554, § 113(c), substituted "5 per centum upon all payments received under plans in cases under chapter 12 or 13" for "five percent upon all payments under plans in cases under chapter 13".

Subsec. (e)(2)(B). Pub.L. 99–554, § 113(c), in cl. (i) substituted "such individual's actual" for "such individual actual" and "of paragraph (1)" for "of this paragraph", and in cl. (ii) added "Subject to the approval of the Attorney General, any or all of the interest earned from the deposit of payments under plans by such individual may be utilized to pay actual, necessary expenses without regard to the percentage limitation contained in subparagraph (d)(1)(B) of this section.".

See Effective Date of 1986 Amendment, etc., notes set out below.

References in Text. Level V of the Executive Schedule, referred to in subsec. (e)(1)(A)(i), is set out in section 5316 of Title 5, Government Organization and Employees.

1990 Amendment. Subsec. (e)(1)(A). Pub.L. 101–509 substituted provision that the Attorney General fix a maximum annual compensation consisting of an amount not to exceed the highest annual rate of basic pay in effect for level V of the Executive Schedule and the cash value of employment benefits comparable to the employment benefits provided by the United States to individuals who are employed by the United States at the same rate of basic pay to perform similar services during the same period of time for provision that the Attorney General fix a maximum annual compensation not to exceed the annual rate of basic pay in effect for step 1 of grade GS–16 of the General Schedule prescribed under section 5332 of title 5.

Effective Date of 1990 Amendment. Section 110(b) of Pub.L. 101–509 provided that: "The amendment made by subsection (a) [amending subsec. (e)(1)(A) of this section] shall apply to any trustee to whom the provisions of section 302(d)(3) of the Bankruptcy Judges, United States Trustees, and Family Farmer Bankruptcy Act of 1986 (Public Law 99–54; 100 Stat. 3121) [section 302(d)(3) of Pub.L. 99–554, set out as a note under section 581 of this title] apply."

Effective Date of 1986 Amendments; Effective Date of 1986 Amendments for Certain Judicial Districts Not Served by United States Trustees and for Judicial

Districts in Alabama and North Carolina; U.S. Trustee System Fund Deposits in Alabama and North Carolina; Effective Date of Title 11 Chapter 15 Repeal as to Northern District of Alabama; Authority of Certain Estate Administrators in Alabama and North Carolina; Effective Date of 1986 Amendments in Pending Cases Where a U.S. Trustee Not Authorized or Where a Trustee Files Final Report or Plan is Confirmed; Quarterly Fees. Amendment by Pub.L. 99–554 effective 30 days after Oct. 27, 1986, except as otherwise provided for, see section 302(a) of Pub.L. 99–554, set out as a note under section 581 of this title.

Amendment by Pub.L. 99–554, § 113, not to become effective in or with respect to judicial districts established for the States of Alabama and North Carolina until, or apply to cases while pending in such district before, such district elects to be included in a bankruptcy region established in section 581(a) of Title 28, as amended by section 111(a) of Pub.L. 99–554, or Oct. 1, 2002, whichever occurs first, and, except as otherwise provided for, with respect to cases under chapters 7, 11, 12, and 13 of Title 11 commenced before 30 days after Oct. 27, 1986, and pending in a judicial district in the States of Alabama or North Carolina before any election made under section 302(d)(3) (A) of Pub.L. 99–554 by such district becomes effective or Oct. 1, 2002, whichever occurs first, amendments by Pub.L. 99–554 not to apply until Oct. 1, 2003, or the expiration of the 1-year period beginning on the date such election becomes effective, whichever occurs first, and further, in any judicial district in Alabama or North Carolina not making the election described in section 302(d)(3)(A) of Pub.L. 99–554, any person appointed under regulations issued by the Judicial Conference to administer estates in cases under Title 11 authorized to establish, etc., a panel of private trustees, and to supervise cases and trustees in cases under chapters 7, 11, 12, and 13 of Title 11, until amendments by sections 201 to 231 of Pub.L. 99–554 effective in such district, see section 302(d)(3)(A) to (F), (I) of Pub.L. 99–554, set out as a note under section 581 of this title.

Amendment by Pub.L. 99–554, § 113, except as otherwise provided, with respect to cases under chapters 7, 11, 12, and 13 of Title 11 commenced before 30 days after Oct. 27, 1986, and pending in a judicial district referred to in section 581(a) of Title 28, as amended by section 111(a) of Pub.L. 99–554, for which a United States trustee is not authorized before 30 days after Oct. 27, 1986 to be appointed, not applicable until the expiration of the 3-year period beginning on Oct. 27, 1986, or of the 1-year period beginning on the date the Attorney General certifies under section 303 of Pub.L. 99–554 the region specified in a paragraph of such section 581(a) that includes, such district, whichever occurs first, see section 302(e)(1), (2) of Pub.L. 99–554, set out as a note under section 581 of this title.

See 1986 Amendment notes set out above.

§ 587. Salaries

Subject to sections 5315 through 5317 of title 5, the Attorney General shall fix the annual salaries of United States trustees and assistant United States trustees at rates of compensation not in excess of the rate of basic compensation provided for Executive Level IV of the Executive Schedule set forth in section 5315 of title 5, United States Code.

Added Pub.L. 95–598, Title II, § 224(a), Nov. 6, 1978, 92 Stat. 2664, and amended Pub.L. 99–554, Title I, § 114(a), Oct. 27, 1986, 100 Stat. 3093.

Historical Note

Effective Date of 1986 Amendment. Amendment by Pub.L. 99–554 effective 30 days after Oct. 27, 1986, except as otherwise provided for, see section 302(a) of Pub.L. 99–554, set out as a note under section 581 of this title.

§ 588. Expenses

Necessary office expenses of the United States trustee shall be allowed when authorized by the Attorney General.

Added Pub.L. 95–598, Title II, § 224(a), Nov. 6, 1978, 92 Stat. 2664.

§ 589.   Staff and other employees

The United States trustee may employ staff and other employees on approval of the Attorney General.

Added Pub.L. 95–598, Title II, § 224(a), Nov. 6, 1978, 92 Stat. 2664.

Historical Note

Temporary Suspension of Limitation on Appointments. Pub.L. 99–554, Title I, § 114(b), Oct. 27, 1986, 100 Stat. 3093, provided that: "During the period beginning on the effective date of this Act [see section 302 of Pub.L. 99–554, set out as a note under section 581 of this title] and ending on October 1, 1989, the provisions of title 5 of the United States Code [Title 5, Government Organization and Employees] governing appointments in the competitive service shall not apply with respect to appointments under section 589 of title 28, United States Code [this section]."

U.S. Trustee System Fund Deposits in Alabama and North Carolina. Deposit in the general receipts of the Treasury of funds collected as a result of the amendments made by section 117 of Pub.L. 99–554 in a judicial district in the States of Alabama or North Carolina under section 1930(a) of Title 28 before the date the amendments made by sections 201 to 231 of Pub.L. 99–554 take effect in such districts, and notwithstanding section 589a of Title 28, see section 302(d)(3)(G) of Pub.L. 99–554, set out as a note under section 581 of this title.

§ 589a.   United States Trustee System Fund

(a) There is hereby established in the Treasury of the United States a special fund to be known as the "United States Trustee System Fund" (hereinafter in this section referred to as the "Fund"). Monies in the Fund shall be available to the Attorney General without fiscal year limitation in such amounts as may be specified in appropriations Acts for the following purposes in connection with the operations of United States trustees—

    (1) salaries and related employee benefits;

    (2) travel and transportation;

    (3) rental of space;

    (4) communication, utilities, and miscellaneous computer charges;

    (5) security investigations and audits;

    (6) supplies, books, and other materials for legal research;

    (7) furniture and equipment;

    (8) miscellaneous services, including those obtained by contract; and

    (9) printing.

(b) There shall be deposited in the Fund—

    (1) one-fourth of the fees collected under section 1930(a)(1) of this title;

    (2) three-fifths of the fees collected under section 1930(a)(3) of this title;

    (3) one-half of the fees collected under section 1930(a)(4) of this title;

    (4) one-half of the fees collected under section 1930(a)(5);

    (5) all of the fees collected under section 1930(a)(6) of this title;

    (6) three-fourths of the fees collected under the last sentence of section 1930(a) of this title; and

    (7) the compensation of trustees received under section 330(d) of title 11 by the clerks of the bankruptcy courts.

(c)(1) Except as provided in paragraph (2), amounts in the Fund which are not currently needed for the purposes specified in subsection (a) shall be kept on deposit or invested in obligations of, or guaranteed by, the United States.

(2) On November 1, 1989, and on November 1 of each year thereafter, the Secretary of the Treasury shall transfer into the general fund of the Treasury the amount, if any, in the Fund that exceeds 110 percent of—

(A) the amount appropriated for the entire current fiscal year for the purposes specified in subsection (a), or

(B) if no appropriation has been made for the entire current fiscal year, the annual equivalent of the aggregate amount appropriated to date for the current fiscal year for the purposes specified in subsection (a).

(d)(1) The Attorney General shall transmit to the Congress, not later than 120 days after the end of each fiscal year, a detailed report on the amounts deposited in the Fund and a description of the expenditures made under this section.

(2) If for each fiscal year in any period of 2 successive fiscal years—

(A) the aggregate amount deposited under subsection (b) in the Fund exceeds 110 percent of expenditures for the purposes specified in subsection (a), or

(B) the costs incurred for the purposes specified in subsection (a) exceed the aggregate amount deposited under subsection (b) in the Fund,

then the Attorney General shall include in such report a recommendation regarding the manner and which the fees payable under section 1930(a) of title 28, United States Code, may be modified to cause the annual amount deposited in the Fund to more closely approximate the annual amount expended from the Fund.

(e) There are authorized to be appropriated to the Fund for any fiscal year such sums as may be necessary to supplement amounts deposited under subsection (b) for the purposes specified in subsection (a).

Added Pub.L. 99–554, Title I, § 115(a), Oct. 27, 1986, 100 Stat. 3094, and amended Pub.L. 101–162, Title IV, § 406(c), Nov. 21, 1989, 103 Stat. 1016.

Historical Note

Effective Date. Enactment by Pub.L. 99–554 effective 30 days after Oct. 27, 1986, except as otherwise provided for, see section 302(a) of Pub.L. 99–554, set out as a note under section 581 of this title.

PART III—COURT OFFICERS AND EMPLOYEES

CHAPTER 41—ADMINISTRATIVE OFFICE OF UNITED STATES COURTS

§ 604.   Duties of Director generally

(a) The Director shall be the administrative officer of the courts, and under the supervision and direction of the Judicial Conference of the United States, shall:

(1) Supervise all administrative matters relating to the offices of clerks and other clerical and administrative personnel of the courts;

(2) Examine the state of the dockets of the courts; secure information as to the courts' need of assistance; prepare and transmit semiannually to the chief judges of the circuits, statistical data and reports as to the business of the courts;

(3) Submit to the annual meeting of the Judicial Conference of the United States, at least two weeks prior thereto, a report of the activities of the Administrative Office and the state of the business of the courts, together with the statistical data submitted to the chief judges of the circuits under paragraph (a)(2) of this section, and the Director's recommendations, which report, data and recommendations shall be public documents.

(4) Submit to Congress and the Attorney General copies of the report, data and recommendations required by paragraph (a)(3) of this section;

(5) Fix the compensation of clerks of court, deputies, librarians, criers, messengers, law clerks, secretaries, stenographers, clerical assistants, and other employees of the courts whose compensation is not otherwise fixed by law;

(6) Determine and pay necessary office expenses of courts, judges, and those court officials whose expenses are by law allowable, and the lawful fees of United States Commissioners;

(7) Regulate and pay annuities to widows and surviving dependent children of justices and judges of the United States, judges of the United States Claims Court, bankruptcy judges, United States magistrates, Directors of the Federal Judicial Center, and Directors of the Administrative Office, and necessary travel and subsistence expenses incurred by judges, court officers and employees, and officers and employees of the Administrative Office, and the Federal Judicial Center, while absent from their official stations on official business, without regard to the per diem allowances and amounts for reimbursement of actual and necessary expenses established by the Administrator of General Services under section 5702 of title 5, except that the reimbursement of subsistence expenses may not exceed that authorized by the Director for judges of the United States under section 456 of this title;

(8) Disburse, directly or through the several United States marshals, moneys appropriated for the maintenance and operation of the courts;

(9) Establish pretrial services pursuant to section 3152 of title 18, United States Code;

(10)(A) Purchase, exchange, transfer, distribute, and assign the custody of lawbooks, equipment, supplies, and other personal property for the judicial branch of Government (except the Supreme Court unless otherwise provided pursuant to paragraph (17)); (B) provide or make available readily to each court appropriate equipment for the interpretation of proceedings in accordance with section 1828 of this title; and (C) enter into and perform contracts and other transactions upon such terms as the Director may deem appropriate as may be necessary to the conduct of the work of the judicial branch of Government (except the Supreme Court unless otherwise provided pursuant to paragraph (17)), and contracts for nonpersonal services providing pretrial services, for the interpretation of proceedings, and for the provision of special interpretation services pursuant to section 1828 of this title may be awarded without regard to section 3709 of the Revised Statutes of the United States (41 U.S.C. 5);

(11) Audit vouchers and accounts of the courts, the Federal Judicial Center, the officers providing pretrial services, and their clerical and administrative personnel;

(12) Provide accommodations for the courts, the Federal Judicial Center, the offices providing pretrial services and their clerical and administrative personnel;

(13) Lay before Congress, annually, statistical tables that will accurately reflect the business transacted by the several bankruptcy courts, and all other pertinent data relating to such courts;

(14) Pursuant to section 1827 of this title, establish a program for the certification and utilization of interpreters in courts of the United States;

(15) Pursuant to section 1828 of this title, establish a program for the provision of special interpretation services in courts of the United States;

(16)(A) In those districts where the Director considers it advisable based on the need for interpreters, authorize the full-time or part-time employment by the court of certified interpreters; (B) where the Director considers it advisable based on the need for interpreters, appoint certified interpreters on a full-time or part-time basis, for services in various courts when he determines that such appointments will result in the economical provision of interpretation services; and (C) pay out of moneys appropriated for the judiciary interpreters' salaries, fees, and expenses, and other costs which may accrue in accordance with the provisions of sections 1827 and 1828 of this title;

(17) In the Director's discretion, (A) accept and utilize voluntary and uncompensated (gratuitous) services, including services as authorized by section 3102(b) of title 5, United States Code; and (B) accept, hold, administer, and utilize gifts and bequests of personal property for the purpose of aiding or facilitating the work of the judicial branch of Government, but gifts or bequests of money shall be covered into the Treasury;

(18) Establish procedures and mechanisms within the judicial branch for processing fines, restitution, forfeitures of bail bonds or collateral, and assessments;

(19) Regulate and pay annuities to bankruptcy judges and United States magistrates in accordance with section 377 of this title and paragraphs (1)(B) and (2) of section 2(c) of the Retirement and Survivors' Annuities for Bankruptcy Judges and Magistrates Act of 1988;

(20) Periodically compile—

(A) the rules which are prescribed under section 2071 of this title by courts other than the Supreme Court;

(B) the rules which are prescribed under section 372(c)(11) of this title; and

(C) the orders which are required to be publicly available under section 372(c)(15) of this title;

so as to provide a current record of such rules and orders;

(21) Establish a program of incentive awards for employees of the judicial branch of the United States Government, other than any judge who is entitled to hold office during good behavior;

(22) Receive and expend, either directly or by transfer to the United States Marshals Service or other Government agency, funds appropriated for the procurement, installation, and maintenance of security equipment and protective services for the United States Courts in courtrooms and adjacent areas, including building ingress/egress control, inspection of packages, directed security patrols, and other similar activities;

(23) Regulate and pay annuities to judges of the United States Claims Court in accordance with section 178 of this title;

(24) [1] Lay before Congress, annually, statistical tables that will accurately reflect the business imposed on the Federal courts by the savings and loan crisis.

(24) Perform such other duties as may be assigned to him by the Supreme Court or the Judicial Conference of the United States.

(b) The clerical and administrative personnel of the courts shall comply with all requests by the Director for information or statistical data as to the state of court dockets.

(c) Inspection of court dockets outside the continental United States may be made through United States officials residing within the jurisdiction where the inspection is made.

(d) The Director, under the supervision and direction of the conference, shall:

(1) supervise all administrative matters relating to the offices of the United States magistrates;

(2) gather, compile, and evaluate all statistical and other information required for the performance of his duties and the duties of the conference with respect to such officers;

(3) lay before Congress annually statistical tables and other information which will accurately reflect the business which has come before the various United States magistrates, including (A) the number of matters in which the parties consented to the exercise of jurisdiction by a magistrate, (B) the number of appeals taken pursuant to the decisions of magistrates and the disposition of such appeals, and (C) the professional background and qualifications of individuals appointed under section 631 of this title to serve as magistrate;

(4) prepare and distribute a manual, with annual supplements and periodic revisions, for the use of such officers, which shall set forth their powers and duties, describe all categories of proceedings that may arise before them, and contain such other information as may be required to enable them to discharge their powers and duties promptly, effectively, and impartially.

(e) The Director may promulgate appropriate rules and regulations approved by the conference and not inconsistent with any provision of law, to assist him in the performance of the duties conferred upon him by subsection (d) of this section. Magistrates shall keep such records and make such reports as are specified in such rules and regulations.

(f) The Director may make, promulgate, issue, rescind, and amend rules and regulations (including regulations prescribing standards of conduct for Administrative Office employees) as may be necessary to carry out the Director's functions, powers, duties, and authority. The Director may publish in the

Federal Register such rules, regulations, and notices for the judicial branch of Government as the Director determines to be of public interest; and the Director of the Federal Register hereby is authorized to accept and shall publish such materials.

(g)(1) When authorized to exchange personal property, the Director may exchange or sell similar items and may apply the exchange allowance or proceeds of sale in such cases in whole or in part payment for the property acquired, but any transaction carried out under the authority of this subsection shall be evidenced in writing.

(2) The Director hereby is authorized to enter into contracts for public utility services and related terminal equipment for periods not exceeding ten years.

(h)(1) The Director shall, out of funds appropriated for the operation and maintenance of the courts, provide facilities and pay necessary expenses incurred by the judicial councils of the circuits and the Judicial Conference under section 372 of this title, including mileage allowance and witness fees, at the same rate as provided in section 1821 of this title. Administrative and professional assistance from the Administrative Office of the United States Courts may be requested by each judicial council and the Judicial Conference for purposes of discharging their duties under section 372 of this title.

(2) The Director of the Administrative Office of the United States Courts shall include in his annual report filed with the Congress under this section a summary of the number of complaints filed with each judicial council under section 372(c) of this title, indicating the general nature of such complaints and the disposition of those complaints in which action has been taken.

June 25, 1948, c. 646, 62 Stat. 914; Aug. 3, 1956, c. 944, § 3, 70 Stat. 1026; Dec. 20, 1967, Pub.L. 90–219, Title II, § 203, 81 Stat. 669; Oct. 17, 1968, Pub.L. 90–578, Title II, § 201, 82 Stat. 1114, 1115; Aug. 22, 1972, Pub.L. 92–397, § 4, 86 Stat. 580; Jan. 3, 1975, Pub.L. 93–619, Title II, § 204, 88 Stat. 2089; Oct. 28, 1978, Pub.L. 95–539, §§ 3, 4, 92 Stat. 2043; Nov. 6, 1978, Pub.L. 95–598, Title II, § 225, 92 Stat. 2665; Oct. 10, 1979, Pub.L. 96–82, § 5, 93 Stat. 645; Oct. 15, 1980, Pub.L. 96–458, § 5, 94 Stat. 2040; Dec. 12, 1980, Pub.L. 96–523, § 1(c)(1), 94 Stat. 3040; Sept. 27, 1982, Pub.L. 97–267, § 7, 96 Stat. 1139; Pub.L. 99–554, Title I, § 116, Oct. 27, 1986, 100 Stat. 3095; Dec. 11, 1987, Pub.L. 100–185, § 2, 101 Stat. 1279; Nov. 15, 1988, Pub.L. 100–659, § 6(a), 102 Stat. 3919; Nov. 19, 1988, Pub.L. 100–702, Title IV, § 402(a), Title X, §§ 1008, 1010, 1011, 1020(a)(2), 102 Stat. 4650, 4667, 4668, 4671; Nov. 19, 1988, Pub.L. 100–702, Title IV, § 402(a)(1), amended Oct. 30, 1990, Pub.L. 101–474, § 5(r), 104 Stat. 1099; Nov. 19, 1988, Pub.L. 100–702, Title IV, § 402(a)(1), amended Dec. 1, 1990, Pub.L. 101–650, Title III, § 306(e)(1)(A), 104 Stat. 5111; Nov. 19, 1988, Pub.L. 100–702, Title X, § 1011, amended Dec. 1, 1990, Pub.L. 101–650, Title III, § 325(c)(1), 104 Stat. 5121; Nov. 29, 1990, Pub.L. 101–647, Title XXV, § 2548, 104 Stat. 4888; Dec. 1, 1990, Pub.L. 101–650, Title III, § 306(e)(1)(B), 104 Stat. 5111.

¹ So in original.

Historical Note

References in Text. Section 2(c) of the Retirement and Survivors' Annuities for Bankruptcy Judges and Magistrates Act of 1988, referred to in subsec. (a)(19), is section 2(c) of Pub.L. 100–659, Nov. 15, 1988, 102 Stat. 3916, which is classified as a note under section 377 of Title 28, U.S.C.A., Judiciary and Judicial Procedure.

Codification. Section 5(r) of Pub.L. 101–474 and section 306(e)(1)(A) of Pub.L. 101–650 amended the directory language of Pub.L. 100–702 § 402(a)(1) by substituting "redesignating paragraph (19)" for "redesignating paragraph (18)", which amendments resulted in the paragraphs of subsection (a) being sequentially numbered (1) to (23).

Section 2548 of Pub.L. 101–647 added a subsec. (a)(24) and section 306(e)(1)(B)(ii) and (iii) of Pub.L. 101–650 added a subsec. (a)(23) and redesignated subsec. (a)(23) as (a)(24) without reference to prior addition of subsec. (a)(24) by Pub.L. 101–647, which for purposes of codification has been set out first.

Effective Date of 1990 Amendment. Amendment by section 306(e)(1) of Pub.L. 101–650 applicable to judges of, and senior judges in active service with, the United States Claims Court on or after Dec. 1, 1990, see section 306(f) of Pub.L. 101–650, set out as a note under section 8331 of Title 5, Government Organization and Employees.

Effective Date of 1988 Amendment. Section 9 of Pub.L. 100–659 provided that the amendments by Pub.L. 100–659 shall take effect on Nov. 15, 1988, and shall apply to bankruptcy judges and magistrates who retire on or after Nov. 15, 1988, with special election provisions for bankruptcy judges, etc., who left office on or after July 31, 1987, and before Nov. 15, 1988.

Section 407 of Pub.L. 100–702 provided that amendment redesignating par. (18) as (23) and adding par. (19) relating to periodical compilation shall take effect on Dec. 1, 1988.

Effective Date of 1986 Amendment. Amendment by Pub.L. 99–554 effective 30 days after Oct. 27, 1986, except as otherwise provided for, see section 302(a) of Pub.L. 99–554, set out as a note under section 581 of this title.

Change of Name of United States Magistrate. United States magistrate appointed under section 631 of this title to be known as United States magistrate judge after Dec. 1, 1990, with any reference to United States magistrate or magistrate in Title 28, in any other Federal statute, etc., deemed a reference to United States magistrate judge appointed under section 631 of this title, see section 321 of Pub.L. 101–650, set out as a note under section 631 of this title.

CHAPTER 44—ARBITRATION

Sec.
651. Authorization of arbitration.
652. Jurisdiction.
653. Powers of arbitrator; arbitration hearing.
654. Arbitration award and judgment.
655. Trial de novo.
656. Certification of arbitrators.
657. Compensation of arbitrators.
658. District courts that may authorize arbitration.

Effective and Termination Dates

Section 907 of Pub.L. 100–702 provided that chapter effective 180 days after Nov. 19, 1988, and section 906 of Pub.L. 100–702 provided that chapter to terminate 5 years after Nov. 19, 1988, except that provisions shall continue to apply through final disposition of all actions referred to arbitration before such date.

§ 651. Authorization of arbitration

(a) **Authority of certain district courts.**—Each United States district court described in section 658 may authorize by local rule the use of arbitration in any civil action, including an adversary proceeding in bankruptcy. A district court described in section 658(1) may refer any such action to arbitration as set forth in section 652(a). A district court described in section 658(2) may refer only such actions to arbitration as are set forth in section 652(a)(1)(A).

(b) **Title 9 not affected.**—This chapter shall not affect title 9.

Added Pub.L. 100–702, Title IX, § 901(a), Nov. 19, 1988, 102 Stat. 4659.

Effective and Termination Dates

Section 907 of Pub.L. 100–702 provided that section effective 180 days after Nov. 19, 1988, and section 906 of Pub.L. 100–702 provided that section to terminate 5 years after Nov. 19, 1988, except that provisions shall continue to apply through final disposition of all actions referred to arbitration before such date.

Historical Notes

Effective Date. Section 907 of Pub.L. 100–702 provided that: "This title and the amendments made by this title [enacting this chapter and the notes set out under this section and Section 652 of this title] shall take effect 180 days after the date of enactment of this Act. [Nov. 19, 1988]."

Model Procedures. Section 902 of Pub.L. 100–702 provides that:

"The Judicial Conference of the United States may develop model rules relating to procedures for arbitration under chapter 44, as added by section 901 of this Act [this chapter]. No model rule may supersede any provision of such chapter 44, this title [enacting this chapter and notes set out under this section and section 652 of this title], or any law of the United States."

Reports. Section 903 of Pub.L. 100–702 provided that:

"(a) Annual Report by Director of Administrative Office of the United States Courts.—The Director of the Administrative Office of the United States Courts shall include in the annual report of the activities of the Administrative Office required under section 604(a)(3), statistical information about the implementation of chapter 44, as added by section 901 of this Act [this chapter].

"(b) Report by Federal Judicial Center.— Not later than 5 years after the date of enactment of this Act [Nov. 19, 1988], the Federal Judicial Center, in consultation with the Director of the Administrative Office of the United States Courts, shall submit to the Congress a report on the implementation of chapter 44, as added by section 901 of this Act, which shall include the following:

"(1) A description of the arbitration programs authorized by such chapter, as conceived and as implemented in the judicial districts in which such programs are authorized.

"(2) A determination of the level of satisfaction with the arbitration programs in those judicial districts by a sampling of court personnel, attorneys, and litigants whose cases have been referred to arbitration.

"(3) A summary of those program features that can be identified as being related to program acceptance both within and across judicial districts.

"(4) A description of the levels of satisfaction relative to the cost per hearing of each program.

"(5) Recommendations to the Congress on whether to terminate or continue chapter 44, or, alternatively, to enact an arbitration provision in title 28, United States Code, authorizing arbitration in all Federal district courts."

Effect on Judicial Rule Making Powers. Section 904 of Pub.L. 100–702 provided that:

"Nothing in this title [enacting this chapter and notes set out under this section and section 652 of this title] or in chapter 44, as added by section 901 of this Act [this chapter], is intended to abridge, modify, or enlarge the rule making powers of the Federal judiciary."

Authorization of Appropriations. Section 905 of Pub.L. 100–702 provided that:

"There are authorized to be appropriated for the fiscal year ending September 30, 1989, and for each of the succeeding 4 fiscal years, to the judicial branch such sums as may be necessary to carry out the purposes of chapter 44, as added by section 901 of this Act [this chapter]. Funds appropriated under this section shall be allocated by the Administrative Office of the United States Courts to Federal judicial districts and the Federal Judicial Center. The funds so appropriated are authorized to remain available until expended, except that such funds may not be expended for the arbitration of actions referred to arbitration after the date of repeal set forth in section 906 of this Act [set out as a note under this section]".

Repeal. Section 906 of Pub.L. 100–702 provided that: "Effective 5 years after the date of the enactment of this Act [Nov. 19, 1988], chapter 44, as added by section 901 of this Act [this chapter], and the item relating to that chapter in the table of chapters at the beginning of part III of such title [preceding section 601 of this title], are repealed, except that the provisions of that chapter shall continue to apply through final disposition of all actions in which referral to arbitration was made before the date of repeal."

§ 652.   Jurisdiction

(a) **Actions that may be referred to arbitration.**—(1) Notwithstanding any provision of law to the contrary and except as provided in subsections (b) and (c) of this section, and section 901(c) of the Judicial Improvements and Access to Justice Act, a district court that authorizes arbitration under section 651 may—

(A) allow the referral to arbitration of any civil action (including any adversary proceeding in bankruptcy) pending before it if the parties consent to arbitration, and

(B) require the referral to arbitration of any civil action pending before it if the relief sought consists only of money damages not in excess of $100,000 or such lesser amount as the district court may set, exclusive of interest and costs.

(2) For purposes of paragraph (1)(B), a district court may presume damages are not in excess of $100,000 unless counsel certifies that damages exceed such amount.

(b) **Actions that may not be referred without consent of parties.**—Referral to arbitration under subsection (a)(1)(B) may not be made—

(1) of an action based on an alleged violation of a right secured by the Constitution of the United States, or

(2) if jurisdiction is based in whole or in part on section 1343 of this title.

(c) **Exceptions from arbitration.**—Each district court shall establish by local rule procedures for exempting, sua sponte or on motion of a party, any case from arbitration in which the objectives of arbitration would not be realized—

(1) because the case involves complex or novel legal issues,

(2) because legal issues predominate over factual issues, or

(3) for other good cause.

(d) **Safeguards in consent cases.**—In any civil action in which arbitration by consent is allowed under subsection (a)(1)(A), the district court shall by local rule establish procedures to ensure that—

(1) consent to arbitration is freely and knowingly obtained, and

(2) no party or attorney is prejudiced for refusing to participate in arbitration.

Added Pub.L. 100–702, Title IX, § 901(a), Nov. 19, 1988, 102 Stat. 6459.

Effective and Termination Dates

Section 907 of Pub.L. 100–702 provided that section effective 180 days after Nov. 19, 1988, and section 906 of Pub.L. 100–702 provided that section to terminate 5 years after Nov. 19, 1988, except that provisions shall continue to apply through final disposition of all actions referred to arbitration before such date.

Historical Notes

References in Text. Section 901(c) of the Judicial Improvements and Access to Justice Act, referred to in subsec. (a), is set out as a note below.

Exception to Limitation on Money Damages. Section 901(c) of Pub.L. 100–702 provided that: "Notwithstanding section 652 (as added by subsection (a) of this section) [this section], establishing a limitation of $100,000 in money damages with respect to cases referred to arbitration, a district court listed in section 658 (as added by subsection (a) of this section) [section 658 of this title], whose local rule on the date of the enactment of this Act [Nov. 19, 1988] provides for a limitation on money damages, with respect to such cases, of not more than $150,000, may continue to apply the higher limitation."

§ 653. Powers of arbitrator; arbitration hearing

(a) **Powers.**—An arbitrator to whom an action is referred under section 652 shall have, within the judicial district of the district court which referred the action to arbitration, the power—

(1) to conduct arbitration hearings,

(2) to administer oaths and affirmations, and

(3) to make awards.

(b) **Time for beginning arbitration hearing.**—An arbitration hearing under this chapter shall begin within a time period specified by the district court, but in no event later than 180 days after the filing of an answer, except that the arbitration proceeding shall not, in the absence of the consent of the parties, commence until 30 days after the disposition by the district court of any motion to dismiss the complaint, motion for judgment on the pleadings, motion to join necessary parties, or motion for summary judgment, if the motion was filed during a time period specified by the district court. The 180-day and 30-day periods specified in the preceding sentence may be modified by the court for good cause shown.

(c) **Subpoenas.**—Rule 45 of the Federal Rules of Civil Procedure (relating to subpoenas) applies to subpoenas for the attendance of witnesses and the production of documentary evidence at an arbitration hearing under this chapter.

Added Pub.L. 100–702, Title IX, § 901(a), Nov. 19, 1988, 102 Stat. 4660.

Effective and Termination Dates

Section 907 of Pub.L. 100–702 provided that section effective 180 days after Nov. 19, 1988, and section 906 of Pub.L. 100–702 provided that section to terminate 5 years after Nov. 19, 1988, except that provisions shall continue to apply through final disposition of all actions referred to arbitration before such date.

§ 654. Arbitration award and judgment

(a) **Filing and effect of arbitration award.**—An arbitration award made by an arbitrator under this chapter, along with proof of service of such award on the other party by the prevailing party or by the plaintiff, shall, promptly after the arbitration hearing is concluded, be filed with the clerk of the district court that referred the case to arbitration. Such award shall be entered as the judgment of the court after the time has expired for requesting a trial de novo under section 655. The judgment so entered shall be subject to the same provisions of law and shall have the same force and effect as a judgment of the court in a civil action, except that the judgment shall not be subject to review in any other court by appeal or otherwise.

   (b) Sealing of arbitration award.—The district court shall provide by local rule that the contents of any arbitration award made under this chapter shall not be made known to any judge who might be assigned to the case—

   (1) except as necessary for the court to determine whether to assess costs or attorney fees under section 655,

   (2) until the district court has entered final judgment in the action or the action has been otherwise terminated, or

   (3) except for purposes of preparing the report required by section 903(b) of the Judicial Improvements and Access to Justice Act.

   (c) Taxation of costs.—The district court may by rule allow for the inclusion of costs as provided in section 1920 of this title as a part of the arbitration award.

Added Pub.L. 100–702, Title IX, § 901(a), Nov. 19, 1988, 102 Stat. 4660.

Effective and Termination Dates

   Section 907 of Pub.L. 100–702 provided that section effective 180 days after Nov. 19, 1988, and section 906 of Pub.L. 100–702 provided that section to terminate 5 years after Nov. 19, 1988, except that provisions shall continue to apply through final disposition of all actions referred to arbitration before such date.

§ 655. Trial de novo

   (a) Time for demand.—Within 30 days after the filing of an arbitration award with a district court under section 654, any party may file a written demand for a trial de novo in the district court.

   (b) Restoration to court docket.—Upon a demand for a trial de novo, the action shall be restored to the docket of the court and treated for all purposes as if it had not been referred to arbitration. In such a case, any right of trial by jury that a party otherwise would have had, as well as any place on the court calendar which is no later than that which a party otherwise would have had, are preserved.

   (c) Limitation on admission of evidence.—The court shall not admit at the trial de novo any evidence that there has been an arbitration proceeding, the nature or amount of any award, or any other matter concerning the conduct of the arbitration proceeding, unless—

   (1) the evidence would otherwise be admissible in the court under the Federal Rules of Evidence, or

   (2) the parties have otherwise stipulated.

   (d) Taxation of arbitration fees as cost.—(1)(A) A district court may provide by rule that, in any trial de novo under this section, arbitrator fees paid under section 657 may be taxed as costs against the party demanding the trial de novo.

(B) Such rule may provide that a party demanding a trial de novo under subsection (a), other than the United States or its agencies or officers, shall deposit a sum equal to such arbitrator fees as advanced payment of such costs, unless the party is permitted to proceed in forma pauperis.

(2) Arbitrator fees shall not be taxed as costs under paragraph (1)(A), and any sum deposited under paragraph (1)(B) shall be returned to the party demanding the trial de novo, if—

(A) the party demanding the trial de novo obtains a final judgment more favorable than the arbitration award, or

(B) the court determines that the demand for the trial de novo was made for good cause.

(3) Any arbitrator fees taxed as costs under paragraph (1)(A), and any sum deposited under paragraph (1)(B) that is not returned to the party demanding the trial de novo, shall be paid to the Treasury of the United States.

(4) Any rule under this subsection shall provide that no penalty for demanding a trial de novo, other than that provided in this subsection, shall be assessed by the court.

(e) **Assessment of costs and attorney fees.**—In any trial de novo demanded under subsection (a) in which arbitration was done by consent of the parties, a district court may assess costs, as provided in section 1920 of this title, and reasonable attorney fees against the party demanding the trial de novo if—

(1) such party fails to obtain a judgment, exclusive of interest and costs, in the court which is substantially more favorable to such party than the arbitration award, and

(2) the court determines that the party's conduct in seeking a trial de novo was in bad faith.

Added Pub.L. 100–702, Title IX, § 901(a), Nov. 19, 1988, 102 Stat. 4661.

Effective and Termination Dates

Section 907 of Pub.L. 100–702 provided that section effective 180 days after Nov. 19, 1988, and section 906 of Pub.L. 100–702 provided that section to terminate 5 years after Nov. 19, 1988, except that provisions shall continue to apply through final disposition of all actions referred to arbitration before such date.

§ 656. Certification of arbitrators

(a) **Standards for certification.**—Each district court listed in section 658 shall establish standards for the certification of arbitrators and shall certify arbitrators to perform services in accordance with such standards and this chapter. The standards shall include provisions requiring that any arbitrator—

(1) shall take the oath or affirmation described in section 453, and

(2) shall be subject to the disqualification rules of section 455.

(b) **Treatment of arbitrator as independent contractor and special government employee.**—An arbitrator is an independent contractor and is subject to the provisions of sections 201 through 211 of title 18 to the same extent as such provisions apply to a special Government employee of the executive branch. A person may not be barred from the practice of law because such person is an arbitrator.

Added Pub.L. 100–702, Title IX, § 901(a), Nov. 19, 1988, 102 Stat. 4662.

Effective and Termination Dates

Section 907 of Pub.L. 100–702 provided that section effective 180 days after Nov. 19, 1988, and section 906 of Pub.L. 100–702 provided that section to terminate 5 years after Nov. 19, 1988, except that provisions shall continue to apply through final disposition of all actions referred to arbitration before such date.

§ 657. Compensation of arbitrators

(a) **Compensation.**—The district court may, subject to limits set by the Judicial Conference of the United States, establish and pay the amount of compensation, if any, that each arbitrator shall receive for services rendered in each case.

(b) **Transportation allowances.**—Under regulations prescribed by the Director of the Administrative Office of the United States Courts, a district court may reimburse arbitrators for actual transportation expenses necessarily incurred in the performance of duties under this chapter.

Added Pub.L. 100–702, Title IX, § 901(a), Nov. 19, 1988, 102 Stat. 4662.

Effective and Termination Dates

Section 907 of Pub.L. 100–702 provided that section effective 180 days after Nov. 19, 1988, and section 906 of Pub.L. 100–702 provided that section to terminate 5 years after Nov. 19, 1988, except that provisions shall continue to apply through final disposition of all actions referred to arbitration before such date.

§ 658. District courts that may authorize arbitration

The district courts for the following judicial districts may authorize the use of arbitration under this chapter:

(1) Northern District of California, Middle District of Florida, Western District of Michigan, Western District of Missouri, District of New Jersey, Eastern District of New York, Middle District of North Carolina, Western District of Oklahoma, Eastern District of Pennsylvania, and Western District of Texas.

(2) Ten additional judicial districts, which shall be approved by the Judicial Conference of the United States. The Judicial Conference shall give notice of the 10 districts approved under this paragraph to the Federal Judicial Center and to the public.

Added Pub.L. 100–702, Title IX, § 901(a), Nov. 19, 1988, 102 Stat. 4663.

Effective and Termination Dates

Section 907 of Pub.L. 100–702 provided that section effective 180 days after Nov. 19, 1988, and section 906 of Pub.L. 100–702 provided that section to terminate 5 years after Nov. 19, 1988, except that provisions shall continue to apply through final disposition of all actions referred to arbitration before such date.

CHAPTER 57—GENERAL PROVISIONS APPLICABLE TO COURT OFFICERS AND EMPLOYEES

§ 959.   Trustees and receivers suable; management; State laws

(a) Trustees, receivers or managers of any property, including debtors in possession, may be sued, without leave of the court appointing them, with respect to any of their acts or transactions in carrying on business connected with such property. Such actions shall be subject to the general equity power of such court so far as the same may be necessary to the ends of justice, but this shall not deprive a litigant of his right to trial by jury.

(b) Except as provided in section 1166 of title 11, a trustee, receiver or manager appointed in any cause pending in any court of the United States, including a debtor in possession, shall manage and operate the property in his possession as such trustee, receiver or manager according to the requirements of the valid laws of the State in which such property is situated, in the same manner that the owner or possessor thereof would be bound to do if in possession thereof.

June 25, 1948, c. 646, 62 Stat. 926; Nov. 6, 1978, Pub.L. 95–598, Title II, § 235, 92 Stat. 2667.

PART IV—JURISDICTION AND VENUE

CHAPTER 85—DISTRICT COURTS; JURISDICTION

§ 1334.   Bankruptcy cases and proceedings

(a) Except as provided in subsection (b) of this section, the district courts shall have original and exclusive jurisdiction of all cases under title 11.

(b) Notwithstanding any Act of Congress that confers exclusive jurisdiction on a court or courts other than the district courts, the district courts shall have original but not exclusive jurisdiction of all civil proceedings arising under title 11, or arising in or related to cases under title 11.

(c)(1) Nothing in this section prevents a district court in the interest of justice, or in the interest of comity with State courts or respect for State law, from abstaining from hearing a particular proceeding arising under title 11 or arising in or related to a case under title 11.

(2) Upon timely motion of a party in a proceeding based upon a State law claim or State law cause of action, related to a case under title 11 but not arising under title 11 or arising in a case under title 11, with respect to which an action could not have been commenced in a court of the United States absent jurisdiction under this section, the district court shall abstain from hearing such proceeding if an action is commenced, and can be timely adjudicated, in a State forum of appropriate jurisdiction. Any decision to abstain or not to abstain made under this subsection is not reviewable by appeal or otherwise by the court of appeals under section 158(d), 1291, or 1292 of this title or by the Supreme Court of the United States under section 1254 of this title. This subsection shall not be construed to limit the applicability of the stay provided for by section 362

of title 11, United States Code, as such section applies to an action affecting the property of the estate in bankruptcy.

(d) The district court in which a case under title 11 is commenced or is pending shall have exclusive jurisdiction of all of the property, wherever located, of the debtor as of the commencement of such case, and of property of the estate.

June 25, 1948, c. 646, 62 Stat. 931; July 10, 1984, Pub.L. 98–353, Title I, § 101(a), 98 Stat. 333; Oct. 27, 1986, Pub.L. 99–554, Title I, § 144(e), 100 Stat. 3096; Dec. 1, 1990, Pub.L. 101–650, Title III, § 309(b), 104 Stat. 5113.

Historical Note

Codification. Section 238 of Pub.L. 95–598, Nov. 6, 1978, 92 Stat. 2667, amended this section to read as follows:

"§ 1334. Bankruptcy appeals

"(a) The district courts for districts for which panels have not been ordered appointed under section 160 of this title shall have jurisdiction of appeals from all final judgments, orders, and decrees of bankruptcy courts.

"(b) The district courts for such districts shall have jurisdiction of appeals from interlocutory orders and decrees of bankruptcy courts, but only by leave of the district court to which the appeal is taken.

"(c) A district court may not refer an appeal under that section to a magistrate or to a special master."

Section 113 of Pub.L. 98–353, July 10, 1984, 98 Stat. 343, (effective June 27, 1984 pursuant to section 122(c) of Pub.L. 98–353) provided that this amendment "shall not be effective". Section 121 of Pub.L. 98–353 (effective on July 10, 1984 pursuant to section 122(a) of Pub.L. 98–353) provided that this amendment shall take effect on July 10, 1984.

Effective Date of 1986 Amendment. Amendment by Pub.L. 99–554 effective 30 days after Oct. 27, 1986, except as otherwise provided for, see section 302(a) of Pub.L. 99–554, set out as a note under section 581 of this title.

Effective Date of 1984 Amendments. For effective date of amendments by Title I of Pub.L. 98–353, see section 122 of Pub.L. 98–353, Title I, July 10, 1984, 98 Stat. 346, set out as an Effective Date of 1984 Amendment note under section 151 of Title 28, Judiciary and Judicial Procedure.

Jurisdiction Over and Transfer of Bankruptcy Cases and Proceedings. Section 115

of Pub.L. 98–353, Title I, July 10, 1984, 98 Stat. 343, provided that:

"(a) On the date of the enactment of this Act [July 10, 1984] the appropriate district court of the United States shall have jurisdiction of—

"(1) cases, and matters and proceedings in cases, under the Bankruptcy Act [former Title 11, Bankruptcy] that are pending immediately before such date in the bankruptcy courts continued by section 404(a) of the Act of November 6, 1978 (Public Law 95–598; 92 Stat. 2687) [Pub.L. 95–598, Title IV, § 404(a), Nov. 6, 1978, 92 Stat. 2683, set out in Transition Provisions] and

"(2) cases under title 11 of the United States Code [Title 11, Bankruptcy], and proceedings arising under title 11 of the United States Code or arising in or related to cases under title 11 of the United States Code, that are pending immediately before such date in the bankruptcy courts continued by section 404(a) of the Act of November 6, 1978 (Public Law 95–598; 92 Stat. 2687).

"(b) On the date of the enactment of this Act [July 10, 1984], there shall be transferred to the appropriate district court of the United States appeals from final judgments, orders, and decrees of the bankruptcy courts pending immediately before such date in the bankruptcy appellate panels appointed under section 405(c) of the Act of November 6, 1978 (Public Law 95–598; 92 Stat. 2685) [Pub.L. 95–598, Title IV, § 405(c), Nov. 6, 1978, 92 Stat. 2685, set out in Transition Provisions]."

[For effective date of amendments by Title I of Pub.L. 98–353, see section 122 of Pub.L. 98–353, Title I, July 10, 1984, 98 Stat. 346, set out as an Effective Date of 1984 Amendment note under section 151 of Title 28, Judiciary and Judicial Procedure.]

CHAPTER 87—DISTRICT COURTS; VENUE

Sec.

1408.   Venue of cases under Title 11.
1409.   Venue of proceedings arising under Title 11 or arising in or related to cases under Title 11.
1410.   Venue of cases ancillary to foreign proceedings.
1411.   Jury trials.
1412.   Change of venue.

Historical Note

Codification. Section 240(b) of Pub.L. 95–598, Nov. 6, 1978, 92 Stat. 2668, amended the table of sections by inserting the following item:

1408.   Bankruptcy appeals.

Section 113 of Pub.L. 98–353, July 10, 1984, 98 Stat. 343, (effective June 27, 1984 pursuant to section 122(c) of Pub.L. 98–353) provided that this amendment "shall not be effective". Section 121 of Pub.L. 98–353 (effective on July 10, 1984 pursuant to section 122(a) of Pub.L. 98–353) provided that this amendment shall take effect on July 10, 1984.

Effective Date of 1984 Amendments. Section 102(b) of Pub.L. 98–353, Title I, July 10, 1984, 98 Stat. 335, added items 1408 to 1412. For effective date of amendments by Title I of Pub.L. 98–353, see section 122 of Pub.L. 98–353, Title I, July 10, 1984, 98 Stat. 346, set out as an Effective Date of 1984 Amendment note under section 151 of Title 28, Judiciary and Judicial Procedure.

§ 1408.   Venue of cases under Title 11

Except as provided in section 1410 of this title, a case under title 11 may be commenced in the district court for the district—

(1) in which the domicile, residence, principal place of business in the United States, or principal assets in the United States, of the person or entity that is the subject of such case have been located for the one hundred and eighty days immediately preceding such commencement, or for a longer portion of such one-hundred-and-eighty-day period than the domicile, residence, or principal place of business, in the United States, or principal assets in the United States, of such person were located in any other district; or

(2) in which there is pending a case under title 11 concerning such person's affiliate, general partner, or partnership.

Added Pub.L. 98–353, Title I, § 102(a), July 10, 1984, 98 Stat. 334.

Historical Note

Codification. Section 240(a) of Pub.L. 95–598, Nov. 6, 1978, 92 Stat. 2668, amended this section to read as follows:

"§ 1408.   Bankruptcy appeals

"An appeal under section 1334 of this title from a judgment, order, or decree of a bankruptcy court may be brought only in the judicial district in which such bankruptcy court is located."

Section 113 of Pub.L. 98–353, July 10, 1984, 98 Stat. 343, (effective June 27, 1984 pursuant to section 122(c) of Pub.L. 98–353) provided that this amendment "shall not be effective". Section 121 of Pub.L. 98–353 (effective on July 10, 1984 pursuant to section 122(a) of Pub.L. 98–353) provided that this amendment shall take effect on July 10, 1984.

Effective Date. For effective date of amendments by Title I of Pub.L. 98–353, see section 122 of Pub.L. 98–353, Title I, July 10, 1984, 98 Stat. 346, set out as an Effective Date of 1984 Amendment note under section 151 of Title 28, Judiciary and Judicial Procedure.

§ 1409. Venue of proceedings arising under Title 11 or arising in or related to cases under Title 11

(a) Except as otherwise provided in subsections (b) and (d), a proceeding arising under title 11 or arising in or related to a case under title 11 may be commenced in the district court in which such case is pending.

(b) Except as provided in subsection (d) of this section, a trustee in a case under title 11 may commence a proceeding arising in or related to such case to recover a money judgment of or property worth less than $1,000 or a consumer debt of less than $5,000 only in the district court for the district in which the defendant resides.

(c) Except as provided in subsection (b) of this section, a trustee in a case under title 11 may commence a proceeding arising in or related to such case as statutory successor to the debtor or creditors under section 541 or 544(b) of title 11 in the district court for the district where the State or Federal court sits in which, under applicable nonbankruptcy venue provisions, the debtor or creditors, as the case may be, may have commenced an action on which such proceeding is based if the case under title 11 had not been commenced.

(d) A trustee may commence a proceeding arising under title 11 or arising in or related to a case under title 11 based on a claim arising after the commencement of such case from the operation of the business of the debtor only in the district court for the district where a State or Federal court sits in which, under applicable nonbankruptcy venue provisions, an action on such claim may have been brought.

(e) A proceeding arising under title 11 or arising in or related to a case under title 11, based on a claim arising after the commencement of such case from the operation of the business of the debtor, may be commenced against the representative of the estate in such case in the district court for the district where the State or Federal court sits in which the party commencing such proceeding may, under applicable nonbankruptcy venue provisions, have brought an action on such claim, or in the district court in which such case is pending.

Added Pub.L. 98–353, Title I, § 102a, July 10, 1984, 98 Stat. 334.

Historical Note

Effective Date. For effective date of amendments by Title I of Pub.L. 98–353, see section 122 of Pub.L. 98–353, Title I, July 10, 1984, 98 Stat. 346, set out as an Effective Date of 1984 Amendment note under section 151 of Title 28, Judiciary and Judicial Procedure.

§ 1410. Venue of cases ancillary to foreign proceedings

(a) A case under section 304 of title 11 to enjoin the commencement or continuation of an action or proceeding in a State or Federal court, or the enforcement of a judgment, may be commenced only in the district court for the district where the State or Federal court sits in which is pending the action or proceeding against which the injunction is sought.

(b) A case under section 304 of title 11 to enjoin the enforcement of a lien against a property, or to require the turnover of property of an estate, may be commenced only in the district court for the district in which such property is found.

(c) A case under section 304 of title 11, other than a case specified in subsection (a) or (b) of this section, may be commenced only in the district court for the district in which is located the principal place of business in the United States, or the principal assets in the United States, of the estate that is the subject of such case.

Added Pub.L. 98–353, Title I, § 102(a), July 10, 1984, 98 Stat. 335.

Historical Note

Effective Date. For effective date of amendments by Title I of Pub.L. 98–353, see section 122 of Pub.L. 98–353, Title I, July 10, 1984, 98 Stat. 346, set out as an Effective Date of 1984 Amendment note under section 151 of Title 28, Judiciary and Judicial Procedure.

§ 1411. Jury trials

(a) Except as provided in subsection (b) of this section, this chapter and title 11 do not affect any right to trial by jury that an individual has under applicable nonbankruptcy law with regard to a personal injury or wrongful death tort claim.

(b) The district court may order the issues arising under section 303 of title 11 to be tried without a jury.

Added Pub.L. 98–353, Title I, § 102(a), July 10, 1984, 98 Stat. 335.

Historical Note

Effective Date. For effective date of amendments by Title I of Pub.L. 98–353, see section 122 of Pub.L. 98–353, Title I, July 10, 1984, 98 Stat. 346, set out as an Effective Date of 1984 Amendment note under section 151 of Title 28, Judiciary and Judicial Procedure.

§ 1412. Change of venue

A district court may transfer a case or proceeding under title 11 to a district court for another district, in the interest of justice or for the convenience of the parties.

Added Pub.L. 98–353, Title I, § 102(a), July 10, 1984, 98 Stat. 335.

Historical Note

Effective Date. For effective date of amendments by Title I of Pub.L. 98–353, see section 122 of Pub.L. 98–353, Title I, July 10, 1984, 98 Stat. 346, set out as an Effective Date of 1984 Amendment note under section 151 of Title 28, Judiciary and Judicial Procedure.

CHAPTER 89—DISTRICT COURTS; REMOVAL OF CASES FROM STATE COURTS

§ 1452. Removal of claims related to bankruptcy cases

(a) A party may remove any claim or cause of action in a civil action other than a proceeding before the United States Tax Court or a civil action by a governmental unit to enforce such governmental unit's police or regulatory power, to the district court for the district where such civil action is pending, if such district court has jurisdiction of such claim or cause of action under section 1334 of this title.

(b) The court to which such claim or cause of action is removed may remand such claim or cause of action on any equitable ground. An order entered under this subsection remanding a claim or cause of action, or a decision to not remand, is not reviewable by appeal or otherwise by the court of appeals under section 158(d), 1291, or 1292 of this title or by the Supreme Court of the United States under section 1254 of this title.

Added Pub.L. 98–353, Title I, § 103(a), July 10, 1984, 98 Stat. 335 and amended Pub.L. 101–650, Title III, § 309(c), Dec. 1, 1990, 104 Stat. 5113.

Historical Note

Effective Date. For effective date of amendments by Title I of Pub.L. 98–353, see section 122 of Pub.L. 98–353, Title I, July 10, 1984, 98 Stat. 346, set out as an Effective Date of 1984 Amendment note under section 151 of Title 28, Judiciary and Judicial Procedure.

PART V—PROCEDURE

CHAPTER 123—FEES AND COSTS

Note: *See also "Judicial Conference Schedule of Fees" following § 1930 below*

§ 1930. Bankruptcy fees

(a) Notwithstanding section 1915 of this title, the parties commencing a case under title 11 shall pay to the clerk of the district court or the clerk of the bankruptcy court, if one has been certified pursuant to section 156(b) of this title, the following filing fees:

(1) For a case commenced under chapter 7 or 13 of title 11, $120.

(2) For a case commenced under chapter 9 of title 11, $300.

(3) For a case commenced under chapter 11 of title 11 that does not concern a railroad, as defined in section 101 of title 11, $500.

(4) For a case commenced under chapter 11 of title 11 concerning a railroad, as so defined, $1000.

(5) For a case commenced under chapter 12 of title 11, $200.

(6) In addition to the filing fee paid to the clerk, a quarterly fee shall be paid to the United States trustee, for deposit in the Treasury, in each case under chapter 11 of title 11 for each quarter (including any fraction thereof) until a plan is confirmed or the case is converted or dismissed, whichever occurs first. The fee shall be $150 for each quarter in which disbursements total less than $15,000; $300 for each quarter in which disbursements total $15,000 or more but less than $150,000; $750 for each quarter in which disbursements total $150,000 or more but less than $300,000; $2,250 for each quarter in which disbursements total $300,000 or more but less than $3,000,000; $3,000 for each quarter in which disbursements total $3,000,000 or more. The fee shall be payable on the last day of the calendar month following the calendar quarter for which the fee is owed.

An individual commencing a voluntary case or a joint case under title 11 may pay such fee in installments. For converting, on request of the debtor, a case under chapter 7, or 13 of title 11, to a case under chapter 11 of title 11, the debtor shall pay to the clerk of the district court or the clerk of the bankruptcy court, if one has been certified pursuant to section 156(b) of this title, a fee of $400.

(b) The Judicial Conference of the United States may prescribe additional fees in cases under title 11 of the same kind as the Judicial Conference prescribes under section 1914(b) of this title.

(c) Upon the filing of any separate or joint notice of appeal or application for appeal or upon the receipt of any order allowing, or notice of the allowance of, an appeal or a writ of certiorari $5 shall be paid to the clerk of the court, by the appellant or petitioner.

(d) Whenever any case or proceeding is dismissed in any bankruptcy court for want of jurisdiction, such court may order the payment of just costs.

(e) The clerk of the court may collect only the fees prescribed under this section.

Added Pub.L. 95–598, Title II, § 246(a), Nov. 6, 1978, 92 Stat. 2671, and amended Pub.L. 98–353, Title I, § 111(a),(b), July 10, 1984, 98 Stat. 342; Pub.L. 99–500, Title I, § 101(b) [Title IV, § 407(b)], Oct. 18, 1986, 100 Stat. 1783–64; Pub.L. 99–554, Title I, §§ 117, 144(f), Oct. 27, 1986, 100 Stat. 3095, 3097; Pub.L. 99–591, Title I, § 101(b) [Title IV, § 407(b)], Oct. 30, 1986, 100 Stat. 3341–64, Pub.L. 101–162, Title IV, § 406(a), Nov. 21, 1989, 103 Stat. 1016.

Historical Note

Codification. Amendment by section 144(f) of Pub.L. 99–554 has been executed in two places in the text of subsec. (a) of this section in view of the directory language of such amendment. See 1986 Amendment note set out below.

1986 Amendment. Subsec. (a). Pub.L. 99–554, § 144(f), substituted "clerk of the district court or the clerk of the bankruptcy court, if one has been certified pursuant to section 156(b) of this title," for "clerk of the court" in two places. See Codification note set out hereunder.

Pub.L. 99–554, § 117, in par. (1) substituted "$90" for "$60", in par. (3) substituted "$500" for "$200", in par. (4) substituted "$1,000" for "$500", added pars. (5) and (6), and added "For converting, on request of the debtor, a case under chapter 7, or 13 of title 11, to a case under chapter 11 of title 11, the debtor shall pay to the clerk of the court a fee of $400.".

Pub.L. 99–500 provided for duplicate amendment to subsec. (a)(1).

See Effective Date of 1986 Amendment, etc., notes set out below.

Effective Date of 1989 Amendment. Section 406(a) of Pub.L. 101–162 provided in part that: "Pursuant to section 1930(b) of title 28 [subsec. (b) of this section], the Judicial Conference of the United States shall prescribe a fee of $60 on motions seeking relief from the automatic stay under 11 U.S.C. section 362(b) [section 362(b) of Title 11, Bankruptcy] and motions to compel abandonment of property of the estate. The fees established pursuant to the preceding two sentences [amending subsec. (a)(1) of this section and enacting this note] shall take effect 30 days after the enactment of this Act [Nov. 21, 1989]."

Effective Date of 1986 Amendments; Effective Date of 1986 Amendments for Certain Judicial Districts Not Served by United States Trustees and for Judicial Districts in Alabama and North Carolina; U.S. Trustee System Fund Deposits in Alabama and North Carolina; Effective Date of Title 11 Chapter 15 Repeal as to Northern District of Alabama; Authority of Certain Estate Administrators in Alabama and North Carolina; Effective Date of 1986 Amendments in Pending Cases Where a U.S. Trustee Not Authorized or Where a Trustee Files Final Report or Plan is Confirmed; Quarterly Fees. Amendment by Pub.L. 99–554 effective 30 days after Oct. 27, 1986, except as otherwise provided for, see section 302(a) of Pub.L. 99–554, set out as a note under section 581 of this title.

Amendment by Pub.L. 99–554, § 117(4), not to become effective in or with respect to certain specified judicial districts until, or apply to cases while pending in such district before, the expiration of the 270–day period beginning 30 days after Oct. 27, 1986, or of the 30–day period beginning on the date the Attorney General certifies under section 303 of Pub.L. 99–554 the region specified in a paragraph of section 581(a) of Title 28, as amended by section 111(a) of Pub.L. 99–554, that includes such district, whichever occurs first, see section 302(d)(1) of Pub.L. 99–554, set out as a note under section 581 of this title.

Amendment by Pub.L. 99–554, § 117(4), not to become effective in or with respect to certain specified judicial districts until, or apply to cases while pending in such district before, the expiration of the 2–year period beginning 30 days after Oct. 27, 1986, or of the 30–day period beginning on the date the Attorney General certifies under section 303 of Pub.L. 99–554 the region specified in a paragraph of section 581(a) of Title 28, as amended by section 111(a) of Pub.L. 99–554, that includes such district, whichever occurs first, see section 302(d)(1) of Pub.L. 99–554, set out as a note under section 581 of this title.

Amendment by Pub.L. 99–554, § 117(4), not to become effective in or with respect to judicial districts established for the States of Alabama and North Carolina until, or apply to cases while pending in such district before, such district elects to be included in a bankruptcy region established in section 581(a) of Title 28, as amended by section 111(a) of Pub.L. 99–554, or Oct. 1, 2002, whichever occurs first, and, except as otherwise provided for, with respect to cases under chapters 7, 11, 12, and 13 of Title 11 commenced before 30 days after Oct. 27, 1986, and pending in a judicial district in the States of Alabama or North Carolina before any election made under section 302(d)(3)(A) of Pub.L. 99–554 by such district becomes effective or Oct. 1, 2002, whichever occurs first, amendments by Pub.L. 99–554 not to apply until Oct. 1, 2003, or the expiration of the 1–year period beginning on the date such election becomes effective, whichever occurs first, and further, in any judicial district in Alabama or North Carolina not making the election described in section 302(d)(3)(A) of Pub.L. 99–554, any person appointed under regulations issued by the Judicial Conference to administer estates in cases under Title 11 authorized to establish, etc., a panel of private trustees, and to supervise cases and trustees in cases under chapters 7, 11, 12, and 13 of Title 11, until amendments by sections 201 to 231 of Pub.L. 99–554 effective in such district, see section 302(d)(3)(A) to

(F), (H), (I) of Pub.L. 99–554, set out as a note under section 581 of this title.

Deposit in the general receipts of the Treasury of funds collected as a result of the amendments made by section 117 of Pub.L. 99–554 in a judicial district in the States of Alabama or North Carolina under section 1930(a) of Title 28 before the date the amendments made by sections 201 to 231 of Pub.L. 99–554 take effect in such districts, and notwithstanding section 589a of Title 28, see section 302(d)(3)(G) of Pub.L. 99–554, set out as a note under section 581 of this title.

Amendment by Pub.L. 99–554, § 117(4), except as otherwise provided, with respect to cases under chapters 7, 11, 12, and 13 of Title 11 commenced before 30 days after Oct. 27, 1986, and pending in a judicial district referred to in section 581(a) of Title 28, as amended by section 111(a) of Pub.L. 99–554, for which a United States trustee is not authorized before 30 days after Oct. 27, 1986 to be appointed, not applicable until the expiration of the 3–year period beginning on Oct. 27, 1986, or of the 1-year period beginning on the date the Attorney General certifies under section 303 of Pub.L. 99–554 the region specified in a paragraph of such section 581(a) that includes, such district, whichever occurs first, see section 302(e)(1), (2) of Pub.L. 99–554, set out as a note under section 581 of this title.

Rule of construction regarding fees for cases under Title 11 for any conduct or period occurring before section 1930(a)(6) of Title 28 becomes effective in the district in which such case is pending, see section 302(e)(3) of Pub.L. 99–554, set out as a note under section 581 of this title.

See 1986 Amendment notes set out above.

Effective Date of 1984 Amendments. For effective date of amendments by Title I of Pub.L. 98–353, see section 122 of Pub.L. 98–353, Title I, July 10, 1984, 98 Stat. 346, set out as an Effective Date of 1984 Amendment note under section 151 of Title 28, Judiciary and Judicial Procedure.

Issuance of Notices to Creditors and Other Interested Parties. Section 403 of Pub.L. 101–162 provided that: "Notwithstanding any other provision of law, for fiscal year 1990 and hereafter, (a) The Administrative Office of the United States Courts, or any other agency or instrumentality of the United States, is prohibited from restricting solely to staff of the Clerks of the United States Bankruptcy Courts the issuance of notices to creditors and other interested parties. (b) The

Administrative Office shall permit and encourage the preparation and mailing of such notices to be performed by or at the expense of the debtors, trustees or such other interested parties as the Court may direct and approve. (c) The Director of the Administrative Office of the United States Courts shall make appropriate provisions for the use of and accounting for any postage required pursuant to such directives."

Collection of Fees in Bankruptcy Cases for Salaries and Other Expenses. Section

404(a) of Pub.L. 101–162 provided that: "For fiscal year 1990 and hereafter, such fees as shall be collected for the preparation and mailing of notices in bankruptcy cases as prescribed by the Judicial Conference of the United States pursuant to 28 U.S.C. 1930(b) [subsec. (b) of this section] shall be deposited to the "Courts of Appeals, District Courts, and Other Judicial Services, Salaries and Expenses" appropriation to be used for salaries and other expenses incurred in providing these services."

JUDICIAL CONFERENCE SCHEDULE OF FEES

The Judicial Conference of the United States at its session on March 7–9, 1979, set forth the schedule of fees to be charged in bankruptcy courts pursuant to this section. That schedule became effective on October 1, 1979. At its sessions in March and September 1980, March, 1981, March, 1987, and March and September, 1988, the Judicial Conference amended the schedule of fees. The Administrative Office of the United States Courts provided for Registry Fund Fees effective June 12, 1989. At its September, 1989 meeting, the Judicial Conference again amended the schedule of fees, such amendments effective pursuant to 1989 Judicial Conference Statement. The schedule of fees was again amended by the Judicial Conference at its March and September, 1990 meetings.

Fees to be charged for services to be performed by clerks of the bankruptcy courts (except that no fees are to be charged for services rendered on behalf of the United States or to bankruptcy administrators appointed under Pub.L. No. 99–554, § 302(d)(3)(I).)

(1) For reproducing any record or paper, 50 cents per page. This fee shall apply to paper copies made from either: (1) original documents; or (2) microfiche or microfilm reproductions of the original records.

(2) For certification or exemplification of any document or paper, whether the certification is made directly on the document, or by separate instrument, $5.00.

(3) For reproduction of magnetic tape recordings, either cassette or reel-to-reel, $15.00 including the cost of materials.

(4) For amendments to a debtor's schedules of creditors or lists of creditors after notice to creditors, $20.00 for each amendment, provided the bankruptcy judge may, for good cause, waive the charge in any case.

(5) For every search of the records of the bankruptcy court conducted by the clerk of the bankruptcy court or a deputy clerk, $15.00 per name or item searched.

(6) For filing a complaint, a fee shall be collected in the same amount as the filing fee prescribed in 28 U.S.C. 1914(a) for instituting any civil action other than a writ of habeas corpus. If the United States, other than a United States Trustee acting as a trustee in a case under Title 11, or a debtor is the plaintiff, no fee is required. If a trustee or debtor in possession is the plaintiff, the fee should be payable only from the estate and to the extent there is any estate realized.

(7) For filing or indexing any paper not in a case or proceeding for which a filing fee has been paid, including registering a judgment from another district, $20.00.

(8) For all notices generated in cases filed under Title 11 of the United States Code, 50 cents each. The fee shall be payable only from the estate and only to the extent there is an estate.

(9) Upon the filing of a notice of appeal with the bankruptcy court in a proceeding arising under the Bankruptcy Act, $5.00 shall be paid to the clerk of the bankruptcy court by the appellant.

(10) For clerical processing of each claim filed in excess of 10, 25 cents each in asset cases filed under Chapters I–VII of the Bankruptcy Act, in cases filed under the relief chapters of the Bankruptcy Act, and in asset cases filed under the Bankruptcy Code.

(11) For transcribing a record of any proceeding by a regularly employed member of the bankruptcy court staff who is not entitled by statute to retain the transcript fees for his or her own account, a charge shall be made at the same rate and conditions established by the Judicial Conference for transcripts prepared and sold to parties by official court reporters. The party requesting the transcript shall pay the charge to the clerk of the bankruptcy court for deposit to the credit of the referees' salary and expense fund if the proceeding is related to a case commenced prior to October 1, 1979, and to the credit of the Treasury if the proceeding is related to a case commenced on or after October 1, 1979. If the trustee in bankruptcy or the debtor in possession requests a transcript in the performance of his official duties, the charge shall be paid from the estate to the extent there is any estate realized.

(12) For each microfiche sheet of film or microfilm jacket copy of any court record, where available, $3.00.

(13) For retrieval of a record from a Federal Records Center, National Archives, or other storage location removed from the place of business of the court, $25.00.

(14) For a check paid into the court which is returned for lack of funds, $25.00.

(15) For providing mailing labels, $5.00 per page or portion thereof.

(16) For docketing a proceeding on appeal or review from a final judgment of a bankruptcy judge pursuant to 28 U.S.C. § 158(a) and (b), $100.00. A separate fee shall be paid by each party filing a notice of appeal in the bankruptcy court, but parties filing a joint notice of appeal in the bankruptcy court are required to pay only one fee.

(17) For filing a petition ancillary to a foreign proceeding under 11 U.S.C. § 304, $500.00.

(18) The court may charge and collect fees, commensurate with the cost of printing, for copies of the local rules of court. The court may also distribute copies of the local rules without charge.

(19) The clerk shall assess a charge of up to three percent for the handling of registry funds, to be assessed from interest earnings and in accordance with the detailed fee schedule issued by the Director of the Administrative Office of the United States Courts.

(20) When a joint case filed under § 302 of title 11 is divided into two separate cases at the request of the debtor(s), a fee shall be charged equal to one-

half the current filing fee for the chapter under which the joint case was commenced.

(21) For filing a motion to terminate, annul, modify, or condition the automatic stay provided under § 362(a) of title 11, a motion to compel abandonment of property of the estate pursuant to Bankruptcy Rule 6007(b), or a motion to withdraw the reference of a case under 28 U.S.C. § 157(d), $60.

(22) For docketing a cross appeal from a bankruptcy court determination, $100.

LANGUAGE TO CLARIFY REOPENED BANKRUPTCY CODE CASES

Filing fees prescribed by 28 U.S.C. § 1930(a) must be collected when a Bankruptcy Code case is reopened, unless the reopening is to correct an administrative error or for actions related to the debtor's discharge. If a Bankruptcy Code case is reopened for any other purpose, the appropriate fee to be charged is the same as the filing fee in effect for commencing a new case on the date of reopening.

STATEMENT RESPECTING 1988 AMENDMENTS FROM ADMINISTRATIVE OFFICE OF UNITED STATES COURTS

The Director of the Administrative Office of the United States Courts in a memorandum to the Chief Judges of the United States Courts of Appeals, United States District Courts, and United States Bankruptcy Courts, dated April 19, 1988, provided in part that: "The amendment establishing a fee for filing a petition ancillary to a foreign proceeding under § 304 of the Bankruptcy Code will become effective May 1, 1988. The amendment expanding the exemption for services rendered 'to the United States' to include services rendered to bankruptcy administrators simply expresses a policy which has been in effect since the creation of the bankruptcy administrator program by Congress in the Bankruptcy Judges, United States Trustees and Family Farmer Bankruptcy Act of 1986. [Pub.L. No. 99–554, § 302(d)(3)(I).]"

STATEMENT FROM 1988 MEETING OF JUDICIAL CONFERENCE

The Judicial Conference, at the September 14, 1988 meeting, provided in part that: "In order to remedy an inadvertent omission when the miscellaneous fee schedules were comprehensively revised in 1987 (March 1987 Session, Conf. Rpt. pp. 11–17), the Conference added language to the miscellaneous fee schedule approved pursuant to . . . 28 U.S.C. 1930 (bankruptcy courts)." The language added to the schedule is set out as par. 18 (above). The Conference further provided that: "The Conference also corrected the reference in the Language to Clarify Reopened and Converted Bankruptcy Code Cases, which follow the numbered items in the Bankruptcy fee schedule, from 28 U.S.C. 1930(b) to 28 U.S.C. 1930(a)."

REGISTRY FUND FEES—ITEM 19
(54 F.R. 20407, May 11, 1989)

Effective June 12, 1989, a fee will be assessed for handling funds deposited in noncriminal proceedings with the court and held in interest bearing accounts or instruments pursuant to 28 U.S.C. § 2041 and Federal Rules of Civil Procedure rule 67. For new accounts, i.e., investments made on or after June 12,

1989, the fee will be equal to the first 45 days income earned on the deposit. Each subsequent deposit of new principal in the same case or proceeding will be subject to the fee. Reinvestment of prior deposits will not be subject to the fee. For existing accounts, i.e., investments held by the court prior to June 12, 1989, a fee will be assessed equal to the first 45 days of income earned beginning 30 days after June 12, 1989. Subsequent deposits of new principal in the same account will be subject to the fee. Subsequent reinvestment of existing deposits will not be subject to the fee.

The fee will apply only once to each sum deposited regardless of the length of time deposits are held and will not exceed income actually earned on the account.

The fee does not apply in the District Courts of Guam, Northern Mariana Islands, the Virgin Islands, the United States Claims Court, or other courts whose fees are not set under 28 U.S.C. § 1930.

STATEMENT FROM 1989 MEETING OF JUDICIAL CONFERENCE

The Judicial Conference, at the September 20, 1989 meeting, provided in part that Item 21 takes effect on December 21, 1989. The Conference further provided that: "The remaining fees, Items 20 and 22, take effect on January 11, 1990, pending approval of the Appropriations Committees."

CHAPTER 131—RULES OF COURTS

§ 2075. Bankruptcy rules

The Supreme Court shall have the power to prescribe by general rules, the forms of process, writs, pleadings, and motions, and the practice and procedure in cases under Title 11.

Such rules shall not abridge, enlarge, or modify any substantive right.

Such rules shall not take effect until they have been reported to Congress by the Chief Justice at or after the beginning of a regular session thereof but not later than the first day of May and until the expiration of ninety days after they have been thus reported.

Added Pub.L. 88–623, § 1, Oct. 3, 1964, 78 Stat. 1001, and amended Pub.L. 95–598, Title II, § 247, Nov. 6, 1978, 92 Stat. 2672.

Historical Note

Application of Certain Bankruptcy Rules; Rules Relating to this Chapter. Applicability of rules prescribed under this section and in effect on Oct. 27, 1986, to cases filed under this chapter, except as otherwise provided, see section 305(b) of Pub.L. 99–554, set out as a note under section 581 of this title.

Dismissal of Liquidation Actions For Nonpayment of Fees and Charges. Pub.L.

98–353, Title III, § 320, July 10, 1984, 98 Stat. 357, provided that: "The Supreme Court shall prescribe general rules implementing the practice and procedure to be followed under section 707(b) of title 11, United States Code. Section 2075 of title 28, United States Code, shall apply with respect to the general rules prescribed under this section."

RULES AND FORMS OF PRACTICE AND PROCEDURE IN BANKRUPTCY

As Amended to January 1, 1991

Table of Rules

Rule

1001.   Scope of Rules and Forms; Short Title

PART I.   COMMENCEMENT OF CASE; PROCEEDINGS RELATING TO PETITION AND ORDER FOR RELIEF

1002.   Commencement of Case
1003.   Involuntary Petition
1004.   Partnership Petition
1005.   Caption of Petition
1006.   Filing Fee
1007.   Lists, Schedules and Statements; Time Limits
1008.   Verification of Petitions and Accompanying Papers
1009.   Amendments of Voluntary Petitions, Lists, Schedules and Statements
1010.   Service of Involuntary Petition and Summons; Petition Commencing Ancillary Case
1011.   Responsive Pleading or Motion in Involuntary and Ancillary Cases
1012.   [Abrogated]
1013.   Hearing and Disposition of Petition in Involuntary Cases
1014.   Dismissal and Change of Venue
1015.   Consolidation or Joint Administration of Cases Pending in Same Court
1016.   Death or Insanity of Debtor
1017.   Dismissal of Case; Suspension
1018.   Contested Involuntary Petitions; Contested Petitions Commencing Ancillary Cases; Proceedings to Vacate Order for Relief; Applicability of Rules in Part VII Governing Adversary Proceedings
1019.   Conversion of Chapter 11 Reorganization Case or Chapter 13 Individual's Debt Adjustment Case to Chapter 7 Liquidation Case

PART II.   OFFICERS AND ADMINISTRATION; NOTICES; MEETINGS; EXAMINATIONS; ELECTIONS; ATTORNEYS AND ACCOUNTANTS

2001.   Appointment of Interim Trustee Before Order for Relief in a Chapter 7 Liquidation Case
2002.   Notices to Creditors, Equity Security Holders, and United States
2003.   Meeting of Creditors or Equity Security Holders
2004.   Examination
2005.   Apprehension and Removal of Debtor to Compel Attendance for Examination
2006.   Solicitation and Voting of Proxies in Chapter 7 Liquidation Cases
2007.   Appointment of Creditors' Committee Organized Before Commencement of the Case
2008.   Notice to Trustee of Selection

503

Rule
2009.   Trustees for Estates When Joint Administration Ordered
2010.   Qualification by Trustee; Proceeding on Bond
2011.   Evidence of Debtor in Possession
2012.   Substitution of Trustee or Successor Trustee; Accounting
2013.   Limitation on Appointment or Employment of Trustees, Examiners, Appraisers and Auctioneers
2014.   Employment of Professional Persons
2015.   Duty of Trustee or Debtor in Possession to Keep Records, Make Reports, and Give Notice of Case
2016.   Compensation for Services Rendered and Reimbursement of Expenses
2017.   Examination of Debtor's Transactions With Debtor's Attorney
2018.   Intervention; Right to Be Heard
2019.   Representation of Creditors and Equity Security Holders in Chapter 9 Municipality and Chapter 11 Reorganization Cases

PART III.   CLAIMS AND DISTRIBUTION TO CREDITORS AND EQUITY INTEREST HOLDERS; PLANS

3001.   Proof of Claim
3002.   Filing Proof of Claim or Interest
3003.   Filing Proof of Claim or Equity Security Interest in Chapter 9 Municipality or Chapter 11 Reorganization Cases
3004.   Filing of Claims by Debtor or Trustee
3005.   Filing of Claim, Acceptance, or Rejection by Guarantor, Surety, Indorser, or Other Codebtor
3006.   Withdrawal of Claim or Acceptance or Rejection of Plan
3007.   Objections to Claims
3008.   Reconsideration of Claims
3009.   Declaration and Payment of Dividends in Chapter 7 Liquidation Cases
3010.   Small Dividends and Payments in Chapter 7 Liquidation and Chapter 13 Individual's Debt Adjustment Cases
3011.   Unclaimed Funds in Chapter 7 Liquidation and Chapter 13 Individual's Debt Adjustment Cases
3012.   Valuation of Security
3013.   Classification of Claims and Interests
3014.   Election Pursuant to § 1111(b) by Secured Creditor in Chapter 9 Municipality and Chapter 11 Reorganization Cases
3015.   Filing of Plan in Chapter 13 Individual's Debt Adjustment Cases
3016.   Filing of Plan and Disclosure Statement in Chapter 9 Municipality and Chapter 11 Reorganization Cases
3017.   Court Consideration of Disclosure Statement in Chapter 9 Municipality and Chapter 11 Reorganization Cases
3018.   Acceptance or Rejection of Plans
3019.   Modification of Accepted Plan Before Confirmation
3020.   Deposit; Confirmation of Plan
3021.   Distribution Under Plan
3022.   Final Decree

PART IV.   THE DEBTOR: DUTIES AND BENEFITS

4001.   Relief From Automatic Stay; Use of Cash Collateral; Obtaining Credit; Agreements
4002.   Duties of Debtor
4003.   Exemptions

Rule

4004. Grant or Denial of Discharge
4005. Burden of Proof in Objecting to Discharge
4006. Notice of No Discharge
4007. Determination of Dischargeability of a Debt
4008. Discharge and Reaffirmation Hearing

PART V. COURTS AND CLERKS

5001. Courts and Clerks' Offices
5002. Restrictions on Appointments
5003. Records Kept by the Clerk
5004. Disqualification
5005. Filing of Papers
5006. Certification of Copies of Papers
5007. Record of Proceedings and Transcripts
5008. Funds of the Estate
5009. Closing Cases
5010. Reopening Cases
5011. Withdrawal and Abstention From Hearing a Proceeding

PART VI. COLLECTION AND LIQUIDATION OF THE ESTATE

6001. Burden of Proof as to Validity of Postpetition Transfer
6002. Accounting by Prior Custodian of Property of the Estate
6003. Disbursement of Money of the Estate
6004. Use, Sale, or Lease of Property
6005. Appraisers and Auctioneers
6006. Assumption, Rejection and Assignment of Executory Contracts
6007. Abandonment or Disposition of Property
6008. Redemption of Property From Lien or Sale
6009. Prosecution and Defense of Proceedings by Trustee or Debtor in Possession
6010. Proceeding to Avoid Indemnifying Lien or Transfer to Surety

PART VII. ADVERSARY PROCEEDINGS

7001. Scope of Rules of Part VII
7002. References to Federal Rules of Civil Procedure
7003. Commencement of Adversary Proceeding
7004. Process; Service of Summons, Complaint
7005. Service and Filing of Pleadings and Other Papers
7007. Pleadings Allowed
7008. General Rules of Pleading
7009. Pleading Special Matters
7010. Form of Pleadings
7012. Defenses and Objections—When and How Presented—By Pleading or Motion—Motion for Judgment on the Pleadings
7013. Counterclaim and Cross-Claim
7014. Third-Party Practice
7015. Amended and Supplemental Pleadings
7016. Pre-Trial Procedure; Formulating Issues
7017. Parties Plaintiff and Defendant; Capacity
7018. Joinder of Claims and Remedies
7019. Joinder of Persons Needed for Just Determination
7020. Permissive Joinder of Parties

505

Rule

7021.   Misjoinder and Non-Joinder of Parties
7022.   Interpleader
7023.   Class Proceedings
7023.1. Derivative Proceedings by Shareholders
7023.2. Adversary Proceedings Relating to Unincorporated Associations
7024.   Intervention
7025.   Substitution of Parties
7026.   General Provisions Governing Discovery
7027.   Depositions Before Adversary Proceedings or Pending Appeal
7028.   Persons Before Whom Depositions May Be Taken
7029.   Stipulations Regarding Discovery Procedure
7030.   Depositions Upon Oral Examination
7031.   Deposition Upon Written Questions
7032.   Use of Depositions in Adversary Proceedings
7033.   Interrogatories to Parties
7034.   Production of Documents and Things and Entry Upon Land for Inspection and Other Purposes
7035.   Physical and Mental Examination of Persons
7036.   Requests for Admission
7037.   Failure to Make Discovery: Sanctions
7040.   Assignment of Cases for Trial
7041.   Dismissal of Adversary Proceedings
7042.   Consolidation of Adversary Proceedings; Separate Trials
7052.   Findings by the Court
7054.   Judgments; Costs
7055.   Default
7056.   Summary Judgment
7062.   Stay of Proceedings to Enforce a Judgment
7064.   Seizure of Person or Property
7065.   Injunctions
7067.   Deposit in Court
7068.   Offer of Judgment
7069.   Execution
7070.   Judgment for Specific Acts; Vesting Title
7071.   Process in Behalf of and Against Persons Not Parties
7087.   Transfer of Adversary Proceeding

PART VIII.   APPEALS TO DISTRICT COURT OR
BANKRUPTCY APPELLATE PANEL

8001.   Manner of Taking Appeal; Voluntary Dismissal
8002.   Time for Filing Notice of Appeal
8003.   Leave to Appeal
8004.   Service of the Notice of Appeal
8005.   Stay Pending Appeal
8006.   Record and Issues on Appeal
8007.   Completion and Transmission of the Record; Docketing of the Appeal
8008.   Filing and Service
8009.   Briefs and Appendix; Filing and Service
8010.   Form of Briefs; Length
8011.   Motions
8012.   Oral Argument

Rule

8013. Disposition of Appeal; Weight Accorded Bankruptcy Judge's Findings of Fact

8014. Costs

8015. Motion for Rehearing

8016. Duties of Clerk of District Court and Bankruptcy Appellate Panel

8017. Stay of Judgment of District Court or Bankruptcy Appellate Panel

8018. Rules by Circuit Councils and District Courts

8019. Suspension of Rules in Part VIII

PART IX. GENERAL PROVISIONS

9001. General Definitions

9002. Meanings of Words in the Federal Rules of Civil Procedure When Applicable to Cases Under the Code

9003. Prohibition of Ex Parte Contacts

9004. General Requirements of Form

9005. Harmless Error

9006. Time

9007. General Authority to Regulate Notices

9008. Service or Notice by Publication

9009. Forms

9010. Representation and Appearances; Powers of Attorney

9011. Signing and Verification of Papers

9012. Oaths and Affirmations

9013. Motions: Form and Service

9014. Contested Matters

9015. [Abrogated]

9016. Subpoena

9017. Evidence

9018. Secret, Confidential, Scandalous, or Defamatory Matter

9019. Compromise and Arbitration

9020. Contempt Proceedings

9021. Entry of Judgment

9022. Notice of Judgment or Order

9023. New Trials; Amendment of Judgments

9024. Relief From Judgment or Order

9025. Security: Proceedings Against Sureties

9026. Exceptions Unnecessary

9027. Removal

9028. Disability of a Judge

9029. Local Bankruptcy Rules

9030. Jurisdiction and Venue Unaffected

9031. Masters Not Authorized

9032. Effect of Amendment of Federal Rules of Civil Procedure

9033. Review of Proposed Findings of Fact and Conclusions of Law in Non-core Proceedings

PART X. UNITED STATES TRUSTEES

X–1001. Applicability of Rules

X–1002. Petitions, Lists, Schedules and Statements

X–1003. Appointment of Interim Trustee Before Order for Relief in a Chapter 7 Liquidation Case

X–1004. Notification to Trustee of Selection; Blanket Bond

Rule

X–1005. Trustees for Estates When Joint Administration Ordered

X–1006. Meetings of Creditors or Equity Security Holders

X–1007. Duty of Trustee or Debtor in Possession to Make Reports, Furnish Information, and Cooperate With United States Trustee

X–1008. Notices to United States Trustee

X–1009. Right to Be Heard; Filing Papers

X–1010. Prohibition of Ex Parte Contacts

OFFICIAL BANKRUPTCY FORMS

[See Separate Table of Forms, infra, page 681.]

RULES OF PRACTICE AND PROCEDURE IN BANKRUPTCY

Rule 1001

SCOPE OF RULES AND FORMS; SHORT TITLE

The Bankruptcy Rules and Forms govern procedure in cases under title 11 of the United States Code. The rules shall be cited as the Bankruptcy Rules and the forms as the Official Bankruptcy Forms. These rules shall be construed to secure the just, speedy, and inexpensive determination of every case and proceeding.

Amended Mar. 30, 1987, eff. Aug. 1, 1987.

Advisory Committee Note

Section 247 of Public Law 95–598, 92 Stat. 2549 amended 28 U.S.C. § 2075 by omitting the last sentence. The effect of the amendment is to require that procedural rules promulgated pursuant to 28 U.S.C. § 2075 be consistent with the bankruptcy statute, both titles 11 and 28 U.S.C. Thus, although Rule 1001 sets forth the scope of the bankruptcy rules and forms, any procedural matters contained in title 11 or 28 U.S.C. with respect to cases filed under 11 U.S.C. would control. See 1 Collier, *Bankruptcy* ¶ 3.04[2][c] (15th ed. 1980).

28 U.S.C. § 151 establishes a United States Bankruptcy Court in each district as an adjunct to the district court. This provision does not, however, become effective until April 1, 1984. Public Law 95–598, § 402(b). From October 1, 1979 through March 31, 1984, the courts of bankruptcy as defined in § 1(10) of the Bankruptcy Act, and created in § 2a of that Act continue to be the courts of bankruptcy. Public Law 95–598, § 404(a). From their effective date these rules and forms are to be applicable in cases filed under chapters 7, 9, 11 and 13 of title 11 regardless of whether the court is established by the Bankruptcy Act or by 28 U.S.C. § 151. Rule 9001 contains a broad and general definition of "bankruptcy court," "court" and "United States Bankruptcy Court" for this purpose.

"Bankruptcy Code" or "Code" as used in these rules means title 11 of the United States Code, the codification of the bankruptcy law. Public Law 95–598, § 101. See Rule 9001.

"Bankruptcy Act" as used in the notes to these rules means the Bankruptcy Act of 1898 as amended which was repealed by §·401(a) of Public Law 95–598.

These rules apply to all cases filed under the Code except as otherwise specifically stated.

The final sentence of the rule is derived from former Bankruptcy Rule 903. The objective of "expeditious and economical administration" of cases under the Code has frequently been recognized by the courts to be "a chief purpose of the bankruptcy laws." See *Katchen* v. *Landy*, 382 U.S. 323, 328 (1966): *Bailey* v. *Glover*, 88 U.S. (21 Wall.) 342, 346–47, (1874): *Ex parte Christy*, 44 U.S. (3 How.) 292, 312–14, 320–22 (1845). The rule also incorporates the wholesome mandate of the last sentence of Rule 1 of the Federal Rules of Civil Procedure. 2 Moore, *Federal Practice* ¶ 1.13 (2d ed. 1980); 4 Wright & Miller, *Federal Practice and Procedure—Civil* § 1029 (1969).

Advisory Committee Notes to 1987 Amendments

Title I of the Bankruptcy Amendments and Federal Judgeship Act of 1984, Pub.L.No. 98–353, 98 Stat. 333 (hereinafter the 1984 amendments), created a new bankruptcy judicial system in which the role of the district court was substantially increased. 28 U.S.C. § 1334 confers on the United States district courts original and exclusive jurisdiction over all cases under title 11 of the United States Code and original but not exclusive jurisdiction over civil proceedings arising under title 11 and civil proceedings arising in or related to a case under title 11.

Pursuant to 28 U.S.C. § 157(a) the district court may but need not refer cases and proceedings within the district court's jurisdiction to the bankruptcy judges for the district. Judgments or orders of the bankruptcy judges entered pursuant to 28 U.S.C. § 157(b)(1) and (c)(2) are subject to appellate review by the district courts or bankruptcy appellate panels under 28 U.S.C. § 158(a).

Rule 81(a)(1) F.R.Civ.P. provides that the civil rules do not apply to proceedings in bankruptcy, except as they may be made applicable by rules promulgated by the Supreme Court, *e.g.*, Part VII of these rules. This amended Bankruptcy Rule 1001 makes the Bankruptcy Rules applicable to cases and proceedings under title 11, whether before the district judges or the bankruptcy judges of the district.

PART I

COMMENCEMENT OF CASE; PROCEEDINGS RELATING TO PETITION AND ORDER FOR RELIEF

Rule

1002. Commencement of Case
1003. Involuntary Petition
1004. Partnership Petition
1005. Caption of Petition
1006. Filing Fee
1007. Lists, Schedules and Statements; Time Limits
1008. Verification of Petitions and Accompanying Papers
1009. Amendments of Voluntary Petitions, Lists, Schedules and Statements
1010. Service of Involuntary Petition and Summons; Petition Commencing Ancillary Case
1011. Responsive Pleading or Motion in Involuntary and Ancillary Cases
1012. [Abrogated]
1013. Hearing and Disposition of Petition in Involuntary Cases
1014. Dismissal and Change of Venue
1015. Consolidation or Joint Administration of Cases Pending in Same Court
1016. Death or Insanity of Debtor
1017. Dismissal of Case; Suspension
1018. Contested Involuntary Petitions; Contested Petitions Commencing Ancillary Cases; Proceedings to Vacate Order for Relief; Applicability of Rules in Part VII Governing Adversary Proceedings
1019. Conversion of Chapter 11 Reorganization Case or Chapter 13 Individual's Debt Adjustment Case to Chapter 7 Liquidation Case

Rule 1002

COMMENCEMENT OF CASE

A petition commencing a case under the Code shall be filed with the clerk. Amended Mar. 30, 1987, eff. Aug. 1, 1987.

Advisory Committee Note

Under §§ 301–303 of the Code, a voluntary or involuntary case is commenced by filing a petition with the bankruptcy court. The voluntary petition may request relief under chapter 7, 9, 11, or 13 whereas an involuntary petition may be filed only under chapter 7 or 11. Section 109 of the Code specifies the types of debtors for whom the different forms of relief are available and § 303(a) indicates the persons against whom involuntary petitions may be filed.

The rule in subdivision (a) is in harmony with the Code in that it requires the filing to be with the bankruptcy court.

The number of copies of the petition to be filed is specified in this rule but a local rule may require additional copies. This rule provides for filing sufficient copies for the court's files and for the trustee in a chapter 7 or 13 case.

511

Official Form No. 1 may be used to seek relief voluntarily under any of the chapters. Only the original need be signed and verified, but the copies must be conformed to the original. See Rules 1008 and 9011(c). As provided in § 362(a) of the Code, the filing of a petition acts as a stay of certain acts and proceedings against the debtor, property of the debtor, and property of the estate.

Advisory Committee Notes to 1987 Amendments

Rules 1002(a), governing a voluntary petition, 1003(a), governing an involuntary petition, and 1003(e), governing a petition in a case ancillary to a foreign proceeding, are combined into this Rule 1002. If a bankruptcy clerk has been appointed for the district, the petition is filed with the bankruptcy clerk. Otherwise, the petition is filed with the clerk of the district court.

The elimination of the reference to the Official Forms of the petition is not intended to change the practice. Rule 9009 provides that the Official Forms "shall be observed and used" in cases and proceedings under the Code.

Subdivision (b) which provided for the distribution of copies of the petition to agencies of the United States has been deleted. Some of these agencies no longer wish to receive copies of the petition, while others not included in subdivision (b) have now requested copies. The Director of the Administrative Office will determine on an ongoing basis which government agencies will be provided a copy of the petition.

The number of copies of a petition that must be filed is a matter for local rule.

Rule 1003

INVOLUNTARY PETITION

(a) Transferor or Transferee of Claim. A transferor or transferee of a claim shall annex to the original and each copy of the petition a copy of all documents evidencing the transfer, whether transferred unconditionally, for security, or otherwise, and a signed statement that the claim was not transferred for the purpose of commencing the case and setting forth the consideration for and terms of the transfer. An entity that has transferred or acquired a claim for the purpose of commencing a case for liquidation under chapter 7 or for reorganization under chapter 11 shall not be a qualified petitioner.

(b) Joinder of Petitioners After Filing. If the answer to an involuntary petition filed by fewer than three creditors avers the existence of 12 or more creditors, the debtor shall file with the answer a list of all creditors with their addresses, a brief statement of the nature of their claims, and the amounts thereof. If it appears that there are 12 or more creditors as provided in § 303(b) of the Code, the court shall afford a reasonable opportunity for other creditors to join in the petition before a hearing is held thereon.

Amended Mar. 30, 1987, eff. Aug. 1, 1987.

Advisory Committee Note

Subdivision (a). Official Form No. 11 (Involuntary Case: Creditors' Petition), is prescribed for use by petitioning creditors to have a debtor's assets liquidated under chapter 7 of the Code or the business reorganized under chapter 11. It contains the required allegations as specified in § 303(b) of the Code. Official Form 12 is prescribed for use by fewer than all the general partners to obtain relief for the partnership as governed by § 303(b)(3) of the Code and Rule 1004(b).

Although the number of copies to be filed is specified in Rule 1002, a local rule may require additional copies.

Only the original need be signed and verified, but the copies must be conformed to the original. See Rules 1008 and 9011(c). The petition must be filed with the bankruptcy court. This provision implements § 303(b) which provides that an involuntary case is commenced by filing the petition with the court.

As provided in § 362 of the Code, the filing of the petition acts as a stay of certain acts and proceedings against the debtor, the debtor's property and property of the estate.

Subdivision (c) retains the explicitness of former Bankruptcy Rule 104(d) that a transfer of a claim for the purpose of commencing a case under the Code is a ground for disqualification of a party to the transfer as a petitioner.

Section 303(b) "is not intended to overrule Bankruptcy Rule 104(d), which places certain restrictions on the transfer of claims for the purpose of commencing an involuntary case." House Report No. 95–595, 95th Cong., 1st Sess. (1977) 322; Senate Report No. 95–989, 95th Cong., 2d Sess. (1978) 33.

The subdivision requires disclosure of any transfer of the petitioner's claim as well as a transfer to the petitioner and applies to transfers for security as well as unconditional transfers. *Cf. In re 69th & Crandon Bldg. Corp.*, 97 F.2d 392, 395 (7th Cir.), cert. denied, 305 U.S. 629 (1938), recognizing the right of a creditor to sign a bankruptcy petition notwithstanding a prior assignment of his claim for the purpose of security. This rule does not, however, qualify the requirement of § 303(b)(1) that a petitioning creditor must have a claim not contingent as to liability.

Subdivision (d). Section 303(c) of the Code permits a creditor to join in the petition at any time before the case is dismissed or relief is ordered. While this rule does not require the court to give all creditors notice of the petition, the list of creditors filed by the debtor affords a petitioner the information needed to enable him to give notice for the purpose of obtaining the co-petitioners required to make the petition sufficient. After a reasonable opportunity has been afforded other creditors to join in an involuntary petition, the hearing on the petition should be held without further delay.

Subdivision (e). This subdivision implements § 304. A petition for relief under § 304 may only be filed by a foreign representative who is defined in § 101(20) generally as a representative of an estate in a foreign proceeding. The term "foreign proceeding" is defined in § 101(19).

Section 304(b) permits a petition filed thereunder to be contested by a party in interest. Subdivision (e)(2) therefore requires that the summons and petition be served on any person against whom the relief permitted by § 304(b) is sought as well as on any other party the court may direct.

The rules applicable to the procedure when an involuntary petition is filed are made applicable generally when a case ancillary to a foreign proceeding is commenced. These rules include Rule 1010 with respect to issuance and service of a summons, Rule 1011 concerning responsive pleadings and motions, and Rule 1018 which makes various rules in Part VII applicable in proceedings on contested petitions.

The venue for a case ancillary to a foreign proceeding is provided in 28 U.S.C. § 1474.

Advisory Committee Notes to 1987 Amendments

The subject matter of subdivisions (a), (b), and (e) has been incorporated in Rules 1002, 1010, 1011, and 1018.

Rule 1004

PARTNERSHIP PETITION

(a) Voluntary Petition. A voluntary petition may be filed on behalf of the partnership by one or more general partners if all general partners consent to the petition.

(b) Involuntary Petition; Notice and Summons. After filing of an involuntary petition under § 303(b)(3) of the Code, (1) the petitioning partners or other petitioners shall cause forthwith a copy of the petition to be sent to or served on each general partner who is not a petitioner; and (2) the clerk shall issue forthwith a summons for service on each general partner who is not a petitioner. Rule 1010 applies to the form and service of the summons.

Advisory Committee Note

This rule is adapted from former Bankruptcy Rule 105 and complements §§ 301 and 303(b)(3) of the Code.

Subdivision (a) specifies that while all general partners must consent to the filing of a voluntary petition, it is not necessary that they all execute the petition. It may be executed and filed on behalf of the partnership by fewer than all.

Subdivision (b) implements § 303(b)(3) of the Code which provides that an involuntary petition may be filed by fewer than all the general partners or, when all the general partners are debtors, by a general partner, trustee of the partner or creditors of the partnership. Rule 1010, which governs service of a petition and summons in an involuntary case, specifies the time and mode of service on the partnership. When a petition is filed against a partnership under § 303(b)(3), this rule requires an additional service on the nonfiling general partners. It is the purpose of this subdivision to protect the interests of the nonpetitioning partners and the partnership.

Rule 1005

CAPTION OF PETITION

The caption of a petition commencing a case under the Code shall contain the name of the court, the title of the case, and the docket number. The title of the case shall include the name, social security number and employer's tax identification number of the debtor and all other names used by the debtor within six years before filing the petition. If the petition is not filed by the debtor, it shall include all names used by the debtor which are known to petitioners.

Amended Mar. 30, 1987, eff. Aug. 1, 1987.

Advisory Committee Note

The title of the case should include all names used by the debtor, such as trade names, former married names and maiden name. See also Official Form No. 1 and the Advisory Committee Note to that Form. Additional names of the debtor are also required to appear in the caption of each notice to creditors. See Rule 2002(m).

Rule 1006

FILING FEE

(a) General Requirement. Every petition shall be accompanied by the prescribed filing fee except as provided in subdivision (b) of this rule.

(b) Payment of Filing Fee in Installments.

(1) Application for Permission to Pay Filing Fee in Installments. A voluntary petition by an individual shall be accepted for filing if accompanied by the debtor's signed application stating that the debtor is unable to pay the filing fee except in installments. The application shall state the proposed terms of the installment payments and that the applicant has neither paid any money nor transferred any property to an attorney for services in connection with the case.

(2) Action on Application. Prior to the meeting of creditors, the court may order the filing fee paid to the clerk or grant leave to pay in installments and fix the number, amount and dates of payment. The number of installments shall not exceed four, and the final installment shall be payable not later than 120 days after filing the petition. For cause shown, the court may extend the time of any installment, provided the last installment is paid not later than 180 days after filing the petition.

(3) Postponement of Attorney's Fees. The filing fee must be paid in full before the debtor or chapter 13 trustee may pay an attorney or any other person who renders services to the debtor in connection with the case.

Amended Mar. 30, 1987, eff. Aug. 1, 1987.

Advisory Committee Note

28 U.S.C. § 1930 specifies the filing fees for petitions under chapters 7, 9, 11 and 13 of the Code. It also permits the payment in installments by individual debtors.

Subdivision (b) is adapted from former Bankruptcy Rule 107. The administrative cost of installments in excess of four is disproportionate to the benefits conferred. Prolonging the period beyond 180 days after the commencement of the case causes undesirable delays in administration. Paragraph (2) accordingly continues the imposition of a maximum of four on the number of installments and retains the maximum period of installment payments allowable on an original application at 120 days. Only in extraordinary cases should it be necessary to give an applicant an extension beyond the four months. The requirement of paragraph (3) that filing fees be paid in full before the debtor may pay an attorney for services in connection with the case codifies the rule declared in *In re Latham*, 271 Fed. 538 (N.D.N.Y.1921), and *In re Darr*, 232 Fed. 415 (N.D.Cal.1916).

Advisory Committee Notes to 1987 Amendments

Subdivision (b)(3) is expanded to prohibit payments by the debtor or the chapter 13 trustee not only to attorneys but to any person who renders services to the debtor in connection with the case.

Rule 1007

LISTS, SCHEDULES AND STATEMENTS; TIME LIMITS

(a) List of Creditors and Equity Security Holders.

(1) *Voluntary Case.* In a voluntary case, the debtor shall file with the petition a list containing the name and address of each creditor unless the petition is accompanied by a schedule of liabilities or a Chapter 13 Statement.

(2) *Involuntary Case.* In an involuntary case, the debtor shall file within 15 days after entry of the order for relief, a list containing the name and address of each creditor unless a schedule of liabilities has been filed.

(3) *Equity Security Holders.* In a chapter 11 reorganization case, unless the court orders otherwise, the debtor shall file within 15 days after entry of the order for relief a list of the debtor's equity security holders of each class showing the number and kind of interests registered in the name of each holder, and the last known address or place of business of each holder.

(4) *Extension of Time.* Any extension of time for the filing of the lists required by this subdivision may be granted only on motion for cause shown and on notice to any trustee, committee appointed under the Code, or other party as the court may direct.

(b) Schedules and Statements Required.

(1) The debtor in a chapter 7 liquidation case or chapter 11 reorganization case, unless the court orders otherwise, shall file with the court schedules of assets and liabilities, prepared as prescribed by Official Form No. 6, a schedule of current income and expenditures, prepared as prescribed by Official Form No. 6A, if appropriate, a statement of financial affairs, prepared as prescribed by Official Form No. 7 or No. 8, whichever is appropriate, and a statement of executory contracts.

(2) The debtor in a chapter 13 individual's debt adjustment case, unless the court orders otherwise, shall file with the court a chapter 13 Statement conforming to Official Form No. 10 and, if the debtor is engaged in business, a statement of financial affairs prepared as prescribed by Official Form No. 8. The budget included in the Chapter 13 Statement shall constitute the schedule of current income and current expenditures.

(3) An individual debtor in a chapter 7 case shall file a statement of intention as required by § 521(2) of the Code, prepared as prescribed by Official Form No. 8A. A copy of the statement of intention shall be served on the trustee and the creditors named in the statement on or before the filing of the statement.

(c) Time Limits. The schedules and statements, other than the statement of intention, shall be filed with the petition in a voluntary case, or if the petition

is accompanied by a list of all the debtor's creditors and their addresses, within 15 days thereafter, except as otherwise provided in subdivisions (d), (e), and (h) of this rule. In an involuntary case the schedules and statements, other than the statement of intention, shall be filed by the debtor within 15 days after entry of the order for relief. Schedules and statements previously filed in a pending chapter 7 case shall be deemed filed in a superseding case unless the court directs otherwise. Any extension of time for the filing of the schedules and statements may be granted only on motion for cause shown and on notice to any committee, trustee, examiner, or other party as the court may direct. Notice of an extension shall be given to any committee, trustee, or other party as the court may direct.

(d) **List of 20 Largest Creditors in Chapter 9 Municipality Case or Chapter 11 Reorganization Case.** In addition to the list required by subdivision (a) of this rule, a debtor in a chapter 9 municipality case or a debtor in a voluntary chapter 11 reorganization case shall file with the petition a list containing the name, address and claim of the creditors that hold the 20 largest unsecured claims, excluding insiders, as prescribed by Official Form No. 9. In an involuntary chapter 11 reorganization case, such list shall be filed by the debtor within 2 days after entry of the order for relief under § 303(h) of the Code.

(e) **List in Chapter 9 Municipality Cases.** The list required by subdivision (a) of this rule shall be filed by the debtor in a chapter 9 municipality case within such time as the court shall fix. If a proposed plan requires a revision of assessments so that the proportion of special assessments or special taxes to be assessed against some real property will be different from the proportion in effect at the date the petition is filed, the debtor shall also file with the court a list showing the name and address of each known holder of title, legal or equitable, to real property adversely affected. On motion for cause shown, the court may modify the requirements of this subdivision and subdivision (a) of this rule.

(f) **[Abrogated]**

(g) **Partnership and Partners.** The general partners of a debtor partnership shall prepare and file the schedules of the assets and liabilities, schedule of current income and expenditures, statement of financial affairs, and statement of executory contracts of the partnership. The court may order any general partner to file a statement of personal assets and liabilities with the court within such time as the court may fix.

(h) **Interests Acquired or Arising After Petition.** If, as provided by § 541(a)(5) of the Code, the debtor acquires or becomes entitled to acquire any interest in property, the debtor shall within 10 days after the information comes to the debtor's knowledge or within such further time the court may allow, file a supplemental schedule in the chapter 7 liquidation case, chapter 11 reorganization case, or chapter 13 individual debt adjustment case. If any of the property required to be reported under this subdivision is claimed by the debtor as exempt, the debtor shall claim the exemptions in the supplemental schedule. The duty to file a supplemental schedule in accordance with this subdivision continues notwithstanding the closing of the case, except that the schedule need not be filed in a chapter 11 or chapter 13 case with respect to property acquired after entry of the order confirming a chapter 11 plan or discharging the debtor in a chapter 13 case.

(i) **Disclosure of List of Security Holders.** After notice and hearing and for cause shown, the court may direct an entity other than the debtor or trustee to disclose any list of security holders of the debtor in its possession or under its control, indicating the name, address and security held by any of them. The entity possessing this list may be required either to produce the list or a true copy thereof, or permit inspection or copying, or otherwise disclose the information contained on the list.

(j) **Impounding of Lists.** On motion of a party in interest and for cause shown the court may direct the impounding of the lists filed under this rule, and may refuse to permit inspection by any entity. The court may permit inspection or use of the lists, however, by any party in interest on terms prescribed by the court.

(k) **Preparation of List, Schedules, or Statements on Default of Debtor.** If a list, schedule, or statement, other than a statement of intention, is not prepared and filed as required by this rule, the court may order the trustee, a petitioning creditor, committee, or other party to prepare and file any of these papers within a time fixed by the court. The court may approve reimbursement of the cost incurred in complying with such an order as an administrative expense.

Amended Mar. 30, 1987, eff. Aug. 1, 1987.

Advisory Committee Note

This rule is an adaptation of former Rules 108, 8–106, 10–108 and 11–11. As specified in the rule, it is applicable in all types of cases filed under the Code.

Subdivision (a) requires at least a list of creditors with their names and addresses to be filed with the petition. This list is needed for notice of the meeting of creditors (Rule 2002) and notice of the order for relief (§ 342 of the Code). The list will also serve to meet the requirements of § 521(1) of the Code. Subdivision (a) recognizes that it may be impossible to file the schedules required by § 521(1) and subdivision (b) of the rule at the time the petition is filed but in order for the case to proceed expeditiously and efficiently it is necessary that the clerk have the names and addresses of creditors. It should be noted that subdivision (d) of the rule requires a special list of the 20 largest unsecured creditors in chapter 9 and 11 cases. That list is for the purpose of selecting a committee of unsecured creditors.

Subdivision (b) is derived from former Rule 11–11 and conforms with § 521. This subdivision indicates the forms to be used. The court may dispense with the filing of schedules and the statement of affairs pursuant to § 521.

Subdivisions (c) and (f) specify the time periods for filing the papers required by the rule as well as the number of copies. The provisions dealing with an involuntary case are derived from former Bankruptcy Rule 108. Under the Code, a chapter 11 case may be commenced by an involuntary petition (§ 303(a)), whereas under the Act, a Chapter XI case could have been commenced only by a voluntary petition. A motion for an extension of time to file the schedules and statements is required to be made on notice to parties, as the court may direct, including a creditors' committee if one has been appointed under § 1102 of the Code and a trustee or examiner if one has been appointed pursuant to § 1104 of the Code. Although written notice is preferable, it is not required by the rule; in proper circumstances the notice may be by telephone or otherwise.

Subdivision (d) is new and requires that a list of the 20 largest unsecured creditors, excluding insiders as defined in § 101(25) of the Code, be filed with the petition. The court, pursuant to § 1102 of the Code, is required to appoint a committee of unsecured creditors as soon as practicable after the order for relief. That committee generally is to consist of the seven largest unsecured creditors who are willing to serve. The list should, as indicated on Official Form No. 9, specify the nature and amount of the claim. It is important for the court to be aware of the different types of claims existing in the case and this form should supply such information.

Subdivision (e) applies only in chapter 9 municipality cases. It gives greater discretion to the court to determine the time for filing a list of creditors and any other matter related to the list. A list of creditors must at some point be filed since one is required by § 924 of the Code. When the plan affects special assessments, the definitions in § 902(2) and (3) for "special tax payer" and "special tax payer affected by the plan" become relevant.

Subdivision (g) is derived from former Rules 108(c) and 11–11. Nondebtor general partners are liable to the partnership's trustee for any deficiency in the partnership's estate to pay creditors in full as provided by § 723 of the Code. Subdivision (g) authorizes the court to require a partner to file a statement of personal assets and liabilities to provide the trustee with the relevant information.

Subdivision (h) is derived from former Bankruptcy Rule 108(e) for chapter 7, 11 and 13 purposes. It implements the provisions in and language of § 541(a)(5) of the Code.

Subdivisions (i) and (j) are adapted from §§ 165 and 166 of the Act and former Rule 10–108(b) and (c) without change in substance. The term "party in interest" is not defined in the Code or the rules, but reference may be made to § 1109(b) of the Code. In the context of this subdivision, the term would include the debtor, the trustee, any indenture trustee, creditor, equity security holder or committee appointed pursuant to § 1102 of the Code.

Subdivision (k) is derived from former Rules 108(d) and 10–108(a).

Advisory Committee Notes to 1987 Amendments

Subdivisons (b), (c), and (g) are amended to provide for the filing of a schedule of current income and current expenditures and the individual debtor's statement of intention. These documents are required by the 1984 amendments to § 521 of the Code. Official Form No. 6A is prescribed for use by an individual debtor for filing a schedule of current income and current expenditures in a chapter 7 or chapter 11 case. Although a partnership or corporation is also required by § 521(1) to file a schedule of current income and current expenditures, no Official Form is prescribed therefor.

The time for filing the statement of intention is governed by § 521(2)(A). A copy of the statement of intention must be served on the trustee and the creditors named in the statement within the same time. The provisions of subdivision (c) governing the time for filing when a chapter 11 or chapter 13 case is converted to a chapter 7 case have been omitted from subdivision (c) as amended. Filing after conversion is now governed exclusively by Rule 1019.

Subdivision (f) has been abrogated. The number of copies of the documents required by this rule will be determined by local rule.

Subdivision (h) is amended to include a direct reference to § 541(a)(5).

Subdivision (k) provides that the court may not order an entity other than the debtor to prepare and file the statement of intention.

Rule 1008

VERIFICATION OF PETITIONS AND ACCOMPANYING PAPERS

All petitions, lists, schedules, statements of financial affairs, statements of executory contracts, Chapter 13 Statements and amendments thereto shall be verified or contain an unsworn declaration as provided in 28 U.S.C. § 1746.

Advisory Committee Note

This rule retains the requirement under the Bankruptcy Act and rules that petitions and accompanying papers must be verified. Only the original need be signed and verified, but the copies must be conformed to the original. See Rule 9011(c).

The verification may be replaced by an unsworn declaration as provided in 28 U.S.C. § 1746. See also, Official Form No. 1 and Advisory Committee Note.

Rule 1009

AMENDMENTS OF VOLUNTARY PETITIONS, LISTS, SCHEDULES AND STATEMENTS

(a) General Right to Amend. A voluntary petition, list, schedule, statement of financial affairs, statement of executory contracts, or Chapter 13 Statement may be amended by the debtor as a matter of course at any time before the case is closed. The debtor shall give notice of the amendment to the trustee and to any entity affected thereby. On motion of a party in interest, after notice and a hearing, the court may order any voluntary petition, list, schedule, statement of financial affairs, statement of executory contracts, or Chapter 13 Statement to be amended and the clerk shall give notice of the amendment to entities designated by the court.

(b) Statement of Intention. The statement of intention may be amended by the debtor at any time before the expiration of the period provided in § 521(2)(B) of the Code. The debtor shall give notice of the amendment to the trustee and to any entity affected thereby.

Amended Mar. 30, 1987, eff. Aug. 1, 1987.

Advisory Committee Note

This rule continues the permissive approach adopted by former Bankruptcy Rule 110 to amendments of voluntary petitions and accompanying papers. Notice of any amendment is required to be given to the trustee. This is particularly important with respect to any amendment of the schedule of property affecting the debtor's claim of exemptions. Notice of any amendment of the schedule of liabilities is to be given to any creditor whose claim is changed or newly listed.

The rule does not continue the provision permitting the court to order an amendment on its own initiative. Absent a request in some form by a party in interest, the court should not be involved in administrative matters affecting the estate.

If a list or schedule is amended to include an additional creditor, the effect on the dischargeability of the creditor's claim is governed by the provisions of § 523(a)(3) of the Code.

Advisory Committee Notes to 1987 Amendments

Subdivision (a) is amended to require notice and a hearing in the event a party in interest other than the debtor seeks to amend. The number of copies of the amendment will be determined by local rule of court.

Subdivision (b) is added to treat amendments of the statement of intention separately from other amendments. The intention of the individual debtor must be performed within 45 days of the filing of the statement, unless the court extends the period. Subdivision (b) limits the time for amendment to the time for performance under § 521(2)(B) of the Code or any extension granted by the court.

Rule 1010

SERVICE OF INVOLUNTARY PETITION AND SUMMONS; PETITION COMMENCING ANCILLARY CASE

On the filing of an involuntary petition or a petition commencing a case ancillary to a foreign proceeding the clerk shall forthwith issue a summons for service. When an involuntary petition is filed, service shall be made on the debtor. When a petition commencing an ancillary case is filed, service shall be made on the parties against whom relief is sought pursuant to § 304(b) of the Code and on such other parties as the court may direct. The summons shall conform to Official Form No. 13 and a copy shall be served with a copy of the petition in the manner provided for service of a summons and complaint by Rule 7004(a) or (b). If service cannot be so made, the court may order the summons and petition to be served by mailing copies to the party's last known address, and by not less than one publication in a manner and form directed by the court. The summons and petition may be served on the party anywhere. Rule 7004(f) and Rule 4(g) and (h) F.R.Civ.P. apply when service is made or attempted under this rule.

Amended Mar. 30, 1987, eff. Aug. 1, 1987.

Advisory Committee Note

This rule provides the procedure for service of the involuntary petition and summons. It does not deal with service of a summons and complaint instituting an adversary proceeding pursuant to Part VII.

While this rule is similar to former Bankruptcy Rule 111, it substitutes the clerk of the bankruptcy court for the clerk of the district court as the person who is to issue the summons.

The modes of service prescribed by the rule are personal or by mail, when service can be effected in one of these ways in the United States. Such service is to be made in the manner prescribed in adversary proceedings by Rule 7004(a) and (b). If service must be made in a foreign country, the mode of service is one of that set forth in Rule 4(i) F.R.Civ.P.

When the methods set out in Rule 7004(a) and (b) cannot be utilized, service by publication coupled with mailing to the last known address is authorized. *Cf.* Rule 7004(c). The court determines the form and manner of publication as provided in Rule 9007. The publication need not set out the petition or the order directing service by publication. In order to apprise the debtor fairly, however, the publication should include all the information required to be in the summons by Official Form No. 13 and a notice indicating how service is being effected and how a copy of the petition may be obtained.

There are no territorial limits on the service authorized by this rule, which continues the practice under the former rules and Act. There must, however, be a basis for jurisdiction pursuant to § 109(a) of the Code for the court to order relief. Venue provisions are set forth in 28 U.S.C. § 1472.

Subdivision (f) of Rule 7004 and subdivisions (g) and (h) of Rule 4 F.R. Civ.P. govern time and proof of service and amendment of process or of proof of service.

Rule 1004 provides for transmission to nonpetitioning partners of a petition filed against the partnership by fewer than all the general partners.

Advisory Committee Notes to 1987 Amendments

The rule has been broadened to include service of a petition commencing a case ancillary to a foreign proceeding, previously included in Rule 1003(e) (2).

Rule 1011

RESPONSIVE PLEADING OR MOTION IN INVOLUNTARY AND ANCILLARY CASES

(a) Who May Contest Petition. The debtor named in an involuntary petition or a party in interest to a petition commencing a case ancillary to a foreign proceeding may contest the petition. In the case of a petition against a partnership under Rule 1004(b), a nonpetitioning general partner, or a person who is alleged to be a general partner but denies the allegation, may contest the petition.

(b) Defenses and Objections; When Presented. Defenses and objections to the petition shall be presented in the manner prescribed by Rule 12 F.R.Civ.P. and shall be filed and served within 20 days after service of the summons, except that if service is made by publication on a party or partner not residing or found within the state in which the court sits, the court shall prescribe the time for filing and serving the response.

(c) Effect of Motion. Service of a motion under Rule 12(b) F.R.Civ.P. shall extend the time for filing and serving a responsive pleading as permitted by Rule 12(a) F.R.Civ.P.

(d) Claims Against Petitioners. A claim against a petitioning creditor may not be asserted in the answer except for the purpose of defeating the petition.

(e) Other Pleadings. No other pleadings shall be permitted, except that the court may order a reply to an answer and prescribe the time for filing and service.

Amended Mar. 30, 1987, eff. Aug. 1, 1987.

Advisory Committee Note

This rule is derived from former Bankruptcy Rule 112. A petition filed by fewer than all the general partners under Rule 1004(b) to have an order for relief entered with respect to the partnership is referred to as a petition against the partnership because of the adversary character of the proceeding it commences. *Cf.* § 303(b)(3) of the Code; 2 Collier *Bankruptcy* ¶ 303.05[5][a] (15th ed. 1981); 2 *id.* ¶¶ 18.33[2], 18.46 (14th ed. 1966). One who denies an allegation of membership in the firm is nevertheless recognized as a party entitled to contest a petition filed against a partnership under subdivision (b) of Rule 1004 in view of the possible consequences to him of an order for relief against the entity alleged to include him as a member. See § 723 of the Code; *Francis* v. *McNeal*, 228 U.S. 695 (1913); *Manson* v. *Williams*, 213 U.S. 453 (1909); *Carter* v. *Whisler*, 275 Fed. 743, 746–747 (8th Cir. 1921). The rule preserves the features of the former Act and Rule 112 and the Code permitting no response by creditors to an involuntary petition or petition against a partnership under Rule 1004(b).

Subdivision (b). Rule 12 F.R.Civ.P. has been looked to by the courts as prescribing the mode of making a defense or objection to a petition in bankruptcy. See *Fada of New York, Inc.* v. *Organization Service Co., Inc.*, 125 F.2d 120 (2d Cir. 1942); *In the Matter of McDougald*, 17 F.R.D. 2, 5 (W.D.Ark.1955); *In the Matter of Miller*, 6 Fed. Rules Serv. 12f.26, Case No. 1 (N.D.Ohio 1942); *Tatum* v. *Acadian Production Corp. of La.*, 35 F.Supp. 40, 50 (E.D.La.1940); 2 Collier, *supra* ¶ 303.07 (15th ed. 1981); 2 *id.* at 134–40 (14th ed. 1966). As pointed out in the Note accompanying former Bankruptcy Rule 915 an objection that a debtor is neither entitled to the benefits of the Code nor amenable to an involuntary petition goes to jurisdiction of the subject matter and may be made at any time consistent with Rule 12(h)(3) F.R.Civ.P. Nothing in this rule recognizes standing in a creditor or any other person not authorized to contest a petition to raise an objection that a person eligible to file a voluntary petition cannot be the subject of an order for relief on an involuntary petition. See Seligson & King, *Jurisdiction and Venue in Bankruptcy*, 36 Ref.J. 36, 38–40 (1962).

As Collier has pointed out with respect to theBankruptcy Act, "the mechanics of the provisions in § 18a and b relating to time for appearance and pleading are unnecessarily confusing. . . . It would seem, though, to be more straightforward to provide, as does Federal Rule 12(a), that the time to respond runs from the date of service rather than the date of issuance of process." 2 Collier, *supra* at 119. The time normally allowed for the service and filing of an answer or motion under Rule 1011 runs from the date of the issuance of the summons. Compare Rule 7012. Service of the summons and petition will ordinarily be made by mail under Rule 1010 and must be made within 10 days of the issuance of the summons under Rule 7004(e), which governs the time of service. When service is made by publication, the court should fix the time for service and filing of the response in the light of all the circumstances so as to afford a fair opportunity to the debtor to enter a defense or objection without unduly delaying the hearing on the petition. *Cf.* Rule 12(a) F.R.Civ.P.

Subdivision (c). Under subdivision (c), the timely service of a motion permitted by Rule 12(b), (e), (f), or (h) F.R.Civ.P. alters the time within which an answer must be filed. If the court denies a motion or postpones its disposition until trial on the merits, the answer must be served within 10 days after notice of the court's action. If the court grants a motion for a more definite statement, the answer may be served any time within 10 days after the service of the more definite statement.

Many of the rules governing adversary proceedings apply to proceedings on a contested petition unless the court otherwise directs as provided in Rule 1018. The specific provisions of this Rule 1011 or 7005, however, govern the filing of an answer or motion responsive to a petition. The rules of Part VII are adaptations of the corresponding Federal Rules of Civil Procedure, and the effect of Rule 1018 is thus to make the provisions of Civil Rules 5, 8, 9, 15, and 56, *inter alia*, generally applicable to the making of defenses and objections to the petition. Rule 1018 follows prior law and practice in this respect. See 2 Collier, *Bankruptcy* ¶¶ 18.39–18.41 (14th ed. 1966).

Subdivision (d). This subdivision adopts the position taken in many cases that an affirmative judgment against a petitioning creditor cannot be sought by a counterclaim filed in an answer to an involuntary petition. See, *e.g., Georgia Jewelers, Inc.,* v. *Bulova Watch Co.,* 302 F.2d 362, 369–70 (5th Cir. 1962); *Associated Electronic Supply Co. of Omaha* v. *C.B.S. Electronic Sales Corp.,* 288 F.2d 683, 684-85 (8th Cir. 1961). The subdivision follows *Harris* v. *Capehart–Farnsworth Corp.,* 225 F.2d 268 (8th Cir. 1955), in permitting the debtor to challenge the standing of a petitioner by filing a counterclaim against him. It does not foreclose the court from rejecting a counterclaim that cannot be determined without unduly delaying the decision upon the petition. See *In the Matter of Bichel Optical Laboratories, Inc.,* 299 F.Supp. 545 (D.Minn.1969).

Subdivision (e). This subdivision makes it clear that no reply needs to be made to an answer, including one asserting a counterclaim, unless the court orders otherwise.

Advisory Committee Notes to 1987 Amendments

The rule has been broadened to make applicable in ancillary cases the provisions concerning responsive pleadings to involuntary petitions.

Rule 1012

[ABROGATED]

Abrogated Mar. 30, 1987, eff. Aug. 1, 1987.

Advisory Committee Note

This rule is adapted from former Bankruptcy Rule 114. Since the provisions in § 303 of the Code apply equally to chapter 7 and 11 cases, the rule applies in both types of cases.

Former Rule 114 was derived from § 3d of the Bankruptcy Act but added the three sanctions in Rule 37, F.R.Civ.P. Former Rule 114 thus differed from the holdings in *In re Richards Discount Jewelers, Inc.*, 303 F.Supp. 517, 518 (S.D.N.Y.1969), and *In the Matter of Shulund*, 210 F.Supp. 195, 199–200 (D.Mont.1962), that § 3d of the Act was inconsistent with Rule 37 and prescribed the only consequence for failure of the bankrupt to appear with his papers and submit to an examination on the issue of insolvency or inability to pay debts.

Rule 2004 deals with examination of the debtor. The last sentence of Rule 1012 is continued in part from former Rule 114 which eliminates doubts as to the availability to petitioning creditors of an examination of the debtor and others in accordance with the practice that developed under § 21a of the Act. See 1 Collier, *Bankruptcy* ¶ 3.208[2] (14th ed. 1961); 2 *id.* ¶ 18.41[7] (1966); 2 *id.* ¶ 21.08 (1964); 2 *id.* ¶¶ 105.04, 343.01–.12, 344.01 *et seq.* (15th ed. 1981); 3 *id.* ¶ 521.13. The discovery procedures of Rules 26–37, F.R.Civ.P., available in proceedings on a contested involuntary petition pursuant to Rule 1018 are explicitly made applicable to the issue of nonpayment of debts by Rule 1012.

Advisory Committee Notes to 1987 Amendments

This rule is abrogated. The discovery rules apply whenever an involuntary petition is contested. Rule 1018.

Rule 1013

HEARING AND DISPOSITION OF PETITION IN INVOLUNTARY CASES

(a) **Contested Petition.** The court shall determine the issues of a contested petition at the earliest practicable time and forthwith enter an order for relief, dismiss the petition, or enter other appropriate orders.

(b) **Default.** If no pleading or other defense to a petition is filed within the time provided by Rule 1011, the court, on the next day, or as soon thereafter as practicable, shall enter an order for the relief prayed for in the petition.

(c) **Order for Relief.** An order for relief shall conform substantially to Official Form No. 14.

Advisory Committee Note

This rule is adapted from former Bankruptcy Rule 115(a) and (c) and applies in chapter 7 and 11 cases. The right to trial by jury under § 19a of the Bankruptcy Act has been abrogated and the availability of a trial by jury is within the discretion of the bankruptcy judge pursuant to 28 U.S.C. § 1480(b). Rule 9015 governs the demand for a jury trial.

Subdivision (b) of Rule 1013 is derived from former Bankruptcy Rule 115(c) and § 18(e) of the Bankruptcy Act. If an order for relief is not entered on default, dismissal will ordinarily be appropriate but the court may postpone definitive action. See also Rule 9024 with respect to setting aside an order for relief on default for cause.

Subdivision (e) of former Bankruptcy Rule 115 has not been carried over because its provisions are covered by § 303(i) of the Code.

Rule 1014

DISMISSAL AND CHANGE OF VENUE

(a) Dismissal and Transfer of Cases.

(1) *Cases Filed in Proper District.* If a petition is filed in a proper district, on timely motion of a party in interest, and after hearing on notice to the petitioners and other entities as directed by the court, the case may be transferred to any other district if the court determines that the transfer is in the interest of justice or for the convenience of the parties.

(2) *Cases Filed in Improper District.* If a petition is filed in an improper district, on timely motion of a party in interest and after hearing on notice to the petitioners and other entities as directed by the court, the case may be dismissed or transferred to any other district if the court determines that transfer is in the interest of justice or for the convenience of the parties.

(b) Procedure When Petitions Involving the Same Debtor or Related Debtors Are Filed in Different Courts.

If petitions commencing cases under the Code are filed in different districts by or against (1) the same debtor, or (2) a partnership and one or more of its general partners, or (3) two or more general partners, or (4) a debtor and an affiliate, on motion filed in the district in which the first petition is filed and after hearing on notice to the petitioners and other entities as directed by the court, the court may determine, in the interest of justice or for the convenience of the parties, the district or districts in which the case or cases should proceed. Except as otherwise ordered by the court in the district in which the first petition is filed, the proceedings on the other petitions shall be stayed by the courts in which they have been filed until the determination is made.

Amended Mar. 30, 1987, eff. Aug. 1, 1987.

Advisory Committee Note

This rule is derived from former Bankruptcy Rule 116 which contained venue as well as transfer provisions. Public Law 95–598, however, placed the venue provisions in 28 U.S.C. § 1472, and no purpose is served by repeating them in this rule. Transfer of cases is provided in 28 U.S.C. § 1475 but this rule adds the procedure for obtaining transfer. Pursuant to 28 U.S.C. § 1472, proper venue for cases filed under the Code is either the district of domicile, residence, principal place of business, or location of principal assets for 180 days or the longer portion thereof immediately preceding the petition. 28 U.S.C. § 1475 permits the court to transfer a case in the interest of justice and for the convenience of the parties. If the venue is improper, the court may retain or transfer the case in the interest of justice and for the convenience of the parties pursuant to 28 U.S.C. § 1477.

Subdivision (a) of the rule is derived from former Bankruptcy Rule 116(b). It implements 28 U.S.C. §§ 1475 and 1477 and clarifies the procedure to be followed in requesting and effecting transfer of a case. Subdivision (a) protects the parties against being subjected to a transfer except on a timely motion of a party in interest. If the transfer would result in fragmentation or duplication of administration, increase expense, or delay closing the estate, such a factor would bear on the timeliness of the motion as well as on the propriety of the transfer under the standards prescribed in subdivision (a). Subdivision (a) of the rule requires the interest of justice and the convenience of the parties to be the grounds of any transfer of a case or of the retention of a case filed in an improper district as does 28 U.S.C. § 1477. *Cf.* 28 U.S.C. § 1404(a) (district court may transfer any civil action "[f]or the convenience of parties and witnesses, in the interest of justice"). It also expressly requires a hearing on notice to the petitioner or petitioners before the transfer of any case may be ordered. Under this rule, a motion by a party in interest is necessary. There is no provision for the court to act on its own initiative.

Subdivision (b) is derived from former Bankruptcy Rule 116(c). It authorizes the court in which the first petition is filed under the Code by or against a debtor to entertain a motion seeking a determination whether the case so commenced should continue or be transferred and consolidated or administered jointly with another case commenced by or against the same or related person in another court under a different chapter of the Code. Subdivision (b) is correlated with 28 U.S.C. § 1472 which authorizes petitioners to file cases involving a partnership and partners or affiliated debtors.

The reference in subdivision (b) to petitions filed "by" a partner or "by" any other of the persons mentioned is to be understood as referring to voluntary petitions. It is not the purpose of this subdivision to permit more than one case to be filed in the same court because a creditor signing an involuntary petition happens to be a partner, a partnership, or an affiliate of a debtor.

Transfers of adversary proceedings in cases under title 11 are governed by Rule 7087 and 28 U.S.C. § 1475.

Advisory Committee Notes to 1987 Amendments

Both paragraphs 1 and 2 of subdivision (a) are amended to conform to the standard for transfer in 28 U.S.C. § 1412. Formerly, 28 U.S.C. § 1477 authorized a court either to transfer or retain a case which had been commenced in a district where venue was improper. However, 28 U.S.C. § 1412, which supersedes 28 U.S.C. § 1477, authorizes only the transfer of a case. The rule is amended to delete the reference to retention of a case commenced in the improper district. Dismissal of a case commenced in the improper district as authorized by 28 U.S.C. § 1406 has been added to the rule. If a timely motion to dismiss for improper venue is not filed, the right to object to venue is waived.

The last sentence of the rule has been deleted as unnecessary.

Rule 1015

CONSOLIDATION OR JOINT ADMINISTRATION OF CASES PENDING IN SAME COURT

(a) Cases Involving Same Debtor. If two or more petitions are pending in the same court by or against the same debtor, the court may order consolidation of the cases.

(b) Cases Involving Two or More Related Debtors. If a joint petition or two or more petitions are pending in the same court by or against (1) a husband and wife, or (2) a partnership and one or more of its general partners, or (3) two or more general partners, or (4) a debtor and an affiliate, the court may order a joint administration of the estates. Prior to entering an order the court shall give consideration to protecting creditors of different estates against potential conflicts of interest. An order directing joint administration of individual cases of a husband and wife shall, if one spouse has elected the exemptions under § 522(b)(1) of the Code and the other has elected the exemptions under § 522(b)(2), fix a reasonable time within which either may amend the election so that both shall have elected the same exemptions. The order shall notify the debtors that unless they elect the same exemptions within the time fixed by the court, they will be deemed to have elected the exemptions provided by § 522(b)(1).

(c) Expediting and Protective Orders. When an order for consolidation or joint administration of a joint case or two or more cases is entered pursuant to this rule, while protecting the rights of the parties under the Code, the court may enter orders as may tend to avoid unnecessary costs and delay.

Amended Mar. 30, 1987, eff. Aug. 1, 1987.

Advisory Committee Note

Subdivision (a) of this rule is derived from former Bankruptcy Rule 117(a). It applies to cases when the same debtor is named in both voluntary and involuntary petitions, when husband and wife have filed a joint petition pursuant to § 302 of the Code, and when two or more involuntary petitions are filed against the same debtor. It also applies when cases are pending in the same court by virtue of a transfer of one or more petitions from another court. Subdivision (c) allows the court discretion regarding the order of trial of issues raised by two or more involuntary petitions against the same debtor.

Subdivision (b) recognizes the propriety of joint administration of estates in certain kinds of cases. The election or appointment of one trustee for two or more jointly administered estates is authorized by Rule 2009. The authority of the court to order joint administration under subdivision (b) extends equally to the situation when the petitions are filed under different sections, *e.g.*, when one petition is voluntary and the other involuntary, and when all of the petitions are filed under the same section of the Code.

Consolidation of cases implies a unitary administration of the estate and will ordinarily be indicated under the circumstances to which subdivision (a) applies. This rule does not deal with the consolidation of cases involving two or more separate debtors. Consolidation of the estates of separate debtors may sometimes be appropriate, as when the affairs of an individual and a corporation owned or controlled by that individual are so intermingled that the court cannot separate their assets and liabilities. Consolidation, as distinguished from joint administration, is neither authorized nor prohibited by this rule since the propriety of consolidation depends on substantive considerations and affects the substantive rights of the creditors of the different estates. For illustrations of the substantive consolidation of separate estates, see *Sampsell* v. *Imperial Paper & Color Corp.*, 313 U.S. 215 (1941). See also *Chemical Bank N.Y. Trust Co.* v. *Kheel*, 369 F.2d 845 (2d Cir. 1966); Seligson & Mandell, *Multi-Debtor Petition—Consolidation of Debtors and Due Process of Law*, 73 Com.L.J. 341 (1968); Kennedy, *Insolvency and the Corporate Veil in the United States* in *Proceedings of the 8th International Symposium on Comparative Law* 232, 248–55 (1971).

Joint administration as distinguished from consolidation may include combining the estates by using a single docket for the matters occurring in the administration, including the listing of filed claims, the combining of notices to creditors of the different estates, and the joint handling of other purely administrative matters that may aid in expediting the cases and rendering the process less costly.

Subdivision (c) is an adaptation of the provisions of Rule 42(a) F.R.Civ.P. for the purposes of administration of estates under this rule. The rule does not deal with filing fees when an order for the consolidation of cases or joint administration of estates is made.

A joint petition of husband and wife, requiring the payment of a single filing fee, is permitted by § 302 of the Code. Consolidation of such a case, however, rests in the discretion of the court; see § 302(b) of the Code.

Advisory Committee Notes to 1987 Amendments

The amendment to subdivision (b) implements the provisions of § 522(b) of the Code, as enacted by the 1984 amendments.

Rule 1016

DEATH OR INSANITY OF DEBTOR

Death or insanity of the debtor shall not abate a liquidation case under chapter 7 of the Code. In such event the estate shall be administered and the case concluded in the same manner, so far as possible, as though the death or insanity had not occurred. If a reorganization or individual's debt adjustment case is pending under chapter 11 or chapter 13, the case may be dismissed; or if further administration is possible and in the best interest of the parties, the case may proceed and be concluded in the same manner, so far as possible, as though the death or insanity had not occurred.

Advisory Committee Note

This rule is derived from former Rules 118 and 11–16. In a chapter 11 reorganization case or chapter 13 individual's debt adjustment case, the likelihood is that the case will be dismissed.

Rule 1017

DISMISSAL OF CASE; SUSPENSION

(a) **Voluntary Dismissal; Dismissal for Want of Prosecution.** Except as provided in §§ 707(b) and 1307(b) of the Code, a petition shall not be dismissed on motion of the petitioner or for want of prosecution or other cause or by consent of the parties prior to a hearing on notice to all creditors as provided in Rule 2002(a). For such notice the debtor shall file a list of all creditors with their addresses within the time fixed by the court unless the list was previously filed. If the debtor fails to file the list, the court may order the preparing and filing by the debtor or other entity.

(b) **Dismissal for Failure to Pay Filing Fee.**

(1) For failure to pay any installment of the filing fee, the court may after hearing on notice to the debtor and the trustee dismiss the petition.

(2) If the petition is dismissed or the case closed without full payment of the filing fee, the installments collected shall be distributed in the same manner and proportions as if the filing fee had been paid in full.

(3) Notice of dismissal for failure to pay the filing fee shall be given within 30 days after the dismissal to creditors appearing on the list of creditors and to those who have filed claims, in the manner provided in Rule 2002.

(c) Suspension. A petition shall not be dismissed or proceedings suspended pursuant to § 305 of the Code prior to a hearing on notice as provided in Rule 2002(a).

(d) Procedure for Dismissal or Conversion. A proceeding to dismiss a case or convert a case to another chapter, except pursuant to §§ 706(a), 707(b), 1112(a), or 1307(a) or (b), is governed by Rule 9014. Conversion or dismissal pursuant to §§ 706(a), 1112(a), or 1307(b) shall be on motion filed and served as required by Rule 9013. A chapter 13 case shall be converted without court order on the filing by the debtor of a notice of conversion pursuant to § 1307(a).

(e) Dismissal of Individual Debtor's Chapter 7 Case for Substantial Abuse. An individual debtor's case under chapter 7 may be dismissed for substantial abuse only after a hearing on notice to the debtor and the trustee and such other parties in interest as the court directs. The notice shall advise the debtor of all matters which the court will consider at the hearing.

Amended Mar. 30, 1987, eff. Aug. 1, 1987.

Advisory Committee Note

Subdivision (a) of this rule is derived from former Bankruptcy Rule 120(a). While the rule applies to voluntary and involuntary cases, the "consent of the parties" referred to is that of petitioning creditors and the debtor in an involuntary case. The last sentence recognizes that the court should not be confined to petitioning creditors in its choice of parties on whom to call for assistance in preparing the list of creditors when the debtor fails to do so. This subdivision implements §§ 303(j), 707, 1112 and 1307 of the Code by specifying the manner of and persons to whom notice shall be given and requiring the court to hold a hearing on the issue of dismissal.

Subdivision (b) is derived from former Bankruptcy Rule 120(b). A dismissal under this subdivision can occur only when the petition has been permitted to be filed pursuant to Rule 1006(b). The provision for notice in paragraph (3) is correlated with the provision in Rule 4006 when there is a waiver, denial, or revocation of a discharge. As pointed out in the Note accompanying Rule 4008, the purpose of notifying creditors of a debtor that no discharge has been granted is to correct their assumption to the contrary so that they can take appropriate steps to protect their claims.

Subdivision (c) is new and specifies the notice required for a hearing on dismissal or suspension pursuant to § 305 of the Code. The suspension to which this subdivision refers is that of the case; it does not concern abstention of the court in hearing an adversary proceeding pursuant to 28 U.S.C. § 1478(b).

Subdivision (d). Any proceeding, whether by a debtor or other party, to dismiss or convert a case under §§ 706, 707, 1112, or 1307 is commenced by a motion pursuant to Rule 9014.

Advisory Committee Notes to 1987 Amendments

Subdivision (d) is amended to provide that dismissal or conversion pursuant to §§ 706(a), 707(b), 1112(a), and 1307(b) is not automatically a contested matter under Rule 9014. Conversion or dismissal under these sections is initiated by the filing and serving of a motion as required by Rule 9013. No hearing is required on these motions unless the court directs.

Conversion of a chapter 13 case to a chapter 7 case as authorized by § 1307(a) is accomplished by the filing of a notice of conversion. The notice of conversion procedure is modeled on the voluntary dismissal provision of Rule 41(a)(1) F.R.Civ.P. Conversion occurs on the filing of the notice. No court order is required.

Subdivision (e) is new and provides the procedure to be followed when a court on its own motion has made a preliminary determination that an individual debtor's chapter 7 case may be dismissed pursuant to § 707(b) of the Code, which was added by the 1984 amendments. A debtor's failure to attend the hearing is not a ground for dismissal pursuant to § 707(b).

Rule 1018

CONTESTED INVOLUNTARY PETITIONS; CONTESTED PETITIONS COMMENCING ANCILLARY CASES; PROCEEDINGS TO VACATE ORDER FOR RELIEF; APPLICABILITY OF RULES IN PART VII GOVERNING ADVERSARY PROCEEDINGS

The following rules in Part VII apply to all proceedings relating to a contested involuntary petition, to proceedings relating to a contested petition commencing a case ancillary to a foreign proceeding, and to all proceedings to vacate an order for relief: Rules 7005, 7008–7010, 7015, 7016, 7024–7026, 7028–7037, 7052, 7054, 7056, and 7062, except as otherwise provided in Part I of these rules and unless the court otherwise directs. The court may direct that other rules in Part VII shall also apply. For the purposes of this rule a reference in the Part VII rules to adversary proceedings shall be read as a reference to proceedings relating to a contested involuntary petition, or contested ancillary petition, or proceedings to vacate an order for relief. Reference in the Federal Rules of Civil Procedure to the complaint shall be read as a reference to the petition.

Amended Mar. 30, 1987, eff. Aug. 1, 1987.

Advisory Committee Note

The rules in Part VII to which this rule refers are adaptations of the Federal Rules of Civil Procedure for the purpose of governing the procedure in adversary proceedings in cases under the Code. See the Note accompanying Rule 7001 *infra*. Because of the special need for dispatch and expedition in the determination of the issues in an involuntary petition, see *Acme Harvester Co.* v. *Beekman Lumber Co.*, 222 U.S. 300, 309 (1911), the objective of some of the Federal Rules of Civil Procedure and their adaptations in Part VII to facilitate the settlement of multiple controversies involving many persons in a single lawsuit is not compatible with the exigencies of bankruptcy administration. See *United States F. & G. Co.* v. *Bray*, 225 U.S. 205, 218 (1912). For that reason Rules 7013, 7014 and 7018–7023 will rarely be appropriate in a proceeding on a contested petition.

Certain terms used in the Federal Rules of Civil Procedure have altered meanings when they are made applicable in cases under the Code by these rules. See Rule 9002 *infra*. This Rule 1018 requires that the terms "adversary proceedings" when used in the rules in Part VII and "complaint" when used in the Federal Rules of Civil Procedure be given altered meanings when they are made applicable to proceedings relating to a contested petition or proceedings to vacate any order for relief. A motion to vacate an order for relief, whether or not made on a petition that was or could have been contested, is governed by the rules in Part VII referred to in this Rule 1018.

Advisory Committee Notes to 1987 Amendments

Rule 1018 is amended to include within its terms a petition commencing an ancillary case when it is contested. This provision was formerly included in Rule 1003(e)(4).

Although this rule does not contain an explicit authorization for the entry of an order for relief when a debtor refuses to cooperate in discovery relating to a contested involuntary petition, the court has ample power under Rule 37(b) F.R.Civ.P., as incorporated by Rule 7037, to enter an order for relief under appropriate circumstances. Rule 37(b) authorizes the court to enter judgment by default or an order that "facts shall be taken as established."

Rule 1019

CONVERSION OF CHAPTER 11 REORGANIZATION CASE OR CHAPTER 13 INDIVIDUAL'S DEBT ADJUSTMENT CASE TO CHAPTER 7 LIQUIDATION CASE

When a chapter 11 or chapter 13 case has been converted or reconverted to a chapter 7 case:

(1) *Filing of Lists, Inventories, Schedules, Statements.*

(A) Lists, inventories, schedules, statements of financial affairs, and statements of executory contracts theretofore filed shall be deemed to be filed in the chapter 7 case, unless the court directs otherwise. If they have not been previously filed, the debtor shall comply with Rule 1007 as if an order for relief had been entered on an involuntary petition on the date of the entry of the order directing that the case continue under chapter 7.

(B) The statement of intention, if required, shall be filed within 30 days following entry of the order of conversion or before the first date set for the meeting of creditors, whichever is earlier. An extension of time may be granted for cause only on motion made before the time has expired. Notice of an extension shall be given to any committee, trustee, or other party as the court may direct.

(2) *Notice of Order of Conversion.* Within 20 days after entry of the order converting the case to a chapter 7 case, notice of the order shall be given to any trustee in the superseded case and to all creditors in the manner provided by Rule 2002 and shall be included in the notice of the meeting of creditors.

(3) *New Filing Periods.* A new time period for filing claims, a complaint objecting to discharge, or a complaint to obtain a determination of dischargeability of any debt shall commence pursuant to Rules 3002, 4004, or 4007, provided that a new time period shall not commence if a chapter 7 case had been converted to a chapter 11 or 13 case and thereafter reconverted to a chapter 7 case and the time for filing claims, a complaint objecting to discharge, or a

complaint to obtain a determination of the dischargeability of any debt, or any extension thereof, expired in the original chapter 7 case.

(4) *Claims Filed in Superseded Case.* All claims actually filed by a creditor in the superseded case shall be deemed filed in the chapter 7 case.

(5) *Turnover of Records and Property.* After qualification of, or assumption of duties by the chapter 7 trustee, any debtor in possession or trustee previously acting in the chapter 11 or 13 case shall, forthwith, unless otherwise ordered, turn over to the chapter 7 trustee all records and property of the estate in the possession or control of the debtor in possession or trustee.

(6) *Filing Final Report and Schedule of Postpetition Debts.* Each debtor in possession or trustee in the superseded case shall file with the court a final report and account within 30 days following the entry of the order of conversion, unless the court directs otherwise. The report shall include a schedule of unpaid debts incurred after commencement of the chapter 11 case. A chapter 13 debtor shall file a schedule of unpaid debts incurred after the commencement of a chapter 13 case. If the conversion order is entered after confirmation of a plan, the debtor shall file with the court (A) a schedule of property not listed in the final report and account acquired after the filing of the original petition but before entry of the conversion order; (B) a schedule of unpaid debts not listed in the final report and account incurred after confirmation but before entry of the conversion order; and (C) a schedule of executory contracts entered into or assumed after the filing of the original petition but before entry of the conversion order.

(7) *Filing of Postpetition Claims; Notice.* On the filing of the schedule of unpaid debts, the court shall order that written notice be given to those entities, including the United States, any state, or any subdivision thereof, that their claims may be filed within 60 days from the entry of the order, pursuant to Rule 3001(a)–(d). The court shall fix the time for filing claims arising from debts not so scheduled or arising from rejection of executory contracts under §§ 348(c) and 365(d) of the Code.

(8) *Extension of Time to File Claims Against Surplus.* Any extension of time for the filing of claims against a surplus granted pursuant to Rule 3002(c) (6), shall apply to holders of claims who failed to file their claims within the time prescribed, or fixed by the court pursuant to paragraph (7) of this rule, and notice shall be given as provided in Rule 2002.

Amended Mar. 30, 1987, eff. Aug. 1, 1987.

Advisory Committee Note

This rule is derived from former Bankruptcy Rule 122 and implements § 348 of the Code. The rule applies to proceedings in a chapter 7 case following supersession of a case commenced under chapter 11 or 13, whether the latter was initiated by an original petition or was converted from a pending chapter 7 or another chapter case. The rule is not intended to invalidate any action taken in the superseded case before its conversion to chapter 7.

Paragraph (1). If requirements applicable in the superseded case respecting the filing of schedules of debts and property, or lists of creditors and inventory, and of statements of financial affairs have been complied with before the order directing conversion to liquidation, these documents will ordinarily provide all the information about the debts, property, financial affairs, and contracts of the debtor needed for the administration of the estate. If the information submitted in the superseded case is inadequate for the purposes of administration, however, the court may direct the preparation of further informational material and the manner and time of its submission pursuant to paragraph (1). If no schedules, lists, inventories, or statements were filed in the superseded case, this paragraph imposes the duty on the debtor to file schedules and a statement of affairs pursuant to Rule 1007 as if an involuntary petition had been filed on the date when the court directed the conversion of the case to a liquidation case.

Paragraphs (2) and (3). Paragraph (2) requires notice to be given to all creditors of the order of conversion. The notice is to be included in the notice of the meeting of creditors and Official Form No. 16 may be adapted for use. A meeting of creditors may have been held in the superseded case as required by § 341(a) of the Code but that would not dispense with the need to hold one in the ensuing liquidation case. Section 701(a) of the Code permits the court to appoint the trustee acting in the chapter 11 or 13 case as interim trustee in the chapter 7 case. Section 702(a) of the Code allows creditors to elect a trustee but only at the meeting of creditors held under § 341. The right to elect a trustee is not lost because the chapter 7 case follows a chapter 11 or 13 case. Thus a meeting of creditors is necessary. The date fixed for the meeting of creditors will control at least the time for filing claims pursuant to Rule 3002(c). That time will remain applicable in the ensuing chapter 7 case except as paragraph (3) provides, if that time had expired in an earlier chapter 7 case which was converted to the chapter 11 or 13 case, it is not revived in the subsequent chapter 7 case. The same is true if the time for filing a complaint objecting to discharge or to determine nondischargeability of a debt had expired. Paragraph (3), however, recognizes that such time may be extended by the court under rule 4004 or 4007 on motion made within the original prescribed time.

Paragraph (4) renders it unnecessary to file anew claims that had been filed in the chapter 11 or 13 case before conversion to chapter 7.

Paragraph (5) contemplates that typically, after the court orders conversion of a chapter case to liquidation, a trustee under chapter 7 will forthwith take charge of the property of the estate and proceed expeditiously to liquidate it. The court may appoint the interim trustee in the chapter 7 case pursuant to § 701(a) of the Code. If creditors do not elect a trustee under § 702, the interim trustee becomes the trustee.

Paragraph (6) requires the trustee or debtor in possession acting in the chapter 11 or 13 case to file a final report and schedule of debts incurred in that case. This schedule will provide the information necessary for giving the notice required by paragraph (7) of the rule.

Paragraph (7) requires that claims that arose in the chapter 11 or 13 case be filed within 60 days after entry of the order converting the case to one under chapter 7. Claims not scheduled pursuant to paragraph (6) of the rule or arising from the rejection of an executory contract entered into during the chapter case may be filed within a time fixed by the court. Pursuant to § 348(c) of the Code, the conversion order is treated as the order for relief to fix the time for the trustee to assume or reject executory contracts under § 365(d).

Paragraph (8) permits the extension of the time for filing claims when claims are not timely filed but only with respect to any surplus that may remain in the estate. See also § 726(a)(2)(C) and (3) of the Code.

Advisory Committee Notes to 1987 Amendments

Paragraph (1) is amended to provide for the filing of a statement of intention in a case converted to chapter 7. Paragraph (1)(B) is added to provide for the filing of the statement of intention when a case is converted to chapter 7. The time for filing the statement of intention and for an extension of that time is governed by § 521(2)(A) of the Code. An extension of time for other required filings is governed by Rule 1007(c), which paragraph (1)(A) incorporates by reference. Because of the amendment to Rule 1007(c), the filing of new lists, schedules, and statements is now governed exclusively by Rule 1019(1).

Paragraph (3) of the rule is expanded to include the effect of conversion of a chapter 11 or 13 case to a chapter 7 case. On conversion of a case from chapter 11 or 13 to a chapter 7 case, parties have a new period within which to file claims or complaints relating to the granting of the discharge or the dischargeability of a debt. This amendment is consistent with the holding and reasoning of the court in *F & M Marquette Nat'l Bank v. Richards*, 780 F.2d 24 (8th Cir. 1985).

Paragraph (4) is amended to deal directly with the status of claims which are properly listed on the schedules filed in a chapter 11 case and deemed filed pursuant to § 1111(a) of the Code. Section 1111(a) is only applicable to the chapter 11 case. On conversion of the chapter 11 case to a chapter 7 case, paragraph (4) governs the status of claims filed in the chapter 11 case. The Third Circuit properly construed paragraph (4) as applicable to claims deemed filed in the superseded chapter 11 case. *In re Crouthamel Potato Chip Co.*, 786 F.2d 141 (3d Cir. 1986).

The amendment to paragraph (4) changes that result by providing that only claims that are actually filed in the chapter 11 case are treated as filed in the superseding chapter 7 case. When chapter 11 cases are converted to chapter 7 cases, difficulties in obtaining and verifying the debtors' records are common. It is unfair to the chapter 7 trustee and creditors to require that they be bound by schedules which may not be subject to verification.

Paragraph (6) is amended to place the obligation on the chapter 13 debtor to file a schedule of unpaid debts incurred during the superseded chapter 13 case.

PART II

OFFICERS AND ADMINISTRATION; NOTICES; MEETINGS; EXAMINATIONS; ELECTIONS; ATTORNEYS AND ACCOUNTANTS

Rule
2001. Appointment of Interim Trustee Before Order for Relief in a Chapter 7 Liquidation Case
2002. Notices to Creditors, Equity Security Holders, and United States
2003. Meeting of Creditors or Equity Security Holders
2004. Examination
2005. Apprehension and Removal of Debtor to Compel Attendance for Examination
2006. Solicitation and Voting of Proxies in Chapter 7 Liquidation Cases
2007. Appointment of Creditors' Committee Organized Before Commencement of the Case
2008. Notice to Trustee of Selection
2009. Trustees for Estates When Joint Administration Ordered
2010. Qualification by Trustee; Proceeding on Bond
2011. Evidence of Debtor in Possession
2012. Substitution of Trustee or Successor Trustee; Accounting
2013. Limitation on Appointment or Employment of Trustees, Examiners, Appraisers and Auctioneers
2014. Employment of Professional Persons
2015. Duty of Trustee or Debtor in Possession to Keep Records, Make Reports, and Give Notice of Case
2016. Compensation for Services Rendered and Reimbursement of Expenses
2017. Examination of Debtor's Transactions With Debtor's Attorney
2018. Intervention; Right to Be Heard
2019. Representation of Creditors and Equity Security Holders in Chapter 9 Municipality and Chapter 11 Reorganization Cases

Rule 2001

APPOINTMENT OF INTERIM TRUSTEE BEFORE ORDER FOR RELIEF IN A CHAPTER 7 LIQUIDATION CASE

(a) **Appointment.** At any time following the commencement of an involuntary liquidation case and before an order for relief, the court on written motion of a party in interest may appoint an interim trustee under § 303(g) of the Code. The motion shall set forth the necessity for the appointment and may be granted only after hearing on notice to the debtor, the petitioning creditors and other parties in interest as the court may designate.

(b) **Bond of Movant.** An interim trustee may not be appointed under this rule unless the movant furnishes a bond in an amount approved by the court, conditioned to indemnify the debtor for costs, attorney's fee, expenses, and damages allowable under § 303(i) of the Code.

(c) **Order of Appointment.** The order appointing the interim trustee shall state the reason the appointment is necessary and shall specify the trustee's duties.

(d) Turnover and Report. Following qualification of the trustee selected under § 702 of the Code, the interim trustee, unless otherwise ordered, shall (1) forthwith deliver to the trustee all the records and property of the estate in possession or subject to control of the interim trustee and, (2) within 30 days thereafter file a final report and account.

Amended Mar. 30, 1987, eff. Aug. 1, 1987.

Advisory Committee Note

This rule is adapted from former Bankruptcy Rule 201. See also former Chapter X Rule 10–201. In conformity with title 11 of the United States Code, this rule substitutes "interim trustee" for "receiver." Subdivision (a) and (e) of Rule 201 are not included because the provisions contained therein are found in detail in § 303(g) of the Code, or they are inconsistent with § 701 of the Code. Similarly, the provisions in Rule 201(d) relating to a debtor's counterbond are not included because of their presence in § 303(g).

Subdivision (a) makes it clear that the court may not on its own motion order the appointment of an interim trustee before an order for relief is entered. Appointment may be ordered only on motion of a party in interest.

Subdivision (b) requires those seeking the appointment of an interim trustee to furnish a bond. The bond may be the same one required of petitioning creditors under § 303(e) of the Code to indemnify the debtor for damages allowed by the court under § 303(i).

Subdivision (c) requires that the order specify which duties enumerated in § 303(g) shall be performed by the interim trustee. Reference should be made to Rule 2015 for additional duties required of an interim trustee including keeping records and filing periodic reports with the court.

Subdivision (d) requires turnover of records and property to the trustee selected under § 702 of the Code, after qualification. That trustee may be the interim trustee who becomes the trustee because of the failure of creditors to elect one under § 702(d) or the trustee elected by creditors under § 702(b), (c).

Rule 2002

NOTICES TO CREDITORS, EQUITY SECURITY HOLDERS, AND UNITED STATES

(a) Twenty-day Notices to Parties in Interest. Except as provided in subdivisions (h), (i) and (k) of this rule, the clerk, or some other person as the court may direct, shall give the debtor, the trustee, all creditors and indenture trustees not less than 20 days notice by mail of (1) the meeting of creditors pursuant to § 341 of the Code; (2) a proposed use, sale, or lease of property of the estate other than in the ordinary course of business, unless the court for cause shown shortens the time or directs another method of giving notice; (3) the hearing on approval of a compromise or settlement of a controversy, unless the court for cause shown directs that notice not be sent; (4) the date fixed for the filing of claims against a surplus in an estate as provided in Rule 3002(c)(6); (5) in a chapter 7 liquidation and a chapter 11 reorganization case, the hearing on the dismissal or conversion of a case to another chapter; (6) the time fixed to accept or reject a proposed modification of a plan; (7) hearings on all applications for compensation or reimbursement of expenses totalling in excess of $500; and (8) the time fixed for filing proofs of claims pursuant to Rule 3003(c).

(b) Twenty-five-day Notices to Parties in Interest. Except as provided in subdivisions (h), (i) and (k) of this rule, the clerk, or some other person as the court may direct, shall give the debtor, the trustee, all creditors and indenture trustees not less than 25 days notice by mail of (1) the time fixed for filing objections and the hearing to consider approval of a disclosure statement; and (2) the time fixed for filing objections and the hearing to consider confirmation of a plan.

(c) Content of Notice.

(1) *Proposed Use, Sale, or Lease of Property.* Subject to Rule 6004 the notice of a proposed use, sale, or lease of property required by subdivision (a)(2) of this rule shall include the time and place of any public sale, the terms and conditions of any private sale and the time fixed for filing objections. The notice of a proposed use, sale, or lease of property, including real estate, is sufficient if it generally describes the property.

(2) *Notice of Hearing on Compensation.* The notice of a hearing on an application for compensation or reimbursement of expenses required by subdivision (a)(7) of this rule shall identify the applicant and the amounts requested.

(d) Notice to Equity Security Holders. In a chapter 11 reorganization case, unless otherwise ordered by the court, the clerk, or some other person as the court may direct, shall in the manner and form directed by the court give notice to all equity security holders of (1) the order for relief; (2) any meeting of equity security holders ordered by the court pursuant to § 341 of the Code; (3) the hearing on the proposed sale of all or substantially all of the debtor's assets; (4) the hearing on the dismissal or conversion of a case to another chapter; (5) the time fixed for filing objections to and the hearing to consider approval of a disclosure statement; (6) the time fixed for filing objections to and the hearing to consider confirmation of a plan; and (7) the time fixed to accept or reject a proposed modification of a plan.

(e) Notice of No Dividend. In a chapter 7 liquidation case, if it appears from the schedules that there are no assets from which a dividend can be paid, the notice of the meeting of creditors may include a statement to that effect; that it is unnecessary to file claims; and that if sufficient assets become available for the payment of a dividend, further notice will be given for the filing of claims.

(f) Other Notices. Except as provided in subdivision (k) of this rule, the clerk, or some other person as the court may direct, shall give the debtor, all creditors and indenture trustees notice by mail of (1) the order for relief; (2) dismissal of the case; (3) the time allowed for filing claims pursuant to Rule 3002; (4) the entry of an order directing that the case be converted to a case under a different chapter; (5) the time fixed for filing a complaint objecting to the debtor's discharge pursuant to § 727 of the Code as provided in Rule 4004; (6) the time fixed for filing a complaint to determine the dischargeability of a debt pursuant to § 523 of the Code as provided in Rule 4007; (7) the waiver, denial, or revocation of a discharge as provided in Rule 4006; (8) entry of an order confirming a chapter 9 or 11 plan; and (9) a summary of the trustee's final report and account in a chapter 7 case if the net proceeds realized exceed $250.

Notice of the time fixed for accepting or rejecting a plan pursuant to Rule 3017(c) shall be given in accordance with Rule 3017(d).

(g) Addresses of Notices. All notices required to be mailed under this rule to a creditor, equity security holder, or indenture trustee shall be addressed as such entity or an authorized agent may direct in a request filed with the court; otherwise, to the address shown in the list of creditors or the schedule whichever is filed later. If a different address is stated in a proof of claim duly filed, that address shall be used unless a notice of no dividend has been given.

(h) Notices to Creditors Whose Claims Are Filed. In a chapter 7 case, the court may, after 90 days following the first date set for the meeting of creditors pursuant to § 341 of the Code, direct that all notices required by subdivision (a) of this rule, except clause (4) thereof, be mailed only to creditors whose claims have been filed and creditors, if any, who are still permitted to file claims by reason of an extension granted under rule 3002(c)(6).

(i) Notices to Committees. Copies of all notices required to be mailed under this rule shall be mailed to the committees appointed pursuant to the Code or to their authorized agents. Notwithstanding the foregoing subdivisions, the court may order that notices required by subdivision (a)(2), (3) and (7) of this rule be mailed only to the committees or to their authorized agents and to the creditors and equity security holders who serve on the trustee or debtor in possession and file with the clerk a request that all notices be mailed to them.

(j) Notices to the United States. Copies of notices required to be mailed to all creditors under this rule shall be mailed (1) in a chapter 11 reorganization case to the Securities and Exchange Commission at Washington, D.C., and at any other place the Commission designates in writing filed with the court if the Commission has filed a notice of appearance in the case or has made a request in writing filed with the court; (2) in a commodity broker case, to the Commodity Futures Trading Commission at Washington, D.C.; (3) in a chapter 11 case to the District Director of Internal Revenue for the district in which the case is pending; (4) if the papers in the case disclose a debt to the United States other than for taxes, to the United States attorney for the district in which the case is pending and to the department, agency, or instrumentality of the United States through which the debtor became indebted; or if the filed papers disclose a stock interest of the United States, to the Secretary of the Treasury at Washington, D.C.

(k) Notice by Publication. The court may order notice by publication if it finds that notice by mail is impracticable or that it is desirable to supplement the notice.

(*l*) Orders Designating Matter of Notices. The court may from time to time enter orders designating the matters in respect to which, the entity to whom, and the form and manner in which notices shall be sent except as otherwise provided by these rules.

(m) Caption. The caption of every notice given under this rule shall comply with Rule 1005.

(n) In a voluntary case commenced by an individual debtor whose debts are primarily consumer debts, the clerk or some other person as the court may direct shall give the trustee and all creditors notice by mail of the order for relief within 20 days from the date thereof.

Amended by Pub.L. 98–353, § 321, July 10, 1984, 98 Stat. 333; amended by Mar. 30, 1987, eff. Aug. 1, 1987.

Advisory Committee Note

Some of the notices required by this rule may be given either by the clerk or as the court may otherwise direct. For example, the court may order the trustee or debtor in possession to transmit one or more of the notices required by this rule, such as, notice of a proposed sale of property. See § 363(b) of the Code. When publication of notices is required or desirable, reference should be made to Rule 9008.

Notice of the order for relief is required to be given by § 342 of the Code and by subdivision (f)(1) of this rule. That notice may be combined with the notice of the meeting of creditors as indicated in Official Form No. 16, the notice and order of the meeting of creditors.

Subdivision (a) sets forth the requirement that 20 days notice be given of the significant events in a case under the Bankruptcy Code. The former Act and Rules provided a ten day notice in bankruptcy and Chapter XI cases, and a 20 day notice in a Chapter X case. This rule generally makes uniform the 20 day notice provision except that subdivision (b) contains a 25 day period for certain events in a chapter 9, 11, or 13 case. Generally, Rule 9006 permits reduction of time periods. Since notice by mail is complete on mailing, the requirement of subdivision (a) is satisfied if the notices are deposited in the mail at least 20 days before the event. See Rule 9006(e). The exceptions referred to in the introductory phrase include the modifications in the notice procedure permitted by subdivision (h) as to non-filing creditors, subdivision (i) as to cases where a committee is functioning, and subdivision (k) where compliance with subdivision (a) is impracticable.

The notice of a proposed sale affords creditors an opportunity to object to the sale and raise a dispute for the court's attention. Section 363(b) of the Code permits the trustee or debtor in possession to sell property, other than in the ordinary course of business, only after notice and hearing. If no objection is raised after notice, § 102(1) provides that there need not be an actual hearing. Thus, absent objection, there would be no court involvement with respect to a trustee's sale. Once an objection is raised, only the court may pass on it.

Prior to the Code the court could shorten the notice period for a proposed sale of property or dispense with notice. This subdivision (a), permits the 20 day period to be shortened in appropriate circumstances but the rule does not contain a provision allowing the court to dispense with notice. The rule is thus consistent with the Code, §§ 363(b) and 102(1)(A) of the Code. See 28 U.S.C. § 2075. It may be necessary, in certain circumstances, however, to use a method of notice other than mail. Subdivision (a) (2) vests the court with discretion, on cause shown, to order a different method. Reference should also be made to Rule 6004 which allows a different type of notice of proposed sales when the property is of little value.

Notice of the hearing on an application for compensation or reimbursement of expenses totalling $100 or less need not be given. In chapter 13 cases relatively small amounts are sometimes allowed for post-confirmation services and it would not serve a useful purpose to require advance notice.

Subdivision (b) is similar to subdivision (a) but lengthens the notice time to 25 days with respect to those events particularly significant in chapter 9, 11 and 13 cases. The additional time may be necessary to formulate objections to a disclosure statement or confirmation of a plan and preparation for the hearing on approval of the disclosure statement or confirmation. The disclosure statement and hearing thereon is only applicable in chapter 9 cases (§ 901(a) of the Code), and chapter 11 cases (§ 1125 of the Code).

Subdivision (c) specifies certain matters that should be included in the notice of a proposed sale of property and notice of the hearing on an application for allowances. Rule 6004 fixes the time within which parties in interest may file objections to a proposed sale of property.

Subdivision (d) relates exclusively to the notices given to equity security holders in chapter 11 cases. Under chapter 11, a plan may impair the interests of the debtor's shareholders or a plan may be a relatively simple restructuring of unsecured debt. In some cases, it is necessary that equity interest holders receive various notices and in other cases there is no purpose to be served. This subdivision indicates that the court is not mandated to order notices but rather that the matter should be treated with some flexibility. The court may decide whether notice is to be given and how it is to be given. Under § 341(b) of the Code, a meeting of equity security holders is not required in each case, only when it is ordered by the court. Thus subdivision (d)(2) requires notice only when the court orders a meeting.

In addition to the notices specified in this subdivision, there may be other events or matters arising in a case as to which equity security holders should receive notice. These are situations left to determination by the court.

Subdivision (e), authorizing a notice of the apparent insufficiency of assets for the payment of any dividend, is correlated with Rule 3002(c)(5), which provides for the issuance of an additional notice to creditors if the possibility of a payment later materializes.

Subdivision (f) provides for the transmission of other notices to which no time period applies. Clause (1) requires notice of the order for relief; this complements the mandate of § 342 of the Code requiring such notice as is appropriate of the order for relief. This notice may be combined with the notice of the meeting of creditors to avoid the necessity of more than one mailing. See Official Form No. 16, notice of meeting of creditors.

Subdivision (g) recognizes that an agent authorized to receive notices for a creditor may, without a court order, designate where notices to the creditor he represents should be addressed. Agent includes an officer of a corporation, an attorney at law, or an attorney in fact if the requisite authority has been given him. It should be noted that Official Forms Nos. 17 and 18 do not include an authorization of the holder of a power of attorney to receive notices for the creditor. Neither these forms nor this rule carries any implication that such an authorization may not be given in a power of attorney or that a request for notices to be addressed to both the creditor or his duly authorized agent may not be filed.

Subdivision (h). After the time for filing claims has expired in a chapter 7 case, creditors who have not filed their claims in accordance with Rule 3002(c) are not entitled to share in the estate except as they may come within the special provisions of § 726 of the Code or Rule 3002(c)(6). The elimination of notice to creditors who have no recognized stake in the estate may permit economies in time and expense. Reduction of the list of creditors to receive notices under this subdivision is discretionary. This subdivision does not apply to the notice of the meeting of creditors.

Subdivision (i) contains a list of matters of which notice may be given a creditors' committee or to its authorized agent in lieu of notice to the creditors. Such notice may serve every practical purpose of a notice to all the creditors and save delay and expense. *In re Schulte-United, Inc.*, 59 F.2d 553, 561 (8th Cir. 1932).

Subdivision (j). The premise for the requirement that the district director of internal revenue receive copies of notices that all creditors receive in a chapter 11 case is that every debtor is potentially a tax debtor of the United States. Notice to the district director alerts him to the possibility that a tax debtor's estate is about to be liquidated or reorganized and that the debtor may be discharged. When other indebtedness to the United States is indicated, the United States attorney is notified as the person in the best position to protect the interests of the government. In addition, the provision requires notice by mail to the head of any department, agency, or instrumentality of the United States through whose action the debtor became indebted to the United States. This rule is not intended to preclude a local rule from requiring a state or local tax authority to receive some or all of the notices to creditors under these rules.

Subdivision (k) specifies two kinds of situations in which notice by publication may be appropriate: (1) when notice by mail is impracticable; and (2) when notice by mail alone is less than adequate. Notice by mail may be impracticable when, for example, the debtor has disappeared or his records have been destroyed and the names and addresses of his creditors are unavailable, or when the number of creditors with nominal claims is very large and the estate to be distributed may be insufficient to defray the costs of issuing the notices. Supplementing notice by mail is also indicated when the debtor's records are incomplete or inaccurate and it is reasonable to believe that publication may reach some of the creditors who would otherwise be missed. Rule 9008 applies when the court directs notice by publication under this rule. Neither clause (2) of subdivision (a) nor subdivision (k) of this rule is concerned with the publication of advertisement to the general public of a sale of property of the estate at public auction under Rule 6004(b). See 3 Collier, *Bankruptcy* 522–23 (14th ed. 1971); 4B *id.* 1165–67 (1967); 2 *id.* ¶ 363.03 (15th ed. 1981).

Subdivision (m). Inclusion in notices to creditors of information as to other names used by the debtor as required by Rule 1005 will assist them in the preparation of their proofs of claim and in deciding whether to file a complaint objecting to the debtor's discharge. Additional names may be listed by the debtor on his statement of affairs when he did not file the petition. The mailing of notices should not be postponed to await a delayed filing of the statement of financial affairs.

Advisory Committee Notes to 1987 Amendments

Subdivision (a) is amended to provide that notice of a hearing on an application for compensation must be given only when the amount requested is in excess of $500.

Subdivision (d). A new notice requirement is added as clause (3). When a proposed sale is of all or substantially all of the debtor's assets, it is appropriate that equity security holders be given notice of the proposed sale. The clauses of subdivision (d) are renumbered to accommodate this addition.

Subdivision (f). Clause (7) is eliminated. Mailing of a copy of the discharge order is governed by Rule 4004(g).

Subdivision (g) is amended to relieve the clerk of the duty to mail notices to the address shown in a proof of claim when a notice of no dividend has been given pursuant to Rule 2002. This amendment avoids the necessity of the clerk searching proofs of claim which are filed in no dividend cases to ascertain whether a different address is shown.

Subdivision (n) was enacted by § 321 of the 1984 amendments.

Rule 2003

MEETING OF CREDITORS OR EQUITY SECURITY HOLDERS

(a) **Date and Place.** The court shall call a meeting of creditors to be held not less than 20 nor more than 40 days after the order for relief. If there is an appeal from or a motion to vacate the order for relief, or if there is a motion to dismiss the case, the court may set a later time for the meeting. The meeting may be held at a regular place for holding court or at any other place designated by the court within the district convenient for the parties in interest. If the court designates a place for the meeting which is not regularly staffed by a clerk who may preside at the meeting, the meeting may be held not more than 60 days after the order for relief.

(b) **Order of Meeting.**

(1) Meeting of Creditors. The clerk shall preside at the meeting of creditors unless (1) the court designates a different person, or (2) the creditors who may vote for a trustee under § 702(a) of the Code and who hold a majority in amount of claims that vote designate a presiding officer. In a chapter 11 reorganization case, if a chairperson has been selected by a creditors' committee appointed pursuant to § 1102(a)(1), the chairperson or the chairperson's designee shall preside. The business of the meeting shall include the examination of the debtor under oath and, in a chapter 7 liquidation case, may include the election of a trustee or of a creditors' committee. The presiding officer shall have the authority to administer oaths. When a trustee is elected, the creditors may recommend the amount of the trustee's bond to be fixed by the court.

(2) Meeting of Equity Security Holders. If the court orders a meeting of equity security holders pursuant to § 341(b) of the Code, the clerk shall preside unless the holders of equity security interests present at the meeting who hold a majority in amount of the interests at the meeting designate a presiding officer.

(3) Right to Vote. In a chapter 7 liquidation case, a creditor is entitled to vote at a meeting if, at or before the meeting, the creditor has filed a proof of claim or a writing setting forth facts evidencing a right to vote pursuant to § 702(a) of the Code unless objection is made to the claim or the proof of claim is insufficient on its face. If the court orders an election of a separate trustee for a general partner's estate under Rule 2009(e)(1), a creditor of the partnership may file a proof of claim or writing evidencing a right to vote for that trustee notwithstanding that a trustee for the partnership has previously qualified. Notwithstanding objection to the amount or allowability of a claim for the

purpose of voting, the court may, after such notice and hearing as it may direct, temporarily allow it for that purpose in an amount that seems proper to the court.

(c) Minutes and Record of Meeting. Minutes of the meeting of creditors or equity security holders shall be prepared by the presiding officer. Any examination under oath shall be recorded verbatim by electronic sound recording equipment or other means of recording.

(d) Report to the Court. The presiding officer shall transmit to the court the name and address of any person elected trustee or entity elected a member of a creditors' committee. If an election is disputed, the presiding officer shall promptly inform the court in writing that a dispute exists. Pending disposition by the court of a disputed election for trustee, the interim trustee shall continue in office. If no motion for the resolution of such election dispute is made to the court within 10 days after the date of the creditors' meeting, the interim trustee shall serve as trustee in the case.

(e) Adjournment. The meeting may be adjourned from time to time by announcement at the meeting of the adjourned date and time without further written notice.

Amended Mar. 30, 1987, eff. Aug. 1, 1987.

Advisory Committee Note

Section 341(a) of the Code requires a meeting of creditors in a chapter 7, 11 or 13 case, and § 341(b) permits the court to order a meeting of equity security holders. A major change from prior law, however, prohibits the judge from attending or presiding over the meeting. Section 341(c).

This rule does not apply either in a case for the reorganization of a railroad or for the adjustment of debts of a municipality. Sections 1161 and 901 render §§ 341 and 343 inapplicable in these types of cases. Section 341 sets the requirement for a meeting of creditors and § 343 provides for the examination of the debtor.

Subdivision (a). The meeting is to be held between 20 and 40 days after the date of the order for relief. In a voluntary case, the date of the order for relief is the date of the filing of the petition (§ 301 of the Code); in an involuntary case, it is the date of an actual order (§ 303(i) of the Code).

Subdivision (b) provides flexibility as to who will preside at the meeting of creditors. The court may designate a person to serve as presiding officer, such as the interim trustee appointed under § 701 of the Code. If the court does not designate anyone, the clerk will preside. In either case, creditors may elect a person of their own choosing. In any event, the clerk may remain to record the proceedings and take appearances. Use of the clerk is not contrary to the legislative policy of § 341(c). The judge remains insulated from any information coming forth at the meeting and any information obtained by the clerk must not be relayed to the judge.

Although the clerk may preside at the meeting, the clerk is not performing any kind of judicial role, nor should the clerk give any semblance of performing such a role. It would be pretentious for the clerk to ascend the bench, don a robe or be addressed as "your honor". The clerk should not appear to parties or others as any type of judicial officer.

In a chapter 11 case, if a committee of unsecured creditors has been appointed pursuant to § 1102(a)(1) of the Code and a chairman has been selected, the chairman will preside or a person, such as the attorney for the committee, may be designated to preside by the chairman.

Since the judge must fix the bond of the trustee but cannot be present at the meeting, the rule allows the creditors to recommend the amount of the bond. They should be able to obtain relevant information concerning the extent of assets of the debtor at the meeting.

Paragraph (1) authorizes the presiding officer to administer oaths. This is important because the debtor's examination must be under oath.

Paragraph (3) of subdivision (b) has application only in a chapter 7 case. That is the only type of case under the Code that permits election of a trustee or committee. In all other cases, no vote is taken at the meeting of creditors. If it is necessary for the court to make a determination with respect to a claim, the meeting may be adjourned until the objection or dispute is resolved.

The second sentence recognizes that partnership creditors may vote for a trustee of a partner's estate along with the separate creditors of the partner. Although § 723(c) gives the trustee of a partnership a claim against a partner's estate for the full amount of partnership creditors' claims allowed, the purpose and function of this provision are to simplify distribution and prevent double proof, not to disfranchise partnership creditors in electing a trustee of an estate against which they hold allowable claims.

Subdivision (c) requires minutes and a record of the meeting to be maintained by the presiding officer. A verbatim record must be made of the debtor's examination but the rule is flexible as to the means used to record the examination.

Subdivision (d) recognizes that the court must be informed immediately about the election or nonelection of a trustee in a chapter 7 case. Pursuant to Rule 2008, the clerk officially informs the trustee of his election or appointment and how he is to qualify. The presiding person has no authority to resolve a disputed election.

For purposes of expediency, the results of the election should be obtained for each alternative presented by the dispute and immediately reported to the court. Thus, when an interested party presents the dispute to the court, its prompt resolution by the court will determine the dispute and a new or adjourned meeting to conduct the election may be avoided. The clerk is not an interested party.

A creditors' committee may be elected only in a chapter 7 case. In chapter 11 cases, a creditors' committee is appointed pursuant to § 1102.

While a final meeting is not required, Rule 2002(f)(10) provides for the trustee's final account to be sent to creditors.

Advisory Committee Notes to 1987 Amendments

Subdivision (a). Many courts schedule meetings of creditors at various locations in the district. Because the clerk must schedule meetings at those locations, an additional 20 days for scheduling the meetings is provided under the amended rule.

Rule 2004

EXAMINATION

(a) **Examination on Motion.** On motion of any party in interest, the court may order the examination of any entity.

(b) **Scope of Examination.** The examination of an entity under this rule or of the debtor under § 343 of the Code may relate only to the acts, conduct, or property or to the liabilities and financial condition of the debtor, or to any matter which may affect the administration of the debtor's estate, or to the debtor's right to a discharge. In an individual's debt adjustment case under chapter 13 or a reorganization case under chapter 11 of the Code, other than for the reorganization of a railroad, the examination may also relate to the operation of any business and the desirability of its continuance, the source of any money or property acquired or to be acquired by the debtor for purposes of consummating a plan and the consideration given or offered therefor, and any other matter relevant to the case or to the formulation of a plan.

(c) **Compelling Attendance and Production of Documentary Evidence.** The attendance of an entity for examination and the production of documentary evidence may be compelled in the manner provided in Rule 9016 for the attendance of witnesses at a hearing or trial.

(d) **Time and Place of Examination of Debtor.** The court may for cause shown and on terms as it may impose order the debtor to be examined under this rule at any time or place it designates, whether within or without the district wherein the case is pending.

(e) **Mileage.** An entity other than a debtor shall not be required to attend as a witness unless lawful mileage and witness fee for one day's attendance shall be first tendered. If the debtor resides more than 100 miles from the place of examination when required to appear for an examination under this rule, the mileage allowed by law to a witness shall be tendered for any distance more than 100 miles from the debtor's residence at the date of the filing of the first petition commencing a case under the Code or the residence at the time the debtor is required to appear for the examination, whichever is the lesser.

Amended Mar. 30, 1987, eff. Aug. 1, 1987.

Advisory Committee Note

Subdivision (a) of this rule is derived from former Bankruptcy Rule 205(a). See generally 2 Collier, *Bankruptcy* ¶¶ 343.02, 343.08, 343.13 (15th ed. 1981). It specifies the manner of moving for an examination. The motion may be heard *ex parte* or it may be heard on notice.

Subdivision (b) is derived from former Bankruptcy Rules 205(d) and 11-26.

Subdivision (c) specifies the mode of compelling attendance of a witness or party for an examination and for the production of evidence under this rule. The subdivision is substantially declaratory of the practice that had developed under § 21a of the Act. See 2 Collier, *supra* ¶ 343.11.

This subdivision will be applicable for the most part to the examination of a person other than the debtor. The debtor is required to appear at the meeting of creditors for examination. The word "person" includes the debtor and this subdivision may be used if necessary to obtain the debtor's attendance for examination.

Subdivision (d) is derived from former Bankruptcy Rule 205(f) and is not a limitation on subdivision (c). Any person, including the debtor, served with a subpoena within the range of a subpoena must attend for examination pursuant to subdivision (c). Subdivision (d) applies only to the debtor and a subpoena need not be issued. There are no territorial limits on the service of an order on the debtor. See, *e.g.*, *In re Totem Lodge & Country Club, Inc.*, 134 F.Supp. 158 (S.D.N.Y.1955).

Subdivision (e) is derived from former Bankruptcy Rule 205(g). The lawful mileage and fee for attendance at a United States court as a witness are prescribed by 28 U.S.C. § 1821.

Definition of Debtor. The word "debtor" as used in this rule includes the persons specified in the definition in Rule 9001(5).

Spousal Privilege. The limitation on the spousal privilege formerly contained in § 21a of the Act is not carried over in the Code. For privileges generally, see Rule 501 of the Federal Rules of Evidence made applicable in cases under the Code by Rule 1101 thereof.

Rule 2005

APPREHENSION AND REMOVAL OF DEBTOR TO COMPEL ATTENDANCE FOR EXAMINATION

(a) **Order to Compel Attendance for Examination.** On motion of any party in interest supported by an affidavit alleging (1) that the examination of the debtor is necessary for the proper administration of the estate and that there is reasonable cause to believe that the debtor is about to leave or has left the debtor's residence or principal place of business to avoid examination, or (2) that the debtor has evaded service of a subpoena or of an order to attend for examination, or (3) that the debtor has willfully disobeyed a subpoena or order to attend for examination, duly served, the court may issue to the marshal, or some other officer authorized by law, an order directing the officer to bring the debtor before the court without unnecessary delay. If, after hearing, the court finds the allegations to be true, the court shall thereupon cause the debtor to be examined forthwith. If necessary, the court shall fix conditions for further examination and for the debtor's obedience to all orders made in reference thereto.

(b) **Removal.** Whenever any order to bring the debtor before the court is issued under this rule and the debtor is found in a district other than that of the court issuing the order, the debtor may be taken into custody under the order and removed in accordance with the following rules:

(1) If taken at a place less than 100 miles from the place of issue of the order, the debtor shall be brought forthwith before the court that issued the order.

(2) If taken at a place 100 miles or more from the place of issue of the order, the debtor shall be brought without unnecessary delay before the nearest United States magistrate, bankruptcy judge, or district judge. If, after hearing, the magistrate, bankruptcy judge, or district judge finds that an order has issued under this rule and that the person in custody is the debtor, or if the person in custody waives a hearing, the magistrate, bankruptcy judge, or district judge shall issue an order of removal and the person in custody shall be released on

conditions assuring prompt appearance before the court which issued the order to compel the attendance.

(c) Conditions of Release. In determining what conditions will reasonably assure attendance or obedience under subdivision (a) of this rule or appearance under subdivision (b) of this rule, the court shall be governed by the provisions and policies of title 18, U.S.C., § 3146(a) and (b).

Amended Mar. 30, 1987, eff. Aug. 1, 1987.

Advisory Committee Note

This rule is derived from former Bankruptcy Rule 206. The rule requires the debtor to be examined as soon as possible if allegations of the movant for compulsory examination under this rule are found to be true after a hearing. Subdivision (b) includes in paragraphs (1) and (2) provisions adapted from subdivisions (a) and (b) of Rule 40 of the Federal Rules of Criminal Procedure, which governs the handling of a person arrested in one district on a warrant issued in another. Subdivision (c) incorporates by reference the features of subdivisions (a) and (b) of 18 U.S.C. § 3146, which prescribe standards, procedures and factors to be considered in determining conditions of release of accused persons in noncapital cases prior to trial. The word "debtor" as used in this rule includes the persons named in Rule 9001(5).

The affidavit required to be submitted in support of the motion may be subscribed by the unsworn declaration provided for in 28 U.S.C. § 1746.

Rule 2006

SOLICITATION AND VOTING OF PROXIES IN CHAPTER 7 LIQUIDATION CASES

(a) Applicability. This rule applies only in a liquidation case pending under chapter 7 of the Code.

(b) Definitions.

(1) *Proxy.* A proxy is a written power of attorney authorizing any entity to vote the claim or otherwise act as the owner's attorney in fact in connection with the administration of the estate.

(2) *Solicitation of Proxy.* The solicitation of a proxy is any communication, other than one from an attorney to a regular client who owns a claim or from an attorney to the owner of a claim who has requested the attorney to represent the owner, by which a creditor is asked, directly or indirectly, to give a proxy after or in contemplation of the filing of a petition by or against the debtor.

(c) Authorized Solicitation.

(1) A proxy may be solicited only by (A) a creditor owning an allowable unsecured claim against the estate on the date of the filing of the petition; (B) a committee elected pursuant to § 705 of the Code; (C) a committee of creditors selected by a majority in number and amount of claims of creditors (i) whose claims are not contingent or unliquidated, (ii) who are not disqualified from voting under § 702(a) of the Code and (iii) who were present or represented at a meeting of which all creditors having claims of over $500 or the 100 creditors having the largest claims had at least five days notice in writing and of which meeting written minutes were kept and are available reporting the names of the

creditors present or represented and voting and the amounts of their claims; or (D) a bona fide trade or credit association, but such association may solicit only creditors who were its members or subscribers in good standing and had allowable unsecured claims on the date of the filing of the petition.

(2) A proxy may be solicited only in writing.

(d) Solicitation Not Authorized. This rule does not permit solicitation (1) in any interest other than that of general creditors; (2) by or on behalf of any custodian; (3) by the interim trustee or by or on behalf of any entity not qualified to vote under § 702(a) of the Code; (4) by or on behalf of an attorney at law; or (5) by or on behalf of a transferee of a claim for collection only.

(e) Data Required From Holders of Multiple Proxies. At any time before the voting commences at any meeting of creditors pursuant to Rule 2003, or at any other time as the court may direct, a holder of two or more proxies shall file with the clerk a verified list of the proxies to be voted and a verified statement of the pertinent facts and circumstances in connection with the execution and delivery of each proxy, including:

(1) a copy of the solicitation;

(2) identification of the solicitor, the forwarder, if the forwarder is neither the solicitor nor the owner of the claim, and the proxyholder, including their connections with the debtor and with each other. If the solicitor, forwarder, or proxyholder is an association, there shall also be included a statement that the creditors whose claims have been solicited and the creditors whose claims are to be voted were members or subscribers in good standing and had allowable unsecured claims on the date of the filing of the petition. If the solicitor, forwarder, or proxyholder is a committee of creditors, the statement shall also set forth the date and place the committee was organized, that the committee was organized in accordance with clause (B) or (C) of paragraph (c)(1) of this rule, the members of the committee, the amounts of their claims, when the claims were acquired, the amounts paid therefor, and the extent to which the claims of the committee members are secured or entitled to priority;

(3) a statement that no consideration has been paid or promised by the proxyholder for the proxy;

(4) a statement as to whether there is any agreement and, if so, the particulars thereof, between the proxyholder and any other entity for the payment of any consideration in connection with voting the proxy, or for the sharing of compensation with any entity, other than a member or regular associate of the proxyholder's law firm, which may be allowed the trustee or any entity for services rendered in the case, or for the employment of any person as attorney, accountant, appraiser, auctioneer, or other employee for the estate;

(5) if the proxy was solicited by an entity other than the proxyholder, or forwarded to the holder by an entity who is neither a solicitor of the proxy nor the owner of the claim, a statement signed and verified by the solicitor or forwarder that no consideration has been paid or promised for the proxy, and whether there is any agreement, and, if so, the particulars thereof, between the solicitor or forwarder and any other entity for the payment of any consideration in connection with voting the proxy, or for sharing compensation with any entity, other than a member or regular associate of the solicitor's or forwarder's law firm which may be allowed the trustee or any entity for services rendered in

the case, or for the employment of any person as attorney, accountant, appraiser, auctioneer, or other employee for the estate;

(6) if the solicitor, forwarder, or proxyholder is a committee, a statement signed and verified by each member as to the amount and source of any consideration paid or to be paid to such member in connection with the case other than by way of dividend on the member's claim.

(f) Enforcement of Restrictions on Solicitation. On motion of any party in interest or on its own initiative, the court may determine whether there has been a failure to comply with the provisions of this rule or any other impropriety in connection with the solicitation or voting of a proxy. After notice and a hearing the court may reject any proxy for cause, vacate any order entered in consequence of the voting of any proxy which should have been rejected, or take any other appropriate action.

Amended Mar. 30, 1987, eff. Aug. 1, 1987.

Advisory Committee Note

This rule is a comprehensive regulation of solicitation and voting of proxies in liquidation cases. It is derived from former Bankruptcy Rule 208. The rule applies only in chapter 7 cases because no voting occurs, other than on a plan, in a chapter 11 case. Former Bankruptcy Rule 208 did not apply to solicitations of acceptances of plans.

Creditor control was a basic feature of the Act and is continued, in part, by the Code. Creditor democracy is perverted and the congressional objective frustrated, however, if control of administration falls into the hands of persons whose principal interest is not in what the estate can be made to yield to the unsecured creditors but in what it can yield to those involved in its administration or in other ulterior objectives.

Subdivision (b). The definition of proxy in the first paragraph of subdivision (b) is derived from former Bankruptcy Rule 208.

Subdivision (c). The purpose of the rule is to protect creditors against loss of control of administration of their debtors' estates to holders of proxies having interests that differ from those of the creditors. The rule does not prohibit solicitation but restricts it to those who were creditors at the commencement of the case or their freely and fairly selected representatives. The special role occupied by credit and trade associations is recognized in the last clause of subdivision (c)(1). On the assumption that members or subscribers may have affiliated with an association in part for the purpose of obtaining its services as a representative in liquidation proceedings, an established association is authorized to solicit its own members, or its regular customers or clients, who were creditors on the date of the filing of the petition. Although the association may not solicit nonmembers or nonsubscribers for proxies, it may sponsor a meeting of creditors at which a committee entitled to solicit proxies may be selected in accordance with clause (C) of subdivision (c)(1).

Under certain circumstances, the relationship of a creditor, creditors' committee, or association to the estate or the case may be such as to warrant rejection of any proxy solicited by such a person or group. Thus a person who is forbidden by the Code to vote his own claim should be equally disabled to solicit proxies from creditors. Solicitation by or on behalf of the debtor has been uniformly condemned, *e.g., In re White,* 15 F.2d 371 (9th Cir.

1926), as has solicitation on behalf of a preferred creditor, *Matter of Law*, 13 Am.B.R. 650 (S.D.Ill.1905). The prohibition on solicitation by a receiver or his attorney made explicit by General Order 39 has been collaterally supported by rulings rejecting proxies solicited by a receiver in equity, *In re Western States Bldg.-Loan Ass'n*, 54 F.2d 415 (S.D.Cal.1931), and by an assignee for the benefit of creditors, *Lines* v. *Falstaff Brewing Co.*, 233 F.2d 927 (9th Cir. 1956).

Subdivision (d) prohibits solicitation by any person or group having a relationship described in the preceding paragraph. It also makes no exception for attorneys or transferees of claims for collection. The rule does not undertake to regulate communications between an attorney and his regular client or between an attorney and a creditor who has asked the attorney to represent him in a proceeding under the Code, but any other communication by an attorney or any other person or group requesting a proxy from the owner of a claim constitutes a regulated solicitation. Solicitation by an attorney of a proxy from a creditor who was not a client prior to the solicitation is objectionable not only as unethical conduct as recognized by such cases as *In the Matter of Darland Company*, 184 F.Supp. 760 (S.D.Iowa 1960) but also and more importantly because the practice carries a substantial risk that administration will fall into the hands of those whose interest is in obtaining fees from the estate rather than securing dividends for creditors. The same risk attaches to solicitation by the holder of a claim for collection only.

Subdivision (e). The regulation of solicitation and voting of proxies is achieved by the rule principally through the imposition of requirements of disclosure on the holders of two or more proxies. The disclosures must be made to the clerk before the meeting at which the proxies are to be voted to afford the clerk or a party in interest an opportunity to examine the circumstances accompanying the acquisition of the proxies in advance of any exercise of the proxies. In the light of the examination the clerk or a party in interest should bring to the attention of the judge any question that arises and the judge may permit the proxies that comply with the rule to be voted and reject those that do not unless the holders can effect or establish compliance in such manner as the court shall prescribe. The holders of single proxies are excused from the disclosure requirements because of the insubstantiality of the risk that such proxies have been solicited, or will be voted, in an interest other than that of general creditors.

Every holder of two or more proxies must include in the submission a verified statement that no consideration has been paid or promised for the proxy, either by the proxyholder or the solicitor or any forwarder of the proxy. Any payment or promise of consideration for a proxy would be conclusive evidence of a purpose to acquire control of the administration of an estate for an ulterior purpose. The holder of multiple proxies must also include in the submission a verified statement as to whether there is any agreement by the holder, the solicitor, or any forwarder of the proxy for the employment of any person in the administration of an estate or for the sharing of any compensation allowed in connection with the administration of the estate. The provisions requiring these statements implement the policy of the Code expressed in § 504 as well as the policy of this rule to deter the acquisition of proxies for the purpose of obtaining a share in the outlays for administration. Finally the facts as to any consideration moving or promised to any member of a committee which functions as a solicitor, forwarder, or proxyholder must be disclosed by the proxyholder. Such information would be of significance to the court in evaluating the purpose of the committee in obtaining, transmitting, or voting proxies.

Subdivision (f) has counterparts in the local rules referred to in the Advisory Committee's Note to former Bankruptcy Rule 208. Courts have been accorded a wide range of discretion in the handling of disputes involving proxies. Thus the referee was allowed to reject proxies and to proceed forthwith to hold a scheduled election at the same meeting. *E.g., In re Portage Wholesale Co.*, 183 F.2d 959 (7th Cir. 1950); *In re McGill*, 106 Fed. 57 (6th Cir. 1901); *In re Deena Woolen Mills, Inc.*, 114 F.Supp. 260, 273 (D.Me. 1953); *In re Finlay*, 3 Am.B.R. 738 (S.D.N.Y.1900). The bankruptcy judge may postpone an election to permit a determination of issues presented by a dispute as to proxies and to afford those creditors whose proxies are rejected an opportunity to give new proxies or to attend an adjourned meeting to vote their own claims. *Cf. In the Matter of Lenrick Sales, Inc.*, 369 F.2d 439, 442–43 (3d Cir.), cert. denied, 389 U.S. 822 (1967); *In the Matter of Construction Supply Corp.* 221 F.Supp. 124, 128 (E.D.Va.1963). This rule is not intended to restrict the scope of the court's discretion in the handling of disputes as to proxies.

Rule 2007

APPOINTMENT OF CREDITORS' COMMITTEE ORGANIZED BEFORE COMMENCEMENT OF THE CASE

(a) Appointment. In a chapter 9 municipality or chapter 11 reorganization case, on application of a party in interest and after notice as the court may direct, the court may appoint as the committee of unsecured creditors required by § 1102(a) of the Code, members of a committee selected before the commencement of the case in accordance with subdivision (b) of this rule.

(b) Selection of Members of Committee. The court may find that a committee selected by unsecured creditors before the commencement of a chapter 9 or chapter 11 case satisfies the requirements of § 1102(b)(1) of the Code if:

(1) it was selected by a majority in number and amount of claims of unsecured creditors who may vote under § 702(a) of the Code and were present in person or represented at a meeting of which all creditors having unsecured claims of over $1,000 or the 100 unsecured creditors having the largest claims had at least five days notice in writing, and of which meeting written minutes reporting the names of the creditors present or represented and voting and the amounts of their claims were kept and are available for inspection;

(2) all proxies voted at the meeting for the elected committee were solicited pursuant to Rule 2006 and the lists and statements required by subdivision (e) thereof have been filed with the court; and

(3) the organization of the committee was in all other respects fair and proper.

Amended Mar. 30, 1987, eff. Aug. 1, 1987.

Advisory Committee Note

Section 1102(b)(1) of the Code permits the court to appoint as the unsecured creditors' committee, the committee that was selected by creditors before the order for relief. This provision recognizes the propriety of continuing a "prepetition" committee in an official capacity. Such a committee, however, must be found to have been fairly chosen and representative of the different kinds of claims to be represented.

Subdivision (a) does not necessarily require a hearing but does require a party in interest to bring to the court's attention the fact that a prepetition committee had been organized and should be appointed. An application would suffice for this purpose. Party in interest would include the committee, any member of the committee, or any of its agents acting for the committee. Whether or not notice of the application should be given to any other party is left to the discretion of the court.

Subdivision (b) implements § 1102(b)(1). The Code provision allows the court to appoint, as the official § 1102(a) committee, a "prepetition" committee if its members were fairly chosen and the committee is representative of the different kinds of claims. This subdivision of the rule indicates some of the factors the court may consider in determining whether the requirements of § 1102(b)(1) have been satisfied. In effect, the subdivision provides various factors which are similar to those set forth in Rule 2006 with respect to the solicitation and voting of proxies in a chapter 7 liquidation case.

Advisory Committee Notes to 1987 Amendments

The rule is amended to conform to the 1984 amendments to § 1102(b)(1) of the Code.

Rule 2008

NOTICE TO TRUSTEE OF SELECTION

The clerk shall immediately notify the person selected as trustee how to qualify and, if applicable, the amount of the trustee's bond. A trustee that has filed a blanket bond pursuant to Rule 2010 and has been selected as trustee in a chapter 7 or chapter 13 case that does not notify the court in writing of rejection of the office within five days after receipt of notice of selection shall be deemed to have accepted the office. Any other person selected as trustee shall notify the court in writing of acceptance of the office within five days after receipt of notice of selection or shall be deemed to have rejected the office.

Amended Mar. 1, 1987, eff. Aug. 1, 1987.

Advisory Committee Note

This rule is adapted from former Bankruptcy Rule 209(c). The remainder of that rule is inapplicable because its provisions are covered by §§ 701–703, 321 of the Code.

If the person selected as trustee accepts the office, he must qualify within five days after his selection, as required by § 322(a) of the Code.

In districts having a standing trustee for chapter 13 cases, a blanket acceptance of the appointment would be sufficient for compliance by the standing trustee with this rule.

Advisory Committee Notes to 1987 Amendments

The rule is amended to eliminate the need for a standing chapter 13 trustee or member of the panel of chapter 7 trustees to accept or reject an appointment.

Rule 2009

TRUSTEES FOR ESTATES WHEN JOINT ADMINISTRATION ORDERED

(a) Election of Single Trustee for Estates Being Jointly Administered. If the court orders a joint administration of two or more estates pursuant to Rule 1015(b), creditors may elect a single trustee for the estates being jointly administered.

(b) Right of Creditors to Elect Separate Trustee. Notwithstanding entry of an order for joint administration pursuant to Rule 1015(b) the creditors of any debtor may elect a separate trustee for the estate of the debtor as provided in § 702 of the Code.

(c) Appointment of Trustees for Estates Being Jointly Administered.

(1) Chapter 7 Liquidation Cases. The court may appoint one or more interim trustees for estates being jointly administered in chapter 7 cases.

(2) Chapter 11 Reorganization Cases. If a trustee is ordered, the court may appoint one or more trustees for estates being jointly administered in chapter 11 cases.

(3) Chapter 13 Individual's Debt Adjustment Cases. The court may appoint one or more trustees for estates being jointly administered in chapter 13 cases.

(d) Potential Conflicts of Interest. On a showing that creditors or equity security holders of the different estates will be prejudiced by conflicts of interest of a common trustee, the court shall order separate trustees for estates being jointly administered.

(e) Trustees for Partnership and Partners' Individual Estates. Notwithstanding the foregoing provisions of this rule, the trustee of a partnership estate may also be the trustee of the individual estate of any general partner if the estates are being jointly administered unless the court, for cause shown, either (1) permits the creditors of a general partner to elect a separate trustee or (2) appoints a separate trustee for the individual estate.

(f) Separate Accounts. The trustee or trustees of estates being jointly administered shall keep separate accounts of the property and distribution of each estate.

Amended Mar. 30, 1987, eff. Aug. 1, 1987.

Advisory Committee Note

This rule is applicable in chapter 7 cases and, in part, in chapter 11 and 13 cases. The provisions in subdivisions (a) and (b) concerning creditor election of a trustee apply only in a chapter 7 case because it is only pursuant to § 702 of the Code that creditors may elect a trustee. Subdivision (c) of the rule applies in chapters 11 and 13 as well as chapter 7 cases; pursuant to § 1104 of the Code, the court may order the appointment of a trustee on application of a party in interest and, pursuant to § 1163 of the Code, the court must appoint a trustee in a railroad reorganization case. Subdivision (c) should not be taken as an indication that more than one trustee may be appointed for a single debtor. Section 1104(c) permits only one trustee for each estate. In a chapter 13 case, if there is no standing trustee, the court is to appoint a person to serve as trustee pursuant to

§ 1302 of the Code.   There is no provision for a trustee in a chapter 9 case, except for a very limited purpose; see § 926 of the Code.

This rule recognizes that economical and expeditious administration of two or more estates may be facilitated not only by the selection of a single trustee for a partnership and its partners, but by such selection whenever estates are being jointly administered pursuant to Rule 1015.   See *In the Matter of International Oil Co.*, 427 F.2d 186, 187 (2d Cir. 1970).   The rule is derived from former § 5c of the Act and former Bankruptcy Rule 210.   The premise of § 5c of the Act was that notwithstanding the potentially of conflict between the interests of the creditors of the partners and those of the creditors of the partnership, the conflict is not sufficiently serious or frequent in most cases to warrant the selection of separate trustees for the firm and the several partners.   Even before the proviso was added to § 5c of the Act in 1938 to permit the creditors of a general partner to elect their separate trustee for his estate, it was held that the court had discretion to permit such an election or to make a separate appointment when a conflict of interest was recognized.   *In re Wood*, 248 Fed. 246, 249–50 (6th Cir.), cert. denied, 247 U.S. 512 (1918); 4 Collier, *Bankruptcy* ¶ 723.04 (15th ed. 1980). The rule retains in subdivision (e) the features of the practice respecting the selection of a trustee that was developed under § 5 of the Act.   Subdivisions (a) and (c) permit the court to authorize election of a single trustee or to make a single appointment when joint administration of estates of other kinds of debtors is ordered, but subdivision (d) requires the court to make a preliminary evaluation of the risks of conflict of interest.   If after the election or appointment of a common trustee a conflict of interest materializes, the court must take appropriate action to deal with it.

Subdivision (f) is derived from § 5e of the Act and former Bankruptcy Rule 210(f) and requires that the common trustee keep a separate account for each estate in all cases that are jointly administered.

Rule 2010

QUALIFICATION BY TRUSTEE; PROCEEDING ON BOND

(a) **Blanket Bond.**   The court may authorize a blanket bond in favor of the United States conditioned on the faithful performance of official duties by the trustee or trustees to cover (1) a person who qualifies as trustee in a number of cases, and (2) a number of trustees each of whom qualifies in a different case.

(b) **Evidence of Qualification.**   A certified copy of the order approving the trustee's bond shall constitute conclusive evidence of qualification.

(c) **Proceeding on Bond.**   A proceeding on the trustee's bond may be brought by any party in interest in the name of the United States for the use of the entity injured by the breach of the condition.

Amended Mar. 30, 1987, eff. Aug. 1, 1987.

Advisory Committe Note

Subdivisions (a) and (b).   Subdivision (a) gives authority for approval by the court of a single bond to cover (1) a person who qualifies as trustee in a number of cases, and (2) a number of trustees each of whom qualifies in a different case.   The cases need not be related in any way.   Substantial economies can be effected if a single bond covering a number of different cases can be issued and approved at one time. When a blanket bond is filed, the trustee qualifies under subdivision (b) of the rule by filing an acceptance of the office.

Subdivision (c) prescribes the evidentiary effect of a certified copy of an order approving the trustee's bond given by a trustee under this rule or, when a blanket bond has been authorized, of a certified copy of acceptance. This rule supplements the Federal Rules of Evidence, which apply in bankruptcy cases. See Rule 1101 of the Federal Rules of Evidence. The order of approval should conform to Official Form No. 25. See, however, § 549(c) of the Code which provides only for the filing of the petition in the real estate records to serve as constructive notice of the pendency of the case. See also Rule 2011 which prescribes the evidentiary effect of a certificate that the debtor is a debtor in possession.

Subdivision (d) is derived from former Bankruptcy Rule 212(f). Reference should be made to § 322(a) and (d) of the Code which requires the bond to be filed with the bankruptcy court and places a two year limitation for the commencement of a proceeding on the bond. A bond filed under this rule should conform to Official Form No. 25. A proceeding on the bond of a trustee is governed by the rules in Part VII. See the Note accompanying Rule 7001. See also Rule 9025.

Advisory Committee Notes to 1987 Amendments

Subdivision (b) is deleted because of the amendment to Rule 2008.

Rule 2011

EVIDENCE OF DEBTOR IN POSSESSION

Whenever evidence is required that a debtor is a debtor in possession, the clerk may so certify and the certificate shall constitute conclusive evidence of that fact.

Advisory Committee Note

This rule prescribes the evidentiary effect of a certificate issued by the clerk that the debtor is a debtor in possession. See Official Form No. 26. Only chapter 11 of the Code provides for a debtor in possession. See § 1107(a) of the Code. If, however, a trustee is appointed in the chapter 11 case, there will not be a debtor in possession. See §§ 1101(1), 1105 of the Code.

Rule 2012

SUBSTITUTION OF TRUSTEE OR SUCCESSOR TRUSTEE; ACCOUNTING

(a) Trustee. A trustee appointed in a chapter 11 case is substituted automatically for the debtor in possession as a party in any pending action, proceeding, or matter.

(b) Successor Trustee. When a trustee dies, resigns, is removed, or otherwise ceases to hold office during the pendency of a case under the Code (1) the successor is automatically substituted as a party in any pending action, proceeding, or matter; and (2) within the time fixed by the court, the successor trustee shall prepare and file with the court an accounting of the prior administration of the estate.

Amended Mar. 30, 1987, eff. Aug. 1, 1987.

Advisory Committee Note

Paragraph (1) of this rule implements § 325 of the Code. It provides that a pending action or proceeding continues without abatement and that the trustee's successor is automatically substituted as a party whether it be another trustee or the debtor returned to possession, as such party.

Paragraph (2) places it within the responsibility of a successor trustee to file an accounting of the prior administration of the estate. If an accounting is impossible to obtain from the prior trustee because of death or lack of cooperation, prior reports submitted in the earlier administration may be updated.

Advisory Committee Notes to 1987 Amendments

Subdivision (a) is new. The subdivision provides for the substitution of a trustee appointed in a chapter 11 case for the debtor in possession in any pending litigation.

The original provisions of the rule are now in subdivision (b).

Rule 2013

LIMITATION ON APPOINTMENT OR EMPLOYMENT OF TRUSTEES, EXAMINERS, APPRAISERS AND AUCTIONEERS

(a) **Limitation on Appointments.** Appointments of trustees and examiners and employment of appraisers and auctioneers shall be made so that the annual aggregate compensation of any person shall not be disproportionate or excessive, giving proper regard to geographic constraints.

(b) **Record to Be Kept.** The clerk shall maintain a public record listing fees awarded by the court (1) to trustees and attorneys, accountants, appraisers, auctioneers and other professionals employed by trustees, and (2) to examiners appointed by the court. The record shall include the name and docket number of the case, the name of the individual or firm receiving the fee and the amount of the fee awarded. The record shall be maintained chronologically and shall be kept current and open to examination by the public without charge.

(c) **Summary of Record.** At the close of each annual period, the clerk shall prepare a summary of the public record by individual or firm name, to reflect total fees awarded during the preceding year. The summary shall be open to examination by the public without charge.

Amended Mar. 30, 1987, eff. Aug. 1, 1987.

Advisory Committee Note

This rule is adapted from former Rule 213. The first sentence of that rule is omitted because of the provisions in 28 U.S.C. §§ 586 and 604(f) creating panels of private trustees.

The rule is not applicable to standing trustees serving in chapter 13 cases. See § 1302 of the Code.

A basic purpose of the rule is to prevent what Congress has defined as "cronyism." Appointment or employment, whether in a chapter 7 or 11 case, should not center among a small select group of individuals unless the circumstances are such that it would be warranted. The public record of appointments to be kept by the clerk will provide a means for monitoring the appointment process.

Subdivision (b) provides a convenient source for public review of fees paid from debtors' estates in the bankruptcy courts. Thus, public recognition of appointments, fairly distributed and based on professional qualifications and expertise, will be promoted and notions of improper favor dispelled. This rule is in keeping with the findings of the Congressional subcommittees as set forth in the House Report of the Committee on the Judiciary, No. 95–595, 95th Cong., 1st Sess. 89–99 (1977). These findings included the observations that there were frequent appointments of the same person, contacts developed between the bankruptcy bar and the courts, and an unusually close relationship between the bar and the judges developed over the years. A major purpose of the new statute is to dilute these practices and instill greater public confidence in the system. Rule 2013 implements that laudatory purpose.

Advisory Committee Notes to 1987 Amendments

In subdivisions (b) and (c) the word awarded is substituted for the word paid. While clerks do not know if fees are paid, they can determine what fees are awarded by the court.

Rule 2014

EMPLOYMENT OF PROFESSIONAL PERSONS

(a) Application for and Order of Employment. An order approving the employment of attorneys, accountants, appraisers, auctioneers, agents, or other professionals pursuant to § 327 or § 1103 of the Code shall be made only on application of the trustee or committee, stating the specific facts showing the necessity for the employment, the name of the person to be employed, the reasons for the selection, the professional services to be rendered, any proposed arrangement for compensation, and, to the best of the applicant's knowledge, all of the person's connections with the debtor, creditors, or any other party in interest, their respective attorneys and accountants. The application shall be accompanied by a verified statement of the person to be employed setting forth the person's connections with the debtor, creditors, or any other party in interest, their respective attorneys and accountants.

(b) Services Rendered by Member or Associate of Firm of Attorneys or Accountants. If, under the Code and this rule, a law partnership or corporation is employed as an attorney, or an accounting partnership or corporation is employed as an accountant, or if a named attorney or accountant is employed, any partner, member, or regular associate of the partnership, corporation or individual may act as attorney or accountant so employed, without further order of the court.

Amended Mar. 30, 1987, eff. Aug. 1, 1987.

Advisory Committee Note

Subdivision (a) is adapted from the second sentence of former Bankruptcy Rule 215(a). The remainder of that rule is covered by § 327 of the Code.

Subdivision (b) is derived from former Bankruptcy Rule 215(f). The compensation provisions are set forth in § 504 of the Code.

Rule 2015

DUTY OF TRUSTEE OR DEBTOR IN POSSESSION TO KEEP RECORDS, MAKE REPORTS, AND GIVE NOTICE OF CASE

(a) Trustee or Debtor in Possession. A trustee or debtor in possession shall (1) in a chapter 7 liquidation case and, if the court directs, in a chapter 11 reorganization case file a complete inventory of the property of the debtor within 30 days after qualifying as a trustee or debtor in possession, unless such an inventory has already been filed; (2) keep a record of receipts and the disposition of money and property received; (3) file the reports and summaries required by § 704(8) of the Code within the times fixed by the court and which shall include a statement, if payments are made to employees, of the amounts of deductions for all taxes required to be withheld or paid for and in behalf of employees and the place where these amounts are deposited; (4) as soon as possible after the commencement of the case, give notice of the case to every entity known to be holding money or property subject to withdrawal or order of the debtor, including every bank, savings or building and loan association, public utility company, and landlord with whom the debtor has a deposit, and to every insurance company which has issued a policy having a cash surrender value payable to the debtor, except that notice need not be given to any entity who has knowledge or has previously been notified of the case; (5) in every county in which real property of the debtor is located file a notice of or a copy of the petition, without schedules, in the office where a transfer of real property may be recorded to perfect such transfer; (6) within 30 days after the date of the order confirming a plan or within such other time as the court may fix, file a report with the court concerning the action taken by the trustee or debtor in possession and the progress made in the consummation of the plan and file further reports as the court may direct until the plan has been consummated; (7) after consummation of a plan, file an application for a final decree showing that the plan has been consummated, and the names and addresses, if known, of the holders of claims or interests which have not been surrendered or released in accordance with the provisions of the plan and the nature and amounts of claims or interests, and other facts as may be necessary to enable the court to pass on the provisions to be included in the final decree.

(b) Chapter 13 Trustee and Debtor.

(1) *Business Cases.* In a chapter 13 individual's debt adjustment case, when the debtor is engaged in business, the debtor shall perform the duties prescribed by clauses (1)–(4) of subdivision (a) of this rule.

(2) *Nonbusiness Cases.* In a chapter 13 individual's debt adjustment case, when the debtor is not engaged in business, the trustee shall perform the duties prescribed by clause (2) of subdivision (a) of this rule.

(c) Transmission of Reports. In a chapter 11 case the court may direct that copies or summaries of annual reports and copies or summaries of other reports shall be mailed to the creditors, equity security holders, and indenture trustees. The court may also direct the publication of summaries of any such reports.

Amended Mar. 30, 1987, eff. Aug. 1, 1987.

Advisory Committee Note

This rule combines the provisions found in former Rules 218, 10–208, 11–30 and 13–208 of the Rules of Bankruptcy Procedure. It specifies various duties which are in addition to those required by §§ 704, 1106, 1302 and 1304 of the Code.

In *subdivision (a)* the times permitted to be fixed by the court in clause (3) for the filing of reports and summaries may be fixed by local rule or order.

Subdivision (b). This subdivision prescribes duties on either the debtor or trustee in chapter 13 cases, depending on whether or not the debtor is engaged in business (§ 1304 of the Code). The duty of giving notice prescribed by subdivision (a)(4) is not included in a nonbusiness case because of its impracticability.

Subdivision (c) is derived from former Chapter X Rule 10–208(c) which, in turn, was derived from § 190 of the Act. The equity security holders to whom the reports should be sent are those of record at the time of transmittal of such reports.

Advisory Committee Notes to 1987 Amendments

Subdivision (a) is amended to add as a duty of the trustee or debtor in possession the filing of a notice of or a copy of the petition. The filing of such notice or a copy of the petition is essential to the protection of the estate from unauthorized post-petition conveyances of real property. Section 549(c) of the Code protects the title of a good faith purchaser for fair equivalent value unless the notice or copy of the petition is filed.

Rule 2016

COMPENSATION FOR SERVICES RENDERED AND REIMBURSEMENT OF EXPENSES

(a) Application for Compensation or Reimbursement. An entity seeking interim or final compensation for services, or reimbursement of necessary expenses, from the estate shall file with the court an application setting forth a detailed statement of (1) the services rendered, time expended and expenses incurred, and (2) the amounts requested. An application for compensation shall include a statement as to what payments have theretofore been made or promised to the applicant for services rendered or to be rendered in any capacity whatsoever in connection with the case, the source of the compensation so paid or promised, whether any compensation previously received has been shared and whether an agreement or understanding exists between the applicant and any other entity for the sharing of compensation received or to be received for services rendered in or in connection with the case, and the particulars of any sharing of compensation or agreement or understanding therefor, except that details of any agreement by the applicant for the sharing of compensation as a member or regular associate of a firm of lawyers or accountants shall not be required. The requirements of this subdivision shall apply to an application for compensation for services rendered by an attorney or accountant even though the application is filed by a creditor or other entity.

(b) Disclosure of Compensation Paid or Promised To Attorney for Debtor. Every attorney for a debtor, whether or not the attorney applies for compensation, shall file with the court within 15 days after the order for relief, or at another time as the court may direct, the statement required by § 329 of the Code including whether the attorney has shared or agreed to share the compensation with any other entity. The statement shall include the particulars of any such sharing or agreement to share by the attorney, but the details of any agreement for the sharing of the compensation with a member or regular associate of the attorney's law firm shall not be required. A supplemental statement shall be filed within 15 days after any payment or agreement not previously disclosed.

Amended Mar. 30, 1987, eff. Aug. 1, 1987.

Advisory Committee Note

This rule is derived from former Rule 219. Many of the former rule's requirements are, however, set forth in the Code. Section 329 requires disclosure by an attorney of transactions with the debtor, § 330 sets forth the bases for allowing compensation, and § 504 prohibits sharing of compensation. This rule implements those various provisions.

Subdivision (a) includes within its provisions a committee, member thereof, agent, attorney or accountant for the committee when compensation or reimbursement of expenses is sought from the estate.

Regular associate of a law firm is defined in Rule 9001(9) to include any attorney regularly employed by, associated with, or counsel to that law firm. Firm is defined in Rule 9001(6) to include a partnership or professional corporation.

Advisory Committee Notes to 1987 Amendments

Subdivision (a) is amended to change "person" to "entity." There are occasions in which a governmental unit may be entitled to file an application under this rule. The requirement that the application contain a "detailed statement of services rendered, time expended and expenses incurred" gives to the court authority to ensure that the application is both comprehensive and detailed. No amendments are made to delineate further the requirements of the application because the amount of detail to be furnished is a function of the nature of the services rendered and the complexity of the case.

Subdivision (b) is amended to require that the attorney for the debtor file the § 329 statement before the meeting of creditors. This will assist the parties in conducting the examination of the debtor. In addition, the amended rule requires the attorney to supplement the § 329 statement if an undisclosed payment is made to the attorney or a new or amended agreement is entered into by the debtor and the attorney.

Rule 2017

EXAMINATION OF DEBTOR'S TRANSACTIONS WITH DEBTOR'S ATTORNEY

(a) Payment or Transfer to Attorney Before Commencement of Case. On motion by any party in interest or on the court's own initiative, the court after notice and a hearing may determine whether any payment of money or any transfer of property by the debtor, made directly or indirectly and in contemplation of the filing of a petition under the Code by or against the debtor, to an attorney for services rendered or to be rendered is excessive.

(b) Payment or Transfer to Attorney After Commencement of Case. On motion by the debtor or on the court's own initiative, the court after notice and a hearing may determine whether any payment of money or any transfer of property, or any agreement therefor, by the debtor to an attorney after the commencement of a case under the Code is excessive, whether the payment or transfer is made or is to be made directly or indirectly, if the payment, transfer, or agreement therefor is for services in any way related to the case.

Title amended Mar. 30, 1987, eff. Aug. 1, 1987.

Advisory Committee Note

This rule is derived from § 60d of the Act and former Bankruptcy Rule 220 and implements § 329 of the Code. Information required to be disclosed by the attorney for a debtor by § 329 of the Code and by the debtor in his Statement of Financial Affairs (Item #15 of Form No. 7, Item #20 of Form No. 8) will assist the court in determining whether to proceed under this rule. Section 60d was enacted in recognition of "the temptation of a failing debtor to deal too liberally with his property in employing counsel to protect him in view of financial reverses and probable failure." *In re Wood & Henderson*, 210 U.S. 246, 253 (1908). This rule, like § 60d of the Act and § 329 of the Code, is premised on the need for and appropriateness of judicial scrutiny of arrangements between a debtor and his attorney to protect the creditors of the estate and the debtor against overreaching by an officer of the court who is in a peculiarly advantageous position to impose on both the creditors and his client. 2 Collier, *Bankruptcy* ¶ 329.02 (15th ed. 1980); MacLachlan, *Bankruptcy* 318 (1956). Rule 9014 applies to any contested matter arising under this rule.

This rule is not to be construed to permit post-petition payments or transfers which may be avoided under other provisions of the Code.

Rule 2018

INTERVENTION; RIGHT TO BE HEARD

(a) Permissive Intervention. In a case under the Code, after hearing on such notice as the court directs and for cause shown, the court may permit any interested entity to intervene generally or with respect to any specified matter.

(b) Intervention by Attorney General of a State. In a chapter 7, 11, or 13 case, the Attorney General of a State may appear and be heard on behalf of consumer creditors if the court determines the appearance is in the public interest, but the Attorney General may not appeal from any judgment, order, or decree in the case.

(c) Chapter 9 Municipality Case. The Secretary of the Treasury of the United States may, or if requested by the court shall, intervene in a chapter 9 case. Representatives of the state in which the debtor is located may intervene in a chapter 9 case with respect to matter specified by the court.

(d) Labor Unions. In a chapter 9 or 11 case, a labor union or employees' association, representative of employees of the debtor, shall have the right to be heard on the economic soundness of a plan affecting the interests of the employees. A labor union or employees' association which exercises its right to be heard under this subdivision shall not be entitled to appeal any judgment, order, or decree relating to the plan, unless otherwise permitted by law.

(e) Service on Entities Covered by This Rule. The court may enter orders governing the service of notice and papers on entities permitted to intervene or be heard pursuant to this rule.

Amended Mar. 30, 1987, eff. Aug. 1, 1987.

Advisory Committee Note

This rule is derived from former Rules 8–210, 9–15 and 10–210 and it implements §§ 1109 and 1164 of the Code.

Pursuant to § 1109 of the Code, parties in interest have a right to be heard and the Securities and Exchange Commission may raise and be heard on any issue but it may not take an appeal. That section is applicable in chapter 9 cases (§ 901 of the Code and in chapter 11 cases, including cases under subchapter IV thereof for the reorganization of a railroad.

In a railroad reorganization case under subchapter IV of chapter 11, § 1164 also gives the right to be heard to the Interstate Commerce Commission, the Department of Transportation and any state or local regulatory commission with jurisdiction over the debtor, but these entities may not appeal.

This rule does not apply in adversary proceedings. For intervention in adversary proceedings, see Rule 7024. The rules do not provide any right of compensation to or reimbursement of expenses for intervenors or others covered by this rule. Section 503(b)(3)(D) and (4) is not applicable to the entities covered by this rule.

Subdivision (a) is derived from former Chapter VIII Rule 8–210 and former Chapter X Rule 10–210. It permits intervention of an entity (see § 101(14), (21) of the Code) not otherwise entitled to do so under the Code or this rule. Such a party seeking to intervene must show cause therefor.

Subdivision (b) specifically grants the appropriate state's Attorney General the right to appear and be heard on behalf of consumer creditors when it is in the public interest. See House Rep. No. 95–595, 95th Cong., 1st Sess. (1977) 189. While "consumer creditor" is not defined in the Code or elsewhere, it would include the type of individual entitled to priority under § 507(a)(5) of the Code, that is, an individual who has deposited money for the purchase, lease or rental of property or the purchase of services for the personal, family, or household use of the individual. It would also include individuals who purchased or leased property for such purposes in connection with which there may exist claims for breach of warranty.

This subdivision does not grant the Attorney General the status of party in interest. In other contexts, the Attorney General will, of course, be a party in interest as for example, in representing a state in connection with a tax claim.

Subdivision (c) recognizes the possible interests of the Secretary of the Treasury or of the state of the debtor's locale when a municipality is the debtor. It is derived from former Chapter IX Rule 9–15 and § 85(d) of the act.

Subdivision (d) is derived from former Chapter X Rule 10–210 which, in turn, was derived from § 206 of the Act. Section 206 has no counterpart in the Code.

Subdivision (e) is derived from former Chapter VIII Rule 8–201(d). It gives the court flexibility in directing the type of future notices to be given intervenors.

Advisory Committee Notes to 1987 Amendments

Subdivision (d) is amended to make it clear that the prohibition against appeals by labor unions is limited only to their participation in connection with the hearings on the plan as provided in subdivision (d). If a labor union would otherwise have the right to file an appeal or to be a party to an appeal, this rule does not preclude the labor union from exercising that right.

Rule 2019

REPRESENTATION OF CREDITORS AND EQUITY SECURITY HOLDERS IN CHAPTER 9 MUNICIPALITY AND CHAPTER 11 REORGANIZATION CASES

(a) Data Required. In a chapter 9 municipality or chapter 11 reorganization case, except with respect to a committee appointed pursuant to § 1102 of the Code, every entity or committee representing more than one creditor or equity security holder and, unless otherwise directed by the court, every indenture trustee, shall file a verified statement with the clerk setting forth (1) the name and address of the creditor or equity security holder; (2) the nature and amount of the claim or interest and the time of acquisition thereof unless it is alleged to have been acquired more than one year prior to the filing of the petition; (3) a recital of the pertinent facts and circumstances in connection with the employment of the entity or indenture trustee, and, in the case of a committee, the name or names of the entity or entities at whose instance, directly or indirectly, the employment was arranged or the committee was organized or agreed to act; and (4) with reference to the time of the employment of the entity, the organization or formation of the committee, or the appearance in the case of any indenture trustee, the amounts of claims or interests owned by the entity, the members of the committee or the indenture trustee, the times when acquired, the amounts paid therefor, and any sales or other disposition thereof. The statement shall include a copy of the instrument, if any, whereby the entity, committee, or indenture trustee is empowered to act on behalf of creditors or equity security holders. A supplemental statement shall be filed promptly, setting forth any material changes in the facts contained in the statement filed pursuant to this subdivision.

(b) Failure to Comply; Effect. On motion of any party in interest or on its own initiative, the court may (1) determine whether there has been a failure to comply with the provisions of subdivision (a) of this rule or with any other applicable law regulating the activities and personnel of any entity, committee, or indenture trustee or any other impropriety in connection with any solicitation and, if it so determines, the court may refuse to permit that entity, committee, or indenture trustee to be heard further or to intervene in the case; (2) examine any representation provision of a deposit agreement, proxy, trust mortgage, trust indenture, or deed of trust, or committee or other authorization, and any claim or interest acquired by any entity or committee in contemplation or in the course of a case under the Code and grant appropriate relief; and (3) hold invalid any authority, acceptance, rejection, or objection given, procured, or received by an entity or committee who has not complied with this rule or with § 1125(b) of the Code.

Amended Mar. 30, 1987, eff. Aug. 1, 1987.

Advisory Committee Note

This rule is a comprehensive regulation of representation in chapter 9 municipality and in chapter 11 reorganization cases. It is derived from §§ 209–213 of the Act and former Chapter X Rule 10–211.

Subdivision (b) is derived from §§ 212, 213 of the Act. As used in clause (2), "other authorization" would include a power or warrant of attorney which are specifically mentioned in § 212 of the Act. This rule deals with representation provisions in mortgages, trust deeds, etc. to protect the beneficiaries from unfair practices and the like. It does not deal with the validation or invalidation of security interests generally. If immediate compliance is not possible, the court may permit a representative to be heard on a specific matter, but there is no implicit waiver of compliance on a permanent basis.

PART III

CLAIMS AND DISTRIBUTION TO CREDITORS AND EQUITY INTEREST HOLDERS; PLANS

Rule
3001. Proof of Claim
3002. Filing Proof of Claim or Interest
3003. Filing Proof of Claim or Equity Security Interest in Chapter 9 Municipality or Chapter 11 Reorganization Cases
3004. Filing of Claims by Debtor or Trustee
3005. Filing of Claim, Acceptance, or Rejection by Guarantor, Surety, Indorser, or Other Codebtor
3006. Withdrawal of Claim or Acceptance or Rejection of Plan
3007. Objections to Claims
3008. Reconsideration of Claims
3009. Declaration and Payment of Dividends in Chapter 7 Liquidation Cases
3010. Small Dividends and Payments in Chapter 7 Liquidation and Chapter 13 Individual's Debt Adjustment Cases
3011. Unclaimed Funds in Chapter 7 Liquidation and Chapter 13 Individual's Debt Adjustment Cases
3012. Valuation of Security
3013. Classification of Claims and Interests
3014. Election Pursuant to § 1111(b) by Secured Creditor in Chapter 9 Municipality and Chapter 11 Reorganization Cases
3015. Filing of Plan in Chapter 13 Individual's Debt Adjustment Cases
3016. Filing of Plan and Disclosure Statement in Chapter 9 Municipality and Chapter 11 Reorganization Cases
3017. Court Consideration of Disclosure Statement in Chapter 9 Municipality and Chapter 11 Reorganization Cases
3018. Acceptance or Rejection of Plans
3019. Modification of Accepted Plan Before Confirmation
3020. Deposit; Confirmation of Plan
3021. Distribution Under Plan
3022. Final Decree

Rule 3001

PROOF OF CLAIM

(a) **Form and Content.** A proof of claim is a written statement setting forth a creditor's claim. A proof of claim for wages, salary, or commissions shall conform substantially to Official Form No. 20 or No. 21; any other proof of claim shall conform substantially to Official Form No. 19.

(b) **Who May Execute.** A proof of claim shall be executed by the creditor or the creditor's authorized agent except as provided in Rules 3004 and 3005.

(c) **Claim Based on a Writing.** When a claim, or an interest in property of the debtor securing the claim, is based on a writing, the original or a duplicate shall be filed with the proof of claim. If the writing has been lost or destroyed, a statement of the circumstances of the loss or destruction shall be filed with the claim.

566

(d) Evidence of Perfection of Security Interest. If a security interest in property of the debtor is claimed, the proof of claim shall be accompanied by evidence that the security interest has been perfected.

(e) Transferred Claim.

(1) Unconditional Transfer Before Proof Filed. If a claim other than one based on a bond or debenture has been unconditionally transferred before proof of the claim has been filed, the proof of claim may be filed only by the transferee. If the claim has been transferred after the filing of the petition, the proof of claim shall be supported by (A) a statement of the transferor acknowledging the transfer and stating the consideration therefor or (B) a statement of the transferee setting forth the consideration for the transfer and why the transferee is unable to obtain the statement from the transferor.

(2) Unconditional Transfer After Proof Filed. If a claim other than one based on a bond or debenture has been unconditionally transferred after the proof of claim has been filed, evidence of the terms of the transfer shall be filed by the transferee. The clerk shall immediately notify the original claimant by mail of the filing of the evidence of transfer and that objection thereto, if any, must be filed with the clerk within 20 days of the mailing of the notice or within any additional time allowed by the court. If the court finds, after a hearing on notice, that the claim has been unconditionally transferred, it shall enter an order substituting the transferee for the original claimant, otherwise the court shall enter such order as may be appropriate.

(3) Transfer of Claim for Security Before Proof Filed. If a claim other than one based on a bond or debenture has been transferred for security before proof of the claim has been filed, the transferor or transferee or both may file a proof of claim for the full amount. The proof shall be supported by a statement setting forth the terms of the transfer. If the claim was transferred after the filing of the petition, the proof shall also be supported by (A) a statement of the transferor acknowledging the transfer and stating the consideration therefor, or (B) a statement of the transferee setting forth the consideration for the transfer and why the transferee is unable to obtain the statement from the transferor. If either the transferor or the transferee files a proof of claim, the clerk shall immediately notify the other by mail of the right to join in the filed claim. If both transferor and transferee file proofs of the same claim, the proofs shall be consolidated. After a hearing on notice, the court shall enter such orders respecting allowance and voting of the claim, payment of dividends thereon, and participation in the administration of the estate as may be appropriate.

(4) Transfer of Claim for Security After Proof Filed. If a claim other than one based on a bond or debenture has been transferred for security after the proof of claim has been filed, evidence of the terms of the transfer shall be filed by the transferee. The clerk shall immediately notify the original claimant by mail of the filing of the evidence of transfer and that objection thereto, if any, must be filed with the clerk within 20 days of the mailing of the notice or within any additional time allowed by the court. After a hearing on notice, the court shall enter such orders respecting allowance and voting of the claim, payment of dividends thereon, and participation in the administration of the estate as may be appropriate.

(5) Service of Objection; Notice of Hearing. A copy of an objection to the evidence of transfer filed pursuant to paragraph (2) or (4) of this subdivision

together with a notice of a hearing shall be mailed or otherwise delivered to the transferee at least 30 days prior to the hearing.

(f) Evidentiary Effect. A proof of claim executed and filed in accordance with these rules shall constitute prima facie evidence of the validity and amount of the claim.

(g) To the extent not inconsistent with the United States Warehouse Act or applicable State law, a warehouse receipt, scale ticket, or similar document of the type routinely issued as evidence of title by a grain storage facility, as defined in section 557 of title 11, shall constitute prima facie evidence of the validity and amount of a claim of ownership of a quantity of grain.

Amended by Pub.L. 93–353, § 354, July 10, 1984, 98 Stat. 333.

Advisory Committee Note

This rule is adapted from former Bankruptcy Rules 301 and 302. The Federal Rules of Evidence, made applicable to cases under the Code by Rule 1101, do not prescribe the evidentiary effect to be accorded particular documents. Subdivision (f) of this rule supplements the Federal Rules of Evidence as they apply to cases under the Code.

Subdivision (c). This subdivision is similar to former Bankruptcy Rule 302(c) and continues the requirement for the filing of any written security agreement and provides that the filing of a duplicate of a writing underlying a claim authenticates the claim with the same effect as the filing of the original writing. *Cf.* Rules 1001(4) and 1003 of F.R. of Evid. Subdivision (d) together with the requirement in the first sentence of subdivision (c) for the filing of any written security agreement, is designed to facilitate the determination whether the claim is secured and properly perfected so as to be valid against the trustee.

Subdivision (d). "Satisfactory evidence" of perfection, which is to accompany the proof of claim, would include a duplicate of an instrument filed or recorded, a duplicate of a certificate of title when a security interest is perfected by notation on such a certificate, a statement that pledged property has been in possession of the secured party since a specified date, or a statement of the reasons why no action was necessary for perfection. The secured creditor may not be required to file a proof of claim under this rule if he is not seeking allowance of a claim for a deficiency. But see § 506(d) of the Code.

Subdivision (e). The rule recognizes the differences between an unconditional transfer of a claim and a transfer for the purpose of security and prescribes a procedure for dealing with the rights of the transferor and transferee when the transfer is for security. The rule clarifies the procedure to be followed when a transfer precedes or follows the filing of the petition. The interests of sound administration are served by requiring the post-petition transferee to file with the proof of claim a statement of the transferor acknowledging the transfer and the consideration for the transfer. Such a disclosure will assist the court in dealing with evils that may arise out of post-bankruptcy traffic in claims against an estate. *Monroe v. Scofield*, 135 F.2d 725 (10th Cir. 1943); *In re Philadelphia & Western Ry.*, 64 F.Supp. 738 (E.D.Pa.1946); *cf. In re Latham Lithographic Corp.*, 107 F.2d 749 (2d Cir. 1939). Both paragraphs (1) and (3) of this subdivision, which deal with a transfer before the filing of a proof of claim, recognize that the transferee may be unable to obtain the required statement from the transferor, but in that event a sound reason for such inability must accompany the proof of claim filed by the transferee.

Paragraphs (3) and (4) clarify the status of a claim transferred for the purpose of security. An assignee for security has been recognized as a rightful claimant in bankruptcy. *Feder v. John Engelhorn & Sons*, 202 F.2d 411 (2d Cir. 1953). An assignor's right to file a claim notwithstanding the assignment was sustained in *In re R & L Engineering Co.*, 182 F.Supp. 317 (S.D.Cal.1960). Facilitation of the filing of proofs by both claimants as holders of interests in a single claim is consonant with equitable treatment of the parties and sound administration. See *In re Latham Lithographic Corp.*, 107 F.2d 749 (2d Cir. 1939).

Paragraphs (2) and (4) of subdivision (e) deal with the transfer of a claim after proof has been filed. Evidence of the terms of the transfer required to be disclosed to the court will facilitate the court's determination of the appropriate order to be entered because of the transfer.

Paragraph (5) describes the procedure to be followed when an objection is made by the transferor to the transferee's filed evidence of transfer.

Advisory Committee Notes to 1984 Amendments

Subdivision (g) was added by § 354 of the 1984 amendments.

Rule 3002

FILING PROOF OF CLAIM OR INTEREST

(a) **Necessity for Filing.** An unsecured creditor or an equity security holder must file a proof of claim or interest in accordance with this rule for the claim or interest to be allowed, except as provided in Rules 1019(4), 3003, 3004 and 3005.

(b) **Place of Filing.** A proof of claim or interest shall be filed in accordance with Rule 5005.

(c) **Time for Filing.** In a chapter 7 liquidation or chapter 13 individual's debt adjustment case, a proof of claim shall be filed within 90 days after the first date set for the meeting of creditors called pursuant to § 341(a) of the Code, except as follows:

(1) On motion of the United States, a state, or subdivision thereof before the expiration of such period and for cause shown, the court may extend the time for filing of a claim by the United States, a state, or subdivision thereof.

(2) In the interest of justice and if it will not unduly delay the administration of the case, the court may extend the time for filing a proof of claim by an infant or incompetent person or the representative of either.

(3) An unsecured claim which arises in favor of an entity or becomes allowable as a result of a judgment may be filed within 30 days after the judgment becomes final if the judgment is for the recovery of money or property from that entity or denies or avoids the entity's interest in property. If the judgment imposes a liability which is not satisfied, or a duty which is not performed within such period or such further time as the court may permit, the claim shall not be allowed.

(4) A claim arising from the rejection of an executory contract of the debtor may be filed within such time as the court may direct.

(5) If notice of insufficient assets to pay a dividend was given to creditors pursuant to Rule 2002(e), and subsequently the trustee notifies the court that payment of a dividend appears possible, the clerk shall notify the creditors of that fact and that they may file proofs of claim within 90 days after the mailing of the notice.

(6) In a chapter 7 liquidation case, if a surplus remains after all claims allowed have been paid in full, the court may grant an extension of time for the filing of claims against the surplus not filed within the time hereinabove prescribed.

Amended Mar. 30, 1987, eff. Aug. 1, 1987.

Advisory Committee Note

Subdivision (a) of this rule is substantially a restatement of the general requirement that claims be proved and filed. The exceptions refer to Rule 3003 providing for the filing of claims in chapter 9 and 11 cases, and to Rules 3004 and 3005 authorizing claims to be filed by the debtor or trustee and the filing of a claim by a contingent creditor of the debtor.

A secured claim need not be filed or allowed under § 502 or § 506(d) unless a party in interest has requested a determination and allowance or disallowance under § 502.

Subdivision (c) is adapted from former Bankruptcy Rule 302(e) but changes the time limits on the filing of claims in chapter 7 and 13 cases from six months to 90 days after the first date set for the meeting of creditors. The special rule for early filing by a secured creditor in a chapter 13 case, in former Rule 13–302(e)(1) is not continued.

Although the claim of a secured creditor may have arisen before the petition, a judgment avoiding the security interest may not have been entered until after the time for filing claims has expired. Under Rule 3002(c)(3) the creditor who did not file a secured claim may nevertheless file an unsecured claim within the time prescribed. A judgment does not become final for the purpose of starting the 30 day period provided for by paragraph (3) until the time for appeal has expired or, if an appeal is taken, until the appeal has been disposed of. *In re Tapp,* 61 F.Supp. 594 (W.D.Ky. 1945).

Paragraph (1) is derived from former Bankruptcy Rule 302(e). The governmental unit may move for an extension of the 90 day period. Pursuant to § 501(c) of the Code, if the government does not file its claim within the proper time period, the debtor or trustee may file on its behalf. An extension is not needed by the debtor or trustee because the right to file does not arise until the government's time has expired.

Paragraph (4) is derived from former chapter rules. See, *e.g.,* Rule 11–33(a)(2)(B). In light of the reduced time it is necessary that a party with a claim arising from the rejection of an executory contract have sufficient time to file that claim. This clause allows the court to fix an appropriate time.

Paragraph (5) of subdivision (c) is correlated with the provision in Rule 2002(e) authorizing notification to creditors of estates from which no dividends are anticipated. The clause permits creditors who have refrained from filing claims after receiving notification to be given an opportunity to file when subsequent developments indicate the possibility of a dividend. The notice required by this clause must be given in the manner provided in

Rule 2002. The information relating to the discovery of assets will usually be obtained by the clerk from the trustee's interim reports or special notification by the trustee.

Provision is made in Rule 2002(a) and (h) for notifying all creditors of the fixing of a time for filing claims against a surplus under paragraph (6). This paragraph does not deal with the distribution of the surplus. Reference must also be made to § 726(a)(2)(C) and (3) which permits distribution on late filed claims.

Paragraph (6) is only operative in a chapter 7 case. In chapter 13 cases, the plan itself provides the distribution to creditors which is not necessarily dependent on the size of the estate.

Advisory Committee Notes to 1987 Amendments

Subdivision (a) is amended by adding a reference to Rule 1019(4). Rule 1019(4) provides that claims actually filed by a creditor in a chapter 11 or 13 case shall be treated as filed in a superseding chapter 7 case. Claims deemed filed in a chapter 11 case pursuant to § 1111(a) of the Code are not considered as filed in a superseding chapter 7 case. The creditor must file a claim in the superseding chapter 7 case.

Rule 3003

FILING PROOF OF CLAIM OR EQUITY SECURITY INTEREST IN CHAPTER 9 MUNICIPALITY OR CHAPTER 11 REORGANIZATION CASES

(a) Applicability of Rule. This rule applies in chapter 9 and 11 cases.

(b) Schedule of Liabilities and List of Equity Security Holders.

(1) Schedule of Liabilities. The schedule of liabilities filed pursuant to § 521(1) of the Code shall constitute prima facie evidence of the validity and amount of the claims of creditors, unless they are scheduled as disputed, contingent, or unliquidated. It shall not be necessary for a creditor or equity security holder to file a proof of claim or interest except as provided in subdivision (c)(2) of this rule.

(2) List of Equity Security Holders. The list of equity security holders filed pursuant to Rule 1007(a)(3) shall constitute prima facie evidence of the validity and amount of the equity security interests and it shall not be necessary for the holders of such interests to file a proof of interest.

(c) Filing Proof of Claim.

(1) Who May File. Any creditor or indenture trustee may file a proof of claim within the time prescribed by subdivision (c)(3) of this rule.

(2) Who Must File. Any creditor or equity security holder whose claim or interest is not scheduled or scheduled as disputed, contingent, or unliquidated shall file a proof of claim or interest within the time prescribed by subdivision (c) (3) of this rule; any creditor who fails to do so shall not be treated as a creditor with respect to such claim for the purposes of voting and distribution.

(3) Time For Filing. The court shall fix and for cause shown may extend the time within which proofs of claim or interest may be filed.

(4) Effect of Filing Claim. A proof of claim or interest executed and filed in accordance with this subdivision shall supersede any scheduling of that claim or interest pursuant to § 521(1) of the Code.

(5) Filing by Indenture Trustee. An indenture trustee may file a claim on behalf of all known or unknown holders of securities issued pursuant to the trust instrument under which it is trustee.

(d) Proof of Right to Record Status. For the purposes of Rules 3017, 3018 and 3021 and for receiving notices, an entity who is not the record holder of a security may file a statement setting forth facts which entitle that entity to be treated as the record holder. An objection to the statement may be filed by any party in interest.

Amended Mar. 30, 1987, eff. Aug. 1, 1987.

Advisory Committee Note

Subdivision (a). This rule applies only in chapter 9 and chapter 11 cases. It is adapted from former Chapter X Rule 10–401 and provides an exception to the requirement for filing proofs of claim and interest as expressed in §§ 925 and 1111(a) of the Code.

Subdivision (b). This general statement implements §§ 925 and 1111(a) of the Code.

Subdivision (c). This subdivision permits, in paragraph (1), the filing of a proof of claim but does not make it mandatory. Paragraph (2) requires, as does the Code, filing when a claim is scheduled as disputed, contingent, or unliquidated as to amount. It is the creditor's responsibility to determine if the claim is accurately listed. Notice of the provision of this rule is provided for in Official Form No. 16, the order for the meeting of creditors. In an appropriate case the court may order creditors whose claims are scheduled as disputed, contingent, or unliquidated be notified of that fact but the procedure is left to the discretion of the court.

Subdivision (d) is derived from former Chapter X Rule 10–401(f).

Except with respect to the need and time for filing claims, the other aspects concerning claims covered by Rules 3001 and 3002 are applicable in chapter 9 and 11 cases.

Holders of equity security interests need not file proofs of interest. Voting and distribution participation is dependent on ownership as disclosed by the appropriate records of a transfer agent or the corporate or other business records at the time prescribed in Rules 3017 and 3021.

Rule 3004

FILING OF CLAIMS BY DEBTOR OR TRUSTEE

If a creditor fails to file a proof of claim on or before the first date set for the meeting of creditors called pursuant to § 341(a) of the Code, the debtor or trustee may do so in the name of the creditor, within 30 days after expiration of the time for filing claims prescribed by Rule 3002(c) or 3003(c), whichever is applicable. The clerk shall forthwith mail notice of the filing to the creditor, the debtor and the trustee. A proof of claim filed by a creditor pursuant to Rule 3002 or Rule 3003(c), shall supersede the proof filed by the debtor or trustee.

Amended Mar. 30, 1987, eff. Aug. 1, 1987.

Advisory Committee Note

This rule is adapted from former Bankruptcy Rule 303 but conforms with the changes made by § 501(c) of the Code. Rule 303 permitted only the filing of tax and wage claims by the debtor. Section 501(c) of the Code, however, permits the filing by the debtor or trustee on behalf of any creditor.

It is the policy of the Code that debtors' estates should be administered for the benefit of creditors without regard to the dischargeability of their claims. After their estates have been closed, however, discharged debtors may find themselves saddled with liabilities, particularly for taxes, which remain unpaid because of the failure of creditors holding nondischargeable claims to file proofs of claim and receive distributions thereon. The result is that the debtor is deprived of an important benefit of the Code without any fault or omission on the debtor's part and without any objective of the Code being served thereby.

Section 501(c) of the Code authorizes a debtor or trustee to file a proof of claim for any holder of a claim. Although all claims may not be nondischargeable, it may be difficult to determine, in particular, whether tax claims survive discharge. See Plumb, *Federal Tax Liens and Priorities in Bankruptcy*, 43 Ref.J. 37, 43–44 (1969); 1 Collier, *Bankruptcy* ¶ 17.14 (14th ed. 1967); 3 *id.* ¶ 523.06 (15th ed. 1979). To eliminate the necessity of the resolution of this troublesome issue, the option accorded the debtor by the Code does not depend on the nondischargeability of the claim. No serious administrative problems and no unfairness to creditors seemed to develop from adoption of Rule 303, the forerunner to § 501(c). The authority to file is conditioned on the creditor's failure to file the proof of claim on or before the first date set for the meeting of creditors, which is the date a claim must ordinarily be filed in order to be voted in a chapter 7 case. Notice to the creditor is provided to enable him to file a proof of claim pursuant to Rule 3002, which proof, when filed, would supersede the proof filed by the debtor or trustee. Notice to the trustee would serve to alert the trustee to the special character of the proof and the possible need for supplementary evidence of the validity and amount of the claim. If the trustee does not qualify until after a proof of claim is filed by the debtor pursuant to this rule, he should be notified as soon as practicable thereafter.

To the extent the claim is allowed and dividends paid thereon, it will be reduced or perhaps paid in full. If the claim is also filed pursuant to Rule 3005, only one distribution thereon may be made. As expressly required by Rule 3005 and by the purpose of this rule such distribution must diminish the claim.

Advisory Committee Notes to 1987 Amendments

Under the rule as amended, the debtor or trustee in a chapter 7 or 13 case has 120 days from the first date set for the meeting of creditors to file a claim for the creditor. During the first 90 days of that period the creditor in a chapter 7 or 13 case may file a claim as provided by Rule 3002(c). If the creditor fails to file a claim, the debtor or trustee shall have an additional 30 days thereafter to file the claim. A proof of claim filed by a creditor supersedes a claim filed by the debtor or trustee only if it is timely filed within the 90 days allowed under Rule 3002(c).

Rule 3005

FILING OF CLAIM, ACCEPTANCE, OR REJECTION BY GUARANTOR, SURETY, INDORSER, OR OTHER CODEBTOR

(a) Filing of Claim. If a creditor has not filed a proof of claim pursuant to Rule 3002 or 3003(c), an entity that is or may be liable with the debtor to that creditor, or who has secured that creditor, may, within 30 days after the expiration of the time for filing claims prescribed by Rule 3002(c) or 3003(c) whichever is applicable, execute and file a proof of claim in the name of the creditor, if known, or if unknown, in the entity's own name. No distribution shall be made on the claim except on satisfactory proof that the original debt will be diminished by the amount of distribution. A proof of claim filed by a creditor pursuant to Rule 3002 or 3003(c) shall supersede the proof of claim filed pursuant to the first sentence of this subdivision.

(b) Filing of Acceptance or Rejection; Substitution of Creditor. An entity which has filed a claim pursuant to the first sentence of subdivision (a) of this rule may file an acceptance or rejection of a plan in the name of the creditor, if known, or if unknown, in the entity's own name but if the creditor files a proof of claim within the time permitted by Rule 3003(c) or files a notice with the court prior to confirmation of a plan of the creditor's intention to act in the creditor's own behalf, the creditor shall be substituted for the obligor with respect to that claim.

Amended Mar. 30, 1987, eff. Aug. 1, 1987.

Advisory Committee Note

This rule is adapted from former Rules 304 and 10–402. Together with § 501(b) of the Code, the rule makes clear that anyone who may be liable on a debt of the debtor, including a surety, guarantor, indorser, or other codebtor, is authorized to file in the name of the creditor of the debtor.

Subdivision (a). Rule 3002(c) provides the time period for filing proofs of claim in chapter 7 and 13 cases; Rule 3003(c) provides the time, when necessary, for filing claims in a chapter 9 or 11 case.

Subdivision (b). This subdivision applies in chapter 9 and 11 cases as distinguished from chapter 7 cases. It permits voting for or against a plan by an obligor who files a claim in place of the creditor.

Rule 3006

WITHDRAWAL OF CLAIM OR ACCEPTANCE OR REJECTION OF PLAN

A creditor may withdraw a claim as of right by filing a notice of withdrawal, except as provided in this rule. If after a creditor has filed a proof of claim an objection is filed thereto or a complaint is filed against that creditor in an adversary proceeding, or the creditor has accepted or rejected the plan or otherwise has participated significantly in the case, the creditor may not withdraw the claim except on order of the court after a hearing on notice to the trustee or debtor in possession, and any creditors' committee selected pursuant to §§ 705(a) or 1102 of the Code. The order of the court shall contain such terms and conditions as the court deems proper. Unless the court orders otherwise, an authorized withdrawal of a claim shall constitute withdrawal of any related acceptance or rejection of a plan.

Advisory Committee Note

This rule is derived from former Rules 305 and 10–404.

Since 1938 it has generally been held that Rule 41 F.R.Civ.P. governs the withdrawal of a proof of claim. *In re Empire Coal Sales Corp.*, 45 F.Supp. 974, 976 (S.D.N.Y.), aff'd sub nom. *Kleid v. Ruthbell Coal Co.*, 131 F.2d 372, 373 (2d Cir. 1942); *Kelso v. MacLaren*, 122 F.2d 867, 870 (8th Cir. 1941); *In re Hills*, 35 F.Supp. 532, 533 (W.D.Wash.1940). Accordingly the cited cases held that after an objection has been filed a proof of claim may be withdrawn only subject to approval by the court. This constitutes a restriction of the right of withdrawal as recognized by some though by no means all of the cases antedating the promulgation of the Federal Rules of Civil Procedure. See 3 Collier, *Bankruptcy* ¶ 57.12 (14th ed. 1961); Note, 20 Bost. U.L.Rev. 121 (1940).

The filing of a claim does not commence an adversary proceeding but the filing of an objection to the claim initiates a contest that must be disposed of by the court. This rule recognizes the applicability of the considerations underlying Rule 41(a) F.R.Civ.P. to the withdrawal of a claim after it has been put in issue by an objection. Rule 41(a)(2) F.R.Civ.P. requires leave of court to obtain dismissal over the objection of a defendant who has pleaded a counterclaim prior to the service of the plaintiff's motion to dismiss. Although the applicability of this provision to the withdrawal of a claim was assumed in *Conway v. Union Bank of Switzerland*, 204 F.2d 603, 608 (2d Cir. 1953), *Kleid v. Ruthbell Coal Co., supra, Kelso v. MacLaren, supra,* and *In re Hills, supra,* this rule vests discretion in the court to grant, deny, or condition the request of a creditor to withdraw, without regard to whether the trustee has filed a merely defensive objection or a complaint seeking an affirmative recovery of money or property from the creditor.

A number of pre-1938 cases sustained denial of a creditor's request to withdraw proof of claim on the ground of estoppel or election of remedies. 2 Remington, *Bankruptcy* 186 (Henderson ed. 1956); *cf.* 3 Collier, *supra* ¶ 57.12, at 201 (1964). Voting a claim for a trustee was an important factor in the denial of a request to withdraw in *Standard Varnish Works v. Haydock*, 143 Fed. 318, 319–20 (6th Cir. 1906), and *In re Cann*, 47 F.2d 661, 662 (W.D. Pa.1931). And it has frequently been recognized that a creditor should not be allowed to withdraw a claim after accepting a dividend. *In re Friedmann*, 1 Am.B.R. 510, 512 (Ref., S.D.N.Y.1899); 3 Collier 205 (1964); *cf. In re O'Gara Coal Co.*, 12 F.2d 426, 429 (7th Cir.), cert. denied, 271 U.S. 683 (1926). It was held in *Industrial Credit Co. v. Hazen*, 222 F.2d 225 (8th Cir. 1955), however, that although a claimant had participated in the first meeting of creditors and in the examination of witnesses, the creditor was entitled under Rule 41(a)(1) F.R.Civ.P. to withdraw the claim as of right by filing a notice of withdrawal before the trustee filed an objection under § 57g of the Act. While this rule incorporates the post-1938 case law referred to in the first paragraph of this note, it rejects the inference drawn in the *Hazen* case that Rule 41(a) F.R.Civ.P. supersedes the pre-1938 case law that vests discretion in the court to deny or restrict withdrawal of a claim by a creditor on the ground of estoppel or election of remedies. While purely formal or technical participation in a case by a creditor who has filed a claim should not deprive the creditor of the right to withdraw the claim, a creditor who has accepted a dividend or who has voted in the election of a trustee or otherwise participated actively in proceedings in a case should be permitted to withdraw only with the approval of the court on terms it deems appropriate after notice to the trustee. 3 Collier 205–06 (1964).

Rule 3007

OBJECTIONS TO CLAIMS

An objection to the allowance of a claim shall be in writing and filed with the court. A copy of the objection with notice of the hearing thereon shall be mailed or otherwise delivered to the claimant, the debtor or debtor in possession and the trustee at least 30 days prior to the hearing. If an objection to a claim is joined with a demand for relief of the kind specified in Rule 7001, it becomes an adversary proceeding.

Advisory Committee Note

This rule is derived from § 47a(8) of the Act and former Bankruptcy Rule 306. It prescribes the manner in which an objection to a claim shall be made and notice of the hearing thereon given to the claimant. The requirement of a writing does not apply to an objection to the allowance of a claim for the purpose of voting for a trustee or creditors' committee in a chapter 7 case. See Rule 2003.

The contested matter initiated by an objection to a claim is governed by Rule 9014, unless a counterclaim by the trustee is joined with the objection to the claim. The filing of a counterclaim ordinarily commences an adversary proceeding subject to the rules in Part VII.

While the debtor's other creditors may make objections to the allowance of a claim, the demands of orderly and expeditious administration have led to a recognition that the right to object is generally exercised by the trustee. Pursuant to § 502(a) of the Code, however, any party in interest may object to a claim. But under § 704 the trustee, if any purpose would be served thereby, has the duty to examine proofs of claim and object to improper claims.

By virtue of the automatic allowance of a claim not objected to, a dividend may be paid on a claim which may thereafter be disallowed on objection made pursuant to this rule. The amount of the dividend paid before the disallowance in such event would be recoverable by the trustee in an adversary proceeding.

Rule 3008

RECONSIDERATION OF CLAIMS

A party in interest may move for reconsideration of an order allowing or disallowing a claim against the estate. The court after a hearing on notice shall enter an appropriate order.

Advisory Committee Note

Section 502(j) of the Code deals only with the reconsideration of allowed claims as did former § 57k of the Act and General Order 21(b). It had sometimes been held that a referee had no jurisdiction to reconsider a disallowed claim, or the amount or priority of an allowed claim, at the instance of the claimant. See *e.g., In re Gouse,* 7 F.Supp. 106 (M.D.Pa.1934); *In re Tomlinson & Dye, Inc.,* 3 F.Supp. 800 (N.D.Okla.1933). This view disregarded § 2a(2) of the Act and the "ancient and elementary power" of a referee as a court to reconsider orders. *In re Pottasch Brow. Co., Inc.,* 79 F.2d 613, 616 (2d Cir. 1935); *Castaner* v. *Mora,* 234 F.2d 710 (1st Cir. 1956). This rule recognizes, as did former Bankruptcy Rule 307, the power of the court to reconsider an order of disallowance on appropriate motion.

Reconsideration of a claim that has been previously allowed or disallowed after objection is discretionary with the court. The right to seek reconsideration of an allowed claim, like the right to object to its allowance, is generally exercised by the trustee if one has qualified and is performing the duties of that office with reasonable diligence and fidelity. A request for reconsideration of a disallowance would, on the other hand, ordinarily come from the claimant.

A proof of claim executed and filed in accordance with the rules in this Part III is prima facie evidence of the validity and the amount of the claim notwithstanding a motion for reconsideration of an order of allowance. Failure to respond does not constitute an admission, though it may be deemed a consent to a reconsideration. *In re Goble Boat Co.,* 190 Fed. 92 (N.D.N.Y.1911). The court may decline to reconsider an order of allowance or disallowance without notice to any adverse party and without affording any hearing to the movant. If a motion to reconsider is granted, notice and hearing must be afforded to parties in interest before the previous action in the claim taken in respect to the claim may be vacated or modified. After reconsideration, the court may allow or disallow the claim, increase or decrease the amount of a prior allowance, accord the claim a priority different from that originally assigned it, or enter any other appropriate order.

The rule expands § 502(j) which provides for reconsideration of an allowance only before the case is closed. Authorities have disagreed as to whether reconsideration may be had after a case has been reopened. Compare 3 Collier, *Bankruptcy* ¶ 57.23[4] (14th ed. 1964), see generally 3 *id.* ¶ 502.10 (15th ed. 1979), with 2 Remington, *Bankruptcy* 498 (Henderson ed. 1956). If a case is reopened as provided in § 350(b) of the Code, reconsideration of the allowance or disallowance of a claim may be sought and granted in accordance with this rule.

Rule 3009

DECLARATION AND PAYMENT OF DIVIDENDS IN CHAPTER 7 LIQUIDATION CASES

In chapter 7 cases, dividends to creditors shall be paid as promptly as practicable in the amounts and at the times as ordered by the court. Dividend checks shall be made payable and mailed to each creditor whose claim has been allowed, unless a power of attorney authorizing another entity to receive dividends has been executed and filed in accordance with Rule 9010. In that event, dividend checks shall be made payable to the creditor and to the other entity and shall be mailed to the other entity.

Amended Mar. 30, 1987, eff. Aug. 1, 1987.

Advisory Committee Note

This rule is derived from former Rules 308 and 11–35(a). The preparation of records showing dividends declared and to whom payable is subject to prescription by the Director of the Administrative Office pursuant to Rule 5003(e). The rule governs distributions to creditors having priority as well as to general unsecured creditors. Notwithstanding the detailed statutory provisions regulating the declaration of dividends, a necessarily wide discretion over this matter has been recognized to reside in the court. See 3A Collier, *Bankruptcy* ¶ 65.03 (14th ed. 1975): 1 *Proceedings of Seminar for Newly Appointed Referees in Bankruptcy* 173 (1964). Although the rule leaves to the discretion of the court the amount and the times of dividend payments, it recognizes the creditors' right to as prompt payment as practicable.

The second and third sentences of the rule make explicit the method of payment of dividends and afford protection of the interests of the creditor and the holder of a power of attorney authorized to receive payment.

The rule does not permit variance at local option. This represents a marked change from former Bankruptcy Rule 308.

Rule 3010

SMALL DIVIDENDS AND PAYMENTS IN CHAPTER 7 LIQUIDATION AND CHAPTER 13 INDIVIDUAL'S DEBT ADJUSTMENT CASES

(a) **Chapter 7 Cases.** In a chapter 7 case no dividend in an amount less than $5 shall be distributed by the trustee to any creditor unless authorized by local rule or order of the court. Any dividend not distributed to a creditor shall be treated in the same manner as unclaimed funds as provided in § 347 of the Code.

(b) **Chapter 13 Cases.** In a chapter 13 case no payment in an amount less than $15 shall be distributed by the trustee to any creditor unless authorized by local rule or order of the court. Funds not distributed because of this subdivision shall accumulate and shall be paid whenever the accumulation aggregates $15. Any funds remaining shall be distributed with the final payment.

Amended Mar. 30, 1987, eff. Aug. 1, 1987.

Advisory Committee Note

This rule permits a court to eliminate the disproportionate expense and inconvenience incurred by the issuance of a dividend check of less than $5 (or $15 in a chapter 13 case). Creditors are more irritated than pleased to receive such small dividends, but the money is held subject to their specific request as are unclaimed dividends under § 347(a) of the Code. When the trustee deposits undistributed dividends pursuant to a direction in accordance with this rule the trustee should file with the clerk a list of the names and addresses, so far as known, of the persons entitled to the money so deposited and the respective amounts payable to them pursuant to Rule 3011. In a chapter 13 case, the small dividend will accumulate and will be payable at the latest, with the final dividend. Local rule or order may change the practice permitted in this rule and, in that connection, the order may be incorporated in the order confirming a chapter 13 plan.

Rule 3011

UNCLAIMED FUNDS IN CHAPTER 7 LIQUIDATION AND CHAPTER 13 INDIVIDUAL'S DEBT ADJUSTMENT CASES

The trustee shall file with the clerk a list of all known names and addresses of the entities and the amounts which they are entitled to be paid from remaining property of the estate that is paid into court pursuant to § 347(a) of the Code.

Amended Mar. 30, 1987, eff. Aug. 1, 1987.

Advisory Committee Note

This rule is derived from former Bankruptcy Rule 310. The operative provisions of that rule, however, are contained in § 347(a) of the Code, requiring the trustee to stop payment of checks remaining unpaid 90 days after distribution. The rule adds the requirement of filing a list of the names and addresses of the persons entitled to these dividends. This rule applies in a chapter 7 or 13 case but not in a chapter 9 or 11 case. The latter cases are governed by § 347(b) of the Code which provides for unclaimed distributions to be returned to the debtor or other entity acquiring the assets of the debtor.

Rule 3012

VALUATION OF SECURITY

The court may determine the value of a claim secured by a lien on property in which the estate has an interest on motion of any party in interest and after a hearing on notice to the holder of the secured claim and any other entity as the court may direct.

Amended Mar. 30, 1987, eff. Aug. 1, 1987.

Advisory Committee Note

Pursuant to § 506(a) of the Code, secured claims are to be valued and allowed as secured to the extent of the value of the collateral and unsecured, to the extent it is enforceable, for the excess over such value. The valuation of secured claims may become important in different contexts, *e.g.*, to determine the issue of adequate protection under § 361, impairment under § 1124, or treatment of the claim in a plan pursuant to § 1129(b) of the Code. This rule permits the issue to be raised on motion by a party in interest. The secured creditor is entitled to notice of the hearing on the motion and the court may direct that others in the case also receive such notice.

An adversary proceeding is commenced when the validity, priority, or extent of a lien is at issue as prescribed by Rule 7001. That proceeding is relevant to the basis of the lien itself while valuation under Rule 3012 would be for the purposes indicated above.

Rule 3013

CLASSIFICATION OF CLAIMS AND INTERESTS

For the purposes of the plan and its acceptance, the court may, on motion after hearing on notice as the court may direct, determine classes of creditors and equity security holders pursuant to §§ 1122 and 1322(b)(1) of the Code.

Advisory Committee Note

Sections 1122 and 1322(b)(1) set the standards for classifying claims and interests but provide that such classification is accomplished in the plan. This rule does not change the standards; rather it recognizes that it may be desirable or necessary to establish proper classification before a plan can be formulated. It provides for a court hearing on such notice as the court may direct.

Rule 3014

ELECTION PURSUANT TO § 1111(b) BY SECURED CREDITOR IN CHAPTER 9 MUNICIPALITY AND CHAPTER 11 REORGANIZATION CASES

An election of application of § 1111(b)(2) of the Code by a class of secured creditors in a chapter 9 or 11 case may be made at any time prior to the conclusion of the hearing on the disclosure statement or within such later time as the court may fix. The election shall be in writing and signed unless made at the hearing on the disclosure statement. The election, if made by the majorities required by § 1111(b)(1)(A)(i), shall be binding on all members of the class with respect to the plan.

Advisory Committee Note

Pursuant to § 1111(b)(1) of the Code, a nonrecourse secured loan is converted, automatically, into a recourse loan thereby entitling the creditor to an unsecured deficiency claim if the value of the collateral is less than the debt. The class, however, may retain the loan as a nonrecourse loan by electing application of § 1111(b)(2) of the majorities stated in § 1111(b)(1)(A)(i). That section does not specify any time periods for making the election.

Rule 3014 provides that if no agreement is negotiated, the election of § 1111(b)(2) of the Code may be made at any time prior to conclusion of the hearing on the disclosure statement. Once the hearing has been concluded, it would be too late for a secured creditor class to demand different treatment unless the court has fixed a later time. This would be the case if, for example, a public class of secured creditors should have an approved disclosure statement prior to electing under § 1111(b).

Generally it is important that the proponent of a plan ascertain the position of the secured creditor class before a plan is proposed. The secured creditor class must know the prospects of its treatment under the plan before it can intelligently determine its rights under § 1111(b). The rule recognizes that there may be negotiations between the proponent of the plan and the secured creditor leading to a representation of desired treatment under § 1111(b). If that treatment is approved by the requisite majorities of the class and culminates in a written signed statement filed with the court, that statement becomes binding and the class may not thereafter demand different treatment under § 1111(b) with respect to that plan. The proponent of the plan is thus enabled to seek approval of the disclosure statement and transmit the plan for voting in anticipation of confirmation. Only if that plan is not confirmed may the class of secured creditors thereafter change its prior election.

While this rule and the Code refer to a class of secured creditors it should be noted that ordinarily each secured creditor is in a separate and distinct class. In that event, the secured creditor has the sole power to determine application of § 1111(b) with respect to that claim.

Rule 3015

FILING OF PLAN IN CHAPTER 13 INDIVIDUAL'S DEBT ADJUSTMENT CASES

The debtor may file a chapter 13 plan with the petition. If a plan is not filed with the petition, it shall be filed within 15 days thereafter and such time shall not be further extended except for cause shown and on notice as the court may direct. Every proposed plan and any modification thereof shall be dated. The clerk shall include the plan or a summary of the plan with each notice of the hearing on confirmation pursuant to Rule 2002(b). If required by the court, the debtor shall furnish a sufficient number of copies to enable the clerk to include a copy of the plan with the notice of the hearing.

Advisory Committee Note

Section 1321 provides only that the "debtor shall file a plan." No time periods are specified, nor is any other detail provided. The rule requires a chapter 3 plan to be filed either with the petition or within 10 days thereafter. The court may, for cause, extend the time. The rule permits a summary of the plan to be transmitted with the notice of the hearing on confirmation. The court may, however, require the plan itself to be transmitted and the debtor to supply enough copies for this purpose. In the former rules under Chapter XIII the plan would accompany the notice of the first meeting of creditors. It is more important for the plan or a summary of its terms to be sent with the notice of the confirmation hearing. At that hearing objections to the plan will be heard by the court.

Rule 3016

FILING OF PLAN AND DISCLOSURE STATEMENT IN CHAPTER 9 MUNICIPALITY AND CHAPTER 11 REORGANIZATION CASES

(a) **Time for Filing Plan.** A party in interest, other than the debtor, who is authorized to file a plan under § 1121(c) of the Code, may file a plan at any time before the conclusion of the hearing on the disclosure statement or thereafter with leave of court.

(b) **Identification of Plan.** Every proposed plan and any modification thereof shall be dated and, in a chapter 11 case, identified with the name of the entity or entities submitting or filing it.

(c) Disclosure Statement. In a chapter 9 or 11 case, a disclosure statement pursuant to § 1125 or evidence showing compliance with § 1126(b) of the Code shall be filed with the plan or within a time fixed by the court.

Amended Mar. 30, 1987, eff. Aug. 1, 1987.

Advisory Committee Note

This rule implements the Code provisions concerning the filing of plans in chapters 9 and 11.

Chapter 9 Cases. Section 941 provides that the debtor may file a plan with the petition or thereafter but within a time fixed by the court. A rule, therefore, is unnecessary to specify the time for filing chapter 9 plans.

Chapter 11 Nonrailroad Cases. Section 1121 contains detailed provisions with respect to who may file a chapter 11 plan and, in part, the time period. Section 1121(a) permits a debtor to file a plan with the petition or at any time during the case. Section 1121(b) and (c) grants exclusive periods of 120 days and 180 days for the debtor to file and obtain acceptance of a plan. Failure to take advantage of these periods or the appointment of a trustee would permit other parties in interest to file a plan. These statutory provisions are not repeated in the rules.

Chapter 11 Railroad Cases. Pursuant to subchapter IV of chapter 11, § 1121 of the Code is applicable in railroad cases; see §§ 1161, 103(g). A trustee, however, is to be appointed in every case; thus, pursuant to § 1121(c), any party in interest may file a plan. See discussion of subdivision (a) of this rule, *infra*.

Subdivision (a). Section 1121(c), while permitting parties in interest a limited right to file plans, does not provide any time limitation. This subdivision sets as the deadline, the conclusion of the hearing on the disclosure statement. The court may, however, grant additional time. It is derived from former Chapter X Rule 10–301(c)(2) which used, as the cut-off time, the conclusion of the hearing on approval of a plan. As indicated, *supra*, § 1121(a) permits a debtor to file a plan at any time during the chapter 11 case. Under § 1121(c), parties other than a debtor may file a plan only after a trustee is appointed or the debtor's exclusive time expires.

Subdivision (b) requires plans to be properly identified.

Subdivision (c). This provision is new. In chapter 9 and 11 cases (including railroad reorganization cases) postpetition solicitation of votes on a plan requires transmittal of a disclosure statement, the contents of which have been approved by the court. See § 1125 of the Code. A prepetition solicitation must either have been in conformity with applicable nonbankruptcy law or, if none, the disclosure must have been of adequate information as set forth in § 1125 of the Code. See § 1126(b). Subdivision (c) of this rule provides the time for filing the disclosure statement or evidence of compliance with § 1126(b) which ordinarily will be with the plan but the court may allow a later time or the court may, pursuant to the last sentence, fix a time certain. Rule 3017 deals with the hearing on the disclosure statement. The disclosure statement, pursuant to § 1125 is to contain adequate information. "Adequate information" is defined in § 1125(a) as information that would permit a reasonable creditor or equity security holder to make an informed judgment on the plan.

Rule 3017

COURT CONSIDERATION OF DISCLOSURE STATEMENT IN CHAPTER 9 MUNICIPALITY AND CHAPTER 11 REORGANIZATION CASES

(a) Hearing on Disclosure Statement and Objections Thereto. Following the filing of a disclosure statement as provided in Rule 3016(c), the court shall hold a hearing on not less than 25 days notice to the debtor, creditors, equity security holders and other parties in interest as provided in Rule 2002 to consider such statement and any objections or modifications thereto. The plan and the disclosure statement shall be mailed with the notice of the hearing only to the debtor, any trustee or committee appointed under the Code, the Securities and Exchange Commission and any party in interest who requests in writing a copy of the statement or plan. Objections to the disclosure statement shall be filed with the court and served on the debtor, the trustee, any committee appointed under the Code and such other entity as may be designated by the court, at any time prior to approval of the disclosure statement or by such earlier date as the court may fix.

(b) Determination on Disclosure Statement. Following the hearing the court shall determine whether the disclosure statement should be approved.

(c) Dates Fixed for Voting on Plan and Confirmation. On or before approval of the disclosure statement, the court shall fix a time within which the holders of claims and interests may accept or reject the plan and may fix a date for the hearing on confirmation.

(d) Transmission and Notice to Creditors and Equity Security Holders. On approval of a disclosure statement, the debtor in possession, trustee, proponent of the plan, or clerk as ordered by the court shall mail to all creditors and equity security holders (1) the plan, or a court approved summary of the plan; (2) the disclosure statement approved by the court; (3) notice of the time within which acceptances and rejections of such plan may be filed; (4) notice of any date fixed for the hearing on confirmation; and (5) such other information as the court may direct including any opinion of the court approving the disclosure statement or a court approved summary of the opinion. In addition, a form of ballot conforming to Official Form No. 30 shall be mailed to creditors and equity security holders entitled to vote on the plan. In the event the opinion of the court is not transmitted or only a summary of the plan is transmitted, the opinion of the court or the plan shall be provided on request of a party in interest at the expense of the proponent of the plan. For the purposes of this subdivision, creditors and equity security holders shall include holders of stock, bonds, debentures, notes, and other securities of record at the date the order approving the disclosure statement was entered.

Amended Mar. 30, 1987, eff. Aug. 1, 1987.

Advisory Committee Note

This rule is adapted from former Rule 10–303 which dealt with the approval of a Chapter X plan by the court. There is no requirement for plan approval in a chapter 9 or 11 case under the Code but there is the requirement that a disclosure statement containing adequate financial information be approved by the court after notice and a hearing before votes on a plan are solicited. Section 1125(b) of the Code is made applicable in chapter 9 cases by § 901(a). It is also applicable in railroad reorganization cases under subchapter IV of chapter 11; see § 1161 of the Code.

Subdivision (a) of this rule provides for the hearing on the disclosure statement. Thus, a hearing would be required in all cases; whether it may be ex parte would depend on the circumstances of the case, but a mere absence of objections would not eliminate the need for a hearing; see § 102(1) of the Code.

No provision similar to former Rule 10–303(f) is included. That subdivision together with former Rule 10–304 prohibited solicitation of votes until after entry of an order approving the plan. Section 1125(b) of the Code explicitly provides that votes on a plan may not be solicited until a disclosure statement approved by the court is transmitted. Pursuant to the change in rulemaking power, a comparable provision in this rule is unnecessary. 28 U.S.C. § 2075.

Copies of the disclosure statement and plan need not be mailed with the notice of the hearing or otherwise transmitted prior to the hearing except with respect to the parties explicitly set forth in the subdivision.

It should be noted that, by construction, the singular includes the plural. Therefore, the phrase "plan or plans" or "disclosure statement or statements" has not been used although the possibility of multiple plans and statements is recognized.

Subdivision (d) permits the court to require a party other than the clerk of the bankruptcy court to bear the responsibility for transmitting the notices and documents specified in the rule when votes on the plan are solicited. Ordinarily the person responsible for such mailing will be the proponent of the plan. In rare cases the clerk may be directed to mail these documents, particularly when the trustee would have the responsibility but there is insufficient money in the estate to enable the trustee to perform this task.

Advisory Committee Notes Accompanying 1987 Amendments

Subdivision (d). Section 1125(c) of the Code requires that the entire approved disclosure statement be provided in connection with voting on a plan. The court is authorized by § 1125(c) to approve different disclosure statements for different classes. Although the rule does not permit the mailing of a summary of the disclosure statement in place of the approved disclosure statement, the court may approve a summary of the disclosure statement to be mailed with the complete disclosure statement to those voting on the plan.

Rule 3018

ACCEPTANCE OR REJECTION OF PLANS

(a) Persons Entitled to Accept or Reject Plan; Time for Acceptance or Rejection. A plan may be accepted or rejected by the following entities within the time fixed by the court pursuant to Rule 3017: (1) any creditor whose claim is deemed allowed pursuant to § 502 of the Code or has been allowed by the court; (2) subject to subdivision (b) of this rule, any creditor who is a security holder of record at the date the order approving the disclosure statement is entered whose claim has not been disallowed; and (3) an equity security holder of record at the date the order approving the disclosure statement is entered whose interest has not been disallowed. For cause shown and within the time fixed for acceptance or rejection of a plan, the court after notice and hearing may permit a creditor or equity security holder to change or withdraw an acceptance or rejection. Notwithstanding objection to a claim or interest, the court after notice and hearing may temporarily allow the claim or interest in an amount which the court deems proper for the purpose of accepting or rejecting a plan.

(b) **Acceptances or Rejections Obtained Before Petition.** Acceptances or rejections of a plan may be obtained before the commencement of a case under the Code and may be filed with the court on behalf of (1) the holder of a claim or interest which is deemed allowed pursuant to § 502 of the Code or allowed by the court; (2) a creditor who is a security holder of record at the date specified in the solicitation for the purposes of such solicitation and whose claim has not been disallowed; and (3) an equity security holder of record at the date specified in the solicitation for the purposes of such solicitation and whose interest has not been disallowed. A holder of a claim or interest who has accepted or rejected a plan before the commencement of the case under the Code shall not be deemed to have accepted or rejected the plan if the court finds after notice and hearing that the plan was not transmitted to substantially all impaired creditors and impaired equity security holders, that an unreasonably short time was prescribed for such creditors and equity security holders to accept or reject the plan, or that the solicitation was not in compliance with § 1126(b) of the Code.

(c) **Form of Acceptance or Rejection.** An acceptance or rejection shall be in writing, identify the plan or plans accepted or rejected, be signed by the creditor or equity security holder or an authorized agent, and conform to Official Form No. 30. If more than one plan is transmitted pursuant to Rule 3017, an acceptance or rejection may be filed by each creditor or equity security holder for any number of plans transmitted and if acceptances are filed for more than one plan, the creditor or equity security holder may indicate a preference or preferences among the plans so accepted.

(d) **Acceptance or Rejection by Partially Secured Creditor.** A creditor whose claim has been allowed in part as a secured claim and in part as an unsecured claim shall be entitled to accept or reject a plan in both capacities.

Amended Mar. 30, 1987, eff. Aug. 1, 1987.

Advisory Committee Note

This rule applies in chapter 9, 11 and 13 cases under the Code. The references in the rule to equity security holders will not, however, be relevant in chapter 9 or 13 cases. The rule will be of little utility in a chapter 13 case because only secured creditors may be requested to vote on a plan; unsecured creditors are not entitled to vote; see § 1325(a)(4), (5) of the Code.

Subdivision (a) is derived from former Rule 10–305(a). It substitutes, in a reorganization case, entry of the order approving the disclosure statement for the order approving a plan in conformity with the differences between Chapter X and chapter 11. In keeping with the underlying theory, it continues to recognize that the lapse time between the filing of the petition and entry of such order will normally be significant and, during that interim, bonds and equity interests can change ownership.

Subdivision (b) recognizes the former Chapter XI practice permitting a plan and acceptances to be filed with the petition, as does § 1126(b) of the Code. However, because a plan under chapter 11 may affect shareholder interests, there should be reference to a record date of ownership. In this instance the appropriate record date is that used in the prepetition solicitation materials because it is those acceptances or rejections which are being submitted to the court.

While § 1126(c), (d), and (e) prohibits use of an acceptance or rejection not procured in good faith, the added provision in subdivision (b) of the rule is somewhat more detailed. It would prohibit use of prepetition acceptances or rejections when some but not all impaired creditors or equity security holders are solicited or when they are not given a reasonable opportunity to submit their acceptances or rejections. This provision together with § 1126(e) gives the court the power to nullify abusive solicitation procedures.

Subdivision (c). It is possible that multiple plans may be before the court for confirmation. Pursuant to § 1129(c) of the Code, the court may confirm only one plan but is required to consider the preferences expressed by those accepting the plans in determining which one to confirm.

Subdivisions (d) and (e) of former Rule 10–305 are not continued since comparable provisions are contained in the statute; see § 1126(c), (d), (e).

It should be noted that while the singular "plan" is used throughout, by construction the plural is included; see § 102(7).

Rule 3019

MODIFICATION OF ACCEPTED PLAN BEFORE CONFIRMATION

After a plan has been accepted and before its confirmation, the proponent may file a modification of the plan. If the court finds after hearing on notice to the trustee, any committee appointed under the Code and any other entity designated by the court that the proposed modification does not adversely change the treatment of the claim of any creditor or the interest of any equity security holder who has not accepted in writing the modification, it shall be deemed accepted by all creditors and equity security holders who have previously accepted the plan.

Amended Mar. 30, 1987, eff. Aug. 1, 1987.

Advisory Committee Note

This rule implements §§ 942, 1127 and 1323 of the Code. For example, § 1127 provides for modification before and after confirmation but does not deal with the minor modifications that do not adversely change any rights. The rule makes clear that a modification may be made, after acceptance of the plan without submission to creditors and equity security holders if their interests are not affected. To come within this rule, the modification should be one that does not change the rights of a creditor or equity security holder as fixed in the plan before modification.

Rule 3020

DEPOSIT; CONFIRMATION OF PLAN

(a) Deposit. In a chapter 11 case, prior to entry of the order confirming the plan, the court may order the deposit with the trustee or debtor in possession of the consideration required by the plan to be distributed on confirmation. Any money deposited shall be kept in a special account established for the exclusive purpose of making the distribution.

(b) Objections to and Hearing on Confirmation.

(1) Objections. Objections to confirmation of the plan shall be filed with the court and served on the debtor, the trustee, any committee appointed under the Code and on any other entity designated by the court, within a time fixed by the court. An objection to confirmation is governed by Rule 9014.

(2) Hearing. The court shall rule on confirmation of the plan after notice and hearing as provided in Rule 2002. If no objection is timely filed, the court may determine that the plan has been proposed in good faith and not by any means forbidden by law without receiving evidence on such issues.

(c) Order of Confirmation. The order of confirmation shall conform to Official Form No. 31 and notice of entry thereof shall be mailed promptly as provided in Rule 2002(f) to the debtor, creditors, equity security holders and other parties in interest.

(d) Retained Power. Notwithstanding the entry of the order of confirmation, the court may enter all orders necessary to administer the estate.

Amended Mar. 30, 1987, eff. Aug. 1, 1987.

Advisory Committee Note

This rule is adapted from former Rules 10–307, 11–38, and 13–213. It applies to cases filed under chapters 9, 11 and 13. Certain subdivisions of the earlier rules have not been included, such as, a subdivision revesting title in the debtor because § 541 of the Code does not transfer title out of the debtor as did § 70a of the Bankruptcy Act; see also §§ 1141(b), 1327(b). Subdivision (b) of former Rule 13–213 is not included because its provisions are contained in the statute; see §§ 1322, 1325(b), 105.

Subdivision (a) gives discretion to the court to require in chapter 11 cases the deposit of any consideration to be distributed on confirmation. If money is to be distributed, it is to be deposited in a special account to assure that it will not be used for any other purpose. The Code is silent in chapter 11 with respect to the need to make a deposit or the person with whom any deposit is to be made. Consequently, there is no statutory authority for any person to act in a capacity similar to the disbursing agent under former Chapter XI practice. This rule provides that only the debtor in possession or trustee should be appointed as the recipient of the deposit. Any consideration other than money, *e.g.,* notes or stock may be given directly to the debtor in possession or trustee and need not be left in any kind of special account. In chapter 9 cases, § 944(b) provides for deposit with a disbursing agent appointed by the court of any consideration to be distributed under the plan.

Subdivision (d) clarifies the authority of the court to conclude matters pending before it prior to confirmation and to continue to administer the estate as necessary, *e.g.,* resolving objections to claims.

Rule 3021

DISTRIBUTION UNDER PLAN

After confirmation of a plan, distribution shall be made to creditors whose claims have been allowed, to holders of stock, bonds, debentures, notes, and other securities of record at the time of commencement of distribution whose claims or equity security interests have not been disallowed and to indenture trustees who have filed claims pursuant to Rule 3003(c)(5) and which have been allowed.

Advisory Committee Note

This rule is derived from former Chapter X Rule 10–405(a). Subdivision (b) of that rule is covered by § 1143 of the Code.

Rule 3022

FINAL DECREE

After an estate is fully administered, including distribution of any deposit required by the plan, the court shall enter a final decree (1) discharging any trustee if not previously discharged and cancelling the trustee's bond; (2) making provision by way of injunction or otherwise as may be equitable; and (3) closing the case.

Amended Mar. 30, 1987, eff. Aug. 1, 1987.

Advisory Committee Note

Section 350 of the Code requires the court to close the case after the estate is fully administered and the trustee has been discharged. Section 1143 places a five year limitation on the surrender of securities when required for participation under a plan but this provision should not delay entry of the final decree.

PART IV

THE DEBTOR: DUTIES AND BENEFITS

Rule
4001. Relief From Automatic Stay; Use of Cash Collateral; Obtaining Credit; Agreements
4002. Duties of Debtor
4003. Exemptions
4004. Grant or Denial of Discharge
4005. Burden of Proof in Objecting to Discharge
4006. Notice of No Discharge
4007. Determination of Dischargeability of a Debt
4008. Discharge and Reaffirmation Hearing

Rule 4001

RELIEF FROM AUTOMATIC STAY; USE OF CASH COLLATERAL; OBTAINING CREDIT; AGREEMENTS

(a) Relief From Stay.

(1) *Motion.* A motion for relief from an automatic stay provided by the Code shall be made in accordance with Rule 9014.

(2) *Final Hearing On Stay.* The stay of any act against property of the estate under § 362(a) of the Code expires 30 days after a final hearing is commenced pursuant to § 362(e) unless before that time expires the court denies the motion for relief from the stay or, after notice and a hearing, orders the stay continued pending conclusion of the final hearing.

(3) *Ex Parte Relief From Stay.* Relief from a stay under § 362(a) may be granted without prior notice to the adverse party only if (A) it clearly appears from specific facts shown by affidavit or by a verified motion that immediate and irreparable injury, loss, or damage will result to the movant before the adverse party or the attorney for the adverse party can be heard in opposition, and (B) the movant's attorney certifies to the court in writing the efforts, if any, which have been made to give notice and the reasons why notice should not be required. The party obtaining relief under this subdivision and § 362(f) shall immediately give oral notice thereof to the trustee or debtor in possession and to the debtor and forthwith mail or otherwise transmit to such adverse party or parties a copy of the order granting relief. On two days notice to the party who obtained relief from the stay without notice or on shorter notice to that party as the court may prescribe, the adverse party may appear and move reinstatement of the stay. In that event, the court shall proceed expeditiously to hear and determine the motion.

(b) Use of Cash Collateral.

(1) *Motion; Service.* A motion for authorization to use cash collateral shall be made in accordance with Rule 9014 and shall be served on any entity which has an interest in the cash collateral, on any committee appointed under the Code or its authorized agent, or, if no committee has been appointed, on the

589

creditors included on the list filed pursuant to Rule 1007(d) and on such other entities as the court may direct.

(2) *Hearing.* The court may commence a final hearing on a motion for authorization to use cash collateral no earlier than 15 days after service of the motion. If the motion so requests, the court may conduct a preliminary hearing before such 15 day period expires, but the court may authorize the use of only that amount of cash collateral as is necessary to avoid immediate and irreparable harm to the estate pending a final hearing.

(3) *Notice.* Notice of hearing pursuant to this subdivision shall be given to the parties on whom service of the motion is required by paragraph (1) of this subdivision and to such other entities as the court may direct.

(c) Obtaining Credit.

(1) *Motion; Service.* A motion for authority to obtain credit shall be made in accordance with Rule 9014 and shall be served on any committee appointed under the Code or its authorized agent, or, if no committee has been appointed, on the creditors listed on the list filed pursuant to Rule 1007(d), and on such other entities as the court may direct. The motion shall be accompanied by a copy of the agreement.

(2) *Hearing.* The court may commence a final hearing on a motion for authority to obtain credit no earlier than 15 days after service of the motion. If the motion so requests, the court may conduct a hearing before such 15 day period expires, but the court may authorize the obtaining of credit only to the extent necessary to avoid immediate and irreparable harm to the estate pending a final hearing.

(3) *Notice.* Notice of hearing pursuant to this subdivision shall be given to the parties on whom service of the motion is required by paragraph (1) of this subdivision and to such other entities as the court may direct.

(d) Agreement Relating to Relief From the Automatic Stay, Providing Adequate Protection, Use of Cash Collateral, and Obtaining Credit.

(1) *Motion; Service.* A motion for approval of an agreement to provide adequate protection, for the modification or termination of the stay provided for in § 362, for the use of cash collateral, or for approval of an agreement between the debtor and an entity that has a lien or interest in property of the estate pursuant to which the entity consents to the creation of a lien senior or equal to the entity's lien or interest in such property shall be served on any committee appointed under the Code or its authorized agent, or, if no committee has been appointed, on the creditors listed on the list filed pursuant to Rule 1007(d) and on such other entities as the court may direct. The motion shall be accompanied by a copy of the agreement.

(2) *Objection.* Notice of the motion and the time within which objections may be filed and served on the debtor in possession or trustee shall be mailed to the parties on whom service is required by paragraph (1) of this subdivision and to such other entities as the court may direct. Unless the court fixes a different time, objections may be filed within 15 days of the mailing of notice.

(3) *Disposition; Hearing.* If no objection is filed, the court may enter an order approving or disapproving the agreement without conducting a hearing. If an objection is filed or if the court determines a hearing is appropriate, the court shall hold a hearing on no less than five days' notice to the objector, the

movant, the parties on whom service is required by paragraph (1) of this subdivision and such other entities as the court may direct.

Amended Mar. 30, 1987, eff. Aug. 1, 1987.

Advisory Committee Note

This rule implements § 362 of the Code which sets forth provisions regarding the automatic stay that arises on the filing of a petition. That section and this rule are applicable in chapter 7, 9, 11 and 13 cases. It also implements § 363(c)(2) concerning use of cash collateral.

Subdivision (a) transforms with respect to the automatic stay what was an adversary proceeding under the former rules to motion practice. The Code provides automatic stays in several sections, *e.g.,* §§ 362(a), 1301(a), and in § 362(d) provides some grounds for relief from the stay. This rule specifies that the pleading seeking relief is by means of a motion. Thus the time period in Rule 7012 to answer a complaint would not be applicable and shorter periods may be fixed. Section 362(e) requires the preliminary hearing to be concluded within 30 days of its inception, rendering ordinary complaint and answer practice inappropriate.

This subdivision also makes clear that a motion under Rule 9014 is the proper procedure for a debtor to seek court permission to use cash collateral. See § 363(c)(2). Pursuant to Rule 5005, the motion should be filed in the court in which the case is pending. The court or local rule may specify the persons to be served with the motion for relief from the stay; see Rule 9013.

Subdivision (b) of the rule fills a procedural void left by § 362. Pursuant to § 362(e), the automatic stay is terminated 30 days after a motion for relief is made unless the court continues the stay as a result of a final hearing or, pending final hearing, after a preliminary hearing. If a preliminary hearing is held, § 362(e) requires the final hearing to be commenced within 30 days after the preliminary hearing. Although the expressed legislative intent is to require expeditious resolution of a secured party's motion for relief, § 362 is silent as to the time within which the final hearing must be concluded. Subdivision (b) imposes a 30 day deadline on the court to resolve the dispute.

At the final hearing, the stay is to be terminated, modified, annulled, or conditioned for cause, which includes, *inter alia,* lack of adequate protection; § 362(d). The burden of proving adequate protection is on the party opposing relief from the stay; § 362(g)(2). Adequate protection is exemplified in § 361.

Subdivision (c) implements § 362(f) which permits ex parte relief from the stay when there will be irreparable damage. This subdivision sets forth the procedure to be followed when relief is sought under § 362(f). It is derived from former Bankruptcy Rule 601(d).

Advisory Committee Notes to 1987 Amendments

The scope of this rule is expanded and the former subdivisions (a), (b) and (c) are now combined in subdivision (a). The new subdivision (a)(2) is amended to conform to the 1984 amendments to § 362(e) of the Code.

Subdivision (b) deals explicitly with the procedures which follow after a motion to use cash collateral is made and served. Filing shall be pursuant to Rule 5005. Service of the motion may be made by any method authorized by Rule 7004 and, if service is by mail, service is complete on mailing. Rule 9006(e). Under subdivision (b)(2), the court may commence a final hearing on the motion within 15 days of service. Rule 9006(f) does not extend this 15 day period when service of the motion is by mail because the party served is not required to act within the 15 day period. In addition to service of the motion, notice of the hearing must be given. Rule 9007 authorizes the court to direct the form and manner of giving notice that is appropriate to the circumstances.

Section 363(c)(3) authorizes the court to conduct a preliminary hearing and to authorize the use of cash collateral "if there is a reasonable likelihood that the trustee will prevail at a final hearing." Subdivision (b)(2) of the rule permits a preliminary hearing to be held earlier than 15 days after service. Any order authorizing the use of cash collateral shall be limited to the amount necessary to protect the estate until a final hearing is held.

The objective of subdivision (b) is to accommodate both the immediate need of the debtor and the interest of the secured creditor in the cash collateral. The time for holding the final hearing may be enlarged beyond the 15 days prescribed when required by the circumstances.

The motion for authority to use cash collateral shall include (1) the amount of cash collateral sought to be used; (2) the name and address of each entity having an interest in the cash collateral; (3) the name and address of the entity in control or having possession of the cash collateral; (4) the facts demonstrating the need to use the cash collateral; and (5) the nature of the protection to be provided those having an interest in the cash collateral. If a preliminary hearing is requested, the motion shall also include the amount of cash collateral sought to be used pending final hearing and the protection to be provided.

Notice of the preliminary and final hearings may be combined. This rule does not limit the authority of the court under § 363(c)(2)(B) and § 102(1).

Subdivision (c) is new. The service, hearing, and notice requirements are similar to those imposed by subdivision (b). The motion to obtain credit shall include the amount and type of the credit to be extended, the name and address of the lender, the terms of the agreement, the need to obtain the credit, and the efforts made to obtain credit from other sources. If the motion is to obtain credit pursuant to § 364(c) or (d), the motion shall describe the collateral, if any, and the protection for any existing interest in the collateral which may be affected by the proposed agreement.

Subdivision (d) is new. In the event the 15 day period for filing objections to the approval of an agreement of the parties described in this subdivision is too long, the parties either may move for a reduction of the period under Rule 9006(c)(1) or proceed under subdivision (b) or (c), if applicable. Rule 9006(c)(1) requires that cause be shown for the reduction of the period in which to object. In applying this criterion the court may consider the option of proceeding under subdivision (b) or (c) and grant a preliminary hearing and relief pending final hearing.

Rule 4002

DUTIES OF DEBTOR

In addition to performing other duties prescribed by the Code and rules, the debtor shall (1) attend and submit to an examination at the times ordered by the court; (2) attend the hearing on a complaint objecting to discharge and testify, if called as a witness; (3) inform the trustee immediately in writing as to the location of real property in which the debtor has an interest and the name and address of every person holding money or property subject to the debtor's withdrawal or order if a schedule of property has not yet been filed pursuant to Rule 1007; (4) cooperate with the trustee in the preparation of an inventory, the examination of proofs of claim, and the administration of the estate, and (5) file a statement of any change of the debtor's address.

Amended Mar. 30, 1987, eff. Aug. 1, 1987.

Advisory Committee Note

This rule should be read together with §§ 343 and 521 of the Code and Rule 1007, all of which impose duties on the debtor. Clause (3) of this rule implements the provisions of Rule 2015(a).

Advisory Committee Notes to 1987 Amendments

New clause (5) of the rule imposes on the debtor the duty to advise the clerk of any change of the debtor's address.

Rule 4003

EXEMPTIONS

(a) **Claim of Exemptions.** A debtor shall list the property claimed as exempt under § 522 of the Code on the schedule of assets required to be filed by Rule 1007. If the debtor fails to claim exemptions or file the schedule within the time specified in Rule 1007, a dependent of the debtor may file the list within 30 days thereafter.

(b) **Objections to Claim of Exemptions.** The trustee or any creditor may file objections to the list of property claimed as exempt within 30 days after the conclusion of the meeting of creditors held pursuant to Rule 2003(a) or the filing of any amendment to the list unless, within such period, further time is granted by the court. Copies of the objections shall be delivered or mailed to the trustee and to the person filing the list and the attorney for such person.

(c) **Burden of Proof.** In any hearing under this rule, the objecting party has the burden of proving that the exemptions are not properly claimed. After hearing on notice, the court shall determine the issues presented by the objections.

(d) **Avoidance by Debtor of Transfers of Exempt Property.** A proceeding by the debtor to avoid a lien or other transfer of property exempt under § 522(f) of the Code shall be by motion in accordance with Rule 9014.

Amended Mar. 30, 1987, eff. Aug. 1, 1987.

Advisory Committee Note

This rule is derived from § 522(1) of the Code and, in part, former Bankruptcy Rule 403. The Code changes the thrust of that rule by making it the burden of the debtor to list his exemptions and the burden of parties in interest to raise objections in the absence of which "the property claimed as exempt on such list is exempt;". § 522(1).

Subdivision (a). While § 522(1) refers to a list of property claimed as exempt, the rule incorporates such a list as part of Official Form No. 6, the schedule of the debtor's assets, rather than requiring a separate list and filing. Rule 1007, to which subdivision (a) refers, requires that schedule to be filed within 15 days after the order for relief, unless the court extends the time.

Section 522(1) also provides that a dependent of the debtor may file the list if the debtor fails to do so. Subdivision (a) of the rule allows such filing from the expiration of the debtor's time until 30 days thereafter. Dependent is defined in § 522(a)(1).

Subdivision (d) provides that a proceeding by the debtor, permitted by § 522(f) of the Code, is a contested matter rather than the more formal adversary proceeding. Proceedings within the scope of this subdivision are distinguished from proceedings brought by the trustee to avoid transfers. The latter are classified as adversary proceedings by Rule 7001.

Rule 4004

GRANT OR DENIAL OF DISCHARGE

(a) Time for Filing Complaint Objecting to Discharge; Notice of Time Fixed. In a chapter 7 liquidation case a complaint objecting to the debtor's discharge under § 727(a) of the Code shall be filed not later than 60 days following the first date set for the meeting of creditors held pursuant to § 341(a). In a chapter 11 reorganization case, such complaint shall be filed not later than the first date set for the hearing on confirmation. Not less than 25 days notice of the time so fixed shall be given to all creditors as provided in Rule 2002(f) and to the trustee and the trustee's attorney.

(b) Extension of Time. On motion of any party in interest, after hearing on notice, the court may extend for cause the time for filing a complaint objecting to discharge. The motion shall be made before such time has expired.

(c) Grant of Discharge. In a chapter 7 case, on expiration of the time fixed for filing a complaint objecting to discharge, the court shall forthwith grant the discharge unless (1) the debtor is not an individual, (2) a complaint objecting to the discharge has been filed, or (3) the debtor has filed a waiver under § 727(a) (10). Notwithstanding the foregoing, on motion of the debtor, the court may defer the entry of an order granting a discharge for 30 days and, on motion within such period, the court may defer entry of the order to a date certain.

(d) Applicability of Rules in Part VII. A proceeding commenced by a complaint objecting to discharge is governed by Part VII of these rules.

(e) Order of Discharge. An order of discharge shall conform to Official Form No. 27.

(f) Registration in Other Districts. An order of discharge that has become final may be registered in any other district by filing a certified copy of the order in the office of the clerk of that district. When so registered the order of discharge shall have the same effect as an order of the court of the district where registered.

(g) Notice of Discharge. The clerk shall promptly mail a copy of the final order of discharge to those specified in subdivision (a) of this rule.

Amended Mar. 30, 1987, eff. Aug. 1, 1987.

Advisory Committee Note

This rule is adapted from former Bankruptcy Rule 404.

Subdivisions (a) and (b) of this rule prescribe the procedure for determining whether a discharge will be granted pursuant to § 727 of the Code. The time fixed by subdivision (a) may be enlarged as provided in subdivision (b).

The notice referred to in subdivision (a) is required to be given by mail and addressed to creditors as provided in Rule 2002.

An extension granted on a motion pursuant to subdivision (b) of the rule would ordinarily benefit only the movant, but its scope and effect would depend on the terms of the extension.

Subdivision (c). If a complaint objecting to discharge is filed, the court's grant or denial of the discharge will be entered at the conclusion of the proceeding as a judgment in accordance with Rule 9021. The inclusion of the clause in subdivision (c) qualifying the duty of the court to grant a discharge when a waiver has been filed is in accord with the construction of the Code. 4 Collier, *Bankruptcy* ¶ 727.12 (15th ed. 1979).

The last sentence of subdivision (c) takes cognizance of § 524(c) of the Code which authorizes a debtor to enter into enforceable reaffirmation agreements only prior to entry of the order of discharge. Immediate entry of that order after expiration of the time fixed for filing complaints objecting to discharge may render it more difficult for a debtor to settle pending litigation to determine the dischargeability of a debt and execute a reaffirmation agreement as part of a settlement.

Subdivision (d). An objection to discharge is required to be made by a complaint, which initiates an adversary proceeding as provided in Rule 7003. Pursuant to Rule 5005, the complaint should be filed in the court in which the case is pending.

Subdivision (e). Official Form No. 27 to which subdivision (e) refers, includes notice of the effects of a discharge specified in § 524(a) of the Code.

Subdivision (f). Registration may facilitate the enforcement of the order of discharge in a district other than that in which it was entered. See 2 Moore's *Federal Practice* ¶ 1.04[2] (2d ed. 1967). Because of the nationwide service of process authorized by Rule 7004, however, registration of the order of discharge is not necessary under these rules to enable a discharged debtor to obtain relief against a creditor proceeding anywhere in the United States in disregard of the injunctive provisions of the order of discharge.

Subdivision (g). Notice of discharge should be mailed promptly after the order becomes final so that creditors may be informed of entry of the order and of its injunctive provisions. Rule 2002 specifies the manner of the notice and persons to whom the notice is to be given.

Rule 4005

BURDEN OF PROOF IN OBJECTING TO DISCHARGE

At the trial on a complaint objecting to a discharge, the plaintiff has the burden of proving the objection.

Amended Mar. 30, 1987, eff. Aug. 1, 1987.

Advisory Committee Note

This rule does not address the burden of going forward with the evidence. Subject to the allocation by the rule of the initial burden of producing evidence and the ultimate burden of persuasion, the rule leaves to the courts the formulation of rules governing the shift of the burden of going forward with the evidence in the light of considerations such as the difficulty of proving the nonexistence of a fact and of establishing a fact as to which the evidence is likely to be more accessible to the debtor than to the objector. *See, e.g., In re Haggerty,* 165 F.2d 977, 979–80 (2d Cir. 1948); *Federal Provision Co.* v. *Ershowsky,* 94 F.2d 574, 575 (2d Cir. 1938); *In re Riceputo,* 41 F.Supp. 926, 927–28 (E.D.N.Y.1941).

Rule 4006

NOTICE OF NO DISCHARGE

If an order is entered denying or revoking a discharge or if a waiver of discharge is filed, the clerk, after the order becomes final or the waiver is filed, shall promptly give notice thereof to all creditors in the manner provided in Rule 2002.

Amended Mar. 30, 1987, eff. Aug. 1, 1987.

Advisory Committee Note

The suspension by § 108(c) of the Code of the statute of limitations affecting any debt of a debtor terminates within 30 days after the debtor is denied a discharge or otherwise loses his right to a discharge. If, however, a debtor's failure to receive a discharge does not come to the attention of his creditors until after the statutes of limitations have run, the debtor obtains substantially the same benefits from his bankruptcy as a debtor who is discharged.

This rule requires the clerk to notify creditors if a debtor fails to obtain a discharge because a waiver of discharge was filed under § 727(a)(10) or as a result of an order denying or revoking the discharge under § 727(a) or (d).

Rule 4007

DETERMINATION OF DISCHARGEABILITY OF A DEBT

(a) Persons Entitled to File Complaint. A debtor or any creditor may file a complaint with the court to obtain a determination of the dischargeability of any debt.

(b) Time for Commencing Proceeding Other Than Under § 523(c) of the Code. A complaint other than under § 523(c) may be filed at any time. A case may be reopened without payment of an additional filing fee for the purpose of filing a complaint to obtain a determination under this rule.

(c) Time for Filing Complaint Under § 523(c) in Chapter 7 Liquidation and Chapter 11 Reorganization Cases; Notice of Time Fixed. A complaint to determine the dischargeability of any debt pursuant to § 523(c) of the Code shall be filed not later than 60 days following the first date set for the meeting of creditors held pursuant to § 341(a). The court shall give all creditors not less than 30 days notice of the time so fixed in the manner provided in Rule 2002. On motion of any party in interest, after hearing on notice, the court may for cause extend the time fixed under this subdivision. The motion shall be made before the time has expired.

(d) Time for Filing Complaint Under § 523(c) in Chapter 13 Individual's Debt Adjustment Cases; Notice of Time Fixed. On motion by a debtor for a discharge under § 1328(b), the court shall enter an order fixing a time for the filing of a complaint to determine the dischargeability of any debt pursuant to § 523(c) and shall give not less than 30 days notice of the time fixed to all creditors in the manner provided in Rule 2002. On motion of any party in interest after hearing on notice the court may for cause extend the time fixed under this subdivision. The motion shall be made before the time has expired.

(e) Applicability of Rules in Part VII. A proceeding commenced by a complaint filed under this rule is governed by Part VII of these rules.

Amended Mar. 30, 1987, eff. Aug. 1, 1987.

Advisory Committee Note

This rule prescribes the procedure to be followed when a party requests the court to determine dischargeability of a debt pursuant to § 523 of the Code.

Although a complaint that comes within § 523(c) must ordinarily be filed before determining whether the debtor will be discharged, the court need not determine the issues presented by the complaint filed under this rule until the question of discharge has been determined under Rule 4004. A complaint filed under this rule initiates an adversary proceeding as provided in Rule 7003.

Subdivision (b) does not contain a time limit for filing a complaint to determine the dischargeability of a type of debt listed as nondischargeable under § 523(a)(1), (3), (5), (7), (8), or (9). Jurisdiction over this issue on these debts is held concurrently by the bankruptcy court and any appropriate nonbankruptcy forum.

Subdivision (c) differs from subdivision (b) by imposing a deadline for filing complaints to determine the issue of dischargeability of debts set out in § 523(a)(2), (4) or (6) of the Code. The bankruptcy court has exclusive jurisdiction to determine dischargeability of these debts. If a complaint is not timely filed, the debt is discharged. See § 523(c).

Subdivision (e). The complaint required by this subdivision should be filed in the court in which the case is pending pursuant to Rule 5005.

Rule 4008

DISCHARGE AND REAFFIRMATION HEARING

Not more than 30 days following the entry of an order granting or denying a discharge, or confirming a plan in a chapter 11 reorganization case concerning an individual debtor and on not less than 10 days notice to the debtor and the trustee, the court shall hold a hearing as provided in § 524(d) of the Code. A motion by the debtor for approval of a reaffirmation agreement shall be filed before or at the hearing.

Advisory Committee Note

Section 524(d) of the Code requires the court to hold a hearing to inform an individual debtor concerning the granting or denial of discharge and the law applicable to reaffirmation agreements.

The notice of the § 524(d) hearing may be combined with the notice of the meeting of creditors or entered as a separate order.

The expression "not more than" contained in the first sentence of the rule is for the explicit purpose of requiring the hearing to occur within that time period and cannot be extended.

PART V

COURTS AND CLERKS

Rule
5001. Courts and Clerks' Offices
5002. Restrictions on Appointments
5003. Records Kept by the Clerk
5004. Disqualification
5005. Filing of Papers
5006. Certification of Copies of Papers
5007. Record of Proceedings and Transcripts
5008. Funds of the Estate
5009. Closing Cases
5010. Reopening Cases
5011. Withdrawal and Abstention From Hearing a Proceeding

Rule 5001

COURTS AND CLERKS' OFFICES

(a) Courts Always Open. The courts shall be deemed always open for the purpose of filing any pleading or other proper paper, issuing and returning process, and filing, making, or entering motions, orders and rules.

(b) Trials and Hearings; Orders in Chambers. All trials and hearings shall be conducted in open court and so far as convenient in a regular court room. All other acts or proceedings may be done or conducted by a judge in chambers and at any place either within or without the district; but no hearing, other than one ex parte, shall be conducted outside the district without the consent of all parties affected thereby.

(c) Clerk's Office. The clerk's office with the clerk or a deputy in attendance shall be open during business hours on all days except Saturdays, Sundays and the legal holidays listed in Rule 6(a) F.R.Civ.P.

Amended Mar. 30, 1987, eff. Aug. 1, 1987.

Advisory Committee Note

This rule is adapted from subdivisions (a), (b) and (c) of Rule 77 F.R. Civ.P.

Advisory Committee Notes to 1987 Amendments

Rule 9001, as amended, defines court to mean the bankruptcy judge or district judge before whom a case or proceeding is pending. Clerk means the bankruptcy clerk, if one has been appointed for the district; if a bankruptcy clerk has not been appointed, clerk means clerk of the district court.

Rule 5002

RESTRICTIONS ON APPOINTMENTS

(a) Appointment of Relatives Prohibited. No individual may be appointed as a trustee or examiner or be employed as an attorney, accountant, appraiser, auctioneer, or other professional person pursuant to § 327 or § 1103 of the Code if the individual is a relative of the bankruptcy judge making the appointment or approving the employment. Whenever under this subdivision an individual is ineligible for appointment or employment, the individual's firm, partnership, corporation, or any other form of business association or relationship, and all members, associates and professional employees thereof are also ineligible for appointment or employment.

(b) Judicial Determination that Appointment or Employment Is Improper. A bankruptcy judge may not appoint a person as a trustee or examiner or approve the employment of a person as an attorney, accountant, appraiser, auctioneer, or other professional person pursuant to § 327 or § 1103 of the Code if that person is or has been so connected with such judge as to render the appointment or employment improper.

Amended Apr. 29, 1985, eff. Aug. 1, 1985.

Advisory Committee Note

This rule is adapted from former Bankruptcy Rule 505(a). The scope of the prohibition on appointment or employment is expanded to include an examiner appointed under § 1104 of the Code and attorneys and other professional persons whose employment must be approved by the court under § 327 or § 1103.

The rule supplements two statutory provisions. Under 18 U.S.C. § 1910, it is a criminal offense for a judge to appoint a relative as a trustee and, under 28 U.S.C. § 458, a person may not be "appointed to or employed in any office or duty in any court" if he is a relative of any judge of that court. The rule prohibits the appointment or employment of a relative of a bankruptcy judge in a case pending before that bankruptcy judge or before other bankruptcy judges sitting within the district.

A relative is defined in § 101(34) of the Code to be an "individual related by affinity or consanguinity within the third degree as determined by the common law, or individual in a step or adoptive relationship within such third degree." Persons within the third degree under the common law system are as follows: first degree—parents, brothers and sisters, and children; second degree—grandparents, uncles and aunts, first cousins, nephews and nieces, and grandchildren; third degree—great grandparents, great uncles and aunts, first cousins once removed, second cousins, grand nephews and nieces, great grandchildren. Rule 9001 incorporates the definitions of § 101 of the Code.

In order for the policy of this rule to be meaningfully implemented, it is necessary to extend the prohibition against appointment or employment to the firm or other business association of the ineligible person and to those affiliated with the firm or business association. "Firm" is defined in Rule 9001 to include a professional partnership or corporation of attorneys or accountants. All other types of business and professional associations and relationships are covered by this rule.

Advisory Committee Notes to 1985 Amendments

The amended rule is divided into two subdivisions. Subdivision (a) applies to relatives of bankruptcy judges and subdivision (b) applies to persons who are or have been connected with bankruptcy judges. Subdivision (a) permits no judicial discretion; subdivision (b) allows judicial discretion. In both subdivisions of the amended rule "bankruptcy judge" has been substituted for "judge." The amended rule makes clear that it only applies to relatives of, or persons connected with, the bankruptcy judge. *See In re Hilltop Sand and Gravel, Inc.*, 35 B.R. 412 (N.D.Ohio 1983).

Subdivision (a). The original rule prohibited all bankruptcy judges in a district from appointing or approving the employment of (i) a relative of any bankruptcy judge serving in the district, (ii) the firm or business association of any ineligible relative and (iii) any member or professional employee of the firm or business association of an ineligible relative. In addition, the definition of relative, the third degree relationship under the common law, is quite broad. The restriction on the employment opportunities of relatives of bankruptcy judges was magnified by the fact that many law and accounting firms have practices and offices spanning the nation.

Relatives are not eligible for appointment or employment when the bankruptcy judge to whom they are related makes the appointment or approves the employment. Canon 3(b)(4) of the Code of Judicial Conduct, which provides that the judge "shall exercise his power of appointment only on the basis of merit, avoiding nepotism and favoritism," should guide a bankruptcy judge when a relative of a judge of the same bankruptcy court is considered for appointment or employment.

Subdivision (b), derived from clause (2) of the original rule, makes a person ineligible for appointment or employment if the person is so connected with a bankruptcy judge making the appointment or approving the employment as to render the appointment or approval of employment improper. The caption and text of the subdivision emphasize that application of the connection test is committed to the sound discretion of the bankruptcy judge who is to make the appointment or approve the employment. All relevant circumstances are to be taken into account by the court. The most important of those circumstances include: the nature and duration of the connection with the bankruptcy judge; whether the connection still exists, and, if not, when it was terminated; and the type of appointment or employment. These and other considerations must be carefully evaluated by the bankruptcy judge.

The policy underlying subdivision (b) is essentially the same as the policy embodied in the Code of Judicial Conduct. Canon 2 of the Code of Judicial Conduct instructs a judge to avoid impropriety and the appearance of impropriety, and Canon 3(b)(4) provides that the judge "should exercise his power of appointment only on the basis of merit, avoiding nepotism and favoritism." Subdivision (b) alerts the potential appointee or employee and party seeking approval of employment to consider the possible relevance or impact of subdivision (b) and indicates to them that appropriate disclosure must be made to the bankruptcy court before accepting appointment or employment. The information required may be made a part of the application for approval of employment. See Rule 2014(a).

Subdivision (b) departs from the former rule in an important respect: a firm or business association is not prohibited from appointment or employment merely because an individual member or employee of the firm or business association is ineligible under subdivision (b).

The emphasis given to the bankruptcy court's judicial discretion in applying subdivision (b) and the absence of a *per se* extension of ineligibility to the firm or business association or any ineligible individual complement the amendments to subdivision (a). The change is intended to moderate the prior limitation on the employment opportunities of attorneys, accountants, and other professional persons who are or who have been connected in some way with the bankruptcy judge. For example, in all but the most unusual situations, serve as a law clerk to a bankruptcy judge is not the type of connection which alone precludes appointment or employment. Even if a bankruptcy judge determines that it is improper to appoint or approve the employment of a former law clerk in the period immediately after completion of the former law clerk's service with the judge, the firm which employs the former law clerk will, absent other circumstances, be eligible for employment. In each instance all the facts must be considered by the bankruptcy judge.

Subdivision (b) applies to persons connected with a bankruptcy judge. "Person" is defined in § 101 of the Bankruptcy Code to include an "individual, partnership and corporation." A partnership or corporation may be appointed or employed to serve in a bankruptcy case. If a bankruptcy judge is connected in some way with a partnership or corporation, it is necessary for the court to determine whether the appointment or employment of that partnership or corporation is proper.

The amended rule does not regulate professional relationships which do not require approval of a bankruptcy judge. Disqualification of the bankruptcy judge pursuant to 28 U.S.C. § 455 may, however, be appropriate. Under Rule 5004(a), a bankruptcy judge may find that disqualification from only some aspect of the case, rather than the entire case, is necessary. A situation may also arise in which the disqualifying circumstance only comes to light after services have been performed. Rule 5004(b) provides that if compensation from the estate is sought for these services, the bankruptcy judge is disqualified from awarding compensation.

Rule 5003

RECORDS KEPT BY THE CLERK

(a) **Bankruptcy Dockets.** The clerk shall keep a docket in each case under the Code and shall enter thereon each judgment, order, and activity in that case as prescribed by the Director of the Administrative Office of the United States Courts. The entry of a judgment or order in a docket shall show the date the entry is made.

(b) **Claims Register.** The clerk shall keep in a claims register a list of claims filed in a case when it appears that there will be a distribution to unsecured creditors.

(c) **Judgments and Orders.** The clerk shall keep, in the form and manner as the Director of the Administrative Office of the United States Courts may prescribe, a correct copy of every final judgment or order affecting title to or lien on real property or for the recovery of money or property, and any other order which the court may direct to be kept. On request of the prevailing party, a correct copy of every judgment or order affecting title to or lien upon real or personal property or for the recovery of money or property shall be kept and indexed with the civil judgments of the district court.

(d) **Index of Cases; Certificate of Search.** The clerk shall keep indices of all cases and adversary proceedings as prescribed by the Director of the Administrative Office of the United States Courts. On request, the clerk shall make a search of any index and papers in the clerk's custody and certify whether a case or proceeding has been filed in or transferred to the court or if a discharge has been entered in its records.

(e) Other Books and Records of the Clerk. The clerk shall also keep such other books and records as may be required by the Director of the Administrative Office of the United States Courts.

Amended Mar. 30, 1987, eff. Aug. 1, 1987.

Advisory Committee Note

This rule consolidates former Bankruptcy Rules 504 and 507. The record-keeping duties of the referee under former Bankruptcy Rule 504 are transferred to the clerk. Subdivisions (a), (c), (d) and (e) are similar to subdivisions (a)–(d) of Rule 79 F.R.Civ.P.

Subdivision (b) requires that filed claims be listed on a claims register only when there may be a distribution to unsecured creditors. Compilation of the list for no asset or nominal asset cases would serve no purpose.

Rule 2013 requires the clerk to maintain a public record of fees paid from the estate and an annual summary thereof.

Former Bankruptcy Rules 507(d) and 508, which made materials in the clerk's office and files available to the public, are not necessary because § 107 of the Code guarantees public access to files and dockets of cases under the Code.

Advisory Committee Notes to 1987 Amendments

Subdivision (a) has been made more specific.

Subdivision (c) is amended to require that on the request of the prevailing party the clerk of the district court shall keep and index bankruptcy judgments and orders affecting title to or lien upon real or personal property or for the recovery of money or property with the civil judgments of the district court. This requirement is derived from former Rule 9021(b). The Director of the Administrative Office will provide guidance to the bankruptcy and district court clerks regarding appropriate paperwork and retention procedures.

Rule 5004

DISQUALIFICATION

(a) Disqualification of Judge. A bankruptcy judge shall be governed by 28 U.S.C. § 455, and disqualified from presiding over the proceeding or contested matter in which the disqualifying circumstance arises or, if appropriate, shall be disqualified from presiding over the case.

(b) Disqualification of Judge From Allowing Compensation. A bankruptcy judge shall be disqualified from allowing compensation to a person who is a relative of the bankruptcy judge or with whom the judge is so connected as to render it improper for the judge to authorize such compensation.

Amended Apr. 29, 1985, eff. Aug. 1, 1985; amended Mar. 30, 1987, eff. Aug. 1, 1987.

Advisory Committee Note

Subdivision (a). Disqualification of a bankruptcy judge is governed by 28 U.S.C. § 455. That section provides that the judge "shall disqualify himself in any proceeding in which his impartiality might reasonably be questioned" or under certain other circumstances. In a case under the Code it is possible that the disqualifying circumstance will be isolated to an adversary proceeding or contested matter. The rule makes it clear that when the disqualifying circumstance is limited in that way the judge need only disqualify himself from presiding over that adversary proceeding or contested matter.

It is possible, however, that even if the disqualifying circumstance arises in connection with an adversary proceeding, the effect will be so pervasive that disqualification from presiding over the case is appropriate. This distinction is consistent with the definition of "proceeding" in 28 U.S.C. § 455(d)(1).

Subdivision (b) precludes a bankruptcy judge from allowing compensation from the estate to a relative or other person closely associated with the judge. The subdivision applies where the judge has not appointed or approved the employment of the person requesting compensation. Perhaps the most frequent application of the subdivision will be in the allowance of administrative expenses under § 503(b)(3)–(5) of the Code. For example, if an attorney or accountant is retained by an indenture trustee who thereafter makes a substantial contribution in a chapter 11 case, the attorney or accountant may seek compensation under § 503(b)(4). If the attorney or accountant is a relative of or associated with the bankruptcy judge, the judge may not allow compensation to the attorney or accountant. Section 101(34) defines relative and Rule 9001 incorporates the definitions of the Code. See the Advisory Committee's Note to Rule 5002.

Advisory Committee Notes to 1985 Amendments

Subdivision (a) was affected by the Bankruptcy Amendments and Federal Judgeship Act of 1984, P.L. 98–353, 98 Stat. 333. The 1978 Bankruptcy Reform Act, P.L. 95–598, included bankruptcy judges in the definition of United States judges in 28 U.S.C. § 451 and they were therefore subject to the provisions of 28 U.S.C. § 455. This was to become effective on April 1, 1984, P.L. 95–598, § 404(b). Section 113 of P.L. 98–353, however, appears to have rendered the amendment to 28 U.S.C. § 451 ineffective. Subdivision (a) of the rule retains the substance and intent of the earlier draft by making bankruptcy judges subject to 28 U.S.C. § 455.

The word "associated" in subdivision (b) has been changed to "connected" in order to conform with Rule 5002(b).

Advisory Committee Notes to 1987 Amendments

The rule is amended to be gender neutral. The bankruptcy judge before whom the matter is pending determines whether disqualification is required.

604

Rule 5005

FILING OF PAPERS

(a) Filing. The proofs of claim or interest, complaints, motions, applications, objections and other papers required to be filed by these rules, except as provided in 28 U.S.C. § 1409, shall be filed with the clerk in the district where the case under the Code is pending. The judge of that court may permit the papers to be filed with the judge, in which event the filing date shall be noted thereon, and they shall be forthwith transmitted to the clerk.

(b) Error in Filing. A paper intended to be filed but erroneously delivered to the trustee, the attorney for the trustee, a bankruptcy judge, a district judge, or the clerk of the district court shall, after the date of its receipt has been noted thereon, be transmitted forthwith to the clerk of the bankruptcy court. In the interest of justice, the court may order that the paper shall be deemed filed as of the date of its original delivery.

Amended Mar. 30, 1987, eff. Aug. 1, 1987.

Advisory Committee Note

Subdivision (a) is an adaptation of Rule 5(e) F.R.Civ.P. Sections 301–304 of the Code and Rules 1002 and 1003 require that cases under the Code be commenced by filing a petition "with the bankruptcy court." Other sections of the Code and other rules refer to or contemplate filing but there is no specific reference to filing with the bankruptcy court. For example, § 501 of the Code requires filing of proofs of claim and Rule 3016(c) requires the filing of a disclosure statement. This subdivision applies to all situations in which filing is required. Except when filing in another district is authorized by 28 U.S.C. § 1473, all papers, including complaints commencing adversary proceedings, must be filed in the court where the case under the Code is pending.

Subdivision (b) is the same as former Bankruptcy Rule 509(c).

Advisory Committee Notes to 1987 Amendments

Subdivision (a) is amended to conform with the 1984 amendments.

Rule 5006

CERTIFICATION OF COPIES OF PAPERS

The clerk shall issue a certified copy of the record of any proceeding in a case under the Code or of any paper filed with the court on payment of any prescribed fee.

Advisory Committee Note

Fees for certification and copying are fixed by the Judicial Conference under 28 U.S.C. § 1930(b).

Rule 1101 F.R.Evid. makes the Federal Rules of Evidence applicable to cases under the Code. Rule 1005 F.R.Evid. allows the contents of an official record or of a paper filed with the court to be proved by a duly certified copy.

A copy certified and issued in accordance with Rule 5006 is accorded authenticity by Rule 902(4) F.R.Evid.

Rule 5007

RECORD OF PROCEEDINGS AND TRANSCRIPTS

(a) Filing of Record or Transcript. The reporter or operator of a recording device shall certify the original notes of testimony, tape recording, or other original record of the proceeding and promptly file them with the clerk. The person preparing any transcript shall promptly file a certified copy with the clerk.

(b) Transcript Fees. The fees for copies of transcripts shall be charged at rates prescribed by the Judicial Conference of the United States. No fee may be charged for the certified copy filed with the clerk.

(c) Admissibility of Record in Evidence. A certified sound recording or a transcript of a proceeding shall be admissible as prima facie evidence to establish the record.

Amended Mar. 30, 1987, eff. Aug. 1, 1987.

Advisory Committee Note

This rule supplements 28 U.S.C. § 773. A record of proceedings before the bankruptcy judge is to be made whenever practicable. By whatever means the record is made, subdivision (a) requires that the preparer of the record certify and file the original notes, tape recording, or other form of sound recording of the proceedings. Similarly, if a transcript is requested, the preparer is to file a certified copy with the clerk.

Subdivision (b) is derived from 28 U.S.C. § 753(f).

Subdivision (c) is derived from former Bankruptcy Rule 511(c). This subdivision extends to a sound recording the same evidentiary status as a transcript under 28 U.S.C. § 773(b).

Rule 5008

FUNDS OF THE ESTATE

(a) Court Approval Required. A deposit or investment for which a bond or deposit of securities is required under § 345(b) of the Code shall not be made until the court, on motion with such notice as the court directs, approves the bond or the deposit of securities.

(b) Report of Deposit or Investment. Promptly after making the initial deposit or investment of the estate's funds and thereafter as the court may direct, the trustee shall file a report which identifies the depository or describes the investment and states the amount of any deposit or investment and whether any portion is insured or guaranteed by the United States or a department, agency, or instrumentality of the United States, or backed by the full faith and credit of the United States.

(c) Deposit of Securities; Agreement. Securities accepted for deposit in lieu of a surety on a depository bond shall be deposited in the custody of the Federal Reserve Bank or branch thereof designated by the court or in the custody of such other person as the court may direct. The securities shall be deposited conditioned on proper accounting for all money deposited or invested and for any return on any such money, prompt repayment of such money and return thereon, and faithful performance of the duties as a depository or entity with whom an investment is made. The entity depositing securities shall execute an agreement for the deposit of securities in favor of the United States which incorporates the foregoing conditions. Securities subject to such an agreement shall be subject to the order of the court.

(d) **Action on Bond or Agreement for Deposit of Securities.** Proceedings on a bond given pursuant to § 345(b) of the Code or on an agreement for deposit of securities required by subdivision (c) of this rule shall be in the name of the United States for the use of the estate or any entity injured by a breach of the condition.

(e) **Prohibition of Deposits When Adequacy of Security Doubtful.** No trustee or other person shall deposit or invest funds received or held as a fiduciary under the Code if there is reasonable cause to believe that the bond or the security therefor or the deposited securities are or may be inadequate in view of existing and expected deposits or investments.

(f) **Reports Required.** Depositories and entities with whom deposits or investments are made shall file reports as prescribed by regulations of the Director of the Administrative Office of the United States Courts.

(g) **Deficiency in Amount of Bond or Deposited Securities.** Whenever the bond and any deposited securities do not or will not constitute adequate security because of existing and expected deposits or investments, the court shall require the depository or entity with whom an investment is made to increase the amount of the bond or the deposited securities within a fixed time. If within the time fixed the depository or entity with whom an investment is made fails to increase the amount of the bond or the deposited securities to an amount adequate for existing and expected deposits or investments, the court shall order immediate payment of all money on deposit or invested with it, with all interest payable thereon.

(h) **Relief From Liability on Bond.** A surety on a bond may move to be relieved from liability with respect to any subsequent default. If after hearing on notice to the depository or entity with whom the investment is made, to other sureties, to trustees and to other representatives of estates having money of the estate protected by the bond, the court determines that the motion may be granted without injury to any party in interest, the surety shall be relieved after a new bond or other appropriate security is submitted and approved.

(i) **Combining of Funds for Deposit.** The court may authorize the deposit or investment of funds from more than one estate in a single account or investment instrument. The trustee shall maintain records identifying separately the money of each estate. The court shall require that a statement of account be filed at least quarterly.

Amended Mar. 30, 1987, eff. Aug. 1, 1987.

Advisory Committee Note

Subdivision (a). Section 345 of the Code permits the trustee to deposit or invest money of the estate without prior approval of the court. The trustee may select any kind of financial institution as a depository and any form of investment instrument. Except when the deposit or investment is backed by the United States, the depository must either post a bond or deposit securities. Section 345(b)(1)(B) requires court approval of the bond. Subdivision (a) requires that the court's approval of the bond be obtained before funds of the estate are deposited or invested. The same requirement of prior court approval is also made applicable to the deposit of securities.

Subdivision (b) requires that the initial deposit or investment of the estate's funds be reported to the court. A local rule or order may require the filing of additional reports concerning the management of the estate's funds. If the deposit or investment is not backed by the United States, the report should identify the order of the court approving the bond or the deposit of securities. The court may direct that the report of initial deposits or investments or other reports be provided to creditors or other parties in interest.

Subdivision (c) is an adaptation of former Bankruptcy Rule 512(b). This subdivision makes the conditions of the bond specified in § 345(b)(1) of the Code applicable to a deposit of securities under § 345(b)(2) and also requires the execution of an agreement for deposit of securities which incorporates these conditions. The first sentence of the subdivision goes beyond the comparable provision in former Bankruptcy Rule 512(b) by specifically authorizing the court to permit the securities to be held by an entity other than the Federal Reserve Bank.

Subdivision (d)–(h) are derived from former Bankruptcy Rule 512.

Subdivision (i) authorizes the court to permit a trustee to combine money of more than one estate for the purposes of deposit or investment. Combined deposits or investments may be particularly beneficial when a standing chapter 13 trustee has a large number of plans to administer. The subdivision requires that at least quarterly statements of account be filed, but leaves to the court the form of the account and whether more frequent reports should be filed.

Rule 5009

CLOSING CASES

When an estate has been fully administered and the court has discharged the trustee, the case shall be closed.

Advisory Committee Note

This rule is the same as § 350(a) of the Code. An estate may be closed even though the period allowed by Rule 3002(c) for filing claims has not expired. The closing of a case may be expedited when a notice of no dividends is given under Rule 2002(e). Dismissal of a case for want of prosecution or failure to pay filing fees is governed by Rule 1017.

Rule 5010

REOPENING CASES

A case may be reopened on motion of the debtor or other party in interest pursuant to § 350(b) of the Code. In a Chapter 7 or 13 case a trustee shall be appointed unless the court determines that a trustee is not necessary to protect the interests of creditors and the debtor or to insure efficient administration of the case.

Amended Mar. 30, 1987, eff. Aug. 1, 1987.

Advisory Committee Note

Section 350(b) of the Code provides: "A case may be reopened in the court in which such case was closed to administer assets, to accord relief to the debtor, or for other cause."

Rule 9024, which incorporates Rule 60 F.R.Civ.P., exempts motions to reopen cases under the Code from the one year limitation of Rule 60(b).

Although a case has been closed the court may sometimes act without reopening the case. Under Rule 9024, clerical errors in judgments, orders, or other parts of the record or errors therein caused by oversight or omission may be corrected. A judgment determined to be non-dischargeable pursuant to Rule 4007 may be enforced after a case is closed by a writ of execution obtained pursuant to Rule 7069.

Advisory Committee Notes to 1987 Amendments

In order to avoid unnecessary cost and delay, the rule is amended to permit reopening of a case without the appointment of a trustee when the services of a trustee are not needed.

Rule 5011

WITHDRAWAL AND ABSTENTION FROM HEARING A PROCEEDING

(a) **Withdrawal.** A motion for withdrawal of a case or proceeding shall be heard by a district judge.

(b) **Abstention From Hearing a Proceeding.** Unless a district judge orders otherwise, a motion for abstention pursuant to 28 U.S.C. § 1334(c) shall be heard by the bankruptcy judge, who shall file a report and recommendation for disposition of the motion. The clerk shall serve forthwith a copy of the report and recommendation on the parties to the proceeding. Within 10 days of being served with a copy of the report and recommendation a party may serve and file with the clerk objections prepared in the manner provided in Rule 9033(b). Review of the report and recommendation by the district court shall be governed by Rule 9033.

(c) **Effect of Filing of Motion for Withdrawal or Abstention.** The filing of a motion for withdrawal of a case or proceeding or for abstention pursuant to 28 U.S.C. § 1334(c) shall not stay the administration of the case or any proceeding therein before the bankruptcy judge except that the bankruptcy judge may stay, on such terms and conditions as are proper, proceedings pending disposition of the motion. A motion for a stay ordinarily shall be presented to the bankruptcy judge. A motion for a stay or relief from a stay filed in the district court shall state why it has not been presented to or obtained from the bankruptcy judge. Relief granted by the district judge shall be on such terms and conditions as the judge deems proper.

Adopted Mar. 30, 1987, eff. Aug. 1, 1987.

Advisory Committee Notes

Motions for withdrawal pursuant to 28 U.S.C. § 157(d) or abstention pursuant to 28 U.S.C. § 1334(c), like all other motions, are to be filed with the clerk as required by Rule 5005(a). If a bankruptcy clerk has been appointed for the district, all motions are filed with the bankruptcy clerk. The method for forwarding withdrawal motions to the district court will be established by administrative procedures.

Subdivision (a). Section 157(d) permits the district court to order withdrawal on its own motion or the motion of a party. Subdivision (a) of this rule makes it clear that the bankruptcy judge will not conduct hearings on a withdrawal motion. The withdrawal decision is committed exclusively to the district court.

Subdivision (b). A decision to abstain under 28 U.S.C. § 1334(c) is not appealable. The district court is vested originally with jurisdiction and the decision to relinquish that jurisdiction must ultimately be a matter for the district court. The bankruptcy judge ordinarily will be in the best position to evaluate the grounds asserted for abstention. This subdivision (b) provides that the initial hearing on the motion is before the bankruptcy judge. The procedure for review of the report and recommendation are governed by Rule 9033.

This rule does not apply to motions under § 305 of the Code for abstention from hearing a case. Judicial decisions will determine the scope of the bankruptcy judge's authority under § 305.

Subdivision (c). Unless the court so orders, proceedings are not stayed when motions are filed for withdrawal or for abstention from hearing a proceeding. Because of the district court's authority over cases and proceedings, the subdivision authorizes the district court to order a stay or modify a stay ordered by the bankruptcy judge.

PART VI

COLLECTION AND LIQUIDATION
OF THE ESTATE

Rule

6001. Burden of Proof as to Validity of Postpetition Transfer
6002. Accounting by Prior Custodian of Property of the Estate
6003. Disbursement of Money of the Estate
6004. Use, Sale, or Lease of Property
6005. Appraisers and Auctioneers
6006. Assumption, Rejection and Assignment of Executory Contracts
6007. Abandonment or Disposition of Property
6008. Redemption of Property From Lien or Sale
6009. Prosecution and Defense of Proceedings by Trustee or Debtor in Possession
6010. Proceeding to Avoid Indemnifying Lien or Transfer to Surety

Rule 6001

BURDEN OF PROOF AS TO VALIDITY
OF POSTPETITION TRANSFER

Any entity asserting the validity of a transfer under § 549 of the Code shall have the burden of proof.

Advisory Committee Note

This rule is derived from former Bankruptcy Rule 603. The Act contained, in § 70d, a provision placing the burden of proof on the same person as did Rule 603. The Code does not contain any directive with respect to the burden of proof. This omission, in all probability, resulted from the intention to leave matters affecting evidence to these rules. See H.Rep. No. 95–595, 95th Cong., 1st Sess. (1977) 293.

Rule 6002

ACCOUNTING BY PRIOR CUSTODIAN OF
PROPERTY OF THE ESTATE

(a) **Accounting Required.** Any custodian required by the Code to deliver property in the custodian's possession or control to the trustee shall promptly file a report and account with the court with respect to the property of the estate and the administration thereof.

(b) **Examination of Administration.** On the filing of the report and account required by subdivision (a) of this rule and after an examination has been made into the superseded administration, after hearing on notice the court shall determine the propriety of the administration, including the reasonableness of all disbursements.

Amended Mar. 30, 1987, eff. Aug. 1, 1987.

Advisory Committee Note

"Custodian" is defined in § 101(10) of the Code. The definition includes a trustee or receiver appointed in proceedings not under the Code, as well as an assignee for the benefit of creditors.

This rule prescribes the procedure to be followed by a custodian who under § 543 of the Code is required to deliver property to the trustee and to account for its disposition. The examination under subdivision (b) may be initiated (1) on the motion of the custodian required to account under subdivision (a) for an approval of his account and discharge thereon, (2) on the motion of, or the filing of an objection to the custodian's account by, the trustee or any other party in interest, or (3) on the court's own initiative. Rule 9014 applies to any contested matter arising under this rule.

Section 543(d) is similar to an abstention provision. It grants the bankruptcy court discretion to permit the custodian to remain in possession and control of the property. In that event, the custodian is excused from complying with § 543(a)–(c) and thus would not be required to turn over the property to the trustee. When there is no duty to turn over to the trustee, Rule 6002 would not be applicable.

Rule 6003

DISBURSEMENT OF MONEY OF THE ESTATE

Disbursement of estate funds shall be by check unless another method is approved by the court. On motion of a party in interest, the court may require countersignatures except that signature by the judge shall not be permitted.

Advisory Committee Note

This rule authorizes the trustee to disburse money of the estate not only by check but by any other method approved by the court. In this latter regard, it continues the flexibility introduced by former Bankruptcy Rule 605(c) to recognize that mechanisms for payments through bank accounts are subject to technological and other changes. Local rule or a court order in a particular case may prescribe record-keeping requirements. The second sentence implements the policy of removing judges from nonjudicial functions.

Rule 6004

USE, SALE, OR LEASE OF PROPERTY

(a) Notice of Proposed Use, Sale, or Lease of Property. Notice of a proposed use, sale, or lease of property, other than cash collateral, not in the ordinary course of business shall be given pursuant to Rule 2002(a)(2), (c)(1), and (i) and, if applicable, in accordance with § 363(b)(2) of the Code.

(b) Objection to Proposal. Except as provided in subdivisions (c) and (d) of this rule, an objection to a proposed use, sale, or lease of property shall be filed and served not less than five days before the date set for the proposed action or within the time fixed by the court. An objection to the proposed use, sale, or lease of property is governed by Rule 9014.

(c) Sale Free and Clear of Liens and Other Interests. A motion for authority to sell property free and clear of liens or other interests shall be made in accordance with Rule 9014 and shall be served on the parties who have liens or other interests in the property to be sold. The notice required by subdivision (a) of this rule shall include the date of the hearing on the motion and the time within which objections may be filed and served on the debtor in possession or trustee.

(d) Sale of Property Under $2,500. Notwithstanding subdivision (a) of this rule, when all of the nonexempt property of the estate has an aggregate gross value less than $2,500, it shall be sufficient to give a general notice of intent to sell such property other than in the ordinary course of business to all creditors, indenture trustees, committees appointed or elected pursuant to the Code and other persons as the court may direct. An objection to any such sale may be filed and served by a party in interest within 15 days of the mailing of the notice, or within the time fixed by the court. An objection is governed by Rule 9014.

(e) Hearing. If a timely objection is made pursuant to subdivision (b) or (d) of the rule, the date of the hearing thereon may be set in the notice given pursuant to subdivision (a) of this rule.

(f) Conduct of Sale Not In The Ordinary Course of Business.

(1) Public or Private Sale. All sales not in the ordinary course of business may be by private sale or by public auction. Unless it is impracticable, an itemized statement of the property sold, the name of each purchaser, and the price received for each item or lot or for the property as a whole if sold in bulk shall be filed with the clerk on completion of a sale. If the property is sold by an auctioneer, the auctioneer shall file the statement and furnish a copy to the trustee, debtor in possession, or chapter 13 debtor. If the property is not sold by an auctioneer, the trustee, debtor in possession, or chapter 13 debtor shall file the statement.

(2) Execution of Instruments. After a sale in accordance with this rule the debtor, the trustee, or debtor in possession, as the case may be, shall execute any instrument necessary or ordered by the court to effectuate the transfer to the purchaser.

Amended Mar. 30, 1987, eff. Aug. 1, 1987.

Advisory Committee Note

Subdivisions (a) and (b). Pursuant to § 363(b) of the Code, a trustee or debtor in possession may use, sell, or lease property other than in the ordinary course of business only after notice and hearing. Rule 2002(a), (c) and (i) specifies the time when notice of sale is to be given, the contents of the notice and the persons to whom notice is to be given of sales of property. Subdivision (a) makes those provisions applicable as well to notices for proposed use and lease of property.

The Code does not provide the time within which parties may file objections to a proposed sale. Subdivision (b) of the rule requires the objection to be in writing and filed not less than five days before the proposed action is to take place. The objection should also be served within that time on the person who is proposing to take the action which would be either the trustee or debtor in possession. This time period is subject to change by the court. In some instances there is a need to conduct a sale in a short period of time and the court is given discretion to tailor the requirements to the circumstances.

Subdivision (c). In some situations a notice of sale for different pieces of property to all persons specified in Rule 2002(a) may be uneconomic and inefficient. This is particularly true in some chapter 7 liquidation cases when there is property of relatively little value which must be sold by the trustee. Subdivision (c) allows a general notice of intent to sell when the aggregate value of the estate's property is less than $2,500. The gross value is the value of the property without regard to the amount of any debt secured by a lien on the property. It is not necessary to give a detailed notice specifying the time and place of a particular sale. Thus, the requirements of Rule 2002(c) need not be met. If this method of providing notice of sales is used, the subdivision specifies that parties in interest may serve and file objections to the proposed sale of any property within the class and the time for service and filing is fixed at not later than 15 days after mailing the notice. The court may fix a different time. Subdivision (c) would have little utility in chapter 11 cases. Pursuant to Rule 2002(i), the court can limit notices of sale to the creditors' committee appointed under § 1102 of the Code and the same burdens present in a small chapter 7 case would not exist.

Subdivision (d). If a timely objection is filed, a hearing is required with respect to the use, sale, or lease of property. Subdivision (d) renders the filing of an objection tantamount to requesting a hearing so as to require a hearing pursuant to §§ 363(b) and 102(1)(B)(i).

Subdivision (e) is derived in part from former Bankruptcy Rule 606(b) but does not carry forward the requirement of that rule that court approval be obtained for sales of property. Pursuant to § 363(b) court approval is not required unless timely objection is made to the proposed sale. The itemized statement or information required by the subdivision is not necessary when it would be impracticable to prepare it or set forth the information. For example, a liquidation sale of retail goods although not in the ordinary course of business may be on a daily ongoing basis and only summaries may be available.

The duty imposed by paragraph (2) does not affect the power of the bankruptcy court to order third persons to execute instruments transferring property purchased at a sale under this subdivision. See, *e.g., In re Rosenberg,* 138 F.2d 409 (7th Cir. 1943).

Advisory Committee Notes to 1987 Amendments

Subdivision (a) is amended to conform to the 1984 amendments to § 363(b)(2) of the Code.

Subdivision (b) is amended to provide that an objection to a proposed use, sale, or lease of property creates a contested matter governed by Rule 9014. A similar amendment is made to subdivision (d), which was formerly subdivision (c).

Subdivision (c) is new. Section 363(f) provides that sales free and clear of liens or other interests are only permitted if one of the five statutory requirements is satisfied. Rule 9013 requires that a motion state with particularity the grounds relied upon by the movant. A motion for approval of a sale free and clear of liens or other interests is subject to Rule 9014, service must be made on the parties holding liens or other interests in the property, and notice of the hearing on the motion and the time for filing objections must be included in the notice given under subdivision (a).

Rule 6005

APPRAISERS AND AUCTIONEERS

The order of the court approving the employment of an appraiser or auctioneer shall fix the amount or rate of his compensation. No officer or employee of the Judicial Branch of the United States or the United States Department of Justice shall be eligible to act as appraiser or auctioneer. No residence or licensing requirement shall disqualify an appraiser or auctioneer from employment.

Amended Mar. 30, 1987, eff. Aug. 1, 1987.

Advisory Committee Note

This rule is derived from former Bankruptcy Rule 606(c) and implements § 327 of the Code. Pursuant to § 327, the trustee or debtor in possession may employ one or more appraisers or auctioneers, subject to court approval. This rule requires the court order approving such employment to fix the amount or rate of compensation. The second sentence of the former rule is retained to continue to safeguard against imputations of favoritism which detract from public confidence in bankruptcy administration. The final sentence is to guard against imposition of parochial requirements not warranted by any consideration having to do with sound bankruptcy administration.

Reference should also be made to Rule 2013(a) regarding the limitation on employment of appraisers and auctioneers, and Rule 2014(a) regarding the application for appointment of an appraiser or auctioneer.

Rule 6006

ASSUMPTION, REJECTION AND ASSIGNMENT OF EXECUTORY CONTRACTS

(a) **Proceeding to Assume, Reject, or Assign.** A proceeding to assume, reject, or assign an executory contract, unexpired lease, or time share interest, other than as part of a plan, is governed by Rule 9014.

(b) **Proceeding to Require Trustee to Act.** A proceeding by a party to an executory contract, unexpired lease, or time share interest in a chapter 9 municipality case, chapter 11 reorganization case, or chapter 13 individual's debt adjustment case, to require the trustee, debtor in possession, or debtor to determine whether to assume or reject the contract, lease, or time share interest is governed by Rule 9014.

(c) **Hearing.** When a motion is made pursuant to subdivision (a) or (b) of this rule, the court shall set a hearing on notice to the other party to the contract and to other parties in interest as the court may direct.

Amended Mar. 30, 1987, eff. Aug. 1, 1987.

Advisory Committee Note

Section 365(a) of the Code requires court approval for the assumption or rejection of an executory contract by the trustee or debtor in possession. The trustee or debtor in possession may also assign an executory contract, § 365(f)(1), but must first assume the contract, § 365(f)(2). Rule 6006 provides a procedure for obtaining court approval. It does not apply to the automatic rejection of contracts which are not assumed in chapter 7 liquidation cases within 60 days after the order for relief, or to the assumption or rejection of contracts in a plan pursuant to § 1123(b)(2) or § 1322(b)(7).

Subdivision (a) by referring to Rule 9014 requires a motion to be brought for the assumption, rejection, or assignment of an executory contract. Normally, the motion will be brought by the trustee, debtor in possession or debtor in a chapter 9 or chapter 13 case. The authorization to assume a contract and to assign it may be sought in a single motion and determined by a single order.

Subdivision (b) makes applicable the same motion procedure when the other party to the contract seeks to require the chapter officer to take some action. Section 365(d)(2) recognizes that this procedure is available to these contractual parties. This provision of the Code and subdivision of the rule apply only in chapter 9, 11 and 13 cases. A motion is not necessary in chapter 7 cases because in those cases a contract is deemed rejected if the trustee does not timely assume it.

Subdivision (c) provides for the court to set a hearing on a motion made under subdivision (a) or (b). The other party to the contract should be given appropriate notice of the hearing and the court may order that other parties in interest, such as a creditors' committee, also be given notice.

Advisory Committee Notes to 1987 Amendments

Subdivisions (a) and (b) are amended to conform to the 1984 amendment to § 365 of the Code, which governs assumption or rejection of time share interests.

Section 1113, governing collective bargaining agreements, was added to the Code in 1984. It sets out requirements that must be met before a collective bargaining agreement may be rejected. The application to reject a collective bargaining agreement referred to in § 1113 shall be made by motion. The motion to reject creates a contested matter under Rule 9014, and service is made pursuant to Rule 7004 on the representative of the employees. The time periods set forth in § 1113(d) govern the scheduling of the hearing and disposition of a motion to reject the agreement.

Rule 6007

ABANDONMENT OR DISPOSITION OF PROPERTY

(a) Notice of Proposed Abandonment or Disposition; Objections. Unless otherwise directed by the court, the trustee or debtor in possession shall give notice of a proposed abandonment or disposition of property to all creditors, indenture trustees and committees appointed or elected pursuant to the Code. An objection may be filed and served by a party in interest within 15 days of the mailing of the notice, or within the time fixed by the court.

616

(b) Motion by Party In Interest. A party in interest may file and serve a motion requiring the trustee or debtor in possession to abandon property of the estate.

(c) Hearing. If a timely objection is made as prescribed by subdivision (a) of this rule, or if a motion is made as prescribed by subdivision (b), the court shall set a hearing on notice to the entities as the court may direct.

Amended Mar. 30, 1987, eff. Aug. 1, 1987.

Advisory Committee Note

Sections 554 and 725 of the Code permit and require abandonment and disposition of property of the estate. Pursuant to § 554, the trustee may abandon property but only after notice and hearing. This section is applicable in chapter 7, 11 and 13 cases. Section 725 requires the trustee to dispose of property in which someone other than the estate has an interest, prior to final distribution. It applies only in chapter 7 cases. Notice and hearing are also required conditions. Section 102(1) provides that "notice and hearing" is construed to mean appropriate notice and an opportunity for a hearing. Neither § 554 nor § 725 specify to whom the notices are to be sent. This rule does not apply to § 554(c). Pursuant to that subsection, property is deemed abandoned if it is not administered. A hearing is not required by the statute.

Subdivision (a) requires the notices to be sent to all creditors, indenture trustees, and committees elected under § 705 or appointed under § 1102 of the Code. This may appear burdensome, expensive and inefficient but the subdivision is in keeping with the Code's requirement for notice and the Code's intent to remove the bankruptcy judge from undisputed matters. The burden, expense and inefficiency can be alleviated in large measure by incorporating the notice into or together with the notice of the meeting of creditors so that separate notices would not be required.

Subdivision (b) implements § 554(b) which specifies that a party in interest may request an order that the trustee abandon property. The rule specifies that the request be by motion and, pursuant to the Code, lists the parties who should receive notice.

Subdivision (c) requires a hearing when an objection under subdivision (a) is filed or a motion under subdivision (b) is made. Filing of an objection is sufficient to require a hearing; a separate or joined request for a hearing is unnecessary since the objection itself is tantamount to such a request.

Rule 6008

REDEMPTION OF PROPERTY FROM LIEN OR SALE

On motion by the debtor, trustee, or debtor in possession and after hearing on notice as the court may direct, the court may authorize the redemption of property from a lien or from a sale to enforce a lien in accordance with applicable law.

Advisory Committee Note

This rule is derived from former Bankruptcy Rule 609. No provision in the Code addresses the trustee's right of redemption. Ordinarily the secured creditor should be given notice of the trustee's motion so that any objection may be raised to the proposed redemption.

The rule applies also to a debtor exercising a right of redemption pursuant to § 722. A proceeding under that section is governed by Rule 9014.

Rule 6009

PROSECUTION AND DEFENSE OF PROCEEDINGS BY TRUSTEE OR DEBTOR IN POSSESSION

With or without court approval, the trustee or debtor in possession may prosecute or may enter an appearance and defend any pending action or proceeding by or against the debtor, or commence and prosecute any action or proceeding in behalf of the estate before any tribunal.

Advisory Committee Note

This rule is derived from former Bankruptcy Rule 610.

Rule 6010

PROCEEDING TO AVOID INDEMNIFYING LIEN OR TRANSFER TO SURETY

If a lien voidable under § 547 of the Code has been dissolved by the furnishing of a bond or other obligation and the surety thereon has been indemnified by the transfer of, or the creation of a lien upon, nonexempt property of the debtor, the surety shall be joined as a defendant in any proceeding to avoid the indemnifying transfer or lien. Such proceeding is governed by the rules in Part VII. If an order is entered for the recovery of indemnifying property in kind or for the avoidance of an indemnifying lien, on motion by any party in interest after notice and hearing the court shall ascertain the value of such property or lien. If the value is less than the amount for which the property or lien is indemnity, the surety may elect to retain the property or lien on payment of the value so ascertained to the trustee or debtor in possession, within the time fixed by the court.

Advisory Committee Note

This rule is derived from former Bankruptcy Rule 612.

PART VII

ADVERSARY PROCEEDINGS

Rule
7001. Scope of Rules of Part VII
7002. References to Federal Rules of Civil Procedure
7003. Commencement of Adversary Proceeding
7004. Process; Service of Summons, Complaint
7005. Service and Filing of Pleadings and Other Papers
7007. Pleadings Allowed
7008. General Rules of Pleading
7009. Pleading Special Matters
7010. Form of Pleadings
7012. Defenses and Objections—When and How Presented—By Pleading or Motion—Motion for Judgment on the Pleadings
7013. Counterclaim and Cross-Claim
7014. Third-Party Practice
7015. Amended and Supplemental Pleadings
7016. Pre-Trial Procedure; Formulating Issues
7017. Parties Plaintiff and Defendant; Capacity
7018. Joinder of Claims and Remedies
7019. Joinder of Persons Needed for Just Determination
7020. Permissive Joinder of Parties
7021. Misjoinder and Non-Joinder of Parties
7022. Interpleader
7023. Class Proceedings
7023.1. Derivative Proceedings by Shareholders
7023.2. Adversary Proceedings Relating to Unincorporated Associations
7024. Intervention
7025. Substitution of Parties
7026. General Provisions Governing Discovery
7027. Depositions Before Adversary Proceedings or Pending Appeal
7028. Persons Before Whom Depositions May Be Taken
7029. Stipulations Regarding Discovery Procedure
7030. Depositions Upon Oral Examination
7031. Deposition Upon Written Questions
7032. Use of Depositions in Adversary Proceedings
7033. Interrogatories to Parties
7034. Production of Documents and Things and Entry Upon Land for Inspection and Other Purposes
7035. Physical and Mental Examination of Persons
7036. Requests for Admission
7037. Failure to Make Discovery: Sanctions
7040. Assignment of Cases for Trial
7041. Dismissal of Adversary Proceedings
7042. Consolidation of Adversary Proceedings; Separate Trials
7052. Findings by the Court
7054. Judgments; Costs
7055. Default
7056. Summary Judgment
7062. Stay of Proceedings to Enforce a Judgment

Rule

7064.   Seizure of Person or Property

7065.   Injunctions

7067.   Deposit in Court

7068.   Offer of Judgment

7069.   Execution

7070.   Judgment for Specific Acts; Vesting Title

7071.   Process in Behalf of and Against Persons Not Parties

7087.   Transfer of Adversary Proceeding

Rule 7001

SCOPE OF RULES OF PART VII

An adversary proceeding is governed by the rules of this Part VII. It is a proceeding (1) to recover money or property, except a proceeding to compel the debtor to deliver property to the trustee, or a proceeding under § 554(b) or § 725 of the Code, Rule 2017, or Rule 6002, (2) to determine the validity, priority, or extent of a lien or other interest in property, other than a proceeding under Rule 4003(d), (3) to obtain approval pursuant to § 363(h) for the sale of both the interest of the estate and of a co-owner in property, (4) to object to or revoke a discharge, (5) to revoke an order of confirmation of a chapter 11 or chapter 13 plan, (6) to determine the dischargeability of a debt, (7) to obtain an injunction or other equitable relief, (8) to subordinate any allowed claim or interest, except when subordination is provided in a chapter 9, 11, or 13 plan, (9) to obtain a declaratory judgment relating to any of the foregoing, or (10) to determine a claim or cause of action removed pursuant to 28 U.S.C. § 1452.

Amended Mar. 30, 1987, eff. Aug. 1, 1987.

Advisory Committee Note

The rules in Part VII govern the procedural aspects of litigation involving the matters referred to in this Rule 7001. Under Rule 9014 some of the Part VII rules also apply to contested matters.

These Part VII rules are based on the premise that to the extent possible practice before the bankruptcy courts and the district courts should be the same. These rules either incorporate or are adaptations of most of the Federal Rules of Civil Procedure. Although the Part VII rules of the former Bankruptcy Rules also relied heavily on the F.R.Civ.P., the former Part VII rules departed from the civil practice in two significant ways: a trial or pretrial conference had to be scheduled as soon as the adversary proceeding was filed and pleadings had to be filed within periods shorter than those established by the F.R.Civ.P. These departures from the civil practice have been eliminated.

The content and numbering of these Part VII rules correlates to the content and numbering of the F.R.Civ.P. Most, but not all, of the F.R.Civ.P. have a comparable Part VII rule. When there is no Part VII rule with a number corresponding to a particular F.R.Civ.P., Parts V and IX of these rules must be consulted to determine if one of the rules in those parts deals with the subject. The list below indicates the F.R.Civ.P., or subdivision thereof, covered by a rule in either Part V or Part IX.

F.R.Civ.P.	Rule in Part V or IX
6	9006
7(b)	9013
10(a)	9004(b)
11	9011
38, 39	9015(a)–(e)
47–51	9015(f)
43, 44, 44.1	9017
45	9016
58	9021
59	9023
60	9024
61	9005
63	9028
77(a), (b), (c)	5001
77(d)	9022(d)
79(a)–(d)	5003
81(c)	9027
83	9029
92	9030

Proceedings to which the rules in Part VII apply directly include those brought to avoid transfers by the debtor under §§ 544, 545, 547, 548 and 549 of the Code; subject to important exceptions, proceedings to recover money or property; proceedings on bonds under Rules 5008(d) and 9025; proceedings under Rule 4004 to determine whether a discharge in a chapter 7 or 11 case should be denied because of an objection grounded on § 727 and proceedings in a chapter 7 or 13 case to revoke a discharge as provided in §§ 727(d) or 1328(e); and proceedings initiated pursuant to § 523(c) of the Code to determine the dischargeability of a particular debt. Those proceedings were classified as adversary proceedings under former Bankruptcy Rule 701.

Also included as adversary proceedings are proceedings to revoke an order of confirmation of a plan in a chapter 11 or 13 case as provided in §§ 1144 and 1330, to subordinate under § 510(c), other than as part of a plan, an allowed claim or interest, and to sell under § 363(h) both the interest of the estate and a co-owner in property.

Declaratory judgments with respect to the subject matter of the various adversary proceedings are also adversary proceedings.

Any claim or cause of action removed to a bankruptcy court pursuant to 28 U.S.C. § 1478 is also an adversary proceeding.

Unlike former Bankruptcy Rule 701, requests for relief from an automatic stay do not commence an adversary proceeding. Section 362(e) of the Code and Rule 4001 establish an expedited schedule for judicial disposition of requests for relief from the automatic stay. The formalities of the adversary proceeding process and the time for serving pleadings are not well suited to the expedited schedule. The motion practice prescribed in Rule 4001 is best suited to such requests because the court has the flexibility to fix hearing dates and other deadlines appropriate to the particular situation.

Clause (1) contains important exceptions. A person with an interest in property in the possession of the trustee or debtor in possession may seek to recover or reclaim that property under § 554(b) or § 725 of the Code. Since many attempts to recover or reclaim property under these two sections do not generate disputes, application of the formalities of the Part VII Rules is not appropriate.   Also excluded from adversary proceedings is litigation arising from an examination under Rule 2017 of a debtor's payments of money or transfers of property to an attorney representing the debtor in a case under the Code or an examination of a superseded administration under Rule 6002.

Exemptions and objections thereto are governed by Rule 4003.   Filing of proofs of claim and the allowances thereof are governed by Rules 3001–3005, and objections to claims are governed by Rule 3007.   When an objection to a claim is joined with a demand for relief of the kind specified in this Rule 7001, the matter becomes an adversary proceeding.   See Rule 3007.

Advisory Committee Notes to 1987 Amendments

Another exception is added to clause (1).   A trustee may proceed by motion to recover property from the debtor.

Rule 7002

REFERENCES TO FEDERAL RULES OF CIVIL PROCEDURE

Whenever a Federal Rule of Civil Procedure applicable to adversary proceedings makes reference to another Federal Rule of Civil Procedure, the reference shall be read as a reference to the Federal Rule of Civil Procedure as modified in this Part VII.

Advisory Committee Note

Rules 5, 12, 13, 14, 25, 27, 30, 41 and 52 F.R.Civ.P. are made applicable to adversary proceedings by Part VII.   Each of those rules contains a cross reference to another Federal Rule; however, the Part VII rule which incorporates the cross-referenced Federal Rule modifies the Federal Rule in some way.   Under this Rule 7002 the cross reference is to the Federal Rule as modified by Part VII.   For example, Rule 5 F.R.Civ.P., which is made applicable to adversary proceedings by Rule 7005, contains a reference to Rule 4 F.R.Civ.P.   Under this Rule 7002, the cross reference is to Rule 4 F.R. Civ.P. as modified by Rule 7004.

Rules 7, 10, 12, 13, 14, 19, 22, 23.2, 24–37, 41, 45, 49, 50, 52, 55, 59, 60, 62 F.R.Civ.P. are made applicable to adversary proceedings by Part VII or generally to cases under the Code by Part IX.   Each of those Federal Rules contains a cross reference to another Federal Rule which is not modified by the Part VII or Part IX rule which makes the cross-referenced Federal Rule applicable.   Since the cross-referenced rule is not modified by a Part VII rule this Rule 7002 does not apply.

Rule 7003

COMMENCEMENT OF ADVERSARY PROCEEDING

Rule 3 F.R.Civ.P. applies in adversary proceedings.

Advisory Committee Note

Rule 5005(a) requires that a complaint commencing an adversary proceeding be filed with the court in which the case under the Code is pending unless 28 U.S.C. § 1473 authorizes the filing of the complaint in another district.

Rule 7004

PROCESS; SERVICE OF SUMMONS, COMPLAINT

(a) **Summons; Service; Proof of Service.** Rule 4(a), (b), (c)(2)(C)(i), (d), (e) and (g)–(j) F.R.Civ.P. applies in adversary proceedings. Personal service pursuant to Rule 4(d) F.R.Civ.P. may be made by any person not less than 18 years of age who is not a party and the summons may be delivered by the clerk to any such person.

(b) **Service by First Class Mail.** In addition to the methods of service authorized by Rule 4(c)(2)(C)(i) and (d) F.R.Civ.P., service may be made within the United States by first class mail postage prepaid as follows:

(1) Upon an individual other than an infant or incompetent, by mailing a copy of the summons and complaint to the individual's dwelling house or usual place of abode or to the place where the individual regularly conducts a business or profession.

(2) Upon an infant or an incompetent person, by mailing a copy of the summons and complaint to the person upon whom process is prescribed to be served by the law of the state in which service is made when an action is brought against such defendant in the courts of general jurisdiction of that state. The summons and complaint in such case shall be addressed to the person required to be served at that person's dwelling house or usual place of abode or at the place where the person regularly conducts a business or profession.

(3) Upon a domestic or foreign corporation or upon a partnership or other unincorporated association, by mailing a copy of the summons and complaint to the attention of an officer, a managing or general agent, or to any other agent authorized by appointment or by law to receive service of process and, if the agent is one authorized by statute to receive service and the statute so requires, by also mailing a copy to the defendant.

(4) Upon the United States, by mailing a copy of the summons and complaint to the United States attorney for the district in which the action is brought and also the Attorney General of the United States at Washington, District of Columbia, and in any action attacking the validity of an order of an officer or an agency of the United States not made a party, by also mailing a copy of the summons and complaint to such officer or agency.

(5) Upon any officer or agency of the United States, by mailing a copy of the summons and complaint to the United States as prescribed in paragraph (4) of this subdivision and also to the officer or agency. If the agency is a corporation, the mailing shall be as prescribed in paragraph (3) of this subdivision of this rule.

(6) Upon a state or municipal corporation or other governmental organization thereof subject to suit, by mailing a copy of the summons and complaint to the person or office upon whom process is prescribed to be served by the law of

the state in which service is made when an action is brought against such a defendant in the courts of general jurisdiction of that state, or in the absence of the designation of any such person or office by state law, then to the chief executive officer thereof.

(7) Upon a defendant of any class referred to in paragraph (1) or (3) of this subdivision of this rule, it is also sufficient if a copy of the summons and complaint is mailed to the entity upon whom service is prescribed to be served by any statute of the United States or by the law of the state in which service is made when an action is brought against such defendant in the court of general jurisdiction of that state.

(8) Upon any defendant, it is also sufficient if a copy of the summons and complaint is mailed to an agent of such defendant authorized by appointment or by law to receive service of process, at the agent's dwelling house or usual place of abode or at the place where the agent regularly carries on a business or profession and, if the authorization so requires, by mailing also a copy of the summons and complaint to the defendant as provided in this subdivision.

(9) Upon the debtor, after a petition has been filed by or served upon the debtor and until the case is dismissed or closed, by mailing copies of the summons and complaint to the debtor at the address shown in the petition or statement of affairs or to such other address as the debtor may designate in writing filed with the court and, if the debtor is represented by an attorney, to the attorney at the attorney's post-office address.

(c) Service by Publication. If a party to an adversary proceeding to determine or protect rights in property in the custody of the court cannot be served as provided in Rule 4(d) or (i) F.R.Civ.P. or subdivision (b) of this rule, the court may order the summons and complaint to be served by mailing copies thereof by first class mail postage prepaid, to the party's last known address and by at least one publication in such manner and form as the court may direct.

(d) Nationwide Service of Process. The summons and complaint and all other process except a subpoena may be served anywhere in the United States.

(e) Service on Debtor and Others in Foreign Country. The summons and complaint and all other process except a subpoena may be served as provided in Rule 4(d)(1) and (d)(3) F.R.Civ.P. in a foreign country (A) on the debtor, any person required to perform the duties of a debtor, any general partner of a partnership debtor, or any attorney who is a party to a transaction subject to examination under Rule 2017; or (B) on any party to an adversary proceeding to determine or protect rights in property in the custody of the court; or (C) on any person whenever such service is authorized by a federal or state law referred to in Rule 4(c)(2)(C)(i) or (e) F.R.Civ.P.

(f) Summons: Time Limit for Service. If service is made pursuant to Rule 4(d)(1)–(6) F.R.Civ.P. it shall be made by delivery of the summons and complaint within 10 days following issuance of the summons. If service is made by any authorized form of mail, the summons and complaint shall be deposited in the mail within 10 days following issuance of the summons. If a summons is not timely delivered or mailed, another summons shall be issued and served.

Amended Mar. 30, 1987, eff. Aug. 1, 1987.

Advisory Committee Note

Subdivision (a) of the rule, by incorporation of Rule 4(a), (b), (d), (e) and (g)–(i) F.R.Civ.P., governs the mechanics of issuance of a summons and its form, the manner of service on parties and their representatives, and service in foreign countries.

Subdivision (b), which is the same as former Rule 704(c), authorizes service of process by first class mail postage prepaid. This rule retains the modes of service contained in former Bankruptcy Rule 704. The former practice, in effect since 1976, has proven satisfactory.

Subdivision (c) is derived from former Bankruptcy Rule 704(d)(2).

Subdivision (d). Nationwide service of process is authorized by subdivision (d).

Subdivision (e) authorizes service by delivery on individuals and corporations in foreign countries if the party to be served is the debtor or any person required to perform the duties of the debtor and certain other persons, the adversary proceeding involves property in the custody of the bankruptcy court, or if federal or state law authorizes such service in a foreign country.

Subdivision (f). The requirement of former Bankruptcy Rule 704 that the summons be served within 10 days is carried over into these rules by subdivision (f).

Advisory Committee Notes to 1987 Amendments

Subdivision (a) is amended to make Rule 4(j) F.R.Civ.P. applicable to service of the summons. If service is not completed within 120 days of the filing of the complaint, the complaint may be dismissed.

Technical amendments are made to subdivisions (a), (b), (e), and (f) to conform to recent amendments to Rule 4 F.R.Civ.P.

Rule 7005

SERVICE AND FILING OF PLEADINGS AND OTHER PAPERS

Rule 5 F.R.Civ.P. applies in adversary proceedings.

Advisory Committee Note

Rule 5 F.R.Civ.P. refers to Rule 4 F.R.Civ.P. Pursuant to Rule 7002 this reference is to Rule 4 F.R.Civ.P. as incorporated and modified by Rule 7004.

Rule 7007

PLEADINGS ALLOWED

Rule 7 F.R.Civ.P. applies in adversary proceedings.

Rule 7008

GENERAL RULES OF PLEADING

(a) Applicability of Rule 8 F.R.Civ.P. Rule 8 F.R.Civ.P. applies in adversary proceedings. The allegation of jurisdiction required by Rule 8(a) shall also contain a reference to the name, number, and chapter of the case under the Code to which the adversary proceeding relates and to the district and division where the case under the Code is pending. In an adversary proceeding before a bankruptcy judge, the complaint, counterclaim, cross-claim, or third-party complaint shall contain a statement that the proceeding is core or non-core and, if non-core, that the pleader does or does not consent to entry of final orders or judgment by the bankruptcy judge.

(b) Attorney's Fees. A request for an award of attorney's fees shall be pleaded as a claim in a complaint, cross-claim, third-party complaint, answer, or reply as may be appropriate.

Amended Mar. 30, 1987, eff. Aug. 1, 1987.

Advisory Committee Notes to 1987 Amendments

Proceedings before a bankruptcy judge are either core or non-core. 28 U.S.C. § 157. A bankruptcy judge may enter a final order or judgment in a core proceeding. In a non-core proceeding, absent consent of the parties, the bankruptcy judge may not enter a final order or judgment but may only submit proposed findings of fact and conclusions of law to the district judge who will enter the final order or judgment. 28 U.S.C. § 157(c)(1). The amendment to subdivision (a) of this rule requires an allegation as to whether a proceeding is core or non-core. A party who alleges that the proceeding is non-core shall state whether the party does or does not consent to the entry of a final order or judgment by the bankruptcy judge. Failure to include the statement of consent does not constitute consent. Only express consent in the pleadings or otherwise is effective to authorize entry of a final order or judgment by the bankruptcy judge in a non-core proceeding. Amendments to Rule 7012 require that the defendant admit or deny the allegation as to whether the proceeding is core or non-core.

Rule 7009

PLEADING SPECIAL MATTERS

Rule 9 F.R.Civ.P. applies in adversary proceedings.

Rule 7010

FORM OF PLEADINGS

Rule 10 F.R.Civ.P. applies in adversary proceedings, except that the caption of each pleading in such a proceeding shall conform substantially to Official Form No. 34.

Rule 7012

DEFENSES AND OBJECTIONS—WHEN AND HOW PRESENTED—BY PLEADING OR MOTION—MOTION FOR JUDGMENT ON THE PLEADINGS

(a) When Presented. If a complaint is duly served, the defendant shall serve an answer within 30 days after the issuance of the summons, except when a different time is prescribed by the court. The court shall prescribe the time for service of the answer when service of a complaint is made by publication or upon a party in a foreign country. A party served with a pleading stating a cross-claim shall serve an answer thereto within 20 days after service. The plaintiff shall serve a reply to a counterclaim in the answer within 20 days after service of the answer or, if a reply is ordered by the court, within 20 days after service of the order, unless the order otherwise directs. The United States or an officer or agency thereof shall serve an answer to a complaint within 35 days after the issuance of the summons, and shall serve an answer to a cross-claim, or a reply to a counterclaim, within 35 days after service upon the United States attorney of the pleading in which the claim is asserted. The service of a motion permitted under this rule alters these periods of time as follows, unless a different time is fixed by order of the court: (1) if the court denies the motion or postpones its disposition until the trial on the merits, the responsive pleading shall be served within 10 days after notice of the court's action; (2) if the court grants a motion for a more definite statement, the responsive pleading shall be served within 10 days after the service of a more definite statement.

(b) Applicability of Rule 12(b)–(h) F.R.Civ.P. Rule 12(b)–(h) F.R.Civ.P. applies in adversary proceedings. A responsive pleading shall admit or deny an allegation that the proceeding is core or non-core. If the response is that the proceeding is non-core, it shall include a statement that the party does or does not consent to entry of final orders or judgment by the bankruptcy judge. In non-core proceedings final orders and judgments shall not be entered on the bankruptcy judge's order except with the express consent of the parties.

Amended Mar. 30, 1987, eff. Aug. 1, 1987.

Advisory Committee Note

Subdivision (a) continues the practice of former Bankruptcy Rule 712(a) by requiring that the answer to a complaint be filed within 30 days after the issuance of the summons. Under Rule 7004(f), the summons must be served within 10 days of issuance. The other pleading periods in adversary proceedings are the same as those in civil actions before the district courts, except that the United States is allowed 35 rather than 60 days to respond.

Rule 12(b)(7) and (h)(2) F.R.Civ.P. refers to Rule 19 F.R.Civ.P. Pursuant to Rule 7002 these references are to Rule 19 F.R.Civ.P. as incorporated and modified by Rule 7019.

Advisory Committee Notes to 1987 Amendments

The amendment to subdivision (b) requires a response to the allegation that the proceeding is core or non-core. A final order of judgment may not be entered in a non-core proceeding heard by a bankruptcy judge unless all parties expressly consent. 28 U.S.C. § 157(c).

Rule 7013

COUNTERCLAIM AND CROSS–CLAIM

Rule 13 F.R.Civ.P. applies in adversary proceedings, except that a party sued by a trustee or debtor in possession need not state as a counterclaim any claim that the party has against the debtor, the debtor's property, or the estate, unless the claim arose after the entry of an order for relief. A trustee or debtor in possession who fails to plead a counterclaim through oversight, inadvertence, or excusable neglect, or when justice so requires, may by leave of court amend the pleading, or commence a new adversary proceeding or separate action.

Amended Mar. 30, 1987, eff. Aug. 1, 1987.

Advisory Committee Note

Rule 13(h) F.R.Civ.P. refers to Rule 19 F.R.Civ.P. Pursuant to Rule 7002 this reference is to Rule 19 F.R.Civ.P. as incorporated and modified by Rule 7019.

Rule 7014

THIRD–PARTY PRACTICE

Rule 14 F.R.Civ.P. applies in adversary proceedings.

Advisory Committee Note

This rule does not purport to deal with questions of jurisdiction. The scope of the jurisdictional grant under 28 U.S.C. § 1471 and whether the doctrines of pendent or ancillary jurisdiction are applicable to adversary proceedings will be determined by the courts.

Rule 14 F.R.Civ.P. refers to Rules 12 and 13 F.R.Civ.P. Pursuant to Rule 7002 those references are to Rules 12 and 13 as incorporated and modified by Rules 7012 and 7013.

Rule 7015

AMENDED AND SUPPLEMENTAL PLEADINGS

Rule 15 F.R.Civ.P. applies in adversary proceedings.

Rule 7016

PRE–TRIAL PROCEDURE; FORMULATING ISSUES

Rule 16 F.R.Civ.P. applies in adversary proceedings.

Rule 7017

PARTIES PLAINTIFF AND DEFENDANT; CAPACITY

Rule 17 F.R.Civ.P. applies in adversary proceedings, except as provided in Rules 2010(d) and 5008(d).

Advisory Committee Note

Rules 2010(d) and 5008(d), which implement §§ 322 and 345 of the Code, authorize a party in interest to prosecute a claim on the bond of a trustee or depository in the name of the United States.

Rule 7018

JOINDER OF CLAIMS AND REMEDIES

Rule 18 F.R.Civ.P. applies in adversary proceedings.

Rule 7019

JOINDER OF PERSONS NEEDED FOR
JUST DETERMINATION

Rule 19 F.R.Civ.P. applies in adversary proceedings, except that (1) if an entity joined as a party raises the defense that the court lacks jurisdiction over the subject matter and the defense is sustained, the court shall dismiss such entity from the adversary proceeding and (2) if an entity joined as a party properly and timely raises the defense of improper venue, the court shall determine, as provided in 28 U.S.C. § 1412, whether that part of the proceeding involving the joined party shall be transferred to another district, or whether the entire adversary proceeding shall be transferred to another district.

Amended Mar. 30, 1987, eff. Aug. 1, 1987.

Advisory Committee Note

This rule addresses a situation different from that encountered by the district court when its jurisdiction is based on diversity of citizenship under 28 U.S.C. § 1332. Joining of a party whose citizenship is the same as that of an adversary destroys the district court's jurisdiction over the entire civil action but under 28 U.S.C. § 1471 the attempted joinder of such a person would not affect the bankruptcy court's jurisdiction over the original adversary proceeding.

Advisory Committee Notes to 1987 Amendments

The rule is amended to delete the reference to retention of the adversary proceeding if venue is improper. See 28 U.S.C. § 1412.

Rule 7020

PERMISSIVE JOINDER OF PARTIES

Rule 20 F.R.Civ.P. applies in adversary proceedings.

Rule 7021

MISJOINDER AND NON–JOINDER OF PARTIES

Rule 21 F.R.Civ.P. applies in adversary proceedings.

Rule 7022

INTERPLEADER

Rule 22(1) F.R.Civ.P. applies in adversary proceedings.

Rule 7023

CLASS PROCEEDINGS

Rule 23 F.R.Civ.P. applies in adversary proceedings.

Rule 7023.1

DERIVATIVE PROCEEDINGS BY SHAREHOLDERS

Rule 23.1 F.R.Civ.P. applies in adversary proceedings.

Rule 7023.2

ADVERSARY PROCEEDINGS RELATING TO UNINCORPORATED ASSOCIATIONS

Rule 23.2 F.R.Civ.P. applies in adversary proceedings.

Rule 7024

INTERVENTION

Rule 24 F.R.Civ.P. applies in adversary proceedings.

Advisory Committee Note

A person may seek to intervene in the case under the Code or in an adversary proceeding relating to the case under the Code. Intervention in a case under the Code is governed by Rule 2018 and intervention in an adversary proceeding is governed by this rule. Intervention in a case and intervention in an adversary proceeding must be sought separately.

Rule 7025

SUBSTITUTION OF PARTIES

Subject to the provisions of Rule 2012, Rule 25 F.R.Civ.P. applies in adversary proceedings.

Advisory Committee Note

Rule 25 F.R.Civ.P. refers to Rule 4 F.R.Civ.P. Pursuant to Rule 7002 that reference is to Rule 4 as incorporated and modified by Rule 7004.

Rule 7026

GENERAL PROVISIONS GOVERNING DISCOVERY

Rule 26 F.R.Civ.P. applies in adversary proceedings.

Rule 7027

DEPOSITIONS BEFORE ADVERSARY PROCEEDINGS OR PENDING APPEAL

Rule 27 F.R.Civ.P. applies to adversary proceedings.

Advisory Committee Note

Rule 27(a)(2) F.R.Civ.P. refers to Rule 4 F.R.Civ.P. Pursuant to Rule 7002 the reference is to Rule 4 F.R.Civ.P. as incorporated and modified by Rule 7004.

Rule 7028

PERSONS BEFORE WHOM DEPOSITIONS MAY BE TAKEN

Rule 28 F.R.Civ.P. applies in adversary proceedings.

Rule 7029

STIPULATIONS REGARDING DISCOVERY PROCEDURE

Rule 29 F.R.Civ.P. applies in adversary proceedings.

Rule 7030

DEPOSITIONS UPON ORAL EXAMINATION

Rule 30 F.R.Civ.P. applies in adversary proceedings.

Advisory Committee Note

Rule 30 F.R.Civ.P. refers to Rule 4 F.R.Civ.P. Pursuant to Rule 7002 that reference is a reference to Rule 4 F.R.Civ.P. as incorporated and modified by Rule 7004.

Rule 7031

DEPOSITION UPON WRITTEN QUESTIONS

Rule 31 F.R.Civ.P. applies in adversary proceedings.

Rule 7032

USE OF DEPOSITIONS IN ADVERSARY PROCEEDINGS

Rule 32 F.R.Civ.P. applies in adversary proceedings.

Rule 7033

INTERROGATORIES TO PARTIES

Rule 33 F.R.Civ.P. applies in adversary proceedings.

Rule 7034

PRODUCTION OF DOCUMENTS AND THINGS AND ENTRY UPON LAND FOR INSPECTION AND OTHER PURPOSES

Rule 34 F.R.Civ.P. applies in adversary proceedings.

Rule 7035

PHYSICAL AND MENTAL EXAMINATION OF PERSONS

Rule 35 F.R.Civ.P. applies in adversary proceedings.

Rule 7036

REQUESTS FOR ADMISSION

Rule 36 F.R.Civ.P. applies in adversary proceedings.

Rule 7037

FAILURE TO MAKE DISCOVERY: SANCTIONS

Rule 37 F.R.Civ.P. applies in adversary proceedings.

Rule 7040

ASSIGNMENT OF CASES FOR TRIAL

Rule 40 F.R.Civ.P. applies in adversary proceedings.

Rule 7041

DISMISSAL OF ADVERSARY PROCEEDINGS

Rule 41 F.R.Civ.P. applies in adversary proceedings, except that a complaint objecting to the debtor's discharge shall not be dismissed at the plaintiff's instance without notice to the trustee and only on order of the court containing terms and conditions which the court deems proper.

Advisory Committee Note

Dismissal of a complaint objecting to a discharge raises special concerns because the plaintiff may have been induced to dismiss by an advantage given or promised by the debtor or someone acting in his interest. Some courts by local rule or order have required the debtor and his attorney or the plaintiff to file an affidavit that nothing has been promised to the plaintiff in consideration of the withdrawal of the objection. By specifically authorizing the court to impose conditions in the order of dismissal this rule permits the continuation of this salutary practice.

Rule 41 F.R.Civ.P. refers to Rule 19 F.R.Civ.P. Pursuant to Rule 7002 that reference is to Rule 19 F.R.Civ.P. as incorporated and modified by Rule 7019.

Rule 7042

CONSOLIDATION OF ADVERSARY PROCEEDINGS; SEPARATE TRIALS

Rule 42 F.R.Civ.P. applies in adversary proceedings.

Rule 7052

FINDINGS BY THE COURT

Rule 52 F.R.Civ.P. applies in adversary proceedings.

Advisory Committee Note

Rule 52(a) F.R.Civ.P. refers to Rule 12 F.R.Civ.P. Pursuant to Rule 7002 this reference is to Rule 12 F.R.Civ.P. as incorporated and modified by Rule 7012.

Rule 7054

JUDGMENTS; COSTS

(a) Judgments. Rule 54(a)–(c) F.R.Civ.P. applies in adversary proceedings.

(b) Costs. The court may allow costs to the prevailing party except when a statute of the United States or these rules otherwise provides. Costs against the United States, its officers and agencies shall be imposed only to the extent permitted by law. Costs may be taxed by the clerk on one day's notice; on motion served within five days thereafter, the action of the clerk may be reviewed by the court.

Rule 7055

DEFAULT

Rule 55 F.R.Civ.P. applies in adversary proceedings.

Rule 7056

SUMMARY JUDGMENT

Rule 56 F.R.Civ.P. applies in adversary proceedings.

Rule 7062

STAY OF PROCEEDINGS TO ENFORCE A JUDGMENT

Rule 62 F.R.Civ.P. applies in adversary proceedings except that an order granting relief from an automatic stay provided by § 362, § 922, or § 1301 of the Code, an order authorizing or prohibiting the use of cash collateral or property of the estate under § 363, and an order authorizing the trustee to obtain credit pursuant to § 364 shall be additional exceptions to Rule 62(a).

Advisory Committee Note

The additional exceptions set forth in this rule make applicable to those matters the consequences contained in Rule 62(c) and (d) with respect to orders in actions for injunctions.

Rule 7064

SEIZURE OF PERSON OR PROPERTY

Rule 64 F.R.Civ.P. applies in adversary proceedings.

Rule 7065

INJUNCTIONS

Rule 65 F.R.Civ.P. applies in adversary proceedings, except that a temporary restraining order or preliminary injunction may be issued on application of a debtor, trustee, or debtor in possession without compliance with Rule 65(c).

Rule 7067

DEPOSIT IN COURT

Rule 67 F.R.Civ.P. applies in adversary proceedings.

Rule 7068

OFFER OF JUDGMENT

Rule 68 F.R.Civ.P. applies in adversary proceedings.

Rule 7069

EXECUTION

Rule 69 F.R.Civ.P. applies in adversary proceedings.

Rule 7070

JUDGMENT FOR SPECIFIC ACTS; VESTING TITLE

Rule 70 F.R.Civ.P. applies in adversary proceedings and the court may enter a judgment divesting the title of any party and vesting title in others whenever the real or personal property involved is within the jurisdiction of the court.

Amended Mar. 30, 1987, eff. Aug. 1, 1987.

Advisory Committee Notes to 1987 Amendments

The reference to court is used in the amendment because the district court may preside over an adversary proceeding.

Rule 7071

PROCESS IN BEHALF OF AND AGAINST PERSONS NOT PARTIES

Rule 71 F.R.Civ.P. applies in adversary proceedings.

Rule 7087

TRANSFER OF ADVERSARY PROCEEDING

On motion and after a hearing, the court may transfer an adversary proceeding or any part thereof to another district pursuant to 28 U.S.C. § 1412, except as provided in Rule 7019(2).

Amended Mar. 30, 1987, eff. Aug. 1, 1987.

Advisory Committee Notes to 1987 Amendments

The reference to the venue section of title 28 is amended to conform to the 1984 amendments to title 28.

PART VIII

APPEALS TO DISTRICT COURT OR BANKRUPTCY APPELLATE PANEL

Rule

8001. Manner of Taking Appeal; Voluntary Dismissal
8002. Time for Filing Notice of Appeal
8003. Leave to Appeal
8004. Service of the Notice of Appeal
8005. Stay Pending Appeal
8006. Record and Issues on Appeal
8007. Completion and Transmission of the Record; Docketing of the Appeal
8008. Filing and Service
8009. Briefs and Appendix; Filing and Service
8010. Form of Briefs; Length
8011. Motions
8012. Oral Argument
8013. Disposition of Appeal; Weight Accorded Bankruptcy Judge's Findings of Fact
8014. Costs
8015. Motion for Rehearing
8016. Duties of Clerk of District Court and Bankruptcy Appellate Panel
8017. Stay of Judgment of District Court or Bankruptcy Appellate Panel
8018. Rules by Circuit Councils and District Courts
8019. Suspension of Rules in Part VIII

Rule 8001

MANNER OF TAKING APPEAL; VOLUNTARY DISMISSAL

(a) **Appeal as of Right; How Taken.** An appeal from a final judgment, order, or decree of a bankruptcy judge to a district court or bankruptcy appellate panel shall be taken by filing a notice of appeal with the clerk within the time allowed by Rule 8002. Failure of an appellant to take any step other than the timely filing of a notice of appeal does not affect the validity of the appeal, but is ground only for such action as the district court or bankruptcy appellate panel deems appropriate, which may include dismissal of the appeal. The notice of appeal shall conform substantially to Official Form No. 35, shall contain the names of all parties to the judgment, order, or decree appealed from and the names, addresses and telephone numbers of their respective attorneys, and be accompanied by the prescribed fee. Each appellant shall file a sufficient number of copies of the notice of appeal to enable the clerk to comply promptly with Rule 8004.

(b) **Appeal by Leave; How Taken.** An appeal from an interlocutory judgment, order or decree of a bankruptcy judge as permitted by 28 U.S.C. § 158(a) shall be taken by filing a notice of appeal, as prescribed in subdivision (a) of this rule, accompanied by a motion for leave to appeal prepared in accordance with Rule 8003 and with proof of service in accordance with Rule 8008.

(c) Voluntary Dismissal.

(1) Before Docketing. If an appeal has not been docketed, the appeal may be dismissed by the bankruptcy judge on the filing of a stipulation for dismissal signed by all the parties, or on motion and notice by the appellant.

(2) After Docketing. If an appeal has been docketed and the parties to the appeal sign and file with the clerk of the district court or the clerk of the bankruptcy appellate panel an agreement that the appeal be dismissed and pay any court costs or fees that may be due, the clerk of the district court or the clerk of the bankruptcy appellate panel shall enter an order dismissing the appeal. An appeal may also be dismissed on motion of the appellant on terms and conditions fixed by the district court or bankruptcy appellate panel.

(d) [Abrogated]

(e) Consent to Appeal to Bankruptcy Appellate Panel. Unless otherwise provided by a rule promulgated pursuant to Rule 8018, consent to have an appeal heard by a bankruptcy appellate panel may be given in a separate statement of consent executed by a party or contained in the notice of appeal or cross appeal. The statement of consent shall be filed before the transmittal of the record pursuant to Rule 8007(b) or within 30 days of the filing of the notice of appeal, whichever is later.

Amended Mar. 30, 1987, eff. Aug. 1, 1987.

Advisory Committee Note

These rules in Part VIII apply only to appeals to the district courts or bankruptcy appellate panels. Subsequent appeals to the courts of appeals, or direct appeals by agreement of the parties under 28 U.S.C. § 1293(b), are governed by Federal Rules of Appellate Procedure.

Subdivisions (a) and (b) require that a notice of appeal be filed whenever a litigant seeks to secure appellate review by the district court or bankruptcy appellate panel. An appeal from an interlocutory order which will be heard only if leave is granted under 28 U.S.C. §§ 1334(b) or 1482(b) is taken by filing a notice of appeal accompanied by a motion for leave to appeal which complies with the requirements set forth in Rule 8003. Rule 8003 also governs other aspects of interlocutory appeals.

Subdivision (c) is an adaptation of Rule 42 F.R.App.P.

Subdivision (d) deals with the situation in which an appellant perfects an appeal to the district court or a bankruptcy appellate panel and also a direct appeal pursuant to 28 U.S.C. § 1293(b) to the court of appeals. This subdivision provides that once the appeal to the court of appeals is taken, a notice of appeal to the district court or bankruptcy appellate panel shall be dismissed and, if the first appeal is to the district court or bankruptcy appellate panel, the first appeal shall be dismissed. Paragraph (3) gives an appellant or cross appellant an opportunity to file an appeal to the district court or bankruptcy appellate panel if the court of appeals dismisses the direct appeal because the judgment, order, or decree appealed from is not final. Since the court of appeals has determined the judgment, order, or decree is not final, the new appeal is an appeal for which leave is necessary.

Advisory Committee Notes to 1987 Amendments

Subdivisions (a) and (b) are amended to conform to the 1984 amendments.

Subdivision (d) is abrogated because there is no direct appeal to the court of appeals under 28 U.S.C. § 158, as enacted by the 1984 amendments.

Subdivision (e) is new. Section 158(b)(1) of title 28 authorizes the circuit councils to establish bankruptcy appellate panels. Appeals may not be heard by these panels unless the district court authorizes the referral and all parties to the appeal consent. This rule requires that the parties consent to such an appeal; however, the method of consenting to an appeal may be the subject of a rule promulgated by a circuit council under Rule 8018.

Rule 8002

TIME FOR FILING NOTICE OF APPEAL

(a) Ten-day Period. The notice of appeal shall be filed with the clerk within 10 days of the date of the entry of the judgment, order, or decree appealed from. If a timely notice of appeal is filed by a party, any other party may file a notice of appeal within 10 days of the date on which the first notice of appeal was filed, or within the time otherwise prescribed by this rule, whichever period last expires. If a notice of appeal is mistakenly filed with the district court or the bankruptcy appellate panel, the clerk of the district court or the clerk of the bankruptcy appellate panel shall note thereon the date on which it was received and transmit it to the clerk and it shall be deemed filed with the clerk on the date so noted.

(b) Effect of Motion on Time for Appeal. If a timely motion is filed by any party: (1) for judgment notwithstanding the verdict under Rule 9015; (2) under Rule 7052(b) to amend or make additional findings of fact, whether or not an alteration of the judgment would be required if the motion is granted; (3) under Rule 9023 to alter or amend the judgment; or (4) under Rule 9023 for a new trial, the time for appeal for all parties shall run from the entry of the order denying a new trial or granting or denying any other such motion. A notice of appeal filed before the disposition of any of the above motions shall have no effect; a new notice of appeal must be filed. No additional fees shall be required for such filing.

(c) Extension of Time for Appeal. The bankruptcy judge may extend the time for filing the notice of appeal by any party for a period not to exceed 20 days from the expiration of the time otherwise prescribed by this rule. A request to extend the time for filing a notice of appeal must be made before the time for filing a notice of appeal has expired, except that a request made no more than 20 days after the expiration of the time for filing a notice of appeal may be granted upon a showing of excusable neglect if the judgment or order appealed from does not authorize the sale of any property or the obtaining of credit or the incurring of debt under § 364 of the Code, or is not a judgment or order approving a disclosure statement, confirming a plan, dismissing a case, or converting the case to a case under another chapter of the Code.

Amended Mar. 30, 1987, eff. Aug. 1, 1987.

Advisory Committee Note

This rule is an adaptation of Rule 4(a) F.R.App.P. The time to appeal from a judgment, order, or decree of a bankruptcy judge is 10 days, rather than 30 days provided for in the civil practice. The shortened time is specified in order to obtain prompt appellate review, often important to the administration of a case under the Code. If a timely notice of appeal is filed, other parties have an additional 10 days within which to file a notice of appeal. A notice of appeal filed within the additional 10 day period by an appellee is a cross appeal, but there is a separate appeal if a non-appellee files a notice of appeal within that 10 day period. The district courts and bankruptcy appellate panels have inherent authority to consolidate appeals.

Subdivision (b) is essentially the same as Rule 4(a)(4) of the F.R.App.P.

Subdivision (c) is similar to former Bankruptcy Rule 802(c). To expedite the disposition of appeals the maximum extension of time is 20 days instead of the 30 days provided by Rule 4(a)(5) of the F.R.App.P. Subject to the exceptions set forth in subdivision (c), the court may extend the time for taking an appeal when a motion for extension is filed after the expiration of the original 10 day period but no later than 20 days after the expiration of the original 10 day period. Orders of the bankruptcy court relating to the sale of property, extension of credit, confirmation of a plan, dismissal or conversion of the case, and approval of the disclosure statement are of such significance to the administration of the case, the parties in interest, and third parties that this subdivision requires that either an appeal or a motion for extension be filed within the original 10 day period.

If a timely notice of appeal is not filed, no appeal may be taken later. Former Bankruptcy Rule 803, which provided that a referee's judgment became final when the appeal period expired, has been omitted as unnecessary.

Rule 8003

LEAVE TO APPEAL

(a) Content of Motion; Answer. A motion for leave to appeal under 28 U.S.C. § 158(a) shall contain: (1) a statement of the facts necessary to an understanding of the questions to be presented by the appeal; (2) a statement of those questions and of the relief sought; (3) a statement of the reasons why an appeal should be granted; and (4) a copy of the judgment, order, or decree complained of and of any opinion or memorandum relating thereto. Within 10 days after service of the motion, an adverse party may file with the clerk an answer in opposition.

(b) Transmittal; Determination of Motion. The clerk shall transmit the notice of appeal, the motion for leave to appeal and any answer thereto to the clerk of the district court or the clerk of the bankruptcy appellate panel as soon as all parties have filed answers or the time for filing an answer has expired. The motion and answer shall be submitted without oral argument unless otherwise ordered.

(c) Appeal Improperly Taken Regarded as a Motion for Leave to Appeal. If a required motion for leave to appeal is not filed, but a notice of appeal is timely filed, the district court or bankruptcy appellate panel may grant leave to appeal or direct that a motion for leave to appeal be filed. The district court or the bankruptcy appellate panel may also deny leave to appeal but in so doing shall consider the notice of appeal as a motion for leave to appeal. Unless an order directing that a motion for leave to appeal be filed provides otherwise, the motion shall be filed within 10 days of entry of the order.

Amended Mar. 30, 1987, eff. Aug. 1, 1987.

Advisory Committee Note

Subdivisions (a) and (b) of this rule are derived from Rules 5 and 6 F.R. App.P. The motion for leave to appeal is addressed to the district court or the bankruptcy appellate panel, although filed with the clerk of the bankruptcy court.

Subdivision (c) provides that if a party mistakenly believes the order appealed from is final and files only a notice of appeal, the appeal is not automatically dismissed. The district court or bankruptcy appellate panel has the options to direct that a motion be filed, to decide exclusively on the papers already filed to grant leave to appeal, or to deny leave to appeal. Cf. 28 U.S.C. § 2103.

Rule 8004

SERVICE OF THE NOTICE OF APPEAL

The clerk shall serve notice of the filing of a notice of appeal by mailing a copy thereof to counsel of record of each party other than the appellant or, if a party is not represented by counsel, to the party's last known address. Failure to serve notice shall not affect the validity of the appeal. The clerk shall note on each copy served the date of the filing of the notice of appeal and shall note in the docket the names of the parties to whom copies are mailed and the date of the mailing.

Amended Mar. 30, 1987, eff. Aug. 1, 1987.

Advisory Committee Note

This rule is an adaptation of Rule 3(d) F.R.App.P.

Rule 8005

STAY PENDING APPEAL

A motion for a stay of the judgment, order, or decree of a bankruptcy judge, for approval of a supersedeas bond, or for other relief pending appeal must ordinarily be presented to the bankruptcy judge in the first instance. Notwithstanding Rule 7062 but subject to the power of the district court and the bankruptcy appellate panel reserved hereinafter, the bankruptcy judge may suspend or order the continuation of other proceedings in the case under the Code or make any other appropriate order during the pendency of an appeal on such terms as will protect the rights of all parties in interest. A motion for such relief, or for modification or termination of relief granted by a bankruptcy judge, may be made to the district court or the bankruptcy appellate panel, but the motion shall show why the relief, modification, or termination was not obtained from the bankruptcy judge. The district court or the bankruptcy appellate panel may condition the relief it grants under this rule on the filing of a bond or other appropriate security with the bankruptcy court. When an appeal is taken by a trustee, a bond or other appropriate security may be required, but when an appeal is taken by the United States or an officer or agency thereof or by direction of any department of the Government of the United States a bond or other security shall not be required.

Amended Mar. 30, 1987, eff. Aug. 1, 1987.

Advisory Committee Note

The first, third, and fourth sentences of this rule are adaptations of Rule 8(a) and (b) F.R.App.P. The second sentence of the rule is derived from § 39(c) of the Bankruptcy Act and confers on the bankruptcy judge discretion respecting the stay or continuation of other proceedings in the case while an appeal is pending.

The last sentence of the rule, which specifically subjects a trustee to the same kind of security requirements as other litigants, is derived from former Bankruptcy Rule 805. The exemption of the United States from the bond or security requirements is the same as the exemption contained in Rule 62(e) F.R.Civ.P.

Sections 363(m) and 364(e) of the Code provide that unless an order approving a sale of property, or authorizing the obtaining of credit or the incurring of debt is stayed pending appeal, the sale of property to a good faith purchaser or a good faith extension of credit, with or without any priority or lien, shall not be affected by the reversal or modification of such order on appeal, whether or not the purchaser or creditor knows of the pendency of the appeal.

Rule 8006

RECORD AND ISSUES ON APPEAL

Within 10 days after filing the notice of appeal as provided by Rule 8001(a) or entry of an order granting leave to appeal the appellant shall file with the clerk and serve on the appellee a designation of the items to be included in the record on appeal and a statement of the issues to be presented. Within seven days after the service of the statement of the appellant the appellee may file and serve on the appellant a designation of additional items to be included in the record on appeal and, if the appellee has filed a cross appeal, the appellee as cross appellant shall file and serve a statement of the issues to be presented on the cross appeal and a designation of additional items to be included in the record. A cross appellee may, within seven days of service of the statement of the cross appellant, file and serve on the cross appellant a designation of additional items to be included in the record. The record on appeal shall include the items so designated by the parties, the notice of appeal, the judgment, order, or decree appealed from, and any opinion, findings of fact, and conclusions of law of the court. If the record designated by any party includes a transcript of any proceeding or a part thereof, the party shall immediately after filing the designation deliver to the reporter and file with the clerk a written request for the transcript and make satisfactory arrangements for payment of its cost. All parties shall take any other action necessary to enable the clerk to assemble and transmit the record.

Amended Mar. 30, 1987, eff. Aug. 1, 1987.

Advisory Committee Note

This rule is an adaptation of Rule 10(b) F.R.App.P. The last sentence of the rule is derived from Rule 11(a) F.R.App.P.

Rule 8007

COMPLETION AND TRANSMISSION OF THE RECORD; DOCKETING OF THE APPEAL

(a) **Duty of Reporter to Prepare and File Transcript.** On receipt of a request for a transcript, the reporter shall acknowledge on the request the date it was received and the date on which the reporter expects to have the transcript completed and shall transmit the request, so endorsed, to the clerk or the clerk of the bankruptcy appellate panel. On completion of the transcript the reporter shall file it with the clerk and, if appropriate, notify the clerk of the bankruptcy appellate panel. If the transcript cannot be completed within 30 days of receipt of the request the reporter shall seek an extension of time from the clerk or the clerk of the bankruptcy appellate panel and the action of the clerk shall be entered in the docket and the parties notified. If the reporter does not file the transcript within the time allowed, the clerk or the clerk of the bankruptcy appellate panel shall notify the bankruptcy judge.

(b) **Duty of Clerk to Transmit Record; Copies of Record; Docketing of Appeal.** When the record is complete for purposes of appeal, the clerk shall transmit it forthwith to the clerk of the district court or the clerk of the bankruptcy appellate panel. If the record is to be retained by the clerk as provided in subdivision (c) of this rule, the clerk shall transmit the notice of appeal and the judgment, order, or decree appealed from, and any opinion, findings of fact and conclusions of law of the court. On receipt of the transmission the clerk of the district court or the clerk of the bankruptcy appellate panel shall enter the appeal in the docket and give notice promptly to all parties to the judgment, order, or decree appealed from of the date on which the appeal was docketed. If the bankruptcy appellate panel directs that additional copies of the record be furnished, the clerk of the bankruptcy appellate panel shall notify the appellant and, if the appellant fails to provide the copies, the clerk shall prepare the copies at the expense of the appellant.

(c) **Retention of Record by the Clerk.** Any part of the record on appeal may be retained by the clerk if the parties to the appeal so stipulate, a rule of the bankruptcy appellate panel so provides, or the bankruptcy judge so orders. The record on appeal for all purposes shall nevertheless be the record as designated under Rule 8006. When the bankruptcy judge has ordered retention, the parties shall provide to the clerk copies of any papers retained and the clerk shall transmit those copies to the clerk of the district court or the bankruptcy appellate panel. If papers have been retained, pursuant to a stipulation of the parties, on request of a party to the stipulation the clerk shall transmit the papers so requested to the clerk of the district court or the clerk of the bankruptcy appellate panel. On order of the district court or the bankruptcy appellate panel the clerk shall transmit any retained papers to the clerk of the district court or the clerk of the bankruptcy appellate panel.

(d) Record for Preliminary Hearing. If prior to the time the record is transmitted a party moves in the district court or before the bankruptcy appellate panel for dismissal, for a stay pending appeal, for additional security on the bond on appeal or on a supersedeas bond, or for any intermediate order, the clerk at the request of any party to the appeal shall transmit to the clerk of the district court or the clerk of the bankruptcy appellate panel the parts of the original record as any party to the appeal shall designate.

Amended Mar. 30, 1987, eff. Aug. 1, 1987.

Advisory Committee Note

Subdivision (a) is an adaptation of Rule 11(b) F.R.App.P.

Subdivision (b) is similar to former Bankruptcy Rule 807. The duty of the clerk of the bankruptcy court to transmit the record as soon as the record is complete is derived from the second paragraph of Rule 11(b) F.R. App.P. The last sentence of the subdivision applies to appeals to bankruptcy appellate panels. Additional copies of the record may be needed when the appendix to the brief required under Rule 8009(b) is not adequate in the judgment of the bankruptcy appellate panel for disposition of the appeal. If additional copies are required, the appellant will arrange for the production of the copies; if the appellant fails to do so, the clerk of the bankruptcy appellate panel shall prepare the copies at the expense of the appellant.

Subdivision (c) is derived from subdivisions (c), (e) and (f) of Rule 11 F.R. App.P. and subdivision (d) is essentially the same as Rule 11(b) F.R.App.P.

Rule 8008

FILING AND SERVICE

(a) Filing. Papers required or permitted to be filed with the clerk of the district court or the clerk of the bankruptcy appellate panel may be filed by mail addressed to the clerk, but filing shall not be timely unless the papers are received by the clerk within the time fixed for filing, except that briefs shall be deemed filed on the day of mailing. An original and one copy of all papers shall be filed when an appeal is to the district court; an original and three copies shall be filed when an appeal is to a bankruptcy appellate panel. The district court or bankruptcy appellate panel may require that additional copies be furnished.

(b) Service of All Papers Required. Copies of all papers filed by any party and not required by these rules to be served by the clerk of the district court or the clerk of the bankruptcy appellate panel shall, at or before the time of filing, be served by the party or a person acting for the party on all other parties to the appeal. Service on a party represented by counsel shall be made on counsel.

(c) Manner of Service. Service may be personal or by mail. Personal service includes delivery of the copy to a clerk or other responsible person at the office of counsel. Service by mail is complete on mailing.

(d) Proof of Service. Papers presented for filing shall contain an acknowledgment of service by the person served or proof of service in the form of a statement of the date and manner of service and of the names of the persons served, certified by the person who made service. The clerk of the district court or the clerk of the bankruptcy appellate panel may permit papers to be filed without acknowledgment or proof of service but shall require the acknowledgment or proof of service to be filed promptly thereafter.

Amended Mar. 30, 1987, eff. Aug. 1, 1987.

Advisory Committee Note

This rule is an adaptation of Rule 25 F.R.App.P. Motions, briefs, appendices when required, statements, and any other filed paper must be accompanied by the specified number of copies. Rules 8001 and 8004 govern the number of copies of the notice of appeal which must be filed.

Rule 8009

BRIEFS AND APPENDIX; FILING AND SERVICE

(a) Briefs. Unless the district court or the bankruptcy appellate panel by local rule or by order excuses the filing of briefs or specifies different time limits:

(1) The appellant shall serve and file a brief within 15 days after entry of the appeal on the docket pursuant to Rule 8007.

(2) The appellee shall serve and file a brief within 15 days after service of the brief of appellant. If the appellee has filed a cross appeal, the brief of the appellee shall contain the issues and argument pertinent to the cross appeal, denominated as such, and the response to the brief of the appellant.

(3) The appellant may serve and file a reply brief within 10 days after service of the brief of the appellee, and if the appellee has cross-appealed, the appellee may file and serve a reply brief to the response of the appellant to the issues presented in the cross appeal within 10 days after service of the reply brief of the appellant. No further briefs may be filed except with leave of the district court or the bankruptcy appellate panel.

(b) Appendix to Brief. If the appeal is to a bankruptcy appellate panel, the appellant shall serve and file with the appellant's brief excerpts of the record as an appendix, which shall include the following:

(1) The complaint and answer or other equivalent pleadings;

(2) Any pretrial order;

(3) The judgment, order, or decree from which the appeal is taken;

(4) Any other orders relevant to the appeal;

(5) The opinion, findings of fact, or conclusions of law filed or delivered orally by the court and citations of the opinion if published;

(6) Any motion and response on which the court rendered decision;

(7) The notice of appeal;

(8) The relevant entries in the bankruptcy docket; and

(9) The transcript or portion thereof, if so required by a rule of the bankruptcy appellate panel.

An appellee may also serve and file an appendix which contains material required to be included by the appellant but omitted by appellant.

Amended Mar. 30, 1987, eff. Aug. 1, 1987.

Advisory Committee Note

Subdivision (a) of this rule is adapted from Rules 28(a) and 31(a) F.R. App.P. The introductory clause of the rule recognizes the desirability of allowing local and individual variation in the filing of briefs. The numbered paragraphs prescribe shorter periods than the corresponding periods allowed by Rule 31(a) F.R.App.P.

Subdivision (b), which is similar to an interim rule for bankruptcy appellate panels promulgated by the Ninth Circuit, applies only when an appeal is to an appellate panel. The appellant must prepare an appendix to the brief which contains the documents relevant to the appeal. With the appendix available to each member of the appellate panel, it is unlikely that multiple copies of the record will be necessary. The last sentence of the subdivision enables the appellee to correct an omission of the appellant.

Rule 30 F.R.App.P., which governs the preparation of the appendix in appeals taken to the courts of appeals, specifies fewer documents which must be included in the appendix but permits the parties to include any other material.

Advisory Committee Notes to 1987 Amendments

The amendment to Rule 8007(c) permits a rule of the bankruptcy appellate panel to provide that the record is to be retained rather than transmitted. The new paragraph (9) of subdivision (b) of this rule complements Rule 8007(c) by authorizing a rule of the panel to require inclusion of the transcript or a portion thereof in the appendix.

Rule 8010

FORM OF BRIEFS; LENGTH

(a) Form of Briefs. Unless the district court or the bankruptcy appellate panel by local rule otherwise provides, the form of brief shall be as follows:

(1) Brief of the Appellant. The brief of the appellant shall contain under appropriate headings and in the order here indicated:

(A) A table of contents, with page references, and a table of cases alphabetically arranged, statutes and other authorities cited, with references to the pages of the brief where they are cited.

(B) A statement of the basis of appellate jurisdiction.

(C) A statement of the issues presented and the applicable standard of appellate review.

(D) A statement of the case. The statement shall first indicate briefly the nature of the case, the course of the proceedings, and the disposition in the court below. There shall follow a statement of the facts relevant to the issues presented for review, with appropriate references to the record.

(E) An argument. The argument may be preceded by a summary. The argument shall contain the contentions of the appellant with respect to the issues presented, and the reasons therefor, with citations to the authorities, statutes and parts of the record relied on.

(F) A short conclusion stating the precise relief sought.

(2) Brief of the Appellee. The brief of the appellee shall conform to the requirements of paragraph (1) (A)–(E) of this subdivision, except that a statement of the basis of appellate jurisdiction, of the issues, or of the case need not be made unless the appellee is dissatisfied with the statement of the appellant.

(b) Reproduction of Statutes, Rules, Regulations, or Similar Material. If determination of the issues presented requires reference to the Code or other statutes, rules, regulations, or similar material, relevant parts thereof shall be reproduced in the brief or in an addendum or they may be supplied to the court in pamphlet form.

(c) Length of Briefs. Unless the district court or the bankruptcy appellate panel by local rule or order otherwise provides, principal briefs shall not exceed 50 pages, and reply briefs shall not exceed 25 pages, exclusive of pages containing the table of contents, tables of citations and any addendum containing statutes, rules, regulations, or similar material.

Advisory Committee Note

This rule is derived from subdivisions (a), (b), (c), and (f) of Rule 28 F.R. App.P.

When an appeal is to a bankruptcy appellate panel and an appendix is filed pursuant to Rule 8009(b) and reference is made in a brief to parts of the record included in the appendix, the reference should be to the appropriate pages of the appendix at which those parts appear.

Rule 8011

MOTIONS

(a) Content of Motions; Response; Reply. A request for an order or other relief shall be made by filing with the clerk of the district court or the clerk of the bankruptcy appellate panel a motion for such order or relief with proof of service on all other parties to the appeal. The motion shall contain or be accompanied by any matter required by a specific provision of these rules governing such a motion, shall state with particularity the grounds on which it is based, and shall set forth the order or relief sought. If a motion is supported by briefs, affidavits or other papers, they shall be served and filed with the motion. Any party may file a response in opposition to a motion other than one for a procedural order within seven days after service of the motion, but the district court or the bankruptcy appellate panel may shorten or extend the time for responding to any motion.

(b) Determination of Motions for Procedural Orders. Notwithstanding subdivision (a) of this rule, motions for procedural orders, including any motion under Rule 9006, may be acted on at any time, without awaiting a response thereto and without hearing. Any party adversely affected by such action may move for reconsideration, vacation, or modification of the action.

(c) Determination of All Motions. All motions will be decided without oral argument unless the court orders otherwise. A motion for a stay, or for other emergency relief may be denied if not presented promptly.

(d) Emergency Motions. Whenever a movant requests expedited action on a motion on the ground that, to avoid irreparable harm, relief is needed in less time than would normally be required for the district court or bankruptcy appellate panel to receive and consider a response, the word "Emergency" shall precede the title of the motion. The motion shall be accompanied by an affidavit setting forth the nature of the emergency. The motion shall state whether all grounds advanced in support thereof were submitted to the bankruptcy judge and, if any grounds relied on were not submitted, why the motion should not be remanded to the bankruptcy judge for reconsideration. The motion shall include the office addresses and telephone numbers of moving and opposing counsel and shall be served pursuant to Rule 8008. Prior to filing the motion, the movant shall make every practicable effort to notify opposing counsel in time for counsel to respond to the motion. The affidavit accompanying the motion shall also state when and how opposing counsel was notified or if opposing counsel was not notified why it was not practicable to do so.

(e) Power of a Single Judge to Entertain Motions. A single judge of a bankruptcy appellate panel may grant or deny any request for relief which under these rules may properly be sought by motion, except that a single judge may not dismiss or otherwise decide an appeal or a motion for leave to appeal. The action of a single judge may be reviewed by the panel.

Advisory Committee Note

Subdivisions (a), (b) and (e) of this rule conform substantially to subdivisions (a), (b) and (c) of Rule 27 F.R.App.P. Subdivisions (c) and (d) are taken from Rule 13(c) and (d) of the Rules of the First Circuit governing appeals to bankruptcy appellate panels.

Rule 8012

ORAL ARGUMENT

Oral argument shall be allowed in all cases unless the district judge or the judges of the bankruptcy appellate panel unanimously determine after examination of the briefs and record, or appendix to the brief, that oral argument is not needed. Any party shall have an opportunity to file a statement setting forth the reason why oral argument should be allowed.

Oral argument will not be allowed if (1) the appeal is frivolous; (2) the dispositive issue or set of issues has been recently authoritatively decided; or (3) the facts and legal arguments are adequately presented in the briefs and record and the decisional process would not be significantly aided by oral argument.

Advisory Committee Note

This rule is derived from Rule 34(a) F.R.App.P. The other details of oral argument which are covered by the remaining subdivisions of Rule 34 F.R. App.P. are not in these rules and are left to local rule or order of the court.

Rule 8013

DISPOSITION OF APPEAL; WEIGHT ACCORDED BANKRUPTCY JUDGE'S FINDINGS OF FACT

On an appeal the district court or bankruptcy appellate panel may affirm, modify, or reverse a bankruptcy judge's judgment, order, or decree or remand with instructions for further proceedings. Findings of fact, whether based on oral or documentary evidence, shall not be set aside unless clearly erroneous, and due regard shall be given to the opportunity of the bankruptcy court to judge the credibility of the witnesses.

Amended Mar. 30, 1987, eff. Aug. 1, 1987.

Advisory Committee Note

This rule accords to the findings of a bankruptcy judge the same weight given the findings of a district judge under Rule 52 F.R.Civ.P. See also Rules 7052(a) and 9014.

Advisory Committee Notes to 1987 Amendments

The amendment to this rule conforms the appellate review standard to Rule 52 F.R.Civ.P., as amended in August 1985.

Rule 8014

COSTS

Except as otherwise provided by law, agreed to by the parties, or ordered by the district court or the bankruptcy appellate panel, costs shall be taxed against the losing party on an appeal. If a judgment is affirmed or reversed in part, or is vacated, costs shall be allowed only as ordered by the court. Costs incurred in the production of copies of briefs, the appendices, and the record and in the preparation and transmission of the record, the cost of the reporter's transcript, if necessary for the determination of the appeal, the premiums paid for cost of supersedeas bonds or other bonds to preserve rights pending appeal and the fee for filing the notice of appeal shall be taxed by the clerk as costs of the appeal in favor of the party entitled to costs under this rule.

Amended Mar. 30, 1987, eff. Aug. 1, 1987.

Advisory Committee Note

This rule is an adaptation of Rule 39(a), (c) and (e) of the F.R.App.P. Under this rule all costs are taxed by the clerk of the bankruptcy court.

Rule 8015

MOTION FOR REHEARING

Unless the district court or the bankruptcy appellate panel by local rule or by court order otherwise provides, a motion for rehearing may be filed within 10 days after entry of the judgment of the district court or the bankruptcy appellate panel. If a timely motion for rehearing is filed, the time for appeal to the court of appeals for all parties shall run from the entry of the order denying rehearing or the entry of a subsequent judgment.

Amended Mar. 30, 1987, eff. Aug. 1, 1987.

Advisory Committee Note

This is an adaptation of the first sentence of Rule 40(a) F.R.App.P. The filing of a motion for rehearing does not toll the time for taking an appeal to the court of appeals from the district court or the bankruptcy appellate panel. Appeals from a district court or a bankruptcy appellate panel are to the appropriate court of appeals. Under Rule 4(a)(4) F.R.App.P. the filing of post-trial motions in the district court has the effect of vitiating any prior notice of appeal and, on the district court's disposition of those post-trial motions, a new appeal period starts. Rule 4 F.R.App.P. does not, however, contain any provision which stays or otherwise alters the time for taking an appeal to the court of appeals when a motion for rehearing is filed under Rule 8015 with the district court or bankruptcy appellate panel.

Advisory Committee Notes to the 1987 Amendments

The amendment, which is derived from Rule 8002(b), Rule 4(a)(4) F.R.App.P., and Rule 11.1 Sup.Ct.R., clarifies the effect of the filing of a timely motion for rehearing. If a timely motion is filed, the appeal period to the court of appeals begins to run on the entry of an order denying the motion or the entry of a subsequent judgment.

Rule 8016

DUTIES OF CLERK OF DISTRICT COURT AND BANKRUPTCY APPELLATE PANEL

(a) Entry of Judgment. The clerk of the district court or the clerk of the bankruptcy appellate panel shall prepare, sign and enter the judgment following receipt of the opinion of the court or the appellate panel or, if there is no opinion, following the instruction of the court or the appellate panel. The notation of a judgment in the docket constitutes entry of judgment.

(b) Notice of Orders or Judgments; Return of Record. Immediately on the entry of a judgment or order the clerk of the district court or the clerk of the bankruptcy appellate panel shall transmit a notice of the entry to each party to the appeal and to the clerk, together with a copy of any opinion respecting the judgment or order, and shall make a note of the transmission in the docket. Original papers transmitted as the record on appeal shall be returned to the clerk on disposition of the appeal.

Amended Mar. 30, 1987, eff. Aug. 1, 1987.

Advisory Committee Note

Subdivision (a) of this rule is adapted from Rule 36 F.R.App.P. Subdivision (b) is similar to subdivisions (c) and (d) of Rule 45 F.R.App.P.

Rule 8017

STAY OF JUDGMENT OF DISTRICT COURT OR BANKRUPTCY APPELLATE PANEL

(a) Automatic Stay of Judgment on Appeal. Judgments of the district court or the bankruptcy appellate panel are stayed until the expiration of 10 days after entry, unless otherwise ordered by the district court or the bankruptcy appellate panel.

(b) Stay Pending Appeal to the Court of Appeals. On motion and notice to the parties to the appeal, the district court or the bankruptcy appellate panel may stay its judgment pending an appeal to the court of appeals. The stay shall not extend beyond 30 days after the entry of the judgment of the district court or the bankruptcy appellate panel unless the period is extended for cause shown. If before the expiration of a stay entered pursuant to this subdivision there is an appeal to the court of appeals by the party who obtained the stay, the stay shall continue until final disposition by the court of appeals. A bond or other security may be required as a condition to the grant or continuation of a stay of the judgment. A bond or other security may be required if a trustee obtains a stay but a bond or security shall not be required if a stay is obtained by the United States or an officer or agency thereof or at the direction of any department of the Government of the United States.

(c) Power of Court of Appeals Not Limited. This rule does not limit the power of a court of appeals or any judge thereof to stay proceedings during the pendency of an appeal or to suspend, modify, restore, or grant an injunction during the pendency of an appeal or to make any order appropriate to preserve the status quo or the effectiveness of the judgment subsequently to be entered.

Advisory Committee Note

This rule is derived from Rule 62 F.R.Civ.P. and Rule 41 F.R.App.P.

Subdivision (a) accords to the parties to an appeal 10 days within which to decide whether to pursue an appeal to the court of appeals. In ordinary civil litigation there is a similar opportunity. Rule 62(a) F.R.Civ.P. automatically stays enforcement of a district court's judgment in a civil action and Rule 41(a) F.R.App.P. provides that the mandate of the court of appeals shall not issue for 21 days, unless the court otherwise directs. The district court or bankruptcy appellate panel may reduce the 10 day period of this subdivision.

Subdivision (b) vests in the district courts and the bankruptcy appellate panels the same authority the courts of appeals have under Rule 41(b) F.R. App.P. to stay their judgments pending appeal. Perfection of an appeal to the court of appeals while a stay entered by the district court or bankruptcy appellate panel is in effect results in the automatic continuation of that stay during the course of the appeal in the court of appeals.

Subdivision (c) is the same as Rule 62(g) F.R.Civ.P.

Rule 8018

RULES BY CIRCUIT COUNCILS AND DISTRICT COURTS

Circuit councils which have authorized bankruptcy appellate panels pursuant to 28 U.S.C. § 158(b) and the district courts may by action of a majority of the judges of the council or district court make and amend rules governing practice and procedure for appeals from orders or judgments of bankruptcy judges to the respective bankruptcy appellate panel or district court, not inconsistent with the rules of this Part VIII. Rule 83 F.R.Civ.P. governs the procedure for making and amending rules to govern appeals. In all cases not provided for by rule, the district court or the bankruptcy appellate panel may regulate its practice in any manner not inconsistent with these rules.

Amended Mar. 30, 1987, eff. Aug. 1, 1987.

Advisory Committee Note

This rule is similar to Rule 47 F.R.App.P. and Rule 83 F.R.Civ.P. Local rules governing procedure before the bankruptcy courts may be promulgated under Rule 9028.

Advisory Committee Notes to 1987 Amendments

Rule 83 F.R.Civ.P. was amended in August 1985 to require greater participation by the public in the rule making process. The amendment to Rule 8018 incorporates Rule 83 F.R.Civ.P. Under 28 U.S.C. § 158(b)(2), appeals may be taken to a bankruptcy appellate panel only if the district court so authorizes. If a district court does not authorize appeals to the bankruptcy appellate panel, appeals will be to the district court. This rule is amended to authorize district courts to promulgate rules for appeals.

Rule 8019

SUSPENSION OF RULES IN PART VIII

In the interest of expediting decision or for other cause, the district court or the bankruptcy appellate panel may suspend the requirements or provisions of the rules in Part VIII, except Rules 8001, 8002, and 8013, and may order proceedings in accordance with the direction.

Amended Mar. 30, 1987, eff. Aug. 1, 1987.

Advisory Committee Note

This rule is derived from Rule 2 F.R.App.P.

PART IX

GENERAL PROVISIONS

Rule
9001. General Definitions
9002. Meanings of Words in the Federal Rules of Civil Procedure When Applicable to Cases Under the Code
9003. Prohibition of Ex Parte Contacts
9004. General Requirements of Form
9005. Harmless Error
9006. Time
9007. General Authority to Regulate Notices
9008. Service or Notice by Publication
9009. Forms
9010. Representation and Appearances; Powers of Attorney
9011. Signing and Verification of Papers
9012. Oaths and Affirmations
9013. Motions: Form and Service
9014. Contested Matters
9015. [Abrogated]
9016. Subpoena
9017. Evidence
9018. Secret, Confidential, Scandalous, or Defamatory Matter
9019. Compromise and Arbitration
9020. Contempt Proceedings
9021. Entry of Judgment
9022. Notice of Judgment or Order
9023. New Trials; Amendment of Judgments
9024. Relief From Judgment or Order
9025. Security: Proceedings Against Sureties
9026. Exceptions Unnecessary
9027. Removal
9028. Disability of a Judge
9029. Local Bankruptcy Rules
9030. Jurisdiction and Venue Unaffected
9031. Masters Not Authorized
9032. Effect of Amendment of Federal Rules of Civil Procedure
9033. Review of Proposed Findings of Fact and Conclusions of Law in Non-Core Proceedings

Rule 9001

GENERAL DEFINITIONS

The definitions of words and phrases in § 101, § 902 and § 1101 and the rules of construction in § 102 of the Code govern their use in these rules. In addition, the following words and phrases used in these rules have the meanings indicated:

(1) "Bankruptcy clerk" means a clerk appointed pursuant to 28 U.S.C. § 156(b).

(2) "Bankruptcy Code" or "Code" means title 11 of the United States Code.

652

(3) "Clerk" means bankruptcy clerk, if one has been appointed, otherwise clerk of the district court.

(4) "Court" or "judge" means the judicial officer before whom a case or proceeding is pending.

(5) "Debtor." When any act is required by these rules to be performed by a debtor or when it is necessary to compel attendance of a debtor for examination and the debtor is not a natural person: (A) if the debtor is a corporation, "debtor" includes, if designated by the court, any or all of its officers, members of its board of directors or trustees or of a similar controlling body, a controlling stockholder or member, or any other person in control; (B) if the debtor is a partnership, "debtor" includes any or all of its general partners or, if designated by the court, any other person in control.

(6) "Firm" includes a partnership or professional corporation of attorneys or accountants.

(7) "Judgment" means any appealable order.

(8) "Mail" means first class, postage prepaid.

(9) "Regular associate" means any attorney regularly employed by, associated with, or counsel to an individual or firm.

(10) "Trustee" includes a debtor in possession in a chapter 11 case.

Amended Mar. 30, 1987, eff. Aug. 1, 1987.

Advisory Committee Notes to 1987 Amendments

The terms "bankruptcy clerk" and "clerk" have been defined to reflect that unless otherwise stated, for the purpose of these rules, the terms are meant to identify the court officer for the bankruptcy records. If a bankruptcy clerk is appointed, all filings are made with the bankruptcy clerk. If one has not been appointed, all filings are with the clerk of the district court. Rule 5005.

The rule is also amended to include a definition of "court or judge." Since a case or proceeding may be before a bankruptcy judge or a judge of the district court, "court or judge" is defined to mean the judicial officer before whom the case or proceeding is pending.

Rule 9002

MEANINGS OF WORDS IN THE FEDERAL RULES OF CIVIL PROCEDURE WHEN APPLICABLE TO CASES UNDER THE CODE

The following words and phrases used in the Federal Rules of Civil Procedure made applicable to cases under the Code by these rules have the meanings indicated unless they are inconsistent with the context:

(1) "Action" or "civil action" means an adversary proceeding or, when appropriate, a contested petition, or proceedings to vacate an order for relief or to determine any other contested matter.

(2) "Appeal" means an appeal as provided by 28 U.S.C. § 158.

(3) "Clerk" or "clerk of the district court" means the court officer responsible for the bankruptcy records in the district.

(4) "District court," "trial court," "court," or "judge" means bankruptcy judge if the case or proceeding is pending before a bankruptcy judge.

(5) "Judgment" includes any order appealable to an appellate court.
Amended Mar. 30, 1987, eff. Aug. 1, 1987.

Rule 9003

PROHIBITION OF EX PARTE CONTACTS

Except as otherwise permitted by applicable law, any party in interest and any attorney, accountant, or employee of a party in interest shall refrain from ex parte meetings and communications with the court concerning matters affecting a particular case or proceeding.
Amended Mar. 30, 1987, eff. Aug. 1, 1987.

Advisory Committee Note

This rule regulates the actions of parties in interest and their attorneys or others employed by parties in interest. This regulation of the conduct of parties in interest and their representative is designed to insure that the bankruptcy system operates fairly and that no appearance of unfairness is created. See H.Rep. No. 95–595, 95th Cong., 1st Sess. 95 et seq. (1977).

This rule is not a substitute for or limitation of any applicable canon of professional responsibility or judicial conduct. See, *e.g.*, Canon 7, EC7–35, Disciplinary Rule 7–110(B) of the Code of Professional Responsibility: "Generally, in adversary proceedings a lawyer should not communicate with a judge relative to a matter pending before, or which is to be brought before, a tribunal over which he presides in circumstances which might have the effect or give the appearance of granting undue advantage to one party;" and Canon 3A(4) of the Code of Judicial Conduct: "A judge should . . . neither initiate nor consider ex parte or other communications concerning a pending or impending proceeding."

Advisory Committee Notes to 1987 Amendments

This rule is amended to apply to both the bankruptcy judges and the district judges of the district.

Rule 9004

GENERAL REQUIREMENTS OF FORM

(a) **Legibility; Abbreviations.** All petitions, pleadings, schedules and other papers shall be clearly legible. Abbreviations in common use in the English language may be used.

(b) **Caption.** Each paper filed shall contain a caption setting forth the name of the court, the title of the case, the bankruptcy docket number, and a brief designation of the character of the paper.

Advisory Committee Note

Subdivision (b). Additional requirements applicable to the caption for a petition are found in Rule 1005, to the caption for notices to creditors in Rule 2002(m), and to the caption for a pleading or other paper filed in an adversary proceeding in Rule 7010. Failure to comply with this or any other rule imposing a merely formal requirement does not ordinarily result in the loss of rights. See Rule 9005.

Rule 9005

HARMLESS ERROR

Rule 61 F.R.Civ.P. applies in cases under the Code. When appropriate, the court may order the correction of any error or defect or the cure of any omission which does not affect substantial rights.

Rule 9006

TIME

(a) Computation. In computing any period of time prescribed or allowed by these rules, by the local rules, by order of court, or by any applicable statute, the day of the act, event, or default from which the designated period of time begins to run shall not be included. The last day of the period so computed shall be included, unless it is a Saturday, a Sunday, or a legal holiday, or, when the act to be done is the filing of a paper in court, a day on which weather or other conditions have made the clerk's office inaccessible, in which event the period runs until the end of the next day which is not one of the aforementioned days. When the period of time prescribed or allowed is less than 8 days, intermediate Saturdays, Sundays, and legal holidays shall be excluded in the computation. As used in this rule and in Rule 5001(c), "legal holiday" includes New Year's Day, Birthday of Martin Luther King, Jr., Washington's Birthday, Memorial Day, Independence Day, Labor Day, Columbus Day, Veterans Day, Thanksgiving Day, Christmas Day, and any other day appointed as a holiday by the President or the Congress of the United States, or by the state in which the court is held.

(b) Enlargement.

(1) In General. Except as provided in paragraphs (2) and (3) of this subdivision, when an act is required or allowed to be done at or within a specified period by these rules or by a notice given thereunder or by order of court, the court for cause shown may at any time in its discretion (1) with or without motion or notice order the period enlarged if the request therefor is made before the expiration of the period originally prescribed or as extended by a previous order or (2) on motion made after the expiration of the specified period permit the act to be done where the failure to act was the result of excusable neglect.

(2) Enlargement Not Permitted. The court may not enlarge the time for taking action under Rules 1007(d), 1017(b)(3), 1019(2), 2003(a) and (d), 7052, 9015(f), 9023, and 9024.

(3) Enlargement Limited. The court may enlarge the time for taking action under Rules 1006(b)(2), 3002(c), 4003(b), 4004(a), 4007(c), 8002, and 9033, only to the extent and under the conditions stated in those rules.

(c) Reduction.

(1) In General. Except as provided in paragraph (2) of this subdivision, when an act is required or allowed to be done at or within a specified time by these rules or by a notice given thereunder or by order of court, the court for

cause shown may in its discretion with or without motion or notice order the period reduced.

(2) Reduction Not Permitted.　The court may not reduce the time for taking action under Rules 2002(a)(4) and (a)(8), 2003(a), 3002(c), 3014, 3015, 4001(b)(2), (c) (2), 4003(a), 4004(a), 4007(c), 8002, and 9033(b).

(d) For Motions—Affidavits.　A written motion, other than one which may be heard ex parte, and notice of any hearing shall be served not later than five days before the time specified for such hearing, unless a different period is fixed by these rules or by order of the court.　Such an order may for cause shown be made on ex parte application.　When a motion is supported by affidavit, the affidavit shall be served with the motion; and, except as otherwise provided in Rule 9023, opposing affidavits may be served not later than one day before the hearing, unless the court permits them to be served at some other time.

(e) Time of Service.　Service of process and service of any paper other than process or of notice by mail is complete on mailing.

(f) Additional Time After Service by Mail.　When there is a right or requirement to do some act or undertake some proceedings within a prescribed period after service of a notice or other paper and the notice or paper other than process is served by mail, three days shall be added to the prescribed period.

(g) Grain Storage Facility Cases.　This rule shall not limit the court's authority under § 557 of the Code to enter orders governing procedures in cases in which the debtor is an owner or operator of a grain storage facility.

Amended Mar. 30, 1987, eff. Aug. 1, 1987; April 25, 1989, eff. Aug. 1, 1989.

Advisory Committee Note

Subdivision (a).　This rule is an adaptation of Rule 6 F.R.　Civ.P.　It governs the time for acts to be done and proceedings to be had in cases under the Code and any litigation arising therein.

Subdivision (b) is patterned after Rule 6(b) F.R.Civ.P. and Rule 26(b) F.R. App.P.

Paragraph (1) of this subdivision confers on the court discretion generally to authorize extensions of time for doing acts required or allowed by these rules or orders of court.　The exceptions to this general authority to extend the time are contained in paragraphs (2) and (3).

In the interest of prompt administration of bankruptcy cases certain time periods may not be extended.　Paragraph (2) lists the rules which establish time periods which may not be extended:　Rule 1007(d), time for filing a list of 20 largest creditors;　Rule 1017(b)(3), 30 day period for sending notice of dismissal for failure to pay the filing fee;　Rule 1019(2), 20 day period for notice of conversion to a chapter 7 case;　Rule 2003(a), meeting of creditors not more than 40 days after order for relief;　Rule 2003(d), 10 days for filing a motion for resolution of an election dispute;　Rule 3014, time for the § 1111(b)(2) election;　Rule 4001(b), expiration of stay 30 days following the commencement of final hearing;　Rule 7052(b), 10 day period to move to amend findings of fact;　Rule 9015(f), 20 day period to move for judgment notwithstanding the verdict;　Rule 9023, 10 day period to move for a new trial;　and Rule 9024, time to move for relief from judgment.

Many rules which establish a time for doing an act also contain a specific authorization and standard for granting an extension of time and, in some cases, limit the length of an extension. In some instances it would be inconsistent with the objective of the rule and sound administration of the case to permit extension under rule 9006(b)(1), but with respect to the other rules it is appropriate that the power to extend time be supplemented by Rule 9006(b)(1). Unless a rule which contains a specific authorization to extend time is listed in paragraph (3) of this subdivision, an extension of the time may be granted under paragraph (1) of this subdivision. If a rule is included in paragraph (3) an extension may not be granted under paragraph (1). The following rules are listed in paragraph (3): Rule 1006(b)(2), time for paying the filing fee in installments; Rule 3002(c), 90 day period for filing a claim in a chapter 7 or 13 case; Rule 4003(b), 30 days for filng objections to a claim of exemption; Rule 4004(a), 60 day period to object to a discharge; Rule 4007(b), 60 day period to file a dischargeability complaint; and Rule 8002, 10 days for filng a notice of appeal.

Subdivision (c). Paragraph (1) of this subdivision authorizes the reduction of the time periods established by these rules or an order of the court. Excluded from this general authority are the time periods established by the rules referred to in paragraph (2) of the subdivision: Rule 2002(a) and (b), 20 day and 25 day notices of certain hearings and actions in the case; Rule 2003(a), meeting of creditors to be not less than 20 days after the order for relief; Rule 3002(c), 90 days for filing a claim in a chapter 7 or 13 case; Rule 3014, time for § 1111(b)(2) election; Rule 3015, 10 day period after filing of petition to file a chapter 13 plan; Rule 4003(a), 15 days for a dependent claim exemptions; Rule 4004(a), 60 day period to object to a discharge; Rule 4007(c), 60 day period to file a dischargeability complaint; and Rule 8002, 10 days for filing a notice of appeal. Reduction of the time periods fixed in the rules referred to in this subdivision would be inconsistent with the purposes of those rules and would cause harmful uncertainty.

Subdivision (d) is derived from Rule 6(d) F.R.Civ.P. The reference is to Rule 9023 instead of to Rule 59(c) F.R.Civ.P. because Rule 9023 incorporates Rule 59 F.R.Civ.P. but excepts therefrom motions to reconsider orders allowing and disallowing claims.

Subdivision (f) is new and is the same as Rule 6(e) F.R.Civ.P.

Advisory Committee Notes to 1987 Amendments

Subdivision (a) is amended to conform to the 1984 amendments to Rule 6 F.R.Civ.P.

Subdivision (b). The reference to Rule 4001(b) in paragraph (3) is deleted because of the amendments made to Rule 4001. Rule 9033, which is new, contains specific provisions governing the extension of time to file objections to proposed findings of fact and conclusions of law. Rule 9033 is added to the rules referred to in paragraph (3).

Subdivision (c). Rule 4001(b)(2) and (c)(2) provide that a final hearing on a motion to use cash collateral or a motion for authority to obtain credit may be held no earlier than 15 days after the filing of the motion. These two rules are added to paragraph (2) to make it clear that the 15 day period may not be reduced. Rule 9033 is also added to paragraph (2).

Subdivision (g) is new. Under § 557 of the Code, as enacted by the 1984 amendments, the court is directed to expedite grain storage facility cases. This subdivision makes it clear this rule does not limit the court's authority under § 557.

The original Advisory Committee Note to this rule included the 25 day notice period of Rule 2002(b) as a time period which may not be reduced under Rule 9006(C)(2). This was an error.

Rule 9007

GENERAL AUTHORITY TO REGULATE NOTICES

When notice is to be given under these rules, the court shall designate, if not otherwise specified herein, the time within which, the entities to whom, and the form and manner in which the notice shall be given. When feasible, the court may order any notices under these rules to be combined.

Amended Mar. 30, 1987, eff. Aug. 1, 1987.

Rule 9008

SERVICE OR NOTICE BY PUBLICATION

Whenever these rules require or authorize service or notice by publication, the court shall, to the extent not otherwise specified in these rules, determine the form and manner thereof, including the newspaper or other medium to be used and the number of publications.

Rule 9009

FORMS

The Official Forms prescribed by the Judicial Conference of the United States shall be observed and used with alterations as may be appropriate. Forms may be combined and their contents rearranged to permit economies in their use. The Director of the Administrative Office of the United States Courts may issue additional forms for use under the Code.

Advisory Committee Note

The rule continues the obligatory character of the Official Forms in the interest of facilitating the processing of the paperwork of bankruptcy administration, but provides that Official Forms will be prescribed by the Judicial Conference of the United States. The Supreme Court and the Congress will thus be relieved of the burden of considering the large number of complex forms used in bankruptcy practice. The use of the Official Forms has generally been held subject to a "rule of substantial compliance" and some of these rules, for example Rule 1002, specifically state that the filed document need only "conform substantially" to the Official Form. See also Rule 9005. The second sentence recognizes the propriety of combining and rearranging Official Forms to take advantage of technological developments and resulting economies.

The Director of the Administrative Office is authorized to issue additional forms for the guidance of the bar.

Rule 9010

REPRESENTATION AND APPEARANCES; POWERS OF ATTORNEY

(a) Authority to Act Personally or by Attorney. A debtor, creditor, equity security holder, indenture trustee, committee or other party may (1) appear in a case under the Code and act either in the entity's own behalf or by an attorney authorized to practice in the court, and (2) perform any act not constituting the practice of law, by an authorized agent, attorney in fact, or proxy.

(b) Notice of Appearance. An attorney appearing for a party in a case under the Code shall file a notice of appearance with the attorney's name, office address and telephone number, unless the attorney's appearance is otherwise noted in the record.

(c) Power of Attorney. The authority of any agent, attorney in fact, or proxy to represent a creditor for any purpose other than the execution and filing of a proof of claim or the acceptance or rejection of a plan shall be evidenced by a power of attorney conforming substantially to Official Form No. 17 or Official Form No. 18. The execution of any such power of attorney shall be acknowledged before one of the officers enumerated in 28 U.S.C. § 459, § 953, Rule 9012, or a person authorized to administer oaths under the laws of the state where the oath is administered.

Amended Mar. 30, 1987, eff. Aug. 1, 1987.

Advisory Committee Note

This rule is substantially the same as former Bankruptcy Rule 910 and does not purport to change prior holdings prohibiting a corporation from appearing *pro se*. See *In re Las Colinas Development Corp.*, 585 F.2d 7 (1st Cir. 1978).

Advisory Committee Notes to 1987 Amendments

Subdivision (c) is amended to include a reference to Rule 9012 which is amended to authorize a bankruptcy judge or clerk to administer oaths.

Rule 9011

SIGNING AND VERIFICATION OF PAPERS

(a) Signature. Every petition, pleading, motion and other paper served or filed in a case under the Code on behalf of a party represented by an attorney, except a list, schedule, statement of financial affairs, statement of executory contracts, statement of intention, Chapter 13 Statement, or amendments thereto, shall be signed by at least one attorney of record in the attorney's individual name, whose office address and telephone number shall be stated. A party who is not represented by an attorney shall sign all papers and state the party's address and telephone number. The signature of an attorney or a party constitutes a certificate that the attorney or party has read the document; that to the best of the attorney's or party's knowledge, information, and belief formed after reasonable inquiry it is well grounded in fact and is warranted by existing law or a good faith argument for the extension, modification, or reversal of existing law; and that it is not interposed for any improper purpose, such as to harass, to cause delay, or to increase the cost of litigation. If a document is not signed, it shall be stricken unless it is signed promptly after the omission is called to the attention of the person whose signature is required. If a document is signed in violation of this rule, the court on motion or on its own initiative, shall impose on the person who signed it, the represented party, or both, an appropriate sanction, which may include an order to pay to the other party or parties the amount of the reasonable expenses incurred because of the filing of the document, including a reasonable attorney's fee.

(b) Verification. Except as otherwise specifically provided by these rules, papers filed in a case under the Code need not be verified. Whenever verification is required by these rules, an unsworn declaration as provided in 28 U.S.C. § 1746 satisfies the requirement of verification.

(c) Copies of Signed or Verified Papers. When these rules require copies of a signed or verified paper, it shall suffice if the original is signed or verified and the copies are conformed to the original.

Amended Mar. 30, 1987, eff. Aug. 1, 1987.

Advisory Committee Note

Subdivision (a). Excepted from the papers which an attorney for a debtor must sign are lists, schedules, statements of financial affairs, statements of executory contracts, Chapter 13 Statements and amendments thereto. Rule 1008 requires that these documents be verified by the debtor. Although the petition must also be verified, counsel for the debtor must sign the petition. See Official Form No. 1. An unrepresented party must sign all papers.

The last sentence of this subdivision authorizes a broad range of sanctions.

The word "document" is used in this subdivision to refer to all papers which the attorney or party is required to sign.

Subdivision (b) extends to all papers filed in cases under the Code the policy of minimizing reliance on the formalities of verification which is reflected in the third sentence of Rule 11 F.R.Civ.P. The second sentence of subdivision (b) permits the substitution of an unsworn declaration for the verification. See 28 U.S.C. § 1746. Rules requiring verification or an affidavit are as follows: Rule 1008, petitions, schedules, statements of financial affairs, Chapter 13 Statements and amendments; Rule 2006(e), list of multiple proxies and statement of facts and circumstances regarding their acquisition; Rule 4001(c), motion for ex parte relief from stay; Rule 7065, incorporating Rule 65(b) F.R.Civ.P. governing issuance of temporary restraining order; Rule 8011(d), affidavit in support of emergency motion on appeal.

Advisory Committee Notes to 1987 Amendments

The statement of intention of the debtor under § 521(2) of the Code is added to the documents which counsel is not required to sign.

Rule 9012

OATHS AND AFFIRMATIONS

(a) Persons Authorized to Administer Oaths. The following persons may administer oaths and affirmations and take acknowledgments: a bankruptcy judge, clerk, deputy clerk, officer authorized to administer oaths in proceedings before the courts of the United States or under the laws of the state where the oath is to be taken, or a diplomatic or consular officer of the United States in any foreign country.

(b) Affirmation in Lieu of Oath. When in a case under the Code an oath is required to be taken, a solemn affirmation may be accepted in lieu thereof.

Amended Mar. 30, 1987, eff. Aug. 1, 1987.

Advisory Committee Note

This rule is derived from Rule 43(d) F.R.Civ.P.

The provisions of former Bankruptcy Rule 912(a) relating to who may administer oaths have been deleted as unnecessary. Bankruptcy judges and the clerks and deputy clerks of bankruptcy courts are authorized by statute to administer oaths and affirmations and to take acknowledgments. 28 U.S.C. §§ 459, 953. A person designated to preside at the meeting of creditors has authority under rule 2003(b)(1) to administer the oath. Administration of the oath at a deposition is governed by Rule 7028.

Advisory Committee Notes to 1987 Amendments

Subdivision (a) has been added to the rule to authorize bankruptcy judges and clerks to administer oaths.

Rule 9013

MOTIONS: FORM AND SERVICE

A request for an order, except when an application is authorized by these rules, shall be by written motion, unless made during a hearing. The motion shall state with particularity the grounds therefor, and shall set forth the relief or order sought. Every written motion other than one which may be considered ex parte shall be served by the moving party on the trustee or debtor in possession and on those entities specified by these rules or, if service is not required or the entities to be served are not specified by these rules, the moving party shall serve the entities the court directs.

Amended Mar. 30, 1987, eff. Aug. 1, 1987.

Advisory Committee Note

This rule is derived from Rule 5(a) and Rule 7(b)(1) F.R.Civ.P. Except when an application is specifically authorized by these rules, for example an application under rule 2014 for approval of the employment of a professional, all requests for court action must be made by motion.

Rule 9014

CONTESTED MATTERS

In a contested matter in a case under the Code not otherwise governed by these rules, relief shall be requested by motion, and reasonable notice and opportunity for hearing shall be afforded the party against whom relief is sought. No response is required under this rule unless the court orders an answer to a motion. The motion shall be served in the manner provided for service of a summons and complaint by Rule 7004, and, unless the court otherwise directs, the following rules shall apply: 7021, 7025, 7026, 7028–7037, 7041, 7042, 7052, 7054–7056, 7062, 7064, 7069, and 7071. The court may at any stage in a particular matter direct that one or more of the other rules in Part VII shall apply. An entity that desires to perpetuate testimony may proceed in the same manner as provided in Rule 7027 for the taking of a deposition before an adversary proceeding. The clerk shall give notice to the parties of the entry of any order directing that additional rules of Part VII are applicable or that certain of the rules of Part VII are not applicable. The notice shall be given within such time as is necessary to afford the parties a reasonable opportunity to comply with the procedures made applicable by the order.

Amended Mar. 30, 1987, eff. Aug. 1, 1987.

Advisory Committee Note

Rules 1017(d), 3020(b)(1), 4001(a), 4003(d), and 6006(a), which govern respectively dismissal or conversion of a case, objections to confirmation of a plan, relief from the automatic stay and the use of cash collateral, avoidance of a lien under § 522(f) of the Code, and the assumption or rejection of executory contracts or unexpired leases, specifically provide that litigation under those rules shall be as provided in Rule 9014. This rule also governs litigation in other contested matters.

Whenever there is an actual dispute, other than an adversary proceeding, before the bankrupty court, the litigation to resolve that dispute is a contested matter. For example, the filing of an objection to a proof of claim, to a claim of exemption, or to a disclosure statement creates a dispute which is a contested matter. Even when an objection is not formally required, there may be a dispute. If a party in interest opposes the amount of compensation sought by a professional, there is a dispute which is a contested matter.

When the rules of Part VII are applicable to a contested matter, reference in the Part VII rules to adversary proceedings is to be read as a reference to a contested matter. See Rule 9002(1).

Rule 9015

[ABROGATED]

Abrogated Mar. 30, 1987, eff. Aug. 1, 1987.

Advisory Committee Note

Subdivisions (a)–(f) of this rule are adaptations of subdivisions of Rules 38 and 39 F.R.Civ.P.

Whether a party is entitled to a jury trial is governed by 28 U.S.C. § 1480(a). Subsection (b) of § 1480 empowers the court to dispense with a jury trial on issues presented by a contested involuntary petition, even when a jury trial is properly demanded. The purpose of § 1480(b) is to insure that contested petitions are decided promptly. The court may under § 1480(b) and subdivision (b)(3) act sua sponte and direct that a contested petition be tried by the court instead of to a jury.

Rule 9027(i) governs the procedure for requesting trial by jury in a matter removed to a bankruptcy court.

Advisory Committee Notes to 1987 Amendments

Former section 1480 of title 28 preserved a right to trial by jury in any case or proceeding under title 11 in which jury trial was provided by statute. Rule 9015 provided the procedure for jury trials in bankruptcy courts. Section 1480 was repealed. Section 1411 added by the 1984 amendments affords a jury trial only for personal injury or wrongful death claims, which 28 U.S.C. § 157(b)(5) requires be tried in the district court. Nevertheless, Rule 9015 has been cited as conferring a right to jury trial in other matters before bankruptcy judges. In light of the clear mandate of 28 U.S.C. § 2075 that the "rules shall not abridge, enlarge, or modify any substantive right," Rule 9015 is abrogated. In the event the courts of appeals or the Supreme Court define a right to a jury trial in any bankruptcy matters, a local rule in substantially the form of Rule 9015 can be adopted pending amendment of these rules.

Rule 9016

SUBPOENA

Rule 45 F.R.Civ.P. applies in cases under the Code.

Amended Mar. 30, 1987, eff. Aug. 1, 1987.

Advisory Committee Note

Although Rule 7004(d) authorizes nationwide service of process, Rule 45 F.R.Civ.P. limits the subpoena power to the judicial district and places outside the district which are within 100 miles of the place of trial or hearing.

Rule 9017

EVIDENCE

The Federal Rules of Evidence and rules 43, 44 and 44.1 F.R.Civ.P. apply in cases under the Code.

Advisory Committee Note

Sections 251 and 252 of Public Law 95–598, amended rule 1101 of the Federal Rules of Evidence to provide that the Federal Rules of Evidence apply in bankruptcy courts and to any case or proceeding under the Code. Rules 43, 44 and 44.1 of the F.R.Civ.P., which supplement the Federal Rules of Evidence, are by this rule made applicable to cases under the Code.

Examples of bankruptcy rules containing matters of an evidentiary nature are: Rule 2011, evidence of debtor retained in possession; Rule 3001(f), proof of claim constitutes prima facie evidence of the amount and validity of a claim; and Rule 5007(c), sound recording of court proceedings constitutes the record of the proceedings.

Rule 9018

SECRET, CONFIDENTIAL, SCANDALOUS, OR DEFAMATORY MATTER

On motion or on its own initiative, with or without notice, the court may make any order which justice requires (1) to protect the estate or any entity in respect of a trade secret or other confidential research, development, or commercial information, (2) to protect any entity against scandalous or defamatory matter contained in any paper filed in a case under the Code, or (3) to protect governmental matters that are made confidential by statute or regulation. If an order is entered under this rule without notice, any entity affected thereby may move to vacate or modify the order, and after a hearing on notice the court shall determine the motion.

Advisory Committee Note

This rule provides the procedure for invoking the court's power under § 107 of the Code.

Rule 9019

COMPROMISE AND ARBITRATION

(a) **Compromise.** On motion by the trustee and after a hearing on notice to creditors, the debtor and indenture trustees as provided in Rule 2002(a) and to such other entities as the court may designate, the court may approve a compromise or settlement.

(b) **Authority to Compromise or Settle Controversies Within Classes.** After a hearing on such notice as the court may direct, the court may fix a class or classes of controversies and authorize the trustee to compromise or settle controversies within such class or classes without further hearing or notice.

(c) **Arbitration.** On stipulation of the parties to any controversy affecting the estate the court may authorize the matter to be submitted to final and binding arbitration.

Amended Mar. 30, 1987, eff. Aug. 1, 1987.

Advisory Committee Note

Subdivisions (a) and (c) of this rule are essentially the same as the provisions of former Bankruptcy Rule 919 and subdivision (b) is the same as former Rule 8–514(b), which was applicable to railroad reorganizations. Subdivision (b) permits the court to deal efficiently with a case in which there may be a large number of settlements.

Rule 9020

CONTEMPT PROCEEDINGS

(a) Contempt Committed in Presence of Bankruptcy Judge. Contempt committed in the presence of a bankruptcy judge may be determined summarily by a bankruptcy judge. The order of contempt shall recite the facts and shall be signed by the bankruptcy judge and entered of record.

(b) Other Contempt. Contempt committed in a case or proceeding pending before a bankruptcy judge, except when determined as provided in subdivision (a) of this rule, may be determined by the bankruptcy judge only after a hearing on notice. The notice shall be in writing, shall state the essential facts constituting the contempt charged and describe the contempt as criminal or civil and shall state the time and place of hearing, allowing a reasonable time for the preparation of the defense. The notice may be given on the court's own initiative or on application of the United States attorney or by an attorney appointed by the court for that purpose. If the contempt charged involves disrespect to or criticism of a bankruptcy judge, that judge is disqualified from presiding at the hearing except with the consent of the person charged.

(c) Service and Effective Date of Order; Review. The clerk shall serve forthwith a copy of the order of contempt on the entity named therein. The order shall be effective 10 days after service of the order and shall have the same force and effect as an order of contempt entered by the district court unless, within the 10 day period, the entity named therein serves and files with the clerk objections prepared in the manner provided in Rule 9033(b). If timely objections are filed, the order shall be reviewed as provided in Rule 9033.

(d) Right to Jury Trial. Nothing in this rule shall be construed to impair the right to jury trial whenever it otherwise exists.

Amended Mar. 30, 1987, eff. Aug. 1, 1987.

Advisory Committee Note

Section 1481 of Title 28 provides that a bankruptcy court "may not . . . punish a criminal contempt not committed in the presence of the judge of the court or warranting a punishment of imprisonment." Rule 9020 does not enlarge the power of bankruptcy courts.

Subdivision (a) is adapted from former Bankruptcy Rule 920 and Rule 42 F.R.Crim.P. Paragraph (1) of the subdivision permits summary imposition of punishment for contempt if the conduct is in the presence of the court and is of such nature that the conduct "obstruct[s] the administration of justice." See 18 U.S.C. § 401(a). Cases interpreting Rule 42(a) F.R.Crim.P. have held that when criminal contempt is in question summary disposition should be the exception: summary disposition should be reserved for situations where it is necessary to protect the judicial institution. 3 Wright, *Federal Practice & Procedure—Criminal* § 707 (1969). Those cases are equally pertinent to the application of this rule and, therefore, contemptuous conduct in the presence of the judge may often be punished only after the notice and hearing requirements of subdivision (b) are satisfied.

If the bankruptcy court concludes it is without power to punish or to impose the proper punishment for conduct which constitutes contempt, subdivision (a)(3) authorizes the bankruptcy court to certify the matter to the district court.

Subdivision (b) makes clear that when a person has a constitutional or statutory right to a jury trial in a criminal contempt matter this rule in no way affects that right. See Frank v. United States, 395 U.S. 147 (1969).

The Federal Rules of Civil Procedures do not specifically provide the procedure for the imposition of civil contempt sanctions. The decisional law governing the procedure for imposition of civil sanctions by the district courts will be equally applicable to the bankruptcy courts.

Advisory Committee Notes to 1987 Amendments

The United States Bankruptcy Courts, as constituted under the Bankruptcy Reform Act of 1978, were courts of law, equity, and admiralty with an inherent contempt power, but former 28 U.S.C. § 1481 restricted the criminal contempt power of bankruptcy judges. Under the 1984 amendments, bankruptcy judges are judicial officers of the district court, 28 U.S.C. §§ 151, 152(a)(1). There are no decisions by the courts of appeals concerning the authority of bankruptcy judges to punish for either civil or criminal contempt under the 1984 amendments. This rule, as amended, recognizes that bankruptcy judges may not have the power to punish for contempt.

Sound judicial administration requires that the initial determination of whether contempt has been committed should be made by the bankruptcy judge. If timely objections are not filed to the bankruptcy judge's order, the order has the same force and effect as an order of the district court. If objections are filed within 10 days of service of the order, the district court conducts a de novo review pursuant to Rule 9033 and any order of contempt is entered by the district court on completion of the court's review of the bankruptcy judge's order.

Rule 9021

ENTRY OF JUDGMENT

Except as otherwise provided herein, Rule 58 F.R.Civ.P. applies in cases under the Code. Every judgment entered in an adversary proceeding or contested matter shall be set forth on a separate document. A judgment is effective when entered as provided in Rule 5003. The reference in Rule 58 F.R.Civ.P. to Rule 79(a) F.R.Civ.P. shall be read as a reference to Rule 5003 of these rules. Amended Mar. 30, 1987, eff. Aug. 1, 1987.

Advisory Committee Note

Subdivision (a). This rule is derived from Rule 58 F.R.Civ.P. The requirement that a judgment entered in an adversary proceeding or contested matter be set forth on a separate document is to eliminate uncertainty as to whether an opinion or memorandum of the court is a judgment. There is no sound reason to require that every order in a case under the Code be evidenced by a separate document.

Subdivision (b) establishes a procedure for entering a judgment of a bankruptcy court for the recovery of money or property in an index of judgments kept by the clerk of the district court. It clarifies the availability of the same remedies for the enforcement of a bankruptcy court judgment as those provided for the enforcement of a district court judgment. See 28 U.S.C. §§ 1961–63. When indexed in accordance with subdivision (b) of this rule a judgment of the bankruptcy court may be found by anyone searching for liens of record in the judgment records of the district court. Certification of a copy of the judgment to the clerk of the district court provides a basis for registration of the judgment pursuant to 28 U.S.C. § 1963 in any other district. When so registered, the judgment may be enforced by issuance of execution and orders for supplementary proceedings that may be served anywhere within the state where the registering court sits. See 7 Moore, Federal Practice 2409–11 (2d ed. 1971). The procedures available in the district court are not exclusive, however, and the holder of a judgment entered by the bankruptcy court may use the remedies under Rules 7069 and 7070 even if the judgment is indexed by the clerk of the district court.

Subdivision (c) makes it clear that when a district court hears a matter reserved to it by 28 U.S.C. §§ 1471, 1481, its judgments are entered in the district court's civil docket and in the docket of the bankruptcy court. When the district court acts as an appellate court, Rule 8016(a) governs the entry of judgments on appeal.

Advisory Committee Notes to 1987 Amendments

Former subdivision (a) was derived from Rule 58 F.R.Civ.P. As amended, Rule 9021 adopts Rule 58. The reference in Rule 58 to Rule 79(a) F.R.Civ.P. is to be read as a reference to Rule 5003.

Rule 9022

NOTICE OF JUDGMENT OR ORDER

(a) Judgment or Order of Bankruptcy Judge. Immediately on the entry of a judgment or order the clerk shall serve a notice of the entry by mail in the manner provided by Rule 7005 on the contesting parties and on other entities as the court directs. Service of the notice shall be noted in the docket. Lack of notice of the entry does not affect the time to appeal or relieve or authorize the court to relieve a party for failure to appeal within the time allowed, except as permitted in Rule 8002.

(b) Judgment or Order of District Judge. Notice of a judgment or order entered by a district judge is governed by Rule 77(d) F.R.Civ.P.

Amended Mar. 30, 1987, eff. Aug. 1, 1987.

Advisory Committee Note

Subdivision (a) of this rule is an adaptation of Rule 77(d) F.R.Civ.P.

Subdivision (b) complements Rule 9021(b). When a district court acts as an appellate court, Rule 8016(b) requires the clerk to give notice of the judgment on appeal.

Rule 9023

NEW TRIALS; AMENDMENT OF JUDGMENTS

Rule 59 F.R.Civ.P. applies in cases under the Code, except as provided in Rule 3008.

Advisory Committee Note

Rule 59 F.R.Civ.P. regulates motions for a new trial and amendment of judgment. Those motions must be served within 10 days of the entry of judgment. No similar time limit is contained in Rule 3008 which governs reconsideration of claims.

Rule 9024

RELIEF FROM JUDGMENT OR ORDER

Rule 60 F.R.Civ.P. applies in cases under the Code except that (1) a motion to reopen a case under the Code or for the reconsideration of an order allowing or disallowing a claim against the estate entered without a contest is not subject to the one year limitation prescribed in Rule 60(b), (2) a complaint to revoke a discharge in a chapter 7 liquidation case may be filed only within the time allowed by § 727(e) of the Code, and (3) a complaint to revoke an order confirming a plan may be filed only within the time allowed by § 1144 or § 1330.

Advisory Committee Note

Motions to reopen cases are governed by Rule 5010. Reconsideration of orders allowing and disallowing claims is governed by Rule 3008. For the purpose of this rule all orders of the bankruptcy court are subject to Rule 60 F.R.Civ.P.

Pursuant to § 727(e) of the Code a complaint to revoke a discharge must be filed within one year of the entry of the discharge or, when certain grounds of revocation are asserted, the later of one year after the entry of the discharge or the date the case is closed. Under § 1144 and § 1330 of the Code a party must file a complaint to revoke an order confirming a chapter 11 or 13 plan within 180 days of its entry. Clauses (2) and (3) of this rule make it clear that the time periods established by §§ 727(e), 1144 and 1330 of the Code may not be circumvented by the invocation of F.R.Civ.P. 60(b).

Rule 9025

SECURITY: PROCEEDINGS AGAINST SURETIES

Whenever the Code or these rules require or permit the giving of security by a party, and security is given in the form of a bond or stipulation or other undertaking with one or more sureties, each surety submits to the jurisdiction of the court, and liability may be determined in an adversary proceeding governed by the rules in Part VII.

Advisory Committee Note

This rule is an adaptation of Rule 65.1 F.R.Civ.P. and applies to any surety on a bond given pursuant to § 303(e) of the Code, Rules 2001, 2010, 5008, 7062, 7065, 8005, or any other rule authorizing the giving of such security.

Rule 9026

EXCEPTIONS UNNECESSARY

Rule 46 F.R.Civ.P. applies in cases under the Code.

Rule 9027

REMOVAL

(a) Application.

(1) Where Filed; Form and Content. An application for removal shall be filed with the clerk for the district and division within which is located the state or federal court where the civil action is pending. The application shall be verified and contain a short and plain statement of the facts which entitle the applicant to remove and be accompanied by a copy of all process and pleadings.

(2) Time for Filing; Civil Action Initiated Before Commencement of the Case Under the Code. If the claim or cause of action in a civil action is pending when a case under the Code is commenced, an application for removal may be filed only within the longest of (A) 90 days after the order for relief in the case under the Code, (B) 30 days after entry of an order terminating a stay, if the claim or cause of action in a civil action has been stayed under § 362 of the Code, or (C) 30 days after a trustee qualifies in a chapter 11 reorganization case but not later than 180 days after the order for relief.

(3) Time for Filing; Civil Action Initiated After Commencement of the Case Under the Code. If a case under the Code is pending when a claim or cause of action is asserted in another court, an application for removal may be filed with the clerk only within the shorter of (A) 30 days after receipt, through service or otherwise, of a copy of the initial pleading setting forth the claim or cause of action sought to be removed or (B) 30 days after receipt of the summons if the initial pleading has been filed with the court but not served with the summons.

(b) Bond. An application for removal, except when the applicant is the trustee, debtor, debtor in possession, or the United States shall be accompanied by a bond with good and sufficient surety conditioned that the party will pay all costs and disbursements incurred by reason of the removal should it be determined that the claim or cause of action was not removable or was improperly removed.

(c) Notice. Promptly after filing the application and the bond, if required, the applicant shall serve a copy of the application on all parties to the removed claim or cause of action.

(d) Filing in Non-bankruptcy Court. Promptly after filing the application and bond, if any, the applicant shall file a copy of the application with the clerk of the court from which the claim or cause of action is removed. Removal of the claim or cause of action is effected on such filing of a copy of the application. The parties shall proceed no further in that court unless and until the claim or cause of action is remanded.

(e) Remand. A motion for remand of the removed claim or cause of action shall be filed with the clerk and served on the parties to the removed claim or cause of action. Unless the district court orders otherwise, a motion for remand shall be heard by the bankruptcy judge, who shall file a report and recommendation for disposition of the motion. The clerk shall serve forthwith a copy of the report and recommendation on the parties. Within 10 days of being served with a copy of the report and recommendation, a party may serve and file with the clerk objections prepared in the manner provided in Rule 9033(b). Review by the district court of the report and recommendation shall be governed by Rule 9033.

(f) Procedure After Removal.

(1) After removal of a claim or cause of action to a district court the district court or, if the case under the Code has been referred to a bankruptcy judge of the district, the bankruptcy judge, may issue all necessary orders and process to bring before it all proper parties whether served by process issued by the court from which the claim or cause of action was removed or otherwise.

(2) The district court or, if the case under the Code has been referred to a bankruptcy judge of the district, the bankruptcy judge, may require the applicant to file with the clerk copies of all records and proceedings relating to the claim or cause of action in the court from which the claim or cause of action was removed.

(g) Process After Removal. If one or more of the defendants has not been served with process, the service has not been perfected prior to removal, or the process served proves to be defective, such process or service may be completed or new process issued pursuant to Part VII of these rules. This subdivision shall not deprive any defendant on whom process is served after removal of the defendant's right to move to remand the case.

(h) Applicability of Part VII. The rules of Part VII apply to a claim or cause of action removed to a district court from a federal or state court and govern procedure after removal. Repleading is not necessary unless the court so orders. In a removed action in which the defendant has not answered, the defendant shall answer or present the other defenses or objections available under the rules of Part VII within 20 days following the receipt through service or otherwise of a copy of the initial pleading setting forth the claim for relief on which the action or proceeding is based, or within 20 days following the service of summons on such initial pleading, or within five days following the filing of the application for removal, whichever period is longest.

(i) [Abrogated]

(j) Record Supplied. When a party is entitled to copies of the records and proceedings in any civil action or proceeding in a federal or a state court, to be used in the removed civil action or proceeding, and the clerk of the federal or state court, on demand accompanied by payment or tender of the lawful fees, fails to deliver certified copies, the court may, on affidavit reciting the facts, direct such record to be supplied by affidavit or otherwise. Thereupon the proceedings, trial and judgment may be had in the court, and all process awarded, as if certified copies had been filed.

(k) Attachment or Sequestration; Securities. When a claim or cause of action is removed to a district court, any attachment or sequestration of property in the court from which the claim or cause of action was removed shall hold the property to answer the final judgment or decree in the same manner as the property would have been held to answer final judgment or decree had it been rendered by the court from which the claim or cause of action was removed. All bonds, undertakings, or security given by either party to the claim or cause of action prior to its removal shall remain valid and effectual notwithstanding such removal. All injunctions issued, orders entered and other proceedings had prior to removal shall remain in full force and effect until dissolved or modified by the court.

Amended Mar. 30, 1987, eff. Aug. 1, 1987.

Advisory Committee Note

Under 28 U.S.C. § 1478(a) "any claim or cause of action in a civil action, other than a proceeding before the United States Tax Court or a civil action by a Government unit to enforce [a] . . . regulatory or police power" may be removed "if the bankruptcy courts have jurisdiction over such claim or cause of action." This rule specifies how removal is accomplished, the procedure thereafter, and the procedure to request remand of the removed claim or cause of action. If the claim or cause of action which is removed to the bankruptcy court is subject to the automatic stay of § 362 of the Code, the litigation may not proceed in the bankruptcy court until relief from the stay is granted.

The subdivisions of this rule conform substantially to 28 U.S.C. §§ 1446–1450 and Rule 81(a) F.R.Civ.P. pertaining to removal to the district courts.

Subdivision (a)(1) is derived from 28 U.S.C. § 1446(a).

Subdivisions (a)(2) and (a)(3) are derived from paragraphs one and two of 28 U.S.C. § 1446(b). Timely exercise of the right to remove is as important in bankruptcy cases as in removals from a state court to a district court.

Subdivision (a)(2) governs the situation in which there is litigation pending and a party to the litigation becomes a debtor under the Code. Frequently, removal would be of little utility in such cases because the pending litigation will be stayed by § 362(a) on commencement of the case under the Code. As long as the stay remains in effect there is no reason to impose a time limit for removal to the bankruptcy court and, therefore, clause (B) of subdivision (a)(2) provides that a removal application maybe filed within 30 days of entry of an order terminating the stay. Parties to stayed litigation will not be required to act immediately on commencement of a case under the Code to protect their right to removal. If the pending litigation is not stayed by § 362(a) of the Code, the removal application must ordinarily be filed within 90 days of the order for relief. Clause (C) contains an alternative period for a chapter 11 case. If a trustee is appointed, the removal application may be filed within 30 days of the trustee's qualification, provided that the removal application is filed not more than 180 days after the order for relief.

The removal application must be filed within the longest of the three possible periods. For example, in a chapter 11 case if the 90 day period expires but a trustee is appointed shortly thereafter, the removal application may be filed within 30 days of the trustee's qualification but not later than 180 days after the order for relief. Nevertheless, if the claim or cause of action in the civil action is stayed under § 362, the application may be filed after the 180 day period expires, provided the application is filed within 30 days of an order terminating the stay.

Subdivision (a)(3) applies to a situation in which the case under the Code is pending when the removable claim or cause of action is asserted in a civil action initiated in other than the bankruptcy court. The time for filing the application for removal begins to run on receipt of the first pleading containing the removable claim or cause of action. Only litigation not stayed by the code or by court order may properly be initiated after the case under the Code is commenced. See *e.g.*, § 362(a).

Subdivision (b). With one exception, this subdivision is the same as 28 U.S.C. § 1446(d). The exemption from the bond requirement is enlarged to include a trustee or debtor in possession. Complete exemption from the bond requirement for removal is appropriate because of the limited resources which may be available at the beginning of a case and the small probability that an action will be improperly removed.

Recovery on the bond is permitted only when the removal was improper. If the removal is proper but the bankruptcy court orders the action remanded on equitable grounds, 28 U.S.C. § 1478(b), there is no recovery on the bond.

Subdivisions (c) and (d) are patterned on 28 U.S.C. § 1446(e).

Subdivision (e). There is no provision in the Federal Rules of Civil Procedure for seeking remand. The first sentence of this subdivision requires that a request for remand be by motion and that the moving party serve all other parties; however, no hearing is required. In recognition of the intrusion of the removal practice on the state and federal courts from which claims or causes of action are removed, the subdivision directs the bankruptcy court to decide remand motions as soon as practicable. The last sentence of this subdivision is derived from 28 U.S.C. § 1446(c).

Subdivisions (f) and (g), with appropriate changes to conform them to the bankruptcy contest, are the same as 28 U.S.C. § 1447(a) and (b) and 28 U.S.C. § 1448, respectively.

Subdivisions (h) and (i) are taken from Rule 81(c) F.R.Civ.P.

Subdivisions (j) and (k) are derived from 28 U.S.C. § 1449 and § 1450, respectively.

Remand orders of bankruptcy judges are not appealable. 28 U.S.C. § 1478(b).

This rule does not deal with the question whether a single plaintiff or defendant may remove a claim or cause of action if there are two or more plaintiffs or defendants. See 28 U.S.C. § 1478.

Advisory Committee Notes to 1987 Amendments

Section 1452 of title 28, with certain exceptions, provides for removal of claims or causes of action in civil actions pending in state or federal courts when the claim or cause of action is within the jurisdiction conferred by 28 U.S.C. § 1334. An order granting or denying a motion for remand is not appealable. 28 U.S.C. § 1452(b). Under subdivision (e), as amended, the district court must enter the order on the remand motion; however, the bankruptcy judge conducts the initial hearing on the motion and files a report and recommendation. The parties may file objections. Review of the report and recommendation is pursuant to Rule 9033.

Subdivision (f) has been amended to provide that if there has been a referral pursuant to 28 U.S.C. § 157(a) the bankruptcy judge will preside over the removed civil action.

Subdivision (i) has been abrogated consistent with the abrogation of Rule 9015.

Rule 9028

DISABILITY OF A JUDGE

Rule 63 F.R.Civ.P. applies in cases under the Code.
Amended Mar. 30, 1987, eff. Aug. 1, 1987.

Advisory Committee Note

This rule is an adaptation of Rule 63 F.R.Civ.P.

Advisory Committee Notes to 1987 Amendments

Rule 9028 has been changed to adopt the procedures contained in Rule 63 of the Federal Rules of Civil Procedure for substituting a judge in the event of disability.

Rule 9029

LOCAL BANKRUPTCY RULES

Each district court by action of a majority of the judges thereof may make and amend rules governing practice and procedure in all cases and proceedings within the district court's bankruptcy jurisdiction which are not inconsistent with these rules. Rule 83 F.R.Civ.P. governs the procedure for making local rules. A district court may authorize the bankruptcy judges of the district, subject to any limitation or condition it may prescribe and the requirements of 83 F.R.Civ.P., to make rules of practice and procedure not inconsistent with these rules. In all cases not provided for by rule, the court may regulate its practice in any manner not inconsistent with these rules or those of the district in which the court acts.
Amended Mar. 30, 1987, eff. Aug. 1, 1987.

Advisory Committee Note

This rule is an adaptation of Rule 83 F.R.Civ.P. and Rule 57(a) F.R.Crim. P. Under this rule bankruptcy courts may make local rules which govern practice before those courts. Circuit councils and district courts are authorized by Rule 8018 to make local rules governing appellate practice.

Advisory Committee Notes to 1987 Amendments

Rule 9029 is amended to authorize the district court to promulgate local rules governing bankruptcy practice. This rule, as amended, permits the district court to authorize the bankruptcy judges to promulgate or recommend local rules for adoption by the district court.

Effective August 1, 1985, Rule 83 F.R.Civ.P., governing adoption of local rules, was amended to achieve greater participation by the bar, scholars, and the public in the rule making process; to authorize the judicial council to abrogate local rules; and to make certain that single-judge standing orders are not inconsistent with these rules or local rules. Rule 9029 has been amended to incorporate Rule 83. The term "court" in the last sentence of the rule includes the judges of the district court and the bankruptcy judges of the district. See Rule 9001(4).

Rule 9030

JURISDICTION AND VENUE UNAFFECTED

These rules shall not be construed to extend or limit the jurisdiction of the courts or the venue of any matters therein.

Amended Mar. 30, 1987, eff. Aug. 1, 1987.

Advisory Committee Note

The rule is an adaptation of Rule 82 F.R.Civ.P.

Rule 9031

MASTERS NOT AUTHORIZED

Rule 53 F.R.Civ.P. does not apply in cases under the Code.

Advisory Committee Note

This rule precludes the appointment of masters in cases and proceedings under the Code.

Rule 9032

EFFECT OF AMENDMENT OF FEDERAL RULES OF CIVIL PROCEDURE

The Federal Rules of Civil Procedure which are incorporated by reference and made applicable by these rules shall be the Federal Rules of Civil Procedure in effect on the effective date of these rules and as thereafter amended, unless otherwise provided by such amendment.

Rule 9033

REVIEW OF PROPOSED FINDINGS OF FACT AND CONCLUSIONS OF LAW IN NON–CORE PROCEEDINGS

(a) **Service.** In non-core proceedings heard pursuant to 28 U.S.C. § 157(c)(1), the bankruptcy judge shall file proposed findings of fact and conclusions of law. The clerk shall serve forthwith copies on all parties by mail and note the date of mailing on the docket.

(b) **Objections: Time for Filing.** Within 10 days after being served with a copy of the proposed findings of fact and conclusions of law a party may serve and file with the clerk written objections which identify the specific proposed findings or conclusions objected to and state the grounds for such objection. A party may respond to another party's objections within 10 days after being served with a copy thereof. A party objecting to the bankruptcy judge's proposed findings or conclusions shall arrange promptly for the transcription of the record, or such portions of it as all parties may agree upon or the bankruptcy judge deems sufficient, unless the district judge otherwise directs.

(c) **Extension of Time.** The bankruptcy judge may for cause extend the time for filing objections by any party for a period not to exceed 20 days from the expiration of the time otherwise prescribed by this rule. A request to extend the time for filing objections must be made before the time for filing objections has expired, except that a request made no more than 20 days after the expiration of the time for filing objections may be granted upon a showing of excusable neglect.

(d) Standard of Review. The district judge shall make a de novo review upon the record or, after additional evidence, of any portion of the bankruptcy judge's findings of fact or conclusions of law to which specific written objection has been made in accordance with this rule. The district judge may accept, reject, or modify the proposed findings of fact or conclusions of law, receive further evidence, or recommit the matter to the bankruptcy judge with instructions.

Adopted Mar. 30, 1987, eff. Aug. 1, 1987.

Advisory Committee Notes

Section 157(c)(1) of title 28 requires a bankruptcy judge to submit proposed findings of fact and conclusions of law to the district court when the bankruptcy judge has heard a non-core proceeding. This rule, which is modeled on Rule 72 F.R.Civ.P., provides the procedure for objecting to, and for review by, the district court of specific findings and conclusions.

Subdivision (a) requires the clerk to serve a copy of the proposed findings and conclusions on the parties. The bankruptcy clerk, or the district court clerk if there is no bankruptcy clerk in the district, shall serve a copy of the proposed findings and conclusions on all parties.

Subdivision (b) is derived from Rule 72(b) F.R.Civ.P. which governs objections to a recommended disposition by a magistrate.

Subdivision (c) is similar to Rule 8002(c) of the Bankruptcy Rules and provides for granting of extensions of time to file objections to proposed findings and conclusions.

Subdivision (d) adopts the de novo review provisions of Rule 72(b) F.R.Civ.P.

PART X

UNITED STATES TRUSTEES

Rule
X–1001. Applicability of Rules
X–1002. Petitions, Lists, Schedules and Statements
X–1003. Appointment of Interim Trustee Before Order for Relief in a Chapter 7 Liquidation Case
X–1004. Notification to Trustee of Selection; Blanket Bond
X–1005. Trustees for Estates When Joint Administration Ordered
X–1006. Meetings of Creditors or Equity Security Holders
X–1007. Duty of Trustee or Debtor in Possession to Make Reports, Furnish Information, and Cooperate With United States Trustee
X–1008. Notices to United States Trustee
X–1009. Right to Be Heard; Filing Papers
X–1010. Prohibition of Ex Parte Contacts

Rule X–1001

APPLICABILITY OF RULES

(a) **Part X Rules.** The rules in Part X apply to cases under the Code filed in or transferred to any district in which a United States trustee is authorized.

(b) **Inapplicability of Rules.** The following rules do not apply in cases under the Code filed in or transferred to any district specified in subdivision (a) of this rule: 2001(a), (c), 2002(a)(1), 2003(a), (b)(1), (2), (d), 2007, 2008, 2009(c), (d), (e), 2010(a), 5008, and the second sentence of 6003.

Advisory Committee Note

Section 1501 of the Code lists the following judicial or "pilot" districts in which United States trustees are to be appointed by the Attorney General pursuant to 28 U.S.C. § 581: Northern District of Alabama, Central District of California, Districts of Colorado, District of Columbia, Delaware, Northern District of Illinois, Districts of Kansas, Maine, Massachusetts, Minnesota, New Hampshire, New Jersey, Southern District of New York, Districts of North Dakota, Rhode Island, South Dakota, Northern District of Texas, and Eastern District of Virginia.

These Part X rules are for use in those districts in connection with the duties and responsibilities of the United States trustees. They are set out separately to facilitate their repeal in the event the United States trustee system is not continued by Congress beyond March 31, 1984. See Pub.L. 95–598, § 408(c).

Subdivision (b) indicates the rules that are not applicable in the pilot districts. Following is a list of the rules in Part X and the rules which they affect, in addition to those listed in Rule X–1001:

Rules in Part X	Rules in Parts I through IX affected by rules in Part X
X–1002	1007(d)
X–1002(a)	1007(a)

676

Rules in Part X	Rules in Parts I through IX affected by rules in Part X
X–1002(b)	1007(a)(4)
	1002(b)
	1003(b)
	1007(f)
X–1003(a)	2001(a)
X–1003(b)	2001(c)
X–1004	2008
	2009(e)
	2013(a)
X–1005	2009(e)
X–1005(a)	2009(c)
X–1006	2007 (as to chapter 11)
X–1006(a)	2003(a)
X–1006(b)(1)	2003(b)(1)
X–1006(b)(2)	2003(b)(2)
X–1006(c)	2003(d)
X–1007(a)	2015(a)(1)
X–1007(b)	4002
X–1008	2002(a), (b)
X–1008(a)	2002(a)(2), (5), (7), (f)

Cross references to rules affected by rules in Part X (in addition to those listed in Rule X–1001)

Rule affected	Rules in Part X
1002(b)	X–1002(b)
1003(b)	X–1002(b)
1007(a)(4)	X–1002(b)
1007(a)	X–1002(a)
1007(d)	X–1002
2002(a)	X–1008
2002(a)(2)	X–1008(a)
2002(a)(5)	X–1008(a)
2002(a)(7)	X–1008(a)
2002(b)	X–1008(a)
2002(f)	X–1007(a)
2015(a)(1)	X–1008(a)

Rule X–1002

PETITIONS, LISTS, SCHEDULES AND STATEMENTS

(a) Petitions and Accompanying Materials.

(1) Number of Copies. In addition to the number of copies required to be filed by local rule, there shall be filed one copy of the petition, the list of creditors, the schedules of assets and liabilities, the schedule of current income and expenditures, the statement of financial affairs, the statement of executory contracts, the statement of intention, and the Chapter 13 Statement and any amendments thereto.

(2) *Transmission to United States Trustee.* The clerk shall forthwith transmit to the United States trustee the additional copies filed pursuant to this subdivision. Written notice of a hearing for an extension of time to file schedules, statements and lists pursuant to Rule 1007(a)(4) and (c) shall be given the United States trustee.

(b) Filing Lists by Debtor in Chapter 11 Reorganization Cases. In chapter 11 cases, the debtor shall file an additional copy of the lists of creditors and of the 20 largest unsecured creditors required by Rule 1007(a) and (d). The lists shall contain additional information as the United States trustee may require and one copy of each shall be transmitted forthwith by the clerk to the United States trustee.

Amended Mar. 30, 1987, eff. Aug. 1, 1987.

Advisory Committee Note

Rule X-1002 requires that a copy of the petition commencing a case under the Code, whether it is a case under chapter 7, 9, 11, or 13, be sent to the United States trustee. This supplements Rules 1002(b) and 1003(b). Sections 301–303 of the Code provide that petitions are to be filed with the bankruptcy court. Nevertheless, the United States trustee should be apprised of the commencement of every case and this is most easily accomplished by providing that office with a copy of the petition.

The clerk also must transmit a copy of the lists of creditors and any schedules and statements that are filed. Rule 1007(d) requires a list of the 20 largest creditors and a list of all creditors to be filed. These lists should be transmitted to the United States trustee.

The clerk should transmit the papers specified in this rule forthwith on their filing because the United States trustee requires the information to perform certain duties, *e.g.*, appointment of an interim trustee, § 15701 of the Code, and appointment of a committee of unsecured creditors, § 151102.

Lists of the largest creditors have frequently been deficient, and have hampered the United States trustee in appointing a creditors' committee. Subdivision (b) of this rule provides the United States trustee with authority to require sufficient information to assemble a creditors' committee that complies with § 1102(b) of the Code.

Advisory Committee Notes to 1987 Amendments

Subdivisions (a) and (b) are amended to conform to the amendments to Rules 1002 and 1007.

Rule X-1003

APPOINTMENT OF INTERIM TRUSTEE BEFORE ORDER FOR RELIEF IN A CHAPTER 7 LIQUIDATION CASE

(a) Appointment. At any time following the commencement of an involuntary liquidation case and before an order for relief, the court on written motion of a party in interest may order the appointment of an interim trustee under § 15303 of the Code. The motion shall set forth the necessity for the appointment and may be granted only after hearing on notice to the debtor, the United States trustee, and other parties in interest as the court may designate.

(b) Form of Order. The order directing the appointment of an interim trustee shall state why the appointment is necessary and shall specify the trustee's duties.

Advisory Committee Note

This rule parallels Rule 2001(a) with minor adjustments to reflect that in a United States trustee district, it is the United States trustee, rather than the court, who appoints interim trustees.

Rule X-1004

NOTIFICATION TO TRUSTEE OF SELECTION; BLANKET BOND

(a) Notification. The United States trustee shall immediately notify the person selected as the trustee how to qualify and, if applicable, the amount of the bond. A trustee that has filed a blanket bond pursuant to subdivision (b) of this rule and has been selected as trustee in a chapter 7 or chapter 13 case that does not notify the court in writing of rejection of the office within five days after receipt of notice of selection shall be deemed to have accepted the office. Any other person selected as trustee shall give written notification to the court and the United States trustee of acceptance of the office within five days after receipt of notice of selection.

(b) Blanket Bond. The United States trustee may authorize a blanket bond in favor of the United States conditioned on the faithful performance of official duties by the trustee or trustees to cover (1) a person who qualifies as trustee in a number of cases, and (2) a number of trustees each of whom qualifies in a different case.

Amended Mar. 30, 1987, eff. Aug. 1, 1987.

Advisory Committee Note

This rule parallels Rules 2008 and 2010, except for adjustments to reflect that in a United States trustee district, it is the United States trustee, rather than the court, who appoints interim trustees and sets the bond.

If a person selected as trustee accepts the office, he should also qualify within five days after the selection as required by § 322(a). A standing trustee appointed for chapter 13 cases may notify the court and the United States trustee of the acceptance of office in advance of the commencement of individual cases.

No bond is required if the United States trustee personally serves as trustee in a case; see § 15322(a).

Advisory Committee Notes to 1987 Amendments

Subdivision (a) is amended to eliminate the need for a standing chapter 13 trustee or member of the panel of chapter 7 trustees to accept or reject an appointment.

Rule X–1005

TRUSTEES FOR ESTATES WHEN JOINT ADMINISTRATION ORDERED

(a) Appointment of Trustees for Estates Being Jointly Administered.

(1) Chapter 7 Liquidation Cases. The United States trustee may appoint one or more interim trustees for estates being jointly administered in chapter 7 cases.

(2) Chapter 11 Reorganization Cases. If a trustee is ordered, the United States trustee may appoint one or more trustees for estates being jointly administered in chapter 11 cases.

(3) Chapter 13 Individual's Debt Adjustment Cases. The United States trustee may appoint one or more trustees for estates being jointly administered in chapter 13 cases.

(b) Potential Conflicts of Interest. On a showing that creditors of the different estates will be prejudiced by conflicts of interest of a common trustee the court shall order the appointment of separate trustees for estates being jointly administered.

Advisory Committee Note

This rule parallels Rule 2009(c) and (d), and differs only in that it makes clear that the United States trustee, rather than the court, has the responsibility for appointing trustees. See §§ 15701, 151104, 151302 of the Code and 28 U.S.C. § 586(b).

If separate trustees are ordered pursuant to subdivision (b), separate and successor trustees should be chosen as prescribed by § 703 of the Code. If the occasion for another election arises, the United States trustee should call a meeting of creditors for this purpose.

Rule 2009(e) is not applicable in pilot districts as a direct restriction on the United States trustee because the exercise of discretion by the executive branch is not subject to advance restriction by rule of court or otherwise. *United States v. Cox,* 342 F.2d 167 (5th Cir. 1965), cert. denied, 365 U.S. 863 (1965); *United States v. Frumento,* 409 F.Supp. 136, 141 (E.D.Pa.), *aff'd,* 563 F.2d 1083 (3d Cir. 1977), cert. denied, 434 U.S. 1072 (1977); *accord, Smith v. United States,* 375 F.2d 243 (5th Cir. 1967); House Report No. 95–595, 95th Cong., 1st Sess. 110 (1977). Any appointment of a trustee by a United States trustee in a case under chapter 11 may be disapproved by the court for cause; see § 151104(c).

Rule X–1006

MEETINGS OF CREDITORS OR EQUITY SECURITY HOLDERS

(a) Date and Place. The United States trustee shall call a meeting of creditors to be held not less than 20 nor more than 40 days after the order for relief. If there is an appeal from or a motion to vacate the order for relief, or if there is a motion to dismiss the case, the United States trustee may set a later time for the meeting. The meeting may be held at a regular place for holding court or at any other place designated by the United States trustee within the district convenient for the parties in interest. If the United States trustee designates a place for the meeting which is not regularly staffed by the United States trustee or an assistant who may preside at the meeting, the meeting may be held not more than 60 days after the order for relief.

(b) Order of Meeting.

(1) Meeting of Creditors. The United States trustee or a designee shall preside at the meeting of creditors. The business of the meeting shall include the examination of the debtor under oath and, in a chapter 7 liquidation case, may include the election of a trustee or of a creditors' committee. The presiding officer shall have the authority to administer oaths.

(2) Meeting of Equity Security Holders. If the court orders a meeting of equity security holders pursuant to § 341(b) of the Code, the United States trustee shall fix a date for the meeting and the trustee or a designee shall preside.

(c) Report to the Court. The United States trustee shall transmit to the court the name and address of any person elected trustee or entity elected a member of a creditors' committee. If an election is disputed, the presiding officer shall promptly inform the court in writing of the dispute. Pending disposition of the dispute by the court, the interim trustee shall continue in office. If no motion for the resolution of the election dispute is made to the court within ten days after the date of the creditors' meeting, the interim trustee shall serve as trustee in the case.

(d) Special Meetings. The United States trustee may call a special meeting of creditors on application or on the United States trustee's own initiative.

(e) Final Meeting. If the United States trustee calls a final meeting of creditors in a case in which the net proceeds realized exceed $250, the clerk shall mail a summary of the trustee's final account to the creditors with the notice of the meeting, together with a statement of the amount of the claims allowed. The trustee or a designee shall attend the final meeting and shall, if requested, report on the administration of the estate.

Amended Mar. 30, 1987, eff. Aug. 1, 1987.

Advisory Committee Note

This rule imposes on the United States trustee the duty to fix the date for the meeting of creditors required by § 341(a) of the Code and the meeting of equity security holders if one is ordered by the Court. Although the United States trustee fixes the date of the meeting, a duty that is parallel to that imposed on the court by Rule 2003(a), the clerk of the bankruptcy court transmits the notice of the meeting unless the court orders otherwise, as prescribed by Rule 2002(a)(1). As indicated in Rule X–1006, there is flexibility with regard to the location of the meeting.

Pursuant to §§ 702 and 705 of the Code, creditors may elect a trustee and a committee in a chapter 7 case. Subdivision (b) of this rule provides that the United States trustee or his designee will preside over any election that is held under those sections. While Rule X–1006 is applicable to cases under chapter 11 and chapter 13, trustees and committees are not elected in these cases.

Subdivision (c) recognizes that the court should be informed immediately about the election or nonelection of a trustee in a chapter 7 case. This subdivision also notes that there may be a disputed election, but in no event may the United States trustee or his designee resolve the dispute. For purposes of expediency, the results of the election could be obtained for each alternative presented by the dispute and reported to the court. Thus, when an interested party (not the United States trustee) moves for resolution of the dispute, the court will determine the issue and another meeting to conduct the election may not be necessary.

Advisory Committee Notes to 1987 Amendments

Subdivision (a) is amended to conform to the amendment to Rule 2003(a). See the Committee Note to Rule 2003.

Rule X–1007

DUTY OF TRUSTEE OR DEBTOR IN POSSESSION TO MAKE REPORTS, FURNISH INFORMATION, AND COOPERATE WITH UNITED STATES TRUSTEE

(a) Duty to File Inventory. A trustee or debtor in possession shall file the inventory required by Rule 2015(a)(1) with the United States trustee and with the court if the court so directs.

(b) Duty to Furnish Information To, and Cooperate With, United States Trustee. The trustee or debtor in possession shall cooperate with the United States trustee by furnishing such information as the United States trustee may reasonably require in supervising the administration of the estate. The trustee or debtor in possession in a chapter 11 reorganization case, and the debtor in a chapter 13 individual's debt adjustment case when the debtor is engaged in business, shall furnish the United States trustee and file with the clerk regular reports of operations as the United States trustee may reasonably require.

Advisory Committee Note

Subdivision (a) supplements Rule 2015(a) and the legislative direction that the administration of cases is under the supervision of the United States trustee. 28 U.S.C. § 586(a)(3). Thus, in the absence of a contest, the court should not become involved in receiving or reviewing interim reports of the assets of a debtor, except under the limited circumstances set forth in § 704(7) of the Code.

The United States trustee is charged with the supervision of the administration of all cases under chapters 7, 11 and 13. 28 U.S.C. § 586(a), and chapter 15 of the Code. Subdivision (b), which is based in part on Rule 4002, makes clear the duties of the parties to assist the United States trustee in performing that function. The timely filing of reports of operations is crucial to the efficient administration of chapter 11 and business chapter 13 cases. Under the former Bankruptcy Act, these reports were regularly filed with the bankruptcy judges, but since the United States trustees unlike courts cannot enter orders, this rule enables the United States trustee to superintend the activities of trustees and debtors in possession.

Rule X-1008

NOTICES TO UNITED STATES TRUSTEE

(a) Notices to Be Furnished to United States Trustees. Unless the United States trustee otherwise requests, the United States trustee shall receive notice of and pleadings relating to:

(1) the matters described in Rule 2002(a)(2), (5), (7), 2002(b), and (f);

(2) applications for approval of the employment of professional persons under Rule 2014;

(3) applications for compensation of professional persons under Rule 2016;

(4) the hearing to consider a disclosure statement pursuant to Rule 3017;

(5) the hearing on the appointment of a trustee or examiner; and

(6) any other matter notice of which is requested by the United States trustee or ordered by the court.

(b) Time for Notice to United States Trustee. Subject to Rule 2002, the United States trustee shall receive notice within sufficient time to permit the United States trustee to participate in the matter.

(c) United States Trustee Need Not Furnish Notice. The United States trustee shall not be required to give any notice provided for in Rule 2002(a) or (b).

Amended Mar. 30, 1987, eff. Aug. 1, 1987.

Advisory Committee Note

This rule supplements Rule 2002 and provides for notice to the United States trustee of those matters within his responsibility. The rule omits those notices described in Rule 2002(a)(1) because a meeting of creditors may be convened only by the United States trustee. Rule X-1008 also omits the notice described in Rule 2002(a)(3) (compromise of controversies), 2002(a)(4) (claims against a surplus), and 2002(a)(6) (acceptance or rejection of proposed modifications of a plan in a case under chapter 11), because these do not relate to matters that generally involve the United States trustee. When the facts are such that the United States trustee should be able to monitor those aspects of a case, the rule provides that the United States trustee may request notices. Similarly, this rule permits a United States trustee in a particular judicial district to request notices in certain categories, or request not to receive notices in other categories when the practice in that district makes that desirable.

Rule X-1009

RIGHT TO BE HEARD; FILING PAPERS

(a) Right to Be Heard. The United States trustee may raise and appear and be heard on any issue relating to the United States trustee's responsibilities in a case under the Code.

(b) Filing of Papers. In the interest of effective administration, the court or the United States trustee may require a party in interest to file with the United States trustee a copy of any paper filed with the court.

Amended Mar. 30, 1987, eff. Aug. 1, 1987.

Advisory Committee Note

Subdivision (a) gives the United States trustee standing to be heard. He should have the opportunity, for example, to object to or support actions proposed to be taken by a chapter 7 trustee. Similarly, he should have the opportunity to move to convert or dismiss a chapter 11 case if the operation of the business or management of the property precludes effective administration of the case under that chapter. This rule does not attempt to expand the authority of the United States trustee to move to convert or dismiss a case under § 1112(b), and leaves the interpretation of that provision to the courts. Subdivision (a) gives effect to the Congressional intent that the United States trustee shall have an active role in cases under the Code.

Subdivision (b) enables the United States trustee to be informed of all developments in a case. It supplements the provisions of Rule X–1008 which requires certain notices and pleadings to be sent to the United States trustee.

Rule X–1010

PROHIBITION OF EX PARTE CONTACTS

The United States trustee and assistants to and agents of the United States trustee shall refrain from ex parte meetings and communications with the court concerning matters affecting a particular case or proceeding. This rule does not preclude communication with the court to discuss general problems of administration and improvement of bankruptcy administration, including the operation of the United States trustee system.

Amended Mar. 30, 1987, eff. Aug. 1, 1987.

Advisory Committee Note

This rule and rule 9003 do not supersede or limit any applicable canon of professional responsibility or judicial conduct. See Advisory Committee Note to Rule 9003.

Communication between the judicial and administrative systems is expressed not prohibited. It may be desirable that the court and the United States trustee cooperatively seek ways to improve the administration of cases under the Code.

Advisory Committee Notes to 1987 Amendments

This rule is amended to conform to the amendment to Rule 9003.

OFFICIAL AND PROCEDURAL BANKRUPTCY FORMS

Editorial Comments

ADDITIONAL FORMS, COMMENTS, AND INSTRUCTIONS

The Forms section that follows includes certain official forms and additional procedural forms, together with accompanying commentary and instructions, as issued by the Administrative Office of the United States Courts in its *Bankruptcy Forms Manual* Volume II, "Forms and Instructions for the Public" (September, 1988). The "Official Forms" as included from this Manual Volume II are Nos. 2, 5, 13, 14, 14A, 15, 24–27, 27J, 27O, 28, 32 and 33, and the "Procedural Forms" are Nos. B 131 through B 265. These new and additional forms are issued pursuant to the authority of Bankruptcy Rule 9009.

1986 AMENDMENTS TO OFFICIAL FORMS

Bankruptcy Rule 9009 provides that the "Official Forms [are] prescribed by the Judicial Conference of the United States." At its September 1986 meeting the Judicial Conference approved amendments to the Official Forms (the 1986 Official Forms).

The initial preparation of the amendments to the Official Forms was done by the Advisory Committee on Bankruptcy Rules. The Advisory Committee circulated for public comment drafts of three new forms and one amended form as part of the November, 1985 Preliminary Draft of Proposed Bankruptcy Rules. At that time, the Advisory Committee stated that the final version of the amendments to the Official Forms would also include amendments to make the Official Forms gender neutral.

The 1986 amended Official Forms include two new forms: Official Form 6A, Individual Debtor's Schedule of Current Income and Current Expenditures, and Official Form 8A, Chapter 7 Individual Debtor's Statement of Intention. Both of the forms are essentially the same as the drafts circulated by the Advisory Committee. The Advisory Committee's proposed Official Form 8B, Schedule of Current Income and Current Expenditures of Corporations and Partnerships, and the Advisory Committee's proposed amendment to Official Form No. 19, the proof of claim form, are not included in the 1986 Official Forms.

Numerous changes in style have been made throughout the forms. Most, but not all, of these stylistic changes result from the elimination of masculine pronouns. The following other amendments are of particular interest to the practitioner:

Abrogated Forms. Former Official Forms Nos. 2 and 3 are combined into a new Official Form No. 2 which is titled "Application and Order to Pay Filing Fees in Installments." As a result, Official Form No. 3 is abrogated.

Official Form No. 22, Order Appointing Interim Trustee and Fixing Amount of Bond, and Official Form No. 23, Order Approving Election of Trustee and Fixing

Amount of Bond, are abrogated. The Administrative Office of United States Courts is to prescribe a substitute form, or forms, for use by bankruptcy judges.

Conforming Official Forms to 1984 Amendments to the Bankruptcy Code. Amendments are made to Official Forms Nos. 6, 9, 11, 12 and 15 to conform these forms to 1984 amendments to the Bankruptcy Code.

Official Form No. 6. The farmers' and fishermen's priority under § 507(a)(5)(A) and (B) of the Code are added to the schedule of priority claims.

Official Form No. 9. The reference to "governmental units" is amended to reflect the change in the definition of "person" in § 101(35) of the Code.

Official Forms Nos. 11 and 12. The allegations of the involuntary petitions are amended to reflect the changes in § 303(b)(1) and § 303(h)(1) of the Code which exclude claims which are subject to a bona fide dispute.

Official Form No. 15. Section 1102(b)(1) of the Code requires that a committee of unsecured creditors must have been formed prior to commencement of the case in order to be eligible for appointment as the Official Committee. The form is amended to conform to this change.

Legislative Amendment to Official Form No. 1. Section 283(aa) of Public Law 99–544, Bankruptcy Judges, United States Trustees and Family Farmer Bankruptcy Act of 1986, amends Official Form No. 1, the Voluntary Petition, to include references to the newly enacted chapter 12.

Effective Date. With one exception, the Official Forms are effective as of the date of approval by the Judicial Conference (September, 1986). Official Forms Nos. 7 and 8 include a deletion of the reference to Bankruptcy Rule 1003; however, this deletion was not effective until the August 1, 1987 effective date of the Bankruptcy Rules amendments.

OFFICIAL AND PROCEDURAL BANKRUPTCY FORMS

As Amended to January 1, 1991

Table of Forms

OFFICIAL FORMS

Form
1. Voluntary Petition
2. Application and Order to Pay Filing Fee in Installments
3. [Order for Payment of Filing Fee in Installments] [Abrogated]
4. Unsworn Declaration Under Penalty of Perjury on Behalf of a Corporation or Partnership
5. Certificate of Commencement of Case
6. Schedules of Assets and Liabilities
6A. Schedule of Current Income and Current Expenditures for Individual Debtor
7. Statement of Financial Affairs for Debtor Not Engaged in Business
8. Statement of Financial Affairs for Debtor Engaged in Business
8A. Chapter 7 Individual Debtor's Statement of Intention
9. List of Creditors Holding 20 Largest Unsecured Claims
10. Chapter 13 Statement
11. Involuntary Case: Creditors' Petition
12. Involuntary Case Against Partnership: Partner's Petition
13. Summons to Debtor in Involuntary Case
14. Order for Relief Under Chapter 7
14A. Order for Relief Under Chapter 11
15. Appointment of Committee of Unsecured Creditors in a Chapter 11 Reorganization Case
16. Order for Meeting of Creditors and Related Orders, Combined With Notice Thereof and of Automatic Stay
17. General Power of Attorney
18. Special Power of Attorney
19. Proof of Claim
20. Proof of Claim for Wages, Salary, or Commissions
21. Proof of Multiple Claims for Wages, Salary, or Commissions
22. [Order Appointing Interim Trustee and Fixing Amount of Bond] [Abrogated]
23. [Order Approving Election of Trustee and Fixing Amount of Bond] [Abrogated]
24. Notice to Trustee of Selection and of Time Fixed for Filing a Complaint Objecting to Discharge of Debtor
25. Bond and Order Approving Bond of Trustee
26. Certificate of Retention of Debtor in Possession
27. Discharge of Debtor
27J. Discharge of Joint Debtors
27JO. Discharge of One Joint Debtor
28. Order and Notice for Hearing on Disclosure Statement
29. Order Approving Disclosure Statement and Fixing Time for Filing Acceptances or Rejections of Plan, Combined With Notice Thereof
30. Ballot for Accepting or Rejecting Plan
31. Order Confirming Plan
32. Notice of Filing of Final Account

OFFICIAL FORMS

Form

33. Final Decree
34. Caption of Adversary Proceedings
35. Notice of Appeal to a District Court or Bankruptcy Appellate Panel From a Judgment of a Bankruptcy Court Entered in an Adversary Proceeding

PROCEDURAL FORMS (Omitted)

B 131. Exemplification Certificate
B 132. Application for Search of Bankruptcy Records
B 200. Required Lists, Schedules, Statements and Fees
B 201. Notice to Individual Consumer Debtor
B 203. Disclosure of Compensation of Attorney for Debtor
B 204. Notice of Need to File Proof of Claim Due to Recovery of Assets
B 205. Notice to Creditors and Other Parties in Interest
B 220A. Order Converting Case Under Chapter 7 to Case Under Chapter 11
B 220B. Order Converting Case Under Chapter 7 to Case Under Chapter 12
B 220C. Order Converting Case Under Chapter 7 to Case Under Chapter 13
B 221A. Order Converting Case Under Chapter 11 to Case Under Chapter 7
B 221B. Order Converting Case Under Chapter 11 to Case Under Chapter 12
B 222. Order Upon Conversion of Case Under Chapter 12 to Case Under Chapter 7 by Debtor
B 223A. Order Upon Conversion of Case Under Chapter 13 to Case Under Chapter 7 by Debtor
B 223B. Order Converting Case Under Chapter 13 to Case Under Chapter 7 on Motion by a Party in Interest
B 224A. Order Dismissing Chapter 12 Case
B 224B. Order Dismissing Chapter 13 Case
B 230A. Order Fixing Time to Object to Confirmation of Modified Chapter 12 Plan
B 230B. Order Fixing Time to Object to the Confirmation of Modified Chapter 13 Plan
B 231A. Order Confirming Chapter 12 Plan
B 231B. Order Confirming Chapter 13 Plan
B 240. Reaffirmation Agreement
B 241. Order Discharging Chapter 12 Debtor
B 242A. Order Discharging Debtor After Completion of Chapter 13 Plan
B 242B. Order Discharging Debtor Before Completion of Chapter 13 Plan
B 250A. Summons in an Adversary Proceeding
B 250B. Summons and Notice of Pretrial Conference in an Adversary Proceeding
B 250C. Summons and Notice of Trial in an Adversary Proceeding
B 250D. Third-Party Summons
B 251A. Deposition Subpoena in a Bankruptcy Case
B 251B. Deposition Subpoena in an Adversary Proceeding
B 252A. Subpoena to Witness in a Bankruptcy Case
B 252B. Subpoena to Witness in an Adversary Proceeding
B 260. Entry of Default
B 261. Judgment by Default
B 262. Notice of Entry of Judgment
B 263. Bill of Costs
B 264. Writ of Execution to the United States Marshal
B 265. Certification of Judgment for Registration in Another District

OFFICIAL FORMS

[NOTE: These official forms should be observed and used with such alterations as may be appropriate to suit the circumstances. See Rule 9009.]

Form No. 1

VOLUNTARY PETITION

UNITED STATES BANKRUPTCY COURT FOR
THE _____ DISTRICT OF _____

In re

_____,

Debtor [set forth here all names including trade names used by Debtor within last 6 years].

Social Security No. _____

and Debtor's Employer's Tax Identification No. _____

Case No. _____

VOLUNTARY PETITION

1. Petitioner's mailing address, including county, is _____
_____.

2. Petitioner has resided [*or* has been domiciled *or* Petitioner's principal place of business has been *or* The principal assets of the petitioner have been] within this district for the preceding 180 days [*or* for a longer portion of the preceding 180 days than in any other district].

3. Petitioner is qualified to file this petition and is entitled to the benefits of title 11, United States Code as a voluntary debtor.

4. [*If appropriate*] A copy of petitioner's proposed plan, dated _____, is attached [*or* Petitioner intends to file a plan pursuant to chapter 11 *or* chapter 13] of title 11, United States Code.

5. [*If petitioner is a corporation*] Exhibit "A" is attached to and made part of this petition.

6. [*If petitioner is an individual whose debts are primarily consumer debts*] Petitioner is aware that [he or she] may proceed under chapter 7, 11, 12 or 13 of title 11, United States Code, understands the relief available under each such chapter, and chooses to proceed under chapter 7 of such title.

7. [*If petitioner is an individual whose debts are primarily consumer debts and such petitioner is represented by an attorney.*] A declaration or an affidavit in the form of Exhibit B is attached to and made a part of this petition.

WHEREFORE, petitioner prays for relief in accordance with chapter 7 [*or* chapter 11 *or* chapter 13] of title 11, United States Code.

Signed: _____,
Attorney for Petitioner.

Address: _____,
_____

[Petitioner signs if not represented by attorney.]

————————————————————————,
Petitioner.

I, ———, the petitioner named in the foregoing petition, declare under penalty of perjury that the foregoing is true and correct.
Executed on ———.

Signature: ————————————————
Petitioner.

Exhibit "A"

[If petitioner is a corporation, this Exhibit "A" shall be completed and attached to the petition pursuant to paragraph 5 thereof.]

[Caption as in Form No. 1]

FOR COURT USE ONLY

————————————————————

Date Petition Filed

————————————————————

Case Number

————————————————————

Bankruptcy Judge

1. Petitioner's employer identification number is ———.

2. If any of petitioner's securities are registered under section 12 of the Securities and Exchange Act of 1934, SEC file number is ———.

3. The following financial data is the latest available information and refers to petitioner's condition on ———.

a. Total assets:	$————————————
b. Total liabilities:	$————————————

		Approximate number of holders
Secured debt, excluding that listed below	$————	————
Debt securities held by more than 100 holders	$————	————
Secured	$————	————
Unsecured	$————	————
Other liabilities, excluding contingent or unliquidated claims	$————	————
Number of shares of common stock	$————	————

Comments, if any: ————————————————

————————————————————————————————

4. Brief description of petitioner's business: _____

_____

_____

5. [*If presently available, supply the following information*] The name of any person who directly or indirectly owns, controls, or holds, with power to vote, 20% or more of the voting securities of petitioner is _____

_____

_____

6. [*If presently available, supply the following information*] The names of all corporations 20% or more of the outstanding voting securities of which are directly or indirectly owned, controlled, or held, with power to vote, by petitioner are _____

_____

_____

_____

Exhibit "B"

[*If petitioner is an individual whose debts are primarily consumer debts, this Exhibit "B" shall be completed and attached to the petition pursuant to paragraph 7 thereof.*]

[*Caption as in Form No. 1*]

_____

FOR COURT USE ONLY

_____

Date Petition Filed

_____

Case Number

_____

Bankruptcy Judge

I, _____, the attorney for the petitioner named in the foregoing petition, declare that I have informed the petitioner that [he or she] may proceed under chapter 7, 11, 12 or 13 of title 11, United States Code, and have explained the relief available under each such chapter.

_____

Executed on

_____

Signature

_____

Attorney for Petitioner

Paragraphs 6 and 7 of Voluntary Petition, and Exhibit "B", added by Sec. 322 of Pub.L. 98–353, July 10, 1984, 98 Stat. 333. Paragraph 2 of Voluntary Petition amended eff. Sept. 19, 1986.

Advisory Committee Note

This form may be used to commence a voluntary case under chapter 7, 11, or 13 of the Bankruptcy Code. A chapter 9 petition requires other allegations (see § 109(c) of the Code) but this form may be adapted for such use.

The title of the case, in the caption of the form, should include all names used by the debtor, such as trade names, names used in doing business, married names and maiden names. This will enable creditors to properly identify the debtor when they receive notices and orders.

A joint petition, available for an individual and spouse, may be filed under chapter 7, 11, or 13. See § 302 of the Code. This form may be adapted for such use.

The unsworn declaration at the end of the petition conforms with 28 U.S.C. § 1746 (1976) which permits the declaration to be made in the manner indicated with the same force and effect as a sworn statement. The form may be adapted for use outside of the United States by adding the words "under the laws of the United States" after the word "perjury".

Exhibit "A" to be attached to the petition of a corporate debtor is for the purpose of supplying the Securities and Exchange Commission with the information it requires at the beginning stages of a chapter 11 case.

Advisory Committee Note to 1986 Amendment

Paragraphs 6 and 7 and Exhibit B were added by § 322 of the 1984 amendments. The references to chapters 11 and 12 of title 11 of the United States Code found in paragraph 6 and Exhibit B were added by § 283(aa) of the 1986 amendments.

Form 2

Form No. 2

APPLICATION AND ORDER TO PAY FILING
FEE IN INSTALLMENTS

B2 (Official Form 2)
(1/87)

United States Bankruptcy Court

_____ District of _____

In re

Bankruptcy Case No.

Debtor

APPLICATION TO PAY FILING FEES IN INSTALLMENTS

In accordance with Bankruptcy Rule 1006, application is made for permission to pay the filing fee on the following terms:

$_____ with the filing of the petition, and the balance of

$_____ in _____ installments, as follows:

$_____ on or before _____

$_____ on or before _____

$_____ on or before _____

$_____ on or before _____ .

I certify that I have not paid any money or transferred any property to an attorney or any other person for services in connection with this case or in connection with any other pending bankruptcy case and that I will not make any payment or transfer any property for services in connection with the case until the filing fee is paid in full.

_____   _____
Date   Applicant

                                              _____
                                              Address of Applicant

                                              _____

ORDER

IT IS ORDERED that the debtor pay the filing fee in installments on the terms set forth in the foregoing application.

IT IS FURTHER ORDERED that until the filing fee is paid in full the debtor shall not pay, and no person shall accept, any money for services in connection with this case, and the debtor shall not relinquish, and no person shall accept, any property as payment for services in connection with this case.

_____   _____
Date   Bankruptcy Judge   [E7834]

694

COMMENTS AND INSTRUCTIONS

Pertinent Law and Rules

1. Section 1930(a) of title 28 of the United States Code requires a fee to be paid upon the filing of a petition in bankruptcy. As of January 1, 1988, this fee is:

    $ 90 for a chapter 7 case,
    $500 for a chapter 11 case,
    $200 for a chapter 12 case,
    $ 90 for a chapter 13 case.

2. Section 1930(a) permits individuals to pay this filing fee in installments.

3. Pursuant to Bankruptcy Rule 1006, when an individual requests court approval to pay the fee in installments, the petition must be:

    accompanied by the debtor's signed application stating that the debtor is unable to pay the filing fee except in installments. The application shall state the proposed terms of the installment payments and that the applicant has neither paid any money nor transferred any property to an attorney for services in connection with the case . . . The number of installments shall not exceed four, and the final installment shall be payable not later than 120 days after filing the petition. For cause shown, the court may extend the time of any installment, provided the last installment is paid not later than 180 days after filing the petition. The filing fee must be paid in full before the debtor or chapter 13 trustee may pay an attorney or any other person who renders services to the debtor in connection with the case.

Instructions

Caption

1. Identify the Judicial District in which the bankruptcy case was filed. Example: Eastern District of California.

2. "In re": Insert the name of the debtor as it appears in the bankruptcy petition.

3. "Bankruptcy Case No.": Insert the bankruptcy case number assigned by the court at the time of filing.

Source of Form

This Official Form and the acompanying commentary and instructions are included as Form B 2 of *Bankruptcy Forms Manual* Volume II, "Forms and Instructions for the Public," as issued by the Division of Bankruptcy, Administrative Office of the United States Courts (September, 1988).

Form No. 3

[ORDER FOR PAYMENT OF FILING FEE IN INSTALLMENTS] [ABROGATED]

Abrogated and combined with Form No. 2 eff. Sept. 19, 1986.

Advisory Committee Note to Former Form No. 3

Issuance of an order permitting payment of the filing fees in installments is governed by Rule 1006.

This form may be adapted for use in a joint case when both petitioners apply to pay the filing fee in installments.

Form No. 4

UNSWORN DECLARATION UNDER PENALTY OF PERJURY ON BEHALF OF A CORPORATION OR PARTNERSHIP

I, _____, [the president *or other officer or* an authorized agent of the corporation] [*or* a member *or* an authorized agent of the partnership] named as petitioner in the foregoing petition, declare under penalty of perjury that the foregoing is true and correct, and that the filing of this petition on behalf of the [corporation] [*or* partnership] has been authorized.

Executed on _____.

Signature: _____

Advisory Committee Note

Rule 1008 requires all petitions to be verified. This form is to be used on behalf of a corporation or partnership. It may be adapted for use in connection with other papers required by these rules to be verified. See the Note to Rule 9011. 28 U.S.C. § 1746 permits an unsworn declaration to be used in lieu of a verification. See Advisory Committee Note to Form No. 1.

Form No. 5

CERTIFICATE OF COMMENCEMENT OF CASE

B5 (Official Form 5)
(1/87)

United States Bankruptcy Court

_____District of_____

In re

                                        Bankruptcy Case No.

Debtor*
Social Security No.   :
Employer Tax I.D. No. :

CERTIFICATE OF COMMENCEMENT OF CASE

I certify that on_____,
                              (date)

☐ the above named debtor filed a petition requesting relief

under chapter _____ of the Bankruptcy Code (title 11

of the United States Code), or

☐ a petition was filed against the above named debtor under

chapter _____ of the Bankruptcy Code (title 11 of the

United States Code), and

☐ that as of the date below the case has not been dismissed.

_____
Clerk of the Bankruptcy Court

_____   By:_____
Date   Deputy Clerk

---

*Set forth all names, including trade names, used by the debtor within the last 6 years. (Bankruptcy Rule 1005). For joint debtors set forth both
social security numbers.   [E7835]

COMMENTS AND INSTRUCTIONS

Advisory Committee Note (1983)

"This form is adapted from certificates that have been in use in several districts. The certificate may be used to alert persons dealing with the debtor or property of the debtor of the pendency of a case under the [Bankruptcy] Code [(title 11 of the United States Code)] before the notice of the [filing of the petition in bankruptcy] is sent [by the court]."

Fee

There is a charge of $5.00 for certification. This amount must be paid by check or money order made payable to "Clerk, U.S. Bankruptcy Court."

Instructions

Caption

1. Identify the Judicial District in which the bankruptcy case was filed. Example: Eastern District of California.

2. "In re": Insert the name of the debtor as it appears in the bankruptcy petition.

3. "Bankruptcy Case No.": Insert the bankruptcy case number assigned at the time of filing.

Source of Form

This Official Form and the accompanying commentary and instructions are included as Form B 5 of *Bankruptcy Forms Manual* Volume II, "Forms and Instructions for the Public," as issued by the Division of Bankruptcy, Administrative Office of the United States Courts (September, 1988).

Form No. 6

SCHEDULES OF ASSETS AND LIABILITIES

[Caption as in Form No. 1]

Schedule A.—Statement of All Liabilities of Debtor

Schedules A–1, A–2 and A–3 must include all the claims against the debtor or the debtor's property as of the date of the filing of the petition by or against the debtor.

Schedule A–1.—Creditors having priority

(1)	(2)	(3)	(4)	(5)
Nature of claim	Name of creditor and complete mailing address including zip code	Specify when claim was incurred and the consideration therefor; when claim is subject to setoff, evidenced by a judgment, negotiable instrument, or other writing, or incurred as partner or joint contractor, so indicate; specify name of any partner or joint contractor on any debt	Indicate if claim is contingent, unliquidated, or disputed	Amount of claim

a. Wages, salary, and commissions, including vacation, severance and sick leave pay owing to employees not exceeding $2,000 to each, earned within 90 days before filing of petition or cessation of business (if earlier specify date). $_____

b. Contributions to employee benefit plans for services rendered within 180 days before filing of petition or cessation of business (if earlier specify date). $_____

c. Claims of farmers, not exceeding $2,000 for each individual, pursuant to 11 U.S.C. § 507(a)(5)(A). $_____

d. Claims of United States fishermen, not exceeding $2,000 for each individual, pursuant to 11 U.S.C. § 507(a)(5)(B). $_____

e. Deposits by individuals, not exceeding $900 for each for purchase, lease, or rental of property or services for personal, family, or household use that were not delivered or provided. $_____

f. Taxes owing [itemize by type of tax and taxing authority]

   (1) To the United States $_____

   (2) To any state $_____

   (3) To any other taxing authority $_____

               Total $_____

Schedule A–2.—Creditors holding security

(1) Name of creditor and complete mailing address including zip code	(2) Description of security and date when obtained by creditor	(3) Specify when claim was incurred and the consideration therefor; when claim is subject to setoff, evidenced by a judgment, negotiable instrument, or other writing, or incurred as partner or joint contractor, so indicate; specify name of any partner or joint contractor on any debt	(4) Indicate if claim is contingent, unliquidated, or disputed	(5) Market Value	(6) Amount of claim without deduction of value of security
				Total	$

Schedule A–3.—Creditors having unsecured claims without priority

(1) Name of creditor [including last known holder of any negotiable instrument] and complete mailing address including zip code	(2) Specify when claim was incurred and the consideration therefor; when claim is contingent, unliquidated, disputed, subject to setoff, evidenced by a judgment, negotiable instrument, or other writing, or incurred as partner or joint contractor, so indicate; specify name of any partner or joint contractor on any debt	(3) Indicate if claim is contingent, unliquidated, or disputed	(4) Amount of claim
		Total	$

Schedule B—Statement of All Property of Debtor

Schedules B–1, B–2, B–3, and B–4 must include all property of the debtor as of the date of the filing of the petition by or against the debtor.

Schedule B–1.—Real Property

Description and location of all real property in which debtor has an interest [including equitable and future interests, interests in estates by the entirety, community property, life estates, leaseholds, and rights and powers exercisable for the debtor's own benefit]	Nature of interest [specify all deeds and written instruments relating thereto]	Market value of debtor's interest without deduction for secured claims listed in Schedule A–2 or exemptions claimed in Schedule B–4
		Total $

Schedule B–2.—Personal Property

Type of Property	Description and Location	Market value of debtor's interest without deduction for secured claims listed on Schedule A–2 or exemptions claimed in Schedule B–4 Total $_____
a. Cash on hand		$ _____
b. Deposits of money with banking institutions, savings and loan associations, brokerage houses, credit unions, public utility companies, landlords and others		
c. Household goods, supplies and furnishings		_____
d. Books, pictures, and other art objects; stamp, coin and other collections		_____
e. Wearing apparel, jewelry, firearms, sports equipment and other personal possessions		_____
f. Automobiles, trucks, trailers and other vehicles		_____
g. Boats, motors and their accessories		_____
h. Livestock, poultry and other animals		_____
i. Farming equipment, supplies and implements		_____
j. Office equipment, furnishings and supplies		_____
k. Machinery, fixtures, equipment and supplies [other than those listed in Items j and l] used in business		_____
l. Inventory		_____
m. Tangible personal property of any other description		_____
n. Patents, copyrights, licenses, franchises and other general intangibles [specify all documents and writings relating thereto]		_____
o. Government and corporate bonds and other negotiable and nonnegotiable instruments		_____
p. Other liquidated debts owing debtor		_____
q. Contingent and unliquidated claims of every nature, including counterclaims of the debtor [give estimated value of each]		_____
r. Interests in insurance policies [name insurance company of each policy and itemize surrender or refund value of each]		_____
s. Annuities [itemize and name each issuer]		_____
t. Stock and interests in incorporated and unincorporated companies [itemize separately]		_____
u. Interests in partnerships		_____
v. Equitable and future interests, life estates, and rights or powers exercisable for the benefit of the debtor (other than those listed in Schedule B–1) [specify all written instruments relating thereto]		
	Total	$_____

Schedule B-3.—Property not otherwise scheduled

Type of Property	Description and Location	Market value of debtor's interest without deduction for secured claims listed in Schedule A-2 or exemption claimed in Schedule B-4
a. Property transferred under assignment for benefit of creditors, within 120 days prior to filing of petition [specify date of assignment, name and address of assignee, amount realized therefrom by the assignee, and disposition of proceeds so far as known to debtor]		$_____
b. Property of any kind not otherwise scheduled		
	Total	$_____

Debtor selects the following property as exempt pursuant to 11 U.S.C. § 522(d) [or the laws of the State of _____.]

Schedule B-4.—Property claimed as exempt

Type of Property	Location, description, and, so far as relevant to the claim of exemption, present use of property	Specify statute creating the exemption	Value claimed exempt
			$_____
		Total	$_____

Summary of debts and property.

[From the statements of the debtor in Schedules A and B]

Schedule		Total
	Debts	
A-1/a,b	Wages, etc. having priority	$_____
A-1(c)	Deposits of money	_____
A-1/d(1)	Taxes owing United States	_____
A-1/d(2)	Taxes owing states	_____

Debts

A–1/d(3)	Taxes owing other taxing authorities	$_____
A–2	Secured claims	
A–3	Unsecured claims without priority	
	Schedule A total	$_____

Property

B–1	Real property [total value]	$_____
B–2/a	Cash on hand	_____
B–2/b	Deposits	_____
B–2/c	Household goods	_____
B–2/d	Books, pictures, and collections	_____
B–2/e	Wearing apparel and personal possessions	_____
B–2/f	Automobiles and other vehicles	_____
B–2/g	Boats, motors, and accessories	_____
B–2/h	Livestock and other animals	_____
B–2/i	Farming supplies and implements	_____
B–2/j	Office equipment and supplies	_____
B–2/k	Machinery, equipment, and supplies used in business	_____
B–2/l	Inventory	_____
B–2/m	Other tangible personal property	_____
B–2/n	Patents and other general intangibles	_____
B–2/o	Bonds and other instruments	_____
B–2/p	Other liquidated debts	_____
B–2/q	Contingent and unliquidated claims	_____
B–2/r	Interests in insurance policies	_____
B–2/s	Annuities	_____
B–2/t	Interests in corporations and unincorporated companies	_____
B–2/u	Interests in partnerships	_____
B–2/v	Equitable and future interests, rights, and powers in personalty	_____
B–3/a	Property assigned for benefit of creditors	_____
B–3/b	Property not otherwise scheduled	_____
	Schedule B total	$_____

UNSWORN DECLARATION UNDER PENALTY OF PERJURY OF INDIVIDUAL TO SCHEDULES A AND B

I, _____, declare under penalty of perjury that I have read the foregoing schedules, consisting of __ sheets, and that they are true and correct to the best of my knowledge, information and belief.

Executed on _____.

Signature: _____

UNSWORN DECLARATION UNDER PENALTY OF PERJURY ON BEHALF OF CORPORATION OR PARTNERSHIP TO SCHEDULES A AND B

I, _____, [the president *or other officer* or an authorized agent of the corporation] [*or* a member *or* an authorized agent of the partnership] named as debtor in this case, declare under penalty of perjury that I have read the foregoing schedules, consisting of __ sheets, and that they are true and correct to the best of my knowledge, information, and belief.

Executed on _____.

Signature: _____

Amended eff. Sept. 19, 1986.

Advisory Committee Note

These schedules may be used pursuant to § 521(1) of the Code.

The unsworn declarations at the end of the form are in conformity with 28 U.S.C. § 1746. See Advisory Committee Note to Form No. 1.

Advisory Committee Note to 1986 Amendment

Paragraphs c and d in Schedule A–1 have been added to reflect new priorities added to § 507 of the Code by the 1984 amendments.

Publisher's Supplementary Note

Note, however, that the Official Form inadvertently fails to make the corresponding revision to the Summary of debts and property that follows immediately after Schedules A and B. Bankruptcy Rule 9009 provides authority and direction to make "alterations as may be appropriate" to the Official Forms. Appropriate alterations to this Form might include relabeling and adding so that the Summary of debts would read as follows:

Schedule		Total
	Debts	
A–1/a, b	Wages, etc. having priority	$_____
A–1/c, d	Claims of farmers and fishermen having priority	_____
A–1/e	Deposits of money	_____
A–1/f(1)	Taxes owing United States	_____
A–1/f(2)	Taxes owing states	_____
A–1/f(3)	Taxes owing other taxing authorities	_____
A–2	Secured claims	_____
A–3	Unsecured claims without priority	_____
	Schedule A total	$_____

Form No. 6A

SCHEDULE OF CURRENT INCOME AND CURRENT EXPENDITURES FOR INDIVIDUAL DEBTOR

[Caption as in Form No. 2]

Schedule of Current Income and Current Expenditures
for Individual Debtor

[Complete this form by answering each question. If your answer to a question is "none" or "not applicable" so state.]

A. Family Status.

1. The debtor is: (check one of the following)

   Married ＿＿ Single ＿＿ Separated ＿＿ Divorced ＿＿

2. The name of the debtor's spouse is ＿＿＿＿＿＿＿＿＿＿＿＿＿.

3. The debtor supports the following dependents (*other than the debtor's spouse*):

Name	Age	Relationship to Debtor
＿＿＿＿＿	＿＿＿＿	＿＿＿＿＿＿＿＿
＿＿＿＿＿	＿＿＿＿	＿＿＿＿＿＿＿＿
＿＿＿＿＿	＿＿＿＿	＿＿＿＿＿＿＿＿
＿＿＿＿＿	＿＿＿＿	＿＿＿＿＿＿＿＿

B. Employment and Occupation.

1. The debtor is employed by ＿＿＿＿＿＿＿, as ＿＿＿＿＿＿.
   (name of employer)   *(nature of position)*

2. The debtor is self-employed as ＿＿＿＿＿＿＿＿＿＿ at the
   (nature of business or profession)
   following principal place of business: ＿＿＿＿＿.
   (address)

3. The debtor's spouse is employed by ＿＿＿＿＿＿＿, as ＿＿＿＿＿
   (name of employer)   *(nature of*
   ＿＿＿＿＿.
   position)

4. The debtor's spouse is self-employed as ＿＿＿＿＿＿＿＿＿, at
   (nature of business or profession)
   the following principal place of business: ＿＿＿＿＿.
   (address)

C. Current Income.

Give estimated average current monthly income of debtor and spouse, consisting of:

		Debtor	Spouse
1.	Gross pay (*wages, salary, or commissions*)	$＿＿＿＿	$＿＿＿＿
2.	Take home pay (*gross pay less all deductions*)	$＿＿＿＿	$＿＿＿＿
3.	Regular income available from the operation of a business or profession	$＿＿＿＿	$＿＿＿＿
4.	Other income:		
	Interest and dividends	$＿＿＿＿	$＿＿＿＿

	Debtor	Spouse
From real estate or personal property	$	$
Social security	$	$
Pension or other retirement income	$	$
Other (*specify*)		
_____	$	$
_____	$	$

5. Alimony, maintenance, or support payments:

Payable to the debtor for the debtor's use	$	$
Payable to the debtor for the support of another (*Attach additional sheet listing the name, age, and relationship to the debtor of persons for whose benefit payments are made.*)	$	$
Total estimated current monthly income	$	$

If you anticipate receiving additional income on other than a monthly basis in the next six months (such as an income tax refund), attach additional sheet of paper and describe.

If you anticipate a substantial change in your income in the immediate future, attach additional sheet of paper and describe.

D. Schedule of Current Expenditures.

Give estimated average current monthly expenditures of debtor and spouse, consisting of:

1. Home expenses:
   a. Rent or home loan payment (*including any assessment or maintenance fee*) $____
   b. Real estate taxes $____
   c. Utilities:
      Electricity $____
      Gas $____
      Water $____
      Telephone $____
      Other (*specify*)
      _____ $____
      Total utilities $____
   d. Home maintenance (repairs and upkeep) $____
      Total, all home expenses $____
2. Other expenses:
   a. Taxes (*not deducted from wages or included in home loan payment or included in real estate taxes*) $____
   b. Alimony, maintenance, or support payments (*attach additional sheet listing name, age, and relationship of beneficiaries*) $____
   c. Insurance (*not deducted from wages*)
      Life $____
      Health $____
      Auto $____
      Homeowner's or Renter's $____

Other (*specify*)

_____ $____

Total insurance expenses $____

d. Installment payments:

Auto $____

Other (*specify*)

_____ $____

_____ $____

e. Transportation (*not including auto payments*) $____

f. Education (*including tuition and school books*) $____

g. Food $____

h. Clothing $____

i. Medical, dental, and medicines $____

j. Laundry and cleaning $____

k. Newspapers, periodicals, and books $____

l. Recreation, clubs, and entertainment $____

m. Charitable contributions $____

n. Other expenses (*specify*)

_____ $____

_____ $____

Total estimated current monthly expenses $____

If you anticipate a substantial change in your expenses in the immediate future attach additional sheet of paper and describe.

UNSWORN DECLARATION UNDER PENALTY OF PERJURY

I, _____, declare under penalty of perjury that I have read the foregoing schedule and any attachment, consisting of _____ sheets in all, and that they are true and correct to the best of my knowledge, information and belief.

_____.

Date   *Signature of Debtor*

Added eff. Sept. 19, 1986.

Advisory Committee Note

Section 521(1), as amended by the 1984 amendments, requires debtors to file a schedule of current income and current expenditures. This form is designed for use by individual debtors and is modeled on Official Form No. 10, the Chapter 13 Statement. No official form is prescribed for partnerships and corporations.

Only the original schedule need be signed and verified, but copies must be conformed to the original. See Bankruptcy Rules 1008 and 9011(c).

Form No. 7

STATEMENT OF FINANCIAL AFFAIRS FOR DEBTOR NOT ENGAGED IN BUSINESS

[Caption as in Form No. 1]

STATEMENT OF FINANCIAL AFFAIRS FOR DEBTOR NOT ENGAGED IN BUSINESS

[Each question shall be answered or the failure to answer explained. If the answer is "none" or "not applicable" so state. If additional space is needed for the answer to any question, a separate sheet, properly identified and made a part hereof, should be used and attached.

The term, "original petition," used in the following questions, shall mean the petition filed under Rule 1002, or 1004.]

1. Name and residence.

a. What is your full name?

b. Have you used, or been known by, any other names within the six years immediately preceding the filing of the original petition herein? (If so, give particulars.)

c. Where do you now reside?

d. Where else have you resided during the six years immediately preceding the filing of the original petition herein?

2. Occupation and income.

a. What is your occupation?

b. Where are you now employed? (Give the name and address of your employer, or the address at which you carry on your trade or profession, and the length of time you have been so employed or engaged.)

c. Have you been in a partnership with anyone, or engaged in any business during the six years immediately preceding the filing of the original petition herein? (If so, give particulars, including names, dates, and places.)

d. What amount of income have you received from your trade or profession during each of the two calendar years immediately preceding the filing of the original petition herein?

e. What amount of income have you received from other sources during each of these two years? (Give particulars, including each source, and the amount received therefrom.)

3. Tax returns and refunds.

a. Where did you file your federal, state and municipal income tax returns for the two years immediately preceding the filing of the original petition herein?

b. What tax refunds (income and other) have you received during the year immediately preceding the filing of the original petition herein?

c. To what tax refunds (income or other), if any, are you, or may you be, entitled? (Give particulars, including information as to any refund payable jointly to you and your spouse or any other person.)

4. Financial accounts, certificates of deposit and safe deposit boxes.

a. What accounts or certificates of deposit or shares in banks, savings and loan, thrift, building and loan and homestead associations, credit unions, brokerage houses, pension funds and the like have you maintained, alone or together with any other person, and in your own or any other name within the two years immediately preceding the filing of the original petition herein? (Give the name and address of each institution, the name and number under which the account or certificate is maintained, and the name and address of every other person authorized to make withdrawals from such account.)

b. What safe deposit box or boxes or other depository or depositories have you kept or used for your securities, cash, or other valuables within the two years immediately preceding the filing of the original petition herein? (Give the name and address of the bank or other depository, the name in which each box or other depository was kept, the name and address of every other person who had the right of access thereto, a brief description of the contents thereof, and, if the box has been surrendered, state when surrendered, or, if transferred, when transferred, and the name and address of the transferee.)

5. Books and records.

a. Have you kept books of account or records relating to your affairs within the two years immediately preceding the filing of the original petition herein?

b. In whose possession are these books or records? (Give names and addresses.)

c. If any of these books or records are not available, explain.

d. Have any books of account or records relating to your affairs been destroyed, lost, or otherwise disposed of within the two years immediately preceding the filing of the original petition herein? (If so, give particulars, including date of destruction, loss, or disposition, and reason therefor.)

6. Property held for another person.

What property do you hold for any other person? (Give name and address of each person, and describe the property, or value thereof, and all writings relating thereto.)

7. Property held by another.

Is any other person holding anything of value in which you have an interest? (Give name and address, location and description of the property, and circumstances of the holding.)

8. Prior bankruptcy.

What cases under the Bankruptcy Act or title 11, United States Code have previously been brought by or against you? (State the location of the bankruptcy court, the nature and number of each case, the date when it was filed, and whether a discharge was granted or denied, the case was dismissed, or a composition, arrangement, or plan was confirmed.)

9. Receiverships, general assignments, and other modes of liquidation.

a. Was any of your property, at the time of the filing of the original petition herein, in the hands of a receiver, trustee, or other liquidating agent? (If so, give a brief description of the property, the name and address of the receiver, trustee, or other agent, and, if the agent was appointed in a court proceeding, the name and location of the court, the title and number of the case, and the nature thereof.)

b. Have you made any assignment of your property for the benefit of your creditors, or any general settlement with your creditors, within one year immediately preceding the filing of the original petition herein? (If so, give dates, the name and address of the assignee, and a brief statement of the terms of assignment or settlement.)

10. Suits, executions, and attachments.

a. Were you a party to any suit pending at the time of the filing of the original petition herein? (If so, give the name and location of the court and the title and nature of the proceeding.)

b. Were you a party to any suit terminated within the year immediately preceding the filing of the original petition herein? (If so, give the name and location of the court, the title and nature of the proceeding, and the result.)

c. Has any of your property been attached, garnished, or seized under any legal or equitable process within the year immediately preceding the filing of the original petition herein? (If so, describe the property seized or person garnished, and at whose suit.)

11. (a) Payment of loans, installment purchases and other debts.

What payments in whole or in part have you made during the year immediately preceding the filing of the original petition herein on any of the following: (1) loans; (2) installment purchases of goods and services; and (3) other debts? (Give the names and addresses of the persons receiving payment, the amounts of the loans or other debts and the purchase price of the goods and services, the dates of the original transactions, the amounts and dates of payments and, if any of the payees are your relatives or insiders, the relationship; if the debtor is a partnership and any of the payees is or was a partner or a relative of a partner, state the relationship; if the debtor is a corporation and any of the payees is or was an officer, director, or stockholder, or a relative of an officer, director, or stockholder, state the relationship.)

(b) Setoffs.

What debts have you owed to any creditor, including any bank, which were set off by that creditor against a debt or deposit owing by the creditor to you during the year immediately preceding the filing of the original petition herein? (Give the names and addresses of the persons setting off such debts, the dates of the setoffs, the amounts of the debts owing by you and to you and, if any of the creditors are your relatives or insiders, the relationship.)

12. Transfers of property.

a. Have you made any gifts, other than ordinary and usual presents to family members and charitable donations, during the year immediately preceding the filing of the original petition herein? (If so, give names and addresses of donees and dates, description, and value of gifts.)

b. Have you made any other transfer, absolute or for the purpose of security, or any other disposition, of real or personal property during the year immediately preceding the filing of the original petition herein? (Give a description of the property, the date of the transfer or disposition, to whom transferred or how disposed of, and, if the transferee is a relative or insider, the relationship, the consideration, if any, received therefor, and the disposition of such consideration.)

13. Repossessions and returns.

Has any property been returned to, or repossessed by, the seller or by a secured party during the year immediately preceding the filing of the original petition herein? (If so, give particulars, including the name and address of the party getting the property and its description and value.)

14. Losses.

a. Have you suffered any losses from fire, theft, or gambling during the year immediately preceding or since the filing of the original petition herein? (If so, give particulars, including dates, names, and places, and the amounts of money or value and general description of property lost.)

b. Was the loss covered in whole or part by insurance? (If so, give particulars.)

15. Payments or transfers to attorneys and other persons.

a. Have you consulted an attorney during the year immediately preceding or since the filing of the original petition herein? (Give dates, name and address.)

b. Have you during the year immediately preceding or since the filing of the original petition herein paid any money or transferred any property to the attorney, to any other person on the attorney's behalf, or to any other person rendering services to you in connection with this case? (If so, give particulars, including amount paid or value of property transferred and date of payment or transfer.)

c. Have you, either during the year immediately preceding or since the filing of the original petition herein, agreed to pay any money or transfer any property to an attorney at law, to any other person on the attorney's behalf, or to any other person rendering services to you in connection with this case? (If so, give particulars, including amount and terms of obligation.)

I, _____, declare under penalty of perjury that I have read the answers contained in the foregoing statement of financial affairs and that they are true and correct to the best of my knowledge, information, and belief.

Executed on _____.

_____,
Debtor.

Amended eff. Sept. 19, 1986; eff. Aug. 1, 1987.

Advisory Committee Note

See Advisory Committee Note to Form No. 1 for discussion of unsworn statement at the end of this form.

Advisory Committee Note to 1986 Amendment

The introduction preceding paragraph 1 is amended to delete the reference to Rule 1003(a), which has been combined into Rule 1002.

Paragraph 15 is amended to implement the amendments to Rule 1006(b), which prohibits payments not only to attorneys but to any other person who renders services to the debtor in connection with the case.

Form No. 8

STATEMENT OF FINANCIAL AFFAIRS FOR DEBTOR ENGAGED IN BUSINESS

[Caption as in Form No. 1]

STATEMENT OF FINANCIAL AFFAIRS FOR DEBTOR ENGAGED IN BUSINESS

[Each question shall be answered or the failure to answer explained. If the answer is "none" or "not applicable," so state. If additional space is needed for the answer to any question, a separate sheet properly identified and made a part hereof, should be used and attached.

If the debtor is a partnership or a corporation, the questions shall be deemed to be addressed to, and shall be answered on behalf of, the partnership or corporation; and the statement shall be certified by a member of the partnership or by a duly authorized officer of the corporation.

The term, "original petition," used in the following questions, shall mean the petition filed under Rule 1002 or 1004.]

1. **Nature, location, and name of business.**

   a. Under what name and where do you carry on your business?

   b. In what business are you engaged? (If business operations have been terminated, give the date of termination.)

   c. When did you commence the business?

   d. Where else, and under what other names, have you carried on business within the six years immediately preceding the filing of the original petition herein? (Give street addresses, the names of any partners, joint adventurers, or other associates, the nature of the business, and the periods for which it was carried on.)

2. **Books and records.**

   a. By whom, or under whose supervision, have your books of account and records been kept during the six years immediately preceding the filing of the original petition herein? (Give names, addresses, and periods of time.)

   b. By whom have your books of account and records been audited during the six years immediately preceding the filing of the original petition herein? (Give names, addresses, and dates of audits.)

   c. In whose possession are your books of account and records? (Give names and addresses.)

   d. If any of these books or records are not available, explain.

   e. Have any books of account or records relating to your affairs been destroyed, lost, or otherwise disposed of within the two years immediately preceding the filing of the original petition herein? (If so, give particulars, including date of destruction, loss, or disposition, and reason therefor.)

3. Financial statements.

Have you issued any written financial statements within the two years immediately preceding the filing of the original petition herein? (Give dates, and the names and addresses of the persons to whom issued, including mercantile and trade agencies.)

4. Inventories.

 a. When was the last inventory of your property taken?

 b. By whom, or under whose supervision, was this inventory taken?

 c. What was the amount, in dollars, of the inventory? (State whether the inventory was taken at cost, market, or otherwise.)

 d. When was the next prior inventory of your property taken?

 e. By whom, or under whose supervision, was this inventory taken?

 f. What was the amount, in dollars, of the inventory? (State whether the inventory was taken at cost, market, or otherwise.)

 g. In whose possession are the records of the two inventories above referred to? (Give names and addresses.)

5. Income other than from operation of business.

What amount of income, other than from operation of your business, have you received during each of the two years immediately preceding the filing of the original petition herein? (Give particulars, including each source, and the amount received therefrom.)

6. Tax returns and refunds.

 a. In whose possession are copies of your federal, state and municipal income tax returns for the three years immediately preceding the filing of the original petition herein?

 b. What tax refunds (income or other) have you received during the two years immediately preceding the filing of the original petition herein?

 c. To what tax refunds (income or other), if any, are you, or may you be, entitled? (Give particulars, including information as to any refund payable jointly to you and your spouse or any other person.)

7. Financial accounts, certificates of deposit and safe deposit boxes.

 a. What accounts or certificates of deposit or shares in banks, savings and loan, thrift, building and loan and homestead associations, credit unions, brokerage houses, pension funds and the like have you maintained, alone or together with any other person, and in your own or any other name, within the two years immediately preceding the filing of the original petition herein? (Give the name and address of each institution, the name and number under which the account or certificate is maintained, and the name and address of every person authorized to make withdrawals from such account.)

 b. What safe deposit box or boxes or other depository or depositories have you kept or used for your securities, cash, or other valuables within the two years immediately preceding the filing of the original petition herein? (Give the name and address of the bank or other depository, the name in which each box or other depository was kept, the name and address of every person who had the right of access thereto, a description of the contents thereof, and, if the box has been surrendered, state when surrendered or, if transferred, when transferred and the name and address of the transferee.)

8. Property held for another person.

What property do you hold for any other person? (Give name and address of each person, and describe the property, the amount or value thereof and all writings relating thereto.)

9. Property held by another person.

Is any other person holding anything of value in which you have an interest? (Give name and address, location and description of the property, and circumstances of the holding.)

10. Prior bankruptcy proceedings.

What cases under the Bankruptcy Act or title 11, United States Code have previously been brought by or against you? (State the location of the bankruptcy court, the nature and number of the case, and whether a discharge was granted or denied, the case was dismissed, or a composition, arrangement, or plan was confirmed.)

11. Receiverships, general assignments, and other modes of liquidation.

a. Was any of your property, at the time of the filing of the original petition herein, in the hands of a receiver, trustee, or other liquidating agent? (If so, give a brief description of the property and the name and address of the receiver, trustee, or other agent, and, if the agent was appointed in a court proceeding, the name and location of the court, the title and number of the case, and the nature thereof.)

b. Have you made any assignment of your property for the benefit of your creditors, or any general settlement with your creditors, within the two years immediately preceding the filing of the original petition herein? (If so, give dates, the name and address of the assignee, and a brief statement of the terms of assignment or settlement.)

12. Suits, executions, and attachments.

a. Were you a party to any suit pending at the time of the filing of the original petition herein? (If so, give the name and location of the court and the title and nature of the proceeding.)

b. Were you a party to any suit terminated within the year immediately preceding the filing of the original petition herein? (If so, give the name and location of the court, the title and nature of the proceeding, and the result.)

c. Has any of your property been attached, garnished, or seized under any legal or equitable process within the year immediately preceding the filing of the original petition herein? (If so, describe the property seized or person garnished, and at whose suit.)

13. a. Payments of loans, installment purchases and other debts.

What payments in whole or in part have you made during the year immediately preceding the filing of the original petition herein on any of the following: (1) loans; (2) installment purchases of goods and services; and (3) other debts? (Give the names and addresses of the persons receiving payment, the amounts of the loans or other debts and of the purchase price of the goods and services, the dates of the original transactions, the amounts and dates of payments, and, if any of the payees are your relatives or insiders, the relationship; if the debtor is a partnership and any of the payees is or was a partner or a relative of a partner, state the relationship; if the debtor is a corporation and any of the payees is or was an officer, director, or stockholder, or a relative of an officer, director, or stockholder, state the relationship.)

b. Setoffs.

What debts have you owed to any creditor, including any bank, which were set off by that creditor against a debt or deposit owing by the creditor to you during the year immediately preceding the filing of the original petition herein? (Give the names and addresses of the persons setting off such debts, the dates of the setoffs, the amounts of the debts owing by you and to you and, if any of the creditors are your relatives or insiders, the relationship.)

14. Transfers of property.

a. Have you made any gifts, other than ordinary and usual presents to family members and charitable donations during the year immediately preceding the filing of the original petition herein? (If so, give names and addresses of donees and dates, description, and value of gifts.)

b. Have you made any other transfer, absolute or for the purpose of security, or any other disposition which was not in the ordinary course of business during the year immediately preceding the filing of the original petition herein? (Give a description of the property, the date of the transfer or disposition, to whom transferred or how disposed of, and state whether the transferee is a relative, partner, shareholder, officer, director, or insider, the consideration, if any, received for the property, and the disposition of such consideration.)

15. Accounts and other receivables.

Have you assigned, either absolutely or as security, any of your accounts or other receivables during the year immediately preceding the filing of the original petition herein? (If so, give names and addresses of assignees.)

16. Repossessions and returns.

Has any property been returned to, or repossessed by, the seller, lessor, or a secured party during the year immediately preceding the filing of the original petition herein? (If so, give particulars, including the name and address of the party getting the property and its description and value.)

17. Business leases.

If you are a tenant of business property, what is the name and address of your landlord, the amount of your rental, the date to which rent had been paid at the time of the filing of the original petition herein, and the amount of security held by the landlord?

18. Losses.

a. Have you suffered any losses from fire, theft, or gambling during the year immediately preceding the filing of the original petition herein? (If so, give particulars, including dates, names, and places, and the amounts of money or value and general description of property lost.)

b. Was the loss covered in whole or part by insurance? (If so, give particulars.)

19. Withdrawals.

a. If you are an individual proprietor of your business, what personal withdrawals of any kind have you made from the business during the year immediately preceding the filing of the original petition herein?

b. If the debtor is a partnership or corporation, what withdrawals, in any form (including compensation, bonuses or loans), have been made or received by any member of the partnership, or by any officer, director, insider, managing executive, or shareholder of the corporation, during the year immediately preceding the filing of the original petition herein? (Give the name and designation or relationship to the debtor of each person, the dates and amounts of withdrawals, and the nature or purpose thereof.)

20. Payments or transfers to attorneys and other persons.

a. Have you consulted an attorney during the year immediately preceding or since the filing of the original petition herein? (Give date, name, and address.)

b. Have you during the year immediately preceding or since the filing of the original petition herein paid any money or transferred any property to the attorney, to any other person on the attorney's behalf, or to any other person rendering services to you in connection with this case? (If so, give particulars, including amount paid or value of property transferred and date of payment or transfer.)

c. Have you, either during the year immediately preceding or since the filing of the original petition herein, agreed to pay any money or transfer any property to an attorney at law, to any other person on the attorney's behalf, or to any other person rendering services to you in connection with this case? (If so, give particulars, including amount and terms of obligation.)

(If the debtor is a partnership or corporation, the following additional questions should be answered.)

21. Members of partnership; officers, directors, managers, and principal stockholders of corporation.

a. What is the name and address of each member of the partnership, or the name, title, and address of each officer, director, insider, and managing executive, and of each stockholder holding 20 percent or more of the issued and outstanding stock, of the corporation?

b. During the year immediately preceding the filing of the original petition herein, has any member withdrawn from the partnership, or any officer, director, insider, or managing executive of the corporation terminated his relationship, or any stockholder holding 20 percent or more of the issued stock disposed of more than 50 percent of the stockholder's holdings? (If so, give name and address and reason for withdrawal, termination, or disposition, if known.)

c. Has any person acquired or disposed of 20 percent or more of the stock of the corporation during the year immediately preceding the filing of the petition? (If so, give name and address and particulars.)

I, _____, declare under penalty of perjury that I have read the answers contained in the foregoing statement of affairs and that they are true and correct to the best of my knowledge, information, and belief.

Executed on _____.

Signature: _____

[*Person declaring for partnership or corporation should indicate position or relationship to debtor.*]

Amended eff. Sept. 19, 1986; eff. Aug. 1, 1987.

Advisory Committee Note

Many of the questions on this form are the same as on Form No. 7, Statement of Financial Affairs for Debtor Not Engaged in Business.

The question regarding loans repaid (# 13) includes installment credit sales of goods or services. The information is helpful with respect to possible preferences.

Information regarding leases (# 17) may be helpful with respect to lease termination or extension and whether the landlord may be holding a deposit.

Advisory Committee Note to 1986 Amendment

Form 8 is amended in the same manner as Form 7.

Form No. 8A
CHAPTER 7 INDIVIDUAL DEBTOR'S STATEMENT
OF INTENTION

[Caption as in Form No. 2]

CHAPTER 7 INDIVIDUAL DEBTOR'S STATEMENT OF INTENTION

1. I, _____, the debtor, have filed a schedule of assets and liabilities which includes consumer debts secured by property of the estate.

2. My intention with respect to the property of the estate which secures those consumer debts is as follows:

   a. *Property to Be Surrendered.*

Description of property	Creditor's name
1. _____	_____
2. _____	_____
3. _____	_____
4. _____	_____
5. _____	_____

   b. *Property to Be Retained.* *[Check applicable statement of debtor's intention]*

Description of property	Creditor's name	The debt will be reaffirmed pursuant to § 524(c)	The property is claimed as exempt and will be redeemed pursuant to § 722	The creditor's lien will be avoided pursuant to § 522(f) and the property will be claimed as exempt
1. _____	_____	_____	_____	_____
2. _____	_____	_____	_____	_____
3. _____	_____	_____	_____	_____
4. _____	_____	_____	_____	_____
5. _____	_____	_____	_____	_____

3. I understand that § 521(2)(B) of the Bankruptcy Code requires that I perform the above stated intention within 45 days of the filing of this statement with the court, or within any extension of the 45 day period which the court may grant.

Date: _____.

_____
Debtor

Added eff. Sept. 19, 1986.

Advisory Committee Note

Section 521(2), as added by the 1984 amendments, requires an individual debtor whose schedule of assests and liabilities includes consumer debts

which are secured by property of the estate to file with the clerk a statement
of the debtor's intention with regard to such property. This form is designed
to implement this requirement.

Form No. 9

LIST OF CREDITORS HOLDING 20 LARGEST UNSECURED CLAIMS

[Caption as in Form No. 2]

LIST OF CREDITORS HOLDING 20 LARGEST UNSECURED CLAIMS

Following is the list of the Debtor's creditors holding the 20 largest unsecured claims which is prepared in accordance with Rule 1007(d) for filing in this chapter 11 [*or* chapter 9] case. The list does not include those (1) persons who come within the definition of insider set forth in 11 U.S.C. § 101(25), (2) secured creditors unless the value of the collateral is such that the unsecured deficiency places the creditor among the holders of the 20 largest unsecured claims, or (3) governmental units not within the definition of "person" in 11 U.S.C. § 101(35).

(1)	(2)	(3)	(4)	(5)
Name of creditor and complete mailing address including zip code	Name, telephone number and complete mailing address including zip code of employee, agent or department of creditor familiar with claim who may be contacted	Nature of claim (trade debt, bank loan, type of judgment, etc.)	Indicate if claim is contingent, unliquidated, disputed or subject to setoff	Amount of claim [if secured also state value of security]

Date: _____.

_____
Debtor.

Amended eff. Sept. 19, 1986.

Advisory Committee Note

This form is for use in chapter 11 reorganization and chapter 9 municipality debt adjustment cases to enable the appointment, pursuant to §§ 1102 and 901 of the Code, of a committee of unsecured creditors. The information contained on the form is to assist in expediting the formation of the committee and to assure adequate creditor representation.

In accordance with § 1102 of the Code, the form indicates that insiders should not be listed. "Insiders" is defined in § 101(25) of the Code to include, *inter alia,* persons who are related to the debtor, are partners, officers, directors, affiliates as further defined in § 101(2) of the Code, or are otherwise in control of the debtor. Reference should be made to § 101 for the complete listing of insiders.

The nature of the claim should be specified to indicate whether it is an institutional debt, a trade debt for merchandise or supplies, a debt based on a judgment and the underlying basis for the judgment, or the like.

In column (2), it is important to provide specific information with respect to the person to be contacted. In order to form the committee it may be necessary to write or telephone the creditors. If the creditor company is a large organization individual contact may otherwise be difficult or impossible.

A secured creditor should be listed among the 20 largest unsecured creditors only if that creditor is sufficiently undersecured so as to fall within that category.

Advisory Committee Note to 1986 Amendment

The form has been amended to reflect the definition of "person" in 11 U.S.C. § 101(35), as modified by the 1984 amendments and renumbered by the 1986 amendments.

Form No. 10

CHAPTER 13 STATEMENT

[Caption as in Form No. 1]

CHAPTER 13 STATEMENT

[Each question shall be answered or the failure to answer explained. If the answer is "none" or "not applicable," so state. If additional space is needed for the answer to any question, a separate sheet, properly identified and made a part hereof, should be used and attached.

The term "original petition," used in the following questions, shall mean the original petition filed under § 301 of the Code or, if the chapter 13 case was converted from another chapter of the Code, shall mean the petition by or against you which originated the first case.

This form must be completed in full whether a single or a joint petition is filed. When information is requested for "each" or "either spouse filing a petition," it should be supplied for both when a joint petition is filed.]

1. *Name and residence.*

a. Give full name.

Husband [*or, if single*, Debtor] _____

Wife _____

b. Where does debtor, if single, or each spouse filing a petition now reside?

(1) Mailing address of husband [*or* debtor]

_____

City or town, state and zip code

_____

_____

(2) Mailing address of wife

_____

City or town, state and zip code

_____

_____

(3) Telephone number including area code

Husband [*or, if single*, Debtor] _____

Wife _____

c. What does debtor, if single, or each spouse filing a petition consider his or her residence, if different from that listed in b, above?

Husband [*or* Debtor] _____

Wife _____

2. *Occupation and income.*

a. Give present occupation of debtor, if single, or each spouse filing a petition. (If more than one, list all for debtor or each spouse filing a petition.)

Husband [*or* Debtor] _____

Wife _____

b. What is the name, address, and telephone number of present employer (or employers) of debtor, if single, or each spouse filing a petition? (Include also any identifying badge or card number with employer.)

Husband [*or* Debtor] _____

_____

Wife _____

_____

c. How long has debtor, if single, or each spouse filing a petition been employed by present employer?

Husband [*or* Debtor] _____

_____

Wife _____

_____

d. If debtor or either spouse filing a petition has not been employed by present employer for a period of one year, state the name of prior employer(s) and nature of employment during that period.

Husband [*or* Debtor] _____

_____

Wife _____

_____

e. Has debtor or either spouse filing a petition operated a business, in partnership or otherwise, during the past three years? (If so, give the particulars, including names, dates, and places.)

Husband [*or* Debtor] _____

_____

Wife _____

_____

f. Answer the following questions for debtor, if single, or each spouse whether single or joint petition is filed unless spouses are separated and a single petition is filed:

(1) What are your gross wages, salary, or commissions per pay period?

	Husband [*or* Debtor]	Wife
(a) Weekly	_____	_____
(b) Semi-monthly	_____	_____
(c) Monthly	_____	_____
(d) Other (specify)	_____	_____

(2) What are your payroll deductions per pay period for:

	Husband [or Debtor]	Wife
(a) Payroll taxes (Including Social Security)	_____	_____
(b) Insurance	_____	_____
(c) Credit union	_____	_____
(d) Union dues	_____	_____
(e) Other (specify)	_____	_____

(3) What is your take-home pay per pay period?

	Husband [or Debtor]	Wife
	_____	_____

(4) What was the amount of your gross income for the last calendar year?

	Husband [or Debtor]	Wife
	_____	_____

(5) Is your employment subject to seasonal or other change?

	Husband [or Debtor]	Wife
	_____	_____

(6) Has either of you made any wage assignments or allotments? (If so, indicate which spouse's wages assigned or allotted, the name and address of the person to whom assigned or allotted, and the amount owing, if any, to such person. If allotment or assignment is to a creditor, the claim should also be listed in Item 11a.)

_____

_____

3. *Dependents.* (To be answered by debtor if unmarried, otherwise for each spouse whether single or joint petition is filed unless spouses are separated and a single petition is filed.)

a. Does either of you pay [or receive] alimony, maintenance, or support? _____ If so, how much per month? _____ For whose support? (Give name, age, and relationship to you.)

Husband [or Debtor] _____

_____

Wife _____

_____

b. List all other dependents, other than present spouse, not listed in a, above. (Give name, age and relationship to you.)

Husband [or Debtor] _____

_____

Wife _____

_____

4. *Budget.*

a. Give your estimated average future monthly income, if unmarried, otherwise for each spouse whether single or joint petition is filed, unless spouses are separated and a single petition is filed.

        (1) Husband's [*or* Debtor's] monthly take-home pay   ————

        (2) Wife's monthly take-home pay   ————

        (3) Other monthly income (specify)   ════

                                  Total   ————

b. Give estimated average future monthly expenses of family (not including debts to be paid under plan), consisting of:

        (1) Rent or home mortgage payment (include lot rental for trailer)   ————

        (2) Utilities (Electricity ————, Heat ————, Water ————, Telephone ————)   ————

        (3) Food   ————

        (4) Clothing   ————

        (5) Laundry and cleaning   ————

        (6) Newspapers, periodicals, and books (including school books)   ————

        (7) Medical and drug expenses   ————

        (8) Insurance (not deducted from wages)

            (a) Auto   ————

            (b) Other   ————

        (9) Transportation (not including auto payments to be paid under plan)   ————

        (10) Recreation   ————

        (11) Dues, union, professional, social or otherwise (not deducted from wages)   ————

        (12) Taxes (not deducted from wages)   ————

        (13) Alimony, maintenance, or support payments   ————

        (14) Other payments for support of dependents not living at home   ————

        (15) Religious and other charitable contributions   ————

        (16) Other (specify)

        _____   ════

        _____   ════

    Total   ————

c. Excess of estimated future monthly income (last line of Item 4a, above) over estimated future expenses (last line of Item 4b, above)   ————

d. Total amount to be paid each month under plan   ————

5. *Payment of attorney.*

a. How much have you agreed to pay or what property have you agreed to transfer to your attorney in connection with this case?   ————

b. How much have you paid or what have you transferred to the attorney?   ————

6. *Tax refunds.* (To be answered by debtor, if unmarried, otherwise for each spouse whether single or joint petition is filed, unless spouses are separated and a single petition is filed.)

To what tax refunds (income or other), if any, is either of you, or may either of you be, entitled? (Give particulars, including information as to any refunds payable jointly to you or any other person. All such refunds should also be listed in Item 13b.)

_____

_____

7. *Financial accounts, certificates of deposit and safe deposit boxes.* (To be answered by debtor, if unmarried, otherwise for each spouse whether single or joint petition is filed unless spouses are separated and a single petition is filed.)

a. Does either of you currently have any accounts or certificates of deposit or shares in banks, savings and loan, thrift, building and loan and homestead associations, credit unions, brokerage houses, pension funds and the like? (If so, give name and address of each institution, number and nature of account, current balance, and name and address of every other person authorized to make withdrawals from the account. Such accounts should also be listed in Item 13b.)

_____

_____

b. Does either of you currently keep any safe deposit boxes or other depositories? (If so, give name and address of bank or other depository, name and address of every other person who has a right of access thereto, and a brief description of the contents thereof, which should also be listed in Item 13b.)

_____

_____

8. *Prior Bankruptcy.* What cases under the Bankruptcy Act or Bankruptcy Code have previously been brought by or against you or either spouse filing a petition? (State the location of the bankruptcy court, the nature and number of each case, the date when it was filed, and whether a discharge was granted or denied, the case was dismissed, or a composition, arrangement, or plan was confirmed.)

_____

_____

9. *Foreclosures, executions, and attachments.* (To be answered by debtor, if unmarried, otherwise for each spouse whether single or joint petition is filed unless spouses are separated and a single petition is filed.)

a. Is any of the property of either of you, including real estate, involved in a foreclosure proceeding, in or out of court? (If so, identify the property and the person foreclosing.)

_____

_____

b. Has any property or income of either of you been attached, garnished, or seized under any legal or equitable process within the 90 days immediately preceding the filing of the original petition herein? (If so, describe the property seized, or person garnished, and at whose suit.)

10. *Repossessions and returns.* (To be answered by debtor, if unmarried, otherwise for each spouse whether single or joint petition is filed unless spouses are separated and a single petition is filed.)

Has any property of either of you been returned to, repossessed, or seized by the seller or by any other party, including a landlord, during the 90 days immediately preceding the filing of the original petition herein? (If so, give particulars, including the name and address of the party taking the property and its description and value.)

11. *Transfers of Property.* (To be answered by debtor, if unmarried, otherwise for each spouse whether single or joint petition is filed unless spouses are separated and a single petition is filed.)

a. Has either of you made any gifts, other than ordinary and usual presents to family members and charitable donations, during the year immediately preceding the filing of the original petition herein? (If so, give names and addresses of donees and dates, description and value of gifts.)

b. Has either of you made any other transfer, absolute or for the purpose of security, or any other disposition, of real or personal property during the year immediately preceding the filing of the original petition herein? (Give a description of the property, the date of the transfer or disposition, to whom transferred or how disposed of, and, if the transferee is a relative or insider, the relationship, the consideration, if any, received therefor, and the disposition of such consideration.)

12. *Debts.* (To be answered by debtor, if unmarried, otherwise for each spouse whether single or joint petition is filed.)

a. *Debts Having Priority.*

(1)	(2)	(3)	(4)	(5)
Nature of claim	Name of creditor and complete mailing address including zip code	Specify when claim was incurred and the consideration therefor; when claim is subject to setoff, evidenced by a judgment, negotiable instrument, or other writing	Indicate if claim is contingent, unliquidated, or disputed	Amount of claim

1. Wages, salary, and commissions, including vacation, severance and sick leave pay owing to employees not exceeding $2,000
to each, earned within 90 days before filing of petition or cessation of business (if earlier specify date). $_____

2. Contributions to employee benefit plans for services rendered
within 180 days before filing of petition or cessation of business (if
earlier specify date). $_____

3. Deposits by individuals, not exceeding $900 for each for
purchase, lease, or rental of property or services for personal,
family, or household use that were not delivered or provided. $_____

4. Taxes owing [itemize by type of tax and taxing authority]
    (A) To the United States $_____
    (B) To any state   _____
    (C) To any other taxing authority   ========
    Total   ========

b. *Secured Debts.* List all debts which are or may be secured by real or personal property. (Indicate in sixth column, if debt payable in installments, the amount of each installment, the installment period (monthly, weekly, or otherwise) and number of installments in arrears, if any. Indicate in last column whether husband or wife solely liable, or whether you are jointly liable.)

Creditor's name, account number and complete mailing address including zip code	Consideration or basis for debt	Amount claimed by creditor	If disputed, amount admitted by debtor	Description of collateral [include year and make of automobile]	Installment amount, period, and number of installments in arrears	Husband or wife solely liable, or jointly liable
		Total secured debts				

[D1989]

731

c. *Unsecured Debts.* List all other debts, liquidated and unliquidated, including taxes, attorneys' fees, and tort claims.

Creditor's name, account number and complete mailing address including zip code	Consideration or basis for debt	Amount claimed by creditor	If disputed, amount admitted by debtor	Husband or wife solely liable, or jointly liable
		Total unsecured debts		

13. *Codebtors.* (To be answered by debtor, if unmarried, otherwise for each spouse whether single or joint petition is filed.)

a. Are any other persons liable, as cosigners, guarantors, or in any other manner, on any of the debts of either of you or is either of you so liable on the debts of others? (If so, give particulars, indicating which spouse is liable and including names of creditors, nature of debt, names and addresses of codebtors, and their relationship, if any, to you.)

b. If so, have the codebtors made any payments on the debts? (Give name of each codebtor and amount paid by codebtor.)

c. Has either of you made any payments on the debts? (If so, specify total amount paid to each creditor, whether paid by husband or wife, and name of codebtor.)

14. *Property and Exemptions.* (To be answered by debtor, if unmarried, otherwise for each spouse whether single or joint petition is filed.)

a. *Real Property.* List all real property owned by either of you at date of filing of original petition herein. (Indicate in last column whether owned solely by husband or wife, or jointly.)

Description and location of property	Name of any co-owner other than spouse	Present market value (without deduction for mortgage or other security interest)	Amount of mortgage or other security interest on this property	Name of mortgagee or other secured creditor	Value claimed exempt (specify federal or state statute creating the exemption)	Owned solely by husband or wife or jointly

[D1991]

733

b. *Personal Property.* List all other property, owned by either of you at date of filing of original petition herein.

Description	Location of property if not at debtor's residence	Name of any co-owner other than spouse	Present market value (without deduction for mortgage or other security interest)	Amount of mortgage or other security interest on this property	Name of mortgagee or other secured creditor	Value claimed exempt (specify federal or state statute creating the exemption)	Owned solely by husband or wife or jointly
Autos [give year, and make]							
Household goods							
Personal effects							
Cash or financial account							
Other [specify]							

[D1993]

734

[To be signed by both spouses when joint petition is filed.]

I, _____, [*if joint petition is filed* and I, _____,] declare under penalty of perjury that I have read the answers contained in the foregoing statement, consisting of __ sheets, and that they are true and complete to the best of my knowledge, information, and belief.

_____

Husband [*or Debtor*]

_____

Wife

Executed on _____.

Amended eff. Sept. 19, 1986.

Advisory Committee Note

This form is adapted from former Chapter XIII Official Form No. 13–5. It may be used whether a single chapter 13 petition is filed or a joint petition is filed by husband and wife as authorized by § 302 of the Code.

Question 4 of the Statement, calling for a detailed family budget is particularly designed to insure that the debtor and the debtor's attorney will have compiled information relative to the feasibility of the plan prior to the creditors' meeting.

Inquiry as to most transactions and developments affecting the financial condition of the debtor is limited to the year preceding the filing of the petition or to a shorter period. The scope of examination at the meeting or at any other time is not restricted by the scope of the inquiries in the Chapter 13 Statement. In Question 14a and b any claim of exempt property should be listed. This information assists the court in comparing the creditors' return under the plan and a possible chapter 7 case. Although Chapter 13 Statements are required by Rule 1007(f) to be filed in the same number as the petition they accompany, only the original need be signed and verified, but the copies must be conformed to the original. See Bankruptcy Rule 9011(c).

Advisory Committee Note to 1986 Amendment

In paragraph 8, the references to "proceedings" have been changed to "cases".

Publisher's Supplementary Note

It appears, however, that the above Official Form has not to date been revised to take into account two new categories of priority claims, those of farmers against grain-storage facilities and those of fishermen against fish-produce storage or processing facilities, up to $2000 each. 11 U.S.C.A. § 507(a)(5). Bankruptcy Rule 9009 provides authority and direction to make "alterations as may be appropriate" to the Official Forms. An appropriate alteration to the above form would be to insert a new item 3 under paragraph 12(a), ("Debts Having Priority,"), as follows, and to renumber existing items "3" and "4" as "4" and "5" in paragraph 12(a):

"3. Claims of farmers against grain-storage facilities and of fishermen against fish-produce storage or processing facilities, not exceeding $2000 for each $_____

Form No. 11

INVOLUNTARY CASE: CREDITORS' PETITION

[Caption as in Form No. 1]

INVOLUNTARY CASE: CREDITORS' PETITION

1. Petitioners, _____, of * _____, and _____, of * _____, and _____, of * _____, are creditors of _____, of * _____ [*include county*], holding claims against the debtor, not contingent as to liability and not subject to bona fide dispute, amounting in the aggregate, in excess of the value of any lien held by them on the debtor's property securing such claims, to at least $5000. The nature and amount of petitioners' claims are as follows: _____

_____

_____

2. The debtor's principal place of business [*or principal assets or domicile or residence*] has been within this district for the 180 days preceding the filing of this petition [*or for a longer portion of the 180 days preceding the filing of this petition than in any other district*].

3. The debtor is a person against whom an order for relief may be entered under title 11, United States Code.

4. [The debtor is generally not paying its debts which are not subject to bona fide dispute as they become due as indicated by the following _____

_____.]

or [Within 120 days preceding the filing of this petition, a custodian was appointed for *or* has taken possession of substantially all of the property of the debtor, as follows: _____

_____

_____.]

WHEREFORE petitioners pray that an order of relief be entered against _____ under chapter 7 [*or* 11] of title 11, United States Code.

Signed: _____
Attorney for Petitioners.

Address: _____

_____

[*Petitioners sign if not represented by attorney*]

_____,

_____,

_____,

Petitioners.

I, _____, one of the petitioners named in the foregoing petition, declare under penalty of perjury that the foregoing is true and correct according to the best of my knowledge, information, and belief.

Executed on _____.

Signature: _____

Petitioner.

* State mailing address.

Amended eff. Sept. 19, 1986.

Advisory Committee Note

The requisites for an involuntary petition are specified in § 303 of the Code.

28 U.S.C. § 1746 permits the unsworn declaration in lieu of a verification. See Advisory Committee Note to Form No. 1.

Advisory Committee Note to 1986 Amendment

The inclusion in paragraphs 1 and 4 of the allegations that the debts are not subject to bona fide dispute reflects the requirements added to §§ 303(b)(i) and 303(h)(i) of the Code by the 1984 amendments.

Form No. 12

INVOLUNTARY CASE AGAINST PARTNERSHIP: PARTNER'S PETITION

[Caption as in Form No. 1]

INVOLUNTARY CASE AGAINST PARTNERSHIP: PARTNER'S PETITION

1. Petitioner, _____, of * _____ is one of the general partners of _____, a partnership, of * _____ [*include county*].

2. The other general partners of the debtor are _____, of * _____ and _____ of * _____.

3. The debtor has had its principal place of business [*or* its principal assets *or* its domicile *or* its residence] within this district for the 180 days preceding the filing of this petition [*or* for a longer portion of the 180 days preceding the filing of this petition than in any other district].

4. The debtor is a person against whom an order for relief may be entered under title 11, United States Code.

5. [The debtor is generally not paying its debts which are not subject to bona fide dispute as they become due as indicated by the following _____.]

or [Within 120 days preceding the filing of this petition, a custodian was appointed for *or* has taken possession of substantially all of the property of the debtor, as follows: _____

_____

_____.]

WHEREFORE, petitioner prays that an order of relief be entered against _____ under chapter 7 [*or* 11] of title 11, United States Code.

Signed: _____
Attorney for Petitioner.

Address: _____,

_____,

[Petitioner signs if not represented by attorney]

_____,
Petitioner.

I, _____, the petitioner named in the foregoing petition, declare under penalty of perjury that the foregoing is true and correct according to the best of my knowledge, information and belief.

Executed on _____.

Signature: _____
Petitioner.

* State mailing address.

Amended eff. Sept. 19, 1986.

Advisory Committee Note

Pursuant to § 303(b)(3)(A) of the Code, a petition by fewer than all of the general partners seeking an order for relief with respect to the partnership is treated as an involuntary petition. It is adversarial in character because not all of the partners are joining in the petition.

Section 303(b)(3)(B) permits a petition against the partnership if relief has been ordered under the Code with respect to all of the general partners. In that event, the petition may be filed by a general partner, a trustee of a general partner's estate, or a creditor of the partnership. This form may be adapted for use in that type of case.

28 U.S.C. § 1472(1) specifies the proper venue alternatives for all persons, including partnerships, as domicile, residence, principal place of business or location of principal assets. These options are set forth in paragraph (3) of the form. The paragraph may be adapted for use when venue is based on a pending case commenced by an affiliate pursuant to 28 U.S.C. § 1472(2).

Advisory Committee Note to 1986 Amendment

The inclusion in paragraph 5 of the allegation that the debts are not subject to a bona fide dispute reflects the requirement added to § 303(h)(1) of the Code by the 1984 amendments.

Form No. 13

SUMMONS TO DEBTOR IN INVOLUNTARY CASE

B13 (Official Form 13)
(Rev. 10/87)

United States Bankruptcy Court

_____ District of _____

In re

Bankruptcy Case No.

Debtor*
Social Security No.   :
Employer Tax I.D. No.:

SUMMONS TO DEBTOR IN INVOLUNTARY CASE

To the above named debtor:

A petition under title 11, United States Code was filed against you on _____
(date)

in this bankruptcy court, requesting an order for relief under chapter _____ of the Bankruptcy Code (title

11 of the United States Code).

YOU ARE SUMMONED and required to submit to the clerk of the bankruptcy court a motion or

answer to the petition within 20 days after the service of this summons. A copy of the petition is attached.

Address of Clerk

At the same time you must also serve a copy of your motion or answer on petitioner's attorney.

Name and Address of Petitioner's Attorney

If you make a motion, your time to serve an answer is governed by Bankruptcy Rule 1011(c).

If you fail to respond to this summons, the order for relief will be entered.

_____
Clerk of the Bankruptcy Court

_____ By: _____
Date   Deputy Clerk

*Set forth all names, including trade names, used by the debtor within the last 6 years. (Bankruptcy Rule 1005). For joint debtors, set forth both social security numbers.   [E7836]

Form 13

B13 (Reverse)
(Rev. 10/87)

CERTIFICATE OF SERVICE

I, _____ , certify that I am, and at all times during the service
             (name)

of process was, not less than 18 years of age and not a party to the matter concerning which service of
process was made. I further certify that the service of this summons and a copy of the complaint was made
_____ by:
   (date)

☐ Mail service: Regular, first class United States mail, postage fully pre-paid, addressed to:

☐ Personal Service: By leaving the process with defendant or with an officer or agent of defendant at:

☐ Residence Service: By leaving the process with the following adult at:

☐ Publication: The defendant was served as follows: [Describe briefly]

☐ State Law: The defendant was served pursuant to the laws of the State of _____ ,
as follows: [Describe briefly]   (name of state)

       Under penalty of perjury, I declare that the foregoing is true and correct.

_____   _____
          Date   *Signature*

Print Name		
Business Address		
City	State	Zip

[E7837]

COMMENTS AND INSTRUCTIONS

Purpose of the Form

Bankruptcy cases can arise in two ways: An individual or business may file a voluntary petition or creditors may file an involuntary petition against an individual or business.

The first step in commencing an involuntary bankruptcy proceeding is the filing of a petition by a creditor or creditors, using Form B 11 or 12. Forms B 11 and 12 are not distributed by the government, but are reprinted in most publications which contain the text of the Rules of Bankruptcy Procedure. They may be purchased at most legal stationery stores.)

The summons is the notice which accompanies the petition, advising of the names of the debtor and the petitioning creditors, the court in which the proceeding was filed, and the time limits for responding to the petition.

Pertinent Law and Rules

1. The primary statutory provisions for an involuntary bankruptcy proceeding are found in Section 303 of the Bankruptcy Code (title 11 of the United States Code). These provisions are complex, and there are substantial penalties for filing an improper involuntary petition. This section should therefore be read in its entirety prior to the filing of an involuntary petition.

2. Section 303(a) limits an involuntary petition to chapters 7 and 11. It further provides that the involuntary debtor may not be a farmer, or a corporation which is not a moneyed, business, or commercial corporation.

3. Section 303(b) provides that each of the petitioning creditors must hold claims against the debtor which are not contingent as to liability and which are not the subject of a bona fide dispute. Although there are several complex criteria, the two basic ones are: 1) if the debtor has fewer than 12 creditors, only one creditor need file the involuntary petition, whereas if the debtor has 12 or more creditors, at least three of the creditors must join in the petition; and 2) the claims of the petitioning creditor or creditors must total at least $5,000.

4. Bankruptcy Rule 1010 states that: "On the filing of an involuntary petition . . . the clerk shall forthwith issue a summons for service . . . on the debtor. The summons shall conform to Official Form No. 13 and a copy shall be served with a copy of the petition in the manner provided for service of a summons and complaint by Rule 7004(a) or (b). If service cannot be so made, the court may order the summons and petition to be served by mailing copies to the party's last known address, and by not less than one publication in a manner and form directed by the court. The summons and petition may be served on the party anywhere. [Bankruptcy] Rule 7004(f) and Rule 4(g) and (h) [of the Federal Rules of Civil Procedure] apply when service is made or attempted under this rule."

5. Bankruptcy Rule 7004(a) adopts portions of Rule 4 of the Federal Rules of Civil Procedure (F.R.C.P.), and sets forth other provisions for the issuance and service of a summons. These rules are detailed and complex, and should be read in their entirety.

6. F.R.C.P. 4(a), as made applicable by Bankruptcy Rule 7004, provides that the clerk shall issue the summons to the petitioning creditor or its attorney. It is then the responsibility of the petitioning creditor or the attorney to serve the summons on the debtor.

7. A copy of the petition must be served with the summons. F.R.C.P. 4(a).

8. It is a good idea to submit several copies of the summons to the court with the petition, so that each copy may be signed by the court: one for the court records, one for service on the debtor, one for each of petitioning creditor's records (or the creditor's attorney's records), and one to be returned to the court after the certificate of service has been completed.

9. The summons and petition may be served in a variety of ways which are set forth in Bankruptcy Rules 1010 and 7004 and F.R.C.P. 4. When the debtor is an individual, other than an infant or incompetent person, the easiest method is for the summons and petition to be mailed by first class mail postage prepaid to the individual's dwelling house or usual place of abode or to the place where the individual regularly conducts a business or profession. Bankruptcy Rule 7004(b)(1).

10. In any event, service must be made by someone who is not a party, and who is at least 18 years of age. Bankruptcy Rule 7004(a).

11. The summons and petition must be served within 10 days of the issuance of the summons. Service is complete upon mailing, not upon delivery by the Postal Service. If more than 10 days pass before service is completed, a new summons must be issued and served. Bankruptcy Rules 7004(f) and 9006(e).

12. If the summons and petition are not served within 120 days of the filing of the complaint, the court may dismiss the action. F.R.C.P. 4(j).

13. On the back of the summons is a certificate of service of the summons. After service has been made, this certificate should be completed, and filed with the court.

14. Bankruptcy Rule 1011 grants the debtor 20 days from the service of the summons to reply to the petition. Under the provisions of Section 303(h), if the debtor fails to timely reply to the involuntary petition, the court will enter an order for relief under the appropriate chapter of the Bankruptcy Code, using Form B 14 or 14A. If the debtor timely files an answer, the court will conduct a trial and will only enter the order for relief if the debtor is not generally paying its undisputed debts as they become due, or if within 120 days before the date of the filing of the petition, a custodian, other than a trustee, receiver, or agent authorized to take charge of less than substantially all of the property of the debtor for the purpose of enforcing a lien against such property, was appointed or took possession. Bankruptcy Rule 1018 sets forth the procedures to be followed in the event of a contested involuntary petition.

15. Section 303(i) authorizes the court to order creditors that file improper involuntary petitions to pay the costs and attorney's fees of the debtor. If the court finds that the involuntary petition was brought in bad faith, it can also order the petitioning creditors to pay for all damages proximately caused by the filing, and may assess punitive damages.

Instructions

Caption

1. Identify the Judicial District in which the bankruptcy case was filed. Example: Eastern District of California.

2. "In re": Insert the name of the debtor as it appears in the bankruptcy petition including Social Security number or Employer Tax ID number, and all names, including trade names, used by the debtor within the last 6 years.

3. "Bankruptcy Case No.": Insert the bankruptcy case number assigned by the court at the time of filing.

Address of Clerk:

Be sure to indicate the proper address for the clerk's office.

Name and Address of Petitioner's Attorney:

The complete mailing address of the attorney for the petitioning creditor must be set forth in the box provided, including zip code. If the street address is different, that must also be stated, including room number. If the petitioning creditor is not represented by an attorney, the petitioning creditor's mailing and street address should be placed in the box.

Certificate of Service

1. Line 1 (name) is to be completed with the full name of the person who served the summons and petition.

2. Line 4 (date) is to be completed with the month, day and year service was perfected.

3. The appropriate box should be checked to show how service was made.

   —If mail service, state the mailing address, city, state and zip code of the place to which the summons and petition were mailed.

   —If personal service, state both the name of the person to whom the summons and petition were given, and the address at which this occurred.

   —If residence service, state both the name of the adult to whom the summons and petition were given, and the address at which this occurred.

   —If service by publication, describe the steps taken to perfect service.

   —If service was made pursuant to state law, fill in the blank with the name of the state under whose laws the summons and petition were served, and describe briefly the method of service, including the name of the person served and the address at which they were served.

4. Date: Insert on this line the month, day and year the certificate is signed.

5. Signature: The person who completed service of the summons and petition must sign. This must be an ORIGINAL signature.

6. In the box directly below the Date and Signature lines, *print or type* the name and address of the person who signed the certificate.

Source of Form

This Official Form and the accompanying commentary and instructions are included as Form B 13 of *Bankruptcy Forms Manual* Volume II, "Forms and Instructions for the Public," as issued by the Division of Bankruptcy, Administrative Office of the United States Courts (September, 1988).

Form 14

OFFICIAL FORMS

Form No. 14

ORDER FOR RELIEF UNDER CHAPTER 7

B14 (Official Form 14)
(1/87)

United States Bankruptcy Court

_____District of_____

In re

Bankruptcy Case No.

Debtor*
Social Security No.   :
Employer Tax I.D. No. :

ORDER FOR RELIEF UNDER CHAPTER 7

On consideration of the petition filed on _____ against the

(date)

above-named debtor, an order for relief under chapter 7 of the Bankruptcy Code (title 11 of the United

States Code) is granted.

_____	_____
Date	Bankruptcy Judge

---

*Set forth all names, including trade names, used by the debtor within the last 6 years. (Bankruptcy Rule 1005). For joint debtors set forth both social security numbers.   [E7838]

Source of Form

This Official Form is included as Form B 14 of *Bankruptcy Forms Manual* Volume II, "Forms and Instructions for the Public," as issued by the Division of Bankruptcy, Administrative Office of the United States Courts (September, 1988).

Form 14A   OFFICIAL FORMS

Form No. 14A
ORDER FOR RELIEF UNDER CHAPTER 11

B14A (Official Form 14A)
(1/87)

United States Bankruptcy Court

_____ District of _____

In re

Bankruptcy Case No.

Debtor*

Social Security No.   :
Employer Tax I.D. No. :

ORDER FOR RELIEF UNDER CHAPTER 11

On consideration of the petition filed on _____ against the

(date)

above-named debtor, an order for relief under chapter 11 of the Bankruptcy Code (title 11 of the United

States Code) is granted.

_____   _____
Date   Bankruptcy Judge

---

*Set forth all names, including trade names, used by the debtor within the last 6 years. (Bankruptcy Rule 1005). For joint debtors set forth both
social security numbers.   [E7839]

748

Source of Form

This Official Form is included as Form B 14A of *Bankruptcy Forms Manual* Volume II, "Forms and Instructions for the Public," as issued by the Division of Bankruptcy, Administrative Office of the United States Courts (September, 1988).

Form No. 15

APPOINTMENT OF COMMITTEE OF UNSECURED CREDITORS IN A CHAPTER 11 REORGANIZATION CASE

B15 (Official Form 15)
(Rev. 10/87)

𝔘nited 𝔖tates 𝔅ankruptcy 𝔈ourt

_____ District of _____ .

In re

Bankruptcy Case No.

Debtor*
Social Security No.   :
Employer Tax I.D. No. :

APPOINTMENT OF COMMITTEE OF UNSECURED CREDITORS IN A CHAPTER 11 REORGANIZATION CASE

☐ The following creditors of the above-named debtor holding the 7 largest unsecured claims and who are willing to serve are appointed to the committee of unsecured creditors:

☐ The following creditors of the above-named debtor who are members of a committee organized by creditors before commencement of this case under chapter 11 of the Bankruptcy Code (title 11 of the United States Code), which was fairly chosen and is representative of the different kinds of claims to be represented, and who are willing to serve, are appointed to the committee of unsecured creditors:

Name and Address	Name and Address	Name and Address
Name and Address	Name and Address	Name and Address
Name and Address	Name and Address	Name and Address

Creditors that are partnerships or corporations should designate contact persons to whom correspondence should be directed. If a contact person is replaced, the court and other committee members must be advised in writing.

_____   _____
Date   Bankruptcy Judge

*Set forth all names, including trade names, used by the debtor within the last 6 years. (Bankruptcy Rule 1005). For joint debtors set forth both social security numbers.   [E7840]

750

Source of Form

This Official Form is included as Form B 15 of *Bankruptcy Forms Manual* Volume II, "Forms and Instructions for the Public," as issued by the Division of Bankruptcy, Administrative Office of the United States Courts (September, 1988).

Form No. 16

ORDER FOR MEETING OF CREDITORS AND RELATED ORDERS, COMBINED WITH NOTICE THEREOF AND OF AUTOMATIC STAY

[Caption as in Form No. 1]

ORDER FOR MEETING OF CREDITORS AND FIXING TIMES FOR FILING OBJECTIONS TO DISCHARGE AND FOR FILING COMPLAINTS TO DETERMINE DISCHARGEABILITY OF CERTAIN DEBTS, COMBINED WITH NOTICE THEREOF AND OF AUTOMATIC STAY

To the debtor, creditors, and other parties in interest:

An order for relief under 11 U.S.C. chapter 7 [*or,* 11, *or* 13] having been entered on a petition filed by [*or* against] _____ of _____, on _____ it is ordered, and notice is hereby given, that:

[MEETING OF CREDITORS]

1. A meeting of creditors pursuant to 11 U.S.C. § 341(a) has been scheduled for _____ at _____ o'clock __. m. at _____.

2. The debtor shall appear in person [*or, if the debtor is a partnership,* by a general partner, *or, if the debtor is a corporation,* by its president *or other executive officer*] at that time and place for the purpose of being examined.

[DEADLINE TO OBJECT TO DISCHARGE OR DETERMINE NONDISCHARGEABILITY OF CERTAIN DEBTS]

3. *[If the debtor is an individual]* _____ is fixed as the last day for the filing of objections to the discharge of the debtor pursuant to 11 U.S.C. § 727.

4. *[If the debtor is an individual]* _____ is fixed as the last day for the filing of a complaint to determine the dischargeability of any debt pursuant to 11 U.S.C. § 523(c).

[ADDITIONAL INFORMATION CONCERNING THE MEETING, THE AUTOMATIC STAY AND THE DISCHARGE]

You are further notified that:

The meeting may be continued or adjourned from time to time by notice at the meeting, without further written notice to creditors.

Attendance by creditors at the meeting is welcomed, but not required. At the meeting the creditors may file their claims, [elect a trustee as permitted by law, designate a person to supervise the meeting, elect a committee of creditors,] examine the debtor, and transact such other business as may properly come before the meeting.

As a result of the filing of the petition, certain acts and proceedings against the debtor and property of the estate and of the debtor are stayed as provided in 11 U.S.C. § 362(a).

[If the debtor is an individual] If no objection to the discharge of the debtor is filed on or before the last day fixed therefor as stated in subparagraph 3 above, the debtor will be granted a discharge. If no complaint to determine the dischargeability of a debt under clause (2), (4), or (6) of 11 U.S.C. § 523(a) is filed within the time fixed therefor as stated in subparagraph 4 above, the debt may be discharged.

[FILING OF CLAIMS]

[For a chapter 7 or 13 case] In order to have a claim allowed so that a creditor may share in any distribution from the estate, a creditor must file a claim, whether or not the creditor is included in the list of creditors filed by the debtor. Claims which are not filed within 90 days following the above date set for the meeting of creditors will not be allowed, except as otherwise provided by law. A claim may be filed in the office of the clerk of the bankruptcy court on an official form prescribed for a proof of claim.

[If a no-asset or nominal asset case, the following paragraph may be used in lieu of the preceding paragraph.] It appears from the schedules of the debtor that there are no assets from which any dividend can be paid to creditors. It is unnecessary for any creditor to file a claim at this time in order to share in any distribution from the estate. If it subsequently appears that there are assets from which a dividend may be paid, creditors will be so notified and given an opportunity to file their claims.

[For a chapter 11 case] The debtor *[or* trustee] has filed or will file a list of creditors and equity security holders pursuant to Rule 1007. Any creditor holding a listed claim which is not listed as disputed, contingent, or unliquidated as to amount, may, but need not, file a proof of claim in this case. Creditors whose claims are not listed or whose claims are listed as disputed, contingent, or unliquidated as to amount and who desire to participate in the case or share in any distribution must file their proofs of claim on or before _____, which date is hereby fixed as the last day for filing a proof of claim *[or, if appropriate,* on or before a date to be later fixed of which you will be notified] . Any creditor who desires to rely on the list has the responsibility for determining that the claim is accurately listed.

[OBJECTION TO CLAIM OF EXEMPTIONS]

Unless the court extends the time, any objection to the debtor's claim of exempt property (Schedule B–4) must be filed within 30 days after the conclusion of the meeting of creditors.

[TRUSTEE]

[If appropriate] _____ of * _____ has been appointed [interim] trustee of the estate of the above-named debtor.

Dated: _____.

BY THE COURT

_____,
Bankruptcy Judge.

* State mailing address.

Amended eff. Sept. 19, 1986.

Advisory Committee Note

This form can be used for cases filed under chapter 7, 11, or 13. It conforms with Rule 2003 which specifies that the court is to call the meeting of creditors even though, under the Code, it may not preside at such meeting.

This form revises former Official Form No. 12. The alternative paragraph is to be used when the court exercises the option under Rule 2002(e) to notify the creditors that no dividends are to be anticipated and no claims need be filed.

Form No. 17

GENERAL POWER OF ATTORNEY

[Caption as in Form No. 2]

GENERAL POWER OF ATTORNEY

To _____ of * _____, and _____ of * _____:

The undersigned claimant hereby authorizes you, or any one of you, as attorney in fact for the undersigned and with full power of substitution, to vote on any question that may be lawfully submitted to creditors of the debtor in the above-entitled case; *[if appropriate]* to vote for a trustee of the estate of the debtor and for a committee of creditors; to receive dividends; and in general to perform any act not constituting the practice of law for the undersigned in all matters arising in this case.

Dated: _____

Signed: _____

[If appropriate]

By _____

as _____

Address: _____

_____

[If executed by an individual] Acknowledged before me on _____.

[If executed on behalf of a partnership] Acknowledged before me on _____, by _____, who says that he *[or she]* is a member of the partnership named above and is authorized to execute this power of attorney in its behalf.

[If executed on behalf of a corporation] Acknowledged before me on _____, by _____, who says that he *[or she]* is _____ of the corporation named above and is authorized to execute this power of attorney in its behalf.

_____,

_____

[Official character.]

* State mailing address.

Amended eff. Sept. 19, 1986.

Advisory Committee Note

Rule 9010(c) requires a general power of attorney to be prepared substantially in conformity with this form which is derived from former Official Form No. 13. While a power of attorney may of course be executed in favor of an attorney at law who is also retained as such to represent the creditor executing the form, the power of attorney does not purport to confer the right to act as an attorney at law. The corollary is that one not an attorney at law may act under a general power of attorney within the limitations prescribed in the form.

Form No. 18
SPECIAL POWER OF ATTORNEY

[Caption as in Form No. 2]

SPECIAL POWER OF ATTORNEY

To _____ of * _____, and _____ of * _____:

The undersigned claimant hereby authorizes you, or any one of you, as attorney in fact for the undersigned [*if desired*: and with full power of substitution,] to attend the meeting of creditors of the debtor or any adjournment thereof, and to vote in my behalf on any question that may be lawfully submitted to creditors at such meeting or adjourned meeting, and for a trustee or trustees of the estate of the debtor.

Dated: _____.

Signed: _____

[If appropriate]

By _____

as _____

Address: _____,

_____

[*If executed by an individual*] Acknowledged before me on _____.

[*If executed on behalf of a partnership*] Acknowledged before me on _____, by _____, who says that he [*or* she] is a member of the partnership named above and is authorized to execute this power of attorney in its behalf.

[*If executed on behalf of a corporation*] Acknowledged before me on _____, by _____, who says that he [*or* she] is _____ of the corporation named above and is authorized to execute this power of attorney in its behalf.

_____

_____

[Official character.]

* State mailing address.

Amended eff. Sept. 19, 1986.

Advisory Committee Note

A special power of attorney shall conform substantially with this official form, as provided in Rule 9010(c), but it may grant either more or less authority in accordance with the language used. The form is derived from former Official Form No. 14.

Form No. 19

PROOF OF CLAIM

[Caption as in Form No. 2]

PROOF OF CLAIM

1. *[If claimant is an individual]* The undersigned, _____ who is the claimant herein, resides at * _____ .

[If claimant is a partnership claiming through a member] The undersigned, _____, who resides at * _____, is a member of _____, a partnership, composed of the undersigned and _____, of * _____, and doing business at * _____, and is authorized to make this proof of claim in behalf of the partnership.

[If claimant is a corporation claiming through an authorized officer] The undersigned, _____, who resides at * _____, is the _____ of _____, a corporation organized under the laws of _____ and doing business at * _____, and is authorized to make this proof of claim on behalf of the corporation.

[If claim is made by agent] The undersigned, _____, who resides at * _____, is the agent of _____, of * _____, and is authorized to make this proof of claim on behalf of the claimant.

2. The debtor was, at the time of the filing of the petition initiating this case, and still is indebted [*or* liable] to this claimant, in the sum of $_____ .

3. The consideration for this debt [*or* ground of liability] is as follows:

_____

_____

[If filed in a chapter 7 or 13 case] This claim consists of $_____ in principal amount and $_____ in additional charges [*or* no additional charges]. *[Itemize all charges in addition to principal amount of debt, state basis for inclusion and computation, and set forth any other consideration relevant to the legality of the charge.]* _____

_____

_____

4. *[If the claim is founded on writing]* The writing on which this claim is founded (or a duplicate thereof) is attached hereto [*or* cannot be attached for the reason set forth in the statement attached hereto].

5. *[If appropriate]* This claim is founded on an open account, which became [*or* will become] due on _____, as shown by the itemized statement attached hereto. Unless it is attached hereto or its absence is explained in an attached statement, no note or other negotiable instrument has been received for the account or any part of it.

6. No judgment has been rendered on the claim except _____

_____

7. The amount of all payments on this claim has been credited and deducted for the purpose of making this proof of claim.

8. This claim is not subject to any setoff or counterclaim except

_____ .

9. No security interest is held for this claim except _____. [*If security interest in property of the debtor is claimed*] The undersigned claims the security interest under the writing referred to in paragraph 4 hereof [*or* under a separate writing which (or a duplicate of which) is attached hereto, *or* under a separate writing which cannot be attached hereto for the reason set forth in the statement attached hereto]. Evidence of perfection of such security interest is also attached hereto.

10. This claim is a general unsecured claim, except to the extent that the security interest, if any, described in paragraph 9 is sufficient to satisfy the claim. [*If priority is claimed, state the amount and basis thereof.*] _____

_____

Dated: _____.

Signed: _____

Penalty for Presenting Fraudulent Claim. Fine of not more than $5,000 or imprisonment for not more than 5 years or both—Title 18, U.S.C., § 152.

* State mailing address.

Amended eff. Sept. 19, 1986.

Advisory Committee Note

This form is derived from former Official Form No. 15. It may be used by any claimant, including a wage earner for whom alternative short forms have been specially prepared (Form Nos. 20 and 21), or by an agent or attorney for any claimant. Such a combined form is commonly used in practice.

If a security interest in the debtor's property is claimed, paragraph 9 requires that any security agreement (if not included in the writing on which the claim is founded and which is required by paragraph 4 to be attached) be attached to the proof of claim or that the reason why it cannot be attached be set forth. Paragraph 9 further requires evidence of perfection of the security interest to be attached to the proof of claim. See the Note to Rule 3001(d) as to what constitutes satisfactory evidence of perfection. The information so required will expedite determination of the validity of any claimed security interest as against the trustee.

Paragraph 10, requiring an explicit statement as to whether the claim is filed as a general, priority, or secured claim, will facilitate administration and minimize troublesome litigation over the question whether a proof of claim was intended as a waiver of security. See, *e.g., United States National Bank* v. *Chase National Bank*, 331 U.S. 28, 35–36 (1947); 3 Collier, *Bankruptcy* ¶ 57.07[3.1] (14th ed. 1961).

Form No. 20

PROOF OF CLAIM FOR WAGES, SALARY, OR COMMISSIONS

[Caption as in Form No. 2]

PROOF OF CLAIM FOR WAGES,
SALARY, OR COMMISSIONS

1. The undersigned, _____, claimant herein resides at _____ and has social security number _____.
2. The debtor owes the claimant computed as follows: $_____
    (a) wages, salary, or commissions for services performed from _____ to _____, at the following rate or rates of compensation _____ $_____

[if appropriate]

    (b) allowances and benefits, such as vacation, severance and sick leave pay [*specify*] _____ $_____
         Total amount claimed $_____

3. The claimant demands priority to the extent permitted by 11 U.S.C. § 507(a)(3).

4. The claimant has received no payment, no security, and no check or other evidence of this debt except as follows: _____
_____

Dated: _____.

Signed: _____
Claimant.

Penalty for Presenting Fraudulent Claim. Fine of not more than $5,000 or imprisonment for not more than 5 years or both—Title 18, U.S.C., § 152.

Advisory Committee Note

This form is an adaptation of former Official Form No. 16 for the exclusive use of claimants for personal earnings in cases under the Code. Its limited purpose permits elimination of recitals that are appropriate for other classes of claimants. Most claimants using the form will be entitled to priority under § 507(a)(3) of the Code. If the claim as filed includes an amount not entitled to priority because, for example, not earned within the applicable 90 day period, reference to payroll records will ordinarily permit determination of the amount of the priority, if any, to which the claimant is entitled. If such records are unavailable, the claimant may be required to supply additional information as a condition to allowance of the claim with priority.

Form No. 21

PROOF OF MULTIPLE CLAIMS FOR WAGES, SALARY, OR COMMISSIONS

[Caption as in Form No. 2]

PROOF OF MULTIPLE CLAIMS FOR WAGES, SALARY, OR COMMISSIONS

1. The undersigned, _____, whose address is * _____, is the agent of the claimants listed in the statement appended to this proof of claim and is authorized to make this proof of claims on their behalf.

2. The debtor owes the claimants $_____, computed as indicated in the appended statement.

3. The claimants demand priority to the extent permitted by 11 U.S.C. § 507(a)(3) and (4).

4. The claimants have received no payment, no security, and no check or other evidence of this debt except as follows: _____

_____

_____

Dated: _____.

Signed: _____

Penalty for Presenting Fraudulent Claim. Fine of not more than $5,000 or imprisonment for not more than 5 years or both—Title 18, U.S.C., § 152.

Statement of Wage Claims

Name, Address, & Social Security Numbers	Dates services rendered, rates of pay, and fringe benefits	Contributions to employee benefit plans	Amounts Claimed

* State mailing address.

Advisory Committee Note

This form is an alternative for Form No. 20 provided for use when there are numerous claimants for wages, salary, or commissions against a debtor's estate and they wish to have their proofs of claim executed and filed by a common agent. Use of the form should not only simplify the filing procedure for the claimants but facilitate the handling of the claims by the court.

Form No. 22

[ORDER APPOINTING INTERIM TRUSTEE AND FIXING AMOUNT OF BOND] [ABROGATED]

Abrogated eff. Sept. 19, 1986.

Advisory Committee Note to Former Form No. 22

This form is for use only in a chapter 7 case. Pursuant to § 701 of the Code, the court is to appoint an interim trustee promptly after the order for relief. The interim trustee becomes the trustee if no trustee is elected. The interim trustee is to be disinterested as defined in § 101(13) and a member of the panel of private trustees established under 28 U.S.C. § 604(f). If the chapter 7 case was converted from chapter 11 or 13 the court may appoint as interim trustee the person serving as trustee in the prior case. Section 322(b) requires the court to determine the amount of the bond and sufficiency of the surety. See Form Nos. 23 and 25.

Advisory Committee Note to 1986 Abrogation

This form may be promulgated by the Director of the Administrative Office pursuant to Rule 9009.

Form No. 23

[ORDER APPROVING ELECTION OF TRUSTEE AND FIXING AMOUNT OF BOND] [ABROGATED]

Abrogated eff. Sept. 19, 1986.

Advisory Committee Note to Former Form No. 23

Creditors may elect a trustee pursuant to § 702 of the Code. If none is elected the interim trustee becomes the trustee.

Advisory Committee Note to 1986 Abrogation

This form may be promulgated by the Director of the Administrative Office pursuant to Rule 9009.

Form No. 24

NOTICE TO TRUSTEE OF SELECTION AND OF TIME FIXED FOR FILING A COMPLAINT OBJECTING TO DISCHARGE OF DEBTOR

B24 (Official Form 24)
(1/87)

United States Bankruptcy Court

_____District of_____

In re

Bankruptcy Case No.

Debtor*

Social Security No.　　:
Employer Tax I.D. No.:

NOTICE TO TRUSTEE OF SELECTION AND OF TIME FIXED FOR FILING A COMPLAINT OBJECTING TO DISCHARGE OF DEBTOR

To:

Name and Address of Trustee

You are notified of your election or appointment as trustee of the estate of the above-named debtor.

Your blanket bond is deemed sufficient. If you decide to reject this office, you are required to notify the clerk of the bankruptcy court in writing within 5 days after receipt of this notice. Such notice should be sent to:

Address of Clerk of the Bankruptcy Court

The amount of your bond has been fixed at $ _____. The last date to file your bond is fixed at:

Date:

You are further notified that the last day for the filing by you or any other party in interest of a complaint objecting to the discharge of the debtor has been fixed at:

Date:

_____
Clerk of the Bankruptcy Court

By: _____

_____
Date

Deputy Clerk

*Set forth all names, including trade names, used by the debtor within the last 6 years. (Bankruptcy Rule 1005). For joint debtors set forth both social security numbers.

[E7841]

763

Source of Form

This form is included as Form B 24 of *Bankruptcy Forms Manual* Volume II, "Forms and Instructions for the Public," as issued by the Division of Bankruptcy, Administrative Office of the United States Courts (September, 1988).

Form No. 25

BOND AND ORDER APPROVING BOND OF TRUSTEE

B25 (Official Form 25)
(1/87)

United States Bankruptcy Court

_____ District of _____

In re

Bankruptcy Case No.

Debtor*

Social Security No.　　:

Employer Tax I.D. No. :

BOND AND ORDER APPROVING BOND OF TRUSTEE

Trustee's Name and Address

as principal, and

Surety's Name and Address

as surety, bind ourselves to the Unted States in the sum of $_____ for the faithful performance by the undersigned principal of official duties as trustee of the estate of the above-named debtor.

_____
Date

_____
Signature of Principal

_____
Signature of Surety

This bond filed by the trustee of the estate of above-named debtor is approved.

_____
Date

_____
Bankruptcy Judge

---

*Set forth all names, including trade names, used by the debtor within the last 6 years. (Bankruptcy Rule 1005). For joint debtors set forth both social security numbers.　　　　[E7842]

Form 25   OFFICIAL FORMS

COMMENTS AND INSTRUCTIONS

Purpose of the Form

This form is designed to serve as both the bond and order approving the bond. If the bond is a separate instrument, it will be necessary to modify the form.

Pertinent Law and Rules

1. Section 322 of the Bankruptcy Code (title 11 of the United States Code) requires each person serving as a trustee in a case to qualify by the filing of a bond in favor of the United States within five days after selection as a trustee.

2. Section 322 requires the bond to be approved by the court or, in districts certified by the Attorney General of the United States, by the United States trustee. In the latter districts, the signature line in this form must be modified.

3. Bankruptcy Rule 2010 authorizes the court to approve a blanket bond when one trustee handles a number of cases, or when a number of trustees qualify in different cases.

4. Pursuant to 31 U.S.C. §§ 9304 and 9305, the surety on the bond must be a corporation approved as a surety by the Secretary of the Treasury. Personal signature bonds are NOT permissible.

Source of Form

This Official Form and the accompanying commentary and instructions are included as Form B 25 of *Bankruptcy Forms Manual* Volume II, "Forms and Instructions for the Public," as issued by the Division of Bankruptcy, Administrative Office of the United States Courts (September, 1988).

Form No. 26

CERTIFICATE OF RETENTION OF DEBTOR IN POSSESSION

B26 (Official Form 26)
(Rev. 10/87)

United States Bankruptcy Court

_____ District of _____

In re

Bankruptcy Case No.

Debtor*

Social Security No.   :
Employer Tax I.D. No. :

CERTIFICATE OF RETENTION
OF DEBTOR IN POSSESSION

    I certify that the above-named debtor continues in possession of its estate as debtor in possession, no trustee having been appointed.

_____
Clerk of the Bankruptcy Court

By: _____

_____
Date

Deputy Clerk

***Set forth all names, including trade names, used by the debtor within the last 6 years. (Bankruptcy Rule 1005). For joint debtors set forth both social security numbers.**

[E7843]

COMMENTS AND INSTRUCTIONS

Advisory Committee Note (1983)

"This form may be used in chapter 11 reorganization cases. Usually, a trustee will not be appointed, in which event the debtor is automatically continued in possession pursuant to § 1101(a) of the [Bankruptcy] Code [(title 11 of the United States Code)].

"When evidence of debtor in possession status is required, this certificate may be used in accordance with [Bankruptcy] Rule 2011."

Pertinent Law and Rules

1. Section 1101 of the Bankruptcy Code (title 11 of the United States Code) states that "debtor in possession means debtor, except when a person that has qualified under section 322 of this title is serving as trustee in this case."

2. Bankruptcy Rule 2011 provides that "Whenever evidence is required that a debtor is a debtor in possession, the clerk may so certify and the certificate shall constitute conclusive evidence of that fact."

Fee

There is a charge of $5.00 for certification. This amount must be paid by check or money order made payable to "Clerk, U.S. Bankruptcy Court." The court will not accept cash.

Source of Form

This Official Form and the accompanying commentary and instructions are included as Form B 26 of *Bankruptcy Forms Manual* Volume II, "Forms and Instructions for the Public," as issued by the Division of Bankruptcy, Administrative Office of the United States Courts (September, 1988).

Form No. 27

DISCHARGE OF DEBTOR

B27 (Official Form 27)
(Rev. 10/87)

United States Bankruptcy Court

_____ District of _____

In re

Bankruptcy Case No.

Debtor*
Social Security No.   :
Employer Tax ID. No. :

DISCHARGE OF DEBTOR

It appears that the person named above filed a petition commencing a case under title 11, United States

Code on _____ , that an order for relief was entered under chapter 7, and that no
(date)

complaint objecting to the discharge of the debtor was filed within the time fixed by the court [*or* that a

complaint objecting to discharge of the debtor was filed and, after due notice and hearing, was not

sustained].

IT IS ORDERED THAT:

1. The above-named debtor is released from all dischargeable debts.

2. Any judgment heretofore or hereafter obtained in any court other than this court is null and void as
   a determination of the personal liability of the debtor with respect to any of the following:

   (a) debts dischargeable under 11 U.S.C. § 523;

   (b) unless heretofore or hereafter determined by order of this court to be nondischargeable, debts
       alleged to be excepted from the discharge under clauses (2), (4) and (6) of 11 U.S.C. § 523 (a);

   (c) debts determined by this court to be discharged.

3. All creditors whose debts are discharged by this order and all creditors whose judgments are declared
   null and void by paragraph 2 above are enjoined from instituting or continuing any action or employing any process or engaging in any act to collect such debts as personal liabilities of the above-named
   debtor.

_____   _____
            Date   Bankruptcy Judge

*Set forth all names, including trade names, used by the debtor within the last 6 years. (Bankruptcy Rule 1005).   [E7844]

Source of Form

This Official Form is included as Form B 27 of *Bankruptcy Forms Manual* Volume II, "Forms and Instructions for the Public," as issued by the Division of Bankruptcy, Administrative Office of the United States Courts (September, 1988).

Form No. 27J

DISCHARGE OF JOINT DEBTORS

B27J (Official Form 27 — Joint Debtors)
(Rev. 10/87)

United States Bankruptcy Court

_____ District of _____

In re

Bankruptcy Case No.

Debtor*
Social Security No.   :
Employer Tax I.D. No. :

DISCHARGE OF JOINT DEBTORS

It appears that the persons named above have filed a petition commencing a joint case under title 11,

United States Code on _____ , that an order for relief was entered under chapter 7, and
(date)

that no complaint objecting to the discharge of the debtors was filed within the time fixed by the court [or

that a complaint objecting to discharge of one or both of the debtors was filed and, after due notice and

hearing, was not sustained].

IT IS ORDERED THAT:

1. The above-named debtors are released from all dischargeable debts.

2. Any judgment heretofore or hereafter obtained in any court other than this court is null and void as
   a determination of the personal liability of the debtors with respect to any of the following:

   (a) debts dischargeable under 11 U.S.C. § 523;

   (b) unless heretofore or hereafter determined by order of this court to be nondischargeable, debts
   alleged to be excepted from the discharge under clauses (2), (4) and (6) of 11 U.S.C. § 523 (a);

   (c) debts determined by this court to be discharged.

3. All creditors whose debts are discharged by this order and all creditors whose judgments are
   declared null and void by paragraph 2 above are enjoined from instituting or continuing any action
   or employing any process or engaging in any act to collect such debts as personal liabilities of the
   above-named debtor.

_____   _____
            Date   Bankruptcy Judge

---

*Set forth all names, including trade names, used by the debtor within the last 6 years. (Bankruptcy Rule 1005). For joint debtors set forth both
social security numbers.   [E7845]

Source of Form

This Official Form is included as Form B #27J of _Bankruptcy Forms Manual_
Volume II, "Forms and Instructions for the Public," as issued by the Division of
Bankruptcy, Administrative Office of the United States Courts (September, 1988).

Form 27JO

Form No. 27JO

DISCHARGE OF ONE JOINT DEBTOR

B27JO (Official Form 27 — One Joint Debtor)
(1/87)

United States Bankruptcy Court

_____ District of _____

In re

Bankruptcy Case No.

Debtor*
Social Security No.   :
Employer Tax I.D. No. :

DISCHARGE OF ONE JOINT DEBTOR

It appears that_____** has joined in a

petition commencing a case under title 11, United States Code, which was filed on _____,
(date)

that an order for relief was entered under chapter 7 and that no complaint objecting to the discharge of such

debtor was filed within the time fixed by the court [*or* that a complaint objecting to discharge of the debtor

was filed and, after due notice and hearing, was not sustained].

IT IS ORDERED THAT:

1. _____** is released from
all dischargeable debts.

2. Any judgment heretofore or hereafter obtained in any court other than this court is null and void as
a determination of the personal liability of_____**
with respect to any of the following:

    (a) debts dischargeable under 11 U.S.C. § 523;

    (b) unless heretofore or hereafter determined by order of this court to be nondischargeable, debts
    alleged to be excepted from the discharge under clauses (2), (4) and (6) of 11 U.S.C. § 523 (a);

    (c) debts determined by this court to be discharged under 11 U.S.C. §523.

3. All creditors whose debts are discharged by this order and all creditors whose judgments are
declared null and void by paragraph 2 above are enjoined from instituting or continuing any action
or employing any process of engaging in any act to collect such debts as personal liabilities of

_____** .

_____	_____
Date	Bankruptcy Judge

*Set forth all names, including trade names, used by the debtor within the last 6 years. (Bankruptcy Rule 1005). For joint debtors set forth both
social security numbers.   [E7846]
**When only one of the debtors in a joint use is discharged, state here the name of the individual debtor being discharged.*

Source of Form

This Official Form is included as Form B 27 of *Bankruptcy Forms Manual*
Volume II, "Forms and Instructions for the Public," as issued by the Division of
Bankruptcy, Administrative Office of the United States Courts (September, 1988).

Form No. 28

ORDER AND NOTICE FOR HEARING
ON DISCLOSURE STATEMENT

B28 (Official Form 28)
(Rev. 6/87)

𝔘𝔫𝔦𝔱𝔢𝔡 𝔖𝔱𝔞𝔱𝔢𝔰 𝔅𝔞𝔫𝔨𝔯𝔲𝔭𝔱𝔠𝔶 ℭ𝔬𝔲𝔯𝔱

_____ District of _____

In re
                                           Bankruptcy Case No.

Debtor*
Social Security No.   :
Employer Tax I.D. No. :

ORDER AND NOTICE FOR HEARING ON DISCLOSURE STATEMENT

To all parties in interest:

A disclosure statement and plan under chapter 11 of the Bankruptcy Code was filed on _____ by:
                                                                                 (date)

> Name and Address of Plan Proponent:

The disclosure statement and plan are on file with the bankruptcy clerk and may be viewed during regular business hours at the Court:

> Address of the Court:

Requests for copies of the disclosure statement and plan should be directed to:

> Name and Address of Attorney for Plan Proponent

IT IS ORDERED AND NOTICE IS GIVEN THAT:

1. The hearing to consider approval of the disclosure statement will be held at the following place and time:

Address	Room
	Date and Time

2. Within ____ days after entry of this order, the proponent of the plan must:
   a. send each party in interest a copy of this order and notice;
   b. send a copy of the disclosure statement and plan to the debtor, trustee, each committee appointed pursuant to §1102 of the code, the Securities and Exchange Commission, the United States Trustee, and any party in interest who requests in writing a copy of the disclosure statement and plan.

3. An objection to the disclosure statement may be filed by any party in interest, pursuant to Bankruptcy Rule 3017(a). The last date to file an objection to the disclosure statement is:

> Date:

_____   _____
             Date   Bankruptcy Judge

*Set forth all names, including trade names, used by the debtor within the last 6 years. (Bankruptcy Rule 1005). For joint debtors, set forth both
social security numbers.*   [E7847]

COMMENTS AND INSTRUCTIONS

Advisory Committee Note (1983)

"This form is . . . related to [Bankruptcy] Rule 3017(a). Section 1125 of the [Bankruptcy] Code [(title 11 of the United States Code)] requires court approval of a disclosure statement before votes may be solicited for or against a plan in . . . chapter 11, reorganization . . . cases. Before the court may approve a disclosure statement it must find that the disclosure statement contains adequate information to enable creditors whose votes will be solicited to make an informed judgment about the plan.

"Objections may be filed to the disclosure statement. [Bankruptcy] Rule 3017(a) specifies that the court may fix a time for filing of objections or they can be filed at any time prior to approval of the statement."

"[Bankruptcy] Rule 3017(a) also specifies the persons who are to receive copies of the statement and plan prior to the hearing. These documents will not be sent to all parties in interest because at this stage of the case it could be unnecessarily expensive and confusing. However, any party in interest may request copies. The request should be made in writing ([Bankruptcy] Rule 3017(a)) . . ."

Source of Form

This Official Form and the accompanying commentary and instructions are included as Form B 28 of *Bankruptcy Forms Manual* Volume II, "Forms and Instructions for the Public," as issued by the Division of Bankruptcy, Administrative Office of the United States Courts (September, 1988).

Form No. 29

ORDER APPROVING DISCLOSURE STATEMENT AND FIXING TIME FOR FILING ACCEPTANCES OR REJECTIONS OF PLAN, COMBINED WITH NOTICE THEREOF

[Caption as in Form No. 1]

ORDER APPROVING DISCLOSURE STATEMENT AND
FIXING TIME FOR FILING ACCEPTANCES OR
REJECTIONS OF PLAN, COMBINED
WITH NOTICE THEREOF

A disclosure statement under chapter 11 of the Bankruptcy Code having been filed by _____, on _____ [*if appropriate,* and by _____, on _____], referring to a plan under chapter 11 of the Code filed by _____, on _____ [*if appropriate,* and by _____, on _____ respectively] [*if appropriate,* as modified by a modification filed on _____]; and

It having been determined after hearing on notice that the disclosure statement [*or* statements] contain[s] adequate information;

It is ordered, and notice is hereby given, that:

A. The disclosure statement filed by _____ dated _____ [*if appropriate,* and by _____, dated _____] is [are] approved.

B. _____ is fixed as the last day for filing written acceptances or rejections of the plan [*or* plans] referred to above.

C. Within _____ days after the entry of this order, the plan [*or* plans] [*or* a summary *or* summaries thereof approved by the court], [*if appropriate* a summary approved by the court of its opinion, if any, dated _____, approving the disclosure statement [*or* statements]], the disclosure statement [*or* statements] and a ballot conforming to Official Form No. 29 shall be transmitted by mail to creditors, equity security holders and other parties in interest as provided in Rule 3017(d).

D. If acceptances are filed for more than one plan, preferences among the plans so accepted may be indicated.

[*If appropriate*] E. _____
is fixed for the hearing on confirmation of the plan [*or* plans].

[*If appropriate*] F. _____
is fixed as the last day for filing and serving pursuant to Rule 3020(b)(1) written objections to confirmation of the plan.

Dated: _____.

BY THE COURT

_____
Bankruptcy Judge.

[*If the court directs that a copy of the opinion should be transmitted in lieu of or in addition to the summary thereof, the appropriate change should be made in paragraph C of this order.*]

Advisory Committee Note

This form is new. As provided in § 1125 of the Code, a disclosure statement must be approved by the court prior to the solicitation of votes to a plan. This form may be used for such approval, to give notice of the time fixed for filing acceptances or rejections and the time fixed for the hearing on confirmation if such a time has been fixed.

Form No. 30

BALLOT FOR ACCEPTING OR REJECTING PLAN

[*Caption as in Form No. 1*]

BALLOT FOR ACCEPTING OR REJECTING PLAN

Filed by _____ on _____.

The plan referred to in this ballot can be confirmed by the court and thereby made binding on you if it is accepted by the holders of two-thirds in amount and more than one-half in number of claims in each class and the holders of two-thirds in amount of equity security interests in each class voting on the plan. In the event the requisite acceptances are not obtained, the court may nevertheless confirm the plan if the court finds that the plan accords fair and equitable treatment to the class rejecting it. To have your vote count you must complete and return this ballot.

[*If equity security holder*] The undersigned, the holder of [*state number*] _____ shares of [*describe type*] _____ stock of the above-named debtor, represented by Certificate(s) No. _____, registered in the name of _____.

[*If bondholder, debenture holder, or other debt security holder*] The undersigned, the holder of [*state unpaid principal amount*] $_____ of [*describe security*] _____ of the above-named debtor, with a stated maturity date of _____ [*if applicable* registered in the name of _____] [*if applicable* bearing serial number(s) _____.]

[*If holder of general claim*] The undersigned, a creditor of the above-named debtor in the unpaid principal amount of $_____,

[Check One Box]

☐   Accepts

☐   Rejects

the plan for the reorganization of the above-named debtor.

[*If more than one plan is accepted, the following may but need not be completed. The undersigned prefers the plans accepted in the following order: [Identify plans]*

1. _____.

2. _____.

Dated: _____.

Print or type name:

Signed: _____

[*If appropriate*]

By: _____

as: _____

Address: _____

_____

Form 30   OFFICIAL FORMS

Return this ballot on or before _____

to:

Name: _____

Address: _____

Advisory Committee Note

This form may be modified as necessary to include identification of as many plans as may have been transmitted on which a vote will be taken.

The form can also be modified to take account of the types of parties who will vote as among equity security holders (see § 101(15) of the Code for definition of equity security), security holders (see § 101(35) for definition of security), secured creditors and unsecured creditors.

Before the form is transmitted, the blanks identifying the plan and the name and address of the person to whom it should be returned should be completed for the information of creditors and equity security holders.

Form No. 31

ORDER CONFIRMING PLAN

[Caption as in Form No. 1]

ORDER CONFIRMING PLAN

The plan under chapter 11 of the Bankruptcy Code filed by _____, on _____ [*if appropriate,* as modified by a modification filed on _____,] or a summary thereof having been transmitted to creditors and equity security holders; and

It having been determined after hearing on notice that:

1. The plan has been accepted in writing by the creditors and equity security holders whose acceptance is required by law; and

2. The provisions of chapter 11 of the Code have been complied with; that the plan has been proposed in good faith and not by any means forbidden by law; and

3. Each holder of a claim or interest has accepted the plan [*or* will receive or retain under the plan property of a value, as of the effective date of the plan, that is not less than the amount that such holder would receive or retain if the debtor were liquidated under chapter 7 of the Code on such date] [*or* The plan does not discriminate unfairly, and is fair and equitable, with respect to each class of claims or interests that is impaired under, and had not accepted the plan]; and

4. All payments made or promised by the debtor or by a person issuing securities or acquiring property under the plan or by any other person for services or for costs and expenses in, or in connection with, the plan and incident to the case, have been fully disclosed to the court and are reasonable or, if to be fixed after confirmation of the plan, will be subject to the approval of the court; and

5. The identity, qualifications, and affiliations of the persons who are to be directors or officers, or voting trustees, if any, of the debtor [and an affiliate of the debtor participating in a joint plan with the debtor] [*or* a successor to the debtor under the plan], after confirmation of the plan, have been fully disclosed, and the appointment of such persons to such offices, or their continuance therein, is equitable, and consistent with the interests of the creditors and equity security holders and with public policy; and

6. The identity of any insider that will be employed or retained by the debtor and his compensation have been fully disclosed; and

7. [*If applicable*] Any regulatory commission with jurisdiction, after confirmation of the plan, over the rates of the debtor has approved any rate change provided for in the plan [*or* any rate change is expressly conditioned on approval of any regulatory agency having jurisdiction over the rates of the debtor]; and

779

8. [*If appropriate*] Confirmation of the plan is not likely to be followed by the liquidation [*or* the need for further financial reorganization, of the debtor or any successor to the debtor under the plan]:

It is ordered that:

The plan filed by _____, on _____, a copy of which plan is attached hereto, is confirmed.

Dated: _____.

BY THE COURT

_____

Bankruptcy Judge.

Advisory Committee Note

The order of confirmation specifies those matters heard and determined by the court at the hearing on confirmation which are required by the Code in order for a plan to be confirmed.

In the case of an individual chapter 11 debtor, Form No. 27 may be adapted for use together with this form.

Form No. 32

NOTICE OF FILING OF FINAL ACCOUNT

B32 (Official Form 32)
(1/87)

United States Bankruptcy Court

_____District of_____

In re

Bankruptcy Case No.

Debtor*

Social Security No.   :
Employer Tax I.D. No. :

NOTICE OF FILING OF FINAL ACCOUNT[S] OF TRUSTEE, OF HEARING ON APPLICATIONS FOR COMPENSATION [AND OF HEARING ON ABANDONMENT OF PROPERTY BY THE TRUSTEE]

TO THE CREDITORS:

1. NOTICE IS GIVEN that the final report and account of the trustee in this case has been filed and a hearing will be held by the court at the following place and time.

Address	Room
	Date and Time

2. The hearing will be held for the purpose of examining and passing on the final report and account of the trustee, acting on applications for compensation, and transacting such other business as may properly come before the court. ATTENDANCE BY THE DEBTOR AND THE CREDITORS IS WELCOMED BUT IS NOT REQUIRED.

3. The following applications for compensation have been filed:

Applicants	Commissions or Fees	Expenses
_____ Trustee	$_____	$_____
_____ Attorney for Trustee	$_____	$_____
_____	$_____	$_____
_____	$_____	$_____
_____	$_____	$_____
_____	$_____	$_____

4. The trustee's account shows total receipts of $_____
               and total disbursements of $_____
               for a balance on hand of $_____

(Continued on reverse side)

---

*Set forth all names, including trade names, used by the debtor within the last 6 years. (Bankruptcy Rule 1005). For joint debtors set forth both social security numbers.
             [E7848]

B32 (Reverse)
(1/87)

5. In addition to the commissions and fees that may be allowed by the court, liens and priority claims which must be paid in advance of general creditors have been allowed in the total amount of

$_____

General unsecured claims have been allowed in the amount of $_____

6. ☐ The debtor has been discharged.

    ☐ The debtor has not been discharged.

7. ☐ The trustee's application to abandon the following property will be heard and acted upon:

    Date   Bankruptcy Judge   [E7849]

Source of Form

This Official Form is included as Form B 32 of *Bankruptcy Forms Manual* Volume II, "Forms and Instructions for the Public," as issued by the Division of Bankruptcy, Administrative Office of the United States Courts (September, 1988).

Form No. 33
FINAL DECREE

B33 (Official Form 33)
(1/87)

United States Bankruptcy Court

_____ District of _____

In re

Bankruptcy Case No.

Debtor*
Social Security No.   :
Employer Tax I.D. No. :

FINAL DECREE

The estate of the above named debtor has been fully administered.

☐ The deposit required by the plan has been distributed.

IT IS ORDERED THAT:

☐ _____
(name of trustee)

is discharged as trustee of the estate of the above-named debtor and the bond is cancelled;

☐ the chapter _____ case of the above named debtor is closed; and

☐ [other provisions as needed]

_____   _____
        Date   Bankruptcy Judge

*_Set forth all names, including trade names, used by the debtor within the last 6 years. (Bankruptcy Rule 1005). For joint debtors set forth both social security numbers._
                                                                    [E7850]

Source of Form

This Official Form is included as Form B 33 of *Bankruptcy Forms Manual* Volume II, "Forms and Instructions for the Public," as issued by the Division of Bankruptcy, Administrative Office of the United States Courts (September, 1988).

Form No. 34

CAPTION OF ADVERSARY PROCEEDINGS

UNITED STATES BANKRUPTCY COURT

_____ DISTRICT OF _____

In re   Case No. _____

_____,

Debtor,

_____,   ADV. PRO. NO. _____

Plaintiff,

v.

_____,

Defendant.

Complaint [*or* other Designation]

Advisory Committee Note

Rule 7010 requires the caption of a pleading in an adversary proceeding to conform substantially to this form.

Form No. 35

NOTICE OF APPEAL TO A DISTRICT COURT OR BANKRUPTCY APPELLATE PANEL FROM A JUDGMENT OF A BANKRUPTCY COURT ENTERED IN AN ADVERSARY PROCEEDING

UNITED STATES BANKRUPTCY COURT
_____ DISTRICT OF _____

In re   Case No. _____

_____,
Debtor,

_____,
Plaintiff,

v.

_____,
Defendant.

ADV. PRO. NO. _____

NOTICE OF APPEAL

_____, the plaintiff [*or* defendant *or* other party] appeals to the district court [*or* the bankruptcy appellate panel], from the final judgment [*or* final order *or* final decree (describe it)] of the bankruptcy court entered in this adversary proceeding on the _____ day of _____. The parties to the judgment [*or* order *or* decree] appealed from and the names and addresses of their respective attorneys are as follows: _____

_____

_____.

Dated: _____.

Signed: _____,
Attorney for Appellant.

Address: _____

Advisory Committee Note

This form is an adaptation of the suggested form of notice of appeal which accompanies the Federal Rules of Appellate Procedure.

If the appeal does not arise in an adversary proceeding the caption should conform to that in Official Form No. 2. This form may be modified for an appeal from an interlocutory order. See Rule 8001(b).

PROPOSED REVISED OFFICIAL BANKRUPTCY FORMS

COMMITTEE ON RULES OF PRACTICE AND PROCEDURE
OF THE
JUDICIAL CONFERENCE OF THE UNITED STATES
WASHINGTON, D.C. 20544

June 28, 1990

JOSEPH F WEIS JR
CHAIRMAN

JAMES E MACKLIN JR
SECRETARY

CHAIRMEN OF ADVISORY COMMITTEES
JON O NEWMAN
APPELLATE RULES
JOHN F GRADY
CIVIL RULES
LELAND C NIELSEN
CRIMINAL RULES
LLOYD D GEORGE
BANKRUPTCY RULES

Honorable Joseph F. Weis, Jr.
Chairman, Committee on Rules of
   Practice and Procedure of the
   Judicial Conference of the United States
Washington, D.C. 20544

Dear Judge Weis:

On behalf of the Advisory Committee on Bankruptcy Rules, I have the honor to transmit for consideration by the Committee on Rules of Practice and Procedure of the Judicial Conference of the United States, proposed revisions to the Official Bankruptcy Forms. These proposals are submitted in conjunction with proposed amendments to the Bankruptcy Rules, which were transmitted earlier.

Many of the proposed revisions to the Official Forms are intended to implement the Bankruptcy Judges, United States Trustees, and Family Farmer Bankruptcy Act of 1986, Pub. L. No. 99-554, signed by the President on October 24, 1986. The 1986 Act made the United States trustee system permanent and nationwide and expanded the role of the United States trustees in bankruptcy cases. In particular, a number of forms have been abrogated as pertaining to functions that have been transferred to the United States trustees. The 1986 Act also created a new chapter 12 of the Bankruptcy Code to provide financial relief to family farmers, and provisions for chapter 12 cases are included in the proposed forms.

Some of the most significant revisions, however, arise from the development of automation in the bankruptcy courts. Two forms in particular -- Form 1, the Voluntary Petition, and Form 9, the Notice of Filing under the Bankruptcy Code, Meeting of Creditors, and Fixing of Dates -- have been revised to make them compatible with electronic systems for docketing and noticing in bankruptcy cases.

The preliminary draft of the proposed revisions to the Official Bankruptcy Forms was published and circulated to members of the bench and bar in January 1990, with a request for written

PROPOSED REVISED FORMS

Honorable Joseph F. Weis, Jr.
Page Two

comments. Comments were received from 61 respondents. The
Advisory Committee considered the comments of each respondent
at meetings in April and May, 1990. In addition, on May 14,
1990, the Advisory Committee met with several publishers of
bankruptcy forms, vendors of computer software for completing
bankruptcy forms, and court automation personnel to discuss
some of the issues raised in the comment letters. As a result
of this discussion and the written comments, the Advisory
Committee has made several changes to the preliminary draft.
The changes are explained in the enclosed memorandum dated
June 25, 1990.

The revising of the Official Bankruptcy Forms has been a
major undertaking to which several members of the Advisory
Committee generously devoted countless hours in addition to
their work on the amendments to the Bankruptcy Rules. Joseph
Patchan, Esquire, served as chairman of the subcommittee which
considered every detail of these proposals. Two other
individuals, not members of the Advisory Committee, also were
instrumental to this project. Patricia S. Channon, Esquire,
of the Administrative Office of the United States Courts,
staffed the forms subcommittee. Peter G. McCabe, Assistant
Director of the Administrative Office, organized and guided
the task force that initially proposed revising the Official
Forms. He has continued to participate with the Advisory
Committee as we developed the proposals we now submit. To all
who worked on this endeavor, I am profoundly grateful.

The revisions proposed to the Official Bankruptcy Forms
have been coordinated with the proposed amendments to the
Bankruptcy Rules and should take effect on the same date as
the amended Bankruptcy Rules. The Advisory Committee,
accordingly, requests the Committee on Rules of Practice and
Procedure to recommend to the Judicial Conference that these
proposed revisions to the Official Bankruptcy Forms be adopted
at the September 1990 session of the Judicial Conference to
become effective on the same date as the amended Bankruptcy
Rules. Adoption at this time, combined with a delayed
effective date, will provide sufficient time for forms
publishers, software vendors, and court automation personnel
to prepare to use the revised Official Forms.

Respectfully submitted,

LLOYD D. GEORGE

PROPOSED REVISED FORMS

COMMITTEE ON RULES OF PRACTICE AND PROCEDURE
OF THE
JUDICIAL CONFERENCE OF THE UNITED STATES
WASHINGTON, D.C. 20544

JOSEPH F WEIS JR
CHAIRMAN

JAMES E MACKLIN JR
SECRETARY

CHAIRMEN OF ADVISORY COMMITTEES
JON O NEWMAN
APPELLATE RULES
JOHN F GRADY
CIVIL RULES
LELAND C NIELSEN
CRIMINAL RULES
LLOYD D GEORGE
BANKRUPTCY RULES

June 28, 1990

TO: Honorable Joseph F. Weis, Jr., Chairman
Committee on Rules of Practice and Procedure

FROM: Honorable Lloyd D. George, Chairman
Advisory Committee on Bankruptcy Rules

SUBJECT: Explanation of Changes Made Subsequent to the
Original Publication of the January 1990
Preliminary Draft of Proposed Official Bankruptcy
Forms

The Advisory Committee on Bankruptcy Rules considered the written comments of more than 50 interested individuals and groups who responded to the Advisory Committee's request for comment. In addition to the changes described below, typographical errors have been corrected, and alterations have been made to language and punctuation in the interest of clarity. The visual elements of some forms have been moved for reasons of both design and practicality.

The significant changes made by the Advisory Committee subsequent to the original publication of the preliminary draft of proposed revisions to the Official Bankruptcy Forms are:

Introduction of General Instructions

Many commentators raised questions concerning perceived format requirements in the preliminary draft. Matters such as type style, type face, and width of columns were mentioned. Both the nature of these letters and the number received indicated to the Advisory Committee that the flexibility of formatting which has always been acceptable in connection with the official forms is not widely known and understood. Accordingly, the Advisory Committee has added, as an introduction to the forms, some general instructions describing the rule of substantial compliance with the official forms and the degree of design freedom permitted. These instructions also cover the formatting flexibility authorized for computer generated forms.

PROPOSED REVISED FORMS

Petitions, Schedules, Statement of Financial Affairs

Form 1, Voluntary Petition. The signature boxes have been rearranged to make it clear that in signing the petition the debtor's attorney is not required make a declaration under penalty of perjury. The debtor's child, parent, and sibling have been deleted from the list of persons whose pending bankruptcy cases the debtor must disclose. If any of these relatives are "affiliates" of the debtor, as defined in § 101(2) of the Code, disclosure is required. The request for information concerning prior addresses of the debtor has been moved to Form 7, the Statement of Financial Affairs. The request for the debtor's social security or tax identification number has been expanded to request disclosure of all tax identification numbers used by the debtor.

Form 5, Involuntary Petition. The requirement to disclose any pending voluntary or involuntary bankruptcy cases involving the alleged debtor's family members, who are not also "affiliates" of the debtor as defined in § 101(2) of the Code, has been deleted.

Form 6, Schedules. The caption at the top of all but the first page of the schedules has been deleted and replaced with an instruction that the caption must appear on the first page of the schedules and of any amendments to the schedules. An instruction has been added to make it clear that each claim is to be reported only once. The schedules and their instructions also have been revised to facilitate the reporting of community property and claims against community property.

Form 7, Statement of Financial Affairs. The request for information concerning prior addresses of the debtor, deleted from the Voluntary Petition, has been inserted. Question 1 has been revised to make it clear that the debtor generally should disclose income for each calendar year. Question 3, concerning payments to creditors, has been narrowed so that the debtor will report only payments on loans and installment debt aggregating more than $600 to any creditor within 90 days prior to the filing of the case. Exclusions have been added to Question 7 for small contributions and reasonable gifts to family members.

Other Forms

Form 3, Application and Order to Pay Filing Fee in Installments. The phrase "by the court" has been inserted above the signature line for the bankruptcy judge to indicate that the order is being signed by a judge exercising the full jurisdiction of bankruptcy court as a unit of the district court.

Form 4, List of Creditors Holding 20 Largest Unsecured Claims. The phrase "government contract" has been added to column three of the form, entitled "nature of claim."

Form 10, Proof of Claim. This form has been revised to make it clear that the address to be provided is the address of the person who should receive furthers notices, distributions, etc. A specific request for the amount of any claimed arrearage and other charges included in the claim has been added.

Form 16A, Caption (Full). The form has been revised to request all tax identification numbers used by the debtor.

Form 18, Discharge. The form has been revised to accommodate debtors receiving a discharge in an involuntary case as well as in a voluntary one.

PROPOSED REVISED FORMS

6/90

OFFICIAL BANKRUPTCY FORMS

1. Voluntary Petition
2. Declaration under Penalty of Perjury on Behalf of a Corporation or Partnership
3. Application and Order to Pay Filing Fee in Installments
4. List of Creditors Holding 20 Largest Unsecured Claims
5. Involuntary Petition
6. Schedules
7. Statement of Financial Affairs
8. Chapter 7 Individual Debtor's Statement of Intention
9. Notice of Filing under the Bankruptcy Code, Meeting of Creditors, and Fixing of Dates
10. Proof of Claim
11A. General Power of Attorney
11B. Special Power of Attorney
12. Order and Notice for Hearing on Disclosure Statement
13. Order Approving Disclosure Statement and Fixing Time for Filing Acceptances or Rejections of Plan, Combined with Notice Thereof
14. Ballot for Accepting or Rejecting Plan
15. Order Confirming Plan
16A. Caption
16B. Caption (Short Title)
16C. Caption of Adversary Proceeding
17. Notice of Appeal to a District Court or Bankruptcy Appellate Panel from a Judgment or Other Final Order of a Bankruptcy Court.
18. Discharge of Debtor

Official Forms

[NOTE: These official forms should be observed and used with such alterations as may be appropriate to suit the circumstances. See Rule 9009.]

PROPOSED REVISED FORMS

INTRODUCTION AND GENERAL INSTRUCTIONS

Rule 9009 of the Federal Rules of Bankruptcy Procedure states that the Official Forms prescribed by the Judicial Conference of the United States "shall be observed and used." The Official Forms, accordingly, are obligatory in character.

Rule 9009 expressly permits the user of the Official Forms to make such "alterations as may be appropriate," and the use of the Official Forms has been held to be subject to a "rule of substantial compliance." Some rules, for example Fed. R. Bankr. P. 3001(a), specifically state that the filed document need only "conform substantially" to the Official Form. A document for which an Official Form is prescribed generally will meet the standard of substantial compliance if the document contains the complete substance, that is, all of the information required by the Official Form.

Rule 9009 also expressly permits the contents of Official Forms to be rearranged, and the format of the Official Forms traditionally has been quite flexible. The forms of the voluntary petition, the schedules, and the statement of financial affairs are printed and sold by private publishers. Design features such as type face, type size, layout, and side and top margins were not prescribed by the Judicial Conference, but rather left to the professional judgment of each publisher.

A great deal of variation, accordingly, has developed. Some publishers also add forms that are not official but which have been drafted by the publisher. A form for a chapter 13 plan, for example, frequently is included with commercially printed packages of forms for filing cases under chapter 13, although there is no Official Form for this purpose. The variety of formats has accelerated since the introduction of computer software for generating the petitions, schedules, and statements of affairs. It is the policy of the Judicial Conference that such diversity is desirable and should be encouraged.

The sheer volume of bankruptcy cases, however, has compelled the Judicial Conference, for the first time, to prescribe the format of certain Official Forms. In particular, the format of Form 1, the Voluntary Petition, now is prescribed. This format is designed to assist the clerk of the bankruptcy court to enter the case in the court's computer database and ensures that all required information is available to both the clerk and the United States trustee at the inception of the case. The rule of substantial compliance continues to apply, however. Accordingly, publishers may vary the size and style of the type and may alter the size and shape of the boxes on the form, within the bounds of that rule.

The Official Forms of the petitions, schedules, and statement of financial affairs, (Forms 1, 5, 6, and 7), are to be printed on one side of the paper only. Each page is to be pre-punched with two holes at the top, and sufficient top margin allowed so that neither caption nor text is destroyed or obs-cured. Compliance with these standards will facilitate both the securing of the papers in the case file and review of the file by the public.

Although Rule 9009 permits alteration, for most of the Official Forms, alteration will be appropriate only in rare circumstances. The special forms for chapter 11 cases, on the other hand, seldom will be used without alterations. Forms 12 through 15, while legally sufficient in any chapter 11 case, are intended by the Judicial Conference, and most often will be used, as a framework for drafting a document specially tailored to the particular case. These alterations generally will take the form of additions to the prescribed elements.

Rule 9009 provides for a balance of prescribed substance, to which full adherence is expected in all but the most unusual cases, and flexible formatting, under which requirements are kept to the minimum necessary for proper operation of the courts and the bankruptcy system. While Rule 9009 recognizes the overall need for flexibility, Rule 9029 makes it clear that the Official Forms must be accepted in every bankruptcy court.

Under Rule 9029, courts may not reject documents presented for filing in novel or unfamiliar formats if those documents contain the substance prescribed by the Official Form and meet the requirements for one-sided printing, pre-punched holes, and adequate top margins. Nor are courts authorized to impose local forms which vary in substance from the Official Forms or reject papers presented for filing on Official Forms on the basis that the proffered documents differ from a locally preferred version.

Special Instructions for Computer-Generated Forms

In Form 1, the Voluntary Petition, if a box contains multi-ple choices, a computer-generated petition that shows only the choice made is acceptable for filing. All sections of the petition must be shown and completed, however, unless instruc-tions on the Official Form of the petition state that the box is applicable only to cases filed under a chapter other than the one selected by the debtor. If the debtor has no information to provide for a particular box, for example if the debtor has no prior bankruptcies to report, a computer-generated petition should so indicate by stating "None."

Form 6, the Schedules, on which the debtor reports all of the debtor's assets and liabilities, has been prescribed in a columnar format. Columns help to organize the information which the debtor is required to report and should be used when the printed schedules are completed on a typewriter. In a computer-ized law office, however, the organizational structure of the schedules can be built into the computer program, and a rigid columnar format may be a hindrance rather than a help. Schedules generated by computer which provide all of the information requested by the prescribed form are fully acceptable, regardless of the format of the printed page. The information must be appropriately labeled, however. In Schedule B, for example, all of the categories of personal property must be printed on the filed document together with the debtor's response to each. The space occupied by each category may be expanded, however, so that attachments are not needed. Instructions provided on the printed forms can simply be built into the computer program; they need not be reprinted on the filed document.

Form 7, the Statement of Financial Affairs, contains a series of questions which direct the debtor to answer by furnishing information. If the answer to a question is "None," or the question is not applicable, an affirmative statement to that effect is required. To assure that the trustee and the creditors can review the debtor's statement properly, the complete text of each question must be printed on the filed document.

Form 9, the Notice of Filing under the Bankruptcy Code, Meeting of Creditors, and Fixing of Dates, will be prepared by the clerk of the bankruptcy court in most cases. The form is designed for use with automated printing and mailing equipment. Two free lines, which do not appear on the printed blank form, have been programmed into the form. Courts may use this space to add local information, such as directions for obtaining copies of the debtor's schedules.

PROPOSED REVISED FORMS

FORM B1
(6/90)

FORM 1. VOLUNTARY PETITION

United States Bankruptcy Court _____ District of _____	VOLUNTARY PETITION

IN RE (Name of debtor — If individual, enter Last, First, Middle)	NAME OF JOINT DEBTOR (Spouse) (Last, First, Middle)
ALL OTHER NAMES used by the debtor in the last 6 years (Include married, maiden and trade names)	ALL OTHER NAMES used by the joint debtor in the last 6 years (Include married, maiden, and trade names)
SOC SEC./TAX I.D. NO (If more than one, state all)	SOC SEC./TAX I.D. NO (If more than one, state all)
STREET ADDRESS OF DEBTOR (No and street, city, state, and zip code)	STREET ADDRESS OF JOINT DEBTOR (No and street, city, state, and zip code)
COUNTY OF RESIDENCE OR PRINCIPAL PLACE OF BUSINESS	COUNTY OF RESIDENCE OR PRINCIPAL PLACE OF BUSINESS
MAILING ADDRESS OF DEBTOR (If different from street address)	MAILING ADDRESS OF JOINT DEBTOR (If different from street address)

LOCATION OF PRINCIPAL ASSETS OF BUSINESS DEBTOR (If different from addresses listed above)	VENUE (Check one box) ☐ Debtor has been domiciled or has had a residence, principal place of business, or principal assets in this District for 180 days immediately preceding the date of this petition or for a longer part of such 180 days than in any other District ☐ There is a bankruptcy case concerning debtor's affiliate, general partner, or partnership pending in this District

INFORMATION REGARDING DEBTOR (Check applicable boxes)

TYPE OF DEBTOR ☐ Individual ☐ Joint (Husband & Wife) ☐ Partnership ☐ Other _____ ☐ Corporation Publicly Held ☐ Corporation Not Publicly Held ☐ Municipality NATURE OF DEBT ☐ Non-Business/Consumer ☐ Business — Complete A & B below A TYPE OF BUSINESS (Check one box) ☐ Farming ☐ Transportation ☐ Commodity Broker ☐ Professional ☐ Manufacturing/ ☐ Construction ☐ Retail/Wholesale Mining ☐ Real Estate ☐ Railroad ☐ Stockbroker ☐ Other Business B. BRIEFLY DESCRIBE NATURE OF BUSINESS	CHAPTER OR SECTION OF BANKRUPTCY CODE UNDER WHICH THE PETITION IS FILED (Check one box) ☐ Chapter 7 ☐ Chapter 11 ☐ Chapter 13 ☐ Chapter 9 ☐ Chapter 12 ☐ Sec. 304 — Case Ancillary to Foreign Proceeding FILING FEE (Check one box) ☐ Filing fee attached ☐ Filing fee to be paid in installments (Applicable to individuals only) Must attach signed application for the court's consideration certifying that the debtor is unable to pay fee except in installments. Rule 1006(b), see Official Form No 3 NAME AND ADDRESS OF LAW FIRM OR ATTORNEY Telephone No NAME(S) OF ATTORNEY(S) DESIGNATED TO REPRESENT THE DEBTOR (Print or Type Names) ☐ Debtor is not represented by an attorney

STATISTICAL/ADMINISTRATIVE INFORMATION (28 U.S.C. § 604)
(Estimates only) (Check applicable boxes)

☐ Debtor estimates that funds will be available for distribution to unsecured creditors

☐ Debtor estimates that, after any exempt property is excluded and administrative expenses paid, there will be no funds available for distribution to unsecured creditors.

THIS SPACE FOR COURT USE ONLY

ESTIMATED NUMBER OF CREDITORS

1-15	16-49	50-99	100-199	200-999	1000-over
☐	☐	☐	☐	☐	☐

ESTIMATED ASSETS (In thousands of dollars)

Under 50	50-99	100-499	500-999	1000-9999	10,000-99,000	100,000-over
☐	☐	☐	☐	☐	☐	☐

ESTIMATED LIABILITIES (In thousands of dollars)

Under 50	50-99	100-499	500-999	1000-9999	10,000-99,000	100,000-over
☐	☐	☐	☐	☐	☐	☐

EST. NO. OF EMPLOYEES—CH. 11 & 12 ONLY

0	1-19	20-99	100-999	1000-over
☐	☐	☐	☐	☐

EST. NO. OF EQUITY SECURITY HOLDERS—CH. 11 & 12 ONLY

0	1-19	20-99	100-499	500-Over
☐	☐	☐	☐	☐

PROPOSED REVISED FORMS

Name of Debtor _____

Case No. _____

(Court use only)

FILING OF PLAN

For Chapter 9, 11, 12 and 13 cases only Check appropriate box

☐ A copy of debtor's proposed plan dated _____ is attached

☐ Debtor intends to file a plan within the time allowed by statute, rule, or order of the court.

PRIOR BANKRUPTCY CASE FILED WITHIN LAST 6 YEARS (If more than one, attach additional sheet)

Location Where Filed	Case Number	Date Filed

PENDING BANKRUPTCY CASE FILED BY ANY SPOUSE, PARTNER, OR AFFILIATE OF THIS DEBTOR (If more than one, attach additional sheet.)

Name of Debtor	Case Number	Date
Relationship	District	Judge

REQUEST FOR RELIEF

Debtor requests relief in accordance with the chapter of title 11, United States Code, specified in this petition.

SIGNATURES

ATTORNEY

X _____   Date _____
Signature

INDIVIDUAL/JOINT DEBTOR(S)	CORPORATE OR PARTNERSHIP DEBTOR
I declare under penalty of perjury that the information provided in this petition is true and correct.	I declare under penalty of perjury that the information provided in this petition is true and correct, and that the filing of this petition on behalf of the debtor has been authorized.
X _____ Signature of Debtor	X _____ Signature of Authorized Individual
Date _____	Print or Type Name of Authorized Individual
X _____ Signature of Joint Debtor	Title of Individual Authorized by Debtor to File this Petition
Date _____	Date _____

EXHIBIT "A" (To be completed if debtor is a corporation requesting relief under chapter 11.)

☐ Exhibit "A" is attached and made a part of this petition.

TO BE COMPLETED BY INDIVIDUAL CHAPTER 7 DEBTOR WITH PRIMARILY CONSUMER DEBTS (See P.L. 98-353 § 322)

I am aware that I may proceed under chapter 7, 11, or 12, or 13 of title 11, United States Code, understand the relief available under each such chapter, and choose to proceed under chapter 7 of such title.

If I am represented by an attorney, exhibit "B" has been completed.

X _____   Date _____
Signature of Debtor

X _____   Date _____
Signature of Joint Debtor

EXHIBIT "B" (To be completed by attorney for individual chapter 7 debtor(s) with primarily consumer debts.)

I, the attorney for the debtor(s) named in the foregoing petition, declare that I have informed the debtor(s) that (he, she, or they) may proceed under chapter 7, 11, 12, or 13 of title 11, United States Code, and have explained the relief available under each such chapter.

X _____   Date _____
Signature of Attorney

796

PROPOSED REVISED FORMS

Form B1XA
4/90

Exhibit "A"

[If debtor is a corporation filing under chapter 11 of the Code, this Exhibit "A" shall be completed and attached to the petition.]

[Caption as in Form 16B]

Exhibit "A" to Voluntary Petition

1. Debtor's employer identification number is _____.

2. If any of debtor's securities are registered under section 12 of the Securities and Exchange Act of 1934, the SEC file number is _____.

3. The following financial data is the latest available information and refers to debtor's condition on _____.

		Approximate number of holders
a. Total assets	$ _____	
b. Total liabilities	$ _____	
Fixed, liquidated secured debt	$ _____	_____
Contingent secured debt	$ _____	_____
Disputed secured claims	$ _____	_____
Unliquidated secured debt	$ _____	_____
Fixed, liquidated unsecured debt	$ _____	_____
Contingent unsecured debt	$ _____	_____
Disputed unsecured claims	$ _____	_____
Unliquidated unsecured debt	$ _____	_____
Number of shares of preferred stock	_____	_____
Number of shares of common stock	_____	_____

Comments, if any: _____
_____
_____

4. Brief description of debtor's business: _____
_____

5. List the name of any person who directly or indirectly owns, controls, or holds, with power to vote, 20% or more of the voting securities of debtor: _____
_____
_____

6. List the names of all corporations 20% or more of the outstanding voting securities of which are directly or indirectly owned, controlled, or held, with power to vote, by debtor: _____
_____
_____

PROPOSED REVISED FORMS

COMMITTEE NOTE

Form 1, the Voluntary Petition, is to be used to commence a voluntary case under chapter 7, 11, 12, or 13 of the Bankruptcy Code. A chapter 9 petition requires other allegations, (see § 109(c) of the Code), but this form may be adapted for such use. The form also may be adapted for use in filing a petition ancillary to a foreign proceeding under § 304 of the Code.

The form departs from the traditional format of a captioned pleading. All of the elements of the caption prescribed in Rule 1005 have been retained. Their placement on the page, however, has been changed to make the form compatible with electronic data processing by the clerk. The form of the caption of the case for use in other documents, formerly incorporated in Official Form No. 1, has been made a separate Form 16A.

All names used by the debtor, including trade names, names used in doing business, married names, and maiden names should be furnished in the spaces provided. If there is not sufficient room for all such names on the form itself, the list should be continued on an additional sheet attached to the petition. A complete list will enable creditors to identify the debtor properly when they receive notices and orders.

Redesign of this form into a box format also is intended to provide the court, the United States trustee, and other interested parties with as much information as possible during the 15-day period provided by Rule 1007(c), when schedules and statements may not have been filed. The box format separates into categories the data provided by the debtor, and enables the form to be used by all voluntary debtors in all chapters.

For the first time, the form requires both a street address and any separate mailing address, as well as any separate addresses used by a joint debtor. Disclosure of prior bankruptcies is new to the petition but formerly was required in the statement of financial affairs; its inclusion in the petition is intended to alert the trustee to cases in which an objection to discharge pursuant to § 727(a)(8) or (a)(9) or a motion to dismiss under § 109(g) may be appropriate. The information about pending related cases, also new to the petition, signals the clerk to assign the case to the judge to whom any related case has been assigned.

Rule 1008 requires all petitions to be verified or contain an unsworn declaration as provided in 28 U.S.C. § 1746. The unsworn declaration on page two of the petition conforms with 28 U.S.C. § 1746, which permits the declaration to be made in the manner indicated with the same force and effect as a sworn statement. The form may be adapted for use outside the United States by adding the words "under the laws of the United States" after the word "perjury."

Exhibit "A," to be attached to the petition of a corporate debtor, is for the purpose of supplying the Securities and Exchange Commission with information it needs at the beginning stages of a chapter 11 case in order to determine how actively to monitor the proceedings. Exhibit "B" was added by § 322 of Pub. L. No. 98-353, the Bankruptcy Amendments and Federal Judgeship Act of 1984. The references to chapters 11 and 12 of the Code found in Exhibit "B" and its related allegations were added by § 283(aa) of the 1986 amendments, (Pub. L. No. 99-554). This exhibit has been included in the form of the petition.

The form effects a merger of the petition and the bankruptcy cover sheet to assist the clerk in providing the statistical information required by the Director of the Administrative Office of the United States Courts pursuant to the Congressional reporting mandates of 28 U.S.C. § 604. The Director is authorized to change the particulars of the statistical portion of the form as needed in the performance of these statutory duties.

PROPOSED REVISED FORMS

Form B2
6/90

Form 2. DECLARATION UNDER PENALTY OF PERJURY
ON BEHALF OF A CORPORATION OR PARTNERSHIP

I, [the president *or* other officer *or* an authorized agent of the corporation] [*or* a member *or* an authorized agent of the partnership] named as the debtor in this case, declare under penalty of perjury that I have read the foregoing [list *or* schedule *or* amendment *or* other document (describe)] and that it is true and correct to the best of my information and belief.

Date _____

Signature _____

_____
(Print Name and Title)

COMMITTEE NOTE

This form is derived from former Official Form No. 4.

Rule 1008 requires that all petitions, lists, schedules, statements, and amendments thereto be verified or contain an unsworn declaration conforming with 28 U.S.C. § 1746. This form or adaptations of the form have been incorporated into the official forms of the petitions, schedules, and statement of financial affairs. See Official Forms 1, 5, 6, and 7. The form has been amended for use in connection with other papers required by these rules to be verified or contain an unsworn declaration.

PROPOSED REVISED FORMS

Form B3
6/90

Form 3. APPLICATION AND ORDER TO PAY FILING FEE IN INSTALLMENTS

[Caption as in Form 16B.]

APPLICATION TO PAY FILING FEES IN INSTALLMENTS

In accordance with Fed. R. Bankr. P. 1006, application is made for permission to pay the filing fee on the following terms:

$ _____ with the filing of the petition, and the balance of

$ _____ in _____ installments, as follows:

$ _____ on or before _____

$ _____ on or before _____

$ _____ on or before _____

$ _____ on or before _____

I certify that I am unable to pay the filing fee except in installments. I further certify that I have not paid any money or transferred any property to an attorney or any other person for services in connection with this case or in connection with any other pending bankruptcy case and that I will not make any payment or transfer any property for services in connection with the case until the filing fee is paid in full.

Date: _____

_____
Applicant

_____
Address of Applicant

ORDER

IT IS ORDERED that the debtor pay the filing fee in installments on the terms set forth in the foregoing application.

IT IS FURTHER ORDERED that until the filing fee is paid in full the debtor shall not pay, and no person shall accept, any money for services in connection with this case, and the debtor shall not relinquish, and no person shall accept, any property as payment for services in connection with this case.

BY THE COURT

Date: _____

_____

COMMITTEE NOTE

This form is derived from former Official Form No. 2.

A statement that the applicant is unable to pay the filing fee except in installments has been added as required by Rule 1006(b).

800

Form B4
6/90

Form 4. LIST OF CREDITORS HOLDING 20 LARGEST UNSECURED CLAIMS

[Caption as in Form 16B]

LIST OF CREDITORS HOLDING 20 LARGEST UNSECURED CLAIMS

Following is the list of the debtor's creditors holding the 20 largest unsecured claims. The list is prepared in accordance with Fed. R. Bankr. P. 1007(d) for filing in this chapter 11 *[or chapter 9]* case. The list does not include (1) persons who come within the definition of "insider" set forth in 11 U.S.C. § 101(30), or (2) secured creditors unless the value of the collateral is such that the unsecured deficiency places the creditor among the holders of the 20 largest unsecured claims.

(1)	(2)	(3)	(4)	(5)
Name of creditor and complete mailing address including zip code	Name, telephone number and complete mailing address, including zip code, of employee, agent, or department of creditor familiar with claim who may be contacted	Nature of claim (trade debt, bank loan, government contract, etc.)	Indicate if claim is contingent, unliquidated, disputed or subject to setoff	Amount of claim [if secured also state value of security]

Date: _____

_____
Debtor

[Declaration as in Form 2]

COMMITTEE NOTE

This form is derived from former Official Form No. 9.

In conformity with Rule 1007(d) and in recognition of the notice function served by this list under Rule 4001, governmental units must be listed if they are among the creditors holding the 20 largest claims.

Rule 1008 requires all lists to be verified or contain an unsworn declaration conforming with 28 U.S.C. § 1746.

PROPOSED REVISED FORMS

FORM 5. INVOLUNTARY PETITION

United States Bankruptcy Court _____District of_____	INVOLUNTARY PETITION

IN RE (Name of Debtor — If Individual Last, First, Middle)	ALL OTHER NAMES used by debtor in the last 6 years (Include married, maiden, and trade names.)
SOC. SEC./TAX I.D. NO. (If more than one, state all.)	
STREET ADDRESS OF DEBTOR (No. and street, city, state, and zip code)	MAILING ADDRESS OF DEBTOR (If different from street address)
COUNTY OF RESIDENCE OR PRINCIPAL PLACE OF BUSINESS	

LOCATION OF PRINCIPAL ASSETS OF BUSINESS DEBTOR (If different from previously listed addresses)

CHAPTER OF BANKRUPTCY CODE UNDER WHICH PETITION IS FILED
☐ Chapter 7   ☐ Chapter 11

INFORMATION REGARDING DEBTOR (Check applicable boxes)

Petitioners believe
☐ Debts are primarily consumer debts
☐ Debts are primarily business debts (complete sections A and B)

TYPE OF DEBTOR
☐ Individual
☐ Partnership
☐ Corporation Publicly Held
☐ Corporation Not Publicly Held
☐ Other: _____

A. TYPE OF BUSINESS (Check one)
☐ Professional   ☐ Transportation   ☐ Commodity Broker
☐ Retail/Wholesale ☐ Manufacturing/   ☐ Construction
☐ Railroad   Mining   ☐ Real Estate
                    ☐ Stockbroker   ☐ Other

B. BRIEFLY DESCRIBE NATURE OF BUSINESS

VENUE

☐ Debtor has been domiciled or has had a residence, principal place of business, or principal assets in the District for 180 days immediately preceding the date of this petition or for a longer part of such 180 days than in any other District.

☐ A bankruptcy case concerning debtor's affiliate, general partner or partnership is pending in this District.

PENDING BANKRUPTCY CASE FILED BY OR AGAINST ANY PARTNER
OR AFFILIATE OF THIS DEBTOR (Report information for any additional cases on attached sheets.)

Name of Debtor	Case Number	Date
Relationship	District	Judge

ALLEGATIONS (Check applicable boxes)	COURT USE ONLY

1. ☐ Petitioner(s) are eligible to file this petition pursuant to 11 U.S.C. § 303(b).
2. ☐ The debtor is a person against whom an order for relief may be entered under title 11 of the United States Code.
3.a. ☐ The debtor is generally not paying such debtor's debts as they become due, unless such debts are the subject of a bona fide dispute;

or

b. ☐ Within 120 days preceding the filing of this petition, a custodian, other than a trustee, receiver, or agent appointed or authorized to take charge of less than substantially all of the property of the debtor for the purpose of enforcing a lien against such property, was appointed or took possession.

PROPOSED REVISED FORMS

Name of Debtor _____

FORM 5. Involuntary Petition
(10/89)

Case No. _____

(Court use only)

TRANSFER OF CLAIM

☐ Check this box if there has been a transfer of any claim against the debtor by or to any petitioner. Attach all documents evidencing the transfer and any statements that are required under Bankruptcy Rule 1003(a).

REQUEST FOR RELIEF

Petitioner(s) request that an order for relief be entered against the debtor under the chapter of title 11, United States Code, specified in this petition.

Petitioner(s) declare under penalty of perjury that the foregoing is true and correct according to the best of their knowledge, information, and belief.

X _____

Signature of Petitioner or Representative (State title)

Name of Petitioner _____

Name & Mailing ▶
Address of Individual
Signing in Representative
Capacity

X _____

Signature of Attorney

Name of Attorney/Firm (If any) _____

Address _____

Telephone No. _____

X _____

Signature of Petitioner or Representative (State title)

Name of Petitioner _____

Name & Mailing ▶
Address of Individual
Signing in Representative
Capacity

X _____

Signature of Attorney

Name of Attorney/Firm (If any) _____

Address _____

Telephone No. _____

X _____

Signature of Petitioner or Representative (State title)

Name of Petitioner _____

Name & Mailing ▶
Address of Individual
Signing in Representative
Capacity

X _____

Signature of Attorney

Name of Attorney/Firm (If any) _____

Address _____

Telephone No. _____

PETITIONING CREDITORS

Name and Address of Petitioner	Nature of Claim	Amount of Claim
Name and Address of Petitioner	Nature of Claim	Amount of Claim
Name and Address of Petitioner	Nature of Claim	Amount of Claim

Note: If there are more than three petitioners, attach additional sheets with the statement under penalty of perjury, petitioner(s) signatures under the statement and the name(s) of attorney(s) and petitioning creditor information in the format above.	Total Amount of Petitioners' Claims

_____ continuation sheets attached

PROPOSED REVISED FORMS

COMMITTEE NOTE

This form has been redesigned in a box format similar to that of Form 1. See Advisory Committee Note to Form 1.

The allegations required under § 303 are grouped together, and a separate section has been provided for additional allegations based upon the prohibitions and requirements set forth in Rule 1003(a) concerning transfer of claims by petitioning creditors. Petitioners may wish to supplement the allegations set forth in the form with a further statement of facts. Additional information concerning any allegation can be requested by the debtor as part of the discovery process.

Each petitioning creditor, by signing on the line provided, signs both the petition and the unsworn declaration which 28 U.S.C. § 1746 permits instead of verification. The addresses as well as the names of individuals signing the petition in a representative capacity are required, together with disclosure of which petitioner is represented by each signatory.

This form is intended to be used in every involuntary case, including that of a partnership. The separate form for a petition by a partner has been abrogated. Pursuant to § 303(b)(3)(A) of the Code, a petition by fewer than all of the general partners seeking an order for relief with respect to the partnership is treated as an involuntary petition. Such a petition is adversarial in character because not all of the partners are joining in the petition.

Section 303(b)(3)(B) permits a petition against the partnership if relief has been ordered under the Code with respect to all of the general partners. In that event, the petition may be filed by a general partner, a trustee of a general partner's estate, or a creditor of the partnership. This form may be adapted for use in that type of case.

28 U.S.C. § 1408(1) specifies the proper venue alternatives for all persons, including partnerships, as domicile, residence, principal place of business, or location of principal assets. Venue also may be based on a pending case commenced by an affiliate, general partner, or partnership pursuant to 28 U.S.C. § 1408(2). Both options are set forth in the block labeled "Venue."

28 U.S.C. § 1746 permits the unsworn declaration instead of a verification. See Committee Note to Form 2.

Form B6
(6/90)

FORM 6. SCHEDULES

Summary of Schedules

Schedule A—Real Property

Schedule B—Personal Property

Schedule C—Property Claimed as Exempt

. Schedule D—Creditors Holding Secured Claims

Schedule E—Creditors Holding Unsecured Priority Claims

Schedule F—Creditors Holding Unsecured Nonpriority Claims

Schedule G—Executory Contracts and Unexpired Leases

Schedule H—Codebtors

Schedule I—Current Income of Individual Debtor(s)

Schedule J—Current Expenditures of Individual Debtor(s)

Unsworn Declaration under Penalty of Perjury

GENERAL INSTRUCTIONS: The first page of the debtor's schedules and the first page of any amendments thereto must contain a caption as in Form 16B. Subsequent pages should be identified with the debtor's name and case number. If the schedules are filed with the petition, the case number should be left blank.

Schedules D, E, and F have been designed for the listing of each claim only once. Even when a claim is secured only in part or entitled to priority only in part, it still should be listed only once. A claim which is secured in whole or in part should be listed on Schedule D only, and a claim which is entitled to priority in whole or in part should be listed on Schedule E only. Do not list the same claim twice. If a creditor has more than one claim, such as claims arising from separate transactions, each claim should be scheduled separately.

Review the specific instructions for each schedule before completing the schedule.

FORM B6—Cont
(6/90)

United States Bankruptcy Court

_____ District of _____

In re _____ ,   Case No. _____
Debtor   (If known)

SUMMARY OF SCHEDULES

Indicate as to each schedule whether that schedule is attached and state the number of pages in each. Report the totals from Schedules A, B, D, E, F, I, and J in the boxes provided. Add the amounts from Schedules A and B to determine the total amount of the debtor's assets. Add the amounts from Schedules D, E, and F to determine the total amount of the debtor's liabilities.

NAME OF SCHEDULE	ATTACHED (YES/NO)	NO. OF SHEETS	AMOUNTS SCHEDULED		
			ASSETS	LIABILITIES	OTHER
A— Real Property			$		
B— Personal Property			$		
C— Property Claimed as Exempt					
D— Creditors Holding Secured Claims				$	
E— Creditors Holding Unsecured Priority Claims				$	
F— Creditors Holding Unsecured Nonpriority Claims				$	
G— Executory Contracts and Unexpired Leases					
H— Codebtors					
I— Current Income of Individual Debtor(s)					$
J— Current Expenditures of Individual Debtor(s)					$
Total Number of Sheets of ALL Schedules ▶					
Total Assets ▶		$			
Total Liabilities ▶			$		

PROPOSED REVISED FORMS

FORM B6A
(10/89)

In re _____,   Case No. _____
Debtor   (If known)

SCHEDULE A—REAL PROPERTY

Except as directed below, list all real property in which the debtor has any legal, equitable, or future interest, including all property owned as a co-tenant, community property, or in which the debtor has a life estate. Include any property in which the debtor holds rights and powers exercisable for the debtor's own benefit. If the debtor is married, state whether husband, wife, or both own the property by placing an "H," "W," "J," or "C" in the column labeled "Husband, Wife, Joint, or Community." If the debtor holds no interest in real property, write "None" under "Description and Location of Property."

Do not include interests in executory contracts and unexpired leases on this schedule. List them in Schedule G—Executory Contracts and Unexpired Leases.

If an entity claims to have a lien or hold a secured interest in any property, state the amount of the secured claim. See Schedule D. If no entity claims to hold a secured interest in the property, write "None" in the column labeled "Amount of Secured Claim."

If the debtor is an individual or if a joint petition is filed, state the amount of any exemption claimed in the property only in Schedule C—Property Claimed as Exempt.

DESCRIPTION AND LOCATION OF PROPERTY	NATURE OF DEBTOR'S INTEREST IN PROPERTY	HUSBAND, WIFE, JOINT, OR COMMUNITY	CURRENT MARKET VALUE OF DEBTOR'S INTEREST IN PROPERTY, WITHOUT DEDUCTING ANY SECURED CLAIM OR EXEMPTION	AMOUNT OF SECURED CLAIM

Total ▶ $ _____

(Report also on Summary of Schedules.)

807

In re _____ ,   Case No. _____
        Debtor   (If known)

SCHEDULE B—PERSONAL PROPERTY

Except as directed below, list all personal property of the debtor of whatever kind. If the debtor has no property in one or more of the categories, place an "x" in the appropriate position in the column labeled "None." If additional space is needed in any category, attach a separate sheet properly identified with the case name, case number, and the number of the category. If the debtor is married, state whether husband, wife, or both own the property by placing an "H," "W," "J," or "C" in the column labeled "Husband, Wife, Joint, or Community." If the debtor is an individual or a joint petition is filed, state the amount of any exemptions claimed only in Schedule C—Property Claimed as Exempt.

Do not list interests in executory contracts and unexpired leases on this schedule. List them in Schedule G—Executory Contracts and Unexpired Leases.

If the property is being held for the debtor by someone else, state that person's name and address under "Description and Location of Property."

TYPE OF PROPERTY	N O N E	DESCRIPTION AND LOCATION OF PROPERTY	HUSBAND, WIFE, JOINT, OR COMMUNITY	CURRENT MARKET VALUE OF DEBTOR'S INTEREST IN PROPERTY, WITHOUT DEDUCTING ANY SECURED CLAIM OR EXEMPTION
1. Cash on hand.				
2. Checking, savings or other financial accounts, certificates of deposit, or shares in banks, savings and loan, thrift, building and loan, and homestead associations, or credit unions, brokerage houses, or cooperatives.				
3. Security deposits with public utilities, telephone companies, landlords, and others.				
4. Household goods and furnishings, including audio, video, and computer equipment.				
5. Books; pictures and other art objects; antiques; stamp, coin, record, tape, compact disc, and other collections or collectibles.				
6. Wearing apparel.				
7. Furs and jewelry.				
8. Firearms and sports, photographic, and other hobby equipment.				
9. Interests in insurance policies. Name insurance company of each policy and itemize surrender or refund value of each.				
10. Annuities. Itemize and name each issuer.				

FORM B6B—Cont
(10/89)

In re _____, Case No. _____
                 Debtor   (If known)

SCHEDULE B—PERSONAL PROPERTY
(Continuation Sheet)

TYPE OF PROPERTY	NONE	DESCRIPTION AND LOCATION OF PROPERTY	HUSBAND, WIFE, JOINT, OR COMMUNITY	CURRENT MARKET VALUE OF DEBTOR'S INTEREST IN PROPERTY, WITHOUT DEDUCTING ANY SECURED CLAIM OR EXEMPTION
11. Interests in IRA, ERISA, Keogh, or other pension or profit sharing plans. Itemize.				
12. Stock and interests in incorporated and unincorporated businesses. Itemize.				
13. Interests in partnerships or joint ventures. Itemize.				
14. Government and corporate bonds and other negotiable and non-negotiable instruments.				
15. Accounts receivable.				
16. Alimony, maintenance, support, and property settlements to which the debtor is or may be entitled. Give particulars.				
17. Other liquidated debts owing debtor including tax refunds. Give particulars.				
18. Equitable or future interests, life estates, and rights or powers exercisable for the benefit of the debtor other than those listed in Schedule of Real Property.				
19. Contingent and noncontingent interests in estate of a decedent, death benefit plan, life insurance policy, or trust.				
20. Other contingent and unliquidated claims of every nature, including tax refunds, counterclaims of the debtor, and rights to setoff claims. Give estimated value of each.				
21. Patents, copyrights, and other intellectual property. Give particulars.				
22. Licenses, franchises, and other general intangibles. Give particulars.				

In re _____, Case No. _____
                 Debtor   (If known)

In re _____ , Case No. _____
　　　　　　Debtor　　　　　　　　　　　　　　　　　　　　(if known)

SCHEDULE B—PERSONAL PROPERTY
(Continuation Sheet)

TYPE OF PROPERTY	N O N E	DESCRIPTION AND LOCATION OF PROPERTY	HUSBAND, WIFE, JOINT, OR COMMUNITY	CURRENT MARKET VALUE OF DEBTOR'S INTEREST IN PROPERTY, WITH-OUT DEDUCTING ANY SECURED CLAIM OR EXEMPTION
23. Automobiles, trucks, trailers, and other vehicles and accessories.				
24. Boats, motors, and accessories.				
25. Aircraft and accessories.				
26. Office equipment, furnishings, and supplies.				
27. Machinery, fixtures, equipment, and supplies used in business.				
28. Inventory.				
29. Animals.				
30. Crops—growing or harvested Give particulars.				
31. Farming equipment and implements.				
32. Farm supplies, chemicals, and feed.				
33. Other personal property of any kind not already listed. Itemize.				

_____ continuation sheets attached　　　　　Total ▶ | $

(Include amounts from any continuation
sheets attached. Report total also on
Summary of Schedules.)

PROPOSED REVISED FORMS

FORM B6C
(6/90)

In re _____,   Case No. _____
                        Debtor   (If known)

SCHEDULE C—PROPERTY CLAIMED AS EXEMPT

Debtor elects the exemptions to which debtor is entitled under:

(Check one box)

☐ 11 U.S.C. § 522(b)(1): Exemptions provided in 11 U.S.C. § 522(d). Note: These exemptions are available only in certain states.

☐ 11 U.S.C. § 522(b)(2): Exemptions available under applicable nonbankruptcy federal laws, state or local law where the debtor's domicile has been located for the 180 days immediately preceding the filing of the petition, or for a longer portion of the 180-day period than in any other place, and the debtor's interest as a tenant by the entirety or joint tenant to the extent the interest is exempt from process under applicable nonbankruptcy law.

DESCRIPTION OF PROPERTY	SPECIFY LAW PROVIDING EACH EXEMPTION	VALUE OF CLAIMED EXEMPTION	CURRENT MARKET VALUE OF PROPERTY WITHOUT DEDUCTING EXEMPTION

PROPOSED REVISED FORMS

FORM B6D
(6/90)

In re _____,   Case No. _____
                    Debtor   (If known)

SCHEDULE D—CREDITORS HOLDING SECURED CLAIMS

State the name, mailing address, including zip code, and account number, if any, of all entities holding claims secured by property of the debtor as of the date of filing of the petition. List creditors holding all types of secured interests such as judgment liens, garnishments, statutory liens, mortgages, deeds of trust, and other security interests. List creditors in alphabetical order to the extent practicable. If all secured creditors will not fit on this page, use the continuation sheet provided.

If any entity other than a spouse in a joint case may be jointly liable on a claim, place an "X" in the column labeled "Codebtor," include the entity on the appropriate schedule of creditors, and complete Schedule H—Codebtors. If a joint petition is filed, state whether husband, wife, both of them, or the marital community may be liable on each claim by placing an "H," "W," "J," or "C" in the column labeled "Husband, Wife, Joint, or Community."

If the claim is contingent, place an "X" in the column labeled "Contingent." If the claim is unliquidated, place an "X" in the column labeled "Unliquidated." If the claim is disputed, place an "X" in the column labeled "Disputed." (You may need to place an "X" in more than one of these three columns.)

Report the total of all claims listed on this schedule in the box labeled "Total" on the last sheet of the completed schedule. Report this total also on the Summary of Schedules.

☐ Check this box if debtor has no creditors holding secured claims to report on this Schedule D.

CREDITOR'S NAME AND MAILING ADDRESS INCLUDING ZIP CODE	CODEBTOR	HUSBAND, WIFE, JOINT, OR COMMUNITY	DATE CLAIM WAS INCURRED, NATURE OF LIEN, AND DESCRIPTION AND MARKET VALUE OF PROPERTY SUBJECT TO LIEN	CONTINGENT	UNLIQUIDATED	DISPUTED	AMOUNT OF CLAIM WITHOUT DEDUCTING VALUE OF COLLATERAL	UNSECURED PORTION, IF ANY
ACCOUNT NO.								
			VALUE $					
ACCOUNT NO.								
			VALUE $					
ACCOUNT NO.								
			VALUE $					
ACCOUNT NO.								
			VALUE $					

_____ continuation sheets attached

Subtotal ▶ $ _____
(Total of this page)
Total ▶ $ _____
(Use only on last page)
(Report total also on Summary of Schedules)

812

FORM B6D—Cont.
(10/89)

In re _____ ,   Case No. _____
     Debtor   (If known)

SCHEDULE D—CREDITORS HOLDING SECURED CLAIMS
(Continuation Sheet)

CREDITOR'S NAME AND MAILING ADDRESS INCLUDING ZIP CODE	CODEBTOR	HUSBAND, WIFE, JOINT, OR COMMUNITY	DATE CLAIM WAS INCURRED, NATURE OF LIEN, AND DESCRIPTION AND MARKET VALUE OF PROPERTY SUBJECT TO LIEN	CONTINGENT	UNLIQUIDATED	DISPUTED	AMOUNT OF CLAIM WITHOUT DEDUCTING VALUE OF COLLATERAL	UNSECURED PORTION, IF ANY
ACCOUNT NO.								
			VALUE $					
ACCOUNT NO.								
			VALUE $					
ACCOUNT NO.								
			VALUE $					
ACCOUNT NO.								
			VALUE $					
ACCOUNT NO.								
			VALUE $					

Sheet no. _____ of _____ continuation sheets attached to Schedule of Creditors Holding Secured Claims   Subtotal ▶ $
                                                        (Total of this page)
                                                        Total ▶ $
                                          (Use only on last page)
                                      (Report total also on Summary of Schedules)

PROPOSED REVISED FORMS

FORM 84E
(6/90)

In re _____,   Case No. _____
                  Debtor   (If known)

SCHEDULE E—CREDITORS HOLDING UNSECURED PRIORITY CLAIMS

A complete list of claims entitled to priority, listed separately by type of priority, is to be set forth on the sheets provided. Only holders of unsecured claims entitled to priority should be listed in this schedule. In the boxes provided on the attached sheets, state the name and mailing address, including zip code, and account number, if any, of all entities holding priority claims against the debtor or the property of the debtor, as of the date of the filing of the petition.

If any entity other than a spouse in a joint case may be jointly liable on a claim, place an "X" in the column labeled "Codebtor," include the entity on the appropriate schedule of creditors, and complete Schedule H—Codebtors. If a joint petition is filed, state whether husband, wife, both of them, or the marital community may be liable on each claim by placing an "H," "W," "J," or "C" in the column labeled "Husband, Wife, Joint, or Community."

If the claim is contingent, place an "X" in the column labeled "Contingent." If the claim is unliquidated, place an "X" in the column labeled "Unliquidated." If the claim is disputed, place an "X" in the column labeled "Disputed." (You may need to place an "X" in more than one of these three columns.)

Report the total of claims listed on each sheet in the box labeled "Subtotal" on each sheet. Report the total of all claims listed on this Schedule E in the box labeled "Total" on the last sheet of the completed schedule. Repeat this total also on the Summary of Schedules.

☐ Check this box if debtor has no creditors holding unsecured priority claims to report on this Schedule E.

TYPES OF PRIORITY CLAIMS (Check the appropriate box(es) below if claims in that category are listed on the attached sheets)

☐ **Extensions of credit in an involuntary case**

Claims arising in the ordinary course of the debtor's business or financial affairs after the commencement of the case but before the earlier of the appointment of a trustee or the order for relief. 11 U.S.C. § 507(a)(2).

☐ **Wages, salaries, and commissions**

Wages, salaries, and commissions, including vacation, severance, and sick leave pay owing to employees, up to a maximum of $2000 per employee, earned within 90 days immediately preceding the filing of the original petition, or the cessation of business, whichever occurred first, to the extent provided in 11 U.S.C. § 507(a)(3).

☐ **Contributions to employee benefit plans**

Money owed to employee benefit plans for services rendered within 180 days immediately preceding the filing of the original petition, or the cessation of business, whichever occurred first, to the extent provided in 11 U.S.C. § 507(a)(4).

☐ **Certain farmers and fishermen**

Claims of certain farmers and fishermen, up to a maximum of $2000 per farmer or fisherman, against the debtor, as provided in 11 U.S.C. § 507(a)(5).

☐ **Deposits by individuals**

Claims of individuals up to a maximum of $900 for deposits for the purchase, lease, or rental of property or services for personal, family, or household use, that were not delivered or provided. 11 U.S.C. § 507(a)(6).

☐ **Taxes and Certain Other Debts Owed to Governmental Units**

Taxes, customs duties, and penalties owing to federal, state, and local governmental units as set forth in 11 U.S.C. § 507(a)(7).

_____ continuation sheets attached

814

PROPOSED REVISED FORMS

FORM B6E—Cont.
(10/89)

In re _____ ,   Case No. _____
         Debtor   (If known)

SCHEDULE E—CREDITORS, HOLDING UNSECURED PRIORITY CLAIMS
(Continuation Sheet)

_____
TYPE OF PRIORITY

CREDITOR'S NAME AND MAILING ADDRESS INCLUDING ZIP CODE	CODEBTOR	HUSBAND, WIFE, JOINT, OR COMMUNITY	DATE CLAIM WAS INCURRED AND CONSIDERATION FOR CLAIM	CONTINGENT	UNLIQUIDATED	DISPUTED	TOTAL AMOUNT OF CLAIM	AMOUNT ENTITLED TO PRIORITY
ACCOUNT NO.								
ACCOUNT NO.								
ACCOUNT NO.								
ACCOUNT NO.								
ACCOUNT NO.								

Sheet no. _____ of _____ sheets attached to Schedule of Creditors
Holding Priority Claims

                          Subtotal ▶ $ _____
                       (Total of this page)
                              Total ▶ $ _____
(Use only on last page of the completed Schedule E.)
(Report total also on Summary of Schedules)

PROPOSED REVISED FORMS

FORM B6F
(10/89)

In re _____,
          Debtor

Case No. _____
               (If known)

SCHEDULE F—CREDITORS
HOLDING
UNSECURED NONPRIORITY CLAIMS

State the name, mailing address, including zip code, and account number, if any, of all entities holding unsecured claims without priority against the debtor or the property of the debtor, as of the date of filing of the petition. Do not include claims listed in Schedules D and E. If all creditors will not fit on this page, use the continuation sheet provided.

If any entity other than a spouse in a joint case may be jointly liable on a claim, place an "X" in the column labeled "Codebtor," include the entity on the appropriate schedule of creditors, and complete Schedule H—Codebtors. If a joint petition is filed, state whether husband, wife, both of them, or the marital community maybe liable on each claim by placing an "H," "W," "J," or "C" in the column labeled "Husband, Wife, Joint, or Community."

If the claim is contingent, place an "X" in the column labeled "Contingent." If the claim is unliquidated, place an "X" in the column labeled "Unliquidated." If the claim is disputed, place an "X" in the column labeled "Disputed." (You may need to place an "X" in more than one of these three columns.)

Report total of all claims listed on this schedule in the box labeled "Total" on the last sheet of the completed schedule. Report this total also on the Summary of Schedules.

☐ Check this box if debtor has no creditors holding unsecured non priority claims to report on this Schedule F.

CREDITOR'S NAME AND MAILING ADDRESS INCLUDING ZIP CODE	CODEBTOR	HUSBAND, WIFE, OR JOINT	DATE CLAIM WAS INCURRED AND CONSIDERATION FOR CLAIM. IF CLAIM IS SUBJECT TO SETOFF, SO STATE.	CONTINGENT	UNLIQUIDATED	DISPUTED	AMOUNT OF CLAIM
ACCOUNT NO.							
ACCOUNT NO.							
ACCOUNT NO.							
ACCOUNT NO.							

_____ continuation sheets attached

Subtotals ► $
Total ► $

(Report total also on Summary of Schedules)

816

PROPOSED REVISED FORMS

FORM B6F
(10/89)

In re _____, Case No. _____
　　　　　　　Debtor　　　　　　　　　　　　　　　　　　　(If known)

SCHEDULE F—CREDITORS HOLDING UNSECURED NONPRIORITY CLAIMS

State the name, mailing address, including zip code, and account number, if any, of all entities holding unsecured claims without priority against the debtor or the property of the debtor, as of the date of filing of the petition. Do not include claims listed in Schedules D and E. If all creditors will not fit on this page, use the continuation sheet provided.

If any entity other than a spouse in a joint case may be jointly liable on a claim, place an "X" in the column labeled "Codebtor," include the entity on the appropriate schedule of creditors, and complete Schedule H—Codebtors. If a joint petition is filed, state whether husband, wife, both of them, or the marital community may be liable on each claim by placing an "H," "W," "J," or "C" in the column labeled "Husband, Wife, Joint, or Community."

If the claim is contingent, place an "X" in the column labeled "Contingent." If the claim is unliquidated, place an "X" in the column labeled "Unliquidated." If the claim is disputed, place an "X" in the column labeled "Disputed." (You may need to place an "X" in more than one of these three columns.)

Report total of all claims listed on this schedule in the box labeled "Total" on the last sheet of the completed schedule. Report this total also on the Summary of Schedules.

☐ Check this box if debtor has no creditors holding unsecured non priority claims to report on this Schedule F.

CREDITOR'S NAME AND MAILING ADDRESS INCLUDING ZIP CODE	CODEBTOR	HUSBAND, WIFE, OR JOINT	DATE CLAIM WAS INCURRED AND CONSIDERATION FOR CLAIM. IF CLAIM IS SUBJECT TO SETOFF, SO STATE.	CONTINGENT	UNLIQUIDATED	DISPUTED	AMOUNT OF CLAIM
ACCOUNT NO							
ACCOUNT NO							
ACCOUNT NO.							
ACCOUNT NO.							

_____ continuation sheets attached

Subtotal ▶ $ _____

Total ▶ $ _____
(Report total also on Summary of Schedules)

PROPOSED REVISED FORMS

FORM B6G
(10/89)

In re _____,　　　　　Case No. _____

Debtor　　　　　　　　　　　　　　　　　　　　　　　　　　　(If known)

SCHEDULE G—EXECUTORY CONTRACTS AND UNEXPIRED LEASES

Describe all executory contracts of any nature and all unexpired leases of real or personal property. Include any timeshare interests.

State nature of debtor's interest in contract, i.e., "Purchaser," "Agent," etc. State whether debtor is the lessor or lessee of a lease.

Provide the names and complete mailing addresses of all other parties to each lease or contract described.

NOTE: A party listed on this schedule will not receive notice of the filing of this case unless the party is also scheduled in the appropriate schedule of creditors.

☐ Check this box if debtor has no executory contracts or unexpired leases.

NAME AND MAILING ADDRESS. INCLUDING ZIP CODE. OF OTHER PARTIES TO LEASE OR CONTRACT.	DESCRIPTION OF CONTRACT OR LEASE AND NATURE OF DEBTOR'S INTEREST. STATE WHETHER LEASE IS FOR NONRESIDENTIAL REAL PROPERTY. STATE CONTRACT NUMBER OF ANY GOVERNMENT CONTRACT.

PROPOSED REVISED FORMS

FORM B6H
(6/90)

In re _____ ,   Case No. _____
                    Debtor   (If known)

SCHEDULE H—CODEBTORS

Provide the information requested concerning any person or entity, other than a spouse in a joint case, that is also liable on any debts listed by debtor in the schedules of creditors. Include all guarantors and co-signers. In community property states, a married debtor not filing a joint case should report the name and address of the nondebtor spouse on this schedule. Include all names used by the nondebtor spouse during the six years immediately preceding the commencement of this case.

☐ Check this box if debtor has no codebtors.

NAME AND ADDRESS OF CODEBTOR	NAME AND ADDRESS OF CREDITOR

FORM B6I
(6/90)

In re _____, Case No. _____
                    Debtor   (If known)

SCHEDULE I—CURRENT INCOME OF INDIVIDUAL DEBTOR(S)

The column labeled "Spouse" must be completed in all cases filed by joint debtors and by a married debtor in a chapter 12 or 13 case whether or not a joint petition is filed, unless the spouses are separated and a joint petition is not filed.

Debtor's Marital Status:	DEPENDENTS OF DEBTOR AND SPOUSE		
	NAMES	AGE	RELATIONSHIP

Employment:	DEBTOR	SPOUSE
Occupation		
Name of Employer		
How long employed		
Address of Employer		

	DEBTOR	SPOUSE
Income: (Estimate of average monthly income)		
Current monthly gross wages, salary, and commissions (pro rate if not paid monthly.)	$_____	$_____
Estimated monthly overtime	$_____	$_____
SUBTOTAL	$_____	$_____
LESS PAYROLL DEDUCTIONS		
a. Payroll taxes and social security	$_____	$_____
b. Insurance	$_____	$_____
c. Union dues	$_____	$_____
d. Other (Specify: _____)	$_____	$_____
SUBTOTAL OF PAYROLL DEDUCTIONS	$_____	$_____
TOTAL NET MONTHLY TAKE HOME PAY	$_____	$_____
Regular income from operation of business or profession or farm (attach detailed statement)	$_____	$_____
Income from real property	$_____	$_____
Interest and dividends	$_____	$_____
Alimony, maintenance or support payments payable to the debtor for the debtor's use or that of dependents listed above.	$_____	$_____
Social security or other government assistance (Specify) _____	$_____	$_____
Pension or retirement income	$_____	$_____
Other monthly income (Specify) _____	$_____	$_____
	$_____	$_____
TOTAL MONTHLY INCOME	$_____	$_____

TOTAL COMBINED MONTHLY INCOME $ _____   (Report also on Summary of Schedules)

Describe any increase or decrease of more than 10% in any of the above categories anticipated to occur within the year following the filing of this document:

FORM B6J
(6/90)

In re _____,   Case No. _____
         Debtor   (if known)

SCHEDULE J—CURRENT EXPENDITURES OF INDIVIDUAL DEBTOR(S)

Complete this schedule by estimating the average monthly expenses of the debtor and the debtor's family. Pro rate any payments made bi-weekly, quarterly, semi-annually, or annually to show monthly rate.

☐ Check this box if a joint petition is filed and debtor's spouse maintains a separate household. Complete a separate schedule of expenditures labeled "Spouse."

Rent or home mortgage payment (include lot rented for mobile home)	$ _____
Are real estate taxes included? Yes _____ No _____	
Is property insurance included? Yes _____ No _____	
Utilities Electricity and heating fuel	$ _____
Water and sewer	$ _____
Telephone	$ _____
Other _____	$ _____
Home maintenance (repairs and upkeep)	$ _____
Food	$ _____
Clothing	$ _____
Laundry and dry cleaning	$ _____
Medical and dental expenses	$ _____
Transportation (not including car payments)	$ _____
Recreation, clubs and entertainment, newspapers, magazines, etc.	$ _____
Charitable contributions	$ _____
Insurance (not deducted from wages or included in home mortgage payments)	
Homeowner's or renter's	$ _____
Life	$ _____
Health	$ _____
Auto	$ _____
Other _____	$ _____
Taxes (not deducted from wages or included in home mortgage payments)	
(Specify) _____	$ _____
Installment payments: (In chapter 12 and 13 cases, do not list payments to be included in the plan)	
Auto	$ _____
Other _____	$ _____
Other _____	$ _____
Alimony, maintenance, and support paid to others	$ _____
Payments for support of additional dependents not living at your home	$ _____
Regular expenses from operation of business, profession, or farm (attach detailed statement)	$ _____
Other _____	$ _____
TOTAL MONTHLY EXPENSES (Report also on Summary of Schedules)	$ _____

[FOR CHAPTER 12 AND 13 DEBTORS ONLY]
Provide the information requested below, including whether plan payments are to be made bi-weekly, monthly, annually, or at some other regular interval.

A. Total projected monthly income	$ _____
B. Total projected monthly expenses	$ _____
C. Excess income (A minus B)	$ _____
D. Total amount to be paid into plan each _____	$ _____
(interval)	

FORM B6—Cont.
(6/90)

In re _____, Case No. _____
         Debtor   (If known)

DECLARATION CONCERNING DEBTOR'S SCHEDULES

DECLARATION UNDER PENALTY OF PERJURY BY INDIVIDUAL DEBTOR

I declare under penalty of perjury that I have read the foregoing summary and schedules, consisting of _____ sheets, and that they are true and correct to the best of my knowledge, information, and belief.   (Total shown on summary page plus 1.)

Date _____   Signature: _____
                                                                    Debtor

Date _____   Signature: _____
                                                          (Joint Debtor, if any)
                                          [If joint case, both spouses must sign.]

DECLARATION UNDER PENALTY OF PERJURY ON BEHALF OF CORPORATION OR PARTNERSHIP

I, the _____ [the president or other officer or an authorized agent of the corporation or a member or an authorized agent of the partnership] of the _____ [corporation or partnership] named as debtor in this case, declare under penalty of perjury that I have read the foregoing summary and schedules, consisting of _____ sheets, and that they are true and correct to the best of my knowledge, information, and belief.   (Total shown on summary page plus 1.)

Date _____

          Signature: _____

                    _____
                    [Print or type name of individual signing on behalf of debtor.]

[An individual signing on behalf of a partnership or corporation must indicate position or relationship to debtor.]

Penalty for making a false statement or concealing property: Fine of up to $500,000 or imprisonment for up to 5 years or both. 18 U.S.C. §§ 152 and 3571.

PROPOSED REVISED FORMS

COMMITTEE NOTE

These schedules shall be used to comply with § 521(1) of the Code and Rule 1007(b). Schedules A, B, D, E, and F constitute the schedule of assets and liabilities. Schedules I and J constitute a schedule of current income and current expenditures for individual and joint debtors. Two new schedules have been created, Schedule G - Executory Contracts and Unexpired Leases, and Schedule H - Codebtors.

The order of the schedules has been arranged with the summary sheet in front and with the schedules of assets appearing first, followed by the schedules of liabilities. This structure corresponds to the customary pattern by which trustees and creditors review these documents and to the format of the accounting profession for balance sheets.

The schedules require a complete listing of assets and liabilities but leave many of the details to investigation by the trustee. Instructions in the former schedules to provide details concerning "written instruments" relating to the debtor's property or debts have been deleted. Section 521(3) of the Code requires the debtor to cooperate with the trustee, who can administer the estate more effectively by requesting any documents from the debtor rather than relying on descriptions in the schedules which may prove to be inaccurate.

Leasehold interests in both real and personal property are to be reported in Schedule G - Executory Contracts and Unexpired Leases. This information should not be repeated in the schedules of assets.

Generally in these schedules, a creditor's claim will be listed only once, even if the claim is secured only in part, or is entitled only in part to priority under § 507(a) of the Code, with the remainder of the claim to be treated as a general unsecured claim. For example, a partially secured creditor whose claim is reported in Schedule D - Creditors Holding Secured Claims will be listed together with the value of the property securing the claim and a notation of the amount of any unsecured portion of the claim. Information concerning the unsecured portion should not be repeated in Schedule F - Creditors Holding Nonpriority Unsecured Claims. Any resulting overstatement of the amounts owed on secured and priority claims as reported on the summary sheet is offset by a corresponding understatement of the amount owed on unsecured claims.

If a debtor has no property or no creditors in a particular category, an affirmative statement to that effect is required. Married debtors should indicate whether property is jointly or separately owned and whether spouses are jointly or separately liable for debts, using the columns provided in the schedules.

823

PROPOSED REVISED FORMS

Former "Schedule B-3. Property not otherwise scheduled," has been deleted and its two questions moved. Schedule B - Personal Property now includes at item 33, " Other personal property of any kind not already listed." The only other question on former Schedule B-3 concerned assignments for the benefit of creditors; it has been moved to the Statement of Financial Affairs.

<u>Schedule A - Real Property.</u> Instructions at the top of the form indicate the scope of the interests in property to be reported on the schedule. Leasehold interests of the debtor are not reported here but on the Schedule of Executory Contracts and Unexpired Leases. The trustee will request copies of deeds or other instruments necessary to the administration of the estate.

<u>Schedule B - Personal Property.</u> This schedule is to be used for reporting all of the debtor's interests in personal property except leases and executory contracts, which are to be listed on the Schedule of Executory Contracts and Unexpired Leases. Several new categories of property have been added to the schedule, i.e., aircraft, and interests in IRA, ERISA, Keogh, or other pension or profit-sharing plans. To minimize the potential for concealment of assets, the debtor must declare whether the debtor has any property in each category on the schedule. The trustee can request copies of any documents concerning the debtor's property necessary to the administration of the estate.

<u>Schedule C - Property Claimed as Exempt.</u> The form of the schedule has been modified to eliminate duplication of information provided elsewhere. The location of property, for example, which formerly was required here, is disclosed in the schedules of real and personal property. The requirement that the debtor state the present use of the property also has been eliminated as best left to inquiry by the trustee. Exemptions in some states are granted by constitutional provisions; accordingly, the requirement that the debtor state the "statute" creating an exemption has been changed to request a statement of the relevant "law."

This schedule adds a new requirement that the debtor state the market value of the property in addition to the amount claimed as exempt.

<u>Schedule D - Creditors Holding Secured Claims.</u> Schedules D, E, and F have been redesigned with address boxes sized to match the number of characters which can be accommodated on the computerized noticing systems used by the courts. The size also closely approximates that of standard mailing labels. Space is designated at the top of the box for the debtor's account number with the creditor. The design of the form is intended to reduce the volume of misdirected creditor mail.

The form requires the debtor to state affirmatively that a claim is disputed, unliquidated, or contingent. The existence of any type of codebtor is to be disclosed, but details are to be provided in Schedule H, as they are not needed here. Duplication of information also has been kept to a minimum by deleting requests that the debtor indicate on this schedule whether a debt has been reduced to judgment and the date on which a creditor repossessed any collateral. Requests for details concerning negotiable instruments and the consideration for a claim, formerly part of the schedule, are left to the trustee's inquiries.

Schedule E - Creditors Holding Unsecured Priority Claims. The schedule lists all of the types of claims entitled to priority and requires the debtor to indicate the existence of claims in each category. Continuation sheets are provided. The type of priority claim is to be noted at the top of the continuation sheet, and each type must be reported on a separate sheet. This schedule also requires the debtor to indicate the existence of any codebtors. As in Schedule D - Creditors Holding Secured Claims, requests for information concerning judgments and negotiable instruments have been deleted.

Schedule F - Creditors Holding Unsecured Nonpriority Claims. This schedule has been revised generally in conformity with the other schedules of creditors. If a claim is subject to setoff, the debtor is required to so state.

Schedule G - Executory Contracts and Unexpired Leases. Rule 1007(b) requires the debtor to file a schedule of executory contracts and unexpired leases, unless the court orders otherwise. All unexpired leases of either real or personal property are to be reported on this schedule. The schedule also requires the debtor to disclose specific information to assist the trustee in identifying leases which must be assumed within 60 days after the order for relief or be deemed rejected under $ 365(d) of the Code.

Schedule H - Schedule of Codebtors. This schedule is designed to provide the trustee and creditors with information about codebtors of all types other than spouses in joint cases. The completed schedule provides information concerning non-debtor parties, such as guarantors and non-debtor spouses having an interest in property as tenants by the entirety. In chapter 12 and chapter 13 cases, the completed schedule also indicates those persons who may be entitled to certain protections from creditor action under $$ 1201 and 1301 of the Code.

Schedule I - Schedule of Current Income of Individual Debtor(s) and Schedule J - Schedule of Current Expenditures of Individual Debtor(s). Former Official Form No. 6A has been divided into a schedule of current income and a separate schedule of current expenditures. The language is substantially the same as in former Official Form No. 6A. In light of the abrogation of Official Form No. 10, the Chapter 13 Statement, style changes have been made so that these schedules can be used by individual and joint debtors in all chapters.

PROPOSED REVISED FORMS

FORM 7. STATEMENT OF FINANCIAL AFFAIRS

UNITED STATES BANKRUPTCY COURT
_____ DISTRICT OF _____

In re: _____,   Case No. _____
        (Name)   (if known)
             Debtor

STATEMENT OF FINANCIAL AFFAIRS

This statement is to be completed by every debtor. Spouses filing a joint petition may file a single statement on which the information for both spouses is combined. If the case is filed under chapter 12 or chapter 13, a married debtor must furnish information for both spouses whether or not a joint petition is filed, unless the spouses are separated and a joint petition is not filed. An individual debtor engaged in business as a sole proprietor, partner, family farmer, or self-employed professional, should provide the information requested on this statement concerning all such activities as well as the individual's personal affairs.

Questions 1 - 15 are to be completed by all debtors. Debtors that are or have been in business, as defined below, also must complete Questions 16 - 21. Each question must be answered. If the answer to any question is "None," or the question is not applicable, mark the box labeled "None." If additional space is needed for the answer to any question, use and attach a separate sheet properly identified with the case name, case number (if known), and the number of the question.

DEFINITIONS

"*In business.*" A debtor is "in business" for the purpose of this form if the debtor is a corporation or partnership. An individual debtor is "in business" for the purpose of this form if the debtor is or has been, within the two years immediately preceding the filing of this bankruptcy case, any of the following: an officer, director, managing executive, or person in control of a corporation; a partner, other than a limited partner, of a partnership; a sole proprietor or self-employed.

"*Insider.*" The term "insider" includes but is not limited to: relatives of the debtor; general partners of the debtor and their relatives; corporations of which the debtor is an officer, director, or person in control; officers, directors, and any person in control of a corporate debtor and their relatives; affiliates of the debtor and insiders of such affiliates; any managing agent of the debtor. 11 U.S.C. § 101(30).

---

1. Income from employment or operation of business

None
☐

    State the gross amount of income the debtor has received from employment, trade, or profession, or from operation of the debtor's business from the beginning of this calendar year to the date this case was commenced. State also the gross amounts received during the two years immediately preceding this calendar year. (A debtor that maintains, or has maintained, financial records on the basis of a fiscal rather than a calendar year may report fiscal year income. Identify the beginning and ending dates of the debtor's fiscal year.) If a joint petition is filed, state income for each spouse separately. (Married debtors filing under chapter 12 or chapter 13 must state income of both spouses whether or not a joint petition is filed, unless the spouses are separated and a joint petition is not filed.)

    AMOUNT   **SOURCE (if more than one)**

PROPOSED REVISED FORMS

2. Income other than from employment or operation of business

☐ None

State the amount of income received by the debtor other than from employment, trade, profession, or operation of the debtor's business during the two years immediately preceding the commencement of this case. Give particulars. If a joint petition is filed, state income for each spouse separately. (Married debtors filing under chapter 12 or chapter 13 must state income for each spouse whether or not a joint petition is filed, unless the spouses are separated and a joint petition is not filed.)

AMOUNT   SOURCE

---

3. Payments to creditors

☐ None

a. List all payments on loans, installment purchases of goods or services, and other debts, aggregating more than $600 to any creditor, made within 90 days immediately preceding the commencement of this case. (Married debtors filing under chapter 12 or chapter 13 must include payments by either or both spouses whether or not a joint petition is filed, unless the spouses are separated and a joint petition is not filed.)

NAME AND ADDRESS OF CREDITOR	DATES OF PAYMENTS	AMOUNT PAID	AMOUNT STILL OWING

☐ None

b. List all payments made within one year immediately preceding the commencement of this case to or for the benefit of creditors who are or were insiders. (Married debtors filing under chapter 12 or chapter 13 must include payments by either or both spouses whether or not a joint petition is filed, unless the spouses are separated and a joint petition is not filed.)

NAME AND ADDRESS OF CREDITOR AND RELATIONSHIP TO DEBTOR	DATE OF PAYMENT	AMOUNT PAID	AMOUNT STILL OWING

---

4. Suits, executions, garnishments and attachments

☐ None

a. List all suits to which the debtor is or was a party within one year immediately preceding the filing of this bankruptcy case. (Married debtors filing under chapter 12 or chapter 13 must include information concerning either or both spouses whether or not a joint petition is filed, unless the spouses are separated and a joint petition is not filed.)

CAPTION OF SUIT AND CASE NUMBER	NATURE OF PROCEEDING	COURT AND LOCATION	STATUS OR DISPOSITION

PROPOSED REVISED FORMS

None ☐ b. Describe all property that has been attached, garnished or seized under any legal or equitable process within one year immediately preceding the commencement of this case. (Married debtors filing under chapter 12 or chapter 13 must include information concerning property of either or both spouses whether or not a joint petition is filed, unless the spouses are separated and a joint petition is not filed.)

NAME AND ADDRESS OF PERSON FOR WHOSE BENEFIT PROPERTY WAS SEIZED	DATE OF SEIZURE	DESCRIPTION AND VALUE OF PROPERTY

5. Repossessions, foreclosures and returns

None ☐ List all property that has been repossessed by a creditor, sold at a foreclosure sale, transferred through a deed in lieu of foreclosure or returned to the seller, within one year immediately preceding the commencement of this case. (Married debtors filing under chapter 12 or chapter 13 must include information concerning property of either or both spouses whether or not a joint petition is filed, unless the spouses are separated and a joint petition is not filed.)

NAME AND ADDRESS OF CREDITOR OR SELLER	DATE OF REPOSSESSION, FORECLOSURE SALE, TRANSFER OR RETURN	DESCRIPTION AND VALUE OF PROPERTY

6. Assignments and receiverships

None ☐ a. Describe any assignment of property for the benefit of creditors made within 120 days immediately preceding the commencement of this case. (Married debtors filing under chapter 12 or chapter 13 must include any assignment by either or both spouses whether or not a joint petition is filed, unless the spouses are separated and a joint petition is not filed.)

NAME AND ADDRESS OF ASSIGNEE	DATE OF ASSIGNMENT	TERMS OF ASSIGNMENT OR SETTLEMENT

None ☐ b. List all property which has been in the hands of a custodian, receiver, or court-appointed official within one year immediately preceding the commencement of this case. (Married debtors filing under chapter 12 or chapter 13 must include information concerning property of either or both spouses whether or not a joint petition is filed, unless the spouses are separated and a joint petition is not filed.)

NAME AND ADDRESS OF CUSTODIAN	NAME AND LOCATION OF COURT CASE TITLE & NUMBER	DATE OF ORDER	DESCRIPTION AND VALUE OF PROPERTY

7. Gifts

None ☐   List all gifts or charitable contributions made within one year immediately preceding the commencement of this case except ordinary and usual gifts to family members aggregating less than $200 in value per individual family member and charitable contributions aggregating less than $100 per recipient. (Married debtors filing under chapter 12 or chapter 13 must include gifts or contributions by either or both spouses whether or not a joint petition is filed, unless the spouses are separated and a joint petition is not filed.)

NAME AND ADDRESS OF PERSON OR ORGANIZATION	RELATIONSHIP TO DEBTOR, IF ANY	DATE OF GIFT	DESCRIPTION AND VALUE OF GIFT

8. Losses

None ☐   List all losses from fire, theft, other casualty or gambling within one year immediately preceding the commencement of this case or since the commencement of this case. (Married debtors filing under chapter 12 or chapter 13 must include losses by either or both spouses whether or not a joint petition is filed, unless the spouses are separated and a joint petition is not filed.)

DESCRIPTION AND VALUE OF PROPERTY	DESCRIPTION OF CIRCUMSTANCES AND, IF LOSS WAS COVERED IN WHOLE OR IN PART BY INSURANCE, GIVE PARTICULARS	DATE OF LOSS

9. Payments related to debt counseling or bankruptcy

None ☐   List all payments made or property transferred by or on behalf of the debtor to any persons, including attorneys, for consultation concerning debt consolidation, relief under the bankruptcy law or preparation of a petition in bankruptcy within one year immediately preceding the commencement of this case.

NAME AND ADDRESS OF PAYEE	DATE OF PAYMENT, NAME OF PAYOR IF OTHER THAN DEBTOR	AMOUNT OF MONEY OR DESCRIPTION AND VALUE OF PROPERTY

10. Other transfers

None

□ a. List all other property, other than property transferred in the ordinary course of the business or financial affairs of the debtor, transferred either absolutely or as security within one year immediately preceding the commencement of this case. (Married debtors filing under chapter 12 or chapter 13 must include transfers by either or both spouses whether or not a joint petition is filed, unless the spouses are separated and a joint petition is not filed.)

NAME AND ADDRESS OF TRANSFEREE, RELATIONSHIP TO DEBTOR	DATE	DESCRIBE PROPERTY TRANSFERRED AND VALUE RECEIVED

---

11. Closed financial accounts

None

□ List all financial accounts and instruments held in the name of the debtor or for the benefit of the debtor which were closed, sold, or otherwise transferred within one year immediately preceding the commencement of this case. Include checking, savings, or other financial accounts, certificates of deposit, or other instruments; shares and share accounts held in banks, credit unions, pension funds, cooperatives, associations, brokerage houses and other financial institutions. (Married debtors filing under chapter 12 or chapter 13 must include information concerning accounts or instruments held by or for either or both spouses whether or not a joint petition is filed, unless the spouses are separated and a joint petition is not filed.)

NAME AND ADDRESS OF INSTITUTION	TYPE AND NUMBER OF ACCOUNT AND AMOUNT OF FINAL BALANCE	AMOUNT AND DATE OF SALE OR CLOSING

12. Safe deposit boxes

None

□ List each safe deposit or other box or depository in which the debtor has or had securities, cash, or other valuables within one year immediately preceding the commencement of this case. (Married debtors filing under chapter 12 or chapter 13 must include boxes or depositories of either or both spouses whether or not a joint petition is filed, unless the spouses are separated and a joint petition is not filed.)

NAME AND ADDRESS OF BANK OR OTHER DEPOSITORY	NAMES AND ADDRESSES OF THOSE WITH ACCESS TO BOX OR DEPOSITORY	DESCRIPTION OF CONTENTS	DATE OF TRANSFER OR SURRENDER, IF ANY

13. Setoffs

None ☐   List all setoffs made by any creditor, including a bank, against a debt or deposit of the debtor within 90 days preceding the commencement of this case. (Married debtors filing under chapter 12 or chapter 13 must include information concerning either or both spouses whether or not a joint petition is filed, unless the spouses are separated and a joint petition is not filed.)

NAME AND ADDRESS OF CREDITOR	DATE OF SETOFF	AMOUNT OF SETOFF

---

14. Property held for another person

None ☐   List all property owned by another person that the debtor holds or controls.

NAME AND ADDRESS OF OWNER	DESCRIPTION AND VALUE OF PROPERTY	LOCATION OF PROPERTY

---

15. Prior address of debtor

None ☐   If the debtor has moved within the two years immediately preceding the commencement of this case, list all premises which the debtor occupied during that period and vacated prior to the commencement of this case. If a joint petition is filed, report also any separate address of either spouse.

ADDRESS	NAME USED	DATES OF OCCUPANCY

PROPOSED REVISED FORMS

The following questions are to be completed by every debtor that is a corporation or partnership and by any individual debtor who is or has been, within the two years immediately preceding the commencement of this case, any of the following: an officer, director, managing executive, or owner of more than 5 percent of the voting securities of a corporation; a partner, other than a limited partner, of a partnership; a sole proprietor or otherwise self-employed.

(An individual or joint debtor should complete this portion of the statement only if the debtor is or has been in business, as defined above, within the two years immediately preceding the commencement of this case.)

16. Nature, location and name of business

None □ a. If the debtor is an individual, list the names and addresses of all businesses in which the debtor was an officer, director, partner, or managing executive of a corporation, partnership, sole proprietorship, or was a self-employed professional within the two years immediately preceding the commencement of this case, or in which the debtor owned 5 percent or more of the voting or equity securities within the two years immediately preceding the commencement of this case.

b. If the debtor is a partnership, list the names and addresses of all businesses in which the debtor was a partner or owned 5 percent or more of the voting securities, within the two years immediately preceding the commencement of this case.

c. If the debtor is a corporation, list the names and addresses of all businesses in which the debtor was a partner or owned 5 percent or more of the voting securities within the two years immediately preceding the commencement of this case.

NAME	ADDRESS	NATURE OF BUSINESS	BEGINNING AND ENDING DATES OF OPERATION

17. Books, records and financial statements

None □ a. List all bookkeepers and accountants who within the six years immediately preceding the filing of this bankruptcy case kept or supervised the keeping of books of account and records of the debtor.

NAME AND ADDRESS	DATES SERVICES RENDERED

None □ b. List all firms or individuals who within the two years immediately preceding the filing of this bankruptcy case have audited the books of account and records, or prepared a financial statement of the debtor.

NAME	ADDRESS	DATES SERVICES RENDERED

832

None ☐   c. List all firms or individuals who at the time of the commencement of this case were in possession of the books of account and records of the debtor. If any of the books of account and records are not available, explain.

NAME   ADDRESS

None ☐   d. List all financial institutions, creditors and other parties, including mercantile and trade agencies, to whom a financial statement was issued within the two years immediately preceding the commencement of this case by the debtor.

NAME AND ADDRESS   DATE ISSUED

---

18. Inventories

None ☐   a. List the dates of the last two inventories taken of your property, the name of the person who supervised the taking of each inventory, and the dollar amount and basis of each inventory.

| | | DOLLAR AMOUNT OF INVENTORY |
| DATE OF INVENTORY | INVENTORY SUPERVISOR | (Specify cost, market or other basis) |

None ☐   b. List the name and address of the person having possession of the records of each of the two inventories reported in a., above.

| | NAME AND ADDRESSES OF CUSTODIAN |
| DATE OF INVENTORY | OF INVENTORY RECORDS |

---

19. Current Partners, Officers, Directors and Shareholders

None ☐   a. If the debtor is a partnership, list the nature and percentage of partnership interest of each member of the partnership.

NAME AND ADDRESS   NATURE OF INTEREST   PERCENTAGE OF INTEREST

None b. If the debtor is a corporation, list all officers and directors of the corporation, and each stockholder who directly or indirectly owns, controls, or holds 5 percent or more of the voting securities of the corporation.

NAME AND ADDRESS	TITLE	NATURE AND PERCENTAGE OF STOCK OWNERSHIP

20. Former partners, officers, directors and shareholders

None a. If the debtor is a partnership, list each member who withdrew from the partnership within one year immediately preceding the commencement of this case.

NAME	ADDRESS	DATE OF WITHDRAWAL

None b. If the debtor is a corporation, list all officers, or directors whose relationship with the corporation terminated within one year immediately preceding the commencement of this case.

NAME AND ADDRESS	TITLE	DATE OF TERMINATION

21. Withdrawals from a partnership or distributions by a corporation

None If the debtor is a partnership or corporation, list all withdrawals or distributions credited or given to an insider, including compensation in any form, bonuses, loans, stock redemptions, options exercised and any other perquisite during one year immediately preceding the commencement of this case.

NAME & ADDRESS OF RECIPIENT, RELATIONSHIP TO DEBTOR	DATE AND PURPOSE OF WITHDRAWAL	AMOUNT OF MONEY OR DESCRIPTION AND VALUE OF PROPERTY

• • • • • •

834

PROPOSED REVISED FORMS

[If completed by an individual or individual and spouse]

I declare under penalty of perjury that I have read the answers contained in the foregoing statement of financial affairs and any attachments thereto and that they are true and correct.

Date _____ Signature _____
                                 of Debtor

Date _____ Signature _____
                                 of Joint Debtor
                                 (if any)

• • • • • • •

[If completed on behalf of a partnership or corporation]

I, declare under penalty of perjury that I have read the answers contained in the foregoing statement of financial affairs and any attachments thereto and that they are true and correct to the best of my knowledge, information and belief.

Date _____ Signature _____

                                 _____
                                 Print Name and Title

[An individual signing on behalf of a partnership or corporation must indicate position or relationship to debtor.]

_____ continuation sheets attached

Penalty for making a false statement: Fine of up to $500,000 or imprisonment for up to 5 years, or both. 18 U.S.C. § 152 and 3571

COMMITTEE NOTE

This form consolidates questions from former Official Forms No. 7, No. 8, and No. 10. This form is to be completed by all debtors. An individual debtor engaged in business as a sole proprietor, partner, family farmer, or self-employed professional should provide the information requested on this statement concerning all such activities as well as the individual's personal affairs.

The Chapter 13 Statement, former Official Form No. 10, has been abrogated. Chapter 13 debtors are to complete this statement and the schedules prescribed in Official Form 6.

All questions have been converted to affirmative directions to furnish information, and each question must be answered. If the answer is "none," or the question is not applicable, the debtor is required to so state by marking the box labeled "None" provided at each question.

See Committee Note to Form 2 for a discussion of the unsworn declaration at the end of this form.

Form B8
6/90

Form 8. CHAPTER 7 INDIVIDUAL DEBTOR'S STATEMENT OF INTENTION

[Caption as in Form 16B]

CHAPTER 7 INDIVIDUAL DEBTOR'S STATEMENT OF INTENTION

1. I, the debtor, have filed a schedule of assets and liabilities which includes consumer debts secured by property of the estate.

2. My intention with respect to the property of the estate which secures those consumer debts is as follows:

    a. *Property to Be Surrendered.*

Description of Property	Creditor's name
1. _____	_____
2. _____	_____
3. _____	_____

    b. *Property to Be Retained.* *[Check applicable statement of debtor's intention concerning reaffirmation, redemption, or lien avoidance.]*

Description of property	Creditor's name	Debt will be reaffirmed pursuant to § 524(c)	Property is claimed as exempt and will be redeemed pursuant to § 722	Lien will be avoided pursuant to § 522(f) and property will be claimed as exempt
1. _____	_____	_____	_____	_____
2. _____	_____	_____	_____	_____
3. _____	_____	_____	_____	_____
4. _____	_____	_____	_____	_____
5. _____	_____	_____	_____	_____

3. I understand that § 521(2)(B) of the Bankruptcy Code requires that I perform the above stated intention within 45 days of the filing of this statement with the court, or within such additional time as the court, for cause, within such 45-day period fixes.

Date: _____

_____
Signature of Debtor

COMMITTEE NOTE

This form is derived from former Official Form No. 8A. Rule 1007(b)(2) requires the debtor to serve a copy of this statement on the trustee and all creditors named in the statement. In a joint case, if the property and debts of both debtors are the same, the form may be adapted for joint use. If joint debtors have separate debts, however, each debtor must use a separate form.

Form B9
6/90

Form 9. NOTICE OF FILING UNDER THE BANKRUPTCY CODE, MEETING OF CREDITORS, AND FIXING OF DATES

9A............Chapter 7, Individual/Joint, No-Asset Case

9B............Chapter 7, Corporation/Partnership, No-Asset Case

9C............Chapter 7, Individual/Joint, Asset Case

9D............Chapter 7, Corporation/Partnership, Asset Case

9E............Chapter 11, Individual/Joint Case

9F............Chapter 11, Corporation/Partnership Case

9G............Chapter 12, Individual/Joint Case

9H............Chapter 12, Corporation/Partnership Case

9I............Chapter 13, Individual/Joint Case

FORM B9A
6/90

United States Bankruptcy Court

Case Number

_____ District of _____

NOTICE OF COMMENCEMENT OF CASE UNDER CHAPTER 7 OF THE BANKRUPTCY CODE, MEETING OF CREDITORS, AND FIXING OF DATES
(Individual or Joint Debtor No Asset Case)

In re (Name of Debtor)	Address of Debtor	Soc. Sec./Tax Id. Nos.
	Date Case Filed (or Converted)	
Name and Address of Attorney for Debtor	Name and Address of Trustee	
Telephone Number		Telephone Number

☐ This is a converted case originally filed under chapter _____ on _____ (date).

DATE, TIME, AND LOCATION OF MEETING OF CREDITORS

DISCHARGE OF DEBTS

Deadline to File a Complaint Objecting to Discharge of the Debtor or to Determine Dischargeability of Certain Types of Debts:

AT THIS TIME THERE APPEAR TO BE NO ASSETS AVAILABLE FROM WHICH PAYMENT MAY BE MADE TO UNSECURED CREDITORS. DO NOT FILE A PROOF OF CLAIM UNTIL YOU RECEIVE NOTICE TO DO SO.

COMMENCEMENT OF CASE. A petition for liquidation under chapter 7 of the Bankruptcy Code has been filed in this court by or against the person or persons named above as the debtor, and an order for relief has been entered. You will not receive notice of all documents filed in this case. All documents filed with the court, including lists of the debtor's property, debts, and property claimed as exempt are available for inspection at the office of the clerk of the bankruptcy court.

CREDITORS MAY NOT TAKE CERTAIN ACTIONS. A creditor is anyone to whom the debtor owes money or property. Under the Bankruptcy Code, the debtor is granted certain protection against creditors. Common examples of prohibited actions by creditors are contacting the debtor to demand repayment, taking action against the debtor to collect money owed to creditors or to take property of the debtor, and starting or continuing foreclosure actions, repossessions, or wage deductions. If unauthorized actions are taken by a creditor against a debtor, the court may penalize that creditor. A creditor who is considering taking action against the debtor or the property of the debtor should review § 362 of the Bankruptcy Code and may wish to seek legal advice. The staff of the clerk of the bankruptcy court is not permitted to give legal advice.

MEETING OF CREDITORS. The debtor (both husband and wife in a joint case) is required to appear at the meeting of creditors on the date and at the place set forth above for the purpose of being examined under oath. Attendance by creditors at the meeting is welcomed, but not required. At the meeting, the creditors may elect a trustee other than the one named above, elect a committee of creditors, examine the debtor, and transact such other business as may properly come before the meeting. The meeting may be continued or adjourned from time to time by notice at the meeting, without further written notice to creditors.

LIQUIDATION OF THE DEBTOR'S PROPERTY. The trustee will collect the debtor's property and turn any that is not exempt into money. At this time, however, it appears from the schedules of the debtor that there are no assets from which any distribution can be paid to creditors. If at a later date it appears that there are assets from which a distribution may be paid, the creditors will be notified and given an opportunity to file claims.

EXEMPT PROPERTY. Under state and federal law, the debtor is permitted to keep certain money or property as exempt. If a creditor believes that an exemption of money or property is not authorized by law, the creditor may file an objection. An objection must be filed not later than 30 days after the conclusion of the meeting of creditors.

DISCHARGE OF DEBTS. The debtor is seeking a discharge of debts. A discharge means that certain debts are made unenforceable against the debtor personally. Creditors whose claims against the debtor are discharged may never take action against the debtor to collect the discharged debts. If a creditor believes that the debtor should not receive any discharge of debts under § 727 of the Bankruptcy Code or that a debt owed to the creditor is not dischargeable under § 523(a)(2), (4), or (6) of the Bankruptcy Code, timely action must be taken in the bankruptcy court by the deadline set forth above in the box labeled "Discharge of Debts." Creditors considering taking such action may wish to seek legal advice.

DO NOT FILE A PROOF OF CLAIM UNLESS YOU RECEIVE A COURT NOTICE TO DO SO

Address of the Clerk of the Bankruptcy Court	For the Court:
	Clerk of the Bankruptcy Court
	Date

PROPOSED REVISED FORMS

FORM B9B 6/90	**United States Bankruptcy Court**	Case Number

District of _____

NOTICE OF COMMENCEMENT OF CASE UNDER CHAPTER 7 OF THE BANKRUPTCY CODE,
MEETING OF CREDITORS, AND FIXING OF DATES
(Corporation/Partnership No Asset Case)

In re (Name of Debtor)	Address of Debtor	Soc. Sec./Tax Id. Nos.
	Date Case Filed (or Converted)	

☐ Corporation   ☐ Partnership

Name and Address of Attorney for Debtor	Name and Address of Trustee	
Telephone Number		Telephone Number

☐ This is a converted case originally filed under chapter _____ on _____ (date).

DATE, TIME, AND LOCATION OF MEETING OF CREDITORS

AT THIS TIME THERE APPEAR TO BE NO ASSETS AVAILABLE FROM WHICH PAYMENT MAY BE MADE TO UNSECURED CREDITORS. DO NOT FILE A PROOF OF CLAIM UNTIL YOU RECEIVE NOTICE TO DO SO.

COMMENCEMENT OF CASE. A petition for liquidation under chapter 7 of the Bankruptcy Code has been filed in this court by or against the debtor named above, and an order for relief has been entered. You will not receive notice of all documents filed in this case. All documents filed with the court, including lists of the debtor's property and debts, are available for inspection at the office of the clerk of the bankruptcy court.

CREDITORS MAY NOT TAKE CERTAIN ACTIONS. A creditor is anyone to whom the debtor owes money or property. Under the Bankruptcy Code, the debtor is granted certain protection against creditors. Common examples of prohibited actions by creditors are contacting the debtor to demand repayment, taking action against the debtor to collect money owed to creditors or to take property of the debtor, and starting or continuing foreclosure actions or repossessions. If unauthorized actions are taken by a creditor against a debtor, the court may penalize that creditor. A creditor who is considering taking action against the debtor or the property of the debtor should review § 362 of the Bankruptcy Code and may wish to seek legal advice. If the debtor is a partnership, remedies otherwise available against general partners are not necessarily affected by the commencement of this partnership case. The staff of the clerk of the bankruptcy court is not permitted to give legal advice.

MEETING OF CREDITORS. The debtor's representative, as specified in Bankruptcy Rule 9001(a)(5), is required to appear at the meeting of creditors on the date and at the place set forth above for the purpose of being examined under oath. Attendance by creditors at the meeting is welcomed, but not required. At the meeting, the creditors may elect a trustee other than the one named above, elect a committee of creditors, examine the debtor, and transact such other business as may properly come before the meeting. The meeting may be continued or adjourned from time to time by notice at the meeting, without further written notice to creditors.

LIQUIDATION OF THE DEBTOR'S PROPERTY. The trustee will collect the debtor's property, if any, and turn it into money. At this time, however, it appears from the schedules of the debtor that there are no assets from which any distribution can be paid to the creditors. If at a later date it appears that there are assets from which a distribution may be paid, the creditors will be notified and given an opportunity to file claims.

DO NOT FILE A PROOF OF CLAIM UNLESS YOU RECEIVE A COURT NOTICE TO DO SO

Address of the Clerk of the Bankruptcy Court	For the Court:
	Clerk of the Bankruptcy Court
	Date

PROPOSED REVISED FORMS

<table>
<tr><td>FORM B9C
6/90</td><td colspan="2" align="center">United States Bankruptcy Court</td><td>Case Number</td></tr>
</table>

——————————— District of ———————————

NOTICE OF COMMENCEMENT OF CASE UNDER CHAPTER 7 OF THE BANKRUPTCY CODE, MEETING OF CREDITORS, AND FIXING OF DATES
(Individual or Joint Debtor Asset Case)

In re (Name of Debtor)	Address of Debtor	Soc. Sec./Tax Id. Nos.
	Date Case Filed (or Converted)	
Name and Address of Attorney for Debtor	Name and Address of Trustee	
Telephone Number		Telephone Number

☐ This is a converted case originally filed under chapter _____ on _____ (date).

FILING CLAIMS

Deadline to file a proof of claim:

DATE, TIME, AND LOCATION OF MEETING OF CREDITORS

DISCHARGE OF DEBTS

Deadline to File a Complaint Objecting to Discharge of the Debtor or to Determine Dischargeability of Certain Types of Debts:

COMMENCEMENT OF CASE. A petition for liquidation under chapter 7 of the Bankruptcy Code has been filed in this court by or against the person or persons named above as the debtor, and an order for relief has been entered. You will not receive notice of all documents filed in this case. All documents filed with the court, including lists of the debtor's property, debts, and property claimed as exempt are available for inspection at the office of the clerk of the bankruptcy court.

CREDITORS MAY NOT TAKE CERTAIN ACTIONS. A creditor is anyone to whom the debtor owes money or property. Under the Bankruptcy Code, the debtor is granted certain protection against creditors. Common examples of prohibited actions by creditors are contacting the debtor to demand repayment, taking action against the debtor to collect money owed to creditors or to take property of the debtor, and starting or continuing foreclosure actions, repossessions, or wage deductions. If unauthorized actions are taken by a creditor against a debtor, the court may penalize that creditor. A creditor who is considering taking action against the debtor or the property of the debtor should review § 362 of the Bankruptcy Code and may wish to seek legal advice. The staff of the clerk of the bankruptcy court is not permitted to give legal advice.

MEETING OF CREDITORS. The debtor (both husband and wife in a joint case) is required to appear at the meeting of creditors on the date and at the place set forth above for the purpose of being examined under oath. Attendance by creditors at the meeting is welcomed, but not required. At the meeting, the creditors may elect a trustee other than the one named above, elect a committee of creditors, examine the debtor, and transact such other business as may properly come before the meeting. The meeting may be continued or adjourned from time to time by notice at the meeting, without further written notice to creditors.

LIQUIDATION OF THE DEBTOR'S PROPERTY. The trustee will collect the debtor's property and turn any that is not exempt into money. If the trustee can collect enough money and property from the debtor, creditors may be paid some or all of the debts owed to them.

EXEMPT PROPERTY. Under state and federal law, the debtor is permitted to keep certain money or property as exempt. If a creditor believes that an exemption of money or property is not authorized by law, the creditor may file an objection. An objection must be filed not later than 30 days after the conclusion of the meeting of creditors.

DISCHARGE OF DEBTS. The debtor is seeking a discharge of debts. A discharge means that certain debts are made unenforceable against the debtor personally. Creditors whose claims against the debtor are discharged may never take action against the debtor to collect the discharged debts. If a creditor believes that the debtor should not receive any discharge of debts under § 727 of the Bankruptcy Code or that a debt owed to the creditor is not dischargeable under § 523(a)(2), (4), or (6) of the Bankruptcy Code, timely action must be taken in the bankruptcy court by the deadline set forth above in the box labeled "Discharge of Debts." Creditors considering taking such action may wish to seek legal advice.

PROOF OF CLAIM. Except as otherwise provided by law, in order to share in any payment from the estate, a creditor must file a proof of claim by the date set forth above in the box labeled "Filing Claims." The place to file the proof of claim, either in person or by mail, is the office of the clerk of the bankruptcy court. Proof of claim forms are available in the clerk's office of any bankruptcy court.

Address of the Clerk of the Bankruptcy Court	For the Court:
	Clerk of the Bankruptcy Court
	Date

PROPOSED REVISED FORMS

United States Bankruptcy Court

Case Number

_____ District of _____

NOTICE OF COMMENCEMENT OF CASE UNDER CHAPTER 7 OF THE BANKRUPTCY CODE,
MEETING OF CREDITORS, AND FIXING OF DATES
(Corporation/Partnership Asset Case)

In re (Name of Debtor)	Address of Debtor	Soc. Sec./Tax Id. Nos.
	Date Case Filed (or Converted)	

☐ Corporation ☐ Partnership

Name and Address of Attorney for Debtor	Name and Address of Trustee
Telephone Number	Telephone Number

☐ This is a converted case originally filed under chapter _____ on _____ (date).

FILING CLAIMS

Deadline to File a Proof of Claim:

DATE, TIME, AND LOCATION OF MEETING OF CREDITORS

COMMENCEMENT OF CASE A petition for liquidation under chapter 7 of the Bankruptcy Code has been filed in this court by or against the debtor named above, and an order for relief has been entered You will not receive notice of all documents filed in this case. All documents filed with the court, including lists of the debtor's property and debts, are available for inspection at the office of the clerk of the bankruptcy court.

CREDITORS MAY NOT TAKE CERTAIN ACTIONS. A creditor is anyone to whom the debtor owes money or property. Under the Bankruptcy Code, the debtor is granted certain protection against creditors. Common examples of prohibited actions by creditors are contacting the debtor to demand repayment, taking action against the debtor to collect money owed to creditors or to take property of the debtor, and starting or continuing foreclosure actions or repossessions. If unauthorized actions are taken by a creditor against a debtor, the court may penalize that creditor. A creditor who is considering taking action against the debtor or the property of the debtor should review § 362 of the Bankruptcy Code and may wish to seek legal advice. If the debtor is a partnership, remedies otherwise available against general partners are not necessarily affected by the commencement of this partnership case. The staff of the clerk of the bankruptcy court is not permitted to give legal advice.

MEETING OF CREDITORS The debtor's representative, as specified in Bankruptcy Rule 9001(a)(5), is required to appear at the meeting of creditors on the date and at the place set forth above for the purpose of being examined under oath Attendance by creditors at the meeting is welcomed, but not required At the meeting, the creditors may elect a trustee other than the one named above, elect a committee of creditors, examine the debtor, and transact such other business as may properly come before the meeting The meeting may be continued or adjourned from time to time by notice at the meeting, without further written notice to creditors.

LIQUIDATION OF THE DEBTOR'S PROPERTY. The trustee will collect the debtor's property, if any, and turn it into money. If the trustee can collect enough money and property from the debtor, creditors may be paid some or all of the debts owed to them.

PROOF OF CLAIM. Except as otherwise provided by law, in order to share in any payment from the estate, a creditor must file a proof of claim by the date set forth above in the box labeled "Filing Claims." The place to file the proof of claim, either in person or by mail, is the office of the clerk of the bankruptcy court. Proof of claim forms are available in the clerk's office of any bankruptcy court.

Address of the Clerk of the Bankruptcy Court	For the Court:
	Clerk of the Bankruptcy Court
	Date

PROPOSED REVISED FORMS

FORM B9E 6/90

United States Bankruptcy Court

Case Number

_____ District of _____

NOTICE OF COMMENCEMENT OF CASE UNDER CHAPTER 11 OF THE BANKRUPTCY CODE, MEETING OF CREDITORS, AND FIXING OF DATES
(Individual or Joint Debtor Case)

In re (Name of Debtor)	Address of Debtor	Soc. Sec./Tax Id. Nos.
	Date Case Filed (or Converted)	
Name and Address of Attorney for Debtor	Name and Address of Trustee	
Telephone Number	Telephone Number	

☐ This is a converted case originally filed under chapter _____ on _____ (date).

DATE, TIME, AND LOCATION OF MEETING OF CREDITORS

DISCHARGE OF DEBTS

Deadline to File a Complaint to Determine Dischargeability of Certain Types of Debts:

COMMENCEMENT OF CASE. A petition for reorganization under chapter 11 of the Bankruptcy Code has been filed in this court by or against the person or persons named above as the debtor, and an order for relief has been entered. You will not receive notice of all documents filed in this case. All documents filed with the court, including lists of the debtor's property, debts, and property claimed as exempt are available for inspection at the office of the clerk of the bankruptcy court.

CREDITORS MAY NOT TAKE CERTAIN ACTIONS. A creditor is anyone to whom the debtor owes money or property. Under the Bankruptcy Code, the debtor is granted certain protection against creditors. Common examples of prohibited actions by creditors are contacting the debtor to demand repayment, taking action against the debtor to collect money owed to creditors or to take property of the debtor, and starting or continuing foreclosure actions, repossessions, or wage deductions. If unauthorized actions are taken by a creditor against a debtor, the court may penalize that creditor. A creditor who is considering taking action against the debtor or the property of the debtor should review § 362 of the Bankruptcy Code and may wish to seek legal advice. The staff of the clerk of the bankruptcy court is not permitted to give legal advice.

MEETING OF CREDITORS. The debtor (both husband and wife in a joint case) is required to appear at the meeting of creditors on the date and at the place set forth above for the purpose of being examined under oath. Attendance by creditors at the meeting is welcomed, but not required. At the meeting, the creditors may examine the debtor and transact such other business as may properly come before the meeting. The meeting may be continued or adjourned from time to time by notice at the meeting, without further written notice to creditors.

EXEMPT PROPERTY. Under state and federal law, the debtor is permitted to keep certain money or property as exempt. If a creditor believes that an exemption of money or property is not authorized by law, the creditor may file an objection. An objection must be filed not later than 30 days after the conclusion of the meeting of creditors.

DISCHARGE OF DEBTS. The debtor may seek a discharge of debts. A discharge means that certain debts are made unenforceable against the debtor personally. Creditors whose claims against the debtor are discharged may never take action against the debtor to collect the discharged debts. If a creditor believes that the debtor should not receive a discharge under § 1141(d)(3)(C) of the Bankruptcy Code, timely action must be taken in the bankruptcy court in accordance with Bankruptcy Rule 4004(a). If a creditor believes that a debt owed to the creditor is not dischargeable under § 523(a)(2), (4), or (6) of the Bankruptcy Code, timely action must be taken in the bankruptcy court by the deadline set forth in the box labeled "Discharge of Debts." Creditors considering taking such action may wish to seek legal advice.

PROOF OF CLAIM. Schedules of creditors have been or will be filed pursuant to Bankruptcy Rule 1007. Any creditor holding a scheduled claim which is not listed as disputed, contingent, or unliquidated as to amount may, but is not required to, file a proof of claim in this case. Creditors whose claims are not scheduled or whose claims are listed as disputed, contingent, or unliquidated as to amount and who desire to participate in the case or share in any distribution must file their proofs of claim. A creditor who desires to rely on the schedules of creditors has the responsibility for determining that the claim is listed accurately. If the court sets a deadline for filing a proof of claim, you will be notified. The place to file a proof of claim, either in person or by mail, is the office of the clerk of the bankruptcy court. Proof of claim forms are available in the clerk's office of any bankruptcy court.

PURPOSE OF CHAPTER 11 FILING. Chapter 11 of the Bankruptcy Code enables a debtor to reorganize pursuant to a plan. A plan is not effective unless approved by the court at a confirmation hearing. Creditors will be given notice concerning any plan, or in the event the case is dismissed or converted to another chapter of the Bankruptcy Code. The debtor will remain in possession of its property and will continue to operate any business unless a trustee is appointed.

Address of the Clerk of the Bankruptcy Court	For the Court:
	Clerk of the Bankruptcy Court
	Date

842

PROPOSED REVISED FORMS

FORM B9F 6/90	**United States Bankruptcy Court**	Case Number

———————————— District of ————————————

NOTICE OF COMMENCEMENT OF CASE UNDER CHAPTER 11 OF THE BANKRUPTCY CODE,
MEETING OF CREDITORS, AND FIXING OF DATES
(Corporation/Partnership Case)

In re (Name of Debtor)	Address of Debtor	Soc. Sec./Tax Id. Nos.
	Date Case Filed (or Converted)	

☐ Corporation   ☐ Partnership

Name and Address of Attorney for Debtor	Name and Address of Trustee
Telephone Number	Telephone Number

☐ This is a converted case originally filed under chapter _____ on _____ (date).

DATE, TIME, AND LOCATION OF MEETING OF CREDITORS

COMMENCEMENT OF CASE. A petition for reorganization under chapter 11 of the Bankruptcy Code has been filed in this court by or against the debtor named above, and an order for relief has been entered. You will not receive notice of all documents filed in this case. All documents filed with the court, including lists of the debtor's property and debts, are available for inspection at the office of the clerk of the bankruptcy court.

CREDITORS MAY NOT TAKE CERTAIN ACTIONS. A creditor is anyone to whom the debtor owes money or property. Under the Bankruptcy Code, the debtor is granted certain protection against creditors. Common examples of prohibited actions by creditors are contacting the debtor to demand repayment, taking action against the debtor to collect money owed to creditors or to take property of the debtor, and starting or continuing foreclosure actions or repossessions. If unauthorized actions are taken by a creditor against a debtor, the court may penalize that creditor. A creditor who is considering taking action against the debtor or the property of the debtor should review § 362 of the Bankruptcy Code and may wish to seek legal advice. If the debtor is a partnership, remedies otherwise available against general partners are not necessarily affected by the filing of this partnership case. The staff of the clerk of the bankruptcy court is not permitted to give legal advice.

MEETING OF CREDITORS. The debtor's representative, as specified in Bankruptcy Rule 9001(a)(5) is required to appear at the meeting of creditors on the date and at the place set forth above for the purpose of being examined under oath. Attendance by creditors at the meeting is welcomed, but not required. At the meeting, the creditors may examine the debtor and transact such other business as may properly come before the meeting. The meeting may be continued or adjourned from time to time by notice at the meeting, without further written notice to creditors.

PROOF OF CLAIM. Schedules of creditors have been or will be filed pursuant to Bankruptcy Rule 1007. Any creditor holding a scheduled claim which is not listed as disputed, contingent, or unliquidated as to amount may, but is not required to, file a proof of claim in this case. Creditors whose claims are not scheduled or whose claims are listed as disputed, contingent, or unliquidated as to amount and who desire to participate in the case or share in any distribution must file their proofs of claim. A creditor who desires to rely on the schedule of creditors has the responsibility for determining that the claim is listed accurately. If the court sets a deadline for filing a proof of claim, you will be notified. The place to file a proof of claim, either in person or by mail, is the office of the clerk of the bankruptcy court. Proof of claim forms are available in the clerk's office of any bankruptcy court.

PURPOSE OF CHAPTER 11 FILING. Chapter 11 of the Bankruptcy Code enables a debtor to reorganize pursuant to a plan. A plan is not effective unless approved by the court at a confirmation hearing. Creditors will be given notice concerning any plan, or in the event the case is dismissed or converted to another chapter of the Bankruptcy Code. The debtor will remain in possession of its property and will continue to operate any business unless a trustee is appointed.

Address of the Clerk of the Bankruptcy Court	For the Court:
	Clerk of the Bankruptcy Court
	Date

843

PROPOSED REVISED FORMS

United States Bankruptcy Court

Case Number

_____ District of _____

NOTICE OF COMMENCEMENT OF CASE UNDER CHAPTER 12 OF THE BANKRUPTCY CODE, MEETING OF CREDITORS, AND FIXING OF DATES
(Individual or Joint Debtor Family Farmer)

In re (Name of Debtor)	Address of Debtor	Soc. Sec./Tax Id. Nos.
	Date Case Filed (or Converted)	
Name and Address of Attorney for Debtor	Name and Address of Trustee	
Telephone Number	Telephone Number	

☐ This is a converted case originally filed under chapter _____ on _____ (date)

FILING CLAIMS
Deadline to file a proof of claim:

DATE, TIME, AND LOCATION OF MEETING OF CREDITORS

FILING OF PLAN AND DATE, TIME, AND LOCATION OF HEARING ON CONFIRMATION OF PLAN
☐ The debtor has filed a plan. The plan or a summary of the plan is enclosed. Hearing on confirmation will be held:
_____ (Date) _____ (Time) _____ (Location)
☐ The debtor has filed a plan. The plan or a summary of the plan and notice of the confirmation hearing will be sent separately.
☐ A plan has not been filed as of this date. Creditors will be given separate notice of the hearing on confirmation of the plan.

DISCHARGE OF DEBTS
Deadline to File a Complaint to Determine Dischargeability of Certain Types of Debts:

COMMENCEMENT OF CASE. A family farmer's debt adjustment case under chapter 12 of the Bankruptcy Code has been filed in this court by the family farmer named above as the debtor, and an order for relief has been entered. You will not receive notice of all documents filed in this case. All documents filed with the court, including lists of the debtor's property and debts are available for inspection at the office of the clerk of the bankruptcy court.

CREDITORS MAY NOT TAKE CERTAIN ACTIONS. A creditor is anyone to whom the debtor owes money or property. Under the Bankruptcy Code, the debtor is granted certain protection against creditors. Common examples of prohibited actions by creditors are contacting the debtor to demand repayment, taking action against the debtor to collect money owed to creditors or to take property of the debtor, and starting or continuing foreclosure actions, repossessions, or wage deductions. Some protection is also given to certain codebtors of consumer debts. If unauthorized actions are taken by a creditor against a debtor, or a protected codebtor, the court may penalize that creditor. A creditor who is considering taking action against the debtor or the property of the debtor, or any codebtor, should review §§ 362 and 1201 of the Bankruptcy Code and may wish to seek legal advice. The staff of the clerk of the bankruptcy court is not permitted to give legal advice.

MEETING OF CREDITORS. The debtor (both husband and wife in a joint case) is required to appear at the meeting of creditors on the date and at the place set forth above for the purpose of being examined under oath. Attendance by creditors at the meeting is welcomed, but not required. At the meeting, the creditors may examine the debtor and transact such other business as may properly come before the meeting. The meeting may be continued or adjourned from time to time by notice at the meeting, without further written notice to creditors.

EXEMPT PROPERTY. Under state and federal law, the debtor is permitted to keep certain money or property as exempt. If a creditor believes that an exemption of money or property is not authorized by law, the creditor may file an objection. An objection must be filed not later than 30 days after the conclusion of the meeting of creditors.

DISCHARGE OF DEBTS. The debtor may seek a discharge of debts. A discharge means that certain debts are made unenforceable against the debtor personally. Creditors whose claims against the debtor are discharged may never take action against the debtor to collect the discharged debts. If a creditor believes a specific debt owed to the creditor is not dischargeable under § 523(a)(2), (4), or (6) of the Bankruptcy Code, timely action must be taken in the bankruptcy court by the deadline set forth above in the box labeled "Discharge of Debts." Creditors considering taking such action may wish to seek legal advice.

PROOF OF CLAIM. Except as otherwise provided by law, in order to share in any payment from the estate, a creditor must file a proof of claim by the date set forth above in the box labeled "Filing Claims." The place to file the proof of claim, either in person or by mail, is the office of the clerk of the bankruptcy court. Proof of claim forms are available in the clerk's office of any bankruptcy court.

PURPOSE OF A CHAPTER 12 FILING. Chapter 12 of the Bankruptcy Code enables family farmers to reorganize pursuant to a plan. A plan is not effective unless approved by the bankruptcy court at a confirmation hearing. Creditors will be given notice in the event the case is dismissed or converted to another chapter of the Bankruptcy Code.

Address of the Clerk of the Bankruptcy Court	For the Court:
	Clerk of the Bankruptcy Court
	Date

FORM B9H
6/90

United States Bankruptcy Court

| | Case Number |

———————— District of ————————

NOTICE OF COMMENCEMENT OF CASE UNDER CHAPTER 12 OF THE BANKRUPTCY CODE, MEETING OF CREDITORS, AND FIXING OF DATES
(Corporation/Partnership Family Farmer)

In re (Name of Debtor)	Address of Debtor	Soc. Sec./Tax Id. Nos.
	Date Case Filed (or Converted)	

☐ Corporation   ☐ Partnership

Name and Address of Attorney for Debtor	Name and Address of Trustee
Telephone Number	Telephone Number

☐ This is a converted case originally filed under chapter _____ on _____ (date).

FILING CLAIMS

Deadline to file a proof of claim:

DATE, TIME, AND LOCATION OF MEETING OF CREDITORS

FILING OF PLAN AND DATE, TIME, AND LOCATION OF HEARING ON CONFIRMATION OF PLAN

☐ The debtor has filed a plan. The plan or a summary of the plan is enclosed. Hearing on confirmation will be held:
_____ (Date) _____ (Time) _____ (Location)
☐ The debtor has filed a plan. The plan or a summary of the plan and notice of the confirmation hearing will be sent separately.
☐ The debtor has not filed a plan as of this date. Creditors will be given separate notice of the hearing on confirmation of the plan.

DISCHARGE OF DEBTS

Deadline to File a Complaint Objecting to Discharge of the Debtor or to Determine Dischargeability of Certain Types of Debts:

COMMENCEMENT OF CASE. A family farmer's debt adjustment case under chapter 12 of the Bankruptcy Code has been filed in this court by the family farmer named above as the debtor, and an order for relief has been entered. You will not receive notice of all documents filed in this case. All documents filed with the court, including lists of the debtor's property and debts, are available for inspection at the office of the clerk of the bankruptcy court.

CREDITORS MAY NOT TAKE CERTAIN ACTIONS. A creditor is anyone to whom the debtor owes money or property. Under the Bankruptcy Code, the debtor is granted certain protection against creditors. Common examples of prohibited actions by creditors are contacting the debtor to demand repayment, taking action against the debtor to collect money owed to creditors or to take property of the debtor, and starting or continuing foreclosure actions or repossessions. Some protection is also given to certain codebtors of consumers debts. If unauthorized actions are taken by a creditor against a debtor or a protected codebtor, the court may penalize that creditor. A creditor who is considering taking action against the debtor, the property of the debtor, or a codebtor, should review §§ 362 and 1201 of the Bankruptcy Code and may wish to seek legal advice. If the debtor is a partnership, remedies otherwise available against general partners are not necessarily affected by the commencement of this partnership case. The staff of the clerk of the bankruptcy court is not permitted to give legal advice.

MEETING OF CREDITORS. The debtor's representative, as specified in Bankruptcy Rule 9001(a)(5), is required to appear at the meeting of creditors on the date and at the place set forth above for the purpose of being examined under oath. Attendance by creditors at the meeting is welcomed, but not required. At the meeting, the creditors may examine the debtor and transact such other business as may properly come before the meeting. The meeting may be continued or adjourned from time to time by notice at the meeting, without further written notice to creditors.

DISCHARGE OF DEBTS. The debtor may seek a discharge of debts. A discharge means that certain debts are made unenforceable against the debtor. Creditors whose claims against the debtor are discharged may never take action against the debtor to collect the discharged debts. If a creditor believes a specific debt owed to the debtor is not dischargeable under § 523(a)(2), (4), or (6) of the Bankruptcy Code, timely action must be taken in the bankruptcy court by the deadline set forth above in the box labeled "Discharge of Debts." Creditors considering taking such action may wish to seek legal advice.

PROOF OF CLAIM. Except as otherwise provided by law, in order to share in any payment from the estate, a creditor must file a proof of claim by the date set forth above in the box labeled "Filing Claims." The place to file the proof of claim, either in person or by mail, is the office of the clerk of the bankruptcy court. Proof of claim forms are available in the clerk's office of any bankruptcy court.

PURPOSE OF A CHAPTER 12 FILING. Chapter 12 of the Bankruptcy Code enables family farmers to reorganize pursuant to a plan. A plan is not effective unless approved by the bankruptcy court at a confirmation hearing. Creditors will be given notice in the event the case is dismissed or converted to another chapter of the Bankruptcy Code.

Address of the Clerk of the Bankruptcy Court	For the Court:
	Clerk of the Bankruptcy Court
	Date

PROPOSED REVISED FORMS

<table>
<tr>
<td>

FORM B91
6-90
</td>
<td align="center">

United States Bankruptcy Court
</td>
<td>Case Number</td>
</tr>
</table>

——————————— District of ———————————

NOTICE OF COMMENCEMENT OF CASE UNDER CHAPTER 13 OF THE BANKRUPTCY CODE, MEETING OF CREDITORS, AND FIXING OF DATES

In re (Name of Debtor)	Address of Debtor	Soc. Sec./Tax Id. Nos.
	Date Case Filed (or Converted)	
Name and Address of Attorney for Debtor	Name and Address of Trustee	
Telephone Number		Telephone Number

☐ This is a converted case originally filed under chapter _____ on _____ (date).

FILING CLAIMS

Deadline to file a proof of claim

DATE, TIME, AND LOCATION OF MEETING OF CREDITORS

FILING OF PLAN AND DATE, TIME, AND LOCATION OF HEARING ON CONFIRMATION OF PLAN

☐ The debtor has filed a plan. The plan or a summary of the plan is enclosed. Hearing on confirmation will be held:
_____ (Date) _____ (Time) _____ (Location)

☐ The debtor has filed a plan. The plan or a summary of the plan and notice of the confirmation hearing will be sent separately.

☐ The debtor has not filed a plan as of this date. Creditors will be given separate notice of the hearing on confirmation of the plan.

COMMENCEMENT OF CASE. An individual's debt adjustment case under chapter 13 of the Bankruptcy Code has been filed in this court by the debtor or debtors named above, and an order for relief has been entered. You will not receive notice of all documents filed in this case. All documents filed with the court, including lists of the debtor's property and debts, are available for inspection at the office of the clerk of the bankruptcy court.

CREDITORS MAY NOT TAKE CERTAIN ACTIONS. A creditor is anyone to whom the debtor owes money. Under the Bankruptcy Code, the debtor is granted certain protection against creditors. Common examples of prohibited actions by creditors are contacting the debtor to demand repayment, taking action against the debtor to collect money owed to creditors or to take property of the debtor, and starting or continuing foreclosure actions, repossessions, or wage deductions. Some protection is also given to certain codebtors of consumer debts. If unauthorized actions are taken by a creditor against a debtor, or a protected codebtor, the court may punish that creditor. A creditor who is considering taking action against the debtor or the property of the debtor, or any codebtor, should review §§ 362 and 1301 of the Bankruptcy Code and may wish to seek legal advice. The staff of the clerk of the bankruptcy court is not permitted to give legal advice.

MEETING OF CREDITORS. The debtor (both husband and wife in a joint case) is required to appear at the meeting of creditors on the date and at the place set forth above in the box labeled "Date, Time, and Location of Meeting of Creditors" for the purpose of being examined under oath. Attendance by creditors at the meeting is welcome, but not required. At the meeting, the creditors may examine the debtor and transact such other business as may properly come before the meeting. The meeting may be continued or adjourned from time to time by notice at the meeting, without further written notice to creditors.

PROOF OF CLAIM. Except as otherwise provided by law, in order to share in any payment from the estate, a creditor must file a proof of claim by the date set forth above in the box labeled "Filing Claims." The place to file the proof of claim, either in person or by mail, is the office of the clerk of the bankruptcy court. Proof of claim forms are available in the clerk's office of any bankruptcy court.

PURPOSE OF A CHAPTER 13 FILING. Chapter 13 of the Bankruptcy Code is designed to enable a debtor to pay debts in full or in part over a period of time pursuant to a plan. A plan is not effective unless approved by the bankruptcy court at a confirmation hearing. Creditors will be given notice in the event the case is dismissed or converted to another chapter of the Bankruptcy Code.

Address of the Clerk of the Bankruptcy Court	For the Court:
	Clerk of the Bankruptcy Court
	Date

COMMITTEE NOTE

The form has been redesigned to facilitate electronic generation of notice to creditors concerning the filing of the petition, the meeting of creditors, and important deadlines in the case. Adoption of a box format, with significant dates highlighted, is intended to assist creditors who may be unfamiliar with bankruptcy cases to understand the data provided. Nine variations of the form, designated 9A through 9I, have been created to meet the specialized notice requirements for chapters 7, 11, 12, and 13, asset and no-asset cases, and the various types of debtors.

PROPOSED REVISED FORMS

(6/90)

United States Bankruptcy Court _____ District of _____	PROOF OF CLAIM
In re (Name of Debtor)	Case Number

NOTE This form should not be used to make a claim for an administrative expense arising after the commencement of the case. A request for payment of an administrative expense may be filed pursuant to 11 U.S.C. § 503.

Name of Creditor _(The person or other entity to whom the debtor owes money or property)_ **Name and Address Where Notices Should Be Sent** Telephone No.	☐ Check box if you are aware that anyone else has filed a proof of claim relating to your claim. Attach copy of statement giving particulars. ☐ Check box if you never received any notices from the bankruptcy court in this case. ☐ Check box if this address differs from the address on the envelope sent to you by the court. **THIS SPACE IS FOR COURT USE ONLY**

ACCOUNT OR OTHER NUMBER BY WHICH CREDITOR IDENTIFIES DEBTOR. Check here if this claim ☐ replaces ☐ amends } a previously filed claim dated _____

1. BASIS FOR CLAIM ☐ Goods sold ☐ Services performed ☐ Money loaned ☐ Personal injury/wrongful death ☐ Taxes ☐ Other (Describe briefly)	☐ Retiree benefits as defined in 11 U.S.C. § 1114(a) ☐ Wages, salaries, and commissions (Fill out below) Your social security number _____ Unpaid compensation for services performed from _____ to _____ (date) (date)
2. DATE DEBT WAS INCURRED	3. IF COURT JUDGMENT, DATE OBTAINED:

4. CLASSIFICATION OF CLAIM. Under the Bankruptcy Code all claims are classified as one or more of the following: (1) Unsecured nonpriority, (2) Unsecured Priority, (3) Secured. It is possible for part of a claim to be in one category and part in another. CHECK THE APPROPRIATE BOX OR BOXES that best describe your claim and STATE THE AMOUNT OF THE CLAIM.

☐ SECURED CLAIM $ _____ Attach evidence of perfection of security interest. Brief Description of Collateral: ☐ Real Estate ☐ Motor Vehicle ☐ Other (Describe briefly) Amount of arrearage and other charges included in secured claim above, if any $ _____ ☐ UNSECURED NONPRIORITY CLAIM $ _____ A claim is unsecured if there is no collateral or lien on property of the debtor securing the claim or to the extent that the value of such property is less than the amount of the claim.	☐ UNSECURED PRIORITY CLAIM $ _____ Specify the priority of the claim. ☐ Wages, salaries, or commissions (up to $2000, earned not more than 90 days before filing of the bankruptcy petition or cessation of the debtor's business, whichever is earlier)—11 U.S.C. § 507(a)(3) ☐ Contributions to an employee benefit plan—11 U.S.C. § 507(a)(4) ☐ Up to $900 of deposits toward purchase, lease, or rental of property or services for personal, family, or household use—11 U.S.C. § 507(a)(6) ☐ Taxes or penalties of governmental units—11 U.S.C. § 507(a)(7) ☐ Other—11 U.S.C. §§ 507(a)(2), (a)(5)—(Describe briefly)

5. TOTAL AMOUNT OF CLAIM AT TIME CASE FILED:	$ _____ (Unsecured)	$ _____ (Secured)	$ _____ Priority	$ _____ (Total)

☐ Check this box if claim includes prepetition charges in addition to the principal amount of the claim. Attach itemized statement of all additional charges.

THIS SPACE IS FOR COURT USE ONLY

6. CREDITS AND SETOFFS: The amount of all payments on this claim has been credited and deducted for the purpose of making this proof of claim. In filing this claim, claimant has deducted all amounts that claimant owes to debtor.

7. SUPPORTING DOCUMENTS: Attach copies of supporting documents, such as promissory notes, purchase orders, invoices, itemized statements of running accounts, contracts, court judgments, or evidence of security interests. If the documents are not available, explain. If the documents are voluminous, attach a summary.

8. TIME-STAMPED COPY: To receive an acknowledgment of the filing of your claim, enclose a stamped, self-addressed envelope and copy of this proof of claim.

Date	Sign and print the name and title, if any, of the creditor or other person authorized to file this claim (attach copy of power of attorney, if any)

Penalty for Presenting Fraudulent Claim: Fine of up to $500,000 or imprisonment for up to 5 years, or both. 18 U.S.C. §§ 152 and 3571.

COMMITTEE NOTE

This form replaces former Official Forms No. 19, No. 20, and No. 21. The box format and simplified language are intended to facilitate completion of the form.

The form directs the claimant to attach documents to support the claim or, if voluminous, a summary of such documents. These include any security agreement (if not included in the writing on which the claim is founded), and evidence of perfection of any security interest. See Committee Note to Rule 3001(d) concerning satisfactory evidence of perfection. If the claim includes prepetition interest or other charges such as attorney fees, a statement giving a detailed breakdown of the elements of the claim is required.

Rule 2002(g) requires the clerk to update the mailing list in the case by substituting the address provided by a creditor on a proof of claim, if that address is different from the one supplied by the debtor. The form contains checkboxes to assist the clerk in performing this duty. The form also alerts the trustee when the claim is an amendment to or replacement for an earlier claim.

847

PROPOSED REVISED FORMS

Form B11A
6/90

Form 11A. GENERAL POWER OF ATTORNEY

[Caption as in Form 16B]

GENERAL POWER OF ATTORNEY

To _____ of * _____, and
_____ of * _____.

The undersigned claimant hereby authorizes you, or any one of you, as attorney in fact for the undersigned and with full power of substitution, to vote on any question that may be lawfully submitted to creditors of the debtor in the above-entitled case; *[if appropriate]* to vote for a trustee of the estate of the debtor and for a committee of creditors; to receive dividends; and in general to perform any act not constituting the practice of law for the undersigned in all matters arising in this case.

Dated: _____

Signed: _____

By _____

as _____

Address: _____

_____

[If executed by an individual] Acknowledged before me on _____.

[If executed on behalf of a partnership] Acknowledged before me on _____
by _____, who says that he *[or she]* is a member of the partnership named above and is authorized to execute this power of attorney in its behalf.

[If executed on behalf of a corporation] Acknowledged before me on _____
by _____, who says that he *[or she]* is _____ of the corporation named above and is authorized to execute this power of attorney in its behalf.

_____

_____
[Official character.]

* State mailing address.

COMMITTEE NOTE

This form previously was numbered Official Form No. 17.

848

PROPOSED REVISED FORMS

Form B11B
4/90

Form 11B. SPECIAL POWER OF ATTORNEY

[Caption as in Form 16B]

SPECIAL POWER OF ATTORNEY

To _____ of * _____ , and
of * _____ .

    The undersigned claimant hereby authorizes you, or any one of you, as attorney in fact for the undersigned *[if desired:* and with full power of substitution,] to attend the meeting of creditors of the debtor or any adjournment thereof, and to vote in my behalf on any question that may be lawfully submitted to creditors at such meeting or adjourned meeting, and for a trustee or trustees of the estate of the debtor.

Dated: _____

                                    Signed: _____

                                      By _____

                                      as _____

                                  Address: _____

                                            _____

[If executed by an individual] Acknowledged before me on _____ .

    [If executed on behalf of a partnership] Acknowledged before me _____ ,
by _____ , who says that he [or she] is a member of the partnership named above and is authorized to execute this power of attorney in its behalf.

    [If executed on behalf of a corporation] Acknowledged before me on _____ ,
by _____ , who says that he [or she] is _____ of the corporation named above and is authorized to execute this power of attorney in its behalf.

                                      _____

                                      [Official character.]

* State mailing address.

COMMITTEE NOTE

This form previously was numbered Official Form No. 18.

849

PROPOSED REVISED FORMS

Form B12
6/90

Form 12. ORDER AND NOTICE FOR HEARING
ON DISCLOSURE STATEMENT

[Caption as in Form 16A]

ORDER AND NOTICE FOR HEARING
ON DISCLOSURE STATEMENT

To the debtor, its creditors, and other parties in interest:

   A disclosure statement and a plan under chapter 11 [or chapter 9] of the Bankruptcy Code having been filed by _____ on _____,
IT IS ORDERED and notice is hereby given, that:

   1. The hearing to consider the approval of the disclosure statement shall be held at: _____, on _____ at _____ o'clock ___.m.

   2. _____ is fixed as the last day for filing and serving in accordance with Fed. R. Bankr. P. 3017(a) written objections to the disclosure statement.

   3. Within _____ days after entry of this order, the disclosure statement and plan shall be distributed in accordance with Fed. R. Bankr. P. 3017(a).

   4. Requests for copies of the disclosure statement and plan shall be mailed to the debtor in possession [or trustee or debtor or _____] at * _____.

Dated: _____

                                                        BY THE COURT

                                        _____
* State mailing address   *United States Bankruptcy Judge*

COMMITTEE NOTE

   This form previously was numbered Official Form No. 28. The form is related to Rule 3017(a). Section 1125 of the Code requires court approval of a disclosure statement before votes may be solicited for or against a plan in either chapter 11 reorganization or chapter 9 municipality cases.

   Objections to the disclosure statement may be filed. Rule 3017(a) specifies that the court may fix a time for the filing of objections or they can be filed at any time prior to approval of the statement.

   Rule 3017(a) also specifies the persons who are to receive copies of the statement and plan prior to the hearing. These documents will not be sent to all parties in interest because at this stage of the case it could be unnecessarily expensive and confusing. However, any party in interest may request copies. The request should be made in writing (Rule 3017(a)), and sent to the person mailing the statement and plan which, as the form indicates, would usually be the proponent of the plan.

   This form may be adapted for use if more than one disclosure statement is to be considered by the court.

PROPOSED REVISED FORMS

Form B13
6/90

Form 13. ORDER APPROVING DISCLOSURE STATEMENT AND FIXING TIME FOR FILING ACCEPTANCES OR REJECTIONS OF PLAN, COMBINED WITH NOTICE THEREOF

[Caption as in Form 16A]

ORDER APPROVING DISCLOSURE STATEMENT AND FIXING TIME FOR FILING ACCEPTANCES OR REJECTIONS OF PLAN, COMBINED WITH NOTICE THEREOF

A disclosure statement under chapter 11 of the Bankruptcy Code having been filed by _____, on _____ [*if appropriate*, and by _____, on _____], referring to a plan under chapter 11 of the Code filed by _____, on _____ [*if appropriate*, and by _____, on _____ respectively] [*if appropriate*, as modified by a modification filed on _____]; and

It having been determined after hearing on notice that the disclosure statement [*or statements*] contains[s] adequate information:

IT IS ORDERED, and notice is hereby given, that:

A. The disclosure statement filed by _____ dated _____ [*if appropriate*, and by _____, dated _____ is [are] approved.

B. _____ is fixed as the last day for filing written acceptances or rejections of the plan [*or plans*] referred to above.

C. Within _____ days after the entry of this order, the plan [*or plans*] *or a summary or* summaries thereof approved by the court, [and [*if appropriate*] a summary approved by the court of its opinion, if any, dated _____, approving the disclosure statement [*or statements*]], the disclosure statement [*or statements*], and a ballot conforming to Official Form 14 shall be mailed to creditors, equity security holders, and other parties in interest, and shall be transmitted to the United States trustee, as provided in Fed. R. Bankr. P. 3017(d).

D. If acceptances are filed for more than one plan, preferences among the plans so accepted may be indicated.

E. *[If appropriate]* _____ is fixed for the hearing on confirmation of the plan [*or plans*].

F. *[If appropriate]* _____ is fixed as the last day for filing and serving pursuant to Fed. R. Bankr. P. 3020(b)(1) written objections to confirmation of the plan.

Dated: _____

BY THE COURT

_____
United States Bankruptcy Judge

[If the court directs that a copy of the opinion should be transmitted in lieu of or in addition to the summary thereof, the appropriate change should be made in paragraph C of this order.]

COMMITTEE NOTE

This form is derived from former Official Form No. 29. The form may be adapted for use if more than one disclosure statement is approved by the court.

PROPOSED REVISED FORMS

Form B14
6/90

Form 14. BALLOT FOR ACCEPTING OR REJECTING PLAN

[Caption as in Form 16A]

BALLOT FOR ACCEPTING OR REJECTING PLAN

Filed By _____
on *[date]* _____ .

The plan referred to in this ballot can be confirmed by the court and thereby made binding on you if it is accepted by the holders of two-thirds in amount and more than one-half in number of claims in each class and the holders of two-thirds in amount of equity security interests in each class voting on the plan. In the event the requisite acceptances are not obtained, the court may nevertheless confirm the plan if the court finds that the plan accords fair and equitable treatment to the class or classes rejecting it and otherwise satisfies the requirements of § 1129(b) of the Code. To have your vote count you must complete and return this ballot.

[If holder of general claim] The undersigned, a creditor of the above-named debtor in the unpaid principal amount of $ _____ .

[If bondholder, debenture holder, or other debt security holder] The undersigned, the holder of *[state unpaid principal amount]* $ _____ of *[describe security]* _____
of the above-named debtor, with a stated maturity date of _____ ,
[if applicable] registered in the name of _____ ,
[if applicable] bearing serial number(s) _____].

[If equity security holder] The undersigned, the holder of *[state number]* _____ shares
of *[describe type]* _____ stock of the above named debtor,
represented by Certificate(s) No. _____ , *[or held in my/our brokerage*
Account No. _____ at *[name of broker-dealer]* _____ ,

[Check One Box]

[ ] Accepts

[ ] Rejects

the plan for the reorganization of the above-named debtor proposed by
[name of proponent] _____ .

and *[if more than one plan is to be voted on]*

[ ] Accepts

[ ] Rejects

the plan for the reorganization of the above-named debtor proposed by
[name of proponent] _____ .

852

PROPOSED REVISED FORMS

[If more than one plan is accepted, the following may but need not be completed.] The undersigned prefers the plans accepted in the following order.

[Identify plans]

1. _____ .

2. _____ .

Dated: _____

Print or type name: _____

Signed: _____

[If appropriate] By: _____

as: _____

Address: _____

Return this ballot on or before _____ to: _____
                                (date)   (name)

Address: _____

_____

COMMITTEE NOTE

This form is derived from former Official Form No. 30. The form has been amended to facilitate the voting of a debtor's shares held in "street name." The form may be adapted to designate the class in which each ballot is to be tabulated. It is intended that a separate ballot will be provided for each class in which a holder may vote.

PROPOSED REVISED FORMS

Form B15
6/90

Form 15. ORDER CONFIRMING PLAN

[Caption as in Form 16A]

ORDER CONFIRMING PLAN

The plan under chapter 11 of the Bankruptcy Code filed by _____,
on _____ [*if applicable*, as modified by a modification filed on _____]
or a summary thereof, having been transmitted to creditors and equity security holders; and

It having been determined after hearing on notice that the requirements for confirmation set forth in
11 U.S.C. § 1129(a) [*or, if appropriate*, 11 U.S.C. § 1129(b)] have been satisfied;

IT IS ORDERED that:

The plan filed by _____, on _____, [*If*
appropriate, include dates and any other pertinent details of modifications to the plan] is confirmed.
A copy of the confirmed plan is attached.

Dated: _____

BY THE COURT

_____
United States Bankruptcy Judge.

COMMITTEE NOTE

This form is derived from former Official Form No. 31. The form
has been simplified to avoid the necessity of repeating the
statutory requirements of 11 U.S.C. § 1129(a). In the case of an
individual chapter 11 debtor, Form 18 may be adapted for use
together with this form.

854

PROPOSED REVISED FORMS

Form B16A
6/90

Form 16A. CAPTION (FULL)

UNITED STATES BANKRUPTCY COURT
_____DISTRICT OF_____

In re _____,)
    [Set forth here all names including married,)
    maiden, and trade names used by debtor within)
    last 6 years.])
                                Debtor)   Case No. _____
)
)   Chapter _____
)
Social Security No(s). _____ and all)
Employer's Tax Identification Nos. _[if any]_ _____)
               _____)

[Designation of Character of Paper]

COMMITTEE NOTE

This form has been transferred from former Official Form No. 1, which included the form of caption for the case. Rule 9004(b) requires a caption to set forth the title of the case. Rule 1005 provides that the title of the case shall include the debtor's name, all other names used by the debtor within six years before the commencement of the case, and the debtor's social security and tax identification numbers. This form of caption is prescribed for use on the petition, the notice of the meeting of creditors, the order of discharge, and the documents relating to a chapter 11 plan, (Official Forms 1, 9, 12, 13, 14, 15, and 18). See Rule 2002(m). In the petition, (Official Form 1), and the notice of the meeting of creditors, (Official Form 9), the information required by Rule 1005 appears in a block format. A notation of the chapter of the Bankruptcy Code under which the case is proceeding has been added to the form.

PROPOSED REVISED FORMS

Form B16B
6/90

Form 16B. CAPTION (SHORT TITLE)

UNITED STATES BANKRUPTCY COURT
_____ DISTRICT OF _____

In re _____,

                 Debtor   Case No. _____

                                    Chapter _____

[Designation of Character of Paper]

COMMITTEE NOTE

This form of caption is prescribed for general use in filing papers in a case under the Bankruptcy Code. Rule 9004(b) requires a caption to set forth the title of the case, and Rule 1005 specifies that the title must include all names used by the debtor within six years before the commencement of the case and the debtor's social security and tax identification numbers. This information is necessary in the petition, the notice of the meeting of creditors, the order of discharge, and the documents relating to the plan in a chapter 11 cases. See Rule 2002(m) and Official Form 16A. In other notices, motions, applications, and papers filed in a case, however, a short title containing simply the name of the debtor or joint debtors may be used. Additional names, such as any under which the debtor has engaged in business, may be included in the short title as needed.

PROPOSED REVISED FORMS

Form B16C
6/90

Form 16C. CAPTION OF ADVERSARY PROCEEDING

UNITED STATES BANKRUPTCY COURT
_____ DISTRICT OF _____

In re _____,
Debtor

Case No. _____

_____,
Plaintiff

Chapter _____

v.

_____,
Defendant

Adv. Proc. No. _____

COMPLAINT [*or other Designation*]

COMMITTEE NOTE

This form previously was numbered Official Form No. 34. A notation of the chapter of the Bankruptcy Code under which the case is proceeding has been added to the form. Rule 7010 refers to this form as providing the caption of a pleading in an adversary proceeding.

PROPOSED REVISED FORMS

Form B17
6/90

Form 17. NOTICE OF APPEAL TO A DISTRICT COURT OR BANKRUPTCY APPELLATE PANEL FROM A JUDGMENT OR OTHER FINAL ORDER OF A BANKRUPTCY COURT

[Caption as in Form 16A, 16B, or Form 16C, as appropriate]

NOTICE OF APPEAL

_____, the plaintiff *[or defendant or other party]* appeals to the district court *[or the bankruptcy appellate panel]*, from the final judgment *[or order or decree (describe)]* of the bankruptcy court entered in this adversary proceeding *[or other proceeding, describe type]* on the _____ day of _____, 19____.

The parties to the judgment *[or order or decree]* appealed from and the names and addresses of their respective attorneys are as follows:

_____

_____

Dated: _____

Signed: _____
                        Attorney for Appellant,

Address: _____

COMMITTEE NOTE

This form is derived from former Official Form No. 35. The form has been amended to indicate that a final order may be entered other than in an adversary proceeding.

PROPOSED REVISED FORMS

Form B18
6/90

Form 18. DISCHARGE OF DEBTOR

[Caption as in Form 16A]

DISCHARGE OF DEBTOR

It appearing that a petition commencing a case under title 11, United States Code, was filed by or against the person named above on _____, and that an order for relief was entered under chapter 7, and that no complaint objecting to the discharge of the debtor was filed within the time fixed by the court [*or* that a complaint objecting to discharge of the debtor was filed and, after due notice and hearing, was not sustained];

IT IS ORDERED that

1. The above-named debtor is released from all dischargeable debts.

2. Any judgment heretofore or hereafter obtained in any court other than this court is null and void as a determination of the personal liability of the debtor with respect to any of the following:

    (a) debts dischargeable under 11 U.S.C. § 523;

    (b) unless heretofore or hereafter determined by order of this court to be nondischargeable, debts alleged to be excepted from discharge under clauses (2), (4) and (6) of 11 U.S.C. § 523(a);

    (c) debts determined by this court to be discharged.

3. All creditors whose debts are discharged by this order and all creditors whose judgments are declared null and void by paragraph 2 above are enjoined from instituting or continuing any action or employing any process or engaging in any act to collect such debts as personal liabilities of the above-named debtor.

Dated: _____

BY THE COURT

_____
United States Bankruptcy Judge.

COMMITTEE NOTE

This form previously was numbered Official Form No. 27. The form has been revised to accommodate cases commenced by the filing of either a voluntary or an involuntary petition.

PROPOSED REVISED FORMS

Former Official Form Number

Form No. 1. Voluntary Petition
[Revised; see new Official Form 1.]

Form No. 2. Application and Order to Pay Filing Fee in Installments
[Renumbered; see new Official Form 3.]

Form No. 3. Order for Payment of Filing Fee in Installments
[Abrogated and combined with Form No. 2; see new Official Form 3.]

Form No. 4. Unsworn Declaration under Penalty of Perjury on Behalf of a Corporation or Partnership
[Renumbered; see new Official Form 2.]

Form No. 5. Certificate of Commencement of Case
[Abrogated.]

Form No. 6. Schedules of Assets and Liabilities
[Revised; see new Official Form 6.]

Form No. 6A. Schedule of Current Income and Current Expenditures for Individual Debtor
[Revised; see new Official Form 6, Schedules I and J.]

Form No. 7. Statement of Financial Affairs for Debtor Not Engaged in Business
[Revised and combined with former Form No. 8; see new Official Form 7.]

Form No. 8. Statement of Financial Affairs for Debtor Engaged in Business
[Revised and combined with former Form No. 7; see new Official Form 7.]

Form No. 8A. Chapter 7 Individual Debtor's Statement of Intention
[Renumbered; see new Official Form 8.]

Form No. 9. List of Creditors Holding 20 Largest Unsecured Claims
[Renumbered; see new Official Form 4.]

Form No. 10. Chapter 13 Statement
[Abrogated; see new Official Forms 6, 7, and 8.]

Form No. 11. Involuntary Case: Creditors' Petition
[Revised, combined with former Form No. 12, and renumbered; see new Official Form 5.]

PROPOSED REVISED FORMS

Form No. 12.   Involuntary Case Against Partnership; Partner's
Petition
[Abrogated and combined with former Form No. 11;
see new Official Form 5.]

Form No. 13.   Summons to Debtor
[Abrogated.]

Form No. 14.   Order for Relief
[Abrogated.]

Form No. 15.   Appointment of Committee of Unsecured Creditors in
Chapter 9 Municipality or Chapter 11 Reorgani-
zation Case
[Abrogated.]

Form No. 16.   Order for Meeting of Creditors and Related Orders,
Combined with Notice Thereof and of Automatic Stay
[Revised and renumbered; see new Official Form 9.]

Form No. 17.   General Power of Attorney
[Renumbered; see new Official Form 11A.]

Form No. 18.   Special Power of Attorney
[Renumbered; see new Official Form No. 11B.]

Form No. 19.   Proof of Claim
[Revised and renumbered; see new Official Form
10.]

Form No. 20.   Proof of Claim for Wages, Salary, or Commissions
[Abrogated and combined with former Form No. 19;
see new Official Form 10.]

Form No. 21.   Proof of Multiple Claims for Wages, Salary, or
Commissions
[Abrogated and combined with former Form No. 19;
see new Official Form No. 10.]

Form No. 22.   Order Appointing Interim Trustee and Fixing Amount
of Bond
[Abrogated.]

Form No. 23.   Order Approving Election of Trustee and Fixing
Amount of Bond
[Abrogated.]

Form No. 24.   Notice to Trustee of Selection and of Time Fixed
for Filing a Complaint Objecting to Discharge of
Debtor
[Abrogated.]

PROPOSED REVISED FORMS

Form No. 25. Bond and Order Approving Bond of Trustee
[Abrogated.]

Form No. 26. Certificate of Retention of Debtor in Possession
[Abrogated.]

Form No. 27. Discharge of Debtor
[Renumbered; see new Official Form 18.]

Form No. 28. Order and Notice for Hearing on Disclosure
Statement
[Renumbered; see new Official Form 12.]

Form No. 29. Order Approving Disclosure Statement and Fixing
Time for Filing Acceptances or Rejections of Plan,
Combined with Notice Thereof
[Renumbered; see new Official Form 13.]

Form No. 30. Ballot for Accepting or Rejecting Plan
[Renumbered; see new Official Form 14.]

Form No. 31. Order Confirming Plan
[Renumbered; see new Official Form 15.]

Form No. 32. Notice of Filing Final Account
[Abrogated.]

Form No. 33. Final Decree
[Abrogated.]

Form No. 34. Caption of Adversary Proceedings
[Renumbered; see new Official Form No. 16C.]

Form No. 35. Notice of Appeal to a District Court or Bankruptcy
Appellate Panel from a Judgment of a Bankruptcy
Court Entered in an Adversary Proceeding
[Revised and renumbered; see new Official Form
17.]

Note Concerning Continued Availability of Certain Abrogated Forms.

Forms No. 5, 13, 14, 26, 32 and 33, although abrogated as
Official Forms, continue to be available as procedural forms
issued by the Director of the Administrative Office of the United
States Courts. Members of the bar and the public may consult the
Bankruptcy Forms Manual, which is available in the clerk's office
at every bankruptcy court location. The contents of the Bankruptcy Forms Manual may be copied without restriction, subject to
any applicable copy fee charged by the clerk.

Forms No. 15, 22, 23, 24 and 25, also abrogated as Official
Forms, pertain to functions now performed by the United States
trustee. Any forms deemed necessary for carrying out those
functions will be issued by the Department of Justice.

TABLE 1

FORMER TITLE 11 U.S.C.—DISPOSITION

Showing disposition of all sections of former Title 11. The sections listed in the second column throughout this Table are sections of new Title 11, U.S.C., except as otherwise designated.

Former Title 11 Sections	New Title 11 Sections	Former Title 11 Sections	New Title 11 Sections
1(1) to (3)	Omitted	23(a)	Omitted
1(4)	See 101(12)	23(b)	See 303(b)
1(5) to (7)	Omitted	23(c) to (f)	Omitted
1(8)	101(8)	23(g)	See 723
1(9), (10)	Omitted	23(h) to (k)	Omitted
1(11)	See 101(9)	24	See 522
1(12), (13)	Omitted	25(a)(1)	See 343, 521(4)
1(14)	See 101(11)	25(a)(2)	Omitted
1(15), (16)	Omitted	25(a)(3)	See 521(2)
1(17)	See 101(17), (18)	25(a)(4)	See 521(3)
1(18)	Omitted	25(a)(5)	See 521(3)
1(19)	101(26)	25(a)(6)	See 521(2)
1(20) to (22)	Omitted	25(a)(7)	See 521(2)
1(23)	101(30)	25(a)(8)	See 521(1)
1(24)	See 101(31)	25(a)(9)	See 521(1)
1(25), (26)	Omitted	25(a)(10)	See 343, 344
1(27)	101(34)	25(a)(11)	See 521(3)
1(28), (29)	Omitted	25(b)	Omitted
1(29a)	101(38)	26	See 541(a)
1(30)	101(40)	27, 28	Omitted
1(31)	Omitted	29(a)	See 362
1(32)	See 101(24)	29(b) to (d)	Omitted
1(33), (34)	Omitted	29(e)	108(a), (b)
1(35)	See 102(7)	29(f)	See 108(c)
11(a)(1)	109(a)	30, 31 [Transferred, see sections 501 to 1103 below]	—
11(a)(2)	See 502(j)		
11(a)(2A)	505(a), (b)	32(a)	See 727(a)(10), 1141(d)(4)
11(a)(3), (4)	Omitted		
11(a)(5)	721	32(b)	See 727(c)
11(a)(6)	Omitted	32(c)(1)	727(a)(2), (4)
11(a)(7)	See 363	32(c)(2)	727(a)(3)
11(a)(8)	See 350	32(c)(3)	727(a)(4)
11(a)(9) to (14)	Omitted	32(c)(4)	727(a)(2)
11(a)(15)	105	32(c)(5)	See 727(a)(8), See 727(a)(9)
11(a)(16)	Omitted		
11(a)(17)	See 324	32(c)(6)	See 727(a)(6)
11(a)(18)	See 303(i)	32(c)(7)	See 727(a)(5)
11(a)(19), (20)	Omitted	32(c)(8)	Omitted
11(a)(21)	See 543(b), (c)	32(d), (e)	Omitted
11(a)(22)	See 305(a)(2)	32(f)	524(a)
11(b)	Omitted	32(g), (h)	Omitted
21	See 303(h)	33	See 727(d), (e), 1328(e)
22	See 109(b)		
22(a)	See 301	34	See 524(e)
22(b)	See 303(a)		

TABLE 1—DISPOSITION

Former Title 11 Sections	New Title 11 Sections	Former Title 11 Sections	New Title 11 Sections
35(a)(1)	See 523(a)(1)	78(m)	322(d)
35(a)(2)	523(a)(2)	78(n)	Omitted
35(a)(3)	523(a)(3)	79 to 81	Omitted
35(a)(4)	See 523(a)(4)	82 [Repealed]	—
35(a)(5), (6)	Omitted	91	See 341
35(a)(7)	See 523(a)(5)	92	See 341
35(a)(8)	See 523(a)(6)	93(a) to (c)	Omitted
35(b)	See 523(b), See 349(a)	93(d)	See 502(a), (c)
35(c)	See 523(c)	93(e)	Omitted
35(c)(4)	See 362	93(f)	See 502(b)
41(a)	Omitted	93(g)	502(d)
41(b)	See 303(d)	93(h)	See 506(a), (b)
41(c) to (e)	Omitted	93(i)	See 501(b), 509
41(f)	See 301	93(j)	See 724(a)
42	See T. 28 § 1480	93(k)	502(j)
43	Omitted	93(l), (m)	Omitted
44(a)	343	93(n)	See 501(a), 726(a)(3)
44(b) to (f)	Omitted	93a [Omitted]	—
44(g)	549(c)	94	See 342
44(h) to (l)	Omitted	95(a)	See 301
45 to 51	Omitted	95(b)	See 303(b)
52, 53 [Repealed]	—	95(c), (d)	Omitted
54	Omitted	95(e)	See 303(b)
55	See T. 28 § 1475	95(f)	See 303(c)
61 to 71	Omitted	95(g)	See 303(j), 707
72(a)	See 702	95(h)	Omitted
72(b)	705	96	See 547
72(c)	See 327(c)	96(a)(4)	See 547(e)(1)(B)
73	321	96(b)	See 550, 551
74	325, See 703(a)	96(c)	547(c)(4), See 553
75(a)(1)	704(1)	96(d)	329
75(a)(2)	See 345	96(e)(1)	See 741
75(a)(3)	704(2)	96(e)(2)	See 745, 751, 752
75(a)(4)	Omitted	96(e)(3)	See 753
75(a)(5)	704(2)	96(e)(5)	See 749
75(a)(6)	Omitted	101	345
75(a)(7)	See 704(3)	101a [Omitted]	—
75(a)(8)	704(4)	102(a)(1)	See 503(b)(2)
75(a)(9)	704(5)	102(a)(2) to (4)	Omitted
75(a)(10)	704(6)	102(b)	Omitted
75(a)(11), (12)	Omitted	102(c)	See 504
75(a)(13)	704(8)	102(d)	Omitted
75(a)(14)	Omitted	103	See 101(4)
75(b), (c)	Omitted	103(a)(9)	See 502(b)(7)
76(a), (b)	Omitted	103(c)	See 365
76(c)	326(a), See 330	103a [Omitted]	—
76(d)	Omitted	104(a)	See 507
76(e)	326(d)	104(a)(1)	503(b)
76(f), (g)	Omitted	104(a)(2)	507(a)(3)
76a	See 330	104(a)(4)	See 502(b)(4), 505(a), (b)
77	See 107	104(b) [Repealed]	—
78(a) [Repealed]	—	105(a) to (c)	Omitted
78(b)	322(a)	105(d)	See 508
78(c)	See 322(b)(1)	105(e)	Omitted
78(d)	See 322(b)(2)	106(a)	347(a)
78(e)	Omitted	106(b) [Repealed]	—
78(f)	See 322(b)(2)	107(a)	See 349(b), 547(b), (d), 551
78(g)	See 322(b)(2)		
78(h)	Omitted	107(b)	545
78(i)	322(c)	107(c)	545
78(j), (k)	Omitted	107(c)(1)(A)	545(1)
78(l) [Repealed]	—		

Former Title 11 Sections	New Title 11 Sections	Former Title 11 Sections	New Title 11 Sections
107(c)(1)(B)	545(2), See 546(b)	301 to 303 [Omitted]	—
107(c)(1)(C)	545(3), (4)	401 [as added Act, Aug. 16, 1937, c. 657, 50 Stat. 654. Omitted]	—
107(c)(2)	See 551		
107(c)(3)	See 724(b)		
107(d)(1)(a) to (c)	Omitted	401(1) [as added Pub. L. 94–260, § 1, Apr. 8, 1976, 90 Stat. 315]	See 101(4)
107(d)(1)(d)	See 101(26)		
107(d)(1)(e)	Omitted		
107(d)(2)	548(a)	401(2) [as added Pub. L. 94–260, § 1, Apr. 8, 1976, 90 Stat. 315]	Omitted
107(d)(3)	See 550		
107(d)(4)	548(b)		
107(d)(5)	548(d)(1)	401(3) [as added Pub. L. 94–260, § 1, Apr. 8, 1976, 90 Stat. 315]	See 101(9)
107(d)(6)	548(c), See 550, 551		
107(d)(7)	Omitted		
107(e), (f)	Omitted	401(4) [as added Pub. L. 94–260, § 1, Apr. 8, 1976, 90 Stat. 315]	Omitted
108	502(b)(3), See 553		
109(a)	See 303(e)		
109(b)	See 303(i)	401(5) [as added Pub. L. 94–260, § 1, Apr. 8, 1976, 90 Stat. 315]	See 101(11)
109(c)	Omitted		
109(d)	See 303(g), 543(b), (c)		
110(a)	See 541(a)	401(6) [as added Pub. L. 94–260, § 1, Apr. 8, 1976, 90 Stat. 315]	See 101(28)
110(a)(3)	See 541(b)		
110(a)(5)	See 522(d)(7), (8)		
110(b)	See 365	401(7) [as added Pub. L. 94–260, § 1, Apr. 8, 1976, 90 Stat. 315]	See 101(30)
110(c)	541(e), 544(a)		
110(d)(1)	549(a)		
110(d)(2)	See 542(c)	401(8) [as added Pub. L. 94–260, § 1, Apr. 8, 1976, 90 Stat. 315]	See 101(12)
110(d)(3)	See 542(c)		
110(d)(4), (5)	Omitted		
110(e)	544(b)	401(9) [as added Pub. L. 94–260, § 1, Apr. 8, 1976, 90 Stat. 315]	Omitted
110(f)	See 363		
110(g)	Omitted		
110(h) [Repealed]	—	401(10) [as added Pub. L. 94–260, § 1, Apr. 8, 1976, 90 Stat. 315]	902(2)
110(i)	Omitted		
111, 112	Omitted		
201, 202 [Transferred, see sections 501 to 1103 below]	—	401(11) [as added Pub. L. 94–260, § 1, Apr. 8, 1976, 90 Stat. 315]	902(3)
202a	Omitted		
203, 203a [Omitted]	—	402 [as added Act Aug. 16, 1937, c. 657, 50 Stat. 654. Omitted]	—
204 [Repealed]	—		
205(a)	Omitted		
205(b)	1171(b), See 1172	402(a) [as added Pub. L. 94–260, § 1, Apr. 8, 1976, 90 Stat. 316]	Omitted
205(c)(1)	See 1163		
205(c)(2)	See 1166		
205(c)(3) to (5)	Omitted		
205(c)(6)	1169		
205(c)(7) to (13)	Omitted	402(b)(1), (2) [as added Pub.L. 94–260, § 1, Apr. 8, 1976, 90 Stat. 316]	See 901
205(d)	Omitted		
205(e)	1173		
205(f) to (i)	Omitted		
205(j)	See 1168		
205(k), (l)	Omitted		
205(m)	101(33)		
205(n)	1167, See 1171(a)		
205(o)	See 1170		
205(p) to (s)	Omitted		
205a	Omitted		
206, 207 [Transferred, see sections 501 to 1103 below]	—		
208	Omitted		

TABLE 1—DISPOSITION

Former Title 11 Sections	New Title 11 Sections	Former Title 11 Sections	New Title 11 Sections
402(b)(3) [as added Pub.L. 94–260, § 1, Apr. 8, 1976, 90 Stat. 316]	Omitted	501, 502	Omitted
402(c) [as added Pub. L. 94–260, § 1, Apr. 8, 1976, 90 Stat. 316]	See 904	506(1)	See 101(4)
		506(2), (3)	Omitted
		506(4)	See 101(9)
		506(5)	See 101(12)
		506(6)	See 101(11)
		506(7)	Omitted
402(d) [as added Pub. L. 94–260, § 1, Apr. 8, 1976, 90 Stat. 316]	See 921(b)	506(8)	See 101(23)
		506(9)	See 101(31)
		506(10)	Omitted
403 [as added Act Aug. 16, 1937, c. 657, 50 Stat. 655. Omitted]	—	506(11)	See 101(35)
		506(12), (13)	Omitted
		507	See 1124
		511, 512	Omitted
403 [as added Pub.L. 94–260, § 1, Apr. 8, 1976, 90 Stat. 316]	903	513	See 362
		514, 515	Omitted
		516(1)	See 365
404 [as added Act Aug. 16, 1937, c. 657, 50 Stat. 659. Repealed]	—	516(2)	See 364
		516(3)	See 363
		516(4)	See 362
		516(5)	1110
		516(6)	1110
404 [as added Pub.L. 94–260, § 1, Apr. 8, 1976, 90 Stat. 317]	See 101(29), 109(c)	517	Omitted
		518 [Repealed]	—
405(a)	921(a), (c) to (f)	519 to 521	Omitted
405(b)	924, See 901	526	See 303(b)
405(c)	Omitted	527	Omitted
405(d)	See 923	528	See T. 28, § 1472
405(e)	See 901	529 to 533	Omitted
405(e)(1)	922(a)	536	See 303(d)
405(f), (g)	Omitted	537	See 303(d)
405(h)	926, See 901	541 to 549	Omitted
406, 407	Omitted	556	See 1104(a)
408(a)	See 925	557	See 327
408(b)	See 901	558	101(13)
408(c)	Omitted	559	See 1105
409	See 901	560	See 324, 1104(c)
410(a)	941, 942	561, 562	Omitted
410(b)	See 942	563	See 1107(a)
411	See 901	564	See 1106(a)(2)
412	See 901	565	Omitted
413	See 901, 943(a)	566	See 107
414(a)	See 901	567(1)	1106(a)(3)
414(b)(1)	943(b)(5), (6)	567(2)	Omitted
414(b)(2)	943(b)(2)	567(3)	1106(a)(4)(A)
414(b)(3)	Omitted	567(4)	Omitted
414(b)(4)	943(b)(3)	567(5)	1106(a)(4)
414(b)(5)	Omitted	567(6)	Omitted
414(b)(6)	943(b)(4)	568	See 1104(b), 1106(b)
415(a)	944(a)	569	1106(a)(5)
415(b)(1)	944(b)	570	See 1121
415(b)(2)	944(c)	571 to 574	Omitted
416(a)	Omitted	575	See 1125(d)
416(b)	See 901	576	See 1125(b)
416(c)	Omitted	577, 578	Omitted
416(d)	347(b), See 901	579	See 1126, 1128(a)
416(e)	945(a)	580	See 1128(b)
416(f)	Omitted	586	See 541(a)
417	946	587	See 1106
418	927	588	See 1107(a)
		589	See 1108
		590	Omitted

Former Title 11 Sections	New Title 11 Sections	Former Title 11 Sections	New Title 11 Sections
591	See 327	656 to 659	Omitted
596	See 501(a), 1111	661	See 108(c)
597	See 1122	662	Omitted
598	See 501(a)	663	See 362
599	1126(a)	664(a)	1145(a)
600, 601	Omitted	664(b)	1145(b)
602	See 502(b)(7)	665, 666	Omitted
603	See 1126(e)	667	1146(c)
604	See 1143	668	346(j)(1)
605	347(b)	669	See 1129(d)
606	1109(b)	670	346(j)(5)
607	See 1109	671, 672	Omitted
608	1109(a)	676	Omitted
609 to 613	Omitted	701, 702	Omitted
616(1)	See 1123(b)(1)	706(1), (2)	Omitted
616(2)	See 1123(a)(5), (b)(4)	706(3)	See 101(12), 109(d)
616(3)	Omitted	706(4)	Omitted
616(4)	See 1123(b)(2)	706(5)	See 101(31)
616(5)	See 1123(a)(3)	707(1)	See 101(9)
616(6)	See 1123(a)(2)	707(2)	See 101(4), (11)
616(7) to (9)	Omitted	708	See 1124
616(10)	1123(a)(5)	711, 712	Omitted
616(11)	1123(a)(7)	713(1)	See 365
616(12)(a)	1123(a)(6)	713(2)	See 363
616(12)(b)	Omitted	713(3)	Omitted
616(13)	See 1123(b)(3)	714	See 362
616(14)	See 1123(b)(5)	715, 716	Omitted
621(1)	See 1129(a)(1)	721 to 728	Omitted
621(2)	See 1129(a)(7), (11)	731 to 733	Omitted
621(3)	See 1129(a)(3)	734	See 341
621(4)	1129(a)(4)	735	See 341
621(5)	1129(a)(5)	735(3)	See 1128(a)
622	See 1127	736	See 341
623	See 1127(d)	736(2)	See 501(a)
624(1)	See 1141(a)	736(3)	See 343
624(2)	See 1129(a)(6), 1142(a)	737(1)	Omitted
624(3), (4)	Omitted	737(2)	See 1129(a)(9)
625	Omitted	737(3)	See 1128(a)
626	See 1141(c)	738	See 1102
627	See 1142(b)	739(1)(a)	See 1103(c)(2)
628(1)	See 1141(d)(1) to (3)	739(1)(b)	See 1103(c)(3)
628(2) to (4)	Omitted	739(1)(c)	See 1103(c)(3)
629(a)	1101(2)	739(1)(d)	See 1103(c)(3)
629(b)	Omitted	739(1)(e)	See 1103(c)(3)
629(c)	See 1127(b)	739(1)(f)	See 1104(c)(5)
636	See 1112(b)	739(2)	See 503(b)(4), 1103(a)
637	Omitted	741	Omitted
638	See 348	742	See 1107(a)
641(1), (2)	Omitted	743	See 1108
641(3)	See 330	744	See 364
641(4)	See 330	751	See 1122
641(5)	See 503(b)(4)	752	Omitted
642(1)	See 503(b)(3), (5)	753	See 502(b)(7)
642(2)	Omitted	754, 755 [Repealed]	—
642(3)	See 503(b)(4)	755a	See 501(a)
643	See 503(b)(3), (4)	756	Omitted
644(1)	See 330	757(1)	Omitted
644(2)	See 503(b)(4)	757(2)	See 1123(b)(2)
644(3)	See 330	757(3) to (7)	Omitted
644(4)	See 503(b)(3), (4)	757(8)	See 1123(b)(5)
645 to 650	Omitted	761	See 1129(a)(3)
		762	Omitted

TABLE 1—DISPOSITION

Former Title 11 Sections	New Title 11 Sections	Former Title 11 Sections	New Title 11 Sections
763	See 1127	844	See 1107(a)
764	See 1127(d)	845	See 1108
765	See 1127(c)	846	See 364
766(1)	See 1129(a)(1)	851	See 501(a), 1111
766(2)	See 1129(a)(7), (11)	852	See 1122
766(3)	See 1129(a)(2)	853	Omitted
766(4)	See 1129(a)(3)	854	See 501(a)
767(1)	See 1141(a)	855 to 857	Omitted
767(2) to (4)	Omitted	858	See 502(b)(7)
768 to 770	Omitted	859 [Repealed]	—
771	See 1141(d)(1) to (3)	861(1) to (3)	Omitted
772	Omitted	861(4)	See 1123(b)(2)
776	See 1112(b)	861(5), (6)	Omitted
777	See 1112(b)	861(7)	See 1123(b)(4)
778	See 348	861(8)	Omitted
779 to 781	Omitted	861(9)	See 1123(a)(3)
786	See 1144	861(10)	See 1123(a)(2)
787(1)	See 1127(b)	861(11)	Omitted
787(2)	See 1127(c)	861(12)	See 1123(a)(5)
787(3)	See 1127(d)	861(13)	See 1123(b)(5)
787(4)	Omitted	866	Omitted
791	See 108(c)	867	See 1129(a)(3)
792	Omitted	868	Omitted
793(a)	1145(a)	869	See 1127(a), (b)
793(b)	1145(b)	870	See 1127(d)
794	Omitted	871	See 1127(c)
795	346(j)(1)	872(1)	See 1129(a)(1)
796	346(j)(5)	872(2)	See 1129(a)(7), (11)
797	Omitted	872(3)	See 1129(a)(2)
799	Omitted	872(4)	See 1129(a)(3)
801, 802	Omitted	872(5)	See 1129(a)(4)
806(1)	Omitted	873(1)	See 1141(a)
806(2)	See 101(4)	873(2)	See 1142(a)
806(3), (4)	Omitted	873(3)	Omitted
806(5)	See 101(9)	874	See 1141(c)
806(6)	See 101(12), 109(d)	875	See 1142(b)
806(7)	See 101(11)	876	See 1141(d)(1) to (3)
806(8)	See 101(23)	877	Omitted
806(9)	See 101(31)	881	See 1112(b)
807	See 1124	882	See 1112(b)
811, 812	Omitted	883	See 348
813(1)	See 365	884 to 886	Omitted
813(2)	See 363	891(1)	Omitted
813(3)	Omitted	891(2), (3)	See 330
814	See 362	892(1)	See 503(b)(3)
815, 816	Omitted	892(2)	Omitted
821 to 827	Omitted	892(3)	See 503(b)(4)
828	See 362	893(1)	Omitted
831	Omitted	893(2)	See 503(b)(4)
832	See 1104(a)	893(3)	See 330
833	Omitted	893(4)	See 503(b)(4)
834	See 341	894 to 898	Omitted
835	See 341, 1128(a)	906 to 909	Omitted
836	See 341	911	See 1144
836(2)	See 501(a)	916	See 108(c)
836(3)	See 343	917	See 362
837(1)	See 1104(a)	918(a)	1145(a)
837(2)	Omitted	918(b)	1145(b)
837(3)	See 1128(a)	919	Omitted
841	Omitted	920	346(j)(1)
842	See 1106	921	See 1129(d)
843	See 348	922	346(j)(5)

FORMER TITLE 11 U.S.C.

Former Title 11 Sections	New Title 11 Sections	Former Title 11 Sections	New Title 11 Sections
923	Omitted	1046(3)	See 1322(a)(2)
926	Omitted	1046(4)	See 1322(a)(1)
1001, 1002	Omitted	1046(5)	See 1329(a)
1006(1)	See 101(4)	1046(6)	See 1322(b)(7)
1006(2)	See 101(9)	1046(7)	See 1322(b)(10)
1006(3)	See 101(12), 109(e)	1051	See 1325(a)(3)
1006(4)	See 101(11)	1052	Omitted
1006(5)	Omitted	1053	See 1323(a)
1006(6)	See 101(31)	1054	See 1323(c)
1006(7)	Omitted	1055	Omitted
1006(8)	See 101(24), 109(e)	1056(a)(1)	See 1325(a)(1)
1007	Omitted	1056(a)(2)	See 1325(a)(6)
1011, 1012	Omitted	1056(a)(3)	Omitted
1013(1)	See 365	1056(a)(4)	See 1325(a)(3)
1013(2)	Omitted	1056(b)	See 502(b)
1014	See 362	1057	See 1327(a)
1015, 1016	Omitted	1058	Omitted
1021 to 1026	Omitted	1059	See 1326(a)
1031	Omitted	1060	See 1328(a), (c), (d)
1032	See 341	1061	1328(b)
1033	See 341	1062	Omitted
1033(1)	See 343, 501(a)	1066	See 348, 1307
1033(2)	See 1321	1067	See 348
1033(5)	See 1324	1068, 1069	Omitted
1036	See 1303	1071	See 1330
1037	Omitted	1076	See 108(c)
1041, 1042	Omitted	1077 to 1079	Omitted
1043 [Repealed]	—	1080	See 1305(a)(1)
1044	Omitted	1086	Omitted
1046(1)	See 1322(b)(1)	1101 to 1103	Omitted
1046(2)	See 1322(b)(2)	1200 to 1255 [Omitted]	—

*

TABLE 2

NEW TITLE 11 U.S.C.—DERIVATION

Showing derivation of all sections of new Title 11, U.S.C. The sections listed in the second column throughout this Table are sections of former Title 11, except as otherwise designated.

New Title 11 Sections	Former Title 11 Sections	New Title 11 Sections	Former Title 11 Sections
101(1) to (3)	—	103	—
101(4)	See 103, 401(1), 506(1), 707(2), 806(2), 1006(1)	104	—
		105	11(a)(15)
101(5) to (7)	—	106	—
101(8)	1(8)	107	See 77 and 566
101(9)	See 1(11), 401(3), 506(4), 707(1), 806(5), 1006(2)	108(a)	29(e)
		108(b)	29(e)
		108(c)	See 29(f), 661, 791, 1076
101(10)	—	109(a)	11(a)(1)
101(11)	See 1(14), 401(5), 506(6), 707(2), 806(7), 1006(4)	109(b)	See 22
		109(c)	See 404
		109(d)	See 706(3), 806(6)
101(12)	See 1(4), 401(8), 506(5), 706(3), 806(6), 1006(3)	109(e)	See 1006(3), (8)
		301	See 22(a), 41(f), 95(a)
101(13)	558	302	—
101(14) to (16)	—	303(a)	See 22(b)
101(17)	See 1(17)	303(b)	See 23(b), 95(b) & (e), 526
101(18)	See 1(17)		
101(19) to (21)	—	303(c)	See 95(f)
101(22)	15 U.S.C. 77ccc(7)	303(d)	See 41(b), 536, 537
101(23)	See 506(8), 806(8)	303(e)	See 109(a)
101(24)	See 1(32), 1006(8)	303(f)	—
101(25)	—	303(g)	See 109(d)
101(26)	1(19), See 107(d)(1)(d)	303(h)	See 21
101(27)	—	303(i)	See 11(a)(18), 109(b)
101(28)	See 401(6)	303(j)	See 95(g)
101(29)	See 404	303(k)	—
101(30)	1(23), See 401(7)	304	—
101(31)	See 1(24), 506(9), 706(5), 806(9), 1006(6)	305(a)(1)	—
		305(a)(2)	See 11(a)(22)
101(32)	—	305(b), (c)	—
101(33)	205(m)	306	—
101(34)	1(27)	321	73, Bankruptcy Rule 209
101(35)	See 506(11)		
101(36)	See UCC 9–105(1)(l)	322(a)	78(b)
101(37)	See UCC 1–201(37)	322(b)(1)	See 78(c)
101(38)	1(29a)	322(b)(2)	See 78(d), (f) and (g)
101(39)	15 U.S.C. 78c(a)(4), (5)	322(c)	78(i)
		322(d)	78(m)
101(40)	1(30)	323	—
102(1) to (6)	—	324	See 11(a)(17), 560
102(7)	See 1(35)	325	74, Bankruptcy Rule 221(b)
102(8)	—		
		326(a)	76(c)

871

TABLE 2—DERIVATION

New Title 11 Sections	Former Title 11 Sections	New Title 11 Sections	Former Title 11 Sections
326(b), (c)	—	503(b)(4)	See 641(5), 642(3), 643, 644(2), (4), 739(2), 892(3), 893(2), (4)
326(d)	See 76(e)		
327	See 557, 591		
327(c)	See 72(c)		
328	—	503(b)(5)	See 642(1)
329	96(d)	504	See 102(c)
330	See 76(c), 76a, 641(3), (4), 644(1), (3), 891(2), (3), 893(3)	505(a), (b)	11(a)(2A), See 104(a)(4)
		505(c)	—
331	—	506(a), (b)	See 93(h)
341	See 91, 92, 734 to 736, 834 to 836, 1032, 1033	506(c), (d)	—
		507	See 104(a)
		507(a)(3)	104(a)(2)
342	See 94	508	See 105(d)
343	44(a), See 25(a)(1), (10), 736(3), 836(3), 1033(1)	509	See 93(i)
		510	—
		521(1)	See 25(a)(8), (9)
344	See 25(a)(10)	521(2)	See 25(a)(3), (6), (7)
345	101, See 75(a)(2)	521(3)	See 25(a)(4), (5), (11)
346(a) to (i)	—	521(4)	See 25(a)(1)
346(j)(1)	668, 795, 920	522	See 24
346(j)(2) to (4)	—	522(d)(1)	Uniform Exemptions Act 4, 5(1)
346(j)(5)	670, 796, 922		
346(j)(6), (7)	—	522(d)(2)	Uniform Exemptions Act 8(c)
347(a)	106(a)		
347(b)	416(d), 605	522(d)(3)	Uniform Exemptions Act 8(a)(1), (2)
348	See 638, 778, 843, 1066, 1067		
		522(d)(4)	Uniform Exemptions Act 8(b)
349(a)	See 35(b)		
349(b)	See 107(a)	522(d)(5)	Uniform Exemptions Act 8(d)
350	See 11(a)(8)		
361	—	522(d)(6)	Uniform Exemptions Act 8(c)
362	See 29(a), 35(c)(4), 513, 516(4), 663, 714, 814, 828, 917, 1014		
		522(d)(7)	Uniform Exemptions Act 7, See 110(a)(5)
363	See 11(a)(7), 110(f), 516(3), 713(2), 813(2)	522(d)(8)	Uniform Exemptions Act 7, See 110(a)(5)
364	See 516(2), 744, 846	522(d)(9)	Uniform Exemptions Act 5(2)
365	See 103(c), 110(b), 516(1), 713(1), 813(1), 1013(1)	522(d)(10)(A)	Uniform Exemptions Act 5(3)
		522(d)(10)(B)	Uniform Exemptions Act 5(5)
366	—	522(d)(10)(C)	Uniform Exemptions Act 6(a)(1)
501(a)	See 93(n), 596, 598, 736(2), 755a, 836(2), 851, 854, 1033(1)		
		522(d)(10)(D)	Uniform Exemptions Act 6(a)(2)
501(b)	See 93(i)		
501(c), (d)	—	522(d)(10)(E)	Uniform Exemptions Act 6(a)(5)
502(a)	See 93(d)		
502(b)	See 93(f), 1056(b)	522(d)(11)(A)	Uniform Exemptions Act 5(6)
502(b)(3)	108		
502(b)(4)	See 104(a)(4)	522(d)(11)(B)	Uniform Exemptions Act 6(a)(3)
502(b)(7)	See 103(a)(9), 602, 753, 858		
		522(d)(11)(C)	Uniform Exemptions Act 6(a)(4)
502(c)	See 93(d)		
502(d)	93(g)	522(d)(11)(D)	Uniform Exemptions Act 6(a)(3)
502(e) to (i)	—		
502(j)	93(k), See 11(a)(2)	522(d)(11)(E)	—
503(a)	—	523(a)(1)	See 35(a)(1)
503(b)	104(a)(1)	523(a)(2)	35(a)(2)
503(b)(2)	See 102(a)(1)	523(a)(3)	35(a)(3)
503(b)(3)	See 642(1), 643, 644(4), 892(1)	523(a)(4)	See 35(a)(4)

New Title 11 Sections	Former Title 11 Sections	New Title 11 Sections	Former Title 11 Sections
523(a)(5)	See 35(a)(7)	704(5)	75(a)(9)
523(a)(6)	See 35(a)(8)	704(6)	75(a)(10)
523(a)(7) to (9)	—	704(7)	—
523(b)	35(b)	704(8)	75(a)(13)
523(c)	See 35(c)	705	72(b)
523(d)	—	706	—
524(a)	32(f)	707	See 95(g)
524(b) to (d)	—	721	11(a)(5)
524(e)	See 34	722	—
525	—	723	See 23(g)
541(a)	See 26, 110(a), 586	724(a)	See 93(j)
541(b)	See 110(a)(3)	724(b)	See 107(c)(3)
541(c), (d)	—	724(c), (d)	—
541(e)	110(c)	725	—
542(a), (b)	—	726(a)(1), (2)	—
542(c)	See 110(d)(2), (3)	726(a)(3)	See 93(n)
542(d), (e)	—	726(a)(4) to (6)	—
543(a)	—	726(b), (c)	—
543(b)	See 11(a)(21), 109(d)	727(a)(1)	—
543(c)	See 11(a)(21), 109(d)	727(a)(2)	32(c)(1), (4)
543(d)	—	727(a)(3)	32(c)(2)
544(a)	110(c)	727(a)(4)	32(c)(1), (3)
544(b)	110(e)	727(a)(5)	See 32(c)(7)
545	107(b), (c)	727(a)(6)	See 32(c)(6)
545(1)	107(c)(1)(A)	727(a)(7)	—
545(2)	107(c)(1)(B)	727(a)(8)	32(c)(5)
545(3), (4)	107(c)(1)(C)	727(a)(9)	See 32(c)(5)
546(a)	—	727(a)(10)	See 32(a)
546(b)	See 107(c)(1)(B)	727(b)	—
546(c)	—	727(c)	See 32(b)
547	See 96	727(d)	See 33
547(b)	See 107(a)	727(e)	See 33
547(c)(4)	96(c)	728	—
547(d)	107(a)	741	See 96(e)(1)
547(e)(1)(B)	See 96(a)(4)	742 to 744	—
548(a)	107(d)(2)	745	See 96(e)(2)
548(b)	107(d)(4)	746 to 748	—
548(c)	107(d)(6)	749	See 96(e)(5)
548(d)(1)	107(d)(5)	750	—
548(d)(2)	—	751	See 96(e)(2)
549(a)	110(d)(1)	752	See 96(e)(2), (3)
549(b)	—	761 to 766	—
549(c)	44(g)	901	See 402(b)(1), (2),
549(d)	—		405(b), (e), (h), 408(b),
550	See 96(b), 107(d)(3), (6)		409, 411, 412, 413,
			414(a), 416(b), (d)
551	See 96(b), 107(a)(3), (c)(2), (d)(6), 110(e)(2)	902(1)	—
552	—	902(2)	401(10)
553	See 96(c), 108	902(3)	401(11)
554	—	902(4)	—
701	—	903	403
702	See 72(a)	904	See 402(c)
702(a)(2)	See Bankruptcy Rule 207(d)	921(a)	405(a)
		921(b)	See 402(d)
703(a)	See 74	921(c) to (f)	405(a)
703(b)	—	922(a)	405(e)(1)
703(c)	—	922(b)	—
704(1)	75(a)(1)	923	See 405(d)
704(2)	75(a)(3), (5)	924	405(b)
704(3)	See 75(a)(7)	925	See 408(a)
704(4)	75(a)(8)	926	405(h)
		927	418

TABLE 2—DERIVATION

New Title 11 Sections	Former Title 11 Sections	New Title 11 Sections	Former Title 11 Sections
941	410(a)	1123(b)(2)	See 616(4), 757(2), 861(4)
942	410(a), See 410(b)	1123(b)(3)	See 616(13)
943(a)	See 413	1123(b)(4)	See 616(2), 861(7)
943(b)(1)	—	1123(b)(5)	See 616(14), 757(8), 861(13)
943(b)(2)	414(b)(2)	1123(c)	—
943(b)(3)	414(b)(4)	1124	See 507, 708, 807
943(b)(4)	414(b)(6)	1125(a)	—
943(b)(5)	414(b)(1)	1125(b)	See 576
943(b)(6)	414(b)(1)	1125(c)	—
944(a)	415(a)	1125(d)	See 575
944(b)	415(b)(1)	1125(e)	—
944(c)	415(b)(2)	1126	See 579
945(a)	416(e)	1126(a)	599
945(b)	—	1126(e)	603
946	417	1127	See 622, 763
1101(1)	—	1127(a)	See 869
1101(2)	629(a)	1127(b)	See 629(c), 787(1), 869
1102	See 738	1127(c)	See 765, 787(2), (3), 871
1103(a)	See 739(2)		
1103(b)	—	1127(d)	See 623, 764, 870
1103(c)(1)	—	1128(a)	See 579, 735(3), 737(3), 835, 837(3)
1103(c)(2)	See 739(1)(a)		
1103(c)(3)	See 739(1)(b) to (e)	1128(b)	See 580
1103(c)(4)	—	1129(a)(1)	See 621(1), 766(1), 872(1)
1103(c)(5)	See 739(1)(f)		
1103(d)	—	1129(a)(2)	See 766(3), 872(3)
1104(a)	See 556, 832, 837(1)	1129(a)(3)	See 621(3), 761, 766(4), 867, 872(4)
1104(b)	See 568		
1104(c)	See 560	1129(a)(4)	621(4), See 872(5)
1105	See 559	1129(a)(5)	621(5)
1106	See 587, 842	1129(a)(6)	See 624(2)
1106(a)(2)	See 564	1129(a)(7)	See 621(2), 766(2), 872(2)
1106(a)(3)	567(1)		
1106(a)(4)	567(5)	1129(a)(8)	—
1106(a)(4)(A)	567(3)	1129(a)(9)	See 737(2)
1106(a)(5)	569	1129(a)(10)	—
1106(b)	See 568	1129(a)(11)	See 621(2), 766(2), 872(2)
1107(a)	See 563, 588, 742, 844		
		1129(b), (c)	—
1107(b)	—	1129(d)	See 669, 921
1108	See 589, 743, 845	1141(a)	See 624(1), 767(1), 873(1)
1109	See 607		
1109(a)	608	1141(b)	—
1109(b)	606	1141(c)	See 626, 874
1110	516(5), (6)	1141(d)(1)–(3)	See 628(1), 771, 876
1111	See 596, 851	1141(d)(4)	See 32(a)
1112(a)	—	1142(a)	See 624(2), 873(2)
1112(b)	See 636, 776, 777, 881, 882	1142(b)	See 627, 875
		1143	See 604
1112(c) to (e)	—	1144	See 786, 911
1121	See 570	1145(a)	664(a), 793(a), 918(a)
1122	See 597, 751 and 852	1145(b)	664(b), 793(b), 918(b)
1123(a)(1)	—	1145(c), (d)	—
1123(a)(2)	See 616(6), 861(10)	1146(a), (b)	—
1123(a)(3)	See 616(5), 861(9)	1146(c)	667
1123(a)(4)	—	1146(d)	—
1123(a)(5)	616(10), See 616(2), 861(12)	1161, 1162	—
1123(a)(6)	616(12)(a)	1163	See 205(c)(1)
1123(a)(7)	616(11)	1164, 1165	—
1123(b)(1)	See 616(1)		

New Title 11 Sections	Former Title 11 Sections	New Title 11 Sections	Former Title 11 Sections
1166	See 205(c)(2)	1322(b)(7)	See 1046(6)
1167	205(n)	1322(b)(8), (9)	—
1168	See 205(j)	1322(b)(10)	See 1046(7)
1169	205(c)(6)	1322(c)	—
1170	See 205(o)	1323(a)	See 1053
1171(a)	See 205(n)	1323(b)	—
1171(b)	205(b)	1323(c)	See 1054
1172	See 205(b)	1324	See 1033(5)
1173	205(e)	1325(a)(1)	See 1056(a)(1)
1174	—	1325(a)(2)	—
1301	—	1325(a)(3)	See 1051, 1056(a)(4)
1302	—	1325(a)(4), (5)	—
1303	See 1036	1325(a)(6)	See 1056(a)(2)
1304	—	1325(b)	—
1305(a)(1)	See 1080	1326(a)	See 1059
1305(a)(2)	—	1326(b)	—
1305(b), (c)	—	1327(a)	See 1057
1306	—	1327(b), (c)	—
1307	See 1066	1328(a)	See 1060
1321	See 1033(2)	1328(b)	1061
1322(a)(1)	See 1046(4)	1328(c), (d)	See 1060
1322(a)(2)	See 1046(3)	1328(e)	See 33
1322(a)(3)	—	1329(a)	See 1046(5)
1322(b)(1)	See 1046(1)	1329(b), (c)	—
1322(b)(2)	See 1046(2)	1330	See 1071
1322(b)(3) to (6)	—	1501 to 151326	—

*

TABLE 3

BANKRUPTCY ACT OF 1898—
DISPOSITION

Showing disposition of sections of the Bankruptcy Act of July 1, 1898, as amended, to former Title 11 U.S.C. and to the new Title 11 U.S.C.

Bankr. Act Sections	Former Title 11 Sections	New Title 11 Sections
1(1) to (3)	1(1) to (3)	Omitted
1(4)	1(4)	See 101(12)
1(5) to (7)	1(5) to (7)	Omitted
1(8)	1(8)	101(8)
1(9), (10)	1(9), (10)	Omitted
1(11)	1(11)	See 101(9)
1(12), (13)	1(12), (13)	Omitted
1(14)	1(14)	See 101(11)
1(15), (16)	1(15), (16)	Omitted
1(17)	1(17)	See 101(17), (18)
1(18)	1(18)	Omitted
1(19)	1(19)	101(26)
1(20) to (22)	1(20) to (22)	Omitted
1(23)	1(23)	101(30)
1(24)	1(24)	See 101(31)
1(25), (26)	1(25), (26)	Omitted
1(27)	1(27)	101(34)
1(28), (29)	1(28), (29)	Omitted
1(29a)	1(29a)	101(38)
1(30)	1(30)	101(40)
1(31)	1(31)	Omitted
1(32)	1(32)	See 101(24)
1(33), (34)	1(33), (34)	Omitted
1(35)	1(35)	See 102(7)
2a(1)	11(a)(1)	109(a)
2a(2)	11(a)(2)	See 502(j)
2a(2A)	11(a)(2A)	505(a), (b)
2a(3), (4)	11(a)(3), (4)	Omitted
2a(5)	11(a)(5)	721
2a(6)	11(a)(6)	Omitted
2a(7)	11(a)(7)	See 363
2a(8)	11(a)(8)	See 350
2a(9) to (14)	11(a)(9) to (14)	Omitted
2a(15)	11(a)(15)	105
2a(16)	11(a)(16)	Omitted
2a(17)	11(a)(17)	See 324

TABLE 3—DISPOSITION

Bankr. Act Sections	Former Title 11 Sections	New Title 11 Sections
2a(18)	11(a)(18)	See 303(i)
2a(19), (20)	11(a)(19), (20)	Omitted
2a(21)	11(a)(21)	See 543(b), (c)
2a(22)	11(a)(22)	See 305(a)(2)
2b	11(b)	Omitted
3	21	See 303(h)
4	22	See 109(b)
4a	22(a)	See 301
4b	22(b)	See 303(a)
5a	23(a)	Omitted
5b	23(b)	See 303(b)
5c to f	23(c) to (f)	Omitted
5g	23(g)	See 723
5h to k	23(h) to (k)	Omitted
6	24	See 522
7a(1)	25(a)(1)	See 343, 521(4)
7a(2)	25(a)(2)	Omitted
7a(3)	25(a)(3)	See 521(2)
7a(4)	25(a)(4)	See 521(3)
7a(5)	25(a)(5)	See 521(3)
7a(6)	25(a)(6)	See 521(2)
7a(7)	25(a)(7)	See 521(2)
7a(8)	25(a)(8)	See 521(1)
7a(9)	25(a)(9)	See 521(1)
7a(10)	25(a)(10)	See 343, 344
7a(11)	25(a)(11)	See 521(3)
7b	25(b)	Omitted
8	26	See 541(a)
9, 10	27, 28	Omitted
11a	29(a)	See 362
11b to d	29(b) to (d)	Omitted
11e	29(e)	108(a), (b)
11f	29(f)	See 108(c)
12, 13	30, 31 [Transferred, see sections 501 to 1103 below]	—
14a	32(a)	See 727(a)(10), 1141(d)(4)
14b	32(b)	See 727(c)
14c(1)	32(c)(1)	727(a)(2), (4)
14c(2)	32(c)(2)	727(a)(3)
14c(3)	32(c)(3)	727(a)(4)
14c(4)	32(c)(4)	727(a)(2)
14c(5)	32(c)(5)	727(a)(8), See 727(a)(9)
14c(6)	32(c)(6)	See 727(a)(6)
14c(7)	32(c)(7)	See 727(a)(5)
14c(8)	32(c)(8)	Omitted
14d, e	32(d), (e)	Omitted
14f	32(f)	524(a)
14g, h	32(g), (h)	Omitted
15	33	See 727(d), (e), 1328(e)
16	34	See 524(e)
17a(1)	35(a)(1)	See 523(a)(1)
17a(2)	35(a)(2)	523(a)(2)
17a(3)	35(a)(3)	523(a)(3)
17a(4)	35(a)(4)	See 523(a)(4)
17a(5), (6)	35(a)(5), (6)	Omitted
17a(7)	35(a)(7)	See 523(a)(5)

BANKRUPTCY ACT OF 1898

Bankr. Act Sections	Former Title 11 Sections	New Title 11 Sections
17a(8)	35(a)(8)	See 523(a)(6)
17b	35(b)	523(b), See 349(a)
17c	35(c)	See 523(c)
17c(4)	35(c)(4)	See 362
18a	41(a)	Omitted
18b	41(b)	See 303(d)
18c to e	41(c) to (e)	Omitted
18f	41(f)	See 301
19	42	See T. 28 § 1480
20	43	Omitted
21a	44(a)	343
21b to f	44(b) to (f)	Omitted
21g	44(g)	549(c)
21h to l	44(h) to (l)	Omitted
22 to 28	45 to 51	Omitted
29, 30	52, 53 [Repealed]	—
31	54	Omitted
32	55	See T. 28 § 1475
33 to 43	61 to 71	Omitted
44a	72(a)	See 702
44b	72(b)	705
44c	72(c)	See 327(c)
45	73	321
46	74	325, See 703(a)
47a(1)	75(a)(1)	704(1)
47a(2)	75(a)(2)	See 345
47a(3)	75(a)(3)	704(2)
47a(4)	75(a)(4)	Omitted
47a(5)	75(a)(5)	704(2)
47a(6)	75(a)(6)	Omitted
47a(7)	75(a)(7)	See 704(3)
47a(8)	75(a)(8)	704(4)
47a(9)	75(a)(9)	704(5)
47a(10)	75(a)(10)	704(6)
47a(11), (12)	75(a)(11), (12)	Omitted
47a(13)	75(a)(13)	704(8)
47a(14)	75(a)(14)	Omitted
47b, c	75(b), (c)	Omitted
48a, b	76(a), (b)	Omitted
48c	76(c)	326(a), See 330
48d	76(d)	Omitted
48e	76(e)	326(d)
48f, g	76(f), (g)	Omitted
49	77	See 107
50a	78(a) [Repealed]	—
50b	78(b)	322(a)
50c	78(c)	See 322(b)(1)
50d	78(d)	See 322(b)(2)
50e	78(e)	Omitted
50f	78(f)	See 322(b)(2)
50g	78(g)	See 322(b)(2)
50h	78(h)	Omitted
50i	78(i)	322(c)
50j, k	78(j), (k)	Omitted
50l	78(l) [Repealed]	—
50m	78(m)	322(d)

TABLE 3—DISPOSITION

Bankr. Act Sections	Former Title 11 Sections	New Title 11 Sections
50n	78(n)	Omitted
51 to 53	79 to 81	Omitted
54	82 [Repealed]	—
55	91	See 341
56	92	See 341
57a to c	93(a) to (c)	Omitted
57d	93(d)	See 502(a), (c)
57e	93(e)	Omitted
57f	93(f)	See 502(b)
57g	93(g)	502(d)
57h	93(h)	See 506(a), (b)
57i	93(i)	See 501(b), 509
57j	93(j)	See 724(a)
57k	93(k)	502(j)
57l, m	93(l), (m)	Omitted
57n	93(n)	See 501(a), 726(a)(3)
58	94	See 342
59a	95(a)	See 301
59b	95(b)	See 303(b)
59c, d	95(c), (d)	Omitted
59e	95(e)	See 303(b)
59f	95(f)	See 303(c)
59g	95(g)	See 303(j), 707
59h	95(h)	Omitted
60	96	See 547
60a(4)	96(a)(4)	See 547(e)(1)(B)
60b	96(b)	See 550, 551
60c	96(c)	547(c)(4), See 553
60d	96(d)	329
60e(1)	96(e)(1)	See 741
60e(2)	96(e)(2)	See 745, 751, 752
60e(3)	96(e)(3)	See 753
60e(5)	96(e)(5)	See 749
61	101	345
62a(1)	102(a)(1)	See 503(b)(2)
62a(2) to (4)	102(a)(2) to (4)	Omitted
62b	102(b)	Omitted
62c	102(c)	See 504
62d	102(d)	Omitted
63	103	See 101(4)
63a(9)	103(a)(9)	See 502(b)(7)
63c	103(c)	See 365
64a	104(a)	See 507
64a(1)	104(a)(1)	503(b)
64a(2)	104(a)(2)	507(a)(3)
64a(4)	104(a)(4)	See 502(b)(4), 505(a), (b)
64b	104(b) [Repealed]	—
65a to c	105(a) to (c)	Omitted
65d	105(d)	See 508
65e	105(e)	Omitted
66a	106(a)	347(a)
66b	106(b) [Repealed]	—
67a	107(a)	See 349(b), 547(b), (d), 551
67b	107(b)	545
67c	107(c)	545
67c(1)(A)	107(c)(1)(A)	545(1)

Bankr. Act Sections	Former Title 11 Sections	New Title 11 Sections
67c(1)(B)	107(c)(1)(B)	545(2), See 546(b)
67c(1)(C)	107(c)(1)(C)	545(3), (4)
67c(2)	107(c)(2)	See 551
67c(3)	107(c)(3)	See 724(b)
67d(1)(a) to (c)	107(d)(1)(a) to (c)	Omitted
67d(1)(d)	107(d)(1)(d)	See 101(26)
67d(1)(e)	107(d)(1)(e)	Omitted
67d(2)	107(d)(2)	548(a)
67d(3)	107(d)(3)	See 550
67d(4)	107(d)(4)	548(b)
67d(5)	107(d)(5)	548(d)(1)
67d(6)	107(d)(6)	548(c), See 550, 551
67d(7)	107(d)(7)	Omitted
67e, f	107(e), (f)	Omitted
68	108	502(b)(3), See 553
69a	109(a)	See 303(e)
69b	109(b)	See 303(i)
69c	109(c)	Omitted
69d	109(d)	See 303(g), 543(b), (c)
70a	110(a)	See 541(a)
70a(3)	110(a)(3)	See 541(b)
70a(5)	110(a)(5)	See 522(d)(7), (8)
70b	110(b)	See 365
70c	110(c)	541(e), 544(a)
70d(1)	110(d)(1)	549(a)
70d(2)	110(d)(2)	See 542(c)
70d(3)	110(d)(3)	See 542(c)
70d(4), (5)	110(d)(4), (5)	Omitted
70e	110(e)	544(b)
70f	110(f)	See 363
70g	110(g)	Omitted
70h	110(h) [Repealed]	—
70i	110(i)	Omitted
71, 72	111, 112	Omitted
73, 74	201, 202 [Transferred, see sections 501 to 1103 below]	—
75	203 [Omitted]	—
76	204 [Repealed]	—
77(a)	205(a)	Omitted
77(b)	205(b)	1171(b), See 1172
77(c)(1)	205(c)(1)	See 1163
77(c)(2)	205(c)(2)	See 1166
77(c)(3) to (5)	205(c)(3) to (5)	Omitted
77(c)(6)	205(c)(6)	1169
77(c)(7) to (13)	205(c)(7) to (13)	Omitted
77(d)	205(d)	Omitted
77(e)	205(e)	1173
77(f) to (i)	205(f) to (i)	Omitted
77(j)	205(j)	See 1168
77(k), (l)	205(k), (l)	Omitted
77(m)	205(m)	101(33)
77(n)	205(n)	1167, See 1171(a)
77(o)	205(o)	See 1170
77(p) to (s)	205(p) to (s)	Omitted
77A, 77B	206, 207 [Transferred, see sections 501 to 1103 below]	—

TABLE 3—DISPOSITION

Bankr. Act Sections	Former Title 11 Sections	New Title 11 Sections
78 to 80	301 to 303 [Omitted]	—
81 [as added Act Aug. 16, 1937, c. 657, 50 Stat. 654]	401 [Omitted]	—
81(1) [as added Pub.L. 94–260, § 1, Apr. 8, 1976, 90 Stat. 315]	401(1)	See 101(4)
81(2) [as added Pub.L. 94–260, § 1, Apr. 8, 1976, 90 Stat. 315]	401(2)	Omitted
81(3) [as added Pub.L. 94–260, § 1, Apr. 8, 1976, 90 Stat. 315]	401(3)	See 101(9)
81(4) [as added Pub.L. 94–260, § 1, Apr. 8, 1976, 90 Stat. 315]	401(4)	Omitted
81(5) [as added Pub.L. 94–260, § 1, Apr. 8, 1976, 90 Stat. 315]	401(5)	See 101(11)
81(6) [as added Pub.L. 94–260, § 1, Apr. 8, 1976, 90 Stat. 315]	401(6)	See 101(28)
81(7) [as added Pub.L. 94–260, § 1, Apr. 8, 1976, 90 Stat. 315]	401(7)	See 101(30)
81(8) [as added Pub.L. 94–260, § 1, Apr. 8, 1976, 90 Stat. 315]	401(8)	See 101(12)
81(9) [as added Pub.L. 94–260, § 1, Apr. 8, 1976, 90 Stat. 315]	401(9)	Omitted
81(10) [as added Pub.L. 94–260, § 1, Apr. 8, 1976, 90 Stat. 315]	401(10)	902(2)
81(11) [as added Pub.L. 94–260, § 1, Apr. 8, 1976, 90 Stat. 315]	401(11)	902(3)
82 [as added Act Aug. 16, 1937, c. 657, 50 Stat. 654]	402 [Omitted]	—
82(a) [as added Pub.L. 94–260, § 1, Apr. 8, 1976, 90 Stat. 316]	402(a)	Omitted
82(b)(1), (2) [as added Pub. L. 94–260, § 1, Apr. 8, 1976, 90 Stat. 316]	402(b)(1), (2)	See 901
82(b)(3) [as added Pub.L. 94–260, § 1, Apr. 8, 1976, 90 Stat. 316]	402(b)(3)	Omitted
82(c) [as added Pub.L. 94–260, § 1, Apr. 8, 1976, 90 Stat. 316]	402(c)	See 904
82(d) [as added Pub.L. 94–260, § 1, Apr. 8, 1976, 90 Stat. 316]	402(d)	See 921(b)

Bankr. Act Sections	Former Title 11 Sections	New Title 11 Sections
83 [as added Act Aug. 16, 1937, c. 657, 50 Stat. 655]	403 [Omitted]	—
83 [as added Pub.L. 94–260, § 1, Apr. 8, 1976, 90 Stat. 316]	403	903
84 [as added Act Aug. 16, 1937, c. 657, 50 Stat. 659]	404 [Repealed]	—
84 [as added Pub.L. 94–260, § 1, Apr. 8, 1976, 90 Stat. 317]	404	See 101(29), 109(c)
85(a)	405(a)	921(a), (c) to (f)
85(b)	405(b)	924, See 901
85(c)	405(c)	Omitted
85(d)	405(d)	See 923
85(e)	405(e)	See 901
85(e)(1)	405(e)(1)	922(a)
85(f), (g)	405(f), (g)	Omitted
85(h)	405(h)	926, See 901
86, 87	406, 407	Omitted
88(a)	408(a)	See 925
88(b)	408(b)	See 901
88(c)	408(c)	Omitted
89	409	See 901
90(a)	410(a)	941, 942
90(b)	410(b)	See 942
91	411	See 901
92	412	See 901
93	413	See 901, 943(a)
94(a)	414(a)	See 901
94(b)(1)	414(b)(1)	943(b)(5), (6)
94(b)(2)	414(b)(2)	943(b)(2)
94(b)(3)	414(b)(3)	Omitted
94(b)(4)	414(b)(4)	943(b)(3)
94(b)(5)	414(b)(5)	Omitted
94(b)(6)	414(b)(6)	943(b)(4)
95(a)	415(a)	944(a)
95(b)(1)	415(b)(1)	944(b)
95(b)(2)	415(b)(2)	944(c)
96(a)	416(a)	Omitted
96(b)	416(b)	See 901
96(c)	416(c)	Omitted
96(d)	416(d)	347(b), See 901
96(e)	416(e)	945(a)
96(f)	416(f)	Omitted
97	417	946
98	418	927
101, 102	501, 502	Omitted
106(1)	506(1)	See 101(4)
106(2), (3)	506(2), (3)	Omitted
106(4)	506(4)	See 101(9)
106(5)	506(5)	See 101(12)
106(6)	506(6)	See 101(11)
106(7)	506(7)	Omitted
106(8)	506(8)	See 101(23)

TABLE 3—DISPOSITION

Bankr. Act Sections	Former Title 11 Sections	New Title 11 Sections
106(9)	506(9)	See 101(31)
106(10)	506(10)	Omitted
106(11)	506(11)	See 101(35)
106(12), (13)	506(12), (13)	Omitted
107	507	See 1124
111, 112	511, 512	Omitted
113	513	See 362
114, 115	514, 515	Omitted
116(1)	516(1)	See 365
116(2)	516(2)	See 364
116(3)	516(3)	See 363
116(4)	516(4)	See 362
116(5)	516(5)	1110
116(6)	516(6)	1110
117	517	Omitted
118	518 [Repealed]	—
119 to 121	519 to 521	Omitted
126	526	See 303(b)
127	527	Omitted
128	528	See T. 28, § 1472
129 to 133	529 to 533	Omitted
136	536	See 303(d)
137	537	See 303(d)
141 to 149	541 to 549	Omitted
156	556	See 1104(a)
157	557	See 327
158	558	101(13)
159	559	See 1105
160	560	See 324, 1104(c)
161, 162	561, 562	Omitted
163	563	See 1107(a)
164	564	See 1106(a)(2)
165	565	Omitted
166	566	See 107
167(1)	567(1)	1106(a)(3)
167(2)	567(2)	Omitted
167(3)	567(3)	1106(a)(4)(A)
167(4)	567(4)	Omitted
167(5)	567(5)	1106(a)(4)
167(6)	567(6)	Omitted
168	568	See 1104(b), 1106(b)
169	569	1106(a)(5)
170	570	See 1121
171 to 174	571 to 574	Omitted
175	575	See 1125(d)
176	576	See 1125(b)
177, 178	577, 578	Omitted
179	579	See 1126, 1128(a)
180	580	See 1128(b)
186	586	See 541(a)
187	587	See 1106
188	588	See 1107(a)
189	589	See 1108
190	590	Omitted
191	591	See 327
196	596	See 501(a), 1111

BANKRUPTCY ACT OF 1898

Bankr. Act Sections	Former Title 11 Sections	New Title 11 Sections
197	597	See 1122
198	598	See 501(a)
199	599	1126(a)
200, 201	600, 601	Omitted
202	602	See 502(b)(7)
203	603	See 1126(e)
204	604	See 1143
205	605	347(b)
206	606	1109(b)
207	607	See 1109
208	608	1109(a)
209 to 213	609 to 613	Omitted
216(1)	616(1)	See 1123(b)(1)
216(2)	616(2)	See 1123(a)(5), (b)(4)
216(3)	616(3)	Omitted
216(4)	616(4)	See 1123(b)(2)
216(5)	616(5)	See 1123(a)(3)
216(6)	616(6)	See 1123(a)(2)
216(7) to (9)	616(7) to (9)	Omitted
216(10)	616(10)	1123(a)(5)
216(11)	616(11)	1123(a)(7)
216(12)(a)	616(12)(a)	1123(a)(6)
216(12)(b)	616(12)(b)	Omitted
216(13)	616(13)	See 1123(b)(3)
216(14)	616(14)	See 1123(b)(5)
221(1)	621(1)	See 1129(a)(1)
221(2)	621(2)	See 1129(a)(7), (11)
221(3)	621(3)	See 1129(a)(3)
221(4)	621(4)	1129(a)(4)
221(5)	621(5)	1129(a)(5)
222	622	See 1127
223	623	See 1127(d)
224(1)	624(1)	See 1141(a)
224(2)	624(2)	See 1129(a)(6), 1142(a)
224(3), (4)	624(3), (4)	Omitted
225	625	Omitted
226	626	See 1141(c)
227	627	See 1142(b)
228(1)	628(1)	See 1141(d)(1) to (3)
228(2) to (4)	628(2) to (4)	Omitted
229(a)	629(a)	1101(2)
229(b)	629(b)	Omitted
229(c)	629(c)	See 1127(b)
236	636	See 1112(b)
237	637	Omitted
238	638	See 348
241(1), (2)	641(1), (2)	Omitted
241(3)	641(3)	See 330
241(4)	641(4)	See 330
241(5)	641(5)	See 503(b)(4)
242(1)	642(1)	See 503(b)(3), (5)
242(2)	642(2)	Omitted
242(3)	642(3)	See 503(b)(4)
243	643	See 503(b)(3), (4)
244(1)	644(1)	See 330
244(2)	644(2)	See 503(b)(4)

TABLE 3—DISPOSITION

Bankr. Act Sections	Former Title 11 Sections	New Title 11 Sections
244(3)	644(3)	See 330
244(4)	644(4)	See 503(b)(3), (4)
245 to 250	645 to 650	Omitted
256 to 259	656 to 659	Omitted
261	661	See 108(c)
262	662	Omitted
263	663	See 362
264(a)	664(a)	1145(a)
264(b)	664(b)	1145(b)
265, 266	665, 666	Omitted
267	667	1146(c)
268	668	346(j)(1)
269	669	See 1129(d)
270	670	346(j)(5)
271, 272	671, 672	Omitted
276	676	Omitted
301, 302	701, 702	Omitted
306(1), (2)	706(1), (2)	Omitted
306(3)	706(3)	See 101(12), 109(d)
306(4)	706(4)	Omitted
306(5)	706(5)	See 101(31)
307(1)	707(1)	See 101(9)
307(2)	707(2)	See 104(4), (11)
308	708	See 1124
311, 312	711, 712	Omitted
313(1)	713(1)	See 365
313(2)	713(2)	See 363
313(3)	713(3)	Omitted
314	714	See 362
315, 316	715, 716	Omitted
321 to 328	721 to 728	Omitted
331 to 333	731 to 733	Omitted
334	734	See 341
335	735	See 341
335(3)	735(3)	See 1128(a)
336	736	See 341
336(2)	736(2)	See 501(a)
336(3)	736(3)	See 343
337(1)	737(1)	Omitted
337(2)	737(2)	See 1129(a)(9)
337(3)	737(3)	See 1128(a)
338	738	See 1102
339(1)(a)	739(1)(a)	See 1103(c)(2)
339(1)(b)	739(1)(b)	See 1103(c)(3)
339(1)(c)	739(1)(c)	See 1103(c)(3)
339(1)(d)	739(1)(d)	See 1103(c)(3)
339(1)(e)	739(1)(e)	See 1103(c)(3)
339(1)(f)	739(1)(f)	See 1104(c)(5)
339(2)	739(2)	See 503(b)(4), 1103(a)
341	741	Omitted
342	742	See 1107(a)
343	743	See 1108
344	744	See 364
351	751	See 1122
352	752	Omitted
353	753	See 502(b)(7)

Bankr. Act Sections	Former Title 11 Sections	New Title 11 Sections
354	754 [Repealed]	—
354 [formerly 355]	755 [Repealed]	—
355	755a	See 501(a)
356	756	Omitted
357(1)	757(1)	Omitted
357(2)	757(2)	See 1123(b)(2)
357(3) to (7)	757(3) to (7)	Omitted
357(8)	757(8)	See 1123(b)(5)
361	761	See 1129(a)(3)
362	762	Omitted
363	763	See 1127
364	764	See 1127(d)
365	765	See 1127(c)
366(1)	766(1)	See 1129(a)(1)
366(2)	766(2)	See 1129(a)(7), (11)
366(3)	766(3)	See 1129(a)(2)
366(4)	766(4)	See 1129(a)(3)
367(1)	767(1)	See 1141(a)
367(2) to (4)	767(2) to (4)	Omitted
368 to 370	768 to 770	Omitted
371	771	See 1141(d)(1) to (3)
372	772	Omitted
376	776	See 1112(b)
377	777	See 1112(b)
378	778	See 348
379 to 381	779 to 781	Omitted
386	786	See 1144
387(1)	787(1)	See 1127(b)
387(2)	787(2)	See 1127(c)
387(3)	787(3)	See 1127(d)
387(4)	787(4)	Omitted
391	791	See 108(c)
392	792	Omitted
393(a)	793(a)	1145(a)
393(b)	793(b)	1145(b)
394	794	Omitted
395	795	346(j)(1)
396	796	346(j)(5)
397	797	Omitted
399	799	Omitted
401, 402	801, 802	Omitted
406(1)	806(1)	Omitted
406(2)	806(2)	See 101(4)
406(3), (4)	806(3), (4)	Omitted
406(5)	806(5)	See 101(9)
406(6)	806(6)	See 101(12), 109(d)
406(7)	806(7)	See 101(11)
406(8)	806(8)	See 101(23)
406(9)	806(9)	See 101(31)
407	807	See 1124
411, 412	811, 812	Omitted
413(1)	813(1)	See 365
413(2)	813(2)	See 363
413(3)	813(3)	Omitted
414	814	See 362
415, 416	815, 816	Omitted

TABLE 3—DISPOSITION

Bankr. Act Sections	Former Title 11 Sections	New Title 11 Sections
421 to 427	821 to 827	Omitted
428	828	See 362
431	831	Omitted
432	832	See 1104(a)
433	833	Omitted
434	834	See 341
435	835	See 341, 1128(a)
436	836	See 341
436(2)	836(2)	See 501(a)
436(3)	836(3)	See 343
437(1)	837(1)	See 1104(a)
437(2)	837(2)	Omitted
437(3)	837(3)	See 1128(a)
441	841	Omitted
442	842	See 1106
443	843	See 348
444	844	See 1107(a)
445	845	See 1108
446	846	See 364
451	851	See 501(a), 1111
452	852	See 1122
453	853	Omitted
454	854	See 501(a)
455 to 457	855 to 857	Omitted
458	858	See 502(b)(7)
459	859 [Repealed]	—
461(1) to (3)	861(1) to (3)	Omitted
461(4)	861(4)	See 1123(b)(2)
461(5), (6)	861(5), (6)	Omitted
461(7)	861(7)	See 1123(b)(4)
461(8)	861(8)	Omitted
461(9)	861(9)	See 1123(a)(3)
461(10)	861(10)	See 1123(a)(2)
461(11)	861(11)	Omitted
461(12)	861(12)	See 1123(a)(5)
461(13)	861(13)	See 1123(b)(5)
466	866	Omitted
467	867	See 1129(a)(3)
468	868	Omitted
469	869	See 1127(a), (b)
470	870	See 1127(d)
471	871	See 1127(c)
472(1)	872(1)	See 1129(a)(1)
472(2)	872(2)	See 1129(a)(7), (11)
472(3)	872(3)	See 1129(a)(2)
472(4)	872(4)	See 1129(a)(3)
472(5)	872(5)	See 1129(a)(4)
473(1)	873(1)	See 1141(a)
473(2)	873(2)	See 1142(a)
473(3)	873(3)	Omitted
474	874	See 1141(c)
475	875	See 1142(b)
476	876	See 1141(d)(1) to (3)
477	877	Omitted
481	881	See 1112(b)
482	882	See 1112(b)

Bankr. Act Sections	Former Title 11 Sections	New Title 11 Sections
483	883	See 348
484 to 486	884 to 886	Omitted
491(1)	891(1)	Omitted
491(2), (3)	891(2), (3)	See 330
492(1)	892(1)	See 503(b)(3)
492(2)	892(2)	Omitted
492(3)	892(3)	See 503(b)(4)
493(1)	893(1)	Omitted
493(2)	893(2)	See 503(b)(4)
493(3)	893(3)	See 330
493(4)	893(4)	See 503(b)(4)
494 to 498	894 to 898	Omitted
506 to 509	906 to 909	Omitted
511	911	See 1144
516	916	See 108(c)
517	917	See 362
518(a)	918(a)	1145(a)
518(b)	918(b)	1145(b)
519	919	Omitted
520	920	346(j)(1)
521	921	See 1129(d)
522	922	346(j)(5)
523	923	Omitted
526	926	Omitted
601, 602	1001, 1002	Omitted
606(1)	1006(1)	See 101(4)
606(2)	1006(2)	See 101(a)
606(3)	1006(3)	See 101(12), 109(e)
606(4)	1006(4)	See 101(11)
606(5)	1006(5)	Omitted
606(6)	1006(6)	See 101(31)
606(7)	1006(7)	Omitted
606(8)	1006(8)	See 101(24), 109(e)
607	1007	Omitted
611, 612	1011, 1012	Omitted
613(1)	1013(1)	See 365
613(2)	1013(2)	Omitted
614	1014	See 362
615, 616	1015, 1016	Omitted
621 to 626	1021 to 1026	Omitted
631	1031	Omitted
632	1032	See 341
633	1033	See 341
633(1)	1033(1)	See 343, 501(a)
633(2)	1033(2)	See 1321
633(5)	1033(5)	See 1324
636	1036	See 1303
637	1037	Omitted
641, 642	1041, 1042	Omitted
643	1043 [Repealed]	—
643 [formerly 644]	1044	Omitted
646(1)	1046(1)	See 1322(b)(1)
646(2)	1046(2)	See 1322(b)(2)
646(3)	1046(3)	See 1322(a)(2)
646(4)	1046(4)	See 1322(a)(1)
646(5)	1046(5)	See 1329(a)

TABLE 3—DISPOSITION

Bankr. Act Sections	Former Title 11 Sections	New Title 11 Sections
646(6)	1046(6)	See 1322(b)(7)
646(7)	1046(7)	See 1322(b)(10)
651	1051	See 1325(a)(3)
652	1052	Omitted
653	1053	See 1323(a)
654	1054	See 1323(c)
655	1055	Omitted
656(a)(1)	1056(a)(1)	See 1325(a)(1)
656(a)(2)	1056(a)(2)	See 1325(a)(6)
656(a)(3)	1056(a)(3)	Omitted
656(a)(4)	1056(a)(4)	See 1325(a)(3)
656(b)	1056(b)	See 502(b)
657	1057	See 1327(a)
658	1058	Omitted
659	1059	See 1326(a)
660	1060	See 1328(a), (c), (d)
661	1061	1328(b)
662	1062	Omitted
666	1066	See 348, 1307
667	1067	See 348
668, 669	1068, 1069	Omitted
671	1071	See 1330
676	1076	See 108(c)
677 to 679	1077 to 1079	Omitted
680	1080	See 1305(a)(1)
686	1086	Omitted
700	1200 [Omitted]	—
701 to 703	1101 to 1103	Omitted
705 to 755	1205 to 1255 [Omitted]	—

TABLE 4

FORMER BANKRUPTCY RULES
AND FORMS

DISPOSITION

Showing disposition of former bankruptcy rules and Forms prescribed by the Supreme Court on April 24, 1973, March 18, 1974, April 28, 1975, and April 26, 1976. The rules and forms listed in the second column throughout this table are rules and forms of the new Bankruptcy Rules and Official Forms prescribed by the Supreme Court on April 25, 1983, except as otherwise designated.

Former Title 1 Bankr.Rule	New Bankr. Rule	Former Title 1 Bankr.Rule	New Bankr. Rule
1	See 1001	202	Omitted
101	Omitted	203	See 2002
102	Omitted	204	See 2003
103	See 1002	205(a)	2004(a)
104(a)	See 1003(a), (b)	205(b)	See 2003(b)(1)
104(b), (c)	Omitted	205(c)	See 2003(b)(1)
104(d)	1003(c)	205(d)	2004(b)
104(e)	See 1003(d)	205(e)	See 2004(c)
105	1004	205(f)	2004(d)
106	See 1005	205(g)	2004(e)
107	1006	206	2005
108	1007	207	See 2003(b)(3)
109	See 1008	208	2006
110	1009	209(a)	See 2003(b)(1)
111	1010	209(b)	See T. 11 § 703(c)
112	1011	209(c)	2008
113	Omitted	209(d)	See T. 11 § 321
114	1012	210	2009
115(a)	1013(a)	211	Omitted
115(b)	See 9015	212(a)	See T. 11 § 322(a)
115(c)	1013(b)	212(b)	See 2010(a)
115(d)	See 1013(c)	212(c)	Omitted
115(e)	See T. 11 § 303(i)	212(d)	See 2010(b)
116(a)	See T. 28 § 1472	212(e)	See T. 11 § 322(b)
116(b)	1014(a)	212(f)	2010(d)
116(c)	1014(b)	212(g)	See 2010(c)
116(d)	Omitted	213	2013
117(a)	1015(a)	214	See T. 11 § 705
117(b)	See 1015(b)	215(a)	2014(a)
117(c)	See 1015(c)	215(b)	See T. 11 § 328(c)
118	1016	215(c)	See T. 11 § 327(c)
119	See T. 11 § 305(a)(2)	215(d)	See T. 11 § 327(b)
120(a)	1017(a)	215(e)	See T. 11 § 327(d)
120(b)	1017(b)	215(f)	2014(b)
120(c)	See T. 11 § 349	216	See T. 11 § 721
121	See 1018	217	Omitted
122	1019	218	2015
201	2001	219(a)	2016(a)

TABLE 4—DISPOSITION

Former Title 1 Bankr.Rule	New Bankr. Rule	Former Title 1 Bankr.Rule	New Bankr. Rule
219(b)	2016(b)	601(a)	See T. 11 § 362(a)
219(c)	See T. 11 § 330(a)	601(b)	See T. 11 § 362(c)
219(d)	See T. 11 § 504	601(c)	See T. 11 § 362(d)
220	2017	601(d)	4001(c)
221(a)	See T. 11 § 324(a)	601(e)	Omitted
221(b)	See 2012	602(a)	See T. 11 § 549(c)
301(a)	3001(a), (b)	602(b)	See T. 11 § 542(c)
301(b)	3001(f)	603	6001
302(a)	See 3002(a)	604	See 6002
302(b)	3002(b)	605(a)	See T. 11 § 704(1)
302(c)	3001(c)	605(b)	See T. 11 § 345(a)
302(d)	3001(e)	605(c)	6003
302(e)	3002(c)	606(a)	See T. 11 § 327
303	3004	606(b)	6004(e)
304	3005	606(c)	6005
305	3006	607	See 6006
306(a)	T. 11 § 704(4)	608	See 6007
306(b)	T. 11 § 502(a)	609	6008
306(c)	3007	610	6009
306(d)	See 3012	611	See T. 11 § 551
307	3008	612	6010
308	3009	701	See 7001
309	See 3010	703	See 7003
310	3011	704(a)	See 7004(a)
401(a)	See T. 11 § 362(a)	704(b)	See 7004(a)
401(b)	See T. 11 § 362(c)	704(c)	7004(b)
401(c)	See T. 11 § 362(e)	704(d)(1)	See 7004(a)
401(d)	See T. 11 § 362(d)	704(d)(2)	7004(c)
401(e)	Omitted	704(e)	7004(f)
402	See 4002	704(f)	See 7004(d)
403	4003	704(g)	See 7004(a)
404	4004	704(h)	See 7004(a)
405	See T. 11 §§ 727(a)(10), 1141(d)(4)	704(i)	See 7004(a)
406	Omitted	705	See 7005
407	See 4005	707	See 7007
408	See 4006	708	See 7008
409(a)(1)	See 4007(a), (b)	709	See 7009
409(a)(2)	See 4007(c)	710	See 7010
409(b)	Omitted	712(a)	7012(a)
409(c)	See 9015	712(b)	See 7012(b)
409(d)	See 4007(e)	713	See 7013
501	See 5001	714	See 7014
502, 503	Omitted	715	See 7015
504	5003	716	See 7016
505(a)	5002	717	See 7017
505(b)	See 5004(a)	718	See 7018
505(c)	See 5004(b)	719	See 7019
506	Omitted	720	See 7020
507	5003	721	See 7021
508	Omitted	722	See 7022
509(a), (b)	See 5005(a)	723	See 7023
509(c)	5005(b)	723.1	See 7023.1
510	See 5006	723.2	See 7023.2
511(a)	See 5007(a)	724	See 7024
511(b)	See 5007(b)	725	See 7025
511(c)	5007(c)	726	See 7026
512	5008(c) to (h)	727	See 7027
513	Omitted	728	See 7028
514	See 5009	729	See 7029
515	See 5010	730	See 7030
		731	See 7031
		732	See 7032

Former Title 1 Bankr.Rule	New Bankr. Rule
733	See 7033
734	See 7034
735	See 7035
736	See 7036
737	See 7037
741	See 7041
742	See 7042
744.1	Abrogated
752	See 7052
754	See 7054
755	See 7055
756	See 7056
762	See 7062
764	See 7064
765	See 7065
767	See 7067
768	See 7068
769	See 7069
770	See 7070
771	See 7071
782	See 7087
801	See 8001
802(a)	See 8002(a)
802(b)	See 8002(b)
802(c)	8002(c)
803	Omitted
804	See 8004
805	8005
806	See 8006
807	8007(b)
808	See 8009
809	See 8012
810	See 8013
811	See 8014
812	See 8015
813	See 8016
814	See 8019
901	See 9001
902	See 9002
903	1001 (last sentence)
904	See 9004
905	See 9005
906	See 9006
907	See 9007
908	See 9008
909	See 9009
910	9010
911	See 9011
912	See 9012
913	See T. 28 § 2256
914	See 9014
915(a)	See 1011(b)
915(b)	Omitted
916	See 9016
917	See 9017
918	See 9018
919	9019(a), (c)
920	9020
921	See 9021
922	See 9022
923	See 9023
924	See 9024

Former Title 1 Bankr.Rule	New Bankr. Rule
925	See 9025
926	See 9026
927	See 9029
928	See 9030

Former Titles II to VII Bankr.Rule	New Bankr. Rule
8–1	See 1001
8–101	Omitted
8–102	See 1002
8–103(a)	See 1003(a), (b)(1)
8–103(b)	See 1003(c)
8–103(c)	See 1003(d)
8–104	See 1005
8–105	See 1006
8–106	1007
8–107	See 1008
8–108	See 1009
8–109	See 1010
8–110	See 1011
8–111(a) to (c)	See 1013
8–111(d)	See T. 11 § 303(i)
8–112(a)	See T. 28 § 1472
8–112(b)	See 1014(a)
8–112(c)	See 1014(b)
8–112(d)	Omitted
8–113	See 1015
8–114	See T. 11 § 305(a)(2)
8–115	See 7001 et seq.
8–201	See 2001
8–202(a)	See T. 11 § 1163
8–202(b)	Omitted
8–202(c)	See T. 11 § 321
8–202(d)	Omitted
8–202(e)	See 2008
8–202(f)	See 2012; T. 11 § 1105
8–202(g)	Omitted
8–203	See 2009
8–204(a)	See T. 11 § 322(a)
8–204(b)	See T. 11 § 322(b)
8–204(c)	See 2010(d); T. 11 § 322(d)
8–204(d)	See 2010(c)
8–205	See 2012
8–206(a)	See 2014(a)
8–206(b)	See T. 11 § 328(c)
8–206(c)	Omitted
8–207	See T. 11 §§ 1107, 1108
8–208	See T. 11 § 1106
8–209	See 2002
8–210	2018
8–211	See 2019
8–212(a)	See 2016(a)
8–212(b)	See T. 11 § 330(a)
8–212(c)	See T. 11 § 330(a)
8–212(d)	See 2016(b)
8–212(e)	See T. 11 § 504
8–213	See 2017
8–214(a)	See 2004(a)

TABLE 4—DISPOSITION

Former Titles II to VII Bankr.Rule	New Bankr. Rule	Former Titles II to VII Bankr.Rule	New Bankr. Rule
8–214(b)	See 2003(b)(1)	8–510	See 6004; T. 11 § 363
8–214(c)	See 2004(b)	8–511	See 6007
8–214(d)	See 2004(c)	8–512	See 6007; T. 11 § 1170
8–214(e)	See 2004(d)	8–513	Omitted
8–214(f)	See 2004(e)	8–514(a)	See 9019(a)
8–215	See 2005	8–514(b)	9019(b)
8–301	See 3016	8–514(c)	See 9019(c)
8–302	See 3013	8–515	See 6008
8–303	Omitted	8–516	See 6009
8–304	See 3017	8–517	See T. 11 § 551
8–305(a)	See 3018(a)	8–601	See 7001
8–305(b)	See 3016; T. 11 § 1125	8–602(a)	See 7003 to 7087
8–306	See 3018	8–602(b)	Omitted
8–307	See 3020	8–701	See 9001
8–308	Omitted	8–702	See 9002
8–309(a)	See T. 11 § 1142(b)	8–703	Omitted
8–309(b)	See 3022	8–704	Omitted
8–310	See 1017(a); T. 11 § 1112(b)	8–705	See 9014
8–401(a)	See 3003(b)	8–706	See 9010
8–401(b)	See 3003(c)	9–1	See 1001
8–401(c)	See 2002	9–2	Omitted
8–401(d)	See 3001(e)	9–3	See 1002
8–401(e)	See T. 11 § 704(4)	9–4(a)	See T. 11 §§ 362(a), 922(a)
8–401(f)	See T. 11 § 502(a)	9–4(b)	See T. 11 §§ 362(c), 922(b)
8–401(g)	See 3007	9–4(c)	See T. 11 §§ 362(d), 922(b)
8–401(h)	See 3008		
8–401(i)	See 3003(d)	9–4(d)	Omitted
8–402	See 3005	9–5	See 1005
8–403	See 3006	9–6	See 1006
8–404(a)	See 3021	9–7	See 1007
8–404(b)	See T. 11 § 1143	9–8	See 1008
8–405(a)	See 3009	9–9	See 1009
8–405(b)	See T. 11 § 347(b)	9–10	See 1011
8–501(a)	See T. 11 § 362(a)	9–11	See 1013
8–501(b)	See T. 11 § 362(c)	9–12(a)	See T. 28 § 1472
8–501(c)	See T. 11 § 362(d)	9–12(b)	See 1014(a)
8–501(d)	See T. 11 § 362(f)	9–13	Omitted
8–501(e)	Omitted	9–14	See 2002
8–502(a)	See T. 11 § 549(c)	9–15	2018
8–502(b)	See T. 11 § 542(c)	9–16	See 2019
8–503	See 6001	9–17	See 2003
8–504	See 6002	9–18(a)	See T. 11 § 345(b)
8–505(a)	See T. 11 § 345(a)	9–18(b)	See 5008(g)
8–505(b)	See T. 11 § 345(a)	9–18(c)	See 5008(e)
8–505(c)	See 5008(a); T. 11 § 345(b)	9–19(a)	See 2016(a)
8–505(d)	See 5008(e)	9–19(b)	See 2016(b)
8–505(e)	See 5008(c), (d)	9–19(c)	See T. 11 § 330(a)
8–505(f)	See 5008(g)	9–19(d)	See T. 11 § 504
8–505(g)	Omitted	9–20	See T. 11 § 330(a)
8–505(h)	See 5008(h)	9–21	See 2017
8–505(i)	See 6003	9–22(a)	See 3003(b)
8–506	See 6006; T. 11 § 365	9–22(b)	See 3003(c)
		9–22(c)	See 3001(e)
8–507	See T. 11 § 1169	9–22(d)	Omitted
8–508(a)	See T. 11 § 327	9–22(e)	See T. 11 § 502(a)
8–508(b)	See 6005	9–22(f)	See 3007
8–509	See 6004; T. 11 § 363	9–22(g)	See 3013
		9–22(h)	See 3008

Former Titles II to VII Bankr.Rule	New Bankr. Rule	Former Titles II to VII Bankr.Rule	New Bankr. Rule
9–22(i)	See 3003(h)	10–202(c)	See T. 11 § 321
9–23	See 3006	10–202(d)	See 2012; T. 11 § 1105
9–24(a)	See 3016(a); T. 11 § 941	10–202(e)	Omitted
9–24(b)	See 2003(e), 3016(c); T. 11 § 1125	10–203	See 2009
		10–204(a)	See T. 11 § 322(a)
9–25	See 3018	10–204(b)	See T. 11 § 322(b)
9–26	See 3019	10–204(c)	See 2010(d); T. 11 § 322(d)
9–27	See 3020		
9–28(a)	See T. 11 § 927(a)	10–204(d)	See 2010(c)
9–28(b)	See T. 11 § 927(b)	10–205	See 2012
9–28(c)	See 2002	10–206(a)	See 2014(a)
9–29(a)	See 3021	10–206(b)	See T. 11 § 328(c)
9–29(b)	See T. 11 § 347(b)	10–207	See T. 11 §§ 1107, 1108
9–30(a)	See 3009		
9–30(b)	See T. 11 § 347(b)	10–208	2015
9–31(a)	See 3020(a)	10–209	See 2002
9–31(b)	See 3022	10–210	2018
9–31(c)	Omitted	10–211	2019
9–32	Omitted	10–212	See 2003
9–33	See 6006; T. 11 § 365	10–213(a)	See 2004(a)
		10–213(b)	See 2003(b)(1)
9–34	See T. 11 § 551	10–213(c)	See 2004(b)
9–35	See 6010	10–213(d)	See 2004(c)
9–36	See 7001	10–213(e)	See 2004(d)
9–37(a)	See 7003 to 7087	10–213(f)	See 2004(e)
9–37(b)	Omitted	10–214	See 2005
9–38	See 9001	10–215(a)	See 2016(a)
9–39	See 9002	10–215(b)	See 2016(b)
9–40, 9–41	Omitted	10–215(c)	See T. 11 § 330(a)
9–42	See 9014	10–215(d)	See T. 11 § 504
9–43	See 9010	10–216	See T. 11 § 330
10–1	See 1001	10–217	See 2017
10–2	See T. 11 § 1101	10–301	See 3016
10–101 to 10–103	Omitted	10–302(a)	See 3013; T. 11 § 1122
10–104(a)	See 1002	10–302(b)	See 3012
10–104(b)	See T. 11 § 362(a)	10–303	3017
10–105(a)	See 1003(a), (b)	10–304	See T. 11 § 1125(b)
10–105(b)	See 1003(c)	10–305(a)	3018(a)
10–105(c)	See 1003(d)	10–305(b)	See 3018(c)
10–105(d)	See T. 11 § 362(a)	10–305(c)	See 3018(d)
10–106	See 1005	10–305(d), (e)	Omitted
10–107	See 1006	10–306(a)	See 3019
10–108	1007	10–306(b), (c)	See T. 11 § 1127(b)
10–109	See 1008	10–307	3020
10–110	See 1009	10–308	See 1017(a), 1019; T. 11 § 1112
10–111	See 1010		
10–112	See 1011	10–309(a)	See T. 11 § 1142(b)
10–113(a) to (c)	See 1013	10–309(b)	See 3022
10–113(d)	See T. 28 § 303(i)	10–401(a)	3003(b)
10–114(a)	See T. 28 § 1472	10–401(b)	3003(c)
10–114(b)	See 1014(a)	10–401(c)	See 3001(e)
10–114(c)	See 1014(b)	10–401(d)	See T. 11 § 1106(a)(1)
10–114(d)	Omitted	10–401(e)	See T. 11 § 502(a)
10–115	See 1015	10–401(f)	See 3007
10–116	See T. 11 § 305(a)(2)	10–401(g)	See 3008
10–117	See 1019	10–401(h)	3003(d)
10–118	Omitted	10–402	3005
10–201	2001	10–403	Omitted
10–202(a)	See T. 11 § 1104	10–404	3006
10–202(b)	See 2008	10–405(a)	3021

TABLE 4—DISPOSITION

Former Titles II to VII Bankr.Rule	New Bankr. Rule
10–405(b)	See T. 11 § 1143
10–406(a)	See 3009
10–406(b)	See T. 11 § 347(b)
10–501	Omitted
10–601(a)	See T. 11 § 362(a)
10–601(b)	See T. 11 § 362(c)
10–601(c)	See T. 11 § 362(d)
10–601(d)	See T. 11 § 362(f)
10–601(e)	Omitted
10–602	See T. 11 §§ 542(c), 549(c)
10–603	See 6001
10–604	See 6002
10–605	See 6003; T. 11 § 345(a)
10–606	See 6006(c)
10–607(a)	See T. 11 § 327
10–607(b)	See 6004(e)
10–607(c)	See 6005
10–608	See 6007
10–609	See 6008
10–610	See 6009
10–611	See T. 11 § 551
10–612	See 6010
10–701	See 7001
10–801	See 8001 to 8019
10–901	See 9001 to 9032
11–1	See 1001
11–2	See T. 11 § 1101
11–3 to 11–5	Omitted
11–6	See 1002(a), (b)(2)
11–7	Omitted
11–8	See 1004
11–9	See 1005
11–10	See 1006
11–11	1007
11–12	See 1008, 1009
11–13(a)	See T. 28 § 1472
11–13(b)	See 1014(a)
11–13(c)	See 1014(b)
11–14	See 1015(b), (c)
11–15	Omitted
11–16	1016
11–17	See T. 11 § 305(a)(2)
11–18(a) to (c)	Omitted
11–18(d)	See T. 11 § 321
11–18(e)	See T. 11 § 324
11–18(f)	See T. 11 § 324
11–18(g)	See 2012
11–19	See 2009
11–20(a)	See T. 11 § 322(a)
11–20(b)	See 2010(a)
11–20(c)	See 2010(b)
11–20(d)	Omitted
11–20(e)	See 2010(d); T. 11 § 322(b), (d)
11–20(f)	See 2010(c)
11–21	See 2013
11–22	See 2014; T. 11 §§ 327(b) to (d), 328(c)
11–23	See T. 11 §§ 1107, 1108
11–24	See 2002
11–25	See 2003
11–26	2004(b)
11–27	See 2007
11–28	See 2006
11–29	See T. 11 § 705
11–30	2015
11–31	See 2016; T. 11 §§ 330(a), 504
11–32	See 2017
11–33(a)	See 3001(a), (b), and (f)
11–33(b)	See 3003
11–33(c)	See 3004
11–33(d)	See 3005
11–33(e)	See 3007, 3012; T. 11 §§ 502(a), 704(4)
11–33(f)	See 3008
11–34	See 3006
11–35(a)	3009
11–35(b)	See T. 11 § 347(a)
11–35(c)	See T. 11 § 347(b)
11–36(a)	See T. 11 § 1121(c)
11–36(b)	See 2003(e)
11–37(a)	See 3017(c)
11–37(b)	See 3018(b)
11–37(c)	See 3018(c)
11–38	3020
11–39	See 3019
11–40	See T. 11 § 1127(b)
11–41	See T. 11 § 1144
11–42	See 1017(a), 1019; T. 11 § 1112
11–43(a)	See T. 11 §§ 1141(d)(1) to (3)
11–43(b)	Omitted
11–44(a)	See T. 11 § 362(a)
11–44(b)	See T. 11 § 362(c)
11–44(c)	See T. 11 § 362(e)
11–44(d)	See T. 11 § 362(d)
11–44(e)	See T. 11 § 362(f)
11–44(f)	Omitted
11–45	See 4002
11–46	See 2005
11–47	See 4003(a)
11–48	See 4007, 9015
11–49	See T. 11 §§ 542(c), 549(c)
11–50	See 6001
11–51	See 6002
11–52	See 6003; T. 11 § 345(a)
11–53	See 6006(c)
11–54(a)	See T. 11 § 327
11–54(b)	See 6004(e)
11–54(c)	See 6005
11–55	See 6007
11–56	See 6008
11–57	See 6009
11–58	See T. 11 § 551

Former Titles II to VII Bankr.Rule	New Bankr. Rule	Former Titles II to VII Bankr.Rule	New Bankr. Rule
11–59	See 6010	12–31(b)	See 3012
11–60	See 5001 to 5010	12–32	See 3005
11–61	See 7001	12–33	Omitted
11–62	See 8001 to 8019	12–34	See 3006
11–63	See 9001 to 9032	12–35(a)	See 3009
12–1	See 1001	12–35(b)	See T. 11 § 347(a)
12–2	See T. 11 § 1101	12–35(c)	See T. 11 § 347(b)
12–3 to 12–5	Omitted	12–36(a)	See T. 11 § 1121(c)
12–6	See 1002(a), (b)(2)	12–36(b)	See 3016(a)
12–7	Omitted	12–36(c)	Omitted
12–8	See 1004	12–36(d)	See 2003(e)
12–9	See 1005	12–37(a)	See 3018(a)
12–10	See 1006	12–37(b)	See 3018(c)
12–11	See 1007	12–37(c)	See 3018(d)
12–12	See 1008, 1009	12–37(d)	Omitted
12–13(a)	See T. 28 § 1472	12–37(e)	See 3018(a)
12–13(b)	See 1014(a)	12–38	See 3020
12–13(c)	See 1014(b)	12–39	See 3019; T. 11 § 1127(b)
12–14	See 1015(b), (c)	12–40	See T. 11 § 1144
12–15	See 1016	12–41	See 1017(a), 1019; T. 11 § 1112
12–16	See T. 11 § 305(a)(2)	12–42(a)	See T. 11 § 1141(d)(1) to (3)
12–17(a)	See T. 11 § 1104(a)	12–42(b)	Omitted
12–17(b), (c)	Omitted	12–43(a)	See T. 11 § 362(a)
12–17(d)	See T. 11 § 321	12–43(b)	See T. 11 § 362(c)
12–17(e)	See T. 11 § 324	12–43(c)	See T. 11 § 362(e)
12–17(f)	See 2012	12–43(d)	See T. 11 § 362(d)
12–18	See 2009	12–43(e)	See T. 11 § 362(f)
12–19(a)	See T. 11 § 322(a)	12–43(f)	Omitted
12–19(b)	See 2010(a)	12–44	See 4002
12–19(c)	See 2010(b)	12–45	See 2005
12–19(d)	Omitted	12–46	See 4003(a)
12–19(e)	See 2010(d); T. 11 § 322(b), (d)	12–47	See 4007, 9015
12–19(f)	See 2010(c)	12–48	See T. 11 §§ 542(c), 549(c)
12–20	See 2013	12–49	See 6001
12–21	See 2014; T. 11 §§ 327(b) to (d), 328(c)	12–50	See 6002
12–22	See T. 11 §§ 1107, 1108	12–51	See 6003; T. 11 § 345(a)
12–23	See 2002	12–52	See 6006(c)
12–24	See 2003	12–53(a)	See T. 11 § 327
12–25	See 2019	12–53(b)	See 6004(e)
12–26	See 2004(b)	12–53(c)	See 6005
12–27	See 2015	12–54	See 6007
12–28(a)	See T. 11 § 330(a)	12–55	See 6008
12–28(b)	Omitted	12–56	See 6009
12–28(c)	See 2016; T. 11 § 504	12–57	See T. 11 § 551
12–28(d), (e)	Omitted	12–58	See 6010
12–29	See 2017	12–59	See 5001 to 5010
12–30(a)	See 3001(f)	12–60	See 7001
12–30(b)	See 3002	12–61	See 8001 to 8019
12–30(c)	See 3001(e)	12–62	See 9001 to 9032
12–30(d)	See T. 11 § 1106(a)(1)	13–1	See 1001
12–30(e)	See T. 11 § 502(a)	13–2	Omitted
12–30(f)	See 3007	13–101, 13–102	Omitted
12–30(g)	See 3008	13–103	See 1002(a), (b)(1)
12–31(a)	See 3013; T. 11 § 1122	13–104	Omitted
		13–105	See 1005
		13–106	See 1006
		13–107	See 1007

TABLE 4—DISPOSITION

Former Titles II to VII Bankr.Rule	New Bankr. Rule	Former Titles II to VII Bankr.Rule	New Bankr. Rule
13–108	See 1008	13–307(d)	See 3012
13–109	See 1009	13–308	See T. 11 § 502(j)
13–110(a)	See T. 28 § 1472	13–309	See T. 11 § 1326
13–110(b)	See 1014(a)	13–310	See T. 11 § 347(a)
13–110(c)	See 1014(b)	13–401(a)	See T. 11 § 362(a)
13–110(d)	Omitted	13–401(b)	See T. 11 § 362(c)
13–111	See 1015(b), (c)	13–401(c)	See T. 11 § 362(e)
13–112	See 1017(a), 1019; T. 11 § 1307	13–401(d)	See T. 11 § 362(d)
		13–401(e)	See T. 11 § 362(f)
13–201	See 3015	13–401(f)	Omitted
13–202(a)	See 3018(a)	13–402	See 4002
13–202(b)	See 3018(c)	13–403	See 4003(a)
13–202(c)	See 3018(d)	13–404	See 4004; T. 11 § 1328
13–203	See 2002		
13–204	See 2003	13–405	See T. 11 § 1328(a)
13–205(a), (b)	See T. 11 § 1302	13–406	See 4006
13–205(c)	See T. 11 § 322(b)	13–407(a)(1)	See 4007(a), (b)
13–205(d)	See T. 11 § 321	13–407(a)(2)	See 4007(c)
13–205(e)	See 2010(d); T. 11 § 322(d)	13–407(b)	Omitted
		13–407(c)	See 9015
13–205(f)	See 2010(c)	13–407(d)	See 4007(e)
13–206(a)	See 2004(a)	13–501	See 5001 to 5010
13–206(b)	See 2003(b)(1)	13–601	See 6001
13–206(c)	See 2003(b)(1)	13–602	See 6002
13–206(d)	See 2004(b)	13–603(a)	See T. 11 § 345(a)
13–206(e)	See 2004(c)	13–603(b)	See 6003
13–206(f)	See 2004(d)	13–604	See 6006(c)
13–206(g)	See 2004(e)	13–605	See 6007
13–207	See 2014, 2016; T. 11 §§ 327(b), (c), (d), 328(c), 330(a), 504	13–606	See 6008
		13–607	See 6009
13–208	2015	13–608	See T. 11 § 551
13–209(a)	See 2016; T. 11 § 504	13–609	See 6010
		13–701	See 7001
13–209(b)	See T. 11 § 330(a)	13–801	See 8001 to 8019
13–209(c)	See T. 11 § 504	13–901	See 9001 to 9032

Former Title I Bankr.Rule	New Bankr. Rule
13–210	See 2017
13–211(a)	See T. 11 § 324
13–211(b)	See 2012
13–212	See 3019; T. 11 § 1323
1	See 1
2	See 2
3	See 3
13–213	3020
13–214(a)	See T. 11 § 1329
13–214(b)	See T. 11 § 1330
13–215	See 1017(a), 1019; T. 11 § 1307
4	See 4
5	See 4
6	See 6
7	See 7
13–301(a)	See 3001(a), (b)
13–301(b)	See 3001(f)
13–302(a)	See 3002(a)
13–302(b)	See 3002(b)
13–302(c)	See 3001(c)
13–302(d)	See 3001(e)
13–302(e)	See 3002(c)
13–302(f)	Omitted
13–303	See 3004
13–304	See 3005
13–305	See T. 11 § 1305
13–306	See 3006
13–307(a)	See T. 11 § 1302(b)(1)
13–307(b)	See T. 11 § 502(a)
13–307(c)	See 3007

Former Title I Bankr.Rule	New Bankr. Rule
8	See 8
9	See 11
10	See 13
11	14
12	16
13	17
14	18
15	19
16	20
16A	See 21
17	See 23
18	See 24
19	See 25
20	See 25
21 to 23	Omitted
24	27

FORMER BANKRUPTCY RULES AND FORMS

Former Title I Bankr.Rule	New Bankr. Rule
25	See 34
26, 27	Omitted
28	See 35
29	32
30	Omitted

Former Titles II to VII Bankr.Form	New Bankr. Form
8–1	See 1
8–2	See 11
8–3	See 13
8–4	See 16
8–5, 8–6	Omitted
8–7	See 30
8–8	See 31
9–F1	See 1
9–F2	See 16
9–F2A, 9–F3	Omitted
9–F4	See 31
9–F5	See 22
9–F6	See 24
9–F7	See 25
9–F8	See 25
9–F9	See 27
10–1	See 1
10–2	See 11
10–3	See 13
10–4	See 26
10–5	See 16
10–6	Omitted
10–7	See 30
10–8	See 29
10–9	See 31
11–F1	See 1
11–F2	Omitted
11–F3	See 4
11–F4	See 4
11–F5	See 6
11–F6	See 7
11–F7	See 8
11–F8	See 22
11–F9	See 24
11–F10	See 25
11–F11	See 25

Former Titles II to VII Bankr.Form	New Bankr. Form
11–F12	See 26
11–F13	See 16
11–F14	See 19
11–F15	See 20
11–F15A	See 21
11–F16	See 17
11–F17	See 29
11–F18	See 31
11–F19	See 27
12–F1	See 1
12–F2	Omitted
12–F3	See 4
12–F4	See 6
12–F5	See 7
12–F6	See 8
12–F7	See 22
12–F8	See 24
12–F9	See 25
12–F10	See 25
12–F11	See 26
12–F12	See 16
12–F13	See 19
12–F14	See 20
12–F15	See 21
12–F16	See 17
12–F17	See 31
12–F18	See 31
12–F19	See 27
13–1	See 1
13–2	See 2
13–3	See 3
13–4	Omitted
13–5	See 10
13–6	Omitted
13–7	See 16
13–8	See 17
13–9	See 19
13–10	See 19
13–11	See 25
13–12	See 25
13–13	Omitted
13–14	See 29
13–15	See 31
13–16	See 27

*

FEDERAL TAX LIEN STATUTES
INTERNAL REVENUE CODE

Selected Sections

Title 26, United States Code

Subtitle F—Procedure and Administration

Chapter 64—Collection

Subchapter C—Lien for Taxes

---

§ 6321. Lien for taxes

If any person liable to pay any tax neglects or refuses to pay the same after demand, the amount (including any interest, additional amount, addition to tax, or assessable penalty, together with any costs that may accrue in addition thereto) shall be a lien in favor of the United States upon all property and rights to property, whether real or personal, belonging to such person.

§ 6322. Period of lien

Unless another date is specifically fixed by law, the lien imposed by section 6321 shall arise at the time the assessment is made and shall continue until the liability for the amount so assessed (or a judgment against the taxpayer arising out of such liability) is satisfied or becomes unenforceable by reason of lapse of time.

§ 6323. Validity and priority against certain persons

(a) **Purchasers, holders of security interests, mechanic's lienors, and judgment lien creditors.**—The lien imposed by section 6321 shall not be valid as against any purchaser, holder of a security interest, mechanic's lienor, or judgment lien creditor until notice thereof which meets the requirements of subsection (f) has been filed by the Secretary.

(b) **Protection for certain interests even though notice filed.**—Even though notice of a lien imposed by section 6321 has been filed, such lien shall not be valid—

(1) **Securities.**—With respect to a security (as defined in subsection (h)(4))—

(A) as against a purchaser of such security who at the time of purchase did not have actual notice or knowledge of the existence of such lien; and

(B) as against a holder of a security interest in such security who, at the time such interest came into existence, did not have actual notice or knowledge of the existence of such lien.

901

(2) **Motor vehicles.**—With respect to a motor vehicle (as defined in subsection (h)(3)), as against a purchaser of such motor vehicle, if—

(A) at the time of the purchase such purchaser did not have actual notice or knowledge of the existence of such lien, and

(B) before the purchaser obtains such notice or knowledge, he has acquired possession of such motor vehicle and has not thereafter relinquished possession of such motor vehicle to the seller or his agent.

(3) **Personal property purchased at retail.**—With respect to tangible personal property purchased at retail, as against a purchaser in the ordinary course of the seller's trade or business, unless at the time of such purchase such purchaser intends such purchase to (or knows such purchase will) hinder, evade, or defeat the collection of any tax under this title.

(4) **Personal property purchased in casual sale.**—With respect to household goods, personal effects, or other tangible personal property described in section 6334(a) purchased (not for resale) in a casual sale for less than $250, as against the purchaser, but only if such purchaser does not have actual notice or knowledge (A) of the existence of such lien, or (B) that this sale is one of a series of sales.

(5) **Personal property subject to possessory lien.**—With respect to tangible personal property subject to a lien under local law securing the reasonable price of the repair or improvement of such property, as against a holder of such a lien, if such holder is, and has been, continuously in possession of such property from the time such lien arose.

(6) **Real property tax and special assessment liens.**—With respect to real property, as against a holder of a lien upon such property, if such lien is entitled under local law to priority over security interests in such property which are prior in time, and such lien secures payment of—

(A) a tax of general application levied by any taxing authority based upon the value of such property;

(B) a special assessment imposed directly upon such property by any taxing authority, if such assessment is imposed for the purpose of defraying the cost of any public improvement; or

(C) charges for utilities or public services furnished to such property by the United States, a State or political subdivision thereof, or an instrumentality of any one or more of the foregoing.

(7) **Residential property subject to a mechanic's lien for certain repairs and improvements.**—With respect to real property subject to a lien for repair or improvement of a personal residence (containing not more than four dwelling units) occupied by the owner of such residence, as against a mechanic's lienor, but only if the contract price on the contract with the owner is not more than $1,000.

(8) **Attorneys' liens.**—With respect to a judgment or other amount in settlement of a claim or of a cause of action, as against an attorney who, under local law, holds a lien upon or a contract enforcible against such judgment or amount, to the extent of his reasonable compensation for obtaining such judgment or procuring such settlement, except that this paragraph shall not apply to any judgment or amount in settlement of a claim or of a cause of action against the United States to the extent that the

United States offsets such judgment or amount against any liability of the taxpayer to the United States.

(9) Certain insurance contracts.—With respect to a life insurance, endowment, or annuity contract, as against the organization which is the insurer under such contract, at any time—

(A) before such organization had actual notice or knowledge of the existence of such lien;

(B) after such organization had such notice or knowledge, with respect to advances required to be made automatically to maintain such contract in force under an agreement entered into before such organization had such notice or knowledge; or

(C) after satisfaction of a levy pursuant to section 6332(b), unless and until the Secretary or his delegate delivers to such organization a notice, executed after the date of such satisfaction, of the existence of such lien.

(10) Passbook loans.—With respect to a savings deposit, share, or other account, evidenced by a passbook, with an institution described in section 581 or 591, to the extent of any loan made by such institution without actual notice or knowledge of the existence of such lien, as against such institution, if such loan is secured by such account and if such institution has been continuously in possession of such passbook from the time the loan is made.

(c) Protection for certain commercial transactions financing agreements, etc.—

(1) In general.—To the extent provided in this subsection, even though notice of a lien imposed by section 6321 has been filed, such lien shall not be valid with respect to a security interest which came into existence after tax lien filing but which—

(A) is in qualified property covered by the terms of a written agreement entered into before tax lien filing and constituting—

(i) a commercial transactions financing agreement,

(ii) a real property construction or improvement financing agreement, or

(iii) an obligatory disbursement agreement, and

(B) is protected under local law against a judgment lien arising, as of the time of tax lien filing, out of an unsecured obligation.

(2) Commercial transactions financing agreement.—For purposes of this subsection—

(A) Definition.—The term "commercial transactions financing agreement" means an agreement (entered into by a person in the course of his trade or business)—

(i) to make loans to the taxpayer to be secured by commercial financing security acquired by the taxpayer in the ordinary course of his trade or business, or

(ii) to purchase commercial financing security (other than inventory) acquired by the taxpayer in the ordinary course of his trade or business;

but such an agreement shall be treated as coming within the term only to the extent that such loan or purchase is made before the 46th day after the date of tax lien filing or (if earlier) before the lender or purchaser had actual notice or knowledge of such tax lien filing.

(B) Limitation on qualified property.—The term "qualified property", when used with respect to a commercial transactions financing agreement, includes only commercial financing security acquired by the taxpayer before the 46th day after the date of tax lien filing.

(C) Commercial financing security defined.—The term "commercial financing security" means (i) paper of a kind ordinarily arising in commercial transactions, (ii) accounts receivable, (iii) mortgages on real property, and (iv) inventory.

(D) Purchaser treated as acquiring security interest.—A person who satisfies subparagraph (A) by reason of clause (ii) thereof shall be treated as having acquired a security interest in commercial financing security.

(3) Real property construction or improvement financing agreement.—For purposes of this subsection—

(A) Definition.—The term "real property construction or improvement financing agreement" means an agreement to make cash disbursements to finance—

(i) the construction or improvement of real property,

(ii) a contract to construct or improve real property, or

(iii) the raising or harvesting of a farm crop or the raising of livestock or other animals.

For purposes of clause (iii), the furnishing of goods and services shall be treated as the disbursement of cash.

(B) Limitation on qualified property.—The term "qualified property", when used with respect to a real property construction or improvement financing agreement, includes only—

(i) in the case of subparagraph (A)(i), the real property with respect to which the construction or improvement has been or is to be made,

(ii) in the case of subparagraph (A)(ii), the proceeds of the contract described therein, and

(iii) in the case of subparagraph (A)(iii), property subject to the lien imposed by section 6321 at the time of tax lien filing and the crop or the livestock or other animals referred to in subparagraph (A)(iii).

(4) Obligatory disbursement agreement.—For purposes of this subsection—

(A) Definition.—The term "obligatory disbursement agreement" means an agreement (entered into by a person in the course of his trade or business) to make disbursements, but such an agreement shall be treated as coming within the term only to the extent of disbursements which are required to be made by reason of the intervention of the rights of a person other than the taxpayer.

(B) Limitation on qualified property.—The term "qualified property", when used with respect to an obligatory disbursement agreement, means property subject to the lien imposed by section 6321 at the time of tax lien filing and (to the extent that the acquisition is directly traceable to the disbursements referred to in subparagraph (A)) property acquired by the taxpayer after tax lien filing.

(C) Special rules for surety agreements.—Where the obligatory disbursement agreement is an agreement ensuring the performance of a contract between the taxpayer and another person—

(i) the term "qualified property" shall be treated as also including the proceeds of the contract the performance of which was ensured, and

(ii) if the contract the performance of which was ensured was a contract to construct or improve real property, to produce goods, or to furnish services, the term "qualified property" shall be treated as also including any tangible personal property used by the taxpayer in the performance of such ensured contract.

(d) 45-day period for making disbursements.—Even though notice of a lien imposed by section 6321 has been filed, such lien shall not be valid with respect to a security interest which came into existence after tax lien filing by reason of disbursements made before the 46th day after the date of tax lien filing, or (if earlier) before the person making such disbursements had actual notice or knowledge of tax lien filing, but only if such security interest—

(1) is in property (A) subject, at the time of tax lien filing, to the lien imposed by section 6321, and (B) covered by the terms of a written agreement entered into before tax lien filing, and

(2) is protected under local law against a judgment lien arising, as of the time of tax lien filing, out of an unsecured obligation.

(e) Priority of interest and expenses.—If the lien imposed by section 6321 is not valid as against a lien or security interest, the priority of such lien or security interest shall extend to—

(1) any interest or carrying charges upon the obligation secured,

(2) the reasonable charges and expenses of an indenture trustee or agent holding the security interest for the benefit of the holder of the security interest,

(3) the reasonable expenses, including reasonable compensation for attorneys, actually incurred in collecting or enforcing the obligation secured,

(4) the reasonable costs of insuring, preserving, or repairing the property to which the lien or security interest relates,

(5) the reasonable costs of insuring payment of the obligation secured, and

(6) amounts paid to satisfy any lien on the property to which the lien or security interest relates, but only if the lien so satisfied is entitled to priority over the lien imposed by section 6321,

to the extent that, under local law, any such item has the same priority as the lien or security interest to which it relates.

(f) Place for filing notice; form.—

(1) Place for filing.—The notice referred to in subsection (a) shall be filed—

(A) Under State laws.—

(i) Real property.—In the case of real property, in one office within the State (or the county, or other governmental subdivision), as designated by the laws of such State, in which the property subject to the lien is situated; and

(ii) Personal property.—In the case of personal property, whether tangible or intangible, in one office within the State (or the county, or other governmental subdivision), as designated by the laws of such State, in which the property subject to the lien is situated, except that State law merely conforming to or reenacting Federal law establishing a national filing system does not constitute a second office for filing as designated by the laws of such State; or

(B) With clerk of district court.—In the office of the clerk of the United States district court for the judicial district in which the property subject to the lien is situated, whenever the State has not by law designated one office which meets the requirements of subparagraph (A); or

(C) With Recorder of Deeds of the District of Columbia.—In the office of the Recorder of Deeds of the District of Columbia, if the property subject to the lien is situated in the District of Columbia.

(2) Situs of property subject to lien.—For purposes of paragraphs (1) and (4), property shall be deemed to be situated—

(A) Real property.—In the case of real property, at its physical location; or

(B) Personal property.—In the case of personal property, whether tangible or intangible, at the residence of the taxpayer at the time the notice of lien is filed.

For purposes of paragraph (2)(B), the residence of a corporation or partnership shall be deemed to be the place at which the principal executive office of the business is located, and the residence of a taxpayer whose residence is without the United States shall be deemed to be in the District of Columbia.

(3) Form.—The form and content of the notice referred to in subsection (a) shall be prescribed by the Secretary. Such notice shall be valid notwithstanding any other provision of law regarding the form or content of a notice of lien.

(4) Indexing required with respect to certain real property.—In the case of real property, if—

(A) under the laws of the State in which the real property is located, a deed is not valid as against a purchaser of the property who (at the time of purchase) does not have actual notice or knowledge of the existence of such deed unless the fact of filing of such deed has been entered and recorded in a public index at the place of filing in such a manner that a reasonable inspection of the index will reveal the existence of the deed, and

(B) there is maintained (at the applicable office under paragraph (1)) an adequate system for the public indexing of Federal tax liens,

then the notice of lien referred to in subsection (a) shall not be treated as meeting the filing requirements under paragraph (1) unless the fact of filing is entered and recorded in the index referred to in subparagraph (B) in such a manner that a reasonable inspection of the index will reveal the existence of the lien.

(5) National filing systems.—The filing of a notice of lien shall be governed solely by this title and shall not be subject to any other Federal law establishing a place or places for the filing of liens or encumbrances under a national filing system.

(g) Refiling of notice.—For purposes of this section—

(1) General rule.—Unless notice of lien is refiled in the manner prescribed in paragraph (2) during the required refiling period, such notice of lien shall be treated as filed on the date on which it is filed (in accordance with subsection (f)) after the expiration of such refiling period.

(2) Place for filing.—A notice of lien refiled during the required refiling period shall be effective only—

(A) if—

(i) such notice of lien is refiled in the office in which the prior notice of lien was filed, and

(ii) in the case of real property, the fact of refiling is entered and recorded in an index to the extent required by subsection (f)(4); and

(B) in any case in which, 90 days or more prior to the date of a refiling of notice of lien under subparagraph (A), the Secretary received written information (in the manner prescribed in regulations issued by the Secretary) concerning a change in the taxpayer's residence, if a notice of such lien is also filed in accordance with subsection (f) in the State in which such residence is located.

(3) Required refiling period.—In the case of any notice of lien, the term "required refiling period" means—

(A) the one-year period ending 30 days after the expiration of 6 years after the date of the assessment of the tax, and

(B) the one-year period ending with the expiration of 6 years after the close of the preceding required refiling period for such notice of lien.

(4) Transitional rule.—Notwithstanding paragraph (3), if the assessment of the tax was made before January 1, 1962, the first required refiling period shall be the calendar year 1967.

(h) Definitions.—For purposes of this section and section 6324—

(1) Security interest.—The term "security interest" means any interest in property acquired by contract for the purpose of securing payment or performance of an obligation or indemnifying against loss or liability. A security interest exists at any time (A), if, at such time, the property is in existence and the interest has become protected under local law against a subsequent judgment lien arising out of an unsecured obligation, and (B) to the extent that, at such time, the holder has parted with money or money's worth.

(2) Mechanic's lienor.—The term "mechanic's lienor" means any person who under local law has a lien on real property (or on the proceeds of a contract relating to real property) for services, labor, or materials furnished in connection with the construction or improvement of such property. For purposes of the preceding sentence, a person has a lien on the earliest date such lien becomes valid under local law against subsequent purchasers without actual notice, but not before he begins to furnish the services, labor, or materials.

(3) Motor vehicle.—The term "motor vehicle" means a self-propelled vehicle which is registered for highway use under the laws of any State or foreign country.

(4) Security.—The term "security" means any bond, debenture, note, or certificate or other evidence of indebtedness, issued by a corporation or a government or political subdivision thereof, with interest coupons or in registered form, share of stock, voting trust certificate, or any certificate of interest or participation in, certificate of deposit or receipt for, temporary or interim certificate for, or warrant or right to subscribe to or purchase, any of the foregoing; negotiable instrument; or money.

(5) Tax lien filing.—The term "tax lien filing" means the filing of notice (referred to in subsection (a)) of the lien imposed by section 6321.

(6) Purchaser.—The term "purchaser" means a person who, for adequate and full consideration in money or money's worth, acquires an interest (other than a lien or security interest) in property which is valid under local law against subsequent purchasers without actual notice. In applying the preceding sentence for purposes of subsection (a) of this section, and for purposes of section 6324—

(A) a lease of property,

(B) a written executory contract to purchase or lease property,

(C) an option to purchase or lease property or any interest therein, or

(D) an option to renew or extend a lease of property, which is not a lien or security interest shall be treated as an interest in property.

(i) Special rules.—

(1) Actual notice or knowledge.—For purposes of this subchapter, an organization shall be deemed for purposes of a particular transaction to have actual notice or knowledge of any fact from the time such fact is brought to the attention of the individual conducting such transaction, and in any event from the time such fact would have been brought to such individual's attention if the organization had exercised due diligence. An organization exercises due diligence if it maintains reasonable routines for communicating significant information to the person conducting the transaction and there is reasonable compliance with the routine. Due diligence does not require an individual acting for the organization to communicate information unless such communication is part of his regular duties or unless he has reason to know of the transaction and that the transaction would be materially affected by the information.

(2) **Subrogation.**—Where, under local law, one person is subrogated to the rights of another with respect to a lien or interest, such person shall be subrogated to such rights for purposes of any lien imposed by section 6321 or 6324.

(3) **Forfeitures.**—For purposes of this subchapter, a forfeiture under local law of property seized by a law enforcement agency of a State, county, or other local governmental subdivision shall relate back to the time of seizure, except that this paragraph shall not apply to the extent that under local law the holder of an intervening claim or interest would have priority over the interest of the State, county, or other local governmental subdivision in the property.

†